A COLLECTION OF
ENGLISH PO
16

A COLLECTION OF ENGLISH POEMS

1660—1800

Selected and Edited by

RONALD S. CRANE

Professor of English, University of Chicago

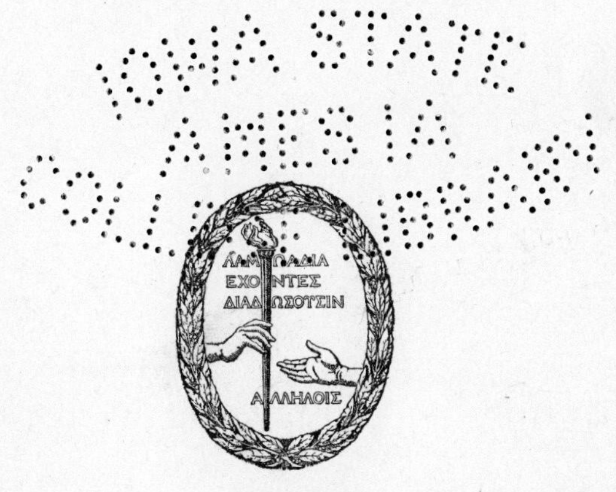

NEW YORK *and* LONDON

HARPER & BROTHERS PUBLISHERS

A COLLECTION OF ENGLISH POEMS

1660-1800

Printed in the United States of America

E-N

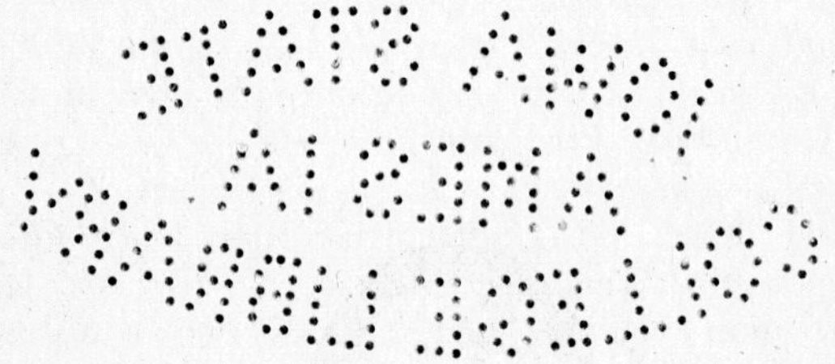

Preface

This book is designed primarily for the convenience of advanced students of Restoration and eighteenth-century literature in American colleges and universities. Its main purpose is to give such students, many of whom cannot rely upon access to adequately equipped libraries, a selection of representative poems published in England and Scotland between 1660 and 1800 sufficiently generous to enable them to judge the achievement of the age, in all its variety of themes and styles, for themselves.

It is an age about which it is increasingly easy to form sympathetic and properly instructed views. The prejudices of a hundred years, to be sure, die hard; and there are many readers and critics among us to whom the verdict pronounced by Romantics and Victorians upon the "classical" school of the eighteenth century remains even yet the final word. That true poetry is always a direct outpouring of personal feeling; that its values are determined by the nature of the emotion which it expresses, the standard being naturally set by the preferences of the most admired poets in the nineteenth-century tradition; that its distinctive effort is "to bring unthinkable thoughts and unsayable sayings within the range of human minds and ears"; that the essence of its art is not statement but suggestion—these are still for many persons self-evident propositions; and their effect is still to fasten a taint of the unpoetic upon even the greatest productions of an age which by principle eschewed personal confessions, which loved wit and cultivated regularity, precision, and a "satisfying completeness" of form, and which drew the substance of its verse from such—to the nineteenth century—prosaic things as the scorn of Tory for Whig or of wit for pedant and dunce, as the coming of a city shower, or as the optimistic theory of the world.

But it is clear that the tyranny of these presuppositions about the nature of poetry and of the inhibitions of taste which they have tended to encourage is far less complete at the present moment than it was even a few years ago. There have of course always been readers who have found in the poetry of Dryden and Pope and Swift and Prior and Johnson a source of unfailing delight. The difference is that today such admirers of "classical" verse need no longer feel themselves isolated in the midst of a hostile world. No more are they on the defensive; it is not they but the surviving disciples of Wordsworth and Matthew Arnold who are out of harmony with the movement of modern criticism and taste. Of this movement in the English-speaking world the most influential spokesman is beyond question Mr. T. S. Eliot; no one has done more than he to make us aware of the limitations of Romantic and Victorian ideas about poetry or to win a respectful hearing for poets who worked in idioms foreign to nineteenth-century taste. His essay on Dryden, inspired by the excellent and no less enthusiastic appraisal of Mr. Van Doren, is a manifesto of revolt. "To enjoy Dryden means to pass beyond the limitations of the nineteenth century into a new freedom." "Dryden [in *Mac Flecknoe*] continually enhances: he makes his object great, in a way contrary to expectation; and the total effect is due to the transformation of the ridiculous into poetry." "The reproach of the prosaic, levelled at Dryden, rests upon a confusion between the emotions considered to be poetic—which is a matter allowing considerable latitude of fashion—and the *result* of personal emotion in poetry. . . ." "Dryden lacked what his master Jonson possessed, a large and unique view of life; he lacked insight, he lacked profundity. But where Dryden fails to satisfy, the nineteenth century does not satisfy us either; and where that century has condemned him, it is itself condemned. In the next revolution of taste it is possible that poets may turn to the study of Dryden. He remains one of those who have set standards for English verse which it is desperate to ignore." That these statements represent a view which has become increasingly prevalent, and that not alone in academic circles, since 1920, there is ample evidence in the mass of recent critical comment not merely on Dryden but on many of his successors in the same tradition—on Pope, on Swift, on Johnson, on Churchill, on the numerous minor poets of the Georgian era who have been so diligently collected by Mr. David Nichol Smith and Mr. Iolo Williams. Not every one would endorse the late Mr. Strachey's enthusiasm for Pope's *Pastorals*; but there are many readers nowadays who appreciate what he means when he speaks of "the enchantment of the heroic couplet," and who would subscribe unreservedly to his emancipated view of the subject-matter of poetry: "If we look at the facts, where do we find poetry? In the wild fantasies of Aristophanes, in the sordid lusts of Baudelaire, in the gentle trivialities of La Fontaine. . . . There is poetry to be found lurking in the metaphysical system of Epicurus, and in the body of a flea. And so need we be surprised if it invests a game of cards, or a gentleman sneezing at Hampton Court?"

Many of the barriers which once stood in the way of a full enjoyment of eighteenth-century poetry have thus been broken down—thanks to the critical revolution of the past decade. But this is not all. Appreciation of the verse contained in this volume is dependent upon other things besides an open mind toward forms of poetry not approved by the nineteenth-century tradition; it demands an adequate conception of the culture, the ruling ideas, and in general the artistic and intellectual history of the age in which it was produced. We stand at present only upon the threshold of a proper understanding of the seventeenth and eighteenth centuries; but progress toward such an understanding has been notably rapid during the last few years, and the student who approaches the period today can do so with the help of much more trustworthy and stimulating guides than would have been available a decade ago.[1] It is not merely that we have for the first time satisfactory texts of a number of important poets (Blake, for example), or that the lives and personalities of others (for instance, Pope) have been put in a fairer light, or that diligent inquiry has told us more than we ever knew before about such topics as the origins of the heroic couplet, the vogue of burlesque and mock-heroic poetry, or the influence of Spenser and Milton on eighteenth-century style. Along with much accumulation of new detail and much fruitful sifting of the old there have come also altered perspectives, and a fresh insight into the complex forces that shaped the period as a whole. In this progress the chief factor has undoubtedly been the renewed concentration by scholars on the relations between eighteenth-century literature and the history of ideas. How vivifying the effect of this form of study can be appears most conspicuously perhaps in the scattered writings of Professor Lovejoy.[2] If we are now beginning to have something like an adequate understanding of the intellectual atmosphere surrounding neo-classical criticism and poetry, if we are on our way toward a more discriminating and genuinely historical conception of the complex of movements which has been commonly called "romanticism," the credit must in very large measure go to him. Others at the same time, but independently, have applied a similar method to more limited problems, with results that are no less illuminating in their way. Thus—to mention only a few examples—a good deal that was formerly obscure in Dryden's religious poems has now been cleared up; many aspects of Thomson have acquired new meaning by being brought into relation with the scientific and religious ideas of his time; Blake no longer stands an isolated and hence unintelligible figure in the later eighteenth century.

In selecting and reprinting the poems which make up this volume I have tried to keep in mind both of these new directions of interest in the verse of the period. I have naturally devoted most space to major figures, such as Dryden, Prior, Swift, Gay, Pope, Thomson, Johnson, Collins, Gray, Goldsmith, Cowper, Blake, and Burns; but I have not neglected their lesser contemporaries, many of whom have left us verse of indubitable excellence in forms or on subjects that would have been inadequately illustrated in a selection

[1] The titles of the most important or useful of these are brought together in the bibliography at the end of the volume.

[2] For a list of his principal papers on eighteenth-century topics see the third and fourth sections of the bibliography.

only from the better-known men. With rare exceptions I have included only complete poems or complete parts of poems, and I have taken the texts of these, whenever possible, from the most authoritative contemporary sources, and have printed them unaltered except for the correction of an occasional misprint or the insertion of an occasional needed mark of punctuation.[3] In arranging them in the volume I have followed an order determined, for the whole work of an author, by the date of his first important publication,[4] and, for the individual poems of an author, by the dates, so far as these could be ascertained, of their first appearance in print.[5]

I suppose that no one who undertakes such a work as this can ever feel entirely happy about the printed result. I have omitted some poems which, could I now plan the collection anew, I should certainly wish to include, and I have given valuable space to others of whose superior claims I am no longer quite convinced. In preparing the texts I have not always, as Johnson confessed on a more momentous occasion, "executed my own scheme, or satisfied my own expectations." The difficulties have been greater than I could anticipate. It has not always been easy, and occasionally it has proved impossible, to determine with certainty what particular form of a poem best represented its author's final intentions. I have been reasonably diligent in my inquiries, but so imperfect still is our knowledge of the textual history of this period that I have been forced, more frequently than I could wish, to content myself with what I feel sure are only approximations. Nor, even when I knew what text I ought to print, has it invariably been possible to act upon the information. Certain poems I have been compelled to reproduce from obviously inferior sources; of a number of others I have been obliged to give texts which, though they have been collated in proof with the proper originals, still retain some of the variations in capitalization and punctuation, though not in wording, characteristic of the modern editions from which they were set.[6] And finally I shall not be surprised to learn, though here again I have taken some pains, that the dates of first publication given in the notes are in some instances incorrect. I can only hope that errors of this sort are not unduly numerous and that users of the collection will have the kindness to inform me of any that they may discover.

[3] The source of the text of each poem is indicated in a footnote, though not always, I am afraid, with all the precision that might be demanded in a work of greater scholarly pretensions. It has seemed unnecessary, for example, to take account of the fact that there were duplicate printings, with some textual variations of minor importance, of Cowley's *Works* of 1668, of Prior's *Poems* of 1718, of the *Gentleman's Magazine* for July, 1731, and possibly of others among the editions which I have used.

[4] This appears as the second of the three dates given in parentheses after the name of the author.

[5] To this latter rule I have admitted a few exceptions. Thus poems printed posthumously have normally been placed according to dates of composition.

[6] These poems are designated in the bibliographical footnotes by the phrase "See Preface."

The debt which this book owes to earlier attempts in the same kind, and especially to the admirable anthologies of Iolo Williams and David Nichol Smith, will be evident to all readers. I have received much kind assistance, at various stages in its preparation, from friends both in this country and England. Messrs. Birrell and Garnett, of London, and Mr. Walter Hill, of Chicago, have generously allowed me to collate certain rare books in their possession. Mr. L. F. Powell, the learned and benevolent librarian of the Taylor Institution, Oxford, Professor F. B. Snyder, of Northwestern University, and Professors Sir William Craigie, George L. Marsh, and George Sherburn, of the University of Chicago, have aided me in the choice and verification of the texts and in the preparation of the appendixes. I am under obligation also to Mr. Geoffrey Keynes and the Nonesuch Press for permission to use the text of Blake contained in the excellent one-volume edition of his poetry and prose published in 1927; to the Cambridge University Press for authorization to include the text of Prior's *Jinny the Just* first printed from manuscript by A. R. Waller in 1907; and to the University of Chicago Press for permission to imitate the cover design of my *New Essays by Oliver Goldsmith.* My chief debt, however, is to my assistant, Mr. W. K. Chandler, from whose advice and criticism, freely given during the whole course of the undertaking, I have profited more than I can adequately say.

Contents

A

Collection of English Poems

1660–1800

Abraham Cowley

(1618-1633-1667)

To Sir William Davenant
Upon His Two First Books of Gondibert, Finished Before His Voyage to America[1]

Methinks *Heroick Poesie* till now
Like some fantastick *Fairy Land* did show,
Gods, Devils, Nymphs, Witches and *Gyants race,*
And all but *Man* in *Mans chief work* had place.
Thou like some worthy *Knight* with sacred Arms
Dost drive the *Monsters* thence, and end the *Charms.*
Instead of those dost *Men* and *Manners* plant,
The things which that rich *Soil* did chiefly want.
Yet ev'en thy *Mortals* do their *Gods* excell,
Taught by thy *Muse* to *Fight* and *Love* so well.
By fatal hands whilst *present Empires* fall,
Thine from the Grave *past Monarchies* recall.
So much more thanks from humane kind does merit
The *Poets Fury,* then the *Zelots Spirit.*
And from the *Grave* thou mak'est this *Empire* rise,
Not like some dreadful *Ghost* t'affright our Eyes,
But with more Lustre and triumphant state,
Then when it *crown'd* at proud *Verona* sate.
So will our *God rebuild* mans perisht frame,
And raise him up much *Better,* yet the *same.*
So *God-like Poets* do past things reherse,
Not *change,* but *Heighten* Nature by their Verse.
With shame, methinks, great *Italy* must see
Her *Conqu'erors* rais'd to *Life* again by *Thee.*
Rais'd by such pow'erful Verse, that ancient *Rome*
May blush no less to see her *Wit o'ercome.*
Some men their *Fancies* like their *Faith* derive,
And think all Ill but that which *Rome* does give.
The Marks of *Old* and *Catholick* would find,
To the same *Chair* would *Truth* and *Fiction* bind.
Thou in those beaten pathes disdain'st to tred,
And scorn'st to *Live* by robbing of the *Dead.*
Since Time does all things change, thou think'st not fit

[1] Published in *The Preface to Gondibert,* Paris, 1650. Text of *Works,* 1668.

This latter *Age* should see *all New but Wit.*
Thy *Fancy* like a *Flame* its way does make,
And leave bright *Tracks* for following Pens to take.
Sure 'twas this noble boldness of the *Muse*
Did thy desire to seek new *Worlds* infuse,
And ne're did Heav'n so much a *Voyage* bless,
If thou canst *Plant* but *there* with like success.

Ode. Of Wit[1]

TELL me, O tell, what kind of thing is *Wit*,
  Thou who *Master* art of it.
For the *First matter* loves *Variety* less;
Less *Women* lov't, either in *Love* or *Dress*.
  A thousand different shapes it bears,
  Comely in thousand shapes appears.
Yonder we saw it plain; and here 'tis now,
Like *Spirits* in a *Place*, we know not *How*.

London that vents of *false Ware* so much store,
  In no *Ware* deceives us more.
For men led by the *Colour*, and the *Shape*,
Like *Zeuxes Birds* fly to the painted *Grape*;
  Some things do through our Judgment pass
  As through a *Multiplying Glass*.
And sometimes, if the *Object* be too far,
We take a *Falling Meteor* for a *Star*.

Hence 'tis a *Wit* that greatest *word* of *Fame*
  Grows such a common Name.
And *Wits* by our *Creation* they become,
Just so, as *Tit'lar Bishops* made at *Rome*.
  'Tis not a *Tale*, 'tis not a *Jest*
  Admir'd with *Laughter* at a feast,
Nor florid *Talk* which can that *Title* gain;
The *Proofs* of *Wit* for ever must remain.

'Tis not to force some lifeless *Verses* meet
  With their five gowty feet.
All ev'ry where, like *Mans*, must be the *Soul*,
And *Reason* the *Inferior Powers* controul.
  Such were the *Numbers* which could call
  The *Stones* into the *Theban* wall.

[1] Published in *Poems*, 1656. Text of *Works*, 1668.

Such *Miracles* are ceast; and now we see
No *Towns* or *Houses* rais'd by *Poetrie*.

Yet 'tis not to adorn, and gild each part;
That shows more *Cost*, then *Art*.
Jewels at *Nose* and *Lips* but ill appear;
Rather then *all things Wit*, let *none* be there.
Several *Lights* will not be seen,
If there be nothing else between.
Men doubt, because they stand so thick i' th' skie,
If those be *Stars* which paint the *Galaxie*.

'Tis not when two like words make up one noise;
Jests for *Dutch Men*, and *English Boys*.
In which who finds out *Wit*, the same may see
In *An'grams* and *Acrostiques Poetrie*.
Much less can that have any place
At which a *Virgin* hides her face,
Such *Dross* the *Fire* must purge away; 'tis just
The *Author blush*, there where the *Reader* must.

'Tis not such *Lines* as almost crack the *Stage*
When *Bajazet* begins to rage.
Nor a tall *Meta'phor* in the *Bombast way*,
Nor the dry chips of short lung'd *Seneca*.
Nor upon all things to obtrude,
And force some odd *Similitude*.
What is it then, which like the *Power Divine*
We only can by *Negatives* define?

In a true piece of *Wit* all things must be,
Yet all things there *agree*.
As in the *Ark*, joyn'd without force or strife,
All *Creatures* dwelt; all *Creatures* that had *Life*.
Or as the *Primitive Forms* of all
(If we compare great things with small)
Which without *Discord* or *Confusion* lie,
In that strange *Mirror* of the *Deitie*.

But *Love* that moulds *One Man* up out of *Two*,
Makes me forget and injure you.
I took *you* for *my self* sure when I thought
That you in any thing were to be *Taught*.
Correct my error with thy Pen;
And if any ask me then,
What thing right *Wit*, and height of *Genius* is,
I'll onely shew your *Lines*, and say, *'Tis This*.

The Chronicle. A Ballad[1]

MARGARITA first possesst,
If I remember well, my brest,
Margarita first of all;
But when a while the wanton Maid
With my restless Heart had plaid,
Martha took the flying Ball.

Martha soon did it resign
To the beauteous *Catharine*.
Beauteous *Catharine* gave place
(Though loth and angry she to part
With the possession of my Heart)
To *Elisa*'s conqu'ering face.

Elisa till this Hour might reign
Had she not *Evil Counsels* ta'ne.
Fundamental Laws she broke,
And still new *Favorites* she chose,
Till up in *Arms* my *Passions* rose,
And cast away her yoke.

Mary then and gentle *Ann*
Both to reign at once began.
Alternately they sway'd,
And sometimes *Mary* was the *Fair*,
And sometimes *Ann* the *Crown* did wear,
And sometimes *Both* I' obey'd.

Another *Mary* then arose
And did rigorous Laws impose.
A mighty *Tyrant* she!
Long, alas, should I have been
Under that *Iron-Scepter'd Queen*,
Had not *Rebecca* set me free.

When fair *Rebecca* set me free,
'Twas then a *golden Time* with me.
But soon those pleasures fled,
For the gracious Princess dy'd
In her Youth and Beauties pride,
And *Judith* reigned in her sted.

[1] Published in *Poems*, 1656. Text of *Works*, 1668.

One Month, three Days, and half an Hour
   Judith held the *Soveraign Power.*
   Wondrous beautiful her Face,
But so weak and small her Wit,
That she to govern was unfit,
   And so *Susanna* took her place.

But when *Isabella* came
   Arm'd with a resistless flame
   And th' Artillery of her Eye;
Whilst she proudly marcht about
Greater Conquests to find out,
   She beat out *Susan* by the By.

But in her place I then obey'd
   Black-ey'd *Besse*, her *Viceroy-Maid*,
   To whom ensu'd a *Vacancy*.
Thousand worse *Passions* then possest
The *Interregnum* of my brest.
   Bless me from such an *Anarchy*!

Gentle *Henriette* than
   And a third *Mary* next began,
   Then *Jone*, and *Jane* and *Audria*.
And then a pretty *Thomasine*,
And then another *Katharine*,
   And then a *long Et cætera*.

But should I now to you relate,
   The strength and riches of their *state*,
   The *Powder*, *Patches*, and the *Pins*,
The *Ribbans*, *Jewels*, and the *Rings*,
The *Lace*, the *Paint*, and *warlike things*
   That make up all their *Magazins*:

If I should tell the politick Arts
   To take and keep mens hearts,
   The Letters, Embassies, and Spies,
The Frowns, and Smiles, and Flatteries,
The Quarrels, Tears, and Perjuries,
   Numberless, *Nameless Mysteries*!

And all the *Little Lime-twigs* laid
   By *Matchavil* the *Waiting-Maid*;
   I more voluminous should grow
(Chiefly if I like them should tell
All Change of *Weathers* that befell)
   Then *Holinshead* or *Stow*.

But I will briefer with them be,
Since few of them were long with Me.
An higher and a nobler strain
My present *Empress* does claim,
Heleonora, First o'th' Name;
Whom *God grant long to reign!*

Anacreontiques: or, Some Copies of Verses Translated Paraphrastically out of Anacreon[1]

Drinking

THE thirsty *Earth* soaks up the *Rain*,
And drinks, and gapes for drink again.
The *Plants* suck in the *Earth*, and are
With constant drinking fresh and fair.
The *Sea* it self, which one would think
Should have but little need of *Drink*,
Drinks ten thousand *Rivers* up,
So fill'd that they or'eflow the *Cup*.
The busie *Sun* (and one would guess
By's drunken fiery face no less)
Drinks up the *Sea*, and when h'as done,
The *Moon* and *Stars* drink up the *Sun*.
They drink and dance by their own light,
They drink and revel all the night.
Nothing in *Nature*'s *Sober* found,
But an eternal *Health* goes round.
Fill up the *Bowl* then, fill it high,
Fill all the *Glasses* there, for why
Should every creature drink but *I*,
Why, *Man* of *Morals*, tell me why?

The Praise of Pindar. In Imitation of Horace his second Ode, B. 4. Pindarum quisquis studet æmulari, &c.[2]

PINDAR is imitable by none;
The *Phœnix Pindar* is a vast *Species alone.*
Who e're but *Dædalus* with waxen wings could fly
And neither *sink* too low, nor *soar* too high?

[1] Published in *Poems*, 1656. Text of *Works*, 1668.
[2] Published in *Poems*, 1656. Text of *Works*, 1668.

What could he who *follow'd* claim,
But of vain *boldness* the unhappy fame,
And by his fall a *Sea* to name?
Pindars unnavigable Song
Like a swoln *Flood* from some steep *Mountain* pours along.
The *Ocean* meets with such a *Voice*
From his enlarged *Mouth,* as drowns the *Oceans* noise.

So *Pindar* does new *Words* and *Figures* roul
Down his impetuous *Dithyrambique Tide,*
Which in no *Channel* deigns t'abide,
Which neither *Banks* nor *Dikes* controul.
Whether th' *Immortal Gods* he sings
In a no less *Immortal strain,*
Or the great Acts of *God-descended Kings,*
Who in his Numbers still survive and *Reign.*
Each rich embroidered *Line,*
Which their triumphant *Brows* around,
By his sacred Hand is bound,
Does all their *starry Diadems* outshine.

Whether at *Pisa*'s race he please
To *carve* in polisht *Verse* the *Conque'rors Images,*
Whether the *Swift*, the *Skilful*, or the *Strong*,
Be crowned in his *Nimble, Artful, Vigorous* Song:
Whether some brave young mans untimely fate
In words worth *Dying for* he celebrate,
Such *mournful*, and such *pleasing* words,
As *joy* to his *Mothers* and his *Mistress grief* affords:
He bids him *Live* and *Grow* in fame,
Among the *Stars* he sticks his *Name*:
The *Grave* can but the *Dross* of him devour,
So *small* is *Deaths*, so *great* the *Poets* power.

Lo, how th'obsequious *Wind*, and swelling *Ayr*
The *Theban Swan* does upwards bear
Into the *walks* of *Clouds*, where he does play,
And with extended *Wings* opens his liquid way.
Whilst, alas, my *tim'erous Muse*
Unambitious tracks pursues;
Does with weak unballast wings,
About the *mossy Brooks* and *Springs*;
About the *Trees* new-blossom'ed *Heads*,
About the *Gardens* painted *Beds*,
About the *Fields* and flowry *Meads*,

And all *inferior beauteous things*
Like the laborious *Bee*,
For little drops of *Honey* flee,
And there with *Humble Sweets* contents her *Industrie.*

To the Royal Society[1]

PHILOSOPHY the great and only Heir
Of all that Human Knowledge which has bin
Unforfeited by Mans rebellious Sin,
Though full of years He do appear,
(Philosophy, I say, and call it, He,
For whatsoe'er the Painters Fancy be,
It a Male-virtue seems to me)
Has still been kept in Nonage till of late,
Nor manag'd or enjoy'd his vast Estate:
Three or four thousand years one would have thought,
To ripeness and perfection might have brought
A Science so well bred and nurst,
And of such hopeful parts too at the first.
But, oh, the Guardians and the Tutors then,
(Some negligent, and some ambitious men)
Would ne're consent to set him Free,
Or his own Natural Powers to let him see,
Lest that should put an end to their Autoritie.

That his own business he might quite forget,
They' amus'd him with the sports of wanton Wit,
With the Desserts of Poetry they fed him,
In stead of solid meats t' encrease his force;
In stead of vigorous exercise they led him
Into the pleasant Labyrinths of ever-fresh Discourse:
In stead of carrying him to see
The Riches which doe hoorded for him lie
In Natures endless Treasurie,
They chose his Eye to entertain
(His curious but not covetous Eye)
With painted Scenes, and Pageants of the Brain.
Some few exalted Spirits this latter Age has shown,
That labour'd to assert the Liberty
(From Guardians, who were now Usurpers grown)
Of this old *Minor* still, Captiv'd Philosophy;
But 'twas Rebellion call'd to fight
For such a long-oppressed Right.

[1] Published in Sprat's *History of the Royal Society*, 1667. Text of *Works*, 1668.

Bacon at last, a mighty Man, arose
Whom a wise King and Nature chose
Lord Chancellour of both their Lawes,
And boldly undertook the injur'd Pupils cause.

Autority, which did a Body boast,
Though 'twas but Air condens'd, and stalk'd about,
Like some old Giants more Gigantic Ghost,
To terrifie the Learned Rout
With the plain Magick of true Reasons Light,
He chac'd out of our sight,
Nor suffer'd Living *Men* to be misled
By the vain shadows of the Dead:
To Graves, from whence it rose, the conquer'd Phantome fled;
He broke that Monstrous God which stood
In midst of th' Orchard, and the whole did claim,
Which with a useless Sith of Wood,
And something else not worth a name,
(Both vast for shew, yet neither fit
Or to Defend, or to Beget;
Ridiculous and senceless Terrors!) made
Children and superstitious Men afraid.
The Orchard's open now, and free;
Bacon has broke that Scare-crow Deitie;
Come, enter, all that will,
Behold the rip'ned Fruit, come gather now your Fill.
Yet still, methinks, we fain would be
Catching at the Forbidden Tree,
We would be like the Deitie,
When Truth and Falshood, Good and Evil, we
Without the Sences aid within our selves would see;
For 'tis God only who can find
All Nature in his Mind.

From Words, which are but Pictures of the Thought,
(Though we our Thoughts from them perversly drew)
To things, the Minds right Object, he it brought,
Like foolish Birds to painted Grapes we flew;
He sought and gather'd for our use the True;
And when on heaps the chosen Bunches lay,
He prest them wisely the Mechanick way,
Till all their juyce did in one Vessel joyn,
Ferment into a Nourishment Divine,
The thirsty Souls refreshing Wine.
Who to the life an exact Piece would make,
Must not from others Work a Copy take;
No, not from *Rubens* or *Vandike*;
Much less content himself to make it like

Th' Idæas and the Images which lie
In his own Fancy, or his Memory.
No, he before his sight must place
The Natural and Living Face;
The real object must command
Each Judgment of his Eye, and Motion of his Hand.

From these and all long Errors of the way,
In which our wandring Prædecessors went,
And like th' old *Hebrews* many years did stray
In Desarts but of small extent,
Bacon, like *Moses*, led us forth at last,
The barren Wilderness he past,
Did on the very Border stand
Of the blest promis'd Land,
And from the Mountains Top of his Exalted Wit,
Saw it himself, and shew'd us it.
But Life did never to one Man allow
Time to Discover Worlds, and Conquer too;
Nor can so short a Line sufficient be
To fadome the vast depths of Natures Sea:
The work he did we ought t' admire,
And were unjust, if we should more require
From his few years, divided 'twixt th' Excess
Of low Affliction, and high Happiness.
For who on things remote can fix his sight,
That's alwayes in a Triumph, or a Fight?

From you, great Champions, we expect to get
These spacious Countries but discover'd yet;
Countries where yet in stead of Nature, we
Her Images and Idols worship'd see:
These large and wealthy Regions to subdue,
Though Learning has whole Armies at command,
Quarter'd about in every Land,
A better Troop she ne're together drew.
Methinks, like *Gideon*'s little Band,
God with Design has pickt out you,
To do these noble Wonders by a Few:
When the whole Host he saw, They are (said he)
Too many to o'rcome for Me;
And now he chuses out his Men,
Much in the way that he did then;
Not those many whom he found
Idely extended on the ground,
To drink with their dejected head

The Stream just so as by their Mouths it fled:
  No, but those Few who took the waters up,
And made of their laborious Hands the Cup.

Thus you prepar'd; and in the glorious Fight
  Their wondrous pattern too you take:
Their old and empty Pitchers first they brake,
And with their Hands then lifted up the Light.
  Io! Sound too the Trumpets here!
Already your victorious Lights appear;
New Scenes of Heaven already we espy,
And Crowds of golden Worlds on high;
Which from the spacious Plains of Earth and Sea;
  Could never yet discover'd be
By Sailers or *Chaldæans* watchful Eye.
Natures great Workes no distance can obscure,
No smalness her near Objects can secure;
  Y' have taught the curious Sight to press
  Into the privatest recess
Of her imperceptible Littleness.
  Y' have learn'd to Read her smallest Hand,
And well begun her deepest Sense to Understand.

Mischief and true Dishonour fall on those
Who would to laughter or to scorn expose
So Virtuous and so Noble a Design,
So Human for its Use, for Knowledge so Divine.
The things which these proud men despise, and call
  Impertinent, and vain, and small,
Those smallest things of Nature let me know,
Rather than all their greatest Actions Doe.
Whoever would Deposed Truth advance
  Into the Throne usurp'd from it,
Must feel at first the Blows of Ignorance,
  And the sharp Points of Envious Wit.
So when by various turns of the Celestial Dance,
  In many thousand years
  A Star, so long unknown, appears,
Though Heaven it self more beauteous by it grow,
It troubles and alarms the World below,
Does to the Wise a Star, to Fools a Meteor show.

With Courage and Success you the bold work begin;
  Your Cradle has not Idle bin:
None e're but *Hercules* and you could be
At five years Age worthy a History.
  And ne're did Fortune better yet

Th' Historian to the Story fit:
As you from all Old Errors free
And purge the Body of Philosophy;
So from all Modern Follies He
Has vindicated Eloquence and Wit.
His candid Stile like a clean Stream does slide,
And his bright Fancy all the way
Does like the Sun-shine in it play;
It does like *Thames*, the best of Rivers, glide,
Where the God does not rudely overturn,
But gently pour the Crystal Urn,
And with judicious hand does the whole Current Guide.
'T has all the Beauties Nature can impart,
And all the comely Dress without the paint of Art.

SIR WILLIAM DAVENANT

(1606-1635-1668)

Gondibert, An Heroick Poem[1]

Book II, Canto V

The House of Astragon; *where in distress*
Of Nature, Gondibert *for Art's redress*
Was by old Ulfin *brought: where Art's hard strife,*
In studying Nature for the aid of Life,
Is by full wealth and conduct easie made;
And Truth much visited, though in her shade.

FROM *Brescia* swiftly o're the bord'ring Plain,
Return we to the House of *Astragon*;
Where *Gondibert*, and his successful Train,
Kindly lament the Victory they won.

But though I Fame's great Book shall open now,
Expect a while, till she that *Decad* reads,
Which does this Dukes eternal Story show,
And aged *Ulfin* cites for special deeds.

Where Friendship is renown'd in *Ulfinore*;
Where th' ancient musick of delightful verse,

[1] Published in 1650. Text of *Works*, 1673.

Does it no less in *Goltho's* Breast adore,
And th' union of their equal hearts reherse.

These weary Victors the descending Sun
Led hither, where swift Night did them surprise;
And where, for valiant toiles, wise *Astragon*,
With sweet rewards of sleep, did fill their Eyes.

When to the needy World Day did appear,
And freely op'd her Treasury of light,
His House (where Art and Nature Tennants were)
The pleasure grew, and bus'ness of their sight.

Where *Ulfin* (who an old Domestick seems,
And rules as Master in the Owners Breast)
Leads *Goltho* to admire what he esteems;
And thus, what he had long observ'd, exprest.

Here Art by such a diligence is serv'd,
As does th' unwearied Planets imitate;
Whose motion (life of Nature) has preserv'd
The world, which God vouchsaf'd but to create.

Those heights, which else Dwarf Life could never reach,
Here, by the wings of diligence they climbe;
Truth (skar'd with Terms from canting Schools) they teach;
And buy it with their best sav'd Treasure, Time,

Here all Men seem Recov'rers of time past;
As busie as intentive *Emmets* are;
As alarm'd Armies that intrench in haste,
Or Cities, whom unlook'd-for sieges skare.

Much it delights the wise Observers Eye,
That all these toiles direct to sev'ral skills;
Some from the Mine to the hot Furnace hie,
And some from flowry Fields to weeping Stills.

The first to hopefull *Chymicks* matter bring,
Where Med'cine they extract for instant cure;
These bear the sweeter burthens of the Spring;
Whose vertues (longer known) though slow, are sure.

See there wet *Divers* from *Fossone* sent!
Who of the Seas deep Dwellers knowledge give;
Which (more unquiet then their Element)
By hungry war, upon each other live.

Pearl to their Lord, and Cordial Coral these
Present; which must in sharpest liquids melt;
He with *Nigella* cures that dull disease
They get, who long with stupid Fish have dwelt.

Others through Quarries dig, deeply below
Where Desart Rivers, cold, and private run;
Where Bodies conservation best they know,
And Mines long growth, and how their veines begun.

He shewes them now Tow'rs of prodigious height,
Where Natures Friends, Philosophers remain
To censure Meteors in their cause and flight,
And watch the Wind's authority on Rain.

Others with Optick Tubes the Moons scant face
(Vaste Tubes, which like long Cedars mounted lie)
Attract through Glasses to so near a space,
As if they came not to survey, but prie.

Nine hasty Centuries are now fulfill'd,
Since Opticks first were known to *Astragon*;
By whom the Moderns are become so skill'd,
They dream of seeing to the Maker's Throne.

And wisely *Astragon*, thus busie grew,
To seek the Stars remote societies;
And judge the walks of th' old, by finding new;
For Nature's law, in correspondence lies.

Man's pride (grown to Religion) he abates,
By moving our lov'd Earth; which we think fix'd;
Think all to it, and it to none relates;
With others motion scorn to have it mix'd;

As if 'twere great and stately to stand still
Whilst other Orbes dance on; or else think all
Those vaste bright Globes (to shew God's needless skill)
Were made but to attend our little Ball.

Now near a sever'd Building they discern'd
(Which seem'd, as in a pleasant shade, retir'd)
A Throng, by whose glad diligence they learn'd,
They came from Toyles which their own choice desir'd.

This they approach, and as they enter it
Their Eyes were stay'd, by reading o'er the Gate,

GREAT NATURES OFFICE, in large letters writ;
  And next, they mark'd who there in office sate.

Old busie Men, yet much for wisdom fam'd;
  Hasty to know, though not by haste beguil'd;
These fitly, NATURE'S REGISTERS were nam'd;
  The Throng were their INTELLIGENCERS stil'd:

Who stop by snares, and by their chace o'retake
  All hidden Beasts the closer Forrest yields;
All that by secret sence their rescue make,
  Or trust their force, or swiftness in the Fields.

And of this Throng, some their imployment have
  In fleeting Rivers, some fix'd Lakes beset;
Where Nature's self, by shifts, can nothing save
  From trifling Angles, or the swal'wing Net.

Some, in the spacious Ayre, their Prey o'retake,
  Cous'ning, with hunger, Falcons of their wings;
Whilst all their patient observations make,
  Which each to NATURE'S OFFICE duely brings.

And there of ev'ry Fish, and Foule, and Beast,
  The wiles these learned *Registers* record,
Courage, and feares, their motion and their rest;
  Which they prepare for their more learned Lord.

From hence to NATURES NURSERY they goe;
  Where seems to grow all that in *Eden* grew;
And more (if Art her mingled *Species* show)
  Then th' Hebrew King, Nature's Historian, knew.

Impatient *Simplers* climbe for Blossomes here;
  When Dewes (Heav'n's secret milk) in unseen show'rs
First feed the early Childhood of the year;
  And in ripe Summer, stoop for Hearbs and Flow'rs.

In Autumn, Seeds and Berries they provide;
  Where Nature a remaining force preserves;
In Winter digg for Roots, where she does hide
  That stock, which if consum'd, the next Spring sterves.

From hence (fresh Nature's flourishing Estate!)
  They to her wither'd Receptacle come;
Where she appears the loathsome Slave of Fate;
  For here her various Dead possess the Room.

This dismall Gall'ry, lofty, long, and wide;
  Was hung with *Skelitons* of ev'ry kinde;
Humane, and all that learned humane pride
  Thinks made t' obey Man's high immortal Minde.

Yet on that Wall hangs he too, who so thought;
  And she dry'd by him, whom that He obey'd;
By her an *El'phant* that with Heards had fought,
  Of which the smallest Beast made her afraid.

Next it, a Whale is high in Cables ty'd,
  Whose strength might Herds of Elephants controul;
Then all, (in payres of ev'ry kinde) they spy'd
  Which Death's wrack leaves, of Fishes, Beasts, and Fowl.

These *Astragon* (to watch with curious Eye
  The diff'rent Tenements of living breath)
Collects, with what far Travailers supply;
  And this was call'd, THE CABINET OF DEATH.

Which some the *Monument of Bodies*, name;
  The Arke, which saves from Graves all dying kindes;
This to a structure led, long known to Fame,
  And call'd, THE MONUMENT OF VANISH'D MINDES.

Where, when they thought they saw in well sought Books,
  Th' assembled soules of all that Men held wise,
It bred such awfull rev'rence in their looks,
  As if they saw the bury'd writers rise.

Such reaps of written thoughts (Gold of the Dead,
  Which Time does still disperse, but not devour)
Made them presume all was from Deluge free'd,
  Which long-liv'd-Authors writ ere *Noah's* Show'r.

They saw *Egyptian* Roles, which vastly great,
  Did like faln Pillars lie, and did display
The tale of Natures life, from her first heat,
  Till by the Flood o'er-cool'd, she felt decay.

And large as these (for Pens were Pencils then)
  Others that *Egypts* chiefest Science show'd;
Whose River forc'd Geometry on Men,
  Which did distinguish what the *Nyle* o're-flow'd.

Near them, in Piles, *Chaldean* Cous'ners lie;
  Who the hid bus'ness of the Stars relate;

Who make a Trade of worship'd Prophesie;
And seem to pick the Cabinet of Fate.

There *Persian Magi* stand; for wisdom prais'd;
Long since wise Statesmen, now *Magicians* thought;
Altars and Arts are soon to fiction rais'd,
And both would have, that miracles are wrought.

In a dark Text, these States-men left their Mindes;
For well they knew, that Monarch's Mistery
(Like that of Priests) but little rev'rence findes,
When they the Curtain op'e to ev'ry Eye.

Behinde this Throng, the talking *Greeks* had place;
Who Nature turn to Art, and Truth disguise,
As skill does native beauty oft deface;
With *Termes* they charm the weak, and pose the wise.

Now they the *Hebrew*, *Greek* and *Roman* spie;
Who for the Peoples ease, yoak'd them with Law;
Whom else, ungovern'd lusts would drive awry;
And each his own way frowardly would draw.

In little Tomes these grave first Lawyers lie,
In Volumes their Interpreters below;
Who first made Law an Art, then Misterie;
So cleerest springs, when troubled, cloudy grow.

But here, the Souls chief Book did all precede;
Our Map tow'rds Heav'n; to common Crowds deny'd;
Who proudly aim to teach, ere they can read;
And all must stray, where each will be a Guide.

About this sacred little Book did stand
Unweildly Volumes, and in number great;
And long it was since any Readers hand
Had reach'd them from their unfrequented Seat.

For a deep Dust (which Time does softly shed,
Where only Time does come) their Covers beare;
On which, grave Spyders, streets of Webbs had spread;
Subtle, and slight, as the grave Writers were.

In these, Heav'ns holy Fire does vainly burn;
Nor warms, nor lights, but is in Sparkles spent;
Where froward Authors, with disputes, have torn
The Garment seamless as the Firmament,

These are the old *Polemicks*, long since read,
 And shut by *Astragon*; who thought it just,
They, like the Authors (Truth's Tormentors) dead,
 Should lie unvisited, and lost in dust.

Here the *Arabian's* Gospel open lay,
 (Men injure Truth, who Fiction nicely hide)
Where they the *Monk*'s audacious stealths survey,
 From the World's first, and greater second Guide.

The Curious much perus'd this, then, new Book;
 As if some secret wayes to Heav'n it taught;
For straying from the old, men newer look,
 And prise the found, not finding those they sought.

We, in Tradition (Heav'n's dark Mapp) descrie
 Heav'n worse, then ancient Mapps farr *India* show;
Therefore in new, we search where Heav'n does lie;
 The Mind's sought Ophir, which we long to know.

Or as a Planter, though good Land he spies,
 Seeks new, and when no more so good he findes,
Doubly esteems the first; so Truth men prise;
 Truth, the discov'ry made by trav'ling Mindes.

And this false Book, till truly understood
 By *Astragon*, was openly display'd;
As counterfeit; false Princes, rather shou'd
 Be shewn abroad, then in close Prison lay'd.

Now to the old *Philosophers* they come;
 Who follow'd Nature with such just despaire,
As some do Kings farr off; and when at home,
 Like Courtiers, boast, that they deep secrets share.

Near them are grave dull *Moralists*, who give
 Counsell to such, as still in publick dwell;
At sea, in Courts, in Camps, and Citties live;
 And scorn experience from th' unpractis'd Cell.

Esop with these stands high, and they below;
 His pleasant wisdome mocks their gravity;
Who Vertue like a tedious Matron show,
 He dresses Nature to invite the Eye.

High skill their *Ethicks* seemes, whilst he stoops down
 To make the People wise; their learned pride

Makes all obscure, that Men may prise the Gown;
With ease he teaches, what with pain they hide.

And next (as if their bus'ness rul'd Mankinde)
Historians stand, bigg as their living looks;
Who thought, swift Time they could in fetters binde;
Till his Confessions they had ta'ne in Books:

But Time oft scap'd them in the shades of Night;
And was in Princes Closets oft conceal'd,
And hid in Battels smoke; so what they Write
Of Courts and Camps, is oft by guess reveal'd.

Near these, *Physitians* stood; who but reprieve
Like life a Judge, whom greater pow'r does awe;
And cannot an Almighty pardon give;
So much yields Subject Art to Nature's Law.

And not weak Art, but Nature we upbraid,
When our frail essence proudly we take ill;
Think we are robb'd, when first we are decay'd,
And those were murder'd whom her law did kill.

Now they refresh, after this long survey,
With pleasant *Poets*, who the Soul sublime;
Fame's *Heraulds*, in whose Triumphs they make way;
And place all those whom Honor helps to climbe.

And he who seem'd to lead this ravish'd Race,
Was Heav'n's lov'd *Laureat*, that in *Jewry* writ;
Whose Harp approach'd Gods Ear, though none his Face
Durst see, and first made inspiration, wit.

And his Attendants, such blest Poets are,
As make unblemish'd Love, Courts best delight;
And sing the prosp'rous Battels of just warre;
By these the loving, Love, and valiant, fight.

O hireless Science! and of all alone
The Liberal! Meanly the rest each State
In pension treats, but this depends on none;
Whose worth they rev'rendly forbear to rate.

SIR JOHN DENHAM

(1615-1642-1669)

Cooper's Hill[1]

SURE there are Poets which did never dream
Upon *Parnassus*, nor did tast the stream
Of *Helicon*, we therefore may suppose
Those made no Poets, but the Poets those.
And as Courts make not Kings, but Kings the Court,
So where the Muses & their train resort,
Parnassus stands; if I can be to thee
A Poet, thou *Parnassus* are to me.
Nor wonder, if (advantag'd in my flight,
By taking wing from thy auspicious height)
Through untrac't ways, and aery paths I fly,
More boundless in my Fancy than my eie:
My eye, which swift as thought contracts the space
That lies between, and first salutes the place
Crown'd with that sacred pile, so vast, so high,
That whether 'tis a part of Earth, or sky,
Uncertain seems, and may be thought a proud
Aspiring mountain, or descending cloud,
Pauls, the late theme of such a Muse whose flight
Has bravely reach't and soar'd above thy height:
Now shalt thou stand though sword, or time, or fire,
Or zeal more fierce than they, thy fall conspire,
Secure, whilst thee the best of Poets sings,
Preserv'd from ruine by the best of Kings.
Under his proud survey the City lies,
And like a mist beneath a hill doth rise;
Whose state and wealth the business and the crowd,
Seems at this distance but a darker cloud:
And is to him who rightly things esteems,
No other in effect than what it seems:
Where, with like hast, though several ways, they run
Some to undo, and some to be undone;
While luxury, and wealth, like war and peace,
Are each the others ruine, and increase;
As Rivers lost in Seas some secret vein
Thence reconveighs, there to be lost again.
Oh happiness of sweet retir'd content!

[1] Published in 1642. Text of *Poems and Translations*, 1668.

To be at once secure, and innocent.
Windsor the next (where *Mars* with *Venus* dwells.
Beauty with strength) above the Valley swells
Into my eye, and doth it self present
With such an easie and unforc't ascent,
That no stupendious precipice denies
Access, no horror turns away our eyes:
But such a Rise, as doth at once invite
A pleasure, and a reverence from the sight.
Thy mighty Masters Embleme, in whose face
Sate meekness, heightned with Majestick Grace
Such seems thy gentle height, made only proud
To be the basis of that pompous load,
Than which, a nobler weight no Mountain bears,
But *Atlas* only that supports the Sphears.
When Natures hand this ground did thus advance,
'Twas guided by a wiser power than Chance;
Mark't out for such a use, as if 'twere meant
T' invite the builder, and his choice prevent.
Nor can we call it choice, when what we chuse,
Folly, or blindness only could refuse.
A Crown of such Majestick towrs doth Grace
The Gods great Mother, when her heavenly race
Do homage to her, yet she cannot boast
Amongst that numerous, and Celestial host,
More *Hero's* than can *Windsor*, nor doth Fames
Immortal book record more noble names.
Not to look back so far, to whom this Isle
Owes the first Glory of so brave a pile,
Whether to *Cæsar, Albanact*, or *Brute*,
The Brittish *Arthur*, or the Danish *Knute*,
(Though this of old no less contest did move,
Then when for *Homers* birth seven Cities strove)
(Like him in birth, thou should'st be like in fame,
As thine his fate, if mine had been his Flame)
But whosoere it was, Nature design'd
First a brave place, and then as brave a mind.
Not to recount those several Kings, to whom
It gave a Cradle, or to whom a Tombe,
But thee (great *Edward*) and thy greater son,
(The lillies which his Father wore, he won)
And thy *Bellona*, who the Consort came
Not only to thy Bed, but to thy Fame,
She to thy Triumph led one Captive King,
And brought that son, which did the second bring.
Then didst thou found that Order (whither love
Or victory thy Royal thoughts did move)
Each was a noble cause, and nothing less,

Than the design, has been the great success:
Which forraign Kings, and Emperors esteem
The second honour to their Diadem.
Had thy great Destiny but given thee skill,
To know as well, as power to act her will,
That from those Kings, who then thy captives were,
In after-times should spring a Royal pair
Who should possess all that thy mighty power,
Or thy desires more mighty, did devour;
To whom their better Fate reserves what ere
The Victor hopes for, or the Vanquisht fear;
That bloud, which thou and thy great Grandsire shed,
And all that since these sister Nations bled,
Had been unspilt, had happy *Edward* known
That all the bloud he spilt, had been his own.
When he that Patron chose, in whom are joyn'd
Souldier and Martyr, and his arms confin'd
Within the Azure Circle, he did seem
But to foretell, and prophesie of him,
Who to his Realms that Azure round hath joyn'd,
Which Nature for their bound at first design'd.
That bound, which to the Worlds extreamest ends,
Endless it self, its liquid arms extends;
Nor doth he need those Emblemes which we paint,
But is himself the Souldier and the Saint.
Here should my wonder dwell, & here my praise,
But my fixt thoughts my wandring eye betrays,
Viewing a neighbouring hill, whose top of late
A Chappel crown'd, till in the Common Fate,
The adjoyning Abby fell: (may no such storm
Fall on our times, where ruine must reform.)
Tell me (my Muse) what monstrous dire offence,
What crime could any Christian King incense
To such a rage? was't Luxury, or Lust?
Was he so temperate, so chast, so just?
Were these their crimes? they were his own much more:
But wealth is Crime enough to him that's poor,
Who having spent the Treasures of his Crown,
Condemns their Luxury to feed his own.
And yet this Act, to varnish o're the shame
Of sacriledge, must bear devotions name.
No Crime so bold, but would be understood
A real, or at least a seeming good.
Who fears not to do ill, yet fears the Name,
And free from Conscience, is a slave to Fame.
Thus he the Church at once protects, & spoils:
But Princes swords are sharper than their stiles.
And thus to th' ages past he makes amends,

Their Charity destroys, their Faith defends.
Then did Religion in a lazy Cell,
In empty, airy contemplations dwell;
And like the block, unmoved lay: but ours,
As much too active, like the stork devours.
Is there no temperate Region can be known,
Betwixt their Frigid, and our Torrid Zone?
Could we not wake from that Lethargick dream,
But to be restless in a worse extream?
And for that Lethargy was there no cure,
But to be cast into a Calenture?
Can knowledge have no bound, but must advance
So far, to make us wish for ignorance?
And rather in the dark to grope our way,
Than led by a false guide to erre by day?
Who sees these dismal heaps, but would demand
What barbarous Invader sackt the land?
But when he hears, no Goth, no Turk did bring
This desolation, but a Christian King;
When nothing, but the Name of Zeal, appears
'Twixt our best actions and the worst of theirs,
What does he think our Sacriledge would spare,
When such th' effects of our devotions are?
Parting from thence 'twixt anger, shame, & fear,
Those for whats past, & this for whats too near:
My eye descending from the Hill, surveys
Where *Thames* amongst the wanton vallies strays.
Thames, the most lov'd of all the Oceans sons,
By his old Sire to his embraces runs,
Hasting to pay his tribute to the Sea,
Like mortal life to meet Eternity.
Though with those streams he no resemblance hold,
Whose foam is Amber, and their Gravel Gold;
His genuine, and less guilty wealth t' explore,
Search not his bottom, but survey his shore;
Ore which he kindly spreads his spacious wing,
And hatches plenty for th' ensuing Spring.
Nor then destroys it with too fond a stay,
Like Mothers which their Infants overlay.
Nor with a sudden and impetuous wave,
Like profuse Kings, resumes the wealth he gave.
No unexpected inundations spoyl
The mowers hopes, nor mock the plowmans toyl:
For God-like his unwearied Bounty flows;
First loves to do, then loves the Good he does.
Nor are his Blessings to his banks confin'd,
But free, and common, as the Sea or Wind;
When he to boast, or to disperse his stores

Full of the tributes of his grateful shores,
Visits the world, and in his flying towers
Brings home to us, and makes both *Indies* ours;
Finds wealth where 'tis, bestows it where it wants
Cities in deserts, woods in Cities plants.
So that to us no thing, no place is strange,
While his fair bosom is the worlds exchange.
O could I flow like thee, and make thy stream
My great example, as it is my theme!
Though deep, yet clear, though gentle, yet not dull,
Strong without rage, without ore-flowing full.
Heaven her *Eridanus* no more shall boast,
Whose Fame in thine, like lesser Currents lost,
Thy Nobler streams shall visit *Jove's* aboads,
To shine amongst the Stars, and bath the Gods.
Here Nature, whether more intent to please
Us or her self, with strange varieties,
(For things of wonder give no less delight
To the wise Maker's, than beholders sight.
Though these delights from several causes move
For so our children, thus our friends we love)
Wisely she knew, the harmony of things,
As well as that of sounds, from discords springs.
Such was the discord, which did first disperse
Form, order, beauty through the Universe;
While driness moysture, coldness heat resists,
All that we have, and that we are, subsists.
While the steep horrid roughness of the Wood
Strives with the gentle calmness of the flood.
Such huge extreams when Nature doth unite,
Wonder from thence results, from thence delight.
The stream is so transparent, pure, and clear,
That had the self-enamour'd youth gaz'd here,
So fatally deceiv'd he had not been,
While he the bottom, not his face had seen.
But his proud head the aery Mountain hides
Among the Clouds; his shoulders, and his sides
A shady mantle cloaths; his curled brows
Frown on the gentle stream, which calmly flows,
While winds and storms his lofty forehead beat:
The common fate of all that's high or great.
Low at his foot a spacious plain is plac't,
Between the mountain and the stream embrac't:
Which shade and shelter from the Hill derives,
While the kind river wealth and beauty gives;
And in the mixture of all these appears
Variety, which all the rest indears.
This scene had some bold Greek, or Brittish Bard

Beheld of old, what stories had we heard,
Of Fairies, Satyrs, and the Nymphs their Dames,
Their feasts, their revels, & their amorous flames:
'Tis still the same, although their aery shape
All but a quick Poetick sight escape.
There *Faunus* and *Sylvanus* keep their Courts,
And thither all the horned hoast resorts,
To graze the ranker mead, that noble heard
On whose sublime and shady fronts is rear'd
Natures great Master-piece; to shew how soon
Great things are made, but sooner are undone.
Here have I seen the King, when great affairs
Give leave to slacken, and unbend his cares,
Attended to the Chase by all the flower
Of youth, whose hopes a Nobler prey devour:
Pleasure with Praise, & danger, they would buy,
And wish a foe that would not only fly.
The stagg now conscious of his fatal Growth,
At once indulgent to his fear and sloth,
To some dark covert his retreat had made,
Where nor mans eye, nor heavens should invade
His soft repose; when th' unexpected sound
Of dogs, and men, his wakeful ear doth wound.
Rouz'd with the noise, he scarce believes his ear,
Willing to think th' illusions of his fear
Had given this false Alarm, but straight his view
Confirms, that more than all he fears is true.
Betray'd in all his strengths, the wood beset,
All instruments, all Arts of ruine met;
He calls to mind his strength, and then his speed,
His winged heels, and then his armed head;
With these t' avoid, with that his Fate to meet:
But fear prevails, and bids him trust his feet.
So fast he flyes, that his reviewing eye
Has lost the chasers, and his ear the cry;
Exulting, till he finds, their Nobler sense
Their disproportion'd speed does recompense.
Then curses his conspiring feet, whose scent
Betrays that safety which their swiftness lent.
Then tries his friends, among the baser herd,
Where he so lately was obey'd, and fear'd,
His safety seeks: the herd, unkindly wise,
Or chases him from thence, or from him flies.
Like a declining States-man, left forlorn
To his friends pity, and pursuers scorn,
With shame remembers, while himself was one
Of the same herd, himself the same had done.
Thence to the coverts, & the conscious Groves,

The scenes of his past triumphs, and his loves;
Sadly surveying where he rang'd alone
Prince of the soyl, and all the herd his own;
And like a bold Knight Errant did proclaim
Combat to all, and bore away the Dame;
And taught the woods to eccho to the stream
His dreadful challenge, and his clashing beam.
Yet faintly now declines the fatal strife;
So much his love was dearer than his life.
Now every leaf, and every moving breath
Presents a foe, and every foe a death.
Wearied, forsaken, and pursu'd, at last
All safety in despair of safety plac'd,
Courage he thence resumes, resolv'd to bear
All their assaults, since 'tis in vain to fear.
And now too late he wishes for the fight
That strength he wasted in Ignoble flight:
But when he sees the eager chase renew'd,
Himself by dogs, the dogs by men pursu'd:
He straight revokes his bold resolve, and more
Repents his courage, than his fear before;
Finds that uncertain waies unsafest are,
And Doubt a greater mischief than Despair.
Then to the stream, when neither friends, nor force,
Nor speed, nor Art avail, he shapes his course;
Thinks not their rage so desperate t' assay
An Element more merciless than they.
But fearless they pursue, nor can the floud
Quench their dire thirst; alas, they thirst for bloud.
So towards a Ship the oarefin'd Gallies ply,
Which wanting Sea to ride, or wind to fly,
Stands but to fall reveng'd on those that dare
Tempt the last fury of extream despair.
So fares the Stagg among th' enraged Hounds,
Repels their force, and wounds returns for wounds.
And as a Hero, whom his baser foes
In troops surround, now these assails, now those,
Though prodigal of life, disdains to die
By common hands; but if he can descry
Some nobler foes approach, to him he calls,
And begs his Fate, and then contented falls.
So when the King a mortal shaft lets fly
From his unerring hand, then glad to dy,
Proud of the wound, to it resigns his bloud,
And stains the Crystal with a Purple floud.
This a more Innocent, and happy chase,
Than when of old, but in the self-same place,
Fair liberty pursu'd, and meant a Prey

To lawless power, here turn'd, and stood at bay.
When in that remedy all hope was plac't
Which was, or should have been at least, the last.
Here was that Charter seal'd, wherein the Crown
All marks of Arbitrary power lays down:
Tyrant and slave, those names of hate and fear,
The happier stile of King and Subject bear:
Happy, when both to the same Center move,
When Kings give liberty, and Subjects love.
Therefore not long in force this Charter stood;
Wanting that seal, it must be seal'd in bloud.
The Subjects arm'd, the more their Princes gave,
Th' advantage only took the more to crave:
Till Kings by giving, give themselves away,
And even that power, that should deny, betray.
"Who gives constrain'd, but his own fear reviles
"Not thank't, but scorn'd; nor are they gifts, but spoils.
Thus Kings, by grasping more than they could hold,
First made their Subjects by oppression bold:
And popular sway, by forcing Kings to give
More than was fit for Subjects to receive,
Ran to the same extreams; and one excess
Made both, by striving to be greater, less.
When a calm River rais'd with sudden rains,
Or Snows dissolv'd, oreflows th' adjoyning Plains,
The Husbandmen with high-rais'd banks secure
Their greedy hopes, and this he can endure.
But if with Bays and Dams they strive to force
His channel to a new, or narrow course;
No longer then within his banks he dwells,
First to a Torrent, then a Deluge swells:
Stronger, and fiercer by restraint he roars,
And knows no bound, but makes his power his shores.

Natura Naturata[1]

WHAT gives us that Fantastick Fit,
That all our Judgment and our Wit
To vulgar custom we submit?

Treason, Theft, Murther, all the rest
Of that foul Legion we so detest,
Are in their proper names exprest.

[1] Published in *Poems and Translations,* 1668. Text of first edition.

Why is it then taught sin or shame,
Those necessary parts to name,
From whence we went, and whence we came?

Nature, what ere she wants, requires;
With Love enflaming our desires,
Finds Engines fit to quench those fires:

Death she abhors; yet when men die,
We are present; but no stander by
Looks on when we that loss supply:

Forbidden Wares sell twice as dear;
Even Sack prohibited last year,
A most abominable rate did bear.

'Tis plain our eyes and ears are nice,
Only to raise by that device,
Of those Commodities the price.

Thus Reason's shadows us betray
By Tropes and Figures led astray,
From Nature, both her Guide and way.

EDMUND WALLER

(1606-1645-1687)

To the King on His Navy[1]

WHERE e're thy Navy spreads her canvas wings,
Homage to thee, and Peace to all she brings.
The *French* and *Spaniard*, when thy Flags appear,
Forget their Hatred, and consent to fear.
So *Jove* from *Ida* did both Hosts survey,
And when he pleas'd to Thunder, part the fray.
Ships heretofore in Seas like Fishes sped,
The mighty still upon the smaller fed.
Thou on the deep imposest Nobler Laws,
And by that Justice hath remov'd the Cause
Of those rude Tempests, which for Rapine sent,

[1] Published in *Poems*, 1645. Text of *Poems, &c. Written upon Several Occasions*, 5th ed., 1686.

Too oft alas, involv'd the innocent.
Now shall the Ocean, as thy *Thames*, be free
From both those fates, of Storms, and Piracy:
But we most happy, who can fear no force
But winged Troops, or Pegasean Horse:
'Tis not so hard for greedy foes to spoil
Another Nation, as to touch our soil.
Should Natures self invade the World again,
And o're the Center spread the liquid Main;
Thy power were safe, and her destructive hand
Would but enlarge the bounds of thy command.
Thy dreadful Fleet would stile thee Lord of all,
And ride in Triumph o're the drowned Ball.
Those Towers of Oak o're fertile plains might go,
And visit Mountains where they once did grow.
  The Worlds Restorer never could endure,
That finish'd *Babel* should those men secure,
Whose Pride design'd that Fabrick to have stood
Above the reach of any second Flood:
To thee his Chosen more indulgent, he
Dares trust such Power with so much Piety.

The Battle of the Summer-Islands[1]

Canto I

What Fruits they have, and how Heaven smiles
Upon those late discovered Isles.

AID me *Bellona*, while the dreadful Fight
Betwixt a Nation and two Whales I write:
Seas stained with goar, I sing, advent'rous toyl,
And how these Monsters did disarm an Isle.
  Bermudas wall'd with Rocks, who does not know,
That happy Island, where huge Lemons grow,
And Orange trees which Golden Fruit do bear,
Th' Hesperian Garden boasts of none so fair?
Where shining Pearl, Coral, and many a pound,
On the rich Shore, of Amber-greece is found:
The lofty Cedar, which to Heaven aspires,
The Prince of Trees, is fewel for their Fires:
The smoak by which their loaded spits do turn,
For incense might, on Sacred Altars burn:

[1] Published in *Poems*, 1645. Text of *Poems, &c. Written upon Several Occasions*, 5th ed., 1686.

Their private Roofs on od'rous Timber born,
Such as might Palaces for Kings adorn.
The sweet *Palmettas* a new *Bacchus* yield,
With Leaves as ample as the broadest shield:
Under the shadow of whose friendly Boughs
They sit carowsing, where their Liquor grows.
Figs there unplanted through the Fields do grow,
Such as fierce *Cato* did the *Romans* show,
With the rare Fruit inviting them to spoil
Carthage the Mistriss of so rich a soil.
The naked Rocks are not unfruitful there,
But at some constant seasons every year,
Their barren tops with luscious Food abound,
And with the eggs of various Fowls are crown'd:
Tobacco is the worst of things, which they
To *English* Land-lords as their Tribute pay:
Such is the Mould, that the Blest Tenant feeds
On precious Fruits, and pays his Rent in Weeds:
With candid Plantines, and the jucy Pine,
On choicest Melons and sweet Grapes they dine;
And with Potatoes fat their wanton Swine.
Nature these Cates with such a lavish hand
Pours out among them, that our courser Land
Tastes of that bounty, and does Cloth return,
Which not for Warmth, but Ornament is worn:
For the king Spring which but salutes us here,
Inhabits there, and courts them all the year:
Ripe Fruits and blossoms on the same Trees live;
At once they promise, what at once they give:
So sweet the Air, so moderate the Clime;
None sickly lives, or dies before his time.
Heaven sure has kept this spot of earth uncurst,
To shew how all things were Created first.
The tardy Plants in our cold Orchards plac'd,
Reserve their Fruit for the next ages taste:
There a small grain in some few Months will be
A firm, a lofty, and a spacious Tree:
The *Palma Christi*, and the fair *Papah*,
Now but a seed (preventing Natures law)
In half the Circle of the hasty year
Project a shade, and lovely fruit do wear:
And as their Trees in our dull Region set
But faintly grow, and no perfection get;
So in this *Northern* Tract our hoarser Throats
Utter unripe and ill-constrained notes:
Where the supporter of the Poets style,
Phœbus, on them eternally does smile.
O how I long! my careless Limbs to lay

Under the Plantanes shade, and all the day
With am'rous Airs my fancy entertain,
Invoke the Muses, and improve my vein!
No passion there in my free breast should move,
None but the sweet and best of passions, Love:
There while I sing, if gentle Love be by
That tunes my Lute, and winds the Strings so high,
With the sweet sound of *Sacharissa*'s name,
I'll make the listning Savages grow tame.
But while I do these pleasing dreams indite,
I am diverted from the promis'd fight.

Canto II

Of their alarm, and how their Foes
Discovered were, this Canto *shows.*

Though Rocks so high about this Island rise,
That well they may the num'rous Turk despise;
Yet is no humane fate exempt from fear,
Which shakes their hearts, while through the Isle they hear
A lasting noise, as horrid and as loud
As Thunder makes, before it breaks the Cloud.
Three days they dread this murmur, e're they know
From what blind cause th' unwonted sound may grow:
At length Two Monsters of unequal size,
Hard by the shoar a Fisher-man espies;
Two mighty Whales, which swelling Seas had tost,
And left them prisoners on the rocky Coast;
One as a Mountain vast, and with her came
A Cub not much inferior to his Dame:
Here in a Pool among the Rocks engag'd,
They roar'd like Lions, caught in toyls, and rag'd:
The man knew what they were, who heretofore
Had seen the like lie murdered on the shore,
By the wild fury of some Tempest cast
The fate of ships and shipwrackt men to taste.
As careless Dames whom Wine and Sleep betray
To frantick dreams their Infants overlay:
So there sometimes the raging Ocean fails,
And her own brood exposes; when the Whales
Against sharp Rocks like reeling vessels quasht,
Though huge as Mountains, are in pieces dasht;
Along the shore their dreadful Limbs lie scatter'd,
Like Hills with Earthquakes shaken, torn & shatter'd.
Hearts sure of Brass they had, who tempted first,
Rude Seas that spare not what themselves have nurst.
The welcome news through all the Nation spread,

To sudden joy and hope converts their dread.
What lately was their publique terror, they
Behold with glad eyes as a certain prey;
Dispose already of th' untaken spoil,
And as the purchase of their future toil,
These share the Bones, and they divide the Oyl;
So was the Huntsman by the Bear opprest,
Whose Hide he sold before he caught the Beast.
  They man their Boats, and all their young men arm
With whatsoever may the Monsters harm;
Pikes, Halberts, Spits, and Darts that wound so far,
The Tools of Peace, and Instruments of War:
Now was the time for vig'rous Lads to show
What love or honor could invite them to;
A goodly Theatre where Rocks are round
With reverend age, and lovely Lasses crown'd:
Such was the Lake which held this dreadful pair
Within the bounds of noble *Warwicks* share:
Warwicks bold Earl, than which no title bears
A greater sound among our British Peers;
And worthy he the memory to renew,
The fate and honor to that title due;
Whose brave adventures have transferr'd his name,
And through the new world spread his growing fame.
  But how they fought, & what their valour gain'd,
  Shall in another Canto be contain'd.

Canto III

The bloody fight, successless toyl,
And how the Fishes sack'd the Isle.

THE Boat which on the first assault did go
Struck with a harping Iron the younger fo;
Who when he felt his side so rudely goar'd,
Loud as the Sea that nourish't him he roar'd.
As a broad Bream to please some curious tast,
While yet alive in boyling water cast,
Vex't with unwonted heat, boyls, flings about
The scorching brass, and hurls the liquor out:
So with the barbed Javeling stung, he raves,
And scourges with his tayl the suffering waves:
Like *Spencer's Talus* with his Iron flayl,
He threatens ruin with his pondrous tayl;
Dissolving at one stroke the battered Boat,
And down the men fall drenched in the Moat:
With every fierce encounter they are forc't

To quit their Boats, and fare like men unhorst.
  The bigger Whale like some huge Carrack lay,
Which wanteth Sea room, with her foes to play;
Slowly she swims, and when provok'd she wo'd
Advance her tail, her head salutes the mud;
The shallow water doth her force infringe,
And renders vain her tails impetuous swinge:
The shining steel her tender sides receive,
And there like Bees they all their weapons leave.
  This sees the Cub, and does himself oppose
Betwixt his cumbred mother and her foes:
With desperate courage he receives her wounds,
And men and boats his active tayl confounds.
Their forces joyn'd, the Seas with billows fill,
And make a tempest, though the winds be still.
  Now would the men with half their hoped prey
Be well content, and wish this Cub away:
Their wish they have; he to direct his dam
Unto the gap through which they thither came,
Before her swims, and quits the hostile Lake,
A pris'ner there, but for his mothers sake.
She by the Rocks compell'd to stay behind,
Is by the vastness of her bulk confin'd.
They shout for joy, and now on her alone
Their fury falls, and all their Darts are thrown.
Their Lances spent; one bolder than the rest
With his broad sword provok'd the sluggish beast:
Her oily side devours both blade and heft,
And there his Steel the bold Bermudian left.
Courage the rest from his example take,
And now they change the colour of the Lake:
Blood flows in Rivers from her wounded side,
As if they would prevent the tardy tide,
And raise the flood to that propitious height,
As might convey her from this fatal streight.
She swims in blood, and blood do's spouting throw
To Heaven, that Heaven mens cruelties might know.
Their fixed Javelins in her side she wears,
And on her back a grove of Pikes appears:
You would have thought, had you the monster seen
Thus drest, she had another Island been.
Roaring she tears the air with such a noise,
(As well resembled the conspiring voice
Of routed Armies, when the field is won)
To reach the ears of her escaped son.
He (though a league removed from the fo)
Hastes to her aid; the pious Trojan so
Neglecting for *Creusas* life his own,

Repeats the danger of the burning Town.
The men amazed blush to see the seed
Of monsters, human piety exceed:
Well proves this kindness what the Grecians sung,
That Loves bright mother from the Ocean sprung.
Their courage droops, and hopeless now they wish
For composition with th' unconquer'd fish:
So she their weapons would restore again,
Through Rocks they'd hew her passage to the main.
But how instructed in each others mind,
Or what commerce can men with monsters find?
Not daring to approach their wounded foe,
Whom her couragious son protected so;
They charge their Muskets, and with hot desire
Of full revenge, renew the fight with fire:
Standing a looff, with lead they bruise the scales,
And tear the flesh of the incensed Whales.
But no success their fierce endeavours found,
Nor this way could they give one fatal wound.
Now to their Fort they are about to send
For the loud Engines which their Isle defend.
But what those pieces fram'd to batter walls
Would have effected on those mighty Whales,
Great *Neptune* will not have us know, who sends
A tyde so high, that it relieves his friends.
And thus they parted with exchange of harms;
Much blood the Monsters lost, and they their Arms.

To Phillis[1]

PHILLIS, why should we delay
Pleasures shorter than the day?
Could we (which we never can)
Stretch our lives beyond their span;
Beauty like a shadow flies,
And our youth before us dies;
Or would youth and beauty stay,
Love hath wings, and will away.
Love hath swifter wings than Time;
Change in love to Heaven does clime.
Gods that never change their state,
Vary oft their love and hate.
Phillis, to this truth we owe,

[1] Published in *Poems,* 1645. Text of *Poems, &c. Written upon Several Occasions,* 5th ed., 1686.

All the love betwixt us two:
Let not you and I require,
What has been our past desire;
On what Shepherds you have smil'd,
Or what Nymphs I have beguil'd;
Leave it to the Planets too,
What we shall hereafter do;
For the joys we now may prove,
Take advice of present love.

On a Girdle[1]

THAT which her slender waste confin'd,
Shall now my joyful Temples bind;
No Monarch but would give his Crown,
His Arms might do what this has done.

It was my Heaven's extreamest Sphear,
The Pale which held that lovely Dear;
My Joy, my Grief, my Hope, my Love,
Did all within this Circle move.

A narrow compass, and yet there
Dwelt all that's good, and all that's fair:
Give me but what this Riban bound,
Take all the rest the Sun goes round.

Song[2]

Go LOVELY Rose,
Tell her that wastes her time and me,
That now she knows,
When I resemble her to thee,
How sweet and fair she seems to be.

Tell her that's young,
And shuns to have her Graces spy'd,
That hadst thou sprung

[1] Published in *Poems,* 1645. Text of *Poems, &c. Written upon Several Occasions,* 5th ed., 1686.

[2] Published in *Poems,* 1645. Text of *Poems, &c. Written upon Several Occasions,* 5th ed., 1686.

In Desarts, where no men abide,
Thou must have uncommended dy'd.

Small is the worth
Of Beauty from the light retir'd;
Bid her come forth,
Suffer her self to be desir'd,
And not blush so to be admir'd.

Then die, that she,
The common fate of all things rare,
May read in thee;
How small a part of time they share,
That are so wondrous sweet and fair.

On St. James's Park, as Lately Improved by His Majesty[1]

OF THE first Paradice there's nothing found,
Plants set by Heav'n are vanisht, & the ground;
Yet the description lasts; who knows the fate
Of lines that shall this Paradice relate?
Instead of Rivers rowling by the side
Of *Eden*'s Garden, here flows in the Tyde;
The Sea which always serv'd his Empire, now
Pays Tribute to our Prince's pleasure too:
Of famous Cities we the Founders know;
But Rivers old, as Seas, to which they go,
Are Nature's bounty; 'tis of more Renown
To make a River than to build a Town.
For future shade young Trees upon the banks
Of the new stream appear in even ranks:
The voice of *Orpheus* or *Amphion*'s hand
In better order could not make them stand;
May they increase as fast, and spread their boughs,
As the high Fame of their great Owner grows!
May he live long enough to see them all
Dark shadows cast, and as his Palace tall.
Methinks I see the love that shall be made,
The Lovers walking in that amorous shade,
The Gallants dancing by the Rivers side,
They bathe in Summer, and in Winter slide.

[1] Published in 1661. Text of *Poems, &c. Written upon Several Occasions*, 5th ed., 1686.

Methinks I hear the Musick in the Boats,
And the loud Eccho which returns the Notes,
Whilst over head a flock of new sprung Fowl
Hangs in the Air, and does the Sun controul:
Darkning the Sky they hover o're, and shrowd
The wanton Sailors with a feather'd cloud:
Beneath a shole of silver Fishes glides,
And plays about the gilded Barges sides;
The Ladies angling in the Chrystal Lake,
Feast on the waters with the prey they take;
At once victorious with their Lines and Eyes
They make the Fishes and the Men their prize;
A thousand *Cupids* on the Billows ride,
And Sea-Nymphs enter with the swelling Tide,
From *Thetis* sent as Spies to make report,
And tell the wonders of her Soveraign's Court,
All that can living feed the greedy Eye,
Or dead the Palat, here you may descry,
The choicest things that furnisht *Noah*'s Ark,
Or *Peter*'s sheet, inhabiting this Park:
All with a border of rich Fruit-trees crown'd,
Whose loaded branches hide the lofty mound.
Such various ways the spacious Allies lead,
My doubtful Muse knows not what path to tread:
Yonder the harvest of cold months laid up,
Gives a fresh coolness to the Royal Cup,
There Ice, like Chrystal, firm, and never lost,
Tempers hot *July* with *Decembers* Frost,
Winters dark Prison, whence he cannot flie,
Though the warm Spring his enemy draws nigh:
Strange! that extremes should thus preserve the snow
High on the *Alps*, or in deep Caves below.
  Here a well-polisht Mall gives us the joy
To see our Prince his matchless force imploy;
His manly posture and his graceful meen
Vigor and Youth in all his motion seen,
His shape so lovely, and his limbs so strong,
Confirm our hopes we shall obey him long:
No sooner has he toucht the flying Ball,
But 'tis already more than half the Mall;
And such a fury from his arm has got
As from a smoaking Culverin 'twere shot.
  Nere this my Muse, what most delights her, sees,
A living Gallery of aged Trees;
Bold Sons of earth that thrust their arms so high,
As if once more they would invade the Sky;

In such green Palaces the first Kings reign'd,
Slept in their shades, and Angels entertain'd:
With such old Counsellors they did advise,
And by frequenting sacred Groves grew wise;
Free from th' impediments of light and noise
Man thus retir'd his nobler thoughts imploys:
Here *Charles* contrives the ordering of his States,
Here he resolves his neighb'ring Princes fates:
What Nation shall have Peace, where War be made
Determin'd is in this oraculous shade;
The World from *India* to the frozen *North*,
Concern'd in what this Solitude brings forth.
His Fancy objects from his view receives,
The prospect thought and contemplation gives:
That seat of Empire here salutes his eye,
To which three Kingdoms do themselves apply,
The structure by a Prelate rais'd, *Whitehall*,
Built with the fortune of *Rome*'s Capitol;
Both disproportion'd to the present State
Of their proud Founders, were approv'd by Fate;
From hence he does that antique Pile behold,
Where Royal heads receive the sacred gold;
It gives them Crowns, and does their ashes keep;
There made like gods, like mortals there they sleep
Making the circle of their Reign complete,
Those Suns of Empire, where they rise they set:
When others fell, this standing did presage
The Crown should triumph over popular rage,
Hard by that House where all our Ills were shap'd,
Th' auspicious Temple stood, and yet escap'd.
So Snow on *Ætna* does unmelted lie,
Whence rowling flames and scatter'd cinders flie;
The distant Countrey in the ruine shares,
What falls from Heav'n the burning Mountain spares.
Next, that capacious Hall he sees the room,
Where the whole Nation does for Justice come.
Under whose large roof flourishes the Gown,
And Judges grave on high Tribunals frown.
Here like the peoples Pastor he does go,
His flock subjected to his view below;
On which reflecting in his mighty mind,
No private passion does Indulgence find;
The pleasures of his Youth suspended are,
And made a Sacrifice to publick care;
Here free from Court compliances he walks,
And with himself, his best adviser, talks;

How peaceful Olive may his Temples shade,
For mending Laws, and for restoring Trade;
Or how his Brows may be with Laurel charg'd,
For Nation's conquer'd, and our Bounds inlarg'd:
Of ancient Prudence here he ruminates,
Of rising Kingdoms, and of falling States:
What ruling *Arts* gave Great *Augustus* Fame,
And how *Alcides* purchas'd such a name:
His eyes upon his native Palace bent
Close by, suggest a greater argument,
His thoughts rise higher when he does reflect
On what the world may from that Star expect
Which at his Birth appear'd to let us see
Day for his sake could with the Night agree;
A Prince on whom such different lights did smile,
Born, the divided world to reconcile:
Whatever Heaven or high extracted blood
Could promise or foretell, he will make good;
Reform these Nations, and improve them more,
Than this fair Park from what it was before.

Of the Last Verses in the Book[1]

WHEN we for Age could neither read nor write,
The Subject made us able to indite.
The Soul with Nobler Resolutions deckt,
The Body stooping, does Herself erect:
No Mortal Parts are requisite to raise
Her, that Unbody'd can her Maker praise.
The Seas are quiet, when the Winds give o're;
So calm are we, when Passions are no more:
For then we know how vain it was to boast
Of fleeting Things, so certain to be lost.
Clouds of Affection from our younger Eyes
Conceal that emptiness, which Age descries.
The Soul's dark Cottage, batter'd and decay'd,
Let's in new Light thrô chinks that time has made.
Stronger by weakness, wiser Men become
As they draw near to their Eternal home:
Leaving the Old, both Worlds at once they view,
That stand upon the Threshold of the New.
—*Miratur Limen Olympi.*
Virgil.

[1] Published in *Poems, &c. Written upon Several Occasions*, 5th ed., 1686. Text of first edition.

Song[1]

CHLORIS farewell; I now must go:
For if with thee I longer stay,
Thy Eyes prevail upon me so,
I shall prove Blind, and lose my Way.

Fame of thy Beauty, and thy Youth,
Among the rest, me hither brought:
Finding this Fame fall short of Truth,
Made me stay longer than I thought.

For I'm engag'd by Word, and Oath,
A Servant to another's Will;
Yet, for thy Love, I'd forfeit both,
Cou'd I be sure to keep it still.

But what Assurance can I take?
When thou, foreknowing this Abuse,
For some more worthy Lover's sake,
May'st leave me with so just Excuse.

For thou may'st say 'twas not thy Fault
That thou didst thus inconstant prove,
Being by my Example taught
To break thy Oath, to mend thy Love.

No *Chloris*, no; I will return,
And raise thy Story to that height,
That Strangers shall at distance burn,
And she distrust me Reprobate.

Then shall my Love this doubt displace,
And gain such trust, that I may come
And banquet sometimes on thy Face,
But make my constant Meals at home.

---

[1] Published in *Poems*, 8th ed., 1711. Text of first edition.

ANDREW MARVELL

(1621-1649-1678)

To His Coy Mistress[1]

HAD we but World enough, and Time,
This coyness Lady were no crime.
We would sit down, and think which way
To walk, and pass our long Loves Day.
Thou by the *Indian Ganges* side
Should'st Rubies find: I by the Tide
Of *Humber* would complain. I would
Love you ten years before the Flood:
And you should if you please refuse
Till the Conversion of the *Jews*.
My vegetable Love should grow
Vaster than Empires, and more slow.
An hundred years should go to praise
Thine Eyes, and on thy Forehead Gaze.
Two hundred to adore each Breast:
But thirty thousand to the rest.
An Age at least to every part,
And the last Age should show your Heart.
For Lady you deserve this State;
Nor would I love at lower rate.
  But at my back I alwaies hear
Times winged Charriot hurrying near:
And yonder all before us lye
Desarts of vast Eternity.
Thy Beauty shall no more be found;
Nor, in thy marble Vault, shall sound
My ecchoing Song: then Worms shall try
That long preserv'd Virginity:
And your quaint Honour turn to dust;
And into ashes all my Lust.
The Grave's a fine and private place,
But none I think do there embrace.
  Now therefore, while the youthful hew
Sits on thy skin like morning lew,
And while thy willing Soul transpires
At every pore with instant Fires,

---

[1] Written cir. 1646-50. Published in *Miscellaneous Poems*, 1681. Text of first edition. I have adopted Margoliouth's emendation of "glew" to "lew" (*i.e.*, 'warmth') in l. 34.

Now let us sport us while we may;
And now, like am'rous birds of prey,
Rather at once our Time devour,
Than languish in his slow chapt pow'r.
Let us roll all our Strength, and all
Our sweetness, up into one Ball:
And tear our Pleasures with rough strife,
Thorough the Iron gates of Life.
Thus, though we cannot make our Sun
Stand still, yet we will make him run.

The Garden[1]

How vainly men themselves amaze
To win the Palm, the Oke, or Bayes;
And their uncessant Labours see
Crown'd from some single Herb or Tree,
Whose short and narrow verged Shade
Does prudently their Toyles upbraid;
While all Flow'rs and all Trees do close
To weave the Garlands of repose.

Fair quiet, have I found thee here,
And Innocence thy Sister dear!
Mistaken long, I sought you then
In busie Companies of Men.
Your sacred Plants, if here below,
Only among the Plants will grow.
Society is all but rude,
To this delicious Solitude.

No white nor red was ever seen
So am'rous as this lovely green.
Fond Lovers, cruel as their Flame,
Cut in these Trees their Mistress name.
Little, Alas, they know, or heed,
How far these Beauties Hers exceed!
Fair Trees! where s'eer your barkes I wound
No Name shall but your own be found.

When we have run our Passions heat,
Love hither makes his best retreat.
The *Gods*, that mortal Beauty chase,

[1] Written cir. 1650-52. Published in *Miscellaneous Poems*, 1681. Text of first edition.

Still in a Tree did end their race.
Apollo hunted *Daphne* so,
Only that She might Laurel grow.
And *Pan* did after *Syrinx* speed,
Not as a Nymph, but for a Reed.

What wond'rous Life in this I lead!
Ripe Apples drop about my head;
The Luscious Clusters of the Vine
Upon my Mouth do crush their Wine;
The Nectaren, and curious Peach,
Into my hands themselves do reach;
Stumbling on Melons, as I pass,
Insnar'd with Flow'rs, I fall on Grass.

Mean while the Mind, from pleasure less,
Withdraws into its happiness:
The Mind, that Ocean where each kind
Does streight its own resemblance find;
Yet it creates, transcending these,
Far other Worlds, and other Seas;
Annihilating all that's made
To a green Thought in a green Shade.

Here at the Fountains sliding foot,
Or at some Fruit-trees mossy root,
Casting the Bodies Vest aside,
My Soul into the boughs does glide:
There like a Bird it sits, and sings,
Then whets, and combs its silver Wings;
And, till prepar'd for longer flight,
Waves in its Plumes the various Light.

Such was that happy Garden-state,
While Man there walk'd without a Mate:
After a Place so pure, and sweet,
What other Help could yet be meet!
But 'twas beyond a Mortal's share
To wander solitary there:
Two Paradises 'twere in one
To live in Paradise alone.

How well the skilful Gardner drew
Of flow'rs and herbes this Dial new;
Where from above the milder Sun
Does through a fragrant Zodiack run;
And, as it works, th' industrious Bee
Computes its time as well as we.

How could such sweet and wholsome Hours
Be reckon'd but with herbs and flow'rs!

Bermudas[1]

WHERE the remote *Bermudas* ride
In th' Oceans bosome unespy'd,
From a small Boat, that row'd along,
The listning Winds receiv'd this Song.
What should we do but sing his Praise
That led us through the watry Maze,
Unto an Isle so long unknown,
And yet far kinder than our own?
Where he the huge Sea-Monsters wracks,
That lift the Deep upon their Backs.
He lands us on a grassy Stage;
Safe from the Storms, and Prelat's rage.
He gave us this eternal Spring,
Which here enamells every thing;
And sends the Fowl's to us in care,
On daily Visits through the Air.
He hangs in shades the Orange bright,
Like golden Lamps in a green Night.
And does in the Pomgranates close,
Jewels more rich than *Ormus* show's.
He makes the Figs our mouths to meet;
And throws the Melons at our feet.
But Apples plants of such a price,
No Tree could ever bear them twice.
With Cedars, chosen by his hand,
From *Lebanon*, he stores the Land.
And makes the hollow Seas, that roar,
Proclaime the Ambergris on shoar.
He cast (of which we rather boast)
The Gospels Pearl upon our Coast.
And in these Rocks for us did frame
A Temple, where to sound his Name.
Oh let our Voice his Praise exalt,
Till it arrive at Heavens Vault:
Which thence (perhaps) rebounding, may
Eccho beyond the *Mexique Bay*.
Thus sung they, in the *English* boat,
An holy and a chearful Note,

[1] Written cir. 1653. Published in *Miscellaneous Poems*, 1681. Text of first edition.

And all the way, to guide their Chime,
With falling Oars they kept the time.

JOHN DRYDEN

(1631-1650-1700)

Upon the Death of the Lord Hastings[1]

MUST Noble *Hastings* Immaturely die,
(The Honour of his ancient Family?)
Beauty and Learning thus together meet,
To bring a *Winding* for a *Wedding-sheet*?
Must *Vertue* prove *Death's* Harbinger? Must She,
With him expiring, feel Mortality?
Is *Death* (Sin's wages) Grace's now? shall Art
Make us more Learned, only to depart?
If Merit be Disease, if Vertue Death;
To be Good, Not to be, who'd then bequeath
Himself to Discipline? Who'd not esteem
Labour a Crime, Study self-murther deem?
Our *Noble Youth* now have pretence to be
Dunces securely, Ign'rant healthfully.
Rare Linguist! whose Worth speaks it self; whose Praise,
Though not his Own, all *Tongues* Besides do raise:
Then Whom Great *Alexander* may seem less,
Who conquer'd Men, but not their Languages.
In his Mouth Nations speak; his Tongue might be
Interpreter to *Greece, France, Italy*.
His native Soyl was the four parts o' th' Earth;
All *Europe* was too narrow for his Birth.
A young Apostle; and (with rev'rence may
I speak 'it) inspir'd with gift of Tongues, as They.
Nature gave him, a Childe, what Men in vain
Oft strive, by Art though further'd, to obtain.
His body was an Orb, his sublime Soul
Did move on Vertue's and on Learning's pole:
Whose Reg'lar Motions better to our view,
Then *Archimedes* Sphere, the Heavens did shew.
Graces and Vertues, Languages and Arts,
Beauty and Learning, fill'd up all the parts.
Heav'ns Gifts, which do, like falling Stars, appear

[1] Published in *Lachrymæ Musarum*, 1650. Text of first edition. See Preface.

Scatter'd in Others; all, as in their Sphear,
Were fix'd and conglobate in's Soul, and thence
Shone th'row his Body with sweet Influence;
Letting their Glories so on each Limb fall,
The whole Frame render'd was Celestial.
Come, learned *Ptolomy*, and tryal make,
If thou this Hero's Altitude canst take;
But that transcends thy skill; thrice happie all,
Could we but prove thus Astronomical.
Liv'd *Tycho* now, struck with this Ray, (which shone
More bright i' th' Morn then others Beam at Noon)
He'd take his *Astrolabe*, and seek out here
What new Star 't was did gild our Hemisphere.
Replenish'd then with such rare Gifts as these,
Where was room left for such a Foul Disease?
The Nations sin hath drawn that Veil which shrouds
Our Day-spring in so sad benighting Clouds.
Heaven would no longer trust its Pledge; but thus
Recall'd it; rapt its *Ganymede* from us.
Was there no milder way but the Small Pox,
The very filth'ness of *Pandora's* Box?
So many Spots, like *næves*, our *Venus* soil?
One Jewel set off with so many a Foil?
Blisters with pride swell'd, which th'row 's flesh did sprout
Like Rose-buds, stuck i' th' Lilly-skin about.
Each little Pimple had a Tear in it,
To wail the fault its rising did commit:
Who, Rebel-like, with their own Lord at strife,
Thus made an Insurrection 'gainst his Life.
Or were these Gems sent to adorn his Skin,
The Cab'net of a richer Soul within?
No Comet need foretel his Change drew on,
Whose Corps might seem a *Constellation*.
O had he di'd of old, how great a strife
Had been, who from his Death should draw their Life?
Who should by one rich draught become whate'er
Seneca, Cato, Numa, Cæsar, were:
Learn'd, Vertuous, Pious, Great, and have by this
An Universal *Metempsuchosis*.
Must all these ag'd Sires in one Funeral
Expire? All die in one so young, so small?
Who, had he liv'd his life out, his great Fame
Had swoln 'bove any *Greek* or *Romane* name?
But hasty Winter, with one blast, hath brought
The hopes of Autumn, Summer, Spring, to nought.
Thus fades the Oak i' th' sprig, i' th' blade the Corn;
Thus, without Young, this *Phœnix* dies, new born.
Must then old three-legg'd gray-beards, with their Gout,

Catarrhs, Rheums, Aches, live three Ages out?
Times Offal, onely fit for th' Hospital,
Or t' hang an Antiquaries room withal;
Must Drunkards, Lechers, spent with Sinning, live
With such helps as Broths, Possits, Physick give?
None live but such as should die? Shall we meet
With none but Ghostly Fathers in the Street?
Grief makes me rail; Sorrow will force its way;
And Show'rs of Tears, Tempestuous Sighs best lay.
The Tongue may fail; but over-flowing Eyes
Will weep out lasting streams of *Elegies*.
  But thou, O *Virgin-widow*, left alone,
Now thy Beloved, Heaven-ravisht *Spouse* is gone,
(Whose skilful Sire in vain strove to apply
Med'cines, when thy Balm was no remedy)
With greater then *Platonick* love, O wed
His Soul, tho' not his Body, to thy Bed:
Let that make thee a Mother; bring thou forth
Th' *Ideas* of his Vertue, Knowledge, Worth;
Transcribe th' Original in new Copies; give
Hastings o' th' better part: so shall he live
In's Nobler Half; and the great Grandsire be
Of an Heroick Divine Progenie:
An Issue which t' Eternity shall last,
Yet but th' Irradiations which he cast.
Erect no *Mausolœums*: for his best
Monument is his Spouses Marble brest.

Heroick Stanzas, Consecrated to the Memory of His Highness, OLIVER, Late Lord Protector of this Commonwealth, &c.[1]

AND now 'tis time; for their officious haste,
  Who would before have born him to the Sky,
Like eager *Romans* e'er all Rites were past,
  Did let too soon the sacred Eagle fly.

Though our best Notes are Treason to his Fame,
  Join'd with the loud Applause of publick Voice,

[1] Published in *Three Poems upon the Death of his late Highnesse Oliver Lord Protector of England* . . . . 1659. Text of *A Poem upon the Death of* . . . *Oliver* . . . . 1659. On the probability that this edition was really printed in 1692, see Dobell, *John Dryden, Bibliographical Memoranda* (London, 1922), pp. 1-4.

Since Heaven, what Praise we offer to his Name,
Hath render'd too Authentick by its Choice.

Though in his Praise no Arts can liberal be,
Since they, whose Muses have the highest flown,
Add not to his Immortal Memory;
But do an Act of Friendship to their own.

Yet 'tis our Duty and our Interest too,
Such Monuments as we can build, to raise;
Lest all the World prevent what we shou'd do,
And claim a Title in him by their Praise.

How shall I then begin, or where conclude,
To draw a Fame so truly Circular?
For in a Round, what Order can be shew'd,
Where all the Parts so equal perfect are?

His Grandeur he derived from Heav'n alone,
For he was great, e'er Fortune made him so;
And Wars, like Mists that rise against the Sun,
Made him but greater seem, not greater grow.

No borrow'd Bays his Temples did adorn,
But to our Crown he did fresh Jewels bring;
Nor was his Vertue poison'd, soon as born,
With the too early Thoughts of being King.

Fortune (that easie Mistress of the Young,
But to her ancient Servants coy and hard)
Him, at that Age, her Favourites ranked among,
When she her best-lov'd *Pompey* did discard.

He, private, marked the Faults of others Sway,
And set as Sea-marks for himself to shun;
Not like rash Monarchs, who their Youth betray
By Acts their Age too late wou'd wish undone.

And yet Dominion was not his Design;
We owe that Blessing not to him, but Heav'n,
Which to fair Acts unsought Rewards did join,
Rewards that less to him, than us, were giv'n.

Our former Chiefs, like Sticklers of the War,
First sought t' inflame the Parties, then to poise:
The Quarrel lov'd, but did the Cause abhor,
And did not strike to hurt, but make a noise.

War, our Consumption, was their gainful Trade;
We inward bled, whilst they prolong'd our Pain;
He fought to end our Fighting, and assay'd
To stench the Blood by breathing of the Vein.

Swift and resistless through the Land he pass'd,
Like that bold *Greek*, who did the East subdue;
And made to Battels such Heroick Haste,
As if on Wings of Victory he flew.

He fought, secure of Fortune, as of fame;
Till by new Maps, the Island might be shown,
Of Conquests, which he strew'd where-e'er he came,
Thick as the *Galaxy* with Stars are sown.

His palms, tho under Weights they did not stand,
Still thriv'd; no Winter could his Laurels fade:
Heaven in his Portraict shew'd a Work-man's Hand
And drew it perfect, yet without a Shade.

Peace was the Prize of all his Toil and Care,
Which War had banish'd and did now restore:
Bolognia's walls thus mounted in the Air,
To seat themselves more surely than before.

Her Safety, rescued *Ireland*, to him owes;
And treacherous Scotland, to no Int'rest true,
Yet bless'd that Fate which did his Arms dispose,
Her Land to civilize, as to subdue.

Nor was he like those Stars which only shine,
When to pale Mariners they Storms portend:
He had his calmer Influence, and his Mien
Did Love and Majesty together blend.

'Tis true, his Count'nance did imprint an Awe,
And naturally all Souls to his did bow;
As Wands of Divination downward draw,
And point to beds where Sov'raign Gold doth grow.

When, past all Off'rings to *Pheretrian Jove*,
He *Mars* depos'd and Arms to Gowns made yield,
Successful Counsels did him soon approve
As fit for close Intrigues as open Field.

To suppliant *Holland* he vouchsaf'd a Peace,
Our once bold Rival in the *British* Main,

Now tamely glad her unjust Claim to cease,
  And buy our Friendship with her Idol, Gain.

Fame of th' asserted Sea, through *Europe* blown,
  Made *France* and *Spain* ambitious of his Love;
Each knew that Side must conquer, he wou'd own;
  And for him fiercely, as for Empire, strove.

No sooner was the *French*-Man's Cause embrac'd,
  That the light *Monsieur* the grave *Don* out-weigh'd:
His Fortune turn'd the Scale where-e'er 'twas cast,
  Tho' *Indian* mines were in the other laid.

When absent, yet we conquer'd in his Right;
  For tho' some meaner Artist's Skill were shown,
In mingling Colours, or in placing Light,
  Yet still the fair Designment was his own.

For from all Tempers he cou'd Service draw
  The worth of each, with its Alloy, he knew;
And, as the Confident of Nature, saw
  How she Complections did divide and brew.

Or he their single Vertues did survey,
  By Intuition, in his own large Breast,
Where all the rich *Idea's* of them lay,
  That were the Rule and Measure to the rest.

When such Heroick Vertue Heaven sets out,
  The Stars, like Commons, sullenly obey;
Because it drains them, when it comes about;
  And therefore is a Tax they seldom pay.

From this high Spring, our Foreign Conquests flow,
  Which yet more glorious Triumphs do portend;
Since their Commencement to his Arms they owe,
  If Springs as high as Fountains may ascend.

He made us Free-men of the Continent,
  Whom Nature did like Captives treat before;
To nobler Preys the *English* Lion sent,
  And taught him first in *Belgian* Walks to roar.

That old unquestion'd Pirate of the Land,
  Proud *Rome,* with Dread the Fate of *Dunkirk* heard;
And trembling, wish'd behind more *Alps* to stand,
  Although an *Alexander* were her Guard.

By his Command we boldly cross'd the Line
  And bravely fought where Southern Stars arise;
We trac'd the far-fetched Gold unto the Mine,
  And that which brib'd our Fathers, made our Prize.

Such was our Prince, yet own'd a Soul above
  The highest Acts it could produce to show:
Thus poor Mechanick Arts in Publick move,
  Whilst the deep Secrets beyond Practice go.

Nor dy'd he when his Ebbing Fame went less,
  But when fresh Laurels courted him to live:
He seem'd but to prevent some new Success,
  As if above what Triumphs Earth could give.

His latest Victories still thickest came,
  As near the Centre, Motion does increase;
Till he, press'd down by his own weighty Name,
  Did, like the Vestal, under Spoils decease.

But first, the Ocean, as a tribute, sent
  That Giant-Prince of all her Watry Herd;
And th' Isle, when her protecting *Genius* went,
  Upon his Obsequies loud Sighs conferr'd.

No Civil Broils have since his Death arose,
  But Faction now, by Habit, does obey;
And Wars have that Respect for his Repose,
  As winds for *Halcyons* when they breed at Sea.

His Ashes in a Peaceful Urn shall rest,
  His Name a great Example stands to show,
How strangely high Endeavours may be bless'd,
  Where Piety and Valour jointly go.

Astræa Redux

A Poem On the Happy Restoration and Return of His Sacred Majesty Charles the Second[1]

Now with a general Peace the World was blest,
While Ours, a World divided from the rest,
A dreadful Quiet felt, and worser far

[1] Published in 1660. Text of *Annus Mirabilis* . . . . , 1688.

Than Armes, a sullen Interval of War:
Thus when black Clouds draw down the lab'ring Skies,
Ere yet abroad the winged Thunder flies,
An horrid Stillness first invades the ear,
And in that silence We the Tempest fear.
Th' Ambitious *Swede* like restless Billows tost,
On this hand gaining what on that he lost,
Though in his life he Blood and Ruine breath'd,
To his now guideless Kingdom Peace bequeath'd.
And Heaven that seem'd regardless of our Fate,
For *France* and *Spain* did Miracles create,
Such mortal Quarrels to compose in Peace
As Nature bred and Int'rest did encrease.
We sigh'd to hear the fair *Iberian* Bride
Must grow a Lilie to the Lilies side,
While Our cross Stars deny'd us *Charles* his Bed
Whom Our first Flames and Virgin Love did wed.
For his long absence Church and State did groan;
Madness the Pulpit, Faction seiz'd the Throne:
Experienc'd Age in deep despair was lost
To see the Rebel thrive, the Loyal crost:
Youth that with Joys had unacquainted been
Envy'd Gray hairs that once good Days had seen:
We thought our Sires, not with their own content,
Had ere we came to age our Portion spent.
Nor could our Nobles hope their bold Attempt
Who ruin'd Crowns would Coronets exempt:
For when by their designing Leaders taught
To strike at Pow'r which for themselves they sought,
The Vulgar gull'd into Rebellion, arm'd,
Their blood to action by the Prize was warm'd.
The Sacred Purple then and Scarlet Gown,
Like sanguine Dye, to Elephants was shewn.
Thus when the bold *Typhoeus* scal'd the Sky,
And forc'd Great *Jove* from his own Heaven to fly,
(What King, what Crown from Treasons reach is free,
If *Jove* and *Heaven* can violated be?)
The lesser Gods that shar'd his prosp'rous State
All suffer'd in the Exil'd Thund'rers Fate.
The Rabble now such Freedom did enjoy,
As Winds at Sea, that use it to destroy:
Blind as the *Cyclops*, and as wild as he,
They own'd a lawless savage Libertie,
Like that our painted Ancestors so priz'd
Ere Empires Arts their Breasts had Civiliz'd.
How Great were then Our *Charles* his Woes, who thus
Was forc'd to suffer for Himself and us!
He toss'd by Fate, and hurried up and down,

Heir to his Fathers Sorrows, with his Crown,
Could taste no sweets of Youths desired Age,
But found his Life too true a Pilgrimage.
Unconquer'd yet in that forlorn Estate
His Manly Courage overcame his Fate.
His Wounds he took like *Romans* on his Breast,
Which by his Virtue were with Laurels drest,
As Souls reach Heav'n while yet in Bodies pent,
So did he live above his Banishment.
That Sun, which we beheld with couz'ned eyes,
Within the Water, mov'd along the Skies.
How easie 'tis when Destiny proves kind,
With full spread Sails, to run before the Wind.
But those that 'gainst stiff Gales laveering go,
Must be at once resolv'd and skilful too.
He would not like soft *Otho* hope prevent,
But stay'd and suffer'd Fortune to repent.
These Virtues *Galba* in a Stranger sought;
And *Piso* to Adopted Empire brought.
How shall I then my doubtful Thoughts express,
That must his Suff'rings both regret and bless!
For when his early Valour Heav'n had crost,
And all at *Worc'ster* but the honour lost,
Forc'd into Exile from his rightful Throne,
He made all Countries where he came his own.
And viewing Monarchs secret Arts of sway
A Royal Factor for their Kingdoms lay.
Thus banish'd *David* spent abroad his time,
When to be Gods Anointed was his Crime,
And when restor'd made his proud Neighbours rue
Those choise Remarks he from his Travels drew:
Nor is he only by Afflictions shewn
To conquer others Realms, but rule his own:
Recov'ring hardly what he lost before,
His Right indears it much, his Purchase more.
Inur'd to suffer ere he came to raign,
No rash procedure will his Actions stain.
To bus'ness ripened by digestive thought,
His future rule is into Method brought:
As they who first Proportion understand,
With easie Practice reach a Master's hand.
Well might the Ancient Poets then confer
On Night, the honour'd name of *Counseller*,
Since struck with rayes of prosp'rous Fortune blind,
We Light alone in dark Afflictions find.
In such adversities to Scepters train'd,
The name of *Great* his famous Grandsire gain'd:
Who yet a King alone in Name and Right,

With hunger, cold and angry *Jove* did fight;
Shock'd by a Covenanting Leagues vast Pow'rs,
As holy and as Catholick as ours:
Till Fortunes fruitless spight had made it known,
Her blows not shook but riveted his Throne.
  Some lazy Ages, lost in Sleep and Ease,
No action leave to busie Chronicles;
Such whose supine felicity but makes
In story *Casmes*, in *Epoche's* mistakes;
O're whom *Time* gently shakes his wings of Down,
Till with his silent Sickle they are mown:
Such is not *Charles* his too too active age,
Which govern'd by the wild distemper'd rage
Of some black Star infecting all the Skies,
Made him at his own cost like *Adam* wise.
Tremble, ye Nations, who secure before,
Laught at those Arms that 'gainst our selves we bore;
Rouz'd by the lash of his own stubborn Tail,
Our Lion now will foreign Foes assail.
With *Alga* who the sacred Altar strows?
To all the Sea-Gods *Charles* an Offering owes:
A Bull to thee, *Portunus*, shall be slain,
A Lamb to you the Tempests of the Main:
For those loud Storms that did against him rore,
Have cast his shipwrack'd Vessel on the Shore.
Yet as wise Artists mix their Colours so,
That by degrees they from each other go,
Black steals unheeded from the neighb'ring white
Without offending the well couz'ned sight:
So on us stole our blessed change; while we
Th' effect did feel, but scarce the manner see.
Frosts that constrain the ground, and birth deny
To Flow'rs, that in its womb expecting lie,
Do seldom their usurping Pow'r withdraw,
But raging Floods persue their hasty Thaw:
Our Thaw was mild, the Cold not chas'd away,
But lost in kindly heat of lengthned day.
Heav'n would no bargain for its Blessings drive,
But what we could not pay for, freely give.
The Prince of Peace would, like himself, confer
A Gift unhop'd without the price of war.
Yet as he knew his Blessings worth, took care
That we should know it by repeated Pray'r;
Which storm'd the Skies and ravish'd *Charles* from thence,
As Heav'n it self is took by violence.
Booth's forward Valour only serv'd to shew,
He durst that duty pay we all did owe:
Th' Attempt was fair; but Heav'ns prefixed hour

Not come; so like the watchful Travellor,
That by the Moons mistaken light did rise,
Lay down again, and clos'd his weary Eyes.
'Twas *MONK* whom Providence design'd to loose
Those real bonds false Freedom did impose.
The blessed Saints that watch'd this turning Scene,
Did from their Stars with joyful wonder lean,
To see small Clues draw vastest weights along,
Not in their bulk but in their order strong.
Thus Pencils can by one slight touch restore,
Smiles to that changed face that wept before.
With ease such fond *Chymæra's* we persue,
As Fancy frames for Fancy to subdue;
But when our selves to action we betake,
It shuns the Mint like Gold that Chymists make:
How hard was then his Task, at once to be,
What in the Body natural we see;
Mans Architect distinctly did ordain
The charge of Muscles, Nerves, and of the Brain,
Through viewless Conduits Spirits to dispense
The Springs of Motion from the Seat of Sense.
'Twas not the hasty product of a day,
But the well ripened Fruit of wise delay.
He like a patient Angler, er'e he stroak,
Would let them play a while upon the hook.
Our healthful food the Stomach labours thus,
At first embracing what it strait doth crush.
Wise Leeches will not vain Receipts obtrude,
While growing Pains pronounce the Humors crude;
Deaf to complaints they wait upon the Ill,
Till some safe *Crisis* authorize their Skill.
Nor could his Acts too close a Vizard wear,
To scape their Eyes whom Guilt had taught to fear,
And guard with caution that polluted nest,
Whence Legion twice before was dispossest.
Once Sacred house, which when they entr'd in,
They thought the place could sanctifie a sin;
Like those that vainly hop'd kind Heav'n would wink,
While to excess on Martyrs Tombs they drink.
And as devouter *Turks* first warn their Souls
To part, before they taste forbidden Bowls,
So these when their black Crimes they went about,
First timely charm'd their useless Conscience out.
Religions Name against it self was made;
The Shadow serv'd the Substance to invade:
Like Zealous Missions, they did Care pretend
Of Souls in shew, but made the Gold their end.
Th' incensed Pow'rs beheld with scorn from high

An Heaven so far distant from the Sky,
Which durst, with horses hoofs that beat the Ground
And Martial Brass, bely the Thunders Sound.
'Twas hence at length just Vengeance thought it fit
To speed their Ruin by their impious wit.
Thus *Sforza*, curs'd with a too fertile brain,
Lost by his Wiles the Pow'r his Wit did gain.
Henceforth their Fogue must spend at lesser rate,
Than in its Flames to wrap a Nations Fate.
Suffer'd to live, they are like *Helots* set,
A virtuous Shame within us to beget.
For by example most we sinn'd before,
And glass-like clearness mixt with frailty bore.
But since reform'd by what we did amiss,
We by our suff'rings learn to prize our bliss.
Like early Lovers whose unpractis'd hearts
Were long the May-game of malicious arts,
When once they find their Jealousies were vain,
With double heat renew their Fires again.
'Twas this produc'd the Joy, that hurried o're
Such swarms of *English* to the Neighb'ring shore,
To fetch that Prize, by which *Batavia* made
So rich amends for our impoverish'd Trade.
Oh had you seen from *Schevelines* barren Shore,
(Crowded with troops, and barren now no more,)
Afflicted *Holland* to his Farewel bring
True Sorrow, *Holland* to regret a King;
While waiting him his Royal Fleet did ride,
And willing Winds to their lowr'd Sails denied.
The wavering Streamers, Flags, and Standart out,
The merry Seamens rude but chearful Shout;
And last the Cannons voice that shook the Skies,
And, as it fares in sudden Extasies,
At once bereft us both of Ears and Eyes.
The *Naseby*, now no longer *Englands* shame,
But better to be lost in *Charles* his name,
(Like some unequal Bride in nobler sheets)
Receives her Lord: The joyful *London* meets
The Princely *York*, himself alone a freight;
The *Swift-sure* groans beneath Great *Glouc'sters* weight.
Secure as when the *Halcyon* breeds, with these,
He that was born to drown might cross the Seas.
Heav'n could not own a Providence, and take
The Wealth three Nations ventur'd at a stake.
The same indulgence *Charles* his Voyage bless'd,
Which in his right had Miracles confess'd.
The Winds that never Moderation knew,

Afraid to blow too much, too faintly blew;
Or out of breath with joy could not enlarge
Their straightned Lungs, or conscious of their Charge.
The British *Amphitryte* smooth and clear,
In richer Azure never did appear;
Proud her returning Prince to entertain
With the submitted Fasces of the Main.
And welcom now (*Great Monarch,*) to your own;
Behold th' approaching Cliffes of *Albion:*
It is no longer Motion cheats your view,
As you meet it, the Land approacheth you.
The Land returns, and in the white it wears
The marks of Penitence and Sorrow bears.
But you, whose Goodness your Descent doth shew,
Your Heav'nly Parentage and Earthly too;
By that same Mildness, which your Fathers Crown
Before did ravish, shall secure your own.
Not ty'd to rules of Policy, you find
Revenge less sweet than a forgiving mind.
Thus when th' Almighty would to *Moses* give
A sight of all he could behold and live;
A Voice before his Entry did proclaim
Long-suffering, Goodness, Mercy in his Name.
Your Pow'r to Justice doth submit your Cause,
Your Goodness only is above the Laws;
Whose rigid Letter while pronounc'd by you
Is softer made. So winds that tempests brew
When through Arabian Groves they take their flight,
Made wanton with rich Odours, lose their spight.
And as those Lees, that trouble it, refine
The agitated Soul of Generous Wine,
So tears of Joy for your returning spilt,
Work out and expiate our former Guilt.
Methinks I see those Crowds on *Dover's* Strand,
Who in their haste to welcom you to Land
Choak'd up the Beach with their still growing store,
And made a wilder Torrent on the Shore.
While spurr'd with eager thoughts of past Delight,
Those who had seen you court a second sight;
Preventing still your Steps, and making hast
To meet you often wheresoe're you past.
How shall I speak of that triumphant Day
When you renew'd the expiring Pomp of *May!*
(A Month that owns an Interest in your Name:
You and the Flow'rs are its peculiar Claim.)
That Star that at your Birth shone out so bright,

It stain'd the duller Suns Meridian light,
Did once again its potent Fires renew,
Guiding our Eyes to find and worship you.
And now times whiter Series is begun,
Which in soft Centuries shall smoothly run;
Those Clouds that overcast your Morn shall fly,
Dispell'd to farthest corners of the Sky.
Our Nation, with united Int'rest blest,
Not now content to poize, shall sway, the rest.
Abroad your Empire shall no Limits know,
But like the Sea in boundless Circles flow.
Your much lov'd Fleet shall with a wide Command
Besiege the petty Monarchs of the Land:
And as Old Time his Off-spring swallow'd down,
Our Ocean in its depths all Seas shall drown.
Their wealthy Trade from Pyrate's Rapine free,
Our Merchants shall no more Advent'rers be:
Nor in the farthest East those Dangers fear
Which humble *Holland* must dissemble here.
Spain to your Gift alone her *Indies* owes,
For what the Pow'rful takes not he bestows.
And *France* that did an Exiles Presence fear
May justly apprehend you still too near.
At home the hateful names of Parties cease
And factious Souls are weary'd into peace.
The discontented now are only they
Whose Crimes before did your Just Cause betray:
Of those your Edicts some reclaim from sins,
But most your Life and Blest Example wins.
Oh happy Prince, whom Heav'n hath taught the way
By paying Vows, to have more Vows to pay!
Oh Happy Age! Oh times like those alone,
By Fate reserv'd for Great *Augustus* Throne!
When the joint growth of Arms and Arts foreshew
The World a Monarch, and that Monarch *You*.

To My Honour'd Friend Dr. Charleton on His Learned and Useful Works; and More Particularly This of Stone-heng, by Him Restored to the True Founders[1]

THE longest Tyranny that ever sway'd
Was that wherein our Ancestors betray'd

[1] Published in Walter Charleton's *Chorea Gigantum*, 1663. Text of first edition.

Their free-born *Reason* to the *Stagirite*,
And made his Torch their universal Light.
So *Truth*, while onely one suppli'd the State,
Grew scarce, and dear, and yet sophisticate.
Until 'twas bought, like Emp'rique Wares, or Charms,
Hard words seal'd up with *Aristotle*'s Armes.
Columbus was the first that shook his Throne;
And found a *Temp'rate* in a *Torrid* Zone:
The fevrish aire fann'd by a cooling breez,
The fruitful Vales set round with shady Trees;
And guiltless *Men*, who danc'd away their time,
Fresh as their *Groves* and *Happy* as their *Clime*.
Had we still paid that homage to a *Name*,
Which onely *God* and *Nature* justly claim;
The *Western* Seas had been our utmost bound,
Where *Poets* still might dream the *Sun* was drown'd:
And all the *Starrs*, that shine in *Southern* Skies,
Had been admir'd by none but *Salvage* Eyes.
  Among th' *Assertors* of free Reason's claim,
Th' *English* are not the least in Worth, or Fame.
The World to *Bacon* does not onely owe
Its *present* Knowledge, but its *future* too.
Gilbert shall live, till *Lode-stones* cease to draw,
Or *British* Fleets the boundless Ocean awe.
And noble *Boyle*, not less in *Nature* seen,
Than his great *Brother* read in *States* and *Men*.
The *Circling* streams, once thought but pools, of blood
(Whether Life's fewel or the Bodie's food)
From dark Oblivion *Harvey*'s name shall save;
While *Ent* keeps all the honour that he gave.
Nor are *You*, Learned Friend, the least renown'd;
Whose Fame, not circumscrib'd with *English* ground,
Flies like the nimble journeys of the Light;
And is, like that, unspent too in its flight.
Whatever *Truths* have been, by *Art*, or *Chance*,
Redeem'd from *Error*, or from *Ignorance*,
Thin in their *Authors*, (like rich veins of Ore)
Your Works unite, and still discover more.
Such is the healing virtue of Your Pen,
To perfect Cures on *Books*, as well as *Men*.
Nor is This Work the least: You well may give
To *Men* new vigour, who makes *Stones* to live.
Through You, the *DANES* (their short Dominion lost)
A longer Conquest than the *Saxons* boast.
STONE-HENG, once thought a *Temple*, You have found
A *Throne*, where Kings, our Earthly Gods, were Crown'd.

Where by their wondring Subjects They were seen,
Joy'd with their Stature and their Princely meen.
Our *Soveraign* here above the rest might stand;
And here be chose again to rule the Land.
These Ruines sheltered once *His* Sacred Head,
Then when from *Wor'sters* fatal Field *He* fled;
Watch'd by the Genius of this Royal place,
And mighty Visions of the Danish Race.
His *Refuge* then was for a *Temple* shown:
But, *He* Restor'd, 'tis now become a *Throne*.

Song[1]

You charm'd me not with that fair face
Though it was all Divine:
To be another's is the Grace,
That makes me wish you mine.
The God's and Fortune take their part
Who like young Monarchs fight;
And boldly dare invade that Heart
Which is another's right.
First mad with hope we undertake
To pull up every Bar;
But once possess'd, we faintly make
A dull defensive War.
Now every friend is turn'd a foe
In hope to get our store:
And passion makes us Cowards grow,
Which made us brave before.

Song[2]

Calm was the Even, and clear was the Sky,
And the new budding Flowers did spring,
When all alone went *Amyntas* and I
To hear the sweet Nightingal sing;
I sate, and he laid him down by me;
But scarcely his breath he could draw;
For when with a fear, he began to draw near,
He was dash'd with A ha ha ha ha!

[1] Published in *An Evening's Love: or, The Mock-Astrologer*, 1668, Act II, Scene i. Text of *Plays*, 1701.

[2] Published in *An Evening's Love: or, The Mock-Astrologer*, 1668, Act IV, Scene i. Text of *Plays*, 1701.

He blush'd to himself, and lay still for a while,
And his modesty curb'd his desire;
But streight I convinc'd all his fear with a smile,
Which added new Flames to his Fire.
O *Sylvia*, said he, you are cruel,
To keep your poor Lover in awe;
Then once more he prest with his hand to my breast,
But was dash'd with A ha ha ha ha!

I knew 'twas his passion that caus'd all his fear;
And therefore I pity'd his Case:
I whisper'd him softly, there's no Body near,
And laid my Cheek close to his Face:
But as he grew bolder and bolder,
A Shepherd came by us and saw;
And just as our bliss we began with a Kiss,
He laugh'd out with A ha ha ha ha!

The Zambra Dance[1]

BENEATH a Myrtle Shade,
Which Love for none but happy Lovers made,
I slept, and straight my Love before me brought
Phillis, the Object of my waking Thought:
Undress'd she came my Flames to meet,
While Love strow'd Flow'rs beneath her Feet;
Flow'rs, which so press'd by her, became more sweet.

From the bright Vision's Head
A careless Veil of Lawn was loosely spread:
From her white Temples fell her shaded Hair,
Like cloudy Sun-shine, not too Brown nor Fair.
Her Hands her Lips did Love inspire;
Her every Grace my Heart did fire:
But most her Eyes, which languish'd with desire.

Ah, Charming Fair, said I,
How long can you my Bliss and yours deny?
By Nature and by Love this lovely Shade
Was for Revenge of suffering Lovers made.
Silence and Shades with Love agree:
Both Shelter you, and Favour me;
You cannot Blush, because I cannot see.

[1] Published in *The Conquest of Granada*, Part I, 1672, Act III, Scene i. Text of *Plays*, 1701.

No, let me Die, she said,
Rather than lose the spotless name of Maid:
Faintly methought she spoke, for all the while
She bid me not believe her, with a Smile.
Then Die, said I, she still deny'd:
And, is it thus, thus, thus she cry'd,
You use a harmless Maid! and so she Dy'd.

I wak'd, and straight I knew
I lov'd so well, it made my Dream prove true:
Fancy, the kinder Mistriss of the two,
Fancy had done what *Phillis* wou'd not do.
Ah, Cruel Nymph! cease your Disdain;
While I can Dream, you scorn in vain:
Asleep or waking, you must ease my pain.

Epilogue[1]

THEY, who have best succeeded on the Stage,
Have still conform'd their Genius to their Age.
Thus *Johnson* did Mechanique humour show,
When Men were dull, and Conversation low.
Then, Comedy was Faultless, but 'twas course:
Cobb's Tankard was a Jest, and *Otter's* Horse.
And as their Comedy, their Love was mean;
Except, by chance, in some one Labour'd Scene,
Which must attone for an ill-written Play.
They rose; but at their height could seldom stay.
Fame then was cheap, and the first comer sped;
And they have kept it since, by being dead.
But were they now to write, when Critiques weigh
Each Line, and ev'ry Word, throughout a Play,
None of 'em, no not *Johnson* in his height,
Could pass, without allowing grains for weight.
Think it not Envy that these Truths are told;
Our Poet's not Malicious, though he's Bold.
'Tis not to brand 'em that their faults are shown,
But, by their Errors, to excuse his own.
If Love and Honour now are higher rais'd,
'Tis not the Poet, but the Age is prais'd.
Wit's new arriv'd to a more high degree;
Our Native Language more refin'd and free.
Our Ladies and our Men now speak more wit
In Conversation, than those Poets writ.

[1] Published in *The Conquest of Granada*, Part II, 1672. Text of *Plays*, 1701.

Then, one of these is, consequently, true;
That what this Poet writes comes short of you,
And imitates you ill, (which most he fears)
Or else his Writing is not worse than theirs.
Yet, though you judge, (as sure the Criticks will)
That some before him writ with greater skill:
In this one Praise he has their Fame surpast,
To please an Age more Gallant than the last.

Song[1]

WHY should a foolish Marriage Vow,
  Which long ago was made,
Oblige us to each other now
  When Passion is decay'd?
We lov'd, and we lov'd, as long as we cou'd,
  Till our Love was lov'd out in us both:
But our Marriage is dead, when the Pleasure is fled:
  'Twas Pleasure first made it an Oath.

If I have Pleasures for a Friend,
  And farther Love in store,
What Wrong has he whose Joys did end,
  And who cou'd give no more?
'Tis a Madness that he should be jealous of me,
  Or that I shou'd bar him of another:
For all we can gain, is to give our selves Pain,
  When neither can hinder the other.

Prologue[2]

OUR Author by experience finds it true,
'Tis much more hard to please himself, than you:
And out of no feign'd Modesty, this day,
Damns his Laborious Trifle of a Play:
Not that its worse than what before he writ,
But he has now another taste of Wit;
And to confess a Truth, (though out of time)
Grows weary of his long-lov'd Mistriss, Rhyme.
Passion's too fierce to be in Fetters bound,
And Nature flies him like Enchanted Ground.

[1] Published in *Marriage A-la Mode*, 1673, Act I, Scene i. Text of *Plays*, 1701.
[2] Published in *Aureng-Zebe: or, The great Mogul*, 1676. Text of *Plays*, 1701.

What Verse can do, he has perform'd in this,
Which he presumes the most correct of his.
But spite of all his Pride, a secret Shame
Invades his Breast at *Shakespear's* sacred Name:
Aw'd when he hears his God-like *Romans* Rage,
He, in a just despair, would quit the Stage.
And to an Age less polish'd, more unskill'd,
Does, with disdain, the foremost Honours yield,
As with the greater dead he dares not strive,
He would not match his Verse with those who live:
Let him retire, betwixt two Ages cast,
The first of this, and hindmost of the Last.
A losing Gamester, let him sneak away;
He bears no ready Money from the Play.
The Fate which governs Poets thought it fit,
He should not raise his Fortunes by his Wit.
The Clergy thrive, and the litigious Bar;
Dull Heroes fatten with the spoils of War;
All Southern Vices, Heav'n be prais'd are here;
But Wit's a Luxury you think too dear.
When you to cultivate the Plant are loth,
'Tis a shrewd sign 'twas never of your growth:
And Wit in Northern Climates will not blow,
Except, like *Orange-Trees* 'tis Hous'd from Snow.
There needs no care to put a Play-House down,
'Tis the most desart Place of all the Town.
Wit and our Neighbours, to speak proudly, are
Like Monarchs, ruin'd with expensive War.
While, like wise *English*, unconcern'd, you sit,
And see us play the Tragedy of Wit.

A Song from the Italian[1]

By a dismal Cypress lying,
Damon cry'd, all pale and dying,
Kind is Death that ends my pain,
But cruel She I lov'd in vain.
The Mossy Fountains
Murmure my trouble,
And hollow Mountains
My groans redouble:
Every Nymph mourns me,
Thus while I languish;

[1] Published in *Limberham: or, The Kind Keeper,* 1678, Act III, Scene i. Text of *Plays,* 1701.

She only scorns me,
Who caus'd my anguish.
No Love returning me, but all hope denying;
By a dismal Cypress lying,
Like a Swan, so sung he dying:
Kind is Death that ends my pain,
But cruel She I lov'd in vain.

Prologue[1]

SEE my lov'd *Britons*, see your *Shakespear* rise,
An awful Ghost confess'd to human Eyes!
Unman'd, methinks, distinguish'd I had been,
From other Shades, by this eternal Green,
About whose Wreaths the vulgar Poets strive,
And with a touch their wither'd Bays revive.
Untaught, unpractis'd in a barbarous Age,
I found not but created first the Stage.
And, if I drain'd no *Greek* or *Latin* store,
'Twas, that my own abundance gave me more.
On Foreign Trade I needed not rely,
Like fruitful *Britan*, rich without supply.
In this my rough-drawn Play, you shall behold
Some Master-strokes, so manly and so bold,
That he, who meant to alter, found 'em such,
He shook; and thought it Sacrilege to touch.
Now, where are the Successors to my Name?
What bring they, to fill out a Poet's Fame?
Weak, short-liv'd Issues of a feeble Age;
Scarce living to be Christen'd on the Stage!
For Humour, Farce; for Love, they Rhyme dispence.
That tolls the Knell for their departed sense.
Dulness might thrive in any Trade but this:
'Twou'd recommend to some fat Benefice.
Dulness, that in a Play-house meets disgrace
Might meet with Reverence in its proper place.
The fulsome clench that nauseates the Town
Wou'd from a Judge or Alderman go down!
Such virtue is there in a Robe and Gown!
And that insipid stuff which here you hate,
Might somewhere else be call'd a grave debate:
Dulness is decent in the Church and State.
But I forget that still 'tis understood,
Bad Plays are best decry'd by showing good:

[1] Published in *Troilus and Cressida*, 1679. Text of *Plays*, 1701.

Sit silent then, that my pleas'd Soul may see
A judging Audience once, and worthy me:
My faithful Scene from true Records shall tell
How *Trojan* Valour did the *Greek* excell;
Your great Forefathers shall their Fame regain,
And *Homer*'s angry Ghost repine in vain.

Song[1]

CAN Life be a blessing,
Or worth the possessing,
Can life be a blessing if love were away?
Ah no! though our love all Night keep us waking,
And though he torment us with Cares all the Day,
Yet he sweetens, he sweetens our pains in the taking.
There's an hour at the last, there's an hour to repay.

In every possessing,
The ravishing blessing,
In every possessing the fruit of our pain,
Poor Lovers forget long Ages of anguish,
Whate'er they have suffer'd and done to obtain;
'Tis a pleasure, a pleasure to sigh and to languish,
When we hope, when we hope to be happy again.

Prologue[2]

IF YET there be a few that take delight
In that which reasonable Men should write,
To them Alone we Dedicate this Night.
The Rest may satisfie their curious Itch
With City Gazets, or some Factious Speech,
Or what-ere Libel, for the Publick Good,
Stirs up the Shrove-tide Crew to Fire and Blood!
Remove your Benches, you apostate Pit,
And take Above, twelve penny-worth of Wit;
Go back to your dear Dancing on the Rope,
Or see what's worse, the Devil and the Pope!
The Plays that take on our Corrupted Stage,
Methinks, resemble the distracted Age;
Noise, Madness, all unreasonable Things,

[1] Published in *Troilus and Cressida*, 1679, Act III, Scene ii. Text of *Plays*, 1701.
[2] Published in Nahum Tate's *The Loyal General*, 1680. Text of first edition.

That strike at Sense, as Rebels do at Kings!
The stile of Forty One our Poets write,
And you are grown to judge like Forty Eight.
Such Censures our mistaking Audience make,
That 'tis almost grown Scandalous to Take!
They talk of Feavours that infect the Brains,
But Non-sence is the new Disease that reigns.
Weak Stomachs, with a long Disease opprest,
Cannot the Cordials of strong Wit digest;
Therefore thin Nourishment of Farce ye choose,
Decoctions of a Barly-water Muse:
A Meal of Tragedy wou'd make ye Sick,
Unless it were a very tender Chick.
Some Scenes in Sippets wou'd be worth our time,
Those wou'd go down; some Love that's poach'd in Rime;
If these shou'd fail—
We must lie down, and, after all our cost,
Keep Holy-day, like Water-men in Frost;
Whilst you turn Players on the Worlds great Stage,
And Act your selves the Farce of your own Age.

Absalom and Achitophel. A Poem[1]

IN PIOUS times, e'r Priest-craft did begin,
Before *Polygamy* was made a Sin;
When Man on many multipli'd his kind,
E'r one to one was cursedly confin'd,
When Nature prompted and no Law deni'd
Promiscuous Use of Concubine and Bride;
Then *Israel's* Monarch, after Heavens own heart,
His vigorous warmth did, variously, impart
To Wives and Slaves: And, wide as his Command,
Scatter'd his Maker's Image through the Land.
Michal,[2] of Royal Blood, the Crown did wear,
A soil ungrateful to the Tiller's care:
Not so the rest; for several Mothers bore
To God-like *David*[3] several sons before.
But since like Slaves his Bed they did ascend,
No True Succession could their Seed attend.
Of all this Numerous Progeny was none
So Beautiful so Brave as *Absalon*:[4]
Whether, inspird by some diviner Lust,

[1] Published in November, 1681. Text of second edition, December, 1681. See Preface.
[2] Queen Katharine.
[3] Charles II.
[4] The Duke of Monmouth.

His father got him with a greater Gust,
Or that his Conscious Destiny made way
By manly Beauty to Imperial Sway.
Early in Foreign Fields he won Renown
With Kings and States allied to *Israel's* Crown:
In Peace the thoughts of War he coud remove
And seem'd as he were onely born for Love.
What e'r he did was done with so much ease,
In him alone, 'twas Natural to please;
His motions all accompanied with grace;
And *Paradise* was open'd in his face.
With secret Joy, indulgent *David* view'd
His Youthful Image in his Son renew'd;
To all his wishes Nothing he deni'd
And made the Charming *Annabel* his Bride.
What faults he had (for who from faults is free?)
His father coud not or he woud not see.
Some warm excesses, which the Law forbore,
Were constru'd Youth that purg'd by boiling o'r:
And *Amnon's* Murther, by a specious Name,
Was call'd a Just Revenge for injur'd Fame.
Thus Prais'd and Lov'd, the Noble Youth remain'd,
While *David*, undisturb'd, in *Sion* reign'd.
But Life can never be sincerely blest:
Heav'n punishes the bad, and proves the best.
The *Jews*, a Headstrong, Moody, Murm'ring race
As ever tri'd th' extent and stretch of grace;
God's pamper'd People, whom, debauch'd with ease,
No King could govern nor no God could please;
(Gods they had tri'd of every shape and size
That God-smiths could produce or Priests devise:)
These *Adam*-wits, too fortunately free,
Began to dream they wanted liberty;
And when no rule, no president was found
Of men, by Laws less circumscrib'd and bound;
They led their wild desires to Woods and Caves;
And thought that all but Savages were Slaves.
They who, when *Saul* was dead, without a blow
Made foolish *Ishbosheth*[5] the Crown forgo;
Who banisht *David* did from *Hebron* bring,
And, with a General shout, proclaim'd him King:
Those very *Jews* who at their very best
Their Humour more than Loyalty exprest,
Now wondred why so long they had obey'd
An Idol-Monarch which their hands had made;
Thought they might ruine him they could create

[5] Richard Cromwell. "*Saul*" is of course Oliver Cromwell.

Or melt him to that Golden Calf, a State.
But these were random Bolts: No form'd Design
Nor Interest made the Factious Croud to join:
The sober part of *Israel*, free from stain,
Well knew the value of a peaceful reign;
And, looking backward with a wise afright,
Saw Seams of wounds, dishonest to the sight:
In contemplation of whose ugly Scars,
They curst the memory of Civil Wars.
The moderate sort of Men, thus qualifi'd,
Inclin'd the Ballance to the better side;
And *David's* mildness manag'd it so well,
The bad found no occasion to Rebel.
But, when to Sin our byast Nature leans,
The careful Devil is still at hand with means;
And providently Pimps for ill desires:
The Good Old Cause, reviv'd, a Plot requires,
Plots, true or false, are necessary things,
To raise up Common-wealths and ruin Kings.
Th' inhabitants of old *Jerusalem*,
Were *Jebusites*;[6] the Town so call'd from them;
And their's the Native right——
But when the chosen People grew more strong,
The rightful cause at length became the wrong;
And every loss the men of *Jebus* bore,
They still were thought God's enemies the more.
Thus, worn and weaken'd, well or ill content,
Submit they must to *David's* Government:
Impoverish't and depriv'd of all Command,
Their Taxes doubled as they lost their Land;
And, what was harder yet to flesh and blood,
Their Gods disgrac'd, and burnt like common Wood.
This set the Heathen Priesthood in a flame,
For Priests of all Religions are the same:
Of whatsoe'er descent their Godhead be,
Stock, Stone, or other homely Pedigree,
In his defence his Servants are as bold,
As if he had been born of beaten Gold.
The *Jewish Rabbins*, though their Enemies,
In this conclude them honest men and wise:
For 'twas their duty, all the Learned think,
T' espouse his Cause by whom they eat and drink.
From hence began that Plot,[7] the Nations Curse,
Bad in itself, but represented worse,
Rais'd in extremes, and in extremes decri'd,
With Oaths affirm'd, with dying Vows deni'd,

[6] The Catholics.
[7] The Popish Plot.

Not weigh'd or winnow'd by the Multitude,
But swallow'd in the Mass, unchewed and crude.
Some Truth there was, but dashed and brew'd with Lies;
To please the Fools, and puzzle all the Wise.
Succeeding Times did equal Folly call
Believing nothing or believing all.
The *Egyptian* Rites the *Jebusites* embrac'd,
Where Gods were recommended by their taste.
Such sav'ry Deities must needs be good
As serv'd at once for Worship and for Food.
By force they could not Introduce these Gods,
For Ten to One in former days was odds.
So Fraud was us'd, (the Sacrificers Trade,)
Fools are more hard to Conquer than Persuade.
Their busie Teachers mingled with the *Jews*
And rak'd for Converts even the Court and Stews:
Which *Hebrew* Priests the more unkindly took,
Because the Fleece accompanies the Flock.
Some thought they God's Anointed meant to slay
By Guns, invented since full many a day:
Our Author swears it not; but who can know
How far the Devil and *Jebusites* may go?
This Plot, which fail'd for want of common Sense,
Had yet a deep and dangerous Consequence;
For as, when raging Fevers boil the Blood
The standing Lake soon floats into a Floud;
And ev'ry hostile Humour which before
Slept quiet in its Channels bubbles o're:
So, several Factions from this first Ferment
Work up to Foam, and threat the Government.
Some by their Friends, more by themselves thought wise,
Oppos'd the Pow'r to which they could not rise.
Some had in Courts been Great and, thrown from thence,
Like Fiends were hardened in Impenitence.
Some, by their Monarch's fatal mercy grown,
From Pardon'd Rebels, Kinsmen to the Throne
Were raised in Pow'r and Publick Office high;
Strong Bands, if Bands ungrateful men coud tie.
Of these the false *Achitophel*[8] was first,
A Name to all succeeding Ages curst.
For close Designs and crooked Counsels fit,
Sagacious, Bold, and Turbulent of wit,
Restless, unfixt in Principles and Place,
In Pow'r unpleased, impatient of Disgrace;
A fiery Soul, which working out its way,
Fretted the Pigmy Body to decay:
And o'r informed the Tenement of Clay.

[8] The first Earl of Shaftesbury.

A daring Pilot in extremity;
Pleas'd with the Danger, when the Waves went high
He sought the Storms; but, for a Calm unfit,
Would Steer too nigh the Sands to boast his Wit.
Great Wits are sure to Madness near alli'd
And thin Partitions do their Bounds divide;
Else, why should he, with Wealth and Honour blest,
Refuse his Age the needful hours of Rest?
Punish a Body which he coud not please,
Bankrupt of Life, yet Prodigal of Ease?
And all to leave what with his Toil he won
To that unfeather'd two-legg'd thing, a Son:
Got, while his Soul did huddled Notions trie;
And born a shapeless Lump, like Anarchy.
In Friendship false, implacable in Hate,
Resolv'd to Ruine or to Rule the State:
To Compass this the Triple Bond he broke;
The Pillars of the Publick Safety shook,
And fitted *Israel* for a Foreign Yoke;
Then, seiz'd with Fear, yet still affecting Fame,
Usurp'd a Patriot's All-attoning Name.
So easie still it proves in Factious Times
With publick Zeal to cancel private Crimes:
How safe is Treason and how sacred ill,
Where none can sin against the Peoples Will,
Where Crouds can wink; and no offence be known,
Since in anothers guilt they find their own.
Yet, Fame deserv'd, no Enemy can grudge;
The Statesman we abhor, but praise the Judge.
In *Israels* courts ne'er sat an *Abbethdin*[9]
With more discerning Eyes or Hands more clean,
Unbrib'd, unsought, the Wretched to redress;
Swift of Dispatch and easie of Access.
Oh, had he been content to serve the Crown
With Vertues onely proper to the Gown,
Or had the rankness of the Soil been freed
From Cockle that opprest the Noble Seed,
David for him his tuneful Harp had strung,
And Heav'n had wanted one Immortal Song.
But wild Ambitión loves to slide, not stand,
And Fortunes Ice prefers to Vertues Land.
Achitophel, grown weary to possess
A lawful Fame, and lazie Happiness,
Disdain'd the Golden Fruit to gather free
And lent the Crowd his Arm to shake the Tree.
Now, manifest of Crimes, contriv'd long since,
He stood at bold Defiance with his Prince:

[9] Lord Chancellor.

Held up the Buckler of the Peoples Cause
Against the Crown; and sculk'd behind the Laws.
The wish'd occasion of the Plot he takes;
Some Circumstances finds, but more he makes.
By buzzing Emissaries, fills the ears
Of listening Crouds, with Jealousies and Fears
Of Arbitrary Counsels brought to light,
And proves the King himself a *Jebusite*.
Weak Arguments! which yet he knew full well,
Were strong with People easie to Rebel.
For, govern'd by the *Moon*, the giddy *Jews*
Tread the same Track when she the Prime renews:
And once in twenty Years, their Scribes record,
By natural Instinct they change their Lord.
Achitophel still wants a Chief, and none
Was found so fit as Warlike *Absalon*:
Not, that he wish'd his Greatness to create,
(For Politicians neither love nor hate:)
But, for he knew his Title not allow'd,
Would keep him still depending on the Croud,
That Kingly pow'r, thus ebbing out, might be
Drawn to the Dregs of a Democracie.
Him he attempts with studied Arts to please
And sheds his Venome in such words as these.
  Auspicious Prince! at whose Nativity
Some Royal Planet rul'd the Southern Sky;
Thy longing Countries Darling and Desire,
Their cloudy Pillar, and their guardian Fire,
Their second *Moses*, whose extended Wand
Divides the Seas and shows the promis'd Land,
Whose dawning Day, in every distant Age,
Has exercised the Sacred Prophets rage,
The Peoples Pray'r, the glad Diviners Theam,
The Young mens Vision and the Old mens Dream!
Thee, *Saviour*, Thee the Nations Vows confess;
And, never satisfi'd with seeing, bless:
Swift, unbespoken Pomps, thy steps proclaim,
And stammering Babes are taught to lisp thy Name.
How long wilt thou the general Joy detain;
Starve, and defraud the People of thy Reign?
Content ingloriously to pass thy days,
Like one of Vertues Fools that Feeds on Praise;
Till thy fresh Glories, which now shine so bright,
Grow Stale and Tarnish with our dayly sight.
Believe me, Royal Youth, thy Fruit must be
Or gather'd Ripe, or rot upon the Tree.
Heav'n has to all allotted, soon or late,
Some lucky Revolution of their Fate:

Whose Motions, if we watch and guide with Skill,
(For humane Good depends on humane Will,)
Our Fortune rolls as from a smooth Descent
And, from the first impression, takes the Bent;
But, if unseiz'd, she glides away like wind;
And leaves repenting Folly far behind.
Now, now she meets you with a glorious prize
And spreads her Locks before her as she flies.
Had thus Old *David*, from whose Loins you spring,
Not dar'd, when Fortune call'd him, to be King,
At *Gath* an Exile he might still remain,
And Heavens Anointing Oil had been in vain.
Let his successful Youth your hopes engage,
But shun th' example of Declining Age.
Behold him setting in his Western Skies,
The Shadows lengthening as the Vapours rise.
He is not now, as when, on *Jordan's* Sand,
The Joyful People throng'd to see him Land,
Cov'ring the *Beach* and blackning all the *Strand*:
But like the Prince of Angels, from his height,
Comes tumbling downward with diminish'd light:
Betray'd by one poor Plot to publick Scorn,
(Our onely blessing since his curst Return,)
Those heaps of People which one Sheaf did bind,
Blown off and scatter'd by a puff of Wind.
What strength can he to your Designs oppose,
Naked of Friends, and round beset with Foes?
If *Pharaoh's*[10] doubtful succour he should use,
A Foreign Aid would more incense the *Jews*:
Proud *Egypt* woud dissembled Friendship bring;
Foment the War, but not support the King:
Nor woud the Royal Party e'r unite
With *Pharaoh's* arms t' assist the *Jebusite*;
Or if they shoud, their Interest soon would break,
And, with such odious Aid, make *David* weak.
All sorts of men, by my successful Arts
Abhorring Kings, estrange their altered Hearts
From *David's* Rule: And 'tis the general Cry,
Religion, Common-wealth, and Liberty.
If you, as Champion of the Publique Good,
Add to their Arms a Chief of Royal Blood;
What may not *Israel* hope, and what Applause
Might such a General gain by such a Cause?
Not barren Praise alone, that Gaudy Flow'r,
Fair onely to the sight, but solid Pow'r:
And Nobler is a limited Command,

[10] Louis XIV.

Giv'n by the Love of all your Native Land,
Than a Successive Title, Long, and Dark,
Drawn from the Mouldy Rolls of *Noah's* ark.
  What cannot Praise effect in Mighty Minds,
When Flattery Sooths and when Ambition Blinds!
Desire of Pow'r, on Earth a Vitious Weed,
Yet, sprung from High is of Cœlestial Seed;
In God 'tis Glory: And when Men Aspire,
'Tis but a Spark too much of Heavenly Fire.
Th' Ambitious Youth, too Covetous of Fame,
Too full of Angels Metal in his Frame,
Unwarily was led from Vertues ways,
Made Drunk with Honour, and debauch'd with Praise.
Half loath and half consenting to the Ill,
(For Loyal Blood within him strugled still,)
He thus repli'd—And what Pretence have I
To take up Arms for Publick Liberty?
My Father Governs with unquestion'd Right;
The Faiths Defender and Mankinds Delight,
Good, Gracious, Just, observant of the Laws;
And Heav'n by Wonders has espous'd his Cause.
Whom has he Wrong'd in all his Peaceful Reign?
Who sues for Justice to his Throne in Vain?
What Millions has he pardoned of his Foes
Whom Just Revenge did to his Wrath expose?
Mild, Easie, Humble, Studious of our Good,
Enclin'd to Mercy, and averse from Blood.
If Mildness Ill with Stubborn *Israel* Suit,
His Crime is God's beloved Attribute.
What could he gain, his People to Betray
Or change his Right, for Arbitrary Sway?
Let Haughty *Pharaoh* Curse with such a Reign
His Fruitful *Nile*, and Yoak a Servile Train.
If *David's* Rule *Jerusalem* Displease,
The *Dog-star* heats their Brains to this Disease.
Why then should I, Encouraging the Bad,
Turn Rebel and run Popularly Mad?
Were he a Tyrant who, by Lawless Might,
Opprest the *Jews* and rais'd the *Jebusite*,
Well might I Mourn; but Nature's holy Bands
Would Curb my Spirits, and Restrain my Hands;
The People might assert their Liberty;
But what was Right in them, were Crime in me.
His Favour leaves me nothing to require;
Prevents my Wishes and out-runs Desire.
What more can I expect while *David* lives?
All but his Kingly Diadem he gives:
And that: But there he paus'd; then Sighing, said,

Is Justly destin'd for a Worthier head.
For when my Father from his Toyls shall Rest
And late Augment the Number of the Blest:
His Lawful Issue shall the Throne ascend,
Or the *Collat'ral* Line, where that shall end.
His Brother, though Opprest with Vulgar Spight,
Yet Dauntless and Secure of Native Right,
Of every Royal Vertue stands possest;
Still Dear to all the Bravest and the Best.
His Courage Foes, his Friends his Truth Proclaim;
His Loyalty the King, the World his Fame.
His Mercy ev'n th' Offending Croud will find,
For sure he comes of a Forgiving Kind.
Why shoud I then Repine at Heavens Decree
Which gives me no Pretence to Royalty?
Yet oh that Fate, Propitiously Inclin'd,
Had rais'd my Birth, or had debas'd my Mind;
To my large Soul, not all her Treasure lent,
And then betrai'd it to a mean Descent.
I find, I find my mounting Spirits Bold,
And *David's* part disdains my Mothers Mold.
Why am I scanted by a Niggard Birth?
My soul Disclaims the Kindred of her Earth:
And, made for Empire, Whispers me within;
Desire of Greatness is a God-like Sin.
  Him Staggering so when Hells dire Agent found,
While fainting Vertue scarce maintain'd her Ground,
He pours fresh Forces in, and thus Replies:
  Th' eternal God, Supreamly Good and Wise,
Imparts not these Prodigious Gifts in vain;
What Wonders are Reserv'd to bless your Reign?
Against your will your Arguments have shown,
Such Vertue's only giv'n to guide a Throne.
Not that your Father's Mildness I contemn,
But manly Force becomes the Diadem.
'Tis true he grants the People all they crave;
And more perhaps than Subjects ought to have:
For Lavish Grants suppose a Monarch tame
And more his Goodness than his Wit proclaim.
But when should People strive their Bonds to break,
If not when Kings are Negligent or Weak?
Let him give on till he can give no more,
The thrifty Sanhedrin shall keep him poor:
And every Sheckle which he can receive
Shall cost a Limb of his Prerogative.
To ply him with new Plots shall be my care;
Or plunge him deep in some Expensive War;
Which, when his Treasure can no more supply,

He must, with the Remains of Kingship, buy.
His faithful Friends our Jealousies and Fears
Call *Jebusites*; and *Pharaoh's* Pensioners,
Whom, when our Fury from his Aid has torn,
He shall be naked left to publick Scorn.
The next Successor, whom I fear and hate,
My Arts have made obnoxious to the State;
Turn'd all his Vertues to his Overthrow,
And gain'd our Elders to pronounce a Foe.
His Right, for Sums of necessary Gold,
Shall first be Pawn'd, and afterwards be Sold;
Till time shall Ever-wanting *David* draw,
To pass your doubtful Title into Law.
If not; the People have a Right Supreme
To make their Kings; for Kings are made for them.
All Empire is no more than Pow'r in Trust,
Which, when resum'd, can be no longer Just.
Succession, for the general Good design'd,
In its own wrong a Nation cannot bind:
If altering that, the People can relieve,
Better one suffer, than a Nation grieve.
The *Jews* well know their pow'r: e'r *Saul*[11] they chose
God was their King, and God they durst Depose.
Urge now your Piety, your Filial Name,
A Father's Right and Fear of future Fame;
The Publick Good, that Universal Call,
To which even Heav'n submitted, answers all.
Nor let his Love enchant your generous Mind;
'Tis Natures trick to propagate her Kind.
Our fond Begetters, who would never die,
Love but themselves in their Posterity.
Or let his Kindness by th' Effects be tried
Or let him lay his vain Pretence aside.
God said he loved your Father; coud he bring
A better Proof than to anoint him King?
It surely shew'd, He lov'd the Shepherd well
Who gave so fair a Flock as *Israel*.
Would *David* have you thought his Darling Son?
What means he then, to Alienate the Crown?
The name of Godly he may blush to bear:
'Tis after Gods own heart to Cheat his Heir.
He to his Brother gives Supreme Command;
To you a Legacie of Barren Land:
Perhaps th' old Harp on which he thrums his Lays:
Or some dull *Hebrew* Ballad in your Praise.
Then the next Heir, a Prince, Severe and Wise,

[11] Oliver Cromwell.

Already looks on you with Jealous Eyes,
Sees through the thin Disguises of your Arts,
And marks your Progress in the Peoples Hearts.
Though now his mighty Soul its Grief contains;
He meditates Revenge who least Complains.
And like a Lion, Slumb'ring in the way,
Or Sleep dissembling, while he waits his Prey,
His fearless Foes within his Distance draws,
Constrains his Roaring, and Contracts his Paws:
Till at the last, his time for Fury found,
He shoots with sudden Vengeance from the Ground:
The Prostrate Vulgar, passes o'r and Spares;
But with a Lordly Rage, his Hunters tears;
Your Case no tame Expedients will afford;
Resolve on Death, or Conquest by the Sword,
Which for no less a Stake than Life, you Draw,
And Self-defence is Natures Eldest Law.
Leave the warm People no Considering time;
For then Rebellion may be thought a Crime.
Prevail your self of what Occasion gives,
But trie your Title while your Father lives;
And, that your Arms may have a fair Pretence,
Proclaim, you take them in the King's Defence;
Whose Sacred Life each minute woud Expose,
To Plots, from seeming Friends and secret Foes.
And who can sound the depth of *David's* Soul?
Perhaps his fear, his kindness may Controul.
He fears his Brother, though he loves his Son,
For plighted Vows too late to be undone.
If so, by Force he wishes to be gain'd,
Like Womens Leachery to seem Constrain'd:
Doubt not; but, when he most affects the Frown,
Commit a pleasing Rape upon the Crown.
Secure his Person to secure your Cause;
They who possess the Prince, possess the Laws.
  He said, And this Advice above the rest
With *Absalon's* Mild Nature suited best;
Unblamed of Life (Ambition set aside,)
Not stain'd with Cruelty, nor puft with pride.
How happy had he been, if Destiny
Had higher placed his Birth, or not so high!
His Kingly Vertues might have claim'd a Throne
And blest all other Countries but his own:
But charming Greatness, since so few refuse;
'Tis Juster to Lament him, than Accuse.
Strong were his hopes a Rival to remove,
With Blandishments to gain the publick Love,
To Head the Faction while their Zeal was hot,

And Popularly Prosecute the Plot.
To farther this, *Achitophel* Unites
The Malecontents of all the *Israelites:*
Whose differing Parties he could wisely Join
For several Ends, to serve the same Design.
The Best, and of the Princes some were such,
Who thought the pow'r of Monarchy too much:
Mistaken Men, and Patriots in their Hearts;
Not Wicked, but seduc'd by Impious Arts.
By these the Springs of Property were bent,
And wound so high, they Crack'd the Government.
The next for Interest sought t' embroil the State,
To sell their Duty at a dearer rate;
And make their *Jewish* Markets of the Throne;
Pretending Publick Good, to serve their own.
Others thought Kings an useless heavy Load,
Who Cost too much, and did too little Good.
These were for laying Honest *David* by
On Principles of pure good Husbandry.
With them join'd all th' Haranguers of the Throng
That thought to get Preferment by the Tongue.
Who follow next, a double danger bring,
Not onely hating *David*, but the King;
The *Solymæan* Rout;[12] well Vers'd of old
In Godly Faction, and in Treason bold;
Cowring and Quaking at a Conqu'ror's Sword,
But Lofty to a Lawful Prince Restored;
Saw with Disdain an *Ethnick* Plot begun
And Scorned by *Jebusites* to be Out-done.
Hot *Levites* Headed these; who pul'd before
From th' *Ark*, which in the Judges days they bore,
Resum'd their Cant, and with a Zealous Crie
Pursu'd their old belov'd Theocracie.
Where Sanhedrin and Priest enslav'd the Nation
And justifi'd their Spoils by Inspiration:
For who so fit for Reign as *Aaron's* Race,
If once Dominion they could found in Grace?
These led the Pack; though not of surest scent,
Yet deepest mouth'd against the Government.
A numerous Host of dreaming Saints succeed;
Of the true old Enthusiastick Breed:
'Gainst Form and Order they their Pow'r imploy;
Nothing to Build, and all things to Destroy.
But far more numerous was the Herd of such,
Who think too little, and who talk too much.
These, out of meer instinct, they knew not why,

[12] London rebels.

Adored their Fathers' God, and Property:
And, by the same blind Benefit of Fate,
The Devil and the *Jebusite* did hate:
Born to be sav'd, even in their own despight;
Because they could not help believing right.
Such were the Tools; but a whole Hydra more
Remains, of sprouting heads too long to score.
Some of their Chiefs were Princes of the Land;
In the first Rank of these did *Zimri*[13] stand:
A man so various, that he seem'd to be
Not one, but all Mankind's Epitome.
Stiff in Opinions, always in the wrong;
Was Every thing by starts, and Nothing long:
But, in the course of one revolving Moon,
Was Chymist, Fidler, States-man, and Buffoon;
Then all for Women, Painting, Rhiming, Drinking,
Besides ten thousand Freaks that died in thinking.
Blest Madman, who coud every hour employ,
With something New to wish, or to enjoy!
Railing and praising were his usual Theams;
And both (to shew his Judgment) in Extreams:
So over Violent, or over Civil,
That every Man, with him, was God or Devil.
In squandring Wealth was his peculiar Art:
Nothing went unrewarded, but Desert.
Begger'd by fools, whom still he found too late:
He had his Jest, and they had his Estate.
He laugh'd himself from Court; then sought Relief
By forming Parties, but could ne'r be Chief:
For, spight of him, the weight of Business fell
On *Absolon* and wise *Achitophel*:
Thus wicked but in Will, of Means bereft,
He left not Faction, but of that was left.
  Titles and Names 'twere tedious to Reherse
Of Lords, below the Dignity of Verse.
Wits, Warriors, Commonwealths-men were the best:
Kind Husbands and meer Nobles all the rest
And, therefore in the name of Dulness, be
The well-hung *Balaam*[14] and cold *Caleb*[15] free;
And Canting *Nadab*[16] let Oblivion damn,
Who made new Porridge for the Paschal Lamb.
Let Friendships holy Band some Names assure,
Some their own Worth, and some let Scorn secure.
Nor shall the Rascal Rabble here have Place,

[13] The Duke of Buckingham.
[14] The Earl of Huntingdon.
[15] Lord Grey.
[16] Lord Howard of Escrick.

Whom Kings no Titles gave, and God no Grace:
Not Bull-fac'd *Jonas*, who coud Statutes draw
To mean Rebellion, and make Treason Law.
But he, though bad, is follow'd by a worse,
The Wretch, who Heav'ns Anointed dar'd to Curse.
Shimei,[17] whose Youth did early Promise bring
Of Zeal to God, and Hatred to his King;
Did wisely from Expensive Sins refrain,
And never broke the Sabbath, but for Gain:
Nor ever was he known an Oath to vent,
Or Curse, unless against the Government.
Thus, heaping Wealth, by the most ready way
Among the *Jews*, which was to Cheat and Pray;
The City, to reward his pious Hate
Against his Master, chose him Magistrate:
His Hand a Vare of Justice did uphold;
His Neck was loaded with a Chain of Gold.
During his Office, Treason was no Crime.
The Sons of *Belial* had a Glorious Time:
For *Shimei*, though not prodigal of pelf,
Yet lov'd his wicked Neighbour as himself:
When two or three were gather'd to declaim
Against the Monarch of *Jerusalem*,
Shimei was always in the midst of them.
And, if they Curst the King when he was by,
Woud rather Curse, than break good Company.
If any durst his Factious Friends accuse,
He pact a jury of dissenting *Jews*:
Whose fellow-feeling, in the godly Cause,
Would free the suff'ring Saint from Humane Laws.
For Laws are onely made to Punish those
Who serve the King, and to protect his Foes.
If any leisure time he had from Pow'r,
(Because 'tis Sin to misimploy an hour;)
His bus'ness was by Writing to persuade
That kings were Useless, and a Clog to Trade:
And that his noble Stile he might refine,
No *Rechabite* more shund the fumes of Wine.
Chaste were his Cellars; and his Shrieval Board
The Grossness of a City Feast abhor'd:
His Cooks, with long disuse, their Trade forgot;
Cool was his Kitchin, though his Brains were hot.
Such frugal Vertue Malice may accuse;
But sure 'twas necessary to the *Jews*:
For Towns once burnt, such Magistrates require
As dare not tempt Gods Providence by Fire.

[17] Slingsley Bethel, one of the sheriffs of London.

With Spiritual Food he fed his Servants well,
But free from Flesh that made the *Jews* rebel:
And *Moses's* Laws he held in more account,
For forty days of Fasting in the Mount.
To speak the rest, who better are forgot,
Would tire a well-breath'd Witness of the Plot:
Yet, *Corah*,[18] thou shalt from Oblivion pass;
Erect thy self thou Monumental Brass:
High as the Serpent of thy Metal made,
While Nations stand secure beneath thy shade.
What though his Birth were base, yet Comets rise
From Earthy Vapours, e'r they shine in Skies.
Prodigious Actions may as well be done
By Weaver's issue as by Prince's son.
This Arch-Attestor for the Publick Good
By that one Deed enobles all his Bloud.
Who'ever ask'd the Witnesses high race
Whose Oath with Martyrdom did *Stephen* grace?
Ours was a *Levite*, and as times went then,
His tribe were God-almighties Gentlemen.
Sunk were his Eyes, his Voice was harsh and loud,
Sure signs he neither Cholerick was, nor Proud:
His long Chin prov'd his Wit; his Saint-like Grace
A Church Vermilion, and a *Moses's* Face.
His Memory, miraculously great,
Coud Plots, exceeding mans belief, repeat;
Which, therefore cannot be accounted Lies,
For humane Wit coud never such devise.
Some future Truths are mingled in his Book;
But where the Witness fail'd, the Prophet spoke:
Some things like Visionary flights appear;
The Spirit caught him up, the Lord knows where:
And gave him his *Rabinical* degree,
Unknown to Foreign University.
His Judgment yet his Mem'ry did excel,
Which piec'd his wondrous Evidence so well:
And suited to the temper of the Times;
Then groaning under *Jebusitick* Crimes.
Let *Israels* foes suspect his Heav'nly call,
And rashly judge his Writ Apocryphal;
Our Laws for such affronts have Forfeits made:
He takes his Life, who takes away his Trade.
Were I myself in Witness *Corah's* place,
The Wretch who did me such a dire disgrace
Should whet my memory, though once forgot,
To make him an Appendix of my Plot.

[18] Titus Oates.

His Zeal to Heav'n, made him his Prince despise,
And load his Person with indignities:
But Zeal peculiar priviledge affords,
Indulging latitude to deeds and words:
And *Corah* might for *Agag's* murther[19] call,
In terms as course as *Samuel* us'd to *Saul*.
What others in his Evidence did join,
(The best that coud be had for love or coin,)
In *Corah's* own predicament will fall
For *Witness* is a Common Name to all.
  Surrounded thus with Friends of every sort,
Deluded *Absolom* forsakes the Court:
Impatient of high hopes, urg'd with renown,
And Fir'd with near possession of a Crown.
The admiring Croud are dazled with surprize
And on his goodly person feed their eyes:
His joy conceal'd, he sets himself to show;
On each side bowing popularly low:
His looks, his gestures, and his words he frames
And with familiar ease repeats their Names.
Thus, form'd by Nature, furnished out with Arts,
He glides unfelt into their secret hearts:
Then with a kind compassionating look,
And sighs, bespeaking pity e'r he spoke,
Few words he said, but easie those and fit,
More slow than Hybla drops, and far more sweet.
  I mourn, my Country-men, your lost Estate,
Though far unable to prevent your Fate:
Behold a Banish'd man, for your dear cause
Expos'd a prey to Arbitrary Laws!
Yet oh! that I alone coud be undone,
Cut off from Empire, and no more a Son!
Now all your Liberties a spoil are made;
Egypt[20] and *Tyrus*[21] intercept your Trade,
And *Jebusites* your Sacred Rites invade.
My Father, whom with reverence yet I name,
Charm'd into Ease, is careless of his Fame:
And, brib'd with petty sums of Foreign Gold,
Is grown in *Bathsheba's*[22] Embraces old:
Exalts his Enemies, his Friends destroys,
And all his pow'r against himself imploys.
He gives, and let him give my right away;
But why should he his own and yours betray?
He onely, he can make the Nation bleed,

[19] The murder of Sir Edmund Bury Godfrey, October, 1678.
[20] France.
[21] Holland.
[22] The Duchess of Portsmouth.

And he alone from my revenge is freed.
Take then my tears (with that he wiped his Eyes)
'Tis all the Aid my present pow'r supplies:
No Court-Informer can these Arms accuse;
These Arms may Sons against their Fathers use;
And, 'tis my wish, the next Successor's reign
May make no other *Israelite* complain.
  Youth, Beauty, Graceful Action seldom fail:
But Common Interest always will prevail:
And pity never Ceases to be shown
To him, who makes the Peoples wrongs his own.
The Croud, (that still believe their Kings oppress,)
With lifted hands their young *Messiah* bless:
Who now begins his Progress to ordain
With Chariots, Horsemen, and a num'rous train;
From East to West his Glories he displays:
And, like the Sun, the Promis'd Land surveys.
Fame runs before him as the Morning-Star,
And shouts of Joy salute him from afar:
Each house receives him as a Guardian God;
And Consecrates the Place of his abode:
But hospitable Treats did most commend
Wise *Issachar*, his wealthy Western Friend.
This moving Court that caught the Peoples Eyes,
And seem'd but Pomp, did other Ends disguise:
Achitophel had form'd it, with intent
To sound the depths, and fathom where it went,
The Peoples hearts distinguish Friends from Foes;
And trie their strength before they came to Blows.
Yet all was colour'd with a smooth pretence
Of specious love, and duty to their Prince.
Religion, and Redress of Grievances,
Two names, that always cheat and always please,
Are often urg'd; and good King *David's* life
Endanger'd by a Brother and a Wife.
Thus, in a Pageant Shew, a Plot is made;
And Peace it self is War in Masquerade.
Oh foolish *Israel*! never warn'd by Ill:
Still the same Bait, and circumvented still!
Did ever men forsake their present ease,
In midst of health imagine a Disease;
Take pains Contingent mischiefs to foresee,
Make Heirs for Monarchs, and for God decree?
What shall we think! Can People give away
Both for themselves and Sons their Native sway?
Then they are left Defenceless, to the Sword
Of each unbounded, Arbitrary Lord:
And Laws are vain, by which we Right enjoy,

If Kings unquestion'd can those Laws destroy.
Yet if the Croud be Judge of Fit and Just,
And Kings are onely Officers in Trust,
Then this resuming Cov'nant was declar'd
When Kings were made, or is for ever bar'd:
If those who gave the Scepter, coud not tie
By their own Deed their own Posterity,
How then coud *Adam* bind his future Race?
How coud his Forfeit on Mankind take place?
Or how coud heavenly Justice damn us all
Who ne'r consented to our Fathers Fall?
Then Kings are Slaves to those whom they command,
And Tenants to their Peoples pleasure stand.
Add that the Pow'r, for Property allow'd,
Is mischievously seated in the Croud;
For who can be secure of private Right,
If Sovereign Sway may be dissolv'd by Might?
Nor is the Peoples Judgment always true:
The Most may err as grosly as the Few.
And faultless Kings run down, by Common Cry,
For Vice, Oppression, and for Tyranny.
What Standard is there in a fickle rout,
Which, flowing to the Mark, runs faster out?
Nor onely crouds, but Sanhedrins may be
Infected with this publick Lunacy:
And Share the madness of Rebellious Times,
To Murther Monarchs for Imagin'd crimes.
If they may Give and Take when e'r they please,
Not Kings alone, (the Godheads Images,)
But Government it self at length must fall
To Natures state, where all have Right to all.
Yet, grant our Lords the People, Kings can make,
What prudent men a setled Throne woud shake?
For whatsoe'r their Sufferings were before,
That Change they Covet makes them suffer more.
All other Errors but disturb a State;
But Innovation is the Blow of Fate.
If ancient Fabricks nod, and threat to fall,
To Patch the Flaws, and Buttress up the Wall,
Thus far 'tis Duty; but here fix the Mark:
For all beyond it is to touch our Ark.
To change Foundations, cast the Frame anew,
Is work for Rebels who base Ends pursue:
At once Divine and Humane Laws controul,
And mend the Parts by ruine of the Whole.
The tamp'ring World is subject to this Curse,
To Physick their Disease into a Worse.
  Now, what Relief can Righteous *David* bring?

How Fatal 'tis to be too good a King!
Friends he has few, so high the madness grows;
Who dare be such, must be the People's Foes:
Yet some there were ev'n in the worst of days;
Some let me name, and Naming is to praise.
  In this short File *Barzillai*[23] first appears;
Barzillai crown'd with Honour and with Years:
Long since, the rising Rebels he withstood
In Regions Waste, beyond the *Jordans* Flood:
Unfortunately Brave to buoy the State;
But sinking underneath his Master's Fate:
In Exile with his God-like Prince he Mourn'd,
For him he Suffer'd, and with him Return'd.
The Court he practis'd, not the Courtier's Art:
Large was his Wealth, but larger was his Heart:
Which, well the Noblest Objects knew to chuse,
The Fighting Warriour, and Recording Muse.
His Bed coud once a Fruitful Issue boast:
Now more than half a Father's Name is lost.
His Eldest Hope, with every Grace adorn'd,
By me (so Heav'n will have it) always Mourn'd
And always honour'd, snatch'd in manhoods prime
B' unequal Fates and Providences crime:
Yet not before the Goal of Honour won,
All Parts fulfill'd of Subject and of Son;
Swift was the Race, but short the Time to run.
Oh Narrow Circle, but of Pow'r Divine,
Scanted in Space, but perfect in thy Line!
By Sea, by Land, thy Matchless Worth was known;
Arms thy Delight, and War was all thy Own:
Thy force, Infus'd, the fainting *Tyrians* prop'd;
And haughty *Pharaoh* found his Fortune stop'd.
Oh Ancient Honour, Oh unconquered Hand,
Whom Foes unpunish'd never coud withstand!
But *Israel* was unworthy of thy Name:
Short is the date of all Immoderate Fame.
It looks as Heav'n our Ruine had design'd,
And durst not trust thy Fortune and thy Mind.
Now, free from Earth, thy disencumbred Soul
Mounts up, and leaves behind the Clouds and Starry Pole:
From thence thy kindred Legions maist thou bring,
To aid the Guardian Angel of thy King.
Here stop my Muse, here cease thy painful flight;
No pinions can pursue Immortal height:
Tell good *Barzillai* thou canst sing no more,
And tell thy Soul she should have fled before;
Or fled she with his life, and left this Verse

[23] The Duke of Ormond.

To hang on her departed Patron's Herse?
Now take thy steepy flight from Heav'n, and see
If thou canst find on Earth another *He*;
Another he would be too hard to find;
See then whom thou canst see not far behind.
Zadock[24] the priest, whom, shunning Pow'r and Place,
His lowly mind advanc'd to *David's* Grace:
With him the *Sagan* of *Jerusalem*,[25]
Of hospitable Soul and noble Stem;
Him of the Western dome, whose weighty sense
Flows in fit words and heavenly eloquence.
The Prophets Sons, by such Example led,
To Learning and to Loyalty were bred:
For *Colleges* on bounteous Kings depend,
And never Rebel was to Arts a Friend.
To these succeed the Pillars of the Laws,
Who best coud plead, and best can judge a Cause.
Next them a train of Loyal Peers ascend:
Sharp judging *Adriel*,[26] the Muses Friend,
Himself a Muse:—In Sanhedrins debate
True to his Prince, but not a Slave of State.
Whom *David's* love with Honours did adorn,
That from his disobedient Son were torn.
Jotham[27] of piercing Wit and pregnant Thought,
Endew'd by nature and by learning taught
To move Assemblies, who but onely tri'd
The worse a while, then chose the better side;
Nor chose alone, but turned the Balance too;
So much the weight of one brave man can do.
Hushai[28] the friend of *David* in distress,
In publick storms of manly stedfastness;
By Foreign Treaties he inform'd his Youth;
And join'd Experience to his Native Truth.
His frugal care suppli'd the wanting Throne;
Frugal for that, but bounteous of his own:
'Tis easie Conduct when Exchequers flow;
But hard the task to manage well the low:
For Sovereign Power is too deprest or high,
When Kings are forced to sell, or Crouds to buy.
Indulge one labour more, my weary Muse,
For *Amiel*;[29] who can *Amiel's* praise refuse?
Of ancient race by birth, but nobler yet
In his own worth, and without Title great:

[24] Archbishop Sancroft.
[25] The Bishop of London.
[26] The Earl of Mulgrave.
[27] The Marquis of Halifax.
[28] Laurence Hyde, Earl of Rochester.
[29] Edward Seymour.

The Sanhedrin long time as Chief he rul'd,
Their Reason guided, and their Passion coold:
So dextrous was he in the Crown's defence,
So form'd to speak a Loyal Nations Sense,
That, as their Band was *Israels* Tribes in small,
So fit was he to represent them all.
Now rasher Charioteers the Seat ascend,
Whose loose Carriers his steady Skill commend:
They, like th' unequal Ruler of the Day,
Misguide the Seasons, and mistake the Way;
While he withdrawn at their mad Labour smiles
And safe enjoys the Sabbath of his Toils.
These were the chief; a small but faithful Band
Of Worthies in the Breach who dar'd to stand
And tempt th' united Fury of the Land.
With grief they view'd such powerful Engines bent
To batter down the lawful Government.
A numerous Faction with pretended frights,
In Sanhedrins to plume the Regal Rights.
The true Successor from the Court removed:
The plot, by hireling Witnesses improv'd.
These Ills they saw, and, as their Duty bound,
They shew'd the King the danger of the Wound:
That no Concessions from the Throne woud please;
But Lenitives fomented the Disease;
That *Absalom*, ambitious of the Crown,
Was made the Lure to draw the People down:
That false *Achitophel's* pernitious Hate
Had turn'd the Plot to ruine Church and State;
The Council violent, the Rabble worse:
That *Shimei* taught *Jerusalem* to Curse.
With all these loads of Injuries opprest,
And long revolving in his careful Brest
Th' event of things; at last his patience tir'd,
Thus from his Royal Throne, by Heav'n inspir'd,
The God-like *David* spoke; with awful fear
His Train their Maker in their Master hear.
Thus long have I by Native Mercy sway'd,
My Wrongs dissembl'd, my Revenge delay'd;
So willing to forgive th' Offending Age;
So much the Father did the King asswage.
But now so far my Clemency they slight,
Th' Offenders question my Forgiving Right.
That one was made for many, they contend;
But 'tis to Rule, for that's a Monarch's End.
They call my tenderness of Blood, my Fear,
Though Manly tempers can the longest bear.
Yet since they will divert my Native course,

'Tis time to show I am not Good by Force.
Those heap'd Affronts that haughty Subjects bring,
Are burdens for a Camel, not a King:
Kings are the publick Pillars of the State,
Born to sustain and prop the Nations weight:
If my young *Sampson* will pretend a Call
To shake the Column, let him share the Fall:
But oh that yet he woud repent and live!
How easie 'tis for Parents to forgive!
With how few Tears a Pardon might be won
From Nature, pleading for a Darling Son!
Poor pitied youth, by my Paternal care,
Rais'd up to all the Height his Frame coud bear:
Had God ordain'd his Fate for Empire born,
He woud have giv'n his Soul another turn:
Gull'd with a Patriot's name, whose Modern sense
Is one that woud by Law supplant his Prince:
The Peoples Brave, the Politicians Tool;
Never was Patriot yet, but was a Fool.
Whence comes it that Religion and the Laws
Should more be *Absalon's* than *David's* Cause?
His old Instructor, e'r he lost his Place,
Was never thought indu'd with so much Grace.
Good heav'ns, how Faction can a Patriot Paint!
My Rebel ever proves my Peoples Saint:
Woud *They* impose an Heir upon the Throne?
Let Sanhedrins be taught to give their Own.
A king's at least a part of Government;
And mine as requisite as their Consent:
Without my leave a future King to choose,
Infers a Right the present to Depose:
True, they petition me t' approve their Choice:
But *Esau's* Hands suit ill with *Jacob's* Voice.
My Pious Subjects for my Safety pray,
Which to Secure, they take my Pow'r away.
From Plots and Treasons Heav'n preserve my Years,
But save me most from my Petitioners.
Unsatiate as the barren Womb or Grave;
God cannot Grant so much as they can Crave.
What then is left but with a Jealous Eye
To guard the Small remains of Royalty?
The Law shall still direct my peaceful Sway,
And the same Law teach Rebels to obey:
Votes shall no more Established Pow'r controul,
Such Votes as make a Part exceed the Whole:
No groundless Clamours shall my Friends remove
Nor Crouds have pow'r to Punish e'r they Prove;
For Gods and God-like kings their Care express,

Still to defend their Servants in distress.
Oh that my Pow'r to Saving were confin'd:
Why am I forc'd, like Heav'n, against my mind,
To make Examples of another Kind?
Must I at length the Sword of Justice draw?
Oh curst Effects of necessary Law!
How ill my Fear they by my Mercy scan,
Beware the Fury of a Patient Man.
Law they require, let Law then shew her Face;
They could not be content to look on Grace,
Her hinder parts, but with a daring Eye
To tempt the terror of her Front, and die.
By their own Arts 'tis Righteously decreed,
Those dire Artificers of Death shall bleed.
Against themselves their Witnesses will Swear,
Till, Viper-like, their Mother Plot they tear,
And suck for Nutriment that bloudy gore
Which was their Principle of Life before.
Their *Belial* with their *Belzebub* will fight;
Thus on my Foes, my Foes shall do me Right.
Nor doubt th' event; for Factious crouds engage
In their first Onset, all their Brutal Rage;
Then let 'em take an unresisted Course;
Retire and Traverse, and Delude their Force:
But when they stand all Breathless, urge the fight,
And rise upon 'em with redoubled might:
For Lawful Pow'r is still Superiour found,
When long driv'n back, at length it stands the ground.
He said. Th' Almighty, nodding, gave consent;
And peals of Thunder shook the Firmament.
Henceforth a Series of new time began,
The mighty Years in long Procession ran:
Once more the God-like *David* was Restor'd,
And willing Nations knew their Lawful Lord.

The Medal. A Satire against Sedition[1]

OF ALL our Antick Sights, and Pageantry
Which *English* Ideots run in crowds to see,
The *Polish Medall* bears the prize alone:
A Monster, more the Favourite of the Town
Than either Fayrs or Theatres have shown.

[1] Published in March, 1682. Text of first edition. The occasion was the striking of a medal in the City to commemorate Shaftesbury's acquittal on a charge of high treason.

Never did Art so well with Nature strive;
Nor ever Idol seem'd so much alive:
So like the Man, so golden to the sight,
So base within, so counterfeit and light.
One side is fill'd with Title and with Face;
And, lest the King shou'd want a regal Place,
On the reverse, a Tow'r the Town surveys;
O'er which our mounting Sun his beams displays.
The Word, pronounc'd aloud by Shrieval voice,
Lætamur, which, in *Polish*, is *rejoyce*.
The Day, Month, Year, to the great Act are join'd:
And a new Canting Holiday design'd.
Five daies he sate, for every cast and look;
Four more than God to finish *Adam* took.
But who can tell what Essence Angels are,
Or how long Heav'n was making *Lucifer?*
Oh, cou'd the Style that copy'd every grace,
And plough'd such furrows for an Eunuch face,
Cou'd it have form'd his ever-changing Will,
The various Piece had tir'd the Graver's Skill!
A Martial Heroe first, with early care,
Blown, like a Pigmee by the Winds, to war.
A beardless Chief, a Rebel, e'r a Man:
(So young his hatred to his Prince began.)
Next this, (How wildly will Ambition steer!)
A Vermin, wriggling in th' Usurper's Ear.
Bart'ring his venal wit for sums of gold
He cast himself into the Saint-like mould;
Groan'd, sigh'd and pray'd, while Godliness was gain;
The lowdest Bagpipe of the squeaking Train.
But, as 'tis hard to cheat a Juggler's Eyes,
His open lewdness he cou'd ne'er disguise.
There split the Saint: for Hypocritique Zeal
Allows no Sins but those it can conceal.
Whoring to Scandal gives too large a scope:
Saints must not trade; but they may interlope.
Th' ungodly Principle was all the same;
But a gross Cheat betrays his Partner's Game.
Besides, their pace was formal, grave and slack:
His nimble Wit outran the heavy Pack.
Yet still he found his Fortune at a stay;
Whole droves of Blockheads choaking up his way;
They took, but not rewarded, his advice;
Villain and Wit exact a double price.
Pow'r was his aym: but, thrown from that pretence,
The Wretch turn'd loyal in his own defence;
And Malice reconcil'd him to his Prince.
Him, in the anguish of his Soul he serv'd;

Rewarded faster still than he deserv'd.
Behold him now exalted into trust;
His Counsel's oft convenient, seldom just.
Ev'n in the most sincere advice he gave
He had a grudging still to be a Knave.
The Frauds he learnt in his Fanatique years
Made him uneasy in his lawfull gears.
At best as little honest as he cou'd:
And, like white Witches, mischievously good.
To his first byass, longingly he leans;
And *rather* wou'd be great by wicked means.
Thus, fram'd for ill, he loos'd our Triple hold;
(Advice unsafe, precipitous, and bold.)
From hence those tears! that *Ilium* of our woe!
Who helps a pow'rfull Friend, fore-arms a Foe.
What wonder if the Waves prevail so far
When He cut down the Banks that made the bar?
Seas follow but their Nature to invade;
But He by Art our native Strength betray'd.
So *Sampson* to his Foe his force confest;
And, to be shorn, lay slumb'ring on her breast.
But, when this fatal Counsel, found too late,
Expos'd its Authour to the publique hate;
When his just Sovereign, by no impious way,
Cou'd be seduc'd to Arbitrary sway;
Forsaken of that hope, he shifts the sayle;
Drives down the Current with a pop'lar gale;
And shews the Fiend confess'd, without a vaile.
He preaches to the Crowd, that Pow'r is lent,
But not convey'd to Kingly Government;
That Claimes successive bear no binding force;
That Coronation Oaths are things of course;
Maintains the Multitude can never err;
And sets the People in the Papal Chair.
The reason's obvious; *Int'rest never lyes;*
The most have still their Int'rest in their eyes;
The pow'r is always theirs, and pow'r is ever wise.
Almighty Crowd, thou shorten'st all dispute;
Pow'r is thy Essence; Wit thy Attribute!
Nor Faith nor Reason make thee at a stay,
Thou leapst o'r all eternal truths, in thy *Pindarique* way!
Athens, no doubt, did righteously decide,
When *Phocion* and when *Socrates* were try'd:
As righteously they did those dooms repent;
Still they were wise, what ever way they went.
Crowds err not, though to both extremes they run;
To kill the Father, and recall the Son.
Some think the Fools were most, as times went then;

But now the World's o'r stock'd with prudent men.
The common Cry is ev'n Religion's Test;
The *Turk*'s is, at *Constantinople*, best;
Idols in *India*, Popery at *Rome*;
And our own Worship onely true at home.
And true, but for the time, 'tis hard to know
How long we please it shall continue so.
This side to day, and that to morrow burns;
So all are God-a'mighties in their turns.
A Tempting Doctrine, plausible and new:
What Fools our Fathers were, if this be true!
Who, to destroy the seeds of Civil War,
Inherent right in Monarchs did declare:
And, that a lawfull Pow'r might never cease,
Secur'd Succession, to secure our Peace.
Thus, Property and Sovereign Sway, at last
In equal Balances were justly cast:
But this new *Jehu* spurs the hot mouth'd horse;
Instructs the Beast to know his native force;
To take the Bit between his teeth and fly
To the next headlong Steep of Anarchy.
Too happy *England*, if our good we knew;
Woud we possess the freedom we pursue!
The lavish Government can give no more:
Yet we repine; and plenty makes us poor.
God try'd us once; our Rebel-fathers fought;
He glutted 'em with all the pow'r they sought:
Till, mastered by their own usurping Brave,
The free-born Subject sunk into a Slave.
We loath our Manna, and we long for Quails;
Ah, what is man, when his own wish prevails!
How rash, how swift to plunge himself in ill;
Proud of his Pow'r, and boundless in his Will!
That Kings can doe no wrong we must believe:
None can they doe, and must they all receive?
Help Heaven! or sadly we shall see an hour,
When neither wrong nor right are in their pow'r!
Already they have lost their best defence,
The benefit of Laws, which they dispence.
No justice to their righteous Cause allow'd;
But baffled by an Arbitrary Crowd.
And Medalls grav'd, their Conquest to record,
The Stamp and Coyn of their adopted Lord.
  The Man who laugh'd but once, to see an Ass
Mumbling to make the cross-grain'd Thistles pass;
Might laugh again, to see a Jury chaw
The prickles of unpalatable Law.
The Witnesses, that, Leech-like, liv'd on bloud,

Sucking for them were med'cinally good;
But, when they fasten'd on *their* fester'd Sore,
Then, Justice and Religion they forswore;
Their Mayden Oaths debauch'd into a Whore.
Thus Men are rais'd by Factions, and decry'd;
And Rogue and Saint distinguish'd by their Side.
They rack ev'n Scripture to confess their Cause;
And plead a Call to preach, in spight of Laws.
But that's no news to the poor injur'd Page;
It has been us'd as ill in every Age:
And is constrain'd, with patience, all to take;
For what defence can Greek and Hebrew make?
Happy who can this talking Trumpet seize;
They make it speak whatever Sense they please!
'Twas fram'd, at first, our Oracle t' enquire;
But, since our Sects in prophecy grow higher,
The Text inspires not them; but they the Text inspire.
London, thou great *Emporium* of our Isle,
O, thou too bounteous, thou too fruitfull *Nile*,
How shall I praise or curse to thy desert!
Or separate thy sound, from thy corrupted part!
I call'd thee *Nile*; the parallel will stand:
Thy tydes of Wealth o'rflow the fattend Land;
Yet Monsters from thy large increase we find;
Engender'd on the Slyme thou leav'st behind.
Sedition has not wholly seiz'd on thee;
Thy nobler Parts are from infection free.
Of *Israel*'s Tribes thou hast a numerous band;
But still the *Canaanite* is in the Land.
Thy military Chiefs are brave and true;
Nor are thy disinchanted Burghers few.
The Head is loyal which thy Heart commands;
But what's a Head with two such gouty Hands?
The wise and wealthy love the surest way;
And are content to thrive and to obey.
But Wisedom is to Sloath too great a Slave;
None are so busy as the Fool and Knave.
Those let me curse; what vengeance will they urge,
Whose Ordures neither Plague nor Fire can purge;
Nor sharp Experience can to duty bring,
Nor angry Heav'n, nor a forgiving King!
In Gospel phrase their Chapmen they betray:
Their Shops are Dens, the Buyer is their Prey.
The Knack of Trades is living on the Spoyl;
They boast, ev'n when each other they beguile.
Customes to steal is such a trivial thing,
That 'tis their Charter, to defraud their King.
All hands unite of every jarring Sect;

They cheat the Country first, and then infect.
They, for God's Cause their Monarchs dare dethrone;
And they'll be sure to make his Cause their own.
Whether the plotting Jesuite lay'd the plan
Of murth'ring Kings, or the *French* Puritan,
Our Sacrilegious Sects their Guides outgo;
And Kings and Kingly Pow'r wou'd murther too.
What means their Trait'rous Combination less,
To plain t' evade, too shamefull to confess.
But Treason is not own'd when tis descry'd;
Successfull Crimes alone are justify'd.
The Men, who no Conspiracy wou'd find,
Who doubts, but had it taken, they had join'd.
Joyn'd, in a mutual Cov'nant of defence;
At first without, at last against their Prince.
If Sovereign Right by Sovereign Pow'r they scan,
The same bold Maxime holds in God and Man:
God were not safe, his Thunder cou'd they shun
He shou'd be forc'd to crown another Son.
Thus, when the Heir was from the Vineyard thrown,
The rich Possession was the Murth'rers own.
In vain to Sophistry they have recourse:
By proving theirs no Plot, they prove 'tis worse;
Unmask'd Rebellion, and audacious Force.
Which, though not Actual, yet all Eyes may see
'Tis working, in th' immediate Pow'r to be;
For, from pretended Grievances they rise,
First to dislike, and after to despise.
Then, *Cyclop*-like in humane Flesh to deal;
Chop up a Minister, at every meal:
Perhaps not wholly to melt down the King;
But clip his regal Rights within the Ring.
From thence, t' assume the pow'r of Peace and War;
And ease him by degrees of publique Care.
Yet, to consult his Dignity and Fame,
He shou'd have leave to exercise the Name;
And hold the Cards, while Commons play'd the game.
For what can Pow'r give more than Food and Drink,
To live at ease, and not be bound to think?
These are the cooler methods of their Crime;
But their hot Zealots think 'tis loss of time;
On utmost bounds of Loyalty they stand;
And grinn and whet like a *Croatian* Band;
That waits impatient for the last Command.
Thus Out-laws open Villany maintain:
They steal not, but in Squadrons scoure the Plain:
And, if their Pow'r the Passengers subdue;
The Most have right, the wrong is in the Few.

Such impious Axiomes foolishly they show;
For, in some Soyles Republiques will not grow:
Our Temp'rate Isle will no extremes sustain,
Of pop'lar Sway, or Arbitrary Reign:
But slides between them both into the best;
Secure in freedom, in a Monarch blest.
And though the Clymate, vex't with various Winds,
Works through our yielding Bodies, on our Minds,
The wholsome Tempest purges what it breeds;
To recommend the Calmness that succeeds.
  But thou, the Pander of the Peoples hearts,
(O Crooked Soul, and Serpentine in Arts,)
Whose blandishments a Loyal Land have whor'd,
And broke the Bonds she plighted to her Lord;
What Curses on thy blasted Name will fall!
Which Age to Age their Legacy shall call;
For all must curse the Woes that must descend on all.
Religion thou hast none: thy *Mercury*
Has pass'd through every Sect, or theirs through Thee.
But what thou giv'st, that Venom still remains;
And the pox'd Nation feels Thee in their Brains.
What else inspires the Tongues, and swells the Breasts
Of all thy bellowing Renegado Priests,
That preach up Thee for God; dispence thy Laws;
And with thy Stumm ferment their fainting Cause?
Fresh Fumes of Madness raise; and toile and sweat
To make the formidable Cripple great.
Yet, shou'd thy Crimes succeed, shou'd lawless Pow'r
Compass those Ends thy greedy Hopes devour,
Thy Canting Friends thy Mortal Foes wou'd be;
Thy God and Theirs will never long agree.
For thine, (if thou hast any,) must be one
That lets the World and Humane-kind alone:
A jolly God, that passes hours too well
To promise Heav'n, or threaten us with Hell.
That unconcern'd can at Rebellion sit;
And Wink at Crimes he did himself commit.
A Tyrant theirs; the Heav'n their Priesthood paints
A Conventicle of gloomy sullen Saints;
A Heav'n, like *Bedlam*, slovenly and sad;
Fore-doom'd for Souls, with false Religion, mad.
  Without a Vision Poets can fore-show
What all but Fools, by common Sense may know:
If true Succession from our Isle shou'd fail,
And Crowds profane, with impious Arms prevail,
Not Thou, nor those thy Factious Arts ingage
Shall reap that Harvest of Rebellious Rage,
With which thou flatter'st thy decrepit Age.

The swelling Poyson of the sev'ral Sects,
Which wanting vent, the Nations Health infects
Shall burst its Bag; and fighting out their way
The various Venoms on each other prey.
The *Presbyter*, puft up with spiritual Pride,
Shall on the Necks of the lewd Nobles ride:
His Brethren damn, the Civil Pow'r defy;
And parcel out Republique Prelacy.
But short shall be his Reign: his rigid Yoke
And Tyrant Pow'r will puny Sects provoke;
And Frogs and Toads, and all the Tadpole Train
Will croak to Heav'n for help, from this devouring Crane.
The Cut-throat Sword and clamorous Gown shall jar,
In shareing their ill-gotten Spoiles of War:
Chiefs shall be grudg'd the part which they pretend;
Lords envy Lords, and Friends with every Friend
About their impious Merit shall contend.
The surly Commons shall respect deny;
And justle Peerage out with Property.
Their Gen'ral either shall his Trust betray,
And force the Crowd to Arbitrary sway;
Or they suspecting his ambitious Aym,
In hate of Kings shall cast anew the Frame;
And thrust out *Collatine* that bore their Name.
  Thus inborn Broyles the Factions wou'd ingage;
Or Wars of Exil'd Heirs, or Foreign Rage,
Till halting Vengeance overtook our Age:
And our wild Labours, wearied into Rest,
Reclin'd us on a rightfull Monarch's Breast.

Mac Flecknoe. Or a Satyr upon the True-Blew Protestant Poet, T. S.[1]

ALL humane things are subject to decay,
And, when Fate summons, Monarchs must obey:
This *Fleckno* found, who, like *Augustus*, young
Was call'd to Empire and had govern'd long:
In Prose and Verse was own'd, without dispute
Through all the realms of Non-sense, absolute.
This aged Prince now flourishing in Peace,
And blest with issue of a large increase,
Worn out with business, did at length debate
To settle the Succession of the State;

[1] Published in October, 1682. Text of second edition, 1684.

And pond'ring which of all his Sons was fit
To Reign, and wage immortal War with Wit,
Cry'd, 'tis resolv'd; for Nature pleads that He
Should onely rule, who most resembles me:
Sh——[2] alone my perfect image bears,
Mature in dullness from his tender years;
Sh—— alone of all my Sons is he
Who stands confirm'd in full stupidity.
The rest to some faint meaning make pretence,
But *Sh*—— never deviates into sense.
Some Beams of Wit on other souls may fall,
Strike through and make a lucid intervall;
But *Sh*——'s genuine night admits no ray,
His rising Fogs prevail upon the Day:
Besides, his goodly Fabrick fills the eye
And seems design'd for thoughtless Majesty:
Thoughtless as Monarch Oakes that shade the plain,
And, spread in solemn state, supinely reign.
Heywood and *Shirley* were but Types of thee,
Thou last great Prophet of Tautology:
Even I, a dunce of more renown than they,
Was sent before but to prepare thy way:
And coarsely clad in *Norwich* Drugget came
To teach the Nations in thy greater name.
My warbling Lute, the Lute I whilom strung,
When to King *John* of *Portugal* I sung,
Was but the prelude to that glorious day,
When thou on silver *Thames* did'st cut thy way,
With well tim'd oars before the Royal Barge,
Swelled with the Pride of thy Celestial charge;
And, big with Hymn, Commander of an Host,
The like was ne'er in *Epsom* blankets tost.
Methinks I see the new *Arion* Sail,
The Lute still trembling underneath thy nail.
At thy well sharpned thumb from Shore to Shore
The Treble squeaks for fear, the Bases roar:
Echoes from Pissing-Ally, *Sh*—— call,
And *Sh*—— they resound from *A*[*ston*] *Hall*.
About thy boat the little Fishes throng,
As at the Morning Toast that Floats along.
Sometimes, as Prince of thy Harmonious band,
Thou wield'st thy Papers in thy threshing hand.
St. *André*'s feet ne'er kept more equal time,
Not ev'n the feet of thy own *Psyche*'s rhime:
Though they in number as in sense excell,
So just, so like tautology they fell

[2] Thomas Shadwell.

That, pale with envy, *Singleton* forswore
The Lute and Sword which he in Triumph bore,
And vow'd he ne'er would act *Villerius* more.
Here stopt the good old Syre; and wept for joy,
In silent raptures of the hopefull boy.
All Arguments, but most his Plays, perswade
That for anointed dulness he was made.
  Close to the Walls which fair *Augusta* bind,
(The fair *Augusta* much to fears inclin'd)
An ancient fabrick raised t' inform the sight,
There stood of yore, and *Barbican* it hight:
A watch Tower once, but now, so Fate ordains,
Of all the Pile an empty name remains.
From its old Ruins Brothel-houses rise,
Scenes of lewd loves, and of polluted joys,
Where their vast Courts the Mother-Strumpets keep,
And, undisturbed by Watch, in silence sleep.
Near these a Nursery erects its head,
Where Queens are formed, and future Hero's bred;
Where unfledged Actors learn to laugh and cry,
Where infant Punks their tender voices try,
And little *Maximins* the Gods defy.
Great *Fletcher* never treads in Buskins here,
Nor greater Johnson dares in Socks appear.
But gentle *Simkin* just reception finds
Amidst this Monument of vanisht minds;
Pure Clinches, the suburbian Muse affords;
And *Panton* waging harmless war with words.
Here *Flecknoe*, as a place to Fame well known,
Ambitiously design'd his *Sh*——'s throne.
For ancient *Decker* prophesi'd long since,
That in this Pile should Reign a mighty Prince,
Born for a scourge of Wit, and flayle of Sense,
To whom true dulness should some *Psyches* owe,
But Worlds of *Misers* from his pen should flow;
Humorists and Hypocrites it should produce,
Whole *Raymond* Families and Tribes of *Bruce*.
  Now Empress Fame had publisht the renown
Of *Sh*——'s Coronation through the Town.
Rows'd by report of Fame, the Nations meet,
From near *Bun-Hill* and distant *Watling-street*.
No *Persian* Carpets spread th' imperial way,
But scatter'd Limbs of mangled Poets lay;
From dusty shops neglected Authors come,
Martyrs of Pies and Reliques of the Bum.
Much *Heywood, Shirley, Ogleby* there lay,
But loads of *Sh*—— almost choakt the way.
Bilk't *Stationers* for Yeomen stood prepar'd

And *H*[*erringman*] was Captain of the Guard.
The hoary Prince in Majesty appear'd,
High on a Throne of his own Labours rear'd.
At his right hand our young *Ascanius* sat
Rome's other hope and Pillar of the State.
His Brows thick fogs, instead of glories, grace,
And lambent dullness plaid around his face.
As *Hannibal* did to the Altars come,
Swore by his Syre a mortal Foe to *Rome*;
So *Sh*—— swore, nor should his Vow bee vain,
That he till Death true dullness would maintain;
And, in his father's Right, and Realms defence,
Ne'er to have Peace with Wit, nor truce with Sense.
The King himself the sacred Unction made,
As King by Office, and as Priest by Trade:
In his sinister hand, instead of Ball,
He placed a mighty Mug of potent Ale;
Love's Kingdom to his right he did convey,
At once his Sceptre and his rule of Sway;
Whose righteous Lore the Prince had practis'd young
And from whose Loyns recorded *Psyche* sprung.
His temples, last, with Poppies were o'erspread,
That nodding seem'd to consecrate his head:
Just at that point of time, if Fame not lye,
On his left hand twelve reverend *Owls* did fly.
So *Romulus*, 'tis sung, by *Tyber*'s *Brook,*
Presage of Sway from twice six Vultures took.
Th' admiring throng loud acclamations make
And Omens of his future Empire take.
The Syre then shook the honours of his head,
And from his brows damps of oblivion shed
Full on the filial dullness: long he stood,
Repelling from his Breast the raging God;
At length burst out in this prophetick mood:
  Heavens bless my Son, from *Ireland* let him reign
To far *Barbadoes* on the Western main;
Of his Dominion may no end be known,
And greater than his Father's be his Throne.
Beyond loves Kingdom let him stretch his Pen;
He paused, and all the people cry'd *Amen.*
Then thus continued he, my son, advance
Still in new Impudence, new Ignorance.
Success let others teach, learn thou from me
Pangs without birth, and fruitless Industry.
Let *Virtuoso*'s in five years be Writ;
Yet not one thought accuse thy toyl of Wit.
Let gentle *George* in triumph tread the stage,
Make *Dorimant* betray, and *Loveit* rage;

Let *Cully, Cockwood, Fopling,* charm the Pit,
And in their folly show the Writers wit.
Yet still thy fools shall stand in thy defence
And justifie their Author's want of sense.
Let 'em be all by thy own model made
Of dulness and desire no foreign aid,
That they to future ages may be known,
Not Copies drawn, but Issue of thy own.
Nay let thy men of wit too be the same,
All full of thee, and differing but in name;
But let no alien *S-dl-y* interpose
To lard with wit thy hungry *Epsom* prose.
And when false flowers of *Rhetorick* thou would'st cull,
Trust Nature, do not labour to be dull;
But write thy best, and top; and in each line
Sir *Formal*'s oratory will be thine.
Sir *Formal*, though unsought, attends thy quill,
And does thy *Northern Dedications* fill.
Nor let false friends seduce thy mind to fame,
By arrogating *Johnson*'s Hostile name.
Let Father *Flecknoe* fire thy mind with praise
And Uncle *Ogleby* thy envy raise.
Thou art my blood, where *Johnson* has no part:
What share have we in Nature or in Art?
Where did his wit on learning fix a brand
And rail at Arts he did not understand?
Where made he love in Prince *Nicander*'s vein,
Or swept the dust in *Psyche*'s humble strain?
Where sold he Bargains, Whip-stitch, kiss my Arse,
Promis'd a Play and dwindled to a Farce?
When did his Muse from *Fletcher* scenes purloin,
As thou whole *Eth'ridg* dost transfuse to thine?
But so transfused as Oyls on waters flow,
His always floats above, thine sinks below.
This is thy Province, this thy wondrous way,
New Humours to invent for each new Play:
This is that boasted Byas of thy mind,
By which one way, to dullness, 'tis inclined,
Which makes thy writings lean on one side still,
And, in all changes, that way bends thy will.
Nor let thy mountain belly make pretence
Of likeness; thine's a tympany of sense.
A Tun of Man in thy large Bulk is writ,
But sure thou 'rt but a Kilderkin of wit.
Like mine thy gentle numbers feebly creep;
Thy Tragick Muse gives smiles, thy Comick sleep.
With whate'er gall thou settst thy self to write,
Thy inoffensive Satyrs never bite.

In thy fellonious heart though Venom lies,
It does but touch thy *Irish* pen, and dyes.
Thy Genius calls thee not to purchase fame
In keen Iambicks, but mild Anagram:
Leave writing Plays, and chuse for thy command
Some peacefull Province in Acrostick Land.
There thou maist wings display, and Altars raise,
And torture one poor word Ten thousand ways;
Or, if thou would'st thy diff'rent talents suit,
Set thy own Songs, and sing them to thy lute.
He said, but his last words were scarcely heard,
For *Bruce* and *Longvil* had a *Trap* prepar'd,
And down they sent the yet declaiming Bard.
Sinking he left his Drugget robe behind,
Borne upwards by a subterranean wind.
The Mantle fell to the young Prophet's part
With double portion of his Father's Art.

From The Second Part of Absalom and Achitophel.[1]

NEXT these, a Troop of buisy Spirits press,
Of little Fortunes and of Conscience Less;
With them the Tribe, whose Luxury had drain'd
Their Banks, in former Sequestrations gain'd:
Who Rich and Great by past Rebellions grew,
And long to fish the troubled Waves anew.
Some future Hopes, some present Payment draws,
To Sell their Conscience and espouse the Cause,
Such Stipends those vile Hirelings best befit,
Priests without Grace, and Poets without wit,
Shall that false *Hebronite* escape our Curse,
Judas[2] that keeps the Rebells Pension-Purse;
Judas that pays the Treason-writers Fee,
Judas that well deserves his Namesake's Tree;
Who at *Jerusalem's* own Gates Erects
His College for a Nursery of Sects.
Young Prophets with an early Care secures,
And with the Dung of his own Arts manures.
What have the Men of *Hebron*[3] here to doe?

[1] Published in November, 1682. Text of the first edition. The "Second Part" is mainly by Nahum Tate. Dryden is known to have contributed lines 310-509, which form part of a description of Achitophel's followers. See Preface.

[2] Robert Ferguson.

[3] Scotland.

What part in *Israels* promis'd Land have you?
Here *Phaleg*[4] the Lay *Hebronite* is come,
Cause like the rest he could not live at Home;
Who from his own Possessions cou'd not drain
An *Omer* even of *Hebronitish* Grain,
Here Struts it like a Patriot, and talks high
Of Injur'd Subjects, alter'd Property:
An Emblem of that buzzing Insect Just,
That mounts the Wheell, and thinks she raises Dust.
Can dry Bones Live? or *Skeletons* produce
The Vital Warmth of Cuckoldizing Juice?
Slim *Phaleg* cou'd, and at the Table fed,
Return'd the gratefull product to the Bed.
A Waiting-man to Trav'ling Nobles chose,
He, his own Laws wou'd Sawcily impose;
Till Bastinado'd back again he went,
To Learn those Manners he to Teach was sent.
Chastiz'd, he ought to have retreated Home,
But He reads politicks to *Absalom*.
For never *Hebronite*, though Kickt and Scorn'd,
To his own Country willingly return'd.
—But leaving famish'd *Phaleg* to be fed
And to talk Treason for his daily Bread,
Let *Hebron*, nay let Hell produce a Man
So made for Mischief as *Ben Jochanan*,[5]
A *Jew* of humble Parentage was He,
By Trade a Levite, though of low Degree:
His Pride no higher than the Desk aspir'd,
But for the Drudgery of Priests was hir'd
To Reade and Pray in Linen Ephod brave,
And pick up single Sheckles from the Grave.
Married at last, and finding Charge come faster,
He cou'd not live by God, but chang'd his Master:
Inspir'd by Want, was made a Factious Tool,
They Got a Villain, and we lost a Fool.
Still Violent, whatever Cause he took,
But most against the Party he forsook,
For Renegadoes, who ne'er turn by halves,
Are bound in Conscience to be double Knaves.
So this Prose-Prophet took most monstrous Pains
To let his Masters see he earn'd his Gains.
But as the Dev'l ows all his Imps a Shame,
He chose th' *Apostate* for his proper Theme;
With little Pains he made the Picture true,
And from Reflexion took the Rogue he drew.

[4] James Forbes.

[5] Samuel Johnson.

A wondrous Work, to prove the *Jewish* nation
In every Age a Murmuring Generation;
To trace 'em from their Infancy of Sinning,
And shew 'em Factious from their First Beginning;
To prove they cou'd Rebell, and Rail, and Mock,
Much to the Credit of the Chosen Flock;
A strong Authority which must Convince,
That Saints own no Allegiance to their Prince.
As 'tis a Leading-Card to make a Whore,
To prove her Mother had turn'd up before.
But tell me, did the Drunken Patriarch Bless
The Son that shew'd his Father's Nakedness?
Such Thanks the present Church thy Pen will give,
Which proves Rebellion was so Primitive.
Must Ancient Failings be Examples made,
Then Murtherers from *Cain* may learn their Trade.
As thou the Heathen and the Saint hast drawn,
Methinks th' Apostate was the better man:
And thy hot *Father* (waving my respect)
Not of a mother church but of a Sect.
And Such he needs must be of thy Inditing,
This Comes of drinking Asses milk and writing.
If *Balack*[6] should be cal'd to leave his place,
(As Profit is the loudest call of Grace,)
His Temple, dispossessed of one, would be
Replenish'd with seven Devils more by thee.
Levi, thou art a load, I'll lay thee down,
And shew Rebellion bare, without a Gown;
Poor Slaves in metre, dull and adle-pated,
Who Rhime below ev'n *David's* Psalms translated.
Some in my Speedy pace I must outrun,
As lame *Mephibosheth*[7] the Wisard's Son;
To make quick way I'll Leap o'er heavy blocks,
Shun rotten *Uzza* as I woud the Pox;
And hasten *Og* and *Doeg* to rehearse,
Two Fools that Crutch their Feeble sense on Verse,
Who by my Muse, to all succeeding times
Shall live in spight of their own Dogrell Rhimes.
Doeg,[8] though without knowing how or why,
Made still a blund'ring kind of Melody;
Spurd boldly on, and Dash'd through Thick and Thin,
Through Sense and Non-sense, never out nor in;
Free from all meaning, whether good or bad,
And in one word, Heroically mad:

---

[6] Gilbert Burnet.
[7] Samuel Pordage.
[8] Elkanah Settle.

He was too warm on Picking-work to dwell,
But Faggotted his Notions as they fell,
And, if they Rhim'd and Rattl'd, all was well.
Spightfull he is not, though he wrote a Satyr,
For still there goes some *thinking* to ill-Nature:
He needs no more than Birds and Beasts to think,
All his occasions are to eat and drink.
If he call Rogue and Rascal from a Garrat,
He means you no more Mischief than a Parat:
The words for Friend and Foe alike were made,
To Fetter 'em in Verse is all his Trade.
For Almonds he'll cry Whore to his own Mother:
And call young *Absalom* King *David's* Brother.
Let him be Gallows-Free by my consent,
And nothing suffer, since he nothing meant:
Hanging Supposes humane Soul and reason,
This Animal's below committing Treason:
Shall he be hang'd who never cou'd Rebell?
That's a preferment for *Achitophel.*
The Woman that Committed Buggary,
Was rightly Sentenc'd by the Law to die;
But 'twas hard Fate that to the Gallows led
The Dog that never heard the Statute read.
Railing in other Men may be a crime,
But ought to pass for mere instinct in him;
Instinct he follows and no farther knows,
For to write Verse with him is to *Transprose.*
'Twere pity treason at his Door to lay
Who *makes Heaven's gate a Lock to its own Key:*
Let him rayl on, let his invective muse
Have four and Twenty letters to abuse,
Which if he Jumbles to one line of Sense,
Indict him of a Capital Offence.
In Fire-works give him leave to vent his spight,
Those are the only Serpents he can write;
The height of his ambition is we know
But to be Master of a Puppet-show;
On that one Stage his works may yet appear,
And a months Harvest keeps him all the Year.
  Now stop your noses, Readers, all and some,
For here's a tun of Midnight work to come,
Og[9] from a Treason Tavern rowling home.
Round as a Globe, and Liquored ev'ry chink,
Goodly and Great he Sayls behind his Link;
With all this Bulk there's nothing lost in *Og*,

[9] Thomas Shadwell.

For ev'ry inch that is not Fool is Rogue:
A Monstrous mass of foul corrupted matter,
As all the Devils had spew'd to make the batter.
When wine has given him courage to Blaspheme,
He curses God, but God before Curst him;
And if man cou'd have reason, none has more,
That made his Paunch so rich and him so poor.
With wealth he was not trusted, for Heav'n knew
What 'twas of Old to pamper up a *Jew*;
To what would he on Quail and Pheasant swell,
That ev'n on Tripe and Carrion cou'd rebell?
But though Heaven made him poor, (with rev'rence speaking,)
He never was a Poet of God's making;
The Midwife laid her hand on his Thick Skull,
With this Prophetick blessing—*Be thou Dull;*
Drink, Swear, and Roar, forbear no lew'd delight
Fit for thy Bulk, doe anything but write.
Thou art of lasting Make, like thoughtless men,
A strong Nativity—but for the Pen;
Eat Opium, mingle Arsenick in thy Drink,
Still thou mayst live, avoiding Pen and Ink.
I see, I see, 'tis Counsell given in vain,
For Treason botcht in Rhime will be thy bane;
Rhime is the Rock on which thou art to wreck,
'Tis fatal to thy Fame and to thy Neck.
Why should thy Metre good King *David* blast?
A Psalm of his will Surely be thy last.
Dar'st thou presume in verse to meet thy foes,
Thou whom the Penny Pamphlet foil'd in prose?
Doeg, whom God for Mankinds mirth has made,
O'er-tops thy tallent in thy very Trade;
Doeg to thee, thy paintings are so Course,
A Poet is, though he's the Poets Horse.
A Double Noose thou on thy Neck dost pull
For writing Treason and for Writing dull;
To die for Faction is a common Evil,
But to be hang'd for Non-sense is the Devil.
Hadst thou the Glories of thy King exprest,
Thy praises had been Satyr at the best;
But thou in Clumsy verse, unlickt, unpointed,
Hast Shamefully defi'd the Lord's Anointed:
I will not rake the Dunghill of thy Crimes,
For who would reade thy Life that reads thy rhimes?
But of King *David*'s Foes be this the Doom,
May all be like the Young-man *Absalom*;
And for my Foes may this their Blessing be,
To talk like *Doeg* and to Write like Thee.

Religio Laici; or, A Layman's Faith. A Poem[1]

DIM, as the borrow'd beams of Moon and Stars
To *lonely, weary, wandring* Travellers,
Is *Reason* to the *Soul:* And as on high,
Those rowling Fires *discover* but the Sky
Not light us *here*; so *Reason's* glimmering Ray
Was lent, not to *assure* our *doubtfull* way,
But *guide* us upward to a *better Day.*
And as those nightly Tapers disappear
When Day's bright Lord ascends our Hemisphere;
So pale grows *Reason* at *Religions* sight;
So *dyes*, and so *dissolves* in *Supernatural Light.*
Some few, whose Lamp shone brighter, have been led
From Cause to Cause, to *Natures* secret head;
And found that *one first principle* must be:
But *what*, or *who*, that *UNIVERSAL HE*;
Whether some *Soul* incompassing this Ball
Unmade, unmov'd; yet *making, moving All*;
Or various *Atom's*, interfering Dance
Leapt into *Form*, (the Noble work of *Chance*;)
Or this great *All* was from *Eternity*;
Not ev'n the *Stagirite* himself could see;
And *Epicurus Guess'd* as well as He:
As *blindly grop'd* they for a *future State*;
As *rashly Judg'd* of *Providence* and *Fate:*
But least of all could their Endeavours find
What most concern'd the good of Humane kind:
For *Happiness* was never to be found;
But vanish'd from 'em, like Enchanted ground.
One thought *Content* the Good to be enjoy'd:
This, every little *Accident* destroy'd:
The *wiser Madmen* did for *Vertue* toyl:
A Thorny, or at best a barren Soil:
In *Pleasure* some their glutton Souls would steep;
But found their Line too short, the Well too deep;
And leaky Vessels which no *Bliss* cou'd keep.
Thus, *anxious Thoughts* in *endless Circles* roul,
Without a *Centre* where to fix the *Soul:*
In this wilde Maze their vain Endeavours end.
How can the *less* the *Greater* comprehend?
Or *finite Reason* reach *Infinity?*
For what cou'd *Fathom GOD* were *more* than *He.*
The *Deist* thinks he stands on firmer ground;
Cries ευρεκα: the mighty Secret's found:

[1] Published in November, 1682. Text of first edition.

God is that *Spring* of *Good*; *Supreme*, and *Best*;
We, made to *serve*, and in that Service *blest*;
If so, some *Rules* of Worship must be given,
Distributed alike to all by Heaven:
Else *God* were *partial*, and to *some* deny'd
The Means his Justice shou'd for *all* provide.
This *general Worship* is to *PRAISE*, and *PRAY:*
One part to *borrow* Blessings, one to *pay:*
And when frail Nature slides into *Offence*,
The *Sacrifice* for *Crimes* is *Penitence.*
Yet, since th' Effects of Providence, we find
Are variously dispens'd to Humane kind;
That *Vice Triumphs*, and *Vertue suffers* here,
(A Brand that Sovereign Justice cannot bear;)
Our Reason prompts us to a *future* State:
The *last Appeal* from *Fortune*, and from *Fate:*
Where God's all-righteous ways will be declar'd;
The *Bad* meet *Punishment*, the *Good, Reward.*
  Thus Man by his own strength to Heaven wou'd soar:
And wou'd not be Oblig'd to God for more.
Vain, wretched Creature, how art thou misled
To think thy Wit these God-like Notions bred!
These Truths are not the product of thy Mind,
But dropt from Heaven, and of a Nobler kind.
Reveal'd Religion first inform'd thy Sight,
And *Reason* saw not, till *Faith* sprung the Light.
Hence all thy *Natural Worship* takes the *Source:*
'Tis *Revelation* what thou thinkst *Discourse.*
Else, how com'st *Thou* to see these truths so clear,
Which so obscure to *Heathens* did appear?
Not *Plato* these, nor *Aristotle* found:
Nor He whose Wisedom *Oracles* renown'd.
Hast thou a Wit so deep, or so sublime,
Or canst thou lower dive, or higher climb?
Canst *Thou*, by *Reason*, more of *God-head* know
Than *Plutarch, Seneca, or Cicero?*
Those Gyant Wits, in happyer Ages born,
(When *Arms*, and *Arts* did *Greece* and *Rome* adorn)
Knew no such *Systeme*: no such Piles cou'd raise
Of *Natural Worship*, built on *Pray'r* and *Praise*,
To One sole GOD.
Nor did Remorse, to Expiate Sin, prescribe:
But slew their fellow Creatures for a Bribe:
The guiltless *Victim* groan'd for their Offence;
And *Cruelty*, and *Blood* was *Penitence.*
If *Sheep* and *Oxen* cou'd Attone for Men
Ah! at how cheap a rate the *Rich* might Sin!
And great Oppressours might Heavens Wrath beguile

By offering his own Creatures for a Spoil!
  Dar'st thou, poor Worm, offend *Infinity?*
And must the Terms of Peace be given by *Thee?*
Then *Thou* art *Justice* in the *last Appeal*;
Thy easie God instructs Thee to *rebell:*
And, like a King remote, and weak, must take
What Satisfaction *Thou* art pleas'd to make.
  But if there be a *Pow'r* too *Just*, and *strong*
To wink at *Crimes*, and bear unpunish'd *Wrong*;
Look humbly upward, see his Will disclose
The *Forfeit* first, and then the *Fine* impose:
A *Mulct thy* Poverty cou'd never pay
Had not *Eternal Wisedom* found the way:
And with Cœlestial Wealth supply'd thy Store:
His Justice makes the *Fine, his Mercy* quits the *Score.*
See God descending in thy Humane Frame;
Th' *offended*, suff'ring in th' *Offenders* Name:
All thy Misdeeds to him imputed see,
And all his Righteousness devolv'd on thee.
  For granting we have Sin'd, and that th' offence
Of *Man*, is made against *Omnipotence*,
Some Price, that bears *proportion*, must be paid;
And *Infinite* with *Infinite* be weigh'd.
See then the *Deist lost: Remorse* for *Vice*,
Not paid, or *paid, inadequate* in price:
What farther means can *Reason* now direct,
Or what Relief from *humane Wit* expect?
That shews us *sick*; and sadly are we sure
Still to be *Sick*, till *Heav'n* reveal the *Cure:*
If then *Heaven's Will* must needs be understood,
(Which must, if we want *Cure*, and *Heaven*, be *Good*)
Let all Records of *Will reveal'd* be shown;
With *Scripture*, all in equal ballance thrown,
And *our one Sacred Book* will be *That one.*
  Proof needs not here, for whether we compare
That Impious, Idle, Superstitious Ware
Of *Rites, Lustrations, Offerings*, (which before,
In various Ages, various Countries bore)
With *Christian Faith* and *Vertues*, we shall find
None answ'ring the great ends of humane kind
But *This one Rule of Life: That* shews us best
How *God* may be *appeas'd*, and *Mortals blest.*
Whether from length of *Time* its worth we draw,
The *World* is scarce more *Ancient* than the *Law:*
Heav'ns early Care prescrib'd for every Age;
First, in the *Soul*, and after, in the *Page.*
Or, whether more abstractedly we look,
Or on the *Writers*, or the *written Book*,

Whence, but from *Heav'n*, cou'd men unskill'd in Arts,
In several Ages born, in several parts,
Weave such *agreeing Truths?* or *how*, or *why*
Shou'd *all* conspire to cheat us with a *Lye?*
Unask'd their *Pains, ungratefull* their *Advice,*
Starving their *Gain*, and *Martyrdom* their *Price.*
  If on the Book it self we cast our view,
Concurrent Heathens prove the Story *True:*
The *Doctrine, Miracles*; which must convince,
For *Heav'n* in *Them* appeals to *humane Sense:*
And though they *prove* not, they *Confirm* the Cause,
When what is *Taught* agrees with *Natures Laws.*
  Then for the *Style*; *Majestick* and *Divine,*
It speaks no less than God in every Line:
Commanding words; whose *Force* is still the same
As the first *Fiat* that produc'd our Frame.
All Faiths *beside*, or did by *Arms* ascend;
Or *Sense* indulg'd has made *Mankind* their *Friend:*
This *onely* Doctrine does our *Lusts* oppose:
Unfed by Natures Soil, in which it grows;
Cross to our *Interests*, curbing Sense, and Sin;
Oppress'd without, and undermin'd within,
It thrives through pain; its own Tormentours tires;
And with a stubborn patience still aspires.
To what can *Reason* such Effects assign
Transcending *Nature,* but to *Laws Divine?*
Which in that Sacred Volume are contain'd;
Sufficient, clear, and for that use ordain'd.
  But stay: the *Deist* here will urge anew,
No *Supernatural Worship* can be *True:*
Because a *general Law* is that alone
Which must to *all*, and every *where* be known:
A Style so large as not *this* Book can claim
Nor ought that bears *reveal'd* Religions *Name.*
'Tis said the sound of a *Messiah*'s *Birth*
Is gone through all the habitable Earth:
But still that Text must be confin'd alone
To what was *Then* inhabited, and known:
And what Provision cou'd from *thence* accrue
To *Indian* Souls, and Worlds discover'd *New?*
In other parts it helps, that Ages past,
The Scriptures there were *known*, and were *imbrac'd*,
Till Sin spread once again the Shades of Night:
What's that to these who never *saw* the Light?
  Of all Objections this indeed is chief
To startle Reason, stagger frail Belief:
We grant, 'tis true, that Heav'n from humane Sense
Has hid the secret paths of *Providence:*

But *boundless Wisedom, boundless Mercy*, may
Find ev'n for those *be-wildred* Souls, a *way:*
If from his *Nature Foes* may Pity claim,
Much more may *Strangers* who ne'er heard his *Name.*
And though *no Name* be for *Salvation* known,
But that of his *Eternal Sons* alone;
Who knows how far transcending Goodness can
Extend the *Merits* of *that Son* to *Man?*
Who knows what *Reasons* may his *Mercy* lead;
Or *Ignorance invincible* may plead?
Not onely *Charity* bids hope the *best*,
But *more* the great Apostle has exprest:
That, if the Gentiles, (whom no Law inspir'd,)
By Nature did what was by *Law requir'd;*
They, who the written Rule had never known,
Were to themselves both Rule and Law alone:
To Natures plain indictment they shall plead;
And, by their Conscience, be condemn'd or freed.
Most righteous Doom! because a *Rule reveal'd*
Is *none* to *Those*, from whom it was *conceal'd.*
Then those who follow'd *Reasons* Dictates right;
Liv'd up, and lifted high their *Natural Light*;
With *Socrates* may see their Maker's Face,
While Thousand *Rubrick-Martyrs* want a place.
  Nor does it baulk my *Charity*, to find
Th' *Egyptian* Bishop of another mind:
For, though his *Creed Eternal Truth* contains,
'Tis hard for *Man* to doom to *endless pains*
All who believ'd not all, his Zeal requir'd;
Unless he first cou'd prove he was inspir'd.
Then let us either think he meant to say
This Faith, where *publish'd*, was the onely way;
Or else conclude that, *Arius* to confute,
The good old Man, too eager in dispute,
Flew high; and as his *Christian* Fury rose
Damn'd all for *Hereticks* who durst *oppose.*

  Thus far my Charity this path has try'd;
(A much unskilfull, but well meaning guide:)
Yet what they are, ev'n these crude thoughts were bred
By reading that, which better thou hast read.
Thy Matchless Author's work: which thou, my Friend,[2]
By well translating better dost commend:
Those youthfull hours which, of thy Equals most
In *Toys* have *squander'd*, or in *Vice* have *lost*,
Those hours hast thou to Nobler use employ'd;

[2] Richard Simon's *Critical History of the Old Testament*, recently translated from the French by Henry Dickinson, to whom Dryden addressed his poem.

And the severe Delights of Truth enjoy'd.
Witness this weighty Book, in which appears
The crabbed Toil of many thoughtfull years,
Spent by thy Authour, in the Sifting Care
Of *Rabbins* old Sophisticated Ware
From Gold Divine; which he who well can sort
May afterwards make *Algebra* a Sport.
A Treasure, which if *Country-Curates* buy,
They *Junius*, and *Tremellius* may defy:
Save pains in various readings, and Translations;
And without *Hebrew* make most learn'd quotations.
A Work so full with various Learning fraught,
So nicely pondred, yet so strongly wrought,
As Natures height and Arts last hand requir'd:
As much as Man cou'd compass, uninspir'd.
Where we may see what *Errours* have been made
Both in the *Copiers* and *Translaters Trade:*
How *Jewish, Popish,* Interests have prevail'd,
And where *Infallibility* has *fail'd.*
  For some, who have his secret meaning ghes'd,
Have found our Authour not too *much* a *Priest:*
For *Fashion-sake* he seems to have recourse
To *Pope*, and *Councils*, and *Traditions* force:
But he that *old* Traditions cou'd subdue,
Cou'd not but find the weakness of the *New:*
If *Scripture*, though deriv'd from *heav'nly birth*,
Has been but carelesly preserv'd on *Earth*;
If *God's own People,* who of *God* before
Knew what we know, and had been promis'd more,
In fuller Terms, of Heaven's assisting Care,
And who did neither *Time*, nor *Study* spare
To keep this Book *untainted, unperplext*;
Let in gross *Errours* to corrupt the *Text:*
Omitted *paragraphs*, embroyl'd the *Sense*;
With vain *Traditions* stopt the gaping Fence,
Which every common hand pull'd up with ease:
What Safety from such *brushwood-helps* as these?
If *written words* from time are not secur'd,
How can we think have *oral Sounds* endur'd?
Which *thus* transmitted, if *one* Mouth has fail'd,
Immortal Lyes on *Ages* are intail'd:
And that some such have been, is prov'd too plain;
If we consider *Interest, Church*, and *Gain.*
  Oh but says one, *Tradition* set aside,
Where can we hope for an *unerring Guid?*
For since th' *original* Scripture has been lost,
All Copies *disagreeing, maim'd* the *most*,

Or *Christian Faith* can have no *certain* ground,
Or *Truth* in *Church Tradition* must be found.

Such an *Omniscient* Church we wish indeed;
'Twere worth *Both Testaments*, and cast in the *Creed:*
But if *this Mother* be a *Guid* so sure,
As can all *doubts resolve*, all *truth secure*,
Then her *Infallibility*, as well
Where Copies are *corrupt*, or *lame*, can tell;
Restore *lost Canon* with as little pains,
As *truly explicate* what still *remains:*
Which yet no *Council* dare *pretend* to doe;
Unless like *Esdras*, they cou'd *write* it new:
Strange Confidence, still to *interpret* true,
Yet not be sure that all they have explain'd,
Is in the blest *Original* contain'd.
More Safe, and much more modest 'tis, to say
God wou'd not leave Mankind without a way:
And that the *Scriptures*, though not *every where*
Free from Corruption, or intire, or clear,
Are uncorrupt, sufficient, clear, intire,
In *all* things which our needfull *Faith* require.
If *others* in the *same Glass better* see
'Tis for *Themselves* they look, but not for *me:*
For *MY* Salvation must its Doom receive
Not from what *OTHERS*, but what *I* believe.

Must *all Tradition* then be set aside?
This to affirm were Ignorance, or Pride.
Are there not many points, some needfull sure
To saving Faith, that Scripture leaves obscure?
Which every Sect will wrest a several way
(For what *one* Sect Interprets, *all* Sects *may:*)
We hold, and say we prove from Scripture plain,
That *Christ* is *GOD*; the bold *Socinian*
From the *same* Scripture urges he's but *MAN*.
Now what Appeal can end th' important Suit;
Both parts *talk* loudly, but the *Rule* is *mute?*

Shall I speak plain, and in a Nation free
Assume an honest *Layman's Liberty?*
I think (according to my little Skill,
To my own Mother-Church submitting still)
That many have been sav'd, and many may,
Who never heard this Question brought in play.
Th' *unletter'd* Christian, who believes in *gross*,
Plods on to *Heaven*; and ne'er is at a loss:
For the *Streight-gate* wou'd be made *streighter* yet,
Were *none* admitted there but men of *Wit*.
The few, by Nature form'd, with Learning fraught,
Born to instruct, as others to be taught,

Must Study well the Sacred Page; and see
Which Doctrine, this, or that, does best agree
With the whole Tenour of the Work Divine:
And plainlyest points to Heaven's reveal'd Design:
Which Exposition flows from *genuine Sense*;
And which is *forc'd* by *Wit* and *Eloquence*.
Not that Traditions parts are useless here:
When general, old, disinteress'd and clear:
That Ancient Fathers thus expound the Page,
Gives *Truth* the reverend Majesty of *Age:*
Confirms its force, by biding every *Test;*
For best *Authority's* next *Rules* are *best.*
And still the nearer to the Spring we go
More limpid, more unsoyl'd the Waters flow.
Thus, *first Traditions* were a proof alone;
Cou'd we be *certain* such they *were*, so *known:*
But since some Flaws in long descent may be,
They make not *Truth* but *Probability*.
Even *Arius* and *Pelagius* durst provoke
To what the *Centuries preceding* spoke.
Such difference is there in an oft-told Tale:
But Truth by its own Sinews will prevail.
Tradition written therefore more commends
Authority, than what from *Voice* descends:
And this, as perfect as its kind can be,
Rouls down to us the Sacred History:
Which, from the *Universal Church receiv'd*,
Is *try'd*, and *after*, for its *self* believ'd.
  The partial *Papists* wou'd infer from hence
Their Church, in last resort, shou'd Judge the *Sense*.
But first they wou'd assume, with wondrous Art,
Themselves to be the *whole*, who are but *part*
Of that vast Frame, the Church; yet grant they were
The handers down, can they from thence infer
A right t' interpret? or wou'd they alone
Who brought the Present, claim it for their own?
The *Book*'s a *Common Largess* to *Mankind*;
Not more for *them*, than *every* Man design'd:
The *welcome News* is in the *Letter* found;
The *Carrier*'s not Commission'd to *expound*.
It *speaks* it *Self*, and what it does contain,
In all things *needfull* to be *known*, is *plain*.
  In times o'ergrown with Rust and Ignorance,
A gainfull Trade their Clergy did advance:
When want of Learning kept the *Laymen* low,
And none but *Priests* were *Authoriz'd* to *know:*
When what small Knowledge was, in them did dwell;
And he a *God* who cou'd but *Reade* or *Spell*;

Then *Mother Church* did mightily prevail:
She parcel'd out the Bible by *retail:*
But still *expounded* what She *sold* or *gave*;
To keep it in *her Power* to *Damn* and *Save:*
Scripture was *scarce*, and as the Market went,
Poor *Laymen* took *Salvation* on *Content*;
As needy men take Money, good or bad:
God's Word they had not, but the *Priests* they had.
Yet, whate'er *false Conveyances* they made,
The *Lawyer* still was *certain* to be paid.
In those dark times they learn'd their knack so well,
That by long use they grew *Infallible:*
At last, a knowing Age began t' enquire
If *they* the *Book*, or *That* did *them* inspire:
And, making narrower search they found, thô late,
That what they thought the *Priest's* was *Their* Estate:
Taught by the *Will produc'd*, (the written Word)
How long they had been *cheated* on *Record*.
Then, every man who saw the Title fair,
Claim'd a Child's part, and put in for a Share:
Consulted Soberly his private good;
And sav'd himself as cheap as e'er he cou'd.
'Tis true, my Friend, (and far be Flattery hence)
This good had full as bad a Consequence:
The Book thus put in every vulgar hand,
Which each presum'd he best cou'd understand,
The *Common Rule* was made the *common Prey*;
And at the mercy of the *Rabble* lay.
The tender Page with horney Fists was gaul'd;
And he was gifted most that loudest baul'd:
The *Spirit* gave the *Doctoral Degree:*
And every member of a *Company*
Was of *his Trade*, and of the *Bible free.*
Plain *Truths* enough for needfull *use* they found;
But men wou'd still be itching to *expound:*
Each was ambitious of th' obscurest place,
No measure ta'n from *Knowledge*, all from *GRACE*.
Study and *Pains* were now no more their Care;
Texts were explain'd by *Fasting*, and by *Prayer:*
This was the Fruit the *private Spirit* brought;
Occasion'd by *great Zeal*, and *little Thought*.
While Crouds unlearn'd, with rude Devotion warm,
About the Sacred Viands buz and swarm.
The *Fly-blown Text* creates a *crawling Brood*;
And turns to *Maggots* what was meant for *Food*.
A Thousand daily Sects rise up, and dye;
A Thousand more the perish'd Race supply:
So all we make of Heavens discover'd Will

Is, not to have it, or to use it ill.
The Danger's much the same; on several Shelves
If *others* wreck *us*, or *we* wreck our *selves*.
 What then remains, but, waving each Extreme,
The Tides of Ignorance, and Pride to stem?
Neither so rich a Treasure to forgo;
Nor proudly seek beyond our pow'r to know:
Faith is not built on disquisitions vain;
The things we *must* believe, are *few*, and *plain*:
But since men *will* believe more than they *need*;
And every man will make *himself* a Creed:
In doubtfull questions 'tis the safest way
To learn what unsuspected Ancients say:
For 'tis not likely *we* shou'd higher Soar
In search of Heav'n, than *all the Church before*:
Nor can we be deceiv'd, unless we see
The *Scripture*, and the *Fathers disagree*.
If after all, they stand suspected still,
(For no man's Faith depends upon his Will;)
'Tis some Relief, that points not clearly known,
Without much hazard may be let alone:
And, after hearing what our Church can say,
If still our Reason runs another way,
That private Reason 'tis more Just to curb,
Than by Disputes the publick Peace disturb.
For points obscure are of small use to learn:
But *Common quiet* is *Mankind's concern*.
 Thus have I made my own Opinions clear:
Yet neither Praise expect, nor Censure fear:
And this unpolish'd, rugged Verse, I chose;
As fittest for Discourse, and nearest Prose:
For, while from *Sacred Truth* I do not swerve,
Tom Sternhold's, or *Tom Sha—ll*'s *Rhimes* will serve.

Epilogue Spoken at Oxford by Mrs. Marshall[1]

OFT has our Poet wisht, this happy Seat
Might prove his fading Muses last retreat.
I wonder'd at his wish, but now I find
He sought for quiet, and content of mind;
Which noiseful Towns, and Courts can never know,
And only in the shades like Laurels grow.
Youth, e'er it sees the World, here studies rest,

[1] Published in *Miscellanies*, 1684. Text of Tonson's edition of Dryden's *Poems*, 1701.

And Age returning thence concludes it best.
What wonder if we court that happiness
Yearly to share, which hourly you possess,
Teaching ev'n you, (while the vext World we show,)
Your Peace to value more, and better know?
'Tis all we can return for favours past,
Whose holy Memory shall ever last,
For Patronage from him whose care presides
O'er every noble Art, and every Science guides:
Bathurst, a name the learn'd with reverence know,
And scarcely more to his own *Virgil* owe.
Whose Age enjoys but what his Youth deserv'd,
To rule those Muses whom before he serv'd:
His Learning, and untainted Manners too
We find (*Athenians*) are deriv'd to you;
Such ancient hospitality there rests,
In yours, as dwelt in the first *Grecian* Breasts,
Whose kindness was Religion to their Guests.
Such Modesty did to our Sex appear,
As had there been no Laws we need not fear,
Since each of you was our Protector here.
Converse so chast, and so strict Virtue shown,
As might *Apollo* with the Muses own.
Till our return we must despair to find
Judges so just, so knowing, and so kind.

To the Memory of Mr. Oldham[1]

FAREWEL, too little and too lately known,
Whom I began to think and call my own;
For sure our Souls were near ally'd, and thine
Cast in the same Poetick mould as mine.
One common Note on either Lyre did strike,
And Knaves and Fools we both abhorr'd alike:
To the same Goal did both our Studies drive,
The last set out the soonest did arrive.
Thus *Nisus* fell upon the slippery place,
Whilst his young Friend perform'd and won the Race.
O early ripe! to thy abundant store
What could advancing Age have added more?
It might (what Nature never gives the young)
Have taught the numbers of thy native Tongue.
But Satyr needs not those, and Wit will shine
Through the harsh cadence of a rugged line.

[1] Published in *The Remains of Mr. John Oldham*, 1684. Text of first edition.

A noble Error, and but seldom made,
When Poets are by too much force betray'd.
Thy generous fruits, though gather'd ere their prime,
Still shew'd a quickness; and maturing time
But mellows what we write to the dull sweets of Rime.
Once more, hail, and farewel; farewel, thou young,
But ah too short, *Marcellus* of our Tongue;
Thy Brows with Ivy, and with Laurels bound;
But Fate and gloomy Night encompass thee around.

Horat. Ode 29. Book 3. Paraphras'd in *Pindarique* Verse[1]

DESCENDED of an ancient Line,
  That long the *Tuscan* Scepter sway'd,
Make haste to meet the generous wine,
  Whose piercing is for thee delay'd:
The rosie wreath is ready made;
  And artful hands prepare
The fragrant *Syrian* Oyl, that shall perfume thy hair.

When the Wine sparkles from a far,
  And the well-natur'd Friend cries, come away;
Make haste, and leave thy business and thy care,
  No mortal int'rest can be worth thy stay.

Leave for a while thy costly Country Seat;
  And, to be Great indeed, forget
The nauseous pleasures of the Great:
  Make haste and come:
Come, and forsake thy cloying store;
  Thy Turret that surveys, from high,
The smoke, and wealth, and noise of *Rome*;
  And all the busie pageantry
That wise men scorn, and fools adore:
Come, give thy Soul a loose, and taste the pleasures of the poor.

Sometimes 'tis grateful to the Rich, to try
A short vicissitude, and fit of Poverty:
  A savoury Dish, a homely Treat,
  Where all is plain, where all is neat,
  Without the stately spacious Room,
The *Persian* Carpet, or the *Tyrian* Loom,
Clear up the cloudy foreheads of the Great.

[1] Published in *Sylvae*, 1685. Text of first edition.

The Sun is in the Lion mounted high;
The *Syrian* Star
Barks from afar;
And with his sultry breath infects the Sky;
The ground below is parch'd, the heav'ns above us fry.
The Shepheard drives his fainting Flock,
Beneath the covert of a Rock;
And seeks refreshing Rivulets nigh:
The *Sylvans* to their shades retire,
Those very shades and streams new shades and streams require;
And want a cooling breeze of wind to fan the raging fire.

Thou, what befits the new Lord May'r,
And what the City Faction dare,
And what the *Gallique* Arms will do,
And what the Quiver bearing Foe,
Art anxiously inquisitive to know:
But God has, wisely, hid from humane sight
The dark decrees of future fate;
And sown their seeds in depth of night;
He laughs at all the giddy turns of State;
When Mortals search too soon, and fear too late.

Enjoy the present smiling hour;
And put it out of Fortunes pow'r:
The tide of bus'ness, like the running stream,
Is sometimes high, and sometimes low,
A quiet ebb, or a tempestuous flow,
And alwayes in extream.
Now with a noiseless gentle course
It keeps within the middle Bed;
Anon it lifts aloft the head,
And bears down all before it, with impetuous force:
And trunks of Trees come rowling down,
Sheep and their Folds together drown:
Both House and Homested into Seas are borne,
And Rocks are from their old foundations torn,
And woods made thin with winds, their scatter'd honours mourn.

Happy the Man, and happy he alone,
He, who can call to day his own:
He, who, secure within, can say,
Tomorrow do thy worst, for I have liv'd today.
Be fair, or foul, or rain, or shine,
The joys I have possest, in spight of fate, are mine.
Not Heav'n it self upon the past has pow'r;
But what has been, has been, and I have had my hour.

Fortune, that with malicious joy,
Does Man her slave oppress,
Proud of her Office to destroy,
Is seldome pleas'd to bless.
Still various, and unconstant still;
But with an inclination to be ill;
Promotes, degrades, delights in strife,
And makes a Lottery of life.
I can enjoy her while she's kind;
But when she dances in the wind,
And shakes her wings, and will not stay,
I puff the Prostitute away:
The little or the much she gave, is quietly resign'd:
Content with poverty, my Soul, I arm;
And Vertue, tho' in rags, will keep me warm.

What is't to me,
Who never sail in her unfaithful Sea,
If Storms arise, and Clouds grow black;
If the Mast split and threaten wreck?
Then let the greedy Merchant fear
For his ill gotten gain;
And pray to Gods that will not hear,
While the debating winds and billows bear
His Wealth into the Main.
For me, secure from Fortunes blows,
(Secure of what I cannot lose,)
In my small Pinnace I can sail,
Contemning all the blustring roar;
And running with a merry gale,
With friendly Stars my safety seek
Within some little winding Creek;
And see the storm a shore.

To the Pious Memory of the Accomplisht Young Lady Mrs. Ann Killigrew. Excellent in the Two Sister-Arts of Poesie, and Painting. An Ode[1]

Thou youngest Virgin-Daughter of the Skies,
Made in the last Promotion of the *Blest;*
Whose Palms, new pluckt from Paradise,

[1] Published in *Poems of Mrs. Anne Killigrew*, 1686. Text of Tonson's edition of Dryden's *Poems*, 1701.

In spreading *Branches* more sublimely rise,
Rich with Immortal Green above the rest:
Whether, adopted to some Neighbouring Star,
Thou rol'st above us, in thy wand'ring Race,
Or, in Procession fixt and regular,
Mov'd with the Heav'ns Majestick Pace;
Or, call'd to more Superiour *Bliss*,
Thou tread'st, with Seraphims, the vast *Abyss*.
What ever happy Region is thy place,
Cease thy Celestial Song a little space;
(Thou wilt have time enough for Hymns Divine,
Since Heav'ns Eternal Year is thine.)
Here then a Mortal Muse thy Praise rehearse,
In no ignoble Verse:
But such as thy own Voice did practise here,
When thy first Fruits of Poesie were giv'n;
To make thy self a welcome Inmate there:
While yet a young Probationer,
And Candidate of Heav'n.

If by Traduction came thy Mind,
Our Wonder is the less to find
A Soul so charming from a Stock so good;
Thy Father was transfus'd into thy *Blood:*
So wert thou born into a tuneful strain,
(An early, rich, and inexhausted Vein.)
But if thy Præexisting Soul
Was form'd, at first, with Myriads more,
It did through all the Mighty Poets roul,
Who *Greek* or *Latine* Laurels wore.
And was that *Sappho* last, which once it was before.
If so, then cease thy flight, *O Heaven-born Mind!*
Thou hast no *Dross* to purge from thy Rich Ore:
Nor can thy Soul a fairer Mansion find,
Than was the Beauteous Frame she left behind:
Return, to fill or mend the Quire, of thy Celestial kind.

May we presume to say, that at thy *Birth*,
New joy was sprung in *Heav'n*, as well as here on *Earth*.
For sure the Milder Planets did combine
On thy *Auspicious* Horoscope to shine,
And ev'n the most Malicious were in Trine.
Thy *Brother-Angels* at thy *Birth*
Strung each his Lyre, and tun'd it high,
That all the People of the Skie
Might know a Poetess was born on Earth.
And then if ever, Mortal Ears
Had heard the Musick of the Spheres!

And if no clust'ring Swarm of *Bees*
On thy sweet Mouth distill'd their golden Dew,
'Twas that, such vulgar Miracles,
Heav'n had not Leasure to renew:
For all the *Blest* Fraternity of Love
Solemniz'd there thy *Birth*, and kept thy Holy day above.

O gracious God! How far have we
Prophan'd thy Heav'nly Gift of Poesy?
Made prostitute and profligate the Muse,
Debas'd to each obscene and impious use,
Whose Harmony was first ordain'd *Above*
For Tongues of *Angels*, and for *Hymns* of *Love?*
O wretched We! why were we hurry'd down
This lubrique and adult'rate Age,
(Nay added fat Pollutions of our own)
T' increase the steaming Ordures of the Stage?
What can we say t' excuse our *Second Fall?*
Let this thy *Vestal*, Heaven, attone for all?
Her *Arethusian* Stream remains unsoil'd,
Unmixt with Forreign Filth, and undefil'd,
Her Wit was more than Man, her Innocence a Child!

Art she had none, yet wanted none:
For Nature did that Want supply,
So rich in Treasures of her Own,
She might our boasted *Stores* defy:
Such Noble Vigour did her Verse adorn,
That it seem'd borrow'd, where 'twas only born.
Her Morals too were in her *Bosom* bred,
By great Examples daily fed,
What in the best of *Books*, her Father's Life, she read.
And to be read her self she need not fear,
Each Test, and ev'ry Light, her Muse will bear,
Though *Epictetus* with his Lamp were there.
Ev'n Love (for Love sometimes her Muse exprest)
Was but a *Lambent-flame* which play'd about her *Breast:*
Light as the Vapours of a Morning Dream,
So cold her self, whilst she such Warmth exprest,
'Twas *Cupid* bathing in *Diana*'s Stream.

Born to the Spacious Empire of the *Nine*,
One wou'd have thought, she shou'd have been content
To manage well that Mighty Government;
But what can young ambitious Souls confine?
To the next Realm she stretcht her Sway
For *Painture* near adjoyning lay,
A plenteous Province, and alluring Prey.

A Chamber of Dependences was fram'd,
(As Conquerors will never want Pretence,
When arm'd, to justifie th' Offence)
And the whole Fief, in right of Poetry, she claim'd.
The Country open lay without Defence:
For Poets frequent In-rodes there had made,
And perfectly cou'd represent
The Shape, the Face, with ev'ry Lineament;
And all the large Demains which the *Dumb-sister* sway'd,
All bow'd beneath her Government,
Receiv'd in Triumph wheresoe're she went.
Her Pencil drew, what e're her Soul design'd,
And of the *happy Draught* surpass'd the *Image* in her *Mind*.
The *Sylvan* Scenes of Herds and Flocks,
And fruitful Plains and barren Rocks,
Of shallow *Brooks* that flow'd so clear,
The bottom did the top appear;
Of deeper too and ampler Floods,
Which as in Mirrors, shew'd the Woods;
Of lofty Trees, with Sacred Shades,
And Perspectives of pleasant Glades,
Where Nymphs of brightest Form appear,
And shaggy Satyrs standing near,
Which them at once admire and fear.
The Ruines too of some Majestick Piece,
Boasting the Pow'r of ancient *Rome* or *Greece*.
Whose Statues, Freezes, Columns broken lie,
And tho' defac'd, the Wonder of the Eye,
What *Nature, Art*, bold *Fiction* e're durst frame,
Her forming Hand gave Feature to the Name.
So strange a Concourse ne're was seen before,
But when the peopl'd *Ark* the whole Creation bore.

The Scene then chang'd, with bold Erected Look
Our Martial King the sight with Reverence strook:
For not content t' express his Outward Part,
Her Hand call'd out the Image of his Heart,
His Warlike Mind, his Soul devoid of Fear,
His High-designing *Thoughts*, were figur'd there,
As when, by Magick, Ghosts are made appear.
Our Phenix Queen was portrai'd too so bright,
Beauty alone cou'd *Beauty* take so right:
Her Dress, her Shape, her Matchless Grace,
Were all observ'd, as well as Heavenly Face.
With such a Peerless Majesty she stands,
As in that Day she took the Crown from Sacred Hands:
Before a Train of Heroins was seen,

In *Beauty* foremost, as in Rank, the Queen!
  Thus nothing to her *Genius* was deny'd,
But like a *Ball* of Fire the further thrown,
  Still with a greater *Blaze* she shone,
And her bright Soul broke out on ev'ry side.
What next she had design'd, Heaven only knows,
To such Immod'rate Growth her Conquest rose,
That Fate alone its Progress cou'd oppose.

  Now all those Charms, that blooming Grace,
The well-proportion'd Shape, and beauteous Face,
Shall never more be seen by Mortal Eyes;
In Earth the much lamented Virgin lies!
  Not Wit, nor Piety cou'd Fate prevent;
  Nor was the cruel *Destiny* content
  To finish all the Murder at a blow,
  To sweep at once her *Life*, and *Beauty* too;
But, like a hardn'd Fellon, took a pride
    To work more Mischievously slow,
    And plunder'd first, and then destroy'd.
O double Sacriledge on things Divine,
To rob the Relique, and deface the Shrine!
    But thus *Orinda* dy'd:
  Heaven, by the same Disease, did both translate,
As equal were their Souls, so equal was their Fate.

  Mean time her *Warlike Brother* on the Seas
  His waving Streams to the Winds displays,
And vows for his Return, with vain Devotion, pays,
    Ah, Generous Youth, that Wish forbear,
    The Winds too soon will waft thee here!
  Slack all thy Sails, and fear to come,
Alas, thou know'st not, thou art wreck'd at home!
No more shalt thou behold thy Sister's Face,
Thou hast already had her last Embrace.
But look aloft, and if thou ken'st from far,
Among the *Pleiad's* a New-kindl'd Star,
If any Sparkles, than the rest, more bright,
'Tis she that shines in that propitious Light.

  When in mid-Air, the Golden Trump shall sound,
    To raise the Nations under Ground;
    When in the Valley of *Jehosaphat*,
The Judging God shall close the Book of Fate;
    And there the last *Assizes* keep,
    For those who Wake, and those who Sleep;
    When ratling *Bones* together fly,
From the four Corners of the Skie,

When Sinews o're the Skeletons are spread,
Those cloath'd with Flesh, and Life inspires the Dead;
The Sacred Poets first shall hear the Sound,
  And formost from the Tomb shall bound:
For they are cover'd with the lightest Ground,
And streight, with in-born Vigour, on the Wing
Like mounting Larks, to the New Morning sing.
There *Thou*, sweet Saint, before the Quire shalt go,
As Harbinger of Heaven, the Way to show,
The Way which thou so well hast learnt below.

The Hind and the Panther[1]

Part I

A MILK white *Hind*,[2] immortal and unchang'd,
Fed on the lawns, and in the forest rang'd;
Without unspotted, innocent within,
She fear'd no danger, for she knew no sin.
Yet had she oft been chas'd with horns and hounds,
And Scythian shafts; and many winged wounds
Aim'd at Her heart; was often forc'd to fly,
And doom'd to death, though fated not to dy.
  Not so her young; for their unequal line
Was Heroe's make, half humane, half divine.
Their earthly mold obnoxious was to fate,
Th' immortal part assum'd immortal state.
Of these a slaughtered army lay in bloud,
Extended o'er the *Caledonian* wood,
Their native walk; whose vocal bloud arose,
And cry'd for pardon on their perjur'd foes;
Their fate was fruitful, and the sanguin seed
Endu'd with souls, encreas'd the sacred breed.
So Captive *Israel* multiply'd in chains,
A numerous Exile; and enjoy'd her pains.
With grief and gladness mixt, their mother view'd
Her martyr'd offspring, and their race renew'd;
Their corps to perish, but their kind to last,
So much the deathless plant the dying fruit surpass'd.
  Panting and pensive now she rang'd alone,
And wander'd in the kingdoms, once Her own.
The common Hunt, though from their rage restrain'd
By sov'reign pow'r, her company disdain'd:

[1] Published in April, 1687. Text of the second edition, 1687.
[2] The Roman Catholic Church.

Grin'd as They pass'd, and with a glaring eye
Gave gloomy signs of secret enmity.
'Tis true, she bounded by, and trip'd so light
They had not time to take a steady sight.
For truth has such a face and such a meen
As to be lov'd needs only to be seen.
The bloudy *Bear*[3] an *Independent* beast,
Unlick'd to form, in groans her hate express'd.
Among the timorous kind the *Quaking Hare*[4]
Profess'd neutrality, but would not swear.
Next her the *Buffoon Ape*,[5] as Atheists use,
Mimick'd all Sects, and had his own to chuse:
Still when the Lyon[6] look'd, his knees he bent,
And pay'd at Church a Courtier's Complement.
The bristl'd *Baptist Boar*,[7] impure as He,
(But whitn'd with the foam of sanctity)
With fat pollutions fill'd the sacred place,
And mountains levell'd in his furious race,
So first rebellion founded was in grace.
But since the mighty ravage which he made
In *German* Forests, had his guilt betrayd,
With broken tusks, and with a borrow'd name
He shun'd the vengeance, and conceal'd the shame;
So lurk'd in Sects unseen. With greater guile
False *Reynard*[8] fed on consecrated spoil:
The graceless beast by *Athanasius* first
Was chas'd from *Nice*; then by *Socinus* nurs'd
His impious race their blasphemy renew'd,
And natures King through natures opticks view'd.
Revers'd they view'd him lessen'd to their eye,
Nor in an Infant could a God descry:
New swarming Sects to this obliquely tend,
Hence they began, and here they all will end.
What weight of antient witness can prevail
If private reason hold the publick scale?
But, gratious God, how well dost thou provide
For erring judgments an unerring Guide?
Thy throne is darkness in th' abyss of light,
A blaze of glory that forbids the sight;
O teach me to believe Thee thus conceal'd,
And search no farther than thy self reveal'd;
But her alone for my Directour take

[3] The Independents.
[4] The Quakers.
[5] The Freethinkers.
[6] The King of England.
[7] The Anabaptists.
[8] The Arians.

Whom thou hast promis'd never to forsake!
My thoughtless youth was wing'd with vain desires,
My manhood, long misled by wandring fires,
Follow'd false lights; and when their glimps was gone,
My pride struck out new sparkles of her own.
Such was I, such by nature still I am,
Be thine the glory, and be mine the shame.
Good life be now my task: my doubts are done,
(What more could fright my faith, than Three in One?)
Can I believe eternal God could lye
Disguis'd in mortal mold and infancy?
That the great maker of the world could dye?
And after that, trust my imperfect sense
Which calls in question his omnipotence?
Can I my reason to my faith compell,
And shall my sight, and touch, and taste rebell?
Superiour faculties are set aside,
Shall their subservient organs be my guide?
Then let the moon usurp the rule of day,
And winking tapers shew the sun his way;
For what my senses can themselves perceive
I need no revelation to believe.
Can they who say the Host should be descry'd
By sense, define a body glorify'd?
Impassible, and penetrating parts?
Let them declare by what mysterious arts
He shot that body through th' opposing might
Of bolts and barrs impervious to the light,
And stood before his train confess'd in open sight.
  For since thus wondrously he pass'd, 'tis plain
One single place two bodies did contain,
And sure the same Omnipotence as well
Can make one body in more places dwell.
Let reason then at Her own quarry fly,
But how can finite grasp Infinity?
  'Tis urg'd again that faith did first commence
By miracles, which are appeals to sense,
And thence concluded that our sense must be
The motive still of credibility.
For latter ages must on former wait,
And what began belief, must propagate.
  But winnow well this thought, and you shall find,
'Tis light as chaff that flies before the wind.
Were all those wonders wrought by pow'r divine
As means or ends of some more deep design?
Most sure as means, whose end was this alone,
To prove the god-head of th' eternal Son.
God thus asserted: man is to believe

Beyond what sense and reason can conceive.
And for mysterious things of faith rely
On the Proponent, heav'ns authority.
If then our faith we for our guide admit,
Vain is the farther search of human wit,
As when the building gains a surer stay,
We take th' unuseful scaffolding away:
Reason by sense no more can understand,
The game is play'd into another hand.
Why chuse we then like *Bilanders* to creep
Along the coast, and land in view to keep,
When safely we may launch into the deep?
In the same vessel which our Saviour bore
Himself the Pilot, let us leave the shoar,
And with a better guide a better world explore.
Could He his god-head veil with flesh and bloud
And not veil these again to be our food?
His grace in both is equal in extent,
The first affords us life, the second nourishment.
And if he can, why all this frantick pain
To construe what his clearest words contain,
And make a riddle what He made so plain?
To take up half on trust, and half to try,
Name it not faith, but bungling biggottry.
Both knave and fool the Merchant we may call
To pay great summs, and to compound the small.
For who wou'd break with heav'n, and wou'd not break for all?
Rest then, my soul, from endless anguish freed;
Nor sciences thy guide, nor sense thy creed.
Faith is the best ensurer of thy bliss;
The Bank above must fail before the venture miss.
But heav'n and heav'n-born faith are far from Thee
Thou first Apostate to Divinity.
Unkennel'd range in thy *Polonian* Plains;
A fiercer foe th' insatiate *Wolf*[9] remains.
  Too boastful *Britain* please thy self no more,
That beasts of prey are banish'd from thy shoar:
The *Bear*, the *Boar*, and every salvage name,
Wild in effect, though in appearance tame,
Lay waste thy woods, destroy thy blissfull bow'r,
And muzl'd though they seem, the mutes devour.
More haughty than the rest the *wolfish* race,
Appear with belly Gaunt, and famish'd face:
Never was so deform'd a beast of Grace.
His ragged tail betwixt his leggs he wears
Close clap'd for shame, but his rough crest he rears,
And pricks up his predestinating ears.

[9] The Presbyterians.

His wild disorder'd walk, his hagger'd eyes,
Did all the bestial citizens surprize.
Though fear'd and hated, yet he rul'd awhile
As Captain or Companion of the spoil.
Full many a year his hatefull head had been
For tribute paid, nor since in *Cambria* seen:
The last of all the Litter scap'd by chance,
And from *Geneva* first infested *France*.
Some Authors thus his Pedigree will trace,
But others write him of an upstart Race:
Because of *Wickliff's* Brood no mark he brings
But his innate Antipathy to Kings.
These last deduce him from th' *Helvetian* kind
Who near the *Leman lake* his Consort lin'd.
That fi'ry *Zuynglius* first th' Affection bred,
And meagre *Calvin* blest the Nuptial Bed.
In *Israel* some believe him whelp'd long since,
When the proud *Sanhedrim* oppres'd the Prince,
Or, since he will be *Jew*, derive him high'r
When *Corah* with his Brethren did conspire,
From *Moyses* Hand the Sov'reign sway to wrest,
And *Aaron* of his Ephod to devest:
Till opening Earth made way for all to pass,
And cou'd not bear the Burd'n of a *class*.
The *Fox* and he came shuffl'd in the Dark,
If ever they were stow'd in *Noah's* Ark:
Perhaps not made; for all their barking train
The Dog (a common species) will contain.
And some wild currs, who from their masters ran,
Abhorring the supremacy of man,
In woods and caves the rebel-race began.
  O happy pair, how well have you encreas'd,
What ills in Church and State have you redress'd!
With Teeth untry'd, and rudiments of Claws
Your first essay was on your native Laws:
Those having torn with Ease, and trampl'd down,
Your Fangs you fasten'd on the miter'd Crown,
And freed from God and Monarchy your Town.
What though your native kennel still be small
Bounded betwixt a Puddle and a Wall,
Yet your Victorious Colonies are sent
Where the North Ocean girds the Continent.
Quickned with fire below your Monsters Breed,
In Fenny *Holland* and in fruitful *Tweed*.
And like the first the last effects to be
Drawn to the dreggs of a Democracy.
As, where in Fields the fairy rounds are seen,

A rank sow'r herbage rises on the Green;
So, springing where these mid-night Elves advance,
Rebellion Prints the Foot-steps of the Dance.
Such are their Doctrines, such contempt they show
To Heaven above, and to their Prince below,
As none but Traytors and Blasphemers know.
God, like the Tyrant of the Skies is plac'd,
And Kings, like slaves, beneath the Croud debas'd.
So fulsome is their food, that Flocks refuse
To bite; and only Dogs for Physick use.
As, where the Lightning runs along the Ground,
No husbandry can heal the blasting Wound,
Nor bladed Grass, nor bearded Corn succeeds,
But Scales of Scurf, and Putrefaction breeds:
Such Warrs, such Waste, such fiery tracks of Dearth
Their Zeal has left, and such a teemless Earth.
But as the Poisons of the deadliest kind
Are to their own unhappy Coasts confin'd,
As only *Indian* Shades of fight deprive,
And Magick Plants will but in *Colchos* thrive;
So Presby'try and Pestilential Zeal
Can only flourish in a Common-weal.
From *Celtique* Woods is chas'd the *wolfish* Crew,
But ah! some Pity e'en to Brutes is due,
Their native Walks, methinks, they might enjoy
Curb'd of their native Malice to destroy.
Of all the Tyrannies on humane kind
The worst is that which Persecutes the mind.
Let us but weigh at what offence we strike,
'Tis but because we cannot think alike.
In punishing of this, we overthrow
The Laws of Nations and of Nature too.
Beasts are the Subjects of Tyrannick sway,
Where still the stronger on the weaker Prey.
Man only of a softer mold is made;
Not for his Fellows ruine, but their Aid.
Created kind, beneficient and free,
The noble Image of the Deity.
One Portion of informing Fire was giv'n
To Brutes, th' Inferiour Family of Heav'n:
The Smith Divine, as with a careless Beat,
Struck out the mute Creation at a Heat:
But when arriv'd at last to humane Race,
The Godhead took a deep consid'ring space:
And, to distinguish Man from all the rest,
Unlock'd the sacred Treasures of his Breast:
And Mercy mixt with reason did impart;
One to his Head, the other to his Heart:

Reason to Rule, but Mercy to forgive:
The first is Law, the last Prerogative.
And like his Mind his outward form appear'd:
When issuing Naked, to the wondring Herd,
He charm'd their Eyes, and for they lov'd, they fear'd.
Not arm'd with horns of arbitrary might,
Or Claws to seize their furry spoils in Fight,
Or with increase of Feet, t'o'ertake 'em in their flight.
Of easie shape, and pliant ev'ry way;
Confessing still the softness of his Clay,
And kind as Kings upon their Coronation-Day:
With open Hands, and with extended space
Of Arms to satisfy a large embrace.
Thus kneaded up with Milk, the new made Man
His Kingdom o'er his Kindred world began:
Till Knowledge mis-apply'd, mis-understood,
And pride of Empire sour'd his Balmy Blood.
Then, first rebelling, his own stamp he coins;
The Murth'rer *Cain* was latent in his Loins;
And Blood began its first and loudest Cry
For diff'ring worship of the Deity.
Thus persecution rose, and farther Space
Produc'd the mighty hunter of his Race.
Not so the blessed *Pan* his flock encreas'd,
Content to fold 'em from the famish'd Beast:
Mild were his laws; the Sheep and harmless Hind
Were never of the persecuting kind.
Such pity now the pious Pastor shows,
Such mercy from the *British* Lyon flows,
That both provide protection for their foes.
  Oh happy Regions, *Italy* and *Spain*,
Which never did those monsters entertain!
The *Wolfe*, the *Bear*, the *Boar*, can there advance
No native claim of just inheritance.
And self-preserving laws, severe in show,
May guard their fences from th' invading foe.
Where birth has plac'd 'em let 'em safely share
The common benefit of vital air.
Themselves unharmful, let them live unharm'd;
Their jaws disabl'd, and their claws disarm'd:
Here, only in nocturnal howlings bold,
They dare not seize the Hind nor leap the fold.
More pow'rful, and as vigilant as they,
The *Lyon* awfully forbids the prey.
Their rage repress'd, though pinch'd with famine sore,
They stand aloof, and tremble at his roar;
Much is their hunger, but their fear is more.
  These are the chief; to number o'er the rest,

And stand, like *Adam*, naming ev'ry beast,
Were weary work; nor will the Muse describe
A slimy-born and sun-begotten Tribe:
Who, far from steeples and their sacred sound,
In fields their sullen conventicles found:
These gross, half animated lumps I leave;
Nor can I think what thoughts they can conceive.
But if they think at all, 'tis sure no high'r
Than matter, put in motion, may aspire.
Souls that can scarce ferment their mass of clay;
So drossy, so divisible are They,
As wou'd but serve pure bodies for allay:
Such souls as *Shards* produce, such beetle things,
As only buz to heav'n with ev'ning wings;
Strike in the dark, offending but by chance,
Such are the blind-fold blows of ignorance.
They know not beings, and but hate a name,
To them the *Hind* and *Panther* are the same.
The *Panther*[10] sure the noblest, next the *Hind*,
And fairest creature of the spotted kind;
Oh, could her in-born stains be wash'd away,
She were too good to be a beast of Prey!
How can I praise, or blame, and not offend,
Or how divide the frailty from the friend!
Her faults and vertues lye so mix'd, that she
Nor wholly stands condemn'd, nor wholly free.
Then, like her injur'd *Lyon*, let me speak,
He cannot bend her, and he would not break.
Unkind already, and estrang'd in part,
The *Wolfe* begins to share her wandring heart.
Though unpolluted yet with actual ill,
She half commits, who sins but in Her will.
If, as our dreaming *Platonists* report,
There could be spirits of a middle sort,
Too black for heav'n, and yet too white for hell,
Who just dropt half way down, nor lower fell;
So pois'd, so gently she descends from high,
It seems a soft dismission from the skie.
Her house not ancient, whatsoe'er pretence
Her clergy Heraulds make in her defence.
A second century not half-way run
Since the new honours of her blood begun.
A *Lyon* old, obscene, and furious made
By lust, compress'd her mother in a shade.
Then, by a left-hand marr'age weds the Dame,
Cov'ring adult'ry with a specious name:

[10] The Church of England.

So schism begot; and sacrilege and she,
A well-match'd pair, got graceless heresie.
God's and Kings rebels have the same good cause,
To trample down divine and humane laws:
Both wou'd be call'd Reformers, and their hate,
Alike destructive both to Church and State:
The fruit proclaims the plant; a lawless Prince
By luxury reform'd incontinence,
By ruins, charity; by riots, abstinence.
Confessions, fasts and penance set aside;
Oh with what ease we follow such a guide!
Where souls are starv'd, and senses gratify'd.
Where marr'age pleasures, midnight pray'r supply,
And mattin bells (a melancholly cry)
Are tun'd to merrier notes, *encrease* and *multiply*.
Religion shows a Rosie colour'd face;
Not hatter'd out with drudging works of grace;
A down-hill Reformation rolls apace.
What flesh and blood wou'd croud the narrow gate
Or, till they waste their pamper'd paunches, wait?
All wou'd be happy at the cheapest rate.
Though our lean faith these rigid laws has giv'n,
The full fed *Musulman* goes fat to heav'n;
For his *Arabian* Prophet with delights
Of sense, allur'd his eastern Proselytes.
The jolly *Luther*, reading him, began
T'interpret Scriptures by his *Alcoran;*
To grub the thorns beneath our tender feet,
And make the paths of *Paradise* more sweet:
Bethought him of a wife e'er half way gone.
(For 'twas uneasie travailing alone,)
And in this masquerade of mirth and love,
Mistook the bliss of heav'n for *Bacchanals* above.
Sure he presum'd of praise, who came to stock
Th' etherial pastures with so fair a flock;
Burnish'd, and bat'ning on their food, to show
The diligence of carefull herds below.
Our *Panther*, though like these she chang'd her head,
Yet, as the mistress of a monarch's bed,
Her front erect with majesty she bore,
The Crozier weilded, and the Miter wore.
Her upper part of decent discipline
Shew'd affectation of an ancient line:
And fathers, councils, church and churches head,
Were on her reverend *Phylacteries* read.
But what disgrac'd and disavow'd the rest,
Was *Calvin*'s brand, that stigmatiz'd the beast.

Thus, like a creature of a double kind,
In her own labyrinth she lives confin'd.
To foreign lands no sounds of Her is come,
Humbly content to be despis'd at home.
Such is her faith, where good cannot be had,
At least she leaves the refuse of the bad.
Nice in her choice of ill, though not of best,
And least deform'd, because reform'd the least.
In doubtful points betwixt her diff'ring friends,
Where one for substance, one for sign contends,
Their contradicting terms she strives to joyn.
Sign shall be substance, substance shall be sign.
A real presence all her sons allow,
And yet 'tis flat Idolatry to bow,
Because the God-head's there they know not how.
Her Novices are taught that bread and wine
Are but the visible and outward sign
Receiv'd by those who in communion joyn.
But th' inward grace, or the thing signify'd,
His blood and body, who to save us dy'd;
The faithful this thing signify'd receive.
What is't those faithful then partake or leave?
For what is signify'd and understood,
Is, by her own confession, flesh and blood.
Then, by the same acknowledgement, we know
They take the sign, and take the substance too.
The lit'ral sense is hard to flesh and blood,
But nonsense never can be understood.
Her wild belief on ev'ry wave is tost,
But sure no Church can better morals boast.
True to her King her principles are found;
Oh that her practice were but half so sound!
Stedfast in various turns of state she stood,
And seal'd her vow'd affection with her blood;
Nor will I meanly tax her constancy,
That int'rest or obligement made the tye,
(Bound to the fate of murdr'd Monarchy:)
(Before the sounding Ax so falls the Vine,
Whose tender branches round the Poplar twine.)
She chose her ruin, and resign'd her life,
In death undaunted as an *Indian* wife:
A rare example: But some souls we see
Grow hard, and stiffen with adversity:
Yet these by fortunes favours are undone,
Resolv'd into a baser form they run,
And bore the wind, but cannot bear the sun.
Let this be natures frailty or her fate,

Or *Isgrim's*[11] counsel, her new chosen mate;
Still she's the fairest of the fallen Crew,
No mother more indulgent but the true.
  Fierce to her foes, yet fears her force to try,
Because she wants innate auctority;
For how can she constrain them to obey
Who has her self cast off the lawful sway?
Rebellion equals all, and those who toil
In common theft, will share the common spoil.
Let her produce the title and the right
Against her old superiours first to fight;
If she reform by Text, ev'n that's as plain
For her own Rebels to reform again.
As long as words a diff'rent sense will bear,
And each may be his own Interpreter,
Our ai'ry faith will no foundation find:
The word's a weathercock for ev'ry wind:
The *Bear*, the *Fox*, the *Wolfe*, by turns prevail,
The most in pow'r supplies the present gale.
The wretched *Panther* crys aloud for aid
To church and councils, whom she first betray'd;
No help from Fathers or traditions train,
Those ancient guides she taught us to disdain.
And by that scripture which she once abus'd
To Reformation, stands her self accus'd.
What bills for breach of laws can she prefer,
Expounding which she owns her self may err?
And, after all her winding ways are try'd,
If doubts arise she slips herself aside,
And leaves the private conscience for the guide.
If then that conscience set th' offender free,
It bars her claim to church auctority.
How can she censure, or what crime pretend,
But Scripture may be constru'd to defend?
Ev'n those whom for rebellion she transmits
To civil pow'r, her doctrine first acquits;
Because no disobedience can ensue,
Where no submission to a Judge is due.
Each judging for himself, by her consent,
Whom thus absolv'd she sends to punishment.
Suppose the Magistrate revenge her cause,
'Tis only for transgressing humane laws.
How answ'ring to its end a church is made,
Whose pow'r is but to counsel and perswade?
O solid rock, on which secure she stands!

[11] The Wolfe.

Eternal house, not built with mortal hands!
O sure defence against th' infernal gate,
A patent during pleasure of the state!
  Thus is the *Panther* neither lov'd nor fear'd,
A meer mock Queen of a divided Herd;
Whom soon by lawful pow'r she might controll,
Her self a part submitted to the whole.
Then, as the Moon who first receives the light
By which she makes our nether regions bright,
So might she shine, reflecting from afar
The rays she borrow'd from a better Star:
Big with the beams which from her mother flow
And reigning o'er the rising tides below:
Now, mixing with a salvage croud, she goes
And meanly flatters her invet'rate foes,
Rul'd while she rules, and losing ev'ry hour
Her wretched remnants of precarious pow'r.
  One evening while the cooler shade she sought,
Revolving many a melancholy thought,
Alone she walk'd, and look'd around in vain,
With ruful visage for her vanish'd train:
None of her sylvan subjects made their court;
Leveés and coucheés pass'd without resort.
So hardly can Usurpers manage well
Those, whom they first instructed to rebel:
More liberty begets desire of more,
The hunger still encreases with the store.
Without respect they brush'd along the wood
Each in his clan, and filled with loathsome food;
Ask'd no permission to the neighb'ring flood,
The *Panther*, full of inward discontent,
Since they wou'd goe, before 'em wisely went:
Supplying want of pow'r by drinking first,
As if she gave 'em leave to quench their thirst.
Among the rest, the *Hind*, with fearful face
Beheld from far the common wat'ring place,
Nor durst approach; till with an awful roar
The sovereign *Lyon* bad her fear no more.
Encourag'd thus she brought her younglings nigh,
Watching the motions of her Patron's eye,
And drank a sober draught; the rest amaz'd
Stood mutely still, and on the stranger gaz'd:
Survey'd her part by part, and sought to find
The ten-horn'd monster in the harmless *Hind*,
Such as the *Wolfe* and *Panther* had design'd.
They thought at first they dream'd, for 'twas offence

With them, to question certitude of sense,
Their guide in faith; but nearer when they drew,
And had the faultless object full in view,
Lord, how they all admir'd her heav'nly hiew!
Some, who before her fellowship disdain'd,
Scarce, and but scarce, from in-born rage restrain'd,
Now frisk'd about her, and old kindred feign'd.
Whether for love or int'rest, ev'ry sect
Of all the salvage nation shew'd respect:
The Vice-roy *Panther* could not awe the herd,
The more the company the less they fear'd.
The surly *Wolfe* with secret envy burst,
Yet cou'd not howl, the *Hind* had seen him first:
But what he durst not speak, the *Panther* durst.
  For when the herd suffis'd, did late repair
To ferney heath, and to their forest lare,
She made a mannerly excuse to stay,
Proff'ring the *Hind* to wait her half the way:
That since the Skie was clear, an hour of talk
Might help her to beguile the tedious walk.
With much good-will the motion was embrac'd,
To chat awhile on their adventures pass'd:
Nor had the grateful *Hind* so soon forgot
Her friend and fellow-suff'rer in the plot.
Yet wondring how of late she grew estrang'd,
Her forehead cloudy, and her count'nance chang'd,
She thought this hour th' occasion would present
To learn her secret cause of discontent,
Which, well she hop'd, might be with ease redress'd,
Consid'ring Her a well-bred civil beast,
And more a Gentlewoman than the rest.
After some common talk what rumours ran,
The Lady of the spotted-muff began.

A Song for St. Cecilia's Day, 1687[1]

FROM Harmony, from Heavenly Harmony
    This Universal Frame began.
  When Nature underneath a heap
    Of jarring Atoms lay,
  And cou'd not heave her Head,
The tuneful Voice was heard from high,
    Arise ye more than dead.

[1] Published in 1687. Text of Tonson's edition of Dryden's *Poems*, 1701.

Then cold, and hot, and moist, and dry,
In order to their stations leap,
And MUSICK's Power obey.
From Harmony, from Heavenly Harmony
This Universal Frame began:
From Harmony to Harmony
Through all the compass of the Notes it ran,
The Diapason closing full in Man.

2.

What Passion cannot MUSICK raise and quell!
When *Jubal* struck the corded Shell,
His list'ning Brethren stood around
And wondring, on their Faces fell
To worship that Celestial Sound.
Less than a God they thought there could not dwell
Within the hollow of that Shell
That spoke so sweetly and so well.
What Passion cannot MUSICK raise and quell!

3.

The TRUMPETS loud Clangor,
Excites us to Arms
With shrill Notes of Anger
And mortal Alarms,
The double double double beat
Of the thundring DRUM
Cries, heark the Foes come;
Charge, Charge, 'tis too late to retreat.

4.

The soft complaining FLUTE
In dying Notes discovers
The Woes of hopeless Lovers,
Whose Dirge is whisper'd by the warbling LUTE.

5.

Sharp VIOLINS proclaim
Their jealous Pangs, and Desperation,
Fury, frantick Indignation,
Depth of Pains, and height of Passion,
For the fair, disdainful Dame.

6.

But oh! what Art can teach
  What human Voice can reach
The sacred ORGANS praise?
Notes inspiring holy Love,
Notes that wing their Heavenly ways
  To mend the Choires above.

7.

Orpheus cou'd lead the savage race;
And Trees unrooted left their place;
    Sequacious of the Lyre:
But bright *CECILIA* rais'd the wonder high'r;
When to her ORGAN, vocal Breath was giv'n
An Angel heard, and straight appear'd
    Mistaking Earth for Heav'n.

Grand CHORUS

As from the pow'r of Sacred Lays
    The Spheres began to Move,
And sung the great Creator's praise
    To all the bless'd above;
So when the last and dreadful hour
This crumbling Pageant shall devour,
The TRUMPET *shall be heard on high,*
The Dead shall live, the Living die,
And MUSICK *shall untune the Sky.*

Lines Printed under the Engraved Portrait of Milton, in Tonson's Folio of the "Paradise Lost," 1688[1]

THREE Poets, in three distant Ages born,
Greece, Italy, and *England* did adorn.
The First in loftiness of thought surpass'd,
The Next in Majesty; in both the Last.
The force of Nature could no farther goe;
To make a Third she joynd the former two.

[1] Published in Tonson's folio edition of *Paradise Lost*, 1688. Text of first edition.

Mercury's Song to Phædra[1]

FAIR *Iris* I love, and hourly I die,
But not for a lip, nor a languishing Eye:
She's fickle and false, and there we agree;
For I am as false and as fickle as she:
We neither believe what either can say;
And, neither believing, we neither betray.

'Tis civil to swear, and say things of course;
We mean not the taking for better for worse.
When present, we love; when absent, agree:
I think not of *Iris*, nor *Iris* of me:
The Legend of Love no Couple can find
So easie to part, or so equally join'd.

Song[2]

Enter *Comus* with three Peasants, who sing the following SONG in Parts.

Com. YOUR Hay it is Mow'd and your Corn is Reap'd;
Your Barns will be full, and your Hovels heap'd:
Come, my Boys, Come;
Come, my Boys, Come;
And merrily Roar out Harvest Home;
Harvest Home,
Harvest Home;
And merrily Roar out Harvest Home.
Chorus. Come, my Boys, come, &c.
1 Man. We ha' cheated the Parson, we'll cheat him agen;
For why shou'd a Blockhead ha' One in Ten?
One in Ten,
One in Ten;
For why shou'd a Blockhead ha' One in Ten?
Chorus. One in Ten,
One in Ten;
For why shou'd a Blockhead ha' One in Ten?
2. For Prating so long like a Book-learn'd Sot,
Till Pudding and Dumplin burn to Pot;
Burn to Pot,
Burn to Pot;

[1] Published in *Amphitryon*, 1691, Act IV, Scene i. Text of *Plays*, 1701.
[2] Published in *King Arthur: or, The British Worthy*, 1691, Act V, Scene i. Text of *Plays*, 1701.

Till Pudding and Dumplin burn to Pot.
Chorus. Burn to Pot, &c.
3. We'll toss off our Ale till we canno' stand,
And Hoigh for the Honour of Old *England:*
Old *England,*
Old *England;*
And Hoigh for the Honour of Old *England.*
Chorus. Old *England,* &c.

The Dance vary'd into a round Country-Dance.

Enter *Venus.*

Venus. Fairest Isle, all Isles Excelling,
Seat of Pleasures, and of Loves;
Venus, here, will chuse her Dwelling,
And forsake her *Cyprian* Groves.

Cupid from his Fav'rite Nation,
Care and Envy will Remove;
Jealousie, that poysons Passion,
And Despair that dies for Love.

Gentle Murmurs, sweet Complaining,
Sighs that blow the Fire of Love;
Soft Repulses, kind Disdaining,
Shall be all the Pains you prove.

Every Swain shall pay his Duty,
Grateful every Nymph shall prove;
And as these Excel in Beauty,
Those shall be Renown'd for Love.

Song[1]

No, NO, poor suff'ring Heart no Change endeavour,
Choose to sustain the smart, rather than leave her;
My ravish'd Eyes behold such Charms about her,
I can dye with her, but not live without her.
One tender Sigh of hers to see me Languish,
Will more than pay the price of my past Anguish:
Beware, O cruel Fair, how you smile on me,
'Twas a kind Look of yours that has undone me.

Love has in store for me one happy Minute,
And She will end my pain who did begin it;

[1] Published in *Cleomenes*, 1692, Act II, Scene ii. Text of *Plays*, 1701.

Then no day void of Bliss, or Pleasure leaving,
Ages shall slide away without perceiving:
Cupid shall guard the Door the more to please us,
And keep out Time and Death when they would seize us:
Time and Death shall depart, and say in flying,
Love has found out a way to Live by Dying.

Veni Creator Spiritus, Translated in Paraphrase[1]

CREATOR Spirit, by whose aid
The World's Foundations first were laid,
Come visit ev'ry pious Mind;
Come pour thy Joys on Humane Kind:
From Sin, and Sorrow set us free;
And make thy Temples worthy Thee.
  O, Source of uncreated Light,
The Father's promis'd *Paraclete!*
Thrice Holy Fount, thrice Holy Fire,
Our Hearts with Heavenly Love inspire;
Come, and thy Sacred Unction bring
To Sanctifie us, while we sing!
  Plenteous of Grace, descend from high,
Rich in thy sev'n-fold Energy!
Thou strength of his Almighty Hand,
Whose Pow'r does Heaven and Earth Command:
Proceeding, Spirit our Defence,
Who do'st the Gift of Tongues dispence,
And crown'st thy Gift, with Eloquence!
  Refine and purge our Earthy Parts;
But, oh, inflame and fire our Hearts!
Our Frailties help, our Vice controul;
Submit the Senses to the Soul;
And when Rebellious they are grown,
Then, lay thy hand, and hold 'em down.
  Chace from our Minds the infernal Foe;
And Peace, the fruit of Love, bestow:
And, lest our Feet shou'd step astray,
Protect, and guide us in the way.
  Make us Eternal Truths receive,
And practise, all that we believe:
Give us thy self, that we may see

[1] Published in *Examen Poeticum*, 1693. Text of Tonson's edition of Dryden's *Poems*, 1701.

The Father and the Son, by thee.
  Immortal Honour, endless Fame
Attend th' Almighty Father's Name:
The Saviour Son, be glorify'd,
Who for lost Man's Redemption dy'd:
And equal Adoration be
Eternal *Paraclete*, to thee.

To My Dear Friend Mr. Congreve, On His Comedy, Call'd, The Double-Dealer[1]

WELL then; the promis'd hour is come at last;
The present Age of Wit obscures the past:
Strong were our Syres; and as they Fought they Writ,
Conqu'ring with force of Arms, and dint of Wit;
Theirs was the Gyant Race, before the Flood;
And thus, when *Charles* Return'd, our Empire stood.
Like *Janus* he the stubborn Soil manur'd,
With Rules of Husbandry the rankness cur'd:
Tam'd us to manners, when the Stage was rude;
And boistrous *English* Wit, with Art indu'd.
Our Age was cultivated thus at length;
But what we gain'd in skill we lost in strength.
Our Builders were, with want of Genius, curst;
The second Temple was not like the first:
Till you, the best *Vitruvius*, come at length;
Our Beauties equal; but excel our strength.
Firm *Dorique* Pillars found Your solid Base:
The Fair *Corinthian* Crowns the higher Space;
Thus all below is Strength, and all above is Grace.
In easie Dialogue is *Fletcher*'s Praise:
He mov'd the mind, but had not power to raise.
Great *Johnson* did by strength of Judgment please:
Yet doubling *Fletcher's* Force, he wants his Ease.
In differing Tallents both adorn'd their Age;
One for the Study, t' other for the Stage.
But both to *Congreve* justly shall submit,
One match'd in Judgment, both o'er-match'd in Wit.
In him all Beauties of this Age we see;
Etherege his Courtship, *Southern's* Purity;
The Satire, Wit, and Strength of Manly *Witcherly*.
All this in blooming Youth you have Atchiev'd;
Now are your foil'd Contemporaries griev'd;

[1] Published in Congreve's *The Double-Dealer*, 1694. Text of Tonson's edition of Dryden's *Poems*, 1701.

So much the sweetness of your manners move,
We cannot envy you because we Love.
Fabius might joy in *Scipio*, when he saw
A Beardless Consul made against the Law,
And joyn his Suffrage to the Votes of *Rome*;
Though He with *Hannibal* was overcome.
Thus old *Romano* bow'd to *Raphel's* Fame;
And Scholar to the Youth he taught, became.
Oh that your Brows my Lawrel had sustain'd,
Well had I been Depos'd, if you had reign'd!
The Father had descended for the Son;
For only You are lineal to the Throne.
Thus when the State one *Edward* did depose;
A Greater *Edward* in his room arose.
But now, not I, but Poetry is curs'd;
For *Tom* the second reigns like *Tom* the first.
But let 'em not mistake my Patron's part;
Nor call his Charity their own desert.
Yet this I Prophecy; Thou shalt be seen,
(Tho' with some short Parenthesis between:)
High on the Throne of Wit; and seated there,
Not mine (that's little) but thy Lawrel wear.
Thy first attempt an early promise made;
That early promise this has more than paid.
So bold, yet so judiciously you dare,
That Your least Praise, is to be Regular.
Time, Place, and Action, may with pains be wrought,
But Genius must be born; and never can be taught.
This is your Portion; this Your Native Store;
Heav'n that but once was Prodigal before,
To *Shakespeare* gave as much; she cou'd not give him more.
Maintain your Post: That's all the Fame You need;
For 'tis impossible you shou'd proceed.
Already I am worn with Cares and Age;
And just abandoning th' Ungrateful Stage:
Unprofitably kept at Heav'ns expence,
I live a Rent-charge on his Providence:
But You, whom ev'ry Muse and Grace adorn,
Whom I foresee to better Fortune born,
Be kind to my Remains; and oh defend,
Against Your Judgment Your departed Friend!
Let not the Insulting Foe my Fame pursue;
But shade those Lawrels which descend to You:
And take for Tribute what these Lines express:
You merit more; nor cou'd my Love do less.

Alexander's Feast; or, The Power of Musique. An Ode, in Honour of St. Cecilia's Day[1]

I.

TWAS at the Royal Feast, for *Persia* won,
By *Philip*'s Warlike Son:
Aloft in awful State
The God-like Heroe sate
On his Imperial Throne:
His valiant Peers were plac'd around;
Their Brows with Roses and with Myrtles bound.
(So shou'd Desert in Arms be Crown'd:)
The Lovely *Thais* by his side,
Sate like a blooming *Eastern* Bride
In Flow'r of Youth and Beauty's Pride.
Happy, happy, happy Pair!
None but the Brave
None but the Brave
None but the Brave deserves the Fair.

CHORUS

Happy, happy, happy Pair!
None but the Brave,
None but the Brave
None but the Brave deserves the Fair.

II.

Timotheus plac'd on high
Amid the tuneful Quire,
With flying Fingers touch'd the Lyre:
The trembling Notes ascend the Sky,
And Heav'nly Joys inspire.
The Song began from *Jove*;
Who left his blissful Seats above,
(Such is the Pow'r of mighty Love.)
A Dragon's fiery Form bely'd the God:
Sublime on Radiant Spires He rode,
When He to fair *Olympia* press'd:
And while He sought her snowy Breast:
Then, round her slender Waist he curl'd,
And stamp'd an Image of himself, a Sov'raign of the World.

[1] Published in 1697. Text of Tonson's edition of Dryden's *Poems*, 1701.

The list'ning Crowd admire the lofty Sound,
A present Deity, they shout around:
A present Deity the vaulted Roofs rebound.
With ravish'd Ears
The Monarch hears,
Assumes the God,
Affects to nod,
And seems to shake the Spheres.

CHORUS

With ravish'd Ears
The Monarch hears,
Assumes the God,
Affects to nod,
And seems to shake the Spheres.

III.

The Praise of *Bacchus* then, the sweet Musician sung;
Of *Bacchus* ever Fair, and ever Young:
The jolly God in Triumph comes;
Sound the Trumpets; beat the Drums;
Flush'd with a purple Grace
He shews his honest Face,
Now gives the Hautboys breath; He comes, He comes.
Bacchus ever Fair and Young,
Drinking Joys did first ordain:
Bacchus Blessings are a Treasure;
Drinking is the Soldiers Pleasure;
Rich the Treasure;
Sweet the Pleasure;
Sweet is Pleasure after Pain.

CHORUS

Bacchus *Blessings are a Treasure;*
Drinking is the Soldier's Pleasure;
Rich the Treasure,
Sweet the Pleasure;
Sweet is Pleasure after Pain.

IV.

Sooth'd with the Sound the King grew vain;
Fought all his Battails o'er again;
And thrice He routed all his Foes; and thrice he slew the slain.
The Master saw the Madness rise;

His glowing Cheeks, his ardent Eyes;
And while He Heav'n and Earth defy'd,
Chang'd his Hand, and check'd his Pride.
He chose a Mournful Muse
Soft Pity to infuse:
He sung *Darius* Great and Good,
By too severe a Fate,
Fallen, fallen, fallen, fallen,
Fallen from his high Estate
And weltring in his Blood:
Deserted at his utmost Need,
By those his former Bounty fed:
On the bare Earth expos'd He lies,
With not a Friend to close his Eyes.
With down-cast Looks the joyless Victor sate,
Revolving in his alter'd Soul
The various Turns of Chance below;
And, now and then, a Sigh he stole;
And Tears began to flow.

CHORUS

Revolving in his alter'd Soul
The various Turns of Chance below;
And, now and then, a Sigh he stole;
And Tears began to flow.

V.

The Mighty Master smil'd to see
That Love was in the next Degree:
'Twas but a Kindred-Sound to move;
For Pity melts the Mind to Love.
Softly sweet in *Lydian* Measures,
Soon he sooth'd his Soul to Pleasures.
War, he sung, is Toil and Trouble;
Honour but an empty Bubble.
Never ending, still beginning,
Fighting still, and still destroying,
If the World be worth thy Winning,
Think, O think, it worth Enjoying.
Lovely *Thais* sits beside thee,
Take the Good the Gods provide thee.
The Many rend the Skies, with loud Applause;
So Love was Crown'd, but Musique won the Cause.
The Prince, unable to conceal his Pain,
Gaz'd on the Fair
Who caus'd his Care,

And sigh'd and look'd, sigh'd and look'd,
Sigh'd and look'd, and sigh'd again:
At length, with Love and Wine at once oppress'd,
The vanquish'd Victor sunk upon her Breast.

CHORUS

The Prince, unable to conceal his Pain,
Gaz'd on the Fair
Who caus'd his Care,
And sigh'd and look'd, sigh'd and look'd,
Sigh'd and look'd, and sigh'd again:
At length, with Love and Wine at once oppress'd,
The vanquish'd Victor sunk upon her Breast.

VI.

Now strike the Golden Lyre again;
A lowder yet, and yet a lowder Strain.
Break his Bands of Sleep asunder,
And rouze him, like a rattling Peal of Thunder.
Hark, hark, the horrid Sound
Has rais'd up his Head,
As awak'd from the Dead,
And amaz'd, he stares around.
Revenge, Revenge, *Timotheus* cries,
See the Furies arise!
See the Snakes that they rear,
How they hiss in their Hair,
And the Sparkles that flash from their Eyes!
Behold a ghastly Band,
Each a Torch in his Hand!
Those are *Grecian* Ghosts, that in Battail were slain,
And unbury'd remain
Inglorious on the Plain.
Give the Vengeance due
To the Valiant Crew.
Behold how they toss their Torches on high,
How they point to the *Persian* Abodes,
And glitt'ring Temples of their Hostile Gods!
The Princes applaud, with a furious Joy;
And the King seiz'd a Flambeau, with Zeal to destroy;
Thais led the Way,
To light him to his Prey,
And, like another *Hellen*, fir'd another *Troy*.

CHORUS

And the King seiz'd a Flambeau, with Zeal to destroy;
Thais *led the Way,*
To light him to his Prey,
And, like another Hellen, *fir'd another* Troy.

VII.

Thus, long ago
'Ere heaving Bellows learn'd to blow,
While Organs yet were mute;
Timotheus, to his breathing Flute,
And sounding Lyre,
Cou'd swell the Soul to rage, or kindle soft Desire.
At last Divine *Cecilia* came,
Inventress of the Vocal Frame;
The sweet Enthusiast, from her Sacred Store,
Enlarg'd the former narrow Bounds,
And added Length to solemn Sounds,
With Nature's Mother-Wit, and Arts unknown before,
Let old *Timotheus* yield the Prize,
Or both divide the Crown;
He rais'd a Mortal to the Skies;
She drew an Angel down.

GRAND CHORUS

At last, Divine Cecilia *came,*
Inventress of the Vocal Frame;
The sweet Enthusiast, from her Sacred Store,
Enlarg'd the former narrow Bounds,
And added Length to solemn Sounds,
With Nature's Mother-Wit, and Arts unknown before.
Let old Timotheus *yield the Prize,*
Or both divide the Crown;
He rais'd a Mortal to the Skies;
She drew an Angel down.

SAMUEL BUTLER

(1613-1663-1680)

Hudibras, Part I[1]

The Argument of the First Canto

Sir Hudibras *his passing worth,*
The manner how he sally'd forth:
His Arms and Equipage are shown;
His Horse's Vertues, and his own.
Th' Adventure of the Bear *and* Fiddle,
Is sung, but breaks off in the middle.

Canto I

WHEN *civil* fury first grew high,
And men fell out they knew not why,
When hard *Words, Jealousies,* and *Fears,*
Set Folks together by the Ears,
And made them fight, like mad or drunk,
For Dame *Religion* as for Punk,
Whose honesty they all durst swear for,
Though not a man of them knew wherefore:
When *Gospel-Trumpeter* surrounded,
With long-ear'd rout to Battel sounded,
And Pulpit, Drum Ecclesiastick,
Was beat with fist, instead of a stick:
Then did Sir *Knight* abandon dwelling,
And out he rode a Colonelling.
A Wight he was, whose very sight wou'd
Entitle him *Mirror of Knighthood;*
That never bent his stubborn knee
To any thing but Chivalry,
Nor put up blow, but that which laid
Right worshipful on Shoulder-blade:
Chief of Domestick Knights and Errant,
Either for Chartel or for Warrant:
Great on the Bench, Great in the Saddle,
That could as well bind o'er, as swaddle.
Mighty he was at both of these,
And styl'd of *War* as well as *Peace.*
(So some Rats of amphibious nature,

[1] Published in 1663. Text of edition of 1678.

Are either for the Land or Water)
But here our Authors make a doubt,
Whether he were more wise, or stout.
Some hold the one, and some the other:
But howsoe'er they make a pother,
The difference was so small, his Brain
Outweigh'd his Rage but half a Grain:
Which made some take him for a Tool
That Knaves do work with, call'd a Fool.
And offer to lay wagers that
As *Mountaigne* playing with his Cat,
Complains she thought him but an Ass,
Much more she would Sir *Hudibras*.
(For that's the Name our valiant Knight
To all his Challenges did write.)
But they're mistaken very much,
'Tis plain enough he was no such.
We grant, although he had much wit,
H' was very shie of using it,
As being loath to wear it out,
And therefore bore it not about.
Unless on Holy-days, or so,
As Men their best Apparel do.
Beside, 'tis known he could speak *Greek*,
As naturally as Pigs squeek:
That *Latine* was no more difficile,
Than to a Black-bird 'tis to whistle.
Being rich in both, he never scanted
His Bounty unto such as wanted;
But much of either would afford,
To many that had not one word.
For *Hebrew* Roots, although th' are found
To flourish most in barren ground,
He had such plenty as suffic'd
To make some think him circumcis'd:
And truely so perhaps, he was
'Tis many a Pious Christians case.
He was in *Logick* a great Critick,
Profoundly skill'd in Analytick.
He could distinguish, and divide
A Hair 'twixt *South* and *South-West* side:
On either which he would dispute,
Confute, change hands, and still confute.
He'd undertake to prove by force
Of Argument, a Man's no Horse.
He'd prove a Buzard is no Fowl,
And that a *Lord* may be an Owl,
A Calf an *Alderman*, a Goose a *Justice*,

And Rooks *Committee-men*, and *Trustees*;
He'd run in Debt by Disputation,
And pay with Ratiocination.
All this by Syllogism, true
In mood and Figure, he would do.
  For *Rhetorick* he could not ope
His mouth, but out there flew a Trope:
And when he hapned to break off
I' th' middle of his speech, or cough,
H' had hard words, ready to shew why,
And tell what Rules he did it by.
Else when with greatest Art he spoke,
You'd think he talk'd like other folk,
For all a Rhetoricians Rules,
Teach nothing but to name his Tools.
His ordinary Rate of Speech
In loftiness of sound was rich,
A *Babylonish* dialect,
Which learned Pedants much affect.
It was a parti-colour'd dress
Of patch'd and pyball'd Languages:
'Twas English cut on *Greek* and *Latin*,
Like Fustian heretofore on Sattin.
It had an odd promiscuous Tone,
As if h' had talk'd three parts in one.
Which made some think when he did gabble,
Th' had heard three Labo'rers of *Babel*;
Or *Cerberus* himself pronounce
A Leash of Languages at once.
This he as volubly would vent
As if his stock would ne'er be spent.
And truly to support that charge
He had supplies as vast and large.
For he could coin or counterfeit
New words with little or no wit:
Words so debas'd and hard, no stone
Was hard enough to touch them on.
And when with hasty noise he spoke 'em,
The Ignorant for currant took 'em.
That had the Orator who once,
Did fill his Mouth with Pibble Stones
When he harangu'd, but known his Phrase,
He would have us'd no other ways.
  In *Mathematicks* he was greater
Than *Tycho Brahe*, or *Erra Pater*:
For he, by *Geometrick* scale,
Could take the size of *Pots of Ale*;
Resolve by Signs and Tangents streight,

If *Bread* or *Butter* wanted weight;
And wisely tell what hour o' th' day
The Clock doth strike, by *Algebra.*
  Beside he was a shrewd *Philosopher,*
And had read every Text and gloss over:
What e'er the crabbed'st Author hath
He understood b' implicit Faith,
What ever *Sceptick* could inquire for;
For every *why* he had a *wherefore;*
Knew more than forty of them do,
As far as words and terms could go.
All which he understood by Rote,
And as occasion serv'd, would quote;
No matter whether right or wrong:
They might be either said or sung.
His Notions fitted things so well,
That which was which he could not tell;
But oftentimes mistook th' one
For th' other, as great Clerks have done.
He could reduce all things to Acts,
And knew their Natures by Abstracts,
Where Entity and Quiddity
The Ghosts of defunct Bodies flie;
Where Truth in Person does appear,
Like words congeal'd in Northern Air.
He knew *what's what,* and that's as high
As *Metaphysick* Wit can fly,
In *School Divinity* as able
As he that hight *Irrefragable;*
Profound in all the Nominal
And real ways beyond them all;
And with as delicate a Hand,
Could twist as tough a Rope of Sand.
And weave fine Cobwebs, fit for Skull
That's empty when the Moon is full;
Such as take Lodgings in a Head
That's to be lett unfurnished.
He could raise Scruples dark and nice,
And after solve 'em in a trice:
As if Divinity had catch'd
The Itch, of purpose to be scratch'd;
Or, like a Mountebank, did wound
And stab her self with doubts profound,
Only to shew with how small pain
The sores of faith are cur'd again;
Although by woful proof we find,
They always leave a Scar behind.
He knew the Seat of Paradise,

Could tell in what degree it lies:
And as he was dispos'd, could prove it,
Below the Moon, or else above it.
What *Adam* dreamt of when his Bride
Came from her Closet in his side:
Whether the Devil tempted her
By a *High Dutch* Interpreter:
If either of them had a Navel;
Who first made Musick malleable:
Whether the Serpent at the fall
Had cloven Feet, or none at all.
All this without a Gloss or Comment,
He would unriddle in a moment:
In proper terms, such as men smatter
When they throw out and miss the matter.
  For his *Religion* it was fit
To match his Learning and his Wit:
'Twas *Presbyterian* true blew,
For he was of that stubborn Crew
Of Errant Saints, whom all men grant
To be the true Church *Militant*:
Such as do build their Faith upon
The holy Text of *Pike* and *Gun*;
Decide all Controversies by
Infallible *Artillery*;
And prove their Doctrine Orthodox
By Apostolick *Blows* and *Knocks*;
Call Fire and Sword and Desolation,
A *godly-thorough-Reformation*,
Which always must be carry'd on,
And still be doing, never done:
As if Religion were intended
For nothing else but to be mended.
A Sect, whose chief Devotion lies
In odd perverse Antipathies;
In falling out with that or this,
And finding somewhat still amiss:
More peevish, cross, and splenetick,
That Dog distract, or Monky sick.
That with more care keep Holy-day
The wrong, than others the right way:
Compound for Sins, they are inclin'd to;
By damning those they have no mind to;
Still so perverse and opposite,
As if they worshipp'd God for spight,
The self-same thing they will abhor
One way, and long another for.
Free-will they one way disavow,

Another, nothing else allow.
All Piety consists therein
In them, in other Men all Sin.
Rather than fail, they will defie
That which they love most tenderly,
Quarrel with *minc'd Pies*, and disparage
Their best and dearest friend, *Plum-porridge*;
Fat *Pig* and *Goose* it self oppose,
And blaspheme *Custard* through the *Nose*.
Th' Apostles of this fierce Religion,
Like *Mahomet*'s, were Ass and Widgeon,
To whom our Knight, by fast instinct
Of Wit and Temper was so linkt,
As if Hipocrisie and Non-sence
Had got th' Advouson of his Conscience.
  Thus was he gifted and accouter'd,
We mean on th' inside, not the outward:
That next of all we shall discuss;
Then listen Sirs, it followeth thus:
  His tawny *Beard* was th' equal grace
Both of his Wisdom and his Face;
In Cut and Dy so like a Tile,
A sudden view it would beguile:
The upper part thereof was Whey,
The nether Orange mixt with Grey.
This hairy Meteor did denounce
The fall of Scepters and of Crowns;
With grizly type did represent
Declining Age of Government;
And tell with Hieroglyphick Spade,
Its own grave and the State's were made.
Like *Sampson*'s Heart-breakers, it grew
In time to make a Nation rue;
Though it contributed its own fall,
To wait upon the publick downfall.
It was Canonick, and did grow
In Holy Orders by strict vow;
Of Rule as sullen and severe,
As that of rigid *Cordeliere*:
'Twas bound to suffer Persecution
And Martyrdome with resolution;
T' oppose it self against the hate
And vengeance of th' incensed State:
In whose defiance it was worn,
Still ready to be pull'd and torn,
With red-hot Irons to be tortur'd,
Revil'd, and spit upon, and martyr'd.
Maugre all which, 'twas to stand fast,

As long as Monarchy should last.
But when the State should hap to reel,
'Twas to submit to fatal Steel,
And fall, as it was consecrate
A Sacrifice to fall of State;
Whose thred of life the fatal Sisters
Did twist together with its Whiskers,
And twine so close, that time should never,
In life or death, their fortunes sever;
But with his rusty Sickle mow
Both down together at a blow.
So learned *Taliacotius* from
The brawny part of Porter's Bum,
Cut supplemental Noses, which
Would last as long as Parent breech:
But when the Date of *Nock* was out,
Off dropt the Sympathetick Snout.
His *Back*, or rather Burthen show'd
As if it stoop'd with its own load.
For as *Æneas* bore his Sire,
Upon his Shoulders through the Fire:
Our Knight did bear no less a Pack
Of his own Buttocks on his Back:
Which now had almost got the Upper-
Hand of his Head, for want of Crupper.
To poize this equally, he bore
A *Paunch* of the same bulk before:
Which still he had a special care
To keep well cramm'd with thrifty fare;
As White-pot, Butter-milk, and Curds,
Such as a Countrey house affords;
With other Victual, which anon,
We further shall dilate upon,
When of his Hose we come to treat,
The Cub-bord where he kept his meat.
His *Doublet* was of sturdy Buff,
And though not Sword, yet Cudgel-proof;
Whereby 'twas fitter for his use,
That fear'd no blows but such as bruise.
His *Breeches* were of rugged Woollen,
And had been at the Siege of *Bullen*,
To old King *Harry* so well known,
Some Writers held they were his own.
Through they were lin'd with many a piece,
Of Ammunition-Bread and Cheese,
And fat Black-puddings, proper food
For Warriers that delight in Blood;
For, as we said, he always chose

To carry Vittle in his Hose.
That often tempted Rats, and Mice,
The Ammunition to surprize:
And when he put a Hand but in
The one or th' other Magazine,
They stoutly in defence on't stood
And from the wounded Foe drew bloud,
And till th' were storm'd and beaten out,
Ne'r left the fortifi'd Redoubt;
And though Knights Errant, as some think,
Of old did neither eat nor drink,
Because when thorough Desarts vast
And Regions Desolate they past,
Where Belly-timber above ground
Or under was not to be found,
Unless they graz'd, there's not one word
Of their Provision, on Record:
Which made some confidently write,
They had no stomachs but to fight,
'Tis false: for *Arthur* wore in Hall
Round Table like a Farthingal,
On which, with Shirt pull'd out behind,
And eke before his good Knights din'd.
Though 'twas no Table, some suppose,
But a huge pair of round Trunk-hose;
In which he carry'd as much meat
As he and all his Knights could eat;
When laying by their Swords and Truncheons,
They took their Breakfasts, or their Nuncheons;
But let that pass at present, lest
We should forget where we digrest;
As learned Authors use, to whom
We leave it, and to th' purpose come,
His Puissant Sword unto his side
Near his undaunted Heart was ty'd,
With Basket-hilt, that wou'd hold broth,
And serve for Fight, and Dinner both.
In it he melted Lead for Bullets,
To shoot at Foes, and sometimes Pullets;
To whom he bore so fell a Grutch,
He ne'er gave quarter t' any such.
The trenchant blade, *Toledo* trusty,
For want of fighting was grown rusty,
And eat into it self, for lack
Of some body to hew and hack.
The peaceful Scabbard where it dwelt,
The Rancor of its Edge had felt:
For of the lower end two handful,

It had devoured 'twas so manful;
And so much scorn'd to lurk in case,
As if it durst not shew its face.
In many desperate Attempts
Of Wars, Exigents, Contempts,
It had appear'd with Courage bolder
Than Sergeant *Bum*, invading shoulder.
Oft had it ta'en possession,
And Pris'ners too, or made them run.
  This Sword a *Dagger* had his Page.
But was but little for his age:
And therefore waited on him so,
As Dwarfs upon Knights Errant do.
It was a serviceable Dudgeon,
Either for fighting or for drudging;
When it had stab'd or broke a head,
It would scrape Trenchers, or chip Bread,
Toast Cheese or Bacon, though it were
To bait a Mouse-trap, 'twould not care.
'Twould make clean shooes, and in the Earth
Set Leeks and Onions, and so forth.
It had been Prentice to a Brewer,
Where this and more it did endure.
But left the Trade, as many more
Have lately done on the same score.
  In th' Holsters, at his Saddle-bow,
Two aged Pistols he did stow,
Among the surplus of such meat
As in his Hose he could not get.
They were upon hard Duty still,
And every night stood Sentinel,
To guard the Magazine i' th' Hose
From two legg'd and from four legg'd Foes.
  Thus clad and fortifi'd, Sir Knight
From peaceful home set forth to fight.
But first with nimble active force
He got on th' outside of his *Horse*.
For having but one stirrup ty'd
T' his Saddle, on the further side,
It was so short, h' had much adoe
To reach it with his desperate Toe.
But after many strains and heaves
He got up to the Saddle eaves.
From whence he vaulted into th' Seat
With so much vigor, strength, and heat,
That he had almost tumbled over
With his own weight, but did recover,
By laying hold of Tail and Mane,

Which oft he us'd instead of Reyn.
  But now we talk of mounting Steed,
Before we further do proceed,
It doth behove us to say something,
Of that which bore our valiant *Bumkin.*
The Beast was sturdy, large and tall,
With Mouth of Meal and Eyes of Wall:
I would say Eye, for h' had but one,
As most agree, though some say none.
He was well stay'd, and in his Gate
Preserv'd a grave majestick state.
At Spur or Switch no more he skipt,
Or mended pace, than *Spaniard* whipt:
And yet so fiery, he would bound,
As if he griev'd to touch the Ground:
That *Cæsar*'s Horse, who, as Fame goes,
Had Corns upon his Feet and Toes,
Was not by half so tender-hooft,
Nor trode upon the ground so soft.
And as that Beast would kneel and stoop,
(Some write) to take his Rider up:
So *Hudibras* his ('tis well known,)
Would often do, to set him down.
We shall not need to say what lack
Of Leather was upon his back:
For that was hidden under pad,
And breech of Knight gall'd full as bad.
His strutting Ribs on both sides show'd
Like furrows he himself had plow'd:
For underneath the skirt of Pannel,
'Twixt every two there was a Channel.
His dragling Tail hung in the Dirt,
Which on his Rider he would flirt
Still as his tender side he prickt,
With arm'd heel or with unarm'd kickt:
For *Hudibras* wore but one Spur,
As wisely knowing, could he stir
To active trot one side of's Horse,
The other would not hang an Arse.
  A Squire he had whose name was *Ralph,*
That in th' adventure went his half.
Though Writers (for more statelier tone)
Do call him *Ralpho,* 'tis all one:
And when we can with Meeter safe,
We'll call him so, if not plain *Ralph,*
For Rhime the Rudder is of Verses,
With which like Ships they stear their courses.
An equal stock of Wit and Valour

He had laid in, by birth a Taylor.
The mighty *Tyrian* Queen that gain'd
With subtle shreds a Tract of Land,
Did leave it with a Castle fair
To his great Ancestor, her Heir:
From him descended cross-leg'd Knights,
Fam'd for their Faith and Warlike Fights
Against the bloudy Caniball,
Whom they destroy'd both great and small.
This sturdy Squire had as well
As the bold *Trojan* Knight, seen hell,
Not with a counterfeited Pass
Of Golden Bough, but true Gold-lace.
His knowledge was not far behind
The Knights, but of another kind,
And he another way came by't,
Some call it *Gift*, and some *New light*;
A liberal Art, that costs no pains
Of Study, Industry, or Brains.
His Wits were sent him for a Token,
But in the Carriage crackt and broken
Like Commendation Nine-pence, crookt
With to and from my Love, it lookt,
He ne'r consider'd it, as loath
To look a Gift-horse in the Mouth;
And very wisely would lay forth
No more upon it than 'twas worth.
But as he got it freely, so
He spent it frank and freely too.
For Saints themselves will sometimes be,
Of Gifts that cost them nothing, free.
By means of this, with *hem* and *cough*,
Prolongers to enlightned Snuff,
He could deep Mysteries unriddle,
As easily as thread a Needle;
For as of Vagabonds we say,
That they are ne'r beside their way:
What e'r men speak by this *New Light*,
Still they are sure to be i' th' right.
'Tis a *Dark-Lanthorn* of the Spirit,
Which none see by but those that bear it.
A Light that falls down from on high,
For Spiritual Trades to couzen by:
An *Ignis Fatuus* that bewitches,
And leads Men into Pools and Ditches,
To make them *dip* themselves, and sound
For Christendom and dirty Pond;
To dive like Wild-foul for Salvation,

And fish to catch Regeneration.
This Light inspires, and plays upon
The nose of Saint like Bag-pipe drone,
And speaks through hollow empty Soul,
As through a Trunk, or whisp'ring hole,
Such language as no mortal Ear
But spiritual Eve-droppers can hear.
So *Phœbus* or some friendly Muse
Into small Poets song infuse;
Which they at second-hand reherse
Through Reed or Bag-pipe, Verse for Verse.
  Thus *Ralph* became infallible,
As three or four-leg'd Oracle,
The ancient Cup, or modern Chair,
Spoke truth point-blank, though unaware:
  For mystick Learning, wondrous able
In Magick *Talisman*, and *Cabal*,
Whose Primitive Tradition reaches
As far as *Adam*'s first green Breeches:
Deep-sighted in Intelligences,
Idea's, Atomes, Influences;
And much of *Terra Incognita*,
Th' intelligible World could say;
A deep occult Philosopher,
As learn'd as the *Wild Irish* are,
Or Sir *Agrippa*, for profound
And solid Lying much renown'd:
He *Anthroposophus*, and *Floud*,
And *Jacob Behmen* understood;
Knew many an Amulet and Charm,
That would do neither good nor harm:
In *Rosy-Crucian* Lore as Learned,
As he that *Veré adeptus* earned.
He understood the speech of Birds
As well as they themselves do words:
Could tell what subtlest *Parrots* mean,
That speak and think contrary clean;
What *Member* 'tis of whom they talk
When they cry *Rope*, and *Walk Knave, walk*.
He'd extract numbers out of matter,
And keep them in a Glass, like water,
Of Sov'raign pow'r to make men wise;
For dropt in blere, thick-sighted Eyes,
They'd make them see in darkest night,
Like Owls, though pur-blind in the light.
By help of these (as he profest)
He had *First Matter* seen undrest:
He took her naked all alone,

Before one Rag of *Form* was on.
The *Chaos* too he had descry'd,
And seen quite through, or else he ly'd:
Not that of Past-board which men shew
For Goats at Fair of *Barthol'mew;*
But its great Gransire, first o' th' name,
Whence that and *Reformation* came:
Both Cousin-Germans, and right able
T' inveigle and draw in the Rabble.
But *Reformation* was, some say,
O' th' younger house to *Puppet-Play*.
He could foretell whats'ever was
By consequence to come to pass.
As Death of Great Men, Alterations,
Diseases, Battels, Inundations.
All this without th' Eclipse of Sun,
Or dreadful Comet, he hath done
By inward Light, a way as good,
And easie to be understood.
But with more lucky hit than those
That use to make the Stars depose,
Like Knights o' th' Post, and falsly charge
Upon themselves what others forge:
As if they were consenting to
All mischief in the World men do:
Or like the Dev'l, did tempt and sway 'em
To Rogueries, and then betray 'em.
They'l search a Planet's house, to know,
Who broke and robb'd a house below:
Examine *Venus*, and the *Moon*
Who stole a Thimble and a Spoon:
And though they nothing will confess,
Yet by their very looks can guess,
And tell what guilty Aspect bodes,
Who stole, and who receiv'd the Goods.
They'l question *Mars*, and by his look
Detect who 'twas that nimm'd a Cloke:
Make *Mercury* confess and peach
Those Thieves which he himself did teach.
They'l find i' th' Phisiognomies
O' th' Planets all mens destinies.
Like him that took the Doctor's Bill,
And swallow'd it instead o' th' Pill.
Cast the Nativity o' th' Question,
And from Positions to be guest on,
As sure as if they knew the Moment
Of Natives birth, tell what will come on 't.
They'l feel the Pulses of the Stars,

To find out Agues, Coughs, Catarrhs;
And tell what *Crysis* does divine
The Rot in Sheep, or Mange in Swine:
In Men what gives or cures the Itch,
What makes them Cuckolds, poor or rich:
What gains or loses, hangs or saves;
What makes men great, what fools or knaves;
But not what wise, for only of those
The Stars (they say) cannot dispose,
No more than can the Astrologians.
There they say right, and like true *Trojans*.
This *Ralpho* knew, and therefore took
The other course, of which we spoke.
  Thus was th' accomplish'd Squire endu'd
With Gifts and Knowledge, per'lous shrew'd.
Never did trusty Squire with Knight,
Or Knight with Squire jump more right.
Their Arms and Equipage did fit,
As well as Virtues, Parts, and Wit.
Their Valors too were of a Rate,
And out they sally'd at the Gate.
Few miles on horseback had they jogged,
But fortune unto them turn'd dogged.
For they a sad adventure met,
Of which we now prepare to Treat:
But e'er we venture to unfold
Atchievements so resolv'd and bold,
We should as learned Poets use,
Invoke the assistance of some *Muse*;
However Criticks count it sillier
Than Juglers talking t' a Familiar.
We think 'tis no great matter which,
They're all alike, yet we shall pitch
On one that fits our purpose most,
Whom therefore thus do we accost.
  Thou that with Ale or viler Liquors,
Didst inspire *Withers*, *Prin*, and *Vickars*,
And force them, though it were in spight
Of Nature, and their Stars, to write;
Who, as we finde in sullen Writs,
And cross-graind Works of modern Wits,
With Vanity, Opinion, Want,
The wonder of the Ignorant,
The Praises of the Author, penn'd
By himself, or wit-ensuring friend,
The Itch of Picture in the Front,
With Bays, and wicked Rhime upon 't
All that is left o' th' forked Hill

To make men scribble without skill,
Canst make a Poet, spight of fate,
And teach all People to translate;
Though out of Languages in which
They understand no Part of Speech:
Assist me but this once, I'mplore,
And I shall trouble thee no more.
  In Western Clime there is a Town
To those that dwell therein well known;
Therefore there needs no more be sed here
We unto them refer our Reader:
For brevity is very good,
When w'are, or are not understood.
To this Town People did repair
On days of Market or of Fair,
And to crack'd Fiddle, and hoarse Tabor
In merriment did drudge and labor:
But now a sport more formidable
Had rak'd together Village rabble.
'Twas an old way of Recreating,
Which learned Butchers call *Bear-baiting*:
A bold advent'rous exercise,
With ancient *Heroe's* in high prize;
For Authors do affirm it came
From *Istmian* or *Nemean* game;
Others derive it from the *Bear*
That's fixt in Northern Hemisphere,
And round about the Pole does make
A circle like a Bear at stake,
That at the Chain's end wheels about,
And over-turns the Rabble-rout.
For after solemn Proclamation
In the Bear's name (as is the fashion,
According to the Law of Arms,
To keep men from inglorious harms)
That none presume to come so near
As forty foot of stake of Bear;
If any yet be so fool-hardy,
T'expose themselves to vain Jeopardy;
If they come wounded off and lame
No honour's got by such a maim.
Although the Bear gain'd much b'ing bound
In honour to make good his ground.
When he's engag'd, and take no notice,
If any press upon him, who 'tis,
But let them know at their own cost
That he intends to keep his post.
This to prevent, and other harms,

Which always wait on feats of Arms,
(For in the hurry of a Fray
'Tis hard to keep out of harm's way)
Thither the Knight his course did stear,
To keep the peace 'twixt *Dog* and *Bear*;
As he believ'd h' was bound to doe,
In Conscience and Commission too.
And therefore thus bespoke the Squire;
  We that are wisely mounted higher
Then Constables, in Curule wit,
When on Tribunal bench we sit,
Like Speculators, should foresee
From *Pharos* of Authority,
Portended Mischiefs farther then
Low Proletarian Tithing-men.
And therefore being inform'd by bruit,
That *Dog* and *Bear* are to dispute;
For so of late men fighting name,
Because they often prove the same;
(For where the first does hap to be
The last does *coincidere*)
Quantum in nobis, have thought good,
To save th' expence of Christian blood,
And try if we by Mediation
Of Treaty and accommodation
Can end the quarrel, and compose
The bloudy Duel without blows.
Are not our Liberties, our Lives,
The Laws, Religion, and our Wives
Enough at once to lie at stake,
For *Cov'nant* and the *Causes* sake;
But in that quarrel *Dogs* and *Bears*
As well as we must venture theirs?
This Feud by *Jesuits* invented,
By *evil Counsel* is fomented,
There is a *Machiavilian* Plot,
(Though ev'ry *Nare olfact* it not)
A deep design in 't to divide
The well-affected that confide,
By setting Brother against Brother,
To claw and curry one another.
Have we not enemies *plus satis*,
That *Cane & angue pejus* hate us?
And shall we turn our fangs and claws
Upon our selves without a cause?
That some occult design doth lie
In bloudy *Cynarctomachy*
Is plain enough to him that knows

How Saints lead Brothers by the Nose.
I wish my self a Pseudo-Prophet,
But sure some mischief will come of it:
Unless by providential wit
Or force we averruncate it.
For what design, what interest
Can Beast have to encounter Beast?
They fight for no espoused *Cause*;
Frail *Priviledge, Fundamental Laws,*
Nor for a *through Reformation*,
Nor *Covenant*, nor *Protestation*;
Nor *Liberty of Consciences*,
Nor Lords and Commons *Ordinances*;
Nor for the *Church*, nor for *Church Lands*,
To get them in their own no Hands;
Nor *evil Counsellors* to bring
To Justice that seduce the King;
Nor for the worship of us men,
Though we have done as much for them.
Th' *Egyptians* worshipp'd *Dogs*, and for
Their faith made fierce and zealous Warr.
Others ador'd a *Rat*, and some
For that Church suffer'd Martyrdome.
The *Indians* fought for the truth
Of th' *Elephant*, and *Monkey*'s Tooth:
And many, to defend that faith,
Fought it out *mordicus* to death.
But no Beast ever was so slight,
For Man, as for his God, to fight.
They have more wit, alas! and know
Themselves and us better than so.
But we, we onely do infuse
The Rage in them like *Boute-feus*.
'Tis our example that instills
In them th' infection of our ills.
For as some late Philosophers
Have well observed, Beasts that converse
With Man, take after him, as Hogs
Get Pigs all th' year, and Bitches Dogs.
Just so by our example Cattle
Learn to give one another Battel.
We read in *Nero*'s time, the Heathen,
When they destroy'd the *Christian Brethren*,
They sow'd them in the skins of Bears,
And then set Dogs about their Ears:
From whence, no doubt, th' invention came
Of this lewd Antichristian Game.
To this, quoth *Ralpho*, Verily,

The Point seems very plain to be.
It is an Antichristian Game,
Unlawful both in thing and name;
First for the *Name*, The word *Bear-baiting*,
Is Carnal, and of man's creating:
For certainly there's no such word
In all the *Scripture* on Record.
Therefore unlawful and a sin,
And so is (secondly) the *thing*.
A vile *Assembly* 'tis, that can
No more be prov'd by Scripture than
Provincial, Classick, National;
Mere humane Creature-Cobwebs all.
Thirdly, it is Idolatrous:
For when men run a-whoring thus
With their Inventions whatsoe'r
The thing be, whether *Dog* or *Bear*,
It is Idolatrous and *Pagan*
No less than worshipping of *Dagon*.
Quoth *Hudibras*, I smell a *Rat*;
Ralpho, thou dost prevaricate.
For though the *Thesis* which thou lay'st
Be true *ad amussim* as thou say'st:
(For that *Bear-baiting* should appear
Jure Divino lawfuller
Than *Synods* are, thou dost deny,
Totidem verbis so do I)
Yet there's a fallacy in this:
For if by sly *Homœosis*,
Thou would'st Sophistically imply
Both are unlawful, I deny.
And I (quoth *Ralpho*) do not doubt
But *Bear-baiting* may be made out
In Gospel-times, as lawful as is
Provincial or *Parochial Classis*:
And that both are so near of kin,
And like in all as well as sin,
That put them in a bag and shake 'em,
Your self o' th' sudden would mistake 'em,
And not know which is which, unless
You measure by their wickedness:
For 'tis not hard t' imagine whether
O' th' two is worst, though I name neither.
Quoth *Hudibras*, thou offer'st much,
But art not able to keep touch.
Mira de lente, as 'tis i' th' Adage,
Id est, to make a Leak a Cabbage.
Thou canst at best but overstrain

A Paradox, and th' own hot brain:
For what can *Synods* have at all
With *Bears* that's Analogical?
Or what relation has debating
Of Church-Affairs with *Bear-baiting*?
A just comparison still is,
Of things *ejusdem generis*.
And then what *Genus* rightly doth,
Include and comprehend them both?
If *Animal*, both of us may
As justly pass for *Bears* as they.
For we are Animals no less,
Although of different *Specieses*.
But, *Ralpho* this is no fit place,
Nor time to argue out the Case:
For now the Field is not far off,
Where we must give the world a proof
Of Deeds, not Words, and such as suit
Another manner of Dispute.
A Controversie that affords
Actions for Arguments, not Words:
Which we must manage at a rate
Of Prowess and Conduct adæquate;
To what our place and fame doth promise,
And all the godly expect from us.
Nor shall they be deceiv'd, unless
W' are slurr'd and outed by success:
Success, the Mark no mortal Wit,
Or surest hand can always hit:
For whatsoe're we perpetrate,
We do but row, we 'are steer'd by Fate,
Which in success oft disinherits,
For spurious Causes, noblest merits.
Great Actions are not always true Sons
Of great and mighty Resolutions:
Nor doth the bold'st attempts bring forth
Events still equal to their worth;
But sometimes fail, and in their stead,
Fortune and Cowardice succeed,
Yet we have no great cause to doubt,
Our actions still have born us out.
Which though th' are known to be so ample,
We need no copy from example,
We' are not the onely person durst
Attempt this Province, nor the first.
In Northern Clime a valorous Knight
Did whilom kill his Bear in fight,

And wound a Fidler: we have both
Of these the objects of our Wroth,
And equal Fame and Glory from
Th' Attempt or Victory to come.
'Tis sung, There is a valiant *Marmaluke*
In foreign Land, yclep'd ——[2]
To whom we have been oft compar'd
For Person, Parts, Address and Beard:
Both equally reputed stout,
And in the same Cause both have fought.
He oft in such Attempts as these
Came off with glory and success.
Nor will we fail in th' execution,
For want of equal Resolution.
Honour is, like a Widow, won
With brisk Attempt and putting on;
With ent'ring manfully, and urging;
Not slow approaches, like a Virgin.
This said, as once the *Phrygian* Knight,
So ours, with rusty steell, did smite
His *Trojan* Horse, and just as much
He mended pace upon the touch;
But from his empty stomach groan'd
Just as that hollow Beast did sound,
And angry answer'd from behind,
With brandish'd Tail and blast of Wind.
So have I seen with armed heel,
A Wight bestride a *Commonweal*;
Whil'st still the more he kick'd and spurr'd,
The less the sullen Jade has stirr'd.

SIR CHARLES SEDLEY

(1639?-1663-1701)

To Cloris[1]

CLORIS, I cannot say your Eyes
Did my unwary Heart surprize;
Nor will I swear it was your Face,

[2] Sir Samuel Luke.

[1] Published in *A Collection of Poems, Written upon Several Occasions*, 1672. Text of *Poetical Works*, ed. Ayloffe, 1707.

Your Shape, or any nameless Grace:
For you are so intirely Fair,
To love a Part, Injustice were;
No drowning Man can know which Drop
Of Water his last Breath did stop;
So when the Stars in Heaven appear,
And joyn to make the Night look clear;
The Light we no one's Bounty call,
But the obliging Gift of all.
He that does Lips or Hands adore,
Deserves them only, and no more;
But I love All, and every Part,
And nothing less can ease my Heart.
Cupid, that Lover, weakly strikes,
Who can express what 'tis he likes.

Song[1]

LOVE still has something of the Sea,
From whence his Mother rose;
No time his Slaves from Doubt can free,
Nor give their Thoughts repose:

They are becalm'd in clearest Days,
And in rough Weather tost;
They wither under cold Delays,
Or are in Tempests lost.

One while they seem to touch the Port,
Then straight into the Main,
Some angry Wind in cruel sport
The Vessel drives again.

At first Disdain and Pride they fear,
Which if they chance to 'scape,
Rivals and Falshood soon appear
In a more dreadful shape.

By such Degrees to Joy they come,
And are so long withstood,
So slowly they receive the Sum,
It hardly does them good.

[1] Published in *A Collection of Poems, Written upon Several Occasions*, 1672. Text of *Poetical Works*, ed. Ayloffe, 1707.

'Tis cruel to prolong a Pain,
  And to defer a Joy;
Believe me, gentle *Celemene*
  Offends the winged Boy.

An hundred thousand Oaths your Fears
  Perhaps would not remove;
And if I gaz'd a thousand Years
  I could no deeper love.

The Indifference[1]

THANKS, fair *Urania*; to your Scorn
I now am free, as I was born,
Of all the Pain that I endur'd
By your late Coldness I am cur'd.

In losing me, proud Nymph, you lose
The humblest Slave your Beauty Knows;
In losing you, I but throw down
A cruel Tyrant from her Throne.

My ranging Love did never find
Such Charms of Person and of Mind;
Y'ave Beauty, Wit, and all things know,
But where you shou'd your Love bestow.

I unawares my Freedom gave,
And to those Tyrants grew a Slave;
Would you have kept what you had won,
You should have more Compassion shewn.

Love is a Burthen, which two Hearts,
When equally they bear their Parts,
With Pleasure carry; but no one,
Alas, can bear it long alone.

I'm not of those who court their Pain,
And make an Idol of Disdain;
My Hope in Love does ne'er expire,
But it extinguishes Desire.

---

[1] Published in *A Collection of Poems, Written upon Several Occasions*, 1672. Text of *Poetical Works*, ed. Ayloffe, 1707.

Nor yet of those who ill receiv'd,
Wou'd have it otherwise believ'd
And, where their Love cou'd not prevail,
Take the vain Liberty to rail.

Whoe'er wou'd make his Victor less,
Must his own weak Defence confess,
And while her Power he does defame,
He poorly doubles his own Shame.

Even that Malice does betray,
And speak Concern another way;
And all such Scorn in Men is but
The Smoke of Fires ill put out.

He's still in Torment, whom the Rage
To Detraction does engage;
In Love Indifference is sure
The only sign of perfect Cure.

Advice to the Old Beaux[1]

SCRAPE no more your harmless Chins,
  Old Beaux, in hope to please;
You shou'd repent your former Sins,
  Not study their Increase;
Young awkard Fops, may shock our Sight,
But you offend by Day and Night.

In vain the Coachman turns about,
  And whips the dappl'd Greys;
When the old Ogler looks out,
  We turn away our Face.
True Love and Youth will ever charm,
But both affected, cannot warm.

Summer-fruits we highly prise,
  They kindly cool the Blood;
But Winter berries we despise,
  And leave 'em in the Wood;
On the Bush they may look well,
But gather'd, lose both taste and smell.

[1] Published in the *Gentleman's Journal*, August, 1693. Text of *Poetical Works*, ed. Ayloffe, 1707.

That you languish, that you dye,
Alas, is but too true;
Yet tax not us with Cruelty,
Who daily pity you.
Nature henceforth alone accuse,
In vain we grant, if she refuse.

Song[1]

SMOOTH was the Water, calm the Air,
The Evening-Sun deprest,
Lawyers dismist the noisie Bar,
The Labourer at rest,

When *Strephon*, with his charming Fair,
Cross'd the proud River *Thames*,
And to a Garden did repair,
To quench their mutual Flames.

The crafty Waiter soon espy'd
Youth sparkling in her Eyes;
He brought no Ham, nor Neats-tongues dry'd,
But Cream and Strawberries.

The amorous *Strephon* ask'd the Maid,
What's whiter than this Cream?
She blush'd, and could not tell, she said:
Thy Teeth, my pretty Lamb.

What's redder than these Berries are?
I know not, she reply'd:
Those lips, which I'll no longer spare,
The burning Shepherd cry'd.

And strait began to hug her:
This Kiss, my Dear,
Is sweater far
Than Strawberries, Cream and Sugar.

[1] Published in *Miscellaneous Works*, ed. Ayloffe, 1702. Text of 1707 edition.

Song[1]

PHILLIS is my only Joy,
Faithless as the Winds or Seas;
Sometimes coming, sometimes coy,
Yet she never fails to please;
If with a Frown
I am cast down,
Phillis smiling,
And beguiling,
Makes me happier than before.

Tho', alas, too late I find,
Nothing can her Fancy fix;
Yet the Moment she is kind,
I forgive her all her Tricks;
Which, tho' I see,
I can't get free;
She deceiving,
I believing;
What need Lovers wish for more?

SIR GEORGE ETHEREGE

(1635?-1664-1691)

Song[2]

IF SHE be not as kind as fair,
But peevish and unhandy,
Leave her, she's only worth the Care
Of some spruce Jack-a-dandy.
I wou'd not have thee such an Ass,
Hadst thou ne're so much leisure,
To sign and whine for such a Lass
Whose Pride's above her Pleasure.

[1] Published in *Miscellaneous Works*, ed. Ayloffe, 1702. Text of 1707 edition.
[2] Published in *Love in a Tub*, 1664, Act II, Scene iii. Text of *Works*, 1704.

To a Lady, Asking Him How Long He would Love Her[1]

IT IS not, *Celia,* in our Power
To say how long our Love will last;
It may be we, within this Hour,
May lose those Joys we now do taste:
The Blessed, that immortal be,
From Change in Love are only free.

Then, since we mortal Lovers are,
Ask not how long our Love will last;
But while it does, let us take care
Each Minute be with Pleasure past:
Were it not Madness to deny
To live, because w' are sure to die?

Song[2]

THE Pleasures of Love, and the Joys of good Wine,
To perfect our Happiness wisely we join.
We to Beauty all Day
Give the Soveraign Sway,
And her Favourite Nymphs devoutly obey.
At the Plays we are constantly making our Court,
And when they are ended we follow the Sport.
To the Mail and the Park,
Where we love 'till 'tis dark;
Then sparkling Champaign
Puts an end to their Reign;
It quickly recovers
Poor languishing Lovers,
Make us frolick and gay, and drowns all our Sorrow.
But alas! we relapse again on the Morrow.
Let ev'ry Man stand
With his Glass in his Hand,
And briskly discharge at the Word of Command.
Here's a Health to all those
Whom to Night we depose.
Wine and Beauty by turns great Souls should inspire.
Present all together, and now Boys give Fire——

[1] Published in 1673. Text of *A Collection of Poems*, third edition, 1716.
[2] Published in *The Man of Mode; or, Sir Fopling Flutter*, 1676, Act IV, Scene i. Text of *Works*, 1704.

To a Very Young Lady[1]

SWEETEST Bud of Beauty, may
No untimely Frost decay
Th' early Glories which we trace,
Blooming in thy matchless Face;
But kindly opening, like the Rose,
Fresh Beauties every day disclose,
Such as by Nature are not shown
In all the Blossoms she has blown.
And then what Conquest shall you make,
Who Hearts already daily take?
Scorch'd in the Morning with thy Beams,
How shall we bear those sad Extremes,
Which must attend thy threatning Eyes,
When thou shalt to thy Noon arise?

CHARLES COTTON

(1630-1670-1687)

The Retirement
Stanzas Irreguliers to Mr. Izaak Walton[2]

FAREWELL thou busie World, and may
We never meet again:
Here I can eat, and sleep, and pray,
And doe more good in one short day,
Than he who his whole Age out-wears
Upon thy most conspicuous Theatres,
Where nought but Vice and Vanity do reign.

Good God! how sweet are all things here!
How beautifull the Fields appear!
How cleanly do we feed and lie!
Lord! what good hours do we keep!
How quietly we sleep!

[1] Published in *A Collection of Poems*, 1701. Text of third edition, 1716.

[2] Published in *The Compleat Angler*, Part II, 1676. Text of *Poems on Several Occasions*, 1689.

What Peace! what Unanimity!
How innocent from the leud Fashion,
Is all our bus'ness, all our Conversation!

Oh how happy here's our leisure!
Oh how innocent our pleasure!
Oh ye Vallies, oh ye Mountains,
Oh ye Groves and Chrystall Fountains,
How I love at liberty,
By turn to come and visit ye!

O Solitude, the Soul's best Friend,
That man acquainted with himself dost make,
And all his Maker's Wonders to intend;
With thee I here converse at will,
And would be glad to do so still;
For it is thou alone that keep'st the Soul awake.

How calm and quiet a delight
It is alone
To read, and meditate, and write,
By none offended, nor offending none;
To walk, ride, sit, or sleep at one's own ease,
And pleasing a man's self, none other to displease!

Oh my beloved Nymph! fair Dove,
Princess of Rivers, how I love
Upon thy flow'ry Banks to lie,
And view thy Silver stream,
When gilded by a Summer's Beam,
And in it all thy wanton Fry
Playing at liberty,
And with my Angle upon them,
The All of Treachery
I ever learn'd to practise and to try!

Such streams *Rome*'s yellow *Tiber* cannot show,
Th' *Iberian Tagus*, nor *Ligurian Po;*
The *Meuse*, the *Danube*, and the *Rhine*,
Are puddle-water all compar'd with thine;
And *Loire*'s pure streams yet too polluted are
With thine much purer to compare:
The rapid *Garonne*, and the winding *Seine*
Are both too mean,
Beloved Dove, with thee
To vie Priority:
Nay, *Tame* and *Isis*, when conjoyn'd, submit,
And lay their Trophies at thy Silver Feet.

Oh my beloved Rocks! that rise
To awe the Earth, and brave the Skies,
From some aspiring Mountain's crown
How dearly do I love,
Giddy with pleasure, to look down,
And from the Vales to view the noble heights above!

Oh my beloved Caves! from Dog-star heats,
And hotter Persecution safe Retreats,
What safety, privacy, what true delight
In the artificial Night
Your gloomy entrails make,
Have I taken, do I take!
How oft, when grief has made me fly
To hide me from Society,
Even of my dearest Friends, have I
In your recesses friendly shade
All my sorrows open laid,
And my most secret woes entrusted to your privacy!

Lord! would men let me alone,
What an over-happy one
Should I think myself to be,
Might I in this desert place,
Which most men by their voice disgrace,
Live but undisturb'd and free!
Here, in this despis'd recess
Would I maugre Winter's cold,
And the Summer's worst excess,
Try to live out to sixty full years old,
And all the while
Without an envious eye
On any thriving under Fortune's smile,
Contented live, and then contented die.

The New Year. To Mr. W. T.[1]

HARK, the Cock crows, and yon, bright Star,
Tells us the day himself's not far;
And see where, breaking from the night,
He guilds the Western hills with light.
With him old *Janus* does appear,
Peeping into the future Year
With such a look as seems to say

[1] Published in *Poems on Several Occasions*, 1689. Text of first edition.

The prospect is not good that way.
Thus do we rise ill sights to see,
And 'gainst our selves to Prophesie,
When the Prophetick fear of things
A more tormenting mischief brings,
More full of Soul-tormenting Gall
Than direst mischiefs can befall.
  But stay! but stay! methinks my sight,
Better inform'd by clearer light,
Discerns sereneness in that brow,
That all contracted seem'd but now:
His reverse face may shew distast,
And frown upon the ills are past;
But that which this way looks is clear,
And smiles upon the New-born year.
He looks too from a place so high,
The year lies open to his eye,
And all the moments open are
To the exact discoverer;
Yet more and more he smiles upon
The happy revolution.
Why should we then suspect or fear
The Influences of a year
So smiles upon us the first morn,
And speaks us good so soon as born?
  Pox on 't! the last was ill enough,
This cannot but make better proof;
Or at the worst, as we brush'd through
The last, why so we may this too;
And then the next in reason shou'd,
Be superexcellently good:
For the worst ills we daily see,
Have no more perpetuity
Than the best Fortunes that do fall;
Which also bring us wherewithall
Longer their being to support,
Than those do of the other sort;
And who has one good year in three,
And yet repines at Destiny,
Appears ingrateful in the case,
And merits not the good he has.
  Then let us welcome the new guest,
With lusty Brimmers of the best;
Mirth always should good Fortune meet,
And renders e'en disaster sweet:
And though the Princess turn her back,
Let us but line ourselves with Sack,

We better shall by far hold out,
Till the next year she face about.

The Angler's Ballad[1]

AWAY to the Brook,
All your Tackle out look,
  Here's a day that is worth a year's wishing;
See that all things be right,
For 'tis a very spight
  To want tools when a man goes a fishing.

Your Rod with tops two,
For the same will not doe
  If your manner of angling you vary;
And full well you may think,
If you troll with a Pink,
  One too weak will be apt to miscarry.

Then Basket, neat made
By a Master in 's trade,
  In a belt at your shoulders must dangle;
For none e'er was so vain
To wear this to disdain,
  Who a true Brother was of the Angle.

Next, Pouch must not fail,
Stuff'd as full as a Mail,
  With Wax, Cruels, Silks, Hair, Furs and Feathers
To make several Flies,
For the several Skies,
  That shall kill in despight of all weathers.

The Boxes and Books
For your Lines and your Hooks,
  And, though not for strict need notwithstanding,
Your Scissors, and your Hone
To adjust your points on,
  With a Net to be sure for your landing.

All these being on,
'Tis high time we were gone,
  Down, and upward, that all may have pleasure;
Till, here meeting at night,

[1] Published in *Poems on Several Occasions*, 1689. Text of first edition.

We shall have the delight
  To discourse of our Fortunes at leisure.

The day's not too bright,
And the wind hits us right,
  And all Nature does seem to invite us;
We have all things at will
For to second our skill,
  As they all did conspire to delight us.

Or stream now, or still,
A large Panier will fill,
  Trout and Grayling to rise are so willing;
I dare venture to say
'Twill be a bloudy day,
  And we all shall be weary of killing.

Away then, away,
We lose sport by delay,
  But first leave all our sorrows behind us;
If misfortune doe come,
We are all gone from home,
  And a fishing she never can find us.

The Angler is free
From the cares that degree
  Finds itself with so often tormented;
And although we should slay
Each a hundred to day,
  'Tis a slaughter needs ne'er be repented.

And though we display
All our Arts to betray
  What were made for man's Pleasure and Diet;
Yet both Princes and States
May, for all our quaint Bates,
  Rule themselves and their People in quiet.

We scratch not our pates,
Nor repine at the Rates
  Our Superiors impose on our living;
But do frankly submit,
Knowing they have more wit
  In demanding, than we have in giving.

Whilst quiet we sit
We conclude all things fit,
  Acquiescing with hearty submission;

For, though simple, we know
That soft murmurs will grow
  At the last unto down-right Sedition.

We care not who says,
And intends it dispraise,
  That an Angler t' a Fool is next neighbour;
Let him prate, what care we,
We're as honest as he,
  And so let him take that for his labour.

We covet no Wealth
But the Blessing of Health,
  And that greater good Conscience within;
Such Devotion we bring
To our God and our King,
  That from either no offers can win.

Whilst we sit and fish,
We do pray as we wish,
  For long life to our King *James* the Second;
Honest Anglers then may,
Or they've very foul play,
  With the best of good Subjects be reckon'd.

CHARLES SACKVILLE, EARL OF DORSET

(1638-1671-1706)

Song;
Written at Sea, in the First Dutch War, 1665, The Night before an Engagement[1]

TO ALL you ladies now at land
  We men at sea indite;
But first wou'd have you understand
  How hard it is to write;
The Muses now, and Neptune too,
We must implore to write to you,
  With a fa, la, la, la, la.

[1] Written in 1665. Text of *Works of the Most Celebrated Minor Poets*, Volume I, 1749.

For tho' the Muses should prove kind,
  And fill our empty brain;
Yet if rough Neptune rouze the wind,
  To wave the azure main,
Our paper, pen, and ink, and we,
Roll up and down our ships at sea,
  With a fa, &c.

Then, if we write not by each post,
  Think not we are unkind;
Nor yet conclude our ships are lost
  By Dutchmen, or by wind:
Our tears we'll send a speedier way,
The tide shall bring 'em twice a day.
  With a fa, &c.

The king with wonder, and surprize,
  Will swear the seas grow bold;
Because the tides will higher rise,
  Than e'er they us'd of old:
But let him know it is our tears
Bring floods of grief to Whitehall stairs.
  With a fa, &c.

Should foggy Opdam chance to know
  Our sad and dismal story;
The Dutch wou'd scorn too weak a foe,
  And quit their fort at Goree:
For what resistance can they find
From men who've left their hearts behind!
  With a fa, &c.

Let wind and weather do its worst,
  Be you to us but kind;
Let Dutchmen vapour, Spaniards curse,
  No sorrow we shall find:
'Tis then no matter how things go,
Or who's our friend, or who's our foe.
  With a fa, &c.

To pass our tedious hours away,
  We throw a merry main;
Or else at serious ombre play;
  But, why should we in vain
Each others ruin thus pursue?
We were undone when we left you.
  With a fa, &c.

But now our fears tempestuous grow,
  And cast our hopes away;
Whilst you, regardless of our woe,
  Sit careless at a play:
Perhaps permit some happier man
To kiss your hand, or flirt your fan.
  With a fa, &c.

When any mournful tune you hear,
  That dies in ev'ry note;
As if it sigh'd with each man's care,
  For being so remote;
Think then how often love we've made
To you, when all those tunes were play'd.
  With a fa, &c.

In justice you cannot refuse,
  To think of our distress;
When we for hopes of honour lose
  Our certain happiness;
All those designs are but to prove
Ourselves more worthy of your love.
  With a fa, &c.

And now we've told you all our loves,
  And likewise all our fears;
In hopes this declaration moves
  Some pity from your tears:
Let's hear of no inconstancy,
We have too much of that at sea.
  With a fa, la, la, la, la.

Song[1]

PHILLIS, for shame let us improve
  A thousand diff'rent ways,
Those few short moments snatch'd by love,
  From many tedious days.

If you want courage to despise
  The censure of the grave,
Though love's a tyrant in your eyes,
  Your heart is but a slave.

[1] Published in *Westminster Drollery*, Volume I, 1671. Text of *A Supplement to the Works of the Most Celebrated Minor Poets*, 1750.

My love is full of noble pride,
Nor can it e'er submit,
To let that fop, discretion, ride
In triumph over it.

False friends I have, as well as you,
Who daily counsel me
Fame and ambition to pursue,
And leave off loving thee.

But when the least regard I shew
To fools, who thus advise,
May I be dull enough to grow
Most miserably wise.

Song[1]

DORINDA's sparkling wit, and eyes,
United, cast too fierce a light,
Which blazes high, but quickly dies,
Pains not the heart, but hurts the sight.

Love is a calmer, gentler joy,
Smooth are his looks, and soft his pace;
Her Cupid is a black-guard boy,
That runs his link full in your face.

Song[2]

METHINKS the poor town has been troubled too long,
With Phillis and Chloris in every song;
By fools, who at once can both love and despair,
And will never leave calling 'em cruel and fair;
Which justly provokes me in rhime to express
The truth that I know of bonny black Bess.

This Bess of my heart, this Bess of my soul,
Has a skin white as milk, and hair black as a coal;
She's plump, yet with ease you may span her round waist,

[1] Published in *The Works of the Most Celebrated Minor Poets,* Volume I, 1749. Text of first edition.

[2] Published in *The Works of the Most Celebrated Minor Poets,* Volume I, 1749. Text of first edition.

But her round swelling thighs can scarce be embrac'd:
Her belly is soft, not a word of the rest;
But I know what I think, when I drink to the best.

The plowman and 'squire, the arranter clown,
At home she subdu'd in her paragon-gown;
But now she adorns both the boxes and pit,
And the proudest town-gallants are forc'd to submit;
All hearts fall a leaping wherever she comes,
And beat day and night, like my lord Craven's Drums.

I dare not permit her to come to Whitehall,
For she'd out-shine the ladies, paint, jewels, and all:
If a lord shou'd but whisper his love in a crowd,
She'd sell him a bargain, and laugh out aloud:
Then the queen over-hearing what Betty did say,
Would send Mr. Roper to take her away.

But to those that have had my dear Bess in their arms,
She's gentle, and knows how to soften her charms;
And to every beauty can add a new grace,
Having learn'd how to lisp, and to trip in her pace;
And with head on one side, and a languishing eye,
To kill us by looking as if she would die.

JOHN WILMOT, EARL OF ROCHESTER

(1647-1672-1680)

A Satyr against Mankind[1]

WERE I, who to my cost already am,
One of those strange, prodigious Creatures *Man*,
A Spirit free, to chuse for my own share,
What sort of Flesh and Blood I pleas'd to wear,
I'd be a Dog, a Monkey or a Bear,
Or any thing, but that vain Animal,
Who is so proud of being rational.
The Senses are too gross; and he'll contrive
A sixth, to contradict the other five:
And before certain Instinct, will preferr
Reason, which fifty times for one does err—

[1] Published in 1675. Text of *Poems*, ed. Rymer, 1691.

Reason, an *Ignis fatuus* of the Mind,
Which leaves the Light of Nature, Sense behind.
Pathless, and dangerous, wand'ring ways, it takes,
Through Errour's fenny Bogs, and thorny Brakes:
Whilst the misguided Follower climbs with pain,
Mountains of Whimseys, heapt in his own Brain,
Stumbling from thought to thought, falls headlong down
Into Doubt's boundless Sea, where like to drown,
Books bear him up a while, and make him try
To swim with Bladders of Philosophy,
In hopes still to o'ertake the skipping Light:
The Vapour dances, in his dazzled sight,
Till spent, it leaves him to eternal night.
Then old Age, and Experience, hand in hand,
Lead him to Death, and make him understand,
After a search so painful, and so long,
That all his Life he has been in the wrong.
Huddled in Dirt, [the] reas'ning Engine lies,
Who was so proud, so witty, and so wise:
Pride drew him in, as Cheats their Bubbles catch,
And made him venture to be made a wretch:
His Wisdom did his Happiness destroy,
Aiming to know the World he should enjoy.
And *Wit* was his vain frivolous pretence,
Of pleasing others at his own expence.
For *Wits* are treated just like *Common Whores*;
First they're enjoy'd, and then kickt out of doors.
The Pleasure past, a threatning Doubt remains,
That frights th' Enjoyer with succeeding Pains.
Women, and *Men of Wit*, are dang'rous Tools,
And ever fatal to admiring Fools.
Pleasure allures, and when the Fops escape,
'Tis not that they're belov'd, but fortunate;
And therefore what they fear, at heart they hate.
But now methinks some formal Band and Beard
Takes me to task; Come on, Sir, I'm prepar'd:
Then by your favour, any thing that's writ
Against this gibing, gingling knack, call'd *Wit*,
Likes me abundantly; but you'll take care
Upon this point, not to be too severe.
Perhaps my Muse were fitter for this part:
For I profess, I can be very smart
On *Wit*, which I abhor with all my heart.
I long to lash it, in some sharp Essay,
But your grand Indiscretion bids me stay,
And turns my Tide of Ink another way;
What Rage ferments in your degen'rate Mind,

To make you rail at Reason and Mankind—
Blest glorious Man, to whom alone kind Heav'n
An everlasting Soul hath freely giv'n;
Whom his great Maker took such care to make,
That from himself he did the Image take,
And this fair Frame in shining Reason drest,
To dignifie his Nature above Beast—
Reason, by whose aspiring Influence,
We take a flight beyond material Sense,
Dive into Mysteries, then soaring pierce
The flaming limits of the Universe,
Search Heav'n and Hell, find out what's acted there,
And give the World true grounds of hope and fear?
  Hold, mighty Man, I cry; all this we know,
From the pathetick Pen of *Ingelo*,
From *Patrick*'s Pilgrim, *Sibb*'s Soliloquies,
And 'tis this very Reason I despise,
This supernat'ral Gift, that makes a Mite
Think he's the Image of the Infinite;
Comparing his short Life, void of all rest,
To the eternal and the ever Blest;
This busie puzling stirrer up of doubt,
That frames deep Mysteries, then finds 'em out,
Filling with frantick Crouds of thinking Fools,
The reverend Bedlams, Colleges and Schools;
Born on whose Wings, each heavy Sot can pierce
The Limits of the boundless Universe:
So charming Ointments make an old Witch fly,
And bear a cripled Carkass through the Sky.
Tis this exalted Pow'r whose Business lies
In Nonsense and Impossibilities:
This made a whimsical Philosopher,
Before the spacious World his Tub prefer:
And we have many modern Coxcombs, who
Retire to think, 'cause they have nought to do.
But Thoughts were giv'n for Actions Government;
Where Action ceases, Thought's impertinent.
Our Sphere of Action is Lifes happiness,
And he that thinks beyond, thinks like an Ass.
Thus whilst against false reas'ning I inveigh,
I own right Reason, which I would obey;
That Reason, which distinguishes by Sense,
And gives us rules of good and ill from thence;
That bounds Desires with a reforming Will,
To keep them more in vigour, not to kill:
Your Reason hinders; mine helps to enjoy,

Renewing Appetites, yours would destroy.
My Reason is my Friend, yours is a Cheat:
Hunger calls out, my Reason bids me eat;
Perversly yours, your Appetite does mock;
This asks for food, that answers what's a Clock?
This plain distinction, Sir, your doubt secures;
'Tis not true Reason I despise, but yours.
Thus, I think Reason righted: But for Man,
I'll ne'er recant, defend him if you can.
For all his Pride, and his Philosophy,
'Tis evident Beasts are, in their degree,
As wise at least, and better far than he.
Those Creatures are the wisest, who attain
By surest means, the ends at which they aim.
If therefore *Jowler* finds, and kills his Hare
Better than *Meres* supplies Committee Chair;
Though one's a Statesman, th' other but a Hound,
Jowler in Justice will be wiser found.
You see how far Man's Wisdom here extends:
Look next if Human Nature makes amends;
Whose Principles are most generous and Just;
And to whose Morals, you wou'd sooner trust.
Be judge your self, I'll bring it to the Test,
Which is the basest Creature, Man, or Beast:
Birds feed on Birds, Beasts on each other prey;
But savage Man alone, does Man betray.
Prest by Necessity, *They* kill for Food;
Man undoes Man, to do himself no good.
With Teeth, and Claws, by Nature arm'd *They* hunt
Nature's allowance, to supply their want:
But Man with Smiles, Embraces, Friendships, Praise,
Inhumanely, his Fellows Life betrays,
With voluntary Pains, works his Distress;
Not through Necessity, but Wantonness.
For Hunger, or for Love *They* bite or tear,
Whilst wretched Man is still in Arms for Fear:
For Fear he arms, and is of Arms afraid;
From Fear, to Fear, successively betray'd.
Base Fear, the Source whence his best Passions came,
His boasted Honour, and his dear-bought Fame,
The Lust of Pow'r, to which he's such a Slave,
And for the which alone he dares be brave:
To which his various Projects are design'd,
Which makes him gen'rous, affable, and kind:
For which he takes such pains to be thought wise,
And scrues his Actions, in a forc'd Disguise:

Leads a most tedious Life, in misery,
Under laborious, mean Hypocrisie.
Look to the bottom of his vast Design,
Wherein Man's Wisdom, Pow'r, and Glory join—
The Good he acts, the Ill he does endure,
'Tis all from Fear, to make himself secure.
Meerly for safety, after Fame they thirst;
For all Men would be Cowards if they durst:
And Honesty's against all common sense—
Men must be Knaves; 'tis in their own defence,
Mankind's dishonest; if they think it fair,
Amongst known Cheats, to play upon the square,
You'll be undone——
Nor can weak Truth, your Reputation save;
The Knaves will all agree to call you Knave.
Wrong'd shall he live, insulted o'er, opprest,
Who dares be less a Villain than the rest.
Thus here you see what Human Nature craves,
Most Men are Cowards, all Men shou'd be Knaves.
The Difference lies, as far as I can see,
Not in the thing it self, but the degree;
And all the subject matter of Debate,
Is only who's a Knave of the first Rate.

Love and Life. A Song[1]

ALL my past Life is mine no more,
  The flying Hours are gone:
Like transitory Dreams giv'n o'er,
Whose Images are kept in store,
  By Memory alone.

The Time that is to come is not;
  How can it then be mine?
The present Moment's all my Lot;
And that, as fast as it is got,
  Phillis, is only thine.

Then talk not of Inconstancy,
  False Hearts, and broken Vows;
If I, by Miracle, can be
This live-long Minute true to thee,
  'Tis all that Heav'n allows.

[1]Published in *Poems*, 1680. Text of *Poems*, ed. Rymer, 1691.

Upon Drinking in a Bowl[1]

VULCAN contrive me such a Cup
  As *Nestor* us'd of old:
Shew all thy Skill to trim it up;
  Damask it round with Gold.

Make it so large that, fill'd with Sack
  Up to the swelling Brim,
Vast Toasts, on the delicious Lake,
  Like Ships at Sea, may swim.

Engrave not Battel on his Cheek;
  With War I've nought to do:
I'm none of those that took *Mastrick*,
  Nor *Yarmouth* Leaguer knew.

Let it no Name of Planets tell,
  Fixt Stars, or Constellations:
For I am no Sir *Sindrophel*,
  Nor none of his Relations.

But carve thereon a spreading Vine;
  Then add two lovely Boys;
Their Limbs in amorous Folds intwine,
  The Type of future Joys.

Cupid and *Bacchus* my Saints are;
  May Drink and Love still reign:
With Wine I wash away my Cares,
  And then to Love again.

THOMAS FLATMAN

(1635-1674-1688)

A Thought of Death[2]

WHEN on my sick Bed I languish,
Full of sorrow, full of anguish,

[1] Published in *Poems*, 1680. Text of *Poems*, ed. Rymer, 1691.
[2] Published in *Poems*, 1674. Text of *Poems*, fourth ed., 1686.

Fainting, gasping, trembling, crying,
Panting, groaning, speechless, dying,
My Soul just now about to take her flight
Into the Regions of eternal night;
Oh tell me you,
That have been long below,
What shall I do!
What shall I think, when cruel Death appears,
That may extenuate my fears!
Methinks I hear some Gentle Spirit say,
Be not fearful, come away!
Think with thy self that now thou shalt be free,
And find thy long expected liberty;
Better thou mayst, but worse thou can'st not be
Than in this Vale of Tears, and Misery.
Like *Cæsar*, with assurance then come on,
And unamaz'd attempt the Laurel Crown,
That lies on th' other side Death's *Rubicon*.

A Dooms-Day Thought
Anno 1659[1]

JUDGMENT! two Syllables can make
The haughtiest Son of *Adam* shake.
Tis coming, and 'twill surely come,
The dawning to that *Day* of *Doom*;
O, th' morning blush of that dread day,
When Heav'n and Earth shall steal away,
Shall in their pristine *Chaos* hide,
Rather than th' angry Judge abide.
'Tis not far off; methinks I see
Among the Stars some dimmer be;
Some tremble, as their Lamps did fear
A neighbouring Extinguisher.
The greater Luminaries fail,
Their Glories by Eclipses vail,
Knowing e're long their borrow'd Light
Must sink in th' Universal Night.
When I behold a Mist arise,
Strait to the same astonish'd Eyes,
Th' ascending Clouds do represent,
A Scene of th' smoaking Firmament.
Oft when I hear a blustering Wind

[1] Published in *Poems*, 1674. Text of *Poems*, fourth ed., 1686.

With a tempestuous murmur joyn'd,
I phancy, *Nature* in this blast,
Practises how to breath her Last,
Or sighs for poor Man's misery,
Or pants for fair Eternity.
  Go to the dull Church-yard and see
Those Hillocks of Mortality.
Where proudest Man is only found
By a small swelling in the Ground?
What Crouds of Carcasses are made
Slaves to the Pickax and the Spade!
Dig but a foot, or two, to make
A Cold Bed, for thy dead Friends sake,
'Tis odds but in that scantling room,
Thou robb'st another of his Tomb,
Or in thy delving smit'st upon
A Shinbone, or a Cranion.
  When th' Prison's full, what next can be
But the Grand Goal-Delivery?
The Great *Assize*, when the pale Clay
Shall gape, and render up its Prey;
When from the Dungeon of the Grave
The meager Throng themselves shall heave,
Shake off their Linnen Chains, and gaze
With wonder, when the world shall blaze,
Then climb the Mountains, scale the Rocks,
Force op'n the Deep's Eternal Locks,
Beseech the Clifts to lend an Ear,
Obdurate they, and will not hear.
What? ne're a Cavern ne're a Grot
To cover from the common Lot?
No quite forgotten Hold, to ly
Obscur'd, and pass the reck'ning by?
No—There's a quick all-piercing Eye
Can through the Earth's dark Center pry,
Search into th' bowels of the Sea,
And comprehend Eternity.
  What shall we do then, when the voice
Of the shrill *Trump* with strong fierce noise
Shall pierce our Ears, and summon all
To th' Universe wide Judgment-Hall?
What shall we do, we cannot hide,
Nor yet that Scrutiny abide:
When enlarg'd Conscience loudly speaks,
And all our bosom-secrets breaks;
When flames surround, and greedy *Hell*
Gapes for a Booty, (*who can dwell*

With everlasting Burnings!) when
Irrevocable words shall pass on Men;
Poor naked Men, who sometimes, thought
These frights perhaps would come to nought!
What shall we do! we cannot run
For Refuge, or the strict Judge shun.
'Tis too late *Then* to think what Course to take;
While we live Here, we must Provision make.

The Batchelors Song[1]

LIKE a Dog with a Bottle, fast ty'd to his tail,
Like Vermin in a Trap, or a Thief in a Jail,
Like a *Tory* in a Bog,
Or an Ape with a Clog:
Such is the man, who when he might go free,
Does his liberty loose,
For a Matrimony noose,
And sells himself into captivity.
The Dog he do's howl, when the Bottle does jog,
The Vermin, the Thief, and the *Tory* in vain
Of the Trap, of the Jail, of the Quagmire complain.
But welfare poor *Pug!* for he plays with his Clog;
And though he would be rid on't rather than his life,
Yet he lugs it, and he hugs it, as a man does his Wife.

The Defiance. Song[2]

BE NOT too proud, imperious Dame,
Your charms are transitory things,
May melt, while you at Heaven aim,
Like *Icarus's* Waxen Wings;
And you a part in his misfortune bear,
Drown'd in a briny Ocean of despair.

You think your beauties are above
The Poets Brain, and Painters Hand,
As if upon the Throne of Love
You only should the World command:
Yet know, though you presume your title true,
There are pretenders, that will Rival you.

[1] Published in *Poems*, 1674. Text of *Poems*, fourth ed., 1686.
[2] Published in *Poems*, 1674. Text of *Poems*, fourth ed., 1686.

There's an experienc'd Rebel, Time,
And in his Squadrons Poverty;
There's Age that brings along with him
A terrible Artillery:
And if against all these thou keep'st thy Crown,
Th' Usurper Death will make thee lay it down.

The Unconcerned. Song[1]

Now that the World is all in a maze,
Drums, and Trumpets rending Heav'ns,
Wounds a bleeding, Mortals dying,
Widows and Orphans piteously crying;
Armies marching, Towns in a blaze,
Kingdoms and States at sixes and sevens:
What should an honest Fellow do,
Whose courage, and fortunes run equally low!
Let him live, say I, till his glass be run,
As easily as he may;
Let the Wine, and the Sand of his Glass flow together,
For Life's but a Winters day.
Alas from Sun to Sun,
The time's very short, very dirty the weather,
And we silently creep away,
Let him nothing do, he could wish undone;
And keep himself safe from the noise of Gun.

Pastoral Dialogue
Castara and Parthenia[2]

PARTHENIA

MY DEAR *Castara*, t'other day
I heard an ancient Shepherd say,
Alas for me! my time draws nigh,
And shortly, shortly I must die!
What meant the man? for lo! apace
Torrents of tears ran down his face.

[1] Published in *Poems*, 1674. Text of *Poems*, fourth ed., 1686.
[2] Published in *Poems*, fourth ed., 1686. Text of first edition.

CASTARA

Poor harmless Maid! why wouldst thou know,
What known, must needs create thee woe?
'Twill cloud the Sunshine of thy days,
And in thy soul such trouble raise,
Thou'lt grieve, and tremble, and complain,
And say that all thy beauty's vain.

PARTHENIA

Ah me! sure 'tis some dreadful thing
That can so great disorder bring,
Yet tell me, prithee tell me, do,
For 'tis some ease the worst to know.

CASTARA

To die, (*Parthenia*) is to quit
The World, and the Suns glorious light,
To leave our flocks, and fields for ever,
To part, and never meet again, O never!
After that cruel hideous hour,
Thou, and I shall sing no more;
In the cold Earth they will thee lay,
And what thou dot'st on shall be Clay.

PARTHENIA

Alas! why will they use me so,
A Virgin that no evil do?

CASTARA

Roses wither, Turtles die,
Fair, and kind as Thou and I.

CHORUS *amb.*

Then, since 'tis appointed to the dust we must go;
Let us innocently live, and vertuously do,
Let us love, let us sing, 'tis no matter, 'tis all one,
If our Lamps be extinguisht at midnight or noon.

THOMAS D'URFEY

(1653-1678-1723)

Solon's Song[1]

TANTIVEE, tivee, tivee, tivee, high and low,
Hark, hark, how the merry merry Horn does blow
As through the Lanes and the Meadows we go;
As Puss has run over the Down:
When *Ringwood*, and *Rockwood*, and *Jowler*, and *Spring*,
And *Thunder* and *Wonder* made all the Woods ring,
And Horsemen, and Footmen, hey ding, a ding, ding,
Who envies the Splendor and State of a Crown.

Then follow, follow, follow, follow, Jolly Boys,
Keep in with the Beagles now whilst the Scent lies,
The fiery-fac'd God is just ready to rise;
Whose Beams all our Pleasure Controuls,
Whilst over the Mountains and Valleys we rowl,
And *Watt*'s fatal knell in each hollow we Toll,
And in the next Cottage top off a brown Bowl,
What Pleasure like Hunting can cherish the Soul.

Scotch Song[2]

JOCKEY was a dowdy Lad;
And *Jemmy* swarth and tawny:
They, my heart no Captive made,
For that was prize to *Sawny*.
Jockey wooes, and sighs and sues,
And *Jemmy* offers Money;
Weel, I see, they both love me,
But I love only *Sawny*.

Jockey high his voice can raise,
And *Jemmy* tunes the Vyol;
But when *Sawny* Pipes sweet Layes
My heart kens no denyal.

[1] Published in *The Marriage-Hater Match'd*, 1692, Act II, Scene i. Text of first edition.

[2] Published in *The Campaigners: or, The Pleasant Adventures at Brussels*, 1698, Act III, Scene i. Text of first edition.

Yen he sings, and t'other strings,
Tho sweet, yet only teize me;
Sawny's Flute can only do't,
And Pipe a Tune to please me.

JOHN OLDHAM

(1653-1679-1683)

Satyrs upon the Jesuits

Prologue[1]

FOR who can longer hold? when every *Press*,
The *Bar* and *Pulpit* too has broke the Peace?
When every scribling *Fool* at the alarms
Has drawn his Pen, and rises up in Arms?
And not a dull *Pretender* of the Town,
But vents his gall in *Pamphlet* up and down?
When all with licence *rail*, and who will not,
Must be almost suspected of the *PLOT*,
And bring his *Zeal* or else his Parts in doubt?
In vain our *Preaching Tribe* attack the *Foes*,
In vain their weak *Artillery* oppose;
Mistaken honest men, who gravely *blame*,
And hope that *gentle Doctrine* should reclaim.
Are *Texts*, and such exploded trifles fit
T'impose, and sham upon a *Jesuit?*
Would they the dull old *Fisher-men* compare
With mighty *Suarez*, and great *Escobar?*
Such thred-bare proofs, and stale *Authorities*
May *Us* poor simple *Hereticks* suffice:
But to a fear'd *Ignatian*'s Conscience,
Harden'd, as his own Face, with Impudence,
Whose Faith in contradiction bore, whom Lies,
Nor Non-sense, nor Impossibilities,
Nor shame, nor death, nor damning can assail:
Not these mild fruitless methods will avail.
'Tis pointed *Satyr*, and the *sharps* of Wit
For such a *prize* are th' only Weapons fit:
Nor needs there *Art*, or *Genius* here to use,
Where *Indignation* can create a muse:

[1] Published in 1679. Text of *Satyrs upon the Jesuits*, third ed., corr., 1685.

Should Parts, and Nature fail, yet very spite
Would make the arrant'st *Wild*, or *Withers* write.
It is resolv'd: henceforth an endless War,
I and my Muse with them, and theirs declare;
Whom neither open *Malice* of the *Foes*,
Nor private *Daggers*, nor St. *Omers Dose*,
Nor all, that *Godfrey* felt, or *Monarchs* fear,
Shall from my vow'd, and sworn revenge deter.
Sooner shall false *Court Favourites* prove just,
And faithful to their Kings, and Countrys trust:
Sooner shall they detect the tricks of *State*,
And knav'ry, suits, and bribes, and flatt'ry hate:
Bawds shall turn *Nuns, Salt* D——s grow chast,
And Paint, and Pride, and Lechery detest:
Popes shall for *Kings Supremacy* decide,
And *Cardinals* for *Huguenots* be try'd:
Sooner (which is the great'st impossible)
Shall the vile Brood of *Loyola*, and *Hell*
Give o'er to Plot, be Villains, and Rebel;
Than I with utmost spite, and vengeance cease
To prosecute, and plague their cursed race.
The rage of *Poets* damn'd, of *Womens Pride*
Contemn'd, and scorn'd, or *proffer'd lust* denied:
The malice of *Religious* angry *Zeal*,
And all, *cashier'd resenting States-men* feel:
What prompts dire *Hags* in their own blood to write
And sell their very souls to Hell for spite:
All this urge on my rank envenom'd spleen,
And with keen Satyr edg my stabbing Pen:
That its each home-set thrust their blood may draw,
Each drop of Ink like *Aquafortis* gnaw.
Red hot with vengeance thus, I'll brand disgrace
So deep, no time shall e'er the marks deface:
Till my severe and exemplary doom
Spread wider than their guilt, till it become
More dreaded than the *Bor*, and frighten worse
Than damning *Pope's Anathema's*, and curse.

The Careless Good Fellow
Written March 9, 1680[1]

A Pox of this fooling, and plotting of late,
What a pother, and stir has it kept in the State?

[1] Published in *Poems and Translations*, 1683. Text of first edition.

Let the Rabble run mad with Suspicions, and Fears,
Let them scuffle, and jar, till they go by the ears:
  Their Grievances never shall trouble my pate,
  So I can enjoy my dear Bottle at quiet.

What Coxcombs were those, who would barter their ease
And their Necks for a Toy, a thin Wafer and Mass?
At old *Tyburn* they never had needed to swing,
Had they been but true Subjects to Drink, and their King;
  A Friend, and a Bottle is all my design;
  He has no room for Treason, that's top-full of Wine.

I mind not the Members and makers of Laws,
Let them sit or Prorogue, as his Majesty please:
Let them damn us to Woollen, I'll never repine
At my Lodging, when dead, so alive I have Wine:
  Yet oft in my Drink I can hardly forbear
  To curse them for making my Claret so dear.

I mind not grave Asses, who idly debate
About Right and Succession, the trifles of State;
We've a good King already: and he deserves laughter
That will trouble his head with who shall come after:
  Come, here's to his Health, and I wish he may be
  As free from all Care, and all Trouble, as we.

What care I how Leagues with the *Hollander* go?
Or Intrigues betwixt *Sidney*, and Monsieur *D' Avaux?*
What concerns it my Drinking, if *Casel* be sold,
If the Conqueror take it by Storming, or Gold?
  Good *Bordeaux* alone is the place that I mind,
  And when the Fleet's coming, I pray for a Wind.

The Bully of *France*, that aspires to Renown
By dull cutting of Throats, and vent'ring his own;
Let him fight and be damn'd, and make Matches and Treat,
To afford the News-mongers, and Coffee-house Chat:
  He's but a brave wretch, while I am more free,
  More safe, and a thousand times happier than He.

Come He, or the Pope, or the Devil to boot,
Or come Faggot, and Stake; I care not a Groat;
Never think that in *Smithfield* I Porters will heat:
No, I swear, Mr. *Fox*, pray excuse me for that.
  I'll drink in defiance of Gibbet, and Halter,
  This is the Profession, that never will alter.

ROBERT GOULD

(?-1680-1709?)

Song
The Hopeless Comfort[1]

NOT though I know she, fondly, lies
  Claspt in my *Rival*'s Arms,
Can free my Heart, or keep my Eyes
  From fixing on her Charms!

Tell me, ye Pow'rs that rule our Fate;
  Why are frail men so vain,
With so much *Zeal* to wish for that
  They never can attain?

Some Comfort 'tis I'me not alone,
  All are like me undone;
And that which does, like Death, spare none,
  Why shou'd I hope to shun?

Song[2]

FAIR, and soft, and gay, and young,
All Charm! she plaid, she danc'd, she sung!
There was no way to scape the Dart,
No care cou'd guard the Lover's Heart.
Ah! why cry'd I, and drop'd a Tear,
(Adoring, yet desparing e'er
To have her to my self alone,)
Was so much sweetness made for One?

But, growing bolder, in her ear
I in soft Numbers told my care:
She heard, and rais'd me from her feet,
And seem'd to glow with equal heat.
Like Heav'ns, too mighty to express,
My Joys cou'd but be known by guess.

[1] Published in *Poems*, 1689. Text of first edition.
[2] Published in *The Rival Sisters*, 1696, Act III. Text of first edition.

Ah! Fools (said I) what have I done,
To wish her made for more than One?

But long she had not been in view,
Before her Eyes their Beams withdrew:
E'er I had reckon'd half her Charms,
She sunk into another's Arms.
But she that once cou'd faithless be,
Will favour him no more than me:
He too, will find he is undone,
And that she was not made for One.

JOHN SHEFFIELD, DUKE OF BUCKINGHAMSHIRE

(1648-1682-1721)

Love's Slavery[1]

GRAVE Fops my Envy now beget,
   Who did my Pity move;
They by the right of wanting Wit,
   Are free from Cares of Love.

Turks honour Fools, because they are
   By that Defect secure
From Slavery and Toils of War,
   Which all the rest endure.

So I, who suffer cold Neglect
   And Wounds from *Celia*'s Eyes,
Begin extremely to respect
   These Fools that seem so wise.

'Tis true, they fondly set their Hearts
   On things of no Delight;
To pass all Day for Men of Parts,
   They pass alone the Night:

But *Celia* never breaks their Rest;
   Such Servants she disdains;
And so the Fops are dully blest,
   While I endure her Chains.

[1] Published in *A Collection of Poems*, 1701. Text of *Works*, ed. Pope, 1723.

The Reconcilement
Song[1]

COME, let us now resolve at last
  To live and love in Quiet;
We'll tie the Knot so very fast,
  That time shall ne'er untie it.

The truest Joys they seldom prove,
  Who free from Quarrels live;
Tis the most tender part of Love,
  Each other to forgive.

When least I seem'd concerned, I took
  No Pleasure, nor no Rest;
And when I feign'd an angry Look,
  Alas, I lov'd you best.

Own but the same to me, you'll find
  How blest will be our Fate;
Oh, to be happy, to be kind,
  Sure never is too late.

To a Coquet Beauty[2]

FROM Wars and Plagues come no such Harms,
As from a Nymph so full of Charms;
So much Sweetness in her Face,
In her Motions such a Grace,
In her kind inviting Eyes
Such a soft Enchantment lies;
That we please our selves too soon,
And are with empty Hopes undone.
  After all her Softness, we
Are but Slaves, while she is free;
Free, alas, from all desire,
Except to set the World on Fire.
  Thou, fair Dissembler, dost but thus
Deceive thy self, as well as us.
Like a restless Monarch, thou
Would'st rather force Mankind to bow,
And venture round the World to roam,

[1] Published in *A Collection of Poems*, 1701. Text of *Works*, ed. Pope, 1723.
[2] Published in *A Collection of Poems*, 1701. Text of *Works*, ed. Pope, 1723.

Than govern peaceably at Home.
But trust me, *Celia*, trust me when
Apollo's self inspires my Pen;
One Hour of Love's Delights outweighs
Whole Years of universal Praise;
And one Adorer kindly us'd,
Gives truer Joys than Crouds refus'd.
For what does Youth and Beauty serve?
Why more than all your Sex deserve?
Why such soft alluring Arts
To charm our Eyes, and melt our Hearts?
By our Loss you nothing gain,
Unless you love, you please in vain.

PHILIP AYRES

(1638-1683-1712)

To Love
A Sonnet[1]

LET others sing of *Mars*, and of his Train,
Of great Exploits, and Honourable Scars,
The many dire Effects of Civil Wars,
Death's Triumphs, and Encomiums of the Slain.
I sing the Conflicts I my self sustain,
With her (Great Love) the Cause of all my Cares,
Who wounds with Looks, and fetters with her Hairs.
This mournful Tale requires a Tragick Strain.
Eyes were the Arms, did first my Peace controul,
Wounded by them, a Source of Tears there sprung,
Running like Blood from my afflicted Soul;
Thou *Love*, to whom this Conquest does belong,
Leave me at least the Comfort to condole,
And as thou wound'st my Heart, inspire my Song.

[1] Published in *Lyric Poems*, 1687. Text of first edition.

To the Winds. A Song[1]

YE WINDS, that in your hasty Flight,
  Just kiss the Leaves, and then away,
The Leaves that tremble with Delight,
  And murmur at so short a stay;
  Stop here, and e're you further goe,
  Give audience to a Lover's Woe.

Condoling Air, to you I speak,
  Since she is deaf to all my Grief,
You see my Heart will quickly break,
  If careless She gives no Relief:
  I'm sure you're troubled at my Pain,
  For when I sigh, you sigh again.

Go, gentle Air, fly to my Dear,
  That thus with Love inflames my Breast,
And whisper softly in her Ear,
  'Tis she that robs my Soul of Rest:
  Express, if possible, such Moans,
  May imitate my dying Groans.

Or with thy rougher Breath make bold
  To toss the Treasure of her Hair,
Till thou dost all those Curls unfold
  Which cunningly Mens Hearts ensnare;
  Try all thy Skill to break the Net,
  That I, like thee, may Freedom get.

Then let some thicker Blasts arise,
  And with her Face so sport, and play,
Till the bright Rays of her fair Eyes
  Be qualify'd, or ta'en away;
  Make all those Charms which Men assail,
  Of lesser force, and less prevail.

[1] Published in *Lyric Poems*, 1687. Text of first edition.

To the Nightingale[1]

Why, Little Charmer of the Air,
Dost thou in Musick spend the Morn?
Whilst I thus languish in Despair,
Opprest by Cynthia'*s Hate and Scorn:*
Why dost thou sing, and hear me cry;
Tell, wanton Songster, tell me why?

WILT thou not cease at my Desire?
Will those small Organs never tire?
Nature did these close Shades prepare,
Not for thy Musick, but my Care:
Then why wilt thou persist to sing,
Thou Beautiful Malitious Thing?
When Kind *Aurora* first appears,
She weeps, in pity to my Tears;
If thus thou think'st to give Relief,
Thou never knew'st a Lover's Grief.
Then, Little Charmer, &c.
That dost in Musick, &c.

Thou Feather'd Atome, where in thee,
Can be compris'd such Harmony?
In whose small Fabrick must remain,
What Composition does contain,
All Griefs but mine are at a stand,
When thy surprising Tunes command?
How can so small a Tongue and Throat
Express so loud, and sweet a Note?
Thou hast more various Points at Will,
Than *Orpheus* had with all his Skill.
Then, Little Charmer, &c.
That dost in Musick, &c.

Great to the Ear, thô Small to Sight,
The Happy Lovers dear Delight,
Fly to the Bow'r where such are lade,
And there bestow thy Serenade.
Haste from my Sorrow, haste away;
Alas, there's Danger in thy Stay,
Lest hearing me so oft complain,
Should make thee change thy cheerful Strain,
Thy Songs cannot my Grief remove,
Thou harmless *Syren* of the Grove.

[1] Published in *Lyric Poems,* 1687. Text of first edition.

Then cease, thou Charmer of the Air,
No more in Musick spend the Morn,
With me that languish in Despair,
Opprest by Cynthia's *Hate and Scorn;*
And do not this Poor Boon deny,
I ask but Silence whilst I dye.

MATTHEW PRIOR

(1664-1687-1721)

On Exodus iii. 14. I am that I am. An Ode Written in 1688, as an Exercise at St. John's College, Cambridge[1]

I.

MAN! Foolish Man!
Scarce know'st Thou how thy self began:
Scarce hast Thou Thought enough to prove Thou art:
Yet steel'd with study'd Boldness, Thou dar'st try
To send thy doubting Reason's dazled Eye
Through the mysterious Gulph of vast Immensity.
Much Thou canst there discern, much thence impart.
Vain Wretch! suppress thy knowing Pride:
Mortifie thy learned Lust:
Vain are thy Thoughts; while Thou thy self are Dust.

II.

Let Wit her Sails, her Oars let Wisdom lend:
The Helm let Politick Experience guide:
Yet cease to hope thy short-liv'd Bark shall ride
Down spreading Fate's unnavigable Tide.
What, tho' still it farther tend?
Still 'tis farther from it's End;
And, in the Bosom of that boundless Sea,
Still finds it's Error lengthen with it's Way.

III.

With daring Pride and insolent Delight
Your Doubts resolv'd you boast, your Labours crown'd;

[1] Published in Dryden's *Miscellany,* Volume III, 1693. Text of *Poems,* 1718.

And, ΕΥΡΗΚΑ! your GOD, forsooth, is found
Incomprehensible and Infinite.
But is He therefore found? Vain Searcher! no:
Let your imperfect Definition show,
That nothing You, the weak Definer, know.

IV.

Say, why should the collected Main
It self within it self contain?
Why to its Caverns should it sometimes creep,
And with delighted Silence sleep
On the lov'd Bosom of it's Parent Deep?
Why shou'd it's num'rous Waters stay
In comely Discipline, and fair Array,
'Till Winds and Tides exert their high Commands?
Then prompt and ready to obey,
Why do the rising Surges spread
Their op'ning Ranks o'er Earth's submissive Head,
Marching thro' different Paths to different Lands?

V.

Why does the constant Sun
With measur'd Steps his radiant Journeys run?
Why does He order the Diurnal Hours
To leave Earth's other Part, and rise in Our's?
Why does He wake the correspondent Moon,
And fill her willing Lamp with liquid Light,
Commanding Her with delegated Pow'rs
To beautifie the World, and bless the Night?
Why does each animated Star
Love the just Limits of it's proper Sphere?
Why does each consenting Sign
With prudent Harmony combine
In Turns to move, and subsequent appear
To gird the Globe, and regulate the Year?

VI.

Man does with dangerous Curiosity
These unfathom'd Wonders try:
With fancy'd Rules and arbitrary Laws
Matter and Motion He restrains;
And study'd Lines, and fictious Circles draws:
Then with imagin'd Soveraignty
Lord of his new *Hypothesis* He reigns.

He reigns? How long? 'till some Usurper rise:
And He too, mighty thoughtful, mighty wise,
Studies new Lines, and other Circles feigns.
  From this last Toil again what Knowledge flows?
    Just as much, perhaps, as shows,
    That all his Predecessor's Rules
  Were empty *Cant*, all *Jargon* of the Schools;
  That he on t'other's Ruin rears his Throne;
And shows his Friend's Mistake, and thence confirms his own.

VII.

On Earth, in Air, amidst the Seas and Skies,
  Mountainous Heaps of Wonders rise;
  Whose tow'ring Strength will ne'er submit
To Reason's Batt'ries, or the Mines of Wit:
Yet still enquiring, still mistaking Man,
Each Hour repuls'd, each Hour dare onward press;
And levelling at GOD his wand'ring Guess
(That feeble Engine of his reasoning War,
Which guides his Doubts, and combats his Despair)
Laws to his Maker the learn'd Wretch can give;
Can bound that Nature, and prescribe that Will,
Whose pregnant Word did either Ocean fill;
Can tell us whence all BEINGS are, and how they move and live.
    Thro' either Ocean (foolish Man!)
    That pregnant Word sent forth again,
  Might to a World extend each ATOM there;
For every Drop call forth a Sea, a Heav'n for every Star.

VIII.

Let cunning Earth her fruitful Wonders hide;
And only lift thy stagg'ring Reason up
To trembling CALVARY's astonish'd Top:
Then mock thy Knowledge, and confound thy Pride,
Explaining how Perfection suffer'd Pain;
Almighty languish'd; and Eternal dy'd:
How by her Patient Victor Death was slain;
And Earth prophan'd, yet bless'd with Deicide.
Then down with all thy boasted Volumes, down:
  Only reserve the Sacred One:
    Low, reverently low,
  Make thy stubborn Knowledge bow;
Weep out thy Reason's, and thy Body's Eyes;
    Deject thy self, that Thou may'st rise;
To look to Heav'n, be blind to all below.

IX.

Then Faith, for Reason's glimmering Light, shall give
  Her Immortal Perspective;
And Grace's Presence Nature's Loss retrieve:
Then thy enliven'd Soul shall see,
That all the Volumes of Philosophy,
With all their Comments, never cou'd invent
  So politick an Instrument,
To reach the Heav'n of Heav'ns, the high Abode,
Where MOSES places his Mysterious GOD,
As was that Ladder which old JACOB rear'd,
When Light Divine had human Darkness clear'd;
And his enlarg'd Ideas found the Road,
Which Faith had dictated, and Angels trod.

The Secretary
Written at the Hague, in the Year 1696[1]

WHILE with labour assid'ous due pleasure I mix,
And in one day atone for the bus'ness of six,
In a little Dutch-chaise on a Saturday night,
On my left hand my HORACE, a NYMPH on my right.
No Memoire to compose, and no Post-Boy to move,
That on Sunday may hinder the softness of love;
For her, neither visits, nor parties of tea,
Nor the long-winded cant of a dull refugée.
This night and the next shall be her's, shall be mine,
To good or ill fortune the third we resign:
Thus scorning the world, and superior to fate,
I drive on my car in processional state;
So with PHIA thro' Athens PYSISTRATUS rode,
Men thought her MINERVA, and him a new GOD.
But why should I stories of Athens rehearse,
Where people knew love, and were partial to verse,
Since none can with justice my pleasures oppose,
In Holland half drowned in int'rest and prose:
By Greece and past ages, what need I be try'd,
When the Hague and the present, are both on my side,
And is it enough, for the joys of the day;
To think what ANACREON, or SAPPHO would say.
When good VANDERGOES, and his provident VROUGH,
As they gaze on my triumph, do freely allow,

[1] Published in *Works*, second ed., 1740. Text of first edition.

That search all the province, you'd find no man there is
So bless'd as the *Englishen Heer SECRETARIS*.

Adriani Morientis ad Animam Suam[1]

ANIMULA, vagula, blandula,
Hospes, Comesque Corporis,
Quæ nunc abibis in loca,
Pallidula, rigida, nudula?
Nec, ut soles, dabis joca.

By Monsieur Fontenelle.

Ma petite Ame, ma Mignonne,
Tu t'en vas donc, ma Fille, & Dieu sçaçhe où Tu vas:
Tu pars seulette, nuë, & tremblotante, Helas!
Que deviendra ton humeur foliçhonne?
Que deviendront tant de jolis ébats?

Imitated.

Poor little, pretty, flutt'ring Thing,
  Must We no longer live together?
And dost Thou prune thy trembling Wing,
  To take thy Flight Thou know'st not whither?

Thy humorous Vein, thy pleasing Folly
  Lyes all neglected, all forgot:
And pensive, wav'ring, melancholy,
  Thou dread'st and hop'st Thou know'st not what.

To a Lady: She Refusing to Continue a Dispute with Me, and Leaving Me in the Argument. An Ode[2]

SPARE, Gen'rous Victor, spare the Slave,
  Who did unequal War pursue;
That more than Triumph He might have,
  In being overcome by You.

In the Dispute whate'er I said,
  My Heart was by my Tongue bely'd;

[1] Published in Dryden's *Miscellany*, Volume V, 1704. Text of *Poems*, 1718.
[2] Published in Dryden's *Miscellany*, Volume V, 1704. Text of *Poems*, 1718.

And in my Looks You might have read,
  How much I argu'd on your side.

You, far from Danger as from Fear,
  Might have sustain'd an open Fight:
For seldom your Opinions err:
  Your Eyes are always in the right.

Why, fair One, would You not rely
  On Reason's Force with Beauty's join'd?
Could I their Prevalence deny;
  I must at once be deaf and blind.

Alas! not hoping to subdue,
  I only to the Fight aspir'd:
To keep the beauteous Foe in view
  Was all the Glory I desir'd.

But She, howe'er of Vict'ry sure,
  Contemns the Wreath too long delay'd;
And, arm'd with more immediate Pow'r,
  Calls cruel Silence to her Aid.

Deeper to Wound, She shuns the Fight:
  She drops her Arms, to gain the Field:
Secures her Conquest by her Flight;
  And triumphs, when She seems to yield.

So when the PARTHIAN turn'd his Steed,
  And from the Hostile Camp withdrew;
With cruel Skill the backward Reed
  He sent; and as He fled, He slew.

To a Child of Quality Five Years Old The Author Suppos'd Forty[1]

LORDS, Knights, and Squires, the num'rous Band
  That wear the Fair Miss *Mary*'s Fetters,
Were summon'd by her high Command,
  To show their Passion by their Letters.

My Pen amongst the rest I took,
  Least those bright Eyes that cannot read

[1] Published in Dryden's *Miscellany*, Volume V, 1704. Text of first edition.

Shou'd dart their kindling Fires, and look
The Pow'r they have to be obey'd.

Nor Quality, nor Reputation,
Forbid me yet my Flame to tell,
Dear Five Years old befriends my Passion,
And I may Write 'till she can Spell.

For while she makes her Silk-worms Beds
With all the tender things I swear,
Whilst all the House my Passion reads,
In Papers round her Baby's Hair.

She may receive and own my Flame,
For tho' the strictest *Prudes* shou'd know it,
She'll pass for a most virtuous Dame,
And I for an unhappy Poet.

Then too, alas, when she shall tear
The Lines some younger Rival sends,
She'll give me leave to Write, I fear,
And we shall still continue Friends.

For as our diff'rent Ages move,
'Tis so ordain'd, wou'd Fate but mend it,
That I shall be past making Love,
When she begins to comprehend it.

A Simile[1]

DEAR Thomas, didst Thou never pop
Thy Head into a Tin-man's Shop?
There, THOMAS, didst Thou never see
('Tis but by way of Simile)
A SQUIRREL spend his little Rage,
In jumping round a rowling Cage?
The Cage, as either Side turn'd up,
Striking a Ring of Bells a-top—?
Mov'd in the Orb, pleas'd with the Chimes,
The foolish Creature thinks he climbs:
But here or there, turn Wood or Wire,
He never gets two Inches higher.
So fares it with those merry Blades,
That frisk it under PINDUS' Shades.

[1] Published in *Poems*, 1707. Text of *Poems*, 1718.

In noble Songs, and lofty Odes,
They tread on Stars, and talk with Gods;
Still Dancing in an airy Round,
Still pleas'd with their own Verses Sound;
Brought back, how fast soe'er they go;
Always aspiring, always low.

An English Padlock[1]

MISS DANAE, when Fair and Young
(As HORACE has divinely sung)
Could not be kept from JOVE's Embrace
By Doors of Steel, and Walls of Brass.
The Reason of the Thing is clear;
Would JOVE the naked Truth aver:
CUPID was with Him of the Party;
And show'd himself sincere and hearty:
For, give That Whipster but his Errand;
He takes my Lord Chief Justice' Warrant:
Dauntless as Death away He walks;
Breaks the Doors open; snaps the Locks;
Searches the Parlour, Chamber, Study;
Nor stops, 'till He has CULPRIT's Body.
  Since This has been Authentick Truth,
By Age deliver'd down to Youth;
Tell us, mistaken Husband, tell us,
Why so Mysterious, why so Jealous?
Does the Restraint, the Bolt, the Bar
Make Us less Curious, Her less Fair?
The Spy, which does this Treasure keep,
Does She ne'er say her Pray'rs, nor sleep?
Does She to no Excess incline?
Does She fly Musick, Mirth, and Wine?
Or have not Gold and Flatt'ry Pow'r,
To purchase One unguarded Hour?
  Your Care does further yet extend:
That Spy is guarded by your Friend.——
But has This Friend nor Eye, nor Heart?
May He not feel the cruel Dart,
Which, soon or late, all Mortals feel?
May He not, with too tender Zeal,
Give the Fair Pris'ner Cause to see,
How much He wishes, She were free?
May He not craftily infer

[1] Published in *Poems*, 1707. Text of *Poems*, 1718.

The Rules of Friendship too severe,
Which chain Him to a hated Trust;
Which make Him Wretched, to be Just?
And may not She, this Darling She,
Youthful and healthy, Flesh and Blood,
Easie with Him, ill-us'd by Thee,
Allow this Logic to be good?
Sir, Will your Questions never end?
I trust to neither Spy nor Friend.
In short, I keep Her from the Sight
Of ev'ry Human Face.——She'll write.——
From Pen and Paper She's debarr'd.——
Has She a Bodkin and a Card?
She'll prick her Mind.——She will, You say:
But how shall She That Mind convey?
I keep Her in one Room: I lock it:
The Key (look here) is in this Pocket.
The Key-hole, is That left? Most certain.
She'll thrust her Letter thro'——Sir MARTIN.
Dear angry Friend, what must be done?
Is there no Way?——There is but One.
Send Her abroad; and let Her see,
That all this mingl'd Mass, which She
Being forbidden longs to know,
Is a dull Farce, an empty Show,
Powder, and Pocket-Glass, and Beau;
A Staple of Romance and Lies,
False Tears, and real Perjuries:
Where Sighs and Looks are bought and sold;
And Love is made but to be told:
Where the fat Bawd, and lavish Heir
The Spoils of ruin'd Beauty share:
And Youth seduc'd from Friends and Fame,
Must give up Age to Want and Shame.
Let Her behold the Frantick Scene,
The Women wretched, false the Men:
And when, these certain Ills to shun,
She would to Thy Embraces run;
Receive Her with extended Arms:
Seem more delighted with her Charms:
Wait on Her to the Park and Play:
Put on good Humour; make Her gay:
Be to her Virtues very kind:
Be to her Faults a little blind:
Let all her Ways be unconfin'd:
And clap your PADLOCK——on her Mind.

In Imitation of Anacreon[1]

LET 'em Censure: what care I?
The Herd of Criticks I defie.
Let the Wretches know, I write
Regardless of their Grace, or Spight.
No, no: the Fair, the Gay, the Young
Govern the Numbers of my Song.
All that They approve is sweet:
And All is Sense, that They repeat.
  Bid the warbling Nine retire:
VENUS, String thy Servant's Lyre:
Love shall be my endless Theme:
Pleasure shall triumph over Fame:
And when these Maxims I decline,
APOLLO, may Thy Fate be Mine:
May I grasp at empty Praise;
And lose the Nymph, to gain the Bays.

An Ode[2]

THE Merchant, to secure his Treasure,
  Conveys it in a borrow'd Name:
EUPHELIA serves to grace my Measure;
  But CLOE is my real Flame.

My softest Verse, my darling Lyre
  Upon EUPHELIA's Toylet lay;
When CLOE noted her Desire,
  That I should sing, that I should play.

My Lyre I tune, my Voice I raise;
  But with my Numbers mix my Sighs:
And whilst I sing EUPHELIA's Praise,
  I fix my Soul on CLOE's Eyes.

Fair CLOE blush'd: EUPHELIA frown'd:
  I sung and gaz'd: I play'd and trembl'd:
And VENUS to the LOVES around
  Remark'd, how ill We all dissembl'd.

[1] Published in *Poems*, 1709. Text of *Poems*, 1718.
[2] Published in *Poems*, 1709. Text of *Poems*, 1718.

A Song[1]

IF WINE and Musick have the Pow'r,
To ease the Sickness of the Soul;
Let PHOEBUS ev'ry String explòre;
And BACCHUS fill the sprightly Bowl.
Let Them their friendly Aid imploy,
To make my CLOE's Absence light;
And seek for Pleasure, to destroy
The Sorrows of this live-long Night.

But She to Morrow will return:
VENUS, be Thou to Morrow great;
Thy Myrtles strow, Thy Odours burn;
And meet Thy Fav'rite Nymph in State.
Kind Goddess, to no other Pow'rs
Let Us to Morrow's Blessings own:
Thy darling LOVES shall guide the Hours;
And all the Day be Thine alone.

Written in the Beginning of Mezeray's History of France[2]

WHATE'ER thy Countrymen have done,
By Law and Wit, by Sword and Gun,
In Thee is faithfully recited:
And all the Living World, that view
Thy Work, give Thee the Praises due:
At once Instructed and Delighted.

Yet for the Fame of all these Deeds,
What Beggar in the *Invalides*,
With Lameness broke, with Blindness smitten,
Wish'd ever decently to die,
To have been either *Mezeray*,
Or any Monarch He has written?

It strange, dear Author, yet it true is,
That down from *Pharamond* to *Loüis*,
All covet Life, yet call it Pain;

[1] Published in *Poems*, 1709. Text of *Poems*, 1718.
[2] Published in *Poems*, 1709. Text of first edition.

All feel the Ill, yet shun the Cure:
Can Sense this Paradox endure?
  Resolve me, *Cambray*, or *Fontaine*.

The Man in graver Tragic known,
Tho' his best Part long since was done,
  Still on the Stage desires to tarry:
And He who play'd the *Harlequin*,
After the Jest still loads the Scene,
  Unwilling to retire, tho' Weary.

A Dutch Proverb[1]

FIRE, Water, Woman, are Man's Ruin;
Says wise Professor VANDER BRÜIN.
By Flames a House I hir'd was lost
Last Year: and I must pay the Cost.
This Spring the Rains o'erflowed my Ground:
And my best Flanders Mare was drown'd.
A Slave I am to CLARA's Eyes:
The Gipsey knows her Pow'r, and flies.
Fire, Water, Woman, are My Ruin:
And great Thy Wisdom, VANDER BRÜIN.

To Cloe Weeping[2]

SEE, whilst Thou weep'st, fair CLOE, see
The World in Sympathy with Thee.
The chearful Birds no longer sing,
Each drops his Head, and hangs his Wing.
The Clouds have bent their Bosom lower,
And shed their Sorrows in a Show'r.
The Brooks beyond their Limits flow;
And louder Murmurs speak their Woe.
The Nymphs and Swains adopt Thy Cares:
They heave Thy Sighs, and weep Thy Tears.
Fantastic Nymph! that Grief should move
Thy Heart, obdurate against Love.
Strange Tears! whose Pow'r can soften All,
But That dear Breast on which they fall.

[1] Published in *Poems*, 1709. Text of *Poems*, 1718.
[2] Published in *Poems*, 1709. Text of *Poems*, 1718.

Picture of Seneca Dying in a Bath. By Jordain. At the Right Honorable the Earl of Exeter's at Burleigh-House[1]

WHILE cruel NERO only drains
The moral SPANIARD's ebbing Veins,
By Study worn, and slack with Age;
How dull, how thoughtless is his Rage!
Heighten'd Revenge He should have took:
He should have burnt his Tutor's Book;
And long have reign'd supream in Vice.
One nobler Wretch can only rise:
'Tis He whose Fury shall deface
The Stoick's Image in this Piece:
For while unhurt, divine JORDAIN,
Thy Work and SENECA's remain:
He still has Body, still has Soul,
And lives and speaks, restor'd and whole.

On Beauty. A Riddle[2]

RESOLVE Me, CLOE, what is THIS:
Or forfeit me One precious Kiss.
'Tis the first Off-spring of the Graces;
Bears diff'rent Forms in diff'rent Places;
Acknowledg'd fine, where-e'er beheld;
Yet fancy'd finer, when conceal'd.
'Twas FLORA's Wealth, and CIRCE's Charm;
PANDORA's Box of Good and Harm:
'Twas MARS's Wish, ENDYMION's Dream;
APELLES' Draught, and OVID's Theme.
THIS guided THESEUS thro' the Maze;
And sent Him home with Life and Praise.
But THIS undid the PHRYGIAN Boy;
And blew the Flames that ruin'd TROY.
THIS shew'd great Kindness to old GREECE,
And help'd rich JASON to the Fleece.
THIS thro' the East just Vengeance hurl'd,
And lost poor ANTHONY the World.
Injur'd, tho' LUCRECE found her Doom;
THIS banish'd Tyranny from ROME.

[1] Published in *Poems*, 1718. Text of first edition.
[2] Published in *Poems*, 1718. Text of first edition.

Appeas'd, tho' LAIS gain'd her Hire;
THIS set PERSEPOLIS on Fire.
For THIS ALCIDES learn'd to Spin;
His club laid down, and Lion's Skin.
For THIS APOLLO deign'd to keep,
With servile Care, a Mortal's Sheep.
For THIS the Father of the Gods,
Content to leave His high Abodes,
In borrow'd Figures loosely ran,
EUROPA's Bull, and LEDA's Swan.
For THIS He reassumes the Nod;
(While SEMELE commands the God)
Launces the Bolt, and shakes the Poles;
Tho' MOMUS laughs, and JUNO scolds.
Here list'ning CLOE smil'd, and said;
Your Riddle is not hard to read:
I Guess it—Fair one, if You do;
Need I, alas! the Theme pursue?
For THIS, Thou see'st, for THIS I leave,
Whate'er the World thinks Wise or Grave,
Ambition, Business, Friendship, News,
My useful Books, and serious Muse.
For THIS I willingly decline
The Mirth of Feasts, and Joys of Wine;
And chuse to sit and talk with Thee,
(As Thy great Orders may decree)
Of Cocks and Bulls, of Flutes and Fiddles,
Of Idle Tales, and foolish Riddles.

Cloe Jealous[1]

FORBEAR to ask Me, why I weep;
Vext CLOE to her Shepherd said:
'Tis for my Two poor stragling Sheep
Perhaps, or for my Squirrel dead.

For mind I what You late have writ?
Your subtle Questions, and Replies;
Emblems, to teach a Female Wit
The Ways, where changing CUPID flies.

Your Riddle, purpos'd to rehearse
The general Pow'r that Beauty has:
But why did no peculiar Verse
Describe one Charm of CLOE's Face?

[1] Published in *Poems*, 1718. Text of first edition.

The Glass, which was at VENUS' Shrine,
  With such Mysterious Sorrow laid:
The Garland (and You call it Mine)
  Which show'd how Youth and Beauty fade.

Ten thousand Trifles light as These
  Nor can my Rage, nor Anger move:
She shou'd be humble, who wou'd please:
  And She must suffer, who can love.

When in My Glass I chanc'd to look;
  Of VENUS what did I implore?
That ev'ry Grace which thence I took,
  Shou'd know to charm my DAMON more.

Reading Thy Verse; who heeds, said I,
  If here or there his Glances flew?
O free for ever be His Eye,
  Whose Heart to Me is always true.

My Bloom indeed, my little Flow'r
  Of Beauty quickly lost it's Pride:
For sever'd from it's Native Bow'r,
  It on Thy glowing Bosom dy'd.

Yet car'd I not, what might presage
  Or withering Wreath, or fleeting Youth:
Love I esteem'd more strong than Age,
  And Time less permanent than Truth.

Why then I weep, forbear to know:
  Fall uncontroll'd my Tears, and free:
O DAMON, 'tis the only Woe,
  I ever yet conceal'd from Thee.

The secret Wound with which I bleed
  Shall lie wrapt up, ev'n in my Herse:
But on my Tomb-stone Thou shalt read
  My Answer to Thy dubious Verse.

A Better Answer (To Cloe Jealous)[1]

DEAR CLOE, how blubber'd is that pretty Face?
  Thy Cheek all on Fire, and Thy Hair all uncurl'd:

[1] Published in *Poems*, 1718. Text of first edition.

Pr'ythee quit this Caprice; and (as old FALSTAF says)
Let Us e'en talk a little like Folks of This World.

How can'st Thou presume, Thou hast leave to destroy
The Beauties, which VENUS but lent to Thy keeping?
Those Looks were design'd to inspire Love and Joy:
More ord'nary Eyes may serve People for weeping.

To be vext at a Trifle or two that I writ,
Your Judgment at once, and my Passion You wrong:
You take that for Fact, which will scarce be found Wit:
Od's Life! must One swear to the Truth of a Song?

What I speak, my fair CLOE, and what I write, shews
The Diff'rence there is betwixt Nature and Art:
I court others in Verse; but I love Thee in Prose:
And They have my Whimsies; but Thou hast my Heart.

The God of us Verse-men (You know Child) the SUN,
How after his Journeys He sets up his Rest:
If at Morning o'er Earth 'tis his Fancy to run;
At Night he reclines on his THETIS's Breast.

So when I am weary'd with wand'ring all Day;
To Thee my Delight in the Evening I come:
No Matter what Beauties I saw in my Way:
They were but my Visits; but Thou art my Home.

Then finish, Dear CLOE, this Pastoral War;
And let us like HORACE and LYDIA agree:
For Thou art a Girl as much brighter than Her,
As He was a Poet sublimer than Me.

Epigram[1]

FRANK Carves very ill, yet will palm all the Meats:
He Eats more than Six; and Drinks more than he Eats.
Four Pipes after Dinner he constantly smokes;
And seasons his Whifs with impertinent Jokes.
Yet sighing, he says, We must certainly break;
And my cruel Unkindness compells him to speak:
For of late I invite Him—but Four Times a Week.

[1] Published in *Poems*, 1718. Text of first edition.

Another[1]

To JOHN I ow'd great Obligation;
But JOHN, unhappily, thought fit
To publish it to all the Nation:
Sure JOHN and I are more than Quit.

Another[2]

YES, every Poet is a Fool:
By Demonstration NED can show it:
Happy, cou'd NED's inverted Rule
Prove every Fool to be a Poet.

Phyllis's Age[3]

How old may PHYLLIS be, You ask,
Whose Beauty thus all Hearts engages?
To Answer is no easie Task;
For She has really two Ages.

Stiff in Brocard, and pinch'd in Stays,
Her Patches, Paint, and Jewels on;
All Day let Envy view her Face;
And PHYLLIS is but Twenty-one.

Paint, Patches, Jewels laid aside,
At Night Astronomers agree,
That Evening has the Day bely'd;
And PHYLLIS is some Forty-three.

[1] Published in *Poems*, 1718. Text of first edition.
[2] Published in *Poems*, 1718. Text of first edition.
[3] Published in *Poems*, 1718. Text of first edition.

An Epitaph[1]

Stet quicunque volet potens
Aulæ culmine lubrico, &c. Senec.

INTERR'D beneath this Marble Stone,
Lie Saunt'ring JACK, and Idle JOAN.
While rolling Threescore Years and One
Did round this Globe their Courses run;
If Human Things went Ill or Well;
If changing Empires rose or fell;
The Morning past, the Evening came,
And found this Couple still the same.
They Walk'd and Eat, good Folks: What then?
Why then They Walk'd and Eat again:
They soundly slept the Night away:
They did just Nothing all the Day:
And having bury'd Children Four,
Wou'd not take Pains to try for more.
Nor Sister either had, nor Brother:
They seem'd just Tally'd for each other.
  Their Moral and Oeconomy
Most perfectly They made agree:
Each Virtue kept it's proper Bound,
Nor Trespass'd on the other's Ground.
Nor Fame, nor Censure They regarded:
They neither Punish'd, nor Rewarded.
He car'd not what the Footmen did:
Her Maids She neither prais'd, nor chid:
So ev'ry Servant took his Course;
And bad at First, They all grew worse.
Slothful Disorder fill'd His Stable;
And sluttish Plenty deck'd Her Table.
Their Beer was strong; Their Wine was *Port*;
Their Meal was large; Their Grace was short.
They gave the Poor the Remnant-meat,
Just when it grew not fit to eat.
  They paid the Church and Parish-Rate;
And took, but read not the Receit:
For which They claim'd their *Sunday*'s Due,
Of slumb'ring in an upper Pew.
  No Man's Defects sought They to know;
So never made Themselves a Foe.
No Man's good Deeds did They commend;
So never rais'd Themselves a Friend.

[1] Published in *Poems*, 1718. Text of first edition.

Nor cherish'd They Relations poor:
That might decrease Their present Store:
Nor Barn nor House did they repair:
That might oblige Their future Heir.
They neither Added, nor Confounded:
They neither Wanted, nor Abounded.
Each *Christmas* They Accompts did clear;
And wound their Bottom round the Year.
Nor Tear, nor Smile did They imploy
At News of Public Grief, or Joy.
When Bells were Rung, and Bonfires made;
If ask'd, They ne'er deny'd their Aid:
Their Jugg was to the Ringers carry'd;
Who ever either Dy'd, or Marry'd.
Their Billet at the Fire was found;
Who ever was Depos'd, or Crown'd.
Nor Good, nor Bad, nor Fools, nor Wise;
They wou'd not learn, nor cou'd advise:
Without Love, Hatred, Joy, or Fear,
They led—a kind of—as it were:
Nor Wish'd, nor Car'd, nor Laugh'd, nor Cry'd:
And so They liv'd; and so They dy'd.

Down-Hall; a Ballad To the Tune of King John, and the Abbot of Canterbury[1]

I SING not old JASON, who Travell'd thro' *Greece*,
To Kiss the fair Maids, and possess the rich *Fleece:*
Nor Sing I ÆNEAS, who led by his Mother,
Got rid of One WIFE, and went far for another,
Derry down, down, hey derry down.

Nor Him who thro' *Asia* and *Europe* did roam,
ULYSSES by Name, who ne'er cry'd to go home;
But rather desir'd to see Cities and Men,
Than return to his Farms, and Converse with old PEN.

Hang HOMER and VIRGIL; their meaning to seek,
A Man must have pok'd in the *Latin* and *Greek*;
Those who Love our own Tongue, we have Reason to hope,
Have read them Translated by DRYDEN and POPE.

[1] Published in 1723. Text of *A New Collection of Poems. . . . By Mr. Prior, and Others*, 1725.

But I sing Exploits, that have lately been done
By Two *British* HEROES, call'd MATTHEW and JOHN:
And how they rid Friendly from fine *London*-Town,
Fair *Essex* to see, and a Place they call *DOWN*.

Now e'er they went out, you may rightly suppose,
How much they Discours'd, both in *Prudence* and *Prose:*
For before this great *Journey* was throughly concerted,
Full often they met; and as often they parted.

And thus *Matthew* said, look you here, my Friend *John*,
I fairly have Travell'd Years Thirty and One;
And tho' I still carry'd my *Soveraign*'s Warrants,
I only have gone upon other Folks Errands.

And now in this *Journey* of Life, I wou'd have
A Place where to Bait, t'wixt the *Court* and the *Grave*;
Where joyful to Live, not unwilling to Die—
Gadzooks, I have just such a Place in my Eye.

There are Gardens so Stately, and Arbors so Thick,
A *Portal* of Stone, and a *Fabrick* of Brick.
The Matter next Week shall be all in your Pow'r;
But the Money, *Gadzooks,* must be Paid in an Hour.

For Things in this World, must by Law be made certain,
We Both must repair unto OLIVER MARTIN;
For he is a *Lawyer* of worthy Renown.
I'll bring You to see; he must fix you at *DOWN*.

Quoth MATTHEW, I know, that from *Berwick* to *Dover*,
You have Sold all our Premisses over and over.
And now if your Buyers and Sellers agree,
You may throw all our Acres into the *South-Sea*.

But a word to the Purpose; To-morrow, dear Friend,
We'll see, what To-night you so highly commend.
And if with a Garden and House I am blest;
Let the *Devil* and *Con—y* go with the rest.

Then answer'd Squire MORLEY, pray get a *Calesch*,
That in *Summer* may Burn, and in *Winter* may Splash:
I love Dirt and Dust; and 'tis always my Pleasure,
To take with me much of the Soil which I Measure.

But *Matthew* thought better: for *Matthew* thought right,
And hired a *Chariot* so trim and so tight,

That extreams both of *Winter* and *Summer* might pass;
For one *Window* was *Canvas*, the t'other was *Glass*.

Draw up quoth Friend *Matthew*; pull down quoth Friend *John*,
We shall be both Hotter and Colder anon.
Thus Talking and Scolding, they forward did Speed;
And RALPHO pac'd by, under NEWMAN the Sweed.

Into an old Inn, did this Equipage roll,
At a Town they call *Hodsdon*, the Sign of the *Bull*,
Near a *Nymph* with an Urn, that divides the High-way,
And into a Puddle throws *Mother of Tea*.

Come here my sweet Landlady, pray how do you do?
Where is *Sisley* so cleanly, and *Prudence* and *Sue?*
And where is the Widow that dwelt here below?
And the Hostler that Sung about Eight Years ago?

And where is your Sister so mild and so dear?
Whose Voice to her Maids like a Trumpet was clear,
By my Troth, She replies, you grow Younger, I think:
And pray Sir, what Wine does the Gentleman drink?

Why now let me Die, Sir, or live upon Trust,
If I know to which Question to answer you first.
Why Things since I saw you, most strangely have vary'd,
And the Hostler is Hang'd, and the Widow is Marry'd.

And PRUE left a Child for the Parish to Nurse;
And SISLEY went off with a Gentleman's Purse;
And as to my Sister so mild and so dear,
She has lain in the Church-yard full many a Year.

Well, Peace to her Ashes; what signifies Grief:
She Roasted red-*Veal*, and she Powder'd lean-*Beef:*
Full nicely she knew to Cook up a fine Dish;
For tough was her *Pullets*, and tender her *Fish*.

For that matter, Sir, be ye Squire, Knight, or Lord,
I'll give you whate'er a good Inn can afford:
I shou'd look on myself as unhappily Sped,
Did I yield to a Sister, or Living, or Dead.

Of *Mutton*, a delicate Neck and a Breast,
Shall Swim in the *Water* in which they were Drest:
And because You great Folks are with Rarities taken,
Addle-*Eggs* shall be next Course, tost up with rank-*Bacon*.

The Supper was Serv'd, and the Sheets they were laid;
And MORLEY most lovingly whisper'd the Maid.
The Maid was She handsome? why truly so, so:
But what MORLEY whisper'd, we never shall know.

Then up rose these *Heroes* as brisk as the Sun,
And their Horses like his, were prepared to Run.
Now when in the Morning MATT. ask'd for the Score,
JOHN kindly had paid it the Evening before.

Their Breakfast so warm to be sure they did Eat:
A Custom in Travellers, mighty Discreet,
And thus with great Friendship and glee they went on
To find out the Place you shall hear of anon,
called Down, *down, hey derry down.*

But what did they talk of from Morning 'till Noon?
Why, of Spots in the *Sun*, and the Man in the *Moon:*
Of the CZAR's gentle Temper, the Stocks in the City,
The Wise Men of *Greece*, and the Secret-*Committee.*

So to HARLOW they came; and hey, where are You all?
Show Us into the Parlor, and mind when I call:
Why, your Maids have no motion, your Men have no life;
Well Master, I hear you have Bury'd your *Wife.*

Come this very instant, take Care to provide
Tea, Sugar, and *Toast*, and a *Horse*, and a *Guide.*
Are the *Harrison*'s here, both the Old and the Young?
And where stands fair DOWN, the delight of my Song?

O Squire, to the Grief of my Heart, I may say,
I have Bury'd Two *Wives* since you Travell'd this way;
And the *Harrison*'s both may be presently here;
And *DOWN* stands, I think where it stood the last Year.

Then JOAN brought the *Tea-pot*, and CALEB the *Toast*;
And the *Wine* was froth'd-out by the Hand of my Host:
But we clear'd our Extempore Banquet so fast,
That the *Harrison*'s both were forgot in the haste.

Now hey for *Down-Hall*; for the Guide he was got:
The *Chariot* was mounted; the *Horses* did trot;
The Guide he did bring us a Dozen Mile round:
But O! all in vain; for no *Down* cou'd be found.

O! thou *Popish* Guide, thou hast led us astray.
Says he; how the Devil shou'd I know the way?

I never yet travell'd this Road in my life:
But *Down* lyes on the left, I was told by my *Wife.*

Thy *Wife,* answer'd MATTHEW, when she went abroad,
Ne'er told Thee of half the bye-ways she had trod:
Perhaps She met Friends, and brought Pence to Thy House
But Thou shalt go home without ever a Souse.

What is this thing, MORLEY, and how can you mean it?
We have lost our Estate here, before we have seen it.
Have Patience, soft MORLEY in anger reply'd:
To find out our way, let us send off our Guide.

O here I spy *Down:* cast your Eye to the *West,*
Where a *Wind-mill* so stately stands plainly Confest.
On the *West* reply'd MATTHEW, no *Wind-mill* I find:
As well Thou may'st tell me, I see the *West-wind.*

Now pardon me, MORLEY, the *Wind-mill* I spy;
But faithful ACHATES, no House is there nigh.
Look again, says mild MORLEY, *Gadzooks* you are blind:
The *Mill* stands before; and the *House* lyes behind.

O now a low ruin'd white Shed I discern,
Untyl'd and unglaz'd; I believe 'tis a *Barn,*
A *Barn?* why you rave: 'Tis a *House* for a Squire,
A Justice of Peace, or a Knight of our Shire.

A House shou'd be Built, or with *Brick,* or with *Stone.*
Why, 'tis *Plaster* and *Lath*; and I think, that's all One.
And such as it is, it has stood with great Fame,
Been called a *Hall,* and has given its Name
To Down, *down, hey derry down.*

O MORLEY, O MORLEY, if that be a *Hall*;
The Fame with the Building will suddenly fall—
With your Friend JIMMY GIBBS about Buildings agree,
My Business is Land; and it matters not me.

I wish you cou'd tell, what a duce your head ails:
I show'd you *Down-Hall*; did you look for *Versailles?*
Then take House and Farm, as JOHN BALLET will let you:
For better for worse, as I took my Dame BETTY.

And now, Sir, a word to the Wise is enough;
You'll make very little of all your Old Stuff:
And to build at your Age, by my Troth, you grow simple.
Are You Young and Rich, like the *Master* of *Wimple*?

If You have these Whims of Apartments and Gardens,
From Twice Fifty Acres you'll ne'er see five Farthings:
And in Yours I shall find the true Gentleman's Fate:
E'er you finish your House, you'll have spent your Estate.

Now let Us touch Thumbs, and be Friends e'er we part.
Here, JOHN, is my Thumb; and here MATT, is my Heart.
To *Halstead* I speed; and You go back to Town.
Thus ends the *First part* of the *Ballad* of *DOWN*.
Derry down, down, hey derry down.

For My Own Monument[1]

As DOCTORS give physic by way of prevention,
MATT alive and in health, of his TOMB-STONE took care,
For delays are unsafe, and his pious intention
May haply be never fulfill'd by his Heir.

Then take MATT's word for it, the SCULPTOR is paid,
That the FIGURE is fine, pray believe your own eye,
Yet credit but lightly what more may be said,
For we flatter our selves, and teach marble to lye.

Yet counting as far as to FIFTY his years,
His virtues and vices were as other men's are,
High hopes he conceiv'd, and he smother'd great fears,
In a life party-colour'd, half pleasure, half care.

Nor to business a drudge, nor to faction a slave,
He strove to make int'rest and freedom agree,
In public employments industrious and grave,
And alone with his friends, Lord how merry was he.

Now in equipage stately, now humbly on foot,
Both fortunes he try'd, but to neither would trust,
And whirl'd in the round, as the wheel turn'd about,
He found riches had wings, and knew man was but dust.

This verse little polish'd, tho' mighty sincere
Sets neither his titles nor merit to view,
It says that his relics collected lie here,
And no mortal yet knows too if this may be true.

[1] Published in *Works*, 1740. Text of *Works*, second ed., 1740.

Fierce robbers there are that infest the highway,
So MATT may be kill'd, and his bones never found,
False witness at court, and fierce tempests at sea,
So MATT may yet chance to be hang'd, or be drown'd.

If his bones lie in earth, roll in sea, fly in air,
To Fate we must yield, and the thing is the same,
And if passing thou giv'st him a smile, or a tear,
He cares not—yet pr'ythee be kind to his FAME.

A Letter to the Honourable Lady Miss Margaret-Cavendish-Holles-Harley[1]

MY NOBLE, lovely, little PEGGY,
Let this, my FIRST-EPISTLE, beg ye,
At dawn of morn, and close of even,
To lift your heart and hands to heaven:
In double beauty say your pray'r,
Our father first, then *notre pere*;
And, dearest CHILD, along the day,
In ev'ry thing you do and say,
Obey and please my LORD and LADY,
So GOD shall love, and ANGELS aid, Ye.

If to these PRECEPTS You attend,
No SECOND-LETTER need I send,
And so I rest Your constant Friend,
M. P.

The Fortune-Teller
To a Young Lady in Search of Her Destiny[2]

YOU, MADAM, may with safety go,
Decrees of destiny to know.
For at your birth kind planets reign'd.
And certain happiness ordain'd:
Such charms as your's are only given
To chosen favourites of heaven.
But such is my uncertain state,
'Tis dangerous to try my fate:

[1] Published in *Works*, 1740. Text of *Works*, second ed., 1740.
[2] Published in *Works*, 1740. Text of *Works*, second ed., 1740.

For I would only know from art,
The future motions of your heart,
And what predestinated doom
Attends my love for years to come;
No secrets else, that mortals learn,
My care deserve, or life concern;
But this will so important be,
I dread to search the dark decree:
For while the smallest hope remains,
Faint joys are mingled with my pains.
Vain distant views my fancy please,
And give some intermitting ease:
But should the stars too plainly show
That you have doom'd my endless woe,
No human force, nor art, could bear
The torment of my wild despair.
  This secret then I dare not know,
And other truths are useless now.
What matters, if unblest in love,
How long or short my life will prove?
To gratify what low desire,
Should I with needless haste enquire,
How great, how wealthy, I shall be?
O! what is wealth or pow'r to me?
If I am happy, or undone,
It must proceed from You alone.

On a Pretty Madwoman[1]

WHILE mad OPHELIA we lament,
  And Her distraction mourn,
Our grief's misplac'd, Our tears mispent,
Since what for Her condition's meant
  More justly fits Our Own.

For if 'tis happiness to be,
  From all the turns of Fate,
From dubious joy, and sorrow free;
OPHELIA then is blest, and we
  Misunderstand Her state.

The Fates may do whate'er they will,
  They can't disturb her mind,
Insensible of good, or ill,

[1] Published in *Works*, 1740. Text of *Works*, second ed., 1740.

OPHELIA is OPHELIA still,
Be Fortune cross or kind.

Then make with reason no more noise,
Since what should give relief,
The quiet of Our mind destroys,
Or with a full spring-tide of joys,
Or a dead-ebb of grief.

Jinny the Just[1]

RELEAS'D from the noise of the Butcher and Baker,
Who, my old Friends be thanked, did seldom forsake her,
And from the soft Duns of my Landlord the Quaker,

From chiding the Footmen and watching the Lasses,
From Nell that burn'd Milk, and Tom that broke Glasses
(Sad mischiefs thro which a good housekeeper passes!)

From some real Care but more fancy'd vexation,
From a life party Colour'd, half reason half passion,
Here lies after all the best Wench in the Nation.

From the Rhine to the Po, from the Thames to the Rhone,
Joanna or Janneton, Jinny or Joan,
Twas all one to her by what name She was known,

For the Idiom of words very little She heeded,
Provided the Matter She drove at succeeded,
She took and gave Languages just as She needed.

So for Kitching and Market, for bargain & Sale,
She paid English or Dutch or French down on the Nail,
But in telling a Story she sometimes did fail;

Then begging Excuse as She happen'd to Stammer,
With respect to her betters but none to her Grammer,
Her blush helpt her out and her Jargon became her.

Her Habit and Mein she endeavor'd to frame
To the different Gout of the place where She came;
Her outside stil chang'd, but her inside the same:

[1] Published in 1907. Text of *Poems*, ed. Waller, 1907. Reprinted by permission of the Cambridge University Press. The punctuation has been supplied.

At the Hague in her Slippers & hair as the Mode is,
At Paris all Falbalow'd fine as a Goddess,
And at censuring London in smock sleeves and Bodice.

She order'd Affairs that few People cou'd tell
In what part about her that mixture did dwell
Of Vrough, or Mistress, or Medemoiselle.

For her Sirname and race let the Heraults e'en Answer;
Her own proper worth was enough to advance her,
And he who lik'd her, little valu'd her Grandsire.

But from what House so ever her lineage may come
I wish my own Jinny but out of her Tomb,
Tho all her Relations were there in her Room.

Of such terrible beauty She never cou'd boast
As with absolute Sway o'er all hearts rules the roast
When J— bawls out to the Chair for a Toast;

But of good Household Features her Person was made,
Nor by Faction cry'd up nor of Censure afraid,
And her beauty was rather for Use than Parade.

Her Blood so well mix't and flesh so well Pasted
That tho her Youth faded her Comliness lasted;
The blew was wore off, but the Plum was well tasted.

Less smooth than her Skin and less white than her breast
Was this pollisht stone beneath which she lyes prest:
Stop, Reader, and Sigh while thou thinkst on the rest.

With a just trim of Virtue her Soul was endu'd,
Not affectedly Pious nor secretly lewd
She cut even between the Cocquet and the Prude.

Her Will with her Duty so equally stood
That seldom oppos'd She was commonly good,
And did pritty well, doing just what she wou'd.

Declining all Pow'r she found means to perswade,
Was then most regarded when most she Obey'd,
The Mistress in truth when she seem'd but the Maid.

Such care of her own proper Actions She took
That on other folks lives She had no time to look,
So Censure and Praise were struck out of her Book.

Her thought stil confin'd to its own little Sphere,
She minded not who did Excell or did Err
But just as the matter related to her.

Then too when her Private Tribunal was rear'd
Her Mercy so mix'd with her judgment appear'd
That her Foes were condemn'd & her friends always clear'd.

Her Religion so well with her learning did suite
That in Practice sincere, and in Controverse Mute,
She shew'd She knew better to live than dispute.

Some parts of the Bible by heart She recited,
And much in historical Chapters delighted,
But in points about Faith She was something short sighted;

So Notions and modes She refer'd to the Schools,
And in matters of Conscience adher'd to Two Rules,
To advise with no Biggots, and jest with no Fools.

And scrupling but little, enough she believ'd,
By Charity ample smal sins She retriev'd,
And when she had New Cloaths She always receiv'd.

Thus stil whilst her Morning unseen fled away
In ord'ring the Linnen and making the Tea
That she scarce cou'd have time for the Psalms of the Day;

And while after Dinner the Night came so soon
That half she propos'd very seldom was done;
With twenty God bless Me's how this day is gone;

While she read and Accounted & payd & abated,
Eat and drank, Play'd & Work't, laught & Cry'd, lov'd & hated,
As answer'd the end of her being Created:

In the midst of her Age came a cruel Desease
Which neither her Julips nor recepts cou'd appease;
So down dropt her Clay, may her Soul be at peace.

Retire from this Sepulchre all the Prophane,
You that love for Debauch, or that marry for gain,
Retire least Ye trouble the Manes of J——

But Thou that know'st Love above Intrest or lust,
Strew the Myrtle and Rose on this once belov'd Dust,
And shed one pious tear upon Jinny the Just.

Tread soft on her Grave, and do right to her honor,
Let neither rude hand nor ill Tongue light upon her,
Do all the smal Favors that now can be done her.

And when what Thou lik't shal return to her Clay,
For so I'm perswaded she must do one Day
What ever fantastic J.... Asgil may say,

When as I have done now, thou shalt set up a Stone
For something however distinguisht or known,
May some Pious Friend the Misfortune bemoan,
And make thy Concern by reflexion his own.

DANIEL DEFOE

(1660-1691-1731)

The True-Born Englishman[1]

Part I

WHERE-EVER God erects a House of Prayer,
The Devil always builds a Chapel there:
And 'twill be found upon Examination,
The latter has the largest Congregation:
For ever since he first debauch'd the Mind,
He made a perfect Conquest of Mankind.
With Uniformity of Service, he
Reigns with a general Aristocracy.
No Nonconforming Sects disturb his Reign,
For of his Yoak there's very few Complain.
He knows the Genius and the Inclination,
And matches proper Sins for ev'ry Nation.
He needs no Standing-Army Government;
He always Rules us by our own Consent:
His Laws are easie, and his gentle Sway
Makes it exceeding pleasant to obey.
The List of his Vice-gerents and Commanders,
Out-does your *Cæsars*, or your *Alexanders*.
They never fail of his infernal Aid,
And he's as certain ne'er to be betray'd.

[1] Published in 1701. Text of *A True Collection of the Writings of the Author of The True-Born Englishman*, 1703.

Thro' all the World they spread his vast Command,
And death's Eternal Empire is maintain'd.
They rule so politickly and so well,
As if they were Lords Justices of Hell.
Duly divided to debauch Mankind,
And plant Infernal Dictates in his Mind.
 Pride, the first Peer, and President of Hell,
To his share *Spain*, the largest Province, fell.
The subtile Prince thought fittest to bestow
On these the Golden Mines of *Mexico*;
With all the Silver Mountains of *Peru*;
Wealth which would in wise hands the World undo:
Because he knew their Genius to be such;
Too Lazy and too Haughty to be Rich.
So proud a People, so above their Fate,
That if reduc'd to beg, they'll beg in State.
Lavish of Money, to be counted Brave,
And proudly starve, because they scorn to save.
Never was Nation in the World before,
So very Rich, and yet so very Poor.
 Lust chose the Torrid Zone of *Italy*,
Where Blood ferments in Rapes and Sodomy:
Where swelling Veins o'erflow with livid Streams,
With Heat impregnate from *Vesuvian* Flames:
Whose flowing Sulphur forms Infernal Lakes,
And humane Body of the Soil partakes.
There Nature ever burns with hot Desires,
Fann'd with Luxuriant Air from Subterranean Fires:
Here undisturb'd in Floods of scalding Lust,
Th' Infernal King reigns with Infernal Gust.
 Drunk'nness, the Darling Favourite of Hell,
Chose *Germany* to Rule; and Rules so well,
No Subjects more obsequiously obey,
None please so well, or are so pleas'd as they.
The cunning Artist manages so well,
He lets them Bow to Heav'n, and Drink to Hell.
If but to Wine and him they Homage pay,
He cares not to what Deity they Pray,
What God they worship most, or in what way.
Whether by *Luther*, *Calvin*, or by *Rome*,
They sail for Heav'n, by Wine he steers them home.
 Ungovern'd Passion settled first in *France*,
Where Mankind Lives in Haste, and Thrives by Chance,
A *Dancing Nation*, Fickle and Untrue:
Have oft undone themselves, and others too:
Prompt the Infernal Dictates to Obey,
And in Hell's Favour none more great than they.

The *Pagan* World he blindly leads away,
And Personally Rules with Arbitrary Sway:
The Mask thrown off, *Plain Devil* his Title stands;
And what elsewhere he Tempts, he there Commands.
There with full Gust th' Ambition of his Mind
Governs, as he of old in Heav'n design'd.
Worship'd as God, his *Painim Altars* smoke,
Embru'd with Blood of those that him Invoke.
The rest by Deputies he Rules as well,
And plants the distant Colonies of Hell.
By them his Secret Power he well maintains,
And binds the World in his Infernal Chains.
By Zeal the *Irish*; and the *Rush* by Folly:
Fury the *Dane*: The *Swede* by Melancholy:
By stupid Ignorance the *Muscovite:*
The *Chinese* by a *Child of Hell*, call'd Wit;
Wealth makes the *Persian* too Effeminate:
And Poverty the *Tartars* Desperate:
The *Turks* and *Moors* by *Mah'met* he subdues:
And God has given him leave to rule the Jews:
Rage rules the *Portuguese*, and Fraud the *Scotch:*
Revenge the *Pole*; and Avarice the *Dutch.*
Satyr be kind, and draw a silent Veil,
Thy *Native England*'s Vices to conceal:
Or if that Task's impossible to do,
At least be just, and show her Vertues too;
Too Great the first, Alas! the last too Few.
England unknown as yet, unpeopled lay;
Happy, had she remain'd so to this Day,
And not to ev'ry Nation been a Prey.
Her open Harbours, and her Fertile Plains,
The Merchants Glory these, and those the Swains,
To ev'ry Barbarous Nation have betray'd her,
Who Conquer her as oft as they Invade her.
So Beauty Guarded but by Innocence,
That Ruins her which should be her Defence.
Ingratitude, a Devil of *Black Renown*,
Possess'd her very early for his own.
An Ugly, Surly, Sullen, Selfish Spirit,
Who Satan'*s worst Perfections does Inherit:*
Second to him in Malice and in Force,
All *Devil without*, and all *within* him *Worse.*
He made her First-born Race to be so rude,
And suffered her to be so oft subdu'd:
By sev'ral Crowds of wand'ring Thieves o'er-run,
Often unpeopl'd, and as oft undone.
While ev'ry Nation that her Powers reduc'd,
Their Languages and Manners introduc'd.

From whose mix'd Relicks our Compounded Breed,
By Spurious Generation does succeed;
Making a Race uncertain and unev'n,
Deriv'd from all the Nations under Heav'n.
The *Romans* first with *Julius Cæsar* came,
Including all the Nations of that Name,
Gauls, *Greeks*, and *Lombards*; and by Computation,
Auxiliaries, or Slaves of ev'ry Nation.
With *Hengist*, *Saxons; Danes* with *Sueno* came,
In search of Plunder, not in search of Fame.
Scots, *Picts*, and *Irish* from th' *Hibernian* Shore;
And Conqu'ring *William* brought the *Normans* o'er.
All these their Barb'rous Off-spring left behind,
The Dregs of Armies, they of all Mankind;
Blended with *Britains* who before were here,
Of whom the *Welsh* ha' blest the Character.
From this Amphibious Ill-born Mob began
That vain ill-natur'd thing, an English-man.
The Customs, Sir-names, Languages, and Manners,
Of all these Nations are their own Explainers:
Whose Relicks are so lasting and so strong,
They ha' left a *Shiboleth* upon our Tongue;
By which with easie search you may distinguish
Your *Roman-Saxon-Danish-Norman* English.
The great Invading *Norman* let us know
What Conquerors in After-Times might do
To ev'ry *Musqueteer* he brought to *Town*,
He gave the Lands which never were his own.
When first the *English* Crown he did obtain,
He did not send his *Dutchmen* home again.
No Re-assumptions in his Reign were known,
Davenant might there ha' let his Book alone.
No Parliament his Army cou'd disband;
He rais'd no Money, for he paid in Land.
He gave his Legions their Eternal Station,
And made them all Free-holders of the Nation.
He Canton'd out the Country to his Men,
And ev'ry Soldier was a Denizen.
The Rascals thus Enrich'd, he call'd them *Lords*,
To please their Upstart Pride with new made Words;
And *Doomsday-Book* his Tyranny Records.
And here begins our Ancient Pedigree
That so exalts our poor Nobility:
'Tis that from some *French* Trooper they derive,
Who with the *Norman* Bastard did arrive:
The Trophies of the Families appear;
Some show the Sword, the Bow, and some the Spear,
Which their Great Ancestor, *forsooth*, did wear.

These in the Herald's Register remain,
Their Noble mean Extraction to explain.
Yet who the Heroe was, no Man can tell,
Whether a Drummer or a Colonel:
The silent Record Blushes to reveal
Their Undescended Dark Original.
But grant the best, How came the Change to pass;
A *True-Born Englishman* of *Norman* Race?
A *Turkish* Horse can show more History,
To prove his Well-descended Family.
Conquest, as by the Moderns 'tis exprest,
May give a Title to the Lands possest:
But that the Longest Sword shou'd be so Civil,
To make a *Frenchman English*, that's the Devil.
These are the Heroes who despise the *Dutch*,
And rail at new-come Foreigners so much;
Forgetting that themselves are all deriv'd
From the most Scoundrel Race that ever liv'd,
A horrid Crowd of Rambling Thieves and Drones,
Who ransack'd Kingdoms, and dispeopled Towns.
The *Pict* and Painted *Britain*, Treach'rous *Scot*,
By Hunger, Theft, and Rapine, hither brought;
Norwegian Pirates, Buccaneering *Danes*,
Whose Red-hair'd Off-spring ev'ry where remains:
Who join'd with *Norman-French* compound the Breed
From whence your *True-Born Englishmen* proceed.
And lest by Length of Time it be pretended,
The Climate may this Modern Breed ha' mended;
Wise Providence to keep us where we are,
Mixes us daily with exceeding Care:
We have been *Europe*'s Sink, *the Jakes* where she
Voids all her Offal Out-cast Progeny.
From our Fifth *Henry*'s time, the Strolling Bands
Of banish'd Fugitives from Neighb'ring Lands,
Have here a certain Sanctuary found:
Th' Eternal Refuge of the Vagabond.
Where in but half a common Age of Time,
Borr'wing new Blood and Manners from the Clime,
Proudly they learn all Mankind to contemn,
And all their Race are *True-Born Englishmen.*
Dutch, Walloons, Flemmings, Irishmen, and *Scots,*
Vaudois and *Valtolins*, and *Hugonots*,
In good Queen *Bess*'s Charitable Reign,
Supply'd us with three hundred thousand Men.
Religion, *God we thank thee*, sent them hither,
Priests, Protestants, the Devil and all together:
Of all Professions, and of ev'ry Trade,
All that were persecuted or afraid;

Whether for Debt, or other Crimes they fled,
David at *Hackelah* was still their Head.
  The Off-spring of this Miscellaneous Crowd,
Had not their new Plantations long enjoy'd,
But they grew *Englishmen*, and rais'd their Votes
At Foreign Shoals of *Interloping Scots*.
The Royal Branch from *Pict-land* did succeed,
With Troops of *Scots*, and Scabs from *North-by-Tweed*.
The Seven first Years of his Pacifick Reign
Made him and half his Nation *Englishmen*.
Scots from the *Northern* Frozen Banks of *Tay*,
With Packs and Plods came *Whigging* all away:
Thick as the Locusts which in *Ægypt* swarm'd,
With Pride and hungry Hopes compleatly arm'd:
With Native *Truth, Diseases*, and no *Money*,
Plunder'd our *Canaan* of the Milk and Honey.
Here they grew quickly Lords and Gentlemen,
And all their Race are *True-Born* Englishmen.
  The Civil Wars, the common Purgative,
Which always use to make the Nation thrive,
Made way for all that strolling Congregation,
Which throng'd in Pious *Ch——s*'s Restoration.
The *Royal Refugee* our Breed restores,
With *Foreign Courtiers*, and with *Foreign Whores*:
And carefully repeopled us again,
Throughout his Lazy, Long, Lascivious Reign;
With such a blest and True-born *English* Fry,
As much Illustrates our Nobility.
A Gratitude which will so black appear,
As future Ages must abhor to hear:
When they look back on all that Crimson Flood,
Which stream'd in *Lindsey*'s, and *Caernarvon*'s Blood:
Bold *Strafford, Cambridge, Capel, Lucas, Lisle*,
Who crown'd in Death his Father's Fun'ral Pile.
The loss of whom, in order to supply,
With *True-Born*-English Nobility,
Six Bastard Dukes survive his Luscious Reign,
The Labours of *Italian Castlemain*,
French Portsmouth, Taby Scot, and *Cambrian*.
Besides the Num'rous Bright and Virgin Throng,
Whose Female Glories shade them from my Song.
  This Off-spring, if one Age they multiply,
May half the House with *English* Peers supply:
There with true *English* Pride they may contemn
Schomberg and *Portland*, new made Noblemen.
  French Cooks, *Scotch* Pedlars, and *Italian* Whores,
Were all made Lords, or Lords Progenitors.

Beggars and Bastards by his new Creation,
Much multiply'd the P——ge of the Nation;
Who will be all, e'er one short Age runs o'er,
As *True-Born* Lords as those we had before.
  Then to recruit the Commons he prepares,
And heal the Latent Breaches of the Wars;
The Pious Purpose better to advance,
H'invites the banish'd Protestants of *France*:
Hither for Gods-sake and their own they fled,
Some for Religion came, and some for Bread:
Two hundred Thousand Pair of Wooden Shooes,
Who, God be thank'd had nothing left to lose;
To Heav'n's great Praise did for Religion fly,
To make us starve our Poor in Charity.
In ev'ry Port they plant their fruitful Train,
To get a Race of *True-Born* Englishmen:
Whose Children will, when Riper Years they see,
Be as Ill-natur'd and as Proud as we:
Call themselves *English*, Foreigners despise,
Be Surly like us all, and just as Wise.
  Thus from a Mixture of all Kinds began,
That Het'rogeneous *Thing, An Englishman*:
In eager Rapes, and furious Lust begot,
Betwixt a Painted *Britain* and a *Scot*.
Whose gend'ring Off-spring quickly learn'd to Bow,
And yoke their Heifers to the *Roman* Plough:
From whence a Mongrel half-Bred Race there came,
With neither Name, nor Nation, Speech or Fame.
In whose hot Veins new Mixtures quickly ran,
Infus'd betwixt a *Saxon* and a *Dane*.
While their Rank Daughters, to their Parents just,
Receiv'd all Nations with Promiscuous Lust.
This Nauseous Brood directly did contain
The well-extracted Blood of *Englishmen*.
  Which Medly canton'd in a Heptarchy,
A Rhapsody of Nations to supply,
Among themselves maintain'd eternal Wars,
And still the Ladies Lov'd the Conquerors.
  The *Western* Angles all the rest subdu'd;
A bloody Nation, barbarous and rude:
Who by the *Tenure* of the Sword possest
One part of *Britain*, and subdu'd the rest.
And as great things denominate the small,
The Conqu'ring part gave *Title* to the whole.
The *Scot, Pict, Britain, Roman, Dane*, submit,
And with the *English-Saxon* all Unite:
And these the mixture have so close pursu'd,

The very Name and Memory's subdu'd:
No *Roman* now, no *Britain* does remain;
Wales strove to separate, but strove in Vain:
The silent Nations undistinguish'd fall,
And *Englishman*'s the common Name for all.
Fate jumbled them together, *God knows how*;
What e'er they were they're *True-Born English* now.
  The Wonder which remains is at our Pride,
To value that which all wise Men deride.
For *Englishmen* to boast of Generation,
Cancels their Knowledge, and Lampoons the Nation.
A *True-Born Englishman*'s a Contradiction,
In Speech an Irony, in Fact a Fiction.
A Banter made to be a test of Fools,
Which those that use it justly ridicules.
A Metaphor invented to express
A Man *a-kin* to all the Universe.
  For as the *Scots*, as Learned Men ha' said,
Throughout the World their Wand'ring Seed ha' spread;
So open-handed *England*, 'tis Believ'd,
Has all the Gleanings of the World Receiv'd.
  Some think of *England* 'twas our Saviour meant,
The Gospel should to all the World be sent:
Since, when the Blessed Sound did hither reach,
They to all Nations might be said to Preach.
  'Tis well that Virtue gives Nobility,
How shall we else the want of Birth and Blood supply?
Since scarce one Family is left alive,
Which does not from some Foreigner derive.
Of sixty thousand *English* Gentlemen,
Whose Names and Arms in Registers remain,
We challenge all our Heralds to declare
Ten Families which *English-Saxons* are.
  France justly boasts the Ancient Noble Line
Of *Bourbon, Mommorency,* and *Lorrain.*
The *Germans* too their House of *Austria* show,
And *Holland* their Invincible *Nassau.*
Lines which in Heraldry were ancient grown,
Before the Name of *Englishman* was known.
Even *Scotland* too, her Elder Glory shows,
Her *Gourdons, Hamiltons*, and her *Monroes*;
Douglas, Mackays, and *Grahams*, Names well known,
Long before Ancient *England* knew her own.
  But *England*, Modern to the last degree,
Borrows or makes her own Nobility,
And yet she boldly boasts of Pedigree:
Repines that Foreigners are put upon her,
And talks of her Antiquity and Honour:

Her *S——lls, S——ls, C——ls, De——la, M——rs,*
M——ns and *M——ues, D—s*, and *V——rs*,
Not one have *English* Names, yet all are *English* Peers.
Your *Houblons, Papillons*, and *Lethuliers*,
Pass now for *True-born-English* Knights and Squires,
And make good Senate Members, or Lord-Mayors.
Wealth, howsoever got, in *England* makes
Lords of Mechanicks, Gentlemen of Rakes:
Antiquity and Birth are needless here;
'Tis Impudence and Money makes a P——r.
  Innumerable City-Knights we know,
From *Blewcoat-Hospitals* and *Bridewel* flow.
Draymen and Porters fill the City Chair,
And Foot-Boys Magisterial Purple wear.
Fate has but very small Distinction set
Betwixt the *Counter* and the Coronet.
Tarpaulin L——ds, Pages of high Renown,
Rise up by Poor Mens Valour, not their own.
Great Families of yesterday we show,
And Lords, whose Parents were *the Lord knows who.*

WILLIAM WALSH

(1663-1691-1708)

The Despairing Lover[1]

DISTRACTED with Care,
For *Phillis* the Fair;
Since nothing cou'd move her,
Poor *Damon*, her Lover,
Resolves in Despair
No longer to languish,
Nor bear so much Anguish;

But, mad with his Love,
To a Precipice goes;
Where, a Leap from above
Wou'd soon finish his Woes.

When in Rage he came there,
Beholding how steep

[1] Published in Dryden's *Miscellany*, Volume V, 1704. Text of first edition.

The Sides did appear,
And the Bottom how deep;
His Torments projecting,
And sadly reflecting,
That a Lover forsaken
A new Love may get;
But a Neck, when once broken,
Can never be set:
And, that he cou'd die
Whenever he wou'd;
But, that he cou'd live
But as long as he cou'd:
How grievous soever
The Torment might grow,
He scorn'd to endeavour
To finish it so.
But Bold, Unconcern'd
At Thoughts of the Pain,
He calmly return'd
To his Cottage again.

To His Book[1]

Go, LITTLE book, and to the world impart,
The faithful image of an am'rous heart;
Those who love's dear, deluding pains have known,
May in my fatal stories read their own.
Those who have liv'd from all its torments free,
May find the thing they never felt, by me;
Perhaps advis'd, avoid the guilded bait,
And, warn'd by my example, shun my fate.
While with calm joy, safe landed on the coast,
I view the waves on which I once was tost.
Love is a medley of endearments, jars,
Suspicions, quarrels, reconcilements, wars;
Then peace again. Oh! wou'd it not be best,
To chase the fatal poison from our breast?
But since so few can live from passion free,
Happy the man, and only happy he,
Who with such lucky stars begins his love,
That his cool judgment does his choice approve.
Ill-grounded passions quickly wear away;
What's built upon esteem, can ne'er decay.

[1] Published in *Works*, 1736. Text of *The Works of the Most Celebrated Minor Poets*, Volume II, 1749.

Elegy
The Unrewarded Lover[1]

LET the dull merchant curse his angry fate,
And from the winds and waves his fortune wait:
Let the loud lawyer break his brains, and be
A slave to wrangling coxcombs for a fee:
Let the rough soldier fight his prince's foes,
And for a livelihood his life expose:
I wage no war, I plead no cause but love's,
I fear no storms, but what Celinda moves.
And what grave censor can my choice despise?
But here, fair charmer, here the diff'rence lies;
The merchant, after all his hazards past,
Enjoys the fruit of his long toils at last;
The soldier high in his king's favour stands,
And after having long obey'd, commands;
The lawyer, to reward his tedious care,
Roars on the bench, that babbled at the bar;
While I take pains to meet a fate more hard,
And reap no fruit, no favour, no reward.

JONATHAN SWIFT

(1667-1691-1745)

To Their Excellencies the Lords Justices of Ireland. The Humble Petition of Frances Harris, Who Must Starve, and Die a Maid if It Miscarries Written in the Year 1701[2]

Humbly sheweth,
THAT I went to warm myself in Lady *Betty*'s Chamber, because I was cold;
And I had in a Purse Seven Pounds, Four Shillings and Six Pence, (besides Farthings,) in Money and Gold;
So, because I had been buying Things for my *Lady* Last Night,

[1] Published in *Works*, 1736. Text of *The Works of the Most Celebrated Minor Poets*, Volume II, 1749.
[2] Written in 1701. Published in 1709. Text of *Works*, Dublin, 1735, Volume II.

I was resolv'd to tell my Money, to see if it was right.
Now you must know, because my Trunk has a very bad Lock,
Therefore all the Money I have, (which, God knows, is a very small Stock,)
I keep in my Pocket, ty'd about my Middle, next my Smock.
So, when I went to put up my Purse, as God would have it, my Smock was unript;
And instead of putting it into my Pocket, down it slipt:
Then the Bell rung, and I went down to put my *Lady* to Bed;
And, God knows, I thought my Money was as safe as my Maidenhead.
So, when I came up again, I found my Pocket feel very light,
But when I search'd, and miss'd my Purse, *Lord!* I thought, I should have sunk outright:
Lord! Madam, says *Mary*, how d'ye do? Indeed, said I, never worse.
But pray, *Mary*, can you tell what I have done with my Purse:
Lord help me, said *Mary*, I never stirr'd out of this Place:
Nay, said I, I had it in Lady *Betty*'s Chamber, that's a plain Case.
So *Mary* got me to Bed, and cover'd me up warm;
However, she stole away my Garters that I might do myself no Harm.
So, I tumbled and toss'd all Night, as you may very well think;
But hardly ever set my Eyes together, or slept a Wink.
So, I was adream'd, methought, that we went and search'd the Folks round:
And in a Corner of Mrs. *Duke*'s Box, ty'd in a Rag, the Money was found.
So, next Morning we told *Whittle*, and he fell a-swearing;
Then my Dame *Wadgar* came, and she, you know, is thick of Hearing:
Dame, said I, as loud as I could bawl, do you know what a Loss I have had?
Nay, said she, my Lord *Collway*'s Folks are all very sad;
For my Lord *Dromedary* comes a *Tuesday* without fail;
Pugh! said I, but that's not the Business that I ail.
Says *Cary*, says he, I have been a Servant this Five and Twenty Years, come Spring;
And in all the Places I liv'd, I never heard of such a Thing.
Yes, says the Steward, I remember, when I was at my Lady *Shrewsbury*'s,
Such a Thing as this happen'd, just about the time of *Gooseberries*.
So I went to the Party suspected, and I found her full of Grief;
(Now you must know, of all things in the World, I hate a Thief.)
However, I was resolv'd to bring the Discourse slily about;
Mrs. *Dukes*, said I, here's an ugly Accident has happen'd out:

'Tis not that I value the Money three Skips of a Louse;
But the Thing I stand upon is, the Credit of the House:
'Tis true, Seven Pounds, Four Shillings, and Six Pence, makes a great Hole in my Wages;
Besides, as they say, Service is no Inheritance in these Ages.
Now, Mrs. *Dukes*, you know, and every Body understands,
That tho' 'tis hard to judge, yet Money can't go without Hands.
The *Devil* take me, said she (blessing her self,) if ever I saw't!
So she roar'd like a *Bedlam*, as tho' I had call'd her all to naught:
So you know, what could I say to her any more:
I e'en left her, and came away as wise as I was before.
Well: But then they would have had me gone to the *Cunning-Man:*
No, said I, 'tis the same Thing, the *Chaplain* will be here anon.
So the *Chaplain* came in. Now the Servants say he is my Sweet-heart,
Because he's always in my Chamber, and I always take his Part;
So, as the *Devil* would have it, before I was aware, out I blunder'd,
Parson, said I, can you cast a *Nativity*, when a Body's plunder'd?
(Now you must know, he hates to be call'd *Parson* like the *Devil.*)
Truly, says he, Mrs. *Nab*, it might become you to be more civil:
If your Money be gone, as a learned *Divine* says, d'ye see,
You are no *Text* for my handling, so take that from me:
I was never taken for a *Conjurer* before, I'd have you to know:
Lord, said I, don't be angry, I am sure I never thought you so:
You know, I honour the Cloth; I design to be a *Parson*'s Wife;
I never took one in *your Coat* for a *Conjurer* in all my Life.
With that, he twisted his Girdle at me like a Rope; as who should say,
Now you may go hang yourself for me; and so went away.
Well; I thought, I should have swoon'd: *Lord*, said I, what shall I do?
I have lost my *Money*; and I shall lose my *True-love* too.
So, my *Lord* call'd me; *Harry*, said my *Lord*, don't cry,
I'll give something towards thy Loss: And says my *Lady*, so will I.
Oh! but said I; what if after all, the Chaplain won't *come to*?
For that, he said, (an't please your *Excellencies*,) I must petition You.

THE Premisses tenderly consider'd; I desire your *Excellencies* Protection:
And that I may have a Share in next *Sunday*'s Collection:
And over and above, that I may have your *Excellencies* Letter,
With an Order for the *Chaplain* aforesaid; or instead of him a better.

And then your poor *Petitioner*, both Night and Day,
Or the *Chaplain* (for 'tis his *Trade,*) as in Duty bound, shall ever *pray.*

Baucis and Philemon[1]

IN ANTIENT Times, as Story tells,
The Saints would often leave their Cells,
And strole about, but hide their Quality,
To try good People's Hospitality.
It happen'd on a Winter Night,
As Authors of the Legend write,
Two Brother Hermits, Saints by Trade,
Taking their *Tour* in Masquerade,
Disguis'd in tatter'd Habits, went
To a small Village down in *Kent*;
Where, in the Strolers canting Strain,
They begg'd from Door to Door in vain;
Try'd ev'ry Tone might Pity win,
But not a Soul would let them in.
Our wand'ring Saints in woful State,
Treated at this ungodly Rate,
Having thro' all the Village pass'd,
To a small Cottage came at last;
Where dwelt a good honest old Yeoman,
Call'd in the Neighbourhood, *Philemon.*
Who kindly did these Saints invite
In his poor Hut to pass the Night:
And then the hospitable Sire
Bid Goody *Baucis* mend the Fire;
While he from out the Chimney took
A Flitch of Bacon off the Hook;
And freely from the fattest Side
Cut out large Slices to be fry'd:
Then stept aside to fetch 'em Drink,
Fill'd a large Jug up to the Brink;
And saw it fairly twice go round:
Yet (what is wonderful) they found
'Twas still replenish'd to the Top,
As if they ne'er had touch'd a Drop.
The good old Couple was amaz'd,
And often on each other gaz'd:
For both were frighted to the Heart,

[1] Written in 1706. Published in *Poetical Miscellanies,* Volume VI, 1709. Text of *Miscellanies,* Volume III, 1728.

And just began to cry,——What art!
Then softly turn'd aside to view,
Whether the Lights were burning blue.
The gentle *Pilgrims* soon aware on't,
Told 'em their Calling, and their Errant:
Good Folks, you need not be afraid,
We are but *Saints*, the Hermits said:
No Hurt shall come to you, or yours;
But, for that Pack of churlish Boors,
Not fit to live on Christian Ground,
They and their Houses shall be drown'd:
Whilst you shall see your Cottage rise,
And grow a Church before your Eyes.
  They scarce had spoke; when fair and soft,
The Roof began to mount aloft;
Aloft rose ev'ry Beam and Rafter,
The heavy Wall climb'd slowly after.
  The Chimney widen'd, and grew higher,
Became a Steeple with a Spire.
  The Kettle to the Top was hoist,
And there stood fast'ned to a Joist;
But with the Upside down, to show
Its Inclination for below:
In vain; for a superior Force
Apply'd at Bottom, stops its Course,
Doom'd ever in Suspence to dwell,
'Tis now no Kettle, but a Bell.
  A wooden Jack, which had almost
Lost, by Disuse, the Art to Roast,
A sudden Alteration feels,
Increas'd by new Intestine Wheels:
And, what exalts the Wonder more,
The Number made the Motion slow'r.
The Flyer, tho't had Leaden Feet,
Turn'd round so quick, you scarce could see't;
But slacken'd by some secret Power,
Now hardly moves an Inch an Hour.
The Jack and Chimney near ally'd,
Had never left each other's Side;
The Chimney to a Steeple grown,
The Jack would not be left alone,
But up against the Steeple rear'd,
Became a Clock, and still adher'd:
And still its Love to Houshold Cares
By a shrill Voice at Noon declares,
Warning the Cook-Maid, not to burn
That Roast-Meat which it cannot turn.

The groaning Chair began to crawl
Like an huge Snail along the Wall;
There stuck aloft, in publick View,
And with small change, a Pulpit grew.
The Porringers, that in a Row
Hung high, and made a glitt'ring Show,
To a less noble Substance chang'd,
Were now but Leathern Buckets rang'd.
The Ballads pasted on the Wall,
Of *Joan* of *France*, and *English Moll*,
Fair *Rosamond*, and *Robin Hood*,
The *Little Children in the Wood*,
Now seem'd to look abundance better,
Improv'd in Picture, Size, and Letter
And high in Order plac'd, describe
The Heraldry of ev'ry Tribe.
A Bedstead of the Antique Mode,
Compact of Timber many a Load,
Such as our Ancestors did use,
Was Metamorphos'd into Pews;
Which still their antient Nature keep,
By lodging Folks dispos'd to Sleep.
The Cottage, by such Feats as these,
Grown to a Church by just Degrees,
The Hermits then desir'd their Host
To ask for what he fancy'd most.
Philemon, having paus'd a while,
Return'd 'em Thanks in homely Style;
Then said, My House is grown so fine,
Methinks I still would call it mine:
I'm old, and fain would live at Ease,
Make me the *Parson*, if you please.
He spoke, and presently he feels
His Grazier's Coat fall down his Heels;
He sees, yet hardly can believe,
About each Arm a Pudding-sleeve;
His Wastcoat to a Cassock grew,
And both assum'd a sable Hue;
But being old, continu'd just
As thread-bare, and as full of Dust.
His Talk was now of *Tythes* and *Dues*;
He smok'd his Pipe, and read the News;
Knew how to preach old Sermons next,
Vamp'd in the Preface and the Text;
At Christ'nings well could act his Part,
And had the Service all by Heart;

Wish'd Women might have Children fast,
And thought whose Sow had farrow'd last:
Against *Dissenters* would repine,
And stood up firm for *Right Divine:*
Found his Head fill'd with many a System,
But Classick Authors,—he ne'er mist 'em.
Thus having furbish'd up a Parson,
Dame *Baucis* next they play'd their Farce on:
Instead of Home-spun Coifs were seen
Good Pinners edg'd with Colberteen:
Her Petticoat transform'd apace,
Became black Sattin flounc'd with Lace.
Plain *Goody* would no longer down,
'Twas *Madam*, in her Grogram Gown.
Philemon was in great Surprize,
And hardly could believe his Eyes,
Amaz'd to see her look so prim;
And she admir'd as much at Him.
Thus, happy in their Change of Life,
Were several Years this Man and Wife:
When on a Day, which prov'd their last,
Discoursing o'er old Stories past,
They went by chance, amidst their Talk,
To the Church-Yard to take a Walk;
When *Baucis* hastily cry'd out,
My Dear, I see your Forehead sprout!
Sprout, quoth the Man, What's this you tell us?
I hope you don't believe me Jealous:
But yet, methinks, I feel it true;
And really, Yours is budding too—
Nay,—now I cannot stir my Foot:
It feels as if 'twere taking Root.
Description would but tire my Muse:
In short, they both were turn'd to *Yews.*
Old Goodman *Dobson* of the Green
Remembers he the Trees has seen;
He'll talk of them from Noon to Night,
And goes with Folks to shew the Sight;
On *Sundays*, after Evening Prayer,
He gathers all the Parish there;
Points out the Place of either *Yew;*
Here *Baucis*, there *Philemon* grew:
Till once, a Parson of our Town,
To mend his Barn, cut *Baucis* down;
At which, 'tis hard to be believ'd,
How much the other Tree was griev'd,

Grew scrubby, dy'd a-top, was stunted:
So, the next Parson stubb'd and burnt it.

On Mrs. Biddy Floyd
Written in the Year 1707[1]

WHEN *Cupid* did his Grandsire *Jove* intreat,
To form some Beauty by a new Receipt;
Jove sent and found far in a Country Scene,
Truth, Innocence, Good-Nature, Look serene;
From which Ingredients, first the dext'rous Boy
Pick'd the Demure, the Aukward, and the Coy:
The *Graces* from the Court did next provide
Breeding, and Wit, and Air, and decent Pride.
These *Venus* cleans'd from e'ery spurious Grain
Of Nice, Coquet, Affected, Pert, and Vain.
Jove mix'd up all, and his best Clay employ'd;
Then call'd the happy Composition *Floyd*.

A Description of the Morning[2]

Now hardly here and there a Hackney-Coach
Appearing, show'd the ruddy Morn's Approach.
Now *Betty* from her Master's Bed had flown,
And softly stole to discompose her own.
The Slip-shod 'Prentice from his Master's Door
Had par'd the Dirt, and sprinkled round the Floor.
Now *Moll* had whirl'd her Mop with dext'rous Airs,
Prepar'd to scrub the Entry and the Stairs.
The Youth with broomy Stumps began to trace
The Kennel-Edge, where Wheels had worn the Place.
The Small-Coal Man was heard with Cadence deep;
Till drown'd in shriller Notes of *Chimney-sweep*.
Duns at his Lordship's Gate began to meet;
And Brick-dust *Moll* had scream'd thro' half a Street.
The Turn-key now his Flock returning sees,
Duly let out a-Nights to steal for Fees.
The watchful Bailiffs take their silent Stands;
And School-boys lag with Satchels in their Hands.

[1] Published in *Poetical Miscellanies*, Volume VI, 1709. Text of *Works*, Dublin, 1735, Volume II.

[2] Published in the *Tatler*, April 30, 1709. Text of *Works*, Dublin, 1735. Volume II.

A Description of a City Shower[1]

CAREFUL Observers may foretel the Hour
(By sure Prognosticks) when to dread a Show'r.
While Rain depends, the pensive Cat gives o'er
Her Frolicks, and pursues her Tail no more.
Returning home at Night you find the Sink
Strike your offended Sense with double Stink.
If you be wise, then go not far to dine,
You spend in Coach-hire more than save in Wine.
A coming Show'r your shooting Corns presage;
Old Aches throb, your hollow Tooth will rage:
Saunt'ring in Coffee-House is *Dulman* seen;
He damns the Climate, and complains of *Spleen*.
MEAN while the South, rising with dabbled Wings,
A sable Cloud athwart the Welkin flings;
That swill'd more Liquor than it could contain,
And like a Drunkard gives it up again.
Brisk *Susan* whips her Linnen from the Rope,
While the first drizzling Show'r is born aslope:
Such is that sprinkling which some careless Quean
Flirts on you from her Mop; but not so clean:
You fly, invoke the Gods; then turning, stop
To rail; she singing, still whirls on her Mop.
Nor yet the Dust had shun'd th' unequal Strife,
But aided by the Wind, fought still for Life;
And wafted with its Foe by vi'lent Gust,
'Twas doubtful which was Rain, and which was Dust.
Ah! where must needy Poet seek for Aid,
When Dust and Rain at once his Coat invade?
Sole Coat, where Dust cemented by the Rain
Erects the Nap, and leaves a cloudy Stain.
Now, in contiguous Drops the Flood comes down,
Threat'ning with Deluge this *devoted* Town.
To Shops in Crowds the daggled Females fly,
Pretend to cheapen Goods; but nothing buy.
The Templer spruce, while ev'ry Spout's abroach,
Stays till 'tis fair, yet *seems* to call a Coach.
The tuck'd-up Sempstress walks with hasty Strides,
While Streams run down her oil'd Umbrella's Sides.
Here various Kinds by various Fortunes led,
Commence Acquaintance underneath a Shed.
Triumphant Tories, and desponding Whigs,
Forget their Feuds, and join to save their Wigs.

[1] Published in the *Tatler*, October 17, 1710. Text of *Works*, Dublin, 1735, Volume II.

Box'd in a Chair the Beau impatient sits,
While Spouts run clatt'ring o'er the Roof by Fits;
And ever and anon with frightful Din
The Leather sounds; he trembles from within.
So when *Troy* Chair-Men bore the wooden Steed,
Pregnant with *Greeks*, impatient to be freed;
(Those Bully *Greeks*, who, as the Moderns do,
Instead of paying Chair-Men, run them thro')
Laocoon struck the Out-side with his Spear,
And each imprison'd Hero quak'd for Fear.
  Now from all Parts the swelling Kennels flow,
And bear their Trophies with them as they go:
Filths of all Hues and Odours, seem to tell
What Streets they sail'd from, by the Sight and Smell.
They, as each Torrent drives with rapid Force
From *Smithfield*, or St. *Pulchre*'s shape their Course;
And in huge Confluent join at *Snow-hill* Ridge,
Fall from the *Conduit* prone to *Holbourn-Bridge*.
Sweepings from Butchers Stalls, Dung, Guts, and Blood,
Drown'd Puppies, stinking Sprats, all drench'd in Mud,
Dead Cats, and Turnip-Tops come tumbling down the Flood.

Horace. Epistle VII. Book I. Imitated and Addressed to the Earl of Oxford[1]

HARLEY, the Nation's great Support,
Returning home one Day from Court;
(His Mind with publick Cares possest,
All *Europe*'s Bus'ness in his Breast.)
Observ'd a *Parson* near *Whitehall*,
Cheap'ning *old* Authors on a Stall.
The Priest was pretty well in Case,
And shew'd some Humour in his Face;
Look'd with an easy careless Mien,
A perfect Stranger to the Spleen;
Of Size that might a Pulpit fill,
But more inclining to sit still.
My Lord, who (if a Man may say't)
Loves Mischief better than his Meat,
Was now dispos'd to crack a Jest;
And bid Friend *Lewis* go in quest;
(This *Lewis* is an arrant Shaver,
And very much in HARLEY's Favour;)
In quest who might this *Parson* be;

[1] Published in 1713. Text of *Works*, Dublin, 1735, Volume II.

What was his Name, of what Degree:
If possible to learn his Story;
And whether he were *Whig* or *Tory?*
LEWIS his Patron's Humour knows,
Away upon his Errand goes;
And quickly did the Matter sift;
Found out that this was Dr. *S——t:*
A Clergyman of special Note,
For shunning those of his own Coat;
Which made his Brethren of the Gown,
Take Care betimes to run him down.
No Libertine, nor over-nice;
Addicted to no Sort of Vice;
Went where he pleas'd, said what he thought;
Not rich; but ow'd no Man a Groat.
In State-Opinions *a-la-Mode*;
He hated *Wharton* like a Toad;
Had giv'n the *Faction* many a Wound,
And libell'd all the *Junta* round:
Kept Company with Men of Wit,
Who often father'd what he writ:
His Works were hawk'd in ev'ry Street,
But seldom rose about a Sheet:
Of late, indeed, the Paper-*Stamp*
Did very much his Genius cramp;
And since he could not spend his Fire,
He now intended to retire.
SAID *Harley*, I desire to know
From his own Mouth, if this be so:
Step to the Doctor straight, and say,
I'd have him dine with me to Day.
S——t seem'd to wonder what he meant,
Nor would believe my Lord had sent;
So never offer'd once to stir;
But coldly said, *Your Servant Sir.*
Does he refuse me? HARLEY cry'd:
He does, with Insolence and Pride.
SOME few Days after, HARLEY spies
The Doctor fasten'd by the Eyes
At *Charing-Cross*, among the Rout,
Where painted Monsters dangle out.
He pull'd the String, and stopt his Coach,
Beck'ning the Doctor to approach.
S——T, who could neither fly nor hide,
Came sneaking to the Chariot-Side,
And offer'd many a lame Excuse:
He never meant the least Abuse——
My Lord—The Honour you design'd——

Extreamly proud——but I had din'd——
I'm sure I never shou'd neglect——
No Man alive has more Respect——
"Well, I shall think of that no more,
"If you'll be sure to come at *Four*.
The Doctor now obeys the Summons;
Likes both his Company and Commons;
Displays his Talent; sits till Ten;
Next Day invited, comes again:
Soon grows domestick; seldom fails
Either at Morning, or at Meals:
Came early, and departed late:
In short, the Gudgeon took the Bait.
My Lord wou'd carry on the Jest,
And down to *Windsor* takes his Guest.
S——t much admires the Place and Air,
And longs to be a *Canon* there;
In Summer, round the Park to ride,
In Winter—never to reside.
A *Canon!* That's a Place too mean;
No, Doctor, you shall be a *Dean*;
Two dozen *Canons* round your Stall,
And you the Tyrant o'er them all:
You need but cross the *Irish Seas*,
To live in Plenty, Power, and Ease.
Poor *S——t* departs; and, what is worse,
With borrow'd Money in his Purse;
Travels, at least, a Hundred Leagues;
And suffers numberless Fatigues.
SUPPOSE him, now, a *Dean* compleat,
Demurely lolling in his Seat;
The Silver Verge, with decent Pride,
Stuck underneath his Cushion Side.
Suppose him gone through all Vexations,
Patents, Instalments, Abjurations,
First-Fruits and Tenths, and Chapter-Treats,
Dues, Payments, Fees, Demands, and — Cheats,
(The wicked Laity's contriving,
To hinder Clergymen from thriving)
Now all the Doctor's Money's spent,
His Tenants wrong him in his Rent;
The Farmers, spightfully combin'd,
Force him to take his Tythes in Kind;
And *Parvisol* discounts Arrears,
By Bills, for Taxes and Repairs.
POOR *S——t*, with all his Losses vext,
Not knowing where to turn him next:
Above a Thousand Pounds in Debt;

Takes Horse, and in a mighty Fret,
Rides Day and Night at such a Rate,
He soon arrives at HARLEY's Gate:
But was so dirty, pale, and thin,
Old *Read* would hardly let him in.
SAID *Harley*, welcome Rev'rend Dean;
What makes your Worship look so lean?
Why sure you won't appear in Town,
In that old Wig, and rusty Gown?
I doubt your Heart is set on Pelf
So much, that you neglect your self.
What? I suppose now Stocks are high,
You've some good Purchase in your Eye;
Or is your Money out at Use?
Truce, good my Lord, I beg a Truce;
(The Doctor in a Passion cry'd,)
Your Raillery is misapply'd:
Experience I have dearly bought,
You know I am not worth a Groat;
But it's a Folly to contest,
When you resolve to have your Jest;
And since you now have done your worst,
Pray leave me where you found me first.

Stella's Birth-Day
Written in the Year 1718[1]

STELLA this Day is Thirty-four,
(We shan't dispute a Year or more:)
However *Stella*, be not troubled,
Although thy Size and Years are doubled,
Since first I saw thee at Sixteen,
The brightest Virgin on the Green.
So little is thy Form declin'd;
Made up so largely in thy Mind.
OH, would it please the Gods, to *split*
Thy Beauty, Size, and Years, and Wit;
No Age could furnish out a Pair
Of Nymphs so graceful, wise, and fair:
With half the Lustre of your Eyes,
With half your Wit, your Years, and Size.
And then, before it grew too late,
How should I beg of gentle Fate,

[1] Published in *Miscellanies*, Volume I, 1727. Text of *Works*, Dublin, 1735, Volume II.

(That either Nymph might have her Swain,)
To split my Worship too in twain.

Stella's Birth-Day
March 13, 1726/7[1]

THIS Day, whate'er the Fates decree,
Shall still be kept with Joy by me:
This Day then, let us not be told,
That you are sick, and I grown old,
Nor think on our approaching Ills,
And talk of Spectacles and Pills;
To morrow will be Time enough
To hear such mortifying Stuff.
Yet, since from Reason may be brought
A better and more pleasing Thought,
Which can, in spite of all Decays,
Support a few remaining Days:
From not the gravest of Divines,
Accept for once some serious Lines.
  Although we now can form no more
Long Schemes of Life, as heretofore;
Yet you, while Time is running fast,
Can look with Joy on what is past.
  Were future Happiness and Pain,
A mere Contrivance of the Brain,
As Atheists argue, to entice,
And fit their Proselytes for Vice;
(The only Comfort they propose,
To have Companions in their Woes.)
Grant this the Case, yet sure 'tis hard,
That Virtue, stil'd its own Reward,
And by all Sages understood
To be the chief of human Good,
Should acting, die, nor leave behind
Some lasting Pleasure in the Mind,
Which by Remembrance will assuage,
Grief, Sickness, Poverty, and Age;
And strongly shoot a radiant Dart,
To shine through Life's declining Part.
  Say, *Stella*, feel you no Content,
Reflecting on a Life well spent?
Your skilful Hand employ'd to save
Despairing Wretches from the Grave;

[1] Published in *Miscellanies*, Volume III, 1728. Text of first edition.

And then supporting, with your Store,
Those whom you dragg'd from Death before:
(So Providence on Mortals waits,
Preserving what it first creates)
Your gen'rous Boldness to defend
An innocent and absent Friend:
That Courage which can make you just
To Merit humbled in the Dust:
The Detestation you express
For Vice in all its glitt'ring Dress:
That Patience under tort'ring Pain,
Where stubborn Stoicks would complain.
  Must these like empty Shadows pass,
Or Forms reflected from a Glass?
Or mere Chimæra's in the Mind,
That fly and leave no Marks behind?
Does not the Body thrive and grow
By Food of twenty Years ago?
And, had it not been still supply'd,
It must a thousand Times have dy'd.
Then, who with Reason can maintain,
That no Effects of Food remain?
And, is not Virtue in Mankind
The Nutriment that feeds the Mind?
Upheld by each good Action past,
And still continued by the last:
Then, who with Reason can pretend,
That all Effects of Virtue end?
  Believe me *Stella*, when you show
That true Contempt for Things below,
Nor prize your Life for other Ends
Than merely to oblige your Friends;
Your former Actions claim their Part,
And join to fortify your Heart.
For Virtue in her daily Race,
Like *Janus*, bears a double Face;
Looks back with Joy where she has gone,
And therefore goes with Courage on.
She at your sickly Couch will wait,
And guide you to a better State.
  O then, whatever Heav'n intends,
Take Pity on your pitying Friends;
Nor let your Ills affect your Mind,
To fancy they can be unkind.
Me, surely me, you ought to spare,
Who gladly would your Suff'rings share;
Or give my Scrap of Life to you,
And think it far beneath your Due;

You, to whose Care so oft I owe,
That I'm alive to tell you so.

In Sickness
Written Soon after the Author's Coming to Live in Ireland, upon the Queen's Death, October 1714[1]

'Tis true,—then why should I repine,
To see my Life so fast decline?
But, why obscurely here alone?
Where I am neither lov'd nor known.
My State of Health none care to learn;
My Life is here no Soul's Concern.
And, those with whom I now converse,
Without a Tear will tend my Herse.
Remov'd from kind *Arbuthnot*'s Aid,
Who knows his Art but not his Trade;
Preferring his Regard for me
Before his Credit or his Fee.
Some formal Visits, Looks, and Words,
What meer Humanity affords,
I meet perhaps from three or four,
From whom I once expected more;
Which those who tend the Sick for Pay,
Can act as decently as they;
But, no obliging, tender Friend
To help at my approaching End.
My Life is now a Burthen grown
To others, e'er it be my own.
  Ye formal Weepers for the Sick,
In your last Offices be quick:
And spare my absent Friends the Grief
To hear, yet give me no Relief;
Expir'd To-day, entomb'd To-morrow,
When known, will save a double Sorrow.

Clever Tom Clinch Going to be Hanged[2]

As clever *Tom Clinch*, while the Rabble was bawling,
Rode stately through *Holbourn*, to die in his Calling;

---

1 Published in *Works*, Dublin, 1735, Volume II. Text of first edition.
2 Written in 1726-27. Published in *Works*, Dublin, 1735, Volume II. Text of first edition.

He stopt at the *George* for a Bottle of Sack,
And promis'd to pay for it when he'd come back.
His Waistcoat and Stockings, and Breeches were white,
His Cap had a new Cherry Ribbon to ty't.
The Maids to the Doors and the Balconies ran,
And said, lack-a-day! he's a proper young Man.
But, as from the Windows the Ladies he spy'd,
Like a Beau in the Box, he bow'd low on each Side;
And when his last Speech the loud Hawkers did cry,
He swore from his Cart, it was all a damn'd Lye.
The Hangman for Pardon fell down on his Knee;
Tom gave him a Kick in the Guts for his Fee.
Then said, I must speak to the People a little,
But I'll see you all damn'd before I will **Whittle*.
My honest Friend †*Wild*, may he long hold his Place,
He lengthen'd my Life with a whole Year of Grace.
Take Courage, dear Comrades, and be not afraid,
Nor slip this Occasion to follow your Trade.
My Conscience is clear, and my spirits are calm,
And thus I go off without Pray'r-Book or Psalm.
Then follow the Practice of clever *Tom Clinch*,
Who hung like a Hero and never would flinch.

The Furniture of a Woman's Mind
Written in the Year 1727[1]

A SET of Phrases learn't by Rote;
A Passion for a Scarlet-Coat;
When at a Play to laugh, or cry,
Yet cannot tell the Reason why:
Never to hold her Tongue a Minute;
While all she prates has nothing in it.
Whole Hours can with a Coxcomb sit,
And take his Nonsense all for Wit:
Her Learning mounts to read a Song;
But, half the Words pronouncing wrong;
Has ev'ry Rapartee in Store,
She spoke ten Thousand Times before.
Can ready Compliments supply
On all Occasions, cut and dry.
Such Hatred to a Parson's Gown,
The Sight will put her in a Swown.

* *A Cant Word for confessing at the Gallows.*
† *The Noted Thief-Catcher.*
[1] Published in *Works*, Dublin, 1735, Volume II. Text of first edition.

For Conversation well endu'd;
She calls it witty to be rude;
And, placing Raillery in Railing,
Will tell aloud your greatest Failing;
Nor makes a Scruple to expose
Your bandy Leg, or crooked Nose.
Can at her Morning Tea, run o'er
The Scandal of the Day before.
Improving hourly in her Skill,
To cheat and wrangle at Quadrille.
  IN chusing Lace a Critick nice,
Knows to a Groat the lowest Price;
Can in her Female Clubs dispute
What Lining best the Silk will suit;
What Colours each Complexion match:
And where with Art to place a Patch.
  IF chance a Mouse creeps in her Sight,
Can finely counterfeit a Fright;
So sweetly screames if it comes near her,
She ravishes all Hearts to hear her.
Can dext'rously her Husband teize,
By taking Fits whene'er she please:
By frequent Practice learns the Trick
At proper Seasons to be sick;
Thinks nothing gives one Airs so pretty;
At once creating Love and Pity.
If *Molly* happens to be careless,
And but neglects to warm her Hair-Lace,
She gets a Cold as sure as Death;
And vows she scarce can fetch her Breath.
Admires how modest Women can
Be so *robustious* like a Man.
  IN Party, furious to her Power;
A bitter Whig, or Tory sow'r;
Her Arguments directly tend
Against the Side she would defend:
Will prove herself a Tory plain,
From Principles the Whigs maintain;
And, to defend the Whiggish Cause,
Her Topicks from the Tories draws.
  O YES! If any Man can find
More Virtues in a Woman's Mind,
Let them be sent to Mrs. **Harding*;
She'll pay the Charges to a Farthing:
Take Notice, she has my Commission
To add them in the next Edition;

* *A Printer.*

They may out-sell a better Thing;
So, Holla Boys; God save the King.

The Beasts Confession To the Priest, On Observing how most Men Mistake Their Own Talents Written in the Year 1732[1]

WHEN beasts could speak (the learned say,
They still can do so every day),
It seems, they had religion then,
As much as now we find in men.
It happen'd, when a plague broke out
(Which therefore made them more devout),
The king of brutes (to make it plain,
Of quadrupeds I only mean)
By proclamation gave command,
That ev'ry subject in the land
Should to the priest confess their sins;
And thus the pious wolf begins;
Good father, I must own with shame,
That often I have been to blame:
I must confess, on *Friday* last,
Wretch that I was! I broke my fast:
But I defy the basest tongue
To prove I did my neighbour wrong;
Or ever went to seek my food
By rapine, theft, or thirst of blood.
  The ass, approaching next, confess'd,
That in his heart he lov'd a jest:
A wag he was he needs must own,
And could not let a dunce alone:
Sometimes his friend he would not spare,
And might perhaps be too severe:
But yet, the worst that could be said,
He was a *wit* both born and bred;
And, if it be a sin or shame,
Nature alone must bear the blame:
One fault he hath, is sorry for't,
His ears are half a foot too short;
Which could he to the standard bring,
He'd shew his face before the king:
Then for his voice, there's none disputes

[1] Published in 1738. Text of *Works*, Volume VII, 1768.

That he's the nightingale of brutes.
  The swine with contrite heart allow'd,
His shape and beauty made him proud:
In diet was perhaps too nice,
But gluttony was ne'er his vice:
In ev'ry turn of life content,
And meekly took what fortune sent:
Enquire through all the parish round,
A better neighbour ne'er was found:
His vigilance might some displease;
'Tis true he hated sloth like pease.
  The mimic ape began his chatter,
How evil tongues his life bespatter:
Much of the cens'ring world complain'd,
Who said, his gravity was feign'd:
Indeed the strictness of his morals
Engag'd him in an hundred quarrels:
He saw, and he was griev'd to see't,
His zeal was sometimes indiscreet:
He found his virtues too severe
For our corrupted times to bear:
Yet, such a lewd licentious age
Might well excuse a Stoic's rage.
  The goat advanc'd with decent pace;
And first excus'd his youthful face;
Forgiveness begg'd that he appear'd
('Twas nature's fault) without a beard.
'Tis true, he was not much inclin'd
To fondness for the female kind;
Not, as his enemies object,
From chance, or natural defect;
Not by his frigid constitution,
But through a pious resolution;
For he had made a holy vow
Of chastity as monks do now;
Which he resolv'd to keep for ever hence,
As strictly too, as doth his reverence.
  Apply the tale, and you shall find,
How just it suits with human-kind.
Some faults we own: but, can you guess?
—Why, virtues carried to excess,
Wherewith our vanity endows us,
Though neither foe nor friend allows us.
  The lawyer swears, you may rely on't,
He never squeez'd a needy client;
And this he makes his constant rule;

For which his brethren call him fool:
His conscience always was so nice,
He freely gave the poor advice;
By which he lost, he may affirm,
A hundred fees last *Easter* term.
While others of the learned robe
Would break the patience of a *Job*;
No pleader at the bar could match
His diligence and quick dispatch;
Ne'er kept a cause, he well may boast,
Above a term or two at most.
  The cringing knave, who seeks a place
Without success, thus tells his case:
Why should he longer mince the matter?
He fail'd, because he could not flatter;
He had not learn'd to turn his coat,
Nor for a party give his vote:
His crime he quickly understood;
Too zealous for the nation's good:
He found the ministers resent it,
Yet could not for his heart repent it.
  The chaplain vows he cannot fawn,
Though it would raise him to the lawn:
He pass'd his hours among his books;
You find it in his meagre looks:
He might, if he were worldly wise,
Preferment get and spare his eyes:
But own'd, he had a stubborn spirit,
That made him trust alone to merit:
Would rise by merit to promotion;
Alas! a mere chimeric notion.
  The doctor, if you will believe him,
Confess'd a sin; and God forgive him!
Call'd up at midnight, ran to save
A blind old beggar from the grave:
But see how *Satan* spreads his snares;
He quite forgot to say his prayers.
He cannot help it for his heart
Sometimes to act the parson's part:
Quotes from the bible many a sentence,
That moves his patients to repentance:
And, when his med'cines do no good,
Supports their minds with heav'nly food,
At which, however well intended,
He hears the clergy are offended;
And grown so bold behind his back,

To call him hypocrite and quack.
In his own church he keeps a seat;
Says grace before and after meat;
And calls, without affecting airs,
His household twice a day to pray'rs.
He shuns apothecaries shops;
And hates to cram the sick with slops:
He scorns to make his art a trade;
Nor bribes my lady's fav'rite maid.
Old nurse-keepers would never hire
To recommend him to the squire;
Which others, whom he will not name,
Have often practis'd to their shame.
The statesman tells you with a *sneer*,
His fault is to be too *sincere*;
And, having no sinister ends,
Is apt to disoblige his friends.
The nation's good, his master's glory,
Without regard to *whig* or *tory*,
Were all the schemes he had in view;
Yet he was seconded by few:
Though some had spread a thousand lyes,
'Twas *he* defeated the EXCISE.
'Twas known, though he had borne aspersion,
That *standing troops* were his aversion:
His practice was, in ev'ry station,
To serve the king, and please the nation.
Though hard to find in ev'ry case
The fittest man to fill a place:
His promises he ne'er forgot,
But took memorials on the spot:
His enemies, for want of charity,
Said, he affected popularity:
'Tis true, the people understood,
That all he did was for their good;
Their kind affections he has try'd;
No love is lost on either side.
He came to court with fortune clear,
Which now he runs out ev'ry year:
Must, at the rate that he goes on,
Inevitably be undone:
Oh! if his majesty would please
To give him but a writ of ease,
Would grant him licence to retire,
As it hath long been his desire,
By fair accounts it would be found,

He's poorer by ten thousand pound.
He owns, and hopes it is no sin,
He ne'er was partial to his kin;
He thought it base for men in stations
To crowd the court with their relations;
His country was his dearest mother,
And ev'ry virtuous man his brother;
Through modesty or aukward shame
(For which he owns himself to blame),
He found the wisest man he cou'd,
Without respect to friends, or blood;
Nor ever acts on private views,
When he hath liberty to chuse.
  The sharper swore he hated play,
Except to pass an hour away:
And well he might; for, to his cost,
By want of skill he always lost;
He heard there was a club of cheats,
Who had contriv'd a thousand feats;
Could change the stock, or cog a dye,
And thus deceive the sharpest eye:
Nor wonder how his fortune sunk,
His brothers fleece him when he's drunk.
  I own the moral not exact;
Besides, the tale is false in fact;
And so absurd, that could I raise up
From fields *Elysian* fabling *Æsop*;
I would accuse him to his face
For libelling the *four-foot* race.
Creatures of ev'ry kind but ours
Well comprehend their natural pow'rs;
While we, whom *reason* ought to sway,
Mistake our talents ev'ry day.
The ass was never known so stupid
To act the part of *Tray* or *Cupid*;
Nor leaps upon his master's lap,
There to be stroak'd, and fed with pap,
As *Æsop* would the world persuade;
He better understands his trade:
Nor comes, whene'er his lady whistles;
But carries loads, and feeds on thistles.
Our author's meaning, I presume, is
A creature *bipes et implumis*;
Wherein the moralist design'd
A compliment on human-kind:
For here he owns, that now and then
Beasts may *degenerate* into men.

Verses on the Death of Dr. Swift, Occasioned by Reading the Following Maxim in Rochefoucault Written in Nov. 1731[1]

Dans l'adversité de nos meilleurs amis nous trouvons toujours quelque chose, qui ne nous deplaist pas.
In the adversity of our best friends we always find something that doth not displease us.

As *Rochefoucault* his maxims drew
From nature, I believe them true:
They argue no corrupted mind
In him; the fault is in mankind.
  This maxim more than all the rest
Is thought too base for human breast:
"In all distresses of our friends
"We first consult our private ends;
"While nature, kindly bent to ease us,
"Points out some circumstance to please us."
  If this perhaps your patience move,
Let reason and experience prove.
  We all behold with envious eyes
Our equal rais'd above our size.
I love my friend as well as you:
But why should he obstruct my view?
Then let me have the higher post;
Suppose it but an inch at most.
If in a battle you should find
One, whom you love of all mankind,
Had some heroick action done,
A champion kill'd, or trophy won;
Rather than thus be overtopt,
Would you not wish his laurels cropt?
Dear honest *Ned* is in the gout,
Lies rack'd with pain, and you without:
How patiently you hear him groan!
How glad, the case is not your own!
  What poet would not grieve to see
His brother write as well as he?
But, rather than they should excell,
Would wish his rivals all in hell?
  Her end when emulation misses,
She turns to envy, stings and hisses:

[1] Published in 1739. Text of *Works*, Volume VI, 1768.

The strongest friendship yields to pride,
Unless the odds be on our side.
  Vain human-kind! fantastick race.
Thy various follies who can trace?
Self-love, ambition, envy, pride,
Their empire in our hearts divide.
Give others riches, power, and station;
'Tis all on me an usurpation;
I have no title to aspire;
Yet, when you sink, I seem the higher.
In *Pope* I cannot read a line,
But with a sigh I wish it mine:
When he can in one couplet fix
More sense, than I can do in six,
It gives me such a jealous fit,
I cry, pox take him and his wit.
I grieve to be outdone by *Gay*
In my own hum'rous biting way.
Arbuthnot is no more my friend,
Who dares to irony pretend,
Which I was born to introduce,
Refin'd it first, and shew'd its use.
St. John, as well as *Pulteney*, knows
That I had some repute for prose;
And, till they drove me out of date,
Could maul a minister of state.
If they have mortify'd my pride,
And made me throw my pen aside;
If with such talents heav'n hath blest 'em,
Have I not reason to detest 'em?
  To all my foes, dear fortune, send
Thy gifts, but never to my friend:
I tamely can endure the first;
But this with envy makes me burst.
  Thus much may serve by way of proem;
Proceed we therefore to our poem.
  The time is not remote, when I
Must by the course of nature die;
When, I foresee, my special friends
Will try to find their private ends:
And, though 'tis hardly understood,
Which way my death can do them good,
Yet thus, methinks, I hear them speak:
See, how the dean begins to break!
Poor gentleman! he droops apace!
You plainly find it in his face.
That old vertigo in his head
Will never leave him, till he's dead.

Besides, his memory decays:
He recollects not what he says;
He cannot call his friends to mind;
Forgets the place where last he din'd:
Plies you with stories o'er and o'er;
He told them fifty times before.
How does he fancy, we can sit
To hear his out-of-fashion wit?
But he takes up with younger folks,
Who for his wine will bear his jokes.
Faith, he must make his stories shorter,
Or change his comrades once a quarter:
In half the time he talks them round:
There must another set be found.
For poetry, he's past his prime;
He takes an hour to find a rhyme:
His fire is out, his wit decay'd,
His fancy sunk, his muse a jade.
I'd have him throw away his pen;—
But there's no talking to some men.
And then their tenderness appears
By adding largely to my years:
He's older than he would be reckon'd,
And well remembers *Charles* the second.
He hardly drinks a pint of wine;
And that, I doubt, is no good sign.
His stomach too begins to fail:
Last year we thought him strong and hale;
But now he's quite another thing:
I wish he may hold out till spring.
They hug themselves, and reason thus;
It is not yet so bad with us.
In such a case they talk in tropes,
And by their fears express their hopes.
Some great misfortune to portend
No enemy can match a friend.
With all the kindness they profess,
The merit of a lucky guess
(When daily how-d'ye's come of course,
And servants answer, "Worse and worse!")
Would please them better, than to tell,
That, God be prais'd! the dean is well.
Then he, who prophesy'd the best,
Approves his foresight to the rest:
"You know I always fear'd the worst,
"And often told you so at first."

He'd rather chuse that I should die,
Than his prediction prove a lie.
Not one foretells, I shall recover,
But all agree to give me over.
  Yet, should some neighbour feel a pain
Just in the parts where I complain;
How many a message would he send?
What hearty prayers, that I should mend?
Inquire what regimen I kept;
What gave me ease, and how I slept?
And more lament, when I was dead,
Than all the sniv'lers round my bed.
  My good companions, never fear;
For though you may mistake a year,
Though your prognosticks run too fast,
They must be verify'd at last.
  Behold the fatal day arrive!
How is the dean? he's just alive.
Now the departing pray'r is read;
He hardly breathes—The dean is dead.
  Before the passing-bell begun,
The news through half the town has run.
Oh! may we all for death prepare!
What has he left? and who's his heir?
I know no more than what the news is;
'Tis all bequeath'd to publick uses.
To publick uses! there's a whim!
What had the publick done for him?
Mere envy, avarice, and pride:
He gave it all—but first he dy'd.
And had the dean in all the nation
No worthy friend, no poor relation?
So ready to do strangers good,
Forgetting his own flesh and blood?
  Now *Grubstreet* wits are all employ'd;
With elegies the town is cloy'd:
Some paragraph in ev'ry paper
To *curse* the *dean*, or *bless* the *drapier*.
The doctors, tender of their fame,
Wisely on me lay all the blame.
We must confess his case was nice;
But he would never take advice.
Had he been rul'd, for ought appears,
He might have lived these twenty years:
For, when we open'd him, we found,
That all his vital parts were sound.

From *Dublin* soon to *London* spread,
'Tis told at court, the dean is dead.
And lady *Suffolk* in the spleen
Runs laughing up to tell the * *
** so gracious, mild, and good,
Cries, "Is he gone! 'tis time he shou'd."

* * * * * * * * *

Now *Chartres*, at sir *Robert's* levee,
Tells with a sneer the tidings heavy:
Why, if he dy'd without his shoes,
(Cries *Bob*) I'm sorry for the news:
Oh, were the wretch but living still,
And in his place my good friend *Will!*
Or had a mitre on his head,
Provided *Bolingbroke* were dead!
Now *Curll* his shop from rubbish drains:
Three genuine tomes of *Swift's* remains!
And then, to make them pass the glibber,
Revis'd by *Tibbalds, Moore,* and *Cibber.*
He'll treat me as he does my betters,
Publish my will, my life, my letters;
Revive the libels born to die;
Which *Pope* must bear, as well as I.
Here shift the scene to represent
How those I love my death lament.
Poor *Pope* will grieve a month, and *Gay*
A week, and *Arbuthnot* a day.
St. John himself will scarce forbear
To bite his pen, and drop a tear.
The rest will give a shrug, and cry,
"I'm sorry—but we all must die!"
Indiff'rence clad in wisdom's guise
All fortitude of mind supplies:
For how can stony bowels melt
In those, who never pity felt?
When we are lash'd, they kiss the rod,
Resigning to the will of God.
The fools my juniors by a year
Are tortur'd with suspence and fear;
Who wisely thought my age a screen,
When death approach'd to stand between:
The screen remov'd, their hearts are trembling;
They mourn for me without dissembling.
My female friends, whose tender hearts
Have better learn'd to act their parts,

Receive the news in doleful dumps:
"The dean is dead (pray, what is trumps?)
"Then, Lord, have mercy on his soul!
"(Ladies, I'll venture for the vole.)
"Six deans, they say, must bear the pall.
"(I wish I knew what king to call.)
"Madam, your husband will attend
"The fun'ral of so good a friend:
"No, madam, 'tis a shocking sight;
"And he's engag'd to-morrow night:
"My lady *Club* will take it ill,
"If he should fail her at quadrille.
"He lov'd the dean—(I lead a heart)
"But dearest friends, they say, must part.
"His time was come; he ran his race;
"We hope he's in a better place."
  Why do we grieve that friends should die?
No loss more easy to supply.
One year is past; a diff'rent scene!
No farther mention of the dean,
Who now, alas! is no more mist,
Than if he never did exist.
Where's now the fav'rite of *Apollo?*
Departed:—*and his works must follow,*
Must undergo the common fate;
His kind of wit is out of date.
  Some country 'squire to *Lintot* goes,
Inquires for *Swift* in verse and prose.
Says *Lintot*, "I have heard the name;
"He dy'd a year ago." The same.
He searches all the shop in vain.
"Sir, you may find them in *Duck-lane:*
"I sent them, with a load of books,
"Last *Monday* to the pastry-cook's.
"To fancy they could live a year!
"I find, you're but a stranger here.
"The dean was famous in his time,
"And had a kind of knack at rhyme.
"His way of writing now is past:
"The town has got a better taste.
"I keep no antiquated stuff;
"But spick and span I have enough.
"Pray, do but give me leave to shew 'em:
"Here's *Colley Cibber's* birth-day poem.
"This ode you never yet have seen
"By *Stephen Duck* upon the queen.
"Then here's a letter finely penn'd

"Against the *Craftsman* and his friend:
"It clearly shews, that all reflection
"On ministers is disaffection.
"Next, here's sir *Robert's* vindication,
"And Mr. *Henley's* last oration.
"The hawkers have not got them yet:
"Your honour please to have a set?"
Suppose me dead; and then suppose
A club assembled at the *Rose*;
Where, from discourse of this and that,
I grow the subject of their chat.
The dean, if we believe report,
Was never ill-receiv'd at court.
Although ironically grave,
He sham'd the fool, and lash'd the knave.
"Sir, I have heard another story;
"He was a most *confounded tory*,
"And grew, or he is much bely'd,
"Extremely *dull*, before he dy'd."
Can we the *Drapier* then forget?
Is not our nation in his debt?
'Twas he that writ the *Drapier's letters!*
"He should have left them for his *betters;*—
"We had a hundred *abler men*,
"Nor need *depend* upon his *pen*.—
"Say what you will about his *reading*,
"You never can *defend* his *breeding*;
"Who, in his *satires* running riot,
"Could never leave the *world* in *quiet*;
"Attacking, when he took the *whim*,
"*Court, city, camp*,—all one to him.—
"But why would he, except he *slobber'd*,
"Offend our *patriot*, great sir *Robert*,
"Whose *counsels* aid the sov'reign pow'r
"To *save* the *nation* ev'ry hour?
"What *scenes* of evil he unravels
"*In satires, libels, lying travels!*
"Not sparing his own *clergy-cloth*,
"But *eats* into it, like a *moth!*"—
Perhaps I may allow, the dean
Had too much satire in his vein,
And seem'd determin'd not to starve it,
Because no age could more deserve it.
Vice, if it e'er can be abash'd,
Must be or *ridicul'd* or *lash'd*.
If you *resent* it, who's to blame?

He neither knew *you*, nor your *name:*
Should *vice* expect to 'scape rebuke,
Because its *owner* is a *duke?*
His friendships, still to few confin'd,
Were always of the middling kind;
No fools of rank or mongrel breed,
Who fain would pass for lords indeed,
Where titles give no right or power,
And peerage is a wither'd flower.
He would have deem'd it a disgrace,
If such a wretch had known his face.
He never thought an honour done him,
Because a peer was proud to own him;
Would rather slip aside, and chuse
To talk with wits in dirty shoes;
And scorn the fools with stars and garters,
So often seen caressing *Chartres*.
He kept with princes due decorum;
Yet never stood in awe before 'em.
He follow'd *David's* lesson just;
In princes never put his trust:
And, would you make him truly sowre,
Provoke him with a slave in power,
"Alas, poor *dean!* his only scope
"Was to be held a *misanthrope*,
"This into gen'ral *odium* drew him,
"Which if he lik'd, *much good may't do him.*
"His *Zeal* was not to lash our *crimes*,
"But *discontent* against the times:
"For, had we made him *timely* offers
"To *raise* his *post*, or *fill* his *coffers*,
"Perhaps he might have truckled down,
"Like other *brethren* of his *gown*.
"For *party* he would scarce have bled:—
"I say no more,—because he's *dead*.—
"What *writings* has he left behind?"—
I hear, they're of a diff'rent kind:
A few in *verse*; but most in prose—
"Some *high-flown pamphlets*, I suppose:—
"All scribbled in the *worst* of *times*,
"To *palliate* his friend *Oxford's* crimes,
"To praise queen *Anne*, nay more, defend her,
"As never fav'ring the *pretender*:—
"Or *libels* yet conceal'd from sight,
"Against the *court* to shew his *spight*:—
"Perhaps his *travels, part the third;*

"A *lye* at ev'ry *second* word—
"Offensive to a *loyal* ear:—
"But—*not one sermon,* you may *swear.*"—
As for his works in verse or prose,
I own myself no judge of those.
Nor can I tell what criticks thought 'em;
But this I know, all people bought 'em,
As with a moral view design'd,
To *please*, and to *reform* mankind:
And, if he often miss'd his aim,
The *world* must own it, to their *shame*,
The *praise* is *his*, and *theirs* the *blame.*
He gave the little wealth he had
To build a house for fools and mad;
To shew, by one satiric touch,
No nation wanted it so much.
And, since you *dread* no farther *lashes*,
Methinks you may *forgive his ashes.*

The Day of Judgement[1]

WITH a whirl of thought oppress'd,
I sunk from reverie to rest.
An horrid vision seiz'd my head,
I saw the graves give up their dead!
Jove, arm'd with terrors, bursts the skies,
And thunder roars, and lightning flies!
Amaz'd, confus'd, its fate unknown,
The world stands trembling at his throne!
While each pale sinner hung his head,
Jove, nodding, shook the heavens, and said:
"Offending race of human-kind,
"By nature, reason, *learning*, blind;
"You who, through frailty, stepp'd aside;
"And you who never fell, *through pride*;
"You who in different sects were shamm'd,
"And come to see each other damn'd;
"(So some folk told you, but they knew
"No more of Jove's designs than you)
"—The world's mad business now is o'er,
"And I resent these pranks no more.
"—I to such blockheads set my wit!
"I damn such fools!—Go, go, you're *bit.*"

[1] Written 1731? Published in *Works*, Volume XVII, 1775. Text of first edition.

Joseph Addison

(1672-1692-1719)

A Letter from Italy, to the Right Honourable Charles Lord Halifax In the Year MDCCI[1]

Salve magna parens frugum Saturnia tellus,
Magna virûm! tibi res antiquæ laudis et artis
Aggredior, sanctos ausus recludere fontes.
Virg. Geor. 2.

While you, my Lord, the rural shades admire,
And from *Britannia*'s publick posts retire,
Nor longer, her ungrateful sons to please,
For their advantage sacrifice your ease;
Me into foreign realms my fate conveys,
Through nations fruitful of immortal lays,
Where the soft season and inviting clime
Conspire to trouble your repose with rhime.
For wheresoe'er I turn my ravish'd eyes,
Gay gilded scenes and shining prospects rise,
Poetick fields encompass me around,
And still I seem to tread on Classic ground;
For here the Muse so oft her Harp has strung,
That not a mountain rears its head unsung,
Renown'd in verse each shady thicket grows,
And ev'ry stream in heavenly numbers flows.
How am I pleas'd to search the hills and woods
For rising springs and celebrated floods!
To view the *Nar*, tumultuous in his course,
And trace the smooth *Clitumnus* to his source,
To see the *Mincio* draw his watry store
Through the long windings of a fruitful shore,
And hoary *Albula*'s infected tide
O'er the warm bed of smoaking sulphur glide.
Fir'd with a thousand raptures I survey
Eridanus through flowery meadows stray,
The king of floods! that rolling o'er the plains
The towering *Alps* of half their moisture drains,
And proudly swoln with a whole winter's snows,

[1] Published in 1703. Text of *Works*, 1721.

Distributes wealth and plenty where he flows.
Sometimes, misguided by the tuneful throng,
I look for streams immortaliz'd in song,
That lost in silence and oblivion lye,
(Dumb are their fountains and their channels dry)
Yet run for-ever by the Muse's skill,
And in the smooth description murmur still.
Sometimes to gentle *Tiber* I retire,
And the fam'd river's Empty shores admire,
That destitute of strength derives its course
From thrifty urns and an unfruitful source;
Yet sung so often in poetick lays,
With scorn the *Danube* and the *Nile* surveys;
So high the deathless Muse exalts her theme!
Such was the *Boin*, a poor inglorious stream,
That in *Hibernian* vales obscurely stray'd,
And unobserv'd in wild *Meanders* play'd;
'Till by Your lines and *Nassau*'s sword renown'd,
Its rising billows through the world resound,
Where-e'er the Heroe's godlike acts can pierce,
Or where the fame of an immortal verse.
Oh cou'd the Muse my ravish'd breast inspire
With warmth like yours, and raise an equal fire,
Unnumber'd beauties in my verse shou'd shine,
And *Virgil*'s *Italy* shou'd yield to mine!
See how the golden groves around me smile,
That shun the coast of *Britain*'s stormy Isle,
Or when transplanted and preserv'd with care,
Curse the cold clime, and starve in northern air.
Here kindly warmth their mounting juice ferments
To nobler tastes, and more exalted scents:
Ev'n the rough rocks with tender Myrtle bloom,
And trodden Weeds send out a rich perfume.
Bear me, some God, to *Baia*'s gentle seats,
Or cover me in *Umbria*'s green retreats;
Where western gales eternally reside,
And all the seasons lavish all their pride:
Blossoms, and fruits, and flowers together rise,
And the whole year in gay confusion lies.
Immortal glories in my mind revive,
And in my soul a thousand passions strive,
When *Rome*'s exalted beauties I descry
Magnificent in piles of ruine lye.
An amphitheater's amazing height
Here fills my eye with terror and delight,
That on its publick shows Unpeopled *Rome*,
And held Uncrowded nations in its womb:

Here pillars rough with sculpture pierce the skies:
And here the proud triumphal arches rise,
Where the old *Romans* deathless acts display'd,
Their base degenerate progeny upbraid:
Whole rivers here forsake the fields below,
And wond'ring at their height through airy channels flow.
  Still to new scenes my wand'ring Muse retires,
And the dumb show of breathing rocks admires;
Where the smooth chissel all its force has shown,
And soften'd into flesh the rugged stone.
In solemn silence, a majestick band,
Heroes, and Gods, and *Roman* Consuls stand,
Stern tyrants, whom their cruelties renown,
And emperors in *Parian* marble frown;
While the bright dames, to whom they humbly su'd,
Still show the charms that their proud hearts subdu'd.
  Fain wou'd I *Raphael*'s godlike art rehearse,
And show th' immortal labours in my verse,
Where from the mingled strength of shade and light
A new creation rises to my sight,
Such heav'nly figures from his pencil flow,
So warm with life his blended colours glow.
From theme to theme with secret pleasure tost,
Amidst the soft variety I'm lost:
Here pleasing airs my ravisht soul confound
With circling notes and labyrinths of sound;
Here domes and temples rise in distant views,
And opening palaces invite my Muse.
  How has kind heav'n adorn'd the happy land,
And scatter'd blessings with a wasteful hand!
But what avail her unexhausted stores,
Her blooming mountains, and her sunny shores,
With all the gifts that heav'n and earth impart,
The smiles of nature, and the charms of art,
While proud Oppression in her vallies reigns,
And Tyranny usurps her happy plains?
The poor inhabitant beholds in vain
The red'ning Orange and the swelling grain:
Joyless he sees the growing Oils and Wines,
And in the Myrtle's fragrant shade repines:
Starves, in the midst of nature's bounty curst,
And in the loaden vineyard dies for thirst.
  Oh Liberty, thou Goddess heavenly bright,
Profuse of bliss, and pregnant with delight!
Eternal pleasures in thy presence reign,
And smiling Plenty leads thy wanton train;

Eas'd of her load Subjection grows more light,
And Poverty looks chearful in thy sight;
Thou mak'st the gloomy face of Nature gay,
Giv'st beauty to the Sun, and pleasure to the Day.
  Thee, Goddess, thee, *Britannia*'s Isle adores;
How has she oft exhausted all her stores,
How oft in fields of death thy presence sought,
Nor thinks the mighty prize too dearly bought!
On foreign mountains may the Sun refine
The Grape's soft juice, and mellow it to wine,
With Citron groves adorn a distant soil,
And the fat Olive swell with floods of oil:
We envy not the warmer clime, that lies
In ten degrees of more indulgent skies,
Nor at the coarseness of our heaven repine,
Tho' o'er our heads the frozen *Pleiads* shine:
'Tis Liberty that crowns *Britannia*'s Isle,
And makes her barren rocks and her bleak mountains smile.
  Others with towering piles may please the sight,
And in their proud aspiring domes delight;
A nicer touch to the stretcht canvas give,
Or teach their animated rocks to live:
'Tis *Britain*'s care to watch o'er *Europe*'s fate,
And hold in balance each contending state,
To threaten bold presumptuous kings with war,
And answer her afflicted neighbours' pray'r.
The *Dane* and *Swede*, rous'd up by fierce alarms,
Bless the wise conduct of her pious arms:
Soon as her fleets appear, their terrors cease,
And all the northern world lies hush'd in peace.
  Th' ambitious *Gaul* beholds with secret dread
Her thunder aim'd at his aspiring head,
And fain her godlike sons wou'd disunite
By foreign gold, or by domestick spite;
But strives in vain to conquer or divide,
Whom *Nassau*'s arms defend and counsels guide.
  Fir'd with the name, which I so oft have found
The distant climes and different tongues resound,
I bridle in my strugling Muse with pain,
That longs to launch into a bolder strain.
  But I've already troubled you too long,
Nor dare attempt a more advent'rous song.
My humble verse demands a softer theme,
A painted meadow, or a purling stream;
Unfit for Heroes; whom immortal lays,
And lines like *Virgil*'s, or like yours, shou'd praise.

The Campaign, a Poem[1]

WHILE crouds of Princes your deserts proclaim,
Proud in their number to enroll your name;
While Emperors to you commit their cause,
And *ANNA*'s praises crown the vast applause;
Accept, great leader, what the Muse recites,
That in ambitious verse attempts your fights,
Fir'd and transported with a theme so new.
Ten thousand wonders op'ning to my view
Shine forth at once; sieges and storms appear,
And wars and conquests fill th' important year,
Rivers of blood I see, and hills of slain,
An Iliad rising out of One campaign.
The haughty *Gaul* beheld, with tow'ring pride,
His ancient bounds enlarg'd on ev'ry side,
Pirene's lofty barriers were subdued,
And in the midst of his wide empire stood;
Ausonia's states, the victor to restrain,
Opposed their *Alpes* and *Appenines* in vain,
Nor found themselves, with strength of rocks immur'd,
Behind their everlasting hills secur'd;
The rising *Danube* its long race began,
And half its course through the new conquests ran;
Amaz'd and anxious for her Soveraign's fates,
Germania trembled through a hundred states;
Great *Leopold* himself was seiz'd with fear;
He gaz'd around, but saw no succour near;
He gaz'd, and half abandon'd to despair
His hopes on heav'n, and confidence in pray'r.
To *Britain*'s Queen the Nations turn their eyes,
On her resolves the western world relies,
Confiding still, amidst its dire alarms,
In *ANNA*'s councils, and in CHURCHILL's arms.
Thrice happy *Britain*, from the kingdoms rent,
To sit the guardian of the continent!
That sees her bravest son advanc'd so high,
And flourishing so near her Prince's eye;
Thy fav'rites grow not up by fortune's sport,
Or from the crimes, or follies of a court;
On the firm basis of desert they rise,
From long-try'd faith, and friendship's holy tyes:
Their Soveraign's well-distinguish'd smiles they share,
Her ornaments in peace, her strength in war;

[1] Published in 1705. Text of *Works*, 1721. The poem is addressed to the Duke of Marlborough on the occasion of his victory at Blenheim, August, 1704.

The nation thanks them with a publick voice,
By show'rs of blessings heaven approves their choice;
Envy it self is dumb, in wonder lost,
And factions strive who shall applaud 'em most.
Soon as soft vernal breezes warm the sky,
Britannia's colours in the zephyrs fly;
Her Chief already has his march begun,
Crossing the provinces himself had won,
'Till the *Moselle*, appearing from afar,
Retards the progress of the moving war.
Delightful stream, had Nature bid her fall
In distant climes, far from the perjur'd *Gaul*;
But now a purchase to the sword she lyes,
Her harvests for uncertain owners rise,
Each vineyard doubtful of its master grows,
And to the victor's bowl each vintage flows.
The discontented shades of slaughter'd hosts,
That wander'd on her banks, her heroes ghosts
Hope'd, when they saw *Britannia*'s arms appear,
The vengeance due to their great deaths was near.
Our god-like leader, ere the stream he past,
The mighty scheme of all his labours cast,
Forming the wond'rous year within his thought;
His bosom glow'd with battles yet unfought.
The long laborious march he first surveys,
And joins the distant *Danube* to the *Maese*,
Between whose floods such pathless forests grow,
Such mountains rise, so many rivers flow:
The toil looks lovely in the heroe's eyes,
And danger serves but to enhance the prize.
Big with the fate of *Europe*, he renews
His dreadful course, and the proud foe pursues:
Infected by the burning Scorpion's heat,
The sultry gales round his chaf'd temples beat,
'Till on the borders of the *Maine* he finds
Defensive shadows, and refreshing winds.
Our *British* youth, with in-born freedom bold,
Unnumber'd scenes of servitude behold,
Nations of slaves, with tyranny debas'd,
(Their maker's image more than half defac'd)
Hourly instructed, as they urge their toil,
To prize their Queen, and love their native soil.
Still to the rising Sun they take their way
Through clouds of dust, and gain upon the day.
When now the *Neckar* on its friendly coast
With cooling streams revives the fainting host,
That chearfully its labours past forgets,

The midnight watches, and the noon-day heats.
  O'er prostrate towns and palaces they pass,
(Now cover'd o'er with weeds, and hid in grass)
Breathing revenge; whilst anger and disdain
Fire ev'ry breast, and boil in ev'ry vein:
Here shatter'd walls, like broken rocks, from far
Rise up in hideous views, the guilt of war,
Whilst here the Vine o'er hills of ruine climbs,
Industrious to conceal great *Bourbon*'s crimes.
  At length the fame of *England*'s heroe drew
Eugenio to the glorious interview.
Great souls by instinct to each other turn,
Demand alliance, and in friendship burn;
A sudden friendship, while with stretch'd-out rays
They meet each other, mingling blaze with blaze.
Polish'd in courts, and harden'd in the field,
Renown'd for conquest, and in council skill'd,
Their courage dwells not in a troubled flood
Of mounting spirits, and fermenting blood;
Lodg'd in the soul, with virtue over-rul'd,
Inflam'd by reason, and by reason cool'd,
In hours of peace content to be unknown,
And only in the field of battel shown:
To souls like these, in mutual friendship join'd,
Heaven dares entrust the cause of human-kind.
  Britannia's graceful sons appear in arms,
Her harras'd troops the heroe's presence warms,
Whilst the high hills and rivers all around
With thund'ring peals of *British* shouts resound:
Doubling their speed they march with fresh delight,
Eager for glory, and require the fight.—
So the stanch Hound the trembling Deer pursues,
And smells his footsteps in the tainted dews,
The tedious track unrav'ling by degrees:
But when the scent comes warm in ev'ry breeze,
Fir'd at the near approach, he shoots away
On his full stretch, and bears upon his prey.
  The march concludes, the various realms are past,
Th' immortal *Schellenberg* appears at last:
Like hills th' aspiring ramparts rise on high,
Like vallies at their feet the trenches lye;
Batt'ries on batt'ries guard each fatal pass,
Threat'ning destruction; rows of hollow brass,
Tube behind tube, the dreadful entrance keep,
Whilst in their wombs ten thousand thunders sleep:
Great CHURCHILL owns, charm'd with the glorious sight,
His march o'er-paid by such a promis'd fight.
  The western Sun now shot a feeble ray,

And faintly scatter'd the remains of day,
Ev'ning approach'd; but oh what hosts of foes
Were never to behold that ev'ning close!
Thick'ning their ranks, and wedg'd in firm array,
The close compacted *Britons* win their way;
In vain the cannon their throng'd war deface'd
With tracts of death, and laid the battel waste;
Still pressing forward to the fight, they broke
Through flames of sulphur, and a night of smoke,
'Till slaughter'd legions fill'd the trench below,—
And bore their fierce avengers to the foe.
  High on the works the mingling hosts engage;
The battel kindled into tenfold rage
With show'rs of bullets and with storms of fire
Burns in full fury; heaps on heaps expire,
Nations with nations mix'd confus'dly die,
And lost in one promiscuous carnage lye.
  How many gen'rous *Britons* meet their doom,—
New to the field, and heroes in the bloom!
Th' illustrious youths, that left their native shore
To march where *Britons* never march'd before,
(O fatal love of fame! O glorious heat
Only destructive to the brave and great!)
After such toils o'ercome, such dangers past,
Stretch'd on *Bavarian* ramparts breathe their last.
But hold, my Muse, may no complaints appear,
Nor blot the day with an ungrateful tear:
While MARLBRÔ lives *Britannia*'s stars dispense
A friendly light, and shine in innocence.
Plunging thro' seas of blood his fiery steed
Where-e'er his friends retire, or foes succeed;
Those he supports, these drives to sudden flight,
And turns the various fortune of the fight.
  Forbear, great man, renown'd in arms, forbear
To brave the thickest terrors of the war,
Nor hazard thus, confus'd in crouds of foes,
Britannia's safety, and the world's repose;
Let nations anxious for thy life abate
This scorn of danger, and contempt of fate:
Thou livest not for thy self; thy Queen demands
Conquest and peace from thy victorious hands;
Kingdoms and empires in thy fortune join,
And *Europe*'s destiny depends on thine.
  At length the long-disputed pass they gain,
By crouded armies fortify'd in vain;
The war breaks in, the fierce *Bavarians* yield,
And see their camp with *British* legions fill'd.
So *Belgian* mounds bear on their shatter'd sides

The sea's whole weight encreas'd with swelling tides;
But if the rushing wave a passage finds,
Enrage'd by wat'ry moons, and warring winds,
The trembling Peasant sees his country round
Cover'd with tempests, and in oceans drown'd.
The few surviving foes disperst in flight,
(Refuse of swords, and gleanings of a fight)
In ev'ry russling wind the victor hear,
And MARLBRÔ's form in every shadow fear,
'Till the dark cope of night with kind embrace
Befriends the rout, and covers their disgrace.
To *Donawert*, with unresisted force,
The gay victorious army bends its course.
The growth of meadows, and the pride of fields,
Whatever spoils *Bavaria*'s summer yields,
(The *Danube*'s great increase) *Britannia* shares,
The food of armies, and support of wars:
With magazines of death, destructive balls,
And cannons doom'd to batter *Landau*'s walls,
The victor finds each hidden cavern stor'd,
And turns their fury on their guilty Lord.
Deluded Prince! how is thy greatness crost,
And all the gaudy dream of empire lost,
That proudly set thee on a fancy'd throne,
And made imaginary realms thy own!
Thy troops, that now behind the *Danube* join,
Shall shortly seek for shelter from the *Rhine*,
Nor find it there: Surrounded with alarms,
Thou hope'st th' assistance of the *Gallic* arms;
The *Gallic* arms in safety shall advance,
And croud thy standards with the power of *France*,
While to exalt thy doom, th' aspiring *Gaul*
Shares thy destruction, and adorns thy fall.
Unbounded courage and compassion join'd,
Temp'ring each other in the victor's mind,
Alternately proclaim him good and great,
And make the Hero and the Man compleat.
Long did he strive th' obdurate foe to gain
By proffer'd grace, but long he strove in vain;
'Till fir'd at length he thinks it vain to spare
His rising wrath, and gives a loose to war.
In vengeance rous'd the soldier fills his hand
With sword and fire, and ravages the land,
A thousand villages to ashes turns,
In crackling flames a thousand harvests burns.
To the thick woods the woolly flocks retreat,
And mixt with bellowing herds confus'dly bleat;
Their trembling lords the common shade partake,

And cries of infants sound in ev'ry brake:
The list'ning soldier fixt in sorrow stands,
Loth to obey his leader's just commands;
The leader grieves, by gen'rous pity sway'd,
To see his just commands so well obey'd.
  But now the trumpet terrible from far
In shriller clangors animates the war,
Confed'rate drums in fuller consort beat,
And echoing hills the loud alarm repeat:
Gallia's proud standards, to *Bavaria*'s join'd,
Unfurl their gilded Lilies in the wind;
The daring Prince his blasted hopes renews,
And while the thick embattled host he views
Stretcht out in deep array, and dreadful length,
His heart dilates, and glories in his strength.
  The fatal day its mighty course began,
That the griev'd world had long desir'd in vain:
States that their new captivity bemoan'd,
Armies of martyrs that in exile groan'd,
Sighs from the depth of gloomy dungeons heard,
And prayers in bitterness of soul prefer'd,
Europe's loud cries, that Providence assail'd,
And *ANNA*'s ardent vows, at length prevail'd;
The day was come when Heaven design'd to show
His care and conduct of the world below.
  Behold in awful march and dread array
The long-extended squadrons shape their way!
Death, in approaching terrible, imparts
An anxious horrour to the bravest hearts;
Yet do their beating breasts demand the strife,
And thirst of glory quells the love of life.
No vulgar fears can *British* minds controul:
Heat of revenge, and noble pride of soul
O'er-look the foe, advantag'd by his post,
Lessen his numbers, and contract his host:
Tho' fens and floods possest the middle space,
That unprovok'd they would have fear'd to pass;
Nor fens nor floods can stop *Britannia*'s bands,
When her proud foe rang'd on their borders stands.
  But O, my Muse, what numbers wilt thou find
To sing the furious troops in battel join'd!
Methinks I hear the drum's tumultuous sound
The victor's shouts and dying groans confound,
The dreadful burst of cannon rend the skies,
And all the thunder of the battel rise.
'Twas then great MARLBRÔ's mighty soul was prov'd,
That, in the shock of charging hosts unmov'd,
Amidst confusion, horror, and despair,

Examin'd all the dreadful scenes of war;
In peaceful thought the field of death survey'd,
To fainting squadrons sent the timely aid,
Inspir'd repuls'd battalions to engage,
And taught the doubtful battel where to rage.
So when an Angel by divine command
With rising tempests shakes a guilty land,
Such as of late o'er pale *Britannia* past,
Calm and serene he drives the furious blast;
And, pleas'd th' Almighty's orders to perform,
Rides in the whirl-wind, and directs the storm.
  But see the haughty houshold-troops advance!
The dread of *Europe*, and the pride of *France*.
The war's whole art each private soldier knows,
And with a Gen'ral's love of conquest glows;
Proudly he marches on, and void of fear
Laughs at the shaking of the *British* spear:
Vain insolence! with native freedom brave
The meanest *Briton* scorns the highest slave;
Contempt and fury fire their souls by turns,
Each nation's glory in each warriour burns,
Each fights, as in his arm th' important day
And all the fate of his great monarch lay:
A thousand glorious actions, that might claim
Triumphant laurels, and immortal fame,
Confus'd in crouds of glorious actions lye,
And troops of heroes undistinguish'd dye.
O *Dormer*, how can I behold thy fate,
And not the wonders of thy youth relate!
How can I see the gay, the brave, the young,
Fall in the cloud of war, and lye unsung!
In joys of conquest he resigns his breath,
And, fill'd with *England*'s glory, smiles in death.
  The rout begins, the *Gallic* squadrons run,
Compell'd in crouds to meet the fate they shun;
Thousands of fiery steeds with wounds transfix'd
Floating in gore, with their dead masters mixt,
Midst heaps of spears and standards driv'n around,
Lie in the *Danube*'s bloody whirl-pools drown'd.
Troops of bold youths, born on the distant *Soane*,
Or sounding borders of the rapid *Rhône*,
Or where the *Seine* her flow'ry fields divides,
Or where the *Loire* through winding vineyards glides;
In heaps the rolling billows sweep away,
And into *Scythian* seas their bloated corps convey.
From *Bleinheim*'s tow'rs the *Gaul*, with wild affright,
Beholds the various havock of the fight;
His waving banners, that so oft had stood

Planted in fields of death, and streams of blood,
So wont the guarded enemy to reach,
And rise triumphant in the fatal breach,
Or pierce the broken foe's remotest lines,
The hardy veteran with tears resigns.
Unfortunate *Tallard!* Oh who can name
The pangs of rage, of sorrow, and of shame,
That with mixt tumult in thy bosom swell'd!
When first thou saw'st thy bravest troops repell'd,
Thine only son pierc'd with a deadly wound,
Choak'd in his blood, and gasping on the ground,
Thy self in bondage by the victor kept!
The Chief, the Father, and the Captive wept.
An *English* Muse is touch'd with gen'rous woe,
And in th' unhappy man forgets the foe.
Greatly distrest! thy loud complaints forbear,
Blame not the turns of fate, and chance of war;
Give thy brave foes their due, nor blush to own
The fatal field by such great leaders won,
The field whence fam'd *Eugenio* bore away
Only the second honours of the day.
With floods of gore that from the vanquisht fell
The marshes stagnate, and the rivers swell.
Mountains of slain lye heap'd upon the ground,
Or 'midst the roarings of the *Danube* drown'd;
Whole captive hosts the conqueror detains
In painful bondage, and inglorious chains;
Ev'n those who 'scape the fetters and the sword,
Nor seek the fortunes of a happier lord,
Their raging King dishonours, to compleat
Marlbrô's great work, and finish the defeat.
From *Memminghen*'s high domes, and *Ausburg*'s walls,
The distant battel drives th' insulting *Gauls*,
Free'd by the terror of the victor's name
The rescu'd states his great protection claim;
Whilst *Ulme* th' approach of her deliverer waits,
And longs to open her obsequious gates.
The hero's breast still swells with great designs,
In ev'ry thought the tow'ring genius shines:
If to the foe his dreadful course he bends,
O'er the wide continent his march extends;
If sieges in his lab'ring thoughts are form'd,
Camps are assaulted, and an army storm'd;
If to the fight his active soul is bent,
The fate of *Europe* turns on its event.
What distant land, what region can afford
An action worthy his victorious sword:
Where will he next the flying *Gaul* defeat,

To make the series of his toils compleat?
  Where the swoln *Rhine* rushing with all its force
Divides the hostile nations in its course,
While each contracts its bounds, or wider grows,
Enlarg'd or straiten'd as the river flows,
On *Gallia*'s side a mighty bulwark stands,
That all the wide extended plain commands;
Twice, since the war was kindled, has it try'd
The victor's rage, and twice has chang'd its side;
As oft whole armies, with the prize o'erjoy'd,
Have the long summer on its walls employ'd.
Hither our mighty Chief his arms directs,
Hence future triumphs from the war expects;
And, tho' the dog-star had its course begun,
Carries his arms still nearer to the Sun:
Fixt on the glorious action, he forgets
The change of seasons, and increase of heats:
No toils are painful that can danger show,
No climes unlovely, that contain a foe.
  The roving *Gaul*, to his own bounds restrain'd,
Learns to encamp within his native land,
But soon as the victorious host he spies,
From hill to hill, from stream to stream he flies:
Such dire impressions in his heart remain
Of MARLBRÔ's sword, and *Hocstet*'s fatal plain:
In vain *Britannia*'s mighty chief besets
Their shady coverts, and obscure retreats;
They fly the conqueror's approaching fame,
That bears the force of armies in his name.
  Austria's young monarch, whose imperial sway
Sceptres and thrones are destin'd to obey,
Whose boasted ancestry so high extends
That in the pagan gods his lineage ends,
Comes from a-far, in gratitude to own
The great supporter of his father's throne:
What tides of glory to his bosom ran,
Clasp'd in th' embraces of the god-like man!
How were his eyes with pleasing wonder fixt
To see such fire with so much sweetness mixt,
Such easie greatness, such a graceful port,
So turn'd and finish'd for the camp or court!
  Achilles thus was form'd with ev'ry grace,
And *Nireus* shone but in the second place;
Thus the great father of Almighty *Rome*
(Divinely flusht with an immortal bloom
That *Cytherea*'s fragrant breath bestow'd)
In all the charms of his bright mother glow'd.
  The royal youth by MARLBRÔ's presence charm'd,

Taught by his counsels, by his actions warm'd,
On *Landau* with redoubled fury falls,
Discharges all his thunder on its walls,
O'er mines and caves of death provokes the fight,
And learns to conquer in the Hero's sight.
  The *British* Chief, for mighty toils renown'd,
Increas'd in titles, and with conquests crown'd,
To *Belgian* coasts his tedious march renews,
And the long windings of the *Rhine* pursues,
Clearing its borders from usurping foes,
And blest by rescu'd nations as he goes.
Treves fears no more, free'd from its dire alarms;
And *Traerbach* feels the terror of his arms,
Seated on rocks her proud foundations shake,
While MARLBRÔ presses to the bold attack,
Plants all his batt'ries, bids his cannon roar,
And shows how *Landau* might have fall'n before.
Scar'd at his near approach, great *Louis* fears
Vengeance reserv'd for his declining years,
Forgets his thirst of universal sway,
And scarce can teach his subjects to obey;
His arms he finds on vain attempts employ'd,
Th' ambitious projects for his race destroy'd,
The work of ages sunk in One campaign,
And lives of millions sacrific'd in vain.
  Such are th' effects of *ANNA*'s royal cares:
By her, *Britannia*, great in foreign wars,
Ranges through nations, wheresoe'er disjoin'd,
Without the wonted aid of sea and wind.
By her th' unfetter'd *Ister*'s states are free,
And taste the sweets of *English* liberty:
But who can tell the joys of those that lye
Beneath the constant influence of her eye!
Whilst in diffusive show'rs her bounties fall
Like heaven's indulgence, and descend on all,
Secure the happy, succour the distrest,
Make ev'ry subject glad, and a whole people blest.
  Thus wou'd I fain *Britannia*'s wars rehearse,
In the smooth records of a faithful verse;
That, if such numbers can o'er time prevail,
May tell posterity the wond'rous tale.
When actions, unadorn'd, are faint and weak,
Cities and Countries must be taught to speak;
Gods may descend in factions from the skies,
And Rivers from their oozy beds arise;
Fiction may deck the truth with spurious rays,
And round the Hero cast a borrow'd blaze.
MARLBRÔ's exploits appear divinely bright,

And proudly shine in their own native light;
Rais'd of themselves, their genuine charms they boast,
And those who paint 'em truest praise 'em most.

Ode[1]

THE Spacious Firmament on high,
With all the blue Etherial Sky,
And spangled Heav'ns, a Shining Frame,
Their great Original proclaim:
Th' unwearied Sun, from Day to Day,
Does his Creator's Power display,
And publishes to every Land
The Work of an Almighty Hand.

Soon as the Evening Shades prevail,
The Moon takes up the wondrous Tale,
And nightly to the listning Earth
Repeats the Story of her Birth:
Whilst all the Stars that round her burn,
And all the Planets, in their turn,
Confirm the Tidings as they rowl,
And spread the Truth from Pole to Pole.

What though, in solemn Silence, all
Move round the dark terrestrial Ball?
What tho' nor real Voice nor Sound
Amid their radiant Orbs be found?
In Reason's Ear they all rejoice,
And utter forth a glorious Voice,
For ever singing, as they shine,
"The Hand that made us is Divine."

WILLIAM CONGREVE

(1670-1693-1729)

A Hue and Cry after Fair Amoret[2]

FAIR *Amoret* is gone astray;
Pursue and seek her, ev'ry Lover;

[1] Published in the *Spectator*, August 23, 1712. Text of first octavo edition.
[2] Published in Dryden's *Miscellany*, Volume V, 1704. Text of first edition.

I'll tell the Signs, by which you may
  The wand'ring Shepherdess discover.

Coquet and Coy at once her Air,
  Both study'd, tho' both seem neglected;
Careless she is with artful Care,
  Affecting to seem unaffected.

With Skill her Eyes dart ev'ry Glance,
  Yet change so soon you'd ne'er suspect 'em;
For she'd persuade they wound by chance,
  Tho' certain Aim and Art direct 'em.

She likes her self, yet others hates
  For that which in her self she prizes;
And while she Laughs at them, forgets
  She is the Thing that she despises.

GEORGE GRANVILLE, LORD LANSDOWNE

(1667-1696-1735)

To Myra[1]

THOUGHTFUL Nights, and restless Waking,
  O the Pains that we endure!
Broken Faith, unkind Forsaking,
  Ever doubting, never sure.
Hopes deceiving, vain Endeavours,
  What a Race has Love to run!
False Protesting, fleeting Favours,
  Ev'ry, ev'ry way, undone.
Still complaining, and defending,
  Both to love, yet not agree,
Fears tormenting, Passion rending,
  O the Pangs of Jealousie!
From such painful Ways of living,
  Ah how sweet, cou'd Love be free!
Still presenting, still receiving
  Fierce, immortal Extasie.

[1] Published in *Poems Upon Several Occasions*, 1712. Text of first edition.

Song. To Myra[1]

THE happiest Mortals once were we,
I lov'd *Myra, Myra* me;
  Each desirous of the Blessing,
  Nothing wanting but Possessing;
I lov'd *Myra, Myra* me,
The happiest Mortals once were we.

But since cruel Fates dissever,
Torn from Love, and torn for ever,
  Tortures end me,
  Death befriend me;
Of all Pains the greatest Pain
Is to love—and love in vain.

COLLEY CIBBER

(1671-1696-1757)

The Blind Boy[2]

O SAY! what is that Thing call'd Light,
  Which I can ne'er enjoy;
What is the Blessing of the Sight,
  O tell your poor Blind Boy?

You talk of wond'rous things you see,
  You say the Sun shines bright:
I feel him warm, but how can he
  Then make it Day, or Night.

My Day, or Night my self I make,
  Whene'er I wake, or play;
And cou'd I ever keep awake,
  It wou'd be always Day.

With heavy sighs, I often hear,
  You mourn my hopeless woe;

[1] Published in *Poems Upon Several Occasions*, 1712. Text of first edition.
[2] Published in *The British Musical Miscellany*, Volume I, 1734. Text of first edition.

But sure with patience I may bear,
A loss I ne'er can know.

Then let not what I cannot have,
My cheer of Mind destroy,
Whilst thus I sing, I am a King,
Altho' a poor Blind Boy!

SAMUEL GARTH

(1661-1699-1719)

The Dispensary[1]

Canto IV

NOT far from that most famous Theater,
Where wandring Punks each Night at five repair;
Where Purple Emperors in Buskins tread,
And Rule imaginary Worlds for Bread;
Where *Bently*, by Old Writers, wealthy grew,
And *Briscoe* lately was undone by New:
There triumphs a *Physician* of Renown,
To scarce a Mortal, but himself, unknown.
None e'er was plac'd more luckily than He,
For th' Exercise of such a Mystery.
When *Bur—ss* deafens all the listning press
With Peals of most Seraphick Emptiness;
Or when Mysterious *F—n* mounts on high,
To preach his Parish to a Lethargy:
This *Æsculapius* waits hard by, to ease
The *Martyrs* of such Christian Cruelties.
Long has this happy Quarter of the Town,
For Lewdness, Wit, and Gallantry been known.
All Sorts meet here, of whatsoe'er Degree,
To blend and justle into Harmony.
The Politicians of *Parnassus* prate,
And Poets canvass the Affairs of State;
The Cits ne'er talk of Trade and Stock, but tell
How *Virgil* writ, how bravely *Turnus* fell,
The Country-Dames drive to *Hippolito*'s,
First find a Spark, and after lose a Nose.

[1] Published in 1699. Text of second edition, 1699.

The Lawyer for Lac'd Coat the Robe does quit,
He grows a Mad-man, and then turns a Wit.
And in the Cloister pensive *Strephon* waits,
Till *Chloe*'s Hackney comes, and then retreats;
And if th' ungenerous Nymph a Shaft lets fly
More fatally than from a sparkling Eye,
Mirmillo, that fam'd *Opifer*, is nigh.
Th' *Apothecaries* thither throng to Dine,
And want of Elbow-room's supply'd in Wine.
Cloy'd with Variety, they surfeit there,
Whilst the wan Patients on thin Gruel fare.
'Twas here the Champions of the Party met,
Of their Heroick Enterprize to treat.
Each Hero a tremendous Air put on,
And stern *Mirmillo* in these Words begun:
'Tis with concern, my Friends, I meet you here;
No Grievance you can know, but I must share.
'Tis plain, my Int'rest you've advanc'd so long,
Each Fee, tho' I was mute, wou'd find a Tongue.
And in return, tho' I have strove to rend
Those Statutes, which on Oath I should defend;
Yet that's a Trifle to a generous Mind,
Great Services, as great Returns should find.
And you'll perceive, this Hand, when Glory calls,
Can brandish Arms as well as Urinals.
Oxford and all her passing Bells can tell,
By this Right Arm, what mighty Numbers fell.
Whilst others meanly ask'd whole Months to slay,
I oft dispatch'd the Patient in a Day:
With Pen in hand I push'd to that degree,
I scarce had left a Wretch to give a Fee.
Some fell by *Laudanum,* and some by *Steel*,
And Death in ambush lay in ev'ry Pill.
For save or slay, this Privilege we claim,
Tho' Credit suffers, the Reward's the same.
What tho' the Art of Healing we pretend,
He that designs it least, is most a Friend.
Into the Right we err, and must confess,
To Oversights we often owe Success.
Thus *Bessus* got the Battel in the *Play*,
His glorious Cowardise restor'd the Day.
So the fam'd *Grecian* Piece ow'd its desert
To Chance, and not the labour'd Stroaks of Art.
Physicians, if they're wise, shou'd never think
Of any other Arms than Pen and Ink:
But th' Enemy, at their expence, shall find,
When Honour calls, I'll scorn to stay behind.
He said; and seal'd th' Engagement with a Kiss,

Which was return'd by Younger *Askaris*;
Who thus advanc'd: Each Word, Sir, you impart,
Has something killing in it, like your Art.
How much we to your boundless Friendship owe,
Our Files can speak, and your Prescriptions show.
Your Ink descends in such excessive Show'rs,
'Tis plain, you can regard no Health but ours.
Whilst poor Pretenders trifle o'er a Case,
You but appear, and give the *Coup de Grace*.
O that near *Xanthus* Banks you had but dwelt,
When *Ilium* first *Achaian* Fury felt,
The Flood had curs'd young *Peleus*'s Arm in vain,
For troubling his choak'd Streams with heaps of slain.
No Trophies you had left for *Greeks* to raise,
Their ten Years Toil, you'd finish'd in ten Days.
Fate smiles on your Attempts, and when you list,
In vain the Cowards fly, or Brave resist.
Then let us Arm, we need not fear Success,
No Labours are too hard for *Hercules*.
Our military Ensigns we'll display;
Conquest pursues, where Courage leads the way.
To this Design sly *Querpo* did agree,
A worthless Member of the Faculty;
Drain'd from an *Elder*'s Loins with awkard gust,
In Lees of Stale Hypocrisie and Lust.
His Sire's pretended pious Steps he treads,
And where the Doctor fails, the Saint succeeds.
A Conventicle flesh'd his greener Years,
And his full age th' envenom'd Rancour shares.
Thus Boys hatch Game-Eggs under Birds o' prey,
To make the Fowl more furious for the Fray.
Dull *Carus* next discover'd his intent,
With much ado explaining what he meant.
His Spirits stagnate like *Cocitus*'s Flood,
And nought but Calentures can warm his Blood.
In his chill Veins the sluggish Puddle flows,
And loads with lazy Fogs his sable Brows.
The brainless Wretch claims a Preeminence
In settling Lunaticks, and helping Sense.
So when Perfumes their fragrant Scent give o're,
Nought can their Odour, like a Jakes, restore.
When for Advice the Vulgar throng, he's found
With lumber of vile Books besieg'd around.
The gazing Fry acknowledge their Surprize,
Consulting less their Reason than their Eyes.
And He perceives it stands in greater stead,
To furnish well his Classes, than his Head.
Thus a weak State, by wise Distrust, enclines

To num'rous Stores, and Strength in Magazines.
So Fools are always most profuse of Words,
And Cowards never fail of longest Swords.
Abandon'd Authors here a Refuge meet,
And from the World, to Dust and Worms retreat.
Here Dregs and Sediment of Auctions reign,
Refuse of Fairs, and Gleanings of *Duck-lane*;
And up these shelves, much *Gothick* Lumber climbs,
With *Swiss* Philosophy, and *Danish* Rhimes.
And hither, rescu'd from the *Grocers*, come
M—— Works entire, and endless Rheams of *Bloom*.
Where wou'd the long neglected *C*——*s* fly,
If bounteous *Carus* should refuse to buy?
But each vile Scribler's happy on this score,
He'll find some *Carus* still to read him o're.
  Nor must we the obsequious *Umbra* spare,
Who, soft by Nature, yet declar'd for War.
But when some Rival Pow'r invades a Right,
Flies set on Flies, and Turtles Turtles fight.
Else courteous *Umbra* to the last had been
Demurely meek, insipidly serene.
With Him, the present still some Virtues have,
The Vain are sprightly, and the Stupid, grave.
The Slothful, negligent; the Foppish neat;
The Lewd are airy, and the Sly discreet.
A Wren's an Eagle, a Baboon a Beau;
C——*t* a *Lycurgus*, and a *Phocion*, *R*——.
  Heroick Ardour now th' Assembly warms,
Each Combatant breaths nothing but Alarms.
For future glory, while the Scheme is laid,
Fam'd *Horoscope* thus offers to disswade;
  Since of each Enterprise th' Event's unknown,
We'll quit the Sword, and hearken to the Gown.
Nigh lives *Vagellius*, one reputed long,
For Strength of Lungs, and Pliancy of Tongue.
Which way He pleases, he can mould a Cause,
The Worst has Merits, and the Best has Flaws.
Five Guinea's make a Criminal to Day,
And ten to Morrow wipe the Stain away.
Whatever he affirms is undeny'd,
Milo's the Lecher, *Clodius* th' Homicide.
Cato pernicious, *Cataline* a Saint,
Or——*rd* suspected, *D*——*comb* innocent.
Let's then to Law, for 'tis by Fate decreed,
Vagellius, and our Mony, shall succeed.
Know, when I first invok'd *Disease* by Charms
T'assist, and be propitious to our Arms;
Ill Omens did the Sacrifice attend,

Nor wou'd the *Sybil* from her *Grott* ascend.
As *Horoscope* urg'd farther to be heard,
He thus was interrupted by a *Bard*;
In vain your Magick Mysteries you use,
Such sounds the *Sybil*'s Sacred Ears abuse.
These Lines the pale Divinity shall raise,
Such is the Pow'r of Sound, and Force of Lays.
Arms meet with Arms, Fauchions with Fauchions clash,
And sparks of Fire struck out from Armour flash.
Thick Clouds of Dust contending Warriours raise,
And hideous War o're all the Region brays.
Some raging ran with huge Herculean *Clubs,*
Some massy Balls of Brass, some mighty Tubs
Of Cynders bore. ——
Naked and half burnt Hulls, with hideous wreck,
Affright the Skies, and fry the Oceans back.
High Rocks of Snow, and sailing Hills of Ice,
Against each other with a mighty crash,
Driven by the Winds, in rude rencounter dash.
Blood, Brains, and Limbs the highest Walls distain,
And all around lay squallid Heaps of Slain.[2]
As he went rumbling on, the *Fury* straight
Crawl'd in, her Limbs cou'd scarce support her Weight.
A noysom Rag her pensive Temples bound,
And faintly her parch'd Lips these Accents found.
Mortal, how dar'st thou with such Lines address
My awful Seat, and trouble my Recess?
In *Essex* Marshy Hundreds is a Cell,
Where lazy Fogs, and drisling Vapours dwell:
Thither raw Damps on drooping Wings repair,
And shiv'ring Quartans shake the sickly Air.
There, when fatigu'd, some silent Hours I pass,
And substitute Physicians in my place.
Then dare not, for the future, once rehearse
Th' offensive Discord of such hideous Verse.
But in your Lines let Energy be found,
And learn to rise in Sense, and sink in Sound.
Harsh words, tho' pertinent, uncouth appear,
None please the Fancy, who offend the Ear.
In Sense and Numbers if you wou'd excel,
Read *W*——*y*, consider *D*——*den* well.
In one, what vigorous Turns of Fancy shine,
In th' other, *Syrens* warble in each Line.
If *D*——*sets* sprightly Muse but touch the Lyre,
The *Smiles* and *Graces* melt in soft desire,
And little *Loves* confess their amorous Fire.

[2] Lines 178-91 are quoted from Sir Richard Blackmore's *King Arthur* and *Prince Arthur*.

The *Tyber* now no gentle *Gallus* sees,
But smiling *Thames* enjoys his *No——bys*.
And gentle *Isis* claims the Ivy Crown,
To bind th' immortal Brows of *A——son*.
As tuneful *C——greve* trys his rural Strains,
Pan quits the Woods, the list'ning Fawns the Plains;
And *Philomel*, in Notes like his, complains.
And *Britain*, since *Pausanias* was writ,
Knows *Spartan* Virtue, and *Athenian* Wit.
When *St——ny* paints the Godlike Acts of Kings,
Or, what *Apollo* dictates, *P——r* sings:
The Banks of *Rhine* a pleas'd Attention show,
And Silver *Sequana* forgets to flow.
Such just Examples carefully read o're,
Slide without falling, without straining soar.
Oft tho' your Stroaks surprize, you shou'd not choose,
A Theme so mighty for a Virgin Muse.
Long did *Appelles* his Fam'd Piece decline,
His *Alexander* was his last Design.
'Tis *M——gue's* rich Vein alone must prove,
None but a *Phidias* shou'd attempt a *Jove*.
The Fury said; and vanishing from Sight,
Cry'd out to Arms; so left the Realms of Light.
The Combatants to th' Enterprize consent,
And the next day smil'd on the great Event.

JOHN POMFRET

(1667-1699-1702)

The Choice[1]

IF HEAV'N the Grateful Liberty wou'd give,
That I might Chuse my Method how to Live,
And all those Hours, propitious Fate should lend,
In blissful Ease, and Satisfaction spend:
Near some fair Town, I'd have a private Seat,
Built Uniform, not Little, nor too Great:
Better, if on a Rising Ground it stood;
Fields on this side, on that a Neighbouring Wood.
It shou'd within no other Things contain,

[1] Published in 1700. Text of *Miscellany Poems*, 1702, with some changes in punctuation.

But what were Useful, Necessary, Plain:
Methinks 'tis Nauseous, and I'd ne'er endure
The needless Pomp of Gaudy Furniture.
A little Garden, Grateful to the Eye,
And a Cool Rivulet run murm'ring by:
On whose delicious Banks a stately Row
Of Shady Limes, or Sycamores, shou'd grow:
At th' End of which a silent Study plac'd,
Shou'd be with all the Noblest Authors Grac'd:
Horace, and *Virgil*, in whose Mighty Lines
Immortal Wit, and Solid Learning shines;
Sharp *Juvenal*, and Am'rous *Ovid* too,
Who all the Turns of Loves soft Passion knew;
He that with Judgment reads his charming Lines,
In which strong Art, with stronger Nature joyns,
Must grant his Fancy does the best Excel,
His Thoughts so tender, and Exprest so well;
With all those Moderns, Men of steady Sense,
Esteem'd for Learning, and for Eloquence.
In some of these, as Fancy shou'd Advise,
I'd always take my Morning Exercise:
For sure no Minutes bring us more Content,
Than those in Pleasing, Useful Studies spent.
  I'd have a Clear, and Competent Estate,
That I might Live Gentilely, but not Great:
As much as I cou'd moderately spend,
A little more, sometimes t' Oblige a Friend.
Nor shou'd the Sons of Poverty Repine
Too much at Fortune, they shou'd Taste of mine;
And all, that Objects of true Pitty were,
Shou'd be Reliev'd with what my Wants cou'd spare.
For that, our Maker has too largely giv'n,
Shou'd be return'd, in Gratitude, to Heav'n.
A frugal Plenty shou'd my Table spread;
With Healthy, not Luxurious Dishes Fed:
Enough to Satisfy, and something more
To Feed the Stranger, and the Neighb'ring Poor.
Strong Meat Indulges Vice, and pampering Food
Creates Diseases, and Inflames the Blood.
But what's sufficient to make Nature strong,
And the bright Lamp of Life continue long,
I'd freely take, and as I did Possess,
The Bounteous Author of my Plenty Bless.
  I'd have a little Vault, but always stor'd
With the Best Wines, each Vintage cou'd afford.
Wine whets the Wit, improves its Native force,
And gives a pleasant Flavour to Discourse;

By making all our Spirits Debonair,
Throws off the Lees, the Sediment of Care.
But as the greatest Blessing, Heaven lends,
May be Debauch'd, and serve Ignoble Ends:
So, but too oft, the Grapes refreshing Juice
Does many Mischievous Effects produce.
My House shou'd no such rude Disorders know,
As from high Drinking consequently flow.
Nor wou'd I use, what was so kindly giv'n,
To the Dishonour of Indulgent Heav'n.
If any Neighbour came, he shou'd be Free,
Us'd with Respect, and not uneasy be,
In my Retreat, or to himself, or me.
What Freedom, Prudence, and right Reason give,
All Men may with Impunity receive:
But the least swerving from their Rule's too much:
For, what's forbidden us, 'tis Death to touch.
  That Life might be more Comfortable yet,
And all my Joys Refin'd, Sincere, and Great;
I'd Chuse two Friends, whose Company wou'd be
A great Advance to my Felicity:
Well Born, of Humours suited to my own,
Discreet, and Men, as well as Books, have known;
Brave, Gen'rous, Witty, and exactly Free
From loose Behaviour, or Formality;
Airy, and Prudent, Merry, but not Light,
Quick in Discerning, and in Judging right.
Secret they shou'd be, Faithful to their Trust;
In Reas'ning Cool, Strong, Temperate, and Just;
Obliging, Open, without Huffing Brave,
Brisk in Gay Talking, and in Sober, Grave;
Close in Dispute, but not Tenacious, try'd
By Solid Reason, and let that Decide;
Not prone to Lust, Revenge, or Envious Hate,
Nor busy Medlers with Intreagues of State;
Strangers to Slander, and sworn Foes to Spight,
Not Quarrelsome, but Stout enough to Fight;
Loyal, and Pious, Friends to *Cæsar* true,
As Dying Martyrs to their Maker too;
In their Society, I cou'd not miss
A Permanent, Sincere, Substantial Bliss.
  Wou'd Bounteous Heav'n once more Indulge, I'd choose,
(For who wou'd so much Satisfaction lose,
As Witty Nymphs, in Conversation, give,)
Near some Obliging, Modest Fair to live;
For there's that Sweetness in a Female Mind,
Which in a Man's we cannot hope to find:

That by a Secret, but a Pow'rful, Art
Winds up the Springs of Life, and does impart
Fresh Vital Heat to the Transported Heart.
I'd have her Reason all her Passions sway;
Easy in Company, in Private Gay:
Coy to a Fop, to the Deserving Free,
Still Constant to her self, and Just to me.
A Soul she shou'd have, for Great Actions fit;
Prudence, and Wisdom to direct her Wit:
Courage to look bold Danger in the Face,
No Fear, but only to be Proud, or Base:
Quick to Advise, by an Emergence prest,
To give good Counsel, or to take the best.
I'd have th' Expression of her Thoughts be such,
She might not seem Reserv'd, nor talk too much;
That shews a want of Judgment and of Sense:
More than Enough is but Impertinence:
Her Conduct Regular, her Mirth Refin'd,
Civil to Strangers, to her Neighbours kind:
Averse to Vanity, Revenge, and Pride,
In all the Methods of Deceit untry'd:
So Faithful to her Friend, and Good to all,
No Censure might upon her Actions fall:
Then wou'd e'en Envy be compell'd to say,
She goes the least of Woman-kind Astray.
To this Fair Creature I'd sometimes Retire;
Her Conversation wou'd new Joys inspire;
Give Life an Edge so keen, no surly Care
Would venture to Assault my Soul, or dare
Near my Retreat to hide one secret Snare.
But so Divine, so Noble a Repast,
I'd seldom, and with Moderation, taste.
For Highest Cordials all their Virtue lose,
By a too frequent, and too bold an Use:
And what wou'd Cheer the Spirits in Distress,
Ruines our Health, when taken to Excess.
I'd be concern'd in no Litigious Jar,
Belov'd by all, not vainly Popular.
What e're Assistance I had Pow'r to bring
T' Oblige my Country, or to Serve my King,
When e're they Call'd, I'd readily afford
My Tongue, my Pen, my Counsel, or my Sword.
Law Suits I'd shun, with as much studious Care,
As I wou'd Dens where hungry Lyons are:
And rather put up Injuries, than be
A Plague to him who'd be a Plague to me.
I value Quiet at a Price too great,
To give for my Revenge so dear a Rate:

For what do we, by all our Bustle, gain,
But Counterfeit Delight, for real Pain?
If Heav'n a Date of many Years wou'd give,
Thus I'd in Pleasure, Ease, and Plenty live.
And as I near approach'd the Verge of Life,
Some kind Relation, (for I'd have no Wife)
Shou'd take upon him all my Worldly Care,
While I did for a better State prepare.
Then I'd not be with any Trouble vex'd,
Nor have the Ev'ning of my days perplex'd;
But by a silent, and a peaceful Death,
Without a Sigh, resign my Aged Breath:
And when committed to the Dust, I'd have
Few Tears, but Friendly, dropt into my Grave.
Then wou'd my Exit so propitious be,
All Men wou'd wish to Live, and Dye like me.

AMBROSE PHILIPS

(1675?-1700-1749)

Pastorals[1]

The Sixth Pastoral

GERON. HOBBINOL. LANQUET.

GERON

How still the Sea! behold; how calm the Sky!
And how, in sportive Chase, the Swallows fly!
My Goats, secure from Harm, no Tendance need,
While high on yonder hanging Rock they feed:
And here below, the banky Shore along,
Your Heifers graze: And I to hear your Song
Dispos'd. As eldest, *Hobbinol*, begin;
And *Lanquet*'s Under-Song by Turns come in.

HOBBINOL

Let others meanly stake upon their Skill,
Or Kid, or Lamb, or Goat, or what they will;
For Praise we sing, nor Wager ought beside:
And, whose the Praise, let *Geron*'s Lips decide.

[1] Published in Dryden's *Miscellany*, Volume VI, 1709. Text of first edition.

LANQUET

To *Geron* I my Voice and Skill commend:
Unbias'd he, to both is equal Friend.

GERON

Begin then, Boys, and vary well your Song;
Nor fear, from *Geron*'s upright Sentence, Wrong.
A boxen Haut-Boy, loud, and sweet of Sound,
All varnish'd, and with brazen Ringlets bound,
I to the Victor give: No small Reward,
If with our usual Country Pipes compar'd.

HOBBINOL

The Snows are melted, and the kindly Rain
Descends on ev'ry Herb, and ev'ry Grain;
Soft balmy Breezes breath along the Sky:
The bloomy Season of the Year is nigh.

LANQUET

The Cuckoo tells aloud her painful Love;
The Turtle's Voice is heard in ev'ry Grove;
The Pastures change; the warbling Linnets sing:
Prepare to welcome in the gawdy Spring.

HOBBINOL

When Locusts in the fearny Bushes cry,
When Ravens pant, and Snakes in Caverns lye;
Then graze in Woods, and quit the burning Plain;
Else shall ye press the spungy Teat in vain.

LANQUET

When Greens to Yellow vary, and you see
The Ground bestrew'd with Fruits off ev'ry Tree,
And stormy Winds are heard; think Winter near,
Nor trust too far to the declining Year.

HOBBINOL

Full fain, O blest *Eliza!* would I praise
Thy Maiden Rule, and *Albion*'s Golden Days.
Then gentle *Sidney* liv'd, the Shepherds Friend:
Eternal Blessings on his Shade attend!

LANQUET

Thrice happy Shepherds now: For *Dorset* loves
The Country Muse, and our delightful Groves;
While *ANNA* reigns. O ever may she reign!
And bring on Earth a Golden Age again.

HOBBINOL

I love in secret all a beauteous Maid,
And have my Love in secret all repaid.
This coming Night she does reserve for me.
Divine her Name; and thou the Victor be.

LANQUET

Mild as the Lamb, and harmless as the Dove,
True as the Turtle, is the Maid I love.
How we in secret love, I shall not say.
Divine her Name; and I give up the Day.

HOBBINOL

Soft, on a Cowslip Bank, my Love and I
Together lay: A Brook ran murm'ring by.
A thousand tender things to me she said;
And I a thousand tender Things repaid.

LANQUET

In Summer Shade, beneath the cocking Hay,
What soft, endearing Words did she not say?
Her Lap, with Apron deck'd, she kindly spread,
And stroak'd my Cheeks, and lull'd my leaning Head.

HOBBINOL

Breath soft, ye Winds, ye Waters gently flow;
Shield her, ye Trees, ye Flowers around her grow;
Ye Swains, I beg you, pass in Silence by;
My Love in yonder Vale asleep does lye.

LANQUET

Once *Delia* slept, on easie Moss reclin'd;
Her lovely Limbs half bare, and rude the Wind:
I smooth'd her Coats, and stole a silent Kiss.
Condemn me, Shepherds, if I did amiss.

HOBBINOL

As *Marian* bath'd, by chance I passed by;
She blush'd, and at me cast a sidelong Eye:
Then swift beneath the crystal Wave she try'd
Her beauteous Form, but all in vain, to hide.

LANQUET

As I, to cool me, bath'd one sultry Day,
Fond *Lydia* lurking in the Sedges lay.
The Wanton laugh'd, and seem'd in haste to fly;
Yet often stopp'd, and often turn'd her Eye.

HOBBINOL

When first I saw, would I had never seen,
Young *Lyset* lead the Dance on yonder Green;
Intent upon her Beauties as she mov'd,
Poor, heedless Wretch, at unawares I lov'd.

LANQUET

When *Lucy* decks with Flow'rs her swelling Breast,
And on her Elbow leans, dissembling Rest;
Unable to refrain my madding Mind,
Nor Sheep nor Pasture worth my Care I find.

HOBBINOL

Come *Rosalind*, O come! For, without thee,
What Pleasure can the Country have for me?
Come *Rosalind*, O come! My brinded Kine,
My snowy Sheep, my Farm and all is thine.

LANQUET

Come *Rosalind*, O come! Here shady Bow'rs,
Here are cool Fountains, and here springing Flow'rs.
Come *Rosalind*: Here ever let us stay,
And sweetly waste our live-long Time away.

HOBBINOL

In vain the Seasons of the Moon I know,
The Force of healing Herbs, and where they grow;
There is no Herb, no Season, may remove
From my fond Heart the racking Pains of Love.

LANQUET

What profits me, that I in Charms have Skill,
And Ghosts and Goblins order as I will;
Yet have, with all my Charms, no Pow'r to lay
The Sprite, that breaks my Quiet Night and Day.

HOBBINOL

O that like *Colin* I had Skill in Rhymes:
To purchase Credit with succeeding Times!
Sweet *Colin Clout*! who never yet had Peer,
Who sung thro' all the Seasons of the Year.

LANQUET

Let me like *Wrenock* sing; his Voice had Pow'r
To free the clipsing Moon at Midnight Hour:
And, as he sung, the Fairies, with their Queen,
In Mantles blue came tripping o'er the Green.

GERON

Here end your pleasing Strife. Both Victors are;
And both with *Colin* may in Rhyme compare.
A Boxen Haut-Boy, loud, and sweet of Sound,
All varnish'd, and with brazen Ringlets bound,
To both I give. A mizling Mist descends
Adown that steepy Rock: And this way tends
Yon distant Rain. Shore-ward the Vessels strive;
And, see, the Boys their Flocks to Shelter drive.

A Winter-Piece
To the Earl of Dorset[1]

Copenhagen, March 9, 1709.

FROM Frozen Climes, and Endless Traks of Snow,
From Streams that Northern Winds forbid to flow;
What Present shall the Muse to *Dorset* bring;
Or how, so near the Pole, attempt to sing?
The hoary Winter here conceals from Sight,
All pleasing Objects that to Verse invite.
The Hills and Dales, and the Delightful Woods,
The Flowry Plains, and Silver Streaming Floods,

[1] Published in the *Tatler*, May 7, 1709. Text of first octavo edition, 1710.

By Snow disguis'd, in bright Confusion lye,
And with one dazling Waste fatigue the Eye.
  No gentle breathing Breeze prepares the Spring,
No Birds within the Desart Region sing.
The Ships unmov'd the boist'rous Winds defy,
While rattling Chariots o'er the Ocean fly.
The vast *Leviathan* wants Room to play,
And spout his Waters in the Face of Day.
The starving Wolves along the main Sea prowl,
And to the Moon in Icy Valleys howl.
For many a shining League the level Main,
Here spreads it self into a Glassy Plain:
There solid Billows of enormous Size,
Alpes of green Ice, in wild Disorder rise.
  And yet but lately have I seen e'en here,
The Winter in a lovely Dress appear.
E'er yet the Clouds let fall the treasur'd Snow,
Or Winds begun thro' hazy Skies to blow.
At Ev'ning a keen Eastern Breeze arose;
And the descending Rain unsullied froze.
Soon as the silent Shades of Night withdrew,
The ruddy Morn disclos'd at once to View
The Face of Nature in a rich Disguise,
And brighten'd ev'ry Object to my Eyes.
For ev'ry Shrub, and ev'ry Blade of Grass,
And ev'ry pointed Thorn, seem'd wrought in Glass.
In Pearls and Rubies rich the Hawthorns show,
While thro' the Ice the Crimson Berries glow.
The thick-sprung Reeds the watry Marshes yield,
Seem polish'd Lances in a hostile Field.
The Stag in limpid Currents with Surprize,
Sees Chrystal Branches on his Forehead rise.
The spreading Oak, the Beech, and tow'ring Pine,
Glaz'd over, in the freezing Æther shine.
The frighted Birds the rattling Branches shun,
That wave and glitter in the distant Sun.
  When if a sudden Gust of Wind arise,
The brittle Forrest into Atoms flies:
The crackling Wood beneath the Tempest bends,
And in a spangled Show'r the Prospect ends.
Or if a Southern Gale the Region warm,
And by Degrees unbind the Wintry Charm;
The Traveller a miry Country sees,
And Journeys sad beneath the dropping Trees.
  Like some deluded Peasant, *Merlin* leads
Thro' fragrant Bow'rs, and thro' delicious Meads;
While here inchanted Gardens to him rise,
And airy Fabricks there attract his Eyes,

His wand'ring Feet the Magick Paths pursue;
And while he thinks the fair Illusion true,
The trackless Scenes disperse in fluid Air,
And Woods and Wilds, and thorny Ways appear:
A tedious Road the weary Wretch returns,
And, as He goes, the transient Vision mourns.

Song[1]

FROM *White*'s and *Will*'s,
To purling Rills
The Love-sick *Strephon* flies;
There, full of Woe,
His Numbers flow,
And all in Rhyme he dies.

The fair Coquett,
With feign'd Regret,
Invites him back to Town;
But when, in Tears,
The Youth appears,
She meets him with a Frown.

Full oft' the Maid
This Prank had play'd,
'Till angry *Strephon* swore;
And, what is strange,
Tho' loath to change,
Would never see her more.

To the Right Honourable Robert Walpole, Esq.[2]

June 15, 1724.

VOTARY to publick zeal,
Minister of *England*'s weal,
Have you leisure for a song,
Tripping lightly o'er the tongue,
Swift and sweet in every measure,
Tell me, *Walpole*, have you leisure?
Nothing lofty will I sing,

[1] Published in Steele's *Poetical Miscellanies*, 1714. Text of first edition.

[2] Published in 1724. Text of *Pastorals, Epistles, Odes, and other Original Poems*, 1765.

Nothing of the favourite king,
Something, rather, sung with ease,
Simply elegant to please.
  Fairy virgin, *British* muse,
Some unhear'd of story chuse:
Chuse the glory of the swain,
Gifted with a magick strain,
Swaging grief of every kind,
Healing, with a verse, the mind:
To him came a man of power,
To him, in a cheerless hour;
When the swain, by Druids taught,
Soon divin'd his irksom thought,
Soon the maple harp he strung,
Soon, with silver accent, sung.
  "Steerer of a mighty realm,
"Pilot, waking o'er the helm,
"Blessing of thy native soil,
"Weary of a thankless toil,
"Cast repining thought behind,
"Give thy trouble to the wind.
"Mortal, destin'd to excel,
"Bear the blame of doing well,
"Like the worthies great of old,
"In the list of fame enroll'd.
"What, though titles thou decline?
"Still the more thy virtues shine.
"Envy, with her serpent eye,
"Marks each praise that soars on high.
"To thy lot resign thy will:
"Every good is mix'd with ill.
"See, the white unblemish'd rose
"On a thorny bramble blows:
"See, the torrent pouring rain
"Does the limpid fountain stain:
"See, the giver of the day
"Urgeth on, through clouds, his way:
"Nothing is, entirely, bless'd;
"Envy does thy worth attest.
  "Pleasing visions, at command,
"Answer to my voice and hand;
"Quick, the blissful scene prepare,
"Sooth the patriot's heavy care:
"Visions, cheering to the sight,
"Give him earnest of delight.
  "Wise disposer of affairs,
"View the end of all thy cares!
"Forward cast thy ravish'd eyes,

"See the gladning harvest rise:
"Lo, the people reap thy pain!
"Thine the labor, theirs the gain.
"Yonder turn, a-while, thy view,
"Turn thee to yon spreading yew,
"Once the gloomy tree of fate,
"Once the plighted virgin's hate:
"Now, no longer, does it grow,
"Parent of the warring bow:
"See, beneath the guiltless shade,
"Peasants shape the plow and spade,
"Rescued, ever, from the fear
"Of the whistling shaft and spear.
"Lo, where plenty comes, with peace!
"Hear the breath of murmur cease:
"See, at last, unclouded days;
"Hear, at last, unenvied praise.
"Nothing shall thy soul molest;
"Labour is the price of rest.
"Mortal, destin'd to excel,
"Bless the toil of doing well!

To Miss Charlotte Pulteney in Her Mother's Arms[1]

May 1, 1724.

TIMELY blossom, infant fair,
Fondling of a happy pair,
Every morn, and every night,
Their solicitous delight,
Sleeping, waking, still at ease,
Pleasing, without skill to please,
Little gossip, blithe and hale,
Tattling many a broken tale,
Singing many a tuneless song,
Lavish of a heedless tongue,
Simple maiden, void of art,
Babbling out the very heart,
Yet abandon'd to thy will,
Yet imagining no ill,
Yet too innocent to blush,
Like the linnet in the bush,
To the mother-linnet's note

[1] Published in *Poems,* Dublin, 1725. Text of *Pastorals, Epistles, Odes, and other Original Poems,* 1765.

Moduling her slender throat,
Chirping forth thy petty joys,
Wanton in the change of toys,
Like the linnet green, in *May*,
Flitting to each bloomy spray,
Wearied then, and glad of rest,
Like the linnet in the nest.
This thy present happy lot,
This, in time, will be forgot:
Other pleasures, other cares,
Ever-busy time prepares;
And thou shalt in thy daughter see,
This picture, once, resembled thee.

To Signora Cuzzoni[1]

May 25, 1724.

LITTLE *Siren* of the stage,
Charmer of an idle age,
Empty warbler, breathing lyre,
Wanton gale of fond desire,
Bane of every manly art,
Sweet enfeebler of the heart,
O, too pleasing in thy strain,
Hence, to southern climes again;
Tuneful mischief, vocal spell,
To this island bid farewel;
Leave us as we ought to be,
Leave the *Britons* rough and free.

To Miss Margaret Pulteney, Daughter of Daniel Pulteney, Esq.; in the Nursery[2]

April 27, 1727.

DIMPLY damsel, sweetly smiling,
All caressing, none beguiling,
Bud of beauty, fairly blowing,
Every charm to nature owing,
This and that new thing admiring,
Much of this and that enquiring,

[1] Published in *The Musical Miscellany*, Vol. V, 1731. Text of *Pastorals, Epistles, Odes, and other Original Poems*, 1765.

[2] Published in 1727. Text of *Pastorals, Epistles, Odes, and other Original Poems*, 1765.

Knowledge by degrees attaining,
Day by day some virtue gaining,
Ten years hence, when I leave chiming,
Beardless poets, fondly rhyming,
(Fescu'd now, perhaps, in spelling,)
On thy riper beauties dwelling,
Shall accuse each killing feature
Of the cruel, charming, creature,
Whom I knew complying, willing,
Tender, and averse to killing.

JOHN PHILIPS

(1676-1701-1709)

The Splendid Shilling. An Imitation of Milton[1]

HAPPY the Man, who void of Cares and Strife,
In Silken, or in Leathern Purse retains
A *Splendid Shilling:* He nor hears with Pain
New Oysters cry'd, nor sighs for chearful Ale;
But with his Friends, when nightly Mists arise,
To *Juniper*'s, *Magpye*, or *Town-Hall* repairs:
Where, mindful of the Nymph, whose wanton Eye
Transfix'd his Soul, and kindled Amorous Flames,
Chloe, or *Phillis*; he each Circling Glass
Wisheth her Health, and Joy, and equal Love.
Mean while he smoaks, and laughs at merry Tale,
Or *Pun* ambiguous, or *Conundrum* quaint.
But I, whom griping Penury surrounds,
And Hunger, sure Attendant upon Want,
With scanty Offals, and small acid Tiff
(Wretched Repast!) my meagre Corps sustain:
Then Solitary walk, or doze at home
In Garret vile, and with a warming puff
Regale chill'd Fingers; or from Tube as black
As Winter-Chimney, or well-polish'd Jet,
Exhale *Mundungus*, ill-perfuming Scent:
Not blacker Tube, nor of a shorter Size
Smoaks *Cambro-Britain* (vers'd in Pedigree,
Sprung from *Cadwalader* and *Arthur*, Kings
Full famous in Romantic tale) when he

[1] Published in 1701. Text of 1705 edition.

O'er many a craggy Hill, and barren Cliff,
Upon a Cargo of fam'd *Cestrian* Cheese,
High over-shadowing rides, with a design
To vend his Wares, or at th' *Arvonian* Mart,
Or *Maridunum*, or the ancient Town
Eclip'd *Brechinia*, or where *Vaga*'s Stream
Encircles *Ariconium*, fruitful Soil,
Whence flow Nectareous Wines, that well may vye
With *Massic*, *Setin*, or renown'd *Falern*.
  Thus while my joyless Minutes tedious flow
With Looks demure, and silent Pace, a *Dunn*,
Horrible Monster! hated by Gods and Men,
To my aerial Citadel ascends;
With Vocal Heel thrice thund'ring at my Gates,
With hideous Accent thrice he calls; I know
The Voice ill-boding, and the solemn Sound.
What shou'd I do? or whither turn? amaz'd,
Confounded, to the dark Recess I fly
Of Woodhole; strait my bristling Hairs erect
Thrô sudden Fear; a chilly Sweat bedews
My shud'ring Limbs, and (wonderful to tell!)
My Tongue forgets her Faculty of Speech;
So horrible he seems! his faded Brow
Entrench'd with many a Frown, and *Conic* Beard,
And spreading Band, admir'd by Modern Saints,
Disastrous Acts forebode; in his Right Hand
Long Scrolls of Paper solemnly he waves,
With Characters, and Figures dire inscrib'd
Grievous to mortal Eyes; (ye Gods avert
Such Plagues from righteous Men!) behind him stalks
Another Monster, not unlike himself,
Sullen of Aspect, by the Vulgar call'd
A *Catchpole*, whose polluted Hands the Gods
With Force incredible, and Magick Charms
Erst have indu'd, if he his ample Palm
Should haply on ill-fated Shoulder lay
Of Debtor, strait his Body, to the Touch
Obsequious, (as whilom Knights were wont)
To some enchanted Castle is convey'd,
Where Gates impregnable, and coercive Chains
In Durance strict detain him, 'till in form
Of Mony, *Pallas* sets the Captive free.
  Beware, ye Debtors, when ye walk beware,
Be circumspect; oft with insidious Ken
This Caitif eyes your Steps aloof, and oft
Lies perdue in a Nook or gloomy Cave,
Prompt to enchant some inadvertent wretch
With his unhallow'd Touch. So (Poets sing)

Grimalkin to Domestick Vermin sworn
An everlasting Foe, with watchful Eye,
Lyes nightly brooding o'er a chinky gap,
Protending her fell Claws, to thoughtless Mice
Sure Ruin. So her disembowell'd Web
Arachne in a Hall, or Kitchin spreads,
Obvious to vagrant Flies: She secret stands
Within her woven Cell; the Humming Prey,
Regardless of their Fate, rush on the toils
Inextricable, nor will aught avail
Their Arts, nor Arms, nor Shapes of lovely Hue.
The Wasp insidious, and the buzzing Drone,
And Butterfly proud of expanded wings
Distinct with Gold, entangled in her Snares,
Useless Resistance make: With eager strides,
She tow'ring flies to her expected Spoils;
Then with envenom'd Jaws the vital Blood
Drinks of reluctant Foes, and to her Cave
Their bulky Carcasses triumphant drags.
  So pass my Days. But when Nocturnal Shades
This World invelop, and th' inclement Air
Persuades Men to repel benumming Frosts,
With pleasant Wines, and crackling blaze of Wood;
Me Lonely sitting, nor the glimmering Light
Of Make-weight Candle, nor the joyous Talk
Of loving Friend delights; distress'd, forlorn,
Amidst the horrors of the tedious Night,
Darkling I sigh, and feed with dismal Thoughts
My anxious Mind; or sometimes mournful Verse
Indite, and sing of Groves and Myrtle Shades,
Or desperate Lady near a purling Stream,
Or Lover pendent on a Willow-Tree:
Mean while I Labour with eternal Drought,
And restless Wish, and Rave; my parched Throat
Finds no Relief, nor heavy Eyes Repose:
But if a Slumber haply does Invade
My weary Limbs, my Fancy's still awake,
Thoughtful of Drink, and Eager in a Dream,
Tipples Imaginary Pots of Ale;
In Vain; awake, I find the settled Thirst
Still gnawing, and the pleasant Phantom curse.
  Thus do I live from Pleasure quite debarr'd,
Nor taste the Fruits that the Sun's genial Rays
Mature, *John-Apple*, nor the downy *Peach*,
Nor *Walnut* in rough-furrow'd Coat secure,
Nor *Medlar*, Fruit delicious in decay;
Afflictions Great! yet Greater still remain:
My *Galligaskins* that have long withstood

The Winter's Fury, and Encroaching Frosts,
By Time subdu'd, (what will not Time subdue!)
An horrid Chasm disclose, with Orifice
Wide, Discontinuous; at which the Winds
Eurus and *Auster*, and the dreadful Force
Of *Boreas*, that congeals the *Cronian* Waves,
Tumultuous enter with dire chilling Blasts,
Portending Agues. Thus a well-fraught Ship
Long sail'd secure, or thrô th' *Ægean* Deep,
Or the *Ionian*, 'till Cruising near
The *Lilybean* Shoar, with hideous Crush
On *Scylla*, or *Charybdis* (dang'rous Rocks)
She strikes rebounding, whence the shatter'd Oak,
So fierce a Shock unable to withstand,
Admits the Sea; in at the gaping Side
The crouding Waves Gush with impetuous Rage,
Resistless, Overwhelming; Horrors seize
The Mariners, Death in their Eyes appears,
They stare, they lave, they pump, they swear, they pray:
(Vain Efforts!) still the battering Waves rush in
Implacable, 'till delug'd by the Foam,
The Ship sinks found'ring in the vast Abyss.

BERNARD MANDEVILLE

(1670-1703-1733)

The Grumbling Hive: or, Knaves turn'd Honest[1]

A SPACIOUS Hive well stockt with Bees,
That liv'd in Luxury and Ease;
And yet as fam'd for Laws and Arms,
As yielding large and early Swarms;
Was counted the great Nursery
Of Sciences and Industry.
No Bees had better Government,
More Fickleness, or less Content:
They were not Slaves to Tyranny,
Nor rul'd by wild *Democracy*;
But Kings, that could not wrong, because
Their Power was circumscrib'd by Laws.
THESE Insects liv'd like Men, and all

[1] Published in 1705. Text of *Fable of the Bees*, 1732.

Our Actions they perform'd in small:
They did whatever's done in Town,
And what belongs to Sword or Gown:
Tho' th' Artful Works, by nimble Slight
Of minute Limbs, 'scap'd Human Sight;
Yet we've no Engines, Labourers,
Ships, Castles, Arms, Artificers,
Craft, Science, Shop, or Instrument,
But they had an Equivalent:
Which, since their Language is unknown,
Must be call'd, as we do our own.
As grant, that among other Things,
They wanted Dice, yet they had Kings;
And those had Guards; from whence we may
Justly conclude, they had some Play;
Unless a Regiment be shewn
Of Soldiers, that make use of none.
  VAST Numbers throng'd the fruitful Hive;
Yet those vast Numbers made 'em thrive;
Millions endeavouring to supply
Each other's Lust and Vanity;
While other Millions were employ'd,
To see their Handy-works destroy'd;
They furnish'd half the Universe;
Yet had more Work than Labourers.
Some with vast Stocks, and little Pains,
Jump'd into Business of great Gains;
And some were damn'd to Sythes and Spades,
And all those hard laborious Trades;
Where willing Wretches daily sweat,
And wear out Strength and Limbs to eat:
While others follow'd Mysteries,
To which few Folks bind 'Prentices;
That want no Stock, but that of Brass,
And may set up without a Cross;
As Sharpers, Parasites, Pimps, Players,
Pick-pockets, Coiners, Quacks, South-sayers,
And all those, that in Enmity,
With downright Working, cunningly
Convert to their own Use the Labour
Of their good-natur'd heedless Neighbour.
These were call'd Knaves, but bar the Name,
The grave Industrious were the same:
All Trades and Places knew some Cheat,
No Calling was without Deceit.
  THE Lawyers, of whose Art the Basis
Was raising Feuds and splitting Cases,
Oppos'd all Registers, that Cheats

Might make more Work with dipt Estates;
As wer't unlawful, that one's own,
Without a Law-Suit, should be known.
They kept off Hearings wilfully,
To finger the refreshing Fee;
And to defend a wicked Cause,
Examin'd and survey'd the Laws,
As Burglars Shops and Houses do,
To find out where they'd best break through.
PHYSICIANS valu'd Fame and Wealth
Above the drooping Patient's Health,
Or their own Skill: The greatest Part
Study'd, instead of Rules of Art,
Grave pensive Looks and dull Behaviour,
To gain th' Apothecary's Favour;
The Praise of Midwives, Priests, and all
That serv'd at Birth or Funeral.
To bear with th' ever-talking Tribe,
And hear my Lady's Aunt prescribe;
With formal Smile, and kind How d'ye,
To fawn on all the Family;
And, which of all the greatest Curse is,
T' endure th' Impertinence of Nurses.
AMONG the many Priests of *Jove*,
Hir'd to draw Blessings from Above,
Some few were Learn'd and Eloquent,
But thousands Hot and Ignorant:
Yet all pass'd Muster that could hide
Their Sloth, Lust, Avarice and Pride;
For which they were as fam'd as Tailors
For Cabbage, or for Brandy Sailors:
Some, meagre-look'd, and meanly clad,
Would mystically pray for Bread,
Meaning by that an ample Store,
Yet lit'rally received no more;
And, while these holy Drudges starv'd,
The lazy Ones, for which they serv'd,
Indulg'd their Ease, with all the Graces
Of Health and Plenty in their Faces.
THE Soldiers, that were forc'd to fight,
If they surviv'd, got Honour by't;
Tho' some, that shunn'd the bloody Fray,
Had Limbs shot off, that ran away:
Some valiant Gen'rals fought the Foe;
Others took Bribes to let them go:
Some ventur'd always where 'twas warm,
Lost now a Leg, and then an Arm;

Till quite disabled, and put by,
They liv'd on half their Salary;
While others never came in Play,
And staid at Home for double Pay.
THEIR Kings were serv'd, but Knavishly,
Cheated by their own Ministry;
Many, that for their Welfare slaved,
Robbing the very Crown they saved:
Pensions were small, and they liv'd high,
Yet boasted of their Honesty.
Calling, whene'er they strain'd their Right,
The slipp'ry Trick a Perquisite;
And when Folks understood their Cant,
They chang'd that for Emolument;
Unwilling to be short or plain,
In any thing concerning Gain;
For there was not a Bee but would
Get more, I won't say, than he should;
But than he dar'd to let them know,
That pay'd for't; as your Gamesters do,
That, tho' at fair Play, ne'er will own
Before the Losers what they've won.
BUT who can all their Frauds repeat?
The very Stuff, which in the Street
They sold for Dirt t'enrich the Ground,
Was often by the Buyers found
Sophisticated with a quarter
Of good-for-nothing Stones and Mortar;
Tho' *Flail* had little Cause to mutter,
Who sold the other Salt for Butter.
JUSTICE her self, fam'd for fair Dealing,
By Blindness had not lost her Feeling;
Her Left Hand, which the Scales should hold,
Had often dropt 'em, brib'd with Gold;
And, tho' she seem'd Impartial,
Where Punishment was corporal,
Pretended to a reg'lar Course,
In Murther, and all Crimes of Force;
Tho' some, first pillory'd for Cheating,
Were hang'd in Hemp of their own beating;
Yet, it was thought, the Sword she bore
Check'd but the Desp'rate and the Poor;
That, urg'd by meer Necessity,
Were ty'd up to the wretched Tree
For Crimes, which not deserv'd that Fate,
But to secure the Rich and Great.
THUS every Part was full of Vice,
Yet the whole Mass a Paradise;

Flatter'd in Peace, and fear'd in Wars,
They were th' Esteem of Foreigners,
And lavish of their Wealth and Lives,
The Balance of all other Hives.
Such were the Blessings of that State;
Their Crimes conspir'd to make them Great:
And Virtue, who from Politicks
Had learn'd a Thousand Cunning Tricks,
Was, by their happy Influence,
Made Friends with Vice: And ever since,
The worst of all the Multitude
Did something for the Common Good.
  THIS was the State's Craft, that maintain'd
The Whole of which each Part complain'd:
This, as in Musick Harmony,
Made Jarrings in the main agree;
Parties directly opposite,
Assist each other, as 'twere for Spight;
And Temp'rance with Sobriety,
Serve Drunkenness and Gluttony.
  THE Root of Evil, Avarice,
That damn'd ill-natur'd baneful Vice,
Was Slave to Prodigality,
That noble Sin; whilst Luxury
Employ'd a Million of the Poor,
And odious Pride a Million more:
Envy it self, and Vanity,
Were Ministers of Industry;
Their darling Folly, Fickleness,
In Diet, Furniture and Dress,
That strange ridic'lous Vice, was made
The very Wheel that turn'd the Trade.
Their Laws and Clothes were equally
Objects of Mutability;
For, what was well done for a time,
In half a Year became a Crime;
Yet while they alter'd thus their Laws,
Still finding and correcting Flaws,
They mended by Inconstancy
Faults, which no Prudence could foresee.
  THUS Vice nurs'd Ingenuity,
Which join'd with Time and Industry,
Had carry'd Life's Conveniencies,
It's real Pleasures, Comforts, Ease,
To such a Height, the very Poor
Liv'd better than the Rich before,
And nothing could be added more.
  How Vain is Mortal Happiness!

Had they but known the Bounds of Bliss;
And that Perfection here below
Is more than Gods can well bestow;
The Grumbling Brutes had been content
With Ministers and Government.
But they, at every ill Success,
Like Creatures lost without Redress,
Curs'd Politicians, Armies, Fleets;
While every one cry'd, *Damn the Cheats,*
And would' tho' conscious of his own,
In others barb'rously bear none.
  ONE, that had got a Princely Store,
By cheating Master, King and Poor,
Dar'd cry aloud, *The Land must sink*
For all its Fraud; And whom d'ye think
The Sermonizing Rascal chid?
A Glover that sold Lamb for Kid.
  THE least thing was not done amiss,
Or cross'd the Publick Business;
But all the Rogues cry'd brazenly,
Good Gods, Had we but Honesty!
Merc'ry smil'd at th' Impudence,
And others call'd it want of Sense,
Always to rail at what they lov'd:
But *Jove* with Indignation mov'd,
At last in Anger swore, *He'd rid*
The bawling Hive of Fraud; and did.
The very Moment it departs
And Honesty fills all their Hearts;
There shews 'em, like th' Instructive Tree,
Those Crimes which they're asham'd to see;
Which now in Silence they confess,
By blushing at their Ugliness:
Like Children, that would hide their Faults,
And by their Colour own their Thoughts:
Imag'ning, when they're look'd upon,
That others see what they have done.
  BUT, Oh ye Gods! What Consternation,
How vast and sudden was th' Alteration!
In half an Hour, the Nation round,
Meat fell a Peny in the Pound.
The Mask Hypocrisy's flung down,
From the great Statesman to the Clown:
And some in borrow'd Looks well known,
Appear'd like Strangers in their own.
The Bar was silent from that Day;

For now the willing Debtors pay,
Ev'n what's by Creditors forgot;
Who quitted them that had it not.
Those, that were in the Wrong, stood mute,
And dropt the patch'd vexatious Suit:
On which since nothing less can thrive,
Than Lawyers in an honest Hive,
All, except those that got enough,
With Inkhorns by their sides troop'd off.
JUSTICE hang'd some, set others free;
And after Goal delivery,
Her Presence being no more requir'd,
With all her Train and Pomp retir'd.
First march'd some Smiths with Locks and Grates,
Fetters, and Doors with Iron Plates:
Next Goalers, Turnkeys and Assistants:
Before the Goddess, at some distance,
Her chief and faithful Minister,
'Squire CATCH, the Law's great Finisher,
Bore not th' imaginary Sword,
But his own Tools, an Ax and Cord:
Then on a Cloud the Hood-wink'd Fair,
JUSTICE her self was push'd by Air:
About her Chariot, and behind,
Were Serjeants, Bums of every kind,
Tip-staffs, and all those Officers,
That squeeze a Living out of Tears.
THO' Physick liv'd, while Folks were ill,
None would prescribe, but Bees of skill,
Which through the Hive dispers'd so wide,
That none of them had need to ride;
Wav'd vain Disputes, and strove to free
The Patients of their Misery;
Left Drugs in cheating Countries grown,
And us'd the Product of their own;
Knowing the Gods sent no Disease
To Nations without Remedies.
THEIR Clergy rous'd from Laziness
Laid not their Charge on Journey-Bees;
But serv'd themselves, exempt from Vice,
The Gods with Pray'r and Sacrifice;
All those, that were unfit, or knew
Their Service might be spar'd, withdrew:
Nor was there Business for so many,
(If th' Honest stand in need of any,)
Few only with the High-Priest staid,
To whom the rest Obedience paid:
Himself employ'd in Holy Cares,

Resign'd to others State-Affairs.
He chas'd no Starv'ling from his Door,
Nor pinch'd the Wages of the Poor;
But at his House the Hungry's fed,
The Hireling finds unmeasur'd Bread,
The needy Trav'ler Board and Bed.
  AMONG the King's great Ministers,
And all th' inferior Officers
The Change was great; for frugally
They now liv'd on their Salary:
That a poor Bee should ten times come
To ask his Due, a trifling Sum,
And by some well-hir'd Clerk be made
To give a Crown, or ne'er be paid,
Would now be call'd a downright Cheat,
Tho' formerly a Perquisite.
All Places managed first by Three,
Who watch'd each other's Knavery,
And often for a Fellow-feeling,
Promoted one another's stealing,
Are happily supply'd by One,
By which some thousands more are gone.
  No HONOUR now could be content,
To live and owe for what was spent;
Liv'ries in Brokers Shops are hung,
They part with Coaches for a Song;
Sell stately Horses by whole Sets;
And Country-Houses, to pay Debts.
  VAIN Cost is shunn'd as much as Fraud;
They have no Forces kept Abroad;
Laugh at th' Esteem of Foreigners,
And empty Glory got by Wars;
They fight, but for their Country's sake,
When Right or Liberty's at Stake.
  Now mind the glorious Hive, and see
How Honesty and Trade agree.
The Shew is gone, it thins apace;
And looks with quite another Face.
For 'twas not only that They went,
By whom vast Sums were Yearly spent;
But Multitudes that liv'd on them,
Were daily forc'd to do the same.
In vain to other Trades they'd fly;
All were o'er-stock'd accordingly.
  THE Price of Land and Houses falls;
Mirac'lous Palaces, whose Walls,
Like those of *Thebes*, were rais'd by Play,

Are to be let; while the once gay,
Well-seated Household Gods would be
More pleas'd to expire in Flames, than see
The mean Inscription on the Door
Smile at the lofty ones they bore.
The building Trade is quite destroy'd,
Artificers are not employ'd;
No Limner for his Art is fam'd,
Stone-cutters, Carvers are not nam'd.
  THOSE, that remain'd, grown temp'rate, strive,
Not how to spend, but how to live,
And, when they paid their Tavern Score,
Resolv'd to enter it no more:
No Vintner's Jilt in all the Hive
Could wear now Cloth of Gold, and thrive;
Nor *Torcol* such vast Sums advance,
For *Burgundy* and *Ortelans*;
The Courtier's gone, that with his Miss
Supp'd at his House on *Christmas* Peas;
Spending as much in two Hours stay,
As keeps a Troop of Horse a Day.
  THE haughty *Chloe*, to live Great,
Had made her Husband rob the State:
But now she sells her Furniture,
Which th' *Indies* had been ransack'd for;
Contracts th' expensive Bill of Fare,
And wears her strong Suit a whole Year:
The slight and fickle Age is past;
And Clothes, as well as Fashions, last.
Weavers, that join'd rich Silk with Plate,
And all the Trades subordinate,
Are gone. Still Peace and Plenty reign,
And every Thing is cheap, tho' plain:
Kind Nature, free from Gard'ners Force,
Allows all Fruits in her own Course;
But Rarities cannot be had,
Where Pains to get them are not paid.
  As Pride and Luxury decrease,
So by degrees they leave the Seas.
Not Merchants now, but Companies
Remove whole Manufactories.
All Arts and Crafts neglected lie;
Content, the Bane of Industry,
Makes 'em admire their homely Store,
And neither seek nor covet more.
  So few in the vast Hive remain,

The hundredth Part they can't maintain
Against th' Insults of numerous Foes;
Whom yet they valiantly oppose:
'Till some well-fenc'd Retreat is found,
And here they die or stand their Ground.
No Hireling in their Army's known;
But bravely fighting for their own,
Their Courage and Integrity
At last were crown'd with Victory.
  THEY triumph'd not without their Cost,
For many Thousand Bees were lost.
Hard'ned with Toils and Exercise,
They counted Ease it self a Vice;
Which so improv'd their Temperance;
That, to avoid Extravagance,
They flew into a hollow Tree,
Blest with Content and Honesty.

The Moral

THEN *leave Complaints: Fools only strive*
To make a Great an Honest Hive
T' enjoy the World's Conveniences,
Be fam'd in War, yet live in Ease,
Without great Vices, is a vain
EUTOPIA *seated in the Brain.*
Fraud, Luxury and Pride must live,
While we the Benefits receive:
Hunger's a dreadful Plague, no doubt,
Yet who digests or thrives without?
Do we not owe the Growth of Wine
To the dry shabby crooked Vine?
Which, while its Shoots neglected stood,
Chok'd other Plants, and ran to Wood;
But blest us with its noble Fruit,
As soon as it was ty'd and cut:
So Vice is beneficial found,
When it's by Justice lopt and bound;
Nay, where the People would be great,
As necessary to the State,
As Hunger is to make 'em eat.
Bare Virtue can't make Nations live
In Splendor; they, that would revive
A Golden Age, must be as free,
For Acorns, as for Honesty.

ISAAC WATTS

(1674-1706-1748)

The Incomprehensible[1]

FAR in the Heav'ns my God retires,
My God, the Mark of my Desires,
And hides his lovely Face;
When he descends within my View
He charms my Reason to pursue,
But leaves it tir'd and fainting in th' unequal Chase.

Or if I reach unusual Height
Till near his Presence brought,
There Floods of Glory check my Flight,
Cramp the bold Pinions of my Wit,
And all untune my Thought;
Plung'd in a Sea of Light I roll,
Where *Wisdom, Justice, Mercy* shines;
Infinite Rays in crossing Lines
Beat thick Confusion on my Sight, and overwhelm my Soul.

Come to my Aid, ye Fellow-minds,
And help me reach the Throne;
(What single Strength in vain Designs
United Force hath done;
Thus Worms may joyn, and grasp the Poles,
Thus Atoms fill the Sea)
But the whole Race of Creature-Souls
Stretch'd to their last Extent of Thought, plunge and are lost in Thee.

Great God, behold my Reason lies
Adoring; yet my Love would rise
On Pinions not her own:
Faith shall direct her humble Flight
Thro' all the trackless Seas of Light
To Thee th' Eternal Fair, the Infinite Unknown.

[1] Published in *Horæ Lyricæ*, 1706. Text of second edition, 1709.

Sincere Praise[1]

ALMIGHTY Maker God!
How wondrous is thy Name!
Thy Glories how diffus'd abroad
Thro' the Creations Frame!

Nature in every Dress
Her humble Homage pays,
And finds a Thousand Ways t'express
Thine undissembled Praise.

In native White and Red
The Rose and Lilly stand,
And free from Pride their Beauties spread
To show thy skilful Hand.

The Lark mounts up the Skie
With unambitious Song,
And bears her Maker's Praise on high
Upon her artless Tongue.

My Soul would rise and sing
To her Creator too,
Fain would my Tongue adore my King
And pay the Worship due.

But Pride that busy Sin
Spoils all that I perform,
Curs'd Pride, that creeps securely in,
And swells a haughty Worm.

Thy Glories I abate,
Or praise thee with Design;
Some of thy Favors I forget,
Or think the Merit mine.

The very Songs I frame
Are faithless to thy Cause,
And steal the Honours of thy Name
To build their own Applause.

Create my Soul anew,
Else all my Worship's vain;
This wretched Heart will ne'er be true
Until 'tis form'd again.

[1] Published in *Horæ Lyricæ*, 1706. Text of second edition, 1709.

Descend Celestial Fire,
And seize me from above,
Melt me in Flames of pure Desire
A Sacrifice to Love.

Let Joy and Worship spend
The Remnant of my Days,
And to my God my Soul ascend
In sweet Perfumes of Praise.

The Day of Judgment. An Ode Attempted in English Sapphick[1]

WHEN the fierce Northwind with his airy Forces
Rears up the *Baltick* to a foaming Fury;
And the red Lightning with a storm of Hail comes
Rushing amain down,

How the poor Sailors stand amaz'd and tremble!
While the hoarse Thunder like a bloody Trumpet
Roars a loud Onset to the gaping Waters
Quick to devour them.

Such shall the Noise be, and the wild Disorder,
(If things Eternal may be like these Earthly)
Such the dire Terror when the great Archangel
Shakes the Creation;

Tears the strong Pillars of the Vault of Heaven,
Breaks up old Marble the Repose of Princes;
See the Graves open, and the Bones arising,
Flames all around 'em.

Hark the shrill Outcries of the guilty Wretches!
Lively bright Horror and amazing Anguish
Stare thro' their Eye-lids, while the living Worm lies
Gnawing within them.

Thoughts like old Vultures prey upon their Heartstrings,
And the smart Twinges, when their Eye beholds the
Lofty Judge frowning, and a Flood of Vengeance
Rolling afore him.

Hopeless Immortals! how they scream and shiver

[1] Published in *Horæ Lyricæ*, 1706. Text of second edition, 1709.
[2] Published in *Horæ Lyricæ*, 1706. Text of second edition, 1709.

While Devils push them to the Pit wide yawning
Hideous and gloomy, to receive them headlong
Down to the Centre.

Stop here my Fancy: (all away ye horrid
Doleful Ideas) come arise to *Jesus*,
How he sits God-like! and the Saints around him
Thron'd, yet adoring!

O may I sit there when he comes Triumphant
Dooming the Nations: then ascend to Glory,
While our *Hosannahs* all along the Passage
Shout the Redeemer.

The Hazard of Loving the Creatures[1]

WHERE e'er my flatt'ring Passions rove
I find a lurking Snare;
'Tis dangerous to let loose our Love
Beneath th' Eternal Fair.

Souls whom the Tye of Friendship binds,
And Partners of our Blood,
Seize a large Portion of our Minds,
And leave the less for God.

Nature has soft but powerful Bands,
And Reason she controuls;
While Children with their little Hands
Hang closest to our Souls.

Thoughtless they act th' old Serpents Part;
What tempting things they be!
Lord, how they twine about our Heart,
And draw it off from thee!

Our hasty Wills rush blindly on
Where rising Passion rolls,
And thus we make our Fetters strong
To bind our slavish Souls.

Dear Sovereign, break these Fetters off,
And set our Spirits free;
God in himself is Bliss enough,
For we have all in thee.

[1] Published in *Horæ Lyricæ*, 1706. Text of second edition, 1709.

Meditation in a Grove[1]

Sweet Muse, descend and bless the Shade,
And bless the Evening Grove;
Business and Noise and Day are fled,
And every Care but Love.

But hence, ye wanton Young and Fair,
Mine is a purer Flame;
No *Phillis* shall infect the Air
With her unhallowed Name.

Jesus has all my Powers possest,
My Hopes, my Fears, my Joys:
He, the dear Sovereign of my Breast
Shall still command my Voice.

Some of the fairest Choirs above
Shall flock around my Song
With Joy to hear the Name they love
Sound from a mortal Tongue.

His Charms shall make my Numbers flow,
And hold the falling Floods,
While Silence sits on every Bough,
And bends the list'ning Woods.

I'll carve our Passion on the Bark,
And every wounded Tree
Shall drop and bear some mystic Mark
That *Jesus* dy'd for me.

The Swains shall wonder when they read
Inscrib'd on all the Grove,
That Heaven it self came down, and bled
To win a Mortals Love.

God's Dominion and Decrees[2]

Keep Silence, all created Things,
And wait your Maker's Nod:
The Muse stands trembling while she sings
The Honours of her God.

[1] Published in *Horæ Lyricæ*, 1706. Text of second edition, 1709.
[2] Published in *Horæ Lyricæ*, second edition, 1709. Text of first edition.

Life, Death, and Hell, and Worlds unknown
Hang on his firm Decree:
He sits on no precarious Throne,
Nor borrows Leave to be.

Th' Almighty Voice bid ancient Night
Her endless Realms resign,
And lo, ten thousand Globes of Light
In Fields of Azure shine.

Now Wisdom with superiour Sway
Guides the vast moving Frame,
Whilst all the Ranks of Being pay
Deep Rev'rence to his Name.

He spake; The Sun obedient stood,
And held the falling Day:
Old *Jordan* backward drives his Flood,
And disappoints the Sea.

Lord of the Armies of the Sky,
He marshals all the Stars;
Red Comets lift their Banners high,
And wide proclaim his Wars.

Chain'd to his Throne a Volume lies
With all the Fates of Men,
With every Angel's Form and Size
Drawn by th' eternal Pen.

His Providence unfolds the Book,
And makes his Counsels shine:
Each opening Leaf and every Stroke
Fulfils some deep Design.

Here he exalts neglected Worms
To Scepters and a Crown;
Anon the following Page he turns,
And treads the Monarchs down.

Not *Gabriel* asks the Reason why,
Nor God the Reason gives,
Nor dares the Favourite-Angel pry
Between the folded Leaves.

My God, I never long'd to see
  My Fate with curious Eyes,
What gloomy Lines are writ for me,
  Or what bright Scenes shall rise.

In thy fair Book of Life and Grace
  May I but find my Name
Recorded in some humble Place
  Beneath my Lord the Lamb.

Against Idleness and Mischief[1]

How doth the little busy Bee
  Improve each shining Hour,
And gather Honey all the Day
  From ev'ry op'ning Flow'r!

How skilfully she builds her Cell!
  How neat she spreads the Wax;
And labours hard to store it well
  With the sweet Food she makes.

In Works of Labour or of Skill
  I would be busy too:
For *Satan* finds some Mischief still
  For idle Hands to do.

In Books, or Work, or healthful Play
  Let my first Years be past,
That I may give for every Day
  Some good Account at last.

The Sluggard[2]

'TIS the Voice of the *Sluggard*; I hear him complain,
You have wak'd me too soon, I must slumber again.
As the Door on its Hinges, so he on his Bed,
Turns his Sides, and his Shoulders, and his Heavy Head.

[1] Published in *Divine Songs*, 1720. Text of ninth edition, 1728.
[2] Published in *Divine Songs*, 1720. Text of ninth edition, 1728.

A little more Sleep, and a little more Slumber,
Thus he wastes half his Days, and his Hours without Number:
And when he gets up, he sits folding his Hands,
Or walks about sauntring, or trifling he stands.

I past by his Garden, and saw the wild Bryar,
The Thorn and the Thistle grow broader and higher:
The Clothes that hang on him are turning to Rags;
And his Money still wastes, till he starves, or he begs.

I made him a Visit, still hoping to find
He had took better Care for improving his Mind:
He told me his Dreams, talk'd of Eating and Drinking;
But he scarce reads his Bible, and never loves Thinking.

Said I then to my Heart, *Here's a Lesson for me,*
That Man's but a Picture of what I might be.
But Thanks to my Friends for their Care in my Breeding,
Who taught me betimes to love Working and Reading.

A Cradle Hymn[1]

Hush! my Dear, lie still and slumber;
Holy Angels guard thy Bed!
Heavenly Blessings without Number
Gently falling on thy Head.

Sleep, my Babe; thy Food and Rayment,
House and Home thy Friends provide;
All without thy Care or Payment,
All thy Wants are well supply'd.

How much better thou 'rt attended
Than the *Son of God* could be,
When from Heaven he descended,
And became a Child like thee?

Soft and easy is thy Cradle;
Coarse and hard thy Saviour lay,
When his Birth-Place was a Stable,
And his softest Bed was Hay.

[1] Published in *Divine Songs*, 1720. Text of ninth edition, 1728.

Blessed Babe! what glorious Features,
Spotless fair, divinely bright!
Must he dwell with brutal Creatures?
How could Angels bear the Sight?

Was there nothing but a Manger
Cursed Sinners could afford,
To receive the heavenly Stranger?
Did they thus affront their Lord?

Soft, my Child; I did not chide thee,
Tho' my Song might sound too hard;
'Tis thy {*Mother / Nurse that} sits beside thee,
And her Arm shall be thy Guard.

Yet to read the shameful Story,
How the *Jews* abus'd their King,
How they serv'd the *Lord of Glory*,
Makes me angry while I sing.

See the kinder Shepherds round him,
Telling Wonders from the Skie;
There they sought him, there they found him,
With his Virgin-Mother by.

See the lovely Babe a dressing;
Lovely Infant, how he smil'd!
When he wept, the Mother's Blessing
Sooth'd and hush'd the holy Child.

Lo, he slumbers in his Manger,
Where the horned Oxen fed;
Peace, my Darling, here's no Danger,
Here's no Ox anear thy Bed.

'Twas to save thee, Child, from dying,
Save my Dear from burning Flame,
Bitter Groans, and endless Crying,
That my blest Redeemer came.

May'st thou live to know and fear Him,
Trust and love him all thy Days!
Then go dwell for ever near him,
See his Face, and sing his Praise!

* Here you may use the words, *Brother, Sister, Neighbour, Friend,* &c.

I could give thee thousand Kisses,
Hoping what I most desire:
Not a Mother's fondest Wishes,
Can to greater Joys aspire.

THOMAS TICKELL

(1686-1706-1740)

To the Earl of Warwick
On the Death of Mr. Addison[1]

IF, DUMB too long, the drooping Muse hath stay'd,
And left her debt to *Addison* unpaid;
Blame not her silence, *Warwick,* but bemoan,
And judge, oh judge, my bosom by your own.
What mourner ever felt poetic fires!
Slow comes the verse, that real woe inspires:
Grief unaffected suits but ill with art,
Or flowing numbers with a bleeding heart.
  Can I forget the dismal night, that gave
My soul's best part for-ever to the grave!
How silent did his old companions tread,
By mid-night lamps, the mansions of the dead,
Through breathing statues, then unheeded things,
Through rowes of warriors, and through walks of kings!
What awe did the slow solemn knell inspire;
The pealing organ, and the pausing choir;
The duties by the lawn-rob'd prelate pay'd;
And the last words, that dust to dust convey'd!
While speechless o'er thy closing grave we bend,
Accept these tears, thou dear departed friend,
Oh gone for-ever, take this long adieu;
And sleep in peace, next thy lov'd *Montagu!*
  To strew fresh laurels let the task be mine,
A frequent pilgrim, at thy sacred shrine;
Mine with true sighs thy absence to bemoan,
And grave with faithful epitaphs thy stone.
If e'er from me thy lov'd memorial part,
May shame afflict this alienated heart;
Of thee forgetful if I form a song,
My lyre be broken, and untun'd my tongue,

[1] Published in Addison's *Works,* 1721. Text of first edition.

My griefs be doubled, from thy image free,
And mirth a torment, unchastised by thee.
  Oft let me range the gloomy Iles alone
(Sad luxury! to vulgar minds unknown)
Along the walls where speaking marbles show
What worthies form the hallow'd mold below:
Proud names, who once the reins of empire held;
In arms who triumph'd; or in arts excell'd;
Chiefs, grac'd with scars, and prodigal of blood;
Stern patriots, who for sacred freedom stood;
Just men, by whom impartial laws were given;
And saints, who taught, and led, the way to heaven.
Ne'er to these chambers, where the mighty rest,
Since their foundation, came a nobler guest,
Nor e'er was to the bowers of bliss convey'd
A fairer spirit, or more welcome shade.
  In what new region, to the just assign'd,
What new employments please th' unbody'd mind?
A winged *Virtue*, through th' ethereal sky,
From world to world unweary'd does he fly?
Or curious trace the long laborious maze
Of heaven's decrees, where wondering angels gaze?
Does he delight to hear bold Seraphs tell
How *Michael* battel'd, and the Dragon fell?
Or, mixt with milder Cherubim, to glow
In hymns of love, not ill essay'd below?
Or do'st thou warn poor mortals left behind,
A task well suited to thy gentle mind?
Oh, if sometimes thy spotless form descend,
To me thy aid, thou guardian Genius, lend!
When rage misguides me, or when fear alarms,
When pain distresses, or when pleasure charms,
In silent whisperings purer thoughts impart,
And turn from Ill a frail and feeble heart;
Lead through the paths thy virtue trode before,
'Till bliss shall join, nor death can part us more.
  That awful form (which, so ye heavens decree,
Must still be lov'd and still deplor'd by me)
In nightly visions seldom fails to rise,
Or, rous'd by fancy, meets my waking eyes.
If business calls, or crowded courts invite,
Th' unblemish'd statesman seems to strike my sight;
If in the stage I seek to soothe my care,
I meet his soul, which breathes in *Cato* there;
If pensive to the rural shades I rove,
His shape o'ertakes me in the lonely grove:
'Twas there of Just and Good he reason'd strong,
Clear'd some great truth, or rais'd some serious song;

There patient show'd us the wise course to steer,
A candid censor, and a friend severe;
There taught us how to live; and (oh! too high
The price for knowledge) taught us how to die.
  Thou Hill, whose brow the antique structures grace,
Rear'd by bold chiefs of *Warwick*'s noble race,
Why, once so lov'd, when-e'er thy bower appears,
O'er my dim eye-balls glance the sudden tears!
How sweet were once thy prospects fresh and fair,
Thy sloping walks, and unpolluted air!
How sweet the gloomes beneath thy aged trees,
Thy noon-tide shadow, and thy evening breeze!
His image thy forsaken bowers restore;
Thy walks and airy prospects charm no more,
No more the summer in thy gloomes allay'd,
Thy evening breezes, and thy noon-day shade.
  From other ills, however fortune frown'd,
Some refuge in the muse's art I found:
Reluctant now I touch the trembling string,
Bereft of him, who taught me how to sing,
And these sad accents, murmur'd o'er his urn,
Betray that absence, they attempt to mourn.
Oh! must I then (now fresh my bosom bleeds,
And *Craggs* in death to *Addison* succeeds)
The verse, begun to one lost friend, prolong,
And weep a second in th' unfinish'd song!
  These works divine, which on his death-bed laid
To thee, O *Craggs*, th' expiring Sage convey'd,
Great, but ill-omen'd monument of fame,
Nor he surviv'd to give, nor thou to claim.
Swift after him thy social spirit flies,
And close to his, how soon! thy coffin lies.
Blest pair! whose union future bards shall tell
In future tongues: each other's boast! farewel.
Farewel! whom join'd in fame, in friendship try'd,
No chance could sever, nor the grave divide.

Colin and Lucy[1]

OF Leinster fam'd for maidens fair,
  Bright LUCY was the grace;
Nor e'er did Liffy's limpid stream
  Reflect a fairer face.

[1] Published in *The Musical Miscellany*, Volume I, 1729. Text of Dodsley's *Collection of Poems*, Volume I, 1748.

'Till luckless love and pining care
  Impair'd her rosy hue,
Her damask cheek, her dainty lip,
  And eyes of glossy blue.

Ah! hast thou seen the lily pale
  When beating rains descend?
So droop'd this slow-consuming maid,
  Her life now near it's end.

But LUCY warn'd, of flatt'ring swains
  Take heed, ye easy fair!
Of vengeance due to broken vows,
  Ye flatt'ring swains, beware!

Three times all in the dead of night
  A bell was heard to ring;
And at her window shrieking thrice,
  The raven flap'd his wing.

Full well the love-lorn maiden knew
  The solemn-boding sound,
And thus in dying words bespoke
  The virgins weeping round.

"I hear the voice you cannot hear,
  "That cries I must not stay;
"I see the hand you cannot see,
  "That beckons me away.

"Of a false swain, and broken heart,
  "In early youth I die:
"Am I to blame, because the bride
  "Is twice as rich as I?

"Ah, COLIN, give not her thy vows,
  "Vows due to me alone!
"Nor thou, rash girl, return his kiss,
  "Nor think him all thy own!

"To-morrow in the church, to wed,
  "Impatient both prepare:
"But know, false man, and know, fond maid,
  "Poor LUCY will be there.

"Then bear my corpse, ye comrades dear,
  "The bridegroom blithe to meet;

"He in his wedding-trim so gay,
"I in my winding-sheet!

She spoke, she dy'd, her corpse was borne
The bride-groom blithe to meet;
He in his wedding-trim so gay,
She in her winding-sheet.

What then was Colin's dismal thought?
How were these nuptials kept?
The bride-men flock'd round Lucy dead,
And all the village wept!

Compassion, shame, remorse, despair,
At once his bosom swell:
The damps of death bedew'd his brow,
He groan'd, he shook, he fell.

From the vain bride, a bride no more,
The varying crimson fled;
When, stretch'd beside her rival's corpse,
She saw her husband dead.

He to his Lucy's new-made grave,
Convey'd by trembling swains;
In the same mould, beneath one sod,
For-ever now remains.

Oft in this place the constant hind
And plighted maid are seen,
With garlands gay, and true-love knots
To deck the sacred green.

But swain forsworn, whoe'er thou art,
This hallow'd ground forbear!
Remember Colin's dismal fate,
And fear to join him there.

GEORGE BERKELEY

(1685-1707-1753)

Verses on the Prospect of Planting Arts and Learning in America[1]

THE Muse, disgusted at an age and clime,
  Barren of every glorious theme,
In distant lands now waits a better time,
  Producing subjects worthy fame:

In happy climes, where from the genial sun
  And virgin earth such scenes ensue,
The force of art by nature seems outdone,
  And fancied beauties by the true:

In happy climes the seat of innocence,
  Where nature guides and virtue rules,
Where men shall not impose for truth and sense,
  The pedantry of courts and schools:

There shall be sung another golden age,
  The rise of empire and of arts,
The good and great inspiring epic rage,
  The wisest heads and noblest hearts.

Not such as Europe breeds in her decay;
  Such as she bred when fresh and young,
When heav'nly flame did animate her clay,
  By future poets shall be sung.

Westward the course of empire takes its way;
  The four first acts already past,
A fifth shall close the drama with the day;
  Time's noblest offspring is the last.

[1] Published in 1752. Text of Dodsley's *Collection*, Volume VI, 1758.

JOHN GAY

(1685-1708-1732)

On a Miscellany of Poems to Bernard Lintott[1]

As WHEN some skilful cook, to please each guest,
Would in one mixture comprehend a feast,
With due proportion and judicious care
He fills each dish with diff'rent sorts of fare,
Fishes and fowl deliciously unite,
To feast at once the taste, the smell, and sight.
So, *Bernard,* must a miscellany be
Compounded of all kinds of poetry;
The muses *O'lio*, which all tastes may fit,
And treat each reader with his darling wit.
Wouldst thou for miscellanies raise thy fame;
And bravely rival *Jacob*'s mighty name,
Let all the muses in the piece conspire,
The lyrick bard must strike th' harmonious lyre;
Heroick strains must here and there be found,
And nervous sense be sung in lofty sound;
Let elegy in moving numbers flow,
And fill some pages with melodious woe;
Let not your am'rous songs too num'rous prove,
Nor glut thy reader with abundant love;
Satyr must interfere, whose pointed rage
May lash the madness of a vicious age;
Satyr, the muse that never fails to hit,
For if there's scandal, to be sure there's wit.
Tire not our patience with pindarick lays,
Those swell the piece, but very rarely please:
Let short-breath'd epigram its force confine,
And strike at follies in a single line.
Translations should throughout the work be sown,
And *Homer*'s godlike muse be made our own;
Horace in useful numbers should be sung,
And *Virgil*'s thoughts adorn the *British* tongue;
Let *Ovid* tell *Corinna*'s hard disdain,
And at her door in melting notes complain;
His tender accents pitying virgins move,
And charm the list'ning ear with tales of love.

[1] Published in *Miscellaneous Poems and Translations*, 1712. Text of third edition, 1720.

Let ev'ry classick in the volume shine,
And each contribute to thy great design:
Through various subjects let the reader range,
And raise his fancy with a grateful change;
Variety's the source of joy below,
From whence still fresh revolving pleasures flow.
In books and love, the mind one end pursues,
And only change th' expiring flame renews.
  Where *Buckingham* will condescend to give,
That honour'd piece to distant times must live;
When noble *Sheffield* strikes the trembling strings,
The little loves rejoyce, and clap their wings;
Anacreon lives, they cry, th' harmonious swain
Retunes the lyre, and tries his wonted strain,
'Tis he—our lost *Anacreon* lives again.
But when th' illustrious poet soars above
The sportive revels of the god of love,
Like *Maro*'s muse he takes a loftier flight,
And towres beyond the wond'ring *Cupid*'s sight.
  If thou wouldst have thy volume stand the test,
And of all others be reputed best,
Let *Congreve* teach the list'ning groves to mourn,
As when he wept o'er fair *Pastora*'s urn.
  Let *Prior*'s muse with soft'ning accents move,
Soft as the strains of constant *Emma*'s love:
Or let his fancy chuse some jovial theme,
As when he told *Hans Carvel*'s jealous dream;
Prior th' admiring reader entertains,
With *Chaucer*'s humour, and with *Spencer*'s strains.
  Waller in *Granville* lives; when *Mira* sings
With *Waller*'s hand he strikes the sounding strings,
With sprightly turns his noble genius shines,
And manly sense adorns his easie lines.
  On *Addison*'s sweet lays attention waits,
And silence guards the place while he repeats;
His muse alike on ev'ry subject charms,
Whether she paints the god of love, or arms:
In him, pathetick *Ovid* sings again,
And *Homer*'s *Iliad* shines in his *Campaign*.
  Whenever *Garth* shall raise his sprightly song,
Sense flows in easie numbers from his tongue;
Great *Phœbus* in his learned son we see,
Alike in physic, as in poetry.
  When *Pope*'s harmonious muse with pleasure roves,
Amidst the plains, the murm'ring streams, and groves,
Attentive echo pleas'd to hear his songs,
Thro' the glad shade each warbling note prolongs;

His various numbers charm our ravish'd ears,
His steady judgment far out-shoots his years,
And early in the youth the God appears.
From these successful bards collect thy strains,
And praise with profit shall reward thy pains:
Then, while calves-leather binding bears the sway,
And sheep-skin to its sleeker gloss gives way;
While neat old *Elzevir* is reckon'd better
Than *Pirate Hill*'s brown sheets, and scurvy letter;
While print admirers careful *Aldus* chuse
Before *John Morphew*, or the weekly news:
So long shall live thy praise in books of fame,
And *Tonson* yield to *Lintott*'s lofty name.

A Contemplation on Night[1]

WHETHER amid the gloom of night I stray,
Or my glad eyes enjoy revolving day,
Still Nature's various face informs my sense,
Of an all-wise, all-pow'rful Providence.
When the gay sun first breaks the shades of night,
And strikes the distant eastern hills with light,
Colour returns, the plains their liv'ry wear,
And a bright verdure cloaths the smiling year;
The blooming flow'rs with op'ning beauties glow,
And grazing flocks their milky fleeces show,
The barren cliffs with chalky fronts arise,
And a pure azure arches o'er the skies.
But when the gloomy reign of night returns,
Stript of her fading pride all nature mourns:
The trees no more their wonted verdure boast,
But weep in dewy tears their beauty lost;
No distant landskips draw our curious eyes,
Wrapt in night's robe the whole creation lies.
Yet still, ev'n now, while darkness cloaths the land,
We view the traces of th' almighty hand;
Millions of stars in heav'n's wide vault appear,
And with new glories hang the boundless sphere:
The silver moon her western couch forsakes,
And o'er the skies her nightly circle makes,
Her solid globe beats back the sunny rays,
And to the world her borrow'd light repays.
Whether those stars that twinkling lustre send,

[1] Published in Steele's *Poetical Miscellanies*, 1714. Text of *Poems on Several Occasions*, 1720.

Are suns, and rolling worlds those suns attend,
Man may conjecture, and new schemes declare,
Yet all his systems but conjectures are;
But this we know, that heav'n's eternal King,
Who bid this universe from nothing spring,
Can at his *Word* bid num'rous worlds appear,
And rising worlds th' all-pow'rful *Word* shall hear.
When to the western main the sun descends,
To other lands a rising day he lends,
The spreading dawn another shepherd spies,
The wakeful flocks from their warm folds arise,
Refresh'd, the peasant seeks his early toil,
And bids the plough correct the fallow soil.
While we in sleep's embraces waste the night,
The climes oppos'd enjoy meridian light;
And when those lands the busie sun forsakes,
With us again the rosie morning wakes;
In lazy sleep the night rolls swift away,
And neither clime laments his absent ray.
When the pure soul is from the body flown,
No more shall night's alternate reign be known:
The sun no more shall rolling light bestow,
But from th' Almighty streams of glory flow.
Oh, may some nobler thought my soul employ,
Than empty, transient, sublunary joy!
The stars shall drop, the sun shall lose his flame,
But thou, O God, for ever shine the same.

The Shepherd's Week[1]

Thursday; or, The Spell

HOBNELIA

HOBNELIA, seated in a dreary vale,
In pensive mood rehears'd her piteous tale,
Her piteous tale the winds in sighs bemoan,
And pining eccho answers groan for groan.
I rue the day, a rueful day I trow,
The woful day, a day indeed of woe!
When *Lubberkin* to town his cattle drove,
A maiden fine bedight he hapt to love;
The maiden fine bedight his love retains,
And for the village he forsakes the plains.

[1] Published in 1714. Text of *Poems on Several Occasions*, 1720.

Return my *Lubberkin*, these ditties hear;
Spells will I try, and spells shall ease my care.
  With my sharp heel I three times mark the ground,
And turn me thrice around, around, around.
  When first the year, I heard the cuckow sing,
And call with welcome note the budding spring,
I straitway set a running with such haste,
Deb'rah that won the smock scarce ran so fast.
'Till spent for lack of breath, quite weary grown,
Upon a rising bank I sat adown,
Then doff'd my shoe, and by my troth, I swear,
Therein I spy'd this yellow frizled hair,
As like to *Lubberkin*'s in curl and hue,
As if upon his comely pate it grew.
  With my sharp heel I three times mark the ground,
And turn me thrice around, around, around.
  At eve last *Midsummer* no sleep I sought,
But to the field a bag of hemp-seed brought,
I scatter'd round the seed on ev'ry side,
And three times in a trembling accent cry'd,
This hemp-seed with my virgin hand I sow,
Who shall my true-love be, the crop shall mow.
I strait look'd back, and if my eyes speak truth,
With his keen scythe behind me came the youth.
  With my sharp heel I three times mark the ground,
And turn me thrice around, around, around.
  Last *Valentine*, the day when birds of kind
Their paramours with mutual chirpings find;
I rearly rose, just at the break of day,
Before the sun had chas'd the stars away;
A-field I went, amid the morning dew
To milk my kine (for so should huswives do)
Thee first I spy'd, and the first swain we see,
In spite of fortune shall our true-love be;
See, *Lubberkin*, each bird his partner take,
And canst thou then thy sweetheart dear forsake?
  With my sharp heel I three times mark the ground,
And turn me thrice around, around, around.
  Last *May-day* fair I search'd to find a snail
That might my secret lover's name reveal;
Upon a gooseberry bush a snail I found,
For always snails near sweetest fruit abound.
I seiz'd the vermine, home I quickly sped,
And on the hearth the milk-white embers spread.
Slow crawl'd the snail, and if I right can spell,
In the soft ashes mark'd a curious *L:*
Oh, may this wondrous omen lucky prove!
For *L* is found in *Lubberkin* and *Love.*

With my sharp heel I three times mark the ground,
And turn me thrice around, around, around.
Two hazel-nuts I threw into the flame,
And to each nut I gave a sweet-heart's name.
This with the loudest bounce me sore amaz'd,
That in a flame of brightest colour blaz'd.
As blaz'd the nut so may thy passion grow,
For 'twas thy nut that did so brightly glow.
With my sharp heel I three times mark the ground,
And turn me thrice around, around, around.
As peascods once I pluck'd, I chanc'd to see
One that was closely fill'd with three times three,
Which when I crop'd I safely home convey'd,
And o'er my door the spell in secret laid,
My wheel I turn'd, and sung a ballad new,
While from the spindle I the fleeces drew;
The latch mov'd up, when who shou'd first come in,
But in his proper person,—*Lubberkin.*
I broke my yarn surpriz'd the sight to see,
Sure sign that he would break his word with me.
Eftsoons I join'd it with my wonted slight,
So may again his love with mine unite!
With my sharp heel I three times mark the ground,
And turn me thrice around, around, around.
This *Lady-fly* I take from off the grass,
Whose spotted back might scarlet red surpass.
Fly, Lady Bird, *North, South, or East or West,*
Fly where the Man is found that I love best.
He leaves my hand, see to the *West* he's flown,
To call my true-love from the faithless town.
With my sharp heel I three times mark the ground,
And turn me thrice around, around, around.
This mellow pippin, which I pare around,
My shepherd's name shall flourish on the ground.
I fling th' unbroken paring o'er my head,
Upon the grass a perfect L is read;
Yet on my heart a fairer L is seen
Than what the paring marks upon the green.
With my sharp heel I three times mark the ground,
And turn me thrice around, around, around.
This pippin shall another tryal make,
See from the core two kernels brown I take;
This on my cheek for *Lubberkin* is worn,
And *Boobyclod* on t'other side is born.
But *Boobyclod* soon drops upon the ground,
A certain token that his love's unsound,
While *Lubberkin* sticks firmly to the last;
Oh were his lips to mine but join'd so fast!

With my sharp heel I three times mark the ground,
And turn me thrice around, around, around.
As *Lubberkin* once slept beneath a tree,
I twitch'd his dangling garter from his knee;
He wist not when the hempen string I drew,
Now mine I quickly doff of inkle blue;
Together fast I tye the garters twain,
And while I knit the knot repeat this strain.
Three times a true-love's knot I tye secure,
Firm be the knot, firm may his love endure.
With my sharp heel I three times mark the ground,
And turn me thrice around, around, around.
As I was wont, I trudg'd last market-day
To town, with new-laid eggs preserv'd in hay.
I made my market long before 'twas night,
My purse grew heavy and my basket light.
Strait to the pothecary's shop I went,
And in love-powder all my mony spent;
Behap what will, next sunday after prayers,
When to the ale-house *Lubberkin* repairs,
These *golden flies* into his mug I'll throw,
And soon the swain with fervent love shall glow.
With my sharp heel I three times mark the ground,
And turn me thrice around, around, around.
But hold—our *Light-foot* barks, and cocks his ears,
O'er yonder stile see *Lubberkin* appears.
He comes, he comes, *Hobnelia*'s not bewray'd,
Nor shall she crown'd with willow die a maid.
He vows, he swears, he'll give me a green gown,
Oh dear! I fall adown, adown, adown!

Friday; or, The Dirge

Bumkinet. Grubbinol.

Bumkinet.

Why, *Grubbinol,* dost thou so wistful seem?
There's sorrow in thy look, if right I deem.
'Tis true, yon oaks with yellow tops appear,
And chilly blasts begin to nip the year;
From the tall elm a show'r of leaves is born,
And their lost beauty riven beeches mourn.
Yet ev'n this season pleasance blithe affords,
Now the squeez'd press foams with our apple hoards.

Come, let us hye, and quaff a cheary bowl,
Let cyder new *wash sorrow from thy soul.*

GRUBBINOL

Ah *Bumkinet!* since thou from hence wert gone,
From these sad plains all merriment is flown;
Should I reveal my grief 'twould spoil thy chear,
And make thine eye o'er-flow with many a tear.

BUMKINET

Hang Sorrow! Let's to yonder hutt repair,
And with trim sonnets *cast away our care.*
Gillian of Croydon well thy pipe can play,
Thou sing'st most sweet, *o'er hills and far away.*
Of *Patient Grissel* I devise to sing,
And catches quaint shall make the vallies ring.
Come, *Grubbinol,* beneath this shelter, come,
From hence we view our flocks securely roam.

GRUBBINOL

Yes, blithesome lad, a tale I mean to sing,
But with my woe shall distant valleys ring.
The tale shall make our kidlings droop their head,
For woe is me!—our *Blouzelind* is dead.

BUMKINET

Is *Blouzelinda* dead? farewel my glee!
No happiness is now reserv'd for me.
As the wood pigeon cooes without his mate,
So shall my doleful dirge bewail her fate.
Of *Blouzelinda* fair I mean to tell,
The peerless maid that did all maids excell.
Henceforth the morn shall dewy sorrow shed,
And ev'ning tears upon the grass be spread;
The rolling streams with watry grief shall flow,
And winds shall moan aloud—when loud they blow.
Henceforth, as oft as autumn shall return,
The dropping trees, whene'er it rains, shall mourn;
This season quite shall strip the country's pride,
For 'twas in autumn *Blouzelinda* dy'd.
Where-e'er I gad, I *Blouzelind* shall view,
Woods, dairy, barn and mows our passion knew.
When I direct my eyes to yonder wood,
Fresh rising sorrow curdles in my blood.

Thither I've often been the damsel's guide,
When rotten sticks our fuel have supply'd;
There I remember how her faggots large,
Were frequently these happy shoulders charge.
Sometimes this crook drew hazel boughs adown,
And stuff'd her apron wide with nuts so brown;
Or when her feeding hogs had miss'd their way,
Or wallowing 'mid a feast of acorns lay;
Th' untoward creatures to the stye I drove,
And whistled all the way—or told my love.
  If by the dairy's hatch I chance to hie,
I shall her goodly countenance espie,
For there her goodly countenance I've seen,
Set off with kerchief starch'd and pinners clean.
Sometimes, like wax, she rolls the butter round,
Or with the wooden lilly prints the pound.
Whilome I've seen her skim the clouted cream,
And press from spongy curds the milky stream.
But now, alas! these ears shall hear no more
The whining swine surround the dairy door,
No more her care shall fill the hollow tray,
To fat the guzzling hogs with floods of whey.
Lament, ye swine, in gruntings spend your grief,
For you, like me, have lost your sole relief.
  When in the barn the sounding flail I ply,
Where from her sieve the chaff was wont to fly,
The poultry there will seem around to stand,
Waiting upon her charitable hand.
No succour meet the poultry now can find,
For they, like me, have lost their *Blouzelind*.
  Whenever by yon barley mow I pass,
Before my eyes will trip the tidy lass.
I pitch'd the sheaves (oh could I do so now)
Which she in rows pil'd on the growing mow.
There ev'ry deale my heart by love was gain'd,
There the sweet kiss my courtship has explain'd.
Ah *Blouzelind!* that mow I ne'er shall see,
But thy memorial will revive in me.
  Lament, ye fields, and rueful symptoms show,
Henceforth let not the smelling primrose grow;
Let weeds instead of butter-flow'rs appear,
And meads, instead of daisies, hemlock bear;
For cowslips sweet let dandelions spread,
For *Blouzelinda*, blithsome maid, is dead!
Lament ye swains, and o'er her grave bemoan,
And spell ye right this verse upon her stone.
Here Blouzelinda *lyes—Alas, alas!*
Weep shepherds—and remember flesh is grass.

Grubbinol

Albeit thy songs are sweeter to mine ear,
Than to the thirsty cattle rivers clear;
Or winter porridge to the lab'ring youth,
Or bunns and sugar to the damsel's tooth;
Yet *Blouzelinda*'s name shall tune my lay,
Of her I'll sing for ever and for aye.
When *Blouzelind* expir'd, the weather's bell
Before the drooping flock toll'd forth her knell;
The solemn death-watch click'd the hour she dy'd,
And shrilling crickets in the chimney cry'd;
The boding raven on her cottage sate,
And with hoarse croaking warn'd us of her fate;
The lambkin, which her wonted tendance bred,
Drop'd on the plains that fatal instant dead;
Swarm'd on a rotten stick the bees I spy'd,
Which erst I saw when goody *Dobson* dy'd.
How shall I, void of tears, her death relate,
While on her dearling's bed her mother sate!
These words the dying *Blouzelinda* spoke,
And *of the dead let none the will revoke.*
Mother, quoth she, let not the poultry need,
And give the goose wherewith to raise her breed,
Be these my sister's care—and ev'ry morn
Amid the ducklings let her scatter corn;
The sickly calf that's hous'd, be sure to tend,
Feed him with milk, and from bleak colds defend.
Yet e'er I die—see, mother yonder shelf,
There secretly I've hid my worldly pelf.
Twenty good shillings in a rag I laid,
Be ten the Parson's, for my sermon paid.
The rest is yours—my spinning-wheel and rake,
Let *Susan* keep for her dear sister's sake;
My new straw-hat that's trimly lin'd with green,
Let *Peggy* wear, for she's a damsel clean.
My leathern bottle, long in harvests try'd,
Be *Grubbinol*'s—this silver ring beside:
Three silver pennies, and a ninepence bent,
A token kind, to *Bumkinet* is sent.
Thus spoke the maiden, while her mother cry'd,
And peaceful, like the harmless lamb, she dy'd.
To show their love, the neighbours far and near,
Follow'd with wistful look the damsel's bier.
Sprigg'd rosemary the lads and lasses bore,
While dismally the Parson walk'd before.
Upon her grave the rosemary they threw,
The daisie, butter-flow'r and endive blue.

After the good man warn'd us from his text,
That none cou'd tell whose turn would be the next;
He said, that heav'n would take her soul, no doubt,
And spoke the hour-glass in her praise—quite out.
To her sweet mem'ry flow'ry garlands strung,
O'er her now empty seat aloft were hung.
With wicker rods we fenc'd her tomb around,
To ward from man and beast the hallow'd ground,
Lest her new grave the Parson's cattle raze,
For both his horse and cow the church-yard graze.
Now we trudg'd homeward to her mother's farm,
To drink new cyder mull'd, with ginger warm.
For gaffer *Tread-well* told us by the by,
Excessive sorrow is exceeding dry.
While bulls bear horns upon their curled brow,
Or lasses with soft stroakings milk the cow;
While padling ducks the standing lake desire,
Or batt'ning hogs roll in the sinking mire;
While moles the crumbled earth in hillocks raise,
So long shall swains tell *Blouzelinda*'s praise.
Thus wail'd the louts in melancholy strain,
'Till bonny *Susan* sped a-cross the plain;
They seiz'd the lass in apron clean array'd,
And to the ale-house forc'd the willing maid;
In ale and kisses they forget their cares,
And *Susan Blouzelinda*'s loss repairs.

A Ballad[1]

'TWAS when the seas were roaring
With hollow blasts of wind;
A damsel lay deploring,
All on a rock reclin'd.
Wide o'er the rolling billows
She cast a wistful look;
Her head was crown'd with willows
That tremble o'er the brook.

Twelve months are gone and over,
And nine long tedious days.
Why didst thou, vent'rous lover,
Why didst thou trust the seas?
Cease, cease, thou cruel ocean,
And let my lover rest:

[1] Published in *The What D'Ye Call It: A Tragi-Comi-Pastoral Farce*, 1715. Text of *Poems on Several Occasions*, 1720.

Ah! what's thy troubled motion
  To that within my breast?

The merchant, rob'd of pleasure,
  Sees tempests in despair;
But what's the loss of treasure
  To losing of my dear?
Should you some coast be laid on
  Where gold and di'monds grow,
You'd find a richer maiden,
  But none that loves you so.

How can they say that nature
  Has nothing made in vain;
Why then beneath the water
  Should hideous rocks remain?
No eyes the rocks discover,
  That lurk beneath the deep,
To wreck the wand'ring lover,
  And leave the maid to weep.

All melancholy lying,
  Thus wail'd she for her dear;
Repay'd each blast with sighing,
  Each billow with a tear;
When, o'er the white wave stooping,
  His floating corpse she spy'd;
Then like a lilly drooping,
  She bow'd her head, and dy'd.

Trivia; or, The Art of Walking the Streets of London[1]

Book I

Of the Implements for walking the Streets, and Signs of the Weather

THROUGH winter streets to steer your course aright,
How to walk clean by day, and safe by night,
How jostling crouds, with prudence to decline,
When to assert the wall, and when resign,
I sing: Thou, *Trivia*, Goddess, aid my song,
Thro' spacious streets conduct thy bard along;

[1] Published in 1716. Text of *Poems on Several Occasions*, 1720.

By thee transported, I securely stray
Where winding alleys lead the doubtful way,
The silent court, and op'ning square explore,
And long perplexing lanes untrod before.
To pave thy realm, and smooth the broken ways,
Earth from her womb a flinty tribute pays;
For thee, the sturdy paver thumps the ground,
Whilst ev'ry stroke his lab'ring lungs resound;
For thee the scavinger bids kennels glide
Within their bounds, and heaps of dirt subside.
My youthful bosom burns with thirst of fame,
From the great theme to build a glorious name,
To tread in paths to ancient bards unknown,
And bind my temples with a Civic crown;
But more, my country's love demands the lays,
My country's be the profit, mine the praise.
  When the black youth at chosen stands rejoice,
And *clean your shoes* resounds from ev'ry voice;
When late their miry sides stage-coaches show,
And their stiff horses through the town move slow;
When all the *Mall* in leafy ruin lies,
And damsels first renew their oyster cries:
Then let the prudent walker shoes provide,
Not of the *Spanish* or *Morocco* hide;
The wooden heel may raise the dancer's bound,
And with the scallop'd top his step be crown'd:
Let firm, well-hammer'd soles protect thy feet
Thro' freezing snows, and rains, and soaking sleet.
Should the big laste extend the shoe too wide,
Each stone will wrench th' unwary step aside:
The sudden turn may stretch the swelling vein,
Thy cracking joint unhinge, or ankle sprain;
And when too short the modish shooes are worn,
You'll judge the seasons by your shooting corn.
  Nor should it prove thy less important care,
To chuse a proper coat for winter's wear.
Now in thy trunk thy *D'oily* habit fold,
The silken drugget ill can fence the cold;
The frieze's spongy nap is soak'd with rain,
And show'rs soon drench the camlet's cockled grain.
True *Witney* broad-cloth with its shag unshorn,
Unpierc'd is in the lasting tempest worn:
Be this the horse-man's fence; for who would wear
Amid the town the spoils of *Russia*'s bear?
Within the *Roquelaure*'s clasp thy hands are pent,
Hands, that stretch'd forth invading harms prevent.
Let the loop'd *Bavaroy* the fop embrace,
Or his deep cloak be spatter'd o'er with lace.

That garment best the winter's rage defends,
Whose shapeless form in ample plaits depends;
By various names in various counties known,
Yet held in all the true *Surtout* alone:
Be thine of *Kersey* firm, though small the cost,
Then brave unwet the rain, unchill'd the frost.
If the strong cane support thy walking hand,
Chairmen no longer shall the wall command;
Ev'n sturdy carr-men shall thy nod obey,
And rattling coaches stop to make thee way:
This shall direct thy cautious tread aright,
Though not one glaring lamp enliven night.
Let beaus their canes with amber tipt produce,
Be theirs for empty show, but thine for use.
In gilded chariots while they loll at ease,
And lazily insure a life's disease;
While softer chairs the tawdry load convey
To Court, to *White*'s, Assemblies, or the Play;
Rosie-complexion'd health thy steps attends,
And exercise thy lasting youth defends.
Imprudent men heav'ns choicest gifts prophane.
Thus some beneath their arm support the cane;
The dirty point oft checks the careless pace,
And miry spots thy clean cravat disgrace:
O! may I never such misfortune meet,
May no such vicious walkers croud the street,
May Providence o'er-shade me with her wings,
While the bold Muse experienc'd dangers sings.
Not that I wander from my native home,
And (tempting perils) foreign cities roam.
Let *Paris* be the theme of *Gallia*'s muse,
Where slav'ry treads the street in wooden shoes;
Nor do I rove in *Belgia*'s frozen clime,
And teach the clumsy boor to skate in rhyme,
Where, if the warmer clouds in rain descend,
No miry ways industrious steps offend,
The rushing flood from sloping pavements pours,
And blackens the canals with dirty show'rs.
Let others *Naples*' smoother streets rehearse,
And with proud *Roman* structures grace their verse,
Where frequent murders wake the night with groans,
And blood in purple torrents dies the stones;
Nor shall the Muse thro' narrow *Venice* stray,
Where *Gondolas* their painted oars display.
O happy streets, to rumbling wheels unknown,
No carts, no coaches shake the floating town!
Thus was of old *Britannia*'s city bless'd,
E'er pride and luxury her sons possess'd:

Coaches and chariots yet unfashion'd lay,
Nor late-invented chairs perplex'd the way:
Then the proud lady trip'd along the town,
And tuck'd up petticoats secur'd her gown,
Her rosie cheek with distant visits glow'd,
And exercise unartful charms bestow'd;
But since in braided gold her foot is bound,
And a long trailing manteau sweeps the ground,
Her shoe disdains the street; the lazy fair
With narrow step affects a limping air.
Now gaudy pride corrupts the lavish age,
And the streets flame with glaring equipage;
The tricking gamester insolently rides,
With *Loves* and *Graces* on his chariot's sides;
In sawcy state the griping broker sits,
And laughs at honesty, and trudging wits:
For you, O honest men, these useful lays
The Muse prepares; I seek no other praise.
   When sleep is first disturb'd by morning cries;
From sure prognosticks learn to know the skies,
Lest you of rheums and coughs at night complain;
Surpriz'd in dreary fogs, or driving rain.
When suffocating mists obscure the morn,
Let thy worst wig, long us'd to storms, be worn;
This knows the powder'd footman, and with care,
Beneath his flapping hat secures his hair.
Be thou, for ev'ry season, justly drest,
Nor brave the piercing frost with open breast;
And when the bursting clouds a deluge pour,
Let thy *Surtout* defend the drenching show'r.
   The changing weather certain signs reveal.
E'er winter sheds her snow, or frosts congeal,
You'll see the coals in brighter flame aspire,
And sulphur tinge with blue the rising fire:
Your tender shins the scorching heat decline,
And at the dearth of coals the poor repine;
Before her kitchen hearth, the nodding dame
In flannel mantle wrapt, enjoys the flame;
Hov'ring, upon her feeble knees she bends,
And all around the grateful warmth ascends.
   Nor do less certain signs the town advise,
Of milder weather, and serener skies.
The ladies gayly dress'd, the *Mall* adorn
With various dyes, and paint the sunny morn;
The wanton fawns with frisking pleasure range,
And chirping sparrows greet the welcome change:
Not that their minds with greater skill are fraught,
Endu'd by instinct, or by reason taught,

The seasons operate on ev'ry breast;
'Tis hence that fawns are brisk, and ladies drest.
When on his box the nodding coachman snores,
And dreams of fancy'd fares; when tavern doors
The chairmen idly croud; then ne'er refuse
To trust thy busie steps in thinner shoes.
  But when the swinging signs your ears offend
With creaking noise, then rainy floods impend;
Soon shall the kennels swell with rapid streams,
And rush in muddy torrents to the *Thames*.
The bookseller, whose shop's an open square,
Foresees the tempest, and with early care
Of learning strips the rails; the rowing crew
To tempt a fare, cloath all their tilts in blue:
On hosier's poles depending stockings ty'd,
Flag with the slacken'd gale, from side to side;
Church-monuments foretell the changing air;
Then *Niobe* dissolves into a tear,
And sweats with secret grief: you'll hear the sounds
Of whistling winds, e'er kennels break their bounds;
Ungrateful odours common-shores diffuse,
And dropping vaults distill unwholesom dews
E'er the tiles rattle with the smoaking show'r,
And spouts on heedless men their torrents pour.
  All superstition from thy breast repel.
Let cred'lous boys, and prattling nurses tell,
How, if the festival of *Paul* be clear,
Plenty from lib'ral horn shall strow the year;
When the dark skies dissolve in snow or rain,
The lab'ring hind shall yoke the steer in vain;
But if the threatning winds in tempests roar,
Then war shall bathe her wasteful sword in gore.
How, if on *Swithin*'s feast the welkin lours,
And ev'ry penthouse streams with hasty show'rs,
Twice twenty days shall clouds their fleeces drain,
And wash the pavements with incessant rain.
Let not such vulgar tales debase thy mind;
Nor *Paul* nor *Swithin* rule the clouds and wind.
  If you the precepts of the Muse despise,
And slight the faithful warning of the skies,
Others you'll see, when all the town's afloat,
Wrapt in th' embraces of a kersey coat,
Or double-button'd frieze; their guarded feet
Defie the muddy dangers of the street,
While you, with hat unloop'd, the fury dread
Of spouts high-streaming, and with cautious tread
Shun ev'ry dashing pool; or idly stop,
To seek the kind protection of a shop.

But bus'ness summons; now with hasty scud
You jostle for the wall; the spatter'd mud
Hides all thy hose behind; in vain you scow'r,
Thy wig alas! uncurl'd, admits the show'r.
So fierce *Alecto*'s snaky tresses fell,
When *Orpheus* charm'd the rig'rous pow'rs of hell,
Or thus hung *Glaucus'* beard, with briny dew
Clotted and strait, when first his am'rous view
Surpriz'd the bathing fair; the frighted maid
Now stands a rock, transform'd by *Circe*'s aid.
  Good houswives all the winter's rage despise,
Defended by the riding-hood's disguise:
Or underneath th' umbrella's oily shed,
Safe thro' the wet on clinking pattens tread.
Let *Persian* dames th' umbrella's ribs display,
To guard their beauties from the sunny ray;
Or sweating slaves support the shady load,
When eastern Monarchs show their state abroad;
Britain in winter only knows its aid,
To guard from chilly show'rs the walking maid.
But, O! forget not, Muse, the patten's praise,
That female implement shall grace thy lays;
Say from what art divine th' invention came,
And from its origine deduce the name.
  Where *Lincoln* wide extends her fenny soil,
A goodly yeoman liv'd grown white with toil;
One onely daughter blest his nuptial bed,
Who from her infant hand the poultry fed:
Martha (her careful mother's name) she bore,
But now her careful mother was no more.
Whilst on her father's knee the damsel play'd,
Patty he fondly call'd the smiling maid;
As years encreas'd, her ruddy beauty grew,
And *Patty*'s fame o'er all the village flew.
  Soon as the gray-ey'd morning streaks the skies,
And in the doubtful day the woodcock flies,
Her cleanly pail the pretty houswife bears,
And singing to the distant field repairs:
And when the plains with ev'ning dews are spread,
The milky burthen smoaks upon her head.
Deep, thro' a miry lane she pick'd her way,
Above her ankle rose the chalky clay.
  Vulcan by chance the bloomy maiden spies,
With innocence and beauty in her eyes,
He saw, he lov'd; for yet he ne'er had known
Sweet innocence and beauty meet in one.
Ah *Mulciber*! recal thy nuptial vows,
Think on the graces of thy *Paphian* spouse,

Think how her eyes dart inexhausted charms,
And canst thou leave her bed for *Patty*'s arms?
  The *Lemnian* Pow'r forsakes the realms above,
His bosom glowing with terrestrial love:
Far in the lane a lonely hut he found,
No tenant ventur'd on th' unwholesome ground.
Here smoaks his forge, he bares his sinewy arm,
And early strokes the sounding anvil warm;
Around his shop the steely sparkles flew,
As for the steed he shap'd the bending shoe.
  When blue-ey'd *Patty* near his window came,
His anvil rests, his forge forgets to flame.
To hear his soothing tales she feigns delays;
What woman can resist the force of praise?
  At first she coyly ev'ry kiss withstood,
And all her cheek was flush'd with modest blood:
With headless nails he now surrounds her shoes,
To save her steps from rains and piercing dews;
She lik'd his soothing tales, his presents wore,
And granted kisses, but would grant no more.
Yet winter chill'd her feet, with cold she pines,
And on her cheek the fading rose declines;
No more her humid eyes their lustre boast,
And in hoarse sounds her melting voice is lost.
  This *Vulcan* saw, and in his heav'nly thought,
A new machine mechanick fancy wrought,
Above the mire her shelter'd steps to raise,
And bear her safely through the wintry ways.
Strait the new engine on his anvil glows,
And the pale virgin on the patten rose.
No more her lungs are shook with dropping rheums,
And on her cheek reviving beauty blooms.
The God obtain'd his suit; though flatt'ry fail,
Presents with female virtue must prevail.
The patten now supports each frugal dame,
Which from the blue-ey'd *Patty* takes the name.

Book II

Of Walking the Streets by Day

THUS far the Muse has trac'd in useful lays,
The proper implements for wintry ways;
Has taught the walker, with judicious eyes,
To read the various warnings of the skies.
Now venture, Muse, from home to range the town,

And for the publick safety risque thy own.
  For ease and for dispatch, the morning's best;
No tides of passengers the street molest.
You'll see a draggled damsel, here and there,
From *Billingsgate* her fishy traffick bear;
On doors the sallow milk-maid chalks her gains;
Ah! how unlike the milk-maid of the plains!
Before proud gates attending asses bray,
Or arrogate with solemn pace the way;
These grave physicians with their milky chear,
The love-sick maid and dwindling beau repair;
Here rows of drummers stand in martial file,
And with their vellom thunder shake the pile,
To greet the new-made bride. Are sounds like these
The proper prelude to a state of peace?
Now industry awakes her busie sons,
Full charg'd with news the breathless hawker runs:
Shops open, coaches roll, carts shake the ground,
And all the streets with passing cries resound.
  If cloath'd in black, you tread the busy town,
Or if distinguish'd by the rev'rend gown,
Three trades avoid; oft in the mingling press,
The barber's apron soils the sable dress;
Shun the perfumer's touch with cautious eye,
Nor let the baker's step advance too nigh:
Ye walkers too that youthful colours wear,
Three sullying trades avoid with equal care;
The little chimney-sweeper skulks along,
And marks with sooty stains the heedless throng;
When small-coal murmurs in the hoarser throat,
From smutty dangers guard thy threaten'd coat:
The dust-man's cart offends thy cloaths and eyes,
When through the street a cloud of ashes flies;
But whether black or lighter dyes are worn,
The chandler's basket, on his shoulder born,
With tallow spots thy coat; resign the way,
To shun the surly butcher's greasy tray,
Butchers, whose hands are dy'd with blood's foul stain,
And always foremost in the hangman's train.
  Let due civilities be strictly paid.
The wall surrender to the hooded maid;
Nor let thy sturdy elbow's hasty rage
Jostle the feeble steps of trembling age:
And when the porter bends beneath his load,
And pants for breath; clear thou the crouded road.
But, above all, the groping blind direct,
And from the pressing throng the lame protect.
You'll sometimes meet a fop, of nicest tread,

Whose mantling peruke veils his empty head,
At ev'ry step he dreads the wall to lose,
And risques, to save a coach, his red-heel'd shoes,
Him, like the miller, pass with caution by,
Lest from his shoulder clouds of powder fly.
But when the bully, with assuming pace,
Cocks his broad hat, edg'd round with tarnish'd lace,
Yield not the way; defie his strutting pride,
And thrust him to the muddy kennel's side;
He never turns again, nor dares oppose,
But mutters coward curses as he goes.
If drawn by bus'ness to a street unknown,
Let the sworn porter point thee through the town;
Be sure observe the signs, for signs remain,
Like faithful land-marks to the walking train.
Seek not from prentices to learn the way,
Those fabling boys will turn thy steps astray;
Ask the grave tradesman to direct thee right,
He ne'er deceives, but when he profits by 't.
Where fam'd *St. Giles*'s ancient limits spread,
An inrail'd column rears its lofty head,
Here to sev'n streets sev'n dials count the day,
And from each other catch the circling ray.
Here oft the peasant, with enquiring face,
Bewilder'd, trudges on from place to place;
He dwells on ev'ry sign with stupid gaze,
Enters the narrow alley's doubtful maze,
Tries ev'ry winding court and street in vain,
And doubles o'er his weary steps again.
Thus hardy *Theseus* with intrepid feet,
Travers'd the dang'rous labyrinth of *Crete*;
But still the wandring passes forc'd his stay,
Till *Ariadne*'s clue unwinds the way.
But do not thou, like that bold chief, confide
Thy ventrous footsteps to a female guide;
She'll lead thee with delusive smiles along,
Dive in thy fob, and drop thee in the throng.
When waggish boys the stunted beesom ply
To rid the slabby pavement; pass not by
E'er thou hast held their hands; some heedless flirt
Will over-spread thy calves with spatt'ring dirt.
Where porters hogsheads roll from carts aslope,
Or brewers down steep cellars stretch the rope,
Where counted billets are by carmen tost
Stay thy rash step, and walk without the post.
What though the gath'ring mire thy feet besmear,
The voice of industry is always near.
Hark! the boy calls thee to his destin'd stand,

And the shoe shines beneath his oily hand.
Here let the Muse, fatig'd amid the throng,
Adorn her precepts with digressive song;
Of shirtless youths the secret rise to trace,
And show the parent of the sable race.
  Like mortal man, great *Jove* (grown fond of change)
Of old was wont this nether world to range
To seek amours; the vice the monarch lov'd
Soon through the wide etherial court improv'd,
And ev'n the proudest Goddess now and then
Would lodge a night among the sons of men;
To vulgar Deitys descends the fashion,
Each, like her betters, had her earthly passion.
Then *Cloacina* (Goddess of the tide
Whose sable streams beneath the city glide)
Indulg'd the modish flame; the town she rov'd,
A mortal scavenger she saw, she lov'd;
The muddy spots that dry'd upon his face,
Like female patches, heighten'd ev'ry grace:
She gaz'd; she sigh'd. For love can beauties spy
In what seems faults to ev'ry common eye.
  Now had the watchman walk'd his second round;
When *Cloacina* hears the rumbling sound
Of her brown lover's cart, for well she knows
That pleasing thunder: swift the Goddess rose,
And through the streets pursu'd the distant noise,
Her bosom panting with expected joys.
With the night-wandring harlot's airs she past,
Brush'd near his side, and wanton glances cast;
In the black form of cinder-wench she came,
When love, the hour, the place had banish'd shame;
To the dark alley arm in arm they move:
O may no link-boy interrupt their love!
  When the pale moon had nine times fill'd her space,
The pregnant Goddess (cautious of disgrace)
Descends to earth; but sought no midwife's aid,
Nor midst her anguish to *Lucina* pray'd;
No cheerful gossip wish'd the mother joy,
Alone, beneath a bulk she dropt the boy.
  The child through various risques in years improv'd,
At first a beggar's brat, compassion mov'd;
His infant tongue soon learnt the canting art,
Knew all the pray'rs and whines to touch the heart.
  Oh happy unown'd youths, your limbs can bear
The scorching dog-star, and the winter's air,
While the rich infant, nurs'd with care and pain,
Thirsts with each heat, and coughs with ev'ry rain!
  The Goddess long had mark'd the child's distress,

And long had sought his suff'rings to redress;
She prays the Gods to take the fondling's part,
To teach his hands some beneficial art
Practis'd in streets; the Gods her suit allow'd,
And made him useful to the walking croud,
To cleanse the miry feet, and o'er the shoe
With nimble skill the glossy black renew.
Each Power contributes to relieve the poor:
With the strong bristles of the mighty boar
Diana forms his brush; the God of day
A tripod gives, amid the crouded way
To raise the dirty foot, and ease his toil;
Kind *Neptune* fills his vase with fetid oil
Prest from th' enormous whale; The God of fire,
From whose dominions smoaky clouds aspire,
Among these gen'rous presents joins his part,
And aids with foot the new japanning art:
Pleas'd she receives the gifts; she downward glides,
Lights in *Fleet-ditch*, and shoots beneath the tides.
Now dawns the morn, the sturdy lad awakes,
Leaps from his stall, his tangled hair he shakes,
Then leaning o'er the rails, he musing stood,
And view'd below the black canal of mud,
Where common-shores a lulling murmur keep,
Whose torrents rush from *Holborn*'s fatal steep:
Pensive through idleness, tears flow'd apace,
Which eas'd his loaded heart, and wash'd his face;
At length he sighing cry'd; That boy was blest,
Whose infant lips have drain'd a mother's breast;
But happier far are those, (if such be known)
Whom both a father and a mother own:
But I, alas! hard fortune's utmost scorn,
Who ne'er knew parent, was an orphan born!
Some boys are rich by birth beyond all wants,
Belov'd by uncles, and kind good old aunts;
When time comes round, a Christmas-box they bear,
And one day makes them rich for all the year.
Had I the precepts of a Father learn'd,
Perhaps I then the coach-man's fare had earn'd,
For lesser boys can drive; I thirsty stand
And see the double flaggon charge their hand,
See them puff off the froth, and gulp amain,
While with dry tongue I lick my lips in vain.
While thus he fervent prays, the heaving tide
In widen'd circles beats on either side;
The Goddess rose amid the inmost round,
With wither'd turnip tops her temples crown'd;
Low reach'd her dripping tresses, lank, and black

As the smooth jet, or glossy raven's back;
Around her waste a circling eel was twin'd,
Which bound her robe that hung in rags behind.
Now beck'ning to the boy; she thus begun,
Thy prayers are granted; weep no more, my son:
Go thrive. At some frequented corner stand,
This brush I give thee, grasp it in thy hand,
Temper the soot within this vase of oil,
And let the little tripod aid thy toil;
On this methinks I see the walking crew
At thy request support the miry shoe,
The foot grows black that was with dirt imbrown'd,
And in thy pocket gingling halfpence sound.
The Goddess plunges swift beneath the flood,
And dashes all around her show'rs of mud:
The youth strait chose his post; the labour ply'd
Where branching streets from *Charing-cross* divide;
His treble voice resounds along the *Meuse*,
And *White-hall* echoes—*Clean your Honour's shoes.*
Like the sweet ballad, this amusing lay
Too long detains the walker on his way;
While he attends, new dangers round him throng;
The busy city asks instructive song.
Where elevated o'er the gaping croud,
Clasp'd in the board the perjur'd head is bow'd,
Betimes retreat; here, thick as hailstones pour,
Turnips, and half-hatch'd eggs, (a mingled show'r)
Among the rabble rain: Some random throw
May with the trickling yolk thy cheek o'erflow.
Though expedition bids, yet never stray
Where no rang'd posts defend the rugged way.
Here laden carts with thundring waggons meet,
Wheels clash with wheels, and bar the narrow street;
The lashing whip resounds, the horses strain,
And blood in anguish bursts the swelling vein.
O barb'rous men, your cruel breasts asswage,
Why vent ye on the gen'rous steed your rage?
Does not his service earn your daily bread?
Your wives, your children, by his labours fed!
If, as the *Samian* taught, the soul revives,
And, shifting seats, in other bodies lives;
Severe shall be the brutal coachman's change,
Doom'd in a hackney horse the town to range:
Carmen, transform'd, the groaning load shall draw,
Whom other tyrants with the lash shall awe.
Who would of *Watling-street* the dangers share,
When the broad pavement of *Cheap-side* is near?
Or who that rugged street would traverse o'er,

That stretches, O *Fleet-ditch*, from thy black shore
To the *Tow'r*'s moated walls? Here steams ascend
That, in mix'd fumes, the wrinkled nose offend.
Where chandlers cauldrons boil; where fishy prey
Hide the wet stall, long absent from the sea;
And where the cleaver chops the heifer's spoil,
And where huge hogsheads sweat with trainy oil,
Thy breathing nostril hold; but how shall I
Pass, where in piles *Cornavian* cheeses lye;
Cheese, that the table's closing rites denies,
And bids me with th' unwilling chaplain rise.
O bear me to the paths of fair *Pell-mell*,
Safe are thy pavements, grateful is thy smell!
At distance rolls along the gilded coach,
Nor sturdy carmen on thy walks encroach;
No lets would bar thy ways were chairs deny'd,
The soft supports of laziness and pride;
Shops breathe perfumes, thro' sashes ribbons glow,
The mutual arms of ladies, and the beau.
Yet still ev'n here, when rains the passage hide,
Oft' the loose stone spirts up a muddy tide
Beneath thy careless foot; and from on high,
Where masons mount the ladder, fragments fly;
Mortar, and crumbled lime in show'rs descend,
And o'er thy head destructive tiles impend.
But sometimes let me leave the noisie roads,
And silent wander in the close abodes
Where wheels ne'er shake the ground; there pensive stray,
In studious thought, the long uncrouded way.
Here I remark each walker's diff'rent face,
And in their look their various bus'ness trace.
The broker here his spacious beaver wears,
Upon his brow sit jealousies and cares;
Bent on some mortgage (to avoid reproach)
He seeks bye streets, and saves th' expensive coach.
Soft, at low doors, old letchers tap their cane,
For fair recluse, who travels *Drury-lane;*
Here roams uncomb'd the lavish rake, to shun
His *Fleet-street* draper's everlasting dun.
Careful observers, studious of the town,
Shun the misfortunes that disgrace the clown;
Untempted, they contemn the jugler's feats,
Pass by the *Meuse*, nor try the thimble's cheats.
When drays bound high, they never cross behind,
Where bubbling yest is blown by gusts of wind:
And when up *Ludgate-hill* huge carts move slow,
Far from the straining steeds securely go,
Whose dashing hoofs behind them fling the mire,

And mark with muddy blots the gazing 'squire.
The *Parthian* thus his jav'lin backward throws,
And as he flies infests pursuing foes.
  The thoughtless wits shall frequent forfeits pay,
Who 'gainst the centry's box discharge their tea.
Do thou some court, or secret corner seek,
Nor flush with shame the passing virgin's cheek.
  Yet let me not descend to trivial song,
Nor vulgar circumstance my verse prolong;
Why should I teach the maid when torrents pour,
Her head to shelter from the sudden show'r?
Nature will best her ready hand inform,
With her spread petticoat to fence the storm.
Does not each walker know the warning sign,
When wisps of straw depend upon the twine
Cross the close street; that then the paver's art
Renews the ways, deny'd to coach and cart?
Who knows not that the coachman lashing by,
Oft with his flourish cuts the heedless eye;
And when he takes his stand, to wait a fare,
His horses foreheads shun the winter's air?
Nor will I roam, when summer's sultry rays
Parch the dry ground, and spread with dust the ways;
With whirling gusts the rapid atoms rise,
Smoak o'er the pavement, and involve the skies.
  Winter my theme confines; whose nitry wind
Shall crust the slabby mire, and kennels bind;
She bids the snow descend in flaky sheets,
And in her hoary mantle cloath the streets.
Let not the virgin tread these slipp'ry roads,
The gath'ring fleece the hollow patten loads;
But if thy footsteps slide with clotted frost,
Strike off the breaking balls against the post.
On silent wheel the passing coaches roll;
Oft' look behind, and ward the threatning pole.
In harden'd orbs the school-boy moulds the snow,
To mark the coachman with a dextrous throw.
Why do ye, boys, the kennel's surface spread,
To tempt with faithless pass the matron's tread?
How can ye laugh to see the damsel spurn,
Sink in your frauds, and her green stocking mourn?
At *White*'s the harness'd chairman idly stands,
And swings around his waste his tingling hands:
The sempstress speeds to *'Change* with red-tipt nose;
The *Belgian* stove beneath her footstool glows;
In half-whipt muslin needles useless lie,
And shuttle-cocks across the counter fly.
These sports warm harmless; why then will ye prove,

Deluded maids, the dang'rous flame of love?
  Where *Covent-garden*'s famous temple stands,
That boasts the work of *Jones'* immortal hands;
Columns with plain magnificence appear,
And graceful porches lead along the square:
Here oft' my course I bend, when lo! from far,
I spy the furies of the foot-ball war:
The 'prentice quits his shop, to join the crew,
Encreasing crouds the flying game pursue.
Thus, as you roll the ball o'er snowy ground,
The gath'ring globe augments with ev'ry round.
But whither shall I run? the throng draws nigh,
The ball now skims the street, now soars on high;
The dextr'ous glazier strong returns the bound,
And gingling sashes on the pent-house sound.
  O roving Muse, recal that wond'rous year,
When winter reign'd in bleak *Britannia*'s air;
When hoary *Thames*, with frosted oziers crown'd,
Was three long moons in icy fetters bound.
The waterman, forlorn along the shore,
Pensive reclines upon his useless oar,
Sees harness'd steeds desert the stony town;
And wander roads unstable, not their own:
Wheels o'er the harden'd waters smoothly glide,
And rase with whiten'd tracks the slipp'ry tide.
Here the fat cook piles high the blazing fire,
And scarce the spit can turn the steer entire.
Booths sudden hide the *Thames*, long streets appear,
And num'rous games proclaim the crouded fair.
So when a gen'ral bids the martial train
Spread their encampment o'er the spacious plain;
Thick-rising tents a canvas city build,
And the loud dice resound thro' all the field.
  'Twas here the matron found a doleful fate:
Let elegiac lay the woe relate,
Soft as the breath of distant flutes, at hours
When silent ev'ning closes up the flow'rs;
Lulling as falling water's hollow noise;
Indulging grief, like *Philomela*'s voice.
  Doll ev'ry day had walk'd these treach'rous roads;
Her neck grew warpt beneath autumnal loads
Of various fruit; she now a basket bore,
That head, alas! shall basket bear no more.
Each booth she frequent past, in quest of gain,
And boys with pleasure heard her shrilling strain,
Ah *Doll!* all mortals must resign their breath,
And industry it self submit to death!
The cracking crystal yields, she sinks, she dyes.

Her head, chopt off, from her lost shoulders flies;
Pippins she cry'd, but death her voice confounds,
And pip-pip-pip along the ice resounds.
So when the *Thracian* furies *Orpheus* tore,
And left his bleeding trunk deform'd with gore,
His sever'd head floats down the silver tide,
His yet warm tongue for his lost consort cry'd;
Eurydice with quiv'ring voice he mourn'd,
And *Heber*'s banks *Eurydice* return'd.
  But now the western gale the flood unbinds,
And black'ning clouds move on with warmer winds,
The wooden town its frail foundation leaves,
And *Thames'* full urn rolls down his plenteous waves;
From ev'ry penthouse streams the fleeting snow,
And with dissolving frost the pavements flow.
  Experienc'd men, inur'd to city ways,
Need not the Calendar to count their days.
When through the town with slow and solemn air,
Led by the nostril, walks the muzled bear;
Behind him moves majestically dull,
The pride of *Hockley-hole*, the surly bull;
Learn hence the periods of the week to name,
Mondays and *Thursdays* are the days of game.
  When fishy stalls with double store are laid;
The golden-belly'd carp, the broad-finn'd maid,
Red-speckled trouts, the salmon's silver joul,
The joynted lobster, and unscaly soale,
And luscious 'scallops, to allure the tastes
Of rigid zealots to delicious fasts;
Wednesdays and *Fridays* you'll observe from hence,
Days, when our sires were doom'd to abstinence.
  When dirty waters from balconies drop,
And dext'rous damsels twirle the sprinkling mop,
And cleanse the spatter'd sash, and scrub the stairs;
Know *Saturday*'s conclusive morn appears.
  Successive crys the seasons change declare,
And mark the monthly progress of the year.
Hark, how the streets with treble voices ring,
To sell the bounteous product of the spring!
Sweet-smelling flow'rs, and elder's early bud,
With nettle's tender shoots, to cleanse the blood:
And when *June*'s thunder cools the sultry skies,
Ev'n *Sundays* are prophan'd by mackrell cries.
  Wallnuts the fruit'rer's hand, in autumn, stain,
Blue plumbs and juicy pears augment his gain;
Next oranges the longing boys entice,
To trust their copper fortunes to the dice.
  When rosemary, and bays the Poet's crown,

Are bawl'd, in frequent cries, through all the town,
Then judge the festival of *Christmas* near,
Christmas, the joyous period of the year.
Now with bright holly all your temples strow,
With lawrel green, and sacred misletoe.
Now, heav'n-born Charity, thy blessings shed;
Bid meagre Want uprear her sickly head:
Bid shiv'ring limbs be warm; let plenty's bowle
In humble roofs make glad the needy soul.
See, see, the heav'n-born maid her blessings shed;
Lo! meagre Want uprears her sickly head;
Cloath'd are the naked, and the needy glad,
While selfish Avarice alone is sad.
  Proud coaches pass, regardless of the moan
Of infant orphans, and the widow's groan;
While Charity still moves the walker's mind,
His lib'ral purse relieves the lame and blind.
Judiciously thy half-pence are bestow'd,
Where the laborious beggar sweeps the road.
Whate'er you give, give ever at demand,
Nor let old-age long stretch his palsy'd hand.
Those who give late, are importun'd each day,
And still are teaz'd, because they still delay.
If e'er the miser durst his farthings spare,
He thinly spreads them through the publick square,
Where, all beside the rail, rang'd beggars lie,
And from each other catch the doleful cry;
With heav'n, for two-pence, cheaply wipes his score,
Lifts up his eyes, and hasts to beggar more.
  Where the brass knocker, wrapt in flannel band,
Forbids the thunder of the footman's hand;
Th' upholder, rueful harbinger of death,
Waits with impatience for the dying breath;
As vultures, o'er a camp, with hov'ring flight,
Snuff up the future carnage of the fight.
Here canst thou pass, unmindful of a pray'r,
That heav'n in mercy may thy brother spare?
  Come, *F* * * * sincere, experienc'd friend,
Thy briefs, thy deeds, and ev'n thy fees suspend;
Come let us leave the *Temple*'s silent walls,
Me bus'ness to my distant lodging calls:
Through the long *Strand* together let us stray:
With thee conversing I forget the way.
Behold that narrow street which steep descends,
Whose building to the slimy shore extends;
Here *Arundel*'s fam'd structure rear'd its frame,
The street alone retains an empty name:
Where *Titian*'s glowing paint the canvas warm'd,

And *Raphael*'s fair design, with judgment, charm'd,
Now hangs the bell-man's song, and pasted here
The colour'd prints of *Overton* appear.
Where statues breath'd, the work of *Phidias*' hands,
A wooden pump, or lonely watch-house stands.
There *Essex*' stately pile adorn'd the shore,
There *Cecil*'s, *Bedford*'s, *Villers*', now no more.
Yet *Burlington*'s fair palace still remains:
Beauty within, without proportion reigns.
Beneath his eye declining art revives,
The wall with animated picture lives;
There *Hendel* strikes the strings, the melting strain
Transports the soul, and thrills through ev'ry vein;
There oft' I enter (but with cleaner shoes)
For *Burlington*'s belov'd by ev'ry Muse.
  O ye associate walkers, O my friends,
Upon your state what happiness attends!
What, though no coach to frequent visit rolls,
Nor for your shilling chairmen sling their poles;
Yet still your nerves rheumatic pains defye,
Nor lazy jaundice dulls your saffron eye;
No wasting cough discharges sounds of death,
Nor wheezing asthma heaves in vain for breath;
Nor from your restless couch is heard the groan
Of burning gout, or sedentary stone.
Let others in the jolting coach confide,
Or in the leaky boat the *Thames* divide;
Or, box'd within the chair, contemn the street,
And trust their safety to another's feet,
Still let me walk; for oft the sudden gale
Ruffles the tide, and shifts the dang'rous sail.
Then shall the passenger too late deplore
The whelming billow, and the faithless oar;
The drunken chairman in the kennel spurns,
The glasses shatters, and his charge o'erturns.
Who can recount the coach's various harms,
The legs disjointed, and the broken arms?
  I've seen a beau, in some ill-fated hour,
When o'er the stones choak'd kennels swell the show'r
In gilded chariot loll; he with disdain
Views spatter'd passengers all drench'd in rain;
With mud fill'd high, the rumbling cart draws near,
Now rule thy prancing steeds, lac'd charioteer!
The dust-man lashes on with spiteful rage,
His pond'rous spokes thy painted wheel engage,
Crush'd is thy pride, down falls the shrieking beau,
The slabby pavement crystal fragments strow,
Black floods of mire th' embroider'd coat disgrace,

And mud enwraps the honours of his face.
So when dread *Jove* the son of *Phœbus* hurl'd,
Scarr'd with dark thunder, to the nether world;
The headstrong coursers tore the silver reins,
And the sun's beamy ruin gilds the plains.
  If the pale walker pant with weak'ning ills,
His sickly hand is stor'd with friendly bills:
From hence he learns the seventh-born doctor's fame,
From hence he learns the cheapest tailor's name.
  Shall the large mutton smoak upon your boards?
Such, *Newgate*'s copious market best affords.
Would'st thou with mighty beef augment thy meal?
Seek *Leaden-hall*; *St. James*'s sends thee veal.
Thames-street gives cheeses; *Covent-garden* fruits;
Moor-fields old books; and *Monmouth-street* old suits.
Hence may'st thou well supply the wants of life,
Support thy family, and cloath thy wife.
  Volumes, on shelter'd stalls expanded lye,
And various science lures the learned eye;
The bending shelves with pond'rous scholiasts groan,
And deep divines to modern shops unknown:
Here, like the bee, that on industrious wing
Collects the various odours of the spring,
Walkers, at leisure, learning's flow'rs may spoil,
Nor watch the wasting of the midnight oil,
May morals snatch from *Plutarch*'s tatter'd page,
A mildew'd *Bacon*, or *Stagyra*'s sage.
Here saunt'ring prentices o'er *Otway* weep,
O'er *Congreve* smile, or over *D* * * sleep;
Pleas'd sempstresses the *Lock*'s fam'd *Rape* unfold,
And *Squirts* read *Garth*, 'till apozems grow cold.
  O *Lintot*, let my labours obvious lie,
Rang'd on thy stall, for ev'ry curious eye;
So shall the poor these precepts gratis know,
And to my verse their future safeties owe.
  What walker shall his mean ambition fix
On the false lustre of a coach and six?
Let the vain virgin, lur'd by glaring show,
Sigh for the liv'ries of th' embroider'd beau.
  See yon bright chariot on its harness swing,
With *Flanders* mares, and on an arched spring;
That wretch to gain an equipage and place,
Betray'd his sister to a lewd embrace.
This coach that with the blazon'd 'scutcheon glows,
Vain of his unknown race, the coxcomb shows.
Here the brib'd lawyer, sunk in velvet, sleeps;
The starving orphan, as he passes, weeps;
There flames a fool, begirt with tinsell'd slaves,

Who wastes the wealth of a whole race of knaves.
That other, with a clustring train behind,
Owes his new honours to a sordid mind.
This next in court-fidelity excells,
The publick rifles, and his country sells.
May the proud chariot never be my fate,
If purchas'd at so mean, so dear a rate;
O rather give me sweet content on foot,
Wrapt in my virtue, and a good *Surtout!*

The Toilette. A Town Eclogue[1]

LYDIA

Now twenty springs had cloath'd the Park with green,
Since *Lydia* knew the blossom of fifteen;
No lovers now her morning hours molest,
And catch her at her Toilette half undrest;
The thund'ring knocker wakes the street no more,
No chairs, no coaches croud her silent door;
Her midnights once at cards and *Hazard* fled,
Which now, alas! she dreams away in bed.
Around her wait Shocks, monkeys and mockaws,
To fill the place of Fops, and perjur'd Beaus;
In these she views the mimickry of man,
And smiles when grinning *Pug* gallants her fan;
When *Poll* repeats, the sounds deceive her ear,
For sounds, like his, once told her *Damon*'s care.
With these alone her tedious mornings pass;
Or at the dumb devotion of her glass,
She smooths her brow, and frizles forth her hairs,
And fancys youthful dress gives youthful airs;
With crimson wooll she fixes ev'ry grace,
That not a blush can discompose her face.
Reclin'd upon her arm she pensive sate,
And curs'd th' inconstancy of youth too late.
O Youth! O spring of life! for ever lost!
No more my name shall reign the fav'rite Toast,
On glass no more the di'mond grave my name,
And rhymes mispell'd record a lover's flame:
Nor shall side-boxes watch my restless eyes,
And as they catch the glance in rows arise
With humble bows; nor white-glov'd Beaus encroach
In crouds behind, to guard me to my coach.

[1] Published in *Court Poems*, 1716. Text of *Poems on Several Occasions*, 1720.

Ah hapless nymph! such conquests are no more,
For *Chloe*'s now what *Lydia* was before!
'Tis true, this *Chloe* boasts the peach's bloom.
But does her nearer whisper breathe perfume?
I own her taper shape is form'd to please.
Yet if you saw her unconfin'd by stays!
She doubly to fifteen may make pretence,
Alike we read it in her face and sense.
Her reputation! but that never yet
Could check the freedoms of a young Coquet.
Why will ye then, vain Fops, her eyes believe?
Her eyes can, like your perjur'd tongues, deceive.
What shall I do? how spend the hateful day?
At chappel shall I wear the morn away?
Who there frequents at these unmodish hours,
But ancient matrons with their frizled tow'rs,
And gray religious maids? my presence there
Amid that sober train would own despair;
Nor am I yet so old; nor is my glance
As yet fixt wholy to devotion's trance.
Strait then I'll dress, and take my wonted range
Through ev'ry *Indian* shop, through all the *Change*;
Where the tall jarr erects his costly pride,
With antic shapes in *China*'s azure dy'd;
There careless lies the rich brocade unroll'd,
Here shines a cabinet with burnish'd gold;
But then remembrance will my grief renew,
'Twas there the raffling dice false *Damon* threw;
The raffling dice to him decide the prize.
'Twas there he first convers'd with *Chloe*'s eyes;
Hence sprung th' ill-fated cause of all my smart,
To me the toy he gave, to her his heart.
But soon thy perj'ry in the gift was found,
The shiver'd *China* dropt upon the ground;
Sure omen that thy vows would faithless prove;
Frail was thy present, frailer is thy love.
O happy *Poll*, in wiry prison pent;
Thou ne'er hast known what love or rivals meant,
And *Pug* with pleasure can his fetters bear,
Who ne'er believ'd the vows that lovers swear!
How am I curst! (unhappy and forlorn)
With perjury, with love, and rival's scorn!
False are the loose Coquet's inveigling airs,
False is the pompous grief of youthful heirs,
False is the cringing courtier's plighted word,
False are the dice when gamesters stamp the board,
False is the sprightly widow's publick tear;

Yet these to *Damon*'s oaths are all sincere.
  Fly from perfidious man, the sex disdain;
Let servile *Chloe* wear the nuptial chain.
Damon is practis'd in the modish life,
Can hate, and yet be civil to a wife.
He games; he swears; he drinks; he fights; he roves;
Yet *Chloe* can believe he fondly loves.
Mistress and wife can well supply his need,
A miss for pleasure, and a wife for breed.
But *Chloe*'s air is unconfin'd and gay,
And can perhaps an injur'd bed repay;
Perhaps her patient temper can behold
The rival of her love adorn'd with gold,
Powder'd with di'monds; free from thought and care,
A husband's sullen humours she can bear.
  Why are these sobs? and why these streaming eyes?
Is love the cause? no, I the sex despise;
I hate, I loath his base perfidious name.
Yet if he should but feign a rival flame?
But *Chloe* boasts and triumphs in my pains,
To her he's faithful, 'tis to me, he feigns.
  Thus love-sick *Lydia* rav'd. Her maid appears;
A band-box in her steady hand she bears.
How well this ribband's gloss becomes your face,
She crys, in raptures! then, so sweet a lace!
How charmingly you look! so bright! so fair!
'Tis to your eyes the head-dress owes its air.
Strait *Lydia* smil'd; the comb adjusts her locks,
And at the Play-house *Harry* keeps her box.

Sweet William's Farewell to Black-Ey'd Susan
A Ballad[1]

ALL in the *Downs* the fleet was moor'd,
  The streamers waving in the wind,
When black-ey'd *Susan* came aboard.
  Oh! where shall I my true love find!
Tell me, ye jovial sailors, tell me true,
If my sweet *William* sails among the crew.

William, who high upon the yard,
  Rock'd with the billow to and fro,

[1] Published in *Poems on Several Occasions*, 1720. Text of first edition.

Soon as her well-known voice he heard,
  He sigh'd, and cast his eyes below:
The cord slides swiftly through his glowing hands,
And, (quick as lightning,) on the deck he stands.

So the sweet lark, high-pois'd in air,
  Shuts close his pinions to his breast,
(If, chance, his mate's shrill call he hear)
  And drops at once into her nest.
The noblest Captain in the *British* fleet,
Might envy *William*'s lip those kisses sweet.

O *Susan, Susan*, lovely dear,
  My vows shall ever true remain;
Let me kiss off that falling tear,
  We only part to meet again.
Change, as ye list, ye winds; my heart shall be
The faithful compass that still points to thee.

Believe not what the landmen say,
  Who tempt with doubts thy constant mind:
They'll tell thee, sailors, when away,
  In ev'ry port a mistress find.
Yes, yes, believe them when they tell thee so,
For thou art present wheresoe'er I go.

If to far *India*'s coast we sail,
  Thy eyes are seen in di'monds bright,
Thy breath is *Africk*'s spicy gale,
  Thy skin is ivory, so white.
Thus ev'ry beauteous object that I view,
Wakes in my soul some charm of lovely *Sue*.

Though battel call me from thy arms,
  Let not my pretty *Susan* mourn;
Though cannons roar, yet safe from harms,
  William shall to his Dear return.
Love turns aside the balls that round me fly,
Lest precious tears should drop from *Susan*'s eye.

The boatswain gave the dreadful word,
  The sails their swelling bosom spread,
No longer must she stay aboard:
  They kiss'd, she sigh'd, he hung his head.
Her less'ning boat, unwilling rows to land:
Adieu, she cries! and wav'd her lilly hand.

Molly Mog: or, The Fair Maid of the Inn[1]

SAYS my Uncle, I pray you discover
  What hath been the Cause of your Woes,
Why you pine, and you whine, like a Lover?
  I have seen *Molly Mog* of the *Rose*.

O Nephew! Your Grief is but Folly,
  In Town you may find better Prog;
Half a Crown there will get you a *Molly*,
  A *Molly* much better than *Mog*.

I know that by Wits 'tis recited,
  That Women at best are a Clog;
But I am not so easily frighted,
  From loving of sweet *Molly Mog*.

The School-Boy's desire is a Play-Day,
  The School-Master's joy is to flog;
The Milk-Maid's delight is on *May-Day*,
  But mine is on sweet *Molly Mog*.

Will-a-wisp leads the Trav'ler a gadding
  Thro' Ditch, and thro' Quagmire and Bog;
But no Light can set me a madding,
  Like the Eyes of my sweet *Molly Mog*.

For Guineas in other Mens Breeches
  Your Gamesters will palm and will cog;
But I envy them none of their Riches,
  So I may win sweet *Molly Mog*.

The Heart, when half-wounded, is changing,
  It here and there leaps like a Frog;
But my Heart can never be ranging,
  'Tis so fix'd upon sweet *Molly Mog*.

Who follows all Ladies of Pleasure,
  In Pleasure is thought but a Hog:
All the Sex cannot give so good measure
  Of Joys, as my sweet *Molly Mog*.

I feel I'm in Love to Distraction,
  My Senses all lost in a Fog;

[1] Published in Mist's *Weekly Journal*, August 27, 1726. Text of *Miscellanies*, Volume III, 1728.

And nothing can give Satisfaction
  But thinking of sweet *Molly Mog.*

A Letter when I am inditing,
  Comes *Cupid* and gives me a Jog,
And I fill all the Paper with writing
  Of nothing but sweet *Molly Mog.*

If I would not give up the three *Graces*
  I wish I were hang'd like a Dog,
And at Court all the Drawing-Room Faces,
  For a Glance of my sweet *Molly Mog.*

Those Faces want Nature and Spirit,
  And seem as cut out of a Log;
Juno, Venus, and *Pallas*'s Merit
  Unite in my sweet *Molly Mog.*

Those who toast all the Family Royal,
  In Bumpers of *Hogan* and *Nog,*
Have Hearts not more true or more loyal
  Than mine to my sweet *Molly Mog.*

Were *Virgil* alive with his *Phillis,*
  And writing another Eclogue;
Both his *Phillis* and fair *Amaryllis*
  He'd give up for sweet *Molly Mog.*

When she smiles on each Guest, like her Liquor.
  Then Jealousy sets me agog.
To be sure she's a Bit for the *Vicar,*
  And so I shall lose *Molly Mog.*

Fables[1]

Introduction to the Fables

The Shepherd *and the* Philosopher.

REMOTE from cities liv'd a Swain,
Unvex'd with all the cares of gain,
His head was silver'd o'er with age,
And long experience made him sage;
In summer's heat and winter's cold

[1] Published in 1727. Text of second edition, 1728.

He fed his flock and pen'd the fold,
His hours in cheerful labour flew,
Nor envy nor ambition knew;
His wisdom and his honest fame
Through all the country rais'd his name.
  A deep Philosopher (whose rules
Of moral life were drawn from schools)
The Shepherd's homely cottage sought,
And thus explor'd his reach of thought.
  Whence is thy learning? Hath thy toil
O'er books consum'd the midnight oil?
Hast thou old *Greece* and *Rome* survey'd,
And the vast sense of *Plato* weigh'd?
Hath *Socrates* thy soul refin'd,
And hast thou fathom'd *Tully*'s mind?
Or, like the wise *Ulysses* thrown
By various fates on realms unknown,
Hast thou through many cities stray'd,
Their customs, laws and manners weigh'd?
  The Shepherd modestly reply'd.
I ne'er the paths of learning try'd,
Nor have I roam'd in foreign parts
To read mankind, their laws and arts;
For man is practis'd in disguise,
He cheats the most discerning eyes:
Who by that search shall wiser grow,
When we ourselves can never know?
The little knowledge, I have gain'd,
Was all from simple nature drain'd;
Hence my life's maxims took their rise,
Hence grew my settled hate to vice.
  The daily labours of the bee
Awake my soul to industry.
Who can observe the careful ant,
And not provide for future want?
My dog (the trustiest of his kind)
With gratitude inflames my mind;
I mark his true, his faithful way,
And in my service copy *Tray*.
In constancy, and nuptial love
I learn my duty from the dove.
The hen, who from the chilly air
With pious wing protects her care,
And ev'ry fowl that flies at large
Instructs me in a parent's charge.
  From nature too I take my rule
To shun contempt and ridicule.
I never with important air

In conversation overbear;
Can grave and formal pass for wise,
When men the solemn owl despise?
My tongue within my lips I rein,
For who talks much must talk in vain;
We from the wordy torrent fly:
Who listens to the chatt'ring pye?
Nor would I with felonious slight
By stealth invade my neighbour's right;
Rapacious animals we hate:
Kites, hawks and wolves deserve their fate.
Do not we just abhorrence find
Against the toad and serpent kind?
But envy, calumny and spite
Bear stronger venom in their bite.
Thus ev'ry object of creation
Can furnish hints to contemplation,
And from the most minute and mean
A virtuous mind can morals glean.
  Thy fame is just, the Sage replies,
Thy virtue proves thee truly wise;
Pride often guides the author's pen,
Books as affected are as men,
But he who studys nature's laws
From certain truth his maxims draws,
And those, without our schools, suffice
To make men moral, good and wise.

Fable XVIII

The Painter *who pleased No body and Every body.*

LEST men suspect your tale untrue,
Keep probability in view.
The trav'ler leaping o'er those bounds,
The credit of his book confounds;
Who with his tongue hath armies routed
Makes ev'n his real courage doubted.
But flatt'ry never seems absurd,
The flatter'd always take your word,
Impossibilities seem just,
They take the strongest praise on trust;
Hyperboles, though ne'er so great,
Will still come short of self-conceit.

  So very like a Painter drew,
That ev'ry eye the picture knew;

He hit complexion, feature, air,
So just, the life itself was there.
No flatt'ry, with his colours laid,
To bloom restor'd the faded maid,
He gave each muscle all its strength,
The mouth, the chin, the nose's length
His honest pencil touch'd with truth,
And mark'd the date of age and youth.
  He lost his friends, his practice fail'd,
Truth should not always be reveal'd;
In dusty piles his pictures lay,
For no one sent the second pay.
  Two bustos, fraught with ev'ry grace,
A *Venus*' and *Apollo*'s face,
He plac'd in view; resol'vd to please,
Whoever sate, he drew from these,
From these corrected ev'ry feature,
And spirited each aukward creature.
  All things were set; the hour was come,
His pallet ready o'er his thumb,
My lord appear'd, and seated right
In proper attitude and light,
The Painter look'd, he sketch'd the piece,
Then dipt his pencil, talk'd of *Greece*,
Of *Titian*'s tints, of *Guido*'s air;
Those eyes, my lord, the spirit there
Might well a *Raphael*'s hand require,
To give them all the native fire;
The features fraught with sense and wit
You'll grant are very hard to hit,
But yet with patience you shall view
As much as paint and art can do.
  Observe the work. My lord reply'd,
'Till now I thought my mouth was wide,
Besides, my nose is somewhat long,
Dear sir, for me, 'tis far too young.
  Oh, pardon me, the artist cry'd,
In this we painters must decide.
The piece ev'n common eyes must strike,
I warrant it extreamly like.
  My lord examin'd it anew;
No looking-glass seem'd half so true.
A lady came, with borrow'd grace
He from his *Venus* form'd her face,
Her lover prais'd the painter's art;
So like the picture in his heart!
To ev'ry age some charm he lent,
Ev'n Beauties were almost content.

Through all the town his art they prais'd,
His custom grew, his price was rais'd.
Had he the real likeness shown,
Would any man the picture own?
But when thus happily he wrought,
Each found the likeness in his thought.

Fable XXVII

The Sick Man *and the* Angel.

Is THERE no hope? the sick man said.
The silent doctor shook his head,
And took his leave, with signs of sorrow,
Despairing of his fee to-morrow.
When thus the Man, with gasping breath.
I feel the chilling wound of death.
Since I must bid the world adieu;
Let me my former life review.
I grant, my bargains well were made.
But all men over-reach in trade;
'Tis self-defence in each profession,
Sure self-defence is no transgression.
The little portion in my hands,
By good security on lands,
Is well encreas'd. If unawares,
My justice to my self and heirs,
Hath let my debtor rot in jail,
For want of good sufficient bail;
If I by writ, or bond, or deed
Reduc'd a family to need,
My will hath made the world amends;
My hope on charity depends.
When I am number'd with the dead,
And all my pious gifts are read,
By heav'n and earth 'twill then be known
My charities were amply shown.
An Angel came. Ah friend, he cry'd,
No more in flatt'ring hope confide.
Can thy good deeds in former times
Outweigh the ballance of thy crimes?
What widow or what orphan prays
To crown thy life with length of days?
A pious action's in thy power,
Embrace with joy the happy hour;
Now, while you draw the vital air,

Prove your intention is sincere:
This instant give a hundred pound;
Your neighbours want, and you abound.
But why such haste, the sick Man whines,
Who knows as yet what Heav'n designs?
Perhaps I may recover still.
That sum and more are in my will.
Fool, says the Vision, now 'tis plain,
Your life, your soul, your heav'n was gain;
From ev'ry side, with all your might,
You scrap'd, and scrap'd beyond your right,
And after death would fain attone,
By giving what is not your own.
Where there is life, there's hope, he cry'd;
Then why such haste? so groan'd and dy'd.

From The Beggar's Opera[1]

Air I. An old Woman cloathed in Gray, *&c.*

THROUGH all the Employments of Life
Each Neighbour abuses his Brother;
Whore and Rogue they call Husband and Wife:
All Professions be-rogue one another.
The Priest calls the Lawyer a Cheat,
The Lawyer be-knaves the Divine;
And the Statesman, because he's so great,
Thinks his Trade as honest as mine.

Air XI. A Soldier and a Sailor.

A Fox may steal your Hens, Sir,
A Whore your Health and Pence, Sir,
Your Daughter rob your Chest, Sir,
Your Wife may steal your Rest, Sir,
A Thief your Goods and Plate.

But this is all but picking,
With Rest, Pence, Chest and Chicken;
It ever was decreed, Sir,
If Lawyer's Hand is fee'd, Sir,
He steals your whole Estate.

[1] Published in 1728. Text of second edition, 1728.

Air XVI. Over the Hills and far away.

Mach. Were I laid on *Greenland's* Coast,
And in my Arms embrac'd my Lass;
Warm amidst eternal Frost,
Too soon the Half Year's Night would pass.
Polly. Were I sold on *Indian* Soil,
Soon as the burning Day was clos'd,
I could mock the sultry Toil,
When on my Charmer's Breast repos'd.
Mach. And I would love you all the Day,
Polly. Every Night would kiss and play,
Mach. If with me you'd fondly stray
Polly. Over the Hills and far away.

Air XX. March in *Rinaldo*, with Drums and Trumpets.

Matt. Let us take the Road.
Hark! I hear the sound of Coaches!
The hour of Attack approaches,
To your Arms, brave Boys, and load,
See the Ball I hold!
Let the Chymists toil like Asses,
Our Fire their Fire surpasses,
And turns all our Lead to Gold.

Air XXI. Would you have a Young Virgin, *&c.*

If the Heart of a Man is deprest with Cares,
The Mist is dispell'd when a Woman appears;
Like the Notes of a Fiddle, she sweetly, sweetly
Raises the Spirits, and charms our Ears,
Roses and Lillies her Cheeks disclose,
But her ripe Lips are more sweet than those.
Press her,
Caress her
With Blisses,
Her Kisses
Dissolve us in Pleasure, and soft Repose.

Air XXII. Cotillon.

Youth's the Season made for Joys,
Love is then our Duty,
She alone who that employs,

Well deserves her Beauty.
Let's be gay,
While we may,
Beauty's a Flower, despised in decay.
Youth's the Season &c.

Let us drink and sport to-day,
Ours is not to-morrow.
Love with Youth flies swift away,
Age is nought but Sorrow.
Dance and sing,
Time's on the Wing,
Life never knows the return of Spring.
CHORUS. Let us drink *&c.*

Air XXVI. Courtiers, Courtiers think it no harm, *&c.*

Man may escape from Rope and Gun;
Nay, some have out-liv'd the Doctor's Pill;
Who takes a Woman must be undon,
That Basilisk is sure to kill.
The Fly that sips Treacle is lost in the Sweets,
So he that tastes Woman, Woman, Woman,
He that tastes Woman, Ruin meets.

ALEXANDER POPE

(1688-1709-1744)

Pastorals[1]

Summer

The Second Pastoral, or Alexis

To Dr. Garth

A SHEPHERD'S BOY (he seeks no better name)
Led forth his flocks along the silver Thame,
Where dancing sun-beams on the waters play'd,

[1] Published, May 2, 1709. Text of *Works*, 1751 (small octavo edition).

And verdant alders form'd a quiv'ring shade.
Soft as he mourn'd, the streams forgot to flow,
The flocks around a dumb compassion show,
The Naiads wept in ev'ry watry bow'r,
And Jove consented in a silent show'r.
Accept, O GARTH, the Muse's early lays,
That adds this wreath of Ivy to thy Bays;
Hear what from Love unpractis'd hearts endure,
From Love, the sole disease thou canst not cure.
Ye shady beeches, and ye cooling streams,
Defence from Phœbus', not from Cupid's beams,
To you I mourn, nor to the deaf I sing,
The woods shall answer, and their echo ring.
The hills and rocks attend my doleful lay,
Why art thou prouder and more hard than they?
The bleating sheep with my complaints agree,
They parch'd with heat, and I inflam'd by thee.
The sultry Sirius burns the thirsty plains,
While in thy heart eternal winter reigns.
Where stray ye Muses, in what lawn or grove,
While your Alexis pines in hopeless love?
In those fair fields where sacred Isis glides,
Or else where Cam his winding vales divides?
As in the crystal spring I view my face,
Fresh rising blushes paint the watry glass;
But since those graces please thy eyes no more,
I shun the fountains which I sought before.
Once I was skill'd in ev'ry herb that grew,
And ev'ry plant that drinks the morning dew;
Ah wretched shepherd, what avails thy art,
To cure thy lambs, but not to heal thy heart!
Let other swains attend the rural care,
Feed fairer flocks, or richer fleeces sheer:
But nigh yon' mountain let me tune my lays,
Embrace my Love, and bind my brows with bays.
That flute is mine which Colin's tuneful breath
Inspir'd when living, and bequeath'd in death;
He said; Alexis, take this pipe, the same
That taught the groves my Rosalinda's name:
But now the reeds shall hang on yonder tree,
For ever silent since despis'd by thee.
Oh! were I made by some transforming pow'r
The captive bird that sings within thy bow'r!
Then might my voice thy list'ning ears employ,
And I those kisses he receives, enjoy.
And yet my numbers please the rural throng,

Rough Satyrs dance, and Pan applauds the song:
The Nymphs, forsaking ev'ry cave and spring,
Their early fruit, and milk-white turtles bring;
Each am'rous nymph prefers her gifts in vain,
On you their gifts are all bestow'd again.
For you the swains the fairest flow'rs design,
And in one garland all their beauties join;
Accept the wreath which you deserve alone,
In whom all beauties are compriz'd in one.
  See what delights in sylvan scenes appear!
Descending Gods have found Elysium here.
In woods bright Venus with Adonis stray'd,
And chaste Diana haunts the forest shade.
Come, lovely nymph, and bless the silent hours,
When swains from sheering seek their nightly bow'rs;
When weary reapers quit the sultry field,
And crown'd with corn their thanks to Ceres yield,
This harmless grove no lurking viper hides,
But in my breast the serpent Love abides.
Here bees from blossoms sip the rosy dew,
But your Alexis knows no sweets but you.
Oh deign to visit our forsaken seats,
The mossy fountains, and the green retreats!
Where'er you walk, cool gales shall fan the glade,
Trees, where you sit, shall croud into a shade:
Where'er you tread, the blushing flow'rs shall rise,
And all things flourish where you turn your eyes.
Oh! how I long with you to pass my days,
Invoke the Muses, and resound your praise!
Your praise the birds shall chant in ev'ry grove,
And winds shall waft it to the pow'rs above.
But would you sing, and rival Orpheus' strain,
The wond'ring forests soon should dance again,
The moving mountains hear the pow'rful call,
And headlong streams hang list'ning in their fall!
  But see, the shepherds shun the noon-day heat,
The lowing herds to murm'ring brooks retreat,
To closer shades the panting flocks remove;
Ye Gods! and is there no relief for Love?
But soon the sun with milder rays descends
To the cool ocean, where his journey ends:
On me love's fiercer flames for ever prey,
By night he scorches, as he burns by day.

An Essay on Criticism[1]

'Tis hard to say, if greater want of skill
Appear in writing or in judging ill;
But, of the two, less dang'rous is th' offence
To tire our patience, than mislead our sense.
Some few in that, but numbers err in this,
Ten censure wrong, for one who writes amiss;
A fool might once himself alone expose,
Now one in verse makes many more in prose.
'Tis with our judgments as our watches, none
Go just alike, yet each believes his own.
In Poets as true genius is but rare,
True Taste as seldom is the Critic's share;
Both must alike from Heav'n derive their light,
These born to judge, as well as those to write.
Let such teach others who themselves excel,
And censure freely who have written well.
Authors are partial to their wit, 'tis true,
But are not Critics to their judgment too?
Yet if we look more closely, we shall find
Most have the seeds of judgment in their mind:
Nature affords at least a glimm'ring light;
The lines, tho' touch'd but faintly, are drawn right.
But as the slightest sketch, if justly trac'd,
Is by ill-colouring but the more disgrac'd,
So by false learning is good sense defac'd:
Some are bewilder'd in the maze of schools,
And some made coxcombs Nature meant but fools.
In search of wit these lose their common sense,
And then turn Critics in their own defence:
Each burns alike, who can, or cannot write,
Or with a Rival's, or an Eunuch's spite.
All fools have still an itching to deride,
And fain would be upon the laughing side.
If Mævius scribble in Apollo's spight,
There are, who judge still worse than he can write.
Some have at first for Wits, then Poets past,
Turn'd Critics next, and prov'd plain fools at last.
Some neither can for Wits nor Critics pass,
As heavy mules are neither horse nor ass.
Those half-learn'd witlings, num'rous in our isle,
As half-form'd insects on the banks of Nile;
Unfinish'd things, one knows not what to call,
Their generation's so equivocal:

[1] Published May 15, 1711. Text of *Works*, 1751.

To tell 'em, would a hundred tongues require,
Or one vain wit's, that might a hundred tire.
  But you who seek to give and merit fame,
And justly bear a Critic's noble name,
Be sure yourself and your own reach to know,
How far your genius, taste, and learning go;
Launch not beyond your depth, but be discreet,
And mark that point where sense and dullness meet.
  Nature to all things fix'd the limits fit,
And wisely curb'd proud man's pretending wit.
As on the land while here the ocean gains,
In other parts it leaves wide sandy plains;
Thus in the soul while memory prevails,
The solid pow'r of understanding fails;
Where beams of warm imagination play,
The memory's soft figures melt away.
One science only will one genius fit;
So vast is art, so narrow human wit:
Not only bounded to peculiar arts,
But oft' in those confin'd to single parts.
Like Kings we lose the conquests gain'd before,
By vain ambition still to make them more;
Each might his sev'ral province well command,
Would all but stoop to what they understand.
  First follow Nature, and your judgment frame
By her just standard, which is still the same:
Unerring Nature, still divinely bright,
One clear, unchang'd, and universal light,
Life, force, and beauty, must to all impart,
At once the source, and end, and test of Art.
Art from that fund each just supply provides,
Works without show, and without pomp presides:
In some fair body thus th' informing soul
With spirits feeds, with vigour fills the whole,
Each motion guides, and ev'ry nerve sustains;
Itself unseen, but in th' effects, remains.
Some, to whom Heav'n in wit has been profuse,
Want as much more to turn it to its use;
For wit and judgment often are at strife,
Tho' meant each other's aid, like man and wife.
'Tis more to guide, than spur the Muse's steed;
Restrain his fury, than provoke his speed;
The winged courser, like a gen'rous horse,
Shows most true mettle when you check his course.
  Those Rules of old discover'd, not devis'd,
Are Nature still, but Nature methodiz'd;
Nature, like Liberty, is but restrain'd
By the same Laws which first herself ordain'd.

Hear how learn'd Greece her useful rules indites,
When to repress, and when indulge our flights:
High on Parnassus' top her sons she show'd,
And pointed out those arduous paths they trod;
Held from afar, aloft, th' immortal prize,
And urg'd the rest by equal steps to rise.
Just precepts thus from great examples giv'n,
She drew from them what they deriv'd from Heav'n.
The gen'rous Critic fann'd the Poet's fire,
And taught the world with reason to admire.
Then Criticism the Muses handmaid prov'd,
To dress her charms, and make her more belov'd:
But following wits from that intention stray'd,
Who cou'd not win the mistress, woo'd the maid;
Against the Poets their own arms they turn'd,
Sure to hate most the men from whom they learn'd.
So modern 'Pothecaries, taught the art
By Doctor's bills to play the Doctor's part,
Bold in the practice of mistaken rules,
Prescribe, apply, and call their masters fools.
Some on the leaves of ancient authors prey,
Nor time nor moths e'er spoil'd so much as they.
Some drily plain, without invention's aid,
Write dull receits how poems may be made.
These leave the sense, their learning to display,
And those explain the meaning quite away.
You then whose judgment the right course would steer,
Know well each ANCIENT's proper character;
His Fable, Subject, scope in ev'ry page;
Religion, Country, genius of his Age:
Without all these at once before your eyes,
Cavil you may, but never criticize.
Be Homer's works your study and delight,
Read them by day, and meditate by night;
Thence form your judgment, thence your maxims bring,
And trace the Muses upward to their spring.
Still with itself compar'd, his text peruse;
And let your comment be the Mantuan Muse.
When first young Maro in his boundless mind
A work t' outlast immortal Rome design'd,
Perhaps he seem'd above the Critic's law,
And but from Nature's fountains scorn'd to draw:
But when t' examine ev'ry part he came,
Nature and Homer were, he found, the same.
Convinc'd, amaz'd, he checks the bold design;
And rules as strict his labour'd work confine,
As if the Stagirite o'erlook'd each line.
Learn hence for ancient rules a just esteem;

To copy nature is to copy them.
  Some beauties yet no Precepts can declare,
For there's a happiness as well as care.
Music resembles Poetry, in each
Are nameless graces which no methods teach,
And which a master-hand alone can reach.
If, where the rules not far enough extend,
(Since rules were made but to promote their end)
Some lucky Licence answer to the full
Th' intent propos'd, that Licence is a rule.
Thus Pegasus, a nearer way to take,
May boldly deviate from the common track;
From vulgar bounds with brave disorder part,
And snatch a grace beyond the reach of art,
Which without passing thro' the judgment, gains
The heart, and all its end at once attains.
In prospects thus, some objects please our eyes,
Which out of nature's common order rise,
The shapeless rock, or hanging precipice.
Great Wits sometimes may gloriously offend,
And rise to faults true Critics dare not mend.
But tho' the Ancients thus their rules invade,
(As Kings dispense with laws themselves have made)
Moderns, beware! or if you must offend
Against the precept, ne'er transgress its End;
Let it be seldom, and compell'd by need;
And have, at least, their precedent to plead.
The Critic else proceeds without remorse,
Seizes your fame, and puts his laws in force.
  I know there are, to whose presumptuous thoughts
Those freer beauties, ev'n in them, seem faults.
Some figures monstrous and mis-shap'd appear,
Consider'd singly, or beheld too near,
Which, but proportion'd to their light, or place,
Due distance reconciles to form and grace.
A prudent chief not always must display
His pow'rs in equal ranks, and fair array,
But with th' occasion and the place comply,
Conceal his force, nay seem sometimes to fly.
Those oft are stratagems which errors seem,
Nor is it Homer nods, but we that dream.
  Still green with bays each ancient Altar stands,
Above the reach of sacrilegious hands;
Secure from Flames, from Envy's fiercer rage,
Destructive War, and all-involving Age.
See, from each clime the learn'd their incense bring!
Hear, in all tongues consenting Pæans ring!
In praise so just let ev'ry voice be join'd,

And fill the gen'ral chorus of mankind.
Hail, Bards triumphant! born in happier days;
Immortal heirs of universal praise!
Whose honours with increase of ages grow,
As streams roll down, enlarging as they flow;
Nations unborn your mighty names shall sound,
And worlds applaud that must not yet be found!
Oh may some spark of your celestial fire,
The last, the meanest of your sons inspire,
(That on weak wings, from far, pursues your flights;
Glows while he reads, but trembles as he writes)
To teach vain Wits a science little known,
T' admire superior sense, and doubt their own!

Of all the Causes which conspire to blind
Man's erring judgment, and misguide the mind,
What the weak head with strongest bias rules,
Is *Pride*, the never-failing vice of fools.
Whatever Nature has in worth deny'd,
She gives in large recruits of needful Pride;
For as in bodies, thus in souls, we find
What wants in blood and spirits, swell'd with wind:
Pride, where Wit fails, steps in to our defence,
And fills up all the mighty Void of sense.
If once right reason drives that cloud away,
Truth breaks upon us with resistless day.
Trust not yourself; but your defects to know,
Make use of ev'ry friend—and ev'ry foe.

A *little learning* is a dang'rous thing;
Drink deep, or taste not the Pierian spring:
There shallow draughts intoxicate the brain,
And drinking largely sobers us again.
Fir'd at first sight with what the Muse imparts,
In fearless youth we tempt the heights of Arts,
While from the bounded level of our mind,
Short views we take, nor see the lengths behind;
But more advanc'd, behold with strange surprize
New distant scenes of endless science rise!
So pleas'd at first the tow'ring Alps we try,
Mount o'er the vales, and seem to tread the sky,
Th' eternal snows appear already past,
And the first clouds and mountains seem the last:
But, those attain'd, we tremble to survey
The growing labours of the lengthen'd way,
Th' increasing prospect tires our wand'ring eyes,
Hills peep o'er hills, and Alps on Alps arise!

A perfect Judge will read each work of Wit
With the same spirit that its author writ:
Survey the WHOLE, nor seek slight faults to find

Where nature moves, and rapture warms the mind;
Nor lose, for that malignant dull delight,
The gen'rous pleasure to be charm'd with wit.
But in such lays as neither ebb, nor flow,
Correctly cold, and regularly low,
That shunning faults, one quiet tenour keep;
We cannot blame indeed—but we may sleep.
In Wit, as Nature, what affects our hearts
Is not th' exactness of peculiar parts;
'Tis not a lip, or eye, we beauty call,
But the joint force and full result of all.
Thus when we view some well-proportion'd dome,
(The world's just wonder, and ev'n thine, O Rome!)
No single parts unequally surprize,
All comes united to th' admiring eyes;
No monstrous height, or breadth, or length appear;
The Whole at once is bold, and regular.
  Whoever thinks a faultless piece to see,
Thinks what ne'er was, nor is, nor e'er shall be.
In ev'ry work regard the writer's End,
Since none can compass more than they intend;
And if the means be just, the conduct true,
Applause, in spight of trivial faults, is due.
As men of breeding, sometimes men of wit,
T' avoid great errors, must the less commit:
Neglect the rules each verbal Critic lays,
For not to know some trifles, is a praise.
Most Critics, fond of some subservient art,
Still make the Whole depend upon a Part:
They talk of principles, but notions prize,
And all to one lov'd Folly sacrifice.
  Once on a time, La Mancha's Knight, they say,
A certain Bard encount'ring on the way,
Discours'd in terms as just, with looks as sage,
As e'er could Dennis, of the Grecian stage;
Concluding all were desp'rate sots and fools,
Who durst depart from Aristotle's rules.
Our Author, happy in a judge so nice,
Produc'd his Play, and begg'd the Knight's advice;
Made him observe the subject, and the plot,
The manners, passions, unities, what not?
All which, exact to rule, were brought about,
Were but a Combat in the lists left out.
"What! leave the Combat out?" exclaims the Knight;
Yes, or we must renounce the Stagirite.
"Not so, by Heav'n" (he answers in a rage)
"Knights, squires, and steeds, must enter on the stage."
So vast a throng the stage can ne'er contain.

"Then build a new, or act it on a plain."
  Thus Critics, of less judgment than caprice,
Curious not knowing, not exact but nice,
Form short Ideas; and offend in arts
(As most in manners) by a love to parts.
  Some to *Conceit* alone their taste confine,
And glitt'ring thoughts struck out at ev'ry line;
Pleas'd with a work where nothing's just or fit;
One glaring Chaos and wild heap of wit.
Poets, like painters, thus, unskill'd to trace
The naked nature and the living grace,
With gold and jewels cover ev'ry part,
And hide with ornaments their want of art.
True Wit is Nature to advantage dress'd,
What oft was thought, but ne'er so well express'd;
Something, whose truth convinc'd at sight we find,
That gives us back the image of our mind.
As shades more sweetly recommend the light,
So modest plainness sets off sprightly wit.
For works may have more wit than does 'em good,
As bodies perish thro' excess of blood.
  Others for *Language* all their care express,
And value books, as women men, for Dress:
Their praise is still,—the Style is excellent:
The Sense, they humbly take upon content.
Words are like leaves; and where they most abound,
Much fruit of sense beneath is rarely found.
False Eloquence, like the prismatic glass,
Its gaudy colours spreads on ev'ry place;
The face of Nature we no more survey,
All glares alike, without distinction gay:
But true Expression, like th' unchanging Sun,
Clears, and improves whate'er it shines upon,
It gilds all objects, but it alters none.
Expression is the dress of thought, and still
Appears more decent, as more suitable;
A vile conceit in pompous words express'd,
Is like a clown in regal purple dress'd:
For diff'rent styles with diff'rent subjects sort,
As several garbs with country, town, and court.
Some by old words to fame have made pretence,
Ancients in phrase, meer moderns in their sense;
Such labour'd nothings, in so strange a style,
Amaze th' unlearn'd, and make the learned smile.
Unlucky, as Fungoso in the Play,
These sparks with aukward vanity display
What the fine gentleman wore yesterday;
And but so mimic ancient wits at best,

As apes our grandsires, in their doublets drest.
In words, as fashions, the same rule will hold;
Alike fantastic, if too new, or old:
Be not the first by whom the new are try'd,
Nor yet the last to lay the old aside.
But most by Numbers judge a Poet's song;
And smooth or rough, with them, is right or wrong:
In the bright Muse tho' thousand charms conspire,
Her Voice is all these tuneful fools admire;
Who haunt Parnassus but to please their ear,
Not mend their minds; as some to Church repair,
Not for the doctrine, but the music there.
These equal syllables alone require,
Tho' oft the ear the open vowels tire;
While expletives their feeble aid do join;
And ten low words oft creep in one dull line:
While they ring round the same unvary'd chimes,
With sure returns of still expected rhymes;
Where-e'er you find "the cooling western breeze,"
In the next line, it "whispers thro' the trees":
If crystal streams "with pleasing murmurs creep,"
The reader's threaten'd (not in vain) with "sleep":
Then, at the last and only couplet fraught
With some unmeaning thing they call a thought,
A needless Alexandrine ends the song,
That, like a wounded snake, drags its slow length along.
Leave such to tune their own dull rhymes, and know
What's roundly smooth, or languishingly slow;
And praise the easy vigour of a line,
Where Denham's strength, and Waller's sweetness join.
True ease in writing comes from art, not chance,
As those move easiest who have learn'd to dance.
'Tis not enough no harshness gives offence,
The sound must seem an Echo to the sense:
Soft is the strain when Zephyr gently blows,
And the smooth stream in smoother numbers flows;
But when loud surges lash the sounding shoar,
The hoarse, rough verse should like the torrent roar:
When Ajax strives some rock's vast weight to throw,
The line too labours, and the words move slow;
Not so, when swift Camilla scours the plain,
Flies o'er th' unbending corn, and skims along the main.
Hear how Timotheus' vary'd lays surprize,
And bid alternate passions fall and rise!
While, at each change, the son of Libyan Jove
Now burns with glory, and then melts with love;
Now his fierce eyes with sparkling fury glow,
Now sighs steal out, and tears begin to flow:

Persians and Greeks like turns of nature found,
And the World's victor stood subdu'd by Sound!
The pow'r of Music all our hearts allow,
And what Timotheus was, is DRYDEN now.
  Avoid Extremes; and shun the fault of such,
Who still are pleas'd too little or too much.
At ev'ry trifle scorn to take offence,
That always shows great pride, or little sense;
Those heads, as stomachs, are not sure the best,
Which nauseate all, and nothing can digest.
Yet let not each gay Turn thy rapture move;
For fools admire, but men of sense approve:
As things seem large which we thro' mists descry,
Dulness is ever apt to magnify.
  Some foreign writers, some our own despise;
The Ancients only, or the Moderns prize.
Thus Wit, like Faith, by each man is apply'd
To one small sect, and all are damn'd beside.
Meanly they seek the blessing to confine,
And force that sun but on a part to shine,
Which not alone the southern wit sublimes,
But ripens spirits in cold northern climes;
Which from the first has shone on ages past,
Enlights the present, and shall warm the last;
Tho' each may feel encreases and decays,
And see now clearer and now darker days.
Regard not then if Wit be old or new,
But blame the false, and value still the true.
  Some ne'er advance a Judgment of their own,
But catch the spreading notion of the Town;
They reason and conclude by precedent,
And own stale nonsense which they ne'er invent.
Some judge of authors names, not works, and then
Nor praise nor blame the writings, but the men.
Of all this servile herd, the worst is he
That in proud dulness joins with Quality.
A constant critic at the great man's board,
To fetch and carry nonsense for my Lord.
What woful stuff this madrigal would be,
In some starv'd hackney sonnetteer, or me?
But let a Lord once own the happy lines,
How the wit brightens! how the style refines!
Before his sacred name flies ev'ry fault,
And each exalted stanza teems with thought!
  The Vulgar thus thro' Imitation err;
As oft the Learn'd by being singular;
So much they scorn the croud, that if the throng
By chance go right, they purposely go wrong:

So Schismatics the plain believers quit,
And are but damn'd for having too much wit.
Some praise at morning what they blame at night;
But always think the last opinion right.
A Muse by these is like a mistress us'd,
This hour she's idoliz'd, the next abus'd;
While their weak heads like towns unfortify'd,
'Twixt sense and nonsense daily change their side.
Ask them the cause; they're wiser still, they say;
And still to-morrow's wiser than to-day.
We think our fathers fools, so wise we grow;
Our wiser sons, no doubt, will think us so.
Once School-divines this zealous isle o'er-spread;
Who knew most Sentences, was deepest read;
Faith, Gospel, all, seem'd made to be disputed,
And none had sense enough to be confuted:
Scotists and Thomists, now, in peace remain,
Amidst their kindred cobwebs in Duck-lane.
If Faith itself has diff'rent dresses worn,
What wonder modes in Wit should take their turn?
Oft', leaving what is natural and fit,
The current folly proves the ready wit;
And authors think their reputation safe,
Which lives as long as fools are pleas'd to laugh.
Some valuing those of their own side or mind,
Still make themselves the measure of mankind:
Fondly we think we honour merit then,
When we but praise ourselves in other men.
Parties in Wit attend on those of State,
And public faction doubles private hate.
Pride, Malice, Folly, against Dryden rose,
In various shapes of Parsons, Critics, Beaus;
But sense surviv'd, when merry jests were past;
For rising merit will buoy up at last.
Might he return, and bless once more our eyes,
New Blackmores and new Milbourns must arise:
Nay should great Homer lift his awful head,
Zoilus again would start up from the dead.
Envy will merit, as its shade, pursue;
But like a shadow, proves the substance true;
For envy'd Wit, like Sol eclips'd, makes known
Th' opposing body's grossness, not its own.
When first that sun too pow'rful beams displays,
It draws up vapours which obscure its rays;
But ev'n those clouds at last adorn its way,
Reflect new glories, and augment the day.
Be thou the first true merit to befriend;
His praise is lost, who stays 'till all commend.

Short is the date, alas, of modern rhymes,
And 'tis but just to let them live betimes.
No longer now that golden age appears,
When Patriarch-wits surviv'd a thousand years:
Now length of Fame (our second life) is lost,
And bare threescore is all ev'n that can boast;
Our sons their fathers failing language see,
And such as Chaucer is, shall Dryden be.
So when the faithful pencil has design'd
Some bright Idea of the master's mind,
Where a new world leaps out at his command,
And ready Nature waits upon his hand;
When the ripe colours soften and unite,
And sweetly melt into just shade and light;
When mellowing years their full perfection give,
And each bold figure just begins to live,
The treach'rous colours the fair art betray,
And all the bright creation fades away!
  Unhappy Wit, like most mistaken things,
Atones not for that envy which it brings.
In youth alone its empty praise we boast,
But soon the short-liv'd vanity is lost:
Like some fair flow'r the early spring supplies,
That gayly blooms, but ev'n in blooming dies.
What is this Wit, which must our cares employ?
The owner's wife, that other men enjoy;
Then most our trouble still when most admir'd,
And still the more we give, the more requir'd;
Whose fame with pains we guard, but lose with ease,
Some sure to vex, but never all to please;
'Tis what the vicious fear, the virtuous shun,
By fools 'tis hated, and by knaves undone!
  If Wit so much from Ign'rance undergo,
Ah let not Learning too commence its foe!
Of old, those met rewards who could excell,
And such were prais'd who but endeavour'd well:
Tho' triumphs were to gen'rals only due,
Crowns were reserv'd to grace the soldiers too.
Now, they who reach Parnassus' lofty crown,
Employ their pains to spurn some others down;
And while self-love each jealous writer rules,
Contending wits become the sport of fools:
But still the worst with most regret commend,
For each ill Author is as bad a Friend.
To what base ends, and by what abject ways,
Are mortals urg'd thro' sacred lust of praise!
Ah ne'er so dire a thirst of glory boast,
Nor in the Critic let the Man be lost.

Good-nature and good-sense must ever join;
To err is human, to forgive, divine.
  But if in noble minds some dregs remain
Not yet purg'd off, of spleen and sour disdain;
Discharge that rage on more provoking crimes,
Nor fear a dearth in these flagitious times.
No pardon vile Obscenity should find,
Tho' wit and art conspire to move your mind;
But Dulness with Obscenity must prove
As shameful sure as Impotence in love.
In the fat age of pleasure, wealth, and ease,
Sprung the rank weed, and thriv'd with large increase:
When love was all an easy Monarch's care;
Seldom at council, never in a war:
Jilts rul'd the state, and statesmen farces writ;
Nay wits had pensions, and young Lords had wit:
The Fair sate panting at a Courtier's play,
And not a Mask went unimprov'd away:
The modest fan was lifted up no more,
And Virgins smil'd at what they blush'd before.
The following licence of a Foreign reign
Did all the dregs of bold Socinus drain;
Then unbelieving Priests reform'd the nation,
And taught more pleasant methods of salvation;
Where Heav'n's free subjects might their rights dispute,
Lest God himself should seem too absolute:
Pulpits their sacred satire learn'd to spare,
And Vice admir'd to find a flatt'rer there!
Encourag'd thus, Wit's Titans brav'd the skies,
And the press groan'd with licens'd blasphemies.
These monsters, Critics! with your darts engage,
Here point your thunder, and exhaust your rage!
Yet shun their fault, who, scandalously nice,
Will needs mistake an author into vice;
All seems infected that th' infected spy,
As all looks yellow to the jaundic'd eye.
LEARN then what MORALS Critics ought to show,
For 'tis but half a Judge's task, to know.
'Tis not enough, taste, judgment, learning, join;
In all you speak, let truth and candour shine:
That not alone what to your sense is due
All may allow; but seek your friendship too.
  Be silent always when you doubt your sense;
And speak, tho' sure, with seeming diffidence:
Some positive, persisting fops we know,
Who, if once wrong, will needs be always so;
But you, with pleasure own your errors past,
And make each day a Critic on the last.

'Tis not enough, your counsel still be true;
Blunt truths more mischief than nice falshoods do;
Men must be taught as if you taught them not,
And things unknown propos'd as things forgot.
Without Good Breeding, truth is disapprov'd;
That only makes superior sense belov'd.
Be niggards of advice on no pretence;
For the worst avarice is that of sense.
With mean complacence ne'er betray your trust,
Nor be so civil as to prove unjust.
Fear not the anger of the wise to raise;
Those best can bear reproof, who merit praise.
'Twere well might Critics still this freedom take,
But Appius reddens at each word you speak,
And stares, tremendous, with a threat'ning eye,
Like some fierce Tyrant in old tapestry.
Fear most to tax an Honourable fool,
Whose right it is, uncensur'd to be dull;
Such, without wit, are Poets when they please,
As without learning they can take Degrees.
Leave dang'rous truths to unsuccessful Satires,
And flattery to fulsome Dedicators,
Whom, when they praise, the world believes no more,
Than when they promise to give scribling o'er.
'Tis best sometimes your censure to restrain,
And charitably let the dull be vain:
Your silence there is better than your spite,
For who can rail so long as they can write?
Still humming on, their drouzy course they keep,
And lash'd so long, like tops, are lash'd asleep.
False steps but help them to renew the race,
As, after stumbling, Jades will mend their pace.
What crouds of these, impenitently bold,
In sounds and jingling syllables grown old,
Still run on Poets, in a raging vein,
Ev'n to the dregs and squeezings of the brain,
Strain out the last dull droppings of their sense,
And rhyme with all the rage of Impotence.
Such shameless Bards we have; and yet 'tis true,
There are as mad, abandon'd Critics too.
The bookful blockhead, ignorantly read,
With loads of learned lumber in his head,
With his own tongue still edifies his ears,
And always list'ning to himself appears.
All books he reads, and all he reads assails,
From Dryden's Fables down to Durfey's Tales.
With him, most authors steal their works, or buy;
Garth did not write his own Dispensary.

Name a new Play, and he's the Poet's friend,
Nay show'd his faults—but when would Poets mend?
No place so sacred from such fops is barr'd,
Nor is Paul's church more safe than Paul's church yard:
Nay, fly to Altars; there they'll talk you dead:
For Fools rush in where Angels fear to tread.
Distrustful sense with modest caution speaks,
It still looks home, and short excursions makes;
But rattling nonsense in full vollies breaks,
And never shock'd, and never turn'd aside,
Bursts out, resistless, with a thund'ring tide.
But where's the man, who counsel can bestow,
Still pleas'd to teach, and yet not proud to know?
Unbias'd, or by favour, or by spite;
Not dully prepossess'd, nor blindly right;
Tho' learn'd, well-bred; and tho' well-bred, sincere;
Modestly bold, and humanly severe:
Who to a friend his faults can freely show,
And gladly praise the merit of a foe?
Blest with a taste exact, yet unconfin'd;
A knowledge both of books and human kind;
Gen'rous converse; a soul exempt from pride;
And love to praise, with reason on his side?
Such once were Critics; such the happy few,
Athens and Rome in better ages knew.
The mighty Stagirite first left the shore,
Spread all his sails, and durst the deeps explore;
He steer'd securely, and discover'd far,
Led by the light of the Mæonian Star.
Poets, a race long unconfin'd, and free,
Still fond and proud of savage liberty,
Receiv'd his laws; and stood convinc'd 'twas fit,
Who conquer'd Nature, should preside o'er Wit.
Horace still charms with graceful negligence,
And without method talks us into sense,
Will, like a friend, familiarly convey
The truest notions in the easiest way.
He, who supreme in judgment, as in wit,
Might boldly censure, as he boldly writ,
Yet judg'd with coolness, tho' he sung with fire;
His Precepts teach but what his works inspire.
Our Critics take a contrary extreme,
They judge with fury, but they write with fle'me:
Nor suffers Horace more in wrong Translations
By Wits, than Critics in as wrong Quotations.
See Dionysius Homer's thoughts refine,
And call new beauties forth from ev'ry line!
Fancy and art in gay Petronius please,

The scholar's learning, with the courtier's ease.
  In grave Quintilian's copious work, we find
The justest rules, and clearest method join'd:
Thus useful arms in magazines we place,
All rang'd in order, and dispos'd with grace,
But less to please the eye, than arm the hand,
Still fit for use, and ready at command.
  Thee, bold Longinus! all the Nine inspire,
And bless their Critic with a Poet's fire.
An ardent Judge, who zealous in his trust,
With warmth gives sentence, yet is always just;
Whose own example strengthens all his laws;
And is himself that great Sublime he draws.
  Thus long succeeding Critics justly reign'd,
Licence repress'd, and useful laws ordain'd.
Learning and Rome alike in empire grew;
And Arts still follow'd where her Eagles flew;
From the same foes, at last, both felt their doom,
And the same age saw Learning fall, and Rome.
With Tyranny, then Superstition join'd,
As that the body, this enslav'd the mind;
Much was believed, but little understood,
And to be dull was constru'd to be good;
A second deluge Learning thus o'er-run,
And the Monks finish'd what the Goths begun.
  At length Erasmus, that great injur'd name,
(The glory of the Priesthood, and the shame!)
Stem'd the wild torrent of a barb'rous age,
And drove those holy Vandals off the stage.
  But see! each Muse, in LEO's golden days,
Starts from her trance, and trims her wither'd bays,
Rome's ancient Genius, o'er its ruins spread,
Shakes off the dust, and rears his rev'rend head.
Then Sculpture and her sister-arts revive;
Stones leap'd to form, and rocks began to live;
With sweeter notes each rising Temple rung;
A Raphael painted, and a Vida sung.
Immortal Vida: on whose honour'd brow
The Poet's bays and Critic's ivy grow:
Cremona now shall ever boast thy name,
As next in place to Mantua, next in fame!
  But soon by impious arms from Latium chas'd,
Their ancient bounds the banish'd Muses pass'd;
Thence Arts o'er all the northern world advance,
But Critic-learning flourish'd most in France:
The rules a nation, born to serve, obeys;
And Boileau still in right of Horace sways.
But we, brave Britons, foreign laws despis'd,

And kept unconquer'd, and unciviliz'd;
Fierce for the liberties of wit, and bold,
We still defy'd the Romans, as of old.
Yet some there were, among the sounder few
Of those who less presum'd, and better knew,
Who durst assert the juster ancient cause,
And here restor'd Wit's fundamental laws.
Such was the Muse, whose rules and practice tell,
"Nature's chief Master-piece is writing well."
Such was Roscommon, not more learn'd than good,
With manners gen'rous as his noble blood;
To him the wit of Greece and Rome was known,
And ev'ry author's merit, but his own.
Such late was Walsh—the Muse's judge and friend.
Who justly knew to blame or to commend;
To failings mild, but zealous for desert;
The clearest head, and the sincerest heart.
This humble praise, lamented shade! receive,
This praise at least a grateful Muse may give:
The Muse, whose early voice you taught to sing,
Prescrib'd her heights, and prun'd her tender wing,
(Her guide now lost) no more attempts to rise,
But in low numbers short excursions trics:
Content, if hence th' unlearn'd their wants may view,
The learn'd reflect on what before they knew:
Careless of censure, nor too fond of fame;
Still pleas'd to praise, yet not afraid to blame;
Averse alike to flatter, or offend;
Not free from faults, nor yet too vain to mend.

The Rape of the Lock[1]

Canto I

WHAT dire offence from am'rous causes springs,
What mighty contests rise from trivial things,
I sing—This verse to CARYL, Muse! is due:
This, ev'n Belinda may vouchsafe to view:
Slight is the subject, but not so the praise,
If She inspire, and He approve my lays.
  Say what strange motive, Goddess! could compel
A well-bred Lord t' assault a gentle Belle?
Oh say what stranger cause, yet unexplor'd,
Could make a gentle Belle reject a Lord?

[1] Published May 20, 1712. Text of *Works*, 1751.

In tasks so bold, can little men engage,
And in soft bosoms dwells such mighty Rage?
Sol thro' white curtains shot a tim'rous ray,
And ope'd those eyes that must eclipse the day:
Now lap-dogs give themselves the rousing shake,
And sleepless lovers, just at twelve, awake:
Thrice rung the bell, the slipper knock'd the ground,
And the press'd watch return'd a silver sound.
Belinda still her downy pillow prest,
Her guardian Sylph prolong'd the balmy rest:
'Twas He had summon'd to her silent bed
The morning dream that hover'd o'er her head.
A Youth more glitt'ring than a Birth-night Beau,
(That ev'n in slumber caus'd her cheek to glow)
Seem'd to her ear his winning lips to lay,
And thus in whispers said, or seem'd to say.
Fairest of mortals, thou distinguish'd care
Of thousand bright Inhabitants of Air!
If e'er one Vision touch thy infant thought,
Of all the Nurse and all the Priest have taught;
Of airy Elves by moonlight shadows seen,
The silver token, and the circled green,
Or virgins visited by Angel-pow'rs,
With golden crowns and wreaths of heav'nly flow'rs;
Hear and believe! thy own importance know,
Nor bound thy narrow views to things below.
Some secret truths, from learned pride conceal'd,
To Maids alone and Children are reveal'd:
What tho' no credit doubting Wits may give?
The Fair and Innocent shall still believe.
Know then, unnumber'd Spirits round thee fly,
The light Militia of the lower sky:
These, tho' unseen, are ever on the wing,
Hang o'er the Box, and hover round the Ring.
Think what an equipage thou hast in Air,
And view with scorn two Pages and a Chair.
As now your own, our beings were of old,
And once inclos'd in Woman's beauteous mould;
Thence, by a soft transition, we repair
From earthly Vehicles to these of air.
Think not, when Woman's transient breath is fled,
That all her vanities at once are dead;
Succeeding vanities she still regards,
And tho' she plays no more, o'erlooks the cards.
Her joy in gilded Chariots, when alive,
And love of Ombre, after death survive.
For when the Fair in all their pride expire,
To their first Elements their Souls retire:

The Sprites of fiery Termagants in Flame
Mount up, and take a Salamander's name.
Soft yielding minds to Water glide away,
And sip, with Nymphs, their elemental Tea.
The graver Prude sinks downward to a Gnome,
In search of mischief still on Earth to roam.
The light Coquettes in Sylphs aloft repair,
And sport and flutter in the fields of Air.
  Know farther yet; whoever fair and chaste
Rejects mankind, is by some Sylph embrac'd:
For Spirits, freed from mortal laws, with ease
Assume what sexes and what shapes they please.
What guards the purity of melting Maids,
In courtly balls, and midnight masquerades,
Safe from the treach'rous friend, the daring spark,
The glance by day, the whisper in the dark,
When kind occasion prompts their warm desires,
When music softens, and when dancing fires?
'Tis but their Sylph, the wise Celestials know,
Tho' Honour is the word with Men below.
  Some nymphs there are, too conscious of their face,
For life predestin'd to the Gnomes embrace.
These swell their prospects and exalt their pride,
When offers are disdain'd, and love deny'd:
Then gay Ideas croud the vacant brain,
While Peers, and Dukes, and all their sweeping train,
And Garters, Stars, and Coronets appear,
And in soft sounds, Your Grace salutes their ear.
'Tis these that early taint the female soul,
Instruct the eyes of young Coquettes to roll,
Teach Infant-cheeks a bidden blush to know,
And little hearts to flutter at a Beau.
  Oft, when the World imagine women stray,
The Sylphs thro' mystic mazes guide their way,
Thro' all the giddy circle they pursue,
And old impertinence expel by new.
What tender maid but must a victim fall
To one man's treat, but for another's ball?
When Florio speaks what virgin could withstand,
If gentle Damon did not squeeze her hand?
With varying vanities, from ev'ry part,
They shift the moving Toyshop of their heart;
Where wigs with wigs, with sword-knots sword-knots strive,
Beaux banish beaux, and coaches coaches drive.
This erring mortals Levity may call,
Oh blind to truth! the Sylphs contrive it all.
  Of these am I, who thy protection claim,
A watchful sprite, and Ariel is my name.

Late, as I rang'd the crystal wilds of air,
In the clear Mirror of thy ruling Star
I saw, alas! some dread event impend,
Ere to the main this morning sun descend,
But heav'n reveals not what, or how, or where:
Warn'd by the Sylph, oh pious maid, beware!
This to disclose is all thy guardian can:
Beware of all, but most beware of Man!
He said; when Shock, who thought she slept too long,
Leap'd up, and wak'd his mistress with his tongue.
'Twas then Belinda, if report say true,
Thy eyes first open'd on a Billet-doux;
Wounds, Charms, and Ardors, were no sooner read,
But all the Vision vanish'd from thy head.
And now, unveil'd, the Toilet stands display'd,
Each silver Vase in mystic order laid.
First, rob'd in white, the Nymph intent adores,
With head uncover'd, the Cosmetic pow'rs.
A heav'nly Image in the glass appears,
To that she bends, to that her eyes she rears;
Th' inferior Priestess, at her altar's side,
Trembling, begins the sacred rites of Pride.
Unnumber'd treasures ope at once, and here
The various off'rings of the world appear;
From each she nicely culls with curious toil,
And decks the Goddess with the glitt'ring spoil.
This casket India's glowing gems unlocks,
And all Arabia breathes from yonder box.
The Tortoise here and Elephant unite,
Transform'd to combs, the speckled, and the white.
Here files of pins extend their shining rows,
Puffs, Powders, Patches, Bibles, Billet-doux.
Now awful Beauty puts on all its arms;
The fair each moment rises in her charms,
Repairs her smiles, awakens ev'ry grace,
And calls forth all the wonders of her face;
Sees by degrees a purer blush arise,
And keener lightnings quicken in her eyes.
The busy Sylphs surround their darling care,
These set the head, and those divide the hair,
Some fold the sleeve, whilst others plait the gown;
And Betty's prais'd for labours not her own.

Canto II

Not with more glories, in th' etherial plain,
The Sun first rises o'er the purpled main,
Than, issuing forth, the rival of his beams

Launch'd on the bosom of the silver Thames.
Fair Nymphs, and well-drest Youths around her shone,
But ev'ry eye was fix'd on her alone.
On her white breast a sparkling Cross she wore,
Which Jews might kiss, and Infidels adore.
Her lively looks a sprightly mind disclose,
Quick as her eyes, and as unfix'd as those:
Favours to none, to all she smiles extends;
Oft she rejects, but never once offends.
Bright as the sun, her eyes the gazers strike,
And, like the sun, they shine on all alike.
Yet graceful ease, and sweetness void of pride
Might hide her faults, if Belles had faults to hide:
If to her share some female errors fall,
Look on her face, and you'll forget 'em all.
  This Nymph, to the destruction of mankind,
Nourish'd two Locks, which graceful hung behind
In equal curls, and well conspir'd to deck
With shining ringlets the smooth iv'ry neck.
Love in these labyrinths his slaves detains,
And mighty hearts are held in slender chains.
With hairy springes we the birds betray,
Slight lines of hair surprize the finny prey,
Fair tresses man's imperial race insnare,
And beauty draws us with a single hair.
  Th' advent'rous Baron the bright locks admir'd;
He saw, he wish'd, and to the prize aspir'd.
Resolv'd to win, he meditates the way,
By force to ravish, or by fraud betray;
For when success a Lover's toil attends,
Few ask, if fraud or force attain'd his ends.
  For this, ere Phœbus rose, he had implor'd,
Propitious heav'n, and ev'ry pow'r ador'd,
But chiefly Love—to Love an Altar built,
Of twelve vast French Romances, neatly gilt.
There lay three garters, half a pair of gloves;
And all the trophies of his former loves;
With tender Billet-doux he lights the pyre,
And breathes three am'rous sighs to raise the fire.
Then prostrate falls, and begs with ardent eyes
Soon to obtain, and long possess the prize:
The pow'rs gave ear, and granted half his pray'r,
The rest, the winds dispers'd in empty air.
  But now secure the painted vessel glides,
The sun-beams trembling on the floating tides:
While melting music steals upon the sky,
And soften'd sounds along the waters die;
Smooth flow the waves, the Zephyrs gently play,

Belinda smil'd, and all the world was gay.
All but the Sylph—with careful thoughts opprest,
Th' impending woe sat heavy on his breast.
He summons strait his Denizens of air;
The lucid squadrons round the sails repair;
Soft o'er the shrouds aërial whispers breathe,
That seem'd but Zephyrs to the train beneath.
Some to the sun their insect-wings unfold,
Waft on the breeze, or sink in clouds of gold;
Transparent forms, too fine for mortal sight,
Their fluid bodies half dissolv'd in light.
Loose to the wind their airy garments flew,
Thin glitt'ring textures of the filmy dew,
Dipt in the richest tincture of the skies,
Where light disports in ever-mingling dyes,
While ev'ry beam new transient colours flings,
Colours that change whene'er they wave their wings.
Amid the circle, on the gilded mast,
Superior by the head, was Ariel plac'd;
His purple pinions op'ning to the sun,
He rais'd his azure wand, and thus begun.
  Ye Sylphs and Sylphids, to your chief give ear,
Fays, Fairies, Genii, Elves, and Dæmons hear!
Ye know the spheres and various tasks assign'd
By laws eternal to th' aërial kind.
Some in the fields of purest Æther play,
And bask and whiten in the blaze of day.
Some guide the course of wand'ring orbs on high,
Or roll the planets thro' the boundless sky.
Some less refin'd, beneath the moon's pale light
Pursue the stars that shoot athwart the night,
Or suck the mists in grosser air below,
Or dip their pinions in the painted bow,
Or brew fierce tempests on the wintry main,
Or o'er the glebe distil the kindly rain.
Others on earth o'er human race preside,
Watch all their ways, and all their actions guide:
Of these the chief the care of Nations own,
And guard with Arms divine the British Throne.
  Our humbler province is to tend the Fair,
Not a less pleasing, tho' less glorious care;
To save the powder from too rude a gale,
Nor let th' imprison'd essences exhale;
To draw fresh colours from the vernal flow'rs;
To steal from rainbows e'er they drop in show'rs
A brighter wash; to curl their waving hairs,
Assist their blushes, and inspire their airs;
Nay oft, in dreams, invention we bestow,

To change a Flounce, or add a Furbelow.
 This day, black Omens threat the brightest Fair
That e'er deserv'd a watchful spirit's care;
Some dire disaster, or by force, or slight;
But what, or where, the fates have wrapt in night.
Whether the nymph shall break Diana's law,
Or some frail China jar receive a flaw;
Or stain her honour, or her new brocade;
Forget her pray'rs, or miss a masquerade;
Or lose her heart, or necklace at a ball;
Or whether Heav'n has doom'd that Shock must fall.
Haste then, ye spirits! to your charge repair:
The flutt'ring fan be Zephyretta's care;
The drops to thee, Brillante, we consign;
And, Momentilla, let the watch be thine;
Do thou, Crispissa, tend her fav'rite Lock;
Ariel himself shall be the guard of Shock.
 To fifty chosen Sylphs, of special note,
We trust th' important charge, the Petticoat:
Oft have we known that seven-fold fence to fail,
Tho' stiff with hoops, and arm'd with ribs of whale;
Form a strong line about the silver bound,
And guard the wide circumference around.
 Whatever spirit, careless of his charge,
His post neglects, or leaves the fair at large,
Shall feel sharp vengeance soon o'ertake his sins,
Be stop'd in vials, or transfix'd with pins;
Or plung'd in lakes of bitter washes lie,
Or wedg'd whole ages in a bodkin's eye:
Gums and Pomatums shall his flight restrain,
While clog'd he beats his silken wings in vain;
Or Alum styptics with contracting pow'r
Shrink his thin essence like a rivel'd flow'r:
Or, as Ixion fix'd, the wretch shall feel
The giddy motion of the whirling Mill,
In fumes of burning Chocolate shall glow,
And tremble at the sea that froths below!
 He spoke; the spirits from the sails descend;
Some, orb in orb, around the nymph extend;
Some thrid the mazy ringlets of her hair;
Some hang upon the pendants of her ear;
With beating hearts the dire event they wait,
Anxious, and trembling for the birth of Fate.

Canto III

CLOSE by those meads, for ever crown'd with flow'rs,
Where Thames with pride surveys his rising tow'rs,

There stands a structure of majestic frame,
Which from the neighb'ring Hampton takes its name.
Here Britain's statesmen oft the fall foredoom
Of foreign Tyrants, and of Nymphs at home;
Here thou, great ANNA! whom three realms obey,
Dost sometimes counsel take—and sometimes Tea.
  Hither the heroes and the nymphs resort,
To taste awhile the pleasures of a Court;
In various talk th' instructive hours they past,
Who gave the ball, or paid the visit last;
One speaks the glory of the British Queen,
And one describes a charming Indian screen;
A third interprets motions, looks, and eyes;
At ev'ry word a reputation dies.
Snuff, or the fan, supply each pause of chat,
With singing, laughing, ogling, *and all that.*
  Mean while, declining from the noon of day,
The sun obliquely shoots his burning ray;
The hungry Judges soon the sentence sign,
And wretches hang that jury-men may dine;
The merchant from th' Exchange returns in peace,
And the long labours of the Toilet cease.
Belinda now, whom thirst of fame invites,
Burns to encounter two advent'rous Knights,
At Ombre singly to decide their doom;
And swells her breast with conquests yet to come.
Strait the three bands prepare in arms to join,
Each band the number of the sacred nine.
Soon as she spreads her hand, th' aërial guard
Descend, and sit on each important card:
First Ariel perch'd upon a Matadore,
Then each, according to the rank they bore;
For Sylphs, yet mindful of their ancient race,
Are, as when women, wondrous fond of place.
  Behold, four Kings in majesty rever'd,
With hoary whiskers and a forky beard;
And four fair Queens whose hands sustain a flow'r,
Th' expressive emblem of their softer pow'r;
Four Knaves in garbs succinct, a trusty band,
Caps on their heads, and halberts in their hand;
And particolour'd troops, a shining train,
Draw forth to combat on the velvet plain.
  The skilful Nymph reviews her force with care:
Let Spades be trumps! she said, and trumps they were.
  Now move to war her sable Matadores,
In show like leaders of the swarthy Moors.
Spadillio first, unconquerable Lord!
Led off two captive trumps, and swept the board.

As many more Manillio forc'd to yield,
And march'd a victor from the verdant field.
Him Basto follow'd, but his fate more hard
Gain'd but one trump and one Plebeian card.
With his broad sabre next, a chief in years,
The hoary Majesty of Spades appears,
Puts forth one manly leg, to sight reveal'd,
The rest, his many-colour'd robe conceal'd.
The rebel Knave, who dares his prince engage,
Proves the just victim of his royal rage.
Ev'n mighty Pam, that Kings and Queens o'erthrew
And mow'd down armies in the fights of Lu,
Sad chance of war! now destitute of aid,
Falls undistinguish'd by the victor Spade!
  Thus far both armies to Belinda yield;
Now to the Baron fate inclines the field.
His warlike Amazon her host invades,
Th' imperial consort of the crown of Spades.
The Club's black Tyrant first her victim dy'd,
Spite of his haughty mien, and barb'rous pride:
What boots the regal circle on his head,
His giant limbs, in state unwieldy spread;
That long behind he trails his pompous robe,
And, of all monarchs, only grasps the globe?
The Baron now his Diamonds pours apace;
Th' embroider'd King who shows but half his face,
And his refulgent Queen, with pow'rs combin'd
Of broken troops an easy conquest find.
Clubs, Diamonds, Hearts, in wild disorder seen,
With throngs promiscuous strow the level green.
Thus when dispers'd a routed army runs,
Of Asia's troops, and Afric's sable sons,
With like confusion different nations fly,
Of various habit, and of various dye,
The pierc'd battalions dis-united fall,
In heaps on heaps; one fate o'erwhelms them all.
  The Knave of Diamonds tries his wily arts,
And wins (oh shameful chance!) the Queen of Hearts.
At this, the blood the virgin's cheek forsook,
A livid paleness spreads o'er all her look;
She sees, and trembles at th' approaching ill,
Just in the jaws of ruin, and Codille.
And now, (as oft in some distemper'd State)
On one nice Trick depends the gen'ral fate.
An Ace of Hearts steps forth: The King unseen
Lurk'd in her hand, and mourn'd his captive Queen:
He springs to vengeance with an eager pace,
And falls like thunder on the prostrate Ace.

The nymph exulting fills with shouts the sky;
The walls, the woods, and long canals reply.
  O thoughtless mortals! ever blind to fate,
Too soon dejected, and too soon elate.
Sudden, these honours shall be snatch'd away,
And curs'd for ever this victorious day.
  For lo! the board with cups and spoons is crown'd,
The berries crackle, and the mill turns round;
On shining Altars of Japan they raise
The silver lamp; the fiery spirits blaze:
From silver spouts the grateful liquors glide,
While China's earth receives the smoaking tide:
At once they gratify their scent and taste,
And frequent cups prolong the rich repaste.
Strait hover round the Fair her airy band;
Some, as she sipp'd, the fuming liquor fann'd,
Some o'er her lap their careful plumes display'd,
Trembling, and conscious of the rich brocade.
Coffee, (which makes the politician wise,
And see thro' all things with his half-shut eyes)
Sent up in vapours to the Baron's brain
New stratagems, the radiant Lock to gain.
Ah cease, rash youth! desist ere 'tis too late,
Fear the just Gods, and think of Scylla's Fate!
Chang'd to a bird, and sent to flit in air,
She dearly pays for Nisus' injur'd hair!
  But when to mischief mortals bend their will,
How soon they find fit instruments of ill?
Just then, Clarissa drew with tempting grace
A two-edg'd weapon from her shining case:
So Ladies in Romance assist their Knight,
Present the spear, and arm him for the fight.
He takes the gift with rev'rence, and extends
The little engine on his finger's ends;
This just behind Belinda's neck he spread,
As o'er the fragrant steams she bends her head.
Swift to the Lock a thousand Sprites repair,
A thousand wings, by turns, blow back the hair;
And thrice they twitch'd the diamond in her ear;
Thrice she look'd back, and thrice the foe drew near.
Just in that instant, anxious Ariel sought
The close recesses of the Virgin's thought;
As on the nosegay in her breast reclin'd,
He watch'd th' Ideas rising in her mind,
Sudden he view'd, in spite of all her art,
An earthly Lover lurking at her heart.
Amaz'd, confus'd, he found his pow'r expir'd,
Resign'd to fate, and with a sigh retir'd.

The Peer now spreads the glitt'ring Forfex wide,
T' inclose the Lock; now joins it, to divide.
Ev'n then, before the fatal engine clos'd,
A wretched Sylph too fondly interpos'd;
Fate urg'd the sheers, and cut the Sylph in twain,
(But airy substance soon unites again)
The meeting points the sacred hair dissever
From the fair head, for ever, and for ever!
Then flash'd the living lightning from her eyes,
And screams of horror rend th' affrighted skies.
Not louder shrieks to pitying heav'n are cast,
When husbands, or when lapdogs breathe their last;
Or when rich China vessels fall'n from high,
In glitt'ring dust, and painted fragments lie!
Let wreaths of triumph now my temples twine,
(The Victor cry'd) the glorious Prize is mine!
While fish in streams, or birds delight in air,
Or in a coach and six the British Fair,
As long as Atalantis shall be read,
Or the small pillow grace a Lady's bed,
While visits shall be paid on solemn days,
When num'rous wax-lights in bright order blaze,
While nymphs take treats, or assignations give,
So long my honour, name, and praise shall live!
What Time would spare, from Steel receives its date,
And monuments, like men, submit to fate!
Steel could the labour of the Gods destroy,
And strike to dust th' imperial tow'rs of Troy;
Steel could the works of mortal pride confound,
And hew triumphal arches to the ground.
What wonder then, fair nymph! thy hairs should feel,
The conqu'ring force of unresisted steel?

Canto IV

BUT anxious cares the pensive nymph oppress'd,
And secret passions labour'd in her breast.
Not youthful kings in battle seiz'd alive,
Not scornful virgins who their charms survive,
Not ardent lovers robb'd of all their bliss,
Not ancient ladies when refus'd a kiss,
Not tyrants fierce that unrepenting die,
Not Cynthia when her manteau's pinn'd awry,
E'er felt such rage, resentment, and despair,
As thou, sad Virgin! for thy ravish'd Hair.
For, that sad moment, when the Sylphs withdrew,
And Ariel weeping from Belinda flew,
Umbriel, a dusky, melancholy sprite,

As ever sully'd the fair face of light,
Down to the central earth, his proper scene,
Repair'd to search the gloomy Cave of Spleen.
Swift on his sooty pinions flits the Gnome,
And in a vapour reach'd the dismal dome.
No chearful breeze this sullen region knows,
The dreaded East is all the wind that blows.
Here in a grotto, shelter'd close from air,
And screen'd in shades from day's detested glare,
She sighs for ever on her pensive bed,
Pain at her side, and Megrim at her head.
Two handmaids wait the throne: alike in place,
But diff'ring far in figure and in face.
Here stood Ill-nature like an ancient maid,
Her wrinkled form in black and white array'd;
With store of pray'rs, for mornings, nights, and noons,
Her hand is fill'd; her bosom with lampoons.
There Affectation, with a sickly mien,
Shows in her cheek the roses of eighteen,
Practis'd to lisp, and hang the head aside,
Faints into airs, and languishes with pride,
On the rich quilt sinks with becoming woe,
Wrapt in a gown, for sickness, and for show.
The fair-ones feel such maladies as these,
When each new night-dress gives a new disease.
A constant Vapour o'er the palace flies;
Strange phantoms rising as the mists arise;
Dreadful, as hermit's dreams in haunted shades,
Or bright, as visions of expiring maids.
Now glaring fiends, and snakes on rolling spires,
Pale spectres, gaping tombs, and purple fires:
Now lakes of liquid gold, Elysian scenes,
And crystal domes, and Angels in machines.
Unnumber'd throngs on ev'ry side are seen,
Of bodies chang'd to various forms by Spleen.
Here living Tea-pots stand, one arm held out,
One bent; the handle this, and that the spout:
A Pipkin there, like Homer's Tripod walks;
Here sighs a Jar, and there a Goose-pye talks;
Men prove with child, as pow'rful fancy works,
And maids turn'd bottles, call aloud for corks.
Safe past the Gnome, thro' this fantastic band,
A branch of healing Spleenwort in his hand.
Then thus address'd the pow'r—Hail wayward Queen!
Who rule the sex to fifty from fifteen:
Parent of vapours and of female wit,
Who give th' hysteric, or poetic fit,
On various tempers act by various ways,

Make some take physic, others scribble plays;
Who cause the proud their visits to delay,
And send the godly in a pet to pray.
A nymph there is, that all thy pow'r disdains,
And thousands more in equal mirth maintains.
But oh! if e'er thy Gnome could spoil a grace,
Or raise a pimple on a beauteous face,
Like Citron-waters matrons cheeks inflame,
Or change complexions at a losing game;
If e'er with airy horns I planted heads,
Or rumpled petticoats, or tumbled beds,
Or caus'd suspicion when no soul was rude,
Or discompos'd the head-dress of a Prude,
Or e'er to costive lap-dog gave disease
Which not the tears of brightest eyes could ease:
Hear me, and touch Belinda with chagrin,
That single act gives half the world the spleen.
  The Goddess with a discontented air
Seems to reject him, tho' she grants his pray'r.
A wond'rous Bag with both her hands she binds,
Like that where once Ulysses held the winds;
There she collects the force of female lungs,
Sighs, sobs, and passions, and the war of tongues.
A Vial next she fills with fainting fears,
Soft sorrows, melting griefs, and flowing tears.
The Gnome rejoicing bears her gifts away,
Spreads his black wings, and slowly mounts to day.
  Sunk in Thalestris' arms the nymph he found,
Her eyes dejected, and her hair unbound.
Full o'er their heads the swelling bag he rent,
And all the Furies issu'd at the vent.
Belinda burns with more than mortal ire,
And fierce Thalestris fans the rising fire.
O wretched maid! she spread her hands, and cry'd,
(While Hampton's echoes, wretched maid! reply'd)
Was it for this you took such constant care
The bodkin, comb, and essence to prepare?
For this your locks in paper durance bound,
For this with tort'ring irons wreath'd around?
For this with fillets strain'd your tender head,
And bravely bore the double loads of lead?
Gods! shall the ravisher display your hair,
While the Fops envy, and the Ladies stare!
Honour forbid! at whose unrival'd shrine
Ease, pleasure, virtue, all our sex resign.
Methinks already I your tears survey,
Already hear the horrid things they say,
Already see you a degraded toast,

And all your honour in a whisper lost!
How shall I, then, your helpless fame defend?
'Twill then be infamy to seem your friend!
And shall this prize, th' inestimable prize,
Expos'd thro' crystal to the gazing eyes,
And heighten'd by the diamond's circling rays,
On that rapacious hand for ever blaze?
Sooner shall grass in Hyde-park Circus grow,
And wits take lodgings in the sound of Bow;
Sooner let earth, air, sea, to Chaos fall,
Men, monkeys, lap-dogs, parrots, perish all!
  She said; then raging to Sir Plume repairs,
And bids her Beau demand the precious hairs:
(Sir Plume of amber snuff-box justly vain,
And the nice conduct of a clouded cane)
With earnest eyes, and round unthinking face,
He first the snuff-box open'd, then the case,
And thus broke out—"My Lord, why, what the devil?
"Z—ds! damn the lock! 'fore Gad, you must be civil!
"Plague on't! 'tis past a jest—nay prithee, pox!
"Give her the hair"—he spoke, and rapp'd his box.
  It grieves me much (reply'd the Peer again)
Who speaks so well should ever speak in vain.
But by this Lock, this sacred Lock I swear,
(Which never more shall join its parted hair;
Which never more its honours shall renew,
Clip'd from the lovely head where late it grew)
That while my nostrils draw the vital air,
This hand, which won it, shall for ever wear.
He spoke, and speaking, in proud triumph spread
The long-contended honours of her head.
  But Umbriel, hateful Gnome! forbears not so;
He breaks the Vial whence the sorrows flow.
Then see! the nymph in beauteous grief appears,
Her eyes half-languishing, half-drown'd in tears;
On her heav'd bosom hung her drooping head,
Which, with a sigh, she rais'd; and thus she said:
  For ever curs'd be this detested day,
Which snatch'd my best, my fav'rite curl away!
Happy! ah ten times happy had I been,
If Hampton-Court these eyes had never seen!
Yet am not I the first mistaken maid
By love of Courts to num'rous ills betray'd.
Oh had I rather un-admir'd remain'd
In some lone isle, or distant Northern land;
Where the gilt Chariot never marks the way,
Where none learn Ombre, none e'er taste Bohea!
There kept my charms conceal'd from mortal eye,

Like roses, that in deserts bloom and die.
What mov'd my mind with youthful Lords to roam?
O had I stay'd, and said my pray'rs at home!
'Twas this, the morning omens seem'd to tell,
Thrice from my trembling hand the patch-box fell;
The tott'ring China shook without a wind,
Nay Poll sat mute, and Shock was most unkind!
A Sylph too warn'd me of the threats of fate,
In mystic visions, now believ'd too late!
See the poor remnants of these slighted hairs!
My hands shall rend what ev'n thy rapine spares:
These in two sable ringlets taught to break,
Once gave new beauties to the snowy neck;
The sister-lock now sits uncouth, alone,
And in its fellow's fate foresees its own;
Uncurl'd it hangs, the fatal sheers demands,
And tempts once more, thy sacrilegious hands.
Oh hadst thou, cruel! been content to seize
Hairs less in sight, or any hairs but these!

Canto V

SHE said: the pitying audience melt in tears.
But Fate and Jove had stopp'd the Baron's ears.
In vain Thalestris with reproach assails,
For who can move when fair Belinda fails?
Not half so fix'd the Trojan could remain,
While Anna begg'd and Dido rag'd in vain.
Then grave Clarissa graceful wav'd her fan;
Silence ensu'd, and thus the nymph began.
Say why are Beauties prais'd and honour'd most,
The wise man's passion, and the vain man's toast?
Why deck'd with all that land and sea afford,
Why Angels call'd, and Angel-like ador'd?
Why round our coaches croud the white-glov'd Beaux,
Why bows the side-box from its inmost rows?
How vain are all these glories, all our pains,
Unless good sense preserve what beauty gains:
That men may say, when we the front-box grace,
Behold the first in virtue as in face!
Oh! if to dance all night, and dress all day,
Charm'd the small-pox, or chas'd old age away;
Who would not scorn what housewife's cares produce,
Or who would learn one earthly thing of use?
To patch, nay ogle, might become a Saint,
Nor could it sure be such a sin to paint.
But since, alas! frail beauty must decay,
Curl'd or uncurl'd, since Locks will turn to grey;

Since painted, or not painted, all shall fade,
And she who scorns a man, must die a maid;
What then remains, but well our pow'r to use,
And keep good-humour still whate'er we lose?
And trust me, dear! good-humour can prevail,
When airs, and flights, and screams, and scolding fail.
Beauties in vain their pretty eyes may roll;
Charms strike the sight, but merit wins the soul.
  So spoke the Dame, but no applause ensu'd;
Belinda frown'd, Thalestris call'd her Prude.
To arms, to arms! the fierce Virago cries,
And swift as lightning to the combat flies.
All side in parties, and begin th' attack;
Fans clap, silks russle, and tough whalebones crack;
Heroes and Heroines shouts confus'dly rise,
And base, and treble voices strike the skies.
No common weapons in their hands are found,
Like Gods they fight, nor dread a mortal wound.
  So when bold Homer makes the Gods engage,
And heav'nly breasts with human passions rage;
'Gainst Pallas, Mars; Latona, Hermes arms;
And all Olympus rings with loud alarms:
Jove's thunder roars, heav'n trembles all around,
Blue Neptune storms, the bellowing deeps resound:
Earth shakes her nodding tow'rs, the ground gives way,
And the pale ghosts start at the flash of day!
  Triumphant Umbriel on a sconce's height
Clap'd his glad wings, and sate to view the fight:
Prop'd on their bodkin spears, the Sprites survey
The growing combat, or assist the fray.
  While thro' the press enrag'd Thalestris flies,
And scatters death around from both her eyes,
A Beau and Witling perish'd in the throng,
One dy'd in metaphor, and one in song.
"Oh cruel nymph! a living death I bear,
Cry'd Dapperwit, and sunk beside his chair.
A mournful glance Sir Fopling upwards cast,
"Those eyes are made so killing—was his last.
Thus on Mæander's flow'ry margin lies
Th' expiring Swan, and as he sings he dies.
  When bold Sir Plume had drawn Clarissa down,
Chloe stepp'd in, and kill'd him with a frown;
She smil'd to see the doughty heroe slain,
But, at her smile, the Beau reviv'd again.
  Now Jove suspends his golden scales in air,
Weighs the Mens wits against the Lady's hair;
The doubtful beam long nods from side to side;
At length the wits mount up, the hairs subside.

See fierce Belinda on the Baron flies,
With more than usual lightning in her eyes:
Nor fear'd the Chief th' unequal fight to try,
Who sought no more than on his foe to die.
But this bold Lord with manly strength endu'd,
She with one finger and a thumb subdu'd:
Just where the breath of life his nostrils drew,
A charge of Snuff the wily virgin threw;
The Gnomes direct, to ev'ry atom just,
The pungent grains of titillating dust.
Sudden, with starting tears each eye o'erflows,
And the high dome re-echoes to his nose.
Now meet thy fate, incens'd Belinda cry'd,
And drew a deadly bodkin from her side.
(The same, his ancient personage to deck,
Her great great grandsire wore about his neck,
In three seal-rings; which after, melted down,
Form'd a vast buckle for his widow's gown:
Her infant grandame's whistle next it grew,
The bells she jingled, and the whistle blew;
Then in a bodkin grac'd her mother's hairs,
Which long she wore, and now Belinda wears.)
Boast not my fall (he cry'd) insulting foe!
Thou by some other shalt be laid as low.
Nor think, to die dejects my lofty mind:
All that I dread is leaving you behind!
Rather than so, ah let me still survive,
And burn in Cupid's flames,—but burn alive.
Restore the Lock! she cries; and all around
Restore the Lock! the vaulted roofs rebound.
Not fierce Othello in so loud a strain
Roar'd for the handkerchief that caus'd his pain.
But see how oft ambitious aims are cross'd,
And chiefs contend 'till all the prize is lost!
The Lock, obtain'd with guilt, and kept with pain,
In ev'ry place is sought, but sought in vain:
With such a prize no mortal must be blest,
So heav'n decrees! with heav'n who can contest?
Some thought it mounted to the Lunar sphere,
Since all things lost on earth are treasur'd there.
There Hero's wits are kept in pond'rous vases,
And Beau's in snuff-boxes and tweezer-cases.
There broken vows, and death-bed alms are found,
And lovers hearts with ends of ribband bound,
The courtier's promises, and sick man's pray'rs,
The smiles of harlots, and the tears of heirs,
Cages for gnats, and chains to yoak a flea,
Dry'd butterflies, and tomes of casuistry.

But trust the Muse—she saw it upward rise,
Tho' mark'd by none, but quick, poetic eyes:
(So Rome's great founder to the heav'ns withdrew,
To Proculus alone confess'd in view)
A sudden Star, it shot thro' liquid air,
And drew behind a radiant trail of hair.
Not Berenice's Locks first rose so bright,
The heav'ns bespangling with dishevel'd light.
The Sylphs behold it kindling as it flies,
And pleas'd pursue its progress thro' the skies.
This the Beau monde shall from the Mall survey,
And hail with music its propitious ray.
This the blest Lover shall for Venus take,
And send up vows from Rosamonda's lake.
This Partridge soon shall view in cloudless skies,
When next he looks thro' Galilæo's eyes;
And hence th' egregious wizard shall foredoom
The fate of Louis, and the fall of Rome.
Then cease, bright Nymph! to mourn thy ravish'd hair,
Which adds new glory to the shining sphere!
Not all the tresses that fair head can boast,
Shall draw such envy as the Lock you lost.
For, after all the murders of your eye,
When, after millions slain, yourself shall die;
When those fair suns shall set, as set they must,
And all those tresses shall be laid in dust,
This Lock, the Muse shall consecrate to fame,
And 'midst the stars inscribe Belinda's name.

Windsor-Forest
To the Right Honourable George Lord Lansdown[1]

THY forests, Windsor! and thy green retreats,
At once the Monarch's and the Muse's seats,
Invite my lays. Be present, sylvan maids!
Unlock your springs, and open all your shades.
GRANVILLE commands; your aid, O Muses, bring!
What Muse for GRANVILLE can refuse to sing?
The Groves of Eden, vanish'd now so long,
Live in description, and look green in song:
These, were my breast inspir'd with equal flame,
Like them in beauty, should be like in fame.
Here hills and vales, the woodland and the plain,
Here earth and water seem to strive again;

[1] Published March 7, 1713. Text of *Works*, 1751.

Not Chaos-like together crush'd and bruis'd,
But, as the world, harmoniously confus'd:
Where order in variety we see,
And where, tho' all things differ, all agree.
Here waving groves a chequer'd scene display,
And part admit, and part exclude the day;
As some coy nymph her lover's warm address
Nor quite indulges, nor can quite repress.
There, interspers'd in lawns and op'ning glades,
Thin trees arise that shun each other's shades.
Here in full light the russet plains extend:
There wrapt in clouds the blueish hills ascend.
Ev'n the wild heath displays her purple dyes,
And 'midst the desart fruitful fields arise,
That crown'd with tufted trees and springing corn,
Like verdant isles the sable waste adorn.
Let India boast her plants, nor envy we
The weeping amber or the balmy tree,
While by our oaks the precious loads are born,
And realms commanded which those trees adorn.
Not proud Olympus yields a nobler sight,
Tho' Gods assembled grace his tow'ring height,
Than what more humble mountains offer here,
Where, in their blessings, all those Gods appear.
See Pan with flocks, with fruits Pomona crown'd,
Here blushing Flora paints th' enamel'd ground,
Here Ceres' gifts in waving prospect stand,
And nodding tempt the joyful reapers hand;
Rich Industry sits smiling on the plains,
And peace and plenty tell, a STUART reigns.
  Not thus the land appear'd in ages past,
A dreary desert, and a gloomy waste,
To savage beasts and savage laws a prey,
And kings more furious and severe than they;
Who claim'd the skies, dispeopled air and floods,
The lonely lords of empty wilds and woods:
Cities laid waste, they storm'd the dens and caves,
(For wiser brutes were backward to be slaves.)
What could be free, when lawless beasts obey'd,
And ev'n the elements a Tyrant sway'd?
In vain kind seasons swell'd the teeming grain,
Soft show'rs distill'd, and suns grew warm in vain;
The swain with tears his frustrate labour yields,
And famish'd dies amidst his ripen'd fields.
What wonder then, a beast or subject slain
Were equal crimes in a despotic reign?
Both doom'd alike, for sportive Tyrants bled,
But while the subject starv'd, the beast was fed.

Proud Nimrod first the bloody chace began,
A mighty hunter, and his prey was man:
Our haughty Norman boasts that barb'rous name,
And makes his trembling slaves the royal game.
The fields are ravish'd from th' industrious swains,
From men their cities, and from Gods their fanes:
The levell'd towns with weeds lie cover'd o'er;
The hollow winds thro' naked temples roar;
Round broken columns clasping ivy twin'd;
O'er heaps of ruin stalk'd the stately hind;
The fox obscene to gaping tombs retires,
And savage howlings fill the sacred quires.
Aw'd by his Nobles, by his Commons curst,
Th' Oppressor rul'd tyrannic where he durst,
Stretch'd o'er the Poor and Church his iron rod,
And serv'd alike his Vassals and his God.
Whom ev'n the Saxon spar'd and bloody Dane,
The wanton victims of his sport remain.
But see, the man who spacious regions gave
A waste for beasts, himself deny'd a grave!
Stretch'd on the lawn his second hope survey,
At once the chaser, and at once the prey:
Lo Rufus, tugging at the deadly dart,
Bleeds in the forest like a wounded hart.
Succeeding monarchs heard the subjects cries,
Nor saw displeas'd the peaceful cottage rise.
Then gath'ring flocks on unknown mountains fed,
O'er sandy wilds were yellow harvests spread,
The forests wonder'd at th' unusual grain,
And secret transport touch'd the conscious swain.
Fair Liberty, Britannia's Goddess, rears
Her chearful head, and leads the golden years.

Ye vig'rous swains! while youth ferments your blood,
And purer spirits swell the sprightly flood,
Now range the hills, the gameful woods beset,
Wind the shrill horn, or spread the waving net.
When milder autumn summer's heat succeeds,
And in the new-shorn field the partridge feeds,
Before his lord the ready spaniel bounds,
Panting with hope, he tries the furrow'd grounds;
But when the tainted gales the game betray,
Couch'd close he lies, and meditates the prey:
Secure they trust th' unfaithful field beset,
'Till hov'ring o'er 'em sweeps the swelling net.
Thus (if small things we may with great compare)
When Albion sends her eager sons to war,
Some thoughtless Town, with ease and plenty blest,
Near, and more near, the closing lines invest;

Sudden they seize th' amaz'd, defenceless prize,
And high in air Britannia's standard flies.
  See! from the brake the whirring pheasant springs,
And mounts exulting on triumphant wings:
Short is his joy; he feels the fiery wound,
Flutters in blood, and panting beats the ground.
Ah! what avail his glossy, varying dyes,
His purple crest, and scarlet-circled eyes,
The vivid green his shining plumes unfold,
His painted wings, and breast that flames with gold?
  Not yet, when moist Arcturus clouds the sky,
The woods and fields their pleasing toils deny.
To plains with well-breath'd beagles we repair,
And trace the mazes of the circling hare:
(Beasts, urg'd by us, their fellow-beasts pursue,
And learn of man each other to undo.)
With slaught'ring guns th' unweary'd fowler roves,
When frosts have whiten'd all the naked groves;
Where doves in flocks the leafless trees o'ershade,
And lonely woodcocks haunt the wat'ry glade.
He lifts the tube, and levels with his eye;
Strait a short thunder breaks the frozen sky:
Oft, as in airy rings they skim the heath,
The clam'rous Lapwings feel the leaden death:
Oft, as the mounting larks their notes prepare,
They fall, and leave their little lives in air.
  In genial spring, beneath the quiv'ring shade,
Where cooling vapours breathe along the mead,
The patient fisher takes his silent stand,
Intent, his angle trembling in his hand:
With looks unmov'd, he hopes the scaly breed,
And eyes the dancing cork, and bending reed.
Our plenteous streams a various race supply,
The bright-ey'd perch with fins of Tyrian dye,
The silver eel, in shining volumes roll'd,
The yellow carp, in scales bedrop'd with gold,
Swift trouts, diversify'd with crimson stains,
And pykes, the tyrants of the watry plains.
  Now Cancer glows with Phoebus' fiery car:
The youth rush eager to the sylvan war,
Swarm o'er the lawns, the forest walks surround,
Rouze the fleet hart, and chear the opening hound.
Th' impatient courser pants in ev'ry vein,
And pawing, seems to beat the distant plain:
Hills, vales, and floods appear already cross'd,
And e'er he starts, a thousand steps are lost.

See the bold youth strain up the threat'ning steep,
Rush thro' the thickets, down the valleys sweep,
Hang o'er their coursers heads with eager speed,
And earth rolls back beneath the flying steed.
Let old Arcadia boast her ample plain,
Th' immortal huntress, and her virgin train;
Nor envy, Windsor! since thy shades have seen
As bright a Goddess, and as chaste a QUEEN;
Whose care, like hers, protects the sylvan reign,
The Earth's fair light, and Empress of the Main.
Here too, 'tis sung, of old Diana stray'd,
And Cynthus' top forsook for Windsor shade;
Here was she seen o'er airy wastes to rove,
Seek the clear spring, or haunt the pathless grove;
Here arm'd with silver bows, in early dawn,
Her buskin'd Virgins trac'd the dewy lawn.
Above the rest a rural nymph was fam'd,
Thy offspring, Thames! the fair Lodona nam'd;
(Lodona's fate, in long oblivion cast,
The Muse shall sing, and what she sings shall last.)
Scarce could the Goddess from her nymph be known,
But by the crescent and the golden zone.
She scorn'd the praise of beauty, and the care;
A belt her waist, a fillet binds her hair;
A painted quiver on her shoulder sounds,
And with her dart the flying deer she wounds.
It chanc'd, as eager of the chace, the maid
Beyond the forest's verdant limits stray'd,
Pan saw and lov'd, and burning with desire
Pursu'd her flight, her flight increas'd his fire.
Not half so swift the trembling doves can fly,
When the fierce eagle cleaves the liquid sky;
Not half so swiftly the fierce eagle moves,
When thro' the clouds he drives the trembling doves;
As from the God she flew with furious pace,
Or as the God, more furious, urg'd the chace.
Now fainting, sinking, pale, the nymph appears;
Now close behind, his sounding steps she hears;
And now his shadow reach'd her as she run,
His shadow lengthen'd by the setting sun;
And now his shorter breath, with sultry air,
Pants on her neck, and fans her parting hair.
In vain on father Thames she calls for aid,
Nor could Diana help her injur'd maid.
Faint, breathless, thus she pray'd, nor pray'd in vain;
"Ah Cynthia! ah—tho' banish'd from thy train,

"Let me, O let me, to the shades repair,
"My native shades—there weep, and murmur there."
She said, and melting as in tears she lay,
In a soft, silver stream dissolv'd away.
The silver stream her virgin coldness keeps,
For ever murmurs, and for ever weeps;
Still bears the name the hapless virgin bore,
And bathes the forest where she rang'd before.
In her chaste current oft the Goddess laves,
And with celestial tears augments the waves.
Oft in her glass the musing shepherd spies
The headlong mountains and the downward skies,
The watry landskip of the pendant woods,
And absent trees that tremble in the floods;
In the clear azure gleam the flocks are seen,
And floating forests paint the waves with green,
Thro' the fair scene roll slow the ling'ring streams,
Then foaming pour along, and rush into the Thames.
  Thou too, great father of the British floods!
With joyful pride survey'st our lofty woods;
Where tow'ring oaks their growing honours rear,
And future navies on thy shores appear,
Not Neptune's self from all her streams receives
A wealthier tribute, than to thine he gives.
No seas so rich, so gay no banks appear,
No lake so gentle, and no spring so clear.
Nor Po so swells the fabling Poet's lays,
While led along the skies his current strays,
As thine, which visits Windsor's fam'd abodes,
To grace the mansion of our earthly Gods:
Nor all his stars above a lustre show,
Like the bright Beauties on thy banks below;
Where Jove, subdu'd by mortal Passion still,
Might change Olympus for a nobler hill.
  Happy the man whom this bright Court approves,
His Sov'reign favours, and his Country loves:
Happy next him, who to these shades retires,
Whom Nature charms, and whom the Muse inspires;
Whom humbler joys of home-felt quiet please,
Successive study, exercise, and ease.
He gathers health from herbs the forest yields,
And of their fragrant physic spoils the fields:
With chymic art exalts the min'ral pow'rs,
And draws the aromatic souls of flow'rs:
Now marks the course of rolling orbs on high;
O'er figur'd worlds now travels with his eye;

Of ancient writ unlocks the learned store,
Consults the dead, and lives past ages o'er:
Or wand'ring thoughtful in the silent wood,
Attends the duties of the wise and good,
T' observe a mean, be to himself a friend,
To follow nature, and regard his end;
Or looks on heav'n with more than mortal eyes,
Bids his free soul expatiate in the skies,
Amid her kindred stars familiar roam,
Survey the region, and confess her home!
Such was the life great Scipio once admir'd,
Thus Atticus, and TRUMBAL thus retir'd.
  Ye sacred Nine! that all my soul possess,
Whose raptures fire me, and whose visions bless,
Bear me, oh bear me to sequester'd scenes,
The bow'ry mazes, and surrounding greens:
To Thames's banks which fragrant breezes fill,
Or where ye Muses sport on COOPER'S HILL.
(On COOPER'S HILL eternal wreaths shall grow,
While lasts the mountain, or while Thames shall flow)
I seem thro' consecrated walks to rove,
I hear soft music die along the grove:
Led by the sound, I roam from shade to shade,
By god-like Poets venerable made:
Here his first lays majestic DENHAM sung;
There the last numbers flow'd from COWLEY'S tongue.
O early lost! what tears the river shed,
When the sad pomp along his banks was led?
His drooping swans on ev'ry note expire,
And on his willows hung each Muse's lyre.
  Since fate relentless stop'd their heav'nly voice,
No more the forests ring, or groves rejoice;
Whom now shall charm the shades, where COWLEY strung
His living harp, and lofty DENHAM sung?
But hark! the groves rejoice, the forest rings!
Are these reviv'd, or is it GRANVILLE sings?
'Tis yours, my Lord, to bless our soft retreats,
And call the Muses to their ancient seats;
To paint anew the flow'ry sylvan scenes,
To crown the forests with immortal greens,
Make Windsor-hills in lofty numbers rise,
And lift her turrets nearer to the skies;
To sing those honours you deserve to wear,
And add new lustre to her silver star.
  Here noble SURREY felt the sacred rage,
SURREY, the GRANVILLE of a former age:

Matchless his pen, victorious was his lance,
Bold in the lists, and graceful in the dance:
In the same shades the Cupids tun'd his lyre,
To the same notes, of love, and soft desire:
Fair Geraldine, bright object of his vow,
Then fill'd the groves, as heav'nly Mira now.
Oh would'st thou sing what Heroes Windsor bore,
What Kings first breath'd upon her winding shore,
Or raise old warriours, whose ador'd remains
In weeping vaults her hallow'd earth contains!
With Edward's acts adorn the shining page,
Stretch his long triumphs down thro' ev'ry age,
Draw Monarch chain'd, and Cressi's glorious field,
The lillies blazing on the regal shield:
Then, from her roofs when Verrio's colours fall,
And leave inanimate the naked wall,
Still in thy song should vanquish'd France appear,
And bleed for ever under Britain's spear.
Let softer strains ill-fated Henry mourn,
And palms eternal flourish round his urn.
Here o'er the Martyr-King the marble weeps,
And fast beside him, once-fear'd Edward sleeps:
Whom not th' extended Albion could contain,
From old Belerium to the northern main,
The grave unites; where ev'n the Great find rest,
And blended lie th' oppressor and th' opprest!
Make sacred Charles's tomb for ever known,
(Obscure the place, and un-inscrib'd the stone)
Oh fact accurst! what tears has Albion shed,
Heav'ns, what new wounds! and how her old have bled?
She saw her sons with purple death expire,
Her sacred domes involv'd in rolling fire,
A dreadful series of intestine wars,
Inglorious triumphs and dishonest scars.
At length great ANNA said—"Let Discord cease!"
She said, the world obey'd, and all was Peace!
In that blest moment from his oozy bed
Old father Thames advanc'd his rev'rend head.
His tresses drop'd with dews, and o'er the stream
His shining horns diffus'd a golden gleam:
Grav'd on his urn appear'd the moon, that guides
His swelling waters, and alternate tides;
The figur'd streams in waves of silver roll'd,
And on their banks Augusta rose in gold.
Around his throne the sea-born brothers stood,
Who swell with tributary urns his flood;

First the fam'd authors of his ancient name,
The winding Isis and the fruitful Tame:
The Kennet swift, for silver eels renown'd;
The Loddon slow, with verdant alders crown'd;
Cole, whose dark streams his flow'ry islands lave;
And chalky Wey, that rolls a milky wave:
The blue, transparent Vandalis appears;
The gulphy Lee his sedgy tresses rears;
And sullen Mole, that hides his diving flood;
And silent Darent, stain'd with Danish blood.
High in the midst, upon his urn reclin'd,
(His sea-green mantle waving with the wind)
The God appear'd: he turn'd his azure eyes
Where Windsor-domes and pompous turrets rise;
Then bow'd and spoke; the winds forget to roar,
And the hush'd waves glide softly to the shore.
Hail, sacred Peace! hail long-expected days,
That Thames's glory to the stars shall raise!
Tho' Tyber's streams immortal Rome behold,
Tho' foaming Hermus swells with tides of gold,
From heav'n itself tho' sev'n-fold Nilus flows,
And harvests on a hundred realms bestows;
These now no more shall be the Muse's themes,
Lost in my fame, as in the sea their streams.
Let Volga's banks with iron squadrons shine,
And groves of lances glitter on the Rhine,
Let barb'rous Ganges arm a servile train;
Be mine the blessings of a peaceful reign.
No more my sons shall die with British blood
Red Iber's sands, or Ister's foaming flood:
Safe on my shore each unmolested swain
Shall tend the flocks, or reap the bearded grain;
The shady empire shall retain no trace
Of war or blood, but in the sylvan chace;
The trumpet sleep, while chearful horns are blown,
And arms employ'd on birds and beasts alone.
Behold! th' ascending Villa's on my side,
Project long shadows o'er the crystal tide,
Behold! Augusta's glitt'ring spires increase,
And Temple's rise, the beauteous works of Peace.
I see, I see, where two fair cities bend
Their ample bow, a new Whitehall ascend!
There mighty Nations shall enquire their doom,
The World's great Oracle in times to come;
There Kings shall sue, and suppliant States be seen
Once more to bend before a BRITISH QUEEN.
Thy trees, fair Windsor! now shall leave their woods,
And half thy forests rush into thy floods,

Bear Britain's thunder, and her Cross display,
To the bright regions of the rising day;
Tempt icy seas, where scarce the waters roll,
Where clearer flames glow round the frozen Pole;
Or under southern skies exalt their sails,
Led by new stars, and borne by spicy gales!
For me the balm shall bleed, and amber flow,
The coral redden, and the ruby glow,
The pearly shell its lucid globe infold,
And Phœbus warm the rip'ning ore to gold.
The time shall come, when free as seas or wind
Unbounded Thames shall flow for all mankind,
Whole nations enter with each swelling tide,
And seas but join the regions they divide;
Earth's distant ends our glory shall behold,
And the new world launch forth to seek the old.
Then ships of uncouth form shall stem the tide,
And feather'd people croud my wealthy side,
And naked youths and painted chiefs admire
Our speech, our colour, and our strange attire!
Oh stretch thy reign, fair Peace! from shore to shore,
'Till Conquest cease, and Slav'ry be no more;
'Till the freed Indians in their native groves
Reap their own fruits, and woo their sable loves,
Peru once more a race of Kings behold,
And other Mexico's be roof'd with gold.
Exil'd by thee from earth to deepest hell,
In brazen bonds, shall barb'rous Discord dwell;
Gigantic Pride, pale Terror, gloomy Care,
And mad Ambition shall attend her there:
There purple Vengeance bath'd in gore retires,
Her weapons blunted, and extinct her fires:
There hateful Envy her own snakes shall feel,
And Persecution mourn her broken wheel:
There Faction roar, Rebellion bite her chain,
And gasping Furies thirst for blood in vain.
  Here cease thy flight, nor with unhallow'd lays
Touch the fair fame of Albion's golden days:
The thoughts of Gods let GRANVILLE's verse recite,
And bring the scenes of op'ning fate to light.
My humble Muse, in unambitious strains
Paints the green forests and the flow'ry plains,
Where Peace descending bids her olives spring,
And scatters blessings from her dove-like wing.
Ev'n I more sweetly pass my careless days,
Pleas'd in the silent shade with empty praise;
Enough for me, that to the list'ning swains
First in these fields I sung the sylvan strains.

Prologue to Mr. Addison's Tragedy of Cato[1]

To WAKE the soul by tender strokes of art,
To raise the genius, and to mend the heart;
To make mankind, in conscious virtue bold,
Live o'er each scene, and be what they behold:
For this the Tragic Muse first trod the stage,
Commanding tears to stream thro' ev'ry age;
Tyrants no more their savage nature kept,
And foes to virtue wonder'd how they wept.
Our author shuns by vulgar springs to move,
The hero's glory, or the virgin's love;
In pitying love we but our weakness show,
And wild ambition well deserves its woe.
Here tears shall flow from a more gen'rous cause,
Such tears, as Patriots shed for dying Laws:
He bids your breasts with ancient ardour rise,
And calls forth *Roman* drops from *British* eyes.
Virtue confess'd in human shape he draws,
What *Plato* thought, and godlike *Cato* was:
No common object to your sight displays,
But what with pleasure heav'n itself surveys;
A brave man struggling in the storms of fate,
And greatly falling with a falling state!
While *Cato* gives his little senate laws,
What bosom beats not in his Country's cause?
Who sees him act, but envies ev'ry deed?
Who hears him groan, and does not wish to bleed?
Ev'n when proud *Cæsar* 'midst triumphal cars,
The spoils of nations, and the pomp of wars,
Ignobly vain and impotently great,
Show'd *Rome* her *Cato*'s figure drawn in state;
As her dead Father's rev'rend image past,
The pomp was darken'd, and the day o'ercast,
The triumph ceas'd—Tears gush'd from ev'ry eye;
The World's great Victor pass'd unheeded by;
Her last good man dejected *Rome* ador'd,
And honour'd *Cæsar*'s less than *Cato*'s sword.
  Britains attend: Be worth like this approv'd,
And show, you have the virtue to be mov'd.
With honest scorn the first fam'd *Cato* view'd
Rome learning arts from *Greece*, whom she subdu'd;
Our scene precariously subsists too long

[1] Published in the *Guardian*, April 18, 1713. Text of *Works*, 1717.

On *French* translation, and *Italian* song.
Dare to have sense your selves; assert the stage,
Be justly warm'd with your own native rage.
Such Plays alone should please a *British* ear,
As *Cato*'s self had not disdain'd to hear.

Ode for Music on St. Cecilia's Day[1]

I.

DESCEND, ye Nine! descend and sing;
The breathing instruments inspire,
Wake into voice each silent string,
And sweep the sounding lyre!
In a sadly-pleasing strain
Let the warbling lute complain:
Let the loud trumpet sound,
'Till the roofs all around
The shrill echos rebound:
While in more lengthen'd notes and slow,
The deep, majestic, solemn organs blow.
Hark! the numbers soft and clear,
Gently steal upon the ear;
Now louder, and yet louder rise
And fill with spreading sounds the skies;
Exulting in triumph now swell the bold notes,
In broken air, trembling, the wild music floats;
'Till, by degrees, remote and small,
The strains decay,
And melt away,
In a dying, dying fall.

II.

By Music, minds an equal temper know,
Nor swell too high, nor sink too low.
If in the breast tumultuous joys arise,
Music her soft, assuasive voice applies;
Or, when the soul is press'd with cares,
Exalts her in enlivening airs.
Warriors she fires with animated sounds;
Pours balm into the bleeding lover's wounds:
Melancholy lifts her head,

[1] Published July 16, 1713. Text of *Works*, 1751.

Morpheus rouzes from his bed,
Sloth unfolds her arms and wakes,
List'ning Envy drops her snakes;
Intestine war no more our Passions wage,
And giddy Factions hear away their rage.

III.

But when our Country's cause provokes to Arms,
How martial music ev'ry bosom warms!
So when the first bold vessel dar'd the seas,
High on the stern the Thracian rais'd his strain,
While Argo saw her kindred trees
Descend from Pelion to the main.
Transported demi-gods stood round,
And men grew heroes at the sound,
Enflam'd with glory's charms:
Each chief his sev'nfold shield display'd,
And half unsheath'd the shining blade:
And seas, and rocks, and skies rebound
To arms, to arms, to arms!

IV.

But when thro' all th' infernal bounds,
Which flaming Phlegeton surrounds,
Love, strong as Death, the Poet led
To the pale nations of the dead,
What sounds were heard,
What scenes appear'd,
O'er all the dreary coasts!
Dreadful gleams,
Dismal screams,
Fires that glow,
Shrieks of woe,
Sullen moans,
Hollow groans,
And cries of tortur'd ghosts!
But hark! he strikes the golden lyre;
And see! the tortur'd ghosts respire,
See, shady forms advance!
Thy stone, O Sysiphus, stands still,
Ixion rests upon his wheel,
And the pale spectres dance!
The Furies sink upon their iron beds,
And snakes uncurl'd hang list'ning round their heads.

V.

By the streams that ever flow,
By the fragrant winds that blow
O'er th' Elysian flow'rs;
By those happy souls who dwell
In yellow meads of Asphodel,
Or Amaranthine bow'rs;
By the hero's armed shades,
Glitt'ring thro' the gloomy glades;
By the youths that dy'd for love,
Wand'ring in the myrtle grove,
Restore, restore Eurydice to life:
Oh take the husband, or return the wife!

He sung, and hell consented
To hear the Poet's prayer:
Stern Proserpine relented,
And gave him back the fair.
Thus song could prevail
O'er death, and o'er hell,
A conquest how hard and how glorious?
Tho' fate had fast bound her
With Styx nine times round her,
Yet music and love were victorious.

VI.

But soon, too soon, the lover turns his eyes:
Again she falls, again she dies, she dies!
How wilt thou now the fatal sisters move?
No crime was thine, if 'tis no crime to love.
Now under hanging mountains,
Beside the falls of fountains,
Or where Hebrus wanders,
Rolling in Mæanders,
All alone,
Unheard, unknown,
He makes his moan;
And calls her ghost,
For ever, ever, ever lost!
Now with Furies surrounded,
Despairing, confounded,
He trembles, he glows,
Amidst Rhodope's snows:
See, wild as the winds, o'er the desart he flies;
Hark! Hæmus resounds with the Bacchanals cries—
Ah see, he dies!

Yet ev'n in death Eurydice he sung,
Eurydice still trembled on his tongue,
Eurydice the woods,
Eurydice the floods,
Eurydice the rocks, and hollow mountains rung.

VII.

Music the fiercest grief can charm,
And fate's severest rage disarm:
Music can soften pain to ease,
And make despair and madness please:
Our joys below it can improve,
And antedate the bliss above.
This the divine Cecilia found,
And to her Maker's praise confin'd the sound.
When the full organ joins the tuneful quire,
Th' immortal pow'rs incline their ear;
Borne on the swelling notes our souls aspire,
While solemn airs improve the sacred fire;
And Angels lean from heav'n to hear.
Of Orpheus now no more let Poets tell,
To bright Cecilia greater power is giv'n;
His numbers rais'd a shade from hell,
Hers lift the soul to heav'n.

A Farewell to London In the Year 1715[1]

Dear, damn'd, distracting town, farewell!
Thy fools no more I'll tease:
This year in peace, ye critics dwell,
Ye harlots, sleep at ease!

Soft B—— and rough C——s adieu,
Earl Warwick make your moan,
The lively H——k and you
May knock up whores alone.

To drink and droll be Rowe allow'd
Till the third watchman's toll;
Let Jervas gratis paint, and Frowde
Save threepence and his soul.

[1] Published in *Additions*, 1776. Text of first edition.

Farewell, Arbuthnot's raillery
  On every learned sot;
And Garth, the best good Christian he,
  Although he knows it not.

Lintot, farewell! thy bard must go;
  Farewell, unhappy Tonson!
Heaven gives thee for thy loss of Rowe,
  Lean Philips and fat Johnson.

Why should I stay? Both parties rage;
  My vixen mistress squalls;
The wits in envious feuds engage:
  And Homer (damn him!) calls.

The love of arts lies cold and dead
  In Halifax's urn:
And not one Muse of all he fed
  Has yet the grace to mourn.

My friends, by turns, my friends confound,
  Betray, and are betrayed:
Poor Y——r's sold for fifty pound,
  And B——ll is a jade.

Why make I friendships with the great,
  When I no favour seek?
Or follow girls, seven hours in eight?
  I us'd but once a week.

Still idle, with a busy air,
  Deep whimsies to contrive;
The gayest valetudinaire,
  Most thinking rake, alive.

Solicitous for others' ends,
  Though fond of dear repose;
Careless or drowsy with my friends,
  And frolic with my foes.

Luxurious lobster-nights, farewell,
  For sober, studious days!
And Burlington's delicious meal,
  For salads, tarts, and pease!

Adieu to all, but Gay alone,
  Whose soul, sincere and free,

Loves all mankind, but flatters none,
And so may starve with me.

From The Sixth Book of the Iliad[1]

THE ARGUMENT

The Episodes of *Glaucus* and *Diomed*, and of *Hector* and *Andromache.*

The Gods having left the field, the Grecians *prevail.* Helenus, *the chief augur of* Troy, *commands* Hector *to return to the city, in order to appoint a solemn procession of the Queen and the* Trojan *matrons to the temple of* Minerva, *to entreat her to remove* Diomed *from the fight. The battel relaxing during the absence of* Hector, Glaucus *and* Diomed *have an interview between the two armies; where coming to the knowledge of the friendship and hospitality past between their ancestors, they make exchange of their arms.* Hector *having performed the orders of* Helenus, *prevail'd upon* Paris *to return to the battel, and taken a tender leave of his wife* Andromache, *hastens again to the field.*

The scene is first in the field of battel, between the rivers Simois *and* Scamander, *and then changes to* Troy.

THE chief reply'd: This time forbids to rest:
The *Trojan* bands by hostile fury prest,
Demand their *Hector*, and his arm require;
The combate urges, and my soul's on fire.
Urge thou thy Knight to march where glory calls,
And timely join me, e're I leave the walls.
E're yet I mingle in the direful fray,
My wife, my infant, claim a moment's stay;
This day (perhaps the last that sees me here)
Demands a parting word, a tender tear:
This day, some God who hates our *Trojan* land
May vanquish *Hector* by a *Grecian* hand.
He said, and past with sad presaging heart
To seek his spouse, his soul's far dearer part;
At home he sought her, but he sought in vain:
She with one maid of all her menial train,
Had thence retir'd; and with her second joy,
The young *Astyanax*, the hope of *Troy*.
Pensive she stood on *Ilion*'s tow'ry height,
Beheld the war, and sicken'd at the sight;
There her sad eyes in vain her Lord explore,
Or weep the wounds her bleeding country bore.
But he who found not whom his soul desir'd,
Whose virtue charm'd him as her beauty fir'd,
Stood in the gates, and ask'd what way she bent

[1] Published March 22, 1716. Text of second edition, 1720.

Her parting step? If to the fane she went,
Where late the mourning matrons made resort;
Or sought her sisters in the *Trojan* court?
Not to the court, (reply'd th' attendant train)
Nor mix'd with matrons to *Minerva*'s fane:
To *Ilion's* steepy tow'r she bent her way,
To mark the fortunes of the doubtful day.
Troy fled, she heard, before the *Grecian* sword;
She heard, and trembled for her absent Lord:
Distracted with surprize, she seem'd to fly,
Fear on her cheek, and sorrow in her eye.
The nurse attended with her infant boy,
The young *Astyanax*, the hope of *Troy*.
  Hector, this heard, return'd without delay;
Swift thro' the town he trod his former way,
Thro' streets of palaces, and walks of state;
And met the mourner at the *Scæan* gate.
With haste to meet him sprung the joyful fair,
His blameless wife, *Aëtions* wealthy heir:
(*Cilician Thebè* great *Aëtion* sway'd,
And *Hippoplacus*' wide-extended shade)
The nurse stood near, in whose embraces prest
His only hope hung smiling at her breast,
Whom each soft charm and early grace adorn,
Fair as the new-born star that gilds the morn.
To this lov'd infant *Hector* gave the name
Scamandrius, from *Scamander*'s honour'd stream;
Astyanax the *Trojans* call'd the boy,
From his great father, the defence of *Troy*.
Silent the warrior smil'd, and pleas'd resign'd
To tender passions all his mighty mind:
His beauteous Princess cast a mournful look,
Hung on his hand, and then dejected spoke;
Her bosom labour'd with a boding sigh,
And the big tear stood trembling in her eye.
  Too daring Prince! ah whither dost thou run?
Ah too forgetful of thy wife and son!
And think'st thou not how wretched we shall be,
A widow I, an helpless orphan he!
For sure such courage length of life denies,
And thou must fall, thy virtue's sacrifice.
Greece in her single heroes strove in vain;
Now Hosts oppose thee, and thou must be slain!
Oh grant me Gods! e're *Hector* meets his doom,
All I can ask of heav'n, an early tomb!
  So shall my days in one sad tenor run,
And end with sorrows as they first begun.
No parent now remains, my griefs to share,

No father's aid, no mother's tender care.
The fierce *Achilles* wrapt our walls in fire,
Lay'd *Thebè* waste, and slew my warlike Sire!
His fate compassion in the victor bred;
Stern as he was, he yet rever'd the dead,
His radiant arms preserv'd from hostile spoil,
And lay'd him decent on the fun'ral pyle;
Then rais'd a mountain where his bones were burn'd,
The mountain nymphs the rural tomb adorn'd,
Jove's sylvan daughters bade their elms bestow
A barren shade, and in his honour grow.
By the same arm my sev'n brave brothers fell,
In one sad day beheld the gates of hell;
While the fat herds and snowy flocks they fed,
Amid their fields the hapless Heroes bled!
My mother liv'd to bear the victor's bands,
The Queen of *Hippoplacia*'s sylvan lands:
Redeem'd too late, she scarce beheld again
Her pleasing empire and her native plain,
When ah! opprest by life-consuming woe,
She fell a victim to *Diana*'s bow.
Yet while my *Hector* still survives, I see
My father, mother, brethren, all, in thee.
Alas! my parents, brothers, kindred, all,
Once more will perish if my *Hector* fall.
Thy wife, thy infant, in thy danger share:
Oh prove a husband's and a father's care!
That quarter most the skilful *Greeks* annoy,
Where yon' wild fig-trees join the wall of *Troy:*
Thou, from this tow'r defend th' important post;
There *Agamemnon* points his dreadful host,
That pass *Tydides, Ajax*, strive to gain,
And there the vengeful *Spartan* fires his train.
Thrice our bold foes the fierce attack have giv'n,
Or led by hopes, or dictated from heav'n.
Let others in the field their arms employ,
But stay my *Hector* here, and guard his *Troy*.
The Chief reply'd: That post shall be my care,
Nor that alone, but all the works of war.
How would the sons of *Troy*, in arms renown'd,
And *Troy*'s proud dames whose garments sweep the ground,
Attaint the lustre of my former name,
Should *Hector* basely quit the field of fame?
My early youth was bred to martial pains,
My soul impells me to th' embattel'd plains:
Let me be foremost to defend the throne,
And guard my father's glories, and my own.
Yet come it will, the day decreed by fates;

(How my heart trembles while my tongue relates!)
The day when thou, imperial *Troy!* must bend,
And see thy warriors fall, thy glories end.
And yet no dire presage so wounds my mind,
My mother's death, the ruin of my kind,
Not *Priam*'s hoary hairs defil'd with gore,
Not all my brothers gasping on the shore;
As thine *Andromache!* thy griefs I dread;
I see thee trembling, weeping, captive led!
In *Argive* looms our battels to design,
And woes, of which so large a part was thine!
To bear the victor's hard commands, or bring
The weight of waters from *Hyperia*'s spring.
There, while you groan beneath the load of life,
They cry, Behold the mighty *Hector*'s wife!
Some haughty *Greek*, who lives thy tears to see,
Embitters all thy woes, by naming me.
The thoughts of glory past, and present shame,
A thousand griefs, shall waken at the name!
May I lay cold before that dreadful day,
Press'd with a load of monumental clay!
Thy *Hector* wrapt in everlasting sleep,
Shall neither hear thee sigh, nor see thee weep.
  Thus having spoke, th' illustrious chief of *Troy*,
Stretch'd his fond arms to clasp the lovely boy.
The babe clung crying to his nurse's breast,
Scar'd at the dazling helm, and nodding crest.
With secret pleasure each fond parent smil'd,
And *Hector* hasted to relieve his child,
The glitt'ring terrors from his brows unbound,
And plac'd the beaming helmet on the ground.
Then kist the child, and lifting high in air,
Thus to the Gods preferr'd a father's pray'r.
  O thou! whose glory fills th' ætherial throne,
And all ye deathless pow'rs! protect my son!
Grant him, like me, to purchase just renown,
To guard the *Trojans*, to defend the crown,
Against his countrey's foes the war to wage,
And rise the *Hector* of the future age!
So when triumphant from successful toils,
Of heroes slain he bears the reeking spoils,
Whole hosts may hail him with deserv'd acclaim,
And say, This chief transcends his father's fame:
While pleas'd amidst the gen'ral shouts of *Troy*,
His mother's conscious heart o'erflows with joy.
  He spoke, and fondly gazing on her charms,
Restor'd the pleasing burthen to her arms;
Soft on her fragrant breast the babe she laid,

Hush'd to repose, and with a smile survey'd.
The troubled pleasure soon chastis'd by fear,
She mingled with the smile a tender tear.
The soften'd chief with kind compassion view'd,
And dry'd the falling drops, and thus pursu'd.
Andromache! my soul's far better part,
Why with untimely sorrows heaves thy heart?
No hostile hand can antedate my doom,
Till fate condemns me to the silent tomb.
Fix'd is the term to all the race of earth,
And such the hard condition of our birth.
No force can then resist, no flight can save,
All sink alike, the fearful and the brave.
No more—but hasten to thy tasks at home,
There guide the spindle, and direct the loom:
Me glory summons to the martial scene,
The field of combate is the sphere for men.
Where heroes war, the foremost place I claim,
The first in danger as the first in fame.
Thus having said, the glorious chief resumes
His tow'ry helmet, black with shading plumes.
His princess parts with a prophetick sigh,
Unwilling parts, and oft reverts her eye
That stream'd at every look: then moving slow,
Sought her own palace, and indulg'd her woe.
There, while her tears deplor'd the godlike man,
Thro' all her train the soft infection ran,
The pious maids their mingled sorrows shed,
And mourn the living *Hector*, as the dead.
But now, no longer deaf to honour's call,
Forth issues *Paris* from the palace wall.
In brazen arms that cast a gleamy ray,
Swift thro' the town the warrior bends his way.
The wanton courser thus, with reins unbound,
Breaks from his stall, and beats the trembling ground;
Pamper'd and proud, he seeks the wonted tides,
And laves, in height of blood, his shining sides;
His head now freed, he tosses to the skies;
His mane dishevel'd o'er his shoulders flies;
He snuffs the females in the distant plain,
And springs, exulting, to his fields again.
With equal triumph, sprightly, bold and gay,
In arms refulgent as the God of day,
The son of *Priam*, glorying in his might,
Rush'd forth with *Hector* to the fields of fight.
And now the warriors passing on the way,
The graceful *Paris* first excus'd his stay.
To whom the noble *Hector* thus reply'd:

O Chief! in blood, and now in arms, ally'd!
Thy pow'r in war with justice none contest;
Known is thy courage, and thy strength confest.
What pity, sloath should seize a soul so brave,
Or godlike *Paris* live a woman's slave!
My heart weeps blood at what the *Trojans* say,
And hopes, thy deeds shall wipe the stain away.
Haste then, in all their glorious labours share;
For much they suffer, for thy sake, in war.
These ills shall cease, whene'er by *Jove*'s decree
We crown the bowl to *Heav'n* and *Liberty:*
While the proud foe his frustrate triumphs mourns,
And *Greece* indignant thro' her seas returns.

Verses to the Memory of an Unfortunate Lady[1]

WHAT beck'ning ghost, along the moonlight shade
Invites my steps, and points to yonder glade?
'Tis she!—but why that bleeding bosom gor'd,
Why dimly gleams the visionary sword?
Oh ever beauteous, ever friendly! tell,
Is it, in heav'n, a crime to love too well?
To bear too tender, or too firm a heart,
To act a Lover's or a *Roman*'s part?
Is there no bright reversion in the sky,
For those who greatly think, or bravely die?
Why bade ye else, ye Pow'rs! her soul aspire
Above the vulgar flight of low desire?
Ambition first sprung from your blest abodes;
The glorious fault of Angels and of Gods:
Thence to their Images on earth it flows,
And in the breasts of Kings and Heroes glows!
Most souls, 'tis true, but peep out once an age,
Dull sullen pris'ners in the body's cage:
Dim lights of life that burn a length of years,
Useless, unseen, as lamps in sepulchres;
Like Eastern Kings a lazy state they keep,
And close confin'd in their own palace sleep.
From these perhaps (e'er nature bade her die)
Fate snatch'd her early to the pitying sky.
As into air the purer spirits flow,
And sep'rate from their kindred dregs below;
So flew the soul to its congenial place,
Nor left one virtue to redeem her Race.

[1] Published in *Works*, June 3, 1717. Text of first edition.

But thou, false guardian of a charge too good,
Thou, mean deserter of thy brother's blood!
See on these ruby lips the trembling breath,
These cheeks, now fading at the blast of death:
Cold is that breast which warm'd the world before,
And those love-darting eyes must roll no more.
Thus, if eternal justice rules the ball,
Thus shall your wives, and thus your children fall:
On all the line a sudden vengeance waits,
And frequent herses shall besiege your gates.
There passengers shall stand, and pointing say,
(While the long fun'rals blacken all the way)
Lo these were they, whose souls the Furies steel'd,
And curs'd with hearts unknowing how to yield.
Thus unlamented pass the proud away,
The gaze of fools, and pageant of a day!
So perish all, whose breast ne'er learn'd to glow
For others good, or melt at others woe.
What can atone (oh ever-injur'd shade!)
Thy fate unpity'd, and thy rites unpaid?
No friend's complaint, no kind domestic tear
Pleas'd thy pale ghost, or grac'd thy mournful bier;
By foreign hands thy dying eyes were clos'd,
By foreign hands thy decent limbs compos'd,
By foreign hands thy humble grave adorn'd,
By strangers honour'd, and by strangers mourn'd!
What tho' no friends in sable weeds appear,
Grieve for an hour, perhaps, then mourn a year,
And bear about the mockery of woe
To midnight dances, and the publick show?
What tho' no weeping Loves thy ashes grace,
Nor polish'd marble emulate thy face?
What tho' no sacred earth allow thee room,
Nor hallow'd dirge be mutter'd o'er thy tomb?
Yet shall thy grave with rising flow'rs be drest,
And the green turf lie lightly on thy breast:
There shall the morn her earliest tears bestow,
There the first roses of the year shall blow;
While Angels with their silver wings o'ershade
The ground, now sacred by thy reliques made.
So peaceful rests, without a stone, a name,
What once had beauty, titles, wealth, and fame.
How lov'd, how honour'd once, avails thee not,
To whom related, or by whom begot;
A heap of dust alone remains of thee;
'Tis all thou art, and all the proud shall be!
Poets themselves must fall, like those they sung;
Deaf the prais'd ear, and mute the tuneful tongue.

Ev'n he, whose soul now melts in mournful lays,
Shall shortly want the gen'rous tear he pays;
Then from his closing eyes thy form shall part,
And the last pang shall tear thee from his heart,
Life's idle business at one gasp be o'er,
The Muse forgot, and thou belov'd no more!

Eloisa to Abelard[1]

ARGUMENT

ABELARD and Eloisa flourished in the twelfth Century; they were two of the most distinguished persons of their age in learning and beauty; but for nothing more famous than for their unfortunate passion. After a long course of calamities, they retired each to a several Convent, and consecrated the remainder of their days to religion. It was many years after this separation, that a letter of Abelard's to a Friend, which contained the history of his misfortune, fell into the hands of Eloisa. This awakening all her tenderness, occasioned those celebrated letters (out of which the following is partly extracted) which give so lively a picture of the struggles of grace and nature, virtue and passion.

IN THESE deep solitudes and awful cells,
Where heav'nly-pensive contemplation dwells,
And ever-musing melancholy reigns;
What means this tumult in a Vestal's veins?
Why rove my thoughts beyond this last retreat?
Why feels my heart its long-forgotten heat?
Yet, yet I love!—From Abelard it came,
And Eloïsa yet must kiss the name.
  Dear fatal name! rest ever unreveal'd,
Nor pass these lips in holy silence seal'd:
Hide it, my heart, within that close disguise,
Where mix'd with God's, his lov'd Idea lies:
O write it not my hand—the name appears
Already written—wash it out, my tears!
In vain lost Eloïsa weeps and prays,
Her heart still dictates, and her hand obeys.
  Relentless walls! whose darksome round contains
Repentant sighs, and voluntary pains:
Ye rugged rocks! which holy knees have worn;
Ye grots and caverns shagg'd with horrid thorn!
Shrines! where their vigils pale-ey'd virgins keep,
And pitying saints, whose statues learn to weep!
Tho' cold like you, unmov'd and silent grown,

[1] Published in *Works*, June 3, 1717. Text of *Works*, 1751.

I have not yet forgot myself to stone.
All is not Heav'n's while Abelard has part,
Still rebel nature holds out half my heart;
Nor pray'rs nor fasts its stubborn pulse restrain,
Nor tears for ages taught to flow in vain.
  Soon as thy letters trembling I unclose,
That well-known name awakens all my woes.
Oh name for ever sad! for ever dear!
Still breath'd in sighs, still usher'd with a tear.
I tremble too, where'er my own I find,
Some dire misfortune follows close behind.
Line after line my gushing eyes o'erflow,
Led thro' a sad variety of woe:
Now warm in love, now with'ring in my bloom,
Lost in a convent's solitary gloom!
There stern Religion quench'd th' unwilling flame,
There dy'd the best of passions, Love and Fame.
  Yet write, oh write me all, that I may join
Griefs to thy griefs, and echo sighs to thine.
Nor foes nor fortune take this pow'r away;
And is my Abelard less kind than they?
Tears still are mine, and those I need not spare,
Love but demands what else were shed in pray'r;
No happier task these faded eyes pursue;
To read and weep is all they now can do.
  Then share thy pain, allow that sad relief;
Ah, more than share it, give me all thy grief.
Heav'n first taught letters for some wretch's aid,
Some banish'd lover, or some captive maid;
They live, they speak, they breathe what love inspires,
Warm from the soul, and faithful to its fires,
The virgin's wish without her fears impart,
Excuse the blush, and pour out all the heart,
Speed the soft intercourse from soul to soul,
And waft a sigh from Indus to the Pole.
  Thou know'st how guiltless first I met thy flame,
When Love approach'd me under Friendship's name;
My fancy form'd thee of angelic kind,
Some emanation of th' all-beauteous Mind.
Those smiling eyes, attemp'ring ev'ry ray,
Shone sweetly lambent with celestial day.
Guiltless I gaz'd; heav'n listen'd while you sung;
And truths divine came mended from that tongue.
From lips like those what precept fail'd to move?
Too soon they taught me 'twas no sin to love:
Back thro' the paths of pleasing sense I ran,
Nor wish'd an Angel whom I lov'd a Man.
Dim and remote the joys of saints I see;

Nor envy them that heav'n I lose for thee.
How oft, when press'd to marriage, have I said,
Curse on all laws but those which Love has made?
Love, free as air, at sight of human ties,
Spreads his light wings, and in a moment flies.
Let wealth, let honour, wait the wedded dame,
August her deed, and sacred be her fame;
Before true passion all those views remove,
Fame, wealth, and honour! what are you to Love?
The jealous God, when we profane his fires,
Those restless passions in revenge inspires,
And bids them make mistaken mortals groan,
Who seek in love for aught but love alone.
Should at my feet the world's great master fall,
Himself, his throne, his world, I'd scorn 'em all:
Not Cæsar's empress would I deign to prove;
No, make me mistress to the man I love;
If there be yet another name more free,
More fond than mistress, make me that to thee!
Oh! happy state! when souls each other draw,
When love is liberty, and nature, law:
All then is full, possessing, and possest,
No craving void left aking in the breast:
Ev'n thought meets thought, ere from the lips it part,
And each warm wish springs mutual from the heart.
This sure is bliss (if bliss on earth there be)
And once the lot of Abelard and me.
Alas how chang'd! what sudden horrors rise!
A naked Lover bound and bleeding lies!
Where, where was Eloïse? her voice, her hand,
Her ponyard had oppos'd the dire command.
Barbarian, stay! that bloody stroke restrain;
The crime was common, common be the pain.
I can no more, by shame, by rage suppress'd,
Let tears, and burning blushes speak the rest.
Canst thou forget that sad, that solemn day,
When victims at yon altar's foot we lay?
Canst thou forget what tears that moment fell,
When, warm in youth, I bade the world farewell?
As with cold lips I kiss'd the sacred veil,
The shrines all trembled, and the lamps grew pale:
Heav'n scarce believ'd the Conquest it survey'd,
And Saints with wonder heard the vows I made.
Yet then, to those dread altars as I drew,
Not on the Cross my eyes were fix'd, but you:
Not grace, or zeal, love only was my call,
And if I lose thy love, I lose my all.
Come! with thy looks, thy words, relieve my woe;

Those still at least are left thee to bestow.
Still on that breast enamour'd let me lie,
Still drink delicious poison from thy eye,
Pant on thy lip, and to thy heart be press'd;
Give all thou canst—and let me dream the rest.
Ah no! instruct me other joys to prize,
With other beauties charm my partial eyes,
Full in my view set all the bright abode,
And make my soul quit Abelard for God.
  Ah think at least thy flock deserves thy care,
Plants of thy hand, and children of thy pray'r.
From the false world in early youth they fled,
By thee to mountains, wilds, and deserts led.
You rais'd these hallow'd walls; the desert smil'd,
And Paradise was open'd in the Wild.
No weeping orphan saw his father's stores
Our shrines irradiate, or emblaze the floors;
No silver saints, by dying misers giv'n,
Here brib'd the rage of ill-requited heav'n:
But such plain roofs as Piety could raise,
And only vocal with the Maker's praise.
In these lone walls (their days eternal bound)
These moss-grown domes with spiry turrets crown'd,
Where awful arches make a noon-day night,
And the dim windows shed a solemn light;
Thy eyes diffus'd a reconciling ray,
And gleams of glory brighten'd all the day.
But now no face divine contentment wears,
'Tis all blank sadness, or continual tears.
See how the force of others pray'rs I try,
(O pious fraud of am'rous charity!)
But why should I on others pray'rs depend?
Come thou, my father, brother, husband, friend!
Ah let thy handmaid, sister, daughter move,
And all those tender names in one, thy love!
The darksome pines that o'er yon rocks reclin'd
Wave high, and murmur to the hollow wind,
The wand'ring streams that shine between the hills,
The grots that echo to the tinkling rills,
The dying gales that pant upon the trees,
The lakes that quiver to the curling breeze;
No more these scenes my meditation aid,
Or lull to rest the visionary maid.
But o'er the twilight groves and dusky caves,
Long-sounding isles, and intermingled graves,
Black Melancholy sits, and round her throws
A death-like silence, and a dread repose:
Her gloomy presence saddens all the scene,

Shades ev'ry flow'r, and darkens ev'ry green,
Deepens the murmur of the falling floods,
And breathes a browner horror on the woods.
Yet here for ever, ever must I stay;
Sad proof how well a lover can obey!
Death, only death, can break the lasting chain;
And here, ev'n then, shall my cold dust remain,
Here all its frailties, all its flames resign,
And wait till 'tis no sin to mix with thine.
Ah wretch! believ'd the spouse of God in vain,
Confess'd within the slave of love and man.
Assist me, heav'n! but whence arose that pray'r?
Sprung it from piety, or from despair?
Ev'n here, where frozen chastity retires,
Love finds an altar for forbidden fires.
I ought to grieve, but cannot what I ought;
I mourn the lover, not lament the fault;
I view my crime, but kindle at the view,
Repent old pleasures, and sollicit new;
Now turn'd to heav'n, I weep my past offence,
Now think of thee, and curse my innocence.
Of all affliction taught a lover yet,
'Tis sure the hardest science to forget!
How shall I lose the sin, yet keep the sense,
And love th' offender, yet detest th' offence?
How dear the object from the crime remove,
Or how distinguish pentitence from love?
Unequal task! a passion to resign,
For hearts so touch'd, so pierc'd, so lost as mine.
Ere such a soul regains its peaceful state,
How often must it love, how often hate!
How often hope, despair, resent, regret,
Conceal, disdain,—do all things but forget.
But let heav'n seize it, all at once 'tis fir'd;
Not touch'd, but rapt; not waken'd, but inspir'd!
Oh come! oh teach me nature to subdue,
Renounce my love, my life, myself—and you.
Fill my fond heart with God alone, for he
Alone can rival, can succeed to thee.
How happy is the blameless Vestal's lot?
The world forgetting, by the world forgot:
Eternal sun-shine of the spotless mind!
Each pray'r accepted, and each wish resign'd;
Labour and rest, that equal periods keep;
"Obedient slumbers that can wake and weep;"
Desires compos'd, affections ever ev'n;
Tears that delight, and sighs that waft to heav'n.
Grace shines around her with serenest beams,

And whisp'ring Angels prompt her golden dreams.
For her th' unfading rose of Eden blooms,
And wings of Seraphs shed divine perfumes,
For her the Spouse prepares the bridal ring,
For her white virgins Hymenæals sing,
To sounds of heav'nly harps she dies away,
And melts in visions of eternal day.
  Far other dreams my erring soul employ,
Far other raptures, of unholy joy:
When at the close of each sad, sorrowing day,
Fancy restores what vengeance snatch'd away,
Then conscience sleeps, and leaving nature free,
All my loose soul unbounded springs to thee.
O curst, dear horrors of all-conscious night!
How glowing guilt exalts the keen delight!
Provoking Dæmons all restraint remove,
And stir within me ev'ry source of love.
I hear thee, view thee, gaze o'er all thy charms,
And round thy phantom glue my clasping arms.
I wake:—no more I hear, no more I view,
The phantom flies me, as unkind as you.
I call aloud; it hears not what I say:
I stretch my empty arms; it glides away.
To dream once more I close my willing eyes;
Ye soft illusions, dear deceits, arise!
Alas, no more! methinks we wand'ring go
Thro' dreary wastes, and weep each other's woe,
Where round some mould'ring tow'r pale ivy creeps,
And low-brow'd rocks hang nodding o'er the deeps.
Sudden you mount, you beckon from the skies;
Clouds interpose, waves roar, and winds arise.
I shriek, start up, the same sad prospect find,
And wake to all the griefs I left behind.
  For thee the fates, severely kind, ordain
A cool suspense from pleasure and from pain;
Thy life a long dead calm of fix'd repose;
No pulse that riots, and no blood that glows.
Still as the sea, ere winds were taught to blow,
Or moving spirit bade the waters flow;
Soft as the slumbers of a saint forgiv'n,
And mild as op'ning gleams of promis'd heav'n.
  Come, Abelard! for what hast thou to dread?
The torch of Venus burns not for the dead.
Nature stands check'd; Religion disapproves;
Ev'n thou art cold—yet Eloïsa loves.
Ah hopeless, lasting flames! like those that burn
To light the dead, and warm th' unfruitful urn.
  What scenes appear where'er I turn my view?

The dear Ideas, where I fly, pursue,
Rise in the grove, before the altar rise,
Stain all my soul, and wanton in my eyes.
I waste the Matin lamp in sighs for thee,
Thy image steals between my God and me,
Thy voice I seem in ev'ry hymn to hear,
With ev'ry bead I drop too soft a tear.
When from the censer clouds of fragrance roll,
And swelling organs lift the rising soul,
One thought of thee puts all the pomp to flight,
Priests, tapers, temples, swim before my sight:
In seas of flame my plunging soul is drown'd,
While Altars blaze, and Angels tremble round.
  While prostrate here in humble grief I lie,
Kind, virtuous drops just gath'ring in my eye,
While praying, trembling, in the dust I roll,
And dawning grace is op'ning on my soul:
Come, if thou dar'st, all charming as thou art!
Oppose thyself to heav'n; dispute my heart;
Come, with one glance of those deluding eyes
Blot out each bright Idea of the skies;
Take back that grace, those sorrows, and those tears;
Take back my fruitless penitence and pray'rs;
Snatch me, just mounting, from the blest abode;
Assist the fiends, and tear me from my God!
  No, fly me, fly me, far as Pole from Pole;
Rise Alps between us! and whole oceans roll!
Ah, come not, write not, think not once of me,
Nor share one pang of all I felt for thee.
Thy oaths I quit, thy memory resign;
Forget, renounce me, hate whate'er was mine.
Fair eyes, and tempting looks (which yet I view!)
Long lov'd, ador'd ideas, all adieu!
O Grace serene! oh virtue heav'nly fair!
Divine oblivion of low-thoughted care!
Fresh blooming Hope, gay daughter of the sky!
And Faith, our early immortality!
Enter, each mild, each amicable guest;
Receive, and wrap me in eternal rest!
  See in her cell sad Eloïsa spread,
Propt on some tomb, a neighbour of the dead.
In each low wind methinks a Spirit calls,
And more than Echoes talk along the walls.
Here, as I watch'd the dying lamps around,
From yonder shrine I heard a hollow sound.
"Come, sister, come! (it said, or seem'd to say)
"Thy place is here, sad sister, come away!
"Once like thyself, I trembled, wept, and pray'd,

"Love's victim then, tho' now a sainted maid:
"But all is calm in this eternal sleep;
"Here grief forgets to groan, and love to weep,
"Ev'n superstition loses ev'ry fear:
"For God, not man, absolves our frailties here."
  I come, I come! prepare your roseate bow'rs,
Celestial palms, and ever-blooming flow'rs.
Thither, where sinners may have rest, I go,
Where flames refin'd in breasts seraphic glow:
Thou, Abelard! the last sad office pay,
And smooth my passage to the realms of day;
See my lips tremble, and my eye-balls roll,
Suck my last breath, and catch my flying soul!
Ah no—in sacred vestments may'st thou stand,
The hallow'd taper trembling in thy hand,
Present the Cross before my lifted eye,
Teach me at once, and learn of me to die.
Ah then, thy once-lov'd Eloïsa see!
It will be then no crime to gaze on me.
See from my cheek the transient roses fly!
See the last sparkle languish in my eye!
'Till ev'ry motion, pulse, and breath be o'er;
And ev'n my Abelard be lov'd no more.
O Death, all-eloquent! you only prove
What dust we doat on, when 'tis man we love.
  Then too, when fate shall thy fair frame destroy,
(That cause of all my guilt, and all my joy)
In trance extatic may thy pangs be drown'd,
Bright clouds descend, and Angels watch thee round,
From op'ning skies may streaming glories shine,
And Saints embrace thee with a love like mine.
  May one kind grave unite each hapless name,
And graft my love immortal on thy fame!
Then, ages hence, when all my woes are o'er,
When this rebellious heart shall beat no more;
If ever chance two wand'ring lovers brings
To Paraclete's white walls and silver springs,
O'er the pale marble shall they join their heads,
And drink the falling tears each other sheds;
Then sadly say, with mutual pity mov'd,
"Oh may we never love as these have lov'd!"
From the full choir when loud Hosannas rise,
And swell the pomp of dreadful sacrifice,
Amid that scene if some relenting eye
Glance on the stone where our cold relicks lie,
Devotion's self shall steal a thought from heav'n,
One human tear shall drop, and be forgiv'n.

And sure if fate some future bard shall join
In sad similitude of griefs to mine,
Condemn'd whole years in absence to deplore,
And image charms he must behold no more;
Sure if there be, who loves so long, so well;
Let him our sad, our tender story tell;
The well-sung woes will sooth my pensive ghost;
He best can paint 'em who shall feel 'em most.

Epistle to Martha Blount on her Leaving the Town after the Coronation[1]

As SOME fond virgin, whom her mother's care
Drags from the town to wholsom country air,
Just when she learns to roll a melting eye,
And hear a spark, yet think no danger nigh;
From the dear man unwilling she must sever,
Yet takes one kiss before she parts for ever.
Thus from the world fair *Zephalinda* flew,
Saw others happy, and with sighs withdrew;
Not that their pleasures caus'd her discontent,
She sigh'd not that They stay'd, but that She went.
  She went, to plain-work and to purling brooks,
Old-fashion'd halls, dull aunts, and croaking rooks,
She went from Op'ra, park, assembly, play,
To morning walks, and pray'rs three hours a day;
To part her time 'twixt reading and Bohea,
To muse, and spill her solitary Tea,
Or o'er cold coffee trifle with the spoon,
Count the slow clock, and dine exact at noon;
Divert her eyes with pictures in the fire,
Hum half a tune, tell stories to the squire;
Up to her godly garret after sev'n,
There starve and pray, for that's the way to heav'n.
  Some Squire, perhaps, you take delight to rack;
Whose game is Whisk, whose treat a toast in sack,
Who visits with a gun, presents you birds,
Then gives a smacking buss, and cries—No words!
Or with his hound comes hollowing from the stable,
Makes love with nods, and knees beneath a table;
Whose laughs are hearty, tho' his jests are coarse,
And loves you best of all things—but his horse.
  In some fair evening, on your elbow laid,

[1] Published in *Works*, June 3, 1717. Text of first edition.

You dream of triumphs in the rural shade;
In pensive thought recall the fancy'd scene,
See Coronations rise on ev'ry green,
Before you pass th' imaginary sights
Of Lords, and Earls, and Dukes, and garter'd Knights;
While the spread Fan o'ershades your closing eyes;
Then give one flirt, and all the vision flies.
Thus vanish sceptres, coronets, and balls,
And leave you in lone woods, or empty walls.
So when your slave, at some dear, idle time,
(Not plagu'd with headachs, or the want of rhime)
Stands in the streets, abstracted from the crew,
And while he seems to study, thinks of you:
Just when his fancy points your sprightly eyes,
Or sees the blush of *Parthenissa* rise,
G——y pats my shoulder, and you vanish quite;
Streets, chairs, and coxcombs, rush upon my sight;
Vext to be still in town, I knit my brow,
Look sow'r, and hum a song—as you may now.

To Robert Earl of Oxford, and Earl Mortimer[1]

SUCH were the Notes thy once-lov'd Poet sung,
'Till Death untimely stop'd his tuneful tongue.
Oh just beheld, and lost! admir'd and mourn'd!
With softest manners, gentlest arts adorn'd!
Blest in each science, blest in ev'ry strain!
Dear to the Muse! to HARLEY dear — in vain!
For him, thou oft hast bid the World attend,
Fond to forget the statesman in the friend;
For SWIFT and him, despis'd the farce of state,
And sober follies of the wise and great;
Dextrous, the craving, fawning croud to quit,
And pleas'd to 'scape from Flattery to Wit.
Absent or dead, still let a friend be dear,
(A sigh the absent claims, the dead a tear)
Recall those nights that clos'd thy toilsome days,
Still hear thy *Parnell* in his living lays,
Who careless now of Int'rest, fame, or fate,
Perhaps forgets that OXFORD e'er was great;
Or deeming meanest what we greatest call,
Beholds thee glorious only in thy *Fall*.

[1] Published in *Poems . . . Written by Dr. Parnell,* December 7, 1721. Text of *Works,* 1743.

And sure, if ought below the seats divine
Can touch Immortals, 'tis a Soul like thine:
A Soul supreme, in each hard instance try'd,
Above all Pain, all Passion, and all Pride,
The rage of Pow'r, the blast of publick breath,
The lust of Lucre, and the dread of Death.
In vain to Desarts thy retreat is made;
The *Muse* attends thee to thy silent shade:
'Tis hers, the brave man's latest steps to trace,
Rejudge his acts, and dignify disgrace.
When Int'rest calls off all her sneaking train
And all th' oblig'd desert, and all the vain;
She waits, or to the scaffold, or the cell,
When the last ling'ring friend has bid farewel.
Ev'n now, she shades thy Ev'ning-walk with bays,
(No hireling she, no prostitute to praise)
Ev'n now, observant of the parting ray,
Eyes the calm Sun-set of thy various Day,
Thro' Fortune's cloud one truely great can see,
Nor fears to tell, that MORTIMER is he.

To Mrs. M. B. on Her Birth-day[1]

OH BE thou blest with all that Heav'n can send,
Long Health, long Youth, long Pleasure, and a Friend:
Not with those Toys the female world admire,
Riches that vex, and Vanities that tire.
With added years if Life bring nothing new,
But like a Sieve let ev'ry blessing thro',
Some joy still lost, as each vain year runs o'er,
And all we gain, some sad Reflection more;
Is that a Birth-day? 'tis alas! too clear,
'Tis but the Fun'ral of the former year.
Let Joy or Ease, let Affluence or Content,
And the gay Conscience of a life well spent,
Calm ev'ry thought, inspirit ev'ry Grace,
Glow in thy heart, and smile upon thy face.
Let day improve on day, and year on year,
Without a Pain, a Trouble, or a Fear;
Till Death unfelt that tender frame destroy,
In some soft Dream, or Extasy of joy;
Peaceful sleep out the Sabbath of the Tomb,
And wake to Raptures in a Life to come.

[1] Published in the *British Journal*, November 14, 1724. Text of *Works*, 1743.

Ode on Solitude[1]

HAPPY the man, whose wish and care
  A few paternal acres bound,
Content to breathe his native air,
    In his own ground.

Whose herds with milk, whose fields with bread,
  Whose flocks supply him with attire,
Whose trees in summer yield him shade,
    In winter fire.

Blest, who can unconcern'dly find,
  Hours, days and years slide soft away,
In health of body, peace of mind,
    Quiet by day,

Sound sleep by night; study and ease,
  Together mixt; sweet recreation;
And innocence which most does please,
    With meditation.

Thus let me live, unseen, unknown,
  Thus unlamented let me die,
Steal from the world, and not a stone
    Tell where I lie.

The Dunciad[2]

Book the First

BOOKS and the Man I sing, the first who brings
The Smithfield Muses to the Ear of Kings.
Say great Patricians! (since your selves inspire
These wond'rous works; so Jove and Fate require)
Say from what cause, in vain decry'd and curst,
Still Dunce the second reigns like Dunce the first?
  In eldest time, e'er mortals writ or read,
E'er Pallas issued from the Thund'rers head,
Dulness o'er all possess'd her antient right,

[1] Published in *Miscellany Poems*, Volume I, fifth edition, 1726. Text of *Works*, 1736.

[2] Published May 18, 1728. Republished with additions, 1729. Text of first quarto edition of 1729.

Daughter of Chaos and eternal Night:
Fate in their dotage this fair idiot gave,
Gross as her sire, and as her mother grave,
Laborious, heavy, busy, bold, and blind,
She rul'd, in native Anarchy, the mind.
  Still her old empire to confirm, she tries,
For born a Goddess, Dulness never dies.
  O thou! whatever Title please thine ear,
Dean, Drapier, Bickerstaff, or Gulliver!
Whether thou chuse Cervantes' serious air,
Or laugh and shake in Rab'lais easy Chair,
Or praise the Court, or magnify Mankind,
Or thy griev'd Country's copper chains unbind;
From thy Bæotia tho' Her Pow'r retires,
Grieve not at ought our sister realms acquire:
Here pleas'd behold her mighty wings out-spread,
To hatch a new Saturnian age of Lead.
  Where wave the tatter'd ensigns of Rag-Fair,
A yawning ruin hangs and nods in air;
Keen, hollow winds howl thro' the bleak recess,
Emblem of Music caus'd by Emptiness:
Here in one bed two shiv'ring sisters lye,
The cave of Poverty and Poetry.
This, the Great Mother dearer held than all
The clubs of Quidnunc's, or her own Guild-hall.
Here stood her Opium, here she nurs'd her Owls,
And destin'd here th' imperial seat of Fools.
Hence springs each weekly Muse, the living boast
Of Curl's chaste press, and Lintot's rubric's post,
Hence hymning Tyburn's elegiac lay,
Hence the soft sing-song on Cecilia's day,
Sepulchral lyes our holy walls to grace,
And New-year Odes, and all the Grubstreet race.
  'Twas here in clouded majesty she shone;
Four guardian Virtues, round, support her Throne;
Fierce champion Fortitude, that knows no fears
Of hisses, blows, or want, or loss of ears:
Calm Temperance, whose blessings those partake
Who hunger, and who thirst, for scribling sake:
Prudence, whose glass presents th' approaching jayl:
Poetic Justice, with her lifted scale;
Where in nice balance, truth with gold she weighs,
And solid pudding against empty praise.
  Here she beholds the Chaos dark and deep,
Where nameless somethings in their causes sleep,
'Till genial Jacob, or a warm Third-day
Call forth each Mass, a poem or a play.
How Hints, like spawn, scarce quick in embryo lie,

How new-born Nonsense first is taught to cry,
Maggots half-form'd, in rhyme exactly meet,
And learn to crawl upon poetic feet.
Here one poor Word a hundred clenches makes,
And ductile dulness new meanders takes;
There motley Images her fancy strike,
Figures ill-pair'd, and Similes unlike.
She sees a Mob of Metaphors advance,
Pleas'd with the Madness of the mazy dance:
How Tragedy and Comedy embrace;
How Farce and Epic get a jumbled race;
How Time himself stands still at her command,
Realms shift their place, and Ocean turns to land.
Here gay Description Ægypt glads with showers;
Or gives to Zembla fruits, to Barca flowers;
Glitt'ring with ice here hoary hills are seen,
There painted vallies of eternal green,
On cold December fragrant chaplets blow,
And heavy harvests nod beneath the snow.
  All these and more, the cloud-compelling Queen
Beholds thro' fogs that magnify the scene:
She, tinsel'd o'er in robes of varying hues,
With self-applause her wild creation views,
Sees momentary monsters rise and fall,
And with her own fools colours gilds them all.
  'Twas on the day, when Thorold, rich and grave,
Like Cimon triumph'd, both on land and wave:
(Pomps without guilt, of bloodless swords and maces,
Glad chains, warm furs, broad banners, and broad faces)
Now Night descending, the proud scene was o'er,
But liv'd, in Settle's numbers, one day more.
Now May'rs and Shrieves all hush'd and satiate lay,
Yet eat in dreams the custard of the day;
While pensive Poets painful vigils keep,
Sleepless themselves to give their readers sleep.
Much to the mindful Queen the feast recalls,
What City-Swans, once sung within the walls;
Much she revolves their arts, their ancient praise,
And sure succession down from Heywood's days.
She saw with joy the line immortal run,
Each sire imprest and glaring in his son;
So watchful Bruin forms with plastic care
Each growing lump, and brings it to a Bear.
She saw old Pryn in restless Daniel shine,
And Eusden eke out Blackmore's endless line;
She saw slow Philips creep like Tate's poor page,
And all the Mighty Mad in Dennis rage.
  In each she marks her image full exprest,

But chief, in Tibbald's monster-breeding breast;
Sees God with Dæmons in strange league ingage,
And earth, and heav'n, and hell her battles wage.
She ey'd the Bard, where supperless he sate,
And pin'd, unconscious of his rising fate;
Studious he sate, with all his books around,
Sinking from thought to thought, a vast profound!
Plung'd for his sense, but found no bottom there;
Then writ, and flounder'd on, in mere despair.
He roll'd his eyes that witness'd huge dismay,
Where yet unpawn'd, much learned lumber lay,
Volumes, whose size the space exactly fill'd;
Or which fond authors were so good to gild;
Or where, by sculpture made for ever known,
The page admires new beauties, not its own.
Here swells the shelf with Ogilby the great:
There, stamp'd with arms, Newcastle shines compleat,
Here all his suff'ring brotherhood retire,
And 'scape the martyrdom of jakes and fire;
A Gothic Vatican! of Greece and Rome
Well-purg'd, and worthy Withers, Quarles, and Blome.
But high above, more solid Learning shone,
The Classicks of an Age that heard of none;
There Caxton slept, with Wynkin at his side,
One clasp'd in wood, and one in strong cow-hide.
There sav'd by spice, like mummies, many a year,
Old Bodies of Philosophy appear.
De Lyra here a dreadful front extends,
And there, the groaning shelves Philemon bends.
Of these twelve volumes, twelve of amplest size,
Redeem'd from tapers and defrauded pyes,
Inspir'd he seizes: These an altar raise:
An hecatomb of pure, unsully'd lays
That altar crowns: A folio Common-place
Founds the whole pyle, of all his works the base;
Quarto's, Octavo's, shape the less'ning pyre,
And last, a little Ajax tips the spire.
Then he. Great Tamer of all human art!
First in my care, and nearest at my heart:
Dulness! whose good old cause I yet defend,
With whom my Muse began, with whom shall end!
O thou, of business the directing soul,
To human heads like byass to the bowl,
Which as more pond'rous makes their aim more true,
Obliquely wadling to the mark in view.
O ever gracious to perplex'd mankind!
Who spread a healing mist before the mind,
And, lest we err by Wit's wild, dancing light,

Secure us kindly in our native night.
Ah! still o'er Britain stretch that peaceful wand,
Which lulls th' Helvetian and Batavian land.
Where rebel to thy throne if Science rise,
She does but shew her coward face and dies:
There, thy good Scholiasts with unweary'd pains
Make Horace flat, and humble Maro's strains;
Here studious I unlucky moderns save,
Nor sleeps one error in its father's grave,
Old puns restore, lost blunders nicely seek,
And crucify poor Shakespear once a week.
For thee I dim these eyes, and stuff this head,
With all such reading as was never read;
For thee supplying, in the worst of days,
Notes to dull books, and prologues to dull plays;
For thee explain a thing till all men doubt it,
And write about it, Goddess, and about it;
So spins the silkworm small its slender store,
And labours, 'till it clouds itself all o'er.
Not that my quill to Critiques was confin'd,
My Verse gave ampler lessons to mankind;
So gravest precepts may successless prove,
But sad examples never fail to move.
As forc'd from wind-guns, lead itself can fly,
And pond'rous slugs cut swiftly thro' the sky;
As clocks to weight their nimble motion owe,
The wheels above urg'd by the load below;
Me, Emptiness and Dulness could inspire,
And were my Elasticity and Fire.
Had heav'n decreed such works a longer date,
Heav'n had decreed to spare the Grubstreet-state.
But see great Settle to the dust descend,
And all thy cause and empire at an end!
Cou'd Troy be sav'd by any single hand,
His gray-goose-weapon must have made her stand.
But what can I? my Flaccus cast aside,
Take up th' Attorney's (once my better) Guide?
Or rob the Roman geese of all their glories,
And save the state by cackling to the Tories?
Yes, to my Country I my pen consign,
Yes, from this moment, mighty Mist! am thine,
And rival, Curtius! of thy fame and zeal,
O'er head and ears plunge for the publick weal.
Adieu my children! better thus expire
Un-stall'd, unsold; thus glorious mount in fire
Fair without spot; than greas'd by grocer's hands,
Or shipp'd with Ward to ape and monkey lands,
Or wafting ginger, round the streets to go,

And visit alehouse where ye first did grow.
  With that, he lifted thrice the sparkling brand,
And thrice he dropt it from his quiv'ring hand:
Then lights the structure, with averted eyes;
The rowling smokes involve the sacrifice.
The opening clouds disclose each work by turns,
Now flames old Memnon, now Rodrigo burns,
In one quick flash see Proserpine expire,
And last, his own cold Æschylus took fire.
Then gush'd the tears, as from the Trojan's eyes
When the last blaze sent Ilion to the skies.
  Rowz'd by the light, old Dulness heav'd the head,
Then snatch'd a sheet of Thulè from her bed;
Sudden she flies, and whelms it o'er the pyre:
Down sink the flames, and with a hiss expire.
  Her ample presence fills up all the place;
A veil of fogs dilates her awful face;
Great in her charms! as when on Shrieves and May'rs
She looks, and breathes her self into their airs.
She bids him wait her to the sacred Dome;
Well-pleas'd he enter'd, and confess'd his Home:
So spirits ending their terrestrial race,
Ascend, and recognize their native place:
Raptur'd, he gazes round the dear retreat,
And in sweet numbers celebrates the seat.
  Here to her Chosen all her works she shows;
Prose swell'd to verse, Verse loitring into prose;
How random Thoughts now meaning chance to find,
Now leave all memory of sense behind:
How Prologues into Prefaces decay,
And these to Notes are fritter'd quite away.
How Index-learning turns no student pale,
Yet holds the Eel of science by the Tail.
How, with less reading than makes felons 'scape,
Less human genius than God gives an ape,
Small thanks to France and none to Rome or Greece,
A past, vamp'd, future, old, reviv'd, new piece,
'Twixt Plautus, Fletcher, Congreve, and Corneille,
Can make a Cibber, Johnson, or Ozell.
  The Goddess then, o'er his anointed head,
With mystic words, the sacred Opium shed;
And lo! her Bird (a monster of a fowl!
Something betwixt a H*** and Owl)
Perch'd on his crown. All hail! and hail again,
My Son! the promis'd land expects thy reign.
Know, Settle, cloy'd with custard and with praise,
Is gather'd to the Dull of antient days,
Safe, where no criticks damn, no duns molest,

Where Gildon, Banks, and high-born Howard rest.
I see a King! who leads my chosen sons
To lands, that flow with clenches and with puns:
'Till each fam'd Theatre my empire own,
'Till Albion, as Hibernia, bless my throne!
I see! I see!—Then rapt, she spoke no more.
God save King Tibbald! Grubstreet alleys roar.
So when Jove's block descended from on high,
(As sings thy great fore-father, Ogilby,)
Loud thunder to its bottom shook the bog,
And the hoarse nation croak'd, God save King Log!

Ode: The Dying Christian to his Soul[1]

Vital spark of heav'nly flame!
Quit, oh quit this mortal frame:
Trembling, hoping, ling'ring, flying,
Oh the pain, the bliss of dying!
Cease, fond Nature, cease thy strife,
And let me languish into life.

Hark! they whisper; Angels say,
Sister Spirit, come away.
What is this absorbs me quite?
Steals my senses, shuts my sight,
Drowns my spirits, draws my breath?
Tell me, my Soul, can this be Death?

The world recedes; it disappears!
Heav'n opens on my eyes! my ears
With sounds seraphic ring:
Lend, lend your wings! I mount! I fly!
O Grave! where is thy Victory?
O Death! where is thy Sting?

Epitaph V

On Mrs. Corbet, Who Dyed of a Cancer in her Breast[2]

Here rests a Woman, good without pretence,
Blest with plain Reason and with sober Sense;

[1] Published in *Miscellaneous Poems*, May 5, 1730. Text of *Works*, 1736.
[2] Published in *Miscellaneous Poems*, May 5, 1730. Text of *Works*, 1735.

No Conquests she, but o'er herself desir'd,
No Arts essay'd, but not to be admir'd.
Passion and Pride were to her soul unknown,
Convinc'd, that Virtue only is our own.
So unaffected, so compos'd a mind,
So firm yet soft, so strong yet so refin'd,
Heav'n, as its purest Gold, by Tortures try'd;
The Saint sustain'd it, but the Woman dy'd.

Epitaph XII

Intended for Sir Isaac Newton, in Westminster-Abbey[1]

ISAACUS NEWTONUS:
Quem Immortalem
Testantur *Tempus, Natura, Cœlum:*
Mortalem
Hoc marmor fatetur.

NATURE and Nature's Laws lay hid in Night:
GOD said, *Let Newton be!* and all was Light.

Epigram II[2]

SHOULD D——s print, how once you robb'd your brother
Traduc'd your monarch, and debauch'd your mother;
Say, what revenge on D——s can be had;
Too dull for laughter, for reply too mad?

Epigram on the Toasts of the Kit-Kat Club, Anno 1716[3]

WHENCE deathless *Kit-Cat* took its name,
Few critics can unriddle;

[1] Published in *The Grub-street Journal*, July 16, 1730. Text of *Works*, 1751.
[2] Published in *The Grub-street Journal*, July 1, 1731. Text of *Works*, 1751.
[3] Published in *Miscellanies, The Third Volume*, October 4, 1732. Text of *Works*, 1751.

Some say from Pastry-cook it came,
And some from Cat and Fiddle.
From no trim beaux its name it boasts,
Gray statesmen or green wits;
But from this pell-mell pack of toasts
Of old "Cats" and young "Kits."

An Essay on Man, in Four Epistles, to H. St. John, Lord Bolingbroke[1]

Epistle I[2]

AWAKE, my ST JOHN! leave all meaner things
To low ambition, and the pride of Kings.
Let us (since Life can little more supply
Than just to look about us and to die)
Expatiate free o'er all this scene of Man;
A mighty maze! but not without a plan;
A Wild, where weeds and flow'rs promiscuous shoot;
Or Garden, tempting with forbidden fruit.
Together let us beat this ample field,
Try what the open, what the covert yield;
The latent tracts, the giddy heights, explore
Of all who blindly creep, or sightless soar;
Eye Nature's walks, shoot Folly as it flies,
And catch the Manners living as they rise;
Laugh where we must, be candid where we can;
But vindicate the ways of God to Man.
I. Say first, of God above, or Man below,
What can we reason, but from what we know?
Of Man, what see we but his station here,
From which to reason, or to which refer?
Thro' worlds unnumber'd tho' the God be known,
'Tis ours to trace him only in our own.
He, who thro' vast immensity can pierce,
See worlds on worlds compose one universe,
Observe how system into system runs,
What other Planets circle other suns,
What vary'd Being peoples ev'ry star,
May tell why Heav'n has made us as we are.
But of this frame the bearings, and the ties,
The strong connections, nice dependencies,
Gradations just, has thy pervading soul

[1] Published 1733-34. Text of *Works*, 1751.
[2] Published February 20, 1733.

Look'd thro'? or can a part contain the whole?
  Is the great chain, that draws all to agree,
And drawn supports, upheld by God, or thee?
  II. Presumptuous Man! the reason wouldst thou find,
Why form'd so weak, so little, and so blind?
First, if thou canst, the harder reason guess,
Why form'd no weaker, blinder, and no less?
Ask of thy mother earth, why oaks are made
Taller or stronger than the weeds they shade?
Or ask of yonder argent fields above,
Why JOVE's Satellites are less than JOVE?
  Of Systems possible, if 'tis confest
That Wisdom infinite must form the best,
Where all must full or not coherent be,
And all that rises, rise in due degree;
Then, in the scale of reas'ning life, 'tis plain,
There must be, somewhere, such a rank as Man:
And all the question (wrangle e'er so long)
Is only this, if God has plac'd him wrong?
  Respecting Man, whatever wrong we call,
May, must be right, as relative to all.
In human works, tho' labour'd on with pain,
A thousand movements scarce one purpose gain;
In God's, one single can it's end produce;
Yet serves to second too some other use.
So Man, who here seems principal alone,
Perhaps acts second to some sphere unknown,
Touches some wheel, or verges to some goal;
'Tis but a part we see, and not a whole.
  When the proud steed shall know why Man restrains
His fiery course, or drives him o'er the plains;
When the dull Ox, why now he breaks the clod,
Is now a victim, and now Ægypt's God:
Then shall Man's pride and dulness comprehend
His actions', passions', being's, use and end;
Why doing, suff'ring, check'd, impell'd; and why
This hour a slave, the next a deity.
  Then say not Man's imperfect, Heav'n in fault;
Say rather, Man's as perfect as he ought:
His knowledge measur'd to his state and place;
His time a moment, and a point his space.
If to be perfect in a certain sphere,
What matter, soon or late, or here or there?
The blest today is as completely so,
As who began a thousand years ago.
  III. Heav'n from all creatures hides the book of Fate,
All but the page prescrib'd, their present state:
From brutes what men, from men what spirits know:

Or who could suffer Being here below?
The lamb thy riot dooms to bleed to-day,
Had he thy Reason, would he skip and play?
Pleas'd to the last, he crops the flow'ry food,
And licks the hand just rais'd to shed his blood.
Oh blindness to the future! kindly given,
That each may fill the circle mark'd by Heav'n:
Who sees with equal eye, as God of all,
A hero perish, or a sparrow fall,
Atoms or systems into ruin hurl'd,
And now a bubble burst, and now a world.
  Hope humbly then; with trembling pinions soar;
Wait the great teacher Death: and God adore.
What future bliss, he gives not thee to know,
But gives that Hope to be thy blessing now.
Hope springs eternal in the human breast:
Man never Is, but always To be blest:
The soul, uneasy and confin'd from home,
Rests and expatiates in a life to come.
  Lo, the poor Indian! whose untutor'd mind
Sees God in clouds, or hears him in the wind;
His soul, proud Science never taught to stray
Far as the solar walk, or milky way;
Yet simple Nature to his hope has giv'n,
Behind the cloud-topt hill, an humbler heav'n;
Some safer world in depth of woods embrac'd,
Some happier island in the wat'ry waste,
Where slaves once more their native land behold,
No fiends torment, no Christians thirst for gold.
To Be, contents his natural desire,
He asks no Angel's wing, no Seraph's fire;
But thinks, admitted to that equal sky,
His faithful dog shall bear him company.
  IV. Go, wiser thou! and, in thy scale of sense,
Weigh thy Opinion against Providence;
Call imperfection what thou fancy'st such,
Say, here he gives too little, there too much:
Destroy all creatures for thy sport or gust,
Yet cry, If Man's unhappy, God's unjust;
If Man alone ingross not Heav'n's high care,
Alone made perfect here, immortal there:
Snatch from his hand the balance and the rod,
Re-judge his justice, be the GOD of GOD.
In Pride, in reas'ning Pride, our error lies;
All quit their sphere, and rush into the skies.
Pride still is aiming at the blest abodes,
Men would be Angels, Angels would be Gods.
Aspiring to be Gods, if Angels fell,

Aspiring to be Angels, Men rebel:
And who but wishes to invert the laws
Of Order, sins against th' Eternal Cause.
  V. Ask for what end the heav'nly bodies shine,
Earth for whose use? Pride answers, "'Tis for mine:
"For me kind Nature wakes her genial pow'r,
"Suckles each herb, and spreads out ev'ry flow'r;
"Annual for me, the grape, the rose, renew,
"The juice nectareous, and the balmy dew;
"For me, the mine a thousand treasures brings;
"For me, health gushes from a thousand springs;
"Seas roll to waft me, suns to light me rise;
"My foot-stool earth, my canopy the skies."
  But errs not Nature from this gracious end,
From burning suns when livid deaths descend,
When earthquakes swallow, or when tempests sweep
Towns to one grave, whole nations to the deep?
"No ('tis reply'd) the first Almighty Cause
"Acts not by partial, but by gen'ral laws;
"Th' exceptions few; some change since all began:
"And what created perfect?"—Why then Man?
If the great end be human Happiness,
Then Nature deviates; and can Man do less?
As much that end a constant course requires
Of show'rs and sun-shine, as of Man's desires;
As much eternal springs and cloudless skies,
As Men for ever temp'rate, calm, and wise.
If plagues or earthquakes break not Heav'n's design,
Why then a Borgia, or a Catiline?
Who knows but he, whose hand the light'ning forms,
Who heaves old Ocean, and who wings the storms;
Pours fierce Ambition in a Cæsar's mind,
Or turns young Ammon loose to scourge mankind?
From pride, from pride, our very reas'ning springs;
Account for moral, as for nat'ral things:
Why charge we Heav'n in those, in these acquit?
In both, to reason right is to submit.
  Better for Us, perhaps, it might appear,
Were there all harmony, all virtue here;
That never air or ocean felt the wind;
That never passion discompos'd the mind.
But ALL subsists by elemental strife;
And Passions are the elements of Life.
The gen'ral Order, since the whole began,
Is kept in Nature, and is kept in Man.
  VI. What would this Man? Now upward will he soar,
And little less than Angel, would be more;
Now looking downwards, just as griev'd appears

To want the strength of bulls, the fur of bears.
Made for his use all creatures if he call,
Say what their use, had he the pow'rs of all?
Nature to these, without profusion, kind,
The proper organs, proper pow'rs assign'd;
Each seeming want compensated of course,
Here with degrees of swiftness, there of force;
All in exact proportion to the state;
Nothing to add, and nothing to abate.
Each beast, each insect, happy in it's own:
Is Heav'n unkind to Man, and Man alone?
Shall he alone, whom rational we call,
Be pleas'd with nothing, if not bless'd with all?
  The bliss of Man (could Pride that blessing find)
Is not to act or think beyond mankind;
No pow'rs of body or of soul to share,
But what his nature and his state can bear.
Why has not Man a microscopic eye?
For this plain reason, Man is not a Fly.
Say what the use, were finer optics giv'n,
T' inspect a mite, not comprehend the heav'n?
Or touch, if tremblingly alive all o'er,
To smart and agonize at ev'ry pore?
Or quick effluvia darting thro' the brain,
Die of a rose in aromatic pain?
If nature thunder'd in his op'ning ears,
And stunn'd him with the music of the spheres,
How would he wish that Heav'n had left him still
The whisp'ring Zephyr, and the purling rill?
Who finds not Providence all good and wise,
Alike in what it gives, and what denies?
  VII. Far as Creation's ample range extends,
The scale of sensual, mental pow'rs ascends:
Mark how it mounts, to Man's imperial race,
From the green myriads in the peopled grass:
What modes of sight betwixt each wide extreme,
The mole's dim curtain, and the lynx's beam:
Of smell, the headlong lioness between,
And hound sagacious on the tainted green:
Of hearing, from the life that fills the flood,
To that which warbles thro' the vernal wood:
The spider's touch, how exquisitely fine!
Feels at each thread, and lives along the line:
In the nice bee, what sense so subtly true
From pois'nous herbs extracts the healing dew?
How Instinct varies in the grov'ling swine,
Compar'd, half-reas'ning elephant, with thine!
'Twixt that, and Reason, what a nice barrier;

For ever sep'rate, yet for ever near!
Remembrance and Reflection how ally'd;
What thin partitions Sense from Thought divide:
And Middle natures, how they long to join,
Yet never pass th' insuperable line!
Without this just gradation, could they be
Subjected, these to those, or all to thee?
The pow'rs of all subdu'd by thee alone,
Is not thy Reason all these pow'rs in one?
VIII. See, thro' this air, this ocean, and this earth,
All matter quick, and bursting into birth.
Above, how high, progressive life may go!
Around, how wide! how deep extend below!
Vast chain of Being! which from God began,
Natures æthereal, human, angel, man,
Beast, bird, fish, insect, what no eye can see,
No glass can reach; from Infinite to thee,
From thee to Nothing.—On superior pow'rs
Were we to press, inferior might on ours:
Or in the full creation leave a void,
Where, one step broken, the great scale's destroy'd:
From Nature's chain whatever link you strike,
Tenth or ten thousandth, breaks the chain alike.
And, if each system in gradation roll
Alike essential to th' amazing Whole,
The least confusion but in one, not all
That system only, but the Whole must fall.
Let Earth unbalanc'd from her orbit fly,
Planets and Suns run lawless thro' the sky;
Let ruling Angels from their spheres be hurl'd,
Being on Being wreck'd, and world on world;
Heav'n's whole foundations to their centre nod,
And Nature trembles to the throne of God.
All this dread ORDER break—for whom? for thee?
Vile worm!—oh Madness! Pride! Impiety!
IX. What if the foot, ordain'd the dust to tread,
Or hand, to toil, aspir'd to be the head?
What if the head, the eye, or ear repin'd
To serve mere engines to the ruling Mind?
Just as absurd for any part to claim
To be another, in this gen'ral frame:
Just as absurd, to mourn the tasks or pains,
The great directing MIND of ALL ordains.
All are but parts of one stupendous whole,
Whose body Nature is, and God the soul;
That, chang'd thro' all, and yet in all the same;
Great in the earth, as in th' æthereal frame;
Warms in the sun, refreshes in the breeze,

Glows in the stars, and blossoms in the trees,
Lives thro' all life, extends thro' all extent,
Spreads undivided, operates unspent;
Breathes in our soul, informs our mortal part,
As full, as perfect, in a hair as heart;
As full, as perfect, in vile Man that mourns,
As the rapt Seraph that adores and burns:
To him no high, no low, no great, no small;
He fills, he bounds, connects, and equals all.
X. Cease then, nor ORDER Imperfection name:
Our proper bliss depends on what we blame.
Know thy own point: This kind, this due degree
Of blindness, weakness, Heav'n bestows on thee.
Submit.—In this, or any other sphere,
Secure to be as blest as thou canst bear:
Safe in the hand of one disposing Pow'r,
Or in the natal, or the mortal hour.
All Nature is but Art, unknown to thee;
All Chance, Direction, which thou canst not see;
All Discord, Harmony not understood;
All partial Evil, universal Good:
And, spite of Pride, in erring Reason's spite,
One truth is clear, WHATEVER IS, IS RIGHT.

Epistle II[1]

I. KNOW then thyself, presume not God to scan;
The proper study of Mankind is Man.
Plac'd on this isthmus of a middle state,
A Being darkly wise, and rudely great:
With too much knowledge for the Sceptic side,
With too much weakness for the Stoic's pride,
He hangs between; in doubt to act, or rest;
In doubt to deem himself a God, or Beast;
In doubt his Mind or Body to prefer;
Born but to die, and reas'ning but to err;
Alike in ignorance, his reason such,
Whether he thinks too little, or too much:
Chaos of Thought and Passion, all confus'd;
Still by himself abus'd, or disabus'd;
Created half to rise, and half to fall;
Great lord of all things, yet a prey to all;
Sole judge of Truth, in endless Error hurl'd:
The glory, jest, and riddle of the world!
Go, wond'rous creature! mount where Science guides,
Go, measure earth, weigh air, and state the tides;
Instruct the planets in what orbs to run,

[1] Published March 29, 1733.

Correct old Time, and regulate the Sun;
Go, soar with Plato to th' empyreal sphere,
To the first good, first perfect, and first fair;
Or tread the mazy round his follow'rs trod,
And quitting sense call imitating God;
As Eastern priests in giddy circles run,
And turn their heads to imitate the Sun.
Go, teach Eternal Wisdom how to rule—
Then drop into thyself, and be a fool!
  Superior beings, when of late they saw
A mortal Man unfold all Nature's law,
Admir'd such wisdom in an earthly shape,
And shew'd a NEWTON as we shew an Ape.
  Could he, whose rules the rapid Comet bind,
Describe or fix one movement of his Mind?
Who saw it's fires here rise, and there descend,
Explain his own beginning, or his end?
Alas what wonder! Man's superior part
Uncheck'd may rise, and climb from art to art;
But when his own great work is but begun,
What Reason weaves, by Passion is undone.
  Trace Science then, with Modesty thy guide;
First strip off all her equipage of Pride;
Deduct what is but Vanity, or Dress,
Or Learning's Luxury, or Idleness;
Or tricks to shew the stretch of human brain,
Mere curious pleasure, or ingenious pain;
Expunge the whole, or lop th' excrescent parts
Of all our Vices have created Arts;
Then see how little the remaining sum,
Which serv'd the past, and must the times to come!
  II. Two Principles in human nature reign;
Self-love, to urge, and Reason, to restrain;
Nor this a good, nor that a bad we call,
Each works it's end, to move or govern all:
And to their proper operation still,
Ascribe all Good; to their improper, Ill.
  Self-love, the spring of motion, acts the soul;
Reason's comparing balance rules the whole.
Man, but for that, no action could attend,
And, but for this, were active to no end:
Fix'd like a plant on his peculiar spot,
To draw nutrition, propagate, and rot;
Or, meteor-like, flame lawless thro' the void,
Destroying others, by himself destroy'd.
  Most strength the moving principle requires;
Active its task, it prompts, impels, inspires.
Sedate and quiet the comparing lies,

Form'd but to check, delib'rate, and advise.
Self-love still stronger, as its objects nigh;
Reason's at distance, and in prospect lie:
That sees immediate good by present sense;
Reason, the future and the consequence.
Thicker than arguments, temptations throng,
At best more watchful this, but that more strong.
The action of the stronger to suspend
Reason still use, to Reason still attend.
Attention, habit and experience gains;
Each strengthens Reason, and Self-love restrains.
Let subtle schoolmen teach these friends to fight,
More studious to divide than to unite;
And Grace and Virtue, Sense and Reason split,
With all the rash dexterity of wit.
Wits, just like Fools, at war about a name,
Have full as oft no meaning, or the same.
Self-love and Reason to one end aspire,
Pain their aversion, Pleasure their desire;
But greedy That, its object would devour,
This taste the honey, and not wound the flow'r:
Pleasure, or wrong or rightly understood,
Our greatest evil, or our greatest good.
III. Modes of Self-love the Passions we may call:
'Tis real good, or seeming, moves them all:
But since not ev'ry good we can divide,
And Reason bids us for our own provide;
Passions, tho' selfish, if their means be fair,
List under Reason, and deserve her care;
Those, that imparted, court a nobler aim,
Exalt their kind, and take some Virtue's name.
In lazy Apathy let Stoics boast
Their Virtue fix'd; 'tis fix'd as in a frost;
Contracted all, retiring to the breast;
But strength of mind is Exercise, not Rest:
The rising tempest puts in act the soul,
Parts it may ravage, but preserves the whole.
On life's vast ocean diversely we sail,
Reason the card, but Passion is the gale;
Nor God alone in the still calm we find,
He mounts the storm, and walks upon the wind.
Passions, like Elements, tho' born to fight,
Yet, mix'd and soften'd, in his work unite:
These 'tis enough to temper and employ;
But what composes Man, can Man destroy?
Suffice that Reason keep to Nature's road,
Subject, compound them, follow her and God.
Love, Hope, and Joy, fair pleasure's smiling train,

Hate, Fear, and Grief, the family of pain,
These mix'd with art, and to due bounds confin'd,
Make and maintain the balance of the mind:
The lights and shades, whose well accorded strife
Gives all the strength and colour of our life.
  Pleasures are ever in our hands or eyes;
And when, in act, they cease, in prospect, rise:
Present to grasp, and future still to find,
The whole employ of body and of mind.
All spread their charms, but charm not all alike;
On diff'rent senses diff'rent objects strike;
Hence diff'rent Passions more or less inflame,
As strong or weak, the organs of the frame;
And hence one MASTER PASSION in the breast,
Like Aaron's serpent, swallows up the rest.
  As Man, perhaps, the moment of his breath,
Receives the lurking principle of death;
The young disease, that must subdue at length,
Grows with his growth, and strengthens with his strength:
So, cast and mingled with his very frame,
The Mind's disease, its RULING PASSION came;
Each vital humour which should feed the whole,
Soon flows to this, in body and in soul:
Whatever warms the heart, or fills the head,
As the mind opens, and its functions spread,
Imagination plies her dang'rous art,
And pours it all upon the peccant part.
  Nature its mother, Habit is its nurse;
Wit, Spirit, Faculties, but make it worse;
Reason itself but gives it edge and pow'r;
As Heav'n's blest beam turns vinegar more sowr;
  We, wretched subjects tho' to lawful sway,
In this weak queen, some fav'rite still obey:
Ah! if she lend not arms, as well as rules,
What can she more than tell us we are fools?
Teach us to mourn our Nature, not to mend,
A sharp accuser, but a helpless friend!
Or from a judge turn pleader, to persuade
The choice we make, or justify it made;
Proud of an easy conquest all along,
She but removes weak passions for the strong:
So, when small humours gather to a gout,
The doctor fancies he has driv'n them out.
  Yes, Nature's road must ever be preferr'd;
Reason is here no guide, but still a guard:
'Tis her's to rectify, not overthrow,
And treat this passion more as friend than foe:
A mightier Pow'r the strong direction sends,

And sev'ral Men impels to sev'ral ends:
Like varying winds, by other passions tost,
This drives them constant to a certain coast.
Let pow'r or knowledge, gold or glory, please,
Or (oft more strong than all) the love of ease;
Thro' life 'tis follow'd, ev'n at life's expence;
The merchant's toil, the sage's indolence,
The monk's humility, the hero's pride,
All, all alike, find Reason on their side.
Th' Eternal Art educing good from ill,
Grafts on this Passion our best principle:
'Tis thus the Mercury of Man is fix'd,
Strong grows the Virtue with his nature mix'd;
The dross cements what else were too refin'd,
And in one interest body acts with mind.
As fruits, ungrateful to the planter's care,
On savage stocks inserted, learn to bear;
The surest Virtues thus from Passions shoot,
Wild Nature's vigor working at the root.
What crops of wit and honesty appear
From spleen, from obstinacy, hate, or fear!
See anger, zeal and fortitude supply;
Ev'n av'rice, prudence; sloth, philosophy;
Lust, thro' some certain strainers well refin'd,
Is gentle love, and charms all womankind;
Envy, to which th' ignoble mind's a slave,
Is emulation in the learn'd or brave;
Nor Virtue, male or female, can we name,
But what will grow on Pride, or grow on Shame.
Thus Nature gives us (let it check our pride)
The virtue nearest to our vice ally'd:
Reason the byas turns to good from ill,
And Nero reigns a Titus, if he will.
The fiery soul abhorr'd in Catiline,
In Decius charms, in Curtius is divine:
The same ambition can destroy or save,
And makes a patriot as it makes a knave.
This light and darkness in our chaos join'd,
What shall divide? The God within the mind.
Extremes in Nature equal ends produce,
In Man they join to some mysterious use;
Tho' each by turns the other's bound invade,
As, in some well-wrought Picture, light and shade,
And oft so mix, the diff'rence is too nice
Where ends the Virtue, or begins the Vice.
Fools! who from hence into the notion fall,
That Vice or Virtue there is none at all.
If white and black blend, soften, and unite

A thousand ways, is there no black or white?
Ask your own heart, and nothing is so plain;
'Tis to mistake them, costs the time and pain.
 Vice is a monster of so frightful mien,
As, to be hated, needs but to be seen;
Yet seen too oft, familiar with her face,
We first endure, then pity, then embrace.
But where th' Extreme of Vice, was ne'er agreed:
Ask where's the North? at York, 'tis on the Tweed;
In Scotland, at the Orcades; and there,
At Greenland, Zembla, or the Lord knows where.
No creature owns it in the first degree,
But thinks his neighbour farther gone than he;
Ev'n those who dwell beneath its very zone,
Or never feel the rage, or never own;
What happier natures shrink at with affright,
The hard inhabitant contends is right.
 Virtuous and vicious ev'ry Man must be,
Few in th' extreme, but all in the degree;
The rogue and fool by fits, is fair and wise;
And ev'n the best, by fits, what they despise.
'Tis but by parts we follow good or ill;
For, Vice or Virtue, Self directs it still;
Each individual seeks a sev'ral goal;
But HEAV'N's great view is One, and that the Whole.
That counter-works each folly and caprice;
That disappoints th' effect of ev'ry vice;
That, happy frailties to all ranks apply'd;
Shame to the virgin, to the matron pride,
Fear to the statesman, rashness to the chief,
To kings presumption, and to crowds belief:
That, Virtue's ends from Vanity can raise,
Which seeks no int'rest, no reward but praise;
And build on wants, and on defects of mind,
The joy, the peace, the glory of Mankind.
 Heav'n forming each on other to depend,
A master, or a servant, or a friend,
Bids each on other for assistance call,
'Till one Man's weakness grows the strength of all.
Wants, frailties, passions, closer still ally
The common int'rest, or endear the tie.
To these we owe true friendship, love sincere,
Each home-felt joy that life inherits here;
Yet from the same we learn, in its decline,
Those joys, those loves, those int'rests to resign;
Taught half by Reason, half by mere decay,
To welcome death, and calmly pass away.
Whate'er the Passion, knowledge, fame, or pelf,

Not one will change his neighbour with himself.
The learn'd is happy nature to explore,
The fool is happy that he knows no more;
The rich is happy in the plenty giv'n,
The poor contents him with the care of Heav'n.
See the blind beggar dance, the cripple sing,
The sot a hero, lunatic a king;
The starving chemist in his golden views
Supremely blest, the poet in his muse.
See some strange comfort ev'ry state attend,
And Pride bestow'd on all, a common friend;
See some fit Passion, ev'ry age supply,
Hope travels thro', nor quits us when we die.
Behold the child, by Nature's kindly law,
Pleas'd with a rattle, tickled with a straw:
Some livelier play-thing gives his youth delight,
A little louder, but as empty quite:
Scarfs, garters, gold, amuse his riper stage;
And beads and pray'r-books are the toys of age:
Pleas'd with this bauble still, as that before;
'Till tir'd he sleeps, and Life's poor play is o'er.
Mean-while Opinion gilds with varying rays
Those painted clouds that beautify our days;
Each want of happiness by Hope supply'd,
And each vacuity of sense by Pride:
These build as fast as knowledge can destroy;
In Folly's cup still laughs the bubble, joy;
One prospect lost, another still we gain;
And not a vanity is giv'n in vain;
Ev'n mean Self-love becomes, by force divine,
The scale to measure others wants by thine.
See! and confess, one comfort still must rise,
'Tis this, Tho' Man's a fool, yet GOD IS WISE.

Epistle III[1]

HERE then we rest: "The Universal Cause
"Acts to one end, but acts by various laws."
In all the madness of superfluous health,
The trim of pride, the impudence of wealth,
Let this great truth be present night and day;
But most be present, if we preach or pray.
Look round our World; behold the chain of Love
Combining all below and all above.
See plastic Nature working to this end,
The single atoms each to other tend,
Attract, attracted to, the next in place

[1] Published May 17, 1733.

Form'd and impell'd its neighbour to embrace.
See Matter next, with various life endu'd,
Press to one centre still, the gen'ral Good.
See dying vegetables life sustain,
See life dissolving vegetate again:
All forms that perish other forms supply,
(By turns we catch the vital breath, and die)
Like bubbles on the sea of Matter born,
They rise, they break, and to that sea return.
Nothing is foreign: Parts relate to whole;
One all-extending, all-preserving Soul
Connects each being, greatest with the least;
Made Beast in aid of Man, and Man of Beast;
All serv'd, all serving: nothing stands alone;
The chains holds on, and where it ends, unknown.
  Has God, thou fool! work'd solely for thy good,
Thy joy, thy pastime, thy attire, thy food?
Who for thy table feeds the wanton fawn,
For him as kindly spread the flow'ry lawn:
Is it for thee the lark ascends and sings?
Joy tunes his voice, joy elevates his wings.
Is it for thee the linnet pours his throat?
Loves of his own and raptures swell the note.
The bounding steed you pompously bestride,
Shares with his lord the pleasure and the pride.
Is thine alone the seed that strews the plain?
The birds of heav'n shall vindicate their grain.
Thine the full harvest of the golden year?
Part pays, and justly, the deserving steer:
The hog, that plows not nor obeys thy call,
Lives on the labours of this lord of all.
  Know, Nature's children all divide her care;
The fur that warms a monarch, warm'd a bear.
While Man exclaims, "See all things for my use!"
"See man for mine!" replies a pamper'd goose:
And just as short of reason He must fall,
Who thinks all made for one, not one for all.
  Grant that the pow'rful still the weak controul;
Be Man the Wit and Tyrant of the whole:
Nature that Tyrant checks; He only knows,
And helps another creature's wants and woes.
Say, will the falcon, stooping from above,
Smit with her varying plumage, spare the dove?
Admires the jay the insect's gilded wings?
Or hears the hawk when Philomela sings?
Man cares for all: to birds he gives his woods,
To beasts his pastures, and to fish his floods;
For some his Int'rest prompts him to provide,

For more his pleasure, yet for more his pride:
All feed on one vain Patron, and enjoy
Th' extensive blessing of his luxury.
That very life his learned hunger craves,
He saves from famine, from the savage saves;
Nay, feasts the animal he dooms his feast,
And, 'till he ends the being, makes it blest;
Which sees no more the stroke, or feels the pain,
Than favour'd Man by touch etherial slain.
The creature had his feast of life before;
Thou too must perish, when thy feast is o'er!
To each unthinking being, Heav'n a friend,
Gives not the useless knowledge of its end:
To Man imparts it; but with such a view
As, while he dreads it, makes him hope it too:
The hour conceal'd, and so remote the fear,
Death still draws nearer, never seeming near.
Great standing miracle! that Heav'n assign'd
Its only thinking thing this turn of mind.
II. Whether with Reason, or with Instinct blest,
Know, all enjoy that pow'r which suits them best;
To bliss alike by that direction tend,
And find the means proportion'd to their end.
Say, where full Instinct is th' unerring guide,
What Pope or Council can they need beside?
Reason, however able, cool at best,
Cares not for service, or but serves when prest,
Stays 'till we call, and then not often near;
But honest Instinct comes a volunteer,
Sure never to o'er-shoot, but just to hit;
While still too wide or short is human Wit;
Sure by quick Nature happiness to gain,
Which heavier Reason labours at in vain.
This too serves always, Reason never long;
One must go right, the other may go wrong.
See then the acting and comparing pow'rs
One in their nature, which are two in ours;
And Reason rise o'er Instinct as you can,
In this 'tis God directs, in that 'tis Man.
Who taught the nations of the field and wood
To shun their poison, and to chuse their food?
Prescient, the tides or tempests to withstand,
Build on the wave, or arch beneath the sand?
Who made the spider parallels design,
Sure as De-moivre, without rule or line?
Who bid the stork, Columbus-like, explore
Heav'ns not his own, and worlds unknown before?

Who calls the council, states the certain day,
Who forms the phalanx, and who points the way?
III. God, in the nature of each being, founds
Its proper bliss, and sets its proper bounds:
But as he fram'd a Whole, the Whole to bless,
On mutual Wants built mutual Happiness:
So from the first, eternal ORDER ran,
And creature link'd to creature, man to man.
Whate'er of life all-quick'ning æther keeps,
Or breathes thro' air, or shoots beneath the deeps,
Or pours profuse on earth, one nature feeds
The vital flame, and swells the genial seeds.
Not Man alone, but all that roam the wood,
Or wing the sky, or roll along the flood,
Each loves itself, but not itself alone,
Each sex desires alike, 'till two are one.
Nor ends the pleasure with the fierce embrace;
They love themselves, a third time, in their race.
Thus beast and bird their common charge attend,
The mothers nurse it, and the sires defend;
The young dismiss'd to wander earth or air,
There stops the Instinct, and there ends the care;
The link dissolves, each seeks a fresh embrace,
Another love succeeds, another race.
A longer care Man's helpless kind demands;
That longer care contracts more lasting bands:
Reflection, Reason, still the ties improve,
At once extend the int'rest, and the love;
With choice we fix, with sympathy we burn:
Each Virtue in each Passion takes its turn;
And still new needs, new helps, new habits rise,
That graft benevolence on charities.
Still as one brood, and as another rose,
These nat'ral love maintain'd, habitual those:
The last, scarce ripen'd into perfect Man,
Saw helpless him from whom their life began:
Mem'ry and fore-cast just returns engage,
That pointed back to youth, this on to age;
While pleasure, gratitude, and hope, combin'd,
Still spread the int'rest, and preserv'd the kind.
IV. Nor think, in NATURE'S STATE they blindly trod;
The state of Nature was the reign of God:
Self-love and Social at her birth began,
Union the bond of all things, and of Man.
Pride then was not; nor Arts, that Pride to aid;
Man walk'd with beast, joint tenant of the shade;
The same his table, and the same his bed;
No murder cloath'd him, and no murder fed.

In the same temple, the resounding wood,
All vocal beings hymn'd their equal God:
The shrine with gore unstain'd, with gold undrest,
Unbrib'd, unbloody, stood the blameless priest:
Heav'n's attribute was Universal Care,
And Man's prerogative to rule, but spare.
Ah! how unlike the man of times to come!
Of half that live the butcher and the tomb;
Who, foe to Nature, hears the gen'ral groan,
Murders their species, and betrays his own.
But just disease to luxury succeeds,
And ev'ry death it's own avenger breeds;
The Fury-passions from that blood began,
And turn'd on Man a fiercer savage, Man.
  See him from Nature rising slow to Art!
To copy Instinct then was Reason's part;
Thus then to Man the voice of Nature spake—
"Go, from the Creatures thy instructions take:
"Learn from the birds what food the thickets yield;
"Learn from the beasts the physic of the field;
"Thy arts of building from the bee receive;
"Learn of the mole to plow, the worm to weave;
"Learn of the little Nautilus to sail,
"Spread the thin oar, and catch the driving gale.
"Here too all forms of social union find,
"And hence let Reason, late, instruct Mankind:
"Here subterranean works and cities see;
"There towns aerial on the waving tree.
"Learn each small People's genius, policies,
"The Ant's republic, and the realm of Bees;
"How those in common all their wealth bestow,
"And Anarchy without confusion know;
"And these for ever, tho' a Monarch reign,
"Their sep'rate cells and properties maintain.
"Mark what unvary'd laws preserve each state,
"Laws wise as Nature, and as fix'd as Fate.
"In vain thy Reason finer webs shall draw,
"Entangle Justice in her net of Law,
"And right, too rigid, harden into wrong;
"Still for the strong too weak, the weak too strong.
"Yet go! and thus o'er all the creatures sway,
"Thus let the wiser make the rest obey;
"And for those Arts mere Instinct could afford,
"Be crown'd as Monarchs, or as Gods ador'd."
  V. Great Nature spoke; observant Men obey'd;
Cities were built, Societies were made:
Here rose one little state; another near
Grew by like means, and join'd, thro' love or fear.

Did here the trees with rudier burdens bend,
And there the streams in purer rills descend?
What War could ravish, Commerce could bestow,
And he return'd a friend, who came a foe.
Converse and Love mankind might strongly draw,
When Love was Liberty, and Nature Law.
Thus States were form'd; the name of King unknown,
'Till common int'rest plac'd the sway in one.
'Twas VIRTUE ONLY (or in arts or arms,
Diffusing blessings, or averting harms)
The same which in a sire the Sons obey'd,
A Prince the Father of a People made.
VI. 'Till then, by Nature crown'd, each Patriarch sate,
King, priest, and parent of his growing state;
On him, their second Providence, they hung,
Their law his eye, their oracle his tongue.
He from the wond'ring furrow call'd the food,
Taught to command the fire, controul the flood,
Draw forth the monsters of th' abyss profound,
Or fetch th' aerial eagle to the ground.
'Till drooping, sick'ning, dying they began
Whom they rever'd as God to mourn as Man:
Then, looking up from sire to sire, explor'd
One great first father, and that first ador'd.
Or plain tradition that this All begun,
Convey'd unbroken faith from sire to son;
The worker from the work distinct was known,
And simple Reason never sought but one:
E'er Wit oblique had broke that steddy light,
Man, like his Maker, saw that all was right;
To Virtue, in the paths of Pleasure, trod,
And own'd a Father when he own'd a God.
LOVE all the faith, and all th' allegiance then;
For Nature knew no right divine in Men,
No ill could fear in God; and understood
A sov'reign being but a sov'reign good.
True faith, true policy, united ran,
That was but love of God, and this of Man.
Who first taught souls enslav'd, and realms undone,
Th' enormous faith of many made for one;
That proud exception to all Nature's laws,
T' invert the world, and counter-work its Cause?
Force first made Conquest, and that conquest, Law;
'Till Superstition taught the tyrant awe,
Then shar'd the Tyranny, then lent it aid,
And Gods of Conqu'rors, Slaves of Subjects made:
She 'midst the light'ning's blaze, and thunder's sound,
When rock'd the mountains, and when groan'd the ground,

She taught the weak to bend, the proud to pray,
To Pow'r unseen, and mightier far than they:
She, from the rending earth and bursting skies,
Saw Gods descend, and fiends infernal rise:
Here fix'd the dreadful, there the blest abodes;
Fear made her Devils, and weak Hope her Gods;
Gods partial, changeful, passionate, unjust,
Whose attributes were Rage, Revenge, or Lust;
Such as the souls of cowards might conceive,
And, form'd like tyrants, tyrants would believe.
Zeal then, not charity, became the guide;
And hell was built on spite, and heav'n on pride.
Then sacred seem'd th' etherial vault no more;
Altars grew marble then, and reek'd with gore:
Then first the Flamen tasted living food;
Next his grim idol smear'd with human blood;
With Heav'n's own thunders shook the world below,
And play'd the God an engine on his foe.
So drives Self-love, thro' just and thro' unjust,
To one Man's pow'r, ambition, lucre, lust:
The same Self-love, in all, becomes the cause
Of what restrains him, Government and Laws.
For, what one likes if others like as well,
What serves one will, when many wills rebel?
How shall he keep, what, sleeping or awake,
A weaker may surprise, a stronger take?
His safety must his liberty restrain:
All join to guard what each desires to gain.
Forc'd into virtue thus by Self-defence,
Ev'n Kings learn'd justice and benevolence:
Self-love forsook the path it first pursu'd,
And found the private in the public good.
'Twas then, the studious head or gen'rous mind,
Follow'r of God or friend of human-kind,
Poet or Patriot, rose but to restore
The Faith and Moral, Nature gave before;
Re-lum'd her ancient light, not kindled new;
If not God's image, yet his shadow drew:
Taught Pow'r's due use to People and to Kings,
Taught nor to slack, nor strain its tender strings,
The less, or greater, set so justly true,
That touching one must strike the other too;
'Till jarring int'rests, of themselves create
Th' according music of a well-mix'd State.
Such is the World's great harmony, that springs
From Order, Union, full Consent of things:
Where small and great, where weak and mighty, made
To serve, not suffer, strengthen, not invade;

More pow'rful each as needful to the rest,
And, in proportion as it blesses, blest;
Draw to one point, and to one center bring
Beast, Man, or Angel, Servant, Lord, or King.
For Forms of Government let fools contest;
Whate'er is best administer'd is best:
For Modes of Faith let graceless zealots fight;
His can't be wrong whose life is in the right:
In Faith and Hope the world will disagree,
But all Mankind's concern is Charity:
All must be false that thwart this One great End;
And all of God, that bless Mankind or mend.
Man, like the gen'rous vine, supported lives;
The strength he gains is from th' embrace he gives.
On their own Axis as the Planets run,
Yet make at once their circle round the Sun;
So two consistent motions act the Soul;
And one regards Itself, and one the Whole.
Thus God and Nature link'd the gen'ral frame,
And bade Self-love and Social be the same.

Epistle IV[1]

OH HAPPINESS! our being's end and aim!
Good, Pleasure, Ease, Content! whate'er thy name:
That something still which prompts th' eternal sigh,
For which we bear to live, or dare to die,
Which still so near us, yet beyond us lies,
O'er-look'd, seen double, by the fool, and wise.
Plant of celestial seed! if dropt below,
Say, in what mortal soil thou deign'st to grow?
Fair op'ning to some Court's propitious shine,
Or deep with di'monds in the flaming mine?
Twin'd with the wreaths Parnassian lawrels yield,
Or reap'd in iron harvests of the field?
Where grows?—where grows it not? If vain our toil,
We ought to blame the culture, not the soil:
Fix'd to no spot is Happiness sincere,
'Tis no where to be found, or ev'ry where;
'Tis never to be bought, but always free,
And fled from monarchs, ST JOHN! dwells with thee.
Ask of the Learn'd the way? The Learn'd are blind;
This bids to serve, and that to shun mankind;
Some place the bliss in action, some in ease,
Those call it Pleasure, and Contentment these;
Some sunk to Beasts, find pleasure end in pain;
Some swell'd to Gods, confess ev'n Virtue vain;

[1] Published January 24, 1734.

Or indolent, to each extreme they fall,
To trust in ev'ry thing, or doubt of all.
  Who thus define it, say they more or less
Than this, that Happiness is Happiness?
  Take Nature's path, and mad Opinion's leave;
All states can reach it, and all heads conceive;
Obvious her goods, in no extreme they dwell;
There needs but thinking right, and meaning well;
And mourn our various portions as we please,
Equal is Common Sense, and Common Ease.
  Remember, Man, "the Universal Cause
"Acts not by partial, but by gen'ral laws;"
And makes what Happiness we justly call,
Subsist not in the good of one, but all.
There's not a blessing Individuals find,
But some way leans and hearkens to the kind:
No Bandit fierce, no Tyrant mad with pride,
No cavern'd Hermit, rests self-satisfy'd:
Who most to shun or hate Mankind pretend,
Seek an admirer, or would fix a friend:
Abstract what others feel, what others think,
All pleasures sicken, and all glories sink:
Each has his share; and who would more obtain,
Shall find, the pleasure pays not half the pain.
  ORDER is Heav'n's first law; and this confest,
Some are, and must be, greater than the rest,
More rich, more wise; but who infers from hence
That such are happier, shocks all common sense.
Heav'n to Mankind impartial we confess,
If all are equal in their Happiness:
But mutual wants this Happiness increase;
All Nature's diff'rence keeps all Nature's peace.
Condition, circumstance is not the thing;
Bliss is the same in subject or in king,
In who obtain defence, or who defend,
In him who is, or him who finds a friend:
Heav'n breathes thro' ev'ry member of the whole
One common blessing, as one common soul.
But Fortune's gifts if each alike possest,
And each were equal, must not all contest?
If then to all Men Happiness was meant,
God in Externals could not place Content.
  Fortune her gifts may variously dispose,
And these be happy call'd, unhappy those;
But Heav'n's just balance equal will appear,
While those are plac'd in Hope, and these in Fear:
Not present good or ill, the joy or curse,
But future views of better, or of worse.

Oh sons of earth! attempt ye still to rise,
By mountains pil'd on mountains, to the skies?
Heav'n still with laughter the vain toil surveys,
And buries madmen in the heaps they raise.
  Know, all the good that individuals find,
Or God and Nature meant to mere Mankind,
Reason's whole pleasure, all the joys of Sense,
Lie in three words, Health, Peace, and Competence.
But Health consists with Temperance alone;
And Peace, oh Virtue! Peace is all thy own.
The good or bad the gifts of Fortune gain;
But these less taste them, as they worse obtain.
Say, in pursuit of profit or delight,
Who risk the most, that take wrong means, or right?
Of Vice or Virtue, whether blest or curst,
Which meets contempt, or which compassion first?
Count all th' advantage prosp'rous Vice attains,
'Tis but what Virtue flies from and disdains:
And grant the bad what happiness they wou'd,
One they must want, which is, to pass for good.
  Oh blind to truth, and God's whole scheme below,
Who fancy Bliss to Vice, to Virtue Woe!
Who sees and follows that great scheme the best,
Best knows the blessing, and will most be blest.
But fools, the Good alone, unhappy call,
For ills or accidents that chance to all.
See FALKLAND dies, the virtuous and the just!
See god-like TURENNE prostrate on the dust!
See SIDNEY bleeds amid the martial strife!
Was this their Virtue, or Contempt of Life?
Say, was it Virtue, more tho' Heav'n ne'er gave,
Lamented DIGBY! sunk thee to the grave?
Tell me, if Virtue made the Son expire,
Why, full of days and honour, lives the Sire?
Why drew Marseille's good bishop purer breath,
When Nature sicken'd, and each gale was death!
Or why so long (in life if long can be)
Lent Heav'n a parent to the poor and me?
  What makes all physical or moral ill?
There deviates Nature, and here wanders Will.
God sends not ill; if rightly understood,
Or partial Ill is universal Good,
Or Change admits, or Nature lets it fall;
Short, and but rare, till Man improv'd it all.
We just as wisely might of Heav'n complain
That righteous Abel was destroy'd by Cain,
As that the virtuous son is ill at ease
When his lewd father gave the dire disease.

Think we, like some weak Prince, th' Eternal Cause,
Prone for his fav'rites to reverse his laws?
  Shall burning Ætna, if a sage requires,
Forget to thunder, and recall her fires?
On air or sea new motions be imprest,
Oh blameless Bethel! to relieve thy breast?
When the loose mountain trembles from on high,
Shall gravitation cease, if you go by?
Or some old temple, nodding to its fall,
For Chartres' head reserve the hanging wall?
  But still this world (so fitted for the knave)
Contents us not. A better shall we have?
A kingdom of the Just then let it be:
But first consider how those Just agree.
The good must merit God's peculiar care;
But who, but God, can tell us who they are?
One thinks on Calvin Heav'n's own spirit fell;
Another deems him instrument of hell;
If Calvin feel Heav'n's blessing, or its rod,
This cries there is, and that, there is no God.
What shocks one part will edify the rest,
Nor with one system can they all be blest.
The very best will variously incline,
And what rewards your Virtue, punish mine.
WHATEVER IS, IS RIGHT.—This world, 'tis true,
Was made for Cæsar—but for Titus too:
And which more blest? who chain'd his country, say,
Or he whose Virtue sigh'd to lose a day?
  "But sometimes Virtue starves, while Vice is fed."
What then? Is the reward of Virtue bread?
That, Vice may merit, 'tis the price of toil;
The knave deserves it, when he tills the soil,
The knave deserves it, when he tempts the main,
Where Folly fights for kings, or dives for gain.
The good man may be weak, be indolent;
Nor is his claim to plenty, but content.
But grant him Riches, your demand is o'er?
"No—shall the good want Health, the good want Pow'r?"
Add Health, and Pow'r, and ev'ry earthly thing,
"Why bounded Pow'r? why private? why no king?"
Nay, why external for internal giv'n?
Why is not Man a God, and Earth a Heav'n?
Who ask and reason thus, will scarce conceive
God gives enough, while he has more to give:
Immense the pow'r immense were the demand;
Say, at what part of nature will they stand?
  What nothing earthly gives, or can destroy,
The soul's calm sun-shine, and the heart-felt joy,

Is Virtue's prize: A better would you fix?
Then give Humility a coach and six,
Justice a Conq'r's sword, or Truth a gown,
Or Public Spirit its great cure, a Crown.
Weak, foolish man! will Heav'n reward us there
With the same trash mad mortals wish for here?
The Boy and Man an individual makes,
Yet sigh'st thou now for apples and for cakes?
Go, like the Indian, in another life,
Expect thy dog, thy bottle, and thy wife:
As well as dream such trifles are assign'd,
As toys and empires, for a god-like mind.
Rewards, that either would to Virtue bring
No joy, or be destructive of the thing:
How oft by these at sixty are undone
The virtues of a saint at twenty-one!
To whom can Riches give Repute, or Trust,
Content, or Pleasure, but the Good and Just?
Judges and Senates have been bought for gold,
Esteem and Love were never to be sold.
Oh fool! to think God hates the worthy mind,
The lover and the love of human-kind,
Whose life is healthful, and whose conscience clear,
Because he wants a thousand pounds a year.
  Honour and shame from no Condition rise;
Act well your part, there all the honour lies.
Fortune in Men has some small diff'rence made,
One flaunts in rags, one flutters in brocade;
The cobler apron'd, and the parson gown'd,
The frier hooded, and the monarch crown'd.
"What differ more (you cry) than crown and cowl?"
I'll tell you, friend! a wise man and a Fool.
You'll find, if once the monarch acts the monk,
Or, cobler-like, the parson will be drunk,
Worth makes the man, and want of it, the fellow;
The rest is all but leather or prunella.
  Stuck o'er with titles and hung round with strings,
That thou may'st be by Kings, or whores of kings.
Boast the pure blood of an illustrious race,
In quiet flow from Lucrece to Lucrece:
But by your father's worth if your's you rate,
Count me those only who were good and great.
Go! if your ancient, but ignoble blood
Has crept thro' scoundrels ever since the flood,
Go! and pretend your family is young;
Nor own, your fathers have been fools so long.
What can ennoble sots, or slaves, or cowards?
Alas! not all the blood of all the HOWARDS.

Look next on Greatness; say where Greatness lies?
"Where, but among the Heroes and the Wise?"
Heroes are much the same, the point's agreed,
From Macedonia's madman to the Swede;
The whole strange purpose of their lives, to find
Or make, an enemy of all mankind!
Not one looks backward, onward still he goes,
Yet ne'er looks forward farther than his nose.
No less alike the Politic and Wise;
All sly slow things, with circumspective eyes:
Men in their loose unguarded hours they take,
Not that themselves are wise, but others weak.
But grant that those can conquer, these can cheat;
'Tis phrase absurd to call a Villain Great:
Who wickedly is wise, or madly brave,
Is but the more a fool, the more a knave.
Who noble ends by noble means obtains,
Or failing, smiles in exile or in chains,
Like good Aurelius let him reign, or bleed
Like Socrates, that Man is great indeed.
What's Fame? a fancy'd life in others breath,
A thing beyond us, ev'n before our death.
Just what you hear, you have, and what's unknown
The same (my Lord) if Tully's, or your own.
All that we feel of it begins and ends
In the small circle of our foes or friends;
To all beside as much an empty shade
An Eugene living, as a Cæsar dead;
Alike or when, or where, they shone, or shine,
Or on the Rubicon, or on the Rhine.
A Wit's a feather, and a Chief a rod;
An honest Man's the noblest work of God.
Fame but from death a villain's name can save,
As Justice tears his body from the grave;
When what t' oblivion better were resign'd,
Is hung on high, to poison half mankind.
All fame is foreign, but of true desert;
Plays round the head, but comes not to the heart:
One self-approving hour whole years out-weighs
Of stupid starers, and of loud huzzas;
And more true joy Marcellus exil'd feels,
Than Cæsar with a senate at his heels.
In Parts superior what advantage lies?
Tell (for You can) what is it to be wise?
'Tis but to know how little can be known;
To see all others faults, and feel our own:
Condemn'd in bus'ness or in arts to drudge,
Without a second, or without a judge:

Truths would you teach, or save a sinking land?
All fear, none aid you, and few understand.
Painful preheminence! yourself to view
Above life's weakness, and its comforts too.
  Bring then these blessings to a strict account;
Make fair deductions; see to what they mount:
How much of other each is sure to cost;
How each for other oft is wholly lost;
How inconsistent greater goods with these;
How sometimes life is risqu'd, and always ease:
Think, and if still the things thy envy call,
Say, would'st thou be the Man to whom they fall?
To sign for ribbands if thou art so silly,
Mark how they grace Lord Umbra, or Sir Billy:
Is yellow dirt the passion of thy life?
Look but on Gripus, or on Gripus' wife:
If Parts allure thee, think how Bacon shin'd,
The wisest, brightest, meanest of mankind:
Or ravish'd with the whistling of a Name,
See Cromwell, damn'd to everlasting fame!
If all, united, thy ambition call,
From ancient story learn to scorn them all.
There, in the rich, the honour'd, fam'd, and great,
See the false scale of Happiness complete!
In hearts of Kings, or arms of Queens who lay,
How happy! those to ruin, these betray.
Mark by what wretched steps their glory grows,
From dirt and sea-weed as proud Venice rose;
In each how guilt and greatness equal ran,
And all that rais'd the Hero, sunk the Man:
Now Europe's laurels on their brows behold,
But stain'd with blood, or ill exchang'd for gold:
Then see them broke with toils, or sunk in ease,
Or infamous for plunder'd provinces.
Oh wealth ill-fated! which no act of fame
E'er taught to shine, or sanctify'd from shame!
What greater bliss attends their close of life?
Some greedy minion, or imperious wife.
The trophy'd arches, story'd halls invade
And haunt their slumbers in the pompous shade.
Alas! not dazzled with their noon-tide ray,
Compute the morn and ev'ning to the day;
The whole amount of that enormous fame,
A Tale, that blends their glory with their shame!
  Know then this truth (enough for Man to know)
"Virtue alone is Happiness below."
The only point where human bliss stands still,
And tastes the good without the fall to ill;

Where only Merit constant pay receives,
Is blest in what it takes, and what it gives;
The joy unequal'd, if its end it gain,
And if it lose, attended with no pain:
Without satiety, tho' e'er so bless'd,
And but more relish'd as the more distress'd:
The broadest mirth unfeeling Folly wears,
Less pleasing far than Virtue's very tears:
Good, from each object, from each place acquir'd,
For ever exercis'd, yet never tir'd;
Never elated, while one man's oppress'd;
Never dejected, while another's bless'd;
And where no wants, no wishes can remain,
Since but to wish more Virtue, is to gain.
  See the sole bliss Heav'n could on all bestow!
Which who but feels can taste, but thinks can know:
Yet poor with fortune, and with learning blind,
The bad must miss; the good, untaught, will find;
Slave to no sect, who takes no private road,
But looks thro' Nature, up to Nature's God;
Pursues that Chain which links th' immense design,
Joins heav'n and earth, and mortal and divine,
Sees, that no Being any bliss can know,
But touches some above, and some below;
Learns, from this union of the rising Whole,
The first, last purpose of the human soul;
And knows where Faith, Law, Morals, all began,
All end, in LOVE OF GOD, and LOVE OF MAN.
  For him alone, Hope leads from goal to goal,
And opens still, and opens on his soul;
'Till lengthen'd on to Faith, and unconfin'd,
It pours the bliss that fills up all the mind.
He sees, why Nature plants in Man alone
Hope of known bliss, and Faith in bliss unknown:
(Nature, whose dictates to no other kind
Are giv'n in vain, but what they seek they find)
Wise is her present; she connects in this
His greatest Virtue with his greatest Bliss;
At once his own bright prospect to be blest,
And strongest motive to assist the rest.
  Self-love thus push'd to social, to divine,
Gives thee to make thy neighbour's blessing thine.
Is this too little for the boundless heart?
Extend it, let thy enemies have part:
Grasp the whole worlds of Reason, Life, and Sense,
In one close system of Benevolence:
Happier as kinder, in whate'er degree,
And height of Bliss but height of Charity.

God loves from Whole to Parts: But human soul
Must rise from Individual to the Whole.
Self-love but serves the virtuous mind to wake,
As the small pebble stirs the peaceful lake;
The centre mov'd, a circle strait succeeds,
Another still, and still another spreads;
Friend, parent, neighbour, first it will embrace;
His country next; and next all human race;
Wide and more wide, th' o'erflowings of the mind
Take ev'ry creature in, of ev'ry kind;
Earth smiles around, with boundless bounty blest,
And Heav'n beholds its image in his breast.
Come then, my Friend! my Genius! come along;
Oh master of the poet, and the song!
And while the Muse now stoops, or now ascends,
To Man's low passions, or their glorious ends,
Teach me, like thee, in various nature wise,
To fall with dignity, with temper rise;
Form'd by thy converse, happily to steer
From grave to gay, from lively to severe;
Correct with spirit, eloquent with ease,
Intent to reason, or polite to please.
Oh! while along the stream of Time thy name
Expanded flies, and gathers all its fame,
Say, shall my little bark attendant sail,
Pursue the triumph, and partake the gale?
When statesmen, heroes, kings, in dust repose,
Whose sons shall blush their fathers were thy foes,
Shall then this verse to future age pretend
Thou wert my guide, philosopher, and friend?
That urg'd by thee, I turn'd the tuneful art
From sounds to things, from fancy to the heart;
For Wit's false mirror held up Nature's light;
Shew'd erring Pride, WHATEVER IS, IS RIGHT;
That REASON, PASSION, answer one great aim;
That true SELF-LOVE and SOCIAL are the same;
That VIRTUE only makes our Bliss below;
And all our Knowledge is, OURSELVES TO KNOW.

Epitaph XI

On Mr. Gay. In Westminster Abbey, 1732[1]

OF MANNERS gentle, of Affections mild;
In Wit, a Man; Simplicity, a Child:

[1] Published in the *Gentleman's Magazine*, June, 1733. Text of *Works*, 1751.

With native Humour temp'ring virtuous Rage,
Form'd to delight at once and lash the age:
Above Temptation in a low Estate,
And uncorrupted, ev'n among the Great:
A safe Companion, and an easy Friend,
Unblam'd thro' Life, lamented in thy End.
These are Thy Honours! not that here thy Bust
Is mix'd with Heroes, or with Kings thy dust;
But that the Worthy and the Good shall say,
Striking their pensive bosoms—*Here* lies GAY.

Moral Essays. Epistle I
To Sir Richard Temple, Lord Cobham.
Of the Knowledge and Characters of Men[1]

YES, you despise the man to Books confin'd,
Who from his study rails at human kind;
Tho' what he learns he speaks, and may advance
Some gen'ral maxims, or be right by chance.
The coxcomb bird, so talkative and grave,
That from his cage cries Cuckold, Whore, and Knave,
Tho' many a passenger he rightly call,
You hold him no Philosopher at all.
 And yet the fate of all extremes is such,
Men may be read, as well as Books, too much.
To observations which ourselves we make,
We grow more partial for th' Observer's sake;
To written Wisdom, as another's less:
Maxims are drawn from Notions, those from Guess.
There's some Peculiar in each leaf and grain,
Some unmark'd fibre, or some varying vein:
Shall only Man be taken in the gross?
Grant but as many sorts of Mind as Moss.
 That each from other differs, first confess;
Next, that he varies from himself no less:
Add Nature's, Custom's, Reason's, Passion's strife,
And all Opinion's colours cast on life.
 Our depths who fathoms, or our shallows finds,
Quick whirls, and shifting eddies, of our minds?
On human actions reason tho' you can,
It may be Reason, but it is not Man:
His Principle of action once explore,
That instant 'tis his Principle no more.

[1] Published January 16, 1734. Text of *Works,* 1751.

Like following life thro' creatures you dissect,
You lose it in the moment you detect.
Yet more; the diff'rence is as great between
The optics seeing, as the objects seen.
All Manners take a tincture from our own;
Or come discolour'd thro' our Passions shown.
Or Fancy's beam enlarges, multiplies,
Contracts, inverts, and gives ten thousand dyes.
Nor will Life's stream for Observation stay,
It hurries all too fast to mark their way:
In vain sedate reflections we wou'd make,
When half our knowledge we must snatch, not take.
Oft, in the Passions' wild rotation tost,
Our spring of action to ourselves is lost:
Tir'd, not determin'd, to the last we yield,
And what comes then is master of the field.
As the last image of that troubled heap,
When Sense subsides, and Fancy sports in sleep,
(Tho' past the recollection of the thought)
Becomes the stuff of which our dream is wrought:
Something as dim to our internal view,
Is thus, perhaps, the cause of most we do.
True, some are open, and to all men known;
Others so very close, they're hid from none;
(So Darkness strikes the sense no less than Light)
Thus gracious CHANDOS is belov'd at sight;
And ev'ry child hates Shylock, tho' his soul
Still sits at squat, and peeps not from its hole.
At half mankind when gen'rous Manly raves,
All know 'tis Virtue, for he thinks them knaves:
When universal homage Umbra pays,
All see 'tis Vice, and itch of vulgar praise.
When Flatt'ry glares, all hate it in a Queen,
While one there is who charms us with his Spleen.
But these plain Characters we rarely find;
Tho' strong the bent, yet quick the turns of mind:
Or puzzling Contraries confound the whole;
Or Affectations quite reverse the soul.
The Dull, flat Falshood serves, for policy;
And in the Cunning, Truth itself's a lye:
Unthought-of Frailties cheat us in the Wise;
The Fool lies hid in inconsistencies.
See the same man, in vigour, in the gout;
Alone, in company; in place, or out;
Early at Bus'ness, and at Hazard late;
Mad at a Fox-chace, wise at a Debate;
Drunk at a Borough, civil at a Ball;
Friendly at Hackney, faithless at Whitehall.

Catius is ever moral, ever grave,
Thinks who endures a knave, is next a knave,
Save just at dinner—then prefers, no doubt,
A Rogue with Ven'son to a Saint without.
Who would not praise Patritio's high desert,
His hand unstain'd, his uncorrupted heart,
His comprehensive head! all Int'rests weigh'd,
All Europe sav'd, yet Britain not betray'd.
He thanks you not, his pride is in Picquette,
New-market-fame, and judgment at a Bett.
What made (say Montagne, or more sage Charron!)
Otho a warrior, Cromwell a buffoon?
A perjur'd Prince a leaden Saint revere,
A godless Regent tremble at a Star?
The throne a Bigot keep, a Genius quit,
Faithless thro' Piety, and dup'd thro' Wit?
Europe a Woman, Child, or Dotard rule,
And just her wisest monarch made a fool?
Know, GOD and NATURE only are the same:
In Man, the judgment shoots at flying game,
A bird of passage! gone as soon as found,
Now in the Moon perhaps, now under ground.
In vain the Sage, with retrospective eye,
Would from th' apparent What conclude the Why,
Infer the Motive from the Deed, and shew,
That what we chanc'd was what we meant to do.
Behold! If Fortune or a Mistress frowns,
Some plunge in bus'ness, others shave their crowns:
To ease the Soul of one oppressive weight,
This quits an Empire, that embroils a State:
The same adust complexion has impell'd
Charles to the Convent, Philip to the Field.
Not always actions shew the man: We find
Who does a kindness, is not therefore kind;
Perhaps Prosperity becalm'd his breast,
Perhaps the Wind just shifted from the east:
Not therefore humble he who seeks retreat,
Pride guides his steps, and bids him shun the great:
Who combats bravely is not therefore brave,
He dreads a death-bed like the meanest slave:
Who reasons wisely is not therefore wise,
His pride in Reas'ning, not in Acting lies.
But grant that Actions best discover man;
Take the most strong, and sort them as you can.
The few that glare each character must mark,
You balance not the many in the dark.
What will you do with such as disagree?
Suppress them, or miscall them Policy?

Must then at once (the character to save)
The plain rough Hero turn a crafty Knave?
Alas! in truth the man but chang'd his mind,
Perhaps was sick, in love, or had not din'd.
Ask why from Britain Cæsar would retreat?
Cæsar himself might whisper he was beat.
Why risk the world's great empire for a Punk?
Cæsar perhaps might answer he was drunk.
But, sage historians! 'tis your task to prove
One action Conduct; one, heroic Love.
'Tis from high Life high Characters are drawn;
A Saint in Crape is twice a Saint in Lawn;
A Judge is just, a Chanc'lor juster still;
A Gownman, learn'd; a Bishop, what you will;
Wise, if a Minister; but, if a King,
More wise, more learn'd, more just, more ev'ry thing.
Court-virtues bear, like Gems, the highest rate,
Born where Heav'n's influence scarce can penetrate:
In life's low vale, the soil the Virtues like,
They please as beauties, here as wonders strike.
Tho' the same Sun with all-diffusive rays
Blush in the Rose, and in the Di'mond blaze,
We prize the stronger effort of his pow'r,
And justly set the Gem above the Flow'r.
'Tis Education forms the common mind,
Just as the Twig is bent, the Tree's inclin'd.
Boastful and rough, your first son is a 'Squire;
The next a Tradesman, meek, and much a lyar;
Tom struts a Soldier, open, bold, and brave;
Will sneaks a Scriv'ner, an exceeding knave:
Is he a Churchman? then he's fond of pow'r:
A Quaker? sly: A Presbyterian? sow'r:
A smart Free-thinker? all things in an hour.
Ask men's Opinions: Scoto now shall tell
How Trade increases, and the World goes well;
Strike off his Pension, by the setting sun,
And Britain, if not Europe, is undone.
That gay Free-thinker, a fine talker once,
What turns him now a stupid silent dunce?
Some God, or Spirit he has lately found;
Or chanc'd to meet a Minister that frown'd.
Judge we by Nature? Habit can efface,
Int'rest o'ercome, or Policy take place:
By Actions? those Uncertainty divides:
By Passions? these Dissimulation hides:
Opinions? they still take a wider range:
Find, if you can, in what you cannot change.

Manners with Fortunes, Humours turn with Climes,
Tenets with Books, and Principles with Times.
Search then the RULING PASSION: There, alone,
The Wild are constant, and the Cunning known;
The Fool consistent, and the False sincere;
Priests, Princes, Women, no dissemblers here.
This clue once found, unravels all the rest,
The prospect clears, and Wharton stands confest.
Wharton, the scorn and wonder of our days,
Whose ruling Passion was the Lust of Praise:
Born with whate'er could win it from the Wise,
Women and Fools must like him or he dies;
Tho' wond'ring Senates hung on all he spoke,
The Club must hail him master of the joke.
Shall parts so various aim at nothing new?
He'll shine a Tully and a Wilmot too.
Then turns repentant, and his God adores
With the same spirit that he drinks and whores;
Enough if all around him but admire,
And now the Punk applaud, and now the Fryer.
Thus with each gift of nature and of art,
And wanting nothing but an honest heart;
Grown all to all, from no one vice exempt;
And most contemptible, to shun contempt;
His Passion still, to covet gen'ral praise,
His Life, to forfeit it a thousand ways;
A constant Bounty which no friend has made;
An angel Tongue, which no Man can persuade;
A Fool, with more of Wit than half mankind,
Too rash for Thought, for Action too refin'd:
A Tyrant to the wife his heart approves;
A Rebel to the very king he loves;
He dies, sad out-cast of each church and state,
And, harder still! flagitious, yet not great.
Ask you why Wharton broke thro' ev'ry rule?
'Twas all for fear the Knaves should call him Fool.
Nature well known, no prodigies remain,
Comets are regular, and Wharton plain.
Yet, in this search, the wisest may mistake,
If second qualities for first they take.
When Catiline by rapine swell'd his store;
When Cæsar made a noble dame a whore;
In this the Lust, in that the Avarice
Were means, not ends; Ambition was the vice.
That very Cæsar, born in Scipio's days,
Had aim'd, like him, by Chastity at praise.
Lucullus, when Frugality could charm,

Had roasted turnips in the Sabin farm.
In vain th' observer eyes the builder's toil,
But quite mistakes the scaffold for the pile.
  In this one Passion man can strength enjoy,
As Fits give vigour, just when they destroy.
Time, that on all things lays his lenient hand,
Yet tames not this; it sticks to our last sand.
Consistent in our follies and our sins,
Here honest Nature ends as she begins.
  Old Politicians chew on wisdom past,
And totter on in bus'ness to the last;
As weak, as earnest; and as gravely out,
As sober Lanesb'row dancing in the gout.
  Behold a rev'rend sire, whom want of grace
Has made the father of a nameless race,
Shov'd from the wall perhaps, or rudely press'd
By his own son, that passes by unbless'd:
Still to his wench he crawls on knocking knees,
And envies ev'ry sparrow that he sees.
  A salmon's belly, Helluo, was thy fate;
The doctor call'd, declares all help too late:
"Mercy! cries Helluo, mercy on my soul!
"Is there no hope?—Alas!—then bring the jowl."
  The frugal Crone, whom praying priests attend,
Still strives to save the hallow'd taper's end,
Collects her breath, as ebbing life retires,
For one puff more, and in that puff expires.
  "Odious! in woollen! 'twould a Saint provoke,
(Were the last words that poor Narcissa spoke)
"No, let a charming Chintz, and Brussels lace
"Wrap my cold limbs, and shade my lifeless face:
"One would not, sure, be frightful when one's dead—
"And—Betty—give this Cheek a little Red."
  The Courtier smooth, who forty years had shin'd
An humble servant to all human kind,
Just brought out this, when scarce his tongue could stir,
"If—where I'm going—I could serve you, Sir?
  "I give and I devise (old Euclio said,
And sigh'd) "my lands and tenements to Ned.
Your money, Sir; "My money, Sir, what all?
"Why,—if I must—(then wept) I give it Paul.
The Manor, Sir?—"The Manor! hold, he cry'd,
"Not that,—I cannot part with that"—and dy'd.
  And you! brave Cobham, to the latest breath
Shall feel your ruling passion strong in death:
Such in those moments as in all the past,
"Oh, save my Country, Heav'n!" shall be your last.

An Epistle from Mr. Pope, to Dr. Arbuthnot[1]

SHUT, shut the door, good John! fatigu'd I said,
Tye up the knocker, say I'm sick, I'm dead.
The Dog-star rages! nay 'tis past a doubt,
All Bedlam, or Parnassus, is let out:
Fire in each eye, and papers in each hand,
They rave, recite, and madden round the land.
What walls can guard me, or what shades can hide?
They pierce my Thickets, thro' my Grot they glide,
By land, by water, they renew the charge,
They stop the chariot, and they board the barge.
No place is sacred, not the Church is free,
Ev'n Sunday shines no Sabbath-day to me:
Then from the Mint walks forth the Man of rhyme,
Happy! to catch me, just at Dinner-time.
Is there a Parson, much be-mus'd in beer,
A maudlin Poetess, a rhyming Peer,
A Clerk, foredoom'd his father's soul to cross,
Who pens a Stanza when he should *engross?*
Is there, who lock'd from ink and paper, scrawls
With desp'rate charcoal round his darken'd walls?
All fly to Twit'nam, and in humble strain
Apply to me, to keep them mad or vain.
Arthur, whose giddy son neglects the Laws,
Imputes to me and my damn'd works the cause:
Poor Cornus sees his frantick wife elope,
And curses Wit, and Poetry, and Pope.
Friend to my Life! (which did not you prolong,
The world had wanted many an idle song)
What *Drop* or *Nostrum* can this plague remove?
Or which must end me, a Fool's wrath or love?
A dire dilemma, either way I'm sped,
If foes, they write, if friends, they read me dead.
Seiz'd and ty'd down to judge, how wretched I!
Who can't be silent, and who will not lye;
To laugh, were want of goodness and of grace,
And to be grave, exceeds all Pow'r of face.
I sit with sad civility, I read
With honest anguish, and an aching head;
And drop at last, but in unwilling ears,
This saving counsel, "Keep your piece nine years."
Nine years! cries he, who high in Drury-lane
Lull'd by soft Zephyrs thro' the broken pane,
Rhymes 'ere he wakes, and prints before *Term* ends,

[1] Published January 2, 1735. Text of *Works,* 1743.

Oblig'd by hunger, and request of friends:
"The piece you think is incorrect? why take it,
"I'm all submission, what you'd have it, make it."
Three things another's modest wishes bound,
My Friendship, and a Prologue, and ten pound.
  Pitholeon sends to me: "You know his Grace,
"I want a Patron; ask him for a Place."
Pitholeon libell'd me—"but here's a letter
"Informs you, Sir, 'twas when he knew no better.
"Dare you refuse him? Curl invites to dine,
"He'll write a *Journal*, or he'll turn Divine."
Bless me! a packet.—" 'Tis a stranger sues,
"A Virgin Tragedy, an Orphan Muse."
If I dislike it, "Furies, death, and rage!
If I approve, "Commend it to the Stage."
There (thank my stars) my whole commission ends,
The Play'rs and I are, luckily, no friends.
Fir'd that the house reject him, "S'death I'll print it,
"And shame the fools—your int'rest, Sir, with Lintot."
Lintot, dull rogue! will think your price too much:
"Not Sir, if you revise it, and retouch."
All my demurs but double his attacks,
At last he whispers, "Do, and we go snacks.
Glad of a quarrel, strait I clap the door,
Sir, let me see your works and you no more.
  'Tis sung, when Midas' Ears began to spring,
(Midas, a sacred person and a King)
His very Minister who spy'd them first,
(Some Say his Queen) was forc'd to speak, or burst.
And is not mine, my friend, a sorer case,
When ev'ry coxcomb perks them in my face?
"Good friend forbear! you deal in dang'rous things,
"I'd never name Queens, Ministers, or Kings;
"Keep close to Ears, and those let asses prick,
" 'Tis nothing."—Nothing? if they bite and kick?
Out with it, *Dunciad!* let the secret pass,
That secret to each fool, that he's an Ass:
The truth once told, (and wherefore shou'd we lie?)
The Queen of Midas slept, and so may I.
  You think this cruel? take it for a rule,
No creature smarts so little as a fool.
Let peals of laughter, Codrus! round thee break,
Thou unconcern'd canst hear the mighty crack:
Pit, box, and gall'ry in convulsions hurl'd,
Thou stand'st unshook amidst a bursting world.
Who shames a Scribler? break one cobweb thro',
He spins the slight, self-pleasing thread a-new:
Destroy his fib or sophistry, in vain,

The creature's at his dirty work again,
Thron'd in the centre of his thin designs,
Proud of a vast extent of flimzy lines!
Whom have I hurt? has Poet yet, or Peer,
Lost the arch'd eye-brow, or Parnassian sneer?
And has not Colly still his lord, and whore?
His butchers Henley, his free-masons Moor?
Does not one table Bavius still admit?
Still to one Bishop Philips seems a wit?
Still Sappho—"Hold! for God sake—you'll offend,
"No Names—be calm—learn prudence of a friend:
"I too could write, and I am twice as tall;
"But foes like these!—One Flatt'rer's worse than all;
Of all mad creatures, if the learn'd are right,
It is the slaver kills, and not the bite.
A fool quite angry is quite innocent,
Alas! 'tis ten times worse when they *repent*.
  One dedicates in high heroic prose,
And ridicules beyond a hundred foes;
One from all Grubstreet will my fame defend,
And more abusive, calls himself my friend.
This prints my *Letters*, that expects a bribe,
And others roar aloud, "Subscribe, subscribe."
  There are, who to my person pay their court,
I cough like *Horace*, and tho' lean, am short,
Ammon's great son one shoulder had too high,
Such *Ovid*'s nose, and "Sir! you have an Eye—
Go on, obliging creatures, make me see
All that disgrac'd my Betters, met in me.
Say for my comfort, languishing in bed,
"Just so immortal *Maro* held his head":
And when I die, be sure you let me know
Great *Homer* dy'd three thousand years ago.
  Why did I write? what sin to me unknown
Dipt me in ink, my parents, or my own?
As yet a child, nor yet a fool to fame,
I lisp'd in numbers, for the numbers came.
I left no calling for this idle trade,
No duty broke, no father disobey'd.
The Muse but serv'd to ease some friend, not Wife,
To help me thro' this long disease, my Life,
To second, ARBUTHNOT! thy Art and Care,
And teach, the Being you preserv'd, to bear.
  But why then publish? *Granville* the polite,
And knowing *Walsh*, would tell me I could write;
Well-natur'd *Garth* inflam'd with early praise,
And *Congreve* lov'd, and *Swift* endur'd my lays;
The courtly *Talbot, Somers, Sheffield* read,

Ev'n mitred *Rochester* would nod the head.
And *St. John*'s self (great *Dryden*'s friend before)
With open arms receiv'd one Poet more.
Happy my studies, when by these approv'd!
Happier their author, when by these belov'd!
From these the world will judge of men and books,
Not from the *Burnets, Oldmixons*, and *Cooks*.
  Soft were my numbers; who could take offence
While pure Description held the place of Sense?
Like gentle *Fanny*'s was my flow'ry theme,
A painted mistress, or a purling stream.
Yet then did *Gildon* draw his venal quill;
I wish'd the man a dinner, and sate still.
Yet then did *Dennis* rave in furious fret;
I never answer'd, I was not in debt.
If want provok'd, or madness made them print,
I wag'd no war with *Bedlam* or the *Mint*.
  Did some more sober Critic come abroad?
If wrong, I smil'd; if right, I kiss'd the rod.
Pains, reading, study, are their just pretence,
And all they want is spirit, taste, and sense.
Comma's and points they set exactly right,
And 'twere a sin to rob them of their mite.
Yet ne'er one sprig of laurel grac'd these ribalds,
From slashing *Bentley* down to pidling *Tibalds*:
Each wight, who reads not, and but scans and spells,
Each Word-catcher, that lives on syllables,
Ev'n such small Critics some regard may claim,
Preserv'd in *Milton*'s or in *Shakespear*'s name.
Pretty! in amber to observe the forms
Of hairs, or straws, or dirt, or grubs, or worms!
The things, we know, are neither rich nor rare,
But wonder how the devil they got there?
  Were others angry? I excus'd them too;
Well might they rage, I gave them but their due.
A man's true merit 'tis not hard to find,
But each man's secret standard in his mind,
That Casting-weight pride adds to emptiness,
This, who can gratify? for who can *guess*?
The Bard whom pilfer'd Pastorals renown,
Who turns a Persian tale for half a crown,
Just writes to make his barrenness appear,
And strains from hard-bound brains, eight lines a year;
He, who still wanting, tho' he lives on theft,
Steals much, spends little, yet has nothing left:
And he, who now to sense, now nonsense leaning,
Means not, but blunders round about a meaning:
And he, whose fustian's so sublimely bad,

It is not Poetry, but prose run mad:
All these, my modest Satire bad *translate*,
And own'd, that nine such Poets made a *Tate*.
How did they fume, and stamp, and roar, and chafe?
And swear, not *Addison* himself was safe.
Peace to all such! but were there One whose fires
True Genius kindles, and fair Fame inspires;
Blest with each talent and each art to please,
And born to write, converse, and live with ease:
Shou'd such a man, too fond to rule alone,
Bear, like the Turk, no brother near the throne,
View him with scornful, yet with jealous eyes,
And hate for arts that caus'd himself to rise;
Damn with faint praise, assent with civil leer,
And without sneering, teach the rest to sneer;
Willing to wound, and yet afraid to strike,
Just hint a fault, and hesitate dislike;
Alike reserv'd to blame, or to commend,
A tim'rous foe, and a suspicious friend:
Dreading ev'n fools, by Flatterers besieg'd,
And so obliging, that he ne'er oblig'd;
Like *Cato*, gave his little Senate laws,
And sit attentive to his own applause;
While Wits and Templers ev'ry sentence raise,
And wonder with a foolish face of praise—
Who but must laugh, if such a man there be?
Who would not weep, if *Atticus* were he!
What tho' my Name stood rubric on the walls,
Or plaister'd posts, with claps in capitals?
Or smoaking forth, a hundred hawkers load,
On wings of winds came flying all abroad?
I sought no homage from the Race that write;
I kept, like *Asian* Monarchs, from their sight:
Poems I heeded (now be-rym'd so long)
No more than thou, great GEORGE! a birth-day song.
I ne'er with wits or witlings past my days,
To spread about the itch of verse and praise;
Nor like a puppy, daggled thro' the town,
To fetch and carry sing-song up and down;
Nor at Rehearsals sweat, and mouth'd, and cry'd,
With handkerchief and orange at my side;
But sick of fops, and poetry, and prate,
To *Bufo* left the whole *Castalian* state.
Proud, as *Apollo* on his forked hill,
Sate full-blown *Bufo*, puff'd by ev'ry quill;
Fed with soft Dedication all day long,

Horace and he went hand in hand in song.
His Library, (where busts of Poets dead
And a true *Pindar* stood without a head)
Receiv'd of wits an undistinguish'd race,
Who first his Judgment ask'd, and then a place:
Much they extoll'd his pictures, much his seat,
And flatter'd ev'ry day, and some days eat:
'Till grown more frugal in his riper days,
He pay'd some bards with port, and some with praise,
To some a dry rehearsal was assign'd,
And others (harder still) he paid in kind.
Dryden alone (what wonder?) came not nigh,
Dryden alone escap'd this judging eye:
But still the great have kindness in reserve,
He help'd to bury whom he help'd to starve.
  May some choise Patron bless each grey goose quill!
May ev'ry *Bavius* have his *Bufo* still!
So when a Statesman wants a day's defence,
Or envy holds a whole week's war with sense,
Or simple Pride for flatt'ry makes demands,
May dunce by dunce be whistled off my hands!
Blest be the *Great!* for those they take away,
And those they left me; For they left me GAY;
Left me to see neglected Genius bloom,
Neglected die, and tell it on his tomb:
Of all thy blameless life the sole return
My Verse, and QUEENSB'RY weeping o'er thy urn!
  Oh let me live my own, and die so too!
("To live and die is all I have to do:)
Maintain a Poet's dignity and ease,
And see what friends, and read what books I please:
Above a Patron, tho' I condescend
Sometimes to call a Minister my friend.
I was not born for Courts or great affairs;
I pay my debts, believe, and say my pray'rs;
Can sleep without a Poem in my head,
Nor know, if *Dennis* be alive or dead.
  Why am I ask'd what next shall see the light;
Heav'n's! was I born for nothing but to write?
Has Life no joys for me? or (to be grave)
Have I no friend to serve, no soul to save?
"I found him close with *Swift*—Indeed? no doubt
"(Cries prating *Balbus*) something will come out.
'Tis all in vain, deny it as I will.
"No, such a Genius never can lie still;
And then for mine obligingly mistakes

The first Lampoon Sir *Will*, or *Bubo* makes.
Poor guiltless I! and can I chuse but smile,
When ev'ry Coxcomb knows me by my *Style?*
  Curst be the verse, how well soe'er it flow,
That tends to make one worthy man my foe,
Give Virtue scandal, Innocence a fear,
Or from the soft-ey'd Virgin steal a tear!
But he who hurts a harmless neighbour's peace,
Insults fall'n worth, or Beauty in distress,
Who loves a Lye, lame slander helps about,
Who writes a Libel, or who copies out:
That Fop, whose pride affects a patron's name,
Yet absent, wounds an author's honest fame:
Who can *your* merit *selfishly* approve,
And show the *sense* of it without the *love*;
Who has the vanity to call you friend,
Yet wants the honour injur'd to defend;
Who tells whate'er you think, whate'er you say,
And, if he lye not, must at least betray;
Who to the *Dean*, and *silver bell* can swear,
And sees at *Cannon*'s what was never there;
Who reads, but with a lust to misapply,
Make Satire a Lampoon, and Fiction Lye.
A lash like mine no honest man shall dread,
But all such babling blockheads in his stead.
  Let *Sporus* tremble—"What? that thing of silk,
"*Sporus*, that mere white curd of Ass's milk?
"Satire or sense alas! can *Sporus* feel?
"Who breaks a butterfly upon a wheel?"
Yet let me flap this bug with gilded wings,
This painted child of dirt, that stinks and stings;
Whose buzz the witty and the fair annoys,
Yet wit ne'er tastes, and beauty ne'er enjoys:
So well-bred spaniels civilly delight
In mumbling of the game they dare not bite.
Eternal smiles his emptiness betray,
As shallow streams run dimpling all the way,
Whether in florid impotence he speaks,
And, as the prompter breathes, the puppet squeaks,
Or at the ear of *Eve*, familiar Toad,
Half froth, half venom, spits himself abroad,
In puns, or politicks, or tales, or lyes,
Or spite, or smut, or rymes, or blasphemies,
His wit all see-saw, between *that* and *this*,
Now high, now low, now master up, now miss,
And he himself one vile Antithesis.
Amphibious thing! that acting either part,

The trifling head, or the corrupted heart,
Fop at the toilet, flatt'rer at the board,
Now trips a Lady, and now struts a Lord.
Eve's tempter thus the Rabbins have exprest,
A Cherub's face, a reptile all the rest,
Beauty that shocks you, parts that none will trust,
Wit that can creep, and pride that licks the dust.
  Not Fortune's worshipper, nor Fashion's fool,
Not Lucre's madman, nor Ambition's tool,
Not proud, nor servile; be one Poet's praise,
That, if he pleas'd, he pleas'd by manly ways;
That Flatt'ry, ev'n to Kings, he held a shame,
And thought a Lye in verse or prose the same.
That not in Fancy's maze he wander'd long,
But stoop'd to Truth, and moraliz'd his song:
That not for Fame, but Virtue's better end,
He stood the furious foe, the timid friend,
The damning critic, half-approving wit,
The coxcomb hit, or fearing to be hit;
Laugh'd at the loss of friends he never had,
The dull, the proud, the wicked, and the mad;
The distant threats of vengeance on his head,
The blow unfelt, the tear he never shed;
The tale reviv'd, the lye so oft o'erthrown,
Th' imputed trash, and dulness not his own;
The morals blacken'd when the writings scape,
The libel'd person, and the pictur'd shape;
Abuse, on all he lov'd, or lov'd him, spread,
A friend in exile, or a father, dead;
The whisper, that to greatness still too near,
Perhaps, yet vibrates on his SOVEREIGN's ear—
Welcome for thee, fair Virtue! all the past:
For thee, fair Virtue! welcome ev'n the *last!*
  "But why insult the poor, affront the great?"
A knave's a knave, to me, in ev'ry state:
Alike my scorn, if he succeed or fail,
Sporus at court, or *Japhet* in a jayl,
A hireling scribbler, or a hireling peer,
Knight of the post corrupt, or of the shire;
If on a Pillory, or near a Throne,
He gain his Prince's ear, or lose his own.
  Yet soft by nature, more a dupe than wit,
Sapho can tell you how this man was bit:
This dreaded Sat'rist *Dennis* will confess
Foe to his pride, but friend to his distress:
So humble, he has knock'd at *Tibbald*'s door,
Has drunk with *Cibber*, nay has rhym'd for *Moor*.

Full ten years slander'd, did he once reply?
Three thousand suns went down on *Welsted*'s lye.
To please a Mistress one aspers'd his life;
He lash'd him not, but let her be his wife:
Let *Budgel* charge low Grubstreet on his quill,
And write whate'er he pleas'd, except his will;
Let the two *Curls* of Town and Court, abuse
His father, mother, body, soul and muse.
Yet why? that Father held it for a rule,
It was a sin to call our neighbour fool:
That harmless Mother thought no wife a whore:
Hear this, and spare his family, *James Moore!*
Unspotted names, and memorable long!
If there be force in Virtue, or in Song.
Of gentle blood (part shed in Honour's cause,
While yet in *Britain* Honour had applause)
Each parent sprung—"What fortune, pray?—Their own,
And better got, than *Bestia*'s from the throne.
Born to no Pride, inheriting no Strife,
Nor marrying Discord in a noble wife,
Stranger to civil and religious rage,
The good man walk'd innoxious thro' his age.
No Courts he saw, no suits would ever try,
Nor dar'd an Oath, nor hazarded a Lye.
Un-learn'd, he knew no schoolman's subtile art,
No language, but the language of the heart.
By Nature honest, by Experience wise,
Healthy by temp'rance, and by exercise;
His life, tho' long, to sickness past unknown,
His death was instant, and without a groan.
O grant me, thus to live, and thus to die!
Who sprung from Kings shall know less joy than I.
O Friend! may each domestic bliss be thine!
Be no unpleasing Melancholy mine:
Me, let the tender office long engage,
To rock the cradle of reposing Age,
With lenient arts extend a Mother's breath,
Make Languor smile, and smooth the bed of Death,
Explore the thought, explain the asking eye,
And keep a while one parent from the sky!
On cares like these if length of days attend,
May heav'n, to bless those days, preserve my Friend,
Preserve him social, chearful, and serene,
And just as rich as when he serv'd a QUEEN.
Whether that blessing be deny'd or giv'n,
Thus far was right, the rest belongs to Heav'n.

To James Craggs, Esq; Secretary of State[1]

A SOUL as full of Worth, as void of Pride,
Which nothing seeks to shew, or needs to hide,
Which nor to Guilt nor Fear, its Caution owes,
And boasts a Warmth that from no Passion flows.
A Face untaught to feign: a judging Eye,
That darts severe upon a rising Lye,
And strikes a blush thro' frontless Flattery.
All this thou wert; and being this before,
Know, Kings and Fortune cannot make thee more.
Then scorn to gain a Friend by servile ways,
Nor wish to lose a Foe these Virtues raise;
But candid, free, sincere, as you began,
Proceed—a Minister, but still a Man.
Be not (exalted to whate'er degree)
Asham'd of any Friend, not ev'n of Me:
The Patriot's plain, but untrod, path pursue;
If not, 'tis I must be asham'd of You.

Imitations of Horace
The First Epistle of the Second Book of Horace
To Augustus[2]

WHILE you,[3] great Patron of Mankind! sustain
The balanc'd World, and open all the Main;
Your Country, chief, in Arms abroad defend,
At home, with Morals, Arts, and Laws amend;
How shall the Muse, from such a Monarch, steal
An hour, and not defraud the Public Weal?
Edward and Henry, now the Boast of Fame,
And Virtuous Alfred, a more sacred Name,
After a Life of gen'rous Toils endur'd,
The Gaul subdu'd, or Property secur'd,
Ambition humbled, mighty Cities storm'd,
Or Laws establish'd, and the world reform'd;
Clos'd their long Glories with a sigh, to find
Th' unwilling Gratitude of base mankind!
All human Virtue, to its latest breath,
Finds Envy never conquer'd, but by Death.

[1] Published in *Works*, July 31, 1735. Text of *Works*, 1743.
[2] Published May 25, 1737. Text of *Works*, 1751.
[3] George II.

The great Alcides, ev'ry Labour past,
Had still this Monster to subdue at last.
Sure fate of all, beneath whose rising ray
Each star of meaner merit fades away!
Oppress'd we feel the beam directly beat,
Those Suns of Glory please not till they set.
To thee, the World its present homage pays,
The Harvest early, but mature the praise:
Great Friend of LIBERTY! in *Kings* a Name
Above all Greek, above all Roman Fame:
Whose Word is Truth, as sacred and rever'd,
As Heav'n's own Oracles from Altars heard.
Wonder of Kings! like whom, to mortal eyes
None e'er has risen, and none e'er shall rise.
Just in one instance, be it yet confest
Your People, Sir, are partial in the rest:
Foes to all living worth except your own,
And Advocates for folly dead and gone.
Authors, like coins, grow dear as they grow old;
It is the rust we value, not the gold.
Chaucer's worst ribaldry is learn'd by rote,
And beastly Skelton Heads of houses quote:
One likes no language but the Faery Queen;
A Scot will fight for Christ's Kirk o' the Green;
And each true Briton is to Ben so civil,
He swears the Muses met him at the Devil.
Tho' justly Greece her eldest sons admires,
Why should not We be wiser than our sires?
In ev'ry Public virtue we excell;
We build, we paint, we sing, we dance as well,
And learned Athens to our art must stoop,
Could she behold us tumbling thro' a hoop.
If Time improve our Wit as well as Wine,
Say at what age a Poet grows divine?
Shall we, or shall we not, account him so,
Who dy'd, perhaps, an hundred years ago?
End all dispute; and fix the year precise
When British bards begin t' immortalize?
"Who lasts a century can have no flaw,
"I hold that Wit a Classic, good in law.
Suppose he wants a year, will you compound?
And shall we deem him Ancient, right and sound,
Or damn to all eternity at once,
At ninety nine, a Modern and a Dunce?
"We shall not quarrel for a year or two;
"By courtesy of England, he may do.
Then, by the rule that made the Horse-tail bare,
I pluck out year by year, as hair by hair,

And melt down Ancients like a heap of snow:
While you, to measure merits, look in Stowe,
And estimating authors by the year,
Bestow a Garland only on a Bier.
  Shakespear (whom you and ev'ry Play-house bill
Style the divine, the matchless, what you will)
For gain, not glory, wing'd his roving flight,
And grew Immortal in his own despight.
Ben, old and poor, as little seem'd to heed
The Life to come, in ev'ry Poet's Creed.
Who now reads Cowley? if he pleases yet,
His Moral pleases, not his pointed wit;
Forgot his Epic, nay Pindaric Art,
But still I love the language of his heart.
  "Yet surely, surely, these were famous men!
"What boy but hears the sayings of old Ben?
"In all debates where Critics bear a part,
"Not one but nods, and talks of Johnson's Art,
"Of Shakespear's Nature, and of Cowley's Wit;
"How Beaumont's judgment check'd what Fletcher writ;
"How Shadwell hasty, Wycherly was slow;
"But, for the Passions, Southern sure and Rowe.
"These, only these, support the crouded stage,
"From eldest Heywood down to Cibber's age."
  All this may be; the People's Voice is odd,
It is, and it is not, the voice of God.
To Gammer Gurton if it give the bays,
And yet deny the Careless Husband praise,
Or say our Fathers never broke a rule;
Why then, I say, the Public is a fool.
But let them own, that greater Faults than we
They had, and greater Virtues, I'll agree.
Spenser himself affects the Obsolete,
And Sydney's verse halts ill on Roman feet:
Milton's strong pinion now not Heav'n can bound,
Now Serpent-like, in prose he sweeps the ground,
In Quibbles, Angel and Archangel join,
And God the Father turns a School-divine.
Not that I'd lop the Beauties from his book,
Like slashing Bentley with his desp'rate hook,
Or damn all Shakespear, like th' affected Fool
At court, who hates whate'er he read at school.
  But for the Wits of either Charles's days,
The Mob of Gentlemen who wrote with Ease;
Sprat, Carew, Sedley, and a hundred more,
(Like twinkling stars the Miscellanies o'er)
One Simile, that solitary shines
In the dry desert of a thousand lines,

Or lengthen'd Thought that gleams through many a page,
Has sactify'd whole poems for an age.
I lose my patience, and I own it too,
When works are censur'd, not as bad but new;
While if our Elders break all reason's laws,
These fools demand not pardon, but Applause.
On Avon's bank, where flow'rs eternal blow,
If I but ask, if any weed can grow?
One Tragic sentence if I dare deride
Which Betterton's grave action dignify'd,
Or well-mouth'd Booth with emphasis proclaims,
(Tho' but, perhaps, a muster-roll of Names)
How will our Fathers rise up in a rage,
And swear, all shame is lost in George's Age!
You'd think no Fools disgrac'd the former reign,
Did not some grave Examples yet remain,
Who scorn a Lad should teach his father skill,
And, having once been wrong, will be so still.
He, who to seem more deep than you or I,
Extols old Bards, or Merlin's Prophecy,
Mistake him not; he envies, not admires,
And to debase the Sons, exalts the Sires.
Had ancient times conspir'd to dis-allow
What then was new, what had been ancient now?
Or what remain'd, so worthy to be read
By learned Critics, of the mighty Dead?
In Days of Ease, when now the weary Sword
Was sheath'd, and *Luxury* with *Charles* restor'd;
In ev'ry taste of foreign Courts improv'd,
"All, by the King's Example, liv'd and lov'd."
Then Peers grew proud in Horsemanship t' excell,
New-market's Glory rose, as Britain's fell;
The Soldier breath'd the Gallantries of France,
And ev'ry flow'ry Courtier writ Romance.
Then Marble, soften'd into life, grew warm,
And yielding Metal flow'd to human form:
Lely on animated Canvas stole
The sleepy Eye, that spoke the melting soul.
No wonder then, when all was Love and sport,
The willing Muses were debauch'd at Court:
On each enervate string they taught the note
To pant, or tremble thro' an Eunuch's throat.
But Britain, changeful as a Child at play,
Now calls in Princes, and now turns away.
Now Whig, now Tory, what we lov'd we hate;
Now all for Pleasure, now for Church and State;
Now for Prerogative, and now for Laws;
Effects unhappy! from a Noble Cause.

Time was, a sober Englishman wou'd knock
His servants up, and rise by five o'clock,
Instruct his Family in ev'ry rule,
And send his Wife to church, his Son to school.
To worship like his Fathers, was his care;
To teach their frugal Virtues to his Heir;
To prove, that Luxury could never hold;
And place, on good Security, his Gold.
Now times are chang'd, and one Poetic Itch
Has seiz'd the Court and City, poor and rich:
Sons, Sires, and Grandsires, all will wear the bays,
Our Wives read Milton, and our Daughters Plays,
To Theatres, and to Rehearsals throng,
And all our Grace at table is a Song.
I, who so oft renounce the Muses, lye,
Not ——'s self e'er tells more *Fibs* than I;
When sick of Muse, our follies we deplore,
And promise our best Friends to rhyme no more;
We wake next morning in a raging fit,
And call for pen and ink to show our Wit.
He serv'd a 'Prenticeship, who sets up shop;
Ward try'd on Puppies, and the Poor, his Drop;
Ev'n Radcliff's Doctors travel first to France,
Nor dare to practise till they've learn'd to dance.
Who builds a Bridge that never drove a pile?
(Should Ripley venture, all the world would smile)
But those who cannot write, and those who can,
All rhyme, and scrawl, and scribble, to a man.
Yet, Sir, reflect, the mischief is not great;
These Madmen never hurt the Church or State:
Sometimes the Folly benefits mankind;
And rarely Av'rice taints the tuneful mind.
Allow him but his plaything of a Pen,
He ne'er rebels, or plots, like other men:
Flight of Cashiers, or Mobs, he'll never mind;
And knows no losses while the Muse is kind.
To cheat a Friend, or Ward, he leaves to Peter;
The good man heaps up nothing but mere metre,
Enjoys his Garden and his book in quiet;
And then—a perfect Hermit in his diet.
Of little use the Man you may suppose,
Who says in verse what others say in prose;
Yet let me show, a Poet's of some weight,
And (tho' no Soldier) useful to the State.
What will a Child learn sooner than a song?
What better teach a Foreigner the tongue?
What's long or short, each accent where to place,
And speak in public with some sort of grace.

I scarce can think him such a worthless thing,
Unless he praise some Monster of a King;
Or Virtue, or Religion turn to sport,
To please a lewd, or unbelieving Court.
Unhappy Dryden!—In all Charles's days,
Roscommon only boasts unspotted bays;
And in our own (excuse some Courtly stains)
No whiter page than Addison remains.
He, from the taste obscene reclaims our youth,
And sets the Passions on the side of Truth,
Forms the soft bosom with the gentlest art,
And pours each human Virtue in the heart.
Let Ireland tell, how Wit upheld her cause,
Her Trade supported, and supplied her Laws;
And leave on SWIFT this grateful verse ingrav'd,
The Rights a Court attack'd, a Poet sav'd.
Behold the hand that wrought a Nation's cure,
Stretch'd to relieve the Idiot and the Poor,
Proud Vice to brand, or injur'd Worth adorn,
And stretch the Ray to Ages yet unborn.
Not but there are, who merit other palms;
Hopkins and Sternhold glad the heart with Psalms:
The Boys and Girls whom charity maintains,
Implore your help in these pathetic strains:
How could Devotion touch the country pews,
Unless the Gods bestow'd a proper Muse?
Verse chears their leisure, Verse assists their work,
Verse prays for peace, or sings down Pope and Turk.
The silenc'd Preacher yields to potent strain,
And feels that grace his pray'r besought in vain;
The blessing thrills thro' all the lab'ring throng,
And Heav'n is won by Violence of Song.
  Our rural Ancestors, with little blest,
Patient of labour when the end was rest,
Indulg'd the day that hous'd their annual grain,
With feasts, and off'rings, and a thankful strain:
The joy their wives, their sons, and servants share,
Ease of their toil, and part'ners of their care:
The laugh, the jest, attendants on the bowl,
Smooth'd ev'ry brow, and open'd ev'ry soul:
With growing years the pleasing Licence grew,
And Taunts alternate innocently flew.
But Times corrupt, and Nature, ill-inclin'd,
Produc'd the point that left a sting behind;
Till friend with friend, and families at strife,
Triumphant Malice rag'd thro' private life.
Who felt the wrong, or fear'd it, took th' alarm,
Appeal'd to Law, and Justice lent her arm.

At length, by wholsome dread of statutes bound,
The Poets learn'd to please, and not to wound:
Most warp'd to Flatt'ry's side; but some, more nice,
Preserv'd the freedom, and forbore the vice.
Hence Satire rose, that just the medium hit,
And heals with Morals what it hurts with Wit.
We conquer'd France, but felt our Captive's charms;
Her Arts victorious triumph'd o'er our Arms;
Britain to soft refinements less a foe,
Wit grew polite, and Numbers learn'd to flow.
Waller was smooth; but Dryden taught to join
The varying verse, the full-resounding line,
The long majestic March, and Energy divine.
Tho' still some traces of our rustic vein
And splay-foot verse, remain'd, and will remain.
Late, very late, correctness grew our care,
When the tir'd Nation breath'd from civil war.
Exact Racine, and Corneille's noble fire,
Show'd us that France had something to admire.
Not but the Tragic spirit was our own,
And full in Shakespear, fair in Otway shone:
But Otway fail'd to polish or refine,
And fluent Shakespear scarce effac'd a line.
Ev'n copious Dryden wanted, or forgot,
The last and greatest Art, the Art to blot.
Some doubt, if equal pains, or equal fire
The humbler Muse of Comedy require.
But in known Images of life, I guess
The labour greater, as th' indulgence less.
Observe how seldom ev'n the best succeed:
Tell me if Congreve's Fools are Fools indeed?
What pert, low Dialogue has Farqu'ar writ!
How Van wants grace, who never wanted wit!
The stage how loosely does Astræa tread,
Who fairly puts all Characters to bed!
And idle Cibber, how he breaks the laws,
To make poor Pinky eat with vast applause!
But fill their purse, our Poet's work is done,
Alike to them, by Pathos or by Pun.
O you! whom Vanity's light bark conveys
On Fame's mad voyage by the wind of praise,
With what a shifting gale your course you ply,
For ever sunk too low, or born too high!
Who pants for glory finds but short repose,
A breath revives him, or a breath o'erthrows.
Farewell the stage! if just as thrives the play,
The silly bard grows fat, or falls away.
There still remains, to mortify a Wit,

The many-headed Monster of the Pit:
A senseless, worthless, and unhonour'd croud;
Who, to disturb their betters mighty proud,
Clatt'ring their sticks before ten lines are spoke,
Call for the Farce, the Bear, or the Black-joke.
What dear delight to Britons Farce affords!
Ever the taste of Mobs, but now of Lords;
(Taste, that eternal wanderer, which flies
From heads to ears, and now from ears to eyes.)
The Play stands still; damn action and discourse,
Back fly the scenes, and enter foot and horse;
Pageants on pageants, in long order drawn,
Peers, Heralds, Bishops, Ermin, Gold and Lawn;
The Champion too! and, to complete the jest,
Old Edward's Armour beams on Cibber's breast.
With laughter sure Democritus had dy'd,
Had he beheld an Audience gape so wide.
Let Bear or Elephant be e'er so white,
The people, sure, the people are the sight!
Ah luckless Poet! stretch thy lungs and roar,
That Bear or Elephant shall heed thee more;
While all its throats the Gallery extends,
And all the Thunder of the Pit ascends!
Loud as the Wolves, on Orcas' stormy steep,
Howl to the roarings of the Northern deep.
Such is the shout, the long-applauding note,
At Quin's high plume, or Oldfield's petticoat;
Or when from Court a birth-day suit bestow'd,
Sinks the lost Actor in the tawdry load.
Booth enters—hark! the Universal peal!
"But has he spoken?" Not a syllable.
What shook the stage, and made the people stare?
Cato's long Wig, flow'r'd gown, and lacquer'd chair.
  Yet lest you think I railly more than teach,
Or praise malignly Arts I cannot reach,
Let me for once presume t' instruct the times,
To know the Poet from the Man of rhymes:
'Tis he, who gives my breast a thousand pains,
Can make me feel each Passion that he feigns;
Inrage, compose, with more than magic Art,
With Pity, and with Terror, tear my heart;
And snatch me, o'er the earth, or thro' the air,
To Thebes, to Athens, when he will, and where.
  But not this Part of the Poetic state
Alone, deserves the favour of the Great:
Think of those Authors, Sir, who would rely
More on a Reader's sense, than Gazer's eye.
Or who shall wander where the Muses sing?

Who climb their mountain, or who taste their spring?
How shall we fill a Library with Wit,
When Merlin's Cave is half unfurnish'd yet?
My Liege! why Writers little claim your thought,
I guess; and, with their leave, will tell the fault:
We Poets are (upon a Poet's word)
Of all mankind, the creatures most absurd:
The season, when to come, and when to go,
To sing, or cease to sing, we never know;
And if we will recite nine hours in ten,
You lose your patience, just like other men.
Then too we hurt ourselves, when to defend
A single verse, we quarrel with a friend;
Repeat unask'd; lament, the Wit's too fine
For vulgar eyes, and point out ev'ry line.
But most, when straining with too weak a wing,
We needs will write Epistles to the King;
And from the moment we oblige the town,
Expect a place, or pension from the Crown;
Or dubb'd Historians by express command,
T' enroll your triumphs o'er the seas and land,
Be call'd to Court to plan some work divine,
As once for LOUIS, Boileau and Racine.
Yet think, great Sir! (so many Virtues shown)
Ah think, what Poet best may make them known?
Or chuse at least some Minister of Grace,
Fit to bestow the Laureat's weighty place.
Charles, to late times to be transmitted fair,
Assign'd his figure to Bernini's care;
And great Nassau to Kneller's hand decreed
To fix him graceful on the bounding Steed;
So well in paint and stone they judg'd of merit:
But Kings in Wit may want discerning Spirit.
The Hero William, and the Martyr Charles,
One knighted Blackmore, and one pension'd Quarles;
Which made old Ben, and surly Dennis swear,
"No Lord's anointed, but a Russian Bear.
Not with such majesty, such bold relief,
The Forms august, of King, or conqu'ring Chief,
E'er swell'd on marble; as in verse have shin'd
(In polish'd verse) the Manners and the Mind.
Oh! could I mount on the Mæonian wing,
Your Arms, your Actions, your Repose to sing!
What seas you travers'd, and what fields you fought!
Your Country's Peace, how oft, how dearly bought!
How barb'rous rage subsided at your word,
And Nations wonder'd while they dropp'd the sword!
How, when you nodded, o'er the land and deep,

Peace stole her wing, and wrapt the world in sleep;
'Till earth's extremes your mediation own,
And Asia's Tyrants tremble at your Throne—
But Verse, alas! your Majesty disdains;
And I'm not us'd to Panegyric strains:
The Zeal of Fools offends at any time,
But most of all, the Zeal of Fools in rhyme.
Besides, a fate attends on all I write,
That when I aim at praise, they say I bite.
A vile Encomium doubly ridicules:
There's nothing blackens like the ink of fools.
If true, a woful likeness; and if lyes,
"Praise undeserv'd is scandal in disguise:"
Well may he blush, who gives it, or receives;
And when I flatter, let my dirty leaves
(Like Journals, Odes, and such forgotten things
As Eusden, Philips, Settle, writ of Kings)
Cloath spice, line trunks, or flutt'ring in a row,
Befringe the rails of Bedlam and Soho.

One Thousand Seven Hundred and Thirty Eight
A Dialogue Something like Horace[1]

FR. Not twice a twelve-month you appear in Print,
And when it comes, the Court see nothing in 't.
You grow correct, that once, with Rapture writ,
And are, besides, too *moral* for a Wit.
Decay of Parts, alas! we all must feel—
Why now, this moment, don't I see you steal?
'Tis all from Horace; Horace long before ye
Said, "Tories call'd him Whig, and Whigs a Tory";
And taught his Romans, in much better metre,
"To laugh at Fools who put their trust in Peter."
  But Horace, Sir, was delicate, was nice;
Bubo observes, he lash'd no sort of *Vice:*
Horace would say, Sir Billy *serv'd the Crown*,
Blunt could *do Bus'ness*, H-ggins *knew the Town*;
In Sappho touch the *Failing of the Sex*,
In rev'rend Bishops note some *small Neglects*,
And own, the Spaniard did a *waggish thing*,
Who cropt our Ears, and sent them to the King.
His sly, polite, insinuating style
Could please at Court, and make AUGUSTUS smile:

[1] This and the following piece were entitled by Warburton "Epilogue to the Satires." Published May 16, 1738. Text of *Works*, 1751.

An artful Manager, that crept between
His Friend and Shame, and was a kind of *Screen.*
But 'faith your very Friends will soon be sore;
Patriots there are, who wish you'd jest no more—
And where's the Glory; 'twill be only thought
The Great man never offer'd you a groat.
Go see Sir ROBERT—
P. See Sir ROBERT!—hum—
And never laugh—for all my life to come?
Seen him I have, but in his happier hour
Of Social Pleasure, ill-exchang'd for Pow'r;
Seen him, uncumber'd with the Venal tribe,
Smile without Art, and win without a Bribe.
Would he oblige me? let me only find,
He does not think me what he thinks mankind.
Come, come, at all I laugh he laughs, no doubt;
The only diff'rence is, I dare laugh out.
F. Why yes: with *Scripture* still you may be free;
A Horse-laugh, if you please, at *Honesty*;
A Joke on JEKYL, or some odd *Old Whig*
Who never chang'd his Principle, or Wig:
A Patriot is a Fool in ev'ry age,
Whom all Lord Chamberlains allow the Stage:
These nothing hurts; they keep their Fashion still,
And wear their strange old Virtue, as they will.
If any ask you, "Who's the Man, so near
"His Prince, that writes in Verse, and has his ear?"
Why, answer, LYTTLETON, and I'll engage
The worthy Youth shall ne'er be in a rage:
But were his Verses vile, his Whisper base,
You'd quickly find him in Lord *Fanny*'s case.
Sejanus, Wolsey, hurt not honest FLEURY,
But well may put some Statesman in a fury.
Laugh then at any, but at Fools or Foes;
These you but anger, and you mend not those.
Laugh at your friends, and, if your Friends are sore,
So much the better, you may laugh the more.
To Vice and Folly to confine the jest,
Sets half the world, God knows, against the rest;
Did not the Sneer of more impartial men
At Sense and Virtue, balance all agen.
Judicious Wits spread wide the Ridicule,
And charitably comfort Knave and Fool.
P. Dear Sir, forgive the Prejudice of Youth:
Adieu Distinction, Satire, Warmth, and Truth!
Come, harmless Characters that no one hit;
Come, Henley's Oratory, Osborn's Wit!
The Honey dropping from Favonio's tongue,

The Flow'rs of Bubo, and the Flow of Y—ng!
The gracious Due of Pulpit Eloquence,
And all the well-whipt Cream of Courtly Sense,
That First was H—vy's, F—'s next, and then
The S—te's, and then H—vy's once agen.
O come, that easy Ciceronian style,
So Latin, yet so English all the while,
As, tho' the Pride of Middleton and Bland,
All Boys may read, and Girls may understand!
Then might I sing, without the least offence,
And all I sung should be the *Nation*'s Sense;
Or teach the Melancholy Muse to mourn,
Hang the sad Verse on CAROLINA's Urn,
And hail her passage to the Realms of Rest,
All Parts perform'd, and *all* her Children blest!
So—Satire is no more—I feel it die—
No *Gazetteer* more innocent than I—
And let, a God's-name, ev'ry Fool and Knave
Be grac'd thro' Life, and flatter'd in his Grave.
F. Why so? if Satire knows its Time and Place,
You still may lash the greatest—in Disgrace:
For Merit will by turns forsake them all;
Would you know when! exactly when they fall.
But let all Satire in all Changes spare
Immortal S—k, and grave De—re.
Silent and soft, as Saints remove to Heav'n,
All Tyes dissolv'd, and ev'ry Sin forgiv'n,
These may some gentle ministerial Wing
Receive, and place for ever near a King!
There, where no Passion, Pride, or Shame transport,
Lull'd with the sweet Nepenthe of a Court;
There, where no Father's, Brother's, Friend's disgrace
Once break their rest, or stir them from their Place:
But past the Sense of human Miseries,
All Tears are wip'd for ever from all eyes;
No cheek is known to blush, no heart to throb,
Save when they lose a Question, or a Job.
P. Good Heav'n forbid, that I should blast their glory,
Who know how like Whig Ministers to Tory,
And when three Sov'reigns dy'd, could scarce be vext,
Consid'ring what a *gracious Prince* was next.
Have I, in silent wonder seen such things
As Pride in Slaves, and Avarice in Kings;
And at a Peer or Peeress, shall I fret,
Who starves a Sister, or forswears a Debt?
Virtue, I grant you, is an empty boast;
But shall the Dignity of *Vice* be lost?
Ye Gods! shall Cibber's Son, without rebuke,

Swear like a Lord, or Rich out-whore a Duke;
A Fav'rite's Porter with his Master vie,
Be brib'd as often, and as often lie?
Shall Ward draw Contracts with a Statesman's skill?
Or Japhet pocket, like his Grace, a Will?
Is it for Bond, or Peter, (paltry things)
To pay their Debts, or keep their Faith, like Kings?
If Blount dispatch'd himself he play'd the man,
And so may'st thou, illustrious Passeran!
But shall a Printer, weary of his life,
Learn, from their Books, to hang himself and Wife?
This, this, my Friend, I cannot, must not bear;
Vice thus abus'd, demands a Nation's care:
This calls the Church to deprecate our Sin,
And hurls the Thunder of the Laws on *Gin.*
  Let modest FOSTER, if he will, excell
Ten Metropolitans in preaching well;
A simple Quaker, or a Quaker's Wife,
Out-do Landaffe in Doctrine,—yea in Life:
Let humble ALLEN, with an aukward Shame,
Do good by stealth, and blush to find it Fame.
Virtue may chuse the high or low Degree,
'Tis just alike to Virtue, and to me;
Dwell in a Monk, or light upon a King,
She's still the same, belov'd, contented thing.
Vice is undone, if she forgets her Birth,
And stoops from Angels to the Dregs of Earth:
But 'tis the *Fall* degrades her to a Whore;
Let *Greatness* own her, and she's mean no more,
Her Birth, her Beauty, Crowds and Courts confess,
Chaste Matrons praise her, and grave Bishops bless;
In golden Chains the willing World she draws,
And hers the Gospel is, and hers the Laws,
Mounts the Tribunal, lifts her scarlet head,
And sees pale Virtue carted in her stead.
Lo! at the wheels of her Triumphal Car,
Old England's Genius, rough with many a Scar,
Dragg'd in the Dust! his arms hang idly round,
His Flag inverted trails along the ground!
Our Youth, all livery'd o'er with foreign Gold,
Before her dance: behind her, crawl the Old!
See thronging Millions to the Pagod run,
And offer Country, Parent, Wife, or Son!
Hear her black Trumpet thro' the Land proclaim,
That NOT TO BE CORRUPTED IS THE SHAME.
In Soldier, Churchman, Patriot, Man in Pow'r,
'Tis Av'rice all, Ambition is no more!
See, all our Nobles begging to be Slaves!

See, all our Fools aspiring to be Knaves!
The Wit of Cheats, the Courage of a Whore,
Are what ten thousand envy and adore:
All, all look up, with reverential Awe,
At Crimes that 'scape, or triumph o'er the Law:
While Truth, Worth, Wisdom, daily they decry—
"Nothing is Sacred now but Villainy."
Yet may this Verse (if such a Verse remain)
Show, there was one who held it in disdain.

One Thousand Seven Hundred and Thirty Eight Dialogue II[1]

FR. 'Tis all a Libel—Paxton (Sir) will say.
P. Not yet, my Friend! to morrow faith it may;
And for that very cause I print to day.
How should I fret to mangle ev'ry line,
In rev'rence to the Sins of *Thirty-nine!*
Vice, with such Giant strides comes on amain,
Invention strives to be before in vain;
Feign what I will, and paint it e'er so strong,
Some rising Genius sins up to my Song.
F. Yet none but you by Name the guilty lash;
Ev'n Guthry saves half Newgate by a Dash.
Spare then the Person, and expose the Vice.
P. How, Sir! not damn the Sharper, but the Dice?
Come on then, Satire! gen'ral, unconfin'd,
Spread thy broad wing, and souce on all the kind.
Ye Statesmen, Priests, of one Religion all!
Ye Tradesmen, vile, in Army, Court, or Hall!
Ye Rev'rend Atheists. F. Scandal! name them, Who?
P. Why that's the thing you bid me not to do.
Who starv'd a Sister, who forswore a Debt,
I never nam'd; the Town's enquiring yet,
The pois'ning Dame—F. You mean—P. I don't. F. You do.
P. See, now I keep the Secret, and not you!
The bribing Statesman—F. Hold, too high you go.
P. The brib'd Elector—F. There you stoop too low.
P. I fain would please you, if I knew with what;
Tell me, which Knave is lawful Game, which not?
Must great Offenders, once escap'd the Crown,
Like Royal Harts be never more run down?
Admit your Law to spare the Knight requires,
As Beasts of Nature may we hunt the Squires?

[1] Published July 18, 1738. Text of *Works*, 1751.

Suppose I censure—you know what I mean—
To save a Bishop, may I name a Dean?
  F. A Dean, Sir? no: his Fortune is not made,
You hurt a man that's rising in the Trade.
  P. If not the Tradesman who set up to day,
Much less the 'Prentice who to morrow may.
Down, down, proud Satire! tho' a Realm be spoil'd,
Arraign no mightier Thief than wretched *Wild*;
Or, if a Court or Country's made a job,
Go drench a Pick-pocket, and join the Mob.
  But, Sir, I beg you (for the Love of Vice!)
The matter's weighty, pray consider twice;
Have you less pity for the needy Cheat,
The poor and friendless Villain, than the Great?
Alas! the small Discredit of a Bribe
Scarce hurts the Lawyer, but undoes the Scribe.
Then better sure it Charity becomes
To tax Directors, who (thank God) have Plums;
Still better, Ministers; or, if the thing
May pinch ev'n there—why lay it on a King.
  F. Stop! stop! P. Must Satire, then, nor rise nor fall?
Speak out, and bid me blame no Rogues at all.
  F. Yes, strike that *Wild*, I'll justify the blow.
  P. Strike? why the man was hang'd ten years ago:
Who now that obsolete Example fears?
Ev'n Peter trembles only for his Ears.
  F. What always Peter? Peter thinks you mad,
You make men desp'rate if they once are bad:
Else might he take to Virtue some years hence—
  P. As S—k, if he lives, will love the PRINCE.
  F. Strange spleen to S—k! P. Do I wrong the Man?
God knows, I praise a Courtier where I can.
When I confess, there is who feels for Fame,
And melts to Goodness, need I SCARB'ROW name?
Pleas'd let me own, in *Esher*'s peaceful Grove
(Where *Kent* and Nature vye for PELHAM'S Love)
The Scene, the Master, opening to my view,
I sit and dream I see my CRAGGS anew!
  Ev'n in a Bishop I can spy Desert;
Secker is decent, *Rundel* has a Heart,
Manners with Candour are to *Benson* giv'n,
To *Berkley*, ev'ry Virtue under Heav'n.
  But does the Court a worthy Man remove?
That instant, I declare, he has my Love:
I shun his Zenith, court his mild Decline;
Thus SOMMERS once, and HALIFAX, were mine.
Oft, in the clear, still Mirrour of Retreat,
I study'd SHREWSBURY, the wise and great:

Carleton's calm Sense, and Stanhope's noble Flame,
Compar'd, and knew their gen'rous End the same:
How pleasing Atterbury's softer hour!
How shin'd the Soul, unconquer'd in the Tow'r!
How can I Pult'ney, Chesterfield forget,
While Roman Spirit charms, and Attic Wit:
Argyll, the State's whole Thunder born to wield,
And shake alike the Senate and the Field:
Or Wyndham, just to Freedom and the Throne,
The Master of our Passions, and his own.
Names, which I long have lov'd, nor lov'd in vain,
Rank'd with their Friends, not number'd with their Train;
And if yet higher the proud List should end,
Still let me say! No Follower, but a Friend.
Yet think not, Friendship only prompts my lays;
I follow *Virtue*; where she shines, I praise:
Point she to Priest or Elder, Whig or Tory,
Or round a Quaker's Beaver cast a Glory.
I never (to my sorrow I declare)
Din'd with the Man of Ross, or my Lord May'r.
Some, in their choice of Friends (nay look not grave)
Have still a secret Byass to a Knave:
To find an honest man I beat about,
And love him, court him, praise him, in or out.
F. Then why so few commended? P. Not so fierce;
Find you the Virtue, and I'll find the Verse.
But random Praise—the task can ne'er be done;
Each Mother asks it for her booby Son,
Each Widow asks it for *the Best of Men*,
For him she weeps, and him she weds agen.
Praise cannot stoop, like Satire, to the ground;
The Number may be hang'd, but not be crown'd.
Enough for half the Greatest of these days,
To 'scape my Censure, not expect my Praise.
Are they not rich? what more can they pretend?
Dare they to hope a Poet for their Friend?
What Richlieu wanted, Louis scarce could gain,
And what young Ammon wish'd, but wish'd in vain.
No Pow'r the Muse's Friendship can command;
No Pow'r, when Virtue claims it, can withstand:
To *Cato, Virgil* pay'd one honest line;
O let my Country's Friends illumin mine!
—What are you thinking? F. Faith the thought's no sin,
I think your Friends are out and would be in.
P. If merely to come in, Sir, they go out,
The way they take is strangely round about.
F. They too may be corrupted, you'll allow?
P. I only call those Knaves who are so now.

Is that too little? Come then, I'll comply—
Spirit of *Arnall!* aid me while I lye.
COBHAM'S a Coward, POLWARTH is a Slave,
And LYTTLETON a dark, designing Knave,
ST. JOHN has ever been a wealthy Fool—
But let me add, Sir ROBERT'S mighty dull,
Has never made a Friend in private life,
And was, besides, a Tyrant to his Wife.
But pray, when others praise him, do I blame?
Call Verres, Wolsey, any odious name?
Why rail they then, if but a Wreath of mine,
Oh All-accomplish'd ST. JOHN! deck thy shrine?
What? shall each spurgall'd Hackney of the day,
When Paxton gives him double Pots and Pay,
Or each new-pension'd Sycophant, pretend
To break my Windows if I treat a Friend?
Then wisely plead, to me they meant no hurt,
But 'twas my Guest at whom they threw the dirt?
Sure, if I spare the Minister, no rules
Of Honour bind me, not to maul his Tools;
Sure, if they cannot cut, it may be said
His Saws are toothless, and his Hatchets Lead.
It anger'd TURENNE, once upon a day,
To see a Footman kick'd that took his pay:
But when he heard th' Affront the Fellow gave,
Knew one a Man of honour, one a Knave;
The prudent Gen'ral turn'd it to a jest,
And begg'd, he'd take the pains to kick the rest:
Which not at present having time to do—
F. Hold Sir! for God's-sake where's th' Affront to you?
Against your worship when had S—k writ?
Or P—ge pour'd forth the Torrent of his Wit?
Or grant the Bard whose distich all commend
[*In Pow'r a Servant, out of Pow'r a friend*]
To W—le guilty of some venial sin;
What's that to you who ne'er was out nor in?
The Priest whose Flattery be-dropt the Crown,
How hurt he you? he only stain'd the Gown.
And how did, pray, the florid Youth offend,
Whose Speech you took, and gave it to a Friend?
P. Faith, it imports not much from whom it came;
Whoever borrow'd, could not be to blame,
Since the whole House did afterwards the same.
Let Courtly Wits to Wits afford supply,
As Hog to Hog in huts of Westphaly;
If one, thro' Nature's Bounty or his Lord's,
Has what the frugal, dirty soil affords,
From him the next receives it, thick or thin,

As pure a mess almost as it came in;
The blessed benefit, not there confin'd,
Drops to the third, who nuzzles close behind;
From tail to mouth, they feed and they carouse:
The last full fairly gives it to the *House*.
F. This filthy simile, this beastly line
Quite turns my stomach— P. So does Flatt'ry mine;
And all your courtly Civet-cats can vent,
Perfume to you, to me is Excrement.
But hear me further—Japhet, 'tis agreed,
Writ not, and Chartres scarce could write or read,
In all the Courts of Pindus guiltless quite;
But Pens can forge, my Friend, that cannot write;
And must no Egg in Japhet's face be thrown,
Because the Deed he forg'd was not my own?
Must never Patriot then declaim at Gin,
Unless, good man! he has been fairly in?
No zealous Pastor blame a failing Spouse,
Without a staring Reason on his brows?
And each Blasphemer quite escape the rod,
Because the insult's not on Man, but God?
Ask you what Provocation I have had?
The strong Antipathy of Good to Bad.
When Truth or Virtue an Affront endures,
Th' Affront is mine, my friend, and should be yours.
Mine, as a Foe profess'd to false Pretence,
Who think a Coxcomb's Honour like his Sense;
Mine, as a Friend to ev'ry worthy mind;
And mine as Man, who feel for all mankind.
F. You're strangely proud. P. So proud, I am no Slave:
So impudent, I own myself no Knave:
So odd, my Country's Ruin makes me grave.
Yes, I am proud; I must be proud to see
Men not afraid of God, afraid of me:
Safe from the Bar, the Pulpit, and the Throne,
Yet touch'd and sham'd by Ridicule alone.
O sacred weapon! left for Truth's defence,
Sole Dread of Folly, Vice, and Insolence!
To all but Heav'n-directed hands deny'd,
The Muse may give thee, but the Gods must guide:
Rev'rent I touch thee! but with honest zeal;
To rouse the Watchmen of the public Weal,
To Virtue's work provoke the tardy Hall,
And goad the Prelate slumb'ring in his Stall.
Ye tinsel Insects! whom a Court maintains,
That counts your Beauties only by your Stains,
Spin all your Cobwebs o'er the Eye of Day!
The Muse's wing shall brush you all away:

All his Grace preaches, all his Lordship sings,
All that makes Saints of Queens, and Gods of Kings.
All, all but Truth, drops dead-born from the Press,
Like the last Gazette, or the last Address.
  When black Ambition stains a public Cause,
A Monarch's sword when mad Vain-glory draws,
Not Waller's Wreath can hide the Nation's Scar,
Nor Boileau turn the Feather to a Star.
  Not so, when diadem'd with rays divine,
Touch'd with the Flame that breaks from *Virtue*'s Shrine,
Her Priestess Muse forbids the Good to die,
And opes the Temple of *Eternity*.
There, other Trophies deck the truly brave,
Than such as Anstis casts into the Grave;
Far other Stars than * and * * wear,
And may descend to Mordington from STAIR:
(Such as on HOUGH's unsully'd Mitre shine,
Or beam, good DIGBY, from a heart like thine)
Let *Envy* howl, while Heav'n's whole Chorus sings,
And bark at Honour not confer'd by Kings;
Let *Flatt'ry* sickening see the Incense rise,
Sweet to the World, and grateful to the Skies:
Truth guards the Poet, sanctifies the line,
And makes immortal, Verse as mean as mine.
  Yes, the last Pen for Freedom let me draw,
When Truth stands trembling on the edge of Law;
Here, Last of Britons! let your Names be read;
Are none, none living? let me praise the Dead,
And for that Cause which made your Fathers shine,
Fall by the Votes of their degen'rate Line.
  Fr. Alas! alas! pray end what you began,
And write next winter more *Essays on Man*.

The Universal Prayer
Deo Opt. Max.[1]

FATHER of All! in ev'ry Age,
  In ev'ry Clime ador'd,
By Saint, by Savage, and by Sage,
  Jehovah, Jove, or Lord!

Thou Great First Cause, least understood:
  Who all my Sense confin'd

[1] Published June 22, 1738. Text of *Works*, 1751.

To know but this, that Thou art Good,
And that myself am blind;

Yet gave me, in this dark Estate,
To see the Good from Ill;
And binding Nature fast in Fate,
Left free the Human Will.

What Conscience dictates to be done,
Or warns me not to do,
This, teach me more than Hell to shun,
That, more than Heav'n pursue.

What Blessings thy free Bounty gives,
Let me not cast away;
For God is pay'd when Man receives,
T' enjoy is to obey.

Yet not to Earth's contracted Span,
Thy Goodness let me bound,
Or think Thee Lord alone of Man,
When thousand Worlds are round:

Let not this weak, unknowing hand
Presume thy bolts to throw,
And deal damnation round the land,
On each I judge thy Foe.

If I am right, thy grace impart,
Still in the right to stay;
If I am wrong, oh teach my heart
To find that better way.

Save me alike from foolish Pride,
Or impious Discontent,
At ought thy Wisdom has deny'd,
Or ought thy Goodness lent.

Teach me to feel another's Woe,
To hide the Fault I see;
That Mercy I to others show,
That Mercy show to me.

Mean tho' I am, not wholly so
Since quick'ned by thy Breath;
Oh lead me wheresoe'er I go,
Thro' this day's Life or Death.

This day, be Bread and Peace my Lot:
All else beneath the Sun,
Thou know'st if best bestow'd or not,
And let Thy Will be done.

To thee, whose Temple is all Space,
Whose Altar, Earth, Sea, Skies!
One Chorus let all Being raise!
All Nature's Incense rise!

On a Certain Lady at Court[1]

I KNOW the thing that's most uncommon;
(Envy be silent, and attend!)
I know a reasonable Woman,
Handsome and witty, yet a Friend.

Not warp'd by Passion, aw'd by Rumour,
Not grave thro' Pride, or gay thro' Folly,
An equal mixture of good Humour,
And sensible soft Melancholy.

"Has she no faults then (Envy says) Sir?"
Yes, she has one, I must aver;
When all the World conspires to praise her,
The Woman's deaf, and does not hear.

THOMAS PARNELL

(1679-1712-1718)

A Hymn to Contentment[2]

LOVELY, lasting Peace of Mind!
Sweet Delight of human kind!
Heavenly born, and bred on high,
To crown the Fav'rites of the Sky
With more of Happiness below,

[1] Published in *Works*, 1751. Text of 1751.
[2] Published in Steele's *Miscellany*, 1714. Text of *Poems on Several Occasions*, 1722.

Than Victors in a Triumph know!
Whither, O whither art thou fled,
To lay thy meek, contented Head?
What happy Region dost thou please
To make the Seat of Calms and Ease?

Ambition searches all its Sphere
Of Pomp and State, to meet thee there.
Encreasing Avarice would find
Thy Presence in its Gold enshrin'd.
The bold Advent'rer ploughs his way,
Thro' Rocks amidst the foaming Sea,
To gain thy Love; and then perceives
Thou wert not in the Rocks and Waves.
The silent Heart which Grief assails,
Treads soft and lonesome o'er the Vales,
Sees Daisies open, Rivers run,
And seeks (as I have vainly done)
Amusing Thought; but learns to know
That Solitude's the Nurse of Woe.
No real Happiness is found
In trailing Purple o'er the Ground:
Or in a Soul exalted high,
To range the Circuit of the Sky,
Converse with Stars above, and know
All Nature in its Forms below;
The Rest it seeks, in seeking dies,
And Doubts at last for Knowledge rise.

Lovely, lasting Peace appear!
This World it self, if thou art here,
Is once again with *Eden* bless'd,
And Man contains it in his Breast.

'Twas thus, as under Shade I stood,
I sung my Wishes to the Wood,
And lost in Thought, no more perceiv'd
The Branches whisper as they wav'd:
It seem'd, as all the quiet Place
Confess'd the Presence of the Grace.
When thus she spoke—Go rule thy Will,
Bid thy wild Passions all be still,
Know God—and bring thy Heart to know,
The Joys which from Religion flow:
Then ev'ry Grace shall prove its Guest,
And I'll be there to crown the rest.

Oh! by yonder Mossy Seat,
In my Hours of sweet Retreat;
Might I thus my Soul employ,
With sense of Gratitude and Joy:
Rais'd as antient Prophets were,
In heavenly Vision, Praise, and Pray'r;
Pleasing all Men, hurting none,
Pleas'd and bless'd with God alone:
Then while the Gardens take my Sight,
With all the Colours of Delight;
While silver Waters glide along,
To please my Ear, and court my Song:
I'll lift my Voice, and tune my String,
And thee, great *Source* of *Nature,* sing.

The Sun that walks his airy Way,
To light the World, and give the Day;
The Moon that shines with borrow'd Light;
The Stars that gild the gloomy Night;
The Seas that roll unnumber'd Waves;
The Wood that spreads its shady Leaves;
The Field whose Ears conceal the Grain,
The yellow Treasure of the Plain;
All of these, and all I see,
Shou'd be sung, and sung by me:
They speak their Maker as they can,
But want and ask the Tongue of Man.

Go search among your idle Dreams,
Your *busy*, or your *vain* Extreams;
And find a Life of equal Bliss,
Or own the *next* begun in *This*.

Song[1]

MY DAYS have been so wond'rous free,
The little Birds that fly
With careless ease from Tree to Tree,
Were but as bless'd as I.

Ask gliding Waters, if a Tear
Of mine encreas'd their Stream?
Or ask the flying Gales, if e'er
I lent one Sigh to them?

[1] Published in Steele's *Miscellany*, 1714. Text of *Poems on Several Occasions*, 1722.

But now my former Days retire,
And I'm by Beauty caught,
The tender Chains of sweet Desire
Are fix't upon my Thought.

Ye Nightingales, ye twisting Pines!
Ye Swains that haunt the Grove!
Ye gentle Echoes, breezy Winds!
Ye close Retreats of Love!

With all of Nature, all of Art,
Assist the dear Design;
O teach a young, unpractic'd Heart,
To make my *Nancy* mine.

The very Thought of Change I hate,
As much as of Despair;
Nor ever covet to be great,
Unless it be for her.

'Tis true, the Passion in my Mind
Is mix'd with soft Distress;
Yet while the Fair I love is kind,
I cannot wish it Less.

An Elegy. To an Old Beauty[1]

IN VAIN, poor Nymph, to please our youthful sight
You sleep in Cream and Frontlets all the Night,
Your Face with Patches soil, with Paint repair,
Dress with gay Gowns, and shade with foreign Hair.
If Truth in spight of Manners must be told,
Why really *Fifty Five* is something old.
Once you were young; or one, whose Life's so long
She might have born my Mother, tells me wrong.
And once (since Envy's dead before you dye,)
The Women own, you play'd a sparkling Eye,
Taught the light Foot a modish little Trip,
And pouted with the prettiest purple Lip—
To some new Charmer are the Roses fled,
Which blew, to damask all thy Cheek with red;
Youth calls the *Graces* there to fix their Reign,
And *Airs* by thousands fill their easy Train.
So parting Summer bids her flow'ry Prime

[1] Published in *Poems on Several Occasions*, 1722. Text of first edition.

Attend the Sun to dress some foreign Clime,
While with'ring Seasons in Succession, here,
Strip the gay Gardens, and deform the Year.
But thou (since Nature bids) the World resign,
'Tis now thy Daughter's Daughter's time to shine.
With more Address, (or such as pleases more)
She runs her Female Exercises o'er,
Unfurls or closes, raps or turns the Fan,
And smiles, or blushes at the Creature Man.
With quicker Life, as guilded Coaches pass,
In sideling Courtesy she drops the Glass.
With better Strength, on Visit-days she bears
To mount her fifty Flights of ample Stairs.
Her Mein, her Shape, her Temper, Eyes and Tongue
Are sure to conquer—for the Rogue is young;
And all that's madly wild, or oddly gay,
We call it only pretty *Fanny*'s way.
Let Time that makes you homely, make you sage,
The Sphere of Wisdom is the Sphere of Age.
'Tis true, when Beauty dawns with early Fire,
And hears the flatt'ring Tongues of soft Desire,
If not from Virtue, from its gravest Ways
The Soul with pleasing Avocation strays.
But Beauty gone, 'tis easier to be wise;
As Harpers better, by the loss of Eyes.
Henceforth retire, reduce your roving Airs,
Haunt less the Plays, and more the publick Pray'rs,
Reject the *Mechlin* Head, and gold Brocade,
Go pray, in sober *Norwich* Crape array'd.
Thy pendent Diamonds let thy *Fanny* take,
(Their trembling Lustre shows how much you shake;)
Or bid her wear thy Necklace row'd with Pearl,
You'll find your *Fanny* an obedient Girl.
So for the rest, with less Incumbrance hung,
You walk thro' Life, unmingled with the young;
And view the *Shade* and *Substance* as you pass
With joint Endeavour trifling at the Glass,
Or *Folly* drest, and rambling all her Days,
To meet her Counterpart, and grow by *Praise:*
Yet still sedate your self, and gravely plain,
You neither fret, nor envy at the Vain.
'Twas thus (if Man with Woman we compare)
The wise *Athenian* crost a glittering Fair,
Unmov'd by Tongues and Sights, he walk'd the place,
Thro' Tape, Toys, Tinsel, Gimp, Perfume, and Lace;
Then bends from *Mars*'s Hill his awful Eyes,
And *What a World I never want?* he cries;
But cries unheard: For *Folly* will be free.

So parts the buzzing gaudy Crowd, and He:
As careless he for them, as they for him;
He wrapt in *Wisdom*, and they whirl'd by *Whim*.

A Night-Piece on Death[1]

By the blue Tapers trembling Light,
No more I waste the wakeful Night,
Intent with endless view to pore
The Schoolmen and the Sages o'er:
Their Books from Wisdom widely stray,
Or point at best the longest Way.
I'll seek a readier Path, and go
Where Wisdom's surely taught *below*.

How deep yon Azure dies the Sky!
Where Orbs of Gold unnumber'd lye,
While thro' their Ranks in silver pride
The nether Crescent seems to glide.
The slumb'ring Breeze forgets to breathe,
The Lake is smooth and clear beneath,
Where once again the spangled Show
Descends to meet our Eyes below.
The Grounds which on the right aspire,
In dimness from the View retire:
The Left presents a Place of Graves,
Whose Wall the silent Water laves.
That Steeple guides thy doubtful sight
Among the livid gleams of Night.
There pass with melancholy State,
By all the solemn Heaps of Fate,
And think, as softly-sad you tread
Above the venerable Dead,
Time was, like thee they Life possest,
And Time shall be, that thou shalt Rest.

Those Graves, with bending Osier bound,
That nameless heave the crumbled Ground,
Quick to the glancing Thought disclose
Where *Toil* and *Poverty* repose.

The flat smooth Stones that bear a Name,
The Chissels slender help to Fame,
(Which e'er our Sett of Friends decay

[1] Published in *Poems on Several Occasions*, 1722. Text of first edition.

Their frequent Steps may wear away.)
A *middle Race* of Mortals own,
Men, half ambitious, all unknown.

The Marble Tombs that rise on high,
Whose Dead in vaulted Arches lye,
Whose Pillars swell with sculptur'd Stones,
Arms, Angels, Epitaphs and Bones,
These (all the poor Remains of State)
Adorn the *Rich*, or praise the *Great*;
Who while on Earth in Fame they live,
Are sensless of the Fame they give.

Ha! while I gaze, pale *Cynthia* fades,
The bursting Earth unveils the Shades!
All slow, and wan, and wrap'd with Shrouds,
They rise in visionary Crouds,
And all with sober Accent cry,
Think, Mortal, what it is to dye.

Now from yon black and fun'ral Yew,
That bathes the Charnel House with Dew,
Methinks I hear a *Voice* begin;
(Ye Ravens, cease your croaking Din,
Ye tolling Clocks, no Time resound
O'er the long Lake and midnight Ground)
It sends a Peal of hollow Groans,
Thus speaking from among the Bones.

When Men my Scythe and Darts supply,
How great a *King* of *Fears* am I!
They view me like the last of Things:
They make, and then they dread, my Stings.
Fools! if you less provok'd your Fears,
No more my Spectre-Form appears.
Death's but a Path that must be trod,
If Man wou'd ever pass to God:
A Port of Calms, a State of Ease
From the rough Rage of swelling Seas.

Why then thy flowing sable Stoles,
Deep pendent Cypress, mourning Poles,
Loose Scarfs to fall athwart thy Weeds,
Long Palls, drawn Herses, cover'd Steeds,
And Plumes of black, that as they tread,
Nod o'er the 'Scutcheons of the Dead?

Nor can the parted Body know,
Nor wants the Soul, these Forms of Woe:
As Men who long in Prison dwell,
With Lamps that glimmer round the Cell,
When e'er their suffering Years are run,
Spring forth to greet the glitt'ring Sun:
Such Joy, tho' far transcending Sense,
Have pious Souls at parting hence.
On Earth, and in the Body plac't,
A few, and evil Years, they wast:
But when their Chains are cast aside,
See the glad Scene unfolding wide,
Clap the glad Wing and tow'r away,
And mingle with the Blaze of Day.

ALLAN RAMSAY

(1685?-1712-1758)

The Young Laird and Edinburgh Katy[1]

Now wat ye wha I met Yestreen
Coming down the Street, my Jo,
My Mistress in her Tartan Screen,
Fow bonny, braw and sweet, my Jo.
My Dear, quoth I, Thanks to the Night,
That never wisht a Lover ill,
Since ye're out of your Mither's Sight,
Let's take a Wauk up to the Hill.

O KATY wiltu gang wi' me,
And leave the dinsome Town a while,
The Blossom's sprouting frae the Tree,
And a' the Summer's gawn to smile;
The Mavis, Nightingale and Lark,
The bleeting Lambs and whistling Hynd,
In ilka Dale, Green, Shaw and Park,
Will nourish Health, and glad ye'r Mind.

Soon as the clear Goodman of Day
Bends his Morning Draught of Dew,
We'll gae to some Burnside and play,
And gather Flowers to busk ye'r Brow.
We'll pou the Dazies on the Green,

[1] Published in *Scots Songs*, 1720. Text of *Poems*, third edition, 1723.

The lucken Gowans frae the Bog;
Between Hands now and then we'll lean,
And sport upo' the Velvet Fog.
  There's up into a pleasant Glen,
A wee Piece frae my Father's Tower,
A canny, saft and flowry Den,
Which circling Birks has form'd a Bower:
When e'er the Sun grows high and warm,
We'll to the cauller Shade remove,
There will I lock thee in mine Arm,
And love and kiss, and kiss and love.

Katy's Answer

MY MITHER's ay glowran o'er me,
Tho she did the same before me,
    I canna get Leave
    To look to my Loove,
Or else she'll be like to devour me.

Right fain wad I take ye'r Offer,
Sweet Sir, but I'll tine my Tocher,
    Then, SANDY, ye'll fret,
    And wyt ye'r poor KATE,
When e'er ye keek in your toom Coffer.

For tho my Father has Plenty
Of Siller and Plenishing dainty,
    Yet he's unco sweer
    To twin wi' his Gear,
And sae we had need to be tenty.

Tutor my Parents wi' Caution,
Be wylie in ilka Motion,
    Brag well o' ye'r Land,
    And there's my leal Hand,
Win them, I'll be at your Devotion.

Polwart on the Green[1]

AT POLWART *on the Green*
If you'll meet me the Morn,
Where Lasses do conveen

[1] Published in *Scots Songs*, 1720. Text of *Poems*, third edition, 1723.

To dance about the Thorn;
A kindly welcome you shall meet
Frae her wha likes to view
A Lover and a Lad complete,
The Lad and Lover you.

Let dorty Dames say *Na*,
As lang as e'er they please,
Seem caulder than the Sna',
While inwardly they Bleez;
But I will frankly shaw my Mind,
And yield my Heart to thee;
Be ever to the Captive kind,
That langs na to be free.

At *Polwart* on the Green,
Amang the new mawn Hay,
With Sangs and dancing keen
We'll pass the heartsome Day:
At Night if Beds be o'er thrang laid,
And thou be twin'd of thine,
Thou shalt be welcome, my dear Lad,
To take a Part of mine.

Up in the Air[1]

Now the Sun's gane out o' Sight,
Beet the Ingle and snuff the Light:
In Glens the Fairies skip and dance,
And Witches wallop o'er to *France*,
Up in the Air
On my bonny gray Mare.
And I see her yet, and I see her yet,
Up in &c.

The Wind's drifting Hail and Sna'
O'er frozen Hags like a Foot Ba',
Nae Starns keek throw the Azure Slit,
'Tis cauld and mirk as ony Pit.
The Man i' the Moon
Is carowsing aboon,
D'ye see, d'ye see, d'ye see him yet.
The Man, &c.

[1] Published in *Scots Songs*, 1720. Text of *Poems*, third edition, 1723.

Take your Glass to clear your Een,
'Tis the *Elixir* hales the Spleen,
Baith Wit and Mirth it will inspire,
And gently puff's the Lover's Fire.
  Up in the Air,
  It drives away Care,
Ha'e wi' ye, ha'e wi' ye, and ha'e wi' ye, Lads, yet.
  Up in &c.

Steek the Doors, keep out the Frost,
Come, *WILLY*, gi'es about ye'r Tost,
Til't Lads and lilt it out,
And let us ha'e a blythsom Bowt.
  Up wi't there,
  Dinna cheat, but drink fair,
Huzza, Huzza, and Huzza Lads yet.
  Up wi't &c.

An Ode to Mr. F ——[1]

Solvitur acris hiems,—HOR.

Now Gowans sprout and Lavrocks sing,
And welcome West-winds warm the Spring,
O'er Hill and Dale they saftly blaw,
And drive the Winter's Cauld awa.
The Ships lang gyzen'd at the Peer,
Now spread their Sails and smoothly steer.
The Nags and Nowt hate wissen'd Strae,
And frisking to the Fields they gae;
Nor Hynds wi' Elson and Hemp Lingle,
Sit solling Shoon out o'er the Ingle.
Now bonny Haughs their Verdure boast,
That late were clade wi' Snaw and Frost.
With her gay Train the *Paphian* Queen
By Moon-light dances on the Green;
She leads, while Nymphs and Graces sing,
And trip around the Fairy Ring.
Mean Time poor *Vulcan* hard at Thrift,
Gets mony a fair and heavy Lift,
Whilst rinnen down, his haff blind Lads
Blaw up the Fire, and thump the Gads.
  Now leave your Fitsted on the Dew,
And busk ye'r sell in Habit new:

[1] Published in *Poems*, 1721. Text of third edition, 1723.

Be gratefu' to the guiding Powers,
And blythly spend your easy Hours.
O canny F——, tutor Time,
And live as lang's ye'r in your Prime:
That ill-bred Death has nae Regard
To King or Cottar, or a Laird:
As soon a Castle he'll attack,
As Waws of Divots roof'd wi' Thack.
Immediately we'll a' take Flight
Into the mirk Realms of Night,
As Stories gang, with Gaists to roam,
In glowmie *Pluto*'s gowsty Dome;
Bid fair Good-day to Pleasure syne
Of bonny Lasses and red Wine.
  Then deem ilk little Care a Crime,
Dares waste an Hour of precious Time;
And since our Life's sae unco short,
Enjoy it a', ye've nae mair for't.

A Poet's Wish: An Ode[1]

Quid dedicatum poscit Apollinem
Vates? —HOR.

Frae great *Apollo*, Poet say,
What is thy Wish, what wadst thou hae,
When thou bows at his Shrine?
Not *Karss* o' *Gowrie*'s fertile Field,
Not a' the Flocks the *Grampians* yield,
  That are baith sleek and fine:
Not costly Things brought frae afar,
  As Ivory, Pearl and Gems;
Nor those fair Straths that water'd are
  With *Tay* and *Tweed*'s smooth Streams,
    Which gentily and daintily
    Eat down the flowry Braes;
    As greatly and quietly
    They wimple to the Seas.

Whaever by his kanny Fate
Is Master of a good Estate,
That can ilk Thing afford,
Let him enjoy't withoutten Care,

[1] Published in *Poems*, 1721. Text of third edition, 1723.

And with the Wale of curious Fare
  Cover his ample Board.
Much dawted by the Gods is he,
  Wha to the *Indian* Plain,
Succussfu' ploughs the wally Sea,
  And safe returns again
    With Riches, that hitches
    Him high aboon the rest
    Of sma' Fowk, and a' Fowk
    That are wi' Poortith prest.

For me I can be well content
To eat my Bannock on the Bent,
And kitchent't wi' fresh Air:
Of Lang-kail I can make a Feast,
And cantily had up my Crest,
  And laugh at Dishes rare.
Nought frae *Apollo* I demand,
  But throu' a lengthen'd Life
My outer Fabrick firm may stand,
  And Saul clear without Strife.
    May he then but gi'e then
    Those Blessings for my Skair,
    I'll fairly and squairly
    Quite a' and seek nae mair.

The Response of the Oracle

To keep thy Saul frae puny Strife,
And heeze thee out of vulgar Life,
We in a Morning-Dream,
Whisper'd our Will concerning thee,
To *Marlus* stretch'd beneath a Tree,
  Hard by a pop'ling Stream;
He full of me shall point the Way,
  Where thou a Star shalt see,
The Influence of whose bright Ray,
  Shall wing thy Muse to flee.
    Mair speer na, and fear na,
    But set thy Mind to Rest:
    Aspire ay still high'r ay,
    And always hope the best.

Give Me a Lass with a Lump of Land[1]

Gi'e me a lass with a lump of land,
And we for life shall gang thegither;
Tho' daft or wise I'll never demand,
Or black or fair it maks na whether.
I'm aff with wit, and beauty will fade,
And blood alane is no worth a shilling;
But she that's rich her market's made,
For ilka charm about her is killing.

Gi'e me a lass with a lump of land,
And in my bosom I'll hug my treasure;
Gin I had anes her gear in my hand,
Should love turn dowf, it will find pleasure.
Laugh on wha likes, but there's my hand,
I hate with poortith, tho' bonny, to meddle;
Unless they bring cash or a lump of land,
They'se never get me to dance to their fiddle.

There's meikle good love in bands and bags,
And siller and gowd's a sweet complexion;
But beauty, and wit, and virtue in rags,
Have tint the art of gaining affection.
Love tips his arrows with woods and parks,
And castles, and riggs, and moors, and meadows;
And naithing can catch our modern sparks,
But well-tocher'd lasses or jointur'd widows.

Sang[2]

My *Peggy* is a young thing,
Just enter'd in her teens,
Fair as the day, and sweet as *May*,
Fair as the day, and always gay:
My *Peggy* is a young thing,
And I'm not very auld,
Yet well I like to meet her at
The wawking of the fauld.

---

[1] Published in *Poems*, Edinburgh, 1728. Text of first edition. See Preface.

[2] Published in *The Gentle Shepherd*, 1734(?), Act I. Text of Edinburgh edition, 1755.

My *Peggy* speaks sae sweetly,
When'er we meet alane,
I wish nae mair to lay my care,
I wish nae mair of a' that's rare:
My *Peggy* speaks sae sweetly,
To a' the lave I'm cauld;
But she gars a' my spirits glow
At wawking of the fauld.

My *Peggy* smiles sae kindly,
Whene'er I whisper love,
That I look down on a' the town,
That I look down upon a crown:
My *Peggy* smiles sae kindly,
It makes me blythe and bauld,
And naithing gi'es me sic delight,
As wawking of the fauld.

My *Peggy* sings sae saftly,
When on my pipe I play,
By a' the rest it is confest,
By a' the rest, that she sings best:
My *Peggy* sings sae saftly,
And in her sangs are tald,
With innocence, the wale of sense,
At wawking of the fauld.

WILLIAM BROOME

(1689-1712-1745)

The Rose-Bud
To a Young Lady[1]

QUEEN of Fragrance, lovely Rose,
The Beauties of thy Leaves disclose!
The Winter's past, the Tempests fly,
Soft Gales breathe gently thro' the Sky;
The Lark sweet warbling on the Wing
Salutes the gay Return of Spring:
The silver Dews, the vernal Show'rs,
Call forth a bloomy Waste of Flow'rs;

[1] Published in *Poems on Several Occasions*, 1727. Text of first edition.

The joyous Fields, the shady Woods,
Are cloath'd with Green, or swell with Buds;
Then haste thy Beauties to disclose,
Queen of Fragrance, lovely Rose!
Thou, beauteous Flow'r, a welcome Guest,
Shalt flourish on the Fair-One's Breast,
Shalt grace her Hand, or deck her Hair,
The Flow'r most sweet, the Nymph most fair;
Breathe soft, ye Winds! be calm, ye Skies!
Arise ye flow'ry Race, arise!
And haste thy Beauties to disclose,
Queen of Fragrance, lovely Rose!
But thou, fair Nymph, thy self survey
In this sweet Offspring of a Day;
That Miracle of Face must fail,
Thy Charms are sweet, but Charms are frail:
Swift as the short-liv'd Flow'r they fly,
At Morn they bloom, at Evening die:
Tho' Sickness yet a while forbears,
Yet Time destroys, what Sickness spares;
Now *Helen* lives alone in Fame,
And *Cleopatra*'s but a Name;
Time must indent that heav'nly Brow,
And thou must be, what *Helen*'s now.
This Moral to the Fair disclose,
Queen of Fragrance, lovely Rose.

Anne Finch, Countess of Winchilsea

(1661-1713-1720)

To the Nightingale[1]

Exert thy Voice, sweet Harbinger of Spring!
This Moment is thy Time to Sing,
This Moment I attend to Praise,
And set my Numbers to thy Layes.
Free as thine shall be my Song;
As thy Musick, short, or long.

Poets, wild as thee, were born,
Pleasing best when unconfin'd,

[1] Published in *Miscellany Poems*, 1713. Text of first edition.

When to Please is least design'd,
Soothing but their Cares to rest;
Cares do still their Thoughts molest,
And still th' unhappy Poet's Breast,
Like thine, when best he sings, is plac'd against a Thorn.

She begins, Let all be still!
Muse, thy Promise now fulfill!
Sweet, oh! sweet, still sweeter yet
Can thy Words such Accents fit,
Canst thou Syllables refine,
Melt a Sense that shall retain
Still some Spirit of the Brain,
Till with Sounds like these it join.
'Twill not be! then change thy Note;
Let Division shake thy Throat.
Hark! Division now she tries;
Yet as far the Muse outflies.
Cease then, prithee, cease thy Tune;
Trifler, wilt thou sing till *June?*
Till thy Bus'ness all lies waste,
And the Time of Building's past!
Thus we Poets that have Speech,
Unlike what thy Forests teach,
If a fluent Vein be shown
That's transcendent to our own,
Criticize, reform, or preach,
Or censure what we cannot reach.

The Tree[1]

Fair *Tree*! for thy delightful Shade
'Tis just that some Return be made:
Sure, some Return is due from me
To thy cool Shadows, and to thee.
When thou to *Birds* do'st Shelter give,
Thou Musick do'st from them receive;
If *Travellers* beneath thee stay,
'Till Storms have worn themselves away,
That Time in praising thee they spend,
And thy protecting Pow'r commend:
The *Shepherd* here, from Scorching freed,
Tunes to thy dancing Leaves his Reed;

[1] Published in *Miscellany Poems*, 1713. Text of first edition.

Whilst his lov'd Nymph, in Thanks, bestows
Her flow'ry Chaplets on thy Boughs.
Shall I then only Silent be,
And no Return be made by me?
No; let this Wish upon thee wait,
And still to flourish be thy Fate,
To future Ages may'st thou stand
Untouch'd by the rash Workman's hand;
'Till that large Stock of Sap is spent,
Which gives thy Summer's Ornament;
'Till the fierce Winds, that vainly strive
To shock thy Greatness whilst alive,
Shall on thy lifeless Hour attend,
Prevent the Axe, and grace thy End;
Their scatter'd Strength together call,
And to the Clouds proclaim thy Fall;
Who then their Ev'ning-Dews may spare,
When thou no longer art their Care;
But shalt, like ancient Heroes, burn,
And some bright Hearth be made thy Urn.

A Nocturnal Reverie[1]

IN SUCH a *Night*, when every louder Wind
Is to its distant Cavern safe confin'd;
And only gentle *Zephyr* fans his Wings,
And lonely *Philomel*, still waking, sings;
Or from some Tree, fam'd for the *Owl*'s delight,
She, hollowing clear, directs the Wand'rer right:
In such a *Night*, when passing Clouds give place,
Or thinly vail the Heav'ns mysterious Face;
When in some River, overhung with Green,
The waving Moon and trembling Leaves are seen;
When freshen'd Grass now bears it self upright,
And makes cool Banks to pleasing Rest invite,
Whence springs the *Woodbind*, and the *Bramble*-Rose,
And where the sleepy *Cowslip* shelter'd grows;
Whilst now a paler Hue the *Foxglove* takes,
Yet checquers still with Red the dusky brakes:
When scatter'd *Glow-worms*, but in Twilight fine,
Shew trivial Beauties watch their Hour to shine;
Whilst *Salisb'ry* stands the Test of every Light,
In perfect Charms, and perfect Virtue bright:
When Odours, which declin'd repelling Day,

[1] Published in *Miscellany Poems*, 1713. Text of first edition.

Thro' temp'rate Air uninterrupted stray;
When darken'd Groves their softest Shadows wear,
And falling Waters we distinctly hear;
When thro' the Gloom more venerable shows
Some ancient Fabrick, awful in Repose,
While Sunburnt Hills their swarthy Looks conceal,
And swelling Haycocks thicken up the Vale:
When the loos'd *Horse* now, as his Pasture leads,
Comes slowly grazing thro' th' adjoining Meads,
Whose stealing Pace, and lengthen'd Shade we fear,
Till torn up Forage in his Teeth we hear:
When nibbling *Sheep* at large pursue their Food,
And unmolested Kine rechew the Cud;
When *Curlews* cry beneath the Village-walls,
And to her straggling Brood the *Partridge* calls;
Their shortliv'd Jubilee the Creatures keep,
Which but endures, whilst Tyrant-*Man* do's sleep;
When a sedate Content the Spirit feels,
And no fierce Light disturbs, whilst it reveals;
But silent Musings urge the Mind to seek
Something, too high for Syllables to speak;
Till the free Soul to a compos'dness charm'd,
Finding the Elements of Rage disarm'd,
O'er all below a solemn Quiet grown,
Joys in th' inferiour World, and thinks it like her Own:
In such a *Night* let Me abroad remain,
Till Morning breaks, and All's confus'd again;
Our Cares, our Toils, our Clamours are renew'd,
Or Pleasures, seldom reach'd, again pursu'd.

A Sigh[1]

Gentle Air, thou Breath of Lovers,
  Vapour from a secret Fire,
Which by Thee it self discovers,
  Ere yet daring to Aspire.

Softest Note of whisper'd Anguish,
  Harmony's refined Part,
Striking, while thou seem'st to Languish,
  Full upon the Listner's Heart.

Safest Messenger of Passion,
  Stealing thro' a Crowd of Spies;

[1] Published in Steele's *Poetical Miscellanies*, 1714. Text of first edition.

Who constrain the outward Fashion,
  Close the Lips, and watch the Eyes.

Shapeless Sigh! we ne'er can show thee,
  Fram'd but to assault the Ear:
Yet, ere to their Cost they know thee,
  Every Nymph may read thee—Here.

EDWARD YOUNG

(1683-1713-1765)

The Complaint: Or Night-Thoughts on Life, Death, and Immortality Night the First[1]

TIR'D Nature's sweet Restorer, balmy *Sleep!*
He, like the World, his ready Visit pays
Where Fortune smiles; the Wretched he forsakes:
Swift on his downy Pinion flies from Woe,
And lights on Lids unsully'd with a Tear.
  From short (as usual) and disturb'd Repose,
I wake: How happy they, who wake no more!
Yet that were vain, if Dreams infest the Grave.
I wake, emerging from a Sea of Dreams
Tumultuous; where my wreck'd, desponding Thought
From Wave to Wave of *fansy'd* Misery,
At random drove, her Helm of Reason lost.
Tho' now restor'd, 'tis only Change of Pain,
(A bitter Change!) severer for severe.
The *Day* too short for my Distress! and *Night*,
Even in the *Zenith* of her dark Domain,
Is Sunshine, to the Colour of my Fate.
  Night, sable Goddess! from her *Ebon* Throne,
In rayless Majesty, now stretches forth
Her leaden Sceptre o'er a slumb'ring World.
Silence, how dead! and Darkness, how profound!
Nor Eye, nor list'ning Ear an Object finds;
Creation sleeps. 'Tis, as the gen'ral Pulse
Of Life stood still, and Nature made a Pause;
An aweful Pause! prophetic of her End.

[1] Published in 1742. Text of the edition of 1750.

And let her Prophecy be soon fulfill'd;
Fate! drop the Curtain; I can lose no more.
  Silence, and *Darkness!* solemn Sisters! Twins
From antient *Night,* who nurse the tender Thought
To *Reason,* and on *Reason* build *Resolve,*
(That Column of true Majesty in Man)
Assist me: I will thank you in the Grave;
The Grave, your Kingdom: *There* this Frame shall fall
A Victim sacred to your dreary Shrine.
But what are ye? THOU, who didst put to Flight
Primæval *Silence,* when the Morning-Stars,
Exulting, shouted o'er the rising Ball;
O THOU! whose Word from solid *Darkness* struck
That Spark, the Sun; strike Wisdom from my Soul;
My Soul, which flies to thee, her Trust, her Treasure,
As Misers to their Gold, while others rest.
  Thro' this Opaque of *Nature,* and of *Soul,*
This double Night, transmit one pitying Ray,
To lighten, and to chear. O lead my Mind,
(A Mind that fain would wander from its Woe)
Lead it thro' various Scenes of *Life,* and *Death;*
And from each Scene, the noblest Truths inspire.
Nor less inspire my *Conduct,* than my *Song;*
Teach my best Reason, Reason; my best Will
Teach Rectitude; and fix my firm Resolve
Wisdom to wed, and pay her long Arrear:
Nor let the Phial of thy Vengeance, pour'd
On this devoted Head, be pour'd in vain.
  The Bell strikes *One.* We take no Note of Time,
But from its Loss. To give it then a Tongue,
Is wise in Man. As if an Angel spoke,
I feel the solemn Sound. If heard aright,
It is the *Knell* of my departed Hours:
Where are they? With the Years beyond the Flood.
It is the *Signal* that demands Dispatch;
How much is to be done? my Hopes and Fears
Start up alarm'd, and o'er Life's narrow Verge
Look down—on what? A fathomless Abyss;
A dread Eternity! how surely *mine!*
And can Eternity belong to me,
Poor Pensioner on the Bounties of an Hour?
  How poor, how rich, how abject, how august,
How complicate, how wonderful, is Man?
How passing wonder HE, who made him such?
Who centred in our Make such strange Extremes?
From diff'rent Natures marvelously mixt,
Connection exquisite of distant Worlds!
Distinguish'd *Link* in Being's endless Chain!

Midway from *Nothing* to the *Deity!*
A Beam etherial sully'd, and absorbt!
Tho' sully'd, and dishonour'd, still Divine!
Dim Miniature of Greatness absolute!
An Heir of Glory! a frail Child of Dust!
Helpless Immortal! Insect *infinite!*
A Worm! a God!—I tremble at myself,
And in myself am lost! At home a Stranger,
Thought wanders up and down, surpris'd, aghast,
And wond'ring at her *own:* How Reason reels!
O what a Miracle to Man is Man,
Triumphantly distress'd! what Joy, what Dread!
Alternately transported, and alarm'd!
What can preserve my Life? or what destroy?
An Angel's Arm can't snatch me from the Grave;
Legions of Angels can't confine me There.
'Tis past Conjecture; all things rise in Proof:
While o'er my Limbs *Sleep*'s soft Dominion spread,
What, tho' my Soul phantastic Measures trod
O'er Fairy Fields; or mourn'd along the Gloom
Of pathless Woods; or down the craggy Steep
Hurl'd headlong, swam with Pain the mantled Pool;
Or scal'd the Cliff; or danc'd on hollow Winds,
With antic Shapes, wild Natives of the Brain?
Her ceaseless Flight, tho' devious, speaks her Nature
Of subtler Essence than the trodden Clod;
Active, aërial, tow'ring, unconfin'd,
Unfetter'd with her gross Companion's Fall.
Ev'n silent Night proclaims my Soul *immortal:*
Ev'n silent Night proclaims eternal Day.
For human Weal, Heav'n husbands all Events,
Dull Sleep instructs, nor sport vain Dreams in vain.
Why then *their* Loss deplore, that are not lost?
Why wanders wretched Thought their Tombs around,
In infidel Distress? Are *Angels* there?
Slumbers, rak'd up in dust, Etherial Fire?
They live! they greatly live a Life on Earth
Unkindled, unconceiv'd; and from an Eye
Of Tenderness, let heav'nly Pity fall
On me, more justly number'd with the Dead.
This is the Desart, *this* the Solitude:
How populous! how vital, is the Grave!
This is Creation's melancholy Vault,
The Vale funereal, the sad *Cypress* Gloom;
The Land of Apparitions, empty Shades!
All, all on Earth is *Shadow*, all beyond
Is *Substance;* the Reverse is Folly's *Creed:*
How solid all, where Change shall be no more?

This is the Bud of Being, the dim Dawn,
The Twilight of our Day, the Vestibule.
Life's Theatre as yet is shut, and Death,
Strong Death, alone can heave the massy Bar,
This gross Impediment of Clay remove,
And make us Embryos of Existence free.
From *real* Life, but little more remote
Is *He*, not yet a Candidate for Light,
The *future* Embryo, slumb'ring in his Sire.
Embryos we must be, till we burst the Shell,
Yon ambient, azure Shell, and spring to Life,
The Life of Gods: O Transport! and of Man.
Yet Man, fool Man! *here* buries all his Thoughts;
Inters celestial Hopes without one Sigh.
Pris'ner of Earth, and pent beneath the Moon,
Here pinions all his Wishes; wing'd by Heav'n
To fly at Infinite; and reach it there,
Where *Seraphs* gather Immortality,
On Life's fair Tree, fast by the Throne of God.
What golden Joys ambrosial clust'ring glow,
In HIS full Beam, and ripen for the Just,
Where momentary Ages are no more!
Where Time, and Pain, and Chance, and Death expire!
And is it in the Flight of threescore Years,
To push Eternity from human Thought,
And smother Souls immortal in the Dust?
A Soul immortal, spending all her Fires,
Wasting her Strength in strenuous Idleness,
Thrown into Tumult, raptur'd, or alarm'd,
At ought this Scene can threaten, or indulge,
Resembles *Ocean* into Tempest wrought,
To waft a Feather, or to drown a Fly.
Where falls this Censure? It o'erwhelms myself.
How was my Heart incrusted by the World!
O how self-fetter'd was my groveling Soul!
How, like a Worm, was I wrapt round and round
In silken Thought, which reptile *Fancy* spun,
Till darken'd *Reason* lay quite clouded o'er
With soft Conceit of endless Comfort *here*,
Nor yet put forth her Wings to reach the Skies!
Night-visions may befriend (as sung above):
Our *waking* Dreams are fatal. How I dreamt
Of things Impossible? (Could Sleep do more?)
Of Joys perpetual in perpetual Change?
Of stable Pleasures on the tossing Wave?
Eternal Sunshine in the Storms of Life?
How richly were my noon-tide Trances hung
With gorgeous Tapestries of pictur'd Joys?

Joy behind Joy, in endless Perspective!
Till at Death's Toll, whose restless Iron Tongue
Calls daily for his Millions at a Meal,
Starting I woke, and found myself undone.
Where now my Frenzy's pompous Furniture?
The *cobweb'd* Cottage, with its ragged Wall
Of mould'ring Mud, is *Royalty* to me!
The *Spider*'s most attenuated Thread
Is Cord, is Cable, to Man's tender Tie
On earthly Bliss; it breaks at ev'ry Breeze.
  O ye blest Scenes of *permanent* Delight!
Full, above measure! lasting, beyond Bound!
A *Perpetuity* of Bliss, is Bliss.
Could you, so rich in Rapture, fear an End,
That ghastly Thought would drink up all your Joy,
And quite unparadise the Realms of Light.
Safe are you lodg'd above these rolling Spheres;
The baleful Influence of whose giddy Dance
Sheds sad Vicissitude on all beneath.
Here teems the Revolutions ev'ry Hour;
And rarely for the better; or the best,
More mortal than the common Births of Fate.
Each *Moment* has its Sickle, emulous
Of *Time*'s enormous Scythe, whose ample Sweep
Strikes Empires from the Root; each *Moment* plays
His little Weapon in the narrower Sphere
Of sweet domestic Comfort, and cuts down
The fairest Bloom of sublunary Bliss.
  Bliss! sublunary Bliss!—Proud Words, and vain!
Implicit Treason to divine Decree!
A bold Invasion of the Rights of Heav'n!
I clasp'd the Phantoms, and I found them Air.
O had I weigh'd it ere my fond Embrace!
What Darts of Agony had miss'd my Heart!
  Death! Great Proprietor of All! 'tis thine
To tread out Empire, and to quench the Stars.
The Sun himself by thy Permission shines;
And, one Day, thou shalt pluck him from his Sphere.
Amid such mighty Plunder, why exhaust
Thy *partial* Quiver on a Mark so *mean?*
Why thy *peculiar* Rancour wreck'd on *me?*
Insatiate Archer! could not *One* suffice?
Thy Shaft flew *thrice*; and *thrice* my Peace was slain;
And thrice, ere thrice yon Moon had fill'd her Horn.
O *Cynthia!* why so pale? Dost thou lament
Thy wretched Neighbour? Grieve to see thy Wheel
Of ceaseless Change outwhirl'd in human Life?
How wanes my *borrow'd* Bliss! from Fortune's Smile,

Precarious Courtesy! not *Virtue*'s sure,
Self-given, *solar*, Ray of sound Delight.
  In ev'ry vary'd Posture, Place, and Hour,
How widow'd ev'ry Thought of ev'ry Joy!
Thought, busy Thought! too busy for my Peace!
Thro' the dark Postern of Time long laps'd,
Led softly, by the Stilness of the Night,
Led, like a Murderer, (and such it proves!)
Strays, wretched Rover! o'er the pleasing *Past*;
In quest of Wretchedness perversely strays;
And finds all desart *now*; and meets the Ghosts
Of my departed Joys; a num'rous Train!
I rue the Riches of my former Fate;
Sweet Comfort's blasted Clusters I lament;
I tremble at the Blessings once so dear;
And ev'ry Pleasure pains me to the Heart.
  Yet why *complain?* or why complain for One?
Hangs out the Sun his Lustre but for me,
The *single* Man? Are Angels all beside?
I mourn for Millions; 'Tis the common Lot;
In *this* Shape, or in *that*, has Fate entail'd
The Mother's Throws on all of Woman born,
Not more the Children, than sure Heirs of *Pain*.
  War, Famine, Pest, Volcano, Storm, and Fire,
Intestine Broils, *Oppression* with her Heart
Wrapt up in triple Brass, besiege Mankind.
God's Image disinherited of Day,
Here, plung'd in Mines, forgets a Sun was made.
There, Beings deathless as their haughty Lord,
Are hammer'd to the galling Oar for Life;
And plough the Winter's Wave, and reap Despair.
Some, for hard Masters, broken under Arms,
In Battle lopt away, with half their Limbs,
Beg bitter Bread thro' Realms their Valour sav'd,
If so the Tyrant, or his Minion, doom.
Want, and incurable *Disease*, (fell Pair!)
On hopeless Multitudes remorseless seize
At once; and make a Refuge of the Grave.
How groaning *Hospitals* eject their Dead!
What Numbers groan for sad Admission there!
What Numbers, once in *Fortune*'s Lap high-fed,
Solicit the cold Hand of Charity!
To shock us more, solicit it in vain!
Ye silken Sons of Pleasure! since in Pains
You rue more modish Visits, visit *here*,
And breathe from your Debauch: *Give*, and reduce
Surfeit's Dominion o'er you; but so great
Your Impudence, you blush at what is Right!

Happy! did Sorrow seize on *such* alone.
Not *Prudence* can defend, or *Virtue* save;
Disease invades the chastest Temperance;
And Punishment the Guiltless; and Alarm
Thro' thickest Shades, pursues the fond of Peace.
Man's Caution often into Danger turns,
And his Guard falling, crushes him to Death.
Not *Happiness* itself makes good her Name;
Our very Wishes give us not our Wish.
How distant oft the Thing we doat on most,
From that for which we doat, *Felicity?*
The *smoothest* Course of Nature has its Pains;
And *truest* Friends, thro' Error, wound our Rest.
Without Misfortune, what Calamities?
And what Hostilities, without a Foe?
Nor are Foes wanting to the best on Earth.
But endless is the List of human Ills,
And Sighs might sooner fail, than Cause to sigh.
A Part how small of the terraqueous Globe
Is tenanted by Man! the Rest a *Waste*,
Rocks, Desarts, frozen Seas, and burning Sands:
Wild Haunts of Monsters, Poisons, Stings, and Death.
Such is Earth's melancholy Map! But, far
More sad! this Earth is a true Map of *Man.*
So bounded are its haughty Lord's *Delights*
To *Woe*'s wide Empire; where deep *Troubles* toss,
Loud *Sorrows* howl, invenom'd *Passions* bite,
Rav'nous *Calamities* our Vitals seize,
And threat'ning *Fate*, wide opens to devour.
What then am I, who sorrow for *myself?*
In Age, in Infancy, from others Aid
Is all our Hope; to teach us to be *kind.*
That, Nature's *first*, *last* Lesson to Mankind;
The selfish Heart deserves the Pain it feels.
More gen'rous Sorrow, while it sinks, exalts;
And conscious Virtue mitigates the Pang.
Nor *Virtue*, more than *Prudence*, bids me give
Swoln Thought a *second* Chanel; who divide,
They weaken too, the Torrent of their Grief.
Take then, O World! thy much-indebted Tear;
How sad a Sight is human Happiness,
To those whose Thought can pierce beyond an Hour!
O thou! whate'er thou art, whose Heart exults!
Wouldst thou I should congratulate thy Fate?
I know thou wouldst; thy Pride demands it from me,
Let thy Pride pardon, what thy Nature needs,
The salutary Censure of a Friend.
Thou happy *Wretch!* by Blindness art thou blest;

By Dotage dandled to perpetual Smiles.
Know, *Smiler!* at thy peril art thou pleas'd;
Thy Pleasure is the Promise of thy Pain.
Misfortune, like a Creditor severe,
But rises in demand for her Delay;
She makes a scourge of past Prosperity,
To sting thee more, and double thy Distress.
  LORENZO, Fortune makes her Court to thee,
Thy fond Heart dances, while the *Siren* sings.
Dear is thy Welfare; think me not unkind;
I would not damp, but to secure thy joys.
Think not that *Fear* is sacred to the Storm,
Stand on thy guard against the *Smiles* of Fate.
Is Heaven tremendous in its Frowns? most sure;
And in its Favours formidable too;
Its favours here are Tryals, not Rewards;
A call to Duty, not discharge from Care;
And should alarm us, full as much as Woes;
Awake us to their *Cause*, and *Consequence*;
And make us tremble, weigh'd with our Desert;
Awe Nature's Tumult, and chastise her Joys,
Lest while we clasp, we kill them; nay invert
To worse than *simple* misery, their Charms.
Revolted Joys, like foes in civil war,
Like bosom friendships to resentment sour'd,
With rage envenom'd rise against our Peace.
Beware what Earth calls Happiness; beware
All joys, but joys that never can expire.
Who builds on less than an *immortal* Base,
Fond as he seems, condemns his joys to Death.
  Mine dy'd with thee, PHILANDER! thy last Sigh
Dissolv'd the charm; the disenchanted Earth
Lost all her Lustre. Where, her glittering Towers?
Her golden Mountains, where? all darken'd down
To naked Waste; a dreary Vale of Tears;
The great Magician's dead! Thou poor, pale Piece
Of out-cast earth, in Darkness! what a Change
From yesterday! Thy darling Hope so near,
(Long-labour'd Prize!) O how Ambition flush'd
Thy glowing Cheek! Ambition truly great,
Of virtuous Praise. Death's subtle Seed within,
(Sly, treach'rous Miner!) working in the Dark,
Smil'd at thy well-concerted Scheme, and beckon'd
The Worm to riot on that Rose so red,
Unfaded ere it fell; one Moment's Prey!
  Man's Foresight is *conditionally* wise;
LORENZO! Wisdom into Folly turns
Oft, the first Instant, its Idea fair

To labouring Thought is born. How dim our Eye!
The *present* Moment terminates our Sight;
Clouds, thick as those on Doomsday, drown the *next*;
We penetrate, we prophesy in vain.
Time is dealt out by Particles; and each,
Ere mingled with the streaming Sands of Life,
By Fate's inviolable Oath is sworn
Deep Silence, "Where Eternity begins."
By Nature's Law, what may be, may be *now*;
There's no Prerogative in human Hours.
In human Hearts what bolder Thought can rise,
Than Man's Presumption on To-morrow's Dawn?
Where is To-morrow? In another World.
For Numbers this is certain; the Reverse
Is sure to none; and yet on this *Perhaps*,
This *Peradventure*, infamous for Lyes,
As on a Rock of Adamant we build
Our mountain Hopes; spin out eternal Schemes,
As we the Fatal Sisters could out-spin,
And, big with Life's Futurities, expire.
Not ev'n PHILANDER had bespoke his Shroud.
Nor had He Cause, a Warning was deny'd;
How many fall as sudden, not as safe!
As sudden, tho' for Years admonisht home.
On human Ills the last Extreme beware,
Beware, LORENZO! a *slow-sudden* Death.
How dreadful that deliberate Surprize!
Be wise To-day; 'tis Madness to defer;
Next Day the fatal Precedent will plead;
Thus on, till Wisdom is push'd out of Life.
Procrastination is the Thief of Time;
Year after Year it steals, till all are fled,
And to the Mercies of a Moment leaves
The vast Concerns of an eternal Scene.
If not so frequent, would not This be strange?
That 'tis so frequent, *This* is stranger still.
Of Man's miraculous Mistakes, this bears
The Palm, "That all Men are about to live,"
For ever on the Brink of being born.
All pay themselves the Compliment to think
They, one Day, shall not drivel; and their Pride
On this Reversion takes up ready Praise;
At least, their own; their future Selves applauds;
How excellent that Life they *ne'er* will lead!
Time lodg'd in their *own* Hands is *Folly*'s Vails;
That lodg'd in *Fate*'s, to *Wisdom* they consign;
The Thing they can't but *purpose*, they *postpone*;
'Tis not in *Folly*, not to scorn a Fool;

And scarce in human *Wisdom* to do more.
All *Promise* is poor dilatory Man,
And that thro' ev'ry Stage: When young, indeed,
In full Content we, sometimes, nobly rest,
Un-anxious for *ourselves*; and only wish,
As duteous Sons, our *Fathers* were more Wise.
At *Thirty* Man *suspects* himself a Fool;
Knows it at *Forty*, and reforms his Plan;
At *Fifty* chides his infamous Delay,
Pushes his prudent Purpose to *Resolve*;
In all the Magnanimity of Thought
Resolves; and re-resolves; then dies the same.
And why? Because he thinks himself Immortal.
All Men think all Men mortal, but Themselves;
Themselves, when some alarming Shock of Fate
Strikes thro' their wounded Hearts the sudden Dread;
But their Hearts wounded, like the wounded Air,
Soon close; where past the Shaft, no Trace is found.
As from the *Wing* no Scar the Sky retains;
The parted Wave no Furrow from the *Keel*;
So dies in human Hearts the Thought of Death.
Ev'n with the tender Tear which Nature sheds
O'er those we love, we drop it in their Grave.
Can I forget PHILANDER? That were strange;
O my full Heart!—But should I give it vent,
The longest Night, tho' longer far, would fail,
And the *Lark* listen to my *Midnight* Song.
The spritely *Lark*'s shrill Matin wakes the Morn;
Grief's sharpest Thorn hard-pressing on my Breast,
I strive, with wakeful Melody to chear
The sullen Gloom, sweet *Philomel!* like Thee,
And call the Stars to listen: Ev'ry Star
If deaf to mine, enamour'd of thy Lay.
Yet be not vain; there are, who thine excell,
And charm thro' distant Ages: Wrapt in Shade,
Pris'ner of Darkness! to the silent *Hours*,
How often I repeat their Rage divine,
To lull my Griefs, and steal my Heart from Woe!
I roll their Raptures, but not catch their Flames.
Dark, tho' not blind, like thee *Mæonides!*
Or *Milton!* thee; ah could I reach your Strain!
Or *His*, who made *Mæonides* our *Own*.[1]
Man too He sung: *Immortal* Man, I sing;
Oft bursts my Song beyond the Bounds of Life;
What, *now,* but Immortality can please?
O had *He* press'd his Theme, pursu'd the Track,

[1] Pope.

Which opens out of Darkness into Day!
O had he mounted on his Wing of Fire,
Soar'd, where I sink, and sung *Immortal* Man!
How had it blest Mankind, and rescu'd me?

HENRY CAREY

(1687?-1713-1743)

The Ballad of Sally in our Alley[1]

OF ALL the Girls that are so smart
  There's none like pretty *Sally*,
She is the Darling of my Heart,
  And she lives in our Alley.
There is no Lady in the Land,
  Is half so sweet as *Sally*,
She is the Darling of my Heart,
  And she lives in our Alley.

Her Father he makes Cabbage-nets,
  And through the Streets does cry 'em;
Her Mother she sells Laces long,
  To such as please to buy 'em:
But sure such Folks could ne'er beget
  So sweet a Girl as *Sally*!
She is the Darling of my Heart,
  And she lives in our Alley.

When she is by I leave my Work,
  (I love her so sincerely)
My Master comes like any Turk,
  And bangs me most severely;
But, let him bang his Belly-full,
  I'll bear it all for *Sally*;
She is the Darling of my Heart,
  And she lives in our Alley.

Of all the Days that's in the Week,
  I dearly love but one Day,
And that's the Day that comes betwixt
  A Saturday and Monday;

[1] Published in *Poems on Several Occasions*, 1729. Text of first edition.

For then I'm dress'd, all in my best,
  To walk abroad with *Sally*;
She is the Darling of my Heart,
  And she lives in our Alley.

My Master carries me to Church,
  And often am I blamed,
Because I leave him in the lurch,
  As soon as Text is named:
I leave the Church in Sermon time,
  And slink away to *Sally*;
She is the Darling of my Heart,
  And she lives in our Alley.

When Christmas comes about again,
  O then I shall have Money;
I'll hoard it up, and Box and all
  I'll give it to my Honey:
And, would it were ten thousand Pounds,
  I'd give it all to *Sally*;
She is the Darling of my Heart,
  And she lives in our Alley.

My Master and the Neighbours all
  Make game of me and *Sally*;
And (but for her) I'd better be
  A Slave and row a Galley:
But when my seven long Years are out,
  O then I'll marry *Sally*!
O then we'll wed and then we'll bed,
  But not in our Alley.

JOHN BYROM

(1692-1714-1763)

Epigram on the Feuds between Handel and Bononcini[1]

SOME say, compar'd to Bononcini,
That Mynheer Handel's but a Ninny;

[1] Published in Swift's *Miscellanies*, 1728. Text of *Miscellaneous Poems*, Volume I, 1773.

Others aver, that he to Handel
Is scarcely fit to hold a Candle:
Strange all this Difference should be,
'Twixt Tweedle-dum and Tweedle-dee!

Contentment: or, The Happy Workman's Song[1]

I AM a poor Workman as rich as a *Jew*,
A strange sort of Tale, but however 'tis true,
Come listen a while, and I'll prove it to you
So as No-body can deny, &c.

I am a poor Workman, you'll easily grant,
And I'm rich as a *Jew*, for there's nothing I want,
I have Meat, Drink, and Cloaths, and am hearty and cant,
Which No-body can deny, &c.

I live in a Cottage, and yonder it stands,
And while I can work with these two honest Hands,
I'm as happy as they that have Houses and Lands,
Which No-body can deny, &c.

I keep to my Workmanship all the Day long,
I sing and I whistle, and this is my Song,
Thank God, that has made me so lusty and strong,
Which No-body can deny, &c.

I never am greedy of delicate Fare,
If he give me enough, tho' 'tis never so bare,
The more is his Love, and the less is my Care,
Which No-body can deny, &c.

My Cloaths on a working Day looken but lean,
But when I can dress me—on Sundays, I mean,
Tho' cheap, they are warm; and tho' coarse, they are clean,
Which No-body can deny, &c.

Folk cry'n out hard Times, but I never regard,
For I ne'er did, nor will set my Heart up o' th' Ward,
So 'tis all one to me, bin they easy or hard,
Which No-body can deny, &c.

I envy not them that have thousands of Pounds,
That sport o'er the Country with Horses and Hounds;

[1] Published in *Miscellaneous Poems*, Volume I, 1773. Text of first edition.

There's nought but *Contentment* can keep within bounds,
Which No-body can deny, &c.

I ne'er lose my Time o'er a Pipe, or a Pot,
Nor cower in a Nook like a sluggardly Sot,
But I buy what is wanting with what I have got,
Which No-body can deny, &c.

And if I have more than I want for to spend,
I help a poor Neighbour or diligent Friend;
He that gives to the Poor, to the Lord he doth lend,
Which No-body can deny, &c.

I grudge not that Gentlefolk dressen so fine;
At their Gold and their Silver I never repine,
But I wish all their Guts were as hearty as mine,
Which No-body can deny, &c.

With Quarrels o' th' Country, and Matters of State,
With *Tories* and *Whigs*, I ne'er puzzle my Pate;
There's some that I love, and there's none that I hate,
Which No-body can deny, &c.

What tho' my Condition be ever so coarse,
I strive to embrace it for better and worse,
And my Heart, I thank God, is as light as my Purse,
Which No-body can deny, &c.

In short, my Condition, whatever it be,
'Tis God that appoints it, as far as I see,
And I'm sure I can never do better than he,
Which No-body can deny, &c.

Careless Content[1]

I AM Content, I do not care,
Wag as it will the World for me;
When Fuss, and Fret was all my Fare,
It got no ground, as I could see:
So when away my Caring went,
I counted Cost, and was Content.

With more of Thanks, and less of Thought,
I strive to make my Matters meet;

[1] Published in *Miscellaneous Poems,* Volume I, 1773. Text of first edition.

To seek what antient Sages sought,
  Physick and Food, in sour and sweet:
To take what passes in good Part,
And keep the Hiccups from the Heart.

With good and gentle-humour'd Hearts,
  I choose to chat where e'er I come;
Whate'er the Subject be that starts;
  But if I get among the Glum,
I hold my Tongue to tell the Troth,
And keep my Breath to cool my Broth.

For Chance or Change, of Peace or Pain;
  For Fortune's Favour, or her Frown;
For Lack or Glut, for Loss or Gain,
  I never dodge, nor up nor down:
But swing what Way the Ship shall swim,
Or tack about, with equal Trim.

I suit not where I shall not speed,
  Nor trace the Turn of ev'ry Tide;
If simple Sense will not succeed,
  I make no Bustling, but abide:
For shining Wealth, or scaring Woe,
I force no Friend, I fear no Foe.

Of *Ups* and *Downs*, of *Ins* and *Outs*,
  Of *they're i' th' wrong*, and *we're i' th' right*,
I shun the Rancours, and the Routs,
  And wishing well to every Wight,
Whatever Turn the Matter takes,
I deem it all but Ducks and Drakes.

With whom I feast I do not fawn,
  Nor if the Folks should flout me, faint;
If wonted Welcome be withdrawn,
  I cook no Kind of a Complaint:
With none dispos'd to disagree,
But like them best, who best like me.

Not that I rate myself the Rule
  How all my Betters should behave;
But Fame shall find me no Man's Fool,
  Nor to a Set of Men a Slave:
I love a Friendship free and frank,
And hate to hang upon a Hank.

Fond of a true and trusty Tie,
  I never loose where'er I link;
Tho' if a Bus'ness budges by,
  I talk thereon just as I think:
My Word, my Work, my Heart, my Hand,
Still, on a Side, together stand.

If Names or Notions make a noise,
  Whatever Hap the Question hath,
The Point impartially I poise,
  And read, or write, but without Wrath;
For should I burn, or break my Brains,
Pray, who will pay me for my Pains?

I love my Neighbour as myself,
  Myself like him too, by his Leave;
Nor to his Pleasure, Pow'r, or Pelf,
  Came I to crouch, as I conceive:
Dame Nature doubtless has design'd
A Man, the Monarch of his Mind.

Now taste and try this Temper, Sirs,
  Mood it, and brood it in your Breast;
Or if ye ween, for worldly Stirs,
  That Man does right to mar his Rest,
Let me be deft, and debonair,
I am Content, I do not care.

Tom the Porter[1]

As *Tom* the Porter went up *Ludgate-Hill*,
A swinging Show'r oblig'd him to stand still;
So, in the Right-hand Passage thro' the Gate,
He pitch'd his Burden down, just by the Grate,
From whence the doleful Accent sounds away,
"Pity—the Poor—and Hungry—Debtors—pray."

To the same Garrison, from *Paul*'s Church-yard,
An half-drown'd Soldier ran to mount the Guard:
Now *Tom*, it seems, the *Ludgateer*, and he
Were old Acquaintance, formerly, all three;
And as the Coast was clear, by cloudy Weather,
They quickly fell into Discourse together.

[1] Published in *Miscellaneous Poems*, Volume I, 1773. Text of first edition.

'Twas in *December*, when the *Highland Clans*
Had got to *Derbyshire* from *Preston Pans;*
And struck all *London* with a general Panic—
But mark the Force of Principles *Britannic.*

The Soldier told 'em fresh the City News,
Just piping hot from *Stockjobbers*, and *Jews;*
Of *French* Fleets landing, and of *Dutch* Neutrality;
Of Jealousies at Court amongst the Quality;
Of *Swarston*-Bridge, that never was pull'd down;
Of all the Rebels in full March to Town;
And of a hundred Things beside, that made
Lord May'r himself, and Aldermen afraid;
Painting with many an Oath the Case in View,
And ask'd the Porter—what he thought to do?

Do? says he, gravely—what I did before;
What I have done these thirty Years, and more;
Carry, as I am like to do, my Pack,
Glad to maintain my Belly by my Back;
If that but hold, I care not; for my Part,
Come as come will, 't shall never break my Heart;
I don't see Folks that fight about their Thrones,
Mind either Soldiers Flesh, or Porters Bones;
Whoe'er gets better, when the Battle's fought,
Thy Pay nor mine will be advanc'd a Groat—
—But to the Purpose—now we are met here,
I'll join, if 't will, for one full Mug of Beer.

The Soldier, touch'd a little with Surprize
To see his Friend's Indifference, replies—
What you say, *Tom*, I own, is very good,
But—OUR RELIGION! (and he d—n'd his Blood)
What will become of OUR RELIGION?—True!
Says the Jail-Bird—and of OUR FREEDOM too?
If the PRETENDER (rapt he out) comes on,
OUR LIBERTIES AND PROPERTIES are gone!

And so the Soldier and the Pris'ner join'd
To work up *Tom* into a better Mind;
He staring, dumb, with Wonder struck and Pity,
Took up his Load, and trudg'd into the City.

The Soul's Tendency Towards Its True Centre[1]

STONES towards the Earth descend;
Rivers to the Ocean roll;
Every Motion has some End:
What is thine, beloved Soul?

Mine is, where my Saviour is;
There with him I hope to dwell:
JESU is the central Bliss;
Love the Force that doth impel.

Truly, thou hast answer'd right:
Now may Heav'n's attractive Grace,
Tow'rds the Source of thy Delight,
Speed along thy quick'ning Pace!

Thank thee for thy gen'rous Care:
Heav'n, that did the Wish inspire,
Through thy instrumental Pray'r,
Plumes the Wings of my Desire.

Now, methinks, aloft I fly:
Now, with Angels bear a Part:
Glory be to God on High!
Peace to ev'ry Christian Heart!

An Hymn on the Omnipresence[2]

OH LORD! thou hast known me, and searched me out,
Thou see'st, at all Times, what I'm thinking about;
When I rise up to Labour, or lye down to Rest,
Thou markest each Motion that works in my Breast;
My Heart has no Secrets, but what thou can'st tell,
Not a Word in my Tongue, but thou knowest it well;
Thou see'st my Intention before it is wrought,
Long before I conceive it, thou knowest my Thought.

Thou art always about me, go whither I will,
All the Paths that I take to, I meet with thee still;
I go forth abroad, and am under thine Eye,
I retire to myself, and behold! thou art by;
How is it that thou hast encompass'd me so

[1] Published in *Miscellaneous Poems*, Volume II, 1773. Text of first edition.
[2] Published in *Miscellaneous Poems*, Volume II, 1773. Text of first edition.

That I cannot escape thee, wherever I go?
Such Knowledge as this is too high to attain,
'Tis a Truth which I feel, tho' I cannot explain.

Whither then shall I flee from thy Spirit, O Lord?
What Shelter can Space from thy Presence afford?
If I climb up to Heav'n, 'tis there is thy Throne,
If I go down to Hell, even there thou art known;
If for Wings I should mount on the Mornings swift Ray,
And remain in the uttermost Parts of the Sea,
Even there, let the Distance be ever so wide,
Thy Hand would support me, thy right Hand would guide.

If I say, peradventure, the Dark may conceal
What Distance, tho' boundless, is forc'd to reveal,
Yet the Dark, at thy Presence, would vanish away,
And my Covering, the Night, would be turn'd into Day:
It is I myself only who could not then see,
Yea, the Darkness, O Lord, is no Darkness to Thee:
The Night, and the Day, are alike in thy Sight,
And the Darkness, to Thee, is as clear as the Light.

LADY MARY WORTLEY MONTAGU

(1689-1716?-1762)

Farewell to Bath[1]

To ALL you Ladies now at *Bath*,
  And eke, ye Beaus, to you,
With aking heart, and wat'ry eyes,
  I bid my last adieu.

Farewel ye Nymphs, who waters sip
  Hot reeking from the pumps,
While music lends her friendly aid,
  To cheer you from the dumps.

Farewel ye wits, who prating stand,
  And criticise the fair;
Yourselves the joke of men of Sense,
  Who hate a coxcomb's air.

[1] Published in the *Gentleman's Magazine*, July, 1731. Text of first edition.

Farewel to *Deard*'s, and all her toys,
  Which glitter in her shop,
Deluding traps to girls and boys,
  The warehouse of the fop.

Lindsay's and *Hayes*'s both farewel,
  Where in the spacious hall,
With bounding steps, and sprightly air,
  I've led up many a ball.

Where *Somerville* of courteous mein,
  Was partner in the dance,
With swimming *Haws*, and *Brownlow* blithe,
  And *Britton* pink of *France*.

Poor *Nash*, farewel! may fortune smile,
  Thy drooping soul revive,
My heart is full I can no more—
  John, bid the Coachman drive.

The Lover: A Ballad[1]

AT LENGTH, by so much importunity press'd,
Take, C——, at once, the inside of my breast;
This stupid indiff'rence so often you blame,
Is not owing to nature, to fear, or to shame:
I am not as cold as a virgin in lead,
Nor is Sunday's sermon so strong in my head:
I know but too well how time flies along,
That we live but few years, and yet fewer are young.

But I hate to be cheated, and never will buy
Long years of repentance for moments of joy.
Oh! was there a man (but where shall I find
Good sense and good nature so equally join'd?)
Would value his pleasure, contribute to mine;
Not meanly would boast, nor would lewdly design;
Not over severe, yet not stupidly vain,
For I would have the power, tho' not give the pain.

No pedant, yet learned; no rake-helly gay,
Or laughing, because he has nothing to say;
To all my whole sex obliging and free,

[1] Published in Dodsley's *Collection of Poems*, Volume III, 1748. Text of fourth edition, 1755.

Yet never be fond of any but me;
In public preserve the decorum that's just,
And shew in his eyes he is true to his trust;
Then rarely approach, and respectfully bow,
But not fulsomely pert, nor yet foppishly low.

But when the long hours of publick are past,
And we meet with champagne and a chicken at last,
May ev'ry fond pleasure that moment endear;
Be banish'd afar both discretion and fear!
Forgetting or scorning the airs of the crowd,
He may cease to be formal, and I to be proud,
Till lost in the joy, we confess that we live,
And he may be rude, and yet I may forgive.

And that my delight may be solidly fix'd,
Let the friend and the lover be handsomely mix'd;
In whose tender bosom my soul may confide,
Whose kindness can sooth me, whose counsel can guide.
From such a dear lover as here I describe,
No danger should fright me, no millions should bribe;
But till this astonishing creature I know,
As I long have liv'd chaste, I will keep myself so.

I never will share with the wanton coquet,
Or be caught by a vain affectation of wit.
The toasters and songsters may try all their art,
But never shall enter the pass of my heart.
I loath the lewd rake, the dress'd fopling despise:
Before such pursuers the nice virgin flies:
And as OVID has sweetly in parable told,
We harden like trees, and like rivers grow cold.

THOMAS WARTON, SR.

(1688?-1718-1745)

An American Love-Ode Taken from the Second Volume of Montagne's Essays[1]

STAY, stay, thou lovely, fearful Snake,
Nor hide thee in yon darksome Brake:

[1] Published in *Poems on Several Occasions*, 1748. Text of first edition.

But let me oft thy Charms review,
Thy glittering Scales, and golden Hue;
From these a Chaplet shall be wove,
To grace the Youth I dearest love.

Then Ages hence, when thou no more,
Shalt creep along the sunny Shore,
Thy copy'd Beauties shall be seen;
Thy Red and Azure mix'd with Green,
In mimic Folds thou shalt display:—
Stay, lovely, fearful Adder stay.

A Runic Ode: Taken from the Second Volume of Sir William Temple's Miscellanies[1]

ARGUMENT

Regner Ladbrog, *a King of one of the Northern Nations, being mortally stung by a Viper, before the Venom had reach'd his Vitals, broke out into the following Verses.*

YES—'tis decreed my Sword no more
Shall smoke and blush with hostile Gore;
To my great Father's Feasts I go,
Where luscious Wines for ever flow,
Which from the hollow Sculls we drain,
Of Kings in furious Combat slain.

Death, to the Brave a blest Resort,
Brings us to awful *Odin*'s Court;
Where with old Warriors mix'd we dwell,
Recount our Wounds, our Triumphs tell;
Me, will they own as bold a Guest,
As e'er in Battle bar'd my Breast.

Another, on the same SUBJECT.

AT length appears the wish'd-for Night,
When my glad Soul shall take her Flight;
Tremble my Limbs, my Eye-balls start,
The Venom's busy at my Heart.
Hark! how the solemn *Sisters call,
And point aloft to *Odin*'s Hall!

[1] Published in *Poems on Several Occasions*, 1748. Text of first edition.
* Call'd by the *Goths, Dysæ.*

I come, I come, prepare full Bowls,
Fit Banquet for heroic Souls:
What's Life—I scorn this idle Breath,
I smile in the Embrace of Death!

JAMES THOMSON

(1700-1720-1748)

A Poem Sacred to the Memory of Sir Isaac Newton[1]

SHALL the great soul of *Newton* quit this earth,
To mingle with his stars; and every muse,
Astonish'd into silence, shun the weight
Of honours due to his illustrious name?
But what can man?—Even now the sons of light,
In strains high-warbled to seraphic lyre,
Hail his arrival on the coast of bliss.
Yet am not I deterr'd, tho' high the theme,
And sung to harps of angels, for with you,
Ethereal Flames! ambitious, I aspire
In Nature's general symphony to join.
  And what new wonders can ye show your guest!
Who, while on this dim spot, where mortals toil
Clouded in dust, from *Motion*'s simple laws,
Could trace the secret hand of *Providence*,
Wide-working thro' this universal frame.
  Have ye not listen'd while he bound the *Suns*,
And *Planets* to their spheres! th' unequal task
Of humankind till then. Oft had they roll'd
O'er erring Man the year, and oft disgrac'd
The pride of schools, before their course was known
Full in its causes and effects to him,
All-piercing sage! who sat not down and dream'd
Romantic schemes, defended by the din
Of specious words, and tyranny of names;
But, bidding his amazing mind attend,
And with heroic patience years on years
Deep-searching, saw at last the *System* dawn,
And shine, of all his race, on him alone.
  What were his raptures then! how pure! how strong!

[1] Published in 1727. Text of *The Seasons* . . . . 1730.

And what the triumphs of old *Greece* and *Rome*,
By his diminish'd, but the pride of boys
In some small fray victorious! when instead
Of shatter'd parcels of this earth usurp'd
By violence unmanly, and sore deeds
Of cruelty and blood, Nature herself
Stood all subdu'd by him, and open laid
Her every latent glory to his view.
  All intellectual eye, our *solar Round*
First gazing thro', he by the blended power
Of *Gravitation* and *Projection* saw
The whole in silent harmony revolve.
From unassisted vision hid, the *Moons*
To chear remoter planets numerous pour'd,
By him in all their mingled tracts were seen.
He also fix'd the wandering *Queen of Night*,
Whether she wanes into a scanty orb,
Or, waxing broad, with her pale shadowy light,
In a soft deluge overflows the sky.
Her every motion clear-discerning, He
Adjusted to the mutual *Main*, and taught
Why now the mighty mass of water swells
Resistless, heaving on the broken rocks,
And the full river turning; till again
The tide revertive, unattracted, leaves
A yellow waste of idle sands behind.
  Then breaking hence, he took his ardent flight
Thro' the blue Infinite; and every *Star*,
Which the clear concave of a winter's night
Pours on the eye, or astronomic tube,
Far-stretching, snatches from the dark abyss,
Or such as farther in successive skies
To fancy shine alone, at his approach
Blaz'd into *Suns*, the living centre each
Of an harmonious system: all combin'd,
And rul'd unerring by that single power,
Which draws the stone projected to the ground.
  O unprofuse magnificence divine!
O *Wisdom* truly perfect! thus to call
From a few causes such a scheme of things,
Effects so various, beautiful, and great,
An universe compleat! and O belov'd
Of heaven! whose well-purg'd penetrative eye,
The mystic veil transpiercing, inly scan'd
The rising, moving, wide-establish'd frame.
  He, first of men, with awful wing pursu'd
The *Comet* thro' the long Eliptic curve,
As round innumerous worlds he wound his way;

Till, to the forehead of our evening sky
Return'd, the blazing wonder glares anew,
And o'er the trembling nations shakes dismay.
The heavens are all his own; from the wild rule
Of whirling *Vortices*, and circling *Spheres*,
To their first great simplicity restor'd.
The schools astonish'd stood; but found it vain
To keep at odds with demonstration strong,
And, unawaken'd, dream beneath the blaze
Of truth. At once their pleasing visions fled,
With the gay shadows of the morning mix'd,
When *Newton* rose, our philosophic sun.
Th' aerial flow of *Sound* was known to him,
From whence it first in wavy circles breaks,
Till the touch'd organ takes the meaning in.
Nor could the darting *Beam*, of speed immense,
Escape his swift pursuit, and measuring eye.
Even *Light itself*, which every thing displays,
Shone undiscover'd, till his brighter mind
Untwisted all the shining robe of day;
And, from the whitening undistinguish'd blaze,
Collecting every ray into his kind,
To the charm'd eye educ'd the gorgeous train
Of *Parent-Colours*. First the flaming *Red*
Sprung vivid forth; the tawny *Orange* next;
And next delicious *Yellow*; by whose side
Fell the kind beams of all-refreshing *Green*.
Then the pure *Blue*, that swells autumnal skies,
Ethereal play'd; and then, of sadder hue,
Emerg'd the deepen'd *Indico*, as when
The heavy-skirted evening droops with frost.
While the last gleamings of refracted light
Dy'd in the fainting *Violet* away.
These, when the clouds distil the rosy shower,
Shine out distinct adown the watry bow;
While o'er our heads the dewy vision bends
Delightful, melting on the fields beneath.
Myriads of mingling dies from these result,
And myriads still remain—Infinite source
Of beauty, ever-flushing, ever-new!
Did ever poet image ought so fair,
Dreaming in whispering groves, by the hoarse brook!
Or prophet, to whose rapture heaven descends!
Even now the setting sun and shifting clouds,
Seen, *Greenwich*, from thy lovely heights, declare
How just, how beauteous the *refractive Law*.

The noiseless *Tide* of *Time*, all bearing down
To vast Eternity's unbounded sea
Where the green islands of the happy shine,
He stem'd alone; and to the source (involv'd
Deep in primæval gloom) ascending, rais'd
His lights at equal distances, to guide
Historian, wilder'd on his darksome way.
But who can number up his labours? who
His high discoveries sing? when but a few
Of the deep-studying race can stretch their minds
To what he knew: in fancy's lighter thought,
How shall the muse then grasp the mighty theme?
What wonder thence that his *Devotion* swell'd
Responsive to his knowledge! for could he,
Whose piercing mental eye diffusive saw
The finish'd University of things,
In all its order, magnitude, and parts,
Forbear incessant to adore that *Power*
Who fills, sustains, and actuates the whole.
Say, ye who best can tell, ye happy few,
Who saw him in the softest lights of life,
All unwith-held, indulging to his friends
The vast unborrow'd treasures of his mind,
Oh speak the wondrous man! how mild, how calm,
How greatly humble, how divinely good;
How firm establish'd on eternal truth;
Fervent in doing well, with every nerve
Still pressing on, forgetful of the past,
And panting for perfection: far above
Those little cares, and visionary joys,
That so perplex the fond impassion'd heart
Of ever-cheated, ever-trusting man.
This, *Conduitt*, from thy rural hours we hope;
As thro' the pleasing shade, where Nature pours
Her every sweet, in studious ease you walk;
The social passions smiling at thy heart,
That glows with all the recollected sage.
And you, ye hopeless gloomy-minded tribe,
You who, unconscious of those nobler flights
That reach impatient at immortal life,
Against the prime endearing privilege
Of Being dare contend, say, can a soul
Of such extensive, deep, tremendous powers,
Enlarging still, be but a finer breath
Of spirits dancing thro' their tubes awhile,
And then for ever lost in vacant air?
But hark! methinks I hear a warning voice,

Solemn as when some awful change is come,
Sound thro' the world—"*'Tis done!—The measure's full*;
"*And I resign my charge*.—Ye mouldering stones,
That build the towering pyramid, the proud
Triumphal arch, the monument effac'd
By ruthless ruin, and whate'er supports
The worship'd name of hoar antiquity,
Down to the dust! what grandeur can ye boast
While *Newton* lifts his column to the skies,
Beyond the waste of time.—Let no weak drop
Be shed for him. The virgin in her bloom
Cut off, the joyous youth, and darling child,
These are the tombs that claim the tender tear,
And Elegiac song. But *Newton* calls
For other notes of gratulation high,
That now he wanders thro' those endless worlds
He here so well descried, and wondering talks,
And hymns their author with his glad compeers.
O *Britain*'s boast! whether with angels thou
Sittest in dread discourse, or fellow-blest,
Who joy to see the honour of their kind;
Or whether, mounted on cherubic wing,
Thy swift career is with the whirling orbs,
Comparing things with things, in rapture lost,
And grateful adoration, for that light
So plenteous ray'd into thy mind below,
From *Light Himself*; Oh look with pity down
On humankind, a frail erroneous race!
Exalt the spirit of a downward world!
O'er thy dejected country chief preside,
And be her *Genius* call'd! her studies raise,
Correct her manners, and inspire her youth.
For, tho' deprav'd and sunk, she brought thee forth,
And glories in thy name; she points thee out
To all her sons, and bids them eye thy star:
While in expectance of the second life,
When Time shall be no more, thy sacred dust
Sleeps with her kings, and dignifies the scene.

Hymn on Solitude[1]

HAIL, mildly pleasing solitude,
Companion of the wise and good;

[1] Published in Ralph's *Miscellaneous Poems*, 1729. Text of *Works*, 1750, Volume II.

But, from whose holy, piercing eye,
The herd of fools, and villains fly.
Oh! how I love with thee to walk,
And listen to thy whisper'd talk,
Which innocence, and truth imparts,
And melts the most obdurate hearts.
  A thousand shapes you wear with ease,
And still in every shape you please.
Now wrapt in some mysterious dream,
A lone philosopher you seem;
Now quick from hill to vale you fly,
And now you sweep the vaulted sky;
A shepherd next, you haunt the plain,
And warble forth your oaten strain;
A lover now, with all the grace
Of that sweet passion in your face:
Then, calm'd to friendship, you assume
The gentle-looking HARFORD's bloom,
As, with her MUSIDORA, she,
(Her MUSIDORA fond of thee)
Amid the long withdrawing vale,
Awakes the rival'd nightingale.
  Thine is the balmy breath of morn,
Just as the dew-bent rose is born;
And while Meridian fervours beat,
Thine is the woodland dumb retreat;
But chief, when evening scenes decay,
And the faint landskip swims away,
Thine is the doubtful soft decline,
And that best hour of musing thine.
  Descending angels bless thy train,
The Virtues of the sage, and swain;
Plain Innocence in white array'd,
Before thee lifts her fearless head:
Religion's beams around thee shine,
And chear thy glooms with light divine:
About thee sports sweet Liberty;
And rapt *Urania* sings to thee.
  Oh, let me pierce thy secret cell!
And in thy deep recesses dwell!
Perhaps from *Norwood*'s oak-clad hill,
When meditation has her fill,
I just may cast my careless eyes
Where *London*'s spiry turrets rise,
Think of its crimes, its cares, its pain,
Then shield me in the woods again.

The Seasons[1]

Winter[2]

THE ARGUMENT

The Subject proposed. Address to Lord WILMINGTON. *First Approach of Winter. According to the natural Course of the Season, various Storms described. Rain. Wind. Snow. The driving of the Snows: A Man perishing among them; whence Reflections on the Wants and Miseries of Human Life. The Wolves descending from the* Alps *and* Apennines. *A Winter-Evening described: as spent by Philosophers; by the Country People; in the City. Frost. A View of Winter within the* polar Circle. *A Thaw. The whole concluding with moral Reflections on a future State.*

SEE, WINTER comes, to rule the vary'd Year,
Sullen, and sad with all his rising Train;
Vapours, and *Clouds*, and *Storms*. Be these my Theme,
These, that exalt the Soul to solemn Thought,
And heavenly Musing. Welcome, kindred Glooms!
Cogenial Horrors, hail! with frequent Foot,
Pleas'd have I, in my chearful Morn of Life,
When nurs'd by careless Solitude I liv'd,
And sung of Nature with unceasing Joy,
Pleas'd have I wander'd thro' your rough Domain;
Trod the pure Virgin-Snows, myself as pure;
Heard the Winds roar, and the big Torrent burst;
Or seen the deep fermenting Tempest brew'd,
In the grim Evening-Sky. Thus pass'd the Time,
Till thro' the lucid Chambers of the South
Look'd out the joyous SPRING, look'd out, and smil'd.
To Thee, the Patron of her first Essay,
The Muse, O WILMINGTON! renews her Song.
Since has she rounded the revolving Year:
Skim'd the gay Spring; on Eagle-Pinions borne,
Attempted thro' the Summer-Blaze to rise;
Then swept o'er Autumn with the shadowy Gale;
And now among the Wintry Clouds again,
Roll'd in the doubling Storm, she tries to soar;
To swell her Note with all the rushing Winds;
To suit her sounding Cadence to the Floods;
As is her Theme, her Numbers wildly great:
Thrice happy! could she fill thy judging Ear
With bold Description, and with manly Thought.
Nor art thou skill'd in awful Schemes alone,

[1] First collected edition in 1730.
[2] Published in 1726. Text of *The Seasons*, 1744.

And how to make a mighty People thrive:
But equal Goodness, sound Integrity,
A firm unshaken uncorrupted Soul
Amid a sliding Age, and burning strong,
Not vainly blazing for thy Country's Weal,
A steady Spirit regularly free;
These, each exalting each, the Statesman light
Into the Patriot; These, the publick Hope
And Eye to thee converting, bid the Muse
Record what Envy dares not Flattery call.
  Now when the chearless Empire of the Sky
To *Capricorn* the *Centaur-Archer* yields,
And fierce *Aquarius*, stains th' inverted Year;
Hung o'er the farthest Verge of Heaven, the Sun
Scarce spreads o'er Ether the dejected Day.
Faint are his Gleams, and ineffectual shoot
His struggling Rays, in horizontal Lines,
Thro' the thick Air; as cloath'd in cloudy Storm,
Weak, wan, and broad, he skirts the Southern Sky;
And, soon descending, to the long dark Night,
Wide-shading All, the prostrate World resigns.
Nor is the Night unwish'd; while vital Heat,
Light, Life, and Joy, the dubious Day forsake.
Mean-time, in sable Cincture, Shadows vast,
Deep-ting'd and damp, and congregated Clouds,
And all the vapoury Turbulence of Heaven
Involve the Face of things. Thus Winter falls,
A heavy Gloom oppressive o'er the World,
Thro' Nature shedding Influence malign,
And rouses up the Seeds of dark Disease.
The Soul of Man dies in him, loathing Life,
And black with more than melancholy Views.
The Cattle droop; and o'er the furrow'd Land,
Fresh from the Plow, the dun discolour'd Flocks,
Untended spreading, crop the wholesome Root.
Along the Woods, along the moorish Fens,
Sighs the sad *Genius* of the coming Storm;
And up among the loose disjointed Cliffs,
And fractur'd Mountains wild, the brawling Brook
And Cave, presageful, send a hollow Moan,
Resounding long in listening Fancy's Ear.
  THEN comes the Father of the Tempest forth,
Wrapt in black Glooms. First joyless Rains obscure
Drive thro' the mingling Skies with Vapour foul;
Dash on the Mountain's Brow, and shake the Woods
That grumbling wave below. Th' unsightly Plane
Lies a brown Deluge; as the low-bent Clouds
Pour Flood on Flood, yet unexhausted still

Combine, and deepening into Night shut up
The Day's fair Face. The Wanderers of Heaven,
Each to his Home, retire; save Those that love
To take their Pastime in the troubled Air,
Or skimming flutter round the dimply Pool.
The Cattle from th' untasted Fields return,
And ask with meaning Lowe, their wonted Stalls,
Or ruminate in the contiguous Shade.
Thither the houshold feathery People croud,
The crested Cock, with all his female Train,
Pensive, and dripping; while the Cottage-Hind
Hangs o'er th' enlivening Blaze, and taleful there
Recounts his simple Frolick: much he talks,
And much he laughs, nor recks the Storm that blows
Without, and rattles on his humble Roof.
  WIDE o'er the Brim, with many a Torrent swell'd,
And the mix'd Ruin of its Banks o'erspread,
At last the rous'd-up River pours along:
Resistless, roaring, dreadful, down it comes,
From the rude Mountain, and the mossy Wild,
Tumbling thro' Locks abrupt, and sounding far;
Then o'er the sanded Valley floating spreads,
Calm, sluggish, silent; till again constrain'd,
Between two meeting Hills it bursts a Way,
Where Rocks and Woods o'erhang the turbid Stream;
There gathering triple Force, rapid, and deep,
It boils, and wheels, and foams, and thunders thro'.
  NATURE! great Parent! whose unceasing Hand
Rolls round the Seasons of the changeful Year,
How mighty, how majestic, are thy Works!
With what a pleasing Dread they swell the Soul!
That sees astonish'd! and astonish'd sings!
Ye too, ye Winds! that now begin to blow,
With boisterous Sweep, I raise my Voice to you.
Where are your Stores, ye powerful Beings! say,
Where your aërial Magazines reserv'd,
To swell the brooding Terrors of the Storm.
In what far-distant Region of the Sky,
Hush'd in dead Silence, sleep you when 'tis calm?
  WHEN from the palid Sky the Sun descends,
With many a Spot, that o'er his glaring Orb
Uncertain wanders, stain'd; red fiery Streaks
Begin to flush around. The reeling Clouds
Stagger with dizzy Poise, as doubting yet
Which Master to obey: while rising slow,
Blank, in the leaden-colour'd East, the Moon
Wears a wan Circle round her blunted Horns.
Seen thro' the turbid fluctuating Air,

The Stars obtuse emit a shivering Ray;
Or frequent seem to shoot athwart the Gloom,
And long behind them trail the whitening Blaze.
Snatch'd in short Eddies, plays the wither'd Leaf;
And on the Flood the dancing Feather floats.
With broaden'd Nostrils to the Sky upturn'd,
The conscious Heifer snuffs the stormy Gale.
Even as the Matron, at her nightly Task,
With pensive Labour draws the flaxen Thread,
The wasted Taper and the crackling Flame
Foretel the Blast. But chief the plumy Race,
The Tenants of the Sky, its Changes speak.
Retiring from the Downs, where all Day long
They pick'd their scanty Fare, a blackning Train
Of clamorous Rooks thick-urge their weary Flight,
And seek the closing Shelter of the Grove.
Assiduous, in his Bower, the wailing Owl
Plies his sad Song. The Cormorant on high
Wheels from the Deep, and screams along the Land.
Loud shrieks the soaring Hern; and with wild Wing
The circling Sea-Fowl cleave the flaky Clouds.
Ocean, unequal press'd with broken Tide
And blind Commotion heaves; while from the Shore,
Eat into Caverns by the restless Wave,
And Forest-rustling Mountain, comes a Voice,
That solemn-sounding bids the World prepare.
Then issues forth the Storm with sudden Burst,
And hurls the whole precipitated Air,
Down, in a Torrent. On the passive Main
Descends th' etherial Force, and with strong Gust
Turns from its Bottom the discolour'd Deep.
Thro' the black Night that sits immense around,
Lash'd into Foam, the fierce conflicting Brine
Seems o'er a Thousand raging Waves to burn;
Mean-time the Mountain-Billows, to the Clouds
In dreadful Tumult swell'd, Surge above Surge,
Burst into Chaos with tremendous Roar,
And anchor'd Navies from their Stations drive,
Wild as the Winds across the howling Waste
Of mighty Waters: now th' inflated Wave
Straining they scale, and now impetuous shoot
Into the secret Chambers of the Deep,
The wintry *Baltick* thundering o'er their Heads.
Emerging thence again, before the Breath
Of full-exerted Heaven they wing their Course,
And dart on distant Coasts; if some sharp Rock,
Or Shoal insidious break not their Career,
And in loose Fragments fling them floating round.

NOR less at Land the loosen'd Tempest reigns.
The Mountain thunders; and its sturdy Sons
Stoop to the Bottom of the Rocks they shade.
Lone on the midnight Steep, and all aghast,
The dark way-faring Stranger breathless toils,
And, often falling, climbs against the Blast.
Low waves the rooted Forest, vex'd, and sheds
What of its tarnish'd Honours yet remain;
Dash'd down, and scatter'd, by the tearing Wind's
Assiduous Fury, its gigantic Limbs.
Thus struggling thro' the dissipated Grove,
The whirling Tempest raves along the Plain;
And on the Cottage thatch'd, or lordly Roof,
Keen-fastening, shakes them to the solid Base.
Sleep frighted flies; and round the rocking Dome,
For Entrance eager, howls the savage Blast.
Then too, they say, thro' all the burthen'd Air,
Long Groans are heard, shrill Sounds, and distant Sighs,
That utter'd by the Demon of the Night,
Warn the devoted Wretch of Woe and Death.
HUGE Uproar lords it wide. The Clouds commix'd
With Stars swift-gliding sweep along the Sky.
All Nature reels. Till Nature's KING, who oft
Amid tempestuous Darkness dwells alone,
And on the Wings of the careering Wind
Walks dreadfully serene, commands a Calm;
Then straight Air, Sea and Earth are hush'd at once.
As yet 'tis Midnight deep. The weary Clouds,
Slow-meeting, mingle into solid Gloom.
Now while the drowsy World lies lost in Sleep,
Let me associate with the serious *Night*,
And *Contemplation* her sedate Compeer;
Let me shake off th' intrusive Cares of Day,
And lay the meddling Senses all aside.
WHERE now, ye lying Vanities of Life!
Ye ever-tempting, ever-cheating Train!
Where are you now? and what is your Amount?
Vexation, Disappointment, and Remorse.
Sad, sickening Thought! and yet deluding Man,
A Scene of crude disjointed Visions past,
And broken Slumbers, rises still resolv'd,
With new-flush'd Hopes, to run the giddy Round.
FATHER of Light and Life! thou GOOD SUPREME!
O teach me what is good! teach me THYSELF!
Save me from Folly, Vanity, and Vice,
From every low Pursuit! and feed my Soul
With Knowledge, conscious Peace, and Virtue pure,
Sacred, substantial, never-fading Bliss!

THE keener Tempests come: and fuming dun
From all the livid East, or piercing North,
Thick Clouds ascend; in whose capacious Womb
A vapoury Deluge lies, to Snow congeal'd.
Heavy they roll their fleecy World along;
And the Sky saddens with the gather'd Storm.
Thro' the hush'd Air the whitening Shower descends,
At first thin-wavering; till at last the Flakes
Fall broad, and wide, and fast, dimming the Day,
With a continual Flow. The cherish'd Fields
Put on their Winter-Robe, of purest White.
'Tis Brightness all; save where the new Snow melts,
Along the mazy Current. Low, the Woods
Bow their hoar Head; and, ere the languid Sun
Faint from the West emits his Evening-Ray,
Earth's universal Face, deep-hid, and chill,
Is one wild dazzling Waste, that buries wide
The Works of Man. Drooping, the Labourer-Ox
Stands cover'd o'er with Snow, and then demands
The Fruit of all his Toil. The Fowls of Heaven,
Tam'd by the cruel Season, croud around
The winnowing Store, and claim the little Boon
Which PROVIDENCE assigns them. One alone,
The Red-Breast, sacred to the houshold Gods,
Wisely regardful of th' embroiling Sky,
In joyless Fields, and thorny Thickets, leaves
His shivering Mates, and pays to trusty Man
His annual Visit. Half-afraid, he first
Against the Window beats; then, brisk, alights
On the warm Hearth; then, hopping o'er the Floor,
Eyes all the smiling Family askance,
And pecks, and starts, and wonders where he is;
Till more familiar grown, the Table Crumbs
Attract his slender Feet. The foodless Wilds
Pour forth their brown Inhabitants. The Hare,
Tho' timorous of Heart, and hard beset
By Death in various Forms, dark Snares, and Dogs,
And more unpitying Men, the Garden seeks,
Urg'd on by fearless Want. The Bleating Kind
Eye the bleak Heaven, and next the glistening Earth,
With Looks of dumb Despair; then, sad dispers'd,
Dig for the wither'd Herb thro' Heaps of Snow.
Now, Shepherds, to your helpless Charge be kind,
Baffle the raging Year, and fill their Pens
With Food at Will; lodge them below the Storm,
And watch them strict: for from the bellowing East,
In this dire Season, oft the Whirlwind's Wing
Sweeps up the Burthen of whole wintry Plains

In one wide Waft, and o'er the hapless Flocks,
Hid in the Hollow of two neighbouring Hills,
The billowy Tempest whelms; till, upward urg'd,
The Valley to a shining Mountain swells,
Tipt with a Wreath, high-curling in the Sky.
As thus the Snows arise; and foul, and fierce,
All Winter drives along the darken'd Air;
In his own loose-revolving Fields, the Swain
Disaster'd stands; sees other Hills ascend,
Of unknown joyless Brow; and other Scenes,
Of horrid Prospect, shag the trackless Plain:
Nor finds the River, nor the Forest, hid
Beneath the formless Wild; but wanders on
From Hill to Dale, still more and more astray;
Impatient flouncing thro' the drifted Heaps,
Stung with the Thoughts of Home; the Thoughts of Home
Rush on his Nerves, and call their Vigor forth
In many a vain Attempt. How sinks his Soul!
What black Despair, what Horror fills his Heart!
When from the dusky Spot, which Fancy feign'd
His tufted Cottage rising thro' the Snow,
He meets the Roughness of the middle Waste,
Far from the Track, and blest Abode of Man:
While round him Night resistless closes fast,
And every Tempest, howling o'er his Head,
Renders the savage Wilderness more wild.
Then throng the busy Shapes into his Mind,
Of cover'd Pits unfathomably deep,
A dire Descent! beyond the Power of Frost,
Of faithless Bogs; of Precipices huge,
Smooth'd up with Snow; and, what is Land unknown,
What Water, of the still unfrozen Spring,
In the loose Marsh or solitary Lake,
Where the fresh Fountain from the Bottom boils.
These check his fearful Steps; and down he sinks
Beneath the Shelter of the shapeless Drift,
Thinking o'er all the Bitterness of Death,
Mix'd with the tender Anguish Nature shoots
Thro' the wrung Bosom of the dying Man,
His Wife, his Children, and his Friends unseen.
In vain for him th' officious Wife prepares
The Fire fair-blazing, and the Vestment warm;
In vain his little Children, peeping out
Into the mingling Storm, demand their Sire,
With Tears of artless Innocence. Alas!
Nor Wife, nor Children, more shall he behold,
Nor Friends, nor sacred Home. On every Nerve
The deadly Winter seizes; shuts up Sense;

And o'er his inmost Vitals creeping cold,
Lays him along the Snow, a stiffen'd Corse,
Stretch'd out, and bleaching in the northern Blast.
  AH little think the gay licentious Proud,
Whom Pleasure, Power, and Affluence surround;
They, who their thoughtless Hours in giddy Mirth,
And wanton, often cruel, Riot waste;
Ah little think they while they dance along,
How many feel, this very Moment, Death
And all the sad Variety of Pain!
How many sink in the devouring Flood,
Or more devouring Flame. How many bleed,
By shameful Variance betwixt Man and Man.
How many pine in Want, and Dungeon Glooms;
Shut from the common Air, and common Use
Of their own Limbs. How many drink the Cup
Of baleful Grief, or eat the bitter Bread
Of Misery. Sore pierc'd by wintry Winds,
How many shrink into the sordid Hut
Of chearless Poverty. How many shake
With all their fiercer Tortures of the Mind,
Unbounded Passion, Madness, Guilt, Remorse;
Whence tumbled headlong from the Height of Life,
They furnish Matter for the Tragic Muse.
Even in the Vale, where Wisdom loves to dwell,
With Friendship, Peace, and Contemplation join'd,
How many, rack'd with honest Passions droop
In deep retir'd Distress. How many stand
Around the Death-Bed of their dearest Friends,
And point the parting Anguish. Thought fond Man
Of these, and all the thousand nameless Ills,
That one incessant Struggle render Life,
One Scene of Toil, of Suffering, and of Fate,
Vice in his high Career would stand appall'd
And heedless rambling Impulse learn to think;
The conscious Heart of Charity would warm,
And her wide Wish Benevolence dilate;
The social Tear would rise, the social Sight;
And into clear Perfection, gradual Bliss,
Refining still the social Passions work.
  AND here can I forget the generous *Band,
Who, touch'd with human Woe, redressive search'd
Into the Horrors of the gloomy Jail?
Unpity'd, and unheard, where Misery moans;
Where Sickness pines; where Thirst and Hunger burn,
And poor Misfortune feels the Lash of Vice.

* *The Jail-Committee, in the Year 1729.*

While in the Land of Liberty, the Land
Whose every Street and public Meeting glow
With open Freedom, little Tyrants rag'd:
Snatch'd the lean Morsel from the starving Mouth;
Tore from cold wintry Limbs the tatter'd Weed;
Even robb'd them of the last of Comforts, Sleep;
The free-born BRITON to the Dungeon chain'd,
Or, as the Lust of Cruelty prevail'd,
At pleasure mark'd him with inglorious Stripes;
And crush'd out Lives, by secret barbarous Ways,
That for their Country would have toil'd, or bled.
O great Design! if executed well,
With patient Care, and Wisdom-temper'd Zeal.
Ye Sons of Mercy! yet resume the Search;
Drag forth the legal Monsters into Light,
Wrench from their Hands Oppression's iron Rod,
And bid the Cruel feel the Pains they give.
Much still untouch'd remains; in this rank Age,
Much is the Patriot's weeding Hand requir'd.
The Toils of Law, (what dark insidious Men
Have cumbrous added to perplex the Truth,
And lengthen simple Justice into Trade)
How glorious were the Day! that saw These broke,
And every Man within the Reach of Right.
  BY wintry Famine rous'd, from all the Tract
Of horrid Mountains which the shining *Alps*,
And wavy *Appenines*, and *Pyrenees*,
Branch out stupendous into distant Lands;
Cruel as Death, and hungry as the Grave!
Burning for Blood! bony, and ghaunt, and grim!
Assembling Wolves in raging Troops descend;
And, pouring o'er the Country, bear along,
Keen as the North-Wind sweeps the glossy Snow.
All is their Prize. They fasten on the Steed,
Press him to Earth, and pierce his mighty Heart.
Nor can the Bull his awful Front defend,
Or shake the murdering Savages away.
Rapacious, at the Mother's Throat they fly,
And tear the screaming Infant from her Breast.
The godlike Face of Man avails him nought.
Even Beauty, Force divine! at whose bright Glance
The generous Lion stands in soften'd Gaze,
Here bleeds, a hapless undistinguish'd Prey.
But if, appriz'd of the severe Attack,
The Country be shut up, lur'd by the Scent,
On Church-Yards drear (inhuman to relate!)
The disappointed Prowlers fall, and dig

The shrouded Body from the Grave; o'er which,
Mix'd with foul Shades, and frighted Ghosts, they howl.
  AMONG those hilly Regions, where embrac'd
In peaceful Vales the happy *Grisons* dwell;
Oft, rushing sudden from the loaded Cliffs,
Mountains of Snow their gathering Terrors roll.
From Steep to Steep, loud-thundering, down they come,
A wintry Waste in dire Commotion all;
And Herds, and Flocks, and Travellers, and Swains,
And sometimes whole Brigades of marching Troops,
Or Hamlets sleeping in the Dead of Night,
Are deep beneath the smothering Ruin whelm'd.
  Now, all amid the Rigours of the Year,
In the wild Depth of Winter, while without
The ceaseless Winds blow Ice, be my Retreat,
Between the groaning Forest and the Shore,
Beat by a boundless Multitude of Waves,
A rural, shelter'd, solitary, Scene;
Where ruddy Fire and beaming Tapers join,
To chear the Gloom. There studious let me sit,
And hold high Converse with the MIGHTY DEAD;
Sages of antient Time, as Gods rever'd,
As Gods beneficent, who blest Mankind
With Arts, and Arms, and humaniz'd a World.
Rous'd at th' inspiring Thought, I throw aside
The long-liv'd Volume; and, deep-musing, hail
The sacred Shades, that slowly-rising pass
Before my wondering Eyes. First SOCRATES,
Who firmly good in a corrupted State,
Against the Rage of Tyrants *single* stood,
Invincible! calm Reason's holy Law,
That *Voice* of GOD within th' attentive Mind,
Obeying, fearless, or in Life, or Death:
Great Moral Teacher! *Wisest of Mankind!*
SOLON the next, who built his Common-Weal
On Equity's wide Base; by *tender* Laws
A lively People curbing, yet undamp'd
Preserving still that quick peculiar Fire,
Whence in the laurel'd Field of finer Arts,
And of bold Freedom, they unequal'd shone,
The Pride of smiling GREECE, and Human-kind.
LYCURGUS then, who bow'd beneath the Force
Of strictest Discipline, *severely wise*,
All human Passions. Following Him, I see,
As at *Thermopylæ* he glorious fell,

The firm *DEVOTED CHIEF, who prov'd by Deeds
The hardest Lesson which the *other* taught.
Then ARISTIDES lifts his honest Front;
Spotless of Heart, to whom th' unflattering Voice
Of Freedom gave the noblest Name of *Just*;
In pure majestic Poverty rever'd;
Who, even his Glory to his Country's Weal
Submitting, swell'd a haughty †*Rival*'s Fame.
Rear'd by his Care, of softer Ray, appears
CIMON sweet-soul'd; whose Genius, rising strong,
Shook off the Load of young Debauch; abroad
The Scourge of *Persian* Pride, at home the Friend
Of every Worth and every splendid Art;
Modest, and simple, in the Pomp of Wealth.
Then the last Worthies of declining GREECE,
Late-call'd to Glory, in *unequal* Times,
Pensive, appear. The fair *Corinthian* Boast,
TIMOLEON, temper'd happy, mild, and firm,
Who wept the *Brother* while the *Tyrant* bled.
And, equal to the Best, the ‡THEBAN PAIR,
Whose Virtues, in *heroic Concord* join'd,
Their Country rais'd to Freedom, Empire, Fame.
He too, with whom *Athenian* Honour sunk,
And left a Mass of sordid Lees behind,
PHOCION the *Good*; in public Life severe,
To Virtue still inexorably firm;
But when, beneath his low illustrious Roof,
Sweet Peace and happy Wisdom smooth'd his Brow,
Not Friendship softer was, nor Love more kind.
And He, the *last* of old LYCURGUS' Sons,
The generous Victim to that vain Attempt,
To save a rotten State, AGIS, who saw
Even SPARTA's self to servile Avarice sunk.
The two *Achaian* Heroes close the Train.
ARATUS, who a while relum'd the Soul
Of fondly-lingering Liberty in GREECE:
And He her Darling as her latest Hope,
The *gallant* PHILOPEMON; who to Arms
Turn'd the luxurious Pomp he could not cure;
Or toiling in his Farm, a simple Swain;
Or, bold and skilful, thundering in the Field.
OF rougher Front, a mighty People come!
A Race of Heroes! in those virtuous Times
Which knew no Stain, save that with partial Flame

* LEONIDAS.
† THEMISTOCLES.
‡ PELOPIDAS, *and* EPAMINONDAS.

Their *dearest* Country they *too fondly* lov'd.
Her *better Founder* first, the Light of Rome,
Numa, who soften'd her rapacious Sons.
Servius the *King*, who laid the solid Base
On which o'er Earth the *vast Republic* spread.
Then the great Consuls venerable rise.
The *Public Father who the *Private* quell'd,
As on the dread Tribunal sternly sad.
He, whom his thankless Country *could not* lose,
Camillus, only vengeful to her Foes.
Fabricius, Scorner of all-conquering Gold:
And Cincinnatus, awful from the Plow.
Thy †willing Victim, *Carthage,* bursting loose
From all that pleading Nature could oppose,
From a whole City's Tears, by rigid Faith
Imperious call'd, and Honour's dire Command.
Scipio, the *gentle Chief*, humanely brave,
Who soon the Race of spotless Glory ran,
And, warm in Youth, to the *Poetic Shade*
With *Friendship* and *Philosophy* retir'd.
Tully, whose powerful Eloquence a while
Restrain'd the *rapid* Fate of rushing Rome.
Unconquer'd Cato, virtuous in *Extreme.*
And thou, unhappy Bbutus, kind of Heart,
Whose steady Arm, by awful Virtue urg'd,
Lifted the *Roman Steel* against thy *Friend.*
Thousands, besides, the Tribute of a Verse
Demand; but who can count the Stars of Heaven?
Who sing their Influence on this lower World?
  Behold, who yonder comes! in sober State,
Fair, mild, and strong, as is a vernal Sun:
'Tis *Phœbus'* self, or else the Mantuan Swain!
Great Homer too appears, of daring Wing,
Parent of Song! and *equal* by his Side,
The British Muse; join'd hand in hand they walk,
Darkling, full up the middle Steep to Fame.
Nor absent are those Shades, whose skilful Hand
Pathetic drew th' impassion'd Heart, and charm'd
Transported *Athens* with the moral Scene:
Nor those who, tuneful, wak'd th' enchanting Lyre.
  First of your Kind! Society divine!
Still visit thus my Nights, for you reserv'd,
And mount my soaring Soul to Thoughts like yours.
Silence, thou lonely Power! the Door be thine;

* Marcus Junius Brutus.
† Regulus.

See on the hallow'd Hour that none intrude,
Save a few chosen Friends, that sometimes deign
To bless my humble Roof, with Sense refin'd,
Learning digested well, exalted Faith,
Unstudy'd Wit, and Humour ever gay.
Or from the Muses' Hill will POPE descend,
To raise the sacred Hour, to bid it smile,
And with the social Spirit warm the Heart:
For tho' not sweeter his own HOMER sings,
Yet is his Life the more endearing Song.
  WHERE art Thou, HAMMOND? Thou the darling Pride,
The Friend and Lover of the tuneful Throng!
Ah why, dear Youth, in all the blooming Prime
Of vernal Genius, where disclosing fast
Each active Worth each manly Virtue lay,
Why wert thou ravish'd from our Hope so soon?
What now avails that noble Thirst of Fame,
Which stung thy fervent Breast? That treasur'd Store
Of Knowledge, early gain'd? That eager Zeal
To serve thy Country, glowing in the Band
Of YOUTHFUL PATRIOTS, who sustain her Name?
What now, alas! that Life-diffusing Charm
Of sprightly Wit? That Rapture for the Muse,
That Heart of Friendship, and that Soul of Joy,
Which bade with softest Light thy Virtues smile?
Ah! only shew'd, to check our fond Pursuits,
And teach our humbled Hopes that Life is vain!
  THUS in some deep Retirement would I pass,
The Winter-Glooms, with Friends of pliant Soul,
Or blithe, or solemn, as the Theme inspir'd:
With them would search, if Nature's boundless Frame
Was call'd, late-rising from the Void of Night,
Or sprung *eternal* from th' ETERNAL MIND,
It's Springs, it's Laws, it's Progress, and it's End.
Hence larger Prospects of the beauteous Whole
Would, gradual, open on our opening Minds;
And each diffusive Harmony unite,
In full Perfection, to th' astonish'd Eye.
Then would we try to scan the *moral World*,
Which, tho' to us it seems embroil'd, moves on
In higher Order; fitted, and impell'd,
By WISDOM's finest Hand, and issuing all
In general Good. The sage Historic Muse
Should next conduct us thro' the Deeps of Time:
Shew us how Empire grew, declin'd, and fell,
In scatter'd States; what makes the Nations smile,

Improves their Soil, and gives them double Suns;
And why they pine beneath the brightest Skies,
In Nature's richest Lap. As thus we talk'd,
Our Hearts would burn within us, would inhale
That Portion of Divinity, that Ray
Of purest Heaven, which lights the public Soul
Of Patriots, and of Heroes. But if doom'd,
In powerless humble Fortune, to repress
These ardent Risings of the kindling Soul;
Then, even superior to Ambition, we
Would learn the private Virtues; how to glide
Thro' Shades and Plains, along the smoothest Stream
Of rural Life: or snatch'd away by Hope,
Thro' the dim Spaces of Futurity,
With earnest Eye anticipate those Scenes
Of Happiness, and Wonder; where the Mind,
In endless Growth and infinite Ascent
Rises from State to State, and World to World.
But when with These the serious Thought is foil'd,
We, shifting for Relief, would play the Shapes
Of frolic Fancy; and incessant form
Those rapid Pictures, that assembled Train
Of fleet Ideas, never join'd before,
Whence lively *Wit* excites to gay Surprize;
Or Folly-painting *Humour*, grave himself,
Calls Laughter forth, deep-shaking every Nerve.
MEAN-TIME the Village rouzes up the Fire;
While well attested, and as well believ'd,
Heard solemn, goes the Goblin-Story round;
Till superstitious Horror creeps o'er all.
Or, frequent in the sounding Hall, they wake
The rural Gambol. Rustic Mirth goes round:
The simple Joke that takes the Shepherd's Heart,
Easily pleas'd; the long loud Laugh, sincere;
The Kiss, snatch'd hasty from the side-long Maid,
On purpose guardless, or pretending Sleep:
The Leap, the Slap, the Haul; and, shook to Notes
Of native Music, the respondent Dance.
Thus jocund fleets with them the Winter-Night.
THE City swarms intense. The public Haunt,
Full of each Theme, and warm with mixt Discourse,
Hums indistinct. The Sons of Riot flow
Down the loose Stream of false inchanted Joy,
To swift Destruction. On the rankled Soul
The gaming Fury falls; and in one Gulph
Of total Ruin, Honour, Virtue, Peace,
Friends, Families, and Fortune, headlong sink.
Up-springs the Dance along the lighted Dome,

Mix'd, and evolv'd, a thousand sprightly ways.
The glittering Court effuses every Pomp;
The Circle deepens: beam'd from gaudy Robes,
Tapers, and sparkling Gems, and radiant Eyes,
A soft Effulgence o'er the Palace waves:
While, a gay Insect in *his* Summer-shine,
The Fop, light fluttering, spreads his mealy Wings.
  DREAD o'er the Scene, the Ghost of HAMLET stalks;
OTHELLO rages; poor MONIMIA mourns;
And BELVIDERA pours her Soul in Love.
Deep-thrilling Terror shakes; the comely Tear
Steals o'er the Cheek: or else the COMIC MUSE
Holds to the World a Picture of itself,
And raises sly the fair impartial Laugh.
Sometimes she lifts her Strain, and paints the Scenes
Of beauteous Life; whate'er can deck Mankind,
Or charm the Heart, in generous *BEVIL shew'd.
  O THOU, whose Wisdom, solid yet refin'd,
Whose Patriot-Virtues, and consummate Skill
To touch the finer Springs that move the World,
Join'd to whate'er the *Graces* can bestow,
And all *Apollo*'s animating Fire,
Give Thee, with pleasing Dignity, to shine
At once the Guardian, Ornament, and Joy,
Of polish'd Life; permit the *Rural Muse*,
O CHESTERFIELD, to grace with Thee her Song!
Ere to the Shades again she humbly flies,
Indulge her fond Ambition, in thy Train,
(For every Muse has in thy Train a Place)
To mark thy various full-accomplish'd Mind:
To mark that Spirit, which, with *British Scorn*,
Rejects th' Allurements of corrupted Power;
That elegant Politeness, which excels
Even in the Judgement of presumptuous *France*,
The boasted Manners of her shining Court;
That Wit, the vivid Energy of Sense,
The Truth of Nature, which, with *Attic* Point,
And kind well-temper'd Satire, smoothly keen,
Steals through the Soul, and without Pain corrects.
Or, rising thence with yet a brighter Flame,
O let me hail Thee on some glorious Day,
When to the listening Senate, ardent, croud
BRITANNIA's Sons to hear her pleaded Cause.
Then drest by Thee, more amiably fair,
Truth the soft Robe of mild Persuasion wears:
Thou to assenting Reason giv'st again

* *A Character in the* CONSCIOUS LOVERS, *written by Sir* RICHARD STEELE.

Her own enlighten'd Thoughts; call'd from the Heart,
Th' obedient Passions on thy Voice attend;
And even reluctant Party feels a while
Thy gracious Power: as thro' the vary'd Maze
Of Eloquence, now smooth, now quick, now strong,
Profound and clear, you roll the copious Flood.
  To thy lov'd Haunt return, my happy Muse:
For now, behold, the joyous Winter-Days,
Frosty, succeed; and thro' the blue Serene,
For Sight too fine, th' etherial Niter flies;
Killing infectious Damps, and the spent Air
Storing afresh with elemental Life.
Close crouds the shining Atmosphere; and binds
Our strengthen'd Bodies in it's cold Embrace,
Constringent; feeds, and animates our Blood;
Refines our Spirits, thro' the new-strung Nerves,
In swifter Sallies darting to the Brain;
Where sits the Soul, intense, collected, cool,
Bright as the Skies, and as the Season keen.
All Nature feels the renovating Force
Of Winter, only to the thoughtless Eye
In Ruin seen. The Frost-concocted Glebe
Draws in abundant vegetable Soul,
And gathers Vigour for the coming Year.
A stronger Glow sits on the lively Cheek
Of ruddy Fire: and luculent along
The purer Rivers flow; their sullen Deeps,
Transparent, open to the Shepherd's Gaze,
And murmur hoarser at the fixing Frost.
  WHAT art thou, Frost? and whence are thy keen Stores
Deriv'd, thou secret all-invading Power,
Whom even th' illusive Fluid cannot fly?
Is not thy potent Energy, unseen,
Myriads of little Salts, or hook'd, or shap'd
Like double Wedges, and diffus'd immense
Thro' Water, Earth, and Ether? Hence at Eve,
Steam'd eager from the red Horizon round,
With the fierce Rage of Winter deep suffus'd,
An icy Gale, oft shifting, o'er the Pool
Breathes a blue Film, and in its mid Career
Arrests the bickering Stream. The loosen'd Ice,
Let down the Flood, and half dissolv'd by Day,
Rustles no more; but to the sedgy Bank
Fast grows, or gathers round the pointed Stone,
A crystal Pavement, by the Breath of Heaven
Cemented firm; till, seiz'd from Shore to Shore,
The whole imprison'd River growls below.
Loud rings the frozen Earth, and hard reflects

A double Noise; while, at his evening Watch,
The Village Dog deters the nightly Thief;
The Heifer lows; the distant Water-fall
Swells in the Breeze; and, with the hasty Tread
Of Traveller, the hollow-sounding Plain
Shakes from afar. The full ethereal Round,
Infinite Worlds disclosing to the View,
Shines out intensely keen; and, all one Cope
Of starry Glitter, glows from Pole to Pole.
From Pole to Pole the rigid Influence falls,
Thro' the still Night, incessant, heavy, strong,
And seizes Nature fast. It freezes on;
Till Morn, late-rising o'er the drooping World,
Lifts her pale Eye unjoyous. Then appears
The various Labour of the silent Night:
Prone from the dripping Eave, and dum Cascade,
Whose idle Torrents only seem to roar,
The pendant Icicle; the Frost-Work fair,
Where transient Hues, and fancy'd Figures rise;
Wide spouted o'er the Hill, the frozen Brook,
A livid Tract, cold-gleaming on the Morn;
The Forest bent beneath the plumy Wave;
And by the Frost refin'd the whiter Snow,
Incrusted hard, and sounding to the Tread
Of early Shepherd, as he pensive seeks
His pining Flock, or from the Mountain-top,
Pleas'd with the slippery Surface, swift descends.
  ON blithsome Frolicks bent, the youthful Swains,
While every Work of Man is laid at rest,
Fond o'er the River croud, in various Sport
And Revelry dissolv'd; where mixing glad,
Happiest of all the Train! the raptur'd Boy
Lashes the whirling Top. Or, where the *Rhine*
Branch'd out in many a long Canal extends,
From every Province swarming, void of Care,
Batavia rushes forth; and as they sweep,
On sounding Skates, a thousand different Ways,
In circling Poise, swift as the Winds, along,
The *then gay* Land is madden'd all to Joy.
Nor less the northern Courts, wide o'er the Snow,
Pour a new Pomp. Eager, on rapid Sleds,
Their vigorous Youth in bold Contention wheel
The long-resounding Course. Meantime, to raise
The manly Strife, with highly-blooming Charms,
Flush'd by the Season, *Scandinavia*'s Dames,
Or *Russia*'s buxom Daughters glow around.
  PURE, quick, and sportful, is the wholesome Day;
But soon elaps'd. The horizontal Sun,

Broad o'er the South, hangs at his utmost Noon;
And, ineffectual, strikes the gelid Cliff.
His azure Gloss the Mountain still maintains,
Nor feels the feeble Touch. Perhaps the Vale
Relents a while to the reflected Ray;
Or from the Forest falls the cluster'd Snow,
Myriads of Gems, that in the waving Gleam
Gay-twinkle as they scatter. Thick around
Thunders the Sport of Those, who with the Gun,
And Dog impatient bounding at the Shot,
Worse than the Season, desolate the Fields;
And, adding to the Ruins of the Year,
Distress the footed or the feather'd Game.
  BUT what is This? Our infant Winter sinks,
Divested of his Grandeur, should our Eye
Astonish'd shoot into the *Frigid Zone*;
Where, for relentless Months, continual Night,
Holds o'er the glittering Waste her starry Reign.
  THERE, thro' the Prison of unbounded Wilds,
Barr'd by the Hand of Nature from Escape,
Wide-roams the *Russian* Exile. Nought around
Strikes his sad Eye, but Desarts lost in Snow;
And heavy-loaded Groves; and solid Floods,
That stretch, athwart the solitary Vast,
Their icy Horrors to the frozen Main;
And chearless Towns far-distant, never bless'd,
Save when it's annual Course the Caravan
Bends to the golden Coast of rich **Cathay*,
With News of Human-kind. Yet there Life glows;
Yet cherish'd there, beneath the shining Waste,
The furry Nations harbour: tipt with Jet,
Fair Ermines, spotless as the Snows they press;
Sables, of glossy Black; and dark-embrown'd,
Or beauteous freakt with many a mingled Hue,
Thousands besides, the costly Pride of Courts.
There, warm together press'd, the trooping Deer
Sleep on the new-fallen Snows; and, scarce his Head
Rais'd o'er the heapy Wreath, the branching Elk
Lies slumbering sullen in the white Abyss.
Nor Dogs, nor Toils, he wants; nor with the Dread
Of sounding Bows the ruthless Hunter drives
The fearful-flying Race; with ponderous Clubs,
As weak against the Mountain-Heaps they push
Their beating Breast in vain, and piteous bray,
He lays them quivering on th' ensanguin'd Snows,
And with loud Shouts rejoicing bears them home.

---

* *The old Name for* China.

There thro' the piny Forest half-absorpt,
Rough Tenant of these Shades, the shapeless Bear,
With dangling Ice all horrid, stalks forlorn;
Slow-pac'd, and sourer as the Storms increase,
He makes his Bed beneath th' inclement Drift,
And, with stern Patience, scorning weak Complaint,
Hardens his Heart against assailing Want.
  WIDE o'er the spacious Regions of the North,
That see *Boötes* urge his tardy Wain,
A boisterous Race, by frosty **Caurus* pierc'd,
Who little Pleasure know, and fear no Pain,
Prolific swarm. They once relum'd the Flame
Of lost Mankind in polish'd Slavery sunk,
Drove martial †Horde on Horse, with dreadful Sweep
Resistless rushing o'er th' enfeebled South,
And gave the vanquish'd World another Form.
Not such the Sons of *Lapland:* wisely They
Despise th' insensate barbarous Trade of War;
They ask no more than simple Nature gives,
They love their Mountains, and enjoy their Storms.
No false Desires, no Pride-created Wants,
Disturb the peaceful Current of their Days;
And thro' the restless ever-tortur'd Maze
Of Pleasure, or Ambition, bid it rage.
Their Rain-Deer form their Riches. These their Tents,
Their Robes, their Beds, and all their homely Wealth
Supply, their wholesome Fare, and chearful Cups.
Obsequious at their Call, the docile Tribe
Yield to the Sled their Necks, and whirl them swift
O'er Hill and Dale, heap'd into one Expanse
Of marbled Snow, or far as Eye can sweep
With a blue Crust of Ice unbounded glaz'd.
By dancing Meteors then, that ceaseless shake
A waving Blaze refracted o'er the Heavens,
And vivid Moons, and Stars that keener play
With doubled Lustre from the radiant Waste,
Even in the Depth of *Polar Night*, they find
A wondrous Day: enough to light the Chace,
Or guide their daring Steps to *Finland*-Fairs.
Wish'd Spring returns; and from the hazy South,
While dim Aurora slowly moves before,
The welcome Sun just verging up at first,
By small Degrees extends the swelling Curve;
Till seen at last for gay rejoicing Months,
Still round and round his spiral Course he winds,
And as he nearly dips his flaming Orb,

* *The North-West Wind.*
† *The wandering* Scythian-Clans.

Wheels up again, and reascends the Sky.
In that glad Season, from the Lakes and Floods,
Where *pure *Niemi*'s fairy Mountains rise,
And fring'd with Roses †*Tenglio* rolls his Stream,
They draw the copious Fry. With these, at Eve,
They chearful-loaded to their Tents repair;
Where, all Day long in useful Cares employ'd,
Their kind unblemish'd Wives the Fire prepare.
Thrice happy Race! by Poverty secur'd
From legal Plunder and rapacious Power:
In whom fell Interest never yet has sown
The Seeds of Vice; whose spotless Swains ne'er knew
Injurious Deed, nor blasted by the Breath
Of faithless Love, their blooming Daughters Woe.
STILL pressing on, beyond *Tornêa*'s Lake,
And *Hecla* flaming thro' a Waste of Snow,
And farthest *Greenland*, to the Pole itself,
Where failing gradual Life at length goes out,
The Muse expands her solitary Flight;
And, hovering o'er the wild stupendous Scene,
Beholds new Seas beneath ‡another Sky.
Thron'd in his Palace of cerulean Ice,
Here WINTER holds his unrejoicing Court;
And thro' his airy Hall the loud Misrule
Of driving Tempest is for ever heard:
Here the grim Tyrant meditates his Wrath;
Here arms his Winds with all-subduing Frost;
Moulds his fierce Hail, and treasures up his Snows,
With which he now oppresses half the Globe.
THENCE winding eastward to the *Tartar*'s Coast,
She sweeps the howling Margin of the Main;
Where undissolving, from the First of Time,
Snows swell on Snows amazing to the Sky;
And icy Mountains, high on Mountains pil'd,
Seem to the shivering Sailor from afar,
Shapeless and white, an Atmosphere of Clouds.
Projected huge, and horrid, o'er the Surge,
Alps frown on Alps; or rushing hideous down,
As if old Chaos was again return'd,
Wide-rend the Deep, and shake the solid Pole.
Ocean itself no longer can resist

* M. de Maupertuis, *in his Book on* the Figure of the Earth, *after having described the beautiful Lake and Mountain of* Niemi *in* Lapland, *says—"From this Height we had Occasion several times to see those Vapours rise from the Lake which the People of the Country call* Haltios, *and which they deem to be the guardian Spirits of the Mountains. We had been frighted with Stories of Bears that haunted this Place, but saw none. It seem'd rather a Place of Resort for* Fairies *and* Genii *than Bears."*

† *The same Author observes—"I was surprized to see upon the Banks of this River,* (*the* Tenglio) *Roses of as lively a Red as any that are in our Gardens."*

‡ *The other Hemisphere.*

The binding Fury; but, in all it's Rage
Of Tempest taken by the boundless Frost,
Is many a Fathom to the Bottom chain'd,
And bid to roar no more: a bleak Expanse,
Shagg'd o'er with wavy Rocks, chearless, and void
Of every Life, that from the dreary Months
Flies conscious southward. Miserable they!
Who, here entangled in the gathering Ice,
Take their last Look of the descending Sun;
While, full of Death, and fierce with tenfold Frost,
The long long Night, incumbent o'er their Heads,
Falls horrible. Such was the *BRITON's Fate,
As with *first* Prow, (What have not BRITONS dar'd!)
He for the Passage sought, attempted since
So much in vain, and seeming to be shut
By jealous Nature with eternal Bars.
In these fell Regions, in *Arzina* caught,
And to the stony Deep his idle Ship
Immediate seal'd, he with his hapless Crew,
Each full exerted at his several Task,
Froze into Statues; to the Cordage glued
The Sailor, and the Pilot to the Helm.
  HARD by these Shores, where scarce his freezing Stream
Rolls the wild *Oby*, live the Last of Men;
And, half-enliven'd by the distant Sun,
That rears and ripens Man, as well as Plants,
Here Human Nature wears it's rudest Form.
Deep from the piercing Season sunk in Caves,
Here by dull Fires, and with unjoyous Chear,
They waste the tedious Gloom. Immers'd in Furs,
Doze the gross Race. Nor sprightly Jest, nor Song,
Nor Tenderness they know; nor aught of Life,
Beyond the kindred Bears that stalk without.
Till Morn at length, her Roses drooping all,
Sheds a long Twilight brightening o'er their Fields,
And calls the quiver'd Savage to the Chace.
  WHAT cannot active Government perform,
New-moulding Man? Wide-stretching from these Shores,
A People savage from remotest Time,
A huge neglected Empire ONE VAST MIND,
By HEAVEN inspir'd, from Gothic Darkness call'd.
Immortal PETER! First of Monarchs! He
His stubborn Country tam'd, her Rocks, her Fens,
Her Floods, her Seas, her ill-submitting Sons;
And while the fierce *Barbarian* he subdu'd,
To more exalted Soul he rais'd the *Man*.

* *Sir* HUGH WILLOUGHBY, *sent by* QUEEN ELIZABETH *to discover the North-East Passage.*

Ye Shades of antient Heroes, ye who toil'd
Thro' long successive Ages to build up
A lab'ring Plan of State, behold at once
The Wonder done! behold the matchless Prince!
Who left his native Throne, where reign'd till then
A mighty Shadow of unreal Power;
Who greatly spurn'd the slothful Pomp of Courts;
And roaming every Land, in every Port,
His Scepter laid aside, with glorious Hand
Unweary'd plying the mechanic Tool,
Gather'd the Seeds of Trade, of useful Arts,
Of Civil Wisdom, and of Martial Skill.
Charg'd with the Stores of *Europe* home he goes!
Then Cities rise amid th' illumin'd Waste;
O'er joyless Desarts smiles the rural Reign;
Far-distant Flood to Flood is social join'd;
Th' astonish'd *Euxine* hears the *Baltic* roar;
Proud Navies ride on Seas that never foam'd
With daring Keel before; and Armies stretch
Each Way their dazzling Files, repressing here
The frantic *Alexander* of the North,
And awing there stern Othman's shrinking Sons.
Sloth flies the Land, and *Ignorance*, and *Vice*,
Of old Dishonour proud; it glows around,
Taught by the Royal Hand that rous'd the Whole,
One Scene of Arts, of Arms, of rising Trade:
For what his Wisdom plann'd, and Power enforc'd,
More potent still, his great *Example* shew'd.

Muttering, the Winds at Eve, with blunted Point,
Blow hollow-blustering from the South. Subdu'd,
The Frost resolves into a trickling Thaw.
Spotted the Mountains shine; loose Sleet descends,
And floods the Country round. The Rivers swell,
Of Bonds impatient. Sudden from the Hills,
O'er Rocks and Woods, in broad brown Cataracts,
A thousand snow-fed Torrents shoot at once;
And, where they rush, the wide-resounding Plain
Is left one slimy Waste. Those sullen Seas,
That wash th' ungenial Pole, will rest no more
Beneath the Shackles of the mighty North;
But, rousing all their Waves, resistless heave——
And hark! the lengthening Roar continuous runs
Athwart the rifted Deep: at once it bursts,
And piles a thousand Mountains to the Clouds.
Ill fares the Bark with trembling Wretches charg'd,
That, tost amid the floating Fragments, moors
Beneath the Shelter of an icy Isle,
While Night o'erwhelms the Sea, and Horror looks

More horrible. Can human Force endure
Th' assembled Mischiefs that besiege them round?
Heart-gnawing Hunger, fainting Weariness,
The Roar of Winds and Waves, the Crush of Ice,
Now ceasing, now renew'd with louder Rage,
And in dire Echoes bellowing round the Main.
More to embroil the Deep, Leviathan
And his unwieldy Train, in dreadful Sport,
Tempest the loosen'd Brine, while thro' the Gloom,
Far, from the bleak inhospitable Shore,
Loading the Winds, is heard the hungry Howl
Of famish'd Monsters, there awaiting Wrecks.
Yet PROVIDENCE, that *ever-waking Eye,*
Looks down with Pity on the feeble Toil
Of Mortals lost to Hope, and lights them safe,
Thro' all his dreary Labyrinth of Fate.
'Tis done!—dread WINTER spreads his latest Glooms,
And reigns tremendous o'er the conquer'd Year.
How dead the Vegetable Kingdom lies!
How dumb the tuneful! Horror wide extends
His melancholy Empire. Here, fond Man!
Behold thy pictur'd Life; pass some few Years,
Thy flowering Spring, thy Summer's ardent Strength,
Thy sober Autumn fading into Age,
And pale concluding Winter comes at last,
And shuts the Scene. Ah! whither now are fled,
Those Dreams of Greatness! those unsolid Hopes
Of Happiness? those Longings after Fame?
Those restless Cares? those busy bustling Days?
Those gay-spent, festive Nights? those veering Thoughts,
Lost between Good and Ill, that shar'd thy Life?
All now are vanish'd! VIRTUE sole survives,
Immortal, never-failing Friend of Man,
His Guide to Happiness on high.—And see!
'Tis come, the glorious Morn! the second Birth
Of Heaven, and Earth! Awakening Nature hears
The *new-creating Word*, and starts to Life,
In every heighten'd Form, from Pain and Death
For ever free. *The great eternal Scheme,*
Involving All, and in a *perfect Whole*
Uniting, as the Prospect wider spreads,
To Reason's Eye refin'd clears up apace.
Ye vainly wise! ye blind Presumptuous! now,
Confounded in the Dust, adore that POWER,
And WISDOM oft arraign'd: see now the Cause,
Why unassuming Worth in secret liv'd,
And dy'd, neglected: why the good Man's Share
In Life was Gall and Bitterness of Soul:

Why the lone Widow, and her Orphans pin'd,
In staring Solitude; while Luxury,
In Palaces, lay straining her low Thought,
To form unreal Wants: why Heaven-born Truth,
And Moderation fair, wore the red Marks
Of Superstition's Scourge: why licens'd Pain,
That cruel Spoiler, that embosom'd Foe,
Imbitter'd all our Bliss. Ye good Distrest!
Ye noble Few! who here unbending stand
Beneath Life's Pressure, yet a little While,
And what your bounded View, which only saw
A little Part, deem'd *Evil* is no more:
The Storms of WINTRY TIME will quickly pass,
And one unbounded SPRING encircle All.

Autumn[1]

THE ARGUMENT

The Subject propos'd. Address'd to Mr. ONSLOW. *A Prospect of the Fields ready for Harvest. Reflexions in praise of Industry rais'd by that View. Reaping. A Tale relative to it. A Harvest Storm. Shooting and Hunting, their Barbarity. A ludicrous Account of Foxhunting. A View of an Orchard. Wall-Fruit. A Vineyard. A Description of Fogs, frequent in the latter part of* Autumn: *whence a Digression, enquiring into the Rise of Fountains and Rivers. Birds of Season considered, that now shift their Habitation. The prodigious Number of them that cover the northern and western Isles of* SCOTLAND. *Hence a View of the Country. A Prospect of the discoloured, fading Woods. After a gentle dusky Day, Moon-light. Autumnal Meteors. Morning: to which succeeds a calm, pure, Sun-shiny Day, such as usually shuts up the Season. The Harvest being gathered in, the Country dissolv'd in Joy. The whole concludes with a Panegyric on a Philosophical Country Life.*

CROWN'D with the Sickle, and the wheaten Sheaf,
While AUTUMN, nodding o'er the yellow Plain,
Comes jovial on; the *Doric* Reed once more,
Well pleas'd, I tune. Whate'er the wintry Frost
Nitrous prepar'd; the various-blossom'd Spring
Put in white Promise forth; and Summer-Suns
Concocted strong, rush boundless now to View,
Full, perfect all, and swell my glorious Theme.
  ONSLOW! the Muse, ambitious of thy Name,
To grace, inspire, and dignify her Song,
Would from the *Public Voice* thy gentle Ear
A while engage. Thy noble Cares she knows,

[1] Published in 1730. Text of *The Seasons*, 1744.

The Patriot-Virtues that distend thy Thought,
Spread on thy Front, and in thy Bosom glow;
While listening Senates hang upon thy Tongue,
Devolving thro' the Maze of Eloquence
A Rowl of Periods, sweeter than her Song.
But she too pants for public Virtue, she,
Tho' weak of Power yet strong in ardent Will,
Whene'er her Country rushes on her Heart,
Assumes a bolder Note, and fondly tries
To mix the Patriot's with the Poet's Flame.
  WHEN the Bright *Virgin* gives the beauteous Days,
And *Libra* weighs in equal Scales the Year;
From Heaven's high Cope the fierce Effulgence shook
Of parting Summer, a serener Blue,
With golden Light enliven'd wide invests
The happy World. Attemper'd Suns arise,
Sweet-beam'd, and shedding oft thro' lucid Clouds
A pleasing Calm; while broad, and brown, below,
Extensive Harvests hang the heavy Head.
Rich, silent, deep, they stand; for not a Gale
Rolls its light Billows o'er the bending Plain;
A Calm of Plenty! till the ruffled Air
Falls from its Poise, and gives the Breeze to blow.
Rent is the fleecy Mantle of the Sky;
The Clouds fly different; and the sudden Sun
By Fits effulgent gilds th' illumin'd Field,
And black by Fits the Shadows sweep along.
A gayly-checker'd Heart-expanding View,
Far as the circling Eye can shoot around,
Unbounded tossing in a Flood of Corn.
  THESE are thy Blessings, INDUSTRY! rough Power!
Whom Labour still attends, and Sweat, and Pain;
Yet the kind Source of every gentle Art,
And all the soft Civility of Life:
Raiser of Human Kind! by Nature cast,
Naked, and helpless, out amid the Woods,
And Wilds, to rude inclement Elements;
With various Seeds of Art deep in the Mind
Implanted, and profusely pour'd around
Materials infinite; but idle all.
Still unexerted, in th' unconscious Breast,
Slept the lethargic Powers; Corruption still,
Voracious, swallow'd what the liberal Hand
Of Bounty scatter'd o'er the savage Year:
And still the sad Barbarian, roving, mix'd
With Beasts of Prey; or for his Acorn-Meal
Fought the fierce tusky Boar; a shivering Wretch!
Aghast, and comfortless, when the bleak North,

With Winter charg'd, let the mix'd Tempest fly,
Hail, Rain, and Snow, and bitter-breathing Frost:
Then to the Shelter of the Hut he fled;
And the wild Season, sordid, pin'd away.
For Home he had not; Home is the Resort
Of Love, of Joy, of Peace and Plenty, where,
Supporting and supported, polish'd Friends,
And dear Relations mingle into Bliss.
But this the rugged Savage never felt,
Even desolate in Crouds; and thus his Days,
Roll'd heavy, dark, and unenjoy'd along;
A Waste of Time! till INDUSTRY approach'd,
And rous'd him from his miserable Sloth:
His Faculties unfolded; pointed out,
Where lavish Nature the directing Hand
Of Art demanded; shew'd him how to raise
His feeble Force by the mechanic Powers,
To dig the Mineral from the vaulted Earth,
On what to turn the piercing Rage of Fire,
On what the Torrent, and the gather'd Blast;
Gave the tall antient Forest to his Ax;
Taught him to chip the Wood, and hew the Stone,
Till by degrees the finish'd Fabric rose;
Tore from his Limbs the Blood-polluted Fur,
And wrapt them in the woolly Vestment warm,
Or bright in glossy Silk, and flowing Lawn;
With wholesome Viands fill'd his Table, pour'd
The generous Glass around, inspir'd to wake
The Life-refining Soul of decent Wit:
Nor stopp'd at barren bare Necessity,
But still advancing bolder, led him on,
To Pomp, to Pleasure, Elegance, and Grace;
And, breathing high Ambition thro' his Soul,
Set Science, Wisdom, Glory, in his View,
And bad him be the *Lord* of all below.

THEN gathering Men their natural Powers combin'd
And form'd a *Public*; to the general Good
Submitting, aiming, and conducting all.
For This the *Patriot-Council* met, the full,
The free, and fairly represented *Whole*;
For This they plann'd the holy Guardian-Laws,
Distinguish'd Orders, animated Arts,
And with joint Force *Oppression* chaining, set
Imperial Justice at the Helm; yet still
To them accountable: nor slavish dream'd
That toiling Millions must resign their Weal,
And all the Honey of their Search, to such
As for themselves alone themselves have rais'd.

HENCE every Form of cultivated Life
In order set, protected, and inspir'd,
Into Perfection wrought. Uniting all,
Society grew numerous, high, polite,
And happy. Nurse of Art! the City rear'd
In beauteous Pride her Tower-encircled Head;
And, stretching Street on Street, by Thousands drew,
From twining woody Haunts, or the tough Yew
To Bows strong-straining, her aspiring Sons.
THEN Commerce brought into the public Walk
The busy Merchant; the big Ware-House built;
Rais'd the strong Crane; choak'd up the loaded Street
With foreign Plenty; and thy Stream, O THAMES,
Large, gentle, deep, majestic, King of Floods!
Than whom no River heaves a fuller Tide,
Chose for his grand Resort. On either hand,
Like a long wintry Forest, Groves of Masts
Shot up their Spires; the bellying Sheet between
Possess'd the breezy Void; the sooty Hulk
Steer'd sluggish on; the splendid Barge along
Row'd, regular, to Harmony; around,
The Boat, light-skimming, stretch'd its oary Wings;
While deep the various Voice of fervent Toil
From Bank to Bank increas'd; whence ribb'd with Oak,
To bear the BRITISH THUNDER, black, and bold,
The roaring Vessel rush'd into the Main.
THEN too the pillar'd Dome, magnific, heav'd
Its ample Roof; and Luxury within
Pour'd out her glittering Stores: the Canvas smooth,
With glowing Life protuberant, to the View
Embodied rose; the Statue seem'd to breathe,
And soften into Flesh, beneath the Touch
Of forming Art, Imagination flush'd.
ALL is the Gift of INDUSTRY; whate'er
Exalts, embellishes, and renders Life
Delightful. Pensive Winter chear'd by him
Sits at the social Fire, and happy hears
Th' excluded Tempest idly rave along;
His harden'd Fingers deck the gaudy Spring;
Without him Summer were an arid Waste;
Nor to th' autumnal Months could thus transmit
Those full, mature, immeasurable Stores,
That, waving round, recal my wandering Song.
SOON as the Morning trembles o'er the Sky,
And, unperceiv'd, unfolds the spreading Day;
Before the ripen'd Field the Reapers stand,
In fair Array; each by the Lass he loves,
To bear the rougher Part, and mitigate

By nameless gentle Offices her Toil.
At once they stoop and swell the lusty Sheaves;
While thro' their chearful Band the rural Talk
The rural Scandal and the rural Jest
Fly harmless, to deceive the tedious Time,
And steal unfelt the sultry Hours away.
Behind the Master walks, builds up the Shocks;
And conscious, glancing oft on every Side
His sated Eye, feels his Heart heave with Joy.
The Gleaners spread around, and here and there,
Spike after Spike, their sparing Harvest pick.
Be not too narrow, Husband-men! but fling
From the full Sheaf, with charitable Stealth,
The liberal Handful. Think, oh grateful think!
How good the GOD OF HARVEST is to you;
Who pours Abundance o'er your flowing Fields;
While these unhappy Partners of your Kind
Wide-hover round you, like the Fowls of Heaven,
And ask their humble Dole. The various Turns
Of Fortune ponder; that your Sons may want
What now, with hard Reluctance, faint, ye give.
  THE lovely young LAVINIA once had Friends;
And Fortune smil'd, deceitful, on her Birth.
For in her helpless Years depriv'd of all,
Of every Stay, save Innocence and HEAVEN,
She with her widow'd Mother, feeble, old
And poor, liv'd in a Cottage, far retir'd
Among the Windings of a woody Vale;
By Solitude and deep surrounding Shades,
But more by bashful Modesty, conceal'd.
Together thus they shunn'd the cruel Scorn
Which Virtue, sunk to Poverty, would meet
From giddy Fashion and low-minded Pride:
Almost on Nature's common Bounty fed,
Like the gay Birds that sung them to Repose,
Content, and careless of to-morrow's Fare.
Her Form was fresher than the Morning Rose,
When the Dew wets it's Leaves; unstain'd, and pure,
As is the Lily, or the Mountain Snow.
The modest Virtues mingled in her Eyes,
Still on the Ground dejected, darting all
Their humid Beams into the blooming Flowers:
Or when the mournful Tale her Mother told,
Of what her faithless Fortune promis'd once,
Thrill'd in her Thought, they, like the dewy Star
Of Evening, shone in Tears. A native Grace
Sat fair-proportion'd on her polish'd Limbs,
Veil'd in a simple Robe, their best Attire,

Beyond the Pomp of Dress; for Loveliness
Needs not the foreign Aid of Ornament,
But is when unadorn'd adorn'd the most.
Thoughtless of Beauty, she was Beauty's Self,
Recluse amid the close-embowering Woods.
As in the hollow Breast of *Appenine*,
Beneath the Shelter of encircling Hills,
A Myrtle rises, far from human Eye,
And breathes it's balmy Fragrance o'er the Wild;
So flourish'd blooming, and unseen by all,
The sweet LAVINIA: till at length, compell'd
By strong Necessity's supreme Command,
With smiling Patience in her Looks, she went
To glean PALEMON's Fields. The Pride of Swains
PALEMON was, the Generous, and the Rich,
Who led the rural Life in all it's Joy,
And Elegance, such as *Arcadian* Song
Transmits from antient uncorrupted Times;
When tyrant Custom had not shackled Man,
But free to follow Nature was the Mode.
He then, his Fancy with Autumnal Scenes
Amusing, chanc'd beside his Reaper-Train
To walk, when poor LAVINIA drew his Eye;
Unconscious of her Power, and turning quick
With unaffected Blushes from his Gaze:
He saw her charming, but he saw not half
The Charms her down-cast Modesty conceal'd.
That very Moment Love and chaste Desire
Sprung in his Bosom, to himself unknown;
For still the World prevail'd, and its dread Laugh,
Which scarce the firm Philosopher can scorn,
Should his Heart own a Gleaner in the Field:
And thus in secret to his Soul he sigh'd.

WHAT pity! that so delicate a Form,
By Beauty kindled, where enlivening Sense,
And more than vulgar Goodness seem to dwell,
Should be devoted to the rude Embrace
Of some indecent Clown? She looks, methinks,
Of old ACASTO's Line; and to my Mind
Recalls that Patron of my happy Life,
From whom my liberal Fortune took its rise;
Now to the Dust gone down; his Houses, Lands,
And once fair-spreading Family dissolv'd.
'Tis said that in some lone obscure Retreat,
Urg'd by Remembrance sad, and decent Pride,
Far from those Scenes which knew their better Days,
His aged Widow and his Daughter live,
Whom yet my fruitless Search could never find.

Romantic Wish, would this the Daughter were!
  WHEN, strict enquiring, from herself he found
She was the same, the Daughter of his Friend,
Of bountiful ACASTO; who can speak
The mingled Passions that surpriz'd his Heart,
And thro' his Nerves in shivering Transport ran?
Then blaz'd his smother'd Flame, avow'd, and bold;
And as he view'd Her, ardent, o'er and o'er,
Love, Gratitude, and Pity wept at once.
Confus'd, and frighten'd at his sudden Tears,
Her rising Beauties flush'd a higher Bloom,
And thus PALEMON, passionate, and just,
Pour'd out the pious Rapture of his Soul.
  AND art thou then ACASTO's dear Remains?
She, whom my restless Gratitude has sought,
So long in vain? Oh yes! the very same,
The soften'd Image of my noble Friend,
Alive, his every Feature, every Look,
More elegantly touch'd. Sweeter than Spring!
Thou sole surviving Blossom from the Root,
That nourish'd up my Fortune, say, ah where,
In what sequester'd Desart, hast thou drawn
The kindest Aspect of delighted Heaven?
Into such Beauty spread, and blown so fair;
Tho' Poverty's cold Wind, and crushing Rain,
Beat keen, and heavy, on thy tender Years?
O let me now, into a richer Soil,
Transplant thee safe! where vernal Suns, and Showers,
Diffuse their warmest, largest Influence;
And of my Garden be the Pride, and Joy!
It ill befits thee, oh it ill befits
ACASTO's Daughter, his, whose open Stores,
Tho' vast, were little to his ampler Heart,
The Father of a Country, thus to pick
The very Refuse of those Harvest-Fields,
Which from his bounteous Friendship I enjoy.
Then throw that shameful Pittance from thy Hand,
But ill apply'd to such a rugged Task;
The Fields, the Master, all, my Fair, are thine;
If to the various Blessings which thy House
Has on me lavish'd, thou wilt add that Bliss,
That dearest Bliss, the Power of blessing Thee!
  HERE ceas'd the Youth: yet still his speaking Eye
Express'd the sacred Triumph of his Soul,
With conscious Virtue, Gratitude, and Love,
Above the vulgar Joy divinely rais'd.
Nor waited he Reply. Won by the Charm
Of Goodness irresistible, and all

In sweet Disorder lost, she blush'd Consent.
The News immediate to her Mother brought,
While pierc'd with anxious Thought, she pin'd away
The lonely Moments for LAVINIA's Fate;
Amaz'd, and scarce believing what she heard,
Joy seiz'd her wither'd Veins, and one bright Gleam
Of setting Life shone on her Evening-Hours:
Not less enraptur'd than the happy Pair;
Who flourish'd long in tender Bliss, and rear'd
A numerous Offspring, lovely like themselves,
And good, the Grace of all the Country round.
  DEFEATING oft the Labours of the Year,
The sultry South collects a potent Blast.
At first, the Groves are scarcely seen to stir
Their trembling Tops; and a still Murmur runs
Along the soft-inclining Fields of Corn:
But as th' aërial Tempest fuller swells,
And in one mighty Stream, invisible,
Immense, the whole excited Atmosphere,
Impetuous rushes o'er the sounding World;
Strain'd to the Root, the stooping Forest pours
A rustling Shower of yet untimely Leaves.
High-beat, the circling Mountains eddy in,
From the bare Wild, the dissipated Storm,
And send it in a Torrent down the Vale.
Expos'd, and naked, to its utmost Rage,
Thro' all the Sea of Harvest rolling round,
The billowy Plain floats wide; nor can evade,
Tho' pliant to the Blast, its seizing Force;
Or whirl'd in Air, or into vacant Chaff
Shook waste. And sometimes too a Burst of Rain,
Swept from the black Horizon, broad, descends
In one continuous Flood. Still over head
The mingling Tempest weaves it's Gloom, and still
The Deluge deepens; till the Fields around
Lie sunk, and flatted, in the sordid Wave.
Sudden, the Ditches swell; the Meadows swim.
Red, from the Hills, innumerable Streams
Tumultuous roar; and high above its Banks
The River lift; before whose rushing Tide,
Herds, Flocks, and Harvests, Cottages, and Swains,
Roll mingled down; all that the Winds had spar'd,
In one wild Moment ruin'd, the big Hopes,
And well-earn'd Treasures of the painful Year.
Fled to some Eminence, the Husbandman,
Helpless beholds the miserable Wreck
Driving along; his drowning Ox at once
Descending, with his Labours scatter'd round,

He sees; and instant o'er his shivering Thought
Comes Winter unprovided, and a Train
Of clamant Children dear. Ye Masters, then,
Be mindful of the rough laborious Hand,
That sinks you soft in Elegance and Ease;
Be mindful of those Limbs, in Russet clad,
Whose Toil to yours is Warmth, and graceful Pride;
And oh be mindful of that sparing Board,
Which covers yours with Luxury profuse,
Makes your Glass sparkle, and your Sense rejoice!
Nor cruelly demand what the deep Rains,
And all-involving Winds have swept away.
  HERE the rude Clamour of the Sportsman's Joy,
The Gun fast-thundering, and the winded Horn,
Would tempt the Muse to sing the *rural Game:*
How, in his Mid-career, the Spaniel struck,
Stiff, by the tainted Gale, with open Nose,
Outstretch'd, and finely sensible, *draws* full,
Fearful, and cautious, on the latent Prey;
As in the Sun the circling Covey bask
Their varied Plumes, and watchful every way
Thro' the rough Stubble turn the secret Eye.
Caught in the meshy Snare, in vain they beat
Their idle Wings, intangled more and more:
Nor on the Surges of the boundless Air,
Tho' borne triumphant, are they safe; the Gun,
Glanc'd just, and sudden, from the Fowler's Eye,
O'ertakes their sounding Pinions; and again,
Immediate, brings them from the towering Wing,
Dead to the Ground; or drives them wide dispers'd,
Wounded, and wheeling various, down the Wind.
  THESE are not Subjects for the peaceful Muse,
Nor will she stain with such her spotless Song;
Then most delighted, when she social sees
The whole mix'd Animal-Creation round
Alive, and happy. 'Tis not Joy to Her,
This falsely chearful barbarous Game of Death;
This Rage of Pleasure, which the restless Youth
Awakes, impatient, with the gleaming Morn;
When Beasts of Prey retire, that all Night long,
Urg'd by Necessity, had rang'd the Dark,
As if their conscious Ravage shun'd the Light,
Asham'd. Not so the steady Tyrant Man,
Who with the thoughtless Insolence of Power
Inflam'd, beyond the most infuriate Wrath
Of the worst Monster that e'er roam'd the Waste
For Sport alone pursues the cruel Chace,
Amid the Beamings of the gentle Days.

Ye ravening Tribes, upbraid our wanton Rage
For Hunger kindles you, and lawless Want;
But lavish fed, in Nature's Bounty roll'd,
To joy at Anguish, and delight in Blood,
Is what your horrid Bosoms never knew.
 POOR is the Triumph o'er the timid Hare!
Scar'd from the Corn, and now to some lone Seat
Retir'd: the rushy Fen; the ragged Furz,
Stretch'd o'er the stony Heath: the Stubble chapt;
The thistly Lawn; the thick entangled Broom;
Of the same friendly Hue, the wither'd Fern:
The fallow Ground laid open to the Sun,
Concoctive; and the nodding sandy Bank,
Hung o'er the Mazes of the Mountain-Brook.
Vain is her best Precaution; tho' she sits
Conceal'd, with folded Ears; unsleeping Eyes,
By Nature rais'd to take th' Horizon in;
And Head couch'd close betwixt her hairy Feet,
In Act to spring away. The scented Dew
Betrays her early Labyrinth; and deep,
In scatter'd sullen Openings, far behind,
With every Breeze she hears the coming Storm.
But nearer, and more frequent, as it loads
The sighing Gale, she springs amaz'd, and all
The savage Soul of Game is up at once:
The Pack full-opening, various; the shrill Horn,
Resounded from the Hills; the neighing Steed,
Wild for the Chace; and the loud Hunter's Shout;
O'er a weak, harmless, flying Creature, all
Mix'd in mad Tumult, and discordant Joy.
 THE Stag too, singled from the Herd, where long
He rang'd the branching Monarch of the Shades,
Before the Tempest drives. At first, in speed
He, sprightly, puts his Faith; and, Fear-arous'd,
Gives all his swift aërial Soul to flight.
Against the Breeze he darts, that Way the more
To leave the lessening murderous Cry behind.
Deception short! tho' fleeter than the Winds
Blown o'er the keen-air'd Mountain by the North,
He bursts the Thickets, glances thro the Glades,
And plunges deep into the wildest Wood.
If slow, yet sure, adhesive to the Track
Hot-steaming, up behind him comes again
Th' inhuman Rout, and from the shady Depth
Expel him, circling thro' his every Shift.
He sweeps the Forest oft; and sobbing sees
The Glades, mild-opening to the golden Day;
Where, in kind Contest, with his butting Friends

He wont to struggle, or his Loves enjoy.
Oft in the full-descending Flood he tries
To lose the Scent, and lave his burning Sides;
Oft seeks the Herd; the watchful Herd, alarm'd,
With selfish Care avoid a Brother's Woe.
What shall he do? His once so vivid Nerves,
So full of buoyant Spirit, now no more
Inspire the Course; but fainting breathless Toil,
Sick, seizes on his Heart: he stands at Bay;
And puts his last weak Refuge in Despair.
The big round Tears run down his dappled Face;
He groans in Anguish; while the growling Pack,
Blood-happy, hang at his fair jutting Chest,
And mark his beauteous chequer'd Sides with Gore.
  OF this enough. But if the silvan Youth
Whose fervent Blood boils into Violence,
Must have the Chace; behold, despising Flight,
The rous'd-up Lion, resolute, and slow,
Advancing full on the protended Spear,
And Coward-Band, that circling wheel aloof.
Slunk from the Cavern, and the troubled Wood,
See the grim Wolf; on him his shaggy Foe
Vindictive fix, and let the Ruffian die:
Or, growling horrid, as the brindled Boar
Grins fell Destruction, to the Monster's Heart
Let the Dart lighten from the nervous Arm.
  THESE BRITAIN knows not; give, ye BRITONS, then
Your sportive Fury, pityless, to pour
Loose on the nightly Robber of the Fold:
Him, from his craggy winding Haunts unearth'd,
Let all the Thunder of the Chace pursue.
Throw the broad Ditch behind you; o'er the Hedge
High-bound, resistless; nor the deep Morass
Refuse, but thro' the shaking Wilderness
Pick your nice Way; into the perilous Flood
Bear fearless, of the raging Instinct full;
And as you ride the Torrent, to the Banks
Your Triumph sound sonorous, running round,
From Rock to Rock, in circling Echo tost;
Then scale the Mountains to their woody Tops;
Rush down the dangerous Steep; and o'er the Lawn,
In Fancy swallowing up the Space between,
Pour all your Speed into the rapid Game,
For happy he! who tops the wheeling Chace;
Has every Maze evolv'd, and every Guile
Disclos'd; who knows the Merits of the Pack;
Who saw the Villain seiz'd, and dying hard,
Without Complaint, tho' by an hundred Mouths

Relentless torn: O glorious he, beyond
His daring Peers! when the retreating Horn
Calls them to ghostly Halls of grey Renown,
With woodland Honours grac'd; the Fox's Fur,
Depending decent from the Roof; and spread
Round the drear Walls, with antick Figures fierce,
The Stag's large Front: he then is loudest heard,
When the Night staggers with severer Toils,
With Feats *Thessalian* Centaurs never knew,
And their repeated Wonders shake the Dome.
  BUT first the fuel'd Chimney blazes wide;
The Tankards foam; and the strong Table groans
Beneath the smoaking Sirloin, stretch'd immense
From side to side; in which, with desperate Knife,
They deep Incision make, and talk the while
Of ENGLAND's Glory, ne'er to be defac'd,
While hence they borrow Vigour: or amain
Into the Pasty plung'd, at Intervals,
If Stomach keen can Intervals allow,
Relating all the Glories of the Chace.
Then sated *Hunger* bids his Brother *Thirst*
Produce the mighty Bowl; the mighty Bowl,
Swell'd high with fiery Juice, steams liberal round
A potent Gale, delicious as the Breath
Of *Maia*, to the love-sick Shepherdess,
On Violets diffus'd, while soft she hears
Her panting Shepherd stealing to her Arms.
Nor wanting is the brown October, drawn
Mature and perfect, from his dark Retreat
Of thirty Years; and now his honest Front
Flames in the Light refulgent, nor afraid
Even with the Vineyard's best Produce to vie.
To cheat the thirsty Moments, Whisk a while
Walks his dull Round, beneath a Cloud of Smoak,
Wreath'd fragrant from the Pipe; or the quick Dice,
In Thunder leaping from the Box, awake
The sounding Gammon: while Romp-loving Miss
Is haul'd about, in Gallantry robust.
  AT last these puling Idlenesses laid
Aside, frequent and full, the dry Divan
Close in firm Circle; and set, ardent, in
For serious Drinking. Nor evasion sly,
Nor sober Shift, is to the puking Wretch
Indulg'd apart; but earnest, brimming Bowls
Lave every Soul, the Table floating round,
And Pavement, faithless to the fuddled Foot.
Thus as they swim in mutual Swill, the Talk,
Vociferous at once from twenty Tongues,

Reels fast from Theme to Theme; from Horses, Hounds,
To Church or Mistress, Politicks or Ghost,
In endless Mazes, intricate, perplex'd.
Mean-time, with sudden Interruption, loud,
Th' impatient Catch bursts from the joyous Heart:
That Moment touch'd is every kindred Soul;
And, opening in a full-mouth'd *Cry* of Joy,
The Laugh, the Slap, the jocund Curse goes round;
While from their Slumbers shook, the kennel'd Hound
Mix in the Music of the Day again.
As when the Tempest, that has vex'd the Deep
The dark Night long with fainter Murmurs falls:
So gradual sinks their Mirth. Their feeble Tongues,
Unable to take up the cumbrous Word,
Lie quite dissolv'd. Before their maudlin Eyes,
Seen dim, and blue, the double Tapers dance,
Like the Sun wading thro' the misty Sky.
Then, sliding soft, they drop. Confus'd above,
Glasses and Bottles, Pipes and Gazetteers,
As if the Table even itself was drunk,
Lie a wet broken Scene; and wide, below,
Is heap'd the social Slaughter: where astride
The *lubber Power* in filthy Triumph sits,
Slumbrous, inclining still from Side to Side,
And steeps them drench'd in potent Sleep till Morn.
Perhaps some Doctor, of tremendous Paunch,
Awful and deep, a black Abyss of Drink,
Out-lives them all; and from his bury'd Flock
Retiring, full of Rumination sad,
Laments the Weakness of these latter Times.
  BUT if the rougher Sex by this fierce Sport
Are hurry'd wild, let not such horrid Joy
E'er stain the Bosom of the BRITISH FAIR.
Far be the Spirit of the Chace from them!
Uncomely Courage, unbeseeming Skill,
To spring the Fence, to rein the prancing Steed,
The Cap, the Whip, the masculine Attire,
In which they roughen to the Sense, and all
The winning Softness of their Sex is lost.
In them 'tis graceful to dissolve at Woe;
With every Motion, every Word, to wave
Quick o'er the kindling Cheek the ready Blush;
And from the smallest Violence to shrink,
Unequal, then the loveliest in their Fears
And by this silent Adulation, soft,
To their Protection more engaging Man.
O may their Eyes no miserable Sight,
Save weeping Lovers, see! a nobler Game,

Thro' Love's enchanting Wiles pursu'd, yet fled,
In Chace ambiguous. May their tender Limbs
Float in the loose Simplicity of Dress!
And, fashion'd all to Harmony, alone
Know they to seize the captivated Soul,
In Rapture warbled from Love-breathing Lips;
To teach the Lute to languish; with smooth Step,
Disclosing Motion in its every Charm,
To swim along, and swell the mazy Dance;
To train the foliage o'er the snowny Lawn;
To guide the Pencil, turn the tuneful Page;
To lend new Flavour to the fruitful Year,
And heighten Nature's Dainties; in their Race
To rear their Graces into second Life;
To give Society its highest Taste;
Well-order'd Home Man's best Delight to make;
And by submissive Wisdom, modest Skill,
With every gentle Care-eluding Art,
To raise the Virtues, animate the Bliss,
Even charm the Pains to something more than Joy,
And sweeten all the Toils of human Life:
This be the female Dignity, and Praise.
  YE Swains now hasten to the Hazel-Bank;
Where, down yon Dale, the wildly-winding Brook
Falls hoarse from Steep to Steep. In close Array,
Fit for the Thickets, and the tangling Shrub,
Ye Virgins, come. For you their latest Song
The Woodlands raise; the clustring Nuts for you
The Lover finds amid the secret Shade;
And, where they burnish on the topmost Bough,
With active Vigour crushes down the Tree;
Or shakes them ripe from the resigning Husk,
A glossy Shower, and of an ardent Brown,
As are the Ringlets of MELINDA's Hair:
MELINDA form'd with every Grace compleat,
Yet These neglecting, above Beauty wise
And far transcending such a vulgar Praise.
  HENCE from the busy Joy-resounding Fields,
In chearful Error, let us tread the Maze
Of Autumn, unconfin'd; and taste, reviv'd,
The Breath of Orchard big with bending Fruit.
Obedient to the Breeze, and beating Ray,
From the deep-loaded Bough a mellow Shower,
Incessant melts away. The juicy Pear
Lies, in a soft Profusion, scatter'd round.
A various Sweetness swells the gentle Race;
In Species different, but in Kind the same,
By Nature's all-refining Hand prepar'd,

Of temper'd Sun, and Water, Earth, and Air,
In ever-changing Composition mixt.
Such, falling frequent thro' the chiller Night,
The fragrant Stores, the wide-projected Heaps
Of Apples, with the lusty-handed Year,
Innumerous, o'er the blushing Orchard shakes.
A various Spirit, fresh, delicious, keen,
Dwells in their gelid Pores; and, active, points
The piercing Cyder for the thirsty Tongue:
Thy *Native* Theme, and boon Inspirer too,
PHILLIPS, *Pomona*'s Bard, the second thou
Who nobly durst, in Rhyme-unfetter'd Verse,
With BRITISH Freedom sing the BRITISH Song;
How, from *Silurian* Vats, high-sparkling Wines
Foam in transparent Floods; some strong, to cheer
The wintry Revels of the labouring Hind;
And tasteful some, to cool the Summer-Hours.
  IN this glad Season, while his sweetest Beams
The Sun sheds equal o'er the meeken'd Day;
Oh lose me in the green delightful Walks
Of, DODINGTON! thy Seat, serene and plain;
Where simple Nature reigns; and every View,
Diffusive, spreads the pure *Dorsetian* Downs,
In boundless Prospect, yonder shagg'd with Wood,
Here rich with Harvest, and there white with Flocks.
Mean time the Grandeur of thy lofty Dome,
Far-splendid, seizes on the ravish'd Eye.
New Beauties rise with each revolving Day;
New Columns swell; and still the fresh Spring finds
New Plants to quicken, and new Groves to green.
Full of thy Genius all! the Muses' Seat;
Where in the secret Bower, and winding Walk,
For virtuous YOUNG and Thee they twine the Bay.
Here wandring oft, fir'd with the restless Thirst
Of thy Applause, I solitary court
Th' inspiring Breeze; and meditate the Book
Of Nature, ever open, aiming thence,
Warm from the Heart, to learn the moral Song.
And, as I steal along the sunny Wall,
Where Autumn basks, with Fruit empurpled deep
My pleasing Theme continual prompts my Thought;
Presents the downy Peach; the shining Plumb,
With a fine bluish Mist of Animals
Clouded; the ruddy Nectarine; and dark,
Beneath his ample Leaf, the luscious Fig.
The Vine too here her curling Tendrils shoots;
Hangs out her Clusters, glowing to the South;
And scarcely wishes for a warmer Sky.

Turn we a Moment Fancy's rapid Flight
To vigorous Soils, and Climes of fair Extent;
Where, by the potent Sun elated high,
The Vineyard swells refulgent on the Day;
Spreads o'er the Vale; or up the Mountain climbs,
Profuse; and drinks amid the sunny Rocks,
From Cliff to Cliff increas'd, the heighten'd Blaze.
Low bend the weighty Boughs. The Clusters clear,
Half thro' the Foliage seen, or ardent flame,
Or shine transparent; while Perfection breathes
White o'er the turgent Film the living Dew.
As thus they brighten with exalted Juice,
Touch'd into Flavour by the mingling Ray;
The rural Youth and Virgins o'er the Field,
Each fond for each to cull th' autumnal Prime,
Exulting rove, and speak the Vintage nigh.
Then comes the crushing Swain; the Country floats,
And foams unbounded with the mashy Flood;
That by degrees fermented, and refin'd,
Round the rais'd Nations pours the Cup of Joy:
The Claret smooth, red as the Lip we press,
In sparkling Fancy, while we drain the Bowl;
The mellow-tasted Burgundy; and quick,
As is the Wit it gives, the gay Champaign.
Now, by the cool declining Year condens'd,
Descend the copious Exhalations, check'd
As up the middle Sky unseen they stole,
And roll the doubling Fogs around the Hill.
No more the Mountain, horrid, vast, sublime,
Who pours a Sweep of Rivers from his Sides,
And high between contending Kingdoms rears
The rocky long Division, fills the View
With great Variety; but in a Night
Of gathering Vapour, from the baffled Sense,
Sinks dark and dreary. Thence expanding far,
The huge Dusk, gradual, swallows up the Plain.
Vanish the Woods. The dim-seen River seems
Sullen, and slow, to rowl the misty Wave.
Even in the Height of Noon opprest, the Sun
Sheds weak, and blunt, his wide-refracted Ray;
Whence glaring oft, with many a broaden'd Orb,
He frights the Nations. Indistinct on Earth,
Seen thro' the turbid Air, beyond the Life,
Objects appear; and, wilder'd, o'er the Waste
The Shepherd stalks gigantic. Till at last
Wreath'd dun around, in deeper Circles still
Successive closing, sits the general Fog
Unbounded o'er the World; and, mingling thick,

A formless grey Confusion covers all.
As when of old (so sung the HEBREW BARD)
Light, uncollected, thro' the Chaos urg'd
It's Infant Way; nor Order yet had drawn
His lovely Train from out the dubious Gloom.
THESE roving Mists, that constant now begin
To smoak along the hilly Country, These,
With weighty Rains, and melted Alpine Snows,
The Mountain-Cisterns fill, those ample Stores
Of Water, scoop'd among the hollow Rocks;
Whence gush the Streams, the ceaseless Fountains play,
And their unfailing Wealth the Rivers draw.
Some Sages say, that, where the numerous Wave
For ever lashes the resounding Shore,
Drill'd thro' the sandy *Stratum*, every Way,
The Waters with the sandy *Stratum* rise;
Amid whose Angles infinitely strain'd,
They joyful leave their jaggy Salts behind,
And clear and sweeten, as they soak along.
Nor stops the restless Fluid, mounting still
Tho' oft amid th' irriguous Vale it springs;
But to the Mountain courted by the Sand,
That leads it darkling on in faithful Maze,
Far from the Parent-Main, it boils again
Fresh into Day; and all the glittering Hill
Is bright with spouting Rills. But hence this vain
Amusive Dream! why should the Waters love
To take so far a Journey to the Hills,
When the sweet Valleys offer to their Toil
Inviting Quiet, and a nearer Bed?
Or if, by blind Ambition led astray,
They must aspire; why should they sudden stop
Among the broken Mountain's rushy Dells,
And, ere they gain it's highest Peak, desert
Th' attractive Sand that charm'd their Course so long?
Besides, the hard agglomerating Salts
The Spoil of Ages, would impervious choak
Their secret Channels; or, by slow Degrees,
High as the Hills protrude the swelling Vales:
Old Ocean too, suck'd thro' the porous Globe,
Had long ere now forsook his horrid Bed,
And brought *Deucalion*'s watry Times again.
SAY then, where lurk the vast eternal Springs,
That, like CREATING NATURE, lie conceal'd
From mortal Eye, yet with their lavish Stores
Refresh the Globe, and all it's joyous Tribes?
O thou pervading *Genius*, given to Man,
To trace the Secrets of the dark Abyss,

O lay the Mountains bare! and wide display
Their hidden Structure to th' astonish'd View!
Strip from the branching *Alps* their piny Load,
The huge Incumbrance of horrific Woods
From *Asian Taurus*, from *Imaüs* stretch'd
Athwart the roving *Tartar*'s sullen Bounds!
Give opening *Hemus* to my searching Eye,
And high **Olympus* pouring many a Stream!
O from the sounding Summits of the North,
The *Dofrine Hills*, thro' *Scandinavia* roll'd
To farthest *Lapland* and the frozen Main;
From lofty *Caucasus*, far-seen by Those
Who in the *Caspian* and black *Euxine* toil;
From cold *Riphean Rocks*, which the wild *Russ*
Believes the †*stony Girdle* of the World;
And all the dreadful Mountains, wrapt in Storm,
Whence wide *Siberia* draws her lonely Floods;
O sweep th' eternal Snows! Hung o'er the Deep,
That ever works beneath his sounding Base,
Bid *Atlas*, propping Heaven, as Poets feign,
His subterranean Wonders spread! unveil
The miny Caverns, blazing on the Day,
Of *Abyssinia*'s Cloud-compelling Cliffs,
And of the bending ‡*Mountains of the Moon!*
O'ertopping all these Giant-Sons of Earth,
Let the dire *Andes*, from the radiant Line
Stretch'd to the stormy Seas that thunder round
The southern Pole, their hideous Deeps unfold!
Amazing Scene! Behold! the Glooms disclose.
I see the Rivers in their infant Beds!
Deep deep I hear them, lab'ring to get free!
I see the leaning *Strata*, artful rang'd;
The gaping Fissures to receive the Rains,
The melting Snows, and ever-dripping Fogs.
Strow'd bibulous above I see the Sands,
The pebbly Gravel next, the Layers then
Of mingled Moulds, of more retentive Earths,
The gutter'd Rocks and mazy running Clefts;
That, while the stealing Moisture they transmit,
Retard it's Motion, and forbid it's Waste.
Beneath th' incessant weeping of these Drains,
I see the rocky Siphons stretch'd immense,
The mighty Reservoirs, of harden'd Chalk,
Or stiff compacted Clay, capacious form'd.

* *The Mountain called by that Name in the lesser Asia.*

† *The* Moscovites *call the* Riphean *Mountains* Weliki Camenypoys, *that is,* the great stony Girdle; *because they suppose them to encompass the whole Earth.*

‡ *A Range of Mountains in* Africa, *that surround almost all* Monomotapa.

O'erflowing thence, the congregated Stores,
The crystal Treasures of the liquid World,
Thro' the stirr'd Sands a bubbling Passage burst;
And welling out, around the middle Steep,
Or from the Bottoms of the bosom'd Hills,
In pure Effusion flow. United, thus,
Th' exhaling Sun, the Vapour-burden'd Air,
The gelid Mountains, that to Rain condens'd
These Vapours in continual Current draw,
And send them, o'er the fair-divided Earth,
In bounteous Rivers to the Deep again,
A social Commerce hold, and firm support
The full-adjusted Harmony of Things.
WHEN Autumn scatters his departing Gleams,
Warn'd of approaching Winter, gather'd, play
The Swallow-People; and toss'd wide around,
O'er the calm Sky, in Convolution swift,
The feather'd Eddy floats: rejoicing once,
Ere to their wintry Slumbers they retire;
In Clusters clung, beneath the mouldring Bank,
And where, unpierc'd by Frost, the Cavern sweats.
Or rather into warmer Climes convey'd,
With other kindred Birds of Season, there
They twitter chearful, till the vernal Months
Invite them welcome back: for, thronging, now
Innumerous Wings are in commotion all.
WHERE the *Rhine* loses his majestic Force
In *Belgian* Plains, won from the raging Deep,
By Diligence amazing, and the strong
Unconquerable Hand of Liberty,
The Stork-Assembly meets; for many a Day,
Consulting deep, and various, ere they take
Their arduous Voyage thro' the liquid Sky.
And now their Rout design'd, their Leaders chose,
Their Tribes adjusted, clean'd their vigorous Wings;
And many a Circle, many a short Essay,
Wheel'd round and round, in Congregation full,
The figur'd Flight ascends; and, riding high
Th' aërial Billows, mixes with the Clouds.
OR where the *Northern* Ocean, in vast Whirls,
Boils round the naked melancholy Isles
Of farthest *Thulè*, and th' *Atlantic* Surge
Pours in among the stormy *Hebrides*;
Who can recount what Transmigrations there
Are annual made? What Nations come and go?
And how the living Clouds on Clouds arise?
Infinite Wings! till all the Plume-dark Air,
And rude resounding Shore are one wild Cry.

Here the plain harmless Native his small Flock,
And Herd diminutive of many Hues,
Tends on the little Island's verdant Swell,
The Shepherd's sea-girt Reign; or, to the Rocks
Dire-clinging, gathers his ovarious Food;
Or sweeps the fishy Shore; or treasures up
The Plumage, rising full, to form the Bed
Of Luxury. And here a while the Muse,
High-hovering o'er the broad cerulean Scene,
Sees Caledonia, in romantic View:
Her airy Mountains, from the waving Main,
Invested with a keen diffusive Sky,
Breathing the Soul acute; her Forests huge,
Incult, robust, and tall, by Nature's Hand
Planted of old; her azure Lakes between,
Pour'd out extensive, and of watry Wealth
Full; winding deep, and green, her fertile Vales;
With many a cool translucent brimming Flood
Wash'd lovely, from the *Tweed* (pure *Parent-Stream*,
Whose pastoral Banks first wak'd my *Doric* Reed,
With, silvan *Jed*, thy tributary Brook)
To where the North-inflated Tempest foams
O'er *Orca*'s or *Betubium*'s highest Peak.
Nurse of a People, in Misfortune's School
Train'd up to hardy Deeds; soon visited
By *Learning*, when before the *Gothic* Rage
She took her western Flight. A manly Race,
Of unsubmitting Spirit, wise, and brave,
Who still thro' bleeding Ages struggled hard,
(As well unhappy Wallace can attest,
Great Patriot-Heroe! ill-requited Chief!)
To hold a generous undiminish'd State:
Too much in vain! Hence of unequal Bounds
Impatient, and by tempting Glory borne
O'er every Land, for every Land their Life
Has flow'd profuse, their piercing Genius plan'd,
And swell'd the Pomp of Peace their faithful Toil.
As from their own clear North, in radiant Streams,
Bright over *Europe* bursts the *Boreal Morn*.

Oh is there not some Patriot, in whose power
That best, that godlike Luxury is plac'd,
Of blessing Thousands, Thousands yet unborn,
Thro' late Posterity? some, large of Soul,
To chear dejected Industry? to give
A double Harvest to the pining Swain?
And teach the labouring Hand the Sweets of Toil?
How, by the finest Art, the native Robe
To weave; how, white as Hyperborean Snow,

To form the lucid Lawn; with venturous Oar,
How to dash wide the Billow; nor look on,
Shamefully passive, while *Batavian* Fleets
Defraud us of the glittering finny Swarms,
That heave our Friths, and croud upon our Shores;
How all-enlivening Trade to rouse, and wing
The prosperous Sail, from every growing Port,
Uninjur'd, round the sea-incircled Globe;
And thus, in Soul united as in Name,
Bid BRITAIN reign the Mistress of the Deep.
  YES, there are such. And full on thee, ARGYLE,
Her Hope, her Stay, her Darling, and her Boast,
From her first Patriots and her Heroes sprung,
Thy fond imploring Country turns her Eye:
In thee with all a Mother's Triumph, sees
Her every Virtue, every Grace combin'd,
Her Genius, Wisdom, her engaging Turn,
Her Pride of Honour and her Courage try'd,
Calm, and intrepid, in the very Throat
Of sulphurous War, on *Tenier*'s dreadful Field.
Nor less the Palm of Peace inwreathes thy Brow:
For, powerful as thy Sword, from thy rich Tongue
Persuasion flows, and wins the high Debate;
While mix'd in thee combine the Charm of Youth,
The Force of Manhood, and the Depth of Age.
Thee, FORBES, too, whom every Worth attends,
As Truth sincere, as weeping Friendship kind,
Thee, truly generous, and in Silence great,
Thy Country feels thro' her reviving Arts,
Plan'd by thy Wisdom, by thy Soul inform'd;
And seldom has she felt a Friend like thee.
  BUT see the fading many-colour'd Woods,
Shade deepening over Shade, the Country round
Imbrown; a crouded Umbrage, dusk, and dun,
Of every Hue, from wan declining Green
To sooty Dark. These now the lonesome Muse,
Low-whispering, lead into their leaf-strown Walks,
And give the Season in its latest View.
  MEAN-TIME, light-shadowing all, a sober Calm
Fleeces unbounded Ether; whose least Wave
Stands tremulous, uncertain where to turn
The gentle Current: while illumin'd wide,
The dewy-skirted Clouds imbibe the Sun,
And thro' their lucid Veil his soften'd Force
Shed o'er the peaceful World. Then is the Time,
For those whom Wisdom and whom Nature charm,
To steal themselves from the degenerate Croud,
And soar above this little Scene of Things;

To tread low-thoughted Vice beneath their Feet;
To sooth the throbbing Passions into Peace;
And woo lone Quiet in her silent Walks.
  THUS solitary, and in pensive Guise,
Oft let me wander o'er the russet Mead,
And thro' the sadden'd Grove, where scarce is heard
One dying Strain, to chear the Woodman's Toil.
Haply some widow'd Songster pours his Plaint,
Far, in faint Warblings, thro' the tawny Copse.
While congregated Trushes, Linnets, Larks,
And each wild Throat, whose artless Strains so late
Swell'd all the Music of the swarming Shades,
Robb'd of their tuneful Souls, now shivering sit
On the dead Tree, a dull despondent Flock!
With not a Brightness waving o'er their Plumes,
And nought save chattering Discord in their Note.
O let not, aim'd from some inhuman Eye,
The Gun the Music of the coming Year
Destroy; and harmless, unsuspecting Harm,
Lay the weak Tribes, a miserable Prey,
In mingled Murder, fluttering on the Ground!
  THE pale descending Year, yet pleasing still,
A gentler Mood inspires; for now the Leaf
Incessant rustles from the mournful Grove,
Oft startling such as, studious, walk below,
And slowly circles thro' the waving Air.
But should a quicker Breeze amid the Boughs
Sob, o'er the Sky the leafy Deluge streams;
Till choak'd, and matted with the dreary Shower,
The Forest-Walks, at every rising Gale,
Roll wide the wither'd Waste, and whistle bleak.
Fled is the blasted Verdure of the Fields;
And, shrunk into their Beds, the flowery Race
Their sunny Robes resign. Even what remain'd
Of bolder Fruits falls from the naked Tree;
And Woods, Fields, Gardens, Orchards, all around
The desolated Prospect thrills the Soul.
  HE comes! he comes! in every Breeze the POWER
Of PHILOSOPHIC MELANCHOLY comes!
His near Approach the sudden-starting Tear,
The glowing Cheek, the mild dejected Air,
The soften'd Feature, and the beating Heart,
Pierc'd deep with many a virtuous Pang, declare.
O'er all the Soul his sacred Influence breathes;
Inflames Imagination; thro' the Breast
Infuses every Tenderness; and far
Beyond dim Earth exalts the swelling Thought.
Ten thousand thousand fleet Ideas, such

As never mingled with the vulgar Dream,
Croud fast into the Mind's creative Eye.
As fast the correspondent Passions rise,
As varied, and as high: Devotion rais'd
To Rapture, and divine Astonishment;
The Love of Nature unconfin'd, and, chief,
Of Human Race; the large ambitious Wish,
To make them blest; the Sigh for suffering Worth,
Lost in Obscurity; the noble Scorn,
Of Tyrant Pride; the fearless great Resolve;
The Wonder which the dying Patriot draws,
Inspiring Glory thro' remotest Time;
Th' awaken'd Throb for Virtue, and for Fame;
The Sympathies of Love, and Friendship dear;
With all the *social Offspring of the Heart.*
 OH bear me then to vast embowering Shades!
To twilight Groves, and visionary Vales!
To weeping Grottoes, and prophetic Glooms!
Where Angel-Forms athwart the solemn Dusk,
Tremendous sweep, or seem to sweep along;
And Voices more than human, thro' the Void
Deep-sounding, seize th' enthusiastic Ear.
 OR is this Gloom too much? Then lead, ye Powers,
That o'er the Garden and the rural Seat
Preside, which shining thro' the chearful Land
In countless Numbers blest BRITANNIA sees;
O lead me to the wide-extended Walks,
The fair Majestic Paradise of STOWE!
Not *Persian Cyrus*, on *Ionia*'s Shore,
E'er saw such silvan Scenes; such various Art
By Genius fir'd, such ardent Genius tam'd
By cool judicious Art; that, in the strife,
All-beauteous Nature fears to be outdone.
And there, O PIT, thy Country's early Boast,
There let me sit beneath the shelter'd Slopes,
Or in that **Temple* where, in future Times,
Thou well shalt merit a distinguish'd Name;
And, with thy Converse blest, catch the last Smiles
Of Autumn beaming o'er the yellow Woods.
While there with Thee th' inchanted Round I walk,
The regulated Wild, gay Fancy then
Will tread in Thought the Groves of *Attic Land*;
Will from thy standard Taste refine her own,
Correct her Pencil to the purest Truth
Of Nature, or, the unimpassion'd Shades
Forsaking, raise it to the human Mind.
O if hereafter she, with *juster* Hand,

* *The Temple of Virtue in* Stowe-Gardens.

Shall draw the Tragic Scene, instruct Her thou,
To mark the vary'd Movements of the Heart,
What every decent Character requires,
And every Passion speaks: O thro' her Strain
Breathe thy pathetic Eloquence! that moulds
Th' attentive Senate, charms, persuades, exalts,
Of honest Zeal th' indignant Lightning throws,
And shakes Corruption on her venal Throne.
While thus we talk, and thro' *Elysian Vales*
Delighted rove, perhaps a Sigh escapes:
What pity, COBHAM, thou thy verdant Files
Of order'd Trees shouldst here inglorious range,
Instead of Squadrons flaming o'er the Field,
And long-embattled Hosts! When the proud Foe
The faithless vain Disturber of Mankind,
Insulting *Gaul*, has rous'd the World to War;
When keen, once more, within their Bounds to press
Those polish'd Robbers, those ambitious Slaves,
The BRITISH YOUTH would hail thy wise Command,
Thy temper'd Ardor and thy veteran Skill.
  THE Western Sun withdraws the shorten'd Day;
And humid Evening, gliding o'er the Sky,
In her chill Progress, to the Ground condens'd
The Vapours throws. Where creeping Waters ooze,
Where Marshes stagnate, and where Rivers wind,
Cluster the rolling Fogs, and swim along
The dusky-mantled Lawn. Mean-while the Moon
Full-orb'd, and breaking thro' the scatter'd Clouds,
Shews her broad Visage in the crimson'd East.
Turn'd to the Sun direct, her spotted Disk,
Where Mountains rise, umbrageous Dales descend,
And Oceans roll, as optic Tube descries,
A smaller Earth, gives all his Blaze again,
Void of it's Flame, and sheds a softer Day.
Now thro' the passing Cloud she seems to stoop,
Now up the pure Cerulean rides sublime.
Wide the pale Deluge floats, and streaming mild
O'er the sky'd Mountain to the shadowy Vale,
While Rocks and Floods reflect the quivering Gleam,
The whole Air whitens with a boundless Tide
Of silver Radiance, trembling round the World.
  BUT when half-blotted from the Sky her Light,
Fainting, permits the starry Fires to burn,
With keener Lustre thro' the Depth of Heaven;
Or quite extinct her deaden'd Orb appears,
And scarce appears, of sickly beamless White;
Oft in this Season, silent from the North
A Blaze of Meteors shoots: ensweeping first

The lower Skies, they all at once converge
High to the Crown of Heaven, and all at once
Relapsing quick as quickly reascend,
And mix, and thwart, extinguish, and renew,
All Ether coursing in a Maze of Light.
  FROM Look to Look, contagious thro' the Croud,
The Pannic runs, and into wondrous Shapes
Th' Appearance throws: Armies in meet Array,
Throng'd with aërial Spears, and Steeds of Fire;
Till the long Lines of full-extended War
In bleeding Fight commixt, the sanguine Flood
Rolls a broad Slaughter o'er the Plains of Heaven.
As thus they scan the visionary Scene,
On all sides swells the superstitious Din,
Incontinent; and busy Frenzy talks
Of Blood and Battle; Cities over-turn'd,
And late at night in swallowing Earthquake sunk,
Or hideous wrapt in fierce ascending Flame;
Of sallow Famine, Inundation, Storm;
Of Pestilence, and every great Distress;
Empires subvers'd, when ruling Fate has struck
Th' unalterable Hour: even Nature's self
Is deem'd to totter on the Brink of Time.
Not so the Man of philosophic Eye,
And Inspect sage; the waving Brightness he
Curious surveys, inquisitive to know
The Causes, and Materials, yet unfix'd,
Of this Appearance beautiful, and new.
  Now black, and deep, the Night begins to fall,
A Shade immense. Sunk in the quenching Gloom,
Magnificent and vast, are Heaven and Earth.
Order confounded lies; all Beauty void;
Distinction lost; and gay Variety
One universal Blot: such the fair Power
Of Light, to kindle and create the Whole.
Drear is the State of the benighted Wretch,
Who then, bewilder'd, wanders thro' the Dark,
Full of pale Fancies, and Chimeras huge;
Nor visited by one directive Ray,
From Cottage-streaming, or from airy Hall.
Perhaps impatient as he stumbles on,
Struck from the Root of slimy Rushes, blue,
The Wild-fire scatters round, or gather'd trails
A Length of Flame deceitful o'er the Moss;
Whither decoy'd by the fantastic Blaze,
Now lost and now renew'd, he sinks absorpt,
Rider and Horse, amid the miry Gulph:
While still, from Day to Day, his pining Wife,

And plaintive Children his Return await,
In wild Conjecture lost. At other Times,
Sent by the *better Genius* of the Night,
Innoxious, gleaming on the Horse's Mane,
The Meteor sits; and shews the narrow Path,
That winding leads thro' Pits of Death, or else
Instructs him how to take the dangerous Ford.
  THE lengthen'd Night elaps'd, the Morning shines
Serene, in all her dewy Beauty bright,
Unfolding fair the last Autumnal Day.
And now the mounting Sun dispels the Fog;
The rigid Hoar-Frost melts before his Beam;
And hung on every Spray, on every Blade
Of Grass, the myriad Dew-Drops twinkle round.
  AH see where robb'd, and murder'd, in that Pit,
Lies the still heaving Hive! at Evening snatch'd,
Beneath the Cloud of Guilt-concealing Night,
And fix'd o'er Sulphur: while, not dreaming Ill,
The happy People, in their waxen Cells,
Sat tending public Cares, and planning Schemes
Of Temperance, for Winter poor; rejoic'd
To mark, full-flowing round, their copious Stores.
Sudden the dark oppressive Steam ascends;
And, us'd to milder Scents, the tender Race,
By thousands, tumbles from their honey'd Domes,
Convolv'd, and agonizing in the Dust.
And was it then for This you roam'd the Spring,
Intent from Flower to Flower? for This you toil'd
Ceaseless the burning Summer-Heats away?
For This in Autumn search'd the blooming Waste,
Nor lost one sunny Gleam? for this sad Fate?
O Man! tyrannic Lord! how long, how long,
Shall prostrate Nature groan beneath your Rage,
Awaiting Renovation? when oblig'd,
Must you destroy? Of their ambrosial Food
Can you not borrow; and, in just Return,
Afford them Shelter from the wintry Winds;
Or, as the sharp Year pinches, with their Own
Again regale them on some smiling Day?
See where the stony Bottom of their Town
Looks desolate, and wild; with here and there
A helpless Number, who the ruin'd State
Survive, lamenting weak, cast out to Death.
Thus a proud City, populous and rich,
Full of the Works of Peace, and high in Joy,
At Theater or Feast, or sunk in Sleep,
(As late, *Palermo*, was thy Fate) is seiz'd
By some dread Earthquake, and convulsive hurl'd,

Sheer from the black Foundation, stench-involv'd,
Into a Gulph of blue sulphureous Flame.
  HENCE every harsher Sight! for now the Day,
O'er Heaven and Earth diffus'd, grows warm, and high,
Infinite Splendor! wide investing All.
How still the Breeze! save what the filmy Threads
Of Dew evaporate brushes from the Plain.
How clear the cloudless Sky! how deeply ting'd
With a peculiar Blue! th' ethereal Arch
How swell'd immense! amid whose azure thron'd
The radiant Sun how gay! how calm below
The gilded Earth! the Harvest-Treasures all
Now gather'd in, beyond the Rage of Storms,
Sure to the Swain; the circling Fence shut up;
And instant Winter's utmost Rage defy'd.
While, loose to festive Joy, the Country round
Laughs with the loud Sincerity of Mirth,
Shook to the Wind their Cares. The Toil-strung Youth
By the quick Sense of Music taught alone,
Leaps wildly graceful in the lively Dance.
Her every Charm abroad, the Village-Toast,
Young, buxom, warm, in native Beauty rich,
Darts not-unmeaning Looks; and, where her Eye
Points an approving Smile, with double Force,
The Cudgel rattles, and the Wrestler twines.
Age too shines out; and, garrulous, recounts
The Feats of Youth. Thus they rejoice; nor think
That, with to-morrow's Sun, their annual Toil
Begins again the never-ceasing Round.
  OH knew he but his Happiness, of Men
The happiest he! who far from public Rage,
Deep in the Vale, with a *choice Few* retir'd,
Drinks the pure Pleasures of the RURAL LIFE.
What tho' the Dome be wanting, whose proud Gate,
Each Morning, vomits out the sneaking Croud
Of Flatterers false, and in their turn abus'd?
Vile Intercourse! What tho' the glittering Robe,
Of every Hue reflected Light can give,
Or floating loose, or stiff with mazy Gold,
The Pride and Gaze of Fools! oppress him not?
What tho', from utmost Land and Sea purvey'd,
For him each rarer tributary Life
Bleeds not, and his insatiate Table heaps
With Luxury, and Death? What tho' his Bowl
Flames not with costly Juice; nor sunk in Beds,
Oft of gay Care, he tosses out the Night,

Or melts the thoughtless Hours in idle State?
What tho' he knows not those fantastick Joys,
That still amuse the Wanton, still deceive;
A Face of Pleasure, but a Heart of Pain;
Their hollow Moments undelighted all?
Sure Peace is his; a solid Life, estrang'd
To Disappointment, and fallacious Hope:
Rich in Content, in Nature's Bounty rich,
In Herbs and Fruits; whatever greens the Spring,
When Heaven descends in Showers; or bends the Bough,
When Summer reddens, and when Autumn beams;
Or in the Wintry Glebe whatever lies
Conceal'd, and fattens with the richest Sap:
These are not wanting; nor the milky Drove,
Luxuriant, spread o'er all the lowing Vale;
Nor bleating Mountains; nor the Chide of Streams,
And Hum of Bees, inviting Sleep sincere
Into the guiltless Breast, beneath the Shade,
Or thrown at large amid the fragrant Hay:
Nor aught besides of Prospect, Grove, or Song,
Dim Grottos, gleaming Lakes, and Fountain clear.
Here too dwells simple Truth; plain Innocence;
Unsully'd Beauty; sound unbroken Youth,
Patient of Labour, with a Little pleas'd;
Health ever-blooming; unambitious Toil;
Calm Contemplation, and poetic Ease.
LET others brave the Flood, in Quest of Gain,
And beat, for joyless Months, the gloomy Wave.
Let such as deem it Glory to destroy
Rush into Blood, the Sack of Cities seek;
Unpierc'd, exulting in the Widow's Wail,
The Virgin's Shriek, and Infant's trembling Cry.
Let some, far-distant from their native Soil,
Urg'd or by Want or harden'd Avarice,
Find other Lands beneath another Sun.
Let This thro' Cities work his eager Way,
By legal Outrage, and establish'd Guile,
The social Sense extinct; and That ferment
Mad into Tumult the seditious Herd,
Or melt them down to Slavery. Let These
Insnare the Wretched in the Toils of Law,
Fomenting Discord, and perplexing Right,
An iron Race! and Those of fairer Front,
But equal Inhumanity, in Courts,
Delusive Pomp, and dark Cabals, delight;
Wreathe the deep Bow, diffuse the lying Smile,
And tread the weary Labyrinth of State.

While He, from all the stormy Passions free
That restless Men involve, hears, and but hears,
At distance safe, the human Tempest roar,
Wrapt close in conscious Peace. The Fall of Kings,
The Rage of Nations, and the Crush of States,
Move not the Man, who from the World escap'd,
In still Retreats, and flowery Solitudes,
To Nature's Voice attends, from Month to Month,
And Day to Day, thro' the revolving Year;
Admiring, sees Her in her every Shape;
Feels all her sweet Emotions at his Heart;
Takes what she liberal gives, nor thinks of more.
He, when young Spring protrudes the bursting Gems,
Marks the first Bud, and sucks the healthful Gale
Into his freshen'd Soul; her genial Hours
He full enjoys; and not a Beauty blows,
And not an opening Blossom breathes in vain.
In Summer he, beneath the living Shade,
Such as o'er frigid *Tempe* wont to wave,
Or *Hemus* cool, reads what the Muse, of These
Perhaps, has in immortal Numbers sung;
Or what she dictates writes; and, oft an Eye
Shot round, rejoices in the vigorous Year.
When Autumn's yellow Lustre gilds the World,
And tempts the sickled Swain into the Field,
Seiz'd by the general Joy, his Heart distends
With gentle Throws; and, thro' the tepid Gleams
Deep-musing, then he *best* exerts his Song.
Even Winter wild to him is full of Bliss.
The mighty Tempest, and the hoary Waste,
Abrupt, and deep, stretch'd o'er the bury'd Earth,
Awake to solemn Thought. At Night the Skies,
Disclos'd, and kindled, by refining Frost,
Pour every Luster on th' exalted Eye.
A Friend, a Book the stealing Hours secure,
And mark them down for Wisdom. With swift Wing,
O'er Land and Sea Imagination roams;
Or Truth, divinely breaking on his Mind,
Elates his Being, and unfolds his Powers;
Or in his Breast heroic Virtue burns.
The Touch of Kindred too and Love he feels;
The modest Eye, whose Beams on His alone
Extatic shine; the little strong Embrace
Of prattling Children, twin'd around his Neck,
And emulous to please him, calling forth
The fond parental Soul. Nor Purpose gay,
Amusement, Dance, or Song, he sternly scorns;
For Happiness and true Philosophy

Are of the social still, and smiling Kind.
This is the Life which those who fret in Guilt,
And guilty Cities, never knew; the Life,
Led by primeval Ages, uncorrupt,
When Angels dwelt, and GOD himself, with Man!
OH NATURE! all-sufficient! over all!
Inrich me with the Knowledge of thy Works!
Snatch me to Heaven; thy rolling Wonders there,
World beyond World, in infinite Extent,
Profusely scatter'd o'er the void Immense,
Shew me; their Motions, Periods, and their Laws,
Give me to scan; thro' the disclosing Deep
Light my blind Way: the mineral *Strata* there;
Thrust, blooming, thence the vegetable World;
O'er that the rising System, more complex,
Of Animals; and higher still, the Mind,
The vary'd Scene of quick-compounded Thought,
And where the mixing Passions endless shift;
These ever open to my ravish'd Eye:
A Search, the Flight of Time can ne'er exhaust!
But if to that unequal; if the Blood,
In sluggish Streams about my Heart, forbid
That *best* Ambition; under closing Shades,
Inglorious, lay me by the lowly Brook,
And whisper to my Dreams. From THEE begin,
Dwell all on THEE, with THEE conclude my Song:
And let me never never stray from THEE!

A Hymn[1]

THESE, as they change, ALMIGHTY FATHER, these,
Are but the *varied* GOD. The rolling Year
Is full of Thee. Forth in the pleasing Spring
THY Beauty walks, THY Tenderness and Love.
Wide-flush the Fields; the softening Air is Balm;
Echo the Mountains round; the Forest smiles;
And every Sense, and every Heart, is Joy.
Then comes THY Glory in the Summer-Months,
With Light and Heat refulgent. Then THY Sun
Shoots full Perfection thro' the swelling Year.
And oft THY Voice in dreadful Thunder speaks;
And oft at Dawn, deep Noon, or falling Eve,
By Brooks and Groves, in hollow-whispering Gales.

[1] Published in *The Seasons*, 1730. Text of *The Seasons*, 1744.

Thy Bounty shines in Autumn unconfin'd,
And spreads a common Feast for all that lives.
In Winter awful Thou! with Clouds and Storms
Around Thee thrown, Tempest o'er Tempest roll'd,
Majestic Darkness! on the Whirlwind's Wing,
Riding sublime, Thou bidst the World adore,
And humblest Nature with Thy northern Blast.
Mysterious Round! what Skill, what Force divine,
Deep-felt, in These appear! a simple Train,
Yet so delightful mix'd, with such kind Art,
Such Beauty and Beneficence combin'd;
Shade, unperceiv'd, so softening into Shade;
And all so forming an harmonious Whole;
That, as they still succeed, they ravish still.
But wandering oft, with brute unconscious Gaze,
Man marks not Thee, marks not the mighty Hand,
That, ever-busy, wheels the silent Spheres;
Works in the secret Deep; shoots, steaming, Thence
The fair Profusion that o'erspreads the Spring:
Flings from the Sun direct the flaming Day;
Feeds every Creature; hurls the Tempest forth;
And, as on Earth this grateful Change revolves,
With Transport touches all the Springs of Life.
Nature, attend! join every living Soul,
Beneath the spacious Temple of the Sky,
In Adoration join; and, ardent, raise
One general Song! To Him, ye vocal Gales,
Breathe soft, whose Spirit in your Freshness breathes:
Oh talk of Him in solitary Glooms!
Where, o'er the Rock, the scarcely-waving Pine
Fills the brown Shade with a religious Awe.
And ye, Whose bolder Note is heard afar,
Who shake th' astonish'd World, lift high to Heaven
Th' impetuous Song, and say from whom you rage.
His Praise, ye Brooks, attune, ye trembling Rills;
And let me catch it as I muse along.
Ye headlong Torrents, rapid, and profound;
Ye softer Floods, that lead the humid Maze
Along the Vale; and thou, majestic Main,
A secret World of Wonders in thyself,
Sound his stupendous Praise; whose greater Voice
Or bids you roar, or bids your Roarings fall.
Soft-roll your Incense, Herbs, and Fruits, and Flowers,
In mingled Clouds to Him; whose Sun exalts,
Whose Breath perfumes you, and whose Pencil paints,
Ye Forests bend, ye Harvests wave, to Him;
Breathe your still Song into the Reaper's Heart,

As home he goes beneath the joyous Moon.
Ye that keep watch in Heaven, as Earth asleep
Unconscious lies, effuse your mildest Beams,
Ye Constellations, while your Angels strike,
Amid the spangled Sky, the Silver Lyre.
Great Source of Day! best Image here below
Of thy Creator, ever pouring wide,
From World to World, the vital Ocean round,
On Nature write with every Beam HIS Praise.
The Thunder rolls: be hush'd the prostrate World;
While Cloud to Cloud returns the solemn Hymn.
Bleat out afresh, ye Hills; ye mossy Rocks,
Retain the Sound: the broad responsive Low,
Ye Valleys, raise; for the GREAT SHEPHERD reigns;
And his *unsuffering* Kingdom yet will come.
Ye Woodlands all, awake: a boundless Song
Burst from the Groves; and when the restless Day,
Expiring, lays the warbling World asleep,
Sweetest of Birds! sweet Philomela, charm
The listening Shades, and teach the Night HIS Praise.
Ye chief, for whom the whole Creation smiles;
At once the Head, the Heart, and Tongue of all,
Crown the great Hymn! in swarming Cities vast,
Assembled Men, to the deep Organ join
The long-resounding Voice, oft-breaking clear,
At solemn Pauses, thro' the swelling Base;
And, as each mingling Flame increases each,
In one united Ardor rise to Heaven.
Or if you rather chuse the rural Shade,
And find a Fane in every sacred Grove;
There let the Shepherd's Flute, the Virgin's Lay,
The prompting Seraph, and the Poet's Lyre,
Still sing the GOD OF SEASONS, as they roll.
For me, when I forget the darling Theme,
Whether the Blossom blows, the Summer-Ray
Russets the Plain, *inspiring* Autumn gleams;
Or Winter rises in the blackening East;
Be my Tongue mute, may Fancy paint no more,
And, dead to Joy, forget my Heart to beat!
SHOULD Fate command me to the farthest Verge
Of the green Earth, to distant barbarous Climes,
Rivers unknown to Song; where first the Sun
Gilds *Indian* Mountains, or his setting Beam
Flames on th' *Atlantic* Isles; 'tis nought to me;
Since GOD is ever present, ever felt,
In the void Waste as in the City full;
And where HE vital spreads there must be Joy.

When even at last the solemn Hour shall come,
And wing my mystic Flight to future Worlds,
I chearful will obey. There, with new Powers,
Will rising Wonders sing: I cannot go
Where UNIVERSAL LOVE not smiles around,
Sustaining all yon Orbs and all their Suns,
From *seeming Evil* still educing *Good*,
And *Better* thence again, and *Better* still,
In infinite Progression.———But I lose
Myself in HIM, in LIGHT INEFFABLE!
Come then, expressive Silence, muse HIS Praise.

Rule Britannia[1]

WHEN *Britain* first, at heaven's command,
Arose from out the azure main;
This was the charter of the land,
And guardian Angels sung *this* strain:
"Rule, *Britannia,* rule the waves;
"*Britons* never will be slaves."

The nations, not so blest as thee,
Must, in their turns, to tyrants fall:
While thou shalt flourish great and free,
The dread and envy of them all.
"Rule, &c.

Still more majestic shalt thou rise,
More dreadful, from each foreign stroke:
As the loud blast that tears the skies,
Serves but to root thy native oak.
"Rule, &c.

Thee haughty tyrants ne'er shall tame:
All their attempts to bend thee down,
Will but arrouse thy generous flame;
But work their woe, and thy renown.
"Rule, &c.

To thee belongs the rural reign;
Thy cities shall with commerce shine:
All thine shall be the subject main,
And every shore it circles thine.
"Rule, &c.

[1] Published in *Alfred: A Masque,* Act ii, 1740. Text of first edition.

The Muses, still with freedom found,
Shall to thy happy coast repair:
Blest isle! with matchless beauty crown'd,
And manly hearts to guard the fair.
"Rule, *Britannia,* rule the waves;
"*Britons* never will be slaves."

The Castle of Indolence[1]

Canto I

The Castle hight of Indolence,
And its false Luxury;
Where for a little Time, alas!
We liv'd right jollily.

I.

O Mortal man, who livest here by toil,
Do not complain of this thy hard estate;
That like an emmet thou must ever moil,
Is a sad sentence of an antient date:
And, certes, there is for it reason great;
For, thou sometimes it makes thee weep and wail,
And curse thy star, and early drudge and late,
Withouten that would come an heavier bale,
Loose life, unruly passions, and diseases pale.

II.

In lowly dale, fast by a river's side,
With woody hill o'er hill encompass'd round,
A most enchanting wizard did abide,
Than whom a fiend more fell is no where found.
It was, I ween, a lovely spot of ground;
And there a season atween June and May,
Half prank't with spring, with summer half imbrown'd,
A listless climate made, where, sooth to say,
No living wight could work, ne cared even for play.

III.

Was nought around but images of rest:
Sleep-soothing groves, and quiet lawns between;
And flowery beds that slumbrous influence kest,[2]

[1] Published in 1748. Text of small octavo edition, 1748.
[2] Cast.

From poppies breath'd; and beds of pleasant green,
Where never yet was creeping creature seen.
Mean time unnumber'd glittering streamlets play'd,
And hurled every-where their waters sheen;
That, as they bicker'd through the sunny glade,
Though restless still themselves, a lulling murmur made.

IV.

Join'd to the prattle of the purling rills,
Were heard the lowing herds along the vale,
And flocks loud-bleating from the distant hills,
And vacant shepherds piping in the dale;
And now and then sweet Philomel would wail,
Or stock-doves plain amid the forest deep,
That drowsy rustled to the sighing gale;
And still a coil the grashopper did keep:
Yet all these sounds yblent inclined all to sleep.

V.

Full in the passage of the vale, above,
A sable, silent, solemn forest stood;
Where nought but shadowy forms were seen to move,
As *Idless* fancy'd in her dreaming mood.
And up the hills, on either side, a wood
Of blackening pines, ay waving to and fro,
Sent forth a sleepy horror through the blood;
And where this valley winded out, below,
The murmuring main was heard, and scarcely heard, to flow.

VI.

A pleasing land of drowsy-hed it was:
Of dreams that wave before the half-shut eye;
And of gay castles in the clouds that pass,
For ever flushing round a summer-sky:
There eke the soft delights, that witchingly
Instil a wanton sweetness through the breast,
And the calm pleasures always hover'd nigh;
But whate'er smack'd of noyance, or unrest,
Was far far off expell'd from this delicious nest.

VII.

The landskip such, inspiring perfect ease,
Where INDOLENCE (for so the wizard hight)
Close-hid his castle mid embowering trees,

That half shut out the beams of Phœbus bright,
And made a kind of checker'd day and night.
Mean while, unceasing at the massy gate,
Beneath a spacious palm, the wicked wight
Was plac'd; and to his lute, of cruel fate,
And labour harsh, complain'd, lamenting man's estate.

VIII.

Thither continual pilgrims crouded still,
From all the roads of earth that pass there by:
For, as they chaunc'd to breathe on neighbouring hill,
The freshness of this valley smote their eye,
And drew them ever and anon more nigh,
'Till clustering round th' enchanter false they hung,
Ymolten with his syren melody;
While o'er th' enfeebling lute his hand he flung,
And to the trembling chords these tempting verses sung:

IX.

"Behold! ye pilgrims of this earth, behold!
"See all but man with unearn'd pleasure gay.
"See her bright robes the butterfly unfold,
"Broke from her wintry tomb in prime of May.
"What youthful bride can equal her array?
"Who can with her for easy pleasure vie?
"From mead to mead with gentle wing to stray,
"From flower to flower on balmy gales to fly,
"Is all she has to do beneath the radiant sky.

X.

"Behold the merry minstrels of the morn,
"The swarming songsters of the careless grove,
"Ten thousand throats! that, from the flowering thorn
"Hymn their good God, and carol sweet of love,
"Such grateful kindly raptures them emove:
"They neither plough, nor sow; ne, fit for flail,
"E'er to the barn the nodding sheaves they drove;
"Yet theirs each harvest dancing in the gale,
"Whatever crowns the hill, or smiles along the vale.

XI.

"Outcast of nature, man! the wretched thrall
"Of bitter-dropping sweat, or sweltry pain,
"Of cares that eat away thy heart with gall,

"And of the vices, an inhuman train,
"That all proceed from savage thirst of gain:
"For when hard-hearted *Interest* first began
"To poison earth, *Astræa* left the plain;
"Guile, violence, and murder seiz'd on man;
"And, for soft milky streams, with blood the rivers ran.

XII.

"Come, ye, who still the cumbrous load of life
"Push hard up hill; but as the farthest steep
"You trust to gain, and put an end to strife,
"Down thunders back the stone with mighty sweep,
"And hurls your labours to the valley deep,
"For-ever vain: come, and, withouten fee,
"I in oblivion will your sorrows steep,
"Your cares, your toils, will steep you in a sea
"Of full delight: O come, ye weary wights, to me!

XIII.

"With me, you need not rise at early dawn,
"To pass the joyless day in various stounds:[3]
"Or, louting low, on upstart fortune fawn,
"And sell fair honor for some paltry pounds;
"Or through the city take your dirty rounds,
"To cheat, and dun, and lye, and visit pay,
"Now flattering base, now giving secret wounds;
"Or proul in courts of law for human prey,
"In venal senate thieve, or rob on broad high-way.

XIV.

"No cocks, with me, to rustic labour call,
"From village on to village sounding clear;
"To tardy swain no shrill-voic'd matrons squall;
"No dogs, no babes, no wives, to stun your ear;
"No hammers thump; no horrid blacksmith fear,
"Ne noisy tradesman your sweet slumbers start,
"With sounds that are a misery to hear:
"But all is calm, as would delight the heart
"Of *Sybarite* of old, all nature, and all art.

XV.

"Here nought but candour reigns, indulgent ease,
"Good-natur'd lounging, sauntering up and down:

[3] Misfortunes, pangs.

"They who are pleas'd themselves must always please;
"On others' ways they never squint a frown,
"Nor heed what haps in hamlet or in town.
"Thus, from the source of tender Indolence,
"With milky blood the heart is overflown,
"Is sooth'd and sweeten'd by the social sense;
"For interest, envy, pride, and strife are banish'd hence.

XVI.

"What, what, is virtue, but repose of mind?
"A pure ethereal calm! that knows no storm;
"Above the reach of wild ambition's wind,
"Above those passions that this world deform,
"And torture man, a proud malignant worm!
"But here, instead, soft gales of passion play,
"And gently stir the heart, thereby to form
"A quicker sense of joy; as breezes stray
"Across th' enliven'd skies, and make them still more gay.

XVII.

"The best of men have ever lov'd repose:
"They hate to mingle in the filthy fray;
"Where the soul sowrs, and gradual rancour grows,
"Imbitter'd more from peevish day to day.
"Even those whom fame has lent her fairest ray,
"The most renown'd of worthy wights of yore,
"From a base world at last have stolen away:
"So SCIPIO, to the soft *Cumæan* shore
"Retiring, tasted joy he never knew before.

XVIII.

"But if a little exercise you chuse,
"Some zest for ease, 'tis not forbidden here.
"Amid the groves you may indulge the muse,
"Or tend the blooms, and deck the vernal year;
"Or softly stealing, with your watry gear,
"Along the brooks, the crimson-spotted fry
"You may delude: the whilst, amus'd, you hear
"Now the hoarse stream, and now the Zephir's sigh,
"Attuned to the birds, and woodland melody.

XIX.

O grievous folly! to heap up estate,
Losing the days you see beneath the sun;

"When, sudden, comes blind unrelenting fate,
"And gives th' untasted portion you have won,
"With ruthless toil, and many a wretch undone,
"To those who mock you gone to *Pluto*'s reign,
"There with sad ghosts to pine, and shadows dun:
"But sure it is of vanities most vain,
"To toil for what you here untoiling may obtain."

XX.

He ceas'd. But still their trembling ears retain'd
The deep vibrations of his witching song;
That, by a kind of magic power, constrain'd
To enter in, pell-mell, the listening throng.
Heaps pour'd on heaps, and yet they slip'd along
In silent ease: as when beneath the beam
Of summer-moons, the distant woods among,
Or by some flood all silver'd with the gleam,
The soft-embodied fays through airy portal stream.

XXI.

By the smooth demon so it order'd was,
And here his baneful bounty first began:
Though some there were who would not further pass,
And his alluring baits suspected han.[4]
The wise distrust the too fair-spoken man.
Yet through the gate they cast a wishful eye:
Not to move on, perdie, is all they can;
For do their very best they cannot fly,
But often each way look, and often sorely sigh.

XXII.

When this the watchful wicked wizard saw,
With sudden spring he leap'd upon them strait;
And soon as touch'd by his unhallow'd paw,
They found themselves within the cursed gate;
Full hard to be repass'd, like that of fate.
Not stronger were of old the giant-crew,
Who sought to pull high *Jove* from regal state;
Though feeble wretch he seem'd, of sallow hue:
Certes, who bides his grasp, will that encounter rue.

XXIII.

For whomsoe'er the villain takes in hand,
Their joints unknit, their sinews melt apace;

[4] Have.

As lithe they grow as any willow-wand,
And of their vanish'd force remains no trace:
So when a maiden fair, of modest grace,
In all her buxom blooming May of charms,
Is seized in some losel's[5] hot embrace,
She waxeth very weakly as she warms,
Then sighing yields her up to love's delicious harms.

XXIV.

Wak'd by the croud, slow from his bench arose
A comely full-spred porter, swoln with sleep:
His calm, broad, thoughtless aspect breath'd repose;
And in sweet torpor he was plunged deep,
Ne could himself from ceaseless yawning keep;
While o'er his eyes the drowsy liquor ran,
Through which his half-wak'd soul would faintly peep.
Then taking his black staff he call'd his man,
And rous'd himself as much as rouse himself he can.

XXV.

The lad leap'd lightly at his master's call.
He was, to weet, a little roguish page,
Save sleep and play who minded nought at all,
Like most the untaught striplings of his age.
This boy he kept each band to disengage,
Garters and buckles, task for him unfit,
But ill-becoming his grave personage,
And which his portly paunch would not permit,
So this same limber page to all performed it.

XXVI.

Mean time the master-porter wide display'd
Great store of caps, of slippers, and of gowns;
Wherewith he those who enter'd in, array'd;
Loose, as the breeze that plays along the downs,
And waves the summer-woods when evening frowns.
O fair undress, best dress! it checks no vein,
But every flowing limb in pleasure drowns,
And heightens ease with grace. This done, right fain
Sir porter sat him down, and turn'd to sleep again.

XXVII.

Thus easy-rob'd, they to the fountain sped,
That in the middle of the court up-threw

[5] A loose idle fellow.

A stream, high-spouting from its liquid bed,
And falling back again in drizzly dew:
There each deep draughts, as deep he thirsted, drew.
It was a fountain of *Nepenthe* rare:
Whence, as Dan HOMER sings, huge pleasaunce grew,
And sweet oblivion of vile earthly care;
Fair gladsome waking thoughts, and joyous dreams more fair.

XXVIII.

This rite perform'd, all inly pleas'd and still,
Withouten tromp, was proclamation made.
"Ye sons of INDOLENCE, do what you will;
"And wander where you list, through hall or glade:
"Be no man's pleasure for another's staid;
"Let each as likes him best his hours employ,
"And curs'd be he who minds his neighbour's trade!
"Here dwells kind ease and unreproving joy;
"He little merits bliss who others can annoy.

XXIX.

Strait of these endless numbers, swarming round,
As thick as idle motes in sunny ray,
Not one eftsoons in view was to be found,
But every man stroll'd off his own glad way.
Wide o'er this ample courts blank area,
With all the lodges that thereto pertain'd,
No living creature could be seen to stray;
While solitude, and perfect silence reign'd:
So that to think you dreamt you almost was constrain'd.

XXX.

As when a shepherd of the *Hebrid-Isles*,
Plac'd far amid the melancholy main,
(Whether it be lone fancy him beguiles;
Or that aerial beings sometimes deign
To stand, embodied, to our senses plain)
Sees on the naked hill, or valley low,
The whilst in ocean *Phœbus* dips his wain,
A vast assembly moving to and fro:
Then all at once in air dissolves the wondrous show.

XXXI.

Ye Gods of quiet, and of sleep profound!
Whose soft dominion o'er this castle sways,

And all the widely-silent places round,
Forgive me, if my trembling pen displays
What never yet was sung in mortal lays.
But how shall I attempt such arduous string?
I who have spent my nights and nightly days,
In this soul-deadening place, loose loitering?
Ah! how shall I for this uprear my moulted wing?

XXXII.

Come on, my muse, nor stoop to low despair,
Thou imp of *Jove*, touch'd by celestial fire!
Thou yet shalt sing of war, and actions fair,
Which the bold sons of BRITAIN will inspire;
Of antient bards thou yet shalt sweep the lyre;
Thou yet shalt tread in tragic pall the stage,
Paint love's enchanting woes, the heroe's ire,
The sage's calm, the patriot's noble rage,
Dashing corruption down through every worthless age.

XXXIII.

The doors, that knew no shrill alarming bell,
Ne cursed knocker ply'd by villain's hand,
Self-open'd into halls, where, who can tell
What elegance and grandeur wide expand
The pride of *Turkey* and of *Persia* land?
Soft quilts on quilts, on carpets carpets spread,
And couches stretch around in seemly band;
And endless pillows rise to prop the head;
So that each spacious room was one full-swelling bed.

XXXIV.

And every where huge cover'd tables stood,
With wines high-flavour'd and rich viands crown'd;
Whatever sprightly juice or tasteful food
On the green bosom of this earth are found,
And all old ocean genders in his round:
Some hand unseen these silently display'd,
Even undemanded, by a sign or sound;
You need but wish, and, instantly obey'd,
Fair-rang'd the dishes rose, and thick the glasses play'd.

XXXV.

Here freedom reign'd, without the least alloy;
Nor gossip's tale, nor ancient maiden's gall,

Nor saintly spleen durst murmur at our joy,
And with envenom'd tongue our pleasures pall.
For why? there was but one great rule for all;
To wit, that each should work his own desire,
And eat, drink, study, sleep, as it may fall,
Or melt the time in love, or wake the lyre,
And carol what, unbid, the muses might inspire.

XXXVI.

The rooms with costly tapestry were hung,
Where was inwoven many a gentle tale;
Such as of old the rural poets sung,
Or of *Arcadian* or *Sicilian* vale:
Reclining lovers, in the lonely dale,
Pour'd forth at large the sweetly-tortur'd heart;
Or, looking tender passion, swell'd the gale,
And taught charm'd echo to resound their smart,
While flocks, woods, streams, around repose and peace impart.

XXXVII.

Those pleas'd the most, where, by a cunning hand,
Depainted was the patriarchal age;
What time Dan *Abraham* left the *Chaldee* land,
And pastur'd on from verdant stage to stage,
Where fields and fountains fresh could best engage.
Toil was not then. Of nothing took they heed,
But with wild beasts the silvan war to wage,
And o'er vast plains their herds and flocks to feed:
Blest sons of nature they! true golden age indeed!

XXXVIII.

Sometimes the pencil, in cool airy halls,
Bade the gay bloom of vernal landskips rise,
Or autumn's varied shades imbrown the walls:
Now the black tempest strikes the astonish'd eyes;
Now down the steep the flashing torrent flies;
The trembling sun now plays o'er ocean blue,
And now rude mountains frown amid the skies;
Whate'er *Lorrain* light-touch'd with softening hue,
Or savage *Rosa* dash'd, or learned *Poussin* drew.

XXXIX.

Each sound too here to languishment inclin'd,
Lull'd the weak bosom, and induced ease.

Aerial music in the warbling wind,
At distance rising oft, by small degrees,
Nearer and nearer came, till o'er the trees
It hung, and breath'd such soul-dissolving airs,
As did, alas! with soft perdition please:
Entangled deep in its enchanting snares,
The listening heart forgot all duties and all cares.

XL.

A certain music, never known before,
Here lull'd the pensive melancholy mind;
Full easily obtain'd. Behoves no more,
But sidelong, to the gently-waving wind,
To lay the well-tun'd instrument reclin'd;
From which, with airy flying fingers light,
Beyond each mortal touch the most refin'd,
The God of winds drew sounds of deep delight:
Whence, with just cause, *The harp of Æolus* it hight.

XLI.

Ah me! what hand can touch the strings so fine?
Who up the lofty diapasan roll
Such sweet, such sad, such solemn airs divine,
Then let them down again into the soul?
Now rising love they fan'd; now pleasing dole
They breath'd, in tender musings, through the heart;
And now a graver sacred strain they stole,
As when seraphic hands an hymn impart:
Wild warbling nature all, above the reach of art!

XLII.

Such the gay splendor, the luxurious state,
Of *Caliphs* old, who on the *Tygris'* shore,
In mighty *Bagdat*, populous and great,
Held their bright court, where was of ladies store;
And verse, love, music still the garland wore:
When sleep was coy, the bard, in waiting there,
Chear'd the lone midnight with the muse's lore;
Composing music bade his dreams be fair,
And music lent new gladness to the morning air.

XLIII.

Near the pavilions where we slept, still ran
Soft-tinkling streams, and dashing waters fell,

And sobbing breezes sigh'd, and oft began
(So work'd the wizard) wintry storms to swell,
As heaven and earth they would together mell:
At doors and windows, threatening, seem'd to call
The demons of the tempest, growling fell,
Yet the least entrance found they none at all;
Whence sweeter grew our sleep, secure in massy hall.

XLIV.

And hither *Morpheus* sent his kindest dreams,
Raising a world of gayer tinct and grace;
O'er which were shadowy cast Elysian gleams,
That play'd, in waving lights, from place to place,
And shed a roseate smile on nature's face.
Not *Titian*'s pencil e'er could so array,
So fleece with clouds the pure etherial space;
Ne could it e'er such melting forms display,
As loose on flowery beds all languishingly lay.

XLV.

No, fair illusions! artful phantoms, no!
My Muse will not attempt your fairy-land:
She has no colours that like you can glow;
To catch your vivid scenes too gross her hand.
But sure it is, was ne'er a subtler band
Than these same guileful angel-seeming sprights,
Who thus in dreams, voluptuous, soft, and bland,
Pour'd all th' *Arabian heaven* upon our nights,
And bless'd them oft besides with more refin'd delights.

XLVI.

They were in sooth a most enchanting train,
Even feigning virtue; skilful to unite
With evil good, and strew with pleasure pain.
But for those fiends, whom blood and broils delight;
Who hurl the wretch, as if to hell outright,
Down down black gulphs, where sullen waters sleep,
Or hold him clambering all the fearful night
On beetling cliffs, or pent in ruins deep:
They, till due time should serve, were bid far hence to keep.

XLVII.

Ye guardian spirits, to whom man is dear,
From these foul demons shield the midnight gloom!

Angels of fancy and of love, be near,
And o'er the blank of sleep diffuse a bloom!
Evoke the sacred shades of *Greece* and *Rome*,
And let them virtue with a look impart!
But chief, a while O lend us from the tomb
Those long-lost friends for whom in love we smart,
And fill with pious awe and joy-mixt woe the heart.

XLVIII.

Or are you sportive—Bid the morn of youth
Rise to new light, and beam afresh the days
Of innocence, simplicity, and truth;
To cares estrang'd, and manhood's thorny ways.
What transport! To retrace our boyish plays,
Our easy bliss, when each thing joy supply'd:
The woods, the mountains, and the warbling maze
Of the wild brooks—But, fondly wandering wide,
My muse, resume the task that yet doth thee abide.

XLIX.

One great amusement of our houshold was,
In a huge crystal magic globe to spy,
Still as you turn'd it, all things that do pass
Upon this ant-hill earth; where constantly
Of idly-busy men the restless fry
Run bustling too and fro with foolish haste,
In search of pleasures vain that from them fly,
Or which obtain'd the caitiffs dare not taste:
When nothing is enjoy'd, can there be greater waste?

L.

Of vanity the mirror this was call'd.
Here you a muckworm of the town might see,
At his dull desk, amid his legers stall'd,
Eat up with carking care and penurie;
Most like to carcase parch'd on gallow-tree.
A penny saved is a penny got:
Firm to this scoundrel maxim keepeth he,
Ne of its rigour will he bate a jot,
Till it has quench'd his fire, and banished his pot.

LI.

Strait from the filth of this low grub, behold!
Comes fluttering forth a gaudy spendthrift heir,

All glossy gay, enamel'd all with gold,
The silly tenant of the summer-air.
In folly lost, of nothing takes he care;
Pimps, lawyers, stewards, harlots, flatterers vile,
And thieving tradesmen him among them share:
His father's ghost from Limbo-lake, the while,
Sees this, which more damnation does upon him pile.

LII.

This globe pourtray'd the race of learned men,
Still at their books, and turning o'er the page,
Backwards and forwards: oft they snatch the pen,
As if inspir'd, and in a *Thespian* rage;
Then write, and blot, as would your ruth engage.
Why, authors, all this scrawl and scribbling sore?
To lose the present, gain the future age,
Praised to be when you can hear no more,
And much enrich'd with fame when useless worldly store.

LIII.

Then would a splendid city rise to view,
With carts, and cars, and coaches roaring all:
Wide-pour'd abroad behold the prowling crew;
See! how they dash along from wall to wall;
At every door, hark! how they thundering call.
Good Lord! what can this giddy rout excite?
Why? On each other with fell tooth to fall;
A neighbour's fortune, fame, or peace to blight,
And make new tiresome parties for the coming night.

LIV.

The puzzling sons of party next appear'd,
In dark cabals and nightly juntos met;
And now they whisper'd close, now shrugging rear'd
Th' important shoulder; then, as if to get
New light, their twinkling eyes were inward set.
No sooner *Lucifer* recalls affairs,
Than forth they various rush in mighty fret;
When lo! push'd up to power, and crown'd their cares,
In comes another set, and kicketh them down stairs.

LV.

But what most shew'd the vanity of life,
Was to behold the nations all on fire,

In cruel broils engag'd, and deadly strife;
Most christian kings, inflam'd by black desire,
With honourable ruffians in their hire,
Cause war to rage, and blood around to pour:
Of this sad work when each begins to tire,
They sit them down just where they were before,
Till for new scenes of woe, peace shall their force restore.

LVI.

To number up the thousands dwelling here,
An useless were, and eke an endless task:
From kings, and those who at the helm appear,
To gipsies brown in summer-glades who bask.
Yea many a man perdie I could unmask,
Whose desk and table make a solemn show,
With tape-ty'd trash, and suits of fools that ask
For place or pension, laid in decent row;
But these I passen by, with nameless numbers moe.

LVII.

Of all the gentle tenants of the place,
There was a man of special grave remark:
A certain tender gloom o'erspread his face,
Pensive not sad, in thought involv'd not dark,
As soot[6] this man could sing as morning-lark,
And teach the noblest morals of the heart:
But these his talents were ybury'd stark;
Of the fine stores he nothing would impart,
Which or boon nature gave, or nature-painting art,

LVIII.

To noontide shades incontinent he ran,
Where purls the brook with sleep-inviting sound;
Or when Dan *Sol* to slope his wheels began,
Amid the broom he bask'd him on the ground,
Where the wild thyme and camomil are found:
There would he linger, till the latest ray
Of light sat trembling on the welkin's bound:
Then homeward through the twilight shadows stray,
Sauntring and slow. So had he passed many a day.

LIX.

Yet not in thoughtless slumber were they past:
For oft the heavenly fire, that lay conceal'd

[6] Sweet.

Beneath the sleeping embers, mounted fast,
And all its native light anew reveal'd;
Oft as he travers'd the Cerulean field,
And mark'd the clouds that drove before the wind,
Ten thousand glorious systems would he build,
Ten thousand great ideas fill'd his mind;
But with the clouds they fled, and left no track behind.

LX.

With him was sometimes join'd, in silent walk,
(Profoundly silent, for they never spoke)
One shyer still, who quite detested talk:
Oft, stung by spleen, at once away he broke,
To groves of pine, and broad o'ershadowing oak;
There, inly thrill'd, he wander'd all alone,
And on himself his pensive fury wroke,
Ne ever utter'd word, save when first shone
The glittering star of eve—"Thank heaven! the day is done."

LXI.

Here lurk'd a wretch, who had not crept abroad
For forty years, ne face of mortal seen;
In chamber brooding like a loathly toad,
And sure his linnen was not very clean;
Through secret loop-hole, that had practis'd been
Near to his bed, his dinner vile he took;
Unkempt, and rough, of squalid face and mein,
Our castle's shame! whence, from his filthy nook,
We drove the villain out for fitter lair to look.

LXII.

One day there chaunc'd into these halls to rove
A joyous youth, who took you at first sight;
Him the wild wave of pleasure higher drove,
Before the sprightly tempest tossing light:
Certes, he was a most engaging wight,
Of social glee, and wit humane though keen,
Turning the night to day and day to night;
For him the merry bells had rung, I ween,
If in this nook of quiet bells had ever been.

LXIII.

But not even pleasure to excess is good,
What most elates then sinks the soul as low;

When spring-tide joy pours in with copious flood,
The higher still th' exulting billows flow,
The farther back again they flagging go,
And leave us groveling on the dreary shore:
Taught by this son of joy, we found it so;
Who, whilst he staid, kept in a gay uproar
Our madden'd castle all, th' abode of sleep no more.

LXIV.

As when in prime of June a burnish'd fly,
Sprung from the meads, o'er which he sweeps along,
Chear'd by the breathing bloom and vital sky,
Tunes up amid these airy halls his song,
Soothing at first the gay reposing throng:
And oft he sips their bowl; or nearly drown'd,
He, thence recovering, drives their beds among,
And scares their tender sleep, with trump profound;
Then out again he flies, to wing his mazy round.

LXV.

Another guest there was, of sense refin'd,
Who felt each worth for every worth he had;
Serene yet warm, humane yet firm his mind,
As little touch'd as any man's with bad:
Him through their inmost walks the muses lad,
To him the sacred love of nature lent,
And sometimes would he make our valley glad;
Whenas we found he would not here be pent,
To him the better sort this friendly message sent.

LXVI.

"Come, dwell with us! true son of virtue, come!
"But if, alas! we cannot thee persuade,
"To lie content beneath our peaceful dome,
"Ne ever more to quit our quiet glade;
"Yet when at last thy toils, but ill apaid,
"Shall dead thy fire, and damp its heavenly spark,
"Thou wilt be glad to seek the rural shade,
"There to indulge the muse, and nature mark:
"We then a lodge for thee will rear in Hagley-Park."

LXVII.

Here whilom ligg'd th' Esopus of the age;
But call'd by fame, in soul ypricked deep,

A noble pride restor'd him to the stage,
And rous'd him like a gyant from his sleep.
Even from his slumbers we advantage reap:
With double force th' enliven'd scene he wakes,
Yet quits not nature's bounds. He knows to keep
Each due decorum: now the heart he shakes,
And now with well-urg'd sense th' enlighten'd judgment takes.

LXVIII.

A bard here dwelt, more fat than bard beseems;
Who void of envy, guile, and lust of gain,
On virtue still, and nature's pleasing themes,
Pour'd forth his unpremeditated strain,
The world forsaking with a calm disdain:
Here laugh'd he careless in his easy seat,
Here quaff'd encircled with the joyous train;
Oft moralizing sage; his ditty sweet
He loathed much to write, ne cared to repeat.

LXIX.

Full oft by holy feet our ground was trod,
Of clerks good plenty here you mote espy.
A little, round, fat, oily man of God,
Was one I chiefly mark'd among the fry:
He had a roguish twinkle in his eye,
And shone all glittering with ungodly dew,
If a tight damsel chaunc'd to trippen by;
Which when observ'd, he shrunk into his mew,
And strait would recollect his piety anew.

LXX.

Nor be forgot a tribe, who minded nought
(Old inmates of the place) but state affairs:
They look'd, perdie, as if they deeply thought;
And on their brow sat every nation's cares.
The world by them is parcel'd out in shares,
When in the *hall of smoak* they congress hold,
And the sage berry sun-burnt *Mocha* bears
Has clear'd their inward eye: then, smoak-enroll'd,
Their oracles break forth mysterious as of old.

LXXI.

Here languid beauty kept her pale-fac'd court:
Bevies of dainty dames, of high degree,

From every quarter hither made resort;
Where, from gross mortal care and business free,
They lay, pour'd out in ease and luxury.
Or should they a vain shew of work assume,
Alas! and well-a-day! what can it be?
To knot, to twist, to range the vernal bloom;
But far is cast the distaff, spinning-wheel, and loom.

LXXII.

Their only labour was to kill the time;
And labour dire it is, and weary woe.
They sit, they loll, turn o'er some idle rhyme;
Then rising sudden, to the glass they go,
Or saunter forth, with tottering step and slow;
This soon too rude an exercise they find;
Strait on the couch their limbs again they throw,
Where hours on hours they sighing lie reclin'd,
And court the vapoury god soft-breathing in the wind.

LXXIII.

Now must I mark the villainy we found,
But ah! too late, as shall eftsoons be shewn,
A place here was, deep, dreary, under ground;
Where still our inmates, when unpleasing grown,
Diseas'd, and loathsome, privily were thrown.
Far from the light of heaven, they languish'd there,
Unpity'd uttering many a bitter groan;
For of these wretches taken was no care:
Fierce fiends, and hags of hell, their only nurses were.

LXXIV.

Alas! the change! from scenes of joy and rest,
To this dark den, where sickness tost alway.
Here *Lethargy*, with deadly sleep opprest,
Stretch'd on his back a mighty lubbard lay,
Heaving his sides, and snored night and day;
To stir him from his traunce it was not eath,
And his half-open'd eyne he shut straightway:
He led, I wot, the softest way to death,
And taught withoutten pain and strife to yield the breath.

LXXV.

Of limbs enormous, but withal unsound,
Soft-swoln and pale, here lay the *Hydropsy*:

Unwieldy man! with belly monstrous round,
For ever fed with watery supply;
For still he drank, and yet he still was dry.
And here a moping mystery did sit,
Mother of spleen, in robes of various dye,
Who vexed was full oft with ugly fit;
And some her frantic deem'd, and some her deem'd a wit.

LXXVI.

A lady proud she was, of ancient blood,
Yet oft her fear her pride made crouchen low:
She felt, or fancy'd in her fluttering mood,
All the diseases which the 'spitals know,
And sought all physick which the shops bestow,
And still new leaches and new drugs would try,
Her humour ever wavering to and fro;
For sometimes she would laugh, and sometimes cry,
Then sudden waxed wroth, and all she knew not why.

LXXVII.

Fast by her side a listless maiden pin'd,
With aching head, and squeamish heart-burnings;
Pale, bloated, cold, she seem'd to hate mankind,
Yet loved in secret all forbidden things.
And here the *Tertian* shakes his chilling wings;
The sleepless *Gout* here counts the crowing cocks,
A wolf now gnaws him, now a serpent stings;
Whilst *Apoplexy* cramm'd intemperance knocks
Down to the ground at once, as butcher felleth ox.

DAVID MALLET

(1705-1720-1765)

William and Margaret[1]

'TWAS at the silent, solemn hour,
When night and morning meet;
In glided MARGARET's grimly ghost,
And stood at WILLIAM's feet.

[1] Published in the *Plain Dealer,* July 24, 1724. Text of *Works,* 1759.

Her face was like an *April* morn,
Clad in a wintry cloud:
And clay-cold was her lilly hand,
That held her sable shroud.

So shall the fairest face appear,
When youth and years are flown:
Such is the robe that kings must wear,
When death has reft their crown.

Her bloom was like the springing flower,
That sips the silver dew;
The rose was budded in her cheek,
Just opening to the view.

But *Love* had, like the canker-worm,
Consum'd her early prime:
The rose grew pale, and left her cheek;
She dy'd before her time.

Awake! *she* cry'd, thy *True Love* calls,
Come from her midnight grave;
Now let thy *Pity* hear the maid,
Thy *Love* refus'd to save.

This is the dumb and dreary hour,
When injur'd ghosts complain;
When yauning graves give up their dead
To haunt the faithless swain.

Bethink thee, WILLIAM, of thy fault,
Thy pledge, and broken oath:
And give me back my maiden vow,
And give me back my troth.

Why did you promise love to me,
And not that promise keep?
Why did you swear my eyes were bright,
Yet leave those eyes to weep?

How could you say my face was fair,
And yet that face forsake?
How could you win my virgin heart,
Yet leave that heart to break?

Why did you say, my lip was sweet,
And made the scarlet pale?

And why did I, young witless maid!
  Believe the flattering tale?

That face, alas! no more is fair;
  Those lips no longer red:
Dark are my eyes, now clos'd in death,
  And every charm is fled.

The hungry *worm* my *sister* is;
  This *winding-sheet* I wear:
And cold and weary lasts our *night*,
  Till that *last morn* appear.

But hark!—the *cock* has warn'd me hence;
  A long and late adieu!
Come, see, false *man*, how low *she* lies,
  Who dy'd for love of you.

The lark sung loud; the morning smil'd,
  With beams of rosy red:
Pale WILLIAM quak'd in every limb,
  And raving left his bed.

He hy'd him to the fatal place
  Where MARGARET's body lay:
And stretch'd him on the grass-green turf,
  That wrap'd her breathless clay.

And thrice he call'd on MARGARET's name,
  And thrice he wept full sore:
Then laid his cheek to her cold grave,
  And word spake never more!

CHARLES MORDAUNT, EARL OF PETERBOROUGH

(1658-1724-1735)

Chloe[1]

I SAID to my Heart, between sleeping and waking,
Thou wild Thing, that ever art leaping or aching,

[1] Published in the *Universal Journal*, January 1, 1724. Text of first edition.

For the Black, for the Fair: In what Clime, in what Nation,
Hast thou not felt a Fit of Pitapatation?

Thus accus'd, the wild Thing gave this serious Reply;
See the Heart without Motion, tho' *Celia* pass by;
Not the Beauty she has, nor the Wit that she borrows,
Gives the Eye any Joys, or the Heart any Sorrows.

When our *Sappho* appears, whose Wit's so refined,
I am forced to admire with the rest of Mankind:
Whatever she says is with Spirit and Fire;
Every Word I attend, but I only admire.

Prudentia, as vainly too, puts in her Claim;
Ever gazing on Heaven, tho' Man is her Aim.
'Tis Love, not Devotion, that turns up her Eyes:
Those Stars of the World are too good for the Skies.

But my *Chloe*, so lovely, so easy, so fair;
Her Wit so genteel, without Art, without Care;
When she comes in my Way, Oh! the Motion and Pain,
The Leapings and Achings, they return all again.

Thou wonderful Creature! A Woman of Reason!
Never grave out of Pride, never gay out of Season!
When so easy to guess, who this Angel should be,
Would one think that my *Chloe* ne'er thought it was she.

William Hamilton of Bangour

(1704-1724-1754)

The Braes of Yarrow, To Lady Jane Home, in Imitation of the Ancient Scottish Manner[1]

A. Busk ye, busk ye, my bony bony bride,
Busk ye, busk ye, my winsome marrow?
Busk ye, busk ye, my bony bony bride,
And think nae mair on the Braes of Yarrow.

[1] Published in *The Tea Table Miscellany*, 1724. Text of *Poems on Several Occasions*, 1760.

B. Where gat ye that bony bony bride?
  Where gat ye that winsome marrow?
A. I gat her where I dare na well be seen,
  Puing the birks on the Braes of Yarrow.

Weep not, weep not, my bony bony bride,
  Weep not, weep not, my winsome marrow,
Nor let thy heart lament to leive
  Puing the birks on the Braes of Yarrow.

B. Why does she weep, thy bony bony bride?
  Why does she weep, thy winsome marrow?
And why dare ye nae mair weil be seen
  Puing the birks on the Braes of Yarrow?

A. Lang maun she weep, lang maun she, maun she weep,
  Lang maun she weep with dule and sorrow,
And lang maun I nae mair weil be seen
  Puing the birks on the Braes of Yarrow.

For she has tint her luver luver dear,
  Her luver dear, the cause of sorrow,
And I hae slain the comliest swain
  That e'er pu'd birks on the Braes of Yarrow.

Why runs thy stream, O Yarrow, Yarrow red?
  Why on thy braes heard the voice of sorrow?
And why yon melancholeous weids
  Hung on the bony birks of Yarrow!

What yonder floats on the rueful rueful flude?
  What's yonder floats? O dule and sorrow!
'Tis he the comely swain I slew
  Upon the duleful Braes of Yarrow.

Wash, O wash his wounds his wounds in tears,
  His wounds in tears, with dule and sorrow,
And wrap his limbs in mourning weids,
  And lay him on the Braes of Yarrow.

Then build, then build, ye sisters sisters sad,
  Ye sisters sad, his tomb with sorrow,
And weep around in waeful wise,
  His helpless fate on the Braes of Yarrow.

Curse ye, curse ye, his useless useless shield,
  My arm that wrought the deed of sorrow,

The fatal spear that pierc'd his breast
His comely breast on the Braes of Yarrow.

Did I not warn thee not to, not to lue,
And warn from fight, but to my sorrow,
O'er rashly bald a stronger arm
Thou met'st, and fell on the Braes of Yarrow.

Sweet smells the birk, green grows, green grows the grass,
Yellow on Yarrow's bank the gowan,
Fair hangs the apple frae the rock,
Sweet the wave of Yarrow flowan.

Flows Yarrow sweet? as sweet, as sweet flows Tweed,
As green its grass, its gowan yellow,
As sweet smells on its braes the birk,
The apple frae the rock as mellow.

Fair was thy luve, fair fair indeed thy luve,
In floury bands thou him did'st fetter,
Tho' he was fair and weil beluv'd again,
Than me, he never lued thee better.

Busk ye, then busk, my bony bony bride,
Busk ye, busk ye, my winsome marrow,
Busk ye, and lue me on the banks of Tweed,
And think nae mair on the Braes of Yarrow.

C. How can I busk a bony bony bride,
How can I busk a winsome marrow,
How lue him on the banks of Tweed,
That slew my luve on the Braes of Yarrow?

O Yarrow fields, may never never rain,
No dew thy tender blossoms cover,
For there was basely slain my luve,
My luve, as he had not been a lover.

The boy put on his robes, his robes of green,
His purple vest, 'twas my awn seuing,
Ah! wretched me! I little little ken'd
He was in these to meet his ruin.

The boy took out his milk-white milk-white steed,
Unheedful of my dule and sorrow,
But e'er the toofal of the night
He lay a corps on the Braes of Yarrow.

Much I rejoic'd that waeful waeful day;
  I sang, my voice the woods returning,
But lang e'er night the spear was flown
  That slew my luve, and left me mourning.

What can my barbarous barbarous father do,
  But with his cruel rage pursue me?
My luver's blood is on thy spear,
  How can'st thou, barbarous man, then woo me?

My happy sisters may be may be proud,
  With cruel, and ungentle scoffin,
May bid me seek on Yarrow Braes
  My luver nailed in his coffin.

My brother Douglas may upbraid,
  And strive with threatning words to muve me,
My luver's blood is on thy spear,
  How can'st thou ever bid me luve thee?

Yes yes, prepare the bed, the bed of luve,
  With bridal sheets my body cover,
Unbar ye bridal maids the door,
  Let in the expected husband lover.

But who the expected husband husband is?
  His hands, methinks, are bath'd in slaughter,
Ah me! what ghastly spectre's yon,
  Comes, in his pale shroud, bleeding after.

Pale as he is, here lay him lay him down,
  O lay his cold head on my pillow;
Take aff take aff these bridal weids,
  And crown my careful head with willow.

Pale tho' thou art, yet best yet best beluv'd,
  O could my warmth to life restore thee,
Yet lye all night between my briests,
  No youth lay ever there before thee.

Pale pale indeed, O lovely lovely youth,
  Forgive, forgive so foul a slaughter,
And lye all night between my briests,
  No youth shall ever lye there after.

A. Return return, O mournful mournful bride,
  Return and dry thy useless sorrow,

Thy luver heeds nought of thy sighs,
He lyes a corps on the Braes of Yarrow.

WILLIAM SOMERVILE

(1675-1725-1742)

Presenting to a Lady a White Rose and a Red, on the Tenth of June[1]

IF THIS pale Rose offend your Sight,
It in your Bosom wear;
'Twill blush to find itself less white,
And turn *Lancastrian* there.

But, *Celia*, should the Red be chose,
With gay Vermilion bright;
'Twou'd sicken at each Blush that glows,
And in Despair turn White.

Let Politicians idly prate,
Their *Babels* build in vain;
As uncontrolable as Fate,
Imperial Love shall reign.

Each haughty Faction shall obey,
And Whigs, and Tories join,
Submit to your Despotick Sway,
Confess your Right Divine.

Yet this (my gracious Monarch) own,
They're Tyrants that oppress;
'Tis Mercy must support your Throne,
And 'tis like Heav'n to Bless.

[1] Published in *Occasional Poems*, 1727. Text of first edition.

An Address to His Elbow-Chair, New Cloath'd[1]

MY DEAR companion, and my faithful friend!
If Orpheus taught the listening oaks to bend;
If stones and rubbish, at Amphion's call,
Danc'd into form, and built the Theban wall;
Why should'st not *thou* attend my humble lays,
And hear my grateful harp resound thy praise?
True, thou art spruce and fine, a very beau;
But what are trappings, and external show?
To real worth alone I make my court;
Knaves are my scorn, and coxcombs are my sport.
Once I beheld thee far less trim and gay;
Ragged, disjointed, and to worms a prey;
The safe retreat of every lurking mouse;
Derided, shun'd; the lumber of my house!
Thy robe, how chang'd from what it was before!
Thy velvet robe, which pleas'd my sires of yore!
'Tis thus capricious Fortune wheels us round;
Aloft we mount—then tumble to the ground.
Yet grateful *then*, my constancy I prov'd;
I knew thy worth; my friend in rags I lov'd!
I lov'd thee, *more;* nor, like a courtier, spurn'd
My benefactor, when the tide was turn'd.
With conscious shame, yet frankly, I confess,
That in my youthful days—I lov'd thee less.
Where vanity, where pleasure call'd, I stray'd;
And every wayward appetite obey'd.
But sage experience taught me how to prize
Myself; and how, this world: she bade me rise
To nobler flights, regardless of a race
Of factious emmets; pointed where to place
My bliss, and lodg'd me in thy soft embrace.
Here on thy yielding down I sit secure,
And, patiently, what heav'n has sent, endure:
From all the futile cares of business free;
Not *fond* of life, but yet content to *be:*
Here mark the fleeting hours; regret the past;
And seriously prepare, to meet the last.
So safe on shore the pension'd sailor lies,
And all the malice of the storm defies:
With ease of body blest, and peace of mind,
Pities the restless crew he left behind;
Whilst, in his cell, he meditates alone
On his great voyage, to the world unknown.

[1] Published in the *Student*, 1750. Text of Dodsley's *Collection of Poems*, Volume V, 1755.

George Bubb Dodington, Lord Melcombe

(1691-1726-1762)

Ode[1]

Love thy Country, wish it well,
  Not with too intense a care,
'Tis enough, that when it fell,
  Thou, it's ruin, didst not share.

Envy's censure, Flattery's praise,
  With unmov'd Indifference, view;
Learn to tread Life's dangerous maze,
  With unerring Virtue's clue.

Void of strong Desires, and Fear,
  Life's wide Ocean trust no more;
Strive thy little Bark to steer,
  With the tide, but near the shore.

Thus prepar'd, thy shorten'd sail
  Shall, whene'er the winds encrease,
Seizing each propitious gale,
  Waft thee to the Port of Peace.

Keep thy conscience from offence,
  And tempestuous passions, free,
So, when thou art call'd from hence,
  Easy shall thy passage be;

Easy shall thy passage be,
  Chearfull, thy allotted stay;
Short th' account twixt God and Thee;
  Hope shall meet thee, on the way;

Truth shall lead thee to the gate,
  Mercy's self shall let thee in;
Where it's never-changing state
  Full perfection shall begin.

[1] Written in 1761. Published in Spence's *Anecdotes*, ed. Singer, 1820. Text of first edition.

JOHN DYER

(1700-1726-1758)

Grongar Hill[1]

SILENT Nymph, with curious eye!
Who, the purple ev'ning, lie
On the mountain's lonely van,
Beyond the noise of busy man,
Painting fair the form of things,
While the yellow linet sings;
Or the tuneful nightingale
Charms the forest with her tale;
Come with all thy various hues,
Come, and aid thy sister Muse;
Now while Phœbus riding high
Gives lustre to the land and sky!
Grongar Hill invites my song,
Draw the landskip bright and strong;
Grongar, in whose mossy cells
Sweetly-musing Quiet dwells;
Grongar, in whose silent shade,
For the modest Muses made,
So oft I have, the evening still,
At the fountain of a rill,
Sate upon a flow'ry bed,
With my hand beneath my head;
While stray'd my eyes o'er Towy's flood,
Over mead, and over wood,
From house to house, from hill to hill,
'Till Contemplation had her fill.
  About his chequer'd sides I wind,
And leave his brooks and meads behind,
And groves, and grottoes where I lay,
And vistoes shooting beams of day:
Wide and wider spreads the vale;
As circles on a smooth canal:
The mountains round, unhappy fate!
Sooner or later, of all height,
Withdraw their summits from the skies,
And lessen as the others rise:
Still the prospect wider spreads,
Adds a thousand woods and meads,

[1] Published in 1726. Text of *Poems*, 1761.

Still it widens, widens still,
And sinks the newly-risen hill.
  Now, I gain the mountain's brow,
What a landskip lies below!
No clouds, no vapours intervene,
But the gay, the open scene
Does the face of nature show,
In all the hues of heaven's bow!
And, swelling to embrace the light,
Spreads around beneath the sight.
  Old castles on the cliffs arise,
Proudly tow'ring in the skies!
Rushing from the woods, the spires
Seem from hence ascending fires!
Half his beams Apollo sheds
On the yellow mountain-heads!
Gilds the fleeces of the flocks:
And glitters on the broken rocks!
  Below me trees unnumber'd rise,
Beautiful in various dyes:
The gloomy pine, the poplar blue,
The yellow beech, the sable yew,
The slender fir, that taper grows,
The sturdy oak with broad-spread boughs.
And beyond the purple grove,
Haunt of Phillis, queen of love!
Gaudy as the op'ning dawn,
Lies a long and level lawn
On which a dark hill, steep and high,
Holds and charms the wand'ring eye!
Deep are his feet in Towy's flood,
His sides are cloath'd with waving wood,
And ancient towers crown his brow,
That cast an aweful look below;
Whose ragged walls the ivy creeps,
And with her arms from falling keeps;
So both a safety from the wind
On mutual dependence find.
  'Tis now the raven's bleak abode;
'Tis now th' apartment of the toad;
And there the fox securely feeds;
And there the pois'nous adder breeds
Conceal'd in ruins, moss and weeds;
While, ever and anon, there falls
Huge heaps of hoary moulder'd walls.
Yet time has seen, that lifts the low,
And level lays the lofty brow,

Has seen this broken pile compleat,
Big with the vanity of state;
But transient is the smile of fate!
A little rule, a little sway,
A sun beam in a winter's day,
Is all the proud and mighty have
Between the cradle and the grave.
  And see the rivers how they run,
Thro' woods and meads, in shade and sun,
Sometimes swift, sometimes slow,
Wave succeeding wave, they go
A various journey to the deep,
Like human life to endless sleep!
Thus is nature's vesture wrought,
To instruct our wand'ring thought;
Thus she dresses green and gay,
To disperse our cares away.
  Ever charming, ever new,
When will the landskip tire the view!
The fountain's fall, the river's flow,
The woody vallies, warm and low;
The windy summit, wild and high,
Roughly rushing on the sky!
The pleasant seat, the ruin'd tow'r,
The naked rock, the shady bow'r;
The town and village, dome and farm,
Each give each a double charm,
As pearls upon an Æthiop's arm.
  See on the mountain's southern side,
Where the prospect opens wide,
Where the evening gilds the tide;
How close and small the hedges lie!
What streaks of meadows cross the eye!
A step methinks may pass the stream,
So little distant dangers seem;
So we mistake the future's face,
Ey'd thro' hope's deluding glass;
As yon summits soft and fair
Clad in colours of the air,
Which to those who journey near,
Barren, brown, and rough appear;
Still we tread the same coarse way,
The present's still a cloudy day.
  O may I with myself agree,
And never covet what I see:
Content me with an humble shade,
My passions tam'd, my wishes laid;
For while our wishes wildly roll,

We banish quiet from the soul:
'Tis thus the busy beat the air;
And misers gather wealth and care.
  Now, ev'n now, my joys run high,
As on the mountain-turf I lie;
While the wanton Zephyr sings,
And in the vale perfumes his wings;
While the waters murmur deep;
While the shepherd charms his sheep;
While the birds unbounded fly,
And with musick fill the sky,
Now, ev'n now, my joys run high.
  Be full, ye courts, be great who will;
Search for Peace with all your skill:
Open wide the lofty door,
Seek her on the marble floor,
In vain you search, she is not there;
In vain ye search the domes of care!
Grass and flowers Quiet treads,
On the meads, and mountain-heads,
Along with Pleasure, close ally'd,
Ever by each other's side:
And often, by the murm'ring rill,
Hears the thrush, while all is still,
Within the groves of Grongar Hill.

ROBERT BLAIR

(1699-1728-1746)

From The Grave[1]

WHILE some affect the sun, and some the shade,
Some flee the city, some the hermitage;
Their aims as various, as the roads they take
In journeying thro' life;—the task be mine,
To paint the gloomy horrors of the TOMB;
Th' appointed place of rendezvous, where all
These travellers meet.—Thy succours I implore,
Eternal King! whose potent arm sustains
The keys of hell and death.—The GRAVE, dread thing!
Men shiver when thou'rt named: Nature appall'd,

[1] Published in 1743. Text of the edition of 1786.

Shakes off her wonted firmness.—Ah! how dark
Thy long extended realms, and rueful wastes!
Where nought but Silence reigns, and Night, dark Night,
Dark as was CHAOS, ere the infant sun
Was roll'd together, or had try'd his beams
Athwart the gloom profound.—The sickly taper,
By glimm'ring thro' thy low-brow'd misty vaults,
(Furr'd round with mouldy damps, and ropy slime,)
Lets fall a supernumerary horror,
And only serves to make thy night more irksome.
Well do I know thee by thy trusty YEW,
Cheerless, unsocial plant! that loves to dwell
'Midst sculls and coffins, epitaphs and worms:
Where light-heel'd ghosts, and visionary shades,
Beneath the wan, cold moon (as fame reports)
Embody'd thick, perform their mystic rounds.
No other merriment, dull tree! is thine.
  SEE yonder hallow'd Fane;—the pious work
Of names once fam'd, now dubious or forgot,
And bury'd 'midst the wreck of things which were;
There lie interr'd the more illustrious dead.
The wind is up:—hark! how it howls!—Methinks,
'Till now, I never heard a sound so dreary:
Doors creak, and windows clap, and night's foul bird,
Rook'd in the spire, screams loud; the gloomy aisles
Black-plaster'd, and hung round with shreds of 'scutcheons,
And tatter'd coats of arms, send back the sound,
Laden with heavier airs, from the low vaults,
The mansions of the dead.—Rous'd from their slumbers,
In grim array the grisly spectres rise,
Grin horrible, and, obstinately sullen,
Pass and repass, hush'd as the foot of Night.
Again the screech-owl shrieks—ungracious sound!
I'll hear no more—it makes one's blood run chill.
  QUITE round the pile, a row of reverend elms
(Coeval near with that), all ragged shew,
Long lash'd by the rude winds. Some rift half down
Their branchless trunks; others so thin at top,
That scarce two crows can lodge in the same tree.
Strange things, the neighbours say, have happen'd here;
Wild shrieks have issued from the hollow tombs;
Dead men have come again, and walk'd about;
And the great bell has toll'd unrung, untouch'd.
(Such tales their cheer at wake or gossipping,
When it draws near to witching time of night.)
  OFT in the lone Church-yard at night I've seen,

By glimpse of moonshine chequering thro' the trees,
The school-boy, with his satchel in his hand,
Whistling aloud to bear his courage up,
And lightly tripping o'er the long flat stones,
(With nettles skirted, and with moss o'ergrown,)
That tell in homely phrase who lie below.
Sudden he starts, and hears, or *thinks* he hears,
The sound of something purring at his heels;
Full fast he flies, and dares not look behind him,
'Till, out of breath, he overtakes his fellows,
Who gather round, and wonder at the tale
Of horrid APPARITION tall and ghastly,
That walks at dead of night, or takes his stand
O'er some new-open'd grave; and (strange to tell!)
Evanishes at crowing of the cock.

. . . .

HERE all the mighty TROUBLERS OF THE EARTH,
Who swam to sov'reign rule thro' seas of blood;
Th' oppressive, sturdy, man-destroying villains,
Who ravag'd kingdoms, and laid empires waste,
And, in a cruel wantonness of power,
Thinn'd states of half their people, and gave up
To want the rest; now, like a storm that's spent,
Lie hush'd, and meanly sneak behind the covert.
Vain thought! to hide thee from the general scorn,
That haunts and doggs them like an injured ghost
Implacable.—Here, too, the PETTY TYRANT,
Whose scant domains GEOGRAPHER ne'er notic'd,
And, well for neighbouring grounds, of arm as short,
Who fix'd his iron talons on the poor,
And grip'd them like some lordly beast of prey;
Deaf to the forceful cries of gnawing Hunger,
And piteous plaintive voice of Misery;
(As if a SLAVE was not a shred of nature,
Of the same common nature with his LORD;)
Now tame and humble, like a child that's whipp'd,
Shakes hands with dust, and calls the worm his kinsman;
Nor pleads his rank and birthright. Under ground,
PRECEDENCY's a jest; Vassal and Lord,
Grossly familiar, side by side consume.
WHEN self-esteem, or other's adulation,
Would cunningly persuade us we are something
Above the common level of our kind;
The *Grave* gainsays the smooth-complection'd flattery,
And with blunt truth acquaints us what we are.

HENRY FIELDING

(1707-1728-1754)

The Roast Beef of Old England[1]

WHEN mighty rost Beef was the *Englishman*'s Food,
It enobled our Hearts, and enriched our Blood;
Our Soldiers were brave, and our Courtiers were good.
Oh the Rost Beef of Old *England*,
And Old *England*'s Rost Beef!

Then, *Britons,* from all nice Dainties refrain,
Which effeminate *Italy*, *France,* and *Spain*;
And mighty Rost Beef shall command on the Main.
Oh the Rost Beef, &c.

Hunting Song[2]

THE dusky Night rides down the Sky,
And ushers in the Morn;
The Hounds all join in glorious Cry,
The Huntsman winds his Horn:
And a Hunting we will go.

The Wife around her Husband throws
Her Arms, and begs his Stay;
My Dear, it rains, and hails, and snows,
You will not hunt to-day.
But a Hunting we will go.

A brushing Fox in yonder Wood,
Secure to find we seek;
For why, I carry'd sound and good
A Cartload there last Week.
And a Hunting we will go.

Away he goes, he flies the Rout,
Their Steeds all spur and switch;

[1] Published in *Don Quixote in England,* 1733. Act. I. Text of first edition.
[2] Published in *Don Quixote in England,* 1733. Act II. Text of first edition.

Some are thrown in, and some thrown out,
And some thrown in the Ditch:
But a Hunting we will go.

At length his Strength to Faintness worn,
Poor *Reynard* ceases Flight;
Then hungry, homeward we return,
To feast away the Night:
Then a Drinking we will go.

A Letter to Sir Robert Walpole[1]

SIR,
WHILE at the helm of state you ride,
Our nation's envy and its pride;
While foreign courts with wonder gaze,
And justly all your counsels praise,
Which, in contempt of faction's force,
Steer, tho' oppos'd, a steady course,
Wou'd you not wonder, Sir, to view
Your bard a greater man than you?
And yet the sequel proves it true.
You know, Sir, certain ancient fellows
Philosophers, and others tell us,
That no alliance e'er between
Greatness and happiness is seen;
If so, may heaven still deny
To you, to be as great as I.
Besides, we're taught, it does behove us,
To think those better who're above us:
Another instance of my glory,
Who live above you twice two story,
And from my garret can look down,
As from an hill, on half the town.
Greatness by poets still is painted,
With many followers acquainted:
This too does in my favour speak,
Your levée is but twice a week,
From mine I can exclude but one day;
My door is quiet on a Sunday.
The distance too at which they bow,
Does my superior greatness shew.
Familiar you to admiration,

[1] Published in *Miscellanies*, Volume I, 1743. Text of Dodsley's *Collection of Poems*, Volume V, 1758.

May be approach'd by all the nation,
While I, like Great Mogul in Indo,
Am never seen but at a window.
  The family that dines the latest,
Is in our street esteem'd the greatest,
But greater him we surely call,
Who hardly deigns to dine at all.
  If with my greatness you're offended,
The fault is easily amended:
You have it, Sir, within your power
To take your humble servant lower.

GEORGE LYTTELTON, BARON LYTTELTON

(1709-1728-1773)

Ode. In Imitation of Pastor Fido
(*O primavera gioventu del anno.*)
Written Abroad, in 1729[1]

PARENT of blooming flowers and gay desires,
  Youth of the tender year, delightful spring,
At whose approach, inspir'd with equal fires,
  The amorous Nightingale and Poet sing.

Again dost thou return, but not with thee
  Return the smiling hours I once possest;
Blessings thou bring'st to others, but to me
  The sad remembrance that I once was blest.

Thy faded charms, which Winter snatch'd away,
  Renew'd in all their former lustre shine;
But ah! no more shall hapless I be gay,
  Or know the vernal joys that have been mine.

Though linnets sing, though flowers adorn the green,
  Though on their wings soft Zephyrs fragrance bear;
Harsh is the musick, joyless is the scene,
  The odour faint; for Delia is not there.

Chearless and cold I feel the genial sun,
  From thee while absent I in exile rove;

[1] Published in Dodsley's *Collection of Poems*, 1748. Text of *Works*, ed. Ayscough, second edition, 1775.

Thy lovely presence, fairest light, alone
Can warm my heart to gladness and to love.

Song. Written in the Year 1732[1]

WHEN Delia on the plain appears,
Aw'd by a thousand tender fears,
I would approach, but dare not move:
Tell me, my heart, if this be love?

Whene'er she speaks, my ravish'd ear
No other voice but hers can hear,
No other wit but hers approve:
Tell me, my heart, if this be love?

If she some other youth commend,
Though I was once his fondest friend,
His instant enemy I prove:
Tell me, my heart, if this be love?

When she is absent, I no more
Delight in all that pleas'd before,
The clearest spring, or shadiest grove:
Tell me, my heart, if this be love?

When, fond of power, of beauty vain,
Her nets she spread for every swain,
I strove to hate, but vainly strove:
Tell me, my heart, if this be love?

Written at Mr. Pope's House at Twickenham, which He Had Lent to Mrs. G——lle. In August, 1735[2]

Go, THAMES, and tell the busy town,
Not all its wealth or pride
Could tempt me from the charms that crown
Thy rural flowery side:

Thy flowery side, where Pope has plac'd
The Muses' green retreat,

[1] Published in *British Musical Miscellany*, Volume I, 1734. Text of *Works*, ed. Ayscough, second edition, 1775.

[2] Published in *Works*, ed. Ayscough, 1775. Text of second edition, 1775.

With every smile of nature grac'd,
  With every art compleat.

But now, sweet bard, thy heavenly song
  Enchants us here no more;
Their darling glory lost too long
  Thy once-lov'd shades deplore.

Yet still, for beauteous G——lle's sake,
  The Muses here remain;
G——lle, whose eyes have power to make
  A Pope of every swain.

ROBERT DODSLEY

(1703-1729-1764)

Song[1]

MAN's a poor deluded bubble,
  Wand'ring in a mist of lies,
Seeing false, or seeing double,
  Who wou'd trust to such weak eyes?
Yet presuming on his senses,
  On he goes most wond'rous wise:
Doubts of truth, believes pretences;
  Lost in error, lives and dies.

The Kings of Europe
A Jest[2]

WHY pray, of late, do Europe's kings
  No jester in their courts admit?
They're grown such stately solemn things.
  To bear a joke they think not fit.

But tho' each court a jester lacks,
  To laugh at monarchs to their face;
All mankind behind their backs
  Supply the honest jester's place.

[1] Published in *Trifles*, 1745. Text of first edition.
[2] Published in *Trifles*, 1745. Text of first edition.

PHILIP DODDRIDGE

(1702-1730-1751)

Hymn[1]

YE GOLDEN Lamps of Heav'n, farewel,
With all your feeble Light:
Farewel, thou ever-changing Moon,
Pale Empress of the Night.

And thou refulgent Orb of Day
In brighter Flames array'd,
My Soul, that springs beyond thy Sphere,
No more demands thine Aid.

Ye Stars are but the shining Dust
Of my divine Abode,
The Pavement of those heav'nly Courts,
Where I shall reign with GOD.

The Father of eternal Light
Shall there his Beams display;
Nor shall one Moment's Darkness mix
With that unvaried Day.

No more the Drops of piercing Grief
Shall swell into mine Eyes;
Nor the Meridian Sun decline
Amidst those brighter Skies.

There all the Millions of his Saints
Shall in one Song unite,
And Each the Bliss of all shall view
With infinite Delight.

[1] Published in *Hymns*, 1755. Text of first edition.

SAMUEL JOHNSON

(1709-1731-1784)

Prologue Spoken by Mr. Garrick at the Opening of the Theatre in Drury-Lane, 1747[1]

WHEN Learning's Triumph o'er her barb'rous Foes
First rear'd the Stage, immortal SHAKESPEAR rose;
Each Change of many-colour'd Life he drew,
Exhausted Worlds, and then imagin'd new:
Existence saw him spurn her bounded Reign,
And panting Time toil'd after him in vain:
His pow'rful Strokes presiding Truth impress'd,
And unresisted Passion storm'd the Breast.
  Then JOHNSON came, instructed from the School,
To please in Method, and invent by Rule;
His studious Patience, and laborious Art,
By regular Approach essay'd the Heart;
Cold Approbation gave the ling'ring Bays,
For those who durst not censure, scarce cou'd praise.
A Mortal born he met the general Doom,
But left, like *Egypt*'s Kings, a lasting Tomb.
  The Wits of *Charles* found easier Ways to Fame,
Nor wish'd for JOHNSON's Art, or SHAKESPEAR's Flame,
Themselves they studied, as they felt, they writ,
Intrigue was Plot, Obscenity was Wit.
Vice always found a sympathetick Friend;
They pleas'd their Age, and did not aim to mend.
Yet Bards like these aspir'd to lasting Praise,
And proudly hop'd to pimp in future Days.
Their Cause was gen'ral, their Supports were strong,
Their Slaves were willing, and their Reign was long;
Till Shame regain'd the Post that Sense betray'd,
And Virtue call'd Oblivion to her Aid.
  Then crush'd by Rules, and weaken'd as refin'd,
For Years the Pow'r of Tragedy declin'd;
From Bard, to Bard, the frigid Caution crept,
Till Declamation roar'd, while Passion slept.
Yet still did Virtue deign the Stage to tread,
Philosophy remain'd, though Nature fled.
But forc'd at length her antient Reign to quit,
She saw great *Faustus* lay the Ghost of Wit:

[1] Published in 1747. Text of first edition.

Exulting Folly hail'd the joyful Day,
And Pantomime, and Song, confirm'd her Sway.
But who the coming Changes can presage,
And mark the future Periods of the Stage?—
Perhaps if Skill could distant Times explore,
New *Behns*, new *Durfeys*, yet remain in Store.
Perhaps, where *Lear* has rav'd, and *Hamlet* dy'd,
On flying Cars new Sorcerers may ride.
Perhaps, for who can guess th' Effects of Chance?
Here *Hunt* may box, or *Mahomet* may dance.
Hard is his Lot, that here by Fortune plac'd,
Must watch the wild Vicissitudes of Taste;
With ev'ry Meteor of Caprice must play,
And chase the new-blown Bubbles of the Day.
Ah! let not Censure term our Fate our Choice,
The Stage but echoes back the publick Voice.
The Drama's Laws the Drama's Patrons give,
For we that live to please, must please to live.
Then prompt no more the Follies you decry,
As Tyrants doom their Tools of Guilt to die;
'Tis yours this Night to bid the Reign commence
Of rescu'd Nature, and reviving Sense;
To chase the Charms of Sound, the Pomp of Show,
For useful Mirth, and salutary Woe;
Bid scenic Virtue form the rising Age,
And Truth diffuse her Radiance from the Stage.

The Vanity of Human Wishes
The Tenth Satire of Juvenal, Imitated[1]

Let observation with extensive view,
Survey mankind, from China to Peru;
Remark each anxious toil, each eager strife,
And watch the busy scenes of crouded life;
Then say how hope and fear, desire and hate,
O'erspread with snares the clouded maze of fate,
Where wav'ring man, betray'd by vent'rous pride,
To tread the dreary paths without a guide;
As treach'rous phantoms in the mist delude,
Shuns fancied ills, or chases airy good.
How rarely reason guides the stubborn choice,
Rules the bold hand, or promps the suppliant voice,
How nations sink, by darling schemes oppress'd,

[1] Published January, 1749. Text of Dodsley's *Collection of Poems*, Volume IV, 1755.

When vengeance listens to the fool's request.
Fate wings with ev'ry wish th' afflictive dart,
Each gift of nature, and each grace of art,
With fatal heat impetuous courage glows,
With fatal sweetness elocution flows,
Impeachment stops the speaker's pow'rful breath,
And restless fire precipitates on death.
But scarce observ'd the knowing and the bold,
Fall in the gen'ral massacre of gold;
Wide-wasting pest! that rages unconfin'd,
And crouds with crimes the records of mankind,
For gold his sword the hireling ruffian draws,
For gold the hireling judge distorts the laws;
Wealth heap'd on wealth, nor truth nor safety buys,
The dangers gather as the treasures rise.
Let hist'ry tell where rival kings command,
And dubious title shakes the madded land,
When statutes glean the refuse of the sword,
How much more safe the vassal than the lord,
Low sculks the hind beneath the rage of pow'r,
And leaves the wealthy traytor in the Tow'r,
Untouch'd his cottage, and his slumbers sound,
Tho' confiscation's vulturs hover round.
The needy traveller, serene and gay,
Walks the wild heath, and sings his toil away.
Does envy seize thee? crush th' upbraiding joy,
Increase his riches and his peace destroy,
New fears in dire vicissitude invade,
The rustling brake alarms, and quiv'ring shade,
Nor light nor darkness bring his pain relief,
One shews the plunder, and one hides the thief.
Yet still one gen'ral cry the skies assails,
And gain and grandeur load the tainted gales;
Few know the toiling statesman's fear or care,
Th' insidious rival and the gaping heir.
Once more, Democritus, arise on earth,
With chearful wisdom and instructive mirth,
See motly life in modern trappings dress'd,
And feed with varied fools th' eternal jest:
Thou who couldst laugh where want enchain'd caprice,
Toil crush'd conceit, and man was of a piece;
Where wealth unlov'd without a mourner dy'd;
And scarce a sycophant was fed by pride;
Where ne'er was known the form of mock debate,
Or seen a new-made mayor's unwieldy state;
Where change of fav'rites made no change of laws,
And senates heard before they judg'd a cause;
How wouldst thou shake at Britain's modish tribe,

Dart the quick taunt, and edge the piercing gibe?
Attentive truth and nature to decry,
And pierce each scene with philosophic eye.
To thee were solemn toys or empty shew,
The robes of pleasure and the veils of woe:
All aid the farce, and all thy mirth maintain,
Whose joys are causeless, or whose griefs are vain.
  Such was the scorn that fill'd the sage's mind,
Renew'd at ev'ry glance on humankind;
How just that scorn ere yet thy voice declare,
Search every state, and canvass ev'ry pray'r.
  Unnumber'd suppliants croud Preferment's gate,
Athirst for wealth, and burning to be great;
Delusive Fortune hears th' incessant call,
They mount, they shine, evaporate, and fall.
On ev'ry stage the foes of peace attend,
Hate dogs their flight, and insult mocks their end.
Love ends with hope, the sinking statesman's door
Pours in the morning worshiper no more;
For growing names the weekly scribbler lies,
To growing wealth the dedicator flies,
From every room descends the painted face,
That hung the bright Palladium of the place,
And smoak'd in kitchens, or in auctions sold,
To better features yields the frame of gold;
For now no more we trace in ev'ry line
Heroic worth, benevolence divine:
The form distorted justifies the fall,
And detestation rids th' indignant wall.
  But will not Britain hear the last appeal,
Sign her foes doom, or guard her fav'rites zeal;
Through Freedom's sons no more remonstrance rings,
Degrading nobles and controuling kings;
Our supple tribes repress their patriot throats,
And ask no questions but the price of votes;
With weekly libels and septennial ale,
Their wish is full to riot and to rail.
  In full-blown dignity, see Wolsey stand,
Law in his voice, and fortune in his hand:
To him the church, the realm, their pow'rs consign,
Thro' him the rays of regal bounty shine,
Still to new heights his restless wishes tow'r,
Claim leads to claim, and pow'r advances pow'r;
Till conquest unresisted ceas'd to please,
And rights submitted, left him none to seize.
At length his sov'reign frowns—the train of state
Mark the keen glance, and watch the sign to hate.
Where-e'er he turns he meets a stranger's eye,

His suppliants scorn him, and his followers fly;
At once is lost the pride of aweful state,
The golden canopy, the glitt'ring plate,
The regal palace, the luxurious board,
The liv'ried army, and the menial lord.
With age, with cares, with maladies oppress'd,
He seeks the refuge of monastic rest.
Grief aids disease, remember'd folly stings,
And his last sighs reproach the faith of kings.
  Speak thou, whose thoughts at humble peace repine,
Shall Wolsey's wealth, with Wolsey's end be thine?
Or liv'st thou now, with safer pride content,
The wisest justice on the banks of Trent?
For why did Wolsey near the steeps of fate,
On weak foundations raise th' enormous weight?
Why but to sink beneath misfortune's blow,
With louder ruin to the gulphs below?
  What gave great Villiers to th' assassin's knife,
And fix'd disease on Harley's closing life?
What murder'd Wentworth, and what exil'd Hyde,
By kings protected, and to kings ally'd?
What but their wish indulg'd in courts to shine,
And pow'r too great to keep, or to resign?
  When first the college rolls receive his name,
The young enthusiast quits his ease for fame;
Through all his veins the fever of renown
Spreads from the strong contagion of the gown;
O'er Bodley's dome his future labours spread,
And Bacon's mansion trembles o'er his head.
Are these thy views? proceed, illustrious youth,
And virtue guard thee to the throne of Truth!
Yet should thy soul indulge the gen'rous heat,
Till captive Science yields her last retreat;
Should Reason guide thee with her brightest ray,
And pour on misty Doubt resistless day;
Should no false Kindness lure to loose delight,
Nor Praise relax, nor Difficulty fright;
Should tempting Novelty thy cell refrain,
And Sloth effuse her opiate fumes in vain;
Should Beauty blunt on fops her fatal dart,
Nor claim the triumph of a letter'd heart;
Should no Disease thy torpid veins invade,
Nor Melancholy's phantoms haunt thy shade;
Yet hope not life from grief or danger free,
Nor think the doom of man revers'd for thee:
Deign on the passing world to turn thine eyes,
And pause awhile from letters, to be wise;
There mark what ills the scholar's life assail,

Toil, envy, want, the patron, and the jail.
See nations slowly wise, and meanly just,
To buried merit raise the tardy bust.
If dreams yet flatter, once again attend,
Hear Lydiat's life, and Galileo's end.
  Nor deem, when learning her last prize bestows
The glitt'ring eminence exempt from foes;
See when the vulgar 'scape, despis'd or aw'd,
Rebellion's vengeful talons seize on Laud.
From meaner minds, tho' smaller fines content
The plunder'd palace or sequester'd rent;
Mark'd out by dangerous parts he meets the shock,
And fatal Learning leads him to the block:
Around his tomb let Art and Genius weep,
But hear his death, ye blockheads, hear and sleep.
  The festal blazes, the triumphal show,
The ravish'd standard, and the captive foe,
The senate's thanks, the gazette's pompous tale,
With force resistless o'er the brave prevail.
Such bribes the rapid Greek o'er Asia whirl'd,
For such the steady Romans shook the world;
For such in distant lands the Britons shine,
And stain with blood the Danube or the Rhine;
This pow'r has praise, that virtue scarce can warm,
Till fame supplies the universal charm.
Yet Reason frowns on War's unequal game,
Where wasted nations raise a single name,
And mortgag'd states their grandsires wreaths regret,
From age to age in everlasting debt;
Wreaths which at last the dear-bought right convey
To rust on medals, or on stones decay.
  On what foundation stands the warrior's pride,
How just his hopes let Swedish Charles decide;
A frame of adamant, a soul of fire,
No dangers fright him, and no labours tire;
O'er love, o'er fear extends his wide domain,
Unconquer'd lord of pleasure and of pain;
No joys to him pacific scepters yield,
War sounds the trump, he rushes to the field;
Behold surrounding kings their pow'r combine,
And one capitulate, and one resign;
Peace courts his hand, but spreads her charms in vain;
"Think nothing gain'd, he cries, till nought remain,
"On Moscow's walls till Gothic standards fly,
"And all be mine beneath the polar sky."
The march begins in military state,
And nations on his eye suspended wait;
Stern Famine guards the solitary coast,

And Winter barricades the realms of Frost;
He comes, not want and cold his course delay;—
Hide, blushing Glory, hide Pultowa's day:
The vanquish'd hero leaves his broken bands,
And shews his miseries in distant lands;
Condemn'd a needy supplicant to wait,
While ladies interpose, and slaves debate.
But did not Chance at length her error mend?
Did no subverted empire mark his end?
Did rival monarchs give the fatal wound?
Or hostile millions press him to the ground?
His fall was destin'd to a barren strand,
A petty fortress, and a dubious hand;
He left the name, at which the world grew pale,
To point a moral, or adorn a tale.
  All times their scenes of pompous woes afford,
From Persia's tyrant to Bavaria's lord.
In gay hostility, and barb'rous pride,
With half mankind embattled at his side,
Great Xerxes comes to seize the certain prey,
And starves exhausted regions in his way;
Attendant Flatt'ry counts his myriads o'er,
Till counted myriads sooth his pride no more;
Fresh praise is try'd till madness fires his mind,
The waves he lashes, and enchains the wind;
New pow'rs are claim'd, new pow'rs are still bestow'd,
Till rude resistance lops the spreading god;
The daring Greeks deride the martial show,
And heap their vallies with the gaudy foe;
Th' insulted sea with humbler thoughts he gains,
A single skiff to speed his flight remains;
Th' incumber'd oar scarce leaves the dreaded coast
Through purple billows and a floating host.
  The bold Bavarian, in a luckless hour,
Tries the dread summits of Cesarean pow'r,
With unexpected legions bursts away,
And sees defenceless realms receive his sway;
Short sway! fair Austria spreads her mournful charms,
The queen, the beauty, sets the world in arms;
From hill to hill the beacons rousing blaze
Spreads wide the hope of plunder and of praise;
The fierce Croatian, and the wild Hussar,
And all the sons of ravage croud the war;
The baffled prince in honour's flatt'ring bloom
Of hasty greatness finds the fatal doom,
His foes derision, and his subjects blame,
And steals to death from anguish and from shame.
  Enlarge my life with multitude of days,

In health, in sickness, thus the suppliant prays;
Hides from himself his state, and shuns to know,
That life protracted is protracted woe.
Time hovers o'er, impatient to destroy,
And shuts up all the passages of joy:
In vain their gifts the bounteous seasons pour,
The fruit autumnal, and the vernal flow'r,
With listless eyes the dotard views the store,
He views, and wonders that they please no more;
Now pall the tastless meats, and joyless wines,
And Luxury with sighs her slave resigns.
Approach, ye minstrels, try the soothing strain,
And yield the tuneful lenitives of pain:
No sounds alas would touch th' impervious ear,
Though dancing mountains witness'd Orpheus near;
Nor lute nor lyre his feeble pow'rs attend,
Nor sweeter musick of a virtuous friend,
But everlasting dictates croud his tongue,
Perversely grave, or positively wrong.
The still returning tale, and ling'ring jest,
Perplex the fawning niece and pamper'd guest,
While growing hopes scarce awe the gath'ring sneer,
And scarce a legacy can bribe to hear;
The watchful guests still hint the last offence,
The daughter's petulance, the son's expence,
Improve his heady rage with treach'rous skill,
And mould his passions till they make his will.
  Unnumber'd maladies his joints invade,
Lay siege to life and press the dire blockade;
But unextinguish'd Av'rice still remains,
And dreaded losses aggravate his pains;
He turns, with anxious heart and cripled hands,
His bonds of debt, and mortgages of lands;
Or views his coffers with suspicious eyes,
Unlocks his gold, and counts it till he dies.
  But grant, the virtues of a temp'rate prime
Bless with an age exempt from scorn or crime;
An age that melts in unperceiv'd decay,
And glides in modest Innocence away;
Whose peaceful day Benevolence endears,
Whose night congratulating Conscience cheers;
The gen'ral fav'rite as the gen'ral friend:
Such age there is, and who could wish its end?
  Yet ev'n on this her load Misfortune flings,
To press the weary minutes flagging wings:
New sorrow rises as the day returns,
A sister sickens, or a daughter mourns.
Now kindred Merit fills the sable bier,

Now lacerated Friendship claims a tear.
Year chases year, decay persues decay,
Still drops some joy from with'ring life away;
New forms arise, and diff'rent views engage,
Superfluous lags the vet'ran on the stage,
Till pitying Nature signs the last release,
And bids afflicted worth retire to peace.
  But few there are whom hours like these await,
Who set unclouded in the gulphs of fate.
From Lydia's monarch should the search descend,
By Solon caution'd to regard his end,
In life's last scene what prodigies surprise,
Fears of the brave, and follies of the wise?
From Marlb'rough's eyes the streams of dotage flow,
And Swift expires a driv'ler and a show.
  The teeming mother, anxious for her race,
Begs for each birth the fortune of a face:
Yet Vane could tell what ills from beauty spring;
And Sedley curs'd the form that pleas'd a king.
Ye nymphs of rosy lips and radiant eyes,
Whom Pleasure keeps too busy to be wise,
Whom Joys with soft varieties invite,
By day the frolick, and the dance by night,
Who frown with vanity, who smile with art,
And ask the latest fashion of the heart,
What care, what rules your heedless charms shall save,
Each nymph your rival, and each youth your slave?
Against your fame with fondness hate combines,
The rival batters, and the lover mines.
With distant voice neglected Virtue calls,
Less heard and less, the faint remonstrance falls;
Tir'd with contempt, she quits the slipp'ry reign,
And Pride and Prudence take her seat in vain.
In croud at once, where none the pass defend,
The harmless Freedom, and the private Friend.
The guardians yield, by force superior ply'd;
By Int'rest, Prudence; and by Flatt'ry, Pride.
Now Beauty falls betray'd, despis'd, distress'd,
And hissing Infamy proclaims the rest.
  Where then shall Hope and Fear their objects find?
Must dull Suspence corrupt the stagnant mind?
Must helpless man, in ignorance sedate,
Roll darkling down the torrent of his fate?
Must no dislike alarm, no wishes rise,
No cries attempt the mercies of the skies?
Enquirer, cease, petitions yet remain,
Which heav'n may hear, nor deem religion vain.
Still raise for good the supplicating voice,

But leave to heav'n the measure and the choice.
Safe in his pow'r, whose eyes discern afar
The secret ambush of a specious pray'r.
Implore his aid, in his decisions rest,
Secure whate'er he gives, he gives the best.
Yet when the sense of sacred presence fires,
And strong devotion to the skies aspires,
Pour forth thy fervours for a healthful mind,
Obedient passions, and a will resign'd;
For love, which scarce collective man can fill;
For patience sov'reign o'er transmuted ill;
For faith, that panting for a happier seat,
Counts death kind Nature's signal of retreat:
These goods for man the laws of heav'n ordain,
These goods he grants, who grants the pow'r to gain;
With these celestial wisdom calms the mind,
And makes the happiness she does not find.

On the Death of Mr. Robert Levet[1]

CONDEMN'D to hope's delusive mine,
  As on we toil from day to day,
By sudden blasts, or slow decline,
  Our social comforts drop away.

Well tried through many a varying year,
  See LEVET to the grave descend;
Officious, innocent, sincere,
  Of every friendless name the friend.

Yet still he fills affection's eye,
  Obscurely wise, and coarsely kind;
Nor, letter'd arrogance, deny
  Thy praise to merit unrefin'd.

When fainting nature call'd for aid,
  And hov'ring death prepar'd the blow,
His vig'rous remedy display'd
  The power of art without the show.

In misery's darkest caverns known,
  His useful care was ever nigh,
Where hopeless anguish pour'd his groan,
  And lonely want retir'd to die.

[1] Published in the *Gentleman's Magazine*, August, 1783. Text of first edition.

No summons mock'd by chill delay,
  No petty gain disdain'd by pride,
The modest wants of ev'ry day
  The toil of ev'ry day supplied.

His virtues walk'd their narrow round,
  Nor made a pause, nor left a void;
And sure th' Eternal Master found
  The single talent well employ'd.

The busy day, the peaceful night,
  Unfelt, uncounted, glided by;
His frame was firm, his powers were bright,
  Tho' now his eightieth year was nigh.

Then with no throbbing fiery pain,
  No cold gradations of decay,
Death broke at once the vital chain,
  And freed his soul the nearest way.

MATTHEW GREEN

(1696-1732?-1737)

From The Spleen
An Epistle to Mr. C—— J——[1]

THIS motly piece to you I send,
Who always were a faithful friend:
Who, if disputes should happen hence,
Can best explain the author's sense;
And, anxious for the publick weal,
Do, what I sing, so often feel.
  The want of method pray excuse,
Allowing for a vapour'd muse;
Nor to a narrow path confin'd,
Hedge in by rules a roving mind.
  The child is genuine; you can trace
Throughout, the sire's transmitted face.
Nothing is stol'n: my muse, tho' mean,
Draws from the spring she finds within;

[1] Published in 1737. Text of Dodsley's *Collection of Poems*, Volume I, fourth edition, 1755.

Nor vainly buys what Gildon sells,
Poetick buckets for dry wells.
School-helps I want, to climb on high,
Where all the antient treasures lie,
And there unseen commit a theft
On wealth, in Greek exchequers left.
Then where? from whom? what can I steal,
Who only with the moderns deal?
This were attempting to put on
Raiment from naked bodies won:
They safely sing before a thief,
They cannot give who want relief;
Some few excepted, names well known,
And justly laurel'd with renown,
Whose stamp of genius marks their ware,
And theft detects: of theft beware;
From Moore so lash'd, example fit,
Shun petty larcency in wit.
First know, my friend, I do not mean
To write a treatise on the Spleen;
Nor to prescribe, when nerves convulse;
Nor mend th' alarum watch, your pulse:
If I am right, your question lay,
What course I take to drive away
The day-mare Spleen, by whose false pleas
Men prove mere suicides in ease;
And how I do myself demean
In stormy world to live serene.
When by it's magick lantern Spleen
With frightful figures spread life's scene,
And threat'ning prospects urg'd my fears,
A stranger to the luck of heirs;
Reason, some quiet to restore,
Shew'd part was substance, shadow more;
With Spleen's dead weight tho' heavy grown,
In life's rough tide I sunk not down,
But swam, till Fortune threw a rope,
Buoyant on bladders fill'd with hope.
I always choose the plainest food
To mend viscidity of blood.
Hail! water-gruel, healing power,
Of easy access to the poor;
Thy help love's confessors implore,
And doctors secretly adore:
To thee I fly, by thee dilute,
Thro' veins my blood doth quicker shoot,
And by swift current throws off clean
Prolifick particles of Spleen.

I never sick by drinking grow,
Nor keep my self a cup too low;
And seldom Cloe's lodgings haunt,
Thrifty of spirits, which I want.
Hunting I reckon very good
To brace the nerves, and stir the blood;
But after no field-honours itch,
Atchiev'd by leaping hedge and ditch.
While Spleen lies soft relax'd in bed,
Or o'er coal fires inclines the head,
Hygeia's sons with hound and horn,
And jovial cry awake the morn:
These see her from her dusky plight,
Smear'd by th' embraces of the night,
With roral wash redeem her face,
And prove herself of Titan's race,
And, mounting in loose robes the skies,
Shed light and fragrance as she flies.
Then horse and hound fierce joy display,
Exulting at the Hark-away,
And in pursuit o'er tainted ground
From lungs robust field-notes resound.
Then, as St. George the dragon slew,
Spleen pierc'd, trod down, and dying view,
While all the spirits are on wing,
And woods, and hills, and vallies ring.
To cure the mind's wrong biass, Spleen;
Some recommend the bowling-green;
Some, hilly walks; all, exercise;
Fling but a stone, the giant dies;
Laugh, and be well. Monkeys have been
Extreme good doctors for the spleen;
And kitten, if the humour hit,
Has harlequin'd away the fit.
Since mirth is good in this behalf,
At some partic'lars let us laugh.
Witlings, brisk fools curs'd with half sense,
That stimulates their impotence,
Who buz in rhime, and, like blind flies,
Err with their wings for want of eyes,
Poor authors worshiping a calf,
Deep tragedies that make us laugh,
A strict dissenter saying grace,
A lect'rer preaching for a place,
Folks, things prophetick to dispense,
Making the past the future tense,
The popish dubbing of a priest,
Fine epitaphs on knaves deceas'd,

Green-apron'd Pythonissa's rage,
Great Æsculapius on his stage,
A miser starving to be rich,
The prior of Newgate's dying speech,
A jointur'd widow's ritual state,
Two Jews disputing tête à tête,
New almanacks compos'd by seers,
Experiments on felons ears,
Disdainful prudes, who ceaseless ply
The superb muscle of the eye,
A coquet's April-weather face,
A Queenb'rough mayor behind his mace,
And fops in military shew,
Are sov'reign for the case in view.
  If Spleen-fogs rise at close of day,
I clear my ev'ning with a play,
Or to some concert take my way.
The company, the shine of lights,
The scenes of humour, musick's flights,
Adjust and set the soul to rights.
  Life's moving pictures, well-wrought plays,
To other's griefs attention raise:
Here, while the tragick fictions glow,
We borrow joy by pitying woe;
There gaily comick scenes delight,
And hold true mirrors to our sight.
Virtue, in charming dress array'd,
Calling the passions to her aid,
When moral scenes just actions join,
Takes shape, and shews her face divine.
  Musick has charms, we all may find,
Ingratiate deeply with the mind.
When art does sound's high pow'r advance,
To musick's pipe the passions dance;
Motions unwill'd its pow'rs have shewn,
Tarantulated by a tune.
Many have held the soul to be
Nearly ally'd to harmony.
Her have I known indulging grief,
And shunning company's relief,
Unveil her face, and looking round,
Own, by neglecting sorrow's wound,
The consanguinity of sound.
  In rainy days keep double guard,
Or Spleen will surely be too hard,
Which, like those fish by sailors met,
Fly highest, while their wings are wet.
In such dull weather, so unfit

To enterprize a work of wit,
When clouds one yard of azure sky,
That's fit for simile, deny,
I dress my face with studious looks,
And shorten tedious hours with books.
But if dull fogs invade the head,
That mem'ry minds not what is read,
I sit in window dark as ark,
And on the drowning world remark:
Or to some coffee-house I stray
For news, the mana of a day,
And from the hipp'd discourses gather,
That politicks go by the weather:
Then seek good-humour'd tavern chums,
And play at cards, but for small sums;
Or with the merry fellows quaff,
And laugh aloud with them that laugh;
Or drink a joco-serious cup
With souls who've took their freedom up,
And let my mind, beguil'd by talk,
In Epicurus' garden walk,
Who thought it heav'n to be serene;
Pain, hell; and purgatory, Spleen.
  Sometimes I dress, with women sit,
And chat away the gloomy fit,
Quit the stiff garb of serious sense,
And wear a gay impertinence,
Nor think, nor speak with any pains,
But lay on fancy's neck the reins;
Talk of unusual swell of waist
In maid of honour loosely lac'd,
And beauty borr'wing Spanish red,
And loving pair with sep'rate bed,
And jewels pawn'd for loss of game,
And then redeem'd by loss of fame;
Of Kitty (aunt left in the lurch
By grave pretence to go to church)
Perceiv'd in hack with lover fine,
Like Will and Mary on the coin:
And thus in modish manner we
In aid of sugar sweeten tea.
  Permit, ye fair, your idol form
Which e'en the coldest heart can warm,
May with its beauties grace my line,
While I bow down before its shrine,
And your throng'd altars with my lays
Perfume, and get by giving praise.
With speech so sweet, so sweet a mien

You excommunicate the spleen,
Which, fiend-like, flies the magick ring
You form with sound, when pleas'd to sing.
Whate'er you say, howe'er you move,
We look, we listen, and approve.
Your touch, which gives to feeling bliss,
Our nerves officious throng to kiss;
By Celia's pat on their report
The grave-air'd soul, inclin'd to sport,
Renounces wisdom's sullen pomp,
And loves the floral game, to romp.
But who can view the pointed rays,
That from black eyes scintillant blaze?
Love on his throne of glory seems
Encompass'd with Satellite beams.
But when blue eyes, more softly bright,
Diffuse benignly humid light,
We gaze, and see the smiling loves,
And Cytherea's gentle doves,
And raptur'd fix in such a face,
Love's mercy-seat, and throne of grace.
Shine but on age, you melt its snow,
Again fires long-extinguish'd glow,
And, charm'd by witchery of eyes,
Blood long congealed liquifies,
True miracle, and fairly done
By heads, which are ador'd while on.
  But oh, what pity 'tis to find
Such beauties both of form and mind,
By modern breeding much debas'd,
In half the female world at least!
Hence I with care such lott'ries shun,
Where, a prize miss'd, I'm quite undone;
And han't by vent'ring on a wife,
Yet run the greatest risk in life.
  Mothers, and guardian aunts, forbear
Your impious pains to form the fair,
Not lay out so much cost and art,
But to deflow'r the virgin heart;
Of ev'ry folly-fost'ring bed
By quick'ning heat of custom bred.
Rather than by your culture spoil'd,
Desist, and give us nature wild,
Delighted with a hoyden soul,
Which truth and innocence controul.
Coquets, leave off affected arts,
Gay fowlers at a flock of hearts;
Woodcocks to shun your snares have skill,

You shew so plain, you strive to kill.
In love the artless catch the game,
And they scarce miss, who never aim.
  The world's great Author did create
The sex to fit the nuptial state,
And meant a blessing in a wife
To solace the fatigues of life;
And old inspired times display,
How wives could love, and yet obey.
Then truth, and patience of controul,
And housewife-arts adorn'd the soul;
And charms, the gift of nature, shone;
And jealousy, a thing unknown:
Veils were the only masks they wore,
Novels (receipts to make a whore)
Nor ombre, nor quadrille they knew,
Nor Pam's puissance felt at loo.
Wise men did not, to be thought gay,
Then compliment their pow'r away:
But lest, by frail desires misled,
The girls forbidden paths should tread,
Of ign'rance rais'd the safe high wall,
But we haw-haws, that shew them all;
Thus we at once solicit sense,
And charge them not to break the fence.
  Now, if untir'd, consider friend,
What I avoid to gain my end.
  I never am at Meeting seen,
Meeting, that region of the Spleen;
The broken heart, the busy fiend,
The inward call, on Spleen depend.
  Law, licens'd breaking of the peace,
To which vacation is disease,
A gypsy diction scarce known well
By th' magi, who law-fortunes tell,
I shun, nor let it breed within
Anxiety, and that the Spleen;
Law, grown a forest, where perplex
The mazes, and the brambles vex,
Where its twelve verd'rers every day
Are changing still the publick way;
Yet if we miss our path and err,
We grievous penalties incur,
And wand'rers tire, and tear their skin,
And then get out where they went in.
  I never game, and rarely bet,
Am loth to lend, or run in debt.
No compter-writs me agitate,

Who moralizing pass the gate,
And there mine eyes on spendthrifts turn,
Who vainly o'er their bondage mourn.
Wisdom, before beneath their care,
Pays her upbraiding visits there,
And forces folly thro' the grate
Her panegyrick to repeat.
This view, profusely when inclin'd,
Enters a caveat in the mind:
Experience join'd with common sense,
To mortals is a providence.
  Passion, as frequently is seen,
Subsiding settles into Spleen.
Hence, as the plague of happy life,
I run away from party-strife.
A prince's cause, a church's claim,
I've known to raise a mighty flame,
And priest, as stoker, very free
To throw in peace and charity.
  That tribe, who practicals decree
Small-beer the deadliest heresy,
Who, fond of pedigree, derive
From the most noted whore alive,
Who own wine's old prophetick aid,
And love the mitre Bacchus made,
Forbid the faithful to depend
On half-pint drinkers for a friend,
And in whose gay red-letter'd face
We read good-living more than grace:
Nor they so pure, and so precise,
Immac'late as their white of eyes,
Who for the spirit hug the Spleen,
Phylacter'd throughout all their mein,
Who their ill-tasted home-brew'd pray'r
To the state's mellow forms prefer,
Who doctrines, as infectious, fear,
Which are not steep'd in vinegar,
And samples of heart-chested grace
Expose to shew-glass of the face,
Did never me as yet provoke,
Either to honour band and cloak,
Or deck my hat with leaves of oak.
  I rail not with mock-patriot grace
At folks, because they are in place,
Nor, hir'd to praise with stallion pen,
Serve the ear-lechery of men;
And to avoid religious jars,
The laws are my expositors,

Which in my doubting mind create
Conformity to church and state.
I go, pursuant to my plan,
To Mecca with the caravan,
And think it right in common sense
Both for diversion and defence.
  Reforming schemes are none of mine,
To mend the world's a vast design,
Like theirs, who tug in little boat
To pull to them the ship afloat,
While, to defeat their labour'd end,
At once both wind and stream contend:
Success herein is seldom seen,
And zeal when baffled, turns to Spleen.
  Happy the man, who, innocent,
Grives not at ills he can't prevent;
His skiff does with the current glide,
Not puffing pull'd against the tide;
He, paddling by the scuffling crowd,
Sees unconcern'd life's wager row'd,
And when he can't prevent foul play,
Enjoys the folly of the fray.

* * *

  Contentment, parent of delight,
So much a stranger to our sight,
Say, goddess, in what happy place
Mortals behold thy blooming face;
Thy gracious auspices impart,
And for thy temple chuse my heart.
They, whom thou deignest to inspire,
Thy science learn, to bound desire;
By happy alchymy of mind
They turn to pleasure all they find;
They both disdain in outward mien
The grave and solemn garb of Spleen,
And meretricious arts of dress
To feign a joy, and hide distress;
Unmov'd when the rude tempest blows,
Without an opiate they repose;
And cover'd by your shield, defy
The whizzing shafts, that round them fly;
Nor, meddling with the gods' affairs,
Concern themselves with distant cares;
But place their bliss in mental rest,
And feast upon the good possess'd.
  Forc'd by soft violence of pray'r,
The blythsome goddess sooths my care,
I feel the deity inspire,

And thus she models my desire.
Two hundred pounds half-yearly paid,
Annuity securely made,
A farm some twenty miles from town,
Small, tight, salubrious, and my own;
Two maids, that never saw the town,
A serving-man not quite a clown,
A boy to help to tread the mow,
And drive, while t'other holds the plough;
A chief of temper form'd to please,
Fit to converse, and keep the keys;
And better to preserve the peace,
Commission'd by the name of niece:
With understandings of a size
To think their master very wise.
May heav'n (it's all I wish for) send
One genial room to treat a friend,
Where decent cup-board, little plate,
Display benevolence, not state.
And may my humble dwelling stand
Upon some chosen spot of land;
A pond before full to the brim,
Where cows may cool, and geese may swim,
Behind, a green like velvet neat,
Soft to the eye, and to the feet,
Where od'rous plants in evening fair
Breathe all around ambrosial air,
From Eurus, foe to kitchen-ground,
Fenc'd by a slope with bushes crown'd,
Fit dwelling for the feather'd throng,
Who pay their quit-rents with a song,
With op'ning views of hill and dale,
Which sense and fancy too regale,
Where the half-cirque, which vision bounds,
Like amphitheatre surrounds:
And woods impervious to the breeze,
Thick phalanx of embodied trees,
From hills thro' plains in dusk array
Extended far repel the day.
Here stillness, height, and solemn shade
Invite, and contemplation aid:
Here nymphs from hollow oaks relate
The dark decrees and will of fate,
And dreams beneath the spreading beech
Inspire, and docile fancy teach,
While soft as breezy breath of wind,
Impulses rustle thro' the mind:
Here Dryads, scorning Phœbus' ray,

While Pan melodious pipes away,
In measur'd motions frisk about,
'Till old Silenus puts them out.
There see the clover, pea, and bean,
Vie in variety of green,
Fresh pastures speckled o'er with sheep,
Brown fields their fallow sabbaths keep,
Plump Ceres golden tresses wear,
And poppy-top-knots deck her hair,
And silver streams through meadows stray.
And Naiads on the margin play,
And lesser nymphs on side of hills
From play-thing urns pour down the rills.
  Thus shelter'd, free from care and strife,
May I enjoy a calm thro' life;
See faction, safe in low degree,
As men at land see storms at sea,
And laugh at miserable elves,
Not kind, so much as to themselves,
Curs'd with such souls of base alloy,
As can possess, but not enjoy,
Debar'd the pleasure to impart
By av'rice, sphincter of the heart,
Who wealth hard earn'd by guilty cares,
Bequeath untouch'd to thankless heirs.
May I, with look ungloom'd by guile,
And wearing virtue's liv'ry-smile,
Prone the distressed to relieve,
And little trespasses forgive,
With income not in fortune's pow'r,
And skill to make a busy hour,
With trips to town life to amuse,
To purchase books, and hear the news,
To see old friends, brush off the clown,
And quicken taste at coming down,
Unhurt by sickness' blasting rage,
And slowly mellowing in age,
When fate extends its gath'ring gripe,
Fall off like fruit grown fully ripe,
Quit a worn being without pain,
Perhaps to blossom soon again.
  But now more serious see me grow,
And what I think, my Memmius, know.
  Th' enthusiast's hopes, and raptures wild
Have never yet my reason foil'd.
His springy soul dilates like air,
When free from weight of ambient care,
And, hush'd in meditations deep,

Slides into dreams, as when asleep.
Then, fond of new discov'ries grown,
Proves a Columbus of her own,
Disdains the narrow bounds of place,
And thro' the wilds of endless space,
Born up on metaphysick wings,
Chases light forms, and shadowy things,
And in the vague excursion caught,
Brings home some rare exotick thought.
The melancholy man such dreams,
As brightest evidence, esteems;
Fain would he see some distant scene
Suggested by his restless Spleen,
And Fancy's telescope applies
With tinctur'd glass to cheat his eyes.
Such thoughts, as love the gloom of night,
I close examine by the light;
For who tho' brib'd by gain to lie,
Dare sun-beam written truths deny,
And execute plain common sense
On faith's mere hearsay evidence?
  That superstition mayn't create,
And club its ills with those of fate,
I many a notion take to task,
Made dreadful by its visor-mask:
Thus scruple, spasm of the mind,
Is cur'd, and certainty I find,
Since optick reason shews me plain,
I dreaded spectres of the brain,
And legendary fears are gone,
Tho' in tenacious childhood sown.
Thus in opinions I commence
Freeholder in the proper sense,
And neither suit nor service do,
Nor homage to pretenders shew,
Who boast themselves by spurious roll,
Lords of the manor of the soul;
Preferring sense, from chin that's bare,
To nonsense thron'd in whisker'd hair.
  To thee, Creator uncreate,
O Entium Ens! divinely great!—
Hold, muse, nor melting pinions try,
Nor near the blazing glory fly,
Nor straining break thy feeble bow,
Unfeather'd arrows far to throw:
Thro' fields unknown nor madly stray,
Where no ideas mark the way,
With tender eyes, and colours faint,

And trembling hands forbear to paint.
Who features veil'd by light can hit?
Where can, what has no outline, sit?
My soul, the vain attempt forego,
Thyself, the fitter subject, know.
He wisely shuns the bold extreme,
Who soon lays by th' unequal theme,
Nor runs, with wisdom's Sirens caught,
On quicksands swall'wing shipwreck'd thought;
But, conscious of his distance, gives
Mute praise, and humble negatives.
In one, no object of our sight,
Immutable and infinite,
Who can't be cruel, or unjust,
Calm and resign'd, I fix my trust;
To him my past and present state
I owe, and must my future fate.
A stranger into life I'm come,
Dying may be our going home,
Transported here by angry fate,
The convicts of a prior state.
Hence I no anxious thoughts bestow
On matters, I can never know;
Thro' life's foul ways, like vagrant pass'd,
He'll grant a settlement at last,
And with sweet ease the wearied crown,
By leave to lay his being down.
If doom'd to dance th' eternal round
Of life no sooner lost but found,
And dissolution soon to come,
Like spunge, wipes out life's present sum,
But can't our state of pow'r bereave
An endless series to receive;
Then, if hard dealt with here by fate
We ballance in another state,
And consciousness must go along,
And sign th' acquittance for the wrong.
He for his creatures must decree
More happiness than misery,
Or be supposed to create,
Curious to try, what 'tis to hate,
And do an act, which rage infers,
'Cause lameness halts, or blindness errs.
  Thus, thus I steer my bark, and sail
On even keel with gentle gale,
At helm I make my reason sit,
My crew of passions all submit.
If dark and blustring prove some nights,

Philosophy puts forth her lights,
Experience holds the cautious glass,
To shun the breakers, as I pass,
And frequent throws the wary lead,
To see what dangers may be hid:
And once in seven years I'm seen,
At Bath, or Tunbridge to careen;
Tho' pleas'd to see the dolphins play,
I mind my compass and my way,
With store sufficient for relief,
And wisely still prepar'd to reef,
Nor wanting the dispersive bowl
Of cloudy weather in the soul,
I make (may heav'n propitious send
Such wind and weather to the end)
Neither becalm'd, nor over-blown,
Life's voyage to the world unknown.

JOHN WESLEY

(1703-1733-1791)

Hymn[1]

THOU hidden love of God, whose height,
  Whose depth unfathom'd no man knows,
I see from far thy beauteous light,
  Inly I sigh for thy repose;
My heart is pain'd, nor can it be
At rest, till it finds rest in thee.

Thy secret voice invites me still,
  The sweetness of thy yoke to prove:
And fain I would: but tho' my will
  Seem fix'd, yet wide my passions rove;
Yet hindrances strew all the way;
I aim at Thee, yet from Thee stray.

'Tis mercy all, that thou hast brought
  My mind to seek her peace in thee;
Yet while I seek, but find thee not,

[1] Published in *Psalms and Hymns*, 1738. Text of *The Oxford Book of Eighteenth Century Verse*.

No peace my wand'ring soul shall see;
O when shall all my wand'rings end,
And all my steps to thee-ward tend!

Is there a thing beneath the sun
That strives with thee my heart to share?
Ah! tear it thence, and reign alone,
The Lord of ev'ry motion there;
Then shall my heart from earth be free,
When it hath found repose in thee.

O hide this self from me, that I
No more, but Christ in me may live;
My vile affections crucify,
Nor let one darling lust survive;
In all things nothing may I see,
Nothing desire or seek but thee.

O Love, thy sov'reign aid impart,
To save me from low-thoughted care:
Chase this self-will thro' all my heart,
Thro' all its latent mazes there:
Make me thy duteous child, that I
Ceaseless may Abba, Father, cry!

Ah no! ne'er will I backward turn:
Thine wholly, thine alone I am!
Thrice happy he who views with scorn
Earth's toys, for thee his constant flame;
O help that I may never move
From the blest footsteps of thy love!

Each moment draw from earth away
My heart that lowly waits thy call:
Speak to my inmost soul, and say,
I am thy love, thy God, thy all!
To feel thy power, to hear thy voice,
To taste thy love, be all my choice.

PHILIP DORMER STANHOPE, EARL OF CHESTERFIELD

(1694-1733-1773)

Verses Written in a Lady's Sherlock "Upon Death"[1]

MISTAKEN fair, lay *Sherlock* by,
His doctrine is deceiving;
For, whilst he teaches us to die,
He cheats us of our living.

To die's a lesson we shall know
Too soon, without a master;
Then let us only study now
How we may live the faster.

To live's to love; to bless, be bless'd
With mutual inclination;
Share then my ardour in your breast,
And kindly meet my passion.

But if thus bless'd I may not live,
And pity you deny,
To me, at least, your *Sherlock* give,
'Tis I must learn to die.

Advice to a Lady in Autumn[2]

ASSES milk, half a pint, take at seven, or before;
Then sleep for an hour or two, and no more.
At nine stretch your arms, and oh! think when alone,
There's no pleasure in bed.—MARY, bring me my gown:
Slip on that ere you rise; let your caution be such,
Keep all cold from your breast, there's already too much.
Your pinners set right, your twitcher ty'd on,
Your prayers at an end, and your breakfast quite done;

[1] Published in *The Gentleman's Magazine*, May, 1733. Text of first edition.
[2] Published in Dodsley's *Collection of Poems*, 1748. Text of fourth edition, 1755, Volume I.

Retire to some author, improving and gay,
And with sense like your own, set your mind for the day.
At twelve you may walk, for at this time o' the year,
The sun, like your wit, is as mild as 'tis clear:
But mark in the meadows the ruin of time;
Take the hint, and let life be improv'd in its prime.
Return not in haste, nor of dressing take heed;
For beauty like yours, no assistance can need.
With an appetite, thus, down to dinner you sit,
Where the chief of the feast is the flow of your wit:
Let this be indulg'd, and let laughter go round;
As it pleases your mind, to your health 'twill redound.
After dinner two glasses at least, I approve;
Name the first to the king, and the last to your love:
Thus cheerful with wisdom, with innocence gay,
And calm with your joys gently glide thro' the day.
The dews of the evening most carefully shun;
Those tears of the sky for the loss of the sun.
Then in chat, or at play, with a dance, or a song,
Let the night, like the day, pass with pleasure along.
All cares, but of love, banish far from your mind;
And those you may end, when you please to be kind.

ANONYMOUS

The Vicar of Bray[1]

IN GOOD King *Charles*'s golden days,
  When Loyalty no harm meant;
A Furious High-Church Man I was,
  And so I gain'd Preferment.
Unto my Flock I daily Preach'd,
  Kings are by God appointed,
And Damn'd are those who dare resist,
  Or touch the Lord's Anointed.
    And this is Law, I will maintain
      Unto my Dying Day, Sir,
    That whatsoever King shall Reign,
      I will be Vicar of *Bray*, Sir!

When Royal *James* possest the Crown,
  And Popery grew in fashion;

[1] Published in *The British Musical Miscellany*, Volume I, 1734. Text of first edition. See Preface.

The Penal Law I houted down,
  And read the Declaration:
The Church of *Rome*, I found would fit
  Full well my Constitution,
And I had been a Jesuit,
  But for the Revolution.
    And this is Law, &c.

When *William* our Deliverer came,
  To heal the Nation's Grievance,
I turned the Cat in Pan again,
  And swore to him Allegiance:
Old Principles I did revoke,
  Set Conscience at a distance,
Passive Obedience is a Joke,
  A Jest is Non-resistance.
    And this is Law, &c.

When glorious *Ann* became our Queen,
  The Church of *England*'s Glory,
Another face of things was seen,
  And I became a Tory:
Occasional Conformists base,
  I Damn'd, and Moderation,
And thought the Church in danger was,
  From such Prevarication.
    And this is Law, &c.

When *George* in Pudding time came o'er,
  And Moderate Men looked big, Sir,
My Principles I chang'd once more,
  And so became a Whig, Sir:
And thus Preferment I procur'd,
  From our Faith's Great Defender,
And almost every day abjur'd
  The Pope, and the Pretender.
    And this is Law, &c.

The Illustrious House of *Hannover*,
  And Protestant Succession,
To these I lustily will swear,
  Whilst they can keep possession:
For in my Faith, and Loyalty,
  I never once will faulter,
But *George*, my Lawful King shall be,
  Except the Times shou'd alter.
    And this is Law, &c.

William Shenstone

(1714-1737-1763)

The School-Mistress. In Imitation of Spenser[1]

Auditæ voces, vagitus & ingens,
Infantumque animæ flentes in limine primo. Virg.

ADVERTISEMENT

What particulars in Spenser were imagined most proper for the author's imitation on this occasion, *are his* language, *his* simplicity, *his manner of* description, *and a peculiar* tenderness *of* sentiment *remarkable throughout his works.*

Ah me! full sorely is my heart forlorn,
To think how modest worth neglected lies;
While partial fame doth with her blasts adorn
Such deeds alone, as pride and pomp disguise;
Deeds of ill sort, and mischievous emprize!
Lend me thy clarion, goddess! let me try
To sound the praise of merit, ere it dies;
Such as I oft have chaunced to espy,
Lost in the dreary shades of dull obscurity.

In ev'ry village mark'd with little spire,
Embow'r'd in trees, and hardly known to fame,
There dwells, in lowly shed, and mean attire,
A matron old, whom we school-mistress name;
Who boasts unruly brats with birch to tame;
They grieven sore, in piteous durance pent,
Aw'd by the pow'r of this relentless dame;
And oft-times, on vagaries idly bent,
For unkempt hair, or task unconn'd, are sorely shent.

And all in sight doth rise a birchen tree,
Which learning near her little dome did stowe;
Whilom a twig of small regard to see,
Tho' now so wide its waving branches flow;
And work the simple vassals mickle woe;
For not a wind might curl the leaves that blew,
But their limbs shudder'd, and their pulse beat low;
And, as they look'd, they found their horror grew,
And shap'd it into rods, and tingled at the view.

---

[1] Published in *Poems upon Various Occasions*, 1737. Text of *Works*, 1764 (much revised).

So have I seen (who has not, may conceive,)
A lifeless phantom near a garden plac'd;
So doth it wanton birds of peace bereave,
Of sport, of song, of pleasure, of repast;
They start, they stare, they wheel, they look aghast:
Sad servitude! such comfortless annoy
May no bold Briton's riper age e'er taste!
Ne superstition clog his dance of joy,
Ne vision empty, vain, his native bliss destroy.

Near to this dome is found a patch so green,
On which the tribe their gambols do display;
And at the door impris'ning board is seen,
Lest weakly wights of smaller size should stray;
Eager, perdie, to bask in sunny day!
The noises intermix'd, which thence resound,
Do learning's little tenement betray:
Where sits the dame, disguis'd in look profound,
And eyes her fairy throng, and turns her wheel around.

Her cap, far whiter than the driven snow,
Emblem right meet of decency does yield:
Her apron dy'd in grain, as blue, I trowe,
As is the hare-bell that adorns the field:
And in her hand, for scepter, she does wield
Tway birchen sprays; with anxious fear entwin'd,
With dark distrust, and sad repentance fill'd;
And stedfast hate, and sharp affliction join'd,
And fury uncontroul'd, and chastisement unkind.

Few but have ken'd, in semblance meet pourtray'd,
The childish faces of old Eol's train;
Libs, Notus, Auster: these in frowns array'd,
How then would fare or earth, or sky, or main,
Were the stern god to give his slaves the rein?
And were not she rebellious breasts to quell,
And were not she her statutes to maintain,
The cott no more, I ween, were deem'd the cell,
Where comely peace of mind, and decent order dwell.

A russet stole was o'er her shoulders thrown;
A russet kirtle fenc'd the nipping air;
'Twas simple russet, but it was her own;
'Twas her own country bred the flock so fair;
'Twas her own labour did the fleece prepare;
And, sooth to say, her pupils, rang'd around,
Thro' pious awe, did term it passing rare;

For they in gaping wonderment abound,
And think, no doubt, she been the greatest wight on ground.

Albeit ne flatt'ry did corrupt her truth,
Ne pompous title did debauch her ear;
Goody, good-woman, gossip, n'aunt, forsooth,
Or dame, the sole additions she did hear;
Yet these she challeng'd, these she held right dear:
Ne would esteem him act as mought behove,
Who should not honour'd eld with these revere:
For never title yet so mean could prove,
But there was eke a mind which did that title love.

One ancient hen she took delight to feed,
The plodding pattern of the busy dame;
Which, ever and anon, impell'd by need,
Into her school, begirt with chickens, came;
Such favour did her past deportment claim:
And, if neglect had lavish'd on the ground
Fragment of bread, she would collect the same;
For well she knew, and quaintly could expound,
What sin it were to waste the smallest crumb she found.

Herbs too she knew, and well of each could speak
That in her garden sip'd the silv'ry dew;
Where no vain flow'r disclos'd a gawdy streak;
But herbs for use, and physick, not a few,
Of grey renown, within those borders grew:
The tufted basil, pun-provoking thyme,
Fresh baum, and mary-gold of chearful hue;
The lowly gill, that never dares to climb;
And more I fain would sing, disdaining here to rhyme.

Yet euphrasy may not be left unsung,
That gives dim eyes to wander leagues around;
And pungent radish, biting infant's tongue;
And plantain ribb'd, that heals the reaper's wound;
And marj'ram sweet, in shepherd's posie found;
And lavender, whose spikes of azure bloom
Shall be, ere-while, in arid bundles bound,
To lurk amidst the labours of her loom,
And crown her kerchiefs clean, with mickle rare perfume.

And here trim rosmarine, that whilom crown'd
The daintiest garden of the proudest peer;
Ere, driven from its envy'd site, it found
A sacred shelter for its branches here;
Where edg'd with gold its glitt'ring skirts appear.

Oh wassel days; O customs meet and well!
Ere this was banish'd from its lofty sphere:
Simplicity then sought this humble cell,
Nor ever would she more with thane and lordling dwell.

Here oft the dame, on sabbath's decent eve,
Hymned such psalms as Sternhold forth did mete,
If winter 'twere, she to her hearth did cleave;
But in her garden found a summer seat:
Sweet melody! to hear her then repeat
How Israel's sons, beneath a foreign king,
While taunting foe-men did a song intreat,
All, for the nonce, untuning ev'ry string,
Up hung their useless lyres—small heart had they to sing.

For she was just, and friend to virtuous lore,
And pass'd much time in truly virtuous deed;
And, in those elfins' ears, would oft deplore
The times, when truth by popish rage did bleed;
And tortious death was true devotion's meed;
And simple faith in iron chains did mourn,
That nould on wooden image place her creed;
And lawny saints in smould'ring flames did burn:
Ah! dearest Lord, forefend, thilk days should e'er return.

In elbow chair, like that of Scottish stem
By the sharp tooth of cank'ring eld defac'd,
In which, when he receives his diadem,
Our sovereign prince and liefest liege is plac'd,
The matron sate; and some with rank she grac'd,
(The source of children's and of courtier's pride!)
Redress'd affronts, for vile affronts there pass'd;
And warn'd them not the fretful to deride,
But love each other dear, whatever them betide.

Right well she knew each temper to descry;
To thwart the proud, and the submiss to raise;
Some with vile copper prize exalt on high,
And some entice with pittance small of praise;
And other some with baleful sprig she 'frays:
Ev'n absent, she the reins of pow'r doth hold,
While with quaint arts the giddy crowd she sways;
Forewarn'd, if little bird their pranks behold,
'Twill whisper in her ear, and all the scene unfold.

Lo now with state she utters the command!
Eftsoons the urchins to their tasks repair;

Their books of stature small they take in hand,
Which with pellucid horn secured are;
To save from finger wet the letters fair:
The work so gay, that on their back is seen,
St. George's high atchievements does declare;
On which thilk wight that has y-gazing been,
Kens the forth-coming rod, unpleasing sight, I ween!

Ah luckless he, and born beneath the beam
Of evil star! it irks me whilst I write!
As erst the bard by Mulla's silver stream,
Oft, as he told of deadly dolorous plight,
Sigh'd as he sung, and did in tears indite.
For brandishing the rod, she doth begin
To loose the brogues, the stripling's late delight!
And down they drop; appears his dainty skin,
Fair as the furry coat of whitest ermilin.

O ruthful scene! when from a nook obscure,
His little sister doth his peril see:
All playful as she sate, she grows demure;
She finds full soon her wonted spirits flee;
She meditates a pray'r to set him free:
Nor gentle pardon could this dame deny,
(If gentle pardon could with dames agree)
To her sad grief that swells in either eye,
And wrings her so that all for pity she could dye.

Nor longer can she now her shrieks command;
And hardly she forbears, thro' aweful fear,
To rushen forth, and, with presumptuous hand,
To stay harsh justice in its mid career.
On thee she calls, on thee her parent dear!
(Ah! too remote to ward the shameful blow!)
She sees no kind domestic visage near,
And soon a flood of tears begins to flow;
And gives a loose at last to unavailing woe.

But ah! what pen his piteous plight may trace?
Or what device his loud laments explain?
The form uncouth of his disguised face?
The pallid hue that dyes his looks amain?
The plenteous show'r that does his cheek distain?
When he, in abject wise, implores the dame,
Ne hopeth aught of sweet reprieve to gain;
Or when from high she levels well her aim,
And, thro' the thatch, his cries each falling stroke proclaim.

The other tribe, aghast, with sore dismay,
Attend, and conn their tasks with mickle care:
By turns, astony'd, ev'ry twig survey,
And, from their fellow's hateful wounds, beware;
Knowing, I wist, how each the same may share;
Till fear has taught them a performance meet,
And to the well-known chest the dame repair;
Whence oft with sugar'd cates she doth 'em greet,
And ginger-bread y-rare; now, certes, doubly sweet!

See to their seats they hye with merry glee,
And in beseemly order sitten there;
All but the wight of bum y-galled, he
Abhorreth bench and stool, and fourm, and chair;
(This hand in mouth y-fix'd, that rends his hair;)
And eke with snubs profound, and heaving breast,
Convulsions intermitting! does declare
His grievous wrong; his dame's unjust behest;
And scorns her offer'd love, and shuns to be caress'd.

His face besprent with liquid crystal shines,
His blooming face that seems a purple flow'r,
Which low to earth its drooping head declines,
All smear'd and sully'd by a vernal show'r.
O the hard bosoms of despotic pow'r!
All, all, but she, the author of his shame,
All, all, but she, regret this mournful hour:
Yet hence the youth, and hence the flow'r, shall claim,
If so I deem aright, transcending worth and fame.

Behind some door, in melancholy thought,
Mindless of food, he, dreary caitiff! pines;
Ne for his fellow's joyaunce careth aught,
But to the wind all merriment resigns;
And deems it shame, if he to peace inclines;
And many a sullen look ascance is sent,
Which for his dame's annoyance he designs;
And still the more to pleasure him she's bent,
The more doth he, perverse, her haviour past resent.

Ah me! how much I fear lest pride it be!
But if that pride it be, which thus inspires,
Beware, ye dames, with nice discernment see,
Ye quench not too the sparks of nobler fires:
Ah! better far than all the muses' lyres,
All coward arts, is valour's gen'rous heat;

The firm fixt breast which fit and right requires,
Like Vernon's patriot soul; more justly great
Than craft that pimps for ill, or flow'ry false deceit.

Yet nurs'd with skill, what dazling fruits appear!
Ev'n now sagacious foresight points to show
A little bench of heedless bishops here,
And there a chancellour in embryo,
Or bard sublime, if bard may e'er be so,
As Milton, Shakespear, names that ne'er shall dye!
Tho' now he crawl along the ground so low,
Nor weeting how the muse shou'd soar on high,
Wisheth, poor starv'ling elf! his paper-kite may fly.

And this perhaps, who, cens'ring the design,
Low lays the house which that of cards doth build,
Shall Dennis be! if rigid fates incline,
And many an epic to his rage shall yield;
And many a poet quit th' Aonian field;
And, sour'd by age, profound he shall appear,
As he who now with 'sdainful fury thrill'd
Surveys mine work; and levels many a sneer,
And furls his wrinkly front, and cries, "What stuff is here?"

But now Dan Phoebus gains the middle skie,
And liberty unbars her prison-door;
And like a rushing torrent out they fly,
And now the grassy cirque han cover'd o'er
With boist'rous revel-rout and wild uproar;
A thousand ways in wanton rings they run,
Heav'n shield their short-liv'd pastimes, I implore!
For well may freedom, erst so dearly won,
Appear to British elf more gladsome than the sun.

Enjoy, poor imps! enjoy your sportive trade;
And chase gay flies, and cull the fairest flow'rs
For when my bones in grass-green sods are laid;
For never may ye taste more careless hours
In knightly castles, or in ladies bow'rs.
O vain to seek delight in earthly thing!
But most in courts where proud ambition tow'rs;
Deluded wight! who weens fair peace can spring
Beneath the pompous dome of kesar or of king.

See in each sprite some various bent appear!
These rudely carol most incondite lay;
Those saunt'ring on the green, with jocund leer
Salute the stranger passing on his way;

Some builden fragile tenements of clay;
Some to the standing lake their courses bend,
With pebbles smooth at duck and drake to play;
Thilk to the huxter's sav'ry cottage tend,
In pastry kings and queens th' allotted mite to spend.

Here, as each season yields a different store,
Each season's stores in order ranged been;
Apples with cabbage-net y-cover'd o'er,
Galling full sore th' unmoney'd wight, are seen;
And goose-b'rie clad in liv'ry red or green;
And here of lovely dye, the cath'rine pear,
Fine pear! as lovely for thy juice, I ween:
O may no wight e'er pennyless come there,
Lest smit with ardent love he pine with hopeless care!

See! cherries here, ere cherries yet abound,
With thread so white in tempting posies ty'd,
Scatt'ring like blooming maid their glances round,
With pamper'd look draw little eyes aside;
And must be bought, tho' penury betide.
The plumb all azure and the nut all brown,
And here each season, do those cakes abide,
Whose honour'd names th' inventive city own,
Rend'ring thro' Britain's isle Salopia's praises known.

Admir'd Salopia! that with venial pride
Eyes her bright form in Severn's ambient wave,
Fam'd for her loyal cares in perils try'd,
Her daughters lovely, and her striplings brave:
Ah! midst the rest, may flowers adorn his grave,
Whose art did first these dulcet cates display!
A motive fair to learning's imps he gave,
Who chearless o'er her darkling region stray;
'Till reason's morn arise, and light them on their way.

Ode to a Young Lady, Somewhat too Sollicitous about Her Manner of Expression[1]

SURVEY, my fair! that lucid stream
Adown the smiling valley stray;
Would art attempt, or fancy dream,
To regulate its winding way?

[1] Published in Dodsley's *Collection of Poems*, Vol. IV, 1755. Text of *Works*, 1764.

So pleas'd I view thy shining hair
  In loose dishevel'd ringlets flow:
Not all thy art, not all thy care
  Can there one single grace bestow.

Survey again that verdant hill,
  With native plants enamel'd o'er;
Say, can the painter's utmost skill
  Instruct one flow'r to please us more?

As vain it were, with artful dye,
  To change the bloom thy cheeks disclose;
And oh may Laura, ere she try,
  With fresh vermilion paint the rose.

Hark, how the wood-lark's tuneful throat
  Can every study'd grace excel;
Let art constrain the rambling note,
  And will she, Laura, please so well?

Oh ever keep thy native ease,
  By no pedantic law confin'd!
For Laura's voice is form'd to please,
  So Laura's words be not unkind.

A Pastoral Ballad, in Four Parts Written 1743[1]

Arbusta humilesque myricæ. Virg.

I. Absence

YE SHEPHERDS so chearful and gay,
  Whose flocks never carelessly roam;
Should Corydon's happen to stray,
  Oh! call the poor wanderers home.
Allow me to muse and to sigh,
  Nor talk of the change that ye find;
None once was so watchful as I:
  —I have left my dear Phyllis behind

Now I know what it is, to have strove
  With the torture of doubt and desire;

[1] Published in Dodsley's *Collection of Poems*, Vol. IV, 1755. Text of *Works*, 1764.

What it is, to admire and to love,
  And to leave her we love and admire.
Ah lead forth my flock in the morn,
  And the damps of each ev'ning repel;
Alas! I am faint and forlorn:
  —I have bade my dear Phyllis farewel.

Since Phyllis vouchsaf'd me a look,
  I never once dreamt of my vine;
May I lose both my pipe and my crook,
  If I knew of a kid that was mine.
I priz'd every hour that went by,
  Beyond all that had pleas'd me before;
But now they are past, and I sigh;
  And I grieve that I priz'd them no more.

But why do I languish in vain?
  Why wander thus pensively here?
Oh! why did I come from the plain,
  Where I fed on the smiles of my dear?
They tell me, my favourite maid,
  The pride of that valley, is flown;
Alas! where with her I have stray'd,
  I could wander with pleasure, alone.

When forc'd the fair nymph to forego,
  What anguish I felt at my heart!
Yet I thought—but it might not be so—
  'Twas with pain that she saw me depart.
She gaz'd, as I slowly withdrew;
  My path I could hardly discern;
So sweetly she bade me adieu,
  I thought that she bade me return.

The pilgrim that journeys all day
  To visit some far-distant shrine,
If he bear but a relique away,
  Is happy, nor heard to repine.
Thus widely remov'd from the fair,
  Where my vows, my devotion, I owe,
Soft hope is the relique I bear,
  And my solace wherever I go.

II. Hope

My banks they are furnish'd with bees,
  Whose murmur invites one to sleep;

My grottos are shaded with trees,
  And my hills are white-over with sheep.
I seldom have met with a loss,
  Such health do my fountains bestow;
My fountains all border'd with moss,
  Where the hare-bells and violets grow.

Not a pine in my grove is there seen,
  But with tendrils of woodbine is bound:
Not a beech's more beautiful green,
  But a sweet-briar entwines it around.
Not my fields, in the prime of the year,
  More charms than my cattle unfold:
Not a brook that is limpid and clear,
  But it glitters with fishes of gold.

One would think she might like to retire
  To the bow'r I have labour'd to rear;
Not a shrub that I heard her admire,
  But I hasted and planted it there.
Oh how sudden the jessamine strove
  With the lilac to render it gay!
Already it calls for my love,
  To prune the wild branches away.

From the plains, from the woodlands and groves,
  What strains of wild melody flow?
How the nightingales warble their loves
  From thickets of roses that blow!
And when her bright form shall appear,
  Each bird shall harmoniously join
In a concert so soft and so clear,
  As—she may not be fond to resign.

I have found out a gift for my fair;
  I have found where the wood-pigeons breed:
But let me that plunder forbear,
  She will say 'twas a barbarous deed.
For he ne'er could be true, she aver'd,
  Who could rob a poor bird of its young:
And I lov'd her the more, when I heard
  Such tenderness fall from her tongue.

I have heard her with sweetness unfold
  How that pity was due to—a dove:
That it ever attended the bold,
  And she call'd it the sister of love.

But her words such a pleasure convey,
  So much I her accents adore,
Let her speak, and whatever she say,
  Methinks I should love her the more.

Can a bosom so gentle remain
  Unmov'd, when her Corydon sighs!
Will a nymph that is fond of the plain,
  These plains and this valley despise?
Dear regions of silence and shade!
  Soft scenes of contentment and ease!
Where I could have pleasingly stray'd,
  If aught, in her absence, could please.

But where does my Phyllida stray?
  And where are her grots and her bow'rs?
Are the groves and the valleys as gay,
  And the shepherds as gentle as ours?
The groves may perhaps be as fair,
  And the face of the valleys as fine;
The swains may in manners compare,
  But their love is not equal to mine.

III. Sollicitude

Why will you my passion reprove?
  Why term it a folly to grieve?
Ere I shew you the charms of my love,
  She is fairer than you can believe.
With her mien she enamours the brave;
  With her wit she engages the free;
With her modesty pleases the grave;
  She is ev'ry way pleasing to me.

O you that have been of her train,
  Come and join in my amorous lays;
I could lay down my life for the swain,
  That will sing but a song in her praise.
When he sings, may the nymphs of the town
  Come trooping, and listen the while;
Nay on him let not Phyllida frown;
  —But I cannot allow her to smile.

For when Paridel tries in the dance
  Any favour with Phyllis to find,
O how, with one trivial glance,
  Might she ruin the peace of my mind!

In ringlets he dresses his hair,
And his crook is be-studded around;
And his pipe—oh may Phyllis beware
Of a magic there is in the sound.

'Tis his with mock passion to glow;
'Tis his in smooth tales to unfold,
"How her face is as bright as the snow,
And her bosom, be sure, is as cold?
How the nightingales labour the strain,
With the notes of his charmer to vie;
How they vary their accents in vain,
Repine at her triumphs, and die."

To the grove or the garden he strays,
And pillages every sweet;
Then, suiting the wreath to his lays
He throws it at Phyllis's feet.
"O Phyllis, he whispers, more fair,
More sweet than the jessamin's flow'r!
What are pinks, in a morn, to compare?
What is eglantine, after a show'r?

Then the lily no longer is white;
Then the rose is depriv'd of its bloom;
Then the violets die with despight,
And the wood-bines give up their perfume."
Thus glide the soft numbers along,
And he fancies no shepherd his peer;
—Yet I never should envy the song,
Were not Phyllis to lend it an ear.

Let his crook be with hyacinths bound,
So Phyllis the trophy despise;
Let his forehead with laurels be crown'd,
So they shine not in Phyllis's eyes.
The language that flows from the heart
Is a stranger to Paridel's tongue;
—Yet may she beware of his art,
Or sure I must envy the song.

IV. Disappointment

Ye shepherds give ear to my lay,
And take no more heed of my sheep:
They have nothing to do, but to stray;
I have nothing to do, but to weep.

Yet do not my folly reprove;
  She was fair—and my passion begun;
She smil'd—and I could not but love;
  She is faithless—and I am undone.

Perhaps I was void of all thought;
  Perhaps it was plain to foresee,
That a nymph so compleat would be sought
  By a swain more engaging than me.
Ah! love ev'ry hope can inspire:
  It banishes wisdom the while;
And the lip of the nymph we admire
  Seems for ever adorn'd with a smile.

She is faithless, and I am undone;
  Ye that witness the woes I endure,
Let reason instruct you to shun
  What it cannot instruct you to cure.
Beware how ye loiter in vain
  Amid nymphs of an higher degree:
It is not for me to explain
  How fair, and how fickle they be.

Alas! from the day that we met,
  What hope of an end to my woes?
When I cannot endure to forget
  The glance that undid my repose.
Yet time may diminish the pain:
  The flow'r, and the shrub, and the tree,
Which I rear'd for her pleasure in vain,
  In time may have comfort for me.

The sweets of a dew-sprinkled rose,
  The sound of a murmuring stream,
The peace which from solitude flows,
  Henceforth shall be Corydon's theme.
High transports are shewn to the sight,
  But we are not to find them our own;
Fate never bestow'd such delight,
  As I with my Phyllis had known.

O ye woods, spread your branches apace;
  To your deepest recesses I fly;
I would hide with the beasts of the chace;
  I would vanish from every eye.
Yet my reed shall resound thro' the grove
  With the same sad complaint it begun;

How she smil'd, and I could not but love;
Was faithless, and I am undone!

Song II. The Landskip[1]

How pleas'd within my native bowers
Erewhile I pass'd the day!
Was ever scene so deck'd with flowers?
Were ever flowers so gay?

How sweetly smil'd the hill, the vale,
And all the landskip round!
The river gliding down the dale!
The hill with beeches crown'd!

But now, when urg'd by tender woes
I speed to meet my dear,
That hill and stream my zeal oppose,
And check my fond career.

No more, since Daphne was my theme,
Their wonted charms I see:
That verdant hill, and silver stream,
Divide my love and me.

Written at an Inn at Henley[2]

To THEE, fair freedom! I retire
From flattery, cards, and dice, and din;
Nor art thou found in mansions higher
Than the low cott, or humble inn.

'Tis here with boundless pow'r I reign;
And ev'ry health which I begin,
Converts dull port to bright champaigne;
Such freedom crowns it, at an inn.

I fly from pomp, I fly from plate!
I fly from falsehood's specious grin!

[1] Published in Dodsley's *Collection of Poems*, Volume V, 1758. Text of *Works*, 1764.

[2] Published in Dodsley's *Collection of Poems*, Volume V, 1758. Text of *Works*, 1764.

Freedom I love, and form I hate,
And chuse my lodgings at an inn.

Here, waiter! take my sordid ore,
Which lacqueys else might hope to win;
It buys, what courts have not in store;
It buys me freedom, at an inn.

Whoe'er has travell'd life's dull round,
Where'er his stages may have been,
May sigh to think he still has found
The warmest welcome, at an inn.

Elegy XI
He Complains how Soon the Pleasing Novelty of Life Is Over. To Mr. J ——[1]

AH ME, my friend! it will not, will not last!
This fairy-scene, that cheats our youthful eyes!
The charm dissolves; th' aerial music's past;
The banquet ceases, and the vision flies.

Where are the splendid forms, the rich perfumes,
Where the gay tapers, where the spacious dome?
Vanish'd the costly pearls, the crimson plumes,
And we, delightless, left to wander home!

Vain now are books, the sage's wisdom vain!
What has the world to bribe our steps astray?
Ere reason learns by study'd laws to reign,
The weaken'd passions, self-subdued, obey.

Scarce has the sun sev'n annual courses roll'd,
Scarce shewn the whole that fortune can supply;
Since, not the miser so caress'd his gold,
As I, for what it gave, was heard to sigh.

On the world's stage I wish'd some sprightly part;
To deck my native fleece with tawdry lace;
'Twas life, 'twas taste, and—oh my foolish heart!
Substantial joy was fix'd in pow'r and place.

And you, ye works of art! allur'd mine eye,
The breathing picture, and the living stone:

[1] Richard Jago. Published in *Works*, 1764. Text of first edition.

"Tho' gold, tho' splendour, heav'n and fate deny,
"Yet might I call one Titian stroke my own!"

Smit with the charms of fame, whose lovely spoil,
The wreath, the garland, fire the poet's pride,
I trim'd my lamp, consum'd the midnight oil—
But soon the paths of health and fame divide!

Oft too I pray'd, 'twas nature form'd the pray'r,
To grace my native scenes, my rural home;
To see my trees express their planter's care,
And gay, on Attic models, raise my dome.

But now 'tis o'er, the dear delusion's o'er!
A stagnant breezeless air becalms my soul:
A fond aspiring candidate no more,
I scorn the palm, before I reach the goal.

O youth! enchanting stage, profusely blest!
Bliss ev'n obtrusive courts the frolic mind;
Of health neglectful, yet by health carest;
Careless of favour, yet secure to find.

Then glows the breast, as op'ning roses fair;
More free, more vivid than the linnet's wing;
Honest as light, transparent ev'n as air,
Tender as buds, and lavish as the spring.

Not all the force of manhood's active might,
Not all the craft to subtle age assign'd,
Not science shall extort that dear delight,
Which gay delusion gave the tender mind.

Adieu soft raptures! transports void of care!
Parent of raptures, dear deceit, adieu!
And you, her daughters, pining with despair,
Why, why so soon her fleeting steps pursue!

Tedious again to curse the drizling day!
Again to trace the wint'ry tracts of snow!
Or, sooth'd by vernal airs, again survey
The self-same hawthorns bud, and cowslips blow!

O life! how soon of ev'ry bliss forlorn!
We start false joys, and urge the devious race:
A tender prey; that chears our youthful morn,
Then sinks untimely, and defrauds the chace.

MARK AKENSIDE

(1721-1737-1770)

Hymn to Science[1]

SCIENCE! thou fair effusive ray
From the great source of mental Day,
Free, generous, and refin'd!
Descend with all thy treasures fraught,
Illumine each bewilder'd thought,
And bless my lab'ring mind.

But first with thy resistless light,
Disperse those phantoms from my sight,
Those mimic shades of thee;
The scholiast's learning, sophist's cant,
The visionary bigot's rant,
The monk's philosophy.

O! let thy powerful charms impart
The patient head, the candid heart,
Devoted to thy sway;
Which no weak passions e'er mislead,
Which still with dauntless steps proceed
Where Reason points the way.

Give me to learn each secret cause;
Let number's, figure's, motion's laws
Reveal'd before me stand;
These to great Nature's scenes apply,
And round the globe, and thro' the sky,
Disclose her working hand.

Next, to thy nobler search resign'd,
The busy, restless, human mind
Thro' ev'ry maze pursue;
Detect Perception where it lies,
Catch the ideas as they rise,
And all their changes view.

Say from what simple springs began
The vast, ambitious thoughts of man,
Which range beyond controul;

[1] Published in the *Gentleman's Magazine*, October, 1739. Text of first edition.

Which seek Eternity to trace,
Dive thro' th' infinity of space,
  And strain to grasp THE WHOLE.

Her secret stores let Memory tell,
Bid Fancy quit her fairy cell,
  In all her colours drest;
While prompt her sallies to controul,
Reason, the judge, recalls the soul
  To Truth's severest test.

Then launch thro' Being's wide extent;
Let the fair scale, with just ascent,
  And cautious steps, be trod;
And from the dead, corporeal mass,
Thro' each progressive order pass
  To Instinct, Reason, GOD.

There, *Science!* veil thy daring eye;
Nor dive too deep, nor soar too high,
  In that divine abyss;
To Faith content thy beams to lend,
Her hopes t' assure, her steps befriend,
  And light her way to bliss.

Then downwards take thy flight agen;
Mix with the policies of men,
  And social nature's ties:
The plan, the genius of each state,
Its interest and its pow'rs relate,
  Its fortunes and its rise.

Thro' private life pursue thy course,
Trace every action to its source,
  And means and motives weigh:
Put tempers, passions in the scale,
Mark what degrees in each prevail,
  And fix the doubtful sway.

That last, best effort of thy skill,
To form the life, and rule the will,
  Propitious pow'r! impart:
Teach me to cool my passion's fires,
Make me the judge of my desires,
  The master of my heart.

Raise me above the vulgar's breath,
Pursuit of fortune, fear of death,
  And all in life that's mean.

Still true to reason be my plan,
Still let my action speak the man,
  Thro' every various scene.

Hail! queen of manners, light of truth;
Hail! charm of age, and guide of youth;
  Sweet refuge of distress:
In business, thou! exact, polite;
Thou giv'st Retirement its delight,
  Prosperity its grace.

Of wealth, pow'r, freedom, thou! the cause;
Foundress of order, cities, laws,
  Of arts inventress, thou!
Without thee what were human kind?
How vast their wants, their thoughts how blind!
  Their joys how mean! how few!

Sun of the soul! thy beams unveil!
Let others spread the daring sail,
  On Fortune's faithless sea;
While undeluded, happier I
From the vain tumult timely fly,
  And sit in peace with Thee.

From The Pleasures of Imagination[1]

Book III

OH! BLEST of heav'n, whom not the languid songs
Of luxury, the Siren! not the bribes
Or sordid wealth, nor all the gaudy spoils
Of pageant honour can seduce to leave
Those ever-blooming sweets, which from the store
Of nature fair imagination culls
To charm th' inliven'd soul! What tho' not all
Of mortal offspring can attain the heights
Of envied life; tho' only few possess
Patrician treasures or imperial state;
Yet nature's care, to all her children just,
With richer treasures and an ampler state
Endows at large whatever happy man
Will deign to use them. His the city's pomp,
The rural honours his. Whate'er adorns

[1] Published in 1744. Text of octavo edition, 1744.

The princely dome, the column and the arch,
The breathing marbles and the sculptur'd gold,
Beyond the proud possessor's narrow claim,
His tuneful breast enjoys. For him, the spring
Distills her dews, and from the silken gem
Its lucid leaves unfolds: for him, the hand
Of autumn tinges every fertile branch
With blooming gold and blushes like the morn,
Each passing hour sheds tribute from her wings;
And still new beauties meet his lonely walk;
And loves unfelt attract him. Not a breeze
Flies o'er the meadow, not a cloud imbibes
The setting sun's effulgence, not a strain
From all the tenants of the warbling shade
Ascends, but whence his bosom can partake
Fresh pleasure, unreprov'd. Nor thence partakes
Fresh pleasure only: for th' attentive mind,
By this harmonious action on her pow'rs,
Becomes herself harmonious: wont so long
In outward things to meditate the charm
Of sacred order, soon she seeks at home
To find a kindred order, to exert
Within herself this elegance of love,
This fair-inspir'd delight: her temper'd pow'rs
Refine at length, and every passion wears
A chaster, milder, more attractive mien.
But if to ampler prospects, if to gaze
On nature's form where negligent of all
These lesser graces, she assumes the port
Of that eternal majesty that weigh'd
The world's foundations, if to these the mind
Exalt her daring eye, then mightier far
Will be the change, and nobler. Would the forms
Of servile custom cramp her gen'rous pow'rs?
Would sordid policies, the barb'rous growth
Of ignorance and rapine bow her down
To tame pursuits, to indolence and fear?
Lo! she appeals to nature, to the winds
And rowling waves, the sun's unwearied course,
The elements and seasons: all declare
For what th' eternal maker has ordain'd
The pow'rs of man: we feel within ourselves
His energy divine: he tells the heart
He meant, he made us to behold and love
What he beholds and loves, the general orb
Of life and being; to be great like him,
Beneficent and active. Thus the men
Whom nature's works can charm, with GOD himself

Hold converse; grow familiar, day by day,
With his conceptions; act upon his plan;
And form to his the relish of their souls.

Ode I
Allusion to Horace[1]

———*Ego, apis Matinæ*
More, modoque, &c. Lib. iv. Od. ii.

AMID the garden's fragrance laid,
Where yonder limes behold their shade
Along the glassy stream,
With HORACE and his tuneful ease
I'll rest from crouds, and care's disease,
And summer's piercing beam.

Behold the busy, wand'ring BEE!
From bloom to bloom, from tree to tree
She sweeps mellifluous dews;
For her the silken gems arise,
For her display their shining dyes,
Their balmy breath diffuse.

Sweet Murmurer! may no rude storm
This pleasurable scene deform
To check thy gladsome toils;
Still may the buds unsullied spring,
Still show'rs and sunshine court thy wing
To these ambrosial spoils.

Nor shall my Muse hereafter fail
Her fellow-lab'rer thus to hail,
And lucky be the strains!
For long ago did nature frame
Your seasons and your arts the same,
Your pleasures and your pains.

Like thee, in lowly, sylvan scenes,
And river-banks and fruitful greens
Delights my vagrant song;
Nor strives by soaring high in air,
Tho' swans and eagles triumph there,
To draw the giddy throng.

[1] Published in *Odes on Several Subjects*, 1745. Text of first edition.

Nor where the raven, where the owl
By night their hateful orgies howl,
  Will she her cares imploy;
But flies from ruins and from graves,
From ghostly cells and monkish caves
  To day-light and to joy.

Nor will she tempt the barren waste;
Nor deigns th' ungrateful stores to taste
  Of any noxious thing;
But leaves with scorn to others' use
The bitter hemlock's baneful juice,
  The nettle's sordid sting.

From all which nature fairest knows,
The vernal blooms, the summer rose,
  She draws her mingled wealth;
And when the lovely task is done,
She consecrates a double boon,
  To pleasure and to health.

Inscription
For a Grotto[1]

To ME, whom in their lays the shepherds call
Actæa, daughter of the neighbouring stream,
This cave belongs. The fig-tree and the vine,
Which o'er the rocky entrance downward shoot,
Were plac'd by Glycon. He with cowslips pale,
Primrose, and purple Lychnis, deck'd the green
Before my threshold, and my shelving walls
With honeysuckle cover'd. Here at noon,
Lull'd by the murmur of my rising fount,
I slumber: here my clustering fruits I tend;
Or from the humid flowers, at break of day,
Fresh garlands weave, and chace from all my bounds
Each thing impure or noxious. Enter-in,
O stranger, undismay'd. Nor bat nor toad
Here lurks: and if thy breast of blameless thoughts
Approve thee, not unwelcome shalt thou tread
My quiet mansion: chiefly, if thy name
Wise Pallas and the immortal Muses own.

[1] Published in Dodsley's *Collection*, Volume VI, 1758. Text of first edition.

Ode to the Evening Star[1]

TO-NIGHT retir'd the queen of heaven
With young Endymion stays:
And now to Hesper is it given
Awhile to rule the vacant sky,
Till she shall to her lamp supply
A stream of brighter rays.

O Hesper, while the starry throng
With awe thy path surrounds,
Oh listen to my suppliant song,
If haply now the vocal sphere
Can suffer thy delighted ear
To stoop to mortal sounds.

So may the bridegroom's genial strain
Thee still invoke to shine:
So may the bride's unmarried train
To Hymen chaunt their flattering vow,
Still that his lucky torch may glow
With lustre pure as thine.

Far other vows must I prefer
To thy indulgent power.
Alas, but now I paid my tear
On fair Olympia's virgin tomb:
And lo, from thence, in quest I roam
Of Philomela's bower.

Propitious send thy golden ray,
Thou purest light above:
Let no false flame seduce to stray
Where gulph or steep lie hid for harm:
But lead where music's healing charm
May sooth afflicted love.

To them, by many a grateful song
In happier seasons vow'd,
These lawns, Olympia's haunt, belong:
Oft by yon silver stream we walk'd,
Or fix'd, while Philomela talk'd,
Beneath yon copses stood.

Nor seldom, where the beachen boughs
That roofless tower invade,

[1] Published in *Poems*, 1772. Text of first edition.

We came while her inchanting Muse
The radiant moon above us held:
Till by a clamorous owl compell'd
  She fled the solemn shade.

But hark; I hear her liquid tone.
  Now, Hesper, guide my feet
Down the red marle with moss o'ergrown,
Through yon wild thicket next the plain,
Whose hawthorns choke the winding lane
  Which leads to her retreat.

See the green space: on either hand
  Inlarg'd it spreads around:
See, in the midst she takes her stand,
Where one old oak his awful shade
Extends o'er half the level mead
  Inclos'd in woods profound.

Hark, how through many a melting note
  She now prolongs her lays:
How sweetly down the void they float!
The breeze their magic path attends:
The stars shine out: the forest bends:
  The wakeful heifers gaze.

Whoe'er thou art whom chance may bring
  To this sequester'd spot,
If then the plaintive Syren sing,
Oh softly tread beneath her bower,
And think of heaven's disposing power,
  Of man's uncertain lot.

Oh think, o'er all this mortal stage,
  What mournful scenes arise:
What ruin waits on kingly rage:
How often virtue dwells with woe:
How many griefs from knowledge flow:
  How swiftly pleasure flies.

O sacred bird, let me at eve,
  Thus wandering all alone,
Thy tender counsel oft receive,
Bear witness to thy pensive airs,
And pity nature's common cares
  Till I forget my own.

Ode XVII
On a Sermon against Glory. MDCCXLVII[1]

I.

COME then, tell me, sage divine,
Is it an offence to own
That our bosoms e'er incline
Toward immortal glory's throne?
For with me nor pomp, nor pleasure,
Bourbon's might, Braganza's treasure,
So can fancy's dream rejoice,
So conciliate reason's choice,
As one approving word of her impartial voice.

II.

If to spurn at noble praise
Be the pass-port to thy heaven,
Follow thou those gloomy ways;
No such law to me was given,
Nor, I trust, shall I deplore me
Faring like my friends before me;
Nor an holier place desire
Than Timoleon's arms acquire,
And Tully's curule chair, and Milton's golden lyre.

CHARLES WESLEY

(1707-1739?-1788)

For Christmas-Day[2]

HARK, how all the welkin rings,
"Glory to the King of kings;
Peace on earth, and mercy mild,
God and sinners reconciled!"

Joyful, all ye nations, rise,
Join the triumph of the skies;

[1] Published in *Poems*, 1772. Text of first edition.
[2] Published in *Hymns and Sacred Poems*, 1739. Text of *Poems*, New York, 1866.

Universal nature say,
"Christ the Lord is born to-day!"

Christ, by highest heaven adored,
Christ, the everlasting Lord:
Late in time behold Him come,
Offspring of a virgin's womb!

Veiled in flesh, the Godhead see,
Hail the incarnate Deity!
Pleased as Man with men to appear,
Jesus, our Immanuel here!

Hail, the heavenly Prince of Peace,
Hail, the Sun of Righteousness!
Light and life to all He brings,
Risen with healing in His wings.

Mild He lays His glory by,
Born that man no more may die;
Born to raise the sons of earth;
Born to give them second birth.

Come, Desire of nations, come,
Fix in us Thy humble home;
Rise, the woman's conquering seed,
Bruise in us the serpent's head.

Now display Thy saving power,
Ruined nature now restore;
Now in mystic union join
Thine to ours, and ours to Thine.

Adam's likeness, Lord, efface,
Stamp Thy image in its place.
Second Adam from above,
Reinstate us in Thy love.

Let us Thee, though lost, regain,
Thee, the Life, the Inner Man:
O, to all Thyself impart,
Formed in each believing heart.

For Easter-Day[1]

"CHRIST the Lord is risen to-day,"
Sons of men and angels say.
Raise your joys and triumphs high;
Sing, ye heavens, and earth reply.

Love's redeeming work is done,
Fought the fight, the battle won.
Lo! our Sun's eclipse is o'er;
Lo! He sets in blood no more.

Vain the stone, the watch, the seal;
Christ has burst the gates of hell!
Death in vain forbids His rise:
Christ has opened Paradise.

Lives again our glorious King;
Where, O Death, is now thy sting?
Dying once, He all doth save;
Where thy victory, O Grave?

Soar we now where Christ has led,
Following our exalted Head:
Made like Him, like Him we rise;
Ours the Cross, the grave, the skies!

What though once we perished all,
Partners in our parents' fall:
Second life we all receive,
In our heavenly Adam live.

Risen with Him, we upward move,
Still we seek the things above,
Still pursue, and kiss the Son,
Seated on His Father's throne.

Scarce on earth a thought bestow;
Dead to all we leave below:
Heaven our aim, and loved abode,
Hid our life with Christ in God.

Hid, till Christ our Life appear,
Glorious in His members here:

[1] Published in *Hymns and Sacred Poems*, 1739. Text of *Poems*, New York, 1866.

Joined to Him, we then shall shine
All immortal, all divine.

Hail, the Lord of earth and heaven!
Praise to Thee by both be given:
Thee we greet triumphant now;
Hail, the Resurrection Thou!

King of glory, Soul of bliss,
Everlasting life is this,
Thee to know, Thy power to prove,
Thus to sing, and thus to love.

A Morning Hymn[1]

CHRIST, whose Glory fills the Skies,
CHRIST, the true, the only Light,
Sun of Righteousness, arise,
  Triumph o'er the Shades of Night:
Day-spring from on High, be near:
Day-star, in my Heart appear.

Dark and Chearless is the Morn
  Unaccompanied by Thee,
Joyless is the Day's Return,
  Till thy Mercy's Beams I see;
Till they Inward Light impart,
Glad my Eyes, and warm my Heart.

Visit then this Soul of mine,
  Pierce the Gloom of Sin, and Grief,
Fill me, Radiancy Divine,
  Scatter all my Unbelief,
More and more Thyself display,
Shining to the Perfect Day.

Wrestling Jacob[2]

COME, O Thou Traveller unknown,
  Whom still I hold, but cannot see,

[1] Published in *Psalms and Hymns*, 1740. Text of *The Oxford Book of Eighteenth Century Verse*.

[2] Published in *Hymns and Sacred Poems*, 1742. Text of *The Oxford Book of Eighteenth Century Verse*.

My Company before is gone,
  And I am left alone with Thee,
With Thee all Night I mean to stay,
And wrestle till the Break of Day.

I need not tell Thee who I am,
  My Misery, or Sin declare,
Thyself hast call'd me by my Name,
  Look on thy Hands, and read it there,
But who, I ask Thee, who art Thou,
Tell me thy Name, and tell me now?

In vain Thou strugglest to get free,
  I never will unloose my Hold:
Art Thou the Man that died for me?
  The Secret of thy Love unfold;
Wrestling I will not let Thee go,
Till I thy Name, thy Nature know.

Wilt Thou not yet to me reveal
  Thy new, unutterable Name?
Tell me, I still beseech Thee, tell,
  To know it Now resolv'd I am;
Wrestling I will not let Thee go,
Till I thy Name, thy Nature know.

'Tis all in vain to hold thy Tongue,
  Or touch the Hollow of my Thigh:
Though every Sinew be unstrung,
  Out of my Arms Thou shalt not fly;
Wrestling I will not let Thee go,
Till I thy Name, thy Nature know.

What tho' my shrinking Flesh complain,
  And murmur to contend so long,
I rise superior to my Pain,
  When I am weak then I am strong,
And when my All of Strength shall fail,
I shall with the GOD-man prevail.

My Strength is gone, my Nature dies,
  I sink beneath thy weighty Hand,
Faint to revive, and fall to rise;
  I fall, and yet by Faith I stand,
I stand, and will not let Thee go,
Till I thy Name, thy Nature know.

Yield to me Now——for I am weak;
  But confident in Self-despair:
Speak to my Heart, in Blessings speak,
  Be conquer'd by my Instant Prayer,
Speak, or Thou never hence shalt move,
And tell me, if thy Name is LOVE.

'Tis Love, 'tis Love! Thou diedst for Me,
  I hear thy Whisper in my Heart.
The Morning breaks, the Shadows flee:
  Pure UNIVERSAL LOVE Thou art,
To me, to All thy Bowels move,
Thy Nature, and thy Name is LOVE.

My Prayer hath Power with GOD; the Grace
  Unspeakable I now receive,
Thro' Faith I see Thee Face to Face,
  I see Thee Face to Face, and live:
In vain I have not wept, and strove,
Thy Nature, and thy Name is LOVE.

I know Thee, Saviour, who Thou art,
  JESUS the feeble Sinner's Friend;
Nor wilt Thou with the Night depart,
  But stay, and love me to the End;
Thy Mercies never shall remove,
Thy Nature, and thy Name is LOVE.

The Sun of Righteousness on Me
  Hath rose with Healing in his Wings,
Wither'd my Nature's Strength; from Thee
  My Soul its Life and Succour brings,
My Help is all laid up above;
Thy Nature, and thy Name is LOVE.

Contented now upon my Thigh
  I halt, till Life's short Journey end;
All Helplessness, all Weakness I,
  On Thee alone for Strength depend,
Nor have I Power, from Thee, to move;
Thy Nature, and thy Name is LOVE.

Lame as I am, I take the Prey,
  Hell, Earth, and Sin with Ease o'ercome;
I leap for Joy, pursue my Way,
  And as a bounding Hart fly home,
Thro' all Eternity to prove
Thy Nature, and thy Name is LOVE.

In Temptation[1]

JESU, Lover of my soul,
Let me to Thy bosom fly,
While the nearer waters roll,
While the tempest still is high.
Hide me, O my Saviour, hide,
Till the storm of life is past:
Safe into the haven guide;
O receive my soul at last.

Other refuge have I none:
Hangs my helpless soul on Thee.
Leave, ah leave me not alone,
Still support and comfort me.
All my trust on Thee is stayed,
All my help from Thee I bring;
Cover my defenceless head
With the shadow of Thy wing.

Wilt Thou not regard my call?
Wilt Thou not accept my prayer?
Lo, I sink, I faint, I fall!
Lo, on Thee I cast my care.
Reach me out Thy gracious hand!
While I of Thy strength receive,
Hoping against hope I stand,
Dying, and behold I live!

Thou, O Christ, art all I want;
More than all in Thee I find.
Raise the fallen, cheer the faint,
Heal the sick, and lead the blind.
Just and holy is Thy Name;
I am all unrighteousness:
False and full of sin I am;
Thou art full of truth and grace.

Plenteous grace with Thee is found,
Grace to cover all my sin:
Let the healing streams abound,
Make and keep me pure within.
Thou of Life the Fountain art:
Freely let me take of Thee:
Spring Thou up within my heart,
Rise to all eternity.

[1] Published in *Hymns and Sacred Poems*, 1749. Text of *Poems*, New York, 1866.

WILLIAM COLLINS

(1721-1739-1759)

Persian Eclogues[1]

THE PREFACE

IT is with the Writings of Mankind, in some Measure, as with their Complexions or their Dress, each Nation hath a Peculiarity in all these, to distinguish it from the rest of the World.

The Gravity of the *Spaniard*, and the Levity of the *Frenchman*, are as evident in all their Productions as in their Persons themselves; and the Stile of my Countrymen is as naturally Strong and Nervous, as that of an *Arabian* or *Persian* is rich and figurative.

There is an Elegancy and Wildness of Thought which recommends all their Compositions; and our Genius's are as much too cold for the Entertainment of such Sentiments, as our Climate is for their Fruits and Spices. If any of these Beauties are to be found in the following *Eclogues*, I hope my Reader will consider them as an Argument of their being Original. I received them at the Hands of a Merchant, who had made it his Business to enrich himself with the Learning, as well as the Silks and Carpets of the *Persians*. The little Information I could gather concerning their Author, was, That his Name was *Mahamed*, and that he was a Native of *Tauris*.

It was in that City that he died of a Distemper fatal in those Parts, whilst he was engag'd in celebrating the Victories of his favourite Monarch, *the great Abbas*. As to the *Eclogues* themselves, they give a very just View of the Miseries, and Inconveniences, as well as the Felicities that attend one of the finest Countries in the East.

The Time of the Writing them was probably in the Beginning of *Sha Sultan Hosseyn's* Reign, the Successor of *Sefi* or *Solyman* the Second.

Whatever Defects, as, I doubt not, there will be many, fall under the Reader's Observation, I hope his Candour will incline him to make the following Reflections:

That the Works of *Orientals* contain many Peculiarities, and that thro' Defect of Language few *European* Translators can do them Justice.

Eclogue the Second
Hassan; or, the Camel driver

Scene, the desart
Time, mid-day

IN SILENT Horror o'er the Desart-Waste
The Driver *Hassan* with his Camels past.
One Cruise of Water on his Back he bore,
And his light Scrip contain'd a scanty Store:
A Fan of painted Feathers in his Hand,

[1] Published in January, 1742. Text of first edition.

To guard his shaded Face from scorching Sand.
The sultry Sun had gain'd the middle Sky,
And not a Tree, and not an Herb was nigh.
The Beasts, with Pain, their dusty Way pursue,
Shrill roar'd the Winds, and dreary was the View!
With desp'rate Sorrow wild th' affrighted Man
Thrice sigh'd, thrice strook his Breast, and thus began:
Sad was the Hour, and luckless was the Day,
When first from Schiraz' *Walls I bent my Way.*

Ah! little thought I of the blasting Wind,
The Thirst or pinching Hunger that I find!
Bethink thee, *Hassan*, where shall Thirst assuage,
When fails this Cruise, his unrelenting Rage?
Soon shall this Scrip its precious Load resign,
Then what but Tears and Hunger shall be thine?

Ye mute Companions of my Toils, that bear
In all my Griefs a more than equal Share!
Here, where no Springs, in Murmurs break away,
Or Moss-crown'd Fountains mitigate the Day:
In vain ye hope the green Delights to know,
Which Plains more blest, or verdant Vales bestow.
Here Rocks alone, and tasteless Sands are found,
And faint and sickly Winds for ever howl around.
Sad was the Hour, &c.

Curst be the Gold and Silver which persuade
Weak Men to follow far-fatiguing Trade.
The Lilly-Peace outshines the silver Store,
And Life is dearer than the golden Ore.
Yet Money tempts us o'er the Desart brown,
To ev'ry distant Mart, and wealthy Town:
Full oft we tempt the Land, and oft the Sea,
And are we only yet repay'd by Thee?
Ah! why was Ruin so attractive made,
Or why fond Man so easily betray'd?
Why heed we not, whilst mad we haste along,
The gentle Voice of Peace, or Pleasure's Song?
Or wherefore think the flow'ry Mountain's Side,
The Fountain's Murmurs, and the Valley's Pride,
Why think we these less pleasing to behold,
Than dreary Desarts, if they lead to Gold?
Sad was the Hour, &c.

O cease, my Fears! all frantic as I go,
When Thought creates unnumber'd Scenes of Woe,
What if the Lion in his Rage I meet!

Oft in the Dust I view his printed Feet:
And fearful! oft, when Day's declining Light
Yields her pale Empire to the Mourner Night,
By Hunger rous'd, he scours the groaning Plain,
Gaunt Wolves and sullen Tygers in his Train:
Before them Death with Shrieks directs their Way,
Fills the wild Yell, and leads them to their Prey.
Sad was the Hour, &c.

At that dead Hour the silent Asp shall creep,
If ought of rest I find, upon my Sleep:
Or some swoln Serpent twist his Scales around,
And wake to Anguish with a burning Wound.
Thrice happy they, the wise contented Poor,
From Lust of Wealth, and Dread of Death secure;
They tempt no Desarts, and no Griefs they find;
Peace rules the Day, where Reason rules the Mind.
Sad was the Hour, &c.

O hapless Youth! for she thy Love hath won,
The tender *Zara*, will be most undone!
Big swell'd my Heart, and own'd the pow'rful Maid,
When fast she dropt her Tears, as thus she said:
"Farewel the Youth whom Sighs could not detain,
"Whom *Zara*'s breaking Heart implor'd in vain;
"Yet as thou go'st, may ev'ry Blast arise,
"Weak and unfelt as these rejected Sighs!
"Safe o'er the Wild, no Perils mayst thou see,
"No Griefs endure, nor weep, false Youth, like me."
O let me safely to the Fair return,
Say with a Kiss, she must not, shall not mourn.
Go teach my Heart, to lose its painful Fears,
Recall'd by Wisdom's Voice, and *Zara*'s Tears.

He said, and call'd on Heav'n to bless the Day,
When back to *Schiraz'* Walls he bent his Way.

Ode to Pity[1]

I.

O THOU, the Friend of Man assign'd,
With balmy Hands his Wounds to bind,
And charm his frantic Woe:

[1] Published in *Odes on Several Descriptive and Allegorical Subjects*, 1747. (December, 1746). Text of first edition.

When first *Distress* with Dagger keen
Broke forth to waste his destin'd Scene,
His wild unsated Foe!

2.

By *Pella's* Bard, a magic Name,
By all the Griefs his Thought could frame,
Receive my humble Rite:
Long, *Pity*, let the Nations view
Thy sky-worn Robes of tend'rest Blue,
And Eyes of dewy Light!

3.

But wherefore need I wander wide
To old *Ilissus'* distant Side,
Deserted Stream, and mute?
Wild *Arun*[2] too has heard thy Strains,
And Echo, 'midst my native Plains,
Been sooth'd by *Pity's* Lute.

4.

There first the Wren thy Myrtles shed
On gentlest *Otway's* infant Head,
To Him thy Cell was shown;
And while He sung the Female Heart,
With Youth's soft Notes unspoil'd by Art,
Thy Turtles mix'd their own.

5.

Come, *Pity*, come, by Fancy's Aid,
Ev'n now my Thoughts, relenting Maid,
Thy Temple's Pride design:
Its Southern Site, its Truth compleat
Shall raise a wild Enthusiast Heat,
In all who view the Shrine.

6.

There Picture's Toils shall well relate,
How Chance, or hard involving Fate,
O'er mortal Bliss prevail:
The Buskin'd Muse shall near her stand,

[2] "The River *Arun* runs by the Village in *Sussex*, where *Otway* had his Birth."—Collins' note.

And sighing prompt her tender Hand,
With each disastrous Tale.

7.

There let me oft, retir'd by Day,
In Dreams of Passion melt away,
Allow'd with Thee to dwell:
There waste the mournful Lamp of Night,
Till, Virgin, Thou again delight
To hear a *British* Shell!

Ode to Fear[1]

Thou, to whom the World unknown
With all its shadowy Shapes is shown;
Who see'st appall'd th' unreal Scene,
While Fancy lifts the Veil between:
Ah *Fear!* Ah frantic *Fear!*
I see, I see Thee near.
I know thy hurried Step, thy haggard Eye!
Like Thee I start, like Thee disorder'd fly.
For lo what *Monsters* in thy Train appear!
Danger, whose Limbs of Giant Mold
What mortal Eye can fix'd behold?
Who stalks his Round, an hideous Form,
Howling amidst the Midnight Storm,
Or throws him on the ridgy Steep
Of some loose hanging Rock to sleep:
And with him thousand Phantoms join'd,
Who prompt to Deeds accurs'd the Mind:
And those, the Fiends, who near allied,
O'er Nature's Wounds, and Wrecks preside;
Whilst *Vengeance*, in the lurid Air,
Lifts her red Arm, expos'd and bare:
On whom that rav'ning Brood of Fate,
Who lap the Blood of Sorrow, wait;
Who, *Fear*, this ghastly Train can see,
And look not madly wild, like Thee?

Epode

In earliest *Grece* to Thee with partial Choice,
The Grief-full Muse addrest her infant Tongue;

[1] Published in *Odes*, 1747. Text of first edition.

The Maids and Matrons, on her awful Voice,
  Silent and pale in wild Amazement hung.

Yet He, the Bard who first invok'd thy Name,[2]
  Disdain'd in *Marathon* its Pow'r to feel:
For not alone he nurs'd the Poet's flame,
  But reach'd from Virtue's Hand the Patriot's Steel.

But who is He whom later Garlands grace,
  Who left a-while o'er *Hybla*'s Dews to rove,
With trembling Eyes thy dreary Steps to trace,
  Where Thou and *Furies* shar'd the baleful Grove?

Wrapt in thy cloudy Veil the *Incestuous Queen*[3]
  Sigh'd the sad Call her Son and Husband hear'd,
When once alone it broke the silent Scene,
  And He the Wretch of *Thebes* no more appear'd.

O *Fear*, I know Thee by my throbbing Heart,
  Thy with'ring Pow'r inspir'd each mournful Line,
Tho' gentle *Pity* claim her mingled Part,
  Yet all the Thunders of the Scene are thine!

Antistrophe

Thou who such weary Lengths hast past,
Where wilt thou rest, mad Nymph, at last?
Say, wilt thou shroud in haunted Cell,
Where gloomy *Rape* and *Murder* dwell?
Or, in some hollow'd Seat,
'Gainst which the big Waves beat,
Hear drowning Sea-men's Cries in Tempests brought!
Dark Pow'r, with shudd'ring meek submitted Thought
Be mine, to read the Visions old,
Which thy awk'ning Bards have told:
And lest thou meet my blasted View,
Hold each strange Tale devoutly true,
Ne'er be I found, by Thee o'eraw'd,
In that thrice-hallow'd Eve abroad,
When Ghosts, as Cottage-Maids believe,
Their pebbled Beds permitted leave,
And *Gobblins* haunt from Fire, or Fen,
Or Mine, or Flood, the Walks of Men!
  O Thou whose Spirit most possest
The sacred Seat of *Shakespear*'s Breast!

---

[2] Æschylus.
[3] Jocasta.

By all that from thy Prophet broke,
In thy Divine Emotions spoke:
Hither again thy Fury deal,
Teach me but once like Him to feel:
His *Cypress Wreath* my Meed decree,
And I, O *Fear*, will dwell with Thee!

Ode to Simplicity[1]

1.

O THOU by *Nature* taught,
To breathe her genuine Thought,
In Numbers warmly pure, and sweetly strong:
Who first on Mountains wild,
In *Fancy* loveliest Child,
Thy Babe, or *Pleasure*'s, nurs'd the Pow'rs of Song!

2.

Thou, who with Hermit Heart
Disdain'st the Wealth of Art,
And Gauds, and pageant Weeds, and trailing Pall:
But com'st a decent Maid
In *Attic* Robe array'd,
O chaste unboastful Nymph, to Thee I call!

3.

By all the honey'd Store
On *Hybla*'s Thymy Shore,
By all her Blooms, and mingled Murmurs dear,
By Her, whose Love-born Woe
In Ev'ning Musings slow
Sooth'd sweetly sad *Electra*'s Poet's Ear:

4.

By old *Cephisus* deep,
Who spread his wavy Sweep
In warbled Wand'rings round thy green Retreat,
On whose enamel'd Side
When holy *Freedom* died
No equal Haunt allur'd thy future Feet.

[1] Published in *Odes*, 1747. Text of first edition.

5.

O Sister meek of Truth,
To my admiring Youth,
Thy sober Aid and native Charms infuse!
The Flow'rs that sweetest breathe,
Tho' Beauty cull'd the Wreath,
Still ask thy Hand to range their order'd Hues.

6.

While *Rome* could none esteem
But Virtue's Patriot Theme,
You lov'd her Hills, and led her Laureate Band:
But staid to sing alone
To one distinguish'd Throne,
And turn'd thy Face, and fled her alter'd Land.

7.

No more, in Hall or Bow'r,
The Passions own thy Pow'r,
Love, only Love her forceless Numbers mean:
For Thou hast left her Shrine,
Nor Olive more, nor Vine,
Shall gain thy Feet to bless the servile Scene.

8.

Tho' Taste, tho' Genius bless,
To some divine Excess,
Faints the cold Work till Thou inspire the whole;
What each, what all supply,
May court, may charm, our Eye,
Thou, only Thou can'st raise the meeting Soul!

9.

Of These let others ask,
To aid some mighty Task,
I only seek to find thy temp'rate Vale:
Where oft my Reed might sound
To Maids and Shepherds round,
And all thy Sons, O *Nature*, learn my Tale.

Ode on the Poetical Character[1]

I.

As ONCE, if not with light Regard,
I read aright that gifted Bard,
(Him whose School above the rest
His Loveliest *Elfin* Queen has blest.)
One, only One, unrival'd Fair,[2]
Might hope the magic Girdle wear,
At solemn Turney hung on high,
The Wish of each love-darting Eye;

Lo! to each other Nymph in turn applied,
As if, in Air unseen, some hov'ring Hand,
Some chaste and Angel-Friend to Virgin-Fame,
With whisper'd Spell had burst the starting Band,
It left unblest her loath'd dishonour'd Side;
Happier hopeless Fair, if never
Her baffled Hand with vain Endeavour
Had touch'd that fatal Zone to her denied!
Young *Fancy* thus, to me Divinest Name,
To whom, prepar'd and bath'd in Heav'n,
The Cest of amplest Pow'r is giv'n:
To few the God-like Gift assigns,
To gird their blest prophetic Loins,
And gaze her Visions wild, and feel unmix'd her Flame!

2.

The Band, as Fairy Legends say,
Was wove on that creating Day,
When He, who call'd with Thought to Birth
Yon tented Sky, this laughing Earth,
And drest with Springs, and Forests tall,
And pour'd the Main engirting all,
Long by the lov'd *Enthusiast* woo'd,
Himself in some Diviner Mood,
Retiring, sate with her alone,
And plac'd her on his Saphire Throne,
The whiles, the vaulted Shrine around,
Seraphic Wires were heard to sound,
Now sublimest Triumph swelling,
Now on Love and Mercy dwelling;
And she, from out the veiling Cloud,
Breath'd her magic Notes aloud:

[1] Published in *Odes*, 1747. Text of first edition.
[2] "Florimel. See Spenser Leg. 4th."—Collins' note.

And Thou, Thou rich-hair'd Youth of Morn,
And all thy subject Life was born!
The dang'rous Passions kept aloof,
Far from the sainted growing Woof:
But near it sate Ecstatic *Wonder*,
List'ning the deep applauding Thunder:
And *Truth*, in sunny Vest array'd,
By whose the Tarsel's Eyes were made;
All the shad'wy Tribes of *Mind*,
In braided Dance their Murmurs join'd,
And all the bright uncounted *Pow'rs*
Who feed on Heav'n's ambrosial Flow'rs.
Where is the Bard, whose Soul can now
Its high presuming Hopes avow?
Where He who thinks, with Rapture blind,
This hallow'd Work for Him design'd?

3.

High on some Cliff, to Heav'n up-pil'd,
Of rude Access, of Prospect wild,
Where, tangled round the jealous Steep,
Strange Shades o'erbrow the Valleys deep,
And holy *Genii* guard the Rock,
Its Gloomes embrown, its Springs unlock,
While on its rich ambitious Head,
An *Eden*, like his own, lies spread.
I view that Oak, the fancied Glades among,
By which as *Milton* lay, His Ev'ning Ear,
From many a Cloud that drop'd Ethereal Dew,
Nigh spher'd in Heav'n its native Strains could hear:
On which that ancient Trump he reach'd was hung;
    Thither oft his Glory greeting,
    From *Waller*'s Myrtle Shades retreating,
With many a Vow from Hope's aspiring Tongue,
My trembling Feet his guiding Steps pursue;
    In vain—Such Bliss to One alone,
    Of all the Sons of Soul was known,
    And Heav'n, and *Fancy*, kindred Pow'rs,
    Have now o'erturn'd th' inspiring Bow'rs,
Or curtain'd close such Scene from ev'ry future View.

Ode, Written in the Beginning of the Year, 1746[1]

How sleep the Brave, who sink to Rest,
By all their Country's Wishes blest!
When *Spring*, with dewy Fingers cold,
Returns to deck their hallow'd Mold,
She there shall dress a sweeter Sod,
Than *Fancy*'s Feet have ever trod.

By Fairy Hands their Knell is rung,
By Forms unseen their Dirge is sung;
There *Honour* comes, a Pilgrim grey,
To bless the Turf that wraps their Clay,
And *Freedom* shall a-while repair,
To dwell a weeping Hermit there!

Ode to Evening[2]

IF OUGHT of oaten stop, or pastoral song,
May hope, chaste EVE, to soothe thy modest ear,
Like thy own solemn springs,
Thy springs, and dying gales,
O NYMPH reserv'd, while now the bright-hair'd sun
Sits in yon western tent, whose cloudy skirts,
With brede ethereal wove,
O'erhang his wavy bed:
Now air is hush'd, save where the weak-ey'd bat,
With short shrill shriek flits by on leathern wing,
Or where the Beetle winds
His small but sullen horn,
As oft he rises 'midst the twilight path,
Against the pilgrim born in heedless hum:
Now teach me, Maid compos'd,
To breathe some soften'd strain,
Whose numbers stealing thro' thy darkning vale,
May not unseemly with its stillness suit,
As musing slow, I hail
Thy genial lov'd return!
For when thy folding star arising shews
His paly circlet, at his warning lamp
The fragrant Hours, and Elves
Who slept in flow'rs the day,

[1] Published in *Odes*, 1747. Text of first edition.
[2] Published in *Odes*, 1747. Text of Dodsley's *Collection of Poems*, 1748.

And many a Nymph who wreaths her brows with sedge,
And sheds the fresh'ning dew, and lovelier still,
The PENSIVE PLEASURES sweet
Prepare thy shadowy car.
Then lead, calm Vot'ress, where some sheety lake
Cheers the lone heath, or some time-hallow'd pile,
Or up-land fallows grey
Reflect its last cool gleam.
But when chill blust'ring winds, or driving rain,
Forbid my willing feet, be mine the hut,
That from the mountain's side,
Views wilds, and swelling floods,
And hamlets brown, and dim-discover'd spires,
And hears their simple bell, and marks o'er all
Thy dewy fingers draw
The gradual dusky veil.
While Spring shall pour his show'rs, as oft he wont,
And bathe thy breathing tresses, meekest Eve!
While Summer loves to sport,
Beneath thy ling'ring light;
While sallow Autumn fills thy lap with leaves;
Or Winter yelling thro' the troublous air,
Affrights thy shrinking train,
And rudely rends thy robes;
So long, sure-found beneath the Sylvan shed,
Shall FANCY, FRIENDSHIP, SCIENCE, rose-lip'd HEALTH,
Thy gentlest influence own,
And hymn thy fav'rite name!

The Passions, An Ode for Music[1]

WHEN Music, Heav'nly Maid, was young,
While yet in early *Greece* she sung,
The Passions oft to hear her Shell,
Throng'd around her magic Cell,
Exulting, trembling, raging, fainting,
Possest beyond the Muse's Painting;
By turns they felt the glowing Mind,
Disturb'd, delighted, rais'd, refin'd.
Till once, 'tis said, when all were fir'd,
Fill'd with Fury, rapt, inspir'd,
From the supporting Myrtles round,
They snatch'd her Instruments of Sound,
And as they oft had heard a-part

[1] Published in *Odes*, 1747. Text of first edition.

Sweet Lessons of her forceful Art,
Each, for Madness rul'd the Hour,
Would prove his own expressive Pow'r.

First *Fear* his Hand, its Skill to try,
Amid the Chords bewilder'd laid,
And back recoil'd he knew not why,
Ev'n at the Sound himself had made.

Next *Anger* rush'd, his Eyes on fire,
In Lightnings own'd his secret Stings,
In one rude Clash he struck the Lyre,
And swept with hurried Hand the Strings.

With woful Measures wan *Despair*
Low sullen Sounds his Grief beguil'd,
A solemn, strange, and mingled Air,
'Twas sad by Fits, by Starts 'twas wild.

But thou, O *Hope*, with Eyes so fair,
What was thy delightful Measure?
Still it whisper'd promis'd Pleasure,
And bad the lovely Scenes at distance hail!

Still would Her Touch the Strain prolong,
And from the Rocks, the Woods, the Vale,
She call'd on Echo still thro' all the Song;
And where Her sweetest Theme She chose,
A soft responsive Voice was heard at ev'ry Close,
And *Hope* enchanted smil'd, and wav'd Her golden Hair.

And longer had She sung,—but with a Frown,
Revenge impatient rose,
He threw his blood-stain'd Sword in Thunder down,
And with a with'ring Look,
The War-denouncing Trumpet took,
And blew a Blast so loud and dread,
Were ne'er Prophetic Sounds so full of Woe.
And ever and anon he beat
The doubling Drum with furious Heat;
And tho' sometimes each dreary Pause between,
Dejected *Pity* at his Side,
Her Soul-subduing Voice applied,
Yet still He kept his wild unalter'd Mien,
While each strain'd Ball of Sight seem'd bursting from his Head.

Thy Numbers, *Jealousy*, to nought were fix'd,
Sad Proof of thy distressful State,

Of diff'ring Themes the veering Song was mix'd,
  And now it courted *Love*, now raving call'd on *Hate*.

With Eyes up-rais'd, as one inspir'd,
Pale *Melancholy* sate retir'd,
And from her wild sequester'd Seat,
In Notes by Distance made more sweet,
Pour'd thro' the mellow *Horn* her pensive Soul:
  And dashing soft from Rocks around,
  Bubbling Runnels join'd the Sound;
Thro' Glades and Glooms the mingled Measure stole,
Or o'er some haunted Stream with fond Delay,
  Round an holy Calm diffusing,
  Love of Peace, and lonely Musing,
In hollow Murmurs died away.
But O how alter'd was its sprightlier Tone!
When *Chearfulness*, a Nymph of healthiest Hue,
  Her Bow a-cross her Shoulder flung,
  Her Buskins gem'd with Morning Dew,
Blew an inspiring Air, that Dale and Thicket rung,
  The Hunter's Call to *Faun* and *Dryad* known!
  The Oak-crown'd *Sisters*, and their chast-eye'd *Queen*,
  Satyrs and sylvan Boys were seen,
  Peeping from forth their Alleys green;
Brown *Exercise* rejoic'd to hear,
  And *Sport* leapt up, and seiz'd his Beechen Spear.

Last came *Joy*'s Ecstatic Trial,
He with viny Crown advancing,
  First to the lively Pipe his Hand addrest,
But soon he saw the brisk awak'ning Viol,
  Whose sweet entrancing Voice he lov'd the best.
  They would have thought who heard the Strain,
  They saw in *Tempe*'s Vale her native Maids,
  Amidst the festal sounding Shades,
To some unwearied Minstrel dancing,
  While as his flying Fingers kiss'd the Strings,
  LOVE fram'd with *Mirth*, a gay fantastic Round,
  Loose were Her Tresses seen, her Zone unbound,
  And HE amidst his frolic Play,
  As if he would the charming Air repay,
  Shook thousand Odours from his dewy Wings.

  O *Music*, Sphere-descended Maid,
  Friend of Pleasure, *Wisdom*'s Aid,
  Why, Goddess, why to us deny'd?
  Lay'st Thou thy antient Lyre aside?
  As in that lov'd *Athenian* Bow'r,

You learn'd an all-commanding Pow'r,
Thy mimic Soul, O Nymph endear'd,
Can well recall what then it heard.
Where is thy native simple Heart,
Devote to Virtue, Fancy, Art?
Arise as in that elder Time,
Warm, Energic, Chaste, Sublime!
Thy Wonders in that God-like Age,
Fill thy recording *Sister*'s Page—
'Tis said, and I believe the Tale,
Thy humblest *Reed* could more prevail,
Had more of Strength, diviner Rage,
Than all which charms this laggard Age,
Ev'n all at once together found,
Cæcilia's mingled World of Sound—
O bid our vain Endeavors cease,
Revive the just Designs of *Greece*,
Return in all thy simple State!
Confirm the Tales Her Sons relate!

A Song from Shakespear's Cymbeline Sung by Guiderus and Arviragus over Fidele, Supposed to be Dead[1]

To FAIR Fidele's grassy tomb
  Soft maids and village hinds shall bring
Each op'ning sweet, of earliest bloom,
  And rifle all the breathing Spring.

No wailing ghost shall dare appear
  To vex with shrieks this quiet grove:
But shepherd lads assemble here,
  And melting virgins own their love.

No wither'd witch shall here be seen,
  No goblins lead their nightly crew:
The female fays shall haunt the green,
  And dress thy grave with pearly dew!

The red-breast oft at ev'ning hours
  Shall kindly lend his little aid:
With hoary moss, and gather'd flow'rs,
  To deck the ground where thou art laid.

[1] Published in the *Gentleman's Magazine*, October, 1749. Text of Dodsley's *Collection of Poems*, Vol. IV, 1755.

When howling winds, and beating rain,
In tempests shake the sylvan cell:
Or 'midst the chace on ev'ry plain,
The tender thought on thee shall dwell.

Each lonely scene shall thee restore,
For thee the tear be duly shed:
Belov'd till life can charm no more,
And mourn'd, till Pity's self be dead.

An Ode on the Popular Superstitions of the Highlands of Scotland, Considered as the Subject of Poetry[1]

I.

H——, thou return'st from Thames, whose Naiads long
Have seen thee ling'ring, with a fond delay,
Mid those soft friends, whose hearts, some future day,
Shall melt, perhaps, to hear thy tragic song.
Go, not unmindful of that cordial youth,
Whom, long endear'd, thou leav'st by Lavant's side;
Together let us wish him lasting truth,
And joy untainted with his destin'd bride.
Go! nor regardless, while these numbers boast
My short-liv'd bliss, forget my social name;
But think far off how, on the southern coast,
I met thy friendship with an equal flame!
Fresh to that soil thou turn'st, whose ev'ry vale
Shall prompt the poet, and his song demand:
To thee thy copious subjects ne'er shall fail;
Thou need'st but take the pencil to thy hand,
And paint what all believe who own thy genial land.

II.

THERE must thou wake perforce thy Doric quill,
'Tis Fancy's land to which thou sett'st thy feet;
Where still, 'tis said, the fairy people meet
Beneath each birken shade on mead or hill.
There each trim lass that skims the milky store
To the swart tribes their creamy bowl allots;

[1] Written about 1749. Published in the *Transactions of the Royal Society of Edinburgh,* 1788. Text of first edition.

By night they sip it round the cottage-door,
  While airy minstrels warble jocund notes.
There every herd, by sad experience, knows
  How, wing'd with fate, their elf-shot arrows fly;
When the sick ewe her summer food foregoes,
  Or, stretch'd on earth, the heart-smit heifers lie.
Such airy beings awe th' untutor'd swain:
  Nor thou, though learn'd, his homelier thoughts neglect;
Let thy sweet muse the rural faith sustain;
  These are the themes of simple, sure effect,
That add new conquests to her boundless reign,
And fill, with double force, her heart-commanding strain.

III.

Ev'n yet preserv'd, how often may'st thou hear,
  Where to the pole the Boreal mountains run,
Taught by the father to his list'ning son
  Strange lays, whose power had charm'd a Spencer's ear.
At ev'ry pause, before thy mind possest,
  Old Runic bards shall seem to rise around,
With uncouth lyres, in many-coloured vest,
  Their matted hair with boughs fantastic crown'd:
Whether thou bid'st the well-taught hind repeat
  The choral dirge that mourns some chieftain brave,
When ev'ry shrieking maid her bosom beat,
  And strew'd with choicest herbs his scented grave;
Or whether, sitting in the shepherd's shiel,
  Thou hear'st some sounding tale of war's alarms;
When at the bugle's call, with fire and steel,
  The sturdy clans pour'd forth their bony swarms,
And hostile brothers met to prove each other's arms.

IV.

'Tis thine to sing, how framing hideous spells
  In Sky's lone isle the gifted wizzard seer,
Lodged in the wintry cave with ———,
  Or in the depth of Uist's dark forests dwells:
How they, whose sight such dreary dreams engross,
  With their own visions oft astonish'd droop,
When o'er the wat'ry strath or quaggy moss
  They see the gliding ghosts unbodied troop.
Or if in sports, or on the festive green,
  Their ——— glance some fated youth descry,
Who, now perhaps in lusty vigour seen
  And rosy health, shall soon lamented die.
For them the viewless forms of air obey,

Their bidding heed, and at their beck repair.
They know what spirit brews the stormful day,
And heartless, oft like moody madness stare
To see the phantom train their secret work prepare.

[Twenty-five lines lost.]

VI.

What though far off, from some dark dell espied
His glimm'ring mazes cheer th' excursive sight,
Yet turn, ye wand'rers, turn your steps aside,
Nor trust the guidance of that faithless light;
For watchful, lurking 'mid th' unrustling reed,
At those mirk hours the wily monster lies,
And listens oft to hear the passing steed,
And frequent round him rolls his sullen eyes,
If chance his savage wrath may some weak wretch surprise.

VII.

Ah, luckless swain, o'er all unblest indeed!
Whom late bewilder'd in the dank, dark fen,
Far from his flocks and smoking hamlet then!
To that sad spot ——————:
On him enrag'd, the fiend, in angry mood,
Shall never look with pity's kind concern,
But instant, furious, raise the whelming flood
O'er its drown'd bank, forbidding all return.
Or, if he meditate his wish'd escape
To some dim hill that seems uprising near,
To his faint eye the grim and grisly shape,
In all its terrors clad, shall wild appear.
Meantime, the wat'ry surge shall around him rise,
Pour'd sudden forth from ev'ry swelling source.
What now remains but tears and hopeless sighs?
His fear-shook limbs have lost their youthly force,
And down the waves he floats, a pale and breathless corse.

VIII.

For him, in vain, his anxious wife shall wait,
Or wander forth to meet him on his way;
For him, in vain, at to-fall of the day,
His babes shall linger at th' unclosing gate.
Ah, ne'er shall he return! Alone, if night
Her travell'd limbs in broken slumbers steep,

With dropping willows drest, his mournful sprite
  Shall visit sad, perchance, her silent sleep:
Then he, perhaps, with moist and wat'ry hand,
  Shall fondly seem to press her shudd'ring cheek,
And with his blue swoln face before her stand,
  And, shiv'ring cold, these piteous accents speak:
Pursue, dear wife, thy daily toils pursue
  At dawn or dusk, industrious as before;
Nor e'er of me one hapless thought renew,
  While I lie welt'ring on the ozier'd shore,
Drown'd by the KAELPIE's wrath, nor e'er shall aid thee more!

IX.

UNBOUNDED is thy range; with varied stile
  Thy muse may, like those feath'ry tribes which spring
From their rude rocks, extend her skirting wing
  Round the moist marge of each cold Hebrid isle,
To that hoar pile which still its ruin shows:
  In whose small vaults a pigmy-folk is found,
Whose bones the delver with his spade upthrows,
  And culls them, wond'ring, from the hallow'd ground!
Or thither where beneath the show'ry west
  The mighty kings of three fair realms are laid:
Once foes, perhaps, together now they rest.
  No slaves revere them, and no wars invade:
Yet frequent now, at midnight's solemn hour,
  The rifted mounds their yawning cells unfold,
And forth the monarchs stalk with sov'reign pow'r
  In pageant robes, and wreath'd with sheeny gold,
And on their twilight tombs aerial council hold.

X.

BUT O! o'er all, forget not KILDA's race,
  On whose bleak rocks, which brave the wasting tides,
Fair Nature's daughter, Virtue, yet abides.
  Go, just, as they, their blameless manners trace!
Then to my ear transmit some gentle song
  Of those whose lives are yet sincere and plain,
Their bounded walks the rugged cliffs along,
  And all their prospect but the wintry main.
With sparing temp'rance, at the needful time,
  They drain the sainted spring, or, hunger-prest,
Along th' Atlantic rock undreading climb,
  And of its eggs despoil the Solan's nest.
Thus blest in primal innocence they live,
  Suffic'd and happy with that frugal fare

Which tasteful toil and hourly danger give.
  Hard is their shallow soil, and bleak and bare;
Nor ever vernal bee was heard to murmur there!

XI.

Nor need'st thou blush, that such false themes engage
  Thy gentle mind, of fairer stores possest;
For not alone they touch the village breast,
  But fill'd in elder time th' historic page.
There Shakespeare's self, with ev'ry garland crown'd,
  In musing hour, his wayward sisters found,
And with their terrors drest the magic scene.
From them he sung, when mid his bold design,
  Before the Scot afflicted and aghast,
The shadowy kings of Banquo's fated line
  Through the dark cave in gleamy pageant past.
Proceed, nor quit the tales which, simply told,
  Could once so well my answ'ring bosom pierce;
Proceed, in forceful sounds and colours bold
  The native legends of thy land rehearse;
To such adapt thy lyre and suit thy powerful verse.

XII.

In scenes like these, which, daring to depart
  From sober truth, are still to nature true,
And call forth fresh delight to fancy's view,
  Th' heroic muse employ'd her Tasso's art!
How have I trembled, when at Tancred's stroke,
  Its gushing blood the gaping cypress pour'd;
When each live plant with mortal accents spoke,
  And the wild blast up-heav'd the vanish'd sword!
How have I sat, when pip'd the pensive wind,
  To hear his harp, by British Fairfax strung.
Prevailing poet, whose undoubting mind
  Believ'd the magic wonders which he sung!
Hence at each sound imagination glows;
Hence his warm lay with softest sweetness flows;
  Melting it flows, pure, num'rous, strong and clear,
And fills th' impassion'd heart, and wins th' harmonious ear.

XIII.

All hail, ye scenes that o'er my soul prevail,
  Ye ——— friths and lakes which, far away,
Are by smooth Annan fill'd, or past'ral Tay,
  Or Don's romantic springs, at distance, hail!

The time shall come when I, perhaps, may tread
  Your lowly glens, o'erhung with spreading broom,
Or o'er your stretching heaths by fancy led:
  Then will I dress once more the faded bow'r,
Where JOHNSON sat in DRUMMOND's —— shade,
  Or crop from Tiviot's dale each ——,
And mourn on Yarrow's banks ——.
Meantime, ye Pow'rs, that on the plains which bore
  The cordial youth, on LOTHIAN's plains attend,
Where'er he dwell, on hill, or lowly muir,
  To him I lose, your kind protection lend,
And, touch'd with love like mine, preserve my absent friend.

JOSEPH WARTON

(1722-1739-1800)

The Enthusiast: or, The Lover of Nature[1]

YE green-rob'd *Dryads*, oft' at dusky Eve
By wondering Shepherds seen, to Forests brown,
To unfrequented Meads, and pathless Wilds,
Lead me from Gardens deckt with Art's vain Pomps.
Can gilt Alcoves, can Marble-mimic Gods,
Parterres embroider'd, Obelisks, and Urns
Of high Relief; can the long, spreading Lake,
Or Vista lessening to the Sight; can *Stow*
With all her *Attic* Fanes, such Raptures raise,
As the Thrush-haunted Copse, where lightly leaps
The fearful Fawn the rustling Leaves along,
And the brisk Squirrel sports from Bough to Bough,
While from an hollow Oak the busy Bees
Hum drowsy Lullabies? The Bards of old,
Fair Nature's Friends, sought such Retreats, to charm
Sweet *Echo* with their Songs; oft' too they met,
In Summer Evenings, near sequester'd Bow'rs,
Or Mountain-Nymph, or Muse, and eager learnt
The moral Strains she taught to mend Mankind.
As to a secret Grot *Ægeria* stole
With Patriot *Numa*, and in silent Night
Whisper'd him sacred Laws, he list'ning sat
Rapt with her virtuous Voice, old *Tyber* leant

[1] Published in 1744. Text of first edition.

Attentive on his Urn, and husht his Waves.
Rich in her weeping Country's Spoils *Versailles*
May boast a thousand Fountains, that can cast
The tortur'd Waters to the distant Heav'ns;
Yet let me choose some Pine-topt Precipice
Abrupt and shaggy, whence a foamy Stream,
Like *Anio*, tumbling roars; or some bleak Heath,
Where straggling stand the mournful Juniper,
Or Yew-tree scath'd; while in clear Prospect round,
From the Grove's Bosom Spires emerge, and Smoak
In bluish Wreaths ascends, ripe Harvests wave,
Herds low, and Straw-rooft Cotts appear, and Streams
Beneath the Sun-beams twinkle—The shrill Lark,
That wakes the Wood-man to his early Task,
Or love-sick *Philomel*, whose luscious Lays
Sooth lone Night-wanderers, the moaning Dove
Pitied by listening Milkmaid, far excell
The deep-mouth'd Viol, the Soul-lulling Lute,
And Battle-breathing Trumpet. Artful Sounds!
That please not like the Choristers of Air,
When first they hail th' Approach of laughing *May*.
Creative *Titian*, can thy vivid Strokes,
Or thine, O graceful *Raphael*, dare to vie
With the rich Tints that paint the breathing Mead?
The thousand-colour'd Tulip, Violet's Bell
Snow-clad and meek, the Vermil-tinctur'd Rose,
And golden Crocus?—Yet with these the Maid,
Phillis or *Phœbe*, at a Feast or Wake,
Her jetty Locks enamels; fairer she,
In Innocence and home-spun Vestments drest,
Than if cœrulean Sapphires at her Ears
Shone pendant, or a precious Diamond-Cross
Heav'd gently on her panting Bosom white.
Yon' Shepherd idly stretcht on the rude Rock,
Listening to dashing Waves, the Sea-Mews Clang
High-hovering o'er his Head, who views beneath
The Dolphin dancing o'er the level Brine,
Feels more true Bliss than the proud Ammiral,
Amid his Vessels bright with burnish'd Gold
And silken Streamers, tho' his lordly Nod
Ten thousand War-worn Mariners revere.
And great *Æneas* gaz'd with more Delight
On the rough Mountain shagg'd with horrid Shades,
(Where Cloud-compelling *Jove*, as Fancy dream'd,
Descending shook his direful *Ægis* black)
Than if he enter'd the high Capitol
On golden Columns rear'd, a conquer'd World
Contributing to deck its stately Head:

More pleas'd he slept in poor *Evander*'s Cott
On shaggy Skins, lull'd by sweet Nightingales,
Than if a *Nero*, in an Age refin'd,
Beneath a gorgeous Canopy had plac'd
His royal Guest, and bade his Minstrels sound
Soft slumb'rous *Lydian* Airs to sooth his Rest.
Happy the first of Men, ere yet confin'd
To smoaky Cities; who in sheltering Groves,
Warm Caves, and deep-sunk Vallies liv'd and lov'd,
By Cares unwounded; what the Sun and Showers,
And genial Earth untillag'd could produce,
They gather'd grateful, or the Acorn brown,
Or blushing Berry; by the liquid Lapse
Of murm'ring Waters call'd to slake their Thirst,
Or with fair Nymphs their Sun-brown Limbs to bathe;
With Nymphs who fondly clasp'd their fav'rite Youths,
Unaw'd by Shame, beneath the Beechen Shade,
Nor Wiles, nor artificial Coyness knew.
Then Doors and Walls were not; the melting Maid
Nor Frowns of Parents fear'd, nor Husband's Threats;
Nor had curs'd Gold their tender Hearts allur'd;
Then Beauty was not venal. Injur'd Love,
O whither, God of Raptures, art thou fled?
While Avarice waves his golden Wand around,
Abhorr'd Magician, and his costly Cup
Prepares with baneful Drugs, t'enchant the Souls
Of each low-thoughted Fair to wed for Gain.
What tho' unknown to those primæval Sires,
The well-arch'd Dome, peopled with breathing Forms
By fair *Italia*'s skilful Hand, unknown
The shapely Column, and the crumbling Busts
Of awful Ancestors in long Descent?
Yet why should Man mistaken deem it nobler
To dwell in Palaces, and high-rooft Halls,
Than in God's Forests, Architect supreme!
Say, is the *Persian* Carpet, than the Field's
Or Meadow's Mantle gay, more richly wov'n;
Or softer to the Votaries of Ease,
Than bladed Grass, perfum'd with dew-dropt Flow'rs?
O Taste corrupt! that Luxury and Pomp
In specious Names of *polish'd Manners* veil'd,
Should proudly banish Nature's simple Charms.
Tho' the fierce North oft smote with Iron Whip
Their shiv'ring Limbs, tho' oft the bristly Boar
Or hungry Lion 'woke them with their Howls,
And scar'd them from their Moss-grown Caves to rove,

Houseless and cold in dark, tempestuous Nights;
Yet were not Myriads in embattled Fields
Swept off at once, nor had the raving Seas
O'erwhelm'd the foundering Bark, and helpless Crew;
In vain the glassy Ocean smil'd to tempt
The jolly Sailor, unsuspecting Harm,
For Commerce was unknown. *Then* Want and Pine
Sunk to the Grave their fainting Limbs; but *Us*
Excess and endless Riot doom to die.
They cropt the poisonous Herb unweetingly,
But wiser we spontaneously provide
Rare powerful Roots, to quench Life's chearful Lamp.
  What are the Lays of artful *Addison*,
Coldly correct, to *Shakespear*'s Warblings wild ?
Whom on the winding *Avon*'s willow'd Banks
Fair Fancy found, and bore the smiling Babe
To a close Cavern: (still the Shepherds shew
The sacred Place, whence with religious Awe
They hear, returning from the Field at Eve,
Strange Whisperings of sweet Music thro' the Air)
Here, as with Honey gather'd from the Rock,
She fed the little Prattler, and with Songs
Oft' sooth'd his wondering Ears, with deep Delight
On her soft Lap he sat, and caught the Sounds.
  Oft' near some crowded City would I walk,
Listening the far-off Noises, rattling Carrs,
Loud Shouts of Joy, sad Shrieks of Sorrow, Knells
Full slowly tolling, Instruments of Trade,
Striking mine Ears with one deep-swelling Hum.
Or wandering near the Sea, attend the Sounds
Of hollow Winds, and ever-beating Waves.
Ev'n when wild Tempests swallow up the Plains,
And *Boreas'* Blasts, big Hail, and Rains combine
To shake the Groves and Mountains, would I sit,
Pensively musing on th' outragious Crimes
That wake Heav'n's Vengeance: at such solemn Hours,
Dæmons and Goblins thro' the dark Air shriek,
While *Hecat* with her black-brow'd Sisters nine,
Rides o'er the Earth, and scatters Woes and Deaths.
Then too, they say, in drear *Ægyptian* Wilds
The Lion and the Tiger prowl for Prey
With Roarings loud! the list'ning Traveller
Starts Fear-struck, while the hollow-echoing Vaults
Of Pyramids encrease the deathful Sounds.
  But let me never fail in cloudless Nights,
When silent *Cynthia* in her silver Car

Thro' the blue Concave slides, when shine the Hills,
Twinkle the Streams, and Woods look tipt with Gold,
To seek some level Mead, and there invoke
Old Midnight's Sister Contemplation sage,
(Queen of the rugged Brow, and stern-fixt Eye)
To lift my Soul above this little Earth,
This Folly-fetter'd World; to purge my Ears,
That I may hear the rolling Planets Song,
And tuneful-turning Spheres: If this debarr'd,
The little *Fayes* that dance in neighbouring Dales,
Sipping the Night-dew, while they laugh and love,
Shall charm me with aërial Notes.—As thus
I wander musing, lo, what awful Forms
Yonder appear! sharp-ey'd *Philosophy*
Clad in dun Robes, an Eagle on his Wrist,
First meets my Eye; next, Virgin *Solitude*
Serene, who blushes at each Gazer's Sight;
Then *Wisdom*'s hoary Head, with Crutch in Hand,
Trembling, and bent with Age; last *Virtue*'s self
Smiling, in White array'd, who with her leads
Fair *Innocence*, that prattles by her Side,
A naked Boy!—Harrass'd with Fear I stop,
I gaze, when *Virtue* thus—'Whoe'er thou art,
'Mortal, by whom I deign to be beheld,
'In these my Midnight-Walks; depart, and say
'That henceforth I and my immortal Train
'Forsake *Britannia*'s Isle; who fondly stoops
'To Vice, her favourite Paramour.'—She spoke,
And as she turn'd, her round and rosy Neck,
Her flowing Train, and long, ambrosial Hair,
Breathing rich Odours, I enamour'd view.
  O who will bear me then to Western Climes,
(Since Virtue leaves our wretched Land) to Shades
Yet unpolluted with *Iberian* Swords;
With simple *Indian* Swains, that I may hunt
The Boar and Tiger thro' *Savannah*'s wild?
There fed on Dates and Herbs, would I despise
The far-fetch'd Cates of Luxury, and Hoards
Of narrow-hearted Avarice; nor heed
The distant Din of the tumultuous World.
So when rude Whirlwinds rouze the roaring Main,
Beneath fair *Thetis* sits, in coral Caves,
Serenely gay, nor sinking Sailors Cries
Disturb her sportive Nymphs, who round her form
The light fantastic Dance, or for her Hair
Weave rosy Crowns, or with according Lutes
Grace the soft Warbles of her honied Voice.

Ode I. To Fancy[1]

O PARENT of each lovely Muse,
Thy spirit o'er my soul diffuse,
O'er all my artless songs preside,
My footsteps to thy temple guide,
To offer at thy turf-built shrine,
In golden cups no costly wine,
No murder'd fatling of the flock,
But flowers and honey from the rock.
O Nymph, with loosely-flowing hair,
With buskin'd leg, and bosom bare,
Thy waist with myrtle-girdle bound,
Thy brows with Indian feathers crown'd,
Waving in thy snowy hand
An all-commanding magic wand,
Of pow'r to bid fresh gardens blow
'Midst chearless Lapland's barren snow,
Whose rapid wings thy flight convey
Thro' air, and over earth and sea,
While the vast, various landscape lies
Conspicuous to thy piercing eyes;
O lover of the desart, hail!
Say, in what deep and pathless vale,
Or on what hoary mountain's side,
'Midst falls of water you reside,
'Midst broken rocks, a rugged scene,
With green and grassy dales between,
'Midst forests dark of aged oak,
Ne'er echoing with the woodman's stroke,
Where never human art appear'd,
Nor ev'n one straw-rooft cott was rear'd,
Where NATURE seems to sit alone,
Majestic on a craggy throne;
Tell me the path, sweet wand'rer, tell,
To thy unknown sequester'd cell,
Where woodbines cluster round the door,
Where shells and moss o'erlay the floor,
And on whose top an hawthorn blows,
Amid whose thickly-woven boughs,
Some nightingale still builds her nest,
Each evening warbling thee to rest;
Then lay me by the haunted stream
Wrapt in some wild, poëtic dream,
In converse while methinks I rove

[1] Published in *Odes on Various Subjects*, 1746. Text of first edition.

With SPENSER thro' a fairy grove;
Till suddenly awoke, I hear
Strange whisper'd music in my ear,
And my glad soul in bliss is drown'd,
By the sweetly-soothing sound!
Me, Goddess, by the right-hand lead,
Sometimes thro' the yellow mead,
Where JOY and white-rob'd PEACE resort,
And VENUS keeps her festive court,
Where MIRTH and YOUTH each evening meet,
And lightly trip with nimble feet,
Nodding their lilly-crowned heads,
Where LAUGHTER rose-lip'd HEBE leads;
Where ECHO walks steep hills among,
List'ning to the shepherd's song:
Or sometimes in thy fiery car
Transport me to the rage of war;
There whirl me o'er the hills of slain,
Where Tumult and Destruction reign;
Where mad with pain, the wounded steed
Tramples the dying and the dead;
Where giant Terror stalks around,
With sullen joy surveys the ground,
And pointing to th' ensanguin'd field,
Shakes his dreadful Gorgon-shield!
Then guide me from this horrid scene
To high-archt walks and alleys green,
Where lovely LAURA walks, to shun
The fervors of the mid-day sun;
The pangs of absence, O remove,
For thou can'st place me near my love,
Can'st fold in visionary bliss,
And let me think I steal a kiss,
While her ruby lips dispense
Luscious nectar's quintessence!
When young-ey'd SPRING profusely throws
From her green lap the pink and rose,
When the soft turtle of the dale,
To SUMMER tells her tender tale,
When AUTUMN cooling caverns seeks,
And stains with wine his jolly cheeks,
When WINTER, like poor pilgrim old,
Shakes his silver beard with cold,
At every season let my ear
Thy solemn whispers, FANCY, hear.
O warm, enthusiastic maid,
Without thy powerful, vital aid,
That breathes an energy divine,

That gives a soul to every line,
Ne'er may I strive with lips profane
To utter an unhallow'd strain,
Nor dare to touch the sacred string,
Save when with smiles thou bid'st me sing.
O hear our prayer, O hither come
From thy lamented SHAKESPEAR's tomb,
On which thou lov'st to sit at eve,
Musing o'er your darling's grave;
O queen of numbers, once again
Animate some chosen swain,
Who fill'd with unexhausted fire,
May boldly smite the sounding lyre,
Who with some new, unequall'd song,
May rise above the rhyming throng,
O'er all our list'ning passions reign,
O'erwhelm our souls with joy and pain,
With terror shake, with pity move,
Rouze with revenge, or melt with love.
O deign t'attend his evening walk,
With him in groves and grottos talk;
Teach him to scorn with frigid art
Feebly to touch th' unraptur'd heart;
Like light'ning, let his mighty verse
The bosom's inmost foldings pierce;
With native beauties win applause,
Beyond cold critic's studied laws:
O let each Muse's fame encrease,
O bid BRITANNIA rival GREECE!

JAMES HAMMOND

(1710-1740-1742)

Love Elegies. Written in the Year 1732[1]

Elegy VII

On Delia's being in the Country where he supposes she stays to see the Harvest

Now DELIA breathes in Woods the fragrant Air,
Dull are the Hearts that still in Town remain,

[1] Published in 1743. Text of Dublin edition, 1747.

Venus her self attends on Delia there,
And Cupid sports amid the sylvan Train.

Oh with what Joy, my Delia to behold,
I'd press the Spade, or weild the weighty Prong,
Guide the slow Plough-share thro' the stubborn Mold,
And patient goad the loit'ring Ox along!

The scorching Heats I'd carelessly despise,
Nor heed the Blisters on my tender Hand;
The great Apollo wore the same Disguise,
Like me subdu'd to Love's supreme Command.

No healing Herbs cou'd sooth their Master's Pain,
The Art of Physick lost and useless lay,
To *Peneus'* Stream, and *Tempe*'s shady Plain,
He drove his Herds beneath the Noon-tide Ray:

Oft with a bleating Lamb in either Arm,
His blushing Sister saw him pace along,
Oft wou'd his Voice the silent Vally charm,
Till lowing Oxen broke the tender Song.

Where are his Triumphs? where his warlike Toil?
Where by his Darts the crested Python slain?
Where are his *Delphi?* his delightful Isle?
The God himself is grown a cottage Swain.

O Ceres, in your golden Fields no more,
With Harvest's chearful Pomp my Fair detain,—
Think what for lost Proserpina you bore,
And in a Mother's Anguish feel my Pain.

Our Wiser Fathers left their Fields unsown,
Their Food was Acorns, Love their sole Imploy,
They met, they lik'd, they stay'd but till alone,
And in each Valley snatch'd the honest Joy:

No wakeful Guard, no Doors to stop Desire,
Thrice happy Times!—but Oh I fondly rave,
Lead me to Delia, all her Eyes inspire
I'll do,—I'll plough or dig as Delia's Slave.

Elegy XII

To Delia

No second Love shall e'er my Heart surprize,
This solemn League did first our Passion bind:

Thou, only thou, canst please thy Lover's Eyes,
Thy Voice alone can sooth his troubled Mind.

Oh that thy Charms were only fair to me,
Displease all Others, and secure my Rest,
No need of Envy,—let me happy be,
I little care that Others know me blest.

With thee in gloomy Deserts let me dwell,
Where never human Footstep mark'd the Ground;
Thou, Light of Life, all Darkness canst expel,
And seem a World with Solitude around.

I say too much—my heedless Words restore,
My Tongue undoes me in this loving Hour,
Thou know'st thy Strength, and thence insulting more,
Will make me feel the Weight of all thy Power:

Whate'er I feel, thy Slave I will remain,
Nor fly the Burthen I am form'd to bear,
In Chains I'll sit me down at VENUS' Fane,
She knows my Wrongs, and will regard my Pray'r.

THOMAS GRAY

(1716-1742-1771)

Ode on the Spring[1]

Lo! WHERE the rosy-bosom'd Hours,
Fair VENUS' train appear,
Disclose the long-expecting flowers,
And wake the purple year!
The Attic warbler pours her throat,
Responsive to the cuckow's note,
The untaught harmony of spring:
While whisp'ring pleasure as they fly,
Cool Zephyrs thro' the clear blue sky
Their gather'd fragrance fling.

Where'er the oak's thick branches stretch
A broader browner shade;

[1] Written in June, 1742. Published in Dodsley's *Collection of Poems*, 1748. Text of *Poems*, 1768.

Where'er the rude and moss-grown beech
O'er-canopies the glade,
Beside some water's rushy brink
With me the Muse shall sit, and think
(At ease reclin'd in rustic state)
How vain the ardour of the Crowd,
How low, how little are the Proud,
How indigent the Great!

Still is the toiling hand of Care:
The panting herds repose:
Yet hark, how thro' the peopled air
The busy murmur glows!
The insect youth are on the wing,
Eager to taste the honied spring,
And float amid the liquid noon:
Some lightly o'er the current skim,
Some shew their gayly-gilded trim
Quick-glancing to the sun.

To Contemplation's sober eye
Such is the race of Man:
And they that creep, and they that fly,
Shall end where they began.
Alike the Busy and the Gay
But flutter thro' life's little day,
In fortune's varying colours drest:
Brush'd by the hand of rough Mischance,
Or chill'd by age, their airy dance
They leave, in dust to rest.

Methinks I hear in accents low
The sportive kind reply:
Poor moralist! and what art thou?
A solitary fly!
Thy Joys no glittering female meets,
No hive hast thou of hoarded sweets,
No painted plumage to display:
On hasty wings thy youth is flown;
Thy sun is set, thy spring is gone——
We frolick, while 'tis May.

Sonnet on the Death of Mr. Richard West[1]

IN VAIN to me the smiling Mornings shine,
And redd'ning Phœbus lifts his golden fire:
The birds in vain their amorous descant join;
Or chearful fields resume their green attire:
These ears, alas! for other notes repine,
A different object do these eyes require.
My lonely anguish melts no heart but mine;
And in my breast the imperfect joys expire.
Yet Morning smiles the busy race to chear,
And new-born pleasure brings to happier men:
The fields to all their wonted tribute bear:
To warm their little loves the birds complain:
I fruitless mourn to him, that cannot hear,
And weep the more, because I weep in vain.

Ode on a Distant Prospect of Eton College[2]

YE DISTANT spires, ye antique towers,
That crown the watry glade,
Where grateful Science still adores
Her HENRY's[3] holy Shade;
And ye, that from the stately brow
Of WINDSOR's heights th' expanse below
Of grove, of lawn, of mead survey,
Whose turf, whose shade, whose flowers among
Wanders the hoary Thames along
His silver-winding way.

Ah happy hills, ah pleasing shade,
Ah fields belov'd in vain,
Where once my careless childhood stray'd,
A stranger yet to pain!
I feel the gales, that from ye blow,
A momentary bliss bestow,
As waving fresh their gladsome wing,
My weary soul they seem to sooth,
And, redolent of joy and youth,
To breathe a second spring.

---

[1] Written in August, 1742. Published in *Poems*, ed. Mason, 1775. Text of first edition.

[2] Written in August, 1742. Published in 1747. Text of *Poems*, 1768.

[3] King Henry the Sixth, Founder of the College.

Say, Father THAMES, for thou hast seen
Full many a sprightly race
Disporting on thy margent green
The paths of pleasure trace,
Who foremost now delight to cleave
With pliant arm thy glassy wave?
The captive linnet which enthrall?
What idle progeny succeed
To chase the rolling circle's speed,
Or urge the flying ball?

While some on earnest business bent
Their murm'ring labours ply
'Gainst graver hours, that bring constraint
To sweeten liberty:
Some bold adventurers disdain
The limits of their little reign,
And unknown regions dare descry:
Still as they run they look behind,
They hear a voice in every wind,
And snatch a fearful joy.

Gay hope is theirs by fancy fed,
Less pleasing when possest;
The tear forgot as soon as shed,
The sunshine of the breast:
Theirs buxom health of rosy hue,
Wild wit, invention ever-new,
And lively chear of vigour born;
The thoughtless day, the easy night,
The spirits pure, the slumbers light,
That fly th' approach of morn.

Alas, regardless of their doom,
The little victims play!
No sense have they of ills to come,
Nor care beyond to-day:
Yet see how all around 'em wait
The Ministers of human fate,
And black Misfortune's baleful train!
Ah, shew them where in ambush stand
To seize their prey the murth'rous band!
Ah, tell them, they are men!

These shall the fury Passions tear,
The vulturs of the mind,
Disdainful Anger, pallid Fear,
And Shame that sculks behind;

Or pineing Love shall waste their youth,
Or Jealousy with rankling tooth,
That inly gnaws the secret heart,
And Envy wan, and faded Care,
Grim-visag'd comfortless Despair,
And Sorrow's piercing dart.

Ambition this shall tempt to rise,
Then whirl the wretch from high,
To bitter Scorn a sacrifice,
And grinning Infamy.
The stings of Falshood those shall try,
And hard Unkindness' alter'd eye,
That mocks the tear it forc'd to flow;
And keen Remorse with blood defil'd,
And moody Madness laughing wild
Amid severest woe.

Lo, in the vale of years beneath
A griesly troop are seen,
The painful family of Death,
More hideous than their Queen:
This racks the joints, this fires the veins,
That every labouring sinew strains,
Those in the deeper vitals rage:
Lo, Poverty, to fill the band,
That numbs the soul with icy hand,
And slow-consuming Age.

To each his suff'rings: all are men,
Condemn'd alike to groan,
The tender for another's pain;
Th' unfeeling for his own.
Yet ah! why should they know their fate?
Since sorrow never comes too late,
And happiness too swiftly flies.
Thought would destroy their paradise.
No more; where ignorance is bliss,
'Tis folly to be wise.

Hymn to Adversity[1]

DAUGHTER of JOVE, relentless Power,
Thou Tamer of the human breast,

[1] Written in August, 1742. Published in *Six Poems*, 1753. Text of *Poems*, 1768.

Whose iron scourge and tort'ring hour,
The Bad affright, afflict the Best!
Bound in thy adamantine chain
The Proud are taught to taste of pain,
And purple Tyrants vainly groan
With pangs unfelt before, unpitied and alone.

When first thy Sire to send on earth
Virtue, his darling Child, design'd,
To thee he gave the heav'nly Birth,
And bad to form her infant mind.
Stern rugged Nurse! thy rigid lore
With patience many a year she bore:
What sorrow was, thou bad'st her know,
And from her own she learn'd to melt at others' woe.

Scared at thy frown terrific, fly
Self-pleasing Folly's idle brood,
Wild Laughter, Noise, and thoughtless Joy,
And leave us leisure to be good.
Light they disperse, and with them go
The summer Friend, the flatt'ring Foe;
By vain Prosperity received,
To her they vow their truth, and are again believed.

Wisdom in sable garb array'd
Immers'd in rapt'rous thought profound,
And Melancholy, silent maid
With leaden eye, that loves the ground,
Still on thy solemn steps attend:
Warm Charity, the gen'ral Friend,
With Justice to herself severe,
And Pity, dropping soft the sadly-pleasing tear.

Oh, gently on thy Suppliant's head,
Dread Goddess, lay thy chast'ning hand!
Not in thy Gorgon terrors clad,
Nor circled with the vengeful Band
(As by the Impious thou art seen)
With thund'ring voice, and threat'ning mien,
With screaming Horror's funeral cry,
Despair, and fell Disease, and ghastly Poverty.

Thy form benign, oh Goddess, wear,
Thy milder influence impart,
Thy philosophic Train be there
To soften, not to wound my heart,

The gen'rous spark extinct revive,
Teach me to love and to forgive,
Exact my own defects to scan,
What others are, to feel, and know myself a Man.

Ode on the Death of a Favourite Cat, Drowned in a Tub of Gold Fishes[1]

'TWAS on a lofty vase's side,
Where China's gayest art had dy'd
The azure flowers, that blow;
Demurest of the tabby kind,
The pensive Selima reclin'd,
Gazed on the lake below.

Her conscious tail her joy declar'd;
The fair round face, the snowy beard,
The velvet of her paws,
Her coat, that with the tortoise vies,
Her ears of jet, and emerald eyes,
She saw; and purr'd applause.

Still had she gaz'd; but 'midst the tide
Two angel forms were seen to glide,
The Genii of the stream:
Their scaly armour's Tyrian hue
Thro' richest purple to the view
Betray'd a golden gleam.

The hapless Nymph with wonder saw:
A whisker first and then a claw,
With many an ardent wish,
She stretch'd in vain to reach the prize.
What female heart can gold despise?
What Cat's averse to fish?

Presumptuous Maid! with looks intent
Again she stretch'd, again she bent,
Nor knew the gulf between.
(Malignant Fate sat by, and smil'd)
The slipp'ry verge her feet beguil'd,
She tumbled headlong in.

[1] Written in 1747. Published in Dodsley's *Collection of Poems*, 1748. Text of *Poems*, 1768.

Eight times emerging from the flood
She mew'd to ev'ry watry God,
  Some speedy aid to send.
No Dolphin came, no Nereid stirr'd:
Nor cruel *Tom*, nor *Susan* heard.
  A Fav'rite has no friend!

From hence, ye Beauties, undeceiv'd,
Know, one false step is ne'er retriev'd,
  And be with caution bold.
Not all that tempts your wand'ring eyes
And heedless hearts, is lawful prize;
  Nor all, that glisters, gold.

The Alliance of Education and Government[1]

. . . Πόταγ', ὦ 'γαθέ; τὰν γὰρ ἀοιδὰν
Οὔτι πω εἰς 'Αΐδαν γε τὸν ἐκλελάθοντα φυλαξεῖς.

THEOCRITUS.

As SICKLY Plants betray a niggard earth,
Whose barren bosom starves her gen'rous birth,
Nor genial warmth, nor genial juice retains
Their roots to feed, and fill their verdant veins:
And as in climes, where Winter holds his reign,
The soil, tho' fertile, will not teem in vain,
Forbids her gems to swell, her shades to rise,
Nor trust her blossoms to the churlish skies.
So draw Mankind in vain the vital airs,
Unform'd, unfriended, by those kindly cares,
That health and vigour to the soul impart,
Spread the young thought, and warm the opening heart:
So fond Instruction on the growing powers
Of nature idly lavishes her stores,
If equal justice with unclouded face
Smile not indulgent on the rising race,
And scatter with a free, tho' frugal, hand
Light golden showers of plenty o'er the land:
But tyranny has fix'd her empire there
To check their tender hopes with chilling fear,
And blast the blooming promise of the year.
  This spacious animated scene survey,
From where the rolling orb, that gives the day,
His sable sons with nearer course surrounds
To either pole, and life's remotest bounds.

[1] Written, cir. 1748. Published in *Poems*, ed. Mason, 1775. Text of first edition.

How rude soe'er th' exteriour form we find,
Howe'er opinion tinge the varied mind,
Alike, to all the kind, impartial heav'n
The sparks of truth and happiness has given:
With sense to feel, with mem'ry to retain,
They follow pleasure, and they fly from pain;
Their judgment mends the plan their fancy draws,
Th' event presages, and explores the cause;
The soft returns of gratitude they know,
By fraud elude, by force repell the foe;
While mutual wishes, mutual woes, endear
The social smile and sympathetic tear.
Say then, thro' ages by what fate confined
To different climes seem different souls assign'd?
Here measured laws and philosophic ease
Fix, and improve the polish'd arts of peace.
There industry and gain their vigils keep,
Command the winds, and tame th' unwilling deep.
Here force and hardy deeds of blood prevail;
There languid pleasure sighs in every gale.
Oft o'er the trembling nations from afar
Has Scythia breath'd the living cloud of war;
And, where the deluge burst, with sweepy sway
Their arms, their kings, their gods were roll'd away.
As oft have issued, host impelling host,
The blue-eyed myriads from the Baltic coast.
The prostrate South to the Destroyer yields
Her boasted titles and her golden fields:
With grim delight the Brood of winter view
A brighter day, and Heav'ns of azure hue,
Scent the new fragrance of the breathing rose,
And quaff the pendent vintage as it grows.
Proud of the yoke, and pliant to the rod,
Why yet does Asia dread a monarch's nod,
While European freedom still withstands
Th' encroaching tide, that drowns her less'ning lands;
And sees far off with an indignant groan
Her native plains, and Empires once her own.
Can opener skies and suns of fiercer flame
O'erpower the fire, that animates our frame;
As lamps, that shed at eve a chearful ray,
Fade and expire beneath the eye of day?
Need we the influence of the Northern star
To string our nerves and steel our hearts to war?
And, where the face of nature laughs around,
Must sick'ning virtue fly the tainted ground?
Unmanly thought! what seasons can controul,

What fancied zone can circumscribe the soul,
Who, conscious of the source from whence she springs,
By reason's light, on resolution's wings,
Spite of her frail companion, dauntless goes
O'er Libya's deserts and thro' Zembla's snows?
She bids each slumb'ring energy awake,
Another touch, another temper take,
Suspends th' inferior laws, that rule our clay:
The stubborn elements confess her sway;
Their little wants, their low desires, refine,
And raise the mortal to a height divine.
Not but the human fabric from the birth
Imbibes a flavour of its parent earth.
As various tracts enforce a various toil,
The manners speak the idiom of their soil.
An iron-race the mountain-cliffs maintain,
Foes to the gentler genius of the plain:
For where unwearied sinews must be found
With side-long plough to quell the flinty ground,
To turn the torrent's swift-descending flood,
To brave the savage rushing from the wood,
What wonder, if to patient valour train'd
They guard with spirit, what by strength they gain'd?
And while their rocky ramparts round they see,
The rough abode of want and liberty,
(As lawless force from confidence will grow)
Insult the plenty of the vales below?
What wonder, in the sultry climes, that spread,
Where Nile redundant o'er his summer-bed
From his broad bosom life and verdure flings,
And broods o'er Ægypt with his wat'ry wings,
If with advent'rous oar and ready sail,
The dusky people drive before the gale;
Or on frail floats to neighb'ring cities ride,
That rise and glitter o'er the ambient tide.

* * * * * *

Elegy Written in a Country Church-yard[1]

THE Curfew tolls the knell of parting day,
The lowing herd wind slowly o'er the lea,
The plowman homeward plods his weary way,
And leaves the world to darkness and to me.

[1] Finished in June, 1750. Published in 1751. Text of *Poems*, 1768.

Now fades the glimmering landscape on the sight,
And all the air a solemn stillness holds,
Save where the beetle wheels his droning flight,
And drowsy tinklings lull the distant folds;

Save that from yonder ivy-mantled tow'r
The mopeing owl does to the moon complain
Of such, as wand'ring near her secret bow'r,
Molest her ancient solitary reign.

Beneath those rugged elms, that yew-tree's shade,
Where heaves the turf in many a mould'ring heap,
Each in his narrow cell for ever laid,
The rude Forefathers of the hamlet sleep.

The breezy call of incense-breathing Morn,
The swallow twitt'ring from the straw-built shed,
The cock's shrill clarion, or the echoing horn,
No more shall rouse them from their lowly bed.

For them no more the blazing hearth shall burn,
Or busy housewife ply her evening care:
No children run to lisp their sire's return,
Or climb his knees the envied kiss to share.

Oft did the harvest to their sickle yield,
Their furrow oft the stubborn glebe has broke;
How jocund did they drive their team afield!
How bow'd the woods beneath their sturdy stroke!

Let not Ambition mock their useful toil,
Their homely joys, and destiny obscure;
Nor Grandeur hear with a disdainful smile,
The short and simple annals of the poor.

The boast of heraldry, the pomp of pow'r,
And all that beauty, all that wealth e'er gave,
Awaits alike th' inevitable hour.
The paths of glory lead but to the grave.

Nor you, ye Proud, impute to These the fault,
If Mem'ry o'er their Tomb no Trophies raise,
Where thro' the long-drawn isle and fretted vault
The pealing anthem swells the note of praise.

Can storied urn or animated bust
Back to its mansion call the fleeting breath?

Can Honour's voice provoke the silent dust,
Or Flatt'ry sooth the dull cold ear of Death?

Perhaps in this neglected spot is laid
Some heart once pregnant with celestial fire;
Hands, that the rod of empire might have sway'd,
Or wak'd to extasy the living lyre.

But Knowledge to their eyes her ample page
Rich with the spoils of time did ne'er unroll;
Chill Penury repress'd their noble rage,
And froze the genial current of the soul.

Full many a gem of purest ray serene,
The dark unfathom'd caves of ocean bear:
Full many a flower is born to blush unseen,
And waste its sweetness on the desert air.

Some village-Hampden, that with dauntless breast
The little Tyrant of his fields withstood;
Some mute inglorious Milton here may rest,
Some Cromwell guiltless of his country's blood.

Th' applause of list'ning senates to command,
The threats of pain and ruin to despise,
To scatter plenty o'er a smiling land,
And read their hist'ry in a nation's eyes,

Their lot forbad: nor circumscrib'd alone
Their growing virtues, but their crimes confin'd;
Forbad to wade through slaughter to a throne,
And shut the gates of mercy on mankind,

The struggling pangs of conscious truth to hide,
To quench the blushes of ingenuous shame,
Or heap the shrine of Luxury and Pride
With incense kindled at the Muse's flame.

Far from the madding crowd's ignoble strife,
Their sober wishes never learn'd to stray;
Along the cool sequester'd vale of life
They kept the noiseless tenor of their way.

Yet ev'n these bones from insult to protect
Some frail memorial still erected nigh,
With uncouth rhimes and shapeless sculpture deck'd,
Implores the passing tribute of a sigh.

Their name, their years, spelt by th' unletter'd muse,
The place of fame and elegy supply:
And many a holy text around she strews,
That teach the rustic moralist to die.

For who to dumb Forgetfulness a prey,
This pleasing anxious being e'er resign'd,
Left the warm precincts of the chearful day,
Nor cast one longing ling'ring look behind?

On some fond breast the parting soul relies,
Some pious drops the closing eye requires;
Ev'n from the tomb the voice of Nature cries,
Ev'n in our Ashes live their wonted Fires.

For thee, who mindful of th' unhonour'd Dead
Dost in these lines their artless tale relate;
If chance, by lonely contemplation led,
Some kindred Spirit shall inquire thy fate,

Haply some hoary-headed Swain may say,
'Oft have we seen him at the peep of dawn
'Brushing with hasty steps the dews away
'To meet the sun upon the upland lawn.

'There at the foot of yonder nodding beech
'That wreathes its old fantastic roots so high,
'His listless length at noontide would he stretch,
'And pore upon the brook that babbles by.

'Hard by yon wood, now smiling as in scorn,
'Mutt'ring his wayward fancies he would rove,
'Now drooping, woeful wan, like one forlorn,
'Or craz'd with care, or cross'd in hopeless love.

'One morn I miss'd him on the custom'd hill,
'Along the heath and near his fav'rite tree;
'Another came; nor yet beside the rill,
'Nor up the lawn, nor at the wood was he;

'The next with dirges due in sad array
'Slow thro' the church-way path we saw him born.
'Approach and read (for thou can'st read) the lay,
'Grav'd on the stone beneath yon aged thorn.'

The Epitaph.

HERE rests his head upon the lap of Earth
A Youth to Fortune and to Fame unknown.

Fair Science frown'd not on his humble birth,
And Melancholy mark'd him for her own.

Large was his bounty, and his soul sincere,
Heav'n did a recompence as largely send:
He gave to Mis'ry all he had, a tear,
He gain'd from Heav'n ('twas all he wish'd) a friend.

No farther seek his merits to disclose,
Or draw his frailties from their dread abode,
(There they alike in trembling hope repose,)
The bosom of his Father and his God.

Ode on the Pleasure Arising from Vicissitude[1]

Now the golden Morn aloft
Waves her dew-bespangled wing,
With vermil cheek, and whisper soft
She wooes the tardy Spring:
Till April starts, and calls around
The sleeping fragrance from the ground;
And lightly o'er the living scene
Scatters his freshest, tenderest green.

New-born flocks, in rustic dance,
Frisking ply their feeble feet;
Forgetful of their wintry trance
The birds his presence greet:
But chief, the Sky-Lark warbles high
His trembling thrilling ecstacy;
And, lessening from the dazzled sight,
Melts into air and liquid light.

Rise, my Soul! on wings of fire,
Rise the rapt'rous Choir among;
Hark! 'tis Nature strikes the Lyre,
And leads the general song:

* * * * * *

Yesterday the sullen year
Saw the snowy whirlwind fly;
Mute was the music of the air,
The herd stood drooping by:
Their raptures now that wildly flow,

[1] Written, 1753-54. Published in *Poems*, ed. Mason, 1775. Text of first edition.

No yesterday, nor morrow know;
'Tis Man alone that joy descries
With forward, and reverted eyes.

Smiles on past Misfortune's brow
Soft Reflection's hand can trace;
And o'er the cheek of Sorrow throw
A melancholy grace;
While Hope prolongs our happier hour,
Or deepest shades, that dimly lower
And blacken round our weary way,
Gilds with a gleam of distant day.

Still, where rosy Pleasure leads,
See a kindred Grief pursue;
Behind the steps that Misery treads,
Approaching Comfort view:
The hues of bliss more brightly glow,
Chastis'd by sabler tints of woe;
And blended form, with artful strife,
The strength and harmony of life.

See the Wretch, that long hast tost
On the thorny bed of pain,
At length repair his vigour lost,
And breathe, and walk again:
The meanest floweret of the vale,
The simplest note that swells the gale,
The common sun, the air, the skies,
To Him are opening Paradise.

Humble Quiet builds her cell,
Near the source whence Pleasure flows;
She eyes the clear chrystalline well,
And tastes it as it goes.

* * * * * *

The Progress of Poesy. A Pindaric Ode[1]

I. 1.

AWAKE, Æolian lyre, awake,
And give to rapture all thy trembling strings.
From Helicon's harmonious springs

[1] Written in 1754. Published in 1757. Text of *Poems*, 1768.

A thousand rills their mazy progress take:
The laughing flowers, that round them blow,
Drink life and fragrance as they flow.
Now the rich stream of music winds along
Deep, majestic, smooth, and strong,
Thro' verdant vales, and Ceres' golden reign:
Now rowling down the steep amain,
Headlong, impetuous, see it pour:
The rocks, and nodding groves rebellow to the roar.

I. 2.

Oh! Sovereign of the willing soul,
Parent of sweet and solemn-breathing airs,
Enchanting shell! the sullen Cares,
And frantic Passions hear thy soft controul.
On Thracia's hills the Lord of War,
Has curb'd the fury of his car,
And drop'd his thirsty lance at thy command.
Perching on the scept'red hand
Of Jove, thy magic lulls the feather'd king
With ruffled plumes, and flagging wing:
Quench'd in dark clouds of slumber lie
The terror of his beak, and light'nings of his eye.

I. 3.

Thee the voice, the dance, obey,
Temper'd to thy warbled lay.
O'er Idalia's velvet-green
The rosy-crowned Loves are seen
On Cytherea's day
With antic Sports, and blue-eyed Pleasures,
Frisking light in frolic measures;
Now pursuing, now retreating,
Now in circling troops they meet:
To brisk notes in cadence beating
Glance their many-twinkling feet.
Slow melting strains their Queen's approach declare:
Where'er she turns the Graces homage pay.
With arms sublime, that float upon the air,
In gliding state she wins her easy way:
O'er her warm cheek, and rising bosom, move
The bloom of young Desire, and purple light of Love.

II. I.

Man's feeble race what Ills await,
Labour, and Penury, the racks of Pain,

Disease, and Sorrow's weeping train,
And Death, sad refuge from the storms of Fate!
The fond complaint, my Song, disprove,
And justify the laws of Jove.
Say, has he giv'n in vain the heav'nly Muse?
Night, and all her sickly dews,
Her Spectres wan, and Birds of boding cry,
He gives to range the dreary sky:
Till down the eastern cliffs afar
Hyperion's march they spy, and glitt'ring shafts of war.

II. 2.

In climes beyond the solar road,
Where shaggy forms o'er ice-built mountains roam,
The Muse has broke the twilight-gloom
To chear the shiv'ring Native's dull abode.
And oft, beneath the od'rous shade
Of Chili's boundless forests laid,
She deigns to hear the savage Youth repeat
In loose numbers wildly sweet
Their feather-cinctured Chiefs, and dusky Loves.
Her track, where'er the Goddess roves,
Glory pursue, and generous Shame,
Th' unconquerable Mind, and Freedom's holy flame.

II. 3.

Woods, that wave o'er Delphi's steep,
Isles, that crown th' Egæan deep,
Fields, that cool Ilissus laves,
Or where Mæander's amber waves
In lingering Lab'rinths creep,
How do your tuneful Echo's languish,
Mute, but to the voice of Anguish?
Where each old poetic Mountain
Inspiration breath'd around:
Ev'ry shade and hallow'd Fountain
Murmur'd deep a solemn sound:
Till the sad Nine in Greece's evil hour
Left their Parnassus for the Latian plains.
Alike they scorn the pomp of tyrant-Power,
And coward Vice, that revels in her chains.
When Latium had her lofty spirit lost,
They sought, oh Albion! next thy sea-encircled coast.

III. 1.

Far from the sun and summer-gale,
In thy green lap was Nature's Darling laid,

What time, where lucid Avon stray'd,
To Him the mighty Mother did unveil
Her aweful face: The dauntless Child
Stretch'd forth his little arms, and smiled.
This pencil take (she said) whose colours clear
Richly paint the vernal year:
Thine too these golden keys, immortal Boy!
This can unlock the gates of Joy;
Of Horrour that, and thrilling Fears,
Or ope the sacred source of sympathetic Tears.

III. 2.

Nor second He, that rode sublime
Upon the seraph-wings of Extasy,
The secrets of th' Abyss to spy.
He pass'd the flaming bounds of Place and Time:
The living Throne, the saphire-blaze,
Where Angels tremble, while they gaze,
He saw; but blasted with excess of light,
Closed his eyes in endless night.
Behold, where Dryden's less presumptuous car,
Wide o'er the fields of Glory bear
Two Coursers of ethereal race,
With necks in thunder cloath'd, and long-resounding pace.

III. 3.

Hark, his hands the lyre explore!
Bright-eyed Fancy hovering o'er
Scatters from her pictured urn
Thoughts, that breath, and words, that burn.
But ah! 'tis heard no more——
Oh! Lyre divine, what daring Spirit
Wakes thee now? tho' he inherit
Nor the pride, nor ample pinion,
That the Theban Eagle bear
Sailing with supreme dominion
Thro' the azure deep of air:
Yet oft before his infant eyes would run
Such forms, as glitter in the Muse's ray
With orient hues, unborrow'd of the Sun:
Yet shall he mount, and keep his distant way
Beyond the limits of a vulgar fate,
Beneath the Good how far—but far above the Great.

The Bard. A Pindaric Ode[1]

I. 1.

'Ruin seize thee, ruthless King!
'Confusion on thy banners wait,
'Tho' fann'd by Conquest's crimson wing
'They mock the air with idle state.
'Helm, nor Hauberk's twisted mail,
'Nor even thy virtues, Tyrant, shall avail
'To save thy secret soul from nightly fears,
'From Cambria's curse, from Cambria's tears!'
Such were the sounds, that o'er the crested pride
Of the first Edward scatter'd wild dismay,
As down the steep of Snowdon's shaggy side
He wound with toilsome march his long array.
Stout Glo'ster stood aghast in speechless trance:
To arms! cried Mortimer, and couch'd his quiv'ring lance.

I. 2.

On a rock, whose haughty brow
Frowns o'er old Conway's foaming flood,
Robed in the sable garb of woe,
With haggard eyes the Poet stood;
(Loose his beard, and hoary hair
Stream'd, like a meteor, to the troubled air)
And with a Master's hand, and Prophet's fire,
Struck the deep sorrows of his lyre.
'Hark, how each giant-oak, and desert cave,
'Sighs to the torrent's aweful voice beneath!
'O'er thee, oh King! their hundred arms they wave,
'Revenge on thee in hoarser murmurs breath;
'Vocal no more, since Cambria's fatal day,
'To high-born Hoel's harp, or soft Llewellyn's lay.

I. 3.

'Cold is Cadwallo's tongue,
'That hush'd the stormy main:
'Brave Urien sleeps upon his craggy bed:
'Mountains, ye mourn in vain
'Modred, whose magic song
'Made huge Plinlimmon bow his cloud-top'd head.
'On dreary Arvon's shore they lie,
'Smear'd with gore, and ghastly pale:

[1] Written between 1754 and 1757. Published in 1757. Text of *Poems*, 1768.

'Far, far aloof th' affrighted ravens sail;
'The famish'd Eagle screams, and passes by.
'Dear lost companions of my tuneful art,
'Dear, as the light that visits these sad eyes,
'Dear, as the ruddy drops that warm my heart,
'Ye died amidst your dying country's cries—
'No more I weep. They do not sleep.
'On yonder cliffs, a griesly band,
'I see them sit, they linger yet,
'Avengers of their native land:
'With me in dreadful harmony they join,
'And weave with bloody hands the tissue of thy line.'

II. 1.

"Weave the warp, and weave the woof,
"The winding-sheet of Edward's race.
"Give ample room, and verge enough
"The characters of hell to trace.
"Mark the year, and mark the night,
"When Severn shall re-eccho with affright
"The shrieks of death, thro' Berkley's roofs that ring,
"Shrieks of an agonizing King![2]
"She-Wolf of France,[3] with unrelenting fangs,
"That tear'st the bowels of thy mangled Mate,
"From thee be born, who o'er thy country hangs
"The scourge of Heav'n.[4] What Terrors round him wait!
"Amazement in his van, with Flight combined,
"And sorrow's faded form, and solitude behind.

II. 2.

"Mighty Victor, mighty Lord,
"Low on his funeral couch he lies!
"No pitying heart, no eye, afford
"A tear to grace his obsequies.
"Is the sable Warriour fled?[5]
"Thy son is gone. He rests among the Dead.
"The Swarm, that in thy noon-tide beam were born?
"Gone to salute the rising Morn.
"Fair laughs the Morn, and soft the Zephyr blows,
"While proudly riding o'er the azure realm
"In gallant trim the gilded Vessel goes;
"Youth on the prow, and Pleasure at the helm;

[2] Edward II, who was murdered in Berkeley Castle.
[3] "Isabel of France, Edward the Second's adulterous Queen."—Gray's note.
[4] Edward III.
[5] Edward the Black Prince.

"Regardless of the sweeping Whirlwind's sway,
"That, hush'd in grim repose, expects his evening-prey.[6]

II. 3.

"Fill high the sparkling bowl,
"The rich repast prepare,
"Reft of a crown, he yet may share the feast:
"Close by the regal chair
"Fell Thirst and Famine scowl
"A baleful smile upon their baffled Guest.
"Heard ye the din of battle bray,
"Lance to lance, and horse to horse?[7]
"Long Years of havock urge their destined course,
"And thro' the kindred squadrons mow their way.
"Ye Towers of Julius, London's lasting shame,
"With many a foul and midnight murther fed,
"Revere his Consort's faith, his Father's fame,[8]
"And spare the meek Usurper's holy head.[9]
"Above, below, the rose of snow,
"Twined with her blushing foe, we spread:
"The bristled Boar in infant-gore
"Wallows beneath the thorny shade.[10]
"Now, Brothers, bending o'er th' accursed loom
"Stamp we our vengeance deep, and ratify his doom.

III. I.

"Edward, lo! to sudden fate
"(Weave we the woof. The thread is spun)
"Half of thy heart we consecrate.
"(The web is wove. The work is done.)"
'Stay, oh stay! nor thus forlorn
'Leave me unbless'd, unpitied, here to mourn:
'In yon bright track, that fires the western skies,
'They melt, they vanish from my eyes.
'But oh! what solemn scenes on Snowdon's height
'Descending slow their glitt'ring skirts unroll?
'Visions of glory, spare my aching sight,
'Ye unborn Ages, crowd not on my soul!
'No more our long-lost Arthur we bewail.
'All-hail, ye genuine Kings, Britannia's Issue, hail![11]

[6] "Magnificence of Richard the Second's reign."—Gray's note.
[7] The Wars of the Roses.
[8] Henry V.
[9] Henry VI.
[10] Richard III.
[11] The house of Tudor.

III. 2.

'Girt with many a Baron bold
'Sublime their starry fronts they rear;
'And gorgeous Dames, and Statesmen old
'In bearded majesty, appear.
'In the midst a Form divine!
'Her eye proclaims her of the Briton-Line;
'Her lyon-port, her awe-commanding face,
'Attemper'd sweet to virgin-grace.[12]
'What strings symphonious tremble in the air,
'What strains of vocal transport round her play!
'Hear from the grave, great Taliessin,[13] hear;
'They breathe a soul to animate thy clay.
'Bright Rapture calls, and soaring, as she sings,
'Waves in the eye of Heav'n her many-colour'd wings.

III. 3.

'The verse adorn again
'Fierce War, and faithful Love,
'And Truth severe, by fairy Fiction drest.
'In buskin'd measures move
'Pale Grief, and pleasing Pain,
'With Horrour, Tyrant of the throbbing breast.[14]
'A Voice, as of the Cherub-Choir,
'Gales from blooming Eden bear;[15]
'And distant warblings lessen on my ear,
'That lost in long futurity expire.[16]
'Fond impious Man, think'st thou, yon sanguine cloud,
'Rais'd by thy breath, has quench'd the Orb of day?
'To-morrow he repairs the golden flood,
'And warms the nations with redoubled ray.
'Enough for me: With joy I see
'The different doom our Fates assign.
'Be thine Despair, and scept'red Care,
'To triumph, and to die, are mine.'
He spoke, and headlong from the mountain's height
Deep in the roaring tide he plung'd to endless night.

---

[12] Queen Elizabeth.

[13] "Taliessin, Chief of the Bards, flourished in the VIth Century. His works are still preserved, and his memory held in high veneration among his Countrymen."—Gray's note.

[14] Shakespeare.

[15] Milton.

[16] "The succession of Poets after Milton's time."—Gray's note.

Sketch of his Own Character[1]

Too poor for a bribe, and too proud to importune;
He had not the method of making a fortune:
Could love, and could hate, so was thought somewhat odd;
NO VERY GREAT WIT, HE BELIEV'D IN A GOD.
A Post or a Pension he did not desire,
But left Church and State to Charles Townshend and Squire.

The Fatal Sisters. An Ode[2]

PREFACE

IN the Eleventh Century *Sigurd*, Earl of the Orkney-Islands, went with a fleet of ships and a considerable body of troops into Ireland, to the assistance of *Sictryg with the silken beard*, who was then making war on his father-in-law *Brian*, King of Dublin: the Earl and all his forces were cut to pieces, and *Sictryg* was in danger of a total defeat; but the enemy had a greater loss by the death of *Brian*, their King, who fell in the action. On Christmas-day, (the day of the battle,) a Native of *Caithness* in Scotland saw at a distance a number of persons on horseback riding full speed towards a hill, and seeming to enter into it. Curiosity led him to follow them, till looking through an opening in the rocks he saw twelve gigantic figures resembling women: they were all employed about a loom; and as they wove, they sung the following dreadful Song; which when they had finished, they tore the web into twelve pieces, and (each taking her portion) galloped Six to the North and as many to the South.

Now the storm begins to lower,
(Haste, the loom of Hell prepare,)
Iron-sleet of arrowy shower
Hurtles in the darken'd air.

Glitt'ring lances are the loom,
Where the dusky warp we strain,
Weaving many a Soldier's doom,
Orkney's woe, and *Randver*'s bane.

See the griesly texture grow,
('Tis of human entrails made,)

[1] Written in 1761. Published in *Poems*, ed. Mason, 1775. Text of first edition.

[2] Written in 1761. Published in *Poems*, 1768. Text of first edition. "The *Valkyriur* were female Divinities, Servants of *Odin* (or *Woden*) in the Gothic mythology. Their name signifies *Chusers of the slain*. They were mounted on swift horses, with drawn swords in their hands; and in the throng of battle selected such as were destined to slaughter, and conducted them to *Valhalla*, the hall of *Odin*, or paradise of the Brave; where they attended the banquet, and served the departed Heroes with horns of mead and ale."—Gray's note.

And the weights, that play below,
Each a gasping Warriour's head.

Shafts for shuttles, dipt in gore,
Shoot the trembling cords along.
Sword, that once a Monarch bore,
Keep the tissue close and strong.

Mista black, terrific Maid,
Sangrida, and *Hilda* see,
Join the wayward work to aid:
'Tis the woof of victory.

Ere the ruddy sun be set,
Pikes must shiver, javelins sing,
Blade with clattering buckler meet,
Hauberk crash, and helmet ring.

(Weave the crimson web of war)
Let us go, and let us fly,
Where our Friends the conflict share,
Where they triumph, where they die.

As the paths of fate we tread,
Wading thro' th' ensanguin'd field:
Gondula, and *Geira*, spread
O'er the youthful King your shield.

We the reins to slaughter give,
Ours to kill, and ours to spare:
Spite of danger he shall live.
(Weave the crimson web of war.)

They, whom once the desart-beach
Pent within its bleak domain,
Soon their ample sway shall stretch
O'er the plenty of the plain.

Low the dauntless Earl is laid,
Gor'd with many a gaping wound:
Fate demands a nobler head;
Soon a King shall bite the ground.

Long his loss shall Eirin weep,
Ne'er again his likeness see;
Long her strains in sorrow steep,
Strains of Immortality!

Horror covers all the heath,
Clouds of carnage blot the sun.
Sisters, weave the web of death;
Sisters, cease, the work is done.

Hail the task, and hail the hands!
Songs of joy and triumph sing!
Joy to the victorious bands;
Triumph to the younger King.

Mortal, thou that hear'st the tale,
Learn the tenour of our song.
Scotland thro' each winding vale
Far and wide the notes prolong.

Sisters, hence with spurs of speed:
Each her thundering faulchion wield;
Each bestride her sable steed.
Hurry, hurry to the field.

The Descent of Odin. An Ode[1]

UPROSE the King of Men with speed,
And saddled strait his coal-black steed;
Down the yawning steep he rode,
That leads to HELA's drear abode.[2]
Him the Dog of Darkness spied,
His shaggy throat he open'd wide,
While from his jaws, with carnage fill'd,
Foam and human gore distill'd:
Hoarse he bays with hideous din,
Eyes that glow, and fangs, that grin;
And long pursues, with fruitless yell,
The Father of the powerful spell.
Onward still his way he takes,
(The groaning earth beneath him shakes,)
Till full before his fearless eyes
The portals nine of hell arise.

Right against the eastern gate,
By the moss-grown pile he sate;
Where long of yore to sleep was laid

[1] Written in 1761. Published in *Poems*, 1768. Text of first edition.

[2] "*Niflheimr*, the hell of the Gothic nations, consisted of nine worlds, to which were devoted all such as died of sickness, old-age, or by any other means than in battle: Over it presided HELA, the Goddess of Death."—Gray's note.

The dust of the prophetic Maid.
Facing to the northern clime,
Thrice he traced the runic rhyme;
Thrice pronounc'd, in accents dread,
The thrilling verse that wakes the Dead;
Till from out the hollow ground
Slowly breath'd a sullen sound.

PR. What call unknown, what charms presume
To break the quiet of the tomb?
Who thus afflicts my troubled sprite,
And drags me from the realms of night?
Long on these mould'ring bones have beat
The winter's snow, the summer's heat,
The drenching dews, and driving rain!
Let me, let me sleep again.
Who is he, with voice unblest,
That calls me from the bed of rest?

O. A Traveller, to thee unknown,
Is he that calls, a Warriour's Son.
Thou the deeds of light shalt know;
Tell me what is done below,
For whom yon glitt'ring board is spread,
Drest for whom yon golden bed.

PR. Mantling in the goblet see
The pure bev'rage of the bee,
O'er it hangs the shield of gold;
'Tis the drink of *Balder* bold:
Balder's head to death is giv'n.
Pain can reach the Sons of Heav'n!
Unwilling I my lips unclose:
Leave me, leave me to repose.

O. Once again my call obey.
Prophetess, arise, and say,
What dangers *Odin*'s Child await,
Who the Author of his fate.

PR. In *Hoder*'s hand the Heroe's doom:
His Brother sends him to the tomb.
Now my weary lips I close:
Leave me, leave me to repose.

O. Prophetess, my spell obey,
Once again arise, and say,

Who th' Avenger of his guilt,
By whom shall *Hoder*'s blood be spilt.

PR. In the caverns of the west,
By *Odin*'s fierce embrace compress,
A wond'rous Boy shall *Rinda* bear,
Who ne'er shall comb his raven-hair,
Nor wash his visage in the stream,
Nor see the sun's departing beam;
Till he on *Hoder*'s corse shall smile
Flaming on the fun'ral pile.
Now my weary lips I close:
Leave me, leave me to repose.

O. Yet a while my call obey.
Prophetess, awake, and say,
What Virgins these, in speechless woe,
That bend to earth their solemn brow,
That their flaxen tresses tear,
And snowy veils, that float in air.
Tell me, whence their sorrows rose:
Then I leave thee to repose.

PR. Ha! no Traveller art thou,
King of Men, I know thee now,
Mightiest of a mighty line——

O. No boding Maid of skill divine
Art thou, nor Prophetess of good;
But Mother of the giant-brood!

PR. Hie thee hence, and boast at home,
That never shall Enquirer come
To break my iron-sleep again;
Till *Lok* has burst his tenfold chain.[3]
Never, till substantial Night
Has reassum'd her ancient right;
Till wrap'd in flames, in ruin hurl'd,
Sinks the fabric of the world.

[3] "*Lok* is the evil Being, who continues in chains till the *Twilight of the Gods* approaches, when he shall break his bonds; the human race, the stars, and sun, shall disappear; the earth sink in the seas, and fire consume the skies: even Odin himself and his kindred-deities shall perish. For a farther explanation of this mythology, see Mallet's Introduction to the History of Denmark, 1755, Quarto."—Gray's note.

The Triumphs of Owen. A Fragment[1]

ADVERTISEMENT

OWEN succeeded his Father GRIFFIN in the Principality of North-Wales, A.D. 1120. This battle was fought near forty years afterwards.

OWEN's praise demands my song,
OWEN swift, and OWEN strong;
Fairest flower of Roderic's stem,
Gwyneth's shield,[2] and Britain's gem.
He nor heaps his brooded stores,
Nor on all profusely pours;
Lord of every regal art,
Liberal hand, and open heart.

Big with hosts of mighty name,
Squadrons three against him came;
This the force of Eirin hiding,
Side by side as proudly riding,
On her shadow long and gay
Lochlin[3] plows the watry way;
There the Norman sails afar
Catch the winds, and join the war:
Black and huge along they sweep,
Burthens of the angry deep.

Dauntless on his native sands
The Dragon-Son of Mona stands;[4]
In glitt'ring arms and glory drest,
High he rears his ruby crest.
There the thund'ring strokes begin,
There the press, and there the din;
Talymalfra's rocky shore
Echoing to the battle's roar.
Where his glowing eye-balls turn,
Thousand Banners round him burn.
Where he points his purple spear,
Hasty, hasty Rout is there,
Marking with indignant eye
Fear to stop, and shame to fly.
There Confusion, Terror's child,
Conflict fierce, and Ruin wild,

---

[1] Written in 1764. Published in *Poems*, 1768. Text of first edition.

[2] Gwyneth is North Wales.

[3] Denmark.

[4] "The red Dragon is the device of Cadwallader, which all his descendents bore on their banners."—Gray's note.

Agony, that pants for breath,
Despair and honourable Death.

* * *

William Shakespeare to Mrs. Anne, Regular Servant to the Rev. Mr. Precentor of York[1]

A MOMENT's patience, gentle Mistris Anne,
(But stint your clack for sweet St. Charitie):
'Tis Willey begs, once a right proper man,
Though now a book, and interleaved you see.
Much have I borne from canker'd critic's spite,
From fumbling baronets, and poets small,
Pert barristers, and parsons nothing bright:
But what awaits me now is worst of all.
'Tis true, our master's temper natural
Was fashion'd fair in meek and dove-like guise;
But may not honey's self be turned to gall
By residence, by marriage, and sore eyes?
If then he wreak on me his wicked will,
Steal to his closet at the hour of prayer;
And (when thou hear'st the organ piping shrill)
Grease his best pen, and all he scribbles, tear.
Better to bottom tarts and cheesecakes nice,
Better the roast meat from the fire to save,
Better be twisted into caps for spice,
Than thus be patch'd and cobbled in one's grave.
So York shall taste what Clouet never knew,
So from our works sublimer fumes shall rise;
While Nancy earns the praise to Shakespeare due,
For glorious puddings and immortal pies.

[1] Written in 1765. Published by Gosse in 1884. Text of *The Letters of Thomas Gray*, ed. D. C. Tovey, London, 1912.

CHRISTOPHER SMART

(1722-1743-1771)

A Song to David[1]

O THOU, that sit'st upon a throne,
With harp of high majestic tone,
  To praise the King of kings;
And voice of heav'n-ascending swell,
Which, while its deeper notes excell,
  Clear, as a clarion, rings:

To bless each valley, grove and coast,
And charm the cherubs to the post
  Of gratitude in throngs;
To keep the days on Zion's mount,
And send the year to his account,
  With dances and with songs:

O Servant of God's holiest charge,
The minister of praise at large,
  Which thou may'st now receive;
From thy blest mansion hail and hear,
From topmost eminence appear
  To this the wreath I weave.

Great, valiant, pious, good, and clean,
Sublime, contemplative, serene,
  Strong, constant, pleasant, wise!
Bright effluence of exceeding grace;
Best man!—the swiftness and the race,
  The peril, and the prize!

Great—from the lustre of his crown,
From Samuel's horn and God's renown,
  Which is the people's voice;
For all the host, from rear to van,
Applauded and embrac'd the man—
  The man of God's own choice.

Valiant—the word, and up he rose—
The fight—he triumph'd o'er the foes,
  Whom God's just laws abhor;

[1] Published in 1763. Text of first edition.

And arm'd in gallant faith he took
Against the boaster, from the brook,
The weapons of the war.

Pious—magnificent and grand;
'Twas he the famous temple plan'd:
(The seraph in his soul)
Foremost to give his Lord his dues,
Foremost to bless the welcome news,
And foremost to condole.

Good—from Jehudah's genuine vein,
From God's best nature good in grain,
His aspect and his heart;
To pity, to forgive, to save,
Witness En-gedi's conscious cave,
And Shimei's blunted dart.

Clean—if perpetual prayer be pure,
And love, which could itself innure
To fasting and to fear—
Clean in his gestures, hands, and feet,
To smite the lyre, the dance compleat,
To play the sword and spear.

Sublime—invention ever young,
Of vast conception, tow'ring tongue,
To God th' eternal theme;
Notes from yon exaltations caught,
Unrival'd royalty of thought,
O'er meaner strains supreme.

Contemplative—on God to fix
His musings, and above the six
The sabbath-day he blest;
'Twas then his thoughts self-conquest prun'd,
And heavenly melancholy tun'd,
To bless and bear the rest.

Serene—to sow the seeds of peace,
Rememb'ring, when he watch'd the fleece,
How sweetly Kidron purl'd—
To further knowledge, silence vice,
And plant perpetual paradise
When God had calm'd the world.

Strong—in the Lord, who could defy
Satan, and all his powers that lie
In sempiternal night;

And hell, and horror, and despair
Were as the lion and the bear
  To his undaunted might.

Constant—in love to God THE TRUTH,
Age, manhood, infancy, and youth—
  To Jonathan his friend
Constant, beyond the verge of death;
And Ziba, and Mephibosheth,
  His endless fame attend.

Pleasant—and various as the year;
Man, soul, and angel, without peer,
  Priest, champion, sage and boy;
In armour, or in ephod clad,
His pomp, his piety was glad;
  Majestic was his joy.

Wise—in recovery from his fall,
Whence rose his eminence o'er all.
  Of all the most revil'd;
The light of Israel in his ways,
Wise are his precepts, prayer and praise,
  And counsel to his child.

His muse, bright angel of his verse,
Gives balm for all the thorns that pierce,
  For all the pangs that rage;
Blest light, still gaining on the gloom,
The more than Michael of his bloom,
  Th' Abishag of his age.

He sung of God—the mighty source
Of all things—the stupendous force
  On which all strength depends;
From whose right arm, beneath whose eyes,
All period, pow'r, and enterprize
  Commences, reigns, and ends.

Angels—their ministry and meed,
Which to and fro with blessings speed,
  Or with their citterns wait;
Where Michael with his millions bows,
Where dwells the seraph and his spouse,
  The cherub and her mate.

Of man—the semblance and effect
Of God and Love—the Saint elect
  For infinite applause—

To rule the land, and briny broad,
To be laborious in his laud,
And heroes in his cause.

The world—the clustring spheres he made,
The glorious light, the soothing shade,
Dale, champaign, grove, and hill;
The multitudinous abyss,
Where secrecy remains in bliss,
And wisdom hides her skill.

Trees, plants, and flow'rs—of virtuous root;
Gem yielding blossom, yielding fruit,
Choice gums and precious balm;
Bless ye the nosegay in the vale,
And with the sweetners of the gale
Enrich the thankful psalm.

Of fowl—e'en ev'ry beak and wing
Which chear the winter, hail the spring,
That live in peace or prey;
They that make music, or that mock,
The quail, the brave domestic cock,
The raven, swan, and jay.

Of fishes—ev'ry size and shape,
Which nature frames of light escape,
Devouring man to shun:
The shells are in the wealthy deep,
The shoals upon the surface leap,
And love the glancing sun.

Of beasts—the beaver plods his task;
While the sleek tygers roll and bask,
Nor yet the shades arouse:
Her cave the mining coney scoops;
Where o'er the mead the mountain stoops,
The kids exult and brouse.

Of gems—their virtue and their price,
Which hid in earth from man's device,
Their darts of lustre sheathe;
The jasper of the master's stamp,
The topaz blazing like a lamp
Among the mines beneath.

Blest was the tenderness he felt
When to his graceful harp he knelt,
  And did for audience call;
When satan with his hand he quell'd,
And in serene suspence he held
  The frantic throes of Saul.

His furious foes no more malign'd
As he such melody divin'd,
  And sense and soul detain'd;
Now striking strong, now soothing soft,
He sent the godly sounds aloft,
  Or in delight refrain'd.

When up to heav'n his thoughts he pil'd,
From fervent lips fair Michael smil'd,
  As blush to blush she stood;
And chose herself the queen, and gave
Her utmost from her heart, 'so brave,
  'And plays his hymns so good.'

The pillars of the Lord are seven,
Which stand from earth to topmost heav'n;
  His wisdom drew the plan;
His WORD accomplish'd the design,
From brightest gem to deepest mine,
  From CHRIST enthron'd to man.

Alpha, the cause of causes, first
In station, fountain, whence the burst
  Of light, and blaze of day;
Whence bold attempt, and brave advance,
Have motion, life, and ordinance,
  And heav'n itself its stay.

Gamma supports the glorious arch
On which angelic legions march,
  And is with sapphires pav'd;
Thence the fleet clouds are sent adrift,
And thence the painted folds, that lift
  The crimson veil, are wav'd.

Eta with living sculpture breathes,
With verdant carvings, flow'ry wreathes
  Of never-wasting bloom;
In strong relief his goodly base
All instruments of labour grace,
  The trowel, spade, and loom.

Next Theta stands to the Supreme—
Who form'd, in number, sign, and scheme,
  Th' illustrious lights that are;
And one address'd his saffron robe,
And one, clad in a silver globe,
  Held rule with ev'ry star.

Iota's tun'd to choral hymns
Of those that fly, while he that swims
  In thankful safety lurks;
And foot, and chapitre, and niche,
The various histories enrich
  Of God's recorded works.

Sigma presents the social droves,
With him that solitary roves,
  And man of all the chief;
Fair on whose face, and stately frame,
Did God impress his hallow'd name,
  For ocular belief.

OMEGA! GREATEST and the BEST,
Stands sacred to the day of rest,
  For gratitude and thought;
Which bless'd the world upon his pole,
And gave the universe his goal,
  And clos'd th' infernal draught.

O DAVID, scholar of the Lord!
Such is thy science, whence reward
  And infinite degree;
O strength, O sweetness, lasting ripe!
God's harp thy symbol, and thy type
  The lion and the bee!

There is but One who ne'er rebell'd,
But One by passion unimpell'd,
  By pleasures unintice't;
He from himself his semblance sent,
Grand object of his own content,
  And saw the God in CHRIST.

Tell them I am, JEHOVA said
To MOSES; while earth heard in dread,
  And smitten to the heart,
At once above, beneath, around,
All nature, without voice or sound,
  Replied, O Lord, THOU ART.

Thou art—to give and to confirm,
For each his talent and his term;
  All flesh thy bounties share:
Thou shalt not call thy brother fool;
The porches of the Christian school
  Are meekness, peace, and pray'r.

Open, and naked of offence,
Man's made of mercy, soul, and sense;
  God arm'd the snail and wilk;
Be good to him that pulls thy plough;
Due food and care, due rest, allow
  For her that yields thee milk.

Rise up before the hoary head,
And God's benign commandment dread,
  Which says thou shalt not die:
'Not as I will, but as thou wilt,'
Pray'd He whose conscience knew no guilt;
  With whose bless'd pattern vie.

Use all thy passions!—love is thine,
And joy, and jealousy divine;
  Thine hope's eternal fort,
And care thy leisure to disturb,
With fear concupiscence to curb,
  And rapture to transport.

Act simply, as occasion asks:
Put mellow wine in season'd casks;
  Till not with ass and bull:
Remember thy baptismal bond;
Keep from commixtures foul and fond,
  Nor work thy flax with wool.

Distribute: pay the Lord his tithe,
And make the widow's heart-strings blithe;
  Resort with those that weep:
As you from all and each expect,
For all and each thy love direct,
  And render as you reap.

The slander and its bearer spurn,
And propagating praise sojourn
  To make thy welcome last;
Turn from old Adam to the New;
By hope futurity pursue;
  Look upwards to the past.

Controul thine eye, salute success,
Honour the wiser, happier bless,
And for thy neighbour feel;
Grutch not of mammon and his leaven,
Work emulation up to heaven
By knowledge and by zeal.

O DAVID, highest in the list
Of worthies, on God's ways insist,
*The genuine word repeat:
Vain are the documents of men,
And vain the flourish of the pen
That keeps the fool's conceit.

PRAISE above all—for praise prevails;
Heap up the measure, load the scales,
And good to goodness add:
The gen'rous soul her Saviour aids,
But peevish obloquy degrades;
The Lord is great and glad.

For ADORATION all the ranks
Of angels yield eternal thanks,
And DAVID in the midst;
With God's good poor, which, last and least
In man's esteem, thou to thy feast,
O blessed bride-groom, bidst.

For ADORATION seasons change,
And order, truth, and beauty range,
Adjust, attract, and fill:
The grass the polyanthus cheques;
And polish'd porphyry reflects,
By the descending rill.

Rich almonds colour to the prime
For ADORATION; tendrils climb,
And fruit-trees pledge their gems;
And †Ivis with her gorgeous vest
Builds for her eggs her cunning nest,
And bell-flowers bow their stems.

With vinous syrups cedars spout;
From rocks pure honey gushing out,
For ADORATION springs:
All scenes of painting croud the map

* Ps. 119.
† Humming-bird.

Of nature; to the mermaid's pap
  The scaled infant clings.

The spotted ounce and playsome cubs
Run rustling 'mongst the flow'ring shrubs,
  And lizards feed the moss;
For ADORATION beasts embark,
While waves upholding halcyon's ark
  No longer roar and toss.

While Israel sits beneath his fig,
With coral root and amber sprig
  The wean'd advent'rer sports;
Where to the palm the jasmin cleaves,
For ADORATION 'mongst the leaves
  The gale his peace reports.

Increasing days their reign exalt,
Nor in the pink and mottled vault
  Th' opposing spirits tilt;
And, by the coasting reader spied,
The silverlings and crusions glide
  For ADORATION gilt.

For ADORATION rip'ning canes
And cocoa's purest milk detains
  The western pilgrim's staff;
Where rain in clasping boughs inclos'd,
And vines with oranges dispos'd,
  Embow'r the social laugh.

Now labour his reward receives,
For ADORATION counts his sheaves
  To peace, her bounteous prince;
The nectarine his strong tint imbibes,
And apples of ten thousand tribes,
  And quick peculiar quince.

The wealthy crops of whit'ning rice,
'Mongst thyine woods and groves of spice,
  For ADORATION grow;
And, marshall'd in the fenced land,
The peaches and pomegranates stand,
  Where wild carnations blow.

The laurels with the winter strive;
The crocus burnishes alive
  Upon the snow-clad earth:

For ADORATION myrtles stay
To keep the garden from dismay,
And bless the sight from dearth.

The pheasant shows his pompous neck;
And ermine, jealous of a speck,
With fear eludes offence:
The sable, with his glossy pride,
For ADORATION is descried,
Where frosts the wave condense.

The chearful holly, pensive yew,
And holy thorn, their trim renew;
The squirrel hoards his nuts:
All creatures batten o'er their stores,
And careful nature all her doors
For ADORATION shuts.

For ADORATION, DAVID's psalms
Lift up the heart to deeds of alms;
And he, who kneels and chants,
Prevails his passions to controul,
Finds meat and med'cine to the soul,
Which for translation pants.

For ADORATION, beyond match,
The scholar bulfinch aims to catch
The soft flute's iv'ry touch;
And, careless on the hazle spray,
The daring redbreast keeps at bay
The damsel's greedy clutch.

For ADORATION, in the skies,
The Lord's philosopher espies
The Dog, the Ram, and Rose;
The planets ring, Orion's sword;
Nor is his greatness less ador'd
In the vile worm that glows.

For ADORATION* on the strings
The western breezes work their wings,
The captive ear to sooth.—
Hark! 'tis a voice—how still, and small—
That makes the cataracts to fall,
Or bids the sea be smooth.

* Æolian harp.

For ADORATION, incense comes
From bezoar, and Arabian gums;
  And on the civet's furr.
But as for prayer, or e're it faints,
Far better is the breath of saints
  Than galbanum and myrrh.

For ADORATION from the down,
Of dam'sins to th' anana's crown,
  God sends to tempt the taste;
And while the luscious zest invites,
The sense, that in the scene delights,
  Commands desire be chaste.

For ADORATION, all the paths
Of grace are open, all the baths
  Of purity refresh;
And all the rays of glory beam
To deck the man of God's esteem,
  Who triumphs o'er the flesh.

For ADORATION, in the dome
Of Christ the sparrows find an home;
  And on his olives perch:
The swallow also dwells with thee,
O man of God's humility,
  Within his Saviour's CHURCH.

Sweet is the dew that falls betimes,
And drops upon the leafy limes;
  Sweet Hermon's fragrant air:
Sweet is the lilly's silver bell,
And sweet the wakeful tapers smell
  That watch for early pray'r.

Sweet the young nurse with love intense,
Which smiles o'er sleeping innocence;
  Sweet when the lost arrive:
Sweet the musician's ardour beats,
While his vague mind's in quest of sweets,
  The choicest flow'rs to hive.

Sweeter in all the strains of love,
The language of thy turtle dove,
  Pair'd to thy swelling chord;
Sweeter with ev'ry grace endu'd,
The glory of thy gratitude,
  Respir'd unto the Lord.

Strong is the horse upon his speed;
Strong in pursuit the rapid glede,
  Which makes at once his game:
Strong the tall ostrich on the ground;
Strong thro' the turbulent profound
  Shoots *xiphias to his aim.

Strong is the lion—like a coal
His eye-ball—like a bastion's mole
  His chest against the foes:
Strong, the gier-eagle on his sail,
Strong against tide, th' enormous whale
  Emerges as he goes.

But stronger still, in earth and air,
And in the sea, the man of pray'r;
  And far beneath the tide;
And in the seat to faith assign'd,
Where ask is have, where seek is find,
  Where knock is open wide.

Beauteous the fleet before the gale;
Beauteous the multitudes in mail,
  Rank'd arms and crested heads:
Beauteous the garden's umbrage mild,
Walk, water, meditated wild,
  And all the bloomy beds.

Beauteous the moon full on the lawn;
And beauteous, when the veil's withdrawn,
  The virgin to her spouse:
Beauteous the temple deck'd and fill'd,
When to the heav'n of heav'ns they build
  Their heart-directed vows.

Beauteous, yea beauteous more than these,
The shepherd king upon his knees,
  For his momentous trust;
With wish of infinite conceit,
For man, beast, mute, the small and great,
  And prostrate dust to dust.

Precious the bounteous widow's mite;
And precious, for extream delight,
  †The largess from the churl:
Precious the ruby's blushing blaze,

* The sword-fish.
† Sam. xxv. 18.

And *alba's blest imperial rays,
  And pure cerulean pearl.

Precious the penitential tear;
And precious is the sigh sincere,
  Acceptable to God:
And precious are the winning flow'rs,
In gladsome Israel's feast of bow'rs,
  Bound on the hallow'd sod.

More precious that diviner part
Of David, ev'n the Lord's own heart,
  Great, beautiful, and new:
In all things where it was intent,
In all extreams, in each event,
  Proof—answ'ring true to true.

Glorious the sun in mid career;
Glorious th' assembled fires appear;
  Glorious the comet's train:
Glorious the trumpet and alarm;
Glorious th' almighty stretch'd-out arm;
  Glorious th' enraptur'd main:

Glorious the northern lights astream;
Glorious the song, when God's the theme
  Glorious the thunder's roar:
Glorious hosanna from the den;
Glorious the catholic amen;
  Glorious the martyr's gore:

Glorious—more glorious is the crown
Of Him that brought salvation down
  By meekness, call'd thy Son;
Thou that stupendous truth believ'd,
And now the matchless deed's atchiev'd,
  DETERMINED, DARED, and DONE.

* Rev. xi. 17.

THOMAS EDWARDS

(1699-1744-1757)

Sonnet
On a Family Picture[1]

WHEN pensive on that Portraiture I gaze,
Where my four Brothers round about me stand,
And four fair Sisters smile with graces bland,
The goodly monument of happier days;
And think how soon insatiate Death, who preys
On all, has cropp'd the rest with ruthless hand;
While only I survive of all that band,
Which one chaste bed did to my Father raise;
It seems that like a Column left alone,
The tottering remnant of some splendid Fane,
Scape'd from the fury of the barbarous Gaul,
And wasting Time, which has the rest o'erthrown;
Amidst our House's ruins I remain
Single, unpropp'd, and nodding to my fall.

EDWARD MOORE

(1712-1744-1757)

Fables for the Ladies[2]

Fable V

The Poet and his Patron

WHY, Cælia, is your spreading waist
So loose, so negligently lac'd?
Why must the wrapping bed-gown hide
Your snowy bosom's swelling pride?
How ill that dress adorns your head,
Distain'd, and rumpled from the bed!

[1] Published in Dodsley's *Collection of Poems,* Volume II, 1748. Text of first edition.

[2] Published in *Poems, Fables, and Plays,* 1756. Text of first edition.

Those clouds, that shade your blooming face,
A little water might displace,
As nature every morn bestows
The crystal dew, to cleanse the rose.
Those tresses, as the raven black,
That wav'd in ringlets down your back,
Uncomb'd, and injur'd by neglect,
Destroy the face, which once they deck'd.
  Whence this forgetfulness of dress?
Pray, madam, are you marry'd? Yes.
Nay, then indeed the wonder ceases,
No matter now how loose your dress is;
The end is won, your fortune's made,
Your sister now may take the trade.
  Alas! what pity 'tis to find
This fault in half the female kind!
From hence proceed aversion, strife,
And all that sours the wedded life.
Beauty can only point the dart,
'Tis neatness guides it to the heart;
Let neatness then, and beauty strive
To keep a wav'ring flame alive.
  'Tis harder far (you'll find it true)
To keep the conquest, than subdue;
Admit us once behind the screen,
What is there farther to be seen?
A newer face may raise the flame,
But every woman is the same.
  Then study chiefly to improve
The charm, that fix'd your husband's love.
Weigh well his humour. Was it dress,
That gave your beauty power to bless?
Pursue it still; be neater seen;
'Tis always frugal to be clean;
So shall you keep alive desire,
And time's swift wing shall fan the fire.

  IN garret high (as stories say)
A Poet sung his tuneful lay;
So soft, so smooth his verse, you'd swear
Apollo, and the muses there.
Through all the town his praises rung,
His sonnets at the playhouse sung;
High waving o'er his lab'ring head,
The goddess Want her pinions spread,
And with poetic fury fir'd,
What Phœbus faintly had inspir'd.

A noble Youth, of taste and wit,
Approv'd the sprightly things he writ,
And sought him in his cobweb dome,
Discharg'd his rent, and brought him home.
Behold him at the stately board,
Who, but the Poet, and my Lord!
Each day deliciously he dines,
And greedy quaffs the gen'rous wines;
His sides were plump, his skin was sleek,
And plenty wanton'd on his cheek;
Astonish'd at the change so new,
Away th' inspiring goddess flew.
Now, dropt for politics, and news,
Neglected lay the drooping muse;
Unmindful whence his fortune came,
He stifled the poetic flame;
Nor tale, nor sonnet, for my lady,
Lampoon, nor epigram was ready.
With just contempt his Patron saw,
(Resolv'd his bounty to withdraw)
And thus, with anger in his look,
The late-repenting fool bespoke.
Blind to the god that courts thee grown,
Whence has the sun of favour shone?
Delighted with thy tuneful art,
Esteem was growing in my heart;
But idly thou reject'st the charm,
That gave it birth, and kept it warm.
Unthinking fools, alone despise
The arts, that taught them first to rise.

Song the Eighth[1]

THAT Jenny's my friend, my delight, and my pride,
I always have boasted, and seek not to hide;
I dwell on her praises wherever I go,
They say I'm in love, but I answer no, no.

At ev'ning oft-times with what pleasure I see
A note from her hand, "I'll be with you at tea!"
My heart how it bounds, when I hear her below!
But say not 'tis love, for I answer no, no.

She sings me a song, and I echo each strain,
Again I cry, Jenny! sweet Jenny, again!

[1] Published in *Poems, Fables, and Plays,* 1756. Text of first edition.

I kiss her soft lips, as if there I could grow,
And fear I'm in love, though I answer no, no.

She tells me her faults, as she sits on my knee,
I chide her, and swear she's an angel to me:
My shoulder she taps, and still bids me think so;
Who knows but she loves, though she tells me no, no?

Yet such is my temper, so dull am I grown,
I ask not Her heart, but would conquer my own:
Her bosom's soft peace shall I seek to o'erthrow,
And wish to persuade, while I answer no, no?

From beauty, and wit, and good-humour, ah! why
Should prudence advise, and compel me to fly?
Thy bounties, O Fortune! make haste to bestow,
And let me deserve her, or still I say no.

Song the Ninth[1]

You tell me I'm handsome, I know not how true,
And easy, and chatty, and good-humour'd too;
That my lips are as red as the rose-bud in June,
And my voice, like the nightingale's, sweetly in tune:
All this has been told me by twenty before,
But he that would win me, must flatter me more.

If beauty from virtue receive no supply,
Or prattle from prudence, how wanting am I!
My ease and good-humour short raptures will bring,
And my voice, like the nightingale's, know but a spring.
For charms such as these then, your praises give o'er,
To love me for life, you must love me for more.

Then talk to me not of a shape or an air,
For Cloe, the wanton, can rival me there:
'Tis virtue alone that makes beauty look gay,
And brightens good-humour, as sunshine the day;
For that if you love me, your flame shall be true,
And I in my turn, may be taught to love too.

[1] Published in *Poems, Fables, and Plays,* 1756. Text of first edition.

THOMAS WARTON, JR.

(1728-1745-1790)

The Pleasures of Melancholy[1]

—Praecipe lugubres
Cantus, Melpomene!—

MOTHER of musings, Contemplation sage,
Whose grotto stands upon the topmost rock
Of Teneriff; 'mid the tempestuous night,
On which, in calmest meditation held,
Thou hear'st with howling winds the beating rain
And drifting hail descend; or if the skies
Unclouded shine, and thro' the blue serene
Pale Cynthia rolls her silver-axled car,
Whence gazing stedfast on the spangled vault
Raptur'd thou sitt'st, while murmurs indistinct
Of distant billows sooth thy pensive ear
With hoarse and hollow sounds; secure, self-blest,
There oft thou listen'st to the wild uproar
Of fleets encount'ring, that in whispers low
Ascends the rocky summit, where thou dwell'st
Remote from man, conversing with the spheres!
O lead me, queen sublime, to solemn glooms
Congenial with my soul; to cheerless shades,
To ruin'd seats, to twilight cells and bow'rs,
Where thoughtful Melancholy loves to muse,
Her fav'rite midnight haunts. The laughing scenes
Of purple Spring, where all the wanton train
Of Smiles and Graces seem to lead the dance
In sportive round, while from their hands they show'r
Ambrosial blooms and flow'rs, no longer charm;
Tempe, no more I court thy balmy breeze,
Adieu green vales! ye broider'd meads, adieu!
  Beneath yon ruin'd abbey's moss-grown piles
Oft let me sit, at twilight hour of eve,
Where thro' some western window the pale moon
Pours her long-levell'd rule of streaming light;
While sullen sacred silence reigns around,
Save the lone screech-owl's note, who builds his bow'r
Amid the mould'ring caverns dark and damp,
Or the calm breeze, that rustles in the leaves
Of flaunting ivy, that with mantle green

[1] Written in 1745. Published in 1747. Text of *Works*, fifth edition, 1802.

Invests some wasted tow'r. Or let me tread
Its neighb'ring walk of pines, where mus'd of old
The cloyster'd brothers: thro' the gloomy void
That far extends beneath their ample arch
As on I pace, religious horror wraps
My soul in dread repose. But when the world
Is clad in Midnight's raven-colour'd robe,
'Mid hollow charnel let me watch the flame
Of taper dim, shedding a livid glare
O'er the wan heaps; while airy voices talk
Along the glimm'ring walls; or ghostly shape
At distance seen, invites with beck'ning hand
My lonesome steps, thro' the far-winding vaults.
Nor undelightful is the solemn noon
Of night, when haply wakeful from my couch
I start: lo, all is motionless around!
Roars not the rushing wind; the sons of men
And every beast in mute oblivion lie;
All nature's hush'd in silence and in sleep.
O then how fearful is it to reflect,
That thro' the still globe's awful solitude,
No being wakes but me! till stealing sleep
My drooping temples bathes in opiate dews.
Nor then let dreams, of wanton folly born,
My senses lead thro' flow'ry paths of joy;
But let the sacred Genius of the night
Such mystic visions send, as Spenser saw,
When thro' bewild'ring Fancy's magic maze,
To the fell house of Busyrane, he led
Th' unshaken Britomart; or Milton knew,
When in abstracted thought he first conceiv'd
All heav'n in tumult, and the Seraphim
Come tow'ring, arm'd in adamant and gold.
Let others love soft Summer's ev'ning smiles,
As list'ning to the distant water-fall,
They mark the blushes of the streaky west;
I choose the pale December's foggy glooms.
Then, when the sullen shades of ev'ning close,
Where thro' the room a blindly-glimm'ring gleam
The dying embers scatter, far remote
From Mirth's mad shouts, that thro' th' illumin'd roof
Resound with festive echo, let me sit,
Blest with the lowly cricket's drowsy dirge.
Then let my thought contemplative explore
This fleeting state of things, the vain delights,
The fruitless toils, that still our search elude,
As thro' the wilderness of life we rove.
This sober hour of silence will unmask

False Folly's smile, that like the dazzling spells
Of wily Comus cheat th' unweeting eye
With blear illusion, and persuade to drink
That charmed cup, which Reason's mintage fair
Unmoulds, and stamps the monster on the man.
Eager we taste, but in the luscious draught
Forget the poisonous dregs that lurk beneath.
  Few know that elegance of soul refin'd,
Whose soft sensation feels a quicker joy
From Melancholy's scenes, than the dull pride
Of tasteless splendor and magnificence
Can e'er afford. Thus Eloise, whose mind
Had languish'd to the pangs of melting love,
More genuine transport found, as on some tomb
Reclin'd, she watch'd the tapers of the dead;
Or thro' the pillar'd iles, amid pale shrines
Of imag'd saints, and intermingled graves,
Mus'd a veil'd votaress; than Flavia feels,
As thro' the mazes of the festive ball,
Proud of her conquering charms, and beauty's blaze,
She floats amid the silken sons of dress,
And shines the fairest of th' assembled fair.
  When azure noontide cheers the dædal globe,
And the blest regent of the golden day
Rejoices in his bright meridian tower,
How oft my wishes ask the night's return,
That best befriends the melancholy mind!
Hail, sacred Night! thou too shalt share my song!
Sister of ebon-scepter'd Hecat, hail!
Whether in congregated clouds thou wrap'st
Thy viewless chariot, or with silver crown
Thy beaming head encirclest, ever hail!
What tho' beneath thy gloom the sorceress-train,
Far in obscured haunt of Lapland moors,
With rhymes uncouth the bloody cauldron bless;
Tho' Murder wan beneath thy shrouding shade
Summons her slow-ey'd vot'ries to devise
Of secret slaughter, while by one blue lamp
In hideous conf'rence sits the list'ning band,
And start at each low wind, or wakeful sound:
What tho' thy stay the pilgrim curseth oft,
As all benighted in Arabian wastes
He hears the wilderness around him howl
With roaming monsters, while on his hoar head
The black-descending tempest ceaseless beats;
Yet more delightful to my pensive mind
Is thy return, than blooming morn's approach,
Ev'n then, in youthful pride of opening May,

When from the portals of the saffron east
She sheds fresh roses, and ambrosial dews.
Yet not ungrateful is the morn's approach,
When dropping wet she comes, and clad in clouds,
While thro' the damp air scowls the louring south,
Blackening the landscape's face, that grove and hill
In formless vapours undistinguish'd swim:
Th' afflicted songsters of the sadden'd groves
Hail not the sullen gloom; the waving elms
That, hoar thro' time, and rang'd in thick array,
Enclose with stately row some rural hall,
Are mute, nor echo with the clamors hoarse
Of rooks rejoicing on their airy boughs;
While to the shed the dripping poultry crowd,
A mournful train: secure the village-hind
Hangs o'er the crackling blaze, nor tempts the storm;
Fix'd in th' unfinish'd furrow rests the plough:
Rings not the high wood with enliven'd shouts
Of early hunter: all is silence drear;
And deepest sadness wraps the face of things.
Thro' POPE's soft song tho' all the Graces breathe,
And happiest art adorn his Attic page;
Yet does my mind with sweeter transport glow,
As at the root of mossy trunk reclin'd,
In magic SPENSER's wildly-warbled song
I see deserted Una wander wide
Thro' wasteful solitudes, and lurid heaths,
Weary, forlorn; than when the fated fair
Upon the bosom bright of silver Thames
Launches in all the lustre of brocade,
Amid the splendors of the laughing Sun.
The gay description palls upon the sense,
And coldly strikes the mind with feeble bliss.
Ye youths of Albion's beauty-blooming isle,
Whose brows have worn the wreath of luckless love,
Is there a pleasure like the pensive mood,
Whose magic wont to soothe your soften'd souls?
O tell how rapturous the joy, to melt
To Melody's assuasive voice; to bend
Th' uncertain step along the midnight mead,
And pour your sorrows to the pitying moon,
By many a slow trill from the bird of woe
Oft interrupted; in embow'ring woods
By darksome brook to muse, and there forget
The solemn dulness of the tedious world,
While Fancy grasps the visionary fair:
And now no more th' abstracted ear attends
The water's murm'ring lapse, th' entranced eye

Pierces no longer thro' th' extended rows
Of thick-rang'd trees; till haply from the depth
The woodman's stroke, or distant tinkling team,
Or heifers rustling thro' the brake, alarms
Th' illuded sense, and mars the golden dream.
These are delights that absence drear has made
Familiar to my soul, e'er since the form
Of young Sapphira, beauteous as the Spring,
When from her vi'let-woven couch awak'd
By frolic Zephyr's hand, her tender cheek
Graceful she lifts, and blushing from her bow'r
Issues to clothe in gladsome-glist'ring green
The genial globe, first met my dazzled sight:
These are delights unknown to minds profane,
And which alone the pensive soul can taste.
The taper'd choir, at the late hour of pray'r,
Oft let me tread, while to th' according voice
The many-sounding organ peals on high,
The clear slow-dittied chaunt, or varied hymn,
Till all my soul is bath'd in ecstasies,
And lapp'd in Paradise. Or let me sit
Far in sequester'd iles of the deep dome,
There lonesome listen to the sacred sounds,
Which, as they lengthen thro' the Gothic vaults,
In hollow murmurs reach my ravish'd ear.
Nor when the lamps expiring yield to night,
And solitude returns, would I forsake
The solemn mansion, but attentive mark
The due clock swinging slow with sweepy sway,
Measuring Time's flight with momentary sound.
Nor let me fail to cultivate my mind
With the soft thrillings of the tragic Muse,
Divine Melpomene, sweet Pity's nurse,
Queen of the stately step, and flowing pall.
Now let Monimia mourn with streaming eyes
Her joys incestuous, and polluted love:
Now let soft Juliet in the gaping tomb
Print the last kiss on her true Romeo's lips,
His lips yet reeking from the deadly draught:
Or Jaffier kneel for one forgiving look.
Nor seldom let the Moor on Desdemone
Pour the misguided threats of jealous rage.
By soft degrees the manly torrent steals
From my swoln eyes; and at a brother's woe
My big heart melts in sympathizing tears.
What are the splendors of the gaudy court,
Its tinsel trappings, and its pageant pomps?
To me far happier seems the banish'd lord,

Amid Siberia's unrejoicing wilds
Who pines all lonesome, in the chambers hoar
Of some high castle shut, whose windows dim
In distant ken discover trackless plains,
Where Winter ever whirls his icy car;
While still repeated objects of his view,
The gloomy battlements, and ivied spires,
That crown the solitary dome, arise;
While from the topmost turret the slow clock,
Far heard along th' inhospitable wastes,
With sad-returning chime awakes new grief;
Ev'n he far happier seems than is the proud,
The potent Satrap, whom he left behind
'Mid Moscow's golden palaces, to drown
In ease and luxury the laughing hours.
  Illustrious objects strike the gazer's mind
With feeble bliss, and but allure the sight,
Nor rouze with impulse quick th' unfeeling heart.
Thus seen by shepherd from Hymettus' brow,
What dædal landscapes smile! here palmy groves,
Resounding once with Plato's voice, arise,
Amid whose umbrage green her silver head
Th' unfading olive lifts; here vine-clad hills
Lay forth their purple store, and sunny vales
In prospect vast their level laps expand,
Amid whose beauties glistering Athens tow'rs.
Tho' thro' the blissful scenes Ilissus roll
His sage-inspiring flood, whose winding marge
The thick-wove laurel shades; tho' roseate Morn
Pour all her splendors on th' empurpled scene;
Yet feels the hoary Hermit truer joys,
As from the cliff, that o'er his cavern hangs,
He views the piles of fall'n Persepolis
In deep arrangement hide the darksome plain.
Unbounded waste! the mould'ring obelisk
Here, like a blasted oak, ascends the clouds;
Here Parian domes their vaulted halls disclose
Horrid with thorn, where lurks th' unpitying thief,
Whence flits the twilight-loving bat at eve,
And the deaf adder wreathes her spotted train,
The dwellings once of elegance and art.
Here temples rise, amid whose hallow'd bounds
Spires the black pine, while thro' the naked street,
Once haunt of tradeful merchants, springs the grass:
Here columns heap'd on prostrate columns, torn
From their firm base, increase the mould'ring mass.
Far as the sight can pierce, appear the spoils
Of sunk magnificence! a blended scene

Of moles, fanes, arches, domes, and palaces,
Where, with his brother Horror, Ruin sits.
O come then, Melancholy, queen of thought!
O come with saintly look and steadfast step,
From forth thy cave embower'd with mournful yew,
Where ever to the curfeu's solemn sound
List'ning thou sitt'st, and with thy cypress bind
Thy votary's hair, and seal him for thy son.
But never let Euphrosyne beguile
With toys of wanton mirth my fixed mind,
Nor in my path her primrose-garland cast.
Tho' 'mid her train the dimpled Hebe bare
Her rosy bosom to th' enamour'd view;
Tho' Venus, mother of the Smiles and Loves,
And Bacchus, ivy-crown'd, in citron bow'r
With her on nectar-streaming fruitage feast:
What tho' 'tis hers to calm the low'ring skies,
And at her presence mild th' embattled clouds
Disperse in air, and o'er the face of heav'n
New day diffusive gleam at her approach;
Yet are these joys that Melancholy gives,
Than all her witless revels happier far;
These deep-felt joys, by Contemplation taught.
Then ever, beauteous Contemplation, hail!
From thee began, auspicious maid, my song,
With thee shall end; for thou art fairer far
Than are the nymphs of Cirrha's mossy grot;
To loftier rapture thou canst wake the thought,
Than all the fabling Poet's boasted pow'rs.
Hail, queen divine! whom, as tradition tells,
Once in his evening walk a Druid found,
Far in a hollow glade of Mona's woods;
And piteous bore with hospitable hand
To the close shelter of his oaken bow'r.
There soon the sage admiring mark'd the dawn
Of solemn musing in your pensive thought;
For when a smiling babe, you lov'd to lie
Oft deeply list'ning to the rapid roar
Of wood-hung Meinai, stream of Druids old.

The Grave of King Arthur[1]

ADVERTISEMENT

KING HENRY the second, having undertaken an expedition into Ireland, to suppress a rebellion raised by Roderick king of Connaught, commonly called

[1] Published in *Poems*, 1777. Text of third edition, 1779.

O Connor Dun, or *the brown monarch of Ireland*, was entertained, in his passage through Wales, with the songs of the Welsh Bards. The subject of their poetry was king Arthur, whose history had been so long disguised by fabulous inventions, that the place of his burial was in general scarcely known or remembered. But in one of these Welsh poems sung before Henry, it was recited, that king Arthur, after the battle of Camlan in Cornwall, was interred at Glastonbury abbey, before the high altar, yet without any external mark or memorial. Afterwards Henry visited the abbey, and commanded the spot, described by the Bard, to be opened: when digging near twenty feet deep, they found the body, deposited under a large stone, inscribed with Arthur's name. This is the ground-work of the following Ode: but for the better accommodation of the story to our present purpose, it is told with some slight variations from the Chronicle of Glastonbury. The castle of Cilgarran, where this discovery is supposed to have been made, now a romantic ruin, stands on a rock descending to the river Teivi in Pembrokeshire: and was built by Roger Montgomery, who led the van of the Normans at Hastings.

STATELY the feast, and high the cheer:
Girt with many an armed peer,
And canopied with golden pall,
Amid CILGARRAN'S castle hall,
Sublime in formidable state,
And warlike splendour, Henry sate;
Prepar'd to stain the briny flood
Of Shannon's lakes with rebel blood.
  Illumining the vaulted roof,
A thousand torches flam'd aloof:
From massy cups, with golden gleam
Sparkled the red metheglin's stream:
To grace the gorgeous festival,
Along the lofty-window'd wall,
The storied tapestry was hung:
With minstrelsy the rafters rung
Of harps, that with reflected light
From the proud gallery glitter'd bright:
While gifted bards, a rival throng,
(From distant Mona, nurse of song,
From Teivi, fring'd with umbrage brown,
From Elvy's vale, and Cader's crown,
From many a shaggy precipice
That shades Ierne's hoarse abyss,
And many a sunless solitude
Of Radnor's inmost mountains rude,)
To crown the banquet's solemn close,
Themes of British glory chose;
And to the strings of various chime
Attemper'd thus the fabling rime.
  "O'er Cornwall's cliffs the tempest roar'd,
"High the screaming sea-mew soar'd;
"On Tintaggel's topmost tower

"Darksom fell the sleety shower;
"Round the rough castle shrilly sung
"The whirling blast, and wildly flung
"On each tall rampart's thundering side
"The surges of the tumbling tide:
"When Arthur rang'd his red-cross ranks
"On conscious Camlan's crimson'd banks:
"By Mordred's faithless guile decreed
"Beneath a Saxon spear to bleed!
"Yet in vain a paynim foe
"Arm'd with fate the mighty blow;
"For when he fell, an elfin queen,
"All in secret, and unseen,
"O'er the fainting hero threw
"Her mantle of ambrosial blue;
"And bade her spirits bear him far,
"In Merlin's agate-axled car,
"To her green isle's enamel'd steep,
"In the navel of the deep.
"O'er his wounds she sprinkled dew
"From flowers that in Arabia grew:
"On a rich, inchanted bed,
"She pillow'd his majestic head;
"O'er his brow, with whispers bland,
"Thrice she wav'd an opiate wand;
"And, to soft music's airy sound,
"Her magic curtains clos'd around.
"There, renew'd the vital spring,
"Again he reigns a mighty king;
"And many a fair and fragrant clime,
"Blooming in immortal prime,
"By gales of Eden ever fann'd,
"Owns the monarch's high command:
"Thence to Britain shall return,
"(If right prophetic rolls I learn)
"Borne on Victory's spreading plume,
"His antient sceptre to resume;
"Once more, in old heroic pride,
"His barbed courser to bestride;
"His knightly table to restore,
"And brave the tournaments of yore."
  They ceas'd: when on the tuneful stage
Advanc'd a bard, of aspect sage;
His silver tresses, thin-besprent,
To age a graceful reverence lent;
His beard, all white as spangles frore
That cloath Plinlimmon's forests hoar,
Down to his harp descending flow'd;

With Time's faint rose his features glow'd;
His eyes diffus'd a soften'd fire,
And thus he wak'd the warbling wire.
"Listen, Henry, to my read!
"Not from fairy realms I lead
"Bright-rob'd Tradition, to relate
"In forged colours Arthur's fate;
"Though much of old romantic lore
"On the blest theme I keep in store:
"But boastful Fiction should be dumb,
"Where Truth the strain might best become.
"If thine ear may still be won
"With songs of Uther's glorious son,
"Henry, I a tale unfold,
"Never yet in rime enroll'd,
"Nor sung nor harp'd in hall or bower;
"Which in my youth's full early flower,
"A minstrel, sprung of Cornish line,
"Who spoke of kings from old Locrine,
"Taught me to chant, one vernal dawn,
"Deep in a cliff-encircled lawn,
"What time the glistening vapours fled
"From cloud-envelop'd Clyder's head;
"And on its sides the torrents gray
"Shone to the morning's orient ray.
"When Arthur bow'd his haughty crest,
"No princess, veil'd in azure vest,
"Snatch'd him, by Merlin's potent spell,
"In groves of golden bliss to dwell;
"Where, crown'd with wreaths of misletoe,
"Slaughter'd kings in glory go:
"But when he fell, with winged speed,
"His champions, on a milk-white steed,
"From the battle's hurricane,
"Bore him to Joseph's towered fane,
"In the fair vale of Avalon:
"There, with chanted orison,
"And the long blaze of tapers clear,
"The stoled fathers met the bier;
"Through the dim iles, in order dread
"Of martial woe, the chief they led,
"And deep intomb'd in holy ground,
"Before the altar's solemn bound.
"Around no dusky banners wave,
"No mouldering trophies mark the grave:
"Away the ruthless Dane has torn
"Each trace that Time's slow touch had worn;
"And long, o'er the neglected stone,

"Oblivion's veil its shade has thrown:
"The faded tomb, with honour due,
"'Tis thine, O Henry, to renew!
"Thither, when Conquest has restor'd
"Yon recreant isle, and sheath'd the sword,
"When Peace with palm has crown'd thy brows,
"Haste thee, to pay thy pilgrim vows.
"There, observant of my lore,
"The pavement's hallow'd depth explore;
"And thrice a fathom underneath
"Dive into the vaults of death.
"There shall thine eye, with wild amaze,
"On his gigantic stature gaze;
"There shalt thou find the monarch laid,
"All in warrior-weeds array'd;
"Wearing in death his helmet-crown,
"And weapons huge of old renown.
"Martial prince, 'tis thine to save
"From dark oblivion Arthur's grave!
"So may thy ships securely stem
"The western frith: thy diadem
"Shine victorious in the van,
"Nor heed the slings of Ulster's clan:
"Thy Norman pike-men win their way
"Up the dun rocks of Harald's bay:
"And from the steeps of rough Kildare
"Thy prancing hoofs the falcon scare:
"So may thy bow's unerring yew
"Its shafts in Roderick's heart embrew."
  Amid the pealing symphony
The spiced goblets mantled high,
With passions new the song impress'd
The listening king's impatient breast:
Flash the keen lightnings from his eyes;
He scorns awhile his bold emprise;
Ev'n now he seems, with eager pace,
The consecrated floor to trace;
And ope, from its tremendous gloom,
The treasure of the wonderous tomb:
Ev'n now, he burns in thought to rear,
From its dark bed, the ponderous spear,
Rough with the gore of Pictish kings:
Ev'n now fond hope his fancy wings,
To poise the monarch's massy blade,
Of magic-temper'd metal made;
And drag to day the dinted shield
That felt the storm of Camlan's field.

O'er the sepulchre profound
Ev'n now, with arching sculpture crown'd,
He plans the chantry's choral shrine,
The daily dirge, and rites divine.

Sonnet III
Written in a Blank Leaf of Dugdale's Monasticon[1]

Deem not, devoid of elegance, the sage,
By Fancy's genuine feelings unbeguil'd,
Of painful Pedantry the poring child;
Who turns, of these proud domes, th' historic page,
Now sunk by Time, and Henry's fiercer rage.
Thinkst thou the warbling Muses never smil'd
On his lone hours? Ingenuous views engage
His thought, on themes, unclassic falsely stil'd,
Intent. While cloister'd Piety displays
Her mouldering roll, the piercing eye explores
New manners, and the pomp of elder days,
Whence culls the pensive bard his pictur'd stores.
Nor rough, nor barren, are the winding ways
Of hoar Antiquity, but strown with flowers.

Sonnet IV
Written at Stonehenge[2]

Thou noblest monument of Albion's isle!
Whether by Merlin's aid, from Scythia's shore,
To Amber's fatal plain Pendragon bore,
Huge frame of giant-hands, the mighty pile,
T'entomb his Britons slain by Hengist's guile:
Or Druid priests, sprinkled with human gore,
Taught mid thy massy maze their mystic lore:
Or Danish chiefs, enrich'd with savage spoil,
To Victory's idol vast, an unhewn shrine,
Rear'd the rude heap: or, in thy hallow'd round,
Repose the kings of Brutus' genuine line;
Or here those kings in solemn state were crown'd:
Studious to trace thy wond'rous origine,
We muse on many an antient tale renown'd.

[1] Published in *Poems*, 1777. Text of third edition, 1779.
[2] Published in *Poems*, 1777. Text of third edition, 1779.

Sonnet IX
To the River Lodon[1]

AH! WHAT a weary race my feet have run,
Since first I trod thy banks with alders crown'd,
And thought my way was all through fairy ground,
Beneath thy azure sky, and golden sun:
Where first my muse to lisp her notes begun!
While pensive memory traces back the round,
Which fills the varied interval between;
Much pleasure, more of sorrow, marks the scene.
Sweet native stream! those skies and suns so pure
No more return, to chear my evening road!
Yet still one joy remains, that not obscure,
Nor useless, all my vacant days have flow'd,
From youth's gay dawn to manhood's prime mature;
Nor with the Muse's laurel unbestow'd.

Ode IV
Solitude, at an Inn
(Written May 15, 1769)[2]

OFT upon the twilight plain,
Circled with thy shadowy train,
While the dove at distance coo'd,
Have I met thee, Solitude!
Then was loneliness to me
Best and true society.
But, ah! how alter'd is thy mien
In this sad deserted scene!
Here all thy classic pleasures cease,
Musing mild, and thoughtful peace:
Here thou com'st in sullen mood,
Not with thy fantastic brood
Of magic shapes and visions airy
Beckon'd from the land of Fairy:
'Mid the melancholy void
Not a pensive charm enjoy'd!
No poetic being here
Strikes with airy sounds mine ear;
No converse here to fancy cold

[1] Published in *Poems*, 1777. Text of third edition, 1779.
[2] Published in *Poems*, fourth edition, 1791. Text of fifth edition, 1802.

With many a fleeting form I hold,
Here all inelegant and rude
Thy presence is, sweet Solitude.

Verses on Sir Joshua Reynolds's Painted Window at New College, Oxford[1]

AH, STAY thy treacherous hand, forbear to trace
Those faultless forms of elegance and grace!
Ah, cease to spread the bright transparent mass,
With Titian's pencil, o'er the speaking glass!
Nor steal, by strokes of art with truth combin'd,
The fond illusions of my wayward mind!
For long, enamour'd of a barbarous age,
A faithless truant to the classic page;
Long have I lov'd to catch the simple chime
Of minstrel-harps, and spell the fabling rime;
To view the festive rites, the knightly play,
That deck'd heroic Albion's elder day;
To mark the mouldering halls of barons bold,
And the rough castle, cast in giant mould;
With Gothic manners Gothic arts explore,
And muse on the magnificence of yore.
  But chief, enraptur'd have I lov'd to roam,
A lingering votary, the vaulted dome,
Where the tall shafts, that mount in massy pride,
Their mingling branches shoot from side to side;
Where elfin sculptors, with fantastic clew,
O'er the long roof their wild embroidery drew;
Where SUPERSTITION with capricious hand
In many a maze the wreathed window plann'd,
With hues romantic ting'd the gorgeous pane,
To fill with holy light the wondrous fane;
To aid the builder's model, richly rude,
By no Vitruvian symmetry subdu'd;
To suit the genius of the mystic pile:
Whilst as around the far-retiring ile,
And fretted shrines, with hoary trophies hung,
Her dark illumination wide she flung,
With new solemnity, the nooks profound,
The caves of death, and the dim arches frown'd.
From bliss long felt unwillingly we part:
Ah, spare the weakness of a lover's heart!
Chase not the phantoms of my fairy dream,

[1] Published in 1782. Text of *Works*, Volume I, fifth edition, 1802.

Phantoms that shrink at Reason's painful gleam!
That softer touch, insidious artist, stay,
Nor to new joys my struggling breast betray!
  Such was a pensive bard's mistaken strain.—
But, oh, of ravish'd pleasures why complain?
No more the matchless skill I call unkind,
That strives to disenchant my cheated mind.
For when again I view thy chaste design,
The just proportion, and the genuine line;
Those native portraitures of Attic art,
That from the lucid surface seem to start;
Those tints, that steal no glories from the day,
Nor ask the sun to lend his streaming ray:
The doubtful radiance of contending dies,
That faintly mingle, yet distinctly rise;
'Twixt light and shade the transitory strife;
The feature blooming with immortal life:
The stole in casual foldings taught to flow,
Not with ambitious ornaments to glow;
The tread majestic, and the beaming eye,
That lifted speaks its commerce with the sky;
Heaven's golden emanation, gleaming mild
O'er the mean cradle of the Virgin's child:
Sudden, the sombrous imagery is fled,
Which late my visionary rapture fed:
Thy powerful hand has broke the Gothic chain,
And brought my bosom back to truth again;
To truth, by no peculiar taste confin'd,
Whose universal pattern strikes mankind;
To truth, whose bold and unresisted aim
Checks frail caprice, and fashion's fickle claim;
To truth, whose charms deception's magic quell,
And bind coy Fancy in a stronger spell.
  Ye brawny Prophets, that in robes so rich,
At distance due, possess the crisped nich;
Ye rows of Patriarchs, that sublimely rear'd
Diffuse a proud primeval length of beard:
Ye Saints, who, clad in crimson's bright array,
More pride than humble poverty display:
Ye Virgins meek, that wear the palmy crown
Of patient faith, and yet so fiercely frown:
Ye Angels, that from clouds of gold recline,
But boast no semblance to a race divine:
Ye tragic Tales of legendary lore,
That draw devotion's ready tear no more;
Ye Martyrdoms of unenlighten'd days,
Ye Miracles, that now no wonder raise:
Shapes, that with one broad glare the gazer strike,

Kings, Bishops, Nuns, Apostles, all alike!
Ye Colours, that th' unwary sight amaze,
And only dazzle in the noontide blaze!
No more the sacred window's round disgrace,
But yield to Grecian groupes the shining space.
Lo, from the canvas Beauty shifts her throne,
Lo, Picture's powers a new formation own!
Behold, she prints upon the crystal plain,
With her own energy, th' expressive stain!
The mighty Master spreads his mimic toil
More wide, nor only blends the breathing oil;
But calls the lineaments of life compleat
From genial alchymy's creative heat;
Obedient forms to the bright fusion gives,
While in the warm enamel Nature lives.
REYNOLDS, 'tis thine, from the broad window's height,
To add new lustre to religious light:
Not of its pomp to strip this ancient shrine,
But bid that pomp with purer radiance shine:
With arts unknown before, to reconcile
The willing Graces to the Gothic pile.

TOBIAS SMOLLETT

(1721-1746-1771)

The Tears of Scotland
Written in the Year MDCCXLVI[1]

MOURN, hapless Caledonia, mourn
Thy banish'd peace, thy laurels torn!
Thy sons, for valour long renown'd,
Lie slaughter'd on their native ground;
Thy hospitable roofs no more
Invite the stranger to the door;
In smoaky ruins sunk they lie,
The monuments of cruelty.

The wretched owner sees, afar,
His all become the prey of war;
Bethinks him of his babes and wife,

[1] Published in Goldsmith's *Beauties of English Poesy*, Volume II, 1767. Text of first edition.

Then smites his breast, and curses life.
Thy swains are famish'd on the rocks,
Where once they fed their wanton flocks:
Thy ravish'd virgins shriek in vain;
Thy infants perish on the plain.

What boots it, then, in ev'ry clime,
Thro' the wide-spreading waste of time,
Thy martial glory, crown'd with praise,
Still shone with undiminish'd blaze?
Thy tow'ring spirit now is broke,
Thy neck is bended to the yoke:
What foreign arms could never quell,
By civil rage and rancour fell.

The rural pipe and merry lay
No more shall chear the happy day:
No social scenes of gay delight
Beguile the dreary winter night:
No strains, but those of sorrow, flow,
And nought be heard but sounds of woe,
While the pale phantoms of the slain
Glide nightly o'er the silent plain.

O baneful cause, oh, fatal morn,
Accurs'd to ages yet unborn!
The sons against their fathers stood;
The parent shed his children's blood.
Yet, when the rage of battle ceas'd,
The victor's soul was not appeas'd:
The naked and forlorn must feel
Devouring flames, and murd'ring steel!

The pious mother doom'd to death,
Forsaken, wanders o'er the heath,
The bleak wind whistles round her head,
Her helpless orphans cry for bread,
Bereft of shelter, food, and friend,
She views the shades of night descend,
And, stretch'd beneath th' inclement skies,
Weeps o'er her tender babes, and dies.

Whilst the warm blood bedews my veins,
And unimpair'd remembrance reigns,
Resentment of my country's fate
Within my filial breast shall beat;
And, spite of her insulting foe,
My sympathizing verse shall flow,

"Mourn, hapless Caledonia, mourn
"Thy banish'd peace, thy laurels torn."

Ode to Leven-Water[1]

On Leven's banks, while free to rove,
And tune the rural pipe to love;
I envied not the happiest swain
That ever trod the Arcadian plain.
Pure stream! in whose transparent wave
My youthful limbs I wont to lave;
No torrents stain thy limpid source;
No rocks impede thy dimpling course,
That sweetly warbles o'er its bed,
With white, round, polish'd pebbles spread;
While, lightly pois'd, the scaly brood
In myriads cleave thy chrystal flood;
The springing trout in speckled pride;
The salmon, monarch of the tide;
The ruthless pike, intent on war;
The silver eel, and mottled par.
Devolving from thy parent lake,
A charming maze thy waters make,
By bowers of birch, and groves of pine,
And edges flower'd with eglantine.
Still on thy banks so gayly green,
May num'rous herds and flocks be seen,
And lasses chanting o'er the pail,
And shepherds piping in the dale,
And ancient faith that knows no guile,
And industry imbrown'd with toil,
And hearts resolv'd, and hands prepar'd,
The blessings they enjoy to guard.

[1] Published in *Plays and Poems*, 1777. Text of first edition.

HORACE WALPOLE, EARL OF ORFORD

(1717-1747-1797)

Countess Temple Appointed Poet Laureate to the King of the Fairies Written at the Desire of Lady Suffolk, January 3, 1763[1]

BY THESE presents be it known,
To all who bend before our throne,
Fays and fairies, elves and sprites,
Beauteous dames and gallant knights,
That we, Oberon the grand,
Emperor of Fairy-land,
King of moonshine, prince of dreams,
Lord of Aganippe's streams,
Baron of the dimpl'd isles
That lie in pretty maiden's smiles,
Arch-treasurer of all the graces
Dispers'd through fifty lovely faces,
Sovereign of the slipper's order,
With all the rites thereon that border,
Defender of the sylphic faith,
Declare—and thus your monarch saith:
  Whereas there is a noble dame,
Whom mortals Countess Temple name,
To whom ourself did erst impart
The choicest secrets of our art,
Taught her to tune th' harmonious line
To our own melody divine,
Taught her the graceful negligence,
Which, scorning art and veiling sense,
Achieves that conquest o'er the heart
Sense seldom gains, and never art:
This lady, 'tis our royal will
Our laureate's vacant seat should fill:
A chaplet of immortal bays
Shall crown her brows and guard her lays;
Of nectar-sack an acorn cup
Be at her board each year fill'd up;
And as each quarter feast comes round,
A silver-penny shall be found

[1] Published in *Works,* Volume IV, 1798. Text of first edition.

Within the compass of her shoe—
And so we bid you all adieu!

Given at our palace of Cowslip-Castle, the shortest night of the year. OBERON.

To Lady Anne Fitzpatrick, When About Five Years Old, with a Present of Shells[1]

O NYMPH, compar'd with whose young bloom
Hebe's herself an ancient fright;
May these gay shells find grace and room
Both in your baby-house and sight!
Shells! What are shells? you ask, admiring
With stare half pleasure half surprise;
And fly with nature's art, enquiring
In dear mamma's all-speaking eyes.
Shells, fairest Anne, are playthings, made
By a brave god call'd Father Ocean,
Whose frown from pole to pole 's obey'd,
Commands the waves, and stills their motion.

From that old sire a daughter came,
As like mamma, as blue to blue;
And, like mamma, the sea-born dame
An urchin bore, not unlike you.
For him fond grand-papa compels
The floods to furnish such a state
Of corals and of cockleshells,
Would turn a little lady's pate.
The chit has tons of bawbles more;
His nurs'ry 's stuff'd with doves and sparrows;
And litter'd is its azure floor
With painted quivers, bows, and arrows.
Spread, spread your frock; you must be friends;
His toys shall fill your lap and breast:
To-day the boy this sample sends,
—And some years hence he'll send the rest.

[1] Published in *Works*, Volume IV, 1798. Text of first edition.

JOHN CUNNINGHAM

(1729-1747-1773)

A Landscape[1]

Rura mihi et irrigui placeant in vallibus omnes. *Virg.*

Now that Summer's ripen'd bloom
Frolics where the Winter frown'd,
Stretch'd upon these banks of broom,
We command the Landscape round.

Nature in the prospect yields
Humble dales and mountains bold,
Meadows, woodlands, heaths—and fields
Yellow'd o'er with waving gold.

Goats upon that frowning steep
Fearless with their kidlings brouse;
Here a flock of snowy sheep,
There an herd of motley cows.

On the uplands ev'ry glade
Brightens in the blaze of day;
O'er the vales the sober shade
Softens to an ev'ning gray.

Where the rill by slow degrees
Swells into a crystal pool,
Shaggy rocks and shelving trees
Shoot to keep the waters cool.

Shiver'd by a thunderstroke
From the mountain's misty ridge,
O'er the brook a ruin'd oak
Near the farm-house forms a bridge.

On her breast the sunny beam
Glitters in meridian pride,
Yonder as the virgin stream
Hastens to the restless tide.—

[1] Published in *Poems*, 1766. Text of *Poems*, 1795.

Where the ships by wanton gales
Wafted o'er the green waves run,
Sweet to see their swelling sails
Whiten'd by the laughing Sun.

High upon the daisy'd hill,
Rising from the slope of trees,
How the wings of yonder mill
Labour in the busy breeze!—

Cheerful as a summer's morn,
Bouncing from her loaded pad,
Where the maid presents her corn,
Smirking to the miller's lad.

O'er the green a festal throng
Gambols in fantastic trim
As the full cart moves along:
Hearken!—'tis the harvest hymn.

Linnets on the crowded sprays
Chorus—and the woodlarks rise,
Soaring with a song of praise
Till the sweet notes reach the skies.

Torrents in extended sheets
Down the cliffs dividing break;
'Twixt the hills the water meets,
Settling in a silver lake.

From his languid flocks the swain,
By the sun-beams sore opprest,
Plunging on the wat'ry plain,
Plows it with his glowing breast.

Where the mantling willows nod
From the green bank's slopy side,
Patient, with his well-thrown rod,
Many an angler breaks the tide.

On the isles, with osiers drest,
Many a fair-plum'd halcyon breeds;
Many a wild bird hides her nest,
Cover'd in yon' crackling reeds.

Fork-tail'd prattlers, as they pass
To their nestlings in the rock,

Darting on the liquid glass,
Seem to kiss the mimic'd flock.

Where the stone-cross lifts its head,
Many a saint and pilgrim hoar
Up the hill was wont to tread
Barefoot in the days of yore.

Guardian of a sacred well,
Arch'd beneath yon' rev'rend shades,
Whilome in that shatter'd cell
Many an hermit told his beads.

Sultry mists surround the heath
Where the Gothic dome appears,
O'er the trembling groves beneath
Tott'ring with a load of years.

Turn to the contrasted scene,
Where, beyond these hoary piles,
Gay upon the rising green,
Many an Attic building smiles.

Painted gardens—grots—and groves,
Intermingling shade and light,
Lengthen'd vistas, green alcoves,
Join to give the eye delight.

Hamlets—villages, and spires,
Scatter'd on the Landscape lie,
Till the distant view retires,
Closing in an azure sky.

The Miller: A Ballad[1]

In a plain pleasant cottage, conveniently neat,
With a mill and some meadows—a freehold estate,
A well-meaning Miller by labour supplies
Those blessings that grandeur to great ones denies:
No passions to plague him, no cares to torment,
His constant companions are Health and Content;
Their Lordships in lace may remark if they will,
He's honest, tho' daub'd with the dust of his Mill.

[1] Published in *Poems*, 1766. Text of *Poems*, 1795.

Ere the lark's early carols salute the new day,
He springs from his cottage as jocund as May;
He cheerfully whistles, regardless of care,
Or sings the last ballad he bought at the fair.
While courtiers are toil'd in the cobwebs of state,
Or bribing elections, in hopes to be great,
No fraud or ambition his bosom e'er fill;
Contented he works if there's grist for his Mill.

On Sunday bedeck'd in his home-spun array,
At church he's the loudest to chant or to pray.
He sits to a dinner of plain English food;
Tho' simple the pudding, his appetite's good.
At night, when the priest and exciseman are gone,
He quaffs at the alehouse with Roger and John,
Then reels to his pillow, and dreams of no ill:
No monarch more bless'd than The Man of the Mill.

RICHARD JAGO

(1715-1753-1781)

The Swallows: An Elegy[1]

Part I

ERE yellow Autumn from our plains retir'd,
  And gave to wintry storms the varied year,
The Swallow-race with prescient gift inspir'd,
  To southern climes prepar'd their course to steer.

On DAMON's roof a large assembly sate,
  His roof a refuge to the feather'd kind!
With serious look he mark'd the grave debate,
  And to his DELIA thus address'd his mind.

Observe yon' twitt'ring flock, my gentle maid!
  Observe, and read the wond'rous ways of Heav'n!
With us thro' Summer's genial reign they stay'd,
  And food, and sunshine to their wants were giv'n.

[1] Published in Dodsley's *Collection of Poems*, Volume V, 1758. Text of *Poems, Moral and Descriptive*, 1784.

But now, by secret instinct taught, they know
  The near approach of elemental strife,
Of blust'ring tempests, and of chilling snow,
  With ev'ry pang, and scourge of tender life.

Thus warn'd they meditate a speedy flight,
  For this ev'n now they prune their vig'rous wing,
For this each other to the toil excite,
  And prove their strength in many a sportive ring.

No sorrow loads their breast, or dims their eye,
  To quit their wonted haunts, or native home,
Nor fear they launching on the boundless sky,
  In search of future settlements to roam.

They feel a pow'r, an impulse all divine,
  That warns them hence, they feel it, and obey,
To this direction all their cares resign,
  Unknown their destin'd stage, unmark'd their way.

Peace to your flight! ye mild, domestic race!
  O! for your wings to travel with the sun!
Health brace your nerves, and zephyrs aid your pace,
  Till your long voyage happily be done.

See, DELIA, on my roof your guests to-day,
  To-morrow on my roof your guests no more,
Ere yet 'tis night with haste they wing away,
  To-morrow lands them on some happier shore.

How just the moral in this scene convey'd!
  And what without a moral? wou'd we read!
Then mark what DAMON tells his gentle maid,
  And with his lesson register the deed.

So youthful joys fly like the Summer's gale,
  So threats the winter of inclement age,
Life's busy plot a short, fantastic tale!
  And Nature's changeful scenes the shifting stage!

And does no friendly pow'r to man dispense
  The joyful tidings of some happier clime?
Find we no guide in gracious Providence
  Beyond the gloomy grave, and short-liv'd time?

Yes, yes the sacred oracles we hear,
  That point the path to realms of endless joy,

That bid our trembling hearts no danger fear,
  Tho' clouds surround, and angry skies annoy.

Then let us wisely for our flight prepare,
  Nor count this stormy world our fixt abode,
Obey the call, and trust our Leader's care,
  To smooth the rough, and light the darksome road.

MOSES, by grant divine, led ISRAEL's host
  Thro' dreary paths to JORDAN's fruitful side;
But we a loftier theme than theirs can boast,
  A better promise, and a nobler guide.

Part II

AT length the Winter's howling blasts are o'er,
  Array'd in smiles the lovely Spring returns,
Now fewel'd hearths attractive blaze no more,
  And ev'ry breast with inward fervor burns.

Again the daisies peep, the violets blow,
  Again the vocal tenants of the grove
Forgot the patt'ring hail, or driving snow,
  Renew the lay to melody, and love.

And see, my DELIA, see o'er yonder stream,
  Where, on the bank, the lambs in gambols play,
Alike attracted by the sunny gleam,
  Again the Swallows take their wonted way.

Welcome, ye gentle tribe, your sports pursue,
  Welcome again to DELIA, and to me,
Your peaceful councils on my roof renew,
  And plan new settlements from danger free.

Again I'll listen to your grave debates,
  Again I'll hear your twitt'ring songs unfold
What policy directs your wand'ring states,
  What bounds are settled, and what tribes enroll'd.

Again I'll hear you tell of distant lands,
  What insect-nations rise from EGYPT's mud,
What painted swarms subsist on LYBIA's sands,
  What GANGES yields, and what th' EUPHRATEAN flood.

Thrice happy race! whom Nature's call invites
  To travel o'er her realms with active wing,

To taste her various stores, her best delights,
The Summer's radiance, and the sweets of Spring.

While we are doom'd to bear the restless change
Of varying seasons, vapours dank, and dry,
Forbid like you in milder climes to range,
When wintry storms usurp the low'ring sky.

Yet know the period to your joys assign'd,
Know ruin hovers o'er this earthly ball,
As lofty tow'rs stoop prostrate to the wind,
Its secret props of adamant shall fall.

But when yon' radiant sun shall shine no more,
The spirit, freed from sin's tyrannic sway,
On lighter pinions borne than yours, shall soar
To fairer realms beneath a brighter ray.

To plains ethereal, and celestial bow'rs,
Where wintry storms no rude access obtain,
Where blasts no lightning, and no tempest low'rs,
But ever-smiling Spring, and Pleasure reign.

JAMES GRAINGER

(1721?-1753-1766)

Solitude. An Ode[1]

O SOLITUDE, romantic maid,
Whether by nodding towers you tread,
Or haunt the desart's trackless gloom,
Or hover o'er the yawning tomb,
Or climb the Andes' clifted side,
Or by the Nile's coy source abide,
Or starting from your half-year's sleep
From Hecla view the thawing deep,
Or Tadmor's marble wastes survey,
Or in yon roofless cloyster stray;
You, Recluse, again I woo,
And again your steps pursue.

[1] Published in Dodsley's *Collection of Poems*, Volume IV, 1755. Text of first edition.

Plum'd Conceit himself surveying,
Folly with her shadow playing,
Purse-proud, elbowing Insolence,
Bloated empirick, puff'd Pretence,
Noise that thro' a trumpet speaks,
Laughter in loud peals that breaks,
Intrusion with a fopling's face,
(Ignorant of time and place)
Sparks of fire Dissention blowing,
Ductile, court-bred Flattery, bowing,
Restraint's stiff neck, Grimace's leer,
Squint-ey'd Censure's artful sneer,
Ambition's buskins steep'd in blood,
Fly thy presence, Solitude.

Sage Reflection bent with years,
Conscious Virtue void of fears,
Muffled Silence wood-nymph shy,
Meditation's piercing eye,
Halcyon Peace on moss reclin'd,
Retrospect that scanns the mind,
Rapt earth-gazing Resvery,
Blushing artless Modesty,
Health that snuffs the morning air,
Full-ey'd Truth with bosom bare,
Inspiration, Nature's child,
Seek the solitary wild.

You with the tragic Muse retir'd
The wise Euripides inspir'd,
You taught the sadly-pleasing air
That Athens sav'd from ruins bare.
You gave the Cean's tears to flow,
And unlock'd the springs of woe;
You penn'd what exil'd Naso thought,
And pour'd the melancholy note.
With Petrarch o'er Valcluse you stray'd,
When Death snatch'd his long-lov'd maid;
You taught the rocks her loss to mourn
You strew'd with flowers her virgin urn.
And late in Hagley you were seen,
With bloodshed eyes, and sombre mien,
Hymen his yellow vestment tore,
And Dirge a wreath of cypress wore.
But chief you own the solemn lay
That wept Narcissa young and gay,
Darkness clap'd her sable wing,
While you touch'd the mournful string,

Anguish left the pathless wild,
Grim-fac'd Melancholy smil'd,
Drowsy Midnight ceas'd to yawn,
The starry host put back the dawn,
Aside their harps ev'n Seraphs flung
To hear thy sweet complaint, O Young.

When all Nature's hush'd asleep,
Nor Love nor Guilt their vigils keep,
Soft you leave your cavern'd den,
And wander o'er the works of men.
But when Phosphor brings the dawn
By her dappled coursers drawn,
Again you to the wild retreat
And the early huntsman meet,
Where as you pensive pace along,
You catch the distant shepherd's song,
Or brush from herbs the pearly dew,
Or the rising primrose view.
Devotion lends her heaven-plum'd wings.
You mount, and Nature with you sings.
But when mid-day fervors glow
To upland airy shades you go,
Where never sunburnt woodman came,
Nor sportsman chas'd the timid game;
And there beneath an oak reclin'd,
With drowsy waterfalls behind,
You sink to rest.
Till the tuneful bird of night
From the neighb'ring poplars height
Wake you with her solemn strain,
And teach pleas'd Echo to complain.

With you roses brighter bloom,
Sweeter every sweet perfume,
Purer every fountain flows
Stronger every wilding grows.

Let those toil for gold who please,
Or for fame renounce their ease,
What is fame? an empty bubble.
Gold? a transient, shining trouble.
Let them for their country bleed,
What was Sidney's, Raleigh's meed?
Man's not worth a moment's pain,
Base, ungrateful, fickle, vain.
Then let me, sequester'd fair,
To your Sibyl grot repair,

On yon hanging cliff it stands
Scoop'd by Nature's salvage hands,
Bosom'd in the gloomy shade
Of cypress not with age decay'd.
Where the owl still-hooting sits,
Where the bat incessant flits,
There in loftier strains I'll sing
Whence the changing seasons spring,
Tell how storms deform the skies,
Whence the waves subside and rise,
Trace the comet's blazing tail,
Weigh the planets in a scale;
Bend, great God, before thy shrine,
The bournless macrocosm's thine.

Save me! what's yon shrouded shade?
That wanders in the dark-brown glade.
It beckons me!—vain fears adieu,
Mysterious ghost, I follow you.
Ah me! too well that gait I know,
My youth's first friend, my manhood's woe!
Its breast it bares! what! stain'd with blood?
Quick let me stanch the vital flood.
Oh spirit, whither art thou flown?
Why left me comfortless alone?
O Solitude on me bestow,
The heart-felt harmony of woe,
Such, such, as on th' Ausonian shore,
Sweet Dorian Moschus trill'd of yore:
No time should cancel thy desert,
More, more, than Bion was, thou wert.

O goddess of the tearful eye,
The never-ceasing stream supply.
Let us with Retirement go
To charnels, and the house of woe,
O'er Friendship's herse low-drooping mourn,
Where the sickly tapers burn,
Where Death and nun-clad Sorrow dwell,
And nightly ring the solemn knell.
The gloom dispels, the charnel smiles,
Light flashes thro' the vaulted iles.
Blow silky soft, thou western gale,
O goddess of the desart, hail!
She bursts from yon cliff-riven cave,
Insulted by the wintry wave;
Her brow an ivy garland binds,
Her tresses wanton with the winds,

A lion's spoils, without a zone,
Around her limbs are careless thrown;
Her right hand wields a knotted mace,
Her eyes roll wild, a stride her pace;
Her left a magic mirror holds,
In which she oft herself beholds.
O goddess of the desart, hail!
And softer blow, thou western gale!
  Since in each scheme of life I've fail'd,
And disappointment seems entail'd;
Since all on earth I valued most,
My guide, my stay, my friend is lost;
You, only you, can make me blest,
And hush the tempest in my breast.
Then gently deign to guide my feet
To your hermit-trodden seat,
Where I may live at last my own,
Where I at last may die unknown.
  I spoke, she twin'd her magic ray,
  And thus she said, or seem'd to say.

  Youth, you're mistaken, if you think to find
In shades a medicine for a troubled mind;
Wan Grief will haunt you wheresoe'er you go,
Sigh in the breeze, and in the streamlet flow.
There pale Inaction pines his life away,
And, satiate, curses the return of day:
There naked Frenzy laughing wild with pain,
Or bares the blade, or plunges in the main:
There Superstition broods o'er all her fears,
And yells of dæmons in the Zephyr hears.
But if a hermit you're resolv'd to dwell,
And bid to social life a last farewel;
'Tis impious.—
God never made an independent man,
'Twould jarr the concord of his general plan:
See every part of that stupendous whole,
"Whose body Nature is, and God the soul;"
To one great end, the general good, conspire,
From matter, brute, to man, to seraph, fire.
Should man thro' Nature solitary roam,
His will his sovereign, every where his home,
What force wou'd guard him from the lion's jaw?
What swiftness wing him from the panther's paw?
Or should Fate lead him to some safer shore,
Where panthers never prowl, nor lions roar;
Where liberal Nature all her charms bestows,
Suns shine, birds sing, flowers bloom, and water flows,

Fool, dost thou think he'd revel on the store,
Absolve the care of Heaven, nor ask for more?
Tho' waters flow'd, flow'rs bloom'd, and Phœbus shone,
He'd sigh, he'd murmur that he was alone.
For know, the Maker on the human breast
A sense of kindred, country, man, imprest;
And social life to better, aid, adorn,
With proper faculties each mortal's born.
  Tho' Nature's works the ruling mind declare,
And well deserve enquiry's serious care,
The God (whate'er Misanthropy may say)
Shines, beams in man with most unclouded ray.
What boots it thee to fly from pole to pole?
Hang o'er the sun, and with the planets roll?
What boots thro' space's furthest bourns to roam?
If thou, O man, a stranger art at home.
Then know thyself, the human mind survey,
The use, the pleasure will the toil repay.
Hence Inspiration plans his manner'd lays,
Hence Homer's crown, and Shakespear hence thy bays.
Hence he, the pride of Athens and the shame,
The best and wisest of mankind became.
Nor study only, practise what you know,
Your life, your knowledge, to mankind you owe.
With Plato's olive wreath the bays entwine;
Those who in study, shou'd in practice shine.
Say, does the learned Lord of Hagley's shade,
Charm man so much by mossy fountains laid,
As when arouz'd, he stems Corruption's course,
And shakes the senate with a Tully's force?
When Freedom gasp'd beneath a Cæsar's feet,
Then Publick Virtue might to shades retreat;
But where she breathes, the least may useful be,
And Freedom, Britain, still belongs to thee.
Tho' man's ungrateful, or tho' Fortune frown;
Is the reward of worth a song, or crown?
Nor yet unrecompens'd are Virtue's pains,
Good Allen lives, and bounteous Brunswick reigns.
On each condition disappointments wait,
Enter the hut, and force the guarded gate.
Nor dare repine, tho' early Friendship bleed,
From love, the world, and all its cares he's freed.
But know, Adversity's the child of God;
Whom Heaven approves of most, most feel her rod.
When smooth old Ocean and each storm's asleep,
Then Ignorance may plough the watery deep;
But when the dæmons of the tempest rave,
Skill must conduct the vessel thro' the wave.

Sidney, what good man envies not thy blow?
Who wou'd not wish Anytus for a foe?
Intrepid Virtue triumphs over Fate,
The good can never be unfortunate.
And be this maxim graven in thy mind,
The height of virtue is to serve mankind.
But when old age has silver'd o'er thy head,
When memory fails, and all thy vigour's fled,
Then may'st thou seek the stillness of retreat,
Then hear aloof the human tempest beat,
Then will I greet thee to my woodland cave,
Allay the pangs of age, and smooth thy grave.

OLIVER GOLDSMITH

(1730?-1757-1774)

An Elegy on that Glory of her Sex, Mrs. Mary Blaize[1]

GOOD people all, with one accord,
Lament for Madam BLAIZE,
Who never wanted a good word—
From those who spoke her praise.

The needy seldom pass'd her door,
And always found her kind;
She freely lent to all the poor,—
Who left a pledge behind.

She strove the neighbourhood to please,
With manners wond'rous winning,
And never follow'd wicked ways,—
Unless when she was sinning.

At church, in silks and sattins new,
With hoop of monstrous size,
She never slumber'd in her pew,—
But when she shut her eyes.

Her love was sought, I do aver,
By twenty beaus and more;
The king himself has follow'd her,—
When she has walk'd before.

[1] Published in *The Bee*, October 27, 1759. Text of first edition.

But now her wealth and finery fled,
  Her hangers-on cut short all;
The doctors found, when she was dead,—
  Her last disorder mortal.

Let us lament, in sorrow sore,
  For Kent-street well may say,
That had she liv'd a twelve-month more,
  She had not dy'd to-day.

The Traveller; or, A Prospect of Society[1]

TO THE REV. HENRY GOLDSMITH

DEAR SIR,

I AM sensible that the friendship between us can acquire no new force from the ceremonies of a Dedication; and perhaps it demands an excuse thus to prefix your name to my attempts, which you decline giving with your own. But as a part of this Poem was formerly written to you from Switzerland, the whole can now, with propriety, be only inscribed to you. It will also throw a light upon many parts of it, when the reader understands, that it is addressed to a man, who, despising Fame and Fortune, has retired early to Happiness and Obscurity, with an income of forty pounds a year.

I now perceive, my dear brother, the wisdom of your humble choice. You have entered upon a sacred office, where the harvest is great, and the labourers are but few; while you have left the field of Ambition, where the labourers are many, and the harvest not worth carrying away. But of all kinds of ambition, what from the refinement of the times, from differing systems of criticism, and from the divisions of party, that which pursues poetical fame is the wildest.

Poetry makes a principal amusement among unpolished nations; but in a country verging to the extremes of refinement, Painting and Music come in for a share. As these offer the feeble mind a less laborious entertainment, they at first rival Poetry, and at length supplant her; they engross all that favour once shewn to her, and though but younger sisters, seize upon the elder's birth-right.

Yet, however this art may be neglected by the powerful, it is still in greater danger from the mistaken efforts of the learned to improve it. What criticisms have we not heard of late in favour of blank verse, and Pindaric odes, chorusses, anapests and iambics, alliterative care and happy negligence! Every absurdity has now a champion to defend it, and as he is generally much in the wrong, so he has always much to say; for error is ever talkative.

But there is an enemy to this art still more dangerous, I mean Party. Party entirely distorts the judgment, and destroys the taste. When the mind is once infected with this disease, it can only find pleasure in what contributes to increase the distemper. Like the tyger that seldom desists from pursuing man after having once preyed upon human flesh, the reader, who has once gratified his appetite with calumny, makes, ever after, the most agreeable feast upon

[1] Published December 19, 1764. Text of sixth edition, 1770.

murdered reputation. Such readers generally admire some half-witted thing, who wants to be thought a bold man, having lost the character of a wise one. Him they dignify with the name of poet; his tawdry lampoons are called satires, his turbulence is said to be force, and his phrenzy fire.

What reception a Poem may find, which has neither abuse, party, nor blank verse to support it, I cannot tell, nor am I sollicitous to know. My aims are right. Without espousing the cause of any party, I have attempted to moderate the rage of all. I have endeavoured to shew, that there may be equal happiness in states, that are differently governed from our own; that every state has a particular principle of happiness, and that this principle in each may be carried to a mischievous excess. There are few can judge, better than yourself, how far these positions are illustrated in this Poem.

I am, dear Sir,

Your most affectionate Brother,

OLIVER GOLDSMITH.

REMOTE, unfriended, melancholy, slow,
Or by the lazy Scheld, or wandering Po;
Or onward, where the rude Carinthian boor
Against the houseless stranger shuts the door;
Or where Campania's plain forsaken lyes,
A weary waste expanding to the skies:
Where'er I roam, whatever realms to see,
My heart untravell'd fondly turns to thee;
Still to my brother turns, with ceaseless pain,
And drags at each remove a lengthening chain.
  Eternal blessings crown my earliest friend,
And round his dwelling guardian saints attend;
Blest be that spot, where chearful guests retire
To pause from toil, and trim their ev'ning fire;
Blest that abode, where want and pain repair,
And every stranger finds a ready chair;
Blest be those feasts with simple plenty crown'd,
Where all the ruddy family around,
Laugh at the jests or pranks that never fail,
Or sigh with pity at some mournful tale,
Or press the bashful stranger to his food,
And learn the luxury of doing good.
  But me, not destin'd such delights to share,
My prime of life in wand'ring spent and care,
Impell'd, with steps unceasing, to pursue
Some fleeting good, that mocks me with the view;
That, like the circle bounding earth and skies,
Allures from far, yet, as I follow, flies;
My fortune leads to traverse realms alone,
And find no spot of all the world my own.
  Even now, where Alpine solitudes ascend,
I sit me down a pensive hour to spend;
And, plac'd on high above the storm's career,
Look downward where an hundred realms appear;

Lakes, forests, cities, plains extending wide,
The pomp of kings, the shepherd's humbler pride.
When thus Creation's charms around combine,
Amidst the store, should thankless pride repine?
Say, should the philosophic mind disdain
That good, which makes each humbler bosom vain?
Let school-taught pride dissemble all it can,
These little things are great to little man;
And wiser he, whose sympathetic mind
Exults in all the good of all mankind.
Ye glitt'ring towns, with wealth and splendour crown'd,
Ye fields, where summer spreads profusion round,
Ye lakes, whose vessels catch the busy gale,
Ye bending swains, that dress the flow'ry vale,
For me your tributary stores combine;
Creation's heir, the world, the world is mine.
As some lone miser visiting his store,
Bends at his treasure, counts, recounts it o'er;
Hoards after hoards his rising raptures fill,
Yet still he sighs, for hoards are wanting still:
Thus to my breast alternate passions rise,
Pleas'd with each good that heaven to man supplies:
Yet oft a sigh prevails, and sorrows fall,
To see the hoard of human bliss so small;
And oft I wish, amidst the scene, to find
Some spot to real happiness consign'd,
Where my worn soul, each wand'ring hope at rest,
May gather bliss to see my fellows blest.
But where to find that happiest spot below,
Who can direct, when all pretend to know?
The shudd'ring tenant of the frigid zone
Boldly proclaims that happiest spot his own,
Extols the treasures of his stormy seas,
And his long nights of revelry and ease;
The naked negroe, panting at the line,
Boasts of his golden sands and palmy wine,
Basks in the glare, or stems the tepid wave,
And thanks his Gods for all the good they gave.
Such is the patriot's boast, where'er we roam,
His first, best country ever is, at home.
And yet, perhaps, if countries we compare,
And estimate the blessings which they share;
Tho' patriots flatter, still shall wisdom find
An equal portion dealt to all mankind,
As different good, by Art or Nature given,
To different nations makes their blessings even.
Nature, a mother kind alike to all,
Still grants her bliss at Labour's earnest call;

With food as well the peasant is supply'd
On Idra's cliffs as Arno's shelvy side;
And though the rocky crested summits frown,
These rocks, by custom, turn to beds of down.
From Art more various are the blessings sent;
Wealth, commerce, honour, liberty, content.
Yet these each other's power so strong contest,
That either seems destructive of the rest.
Where wealth and freedom reign contentment fails,
And honour sinks where commerce long prevails.
Hence every state to one lov'd blessing prone,
Conforms and models life to that alone.
Each to the favourite happiness attends,
And spurns the plan that aims at other ends;
'Till, carried to excess in each domain,
This favourite good begets peculiar pain.
  But let us try these truths with closer eyes,
And trace them through the prospect as it lies:
Here for a while my proper cares resign'd,
Here let me sit in sorrow for mankind,
Like yon neglected shrub at random cast,
That shades the steep, and sighs at every blast.
  Far to the right where Appenine ascends,
Bright as the summer, Italy extends;
Its uplands sloping deck the mountain's side,
Woods over woods in gay theatric pride;
While oft some temple's mould'ring tops between,
With venerable grandeur mark the scene.
  Could Nature's bounty satisfy the breast,
The sons of Italy were surely blest.
Whatever fruits in different climes were found,
That proudly rise, or humbly court the ground;
Whatever blooms in torrid tracts appear,
Whose bright succession decks the varied year;
Whatever sweets salute the northern sky
With vernal lives that blossom but to die;
These here disporting own the kindred soil,
Nor ask luxuriance from the planter's toil;
While sea-born gales their gelid wings expand
To winnow fragrance round the smiling land.
  But small the bliss that sense alone bestows,
And sensual bliss is all the nation knows.
In florid beauty groves and fields appear,
Man seems the only growth that dwindles here.
Contrasted faults through all his manners reign,
Though poor, luxurious, though submissive, vain,
Though grave, yet trifling, zealous, yet untrue,
And ev'n in penance planning sins anew.

All evils here contaminate the mind,
That opulence departed leaves behind;
For wealth was theirs, nor far remov'd the date,
When commerce proudly flourish'd through the state;
At her command the palace learnt to rise,
Again the long-fallen column sought the skies;
The canvass glow'd beyond ev'n Nature warm,
The pregnant quarry teem'd with human form.
Till, more unsteady than the southern gale,
Commerce on other shores display'd her sail;
While nought remain'd of all that riches gave,
But towns unman'd, and lords without a slave:
And late the nation found with fruitless skill
Its former strength was but plethoric ill.
Yet, still the loss of wealth is here supplied
By arts, the splendid wrecks of former pride;
From these the feeble heart and long-fall'n mind
An easy compensation seem to find.
Here may be seen, in bloodless pomp array'd,
The paste-board triumph and the cavalcade;
Processions form'd for piety and love,
A mistress or a saint in every grove.
By sports like these are all their cares beguil'd,
The sports of children satisfy the child;
Each nobler aim represt by long controul,
Now sinks at last, or feebly mans the soul;
While low delights, succeeding fast behind,
In happier meanness occupy the mind:
As in those domes, where Cæsars once bore sway,
Defac'd by time and tottering in decay,
There in the ruin, heedless of the dead,
The shelter-seeking peasant builds his shed,
And, wond'ring man could want the larger pile,
Exults, and owns his cottage with a smile.
My soul turn from them, turn we to survey
Where rougher climes a nobler race display,
Where the bleak Swiss their stormy mansions tread,
And force a churlish soil for scanty bread;
No product here the barren hills afford,
But Man and steel, the soldier and his sword.
No vernal blooms their torpid rocks array,
But winter ling'ring chills the lap of May;
No Zephyr fondly sues the mountain's breast,
But meteors glare, and stormy glooms invest.
Yet still, even here, content can spread a charm,
Redress the clime, and all its rage disarm.
Though poor the peasant's hut, his feasts though small,
He sees his little lot the lot of all;

Sees no contiguous palace rear its head
To shame the meanness of his humble shed;
No costly lord the sumptuous banquet deal
To make him loath his vegetable meal;
But calm, and bred in ignorance and toil,
Each wish contracting, fits him to the soil.
Chearful at morn he wakes from short repose,
Breasts the keen air, and carrols as he goes;
With patient angle trolls the finny deep,
Or drives his venturous plow-share to the steep;
Or seeks the den where snow-tracks mark the way,
And drags the struggling savage into day.
At night returning, every labour sped,
He sits him down the monarch of a shed;
Smiles by his chearful fire, and round surveys
His childrens looks, that brighten at the blaze;
While his lov'd partner, boastful of her hoard,
Displays her cleanly platter on the board:
And haply too some pilgrim, thither led,
With many a tale repays the nightly bed.
  Thus every good his native wilds impart,
Imprints the patriot passion on his heart,
And even those ills, that round his mansion rise,
Enhance the bliss his scanty fund supplies.
Dear is that shed to which his soul conforms,
And dear that hill which lifts him to the storms;
And as a child, when scaring sounds molest,
Clings close and closer to the mother's breast,
So the loud torrent, and the whirlwind's roar,
But bind him to his native mountains more.
  Such are the charms to barren states assign'd;
Their wants but few, their wishes all confin'd.
Yet let them only share the praises due,
If few their wants, their pleasures are but few;
For every want that stimulates the breast,
Becomes a source of pleasure when redrest.
Whence from such lands each pleasing science flies,
That first excites desire, and then supplies;
Unknown to them, when sensual pleasures cloy,
To fill the languid pause with finer joy;
Unknown those powers that raise the soul to flame,
Catch every nerve, and vibrate through the frame.
Their level life is but a smould'ring fire,
Unquench'd by want, unfann'd by strong desire;
Unfit for raptures, or, if raptures cheer
On some high festival of once a year,
In wild excess the vulgar breast takes fire,
Till, buried in debauch, the bliss expire.

But not their joys alone thus coarsely flow:
Their morals, like their pleasures, are but low,
For, as refinement stops, from sire to son
Unalter'd, unimprov'd the manners run,
And love's and friendship's finely pointed dart
Fall blunted from each indurated heart.
Some sterner virtues o'er the mountain's breast
May sit, like falcons cowring on the nest;
But all the gentler morals, such as play
Through life's more cultur'd walks, and charm the way,
These far dispers'd, on timorous pinions fly,
To sport and flutter in a kinder sky.
To kinder skies, where gentler manners reign,
I turn; and France displays her bright domain.
Gay sprightly land of mirth and social ease,
Pleas'd with thyself, whom all the world can please,
How often have I led thy sportive choir,
With tuneless pipe, beside the murmuring Loire?
Where shading elms along the margin grew,
And freshen'd from the wave the Zephyr flew;
And haply, though my harsh touch faltering still,
But mock'd all tune, and marr'd the dancer's skill;
Yet would the village praise my wonderous pow'r,
And dance, forgetful of the noon-tide hour.
Alike all ages. Dames of ancient days
Have led their children through the mirthful maze,
And the gay grandsire, skill'd in gestic lore,
Has frisk'd beneath the burthen of threescore.
So blest a life these thoughtless realms display,
Thus idly busy rolls their world away:
Theirs are those arts that mind to mind endear,
For honour forms the social temper here.
Honour, that praise which real merit gains,
Or even imaginary worth obtains,
Here passes current; paid from hand to hand,
It shifts in splendid traffic round the land:
From courts, to camps, to cottages it strays,
And all are taught an avarice of praise;
They please, are pleas'd, they give to get esteem,
Till, seeming blest, they grow to what they seem.
But while this softer art their bliss supplies,
It gives their follies also room to rise;
For praise too dearly lov'd, or warmly sought,
Enfeebles all internal strength of thought.
And the weak soul, within itself unblest,
Leans for all pleasure on another's breast.
Hence ostentation here, with tawdry art,
Pants for the vulgar praise which fools impart;

Here vanity assumes her pert grimace,
And trims her robes of frize with copper lace,
Here beggar pride defrauds her daily cheer,
To boast one splendid banquet once a year;
The mind still turns where shifting fashion draws,
Nor weighs the solid worth of self applause.
To men of other minds my fancy flies,
Embosom'd in the deep where Holland lies,
Methinks her patient sons before me stand,
Where the broad ocean leans against the land,
And, sedulous to stop the coming tide,
Lift the tall rampire's artificial pride.
Onward methinks, and diligently flow
The firm connected bulwark seems to grow.
Spreads its long arms amidst the watry roar,
Scoops out an empire, and usurps the shore.
While the pent ocean rising o'er the pile,
Sees an amphibious world beneath him smile;
The slow canal, the yellow blossom'd vale,
The willow tufted bank, the gliding sail,
The crowded mart, the cultivated plain,
A new creation rescu'd from his reign.
Thus, while around the wave-subjected soil
Impels the native to repeated toil,
Industrious habits in each bosom reign,
And industry begets a love of gain.
Hence all the good from opulence that springs,
With all those ills superfluous treasure brings,
Are here display'd. Their much-lov'd wealth imparts
Convenience, plenty, elegance, and arts;
But view them closer, craft and fraud appear,
Even liberty itself is barter'd here.
At gold's superior charms all freedom flies,
The needy sell it, and the rich man buys;
A land of tyrants, and a den of slaves,
Here wretches seek dishonourable graves,
And calmly bent, to servitude conform,
Dull as their lakes that slumber in the storm.
Heavens! how unlike their Belgic sires of old!
Rough, poor, content, ungovernably bold;
War in each breast, and freedom on each brow;
How much unlike the sons of Britain now!
Fir'd at the sound my genius spreads her wing,
And flies where Britain courts the western spring;
Where lawns extend that scorn Arcadian pride,
And brighter streams than fam'd Hydaspis glide.
There all around the gentlest breezes stray,
There gentle music melts on every spray;

Creation's mildest charms are there combin'd.
Extremes are only in the master's mind!
Stern o'er each bosom reason holds her state.
With daring aims irregularly great,
Pride in their port, defiance in their eye,
I see the lords of human kind pass by,
Intent on high designs, a thoughtful band,
By forms unfashion'd, fresh from Nature's hand;
Fierce in their native hardiness of soul,
True to imagin'd right, above controul,
While even the peasant boasts these rights to scan,
And learns to venerate himself as man.
  Thine, Freedom, thine the blessings pictur'd here,
Thine are those charms that dazzle and endear;
Too blest indeed, were such without alloy,
But foster'd even by Freedom ills annoy:
That independence Britons prize too high,
Keeps man from man, and breaks the social tie;
The self-dependent lordlings stand alone,
All claims that bind and sweeten life unknown;
Here by the bonds of nature feebly held,
Minds combat minds, repelling and repell'd.
Ferments arise, imprison'd factions roar,
Represt ambition struggles round her shore,
Till over-wrought, the general system feels
Its motions stopt, or phrenzy fire the wheels.
  Nor this the worst. As nature's ties decay,
As duty, love, and honour fail to sway,
Fictitious bonds, the bonds of wealth and law,
Still gather strength, and force unwilling awe.
Hence all obedience bows to these alone,
And talent sinks, and merit weeps unknown;
Till time may come, when stript of all her charms,
The land of scholars, and the nurse of arms;
Where noble stems transmit the patriot flame,
Where kings have toil'd, and poets wrote for fame;
One sink of level avarice shall lie,
And scholars, soldiers, kings, unhonour'd die.
  Yet think not, thus when Freedom's ills I state,
I mean to flatter kings, or court the great;
Ye powers of truth that bid my soul aspire,
Far from my bosom drive the low desire;
And thou fair Freedom, taught alike to feel
The rabble's rage, and tyrant's angry steel;
Thou transitory flower, alike undone
By proud contempt, or favour's fostering sun,
Still may thy blooms the changeful clime endure,
I only would repress them to secure:

For just experience tells; in every soil,
That those who think must govern those that toil;
And all that freedom's highest aims can reach,
Is but to lay proportion'd loads on each.
Hence, should one order disproportion'd grow,
Its double weight must ruin all below.
O then how blind to all that truth requires,
Who think it freedom when a part aspires!
Calm is my soul, nor apt to rise in arms,
Except when fast approaching danger warms:
But when contending chiefs blockade the throne,
Contracting regal power to stretch their own,
When I behold a factious band agree
To call it freedom when themselves are free;
Each wanton judge new penal statutes draw,
Laws grind the poor, and rich men rule the law;
The wealth of climes, where savage nations roam,
Pillag'd from slaves to purchase slaves at home;
Fear, pity, justice, indignation start,
Tear off reserve, and bare my swelling heart;
'Till half a patriot, half a coward grown,
I fly from petty tyrants to the throne.
Yes, brother, curse with me that baleful hour,
When first ambition struck at regal power;
And thus polluting honour in its source,
Gave wealth to sway the mind with double force.
Have we not seen, round Britain's peopled shore,
Her useful sons exchang'd for useless ore?
Seen all her triumphs but destruction haste,
Like flaring tapers brightening as they waste;
Seen opulence, her grandeur to maintain,
Lead stern depopulation in her train,
And over fields where scatter'd hamlets rose,
In barren solitary pomp repose?
Have we not seen at pleasure's lordly call,
The smiling long-frequented village fall;
Beheld the duteous son, the sire decay'd,
The modest matron, and the blushing maid,
Forc'd from their homes, a melancholy train,
To traverse climes beyond the western main;
Where wild Oswego spreads her swamps around,
And Niagara stuns with thund'ring sound?
Even now, perhaps, as there some pilgrim strays
Through tangled forests, and through dangerous ways;
Where beasts with man divided empire claim,
And the brown Indian marks with murderous aim;
There, while above the giddy tempest flies,
And all around distressful yells arise,

The pensive exile, bending with his woe,
To stop too fearful, and too faint to go,
Casts a long look where England's glories shine,
And bids his bosom sympathize with mine.
  Vain, very vain, my weary search to find
That bliss which only centers in the mind:
Why have I stray'd, from pleasure and repose,
To seek a good each government bestows?
In every government, though terrors reign,
Though tyrant kings, or tyrant laws restrain,
How small of all that human hearts endure,
That part which laws or kings can cause or cure.
Still to ourselves in every place consign'd,
Our own felicity we make or find:
With secret course, which no loud storms annoy,
Glides the smooth current of domestic joy.
The lifted ax, the agonizing wheel,
Luke's iron crown, and Damien's bed of steel,
To men remote from power but rarely known,
Leave reason, faith, and conscience, all our own.

Edwin and Angelina. A Ballad[1]

"TURN, gentle hermit of the dale,
   And guide my lonely way,
To where yon taper cheers the vale,
   With hospitable ray.

"For here, forlorn and lost I tread,
   With fainting steps and slow;
Where wilds immeasurably spread,
   Seem lengthening as I go."

"Forbear, my son," the hermit cries,
   "To tempt the dangerous gloom;
For yonder faithless phantom flies
   To lure thee to thy doom.

"Here to the houseless child of want,
   My door is open still;
And though my portion is but scant,
   I give it with goodwill.

[1] Privately printed, 1765. Published in *The Vicar of Wakefield*, 1766. Text of the fifth edition of *The Vicar*, 1773.

"Then turn to-night, and freely share
  Whate'er my cell bestows;
My rushy couch, and frugal fare,
  My blessing and repose.

"No flocks that range the valley free,
  To slaughter I condemn:
Taught by that power that pities me,
  I learn to pity them.

"But from the mountain's grassy side
  A guiltless feast I bring;
A scrip with herbs and fruits supply'd,
  And water from the spring.

"Then, pilgrim, turn, thy cares forego;
  All earth-born cares are wrong:
Man wants but little here below,
  Nor wants that little long."

Soft as the dew from heav'n descends,
  His gentle accents fell:
The modest stranger lowly bends,
  And follows to the cell.

Far in a wilderness obscure
  The lonely mansion lay,
A refuge to the neighbouring poor
  And strangers led astray.

No stores beneath its humble thatch
  Requir'd a master's care;
The wicket opening with a latch,
  Receiv'd the harmless pair.

And now when busy crowds retire
  To take their evening rest,
The hermit trimm'd his little fire,
  And cheer'd his pensive guest;

And spread his vegetable store,
  And gayly prest and smil'd,
And skill'd in legendary lore,
  The lingering hours beguil'd.

Around in sympathetic mirth
  Its tricks the kitten tries,

The cricket chirrups in the hearth;
  The crackling faggot flies.

But nothing could a charm impart
  To sooth the stranger's woe;
For grief was heavy at his heart,
  And tears began to flow.

His rising cares the hermit spy'd,
  With answering care opprest:
And "whence, unhappy youth," he cry'd,
  "The sorrows of thy breast?

"From better habitations spurn'd,
  Reluctant dost thou rove;
Or grieve for friendship unreturn'd,
  Or unregarded love?

"Alas! the joys that fortune brings
  Are trifling, and decay;
And those who prize the paltry things,
  More trifling still than they.

"And what is friendship but a name,
  A charm that lulls to sleep;
A shade that follows wealth or fame,
  But leaves the wretch to weep?

"And love is still an emptier sound,
  The modern fair one's jest,
On earth unseen, or only found
  To warm the turtle's nest.

"For shame, fond youth, thy sorrows hush,
  And spurn the sex," he said:
But, while he spoke, a rising blush
  His love-lorn guest betray'd.

Surpriz'd he sees new beauties rise
  Swift mantling to the view,
Like colours o'er the morning skies,
  As bright, as transient too.

The bashful look, the rising breast,
  Alternate spread alarms,
The lovely stranger stands confest
  A maid in all her charms.

And "Ah! forgive a stranger rude,
A wretch forlorn," she cry'd,
"Whose feet unhallow'd thus intrude
Where heav'n and you reside.

"But let a maid thy pity share,
Whom love has taught to stray;
Who seeks for rest, but finds despair
Companion of her way.

"My father liv'd beside the Tyne,
A wealthy lord was he;
And all his wealth was mark'd as mine,
He had but only me.

"To win me from his tender arms,
Unnumber'd suitors came;
Who prais'd me for imputed charms,
And felt or feign'd a flame.

"Each hour a mercenary crowd
With richest proffers strove:
Among the rest young Edwin bow'd,
But never talk'd of love.

"In humble simplest habit clad,
No wealth nor power had he;
Wisdom and worth were all he had,
But these were all to me.

"The blossom opening to the day,
The dews of heav'n refin'd,
Could nought of purity display,
To emulate his mind.

"The dew, the blossom on the tree,
With charms inconstant shine;
Their charms were his, but woe to me,
Their constancy was mine.

"For still I try'd each fickle art,
Importunate and vain;
And while his passion touch'd my heart,
I triumph'd in his pain.

"Till quite dejected with my scorn,
He left me to my pride;

And sought a solitude forlorn,
In secret where he died.

"But mine the sorrow, mine the fault,
And well my life shall pay,
I'll seek the solitude he sought,
And stretch me where he lay.—

"And there forlorn despairing hid,
I'll lay me down and die:
'Twas so for me that Edwin did,
And so for him will I."

"Forbid it, heaven!" the hermit cry'd,
And clasp'd her to his breast:
The wondering fair one turn'd to chide,
'Twas Edwin's self that prest.

"Turn, Angelina, ever dear,
My charmer turn to see,
Thy own, thy long-lost Edwin here,
Restor'd to love and thee.

"Thus let me hold thee to my heart,
And ev'ry care resign:
And shall we never, never part,
My life,—my all that's mine.

"No, never, from this hour to part,
We'll live and love so true;
The sigh that rends thy constant heart,
Shall break thy Edwin's too."

An Elegy on the Death of a Mad Dog[1]

GOOD people all, of every sort,
Give ear unto my song;
And if you find it wond'rous short,
It cannot hold you long.

In Isling town there was a man,
Of whom the world might say,
That still a godly race he ran,
Whene'er he went to pray.

[1] Published in *The Vicar of Wakefield*, 1766. Text of the fifth edition, 1773.

A kind and gentle heart he had,
  To comfort friends and foes;
The naked every day he clad,
  When he put on his cloaths.

And in that town a dog was found,
  As many dogs there be,
Both mungrel, puppy, whelp and hound,
  And curs of low degree.

This dog and man at first were friends;
  But when a pique began,
The dog, to gain some private ends,
  Went mad and bit the man.

Around from all the neighbouring streets,
  The wond'ring neighbours ran,
And swore the dog had lost his wits,
  To bite so good a man.

The wound it seem'd both sore and sad,
  To every christian eye;
And while they swore the dog was mad,
  They swore the man would die.

But soon a wonder came to light,
  That shew'd the rogues they lied,
The man recover'd of the bite,
  The dog it was that dy'd.

Song[1]

WHEN lovely woman stoops to folly,
  And finds too late that men betray,
What charm can soothe her melancholy,
  What art can wash her guilt away?

The only art her guilt to cover,
  To hide her shame from every eye,
To give repentance to her lover,
  And wring his bosom—is to die.

[1] Published in *The Vicar of Wakefield*, 1766. Text of the fifth edition, 1773.

The Deserted Village, A Poem[1]

TO SIR JOSHUA REYNOLDS

DEAR SIR,

I can have no expectations in an address of this kind, either to add to your reputation, or to establish my own. You can gain nothing from my admiration, as I am ignorant of that art in which you are said to excel; and I may lose much by the severity of your judgment, as few have a juster taste in poetry than you. Setting interest therefore aside, to which I never paid much attention, I must be indulged at present in following my affections. The only dedication I ever made was to my brother, because I loved him better than most other men. He is since dead. Permit me to inscribe this Poem to you.

How far you may be pleased with the versification and mere mechanical parts of this attempt, I don't pretend to enquire; but I know you will object (and indeed several of our best and wisest friends concur in the opinion) that the depopulation it deplores is no where to be seen, and the disorders it laments are only to be found in the poet's own imagination. To this I can scarce make any other answer than that I sincerely believe what I have written; that I have taken all possible pains, in my country excursions, for these four or five years past, to be certain of what I alledge; and that all my views and enquiries have led me to believe those miseries real, which I here attempt to display. But this is not the place to enter into an enquiry, whether the country be depopulating, or not; the discussion would take up much room, and I should prove myself, at best, an indifferent politician, to tire the reader with a long preface, when I want his unfatigued attention to a long poem.

In regretting the depopulation of the country, I inveigh against the encrease of our luxuries; and here also I expect the shout of modern politicians against me. For twenty or thirty years past, it has been the fashion to consider luxury as one of the greatest national advantages; and all the wisdom of antiquity in that particular, as erroneous. Still however, I must remain a professed ancient on that head, and continue to think those luxuries prejudicial to states, by which so many vices are introduced, and so many kingdoms have been undone. Indeed so much has been poured out of late on the other side of the question, that, merely for the sake of novelty and variety, one would sometimes wish to be in the right.

I am,
Dear Sir,
Your sincere friend,
and ardent admirer,
OLIVER GOLDSMITH.

SWEET AUBURN, loveliest village of the plain,
Where health and plenty cheared the labouring swain,
Where smiling spring its earliest visit paid,
And parting summer's lingering blooms delayed,
Dear lovely bowers of innocence and ease,
Seats of my youth, when every sport could please,
How often have I loitered o'er thy green,
Where humble happiness endeared each scene;

[1] Published May 26, 1770. Text of fourth edition, 1770.

How often have I paused on every charm,
The sheltered cot, the cultivated farm,
The never failing brook, the busy mill,
The decent church that topt the neighbouring hill,
The hawthorn bush, with seats beneath the shade,
For talking age and whispering lovers made;
How often have I blest the coming day,
When toil remitting lent its turn to play,
And all the village train, from labour free,
Led up their sports beneath the spreading tree;
While many a pastime circled in the shade,
The young contending as the old surveyed;
And many a gambol frolicked o'er the ground,
And slights of art and feats of strength went round;
And still as each repeated pleasure tired,
Succeeding sports the mirthful band inspired;
The dancing pair that simply sought renown
By holding out to tire each other down;
The swain mistrustless of his smutted face,
While secret laughter tittered round the place;
The bashful virgin's side-long looks of love,
The matron's glance that would those looks reprove:
These were thy charms, sweet village; sports like these,
With sweet succession, taught even toil to please;
These round thy bowers their chearful influence shed,
These were thy charms—But all these charms are fled.
  Sweet smiling village, loveliest of the lawn,
Thy sports are fled, and all thy charms withdrawn;
Amidst thy bowers the tyrant's hand is seen,
And desolation saddens all thy green:
One only master grasps the whole domain,
And half a tillage stints thy smiling plain;
No more thy glassy brook reflects the day,
But choaked with sedges, works its weedy way.
Along thy glades, a solitary guest,
The hollow sounding bittern guards its nest;
Amidst thy desert walks the lapwing flies,
And tires their ecchoes with unvaried cries.
Sunk are thy bowers, in shapeless ruin all,
And the long grass o'ertops the mouldering wall,
And trembling, shrinking from the spoiler's hand,
Far, far away thy children leave the land.
  Ill fares the land, to hastening ills a prey,
Where wealth accumulates, and men decay:
Princes and lords may flourish, or may fade;
A breath can make them, as a breath has made;
But a bold peasantry, their country's pride,
When once destroyed, can never be supplied.

A time there was, ere England's griefs began,
When every rood of ground maintained its man;
For him light labour spread her wholesome store,
Just gave what life required, but gave no more:
His best companions, innocence and health;
And his best riches, ignorance of wealth.
But times are altered; trade's unfeeling train
Usurp the land and dispossess the swain;
Along the lawn, where scattered hamlets rose,
Unwieldy wealth, and cumbrous pomp repose;
And every want to oppulence allied,
And every pang that folly pays to pride.
These gentle hours that plenty bade to bloom,
Those calm desires that asked but little room,
Those healthful sports that graced the peaceful scene,
Lived in each look, and brightened all the green;
These far departing seek a kinder shore,
And rural mirth and manners are no more.
Sweet AUBURN! parent of the blissful hour,
Thy glades forlorn confess the tyrant's power.
Here as I take my solitary rounds,
Amidst thy tangling walks, and ruined grounds,
And, many a year elapsed, return to view
Where once the cottage stood, the hawthorn grew,
Remembrance wakes with all her busy train,
Swells at my breast, and turns the past to pain.
In all my wanderings round this world of care,
In all my griefs—and GOD has given my share—
I still had hopes my latest hours to crown,
Amidst these humble bowers to lay me down;
To husband out life's taper at the close,
And keep the flame from wasting by repose.
I still had hopes, for pride attends us still,
Amidst the swains to shew my book-learned skill,
Around my fire an evening groupe to draw,
And tell of all I felt, and all I saw;
And, as an hare whom hounds and horns pursue,
Pants to the place from whence at first she flew,
I still had hopes, my long vexations past,
Here to return—and die at home at last.
O blest retirement, friend to life's decline,
Retreats from care that never must be mine,
How happy he who crowns in shades like these,
A youth of labour with an age of ease;
Who quits a world where strong temptations try,
And, since 'tis hard to combat, learns to fly.
For him no wretches, born to work and weep,
Explore the mine, or tempt the dangerous deep;

No surly porter stands in guilty state
To spurn imploring famine from the gate,
But on he moves to meet his latter end,
Angels around befriending virtue's friend;
Bends to the grave with unperceived decay,
While resignation gently slopes the way;
And all his prospects brightening to the last,
His Heaven commences ere the world be past!
  Sweet was the sound when oft at evening's close,
Up yonder hill the village murmur rose;
There as I past with careless steps and slow,
The mingling notes came softened from below;
The swain responsive as the milk-maid sung,
The sober herd that lowed to meet their young,
The noisy geese that gabbled o'er the pool,
The playful children just let loose from school,
The watch-dog's voice that bayed the whispering wind,
And the loud laugh that spoke the vacant mind,
These all in sweet confusion sought the shade,
And filled each pause the nightingale had made.
But now the sounds of population fail,
No chearful murmurs fluctuate in the gale,
No busy steps the grass-grown foot-way tread,
For all the bloomy flush of life is fled.
All but yon widowed, solitary thing
That feebly bends beside the plashy spring;
She, wretched matron, forced, in age, for bread,
To strip the brook with mantling cresses spread,
To pick her wintry faggot from the thorn,
To seek her nightly shed, and weep till morn;
She only left of all the harmless train,
The sad historian of the pensive plain.
  Near yonder copse, where once the garden smil'd,
And still where many a garden flower grows wild;
There, where a few torn shrubs the place disclose,
The village preacher's modest mansion rose.
A man he was, to all the country dear,
And passing rich with forty pounds a year;
Remote from towns he ran his godly race,
Nor e'er had changed, nor wished to change his place;
Unpractised he to fawn, or seek for power,
By doctrines fashioned to the varying hour;
Far other aims his heart had learned to prize,
More skilled to raise the wretched than to rise.
His house was known to all the vagrant train,
He chid their wanderings, but relieved their pain;
The long remembered beggar was his guest,
Whose beard descending swept his aged breast;

The ruined spendthrift, now no longer proud,
Claimed kindred there, and had his claims allowed;
The broken soldier, kindly bade to stay,
Sate by his fire, and talked the night away;
Wept o'er his wounds, or tales of sorrow done,
Shouldered his crutch, and shewed how fields were won.
Pleased with his guests, the good man learned to glow,
And quite forgot their vices in their woe;
Careless their merits, or their faults to scan,
His pity gave ere charity began.
  Thus to relieve the wretched was his pride,
And even his failings leaned to Virtue's side;
But in his duty prompt at every call,
He watched and wept, he prayed and felt, for all.
And, as a bird each fond endearment tries,
To tempt its new fledged offspring to the skies;
He tried each art, reproved each dull delay,
Allured to brighter worlds, and led the way.
  Beside the bed where parting life was layed,
And sorrow, guilt, and pain, by turns dismayed,
The reverend champion stood. At his control,
Despair and anguish fled the struggling soul;
Comfort came down the trembling wretch to raise,
And his last faultering accents whispered praise.
  At church, with meek and unaffected grace,
His looks adorned the venerable place;
Truth from his lips prevailed with double sway,
And fools, who came to scoff, remained to pray.
The service past, around the pious man,
With steady zeal each honest rustic ran;
Even children followed with endearing wile,
And plucked his gown, to share the good man's smile.
His ready smile a parent's warmth exprest,
Their welfare pleased him, and their cares distrest;
To them his heart, his love, his griefs were given,
But all his serious thoughts had rest in Heaven.
As some tall cliff that lifts its awful form,
Swells from the vale, and midway leaves the storm,
Tho' round its breast the rolling clouds are spread,
Eternal sunshine settles on its head.
  Beside yon straggling fence that skirts the way,
With blossomed furze unprofitably gay,
There, in his noisy mansion, skill'd to rule,
The village master taught his little school;
A man severe he was, and stern to view,
I knew him well, and every truant knew;
Well had the boding tremblers learned to trace
The day's disasters in his morning face;

Full well they laugh'd with counterfeited glee,
At all his jokes, for many a joke had he;
Full well the busy whisper circling round,
Conveyed the dismal tidings when he frowned;
Yet he was kind, or if severe in aught,
The love he bore to learning was in fault;
The village all declared how much he knew;
'Twas certain he could write, and cypher too;
Lands he could measure, terms and tides presage,
And even the story ran that he could gauge.
In arguing too, the parson owned his skill,
For even tho' vanquished, he could argue still;
While words of learned length, and thundering sound,
Amazed the gazing rustics ranged around;
And still they gazed, and still the wonder grew,
That one small head could carry all he knew.
  But past is all his fame. The very spot
Where many a time he triumphed, is forgot.
Near yonder thorn, that lifts its head on high,
Where once the sign-post caught the passing eye,
Low lies that house where nut-brown draughts inspired,
Where grey-beard mirth and smiling toil retired,
Where village statesmen talked with looks profound,
And news much older than their ale went round.
Imagination fondly stoops to trace
The parlour splendours of that festive place;
The white-washed wall, the nicely sanded floor,
The varnished clock that clicked behind the door;
The chest contrived a double debt to pay,
A bed by night, a chest of drawers by day;
The pictures placed for ornament and use,
The twelve good rules, the royal game of goose;
The hearth, except when winter chill'd the day,
With aspen boughs, and flowers, and fennel gay,
While broken tea-cups, wisely kept for shew,
Ranged o'er the chimney, glistened in a row.
  Vain transitory splendours! Could not all
Reprieve the tottering mansion from its fall!
Obscure it sinks, nor shall it more impart
An hour's importance to the poor man's heart;
Thither no more the peasant shall repair
To sweet oblivion of his daily care;
No more the farmer's news, the barber's tale,
No more the wood-man's ballad shall prevail;
No more the smith his dusky brow shall clear,
Relax his ponderous strength, and lean to hear;
The host himself no longer shall be found
Careful to see the mantling bliss go round;

Nor the coy maid, half willing to be prest,
Shall kiss the cup to pass it to the rest.
Yes! let the rich deride, the proud disdain,
These simple blessings of the lowly train;
To me more dear, congenial to my heart,
One native charm, than all the gloss of art;
Spontaneous joys, where Nature has its play,
The soul adopts, and owns their first born sway;
Lightly they frolic o'er the vacant mind,
Unenvied, unmolested, unconfined.
But the long pomp, the midnight masquerade,
With all the freaks of wanton wealth arrayed,
In these, ere triflers half their wish obtain,
The toiling pleasure sickens into pain;
And, even while fashion's brightest arts decoy,
The heart distrusting asks, if this be joy.
Ye friends to truth, ye statesmen, who survey
The rich man's joys encrease, the poor's decay,
'Tis yours to judge, how wide the limits stand
Between a splendid and an happy land.
Proud swells the tide with loads of freighted ore,
And shouting Folly hails them from her shore;
Hoards, even beyond the miser's wish abound,
And rich men flock from all the world around.
Yet count our gains. This wealth is but a name
That leaves our useful products still the same.
Not so the loss. The man of wealth and pride,
Takes up a space that many poor supplied;
Space for his lake, his park's extended bounds,
Space for his horses, equipage, and hounds;
The robe that wraps his limbs in silken sloth,
Has robbed the neighbouring fields of half their growth;
His seat, where solitary sports are seen,
Indignant spurns the cottage from the green;
Around the world each needful product flies,
For all the luxuries the world supplies.
While thus the land adorned for pleasure, all
In barren splendour feebly waits the fall.
As some fair female unadorned and plain,
Secure to please while youth confirms her reign,
Slights every borrowed charm that dress supplies,
Nor shares with art the triumph of her eyes.
But when those charms are past, for charms are frail,
When time advances, and when lovers fail,
She then shines forth, sollicitous to bless,
In all the glaring impotence of dress.
Thus fares the land, by luxury betrayed;
In nature's simplest charms at first arrayed;

But verging to decline, its splendours rise,
Its vistas strike, its palaces surprize;
While scourged by famine from the smiling land,
The mournful peasant leads his humble band;
And while he sinks without one arm to save,
The country blooms—a garden, and a grave.
  Where then, ah where, shall poverty reside,
To scape the pressure of contiguous pride?
If to some common's fenceless limits strayed,
He drives his flock to pick the scanty blade,
Those fenceless fields the sons of wealth divide,
And even the bare-worn common is denied.
  If to the city sped—What waits him there?
To see profusion that he must not share;
To see ten thousand baneful arts combined
To pamper luxury, and thin mankind;
To see those joys the sons of pleasure know,
Extorted from his fellow-creature's woe.
Here, while the courtier glitters in brocade,
There the pale artist plies the sickly trade;
Here, while the proud their long-drawn pomps display,
There the black gibbet glooms beside the way.
The dome where Pleasure holds her midnight reign,
Here, richly deckt, admits the gorgeous train;
Tumultuous grandeur crowds the blazing square,
The rattling chariots clash, the torches glare.
Sure scenes like these no troubles e'er annoy!
Sure these denote one universal joy!
Are these thy serious thoughts?—Ah, turn thine eyes
Where the poor houseless shivering female lies.
She once, perhaps, in village plenty blest,
Has wept at tales of innocence distrest;
Her modest looks the cottage might adorn,
Sweet as the primrose peeps beneath the thorn;
Now lost to all; her friends, her virtue fled,
Near her betrayer's door she lays her head,
And pinch'd with cold, and shrinking from the shower,
With heavy heart deplores that luckless hour
When idly first, ambitious of the town,
She left her wheel and robes of country brown.
  Do thine, sweet AUBURN, thine, the loveliest train,
Do thy fair tribes participate her pain?
Even now, perhaps, by cold and hunger led,
At proud men's doors they ask a little bread!
  Ah, no. To distant climes, a dreary scene,
Where half the convex world intrudes between,
Through torrid tracts with fainting steps they go,
Where wild Altama murmurs to their woe.

Far different there from all that charm'd before,
The various terrors of that horrid shore;
Those blazing suns that dart a downward ray,
And fiercely shed intolerable day;
Those matted woods where birds forget to sing,
But silent bats in drowsy clusters cling,
Those poisonous fields with rank luxuriance crowned,
Where the dark scorpion gathers death around;
Where at each step the stranger fears to wake
The rattling terrors of the vengeful snake;
Where crouching tigers wait their hapless prey,
And savage men, more murderous still than they;
While oft in whirls the mad tornado flies,
Mingling the ravaged landschape with the skies.
Far different these from every former scene,
The cooling brook, the grassy vested green,
The breezy covert of the warbling grove,
That only sheltered thefts of harmless love.
Good Heaven! what sorrows gloom'd that parting day,
That called them from their native walks away;
When the poor exiles, every pleasure past,
Hung round their bowers, and fondly looked their last,
And took a long farewell, and wished in vain
For seats like these beyond the western main;
And shuddering still to face the distant deep,
Returned and wept, and still returned to weep.
The good old sire, the first prepared to go
To new found worlds, and wept for others woe.
But for himself, in conscious virtue brave,
He only wished for worlds beyond the grave.
His lovely daughter, lovelier in her tears,
The fond companion of his helpless years,
Silent went next, neglectful of her charms,
And left a lover's for a father's arms.
With louder plaints the mother spoke her woes,
And blest the cot where every pleasure rose;
And kist her thoughtless babes with many a tear,
And claspt them close in sorrow doubly dear;
Whilst her fond husband strove to lend relief
In all the silent manliness of grief.
O luxury! Thou curst by Heaven's decree,
How ill exchanged are things like these for thee!
How do thy potions, with insidious joy,
Diffuse their pleasures only to destroy!
Kingdoms, by thee, to sickly greatness grown,
Boast of a florid vigour not their own;
At every draught more large and large they grow,
A bloated mass of rank unwieldy woe;

Till sapped their strength, and every part unsound,
Down, down they sink, and spread a ruin round.
 Even now the devastation is begun,
And half the business of destruction done;
Even now, methinks, as pondering here I stand,
I see the rural virtues leave the land:
Down where yon anchoring vessel spreads the sail,
That idly waiting flaps with every gale,
Downward they move, a melancholy band,
Pass from the shore, and darken all the strand.
Contented toil, and hospitable care,
And kind connubial tenderness, are there;
And piety, with wishes placed above,
And steady loyalty, and faithful love:
And thou, sweet Poetry, thou loveliest maid,
Still first to fly where sensual joys invade;
Unfit in these degenerate times of shame,
To catch the heart, or strike for honest fame;
Dear charming nymph, neglected and decried,
My shame in crowds, my solitary pride;
Thou source of all my bliss, and all my woe,
That found'st me poor at first, and keep'st me so;
Thou guide by which the nobler arts excell,
Thou nurse of every virtue, fare thee well.
Farewell, and O where'er thy voice be tried,
On Torno's cliffs, or Pambamarca's side,
Whether where equinoctial fervours glow,
Or winter wraps the polar world in snow,
Still let thy voice prevailing over time,
Redress the rigours of the inclement clime;
Aid slighted truth, with thy persuasive strain
Teach erring man to spurn the rage of gain;
Teach him that states of native strength possest,
Tho' very poor, may still be very blest;
That trade's proud empire hastes to swift decay,
As ocean sweeps the labour'd mole away;
While self-dependent power can time defy,
As rocks resist the billows and the sky.

The Haunch of Venison, A Poetical Epistle to Lord Clare[1]

THANKS, my Lord, for your Ven'son; for finer, or fatter,
Never rang'd in a forest, or smok'd on a platter:

[1] Written in 1771. Published in 1776. Text of first edition.

The Haunch was a picture for Painters to study;
The white was so white, and the red was so ruddy!
I had thoughts, in my chamber to hang it in view,
To be shown to my Friends as a piece of *Virtù*;
As in some *Irish* Houses, where things are so-so,
One Gammon of Bacon hangs up for a show;
But, for eating a rasher of what they take pride in,
They'd as soon think of eating the pan it is fry'd in.
But hold—let us pause—Don't I hear you pronounce
This tale of the Bacon a damnable bounce?
Well, suppose it a bounce; sure a Poet may try,
By a bounce now and then, to get courage to fly:
But, my Lord, it's no bounce: I protest, in my turn,
It's a truth; and your Lordship may ask Mr. BURNE.
  To go on with my tale—As I gaz'd on the Haunch,
I thought of a Friend that was trusty and staunch:
So I cut it, and sent it to REYNOLDS undrest,
To paint it, or eat it, just as he lik'd best.
Of the Neck and the Breast I had next to dispose;
'Twas a neck and a breast—that might rival MONROE's:
But in parting with these I was puzzled again,
With the *how*, and the *who*, and the *where*, and the *when:*
There's COLEY, and WILLIAMS, and HOWARD, and HIFF—
I think they love Ven'son; I know they love Beef:
But—hang it!—to Poets, that seldom can eat,
Your very good Mutton's a very good treat:
Such dainties to them! It *would* look like a flirt,
Like sending 'em Ruffles when wanting a Shirt.
  While thus I debated, in *reverie* center'd,
An Acquaintance, a Friend—as he call'd himself, enter'd;
A fine-spoken Custom-house Officer he,
Who smil'd as he gaz'd on the Ven'son and me.
"What have we got here?—Aye, this is *good eating!*
"Your own, I suppose—or is it in waiting?"
Why, whose should it be, Sir? cry'd I, with a flounce;
I get these things often—But that was a bounce.
"If that be the case then," cry'd he very gay,
"I'm glad I have taken this house in my way.
"To-morrow you take a poor dinner with me:
"No words—I insist on't—precisely at three.
"And now that I think on't, as I am a sinner,
"We wanted this Ven'son to make up the dinner.
"I'll take no denial—you shall, and you must;
"And my Wife, little *Kitty*, is famous for Crust.
"We'll have JOHNSON and BURKE; all the Wits will be there;
"My acquaintance is slight, or I'd ask my Lord CLARE.
"Here, Porter! this Ven'son with me to *Mile-end*—
"No words, my dear GOLDSMITH! my very good Friend!"

Thus, seizing his hat, he brush'd off like the wind,
And the Porter and Eatables follow'd behind.
Left alone to reflect, having empty'd my shelf,
And nobody with me at sea, but myself;
Though I could not help thinking my Gentleman hasty,
Yet JOHNSON and BURKE, and a good Ven'son Pasty,
Were things that I never dislik'd in my life,
Though clogg'd with a Coxcomb, and *Kitty* his Wife.
So next day, in due splendor to make my approach,
I drove to his door in my own Hackney-coach.
When come to the place where we all were to dine,
(A chair-lumber'd Closet, just twelve feet by nine)
My Friend bid me welcome, but struck me quite dumb
With tidings *that* JOHNSON and BURKE could not come:
"And I knew it," he cry'd; "both eternally fail;
"The one at the House, and the other with THRALE.
"But, I warrant for me, we shall make up the Party,
"With two full as clever, and ten times as hearty.
"The one is a *Scotchman*, the other a *Jew*,
"Who dabble and write in the Papers—like you:
"The one writes the *Snarler;* the other, the *Scourge:*
"Some think he writes *Cinna*—he owns to *Panurge.*"
While thus he describ'd them by Trade and by Name,
They enter'd; and Dinner was serv'd as they came:
At the top a fry'd Liver and Bacon was seen;
At the bottom was Tripe in a swinging terrene;
At the sides there was Spinage and Pudding made hot;
In the middle—a place, where the Ven'son was not.
Now, my Lord, as for Tripe, it's my utter aversion;
And your Bacon I hate, like a *Turk*, or a *Persian:*
But what vex'd me most was that damn'd *Scottish* Rogue,
With his long-winded speeches, and smiles, and his brogue:
"And, Madam," says he, "may this bit be my poison
"If a prettier Dinner I ever set eyes on!
"Pray, a slice of your Liver;—but may I be curst,
"But I've eat of your Tripe till I'm ready to burst."
'Your Tripe!' quoth the *Jew*, 'if the truth I may speak,
'I could eat of this Tripe seven days in the week:
'I like these *here* Dinners, so pretty and small;
'But your Friend there, the Doctor, eats nothing at all.'
"O ho!" quoth my Friend, "he'll come on in a trice;
"He's keeping a corner for something that's nice:
"There's a Pasty."—'A Pasty!' returned the *Scot*;
'I don't care if I keep a corner for *thot.*'
"We'll all keep a corner," the Lady cry'd out:
We'll all keep a corner, was eccho'd about.
While thus we resolv'd, and the Pasty delay'd,
With looks quite astonishing enter'd the Maid:

A visage so sad, and so pale with affright!
Wak'd PRIAM, by drawing his curtains by night.
But too soon we found out (for who could mistake her?)
That she came with some terrible news from the Baker;
And so it fell out; for that negligent Sloven
Had shut out the Pasty on shutting his Oven.
  Sad *Philomel* thus—but let similes drop;
And now, that I think on't, the story may stop.
To be plain, my good Lord, 'tis but labour misplac'd
To send such good Verses to one of your taste:
You've got an odd something, a kind of discerning,
A relish, a taste, sicken'd over by learning;
At least it's your temper, 'tis very well known,
That you think very slightly of all that's your own:
So perhaps, in your habits of thinking amiss,
You may make a Mistake—and think slightly of This.

Retaliation: A Poem[1]

OF OLD, when Scarron his companions invited,
Each guest brought his dish, and the feast was united;
If our (*a*) landlord supplies us with beef, and with fish,
Let each guest bring himself, and he brings the best dish:
Our (*b*) Dean shall be venison, just fresh from the plains;
Our (*c*) Burke shall be tongue, with a garnish of brains;
Our (*d*) Will shall be wild fowl, of excellent flavour,
And (*e*) Dick with his pepper, shall heighten their flavour:
Our (*f*) Cumberland's sweet-bread its place shall obtain,
And (*g*) Douglas is pudding, substantial and plain:
Our (*h*) Garrick's a sallad, for in him we see

[1] Published in 1774. Text of sixth edition, 1774.

(*a*) The Master of the St. James's Coffee-house, where the Doctor [Goldsmith], and the Friends he has characterized in this Poem, held an occasional Club. [These notes appeared in the first edition of the poem, a fortnight after Goldsmith's death. A few that are merely repetitions or cross references have been omitted.]

(*b*) Doctor Barnard, Dean of Derry in Ireland, author of many ingenious pieces.

(*c*) Mr. Edmund Burke, member for Wendover, and one of the greatest orators in this kingdom.

(*d*) Mr. William Burke, late secretary to General Conway, and member for Bedwin.

(*e*) Mr. Richard Burke, collector of Granada, no less remarkable in the walks of wit and humour than his brother Edmund Burke is justly distinguished in all the branches of useful and polite literature.

(*f*) Author of the West Indian, Fashionable Lover, the Brothers, and other dramatic pieces.

(*g*) Doctor Douglas, Canon of Windsor, an ingenious Scotch gentleman, who has no less distinguished himself as a *Citizen of the World*, than a *sound Critic* in detecting several literary mistakes (or rather *forgeries*) of his countrymen: particularly Lauder on Milton and *Bower's History of the Popes*.

(*h*) David Garrick, Esq; joint Patentee and acting Manager of the Theatre-Royal, Drury-lane. For the *other parts* of his character, *vide* the Poem.

Oil, vinegar, sugar, and saltness agree:
To make out the dinner, full certain I am,
That (*i*) Ridge is anchovy, and (*k*) Reynolds is lamb;
That (*l*) Hickey's a capon, and by the same rule,
Magnanimous Goldsmith, a goosberry fool:
At a dinner so various, at such a repast,
Who'd not be a glutton, and stick to the last:
Here, waiter, more wine, let me sit while I'm able,
'Till all my companions sink under the table;
Then with chaos and blunders encircling my head,
Let me ponder, and tell what I think of the dead.
Here lies the good Dean, re-united to earth,
Who mixt reason with pleasure, and wisdom with mirth:
If he had any faults, he has left us in doubt,
At least, in six weeks, I could not find 'em out;
Yet some have declar'd, and it can't be denied 'em,
That sly-boots was cursedly cunning to hide 'em.
Here lies our good Edmund, whose genius was such,
We scarcely can praise it, or blame it too much;
Who, born for the Universe, narrow'd his mind,
And to party gave up, what was meant for mankind.
Tho' fraught with all learning, yet straining his throat,
To persuade (*o*) Tommy Townsend to lend him a vote;
Who, too deep for his hearers, still went on refining,
And thought of convincing, while they thought of dining;
Tho' equal to all things, for all things unfit,
Too nice for a statesman, too proud for a wit:
For a patriot too cool; for a drudge, disobedient,
And too fond of the *right* to pursue the *expedient*.
In short, 'twas his fate, unemploy'd, or in place, Sir,
To eat mutton cold, and cut blocks with a razor.
Here lies honest William, whose heart was a mint,
While the owner ne'er knew half the good that was in't;
The pupil of impulse, it forc'd him along,
His conduct still right, with his argument wrong;
Still aiming at honour, yet fearing to roam,
The coachman was tipsy, the chariot drove home;
Would you ask for his merits, alas! he had none,
What was good was spontaneous, his faults were his own.
Here lies honest Richard, whose fate I must sigh at,
Alas, that such frolic should now be so quiet!
What spirits were his, what wit and what whim,

(*i*) Counsellor John Ridge, a gentleman belonging to the Irish bar, the *relish* of whose agreeable and pointed conversation is admitted, by all his acquaintance, to be very properly compared to the above sauce.

(*k*) Sir Joshua Reynolds, President of the Royal Academy.

(*l*) An eminent Attorney, whose hospitality and good-humour have acquired him, in this Club, the title of 'honest Tom Hickey.'

(*o*) Mr. T. Townsend, Member for Whitchurch.

(*q*) Now breaking a jest, and now breaking a limb;
Now wrangling and grumbling to keep up the ball,
Now teazing and vexing, yet laughing at all?
In short so provoking a Devil was Dick,
That we wish'd him full ten times a day at Old Nick.
But missing his mirth and agreeable vein,
As often we wish'd to have Dick back again.
  Here Cumberland lies having acted his parts,
The Terence of England, the mender of hearts;
A flattering painter, who made it his care
To draw men as they ought to be, not as they are.
His gallants are all faultless, his women divine,
And comedy wonders at being so fine;
Like a tragedy queen he has dizen'd her out,
Or rather like tragedy giving a rout.
His fools have their follies so lost in a croud
Of virtues and feelings, that folly grows proud
And coxcombs alike in their failings alone,
Adopting his portraits are pleas'd with their own.
Say, where has our poet this malady caught,
Or wherefore his characters thus without fault?
Say was it that vainly directing his view,
To find out mens virtues and finding them few,
Quite sick of pursuing each troublesome elf,
He grew lazy at last and drew from himself?
  Here Douglas retires from his toils to relax,
The scourge of impostors, the terror of quacks:
Come all ye quack bards, and ye quacking divines,
Come and dance on the spot where your tyrant reclines,
When Satire and Censure encircl'd his throne,
I fear'd for your safety, I fear'd for my own;
But now he is gone, and we want a detector,
Our (*t*) Dodds shall be pious, our (*u*) Kenricks shall lecture;
(*x*) Macpherson write bombast, and call it a style,
Our Townshend make speeches, and I shall compile;
New Lauders and Bowers the Tweed shall cross over,
No countryman living their tricks to discover;
Detection her taper shall quench to a spark,
And Scotchman meet Scotchman and cheat in the dark.
  Here lies David Garrick, describe me who can,

(*q*) Mr. Richard Burke. . . . This gentleman having slightly fractured one of his arms and legs, at different times, the Doctor has rallied him on those accidents, as a kind of *retributive* justice for breaking his jests upon other people.

(*t*) The Rev. Dr. Dodd.

(*u*) Mr. Kenrick lately read lectures at the Devil Tavern, under the Title of 'The School of Shakespeare.'

(*x*) James Macpherson, Esq; who lately, from the mere *force of his style*, wrote down the first poet of all antiquity.

An abridgment of all that was pleasant in man;
As an actor, confest without rival to shine,
As a wit, if not first, in the very first line,
Yet with talents like these, and an excellent heart,
The man had his failings, a dupe to his art;
Like an ill-judging beauty, his colours he spread,
And beplaister'd, with rouge, his own natural red.
On the stage he was natural, simple, affecting,
'Twas only that, when he was off, he was acting:
With no reason on earth to go out of his way,
He turn'd and he varied full ten times a-day;
Tho' secure of our hearts, yet confoundedly sick,
If they were not his own by finessing and trick;
He cast off his friends, as a huntsman his pack,
For he knew when he pleas'd he could whistle them back.
Of praise a mere glutton, he swallow'd what came,
And the puff of a dunce, he mistook it for fame;
'Till his relish grown callous, almost to disease,
Who pepper'd the highest, was surest to please.
But let us be candid, and speak out our mind,
If dunces applauded, he paid them in kind.
Ye Kenricks, ye (*c*) Kellys, and (*d*) Woodfalls so grave,
What a commerce was yours, while you got and you gave?
How did Grub-street re-echo the shouts that you rais'd,
While he was beroscius'd, and you were beprais'd?
But peace to his spirit, wherever it flies,
To act as an angel, and mix with the skies:
Those poets, who owe their best fame to his skill,
Shall still be his flatterers, go where he will.
Old Shakespeare, receive him, with praise and with love,
And Beaumonts and Bens be his Kellys above.
  Here Hickey reclines, a most blunt, pleasant creature,
And slander itself must allow him good-nature:
He cherish'd his friend, and he relish'd a bumper;
Yet one fault he had, and that one was a thumper:
Perhaps you may ask if the man was a miser?
I answer, no, no, for he always was wiser;
Too courteous, perhaps, or obligingly flat;
His very worst foe can't accuse him of that.
Perhaps he confided in men as they go,
And so was too foolishly honest; ah no!
Then what was his failing? come tell it, and burn ye,
He was, could he help it? a special attorney.

(*c*) Hugh Kelly, Esq; Author of False Delicacy, Word to the Wise, Clementina, School for Wives, &c. &c.

(*d*) Mr. William Woodfall, Printer of the Morning Chronicle.

Here Reynolds is laid, and, to tell you my mind,
He has not left a wiser or better behind;
His pencil was striking, resistless and grand,
His manners were gentle, complying and bland;
Still born to improve us in every part,
His pencil our faces, his manners our heart:
To coxcombs averse, yet most civilly steering,
When they judg'd without skill he was still hard of hearing:
When they talk'd of their Raphaels, Corregios and stuff,
He shifted his (*h*) trumpet, and only took snuff.

THOMAS PERCY

(1729-1758-1811)

A Song[1]

O NANCY, wilt thou go with me,
  Nor sigh to leave the flaunting town:
Can silent glens have charms for thee,
  The lowly cot and russet gown?
No longer dress'd in silken sheen,
  No longer deck'd with jewels rare,
Say can'st thou quit each courtly scene,
  Where thou wert fairest of the fair?

O Nancy! when thou'rt far away,
  Wilt thou not cast a wish behind?
Say canst thou face the parching ray,
  Nor shrink before the wintry wind?
O can that soft and gentle mien
  Extremes of hardship learn to bear,
Nor sad regret each courtly scene,
  Where thou wert fairest of the fair?

O Nancy! can'st thou love so true,
  Thro' perils keen with me to go,

(*h*) Sir Joshua Reynolds is so remarkably deaf as to be under the necessity of using an ear trumpet in company; he is, at the same time, equally remarkable for taking a great quantity of snuff: his manner in both of which, taken in the point of time described, must be allowed, by those who have been witnesses of such a scene. to be as happily given upon *paper*, as that great Artist himself, perhaps, could have exhibited upon *canvas*.

[1] Published in Dodsley's *Collection of Poems*, Volume VI, 1758. Text of first edition.

Or when thy swain mishap shall rue,
  To share with him the pang of woe?
Say should disease or pain befal,
  Wilt thou assume the nurse's care,
Nor wistful those gay scenes recall
  Where thou wert fairest of the fair?

And when at last thy love shall die,
  Wilt thou receive his parting breath?
Wilt thou repress each struggling sigh,
  And chear with smiles the bed of death?
And wilt thou o'er his breathless clay
  Strew flow'rs, and drop the tender tear,
Nor *then* regret those scenes so gay,
  Where thou were fairest of the fair?

The Friar of Orders Gray[1]

Dispersed thro' Shakespeare's plays are innumerable little fragments of ancient ballads, the intire copies of which, could not be recovered. Many of these being of the most beautiful and pathetic simplicity, the Editor was tempted to select some of them, and with a few supplemental stanzas to connect them together and form them into a little TALE, *which is here submitted to the Reader's candour.*

One small fragment was taken from Beaumont and Fletcher.

IT WAS a friar of orders gray,
  Walkt forth to tell his beades;
And he met with a lady faire,
  Clad in a pilgrime's weedes.

Now Christ thee save, thou reverend friar,
  I pray thee tell to me,
If ever at yon holy shrine
  My true love thou didst see.

And how should I know your true love,
  From many another one?
O by his cockle hat, and staff,
  And by his sandal shoone.

But chiefly by his face and mien,
  That were so fair to view;
His flaxen locks that sweetly curl'd,
  And eyne of lovely blue.

[1] Published in Percy's *Reliques*, Volume I, 1765. Text of first edition.

O lady, he is dead and gone!
  Lady, he's dead and gone!
And at his head a green grass turfe,
  And at his heels a stone.

Within these holy cloysters long
  He languisht, and he dyed,
Lamenting of a ladyes love,
  And 'playning of her pride.

Here bore him barefac'd on his bier
  Six proper youths and tall,
And many a tear bedew'd his grave
  Within yon kirk-yard wall.

And art thou dead, thou gentle youth!
  And art thou dead and gone!
And didst thou dye for love of me!
  Break, cruel heart of stone!

O weep not, lady, weep not soe;
  Some ghostly comfort seek:
Let not vain sorrow rive thy heart,
  Ne teares bedew thy cheek.

O do not, do not, holy friar,
  My sorrow now reprove;
For I have lost the sweetest youth,
  That e'er wan ladyes love.

And nowe, alas! for thy sad losse,
  I'll evermore weep and sigh;
For thee I only wisht to live,
  For thee I wish to dye.

Weep no more, lady, weep no more,
  Thy sorrowe is in vaine:
For, violets pluckt the sweetest showers
  Will ne'er make grow againe.

Our joys as winged dreams doe flye,
  Why then should sorrow last?
Since grief but aggravates thy losse,
  Grieve not for what is past.

O say not soe, thou holy friar;
  I pray thee, say not soe:

For since my true-love dyed for mee,
'Tis meet my tears should flow.

And will he ne'er come again?
Will he ne'er come again?
Ah! no, he is dead and laid in his grave,
For ever to remain.

His cheek was redder than the rose,
The comliest youth was he:—
But he is dead and laid in his grave:
Alas, and woe is me!

Sigh no more, lady, sigh no more,
Men were deceivers ever:
One foot on sea and one on land,
To one thing constant never.

Hadst thou been fond, he had been false,
And left thee sad and heavy;
For young men ever were fickle found,
Since summer trees were leafy.

Now say not so, thou holy friar,
I pray thee say not soe:
My love he had the truest heart:
O he was ever true!

And art thou dead, thou much-lov'd youth,
And didst thou dye for mee?
Then farewell home; for, ever-more
A pilgrim I will bee.

But first upon my true-loves grave
My weary limbs I'll lay,
And thrice I'll kiss the green-grass turf,
That wraps his breathless clay.

Yet stay, fair lady; rest awhile
Beneath this cloyster wall:
See through the hawthorn blows the cold wind,
And drizzly rain doth fall.

O stay me not, thou holy friar;
O stay me not I pray:
No drizzly rain that falls on me,
Can wash my fault away.

Yet stay, fair lady, turn again,
  And dry those pearly tears;
For see beneath this gown of gray
  Thy owne true-love appears.

Here forc'd by grief, and hopeless love,
  These holy weeds I sought;
And here amid these lonely walls
  To end my days I thought.

But haply for my year of grace
  Is not yet past away,
Might I still hope to win thy love,
  No longer would I stay.

Now farewell grief, and welcome joy
  Once more unto my heart:
For since I have found thee, lovely youth,
  We never more will part.

JAMES MACPHERSON

(1736-1758-1796)

The Songs of Selma[1]

ARGUMENT

Address to the evening star. An apostrophe to Fingal and his times. Minona sings before the king the song of the unfortunate Colma; and the bards exhibit other specimens of their poetical talents; according to an annual custom established by the monarchs of the ancient Caledonians.

STAR of descending night! fair is thy light in the west! thou liftest thy unshorn head from thy cloud: thy steps are stately on thy hill. What dost thou behold in the plain? The stormy winds are laid. The murmur of the torrent comes from afar. Roaring waves climb the distant rock. The flies of evening are on their feeble wings; the hum of their course is on the field. What dost thou behold, fair light? But thou dost smile and depart. The waves come with joy around thee: they bathe thy lovely hair. Farewel, thou silent beam! Let the light of Ossian's soul arise!

AND it does arise in its strength! I behold my departed friends.

[1] Published in *Fingal*, 1762. Text of *Poems of Ossian*, 1784.

Their gathering is on Lora, as in the days of other years. Fingal comes like a watry column of mist; his heroes are around: And see the bards of song, grey-haired Ullin! stately Ryno! Alpin, with the tuneful voice! the soft complaint of Minona! How are ye changed, my friends, since the days of Selma's feast? when we contended, like gales of spring, as they fly along the hill, and bend by turns the feebly-whistling grass.

MINONA came forth in her beauty; with down-cast look and tearful eye. Her hair flew slowly on the blast, that rushed unfrequent from the hill. The souls of the heroes were sad when she raised the tuneful voice. Often had they seen the grave of Salgar, the dark dwelling of white-bosomed Colma. Colma left alone on the hill, with all her voice of song! Salgar promised to come: but the night descended around. Hear the voice of Colma, when she sat alone on the hill!

COLMA

IT IS night; I am alone, forlorn on the hill of storms. The wind is heard in the mountain. The torrent pours down the rock. No hut receives me from the rain; forlorn on the hill of winds!

RISE, moon! from behind thy clouds. Stars of the night arise! Lead me, some light, to the place, where my love rests from the chace alone! his bow near him, unstrung: his dogs panting around him. But here I must sit alone, by the rock of the mossy stream. The stream and the wind roar aloud. I hear not the voice of my love! Why delays my Salgar, why the chief of the hill, his promise? Here is the rock, and here the tree! here is the roaring stream! Thou didst promise with night to be here. Ah! whither is my Salgar gone? With thee I would fly, from my father; with thee, from my brother of pride. Our race have long been foes; we are not foes, O Salgar!

CEASE a little while, O wind! stream, be thou silent a while! let my voice be heard around. Let my wanderer hear me! Salgar! it is Colma who calls. Here is the tree, and the rock. Salgar, my love! I am here. Why delayest thou thy coming? Lo! the calm moon comes forth. The flood is bright in the vale. The rocks are grey on the steep. I see him not on the brow. His dogs come not before him, with tidings of his near approach. Here I must sit alone!

WHO lie on the heath beside me? Are they my love and my brother? Speak to me, O my friends! To Colma they give no reply. Speak to me: I am alone! My soul is tormented with fears! Ah! they are dead! Their swords are red from the fight. O my brother! my brother! why hast thou slain my Salgar? why, O Salgar! hast thou slain my brother? Dear were ye both to me! what shall I say in your praise? Thou wert fair on the hill among thousands! he was terrible in fight. Speak to me; hear my voice;

hear me, sons of my love! They are silent; silent for ever! Cold, cold are their breasts of clay! Oh! from the rock on the hill; from the top of the windy steep, speak, ye ghosts of the dead! speak, I will not be afraid! Whither are ye gone to rest? In what cave of the hill shall I find the departed? No feeble voice is on the gale: no answer half-drowned in the storm!

I SIT in my grief! I wait for morning in my tears! Rear the tomb, ye friends of the dead. Close it not till Colma come. My life flies away like a dream: why should I stay behind? Here shall I rest with my friends, by the stream of the sounding rock. When night comes on the hill; when the loud winds arise; my ghost shall stand in the blast, and mourn the death of my friends. The hunter shall hear from his booth. He shall fear but love my voice! For sweet shall my voice be for my friends: pleasant were her friends to Colma!

SUCH was thy song, Minona, softly-blushing daughter of Torman. Our tears descended for Colma, and our souls were sad! Ullin came with his harp; he gave the song of Alpin. The voice of Alpin was pleasant: the soul of Ryno was a beam of fire! But they had rested in the narrow house: their voice had ceased in Selma. Ullin had returned, one day, from the chace, before the heroes fell. He heard their strife on the hill; their song was soft but sad! They mourned the fall of Morar, first of mortal men! His soul was like the soul of Fingal; his sword like the sword of Oscar. But he fell, and his father mourned: his sister's eyes were full of tears. Minona's eyes were full of tears, the sister of carborne Morar. She retired from the song of Ullin, like the moon in the west, when she foresees the shower, and hides her fair head in a cloud. I touched the harp, with Ullin; the song of mourning rose!

RYNO

THE wind and the rain are past: calm is the noon of day. The clouds are divided in heaven. Over the green hills flies the inconstant sun. Red through the stony vale comes down the stream of the hill. Sweet are thy murmurs, O stream! but more sweet is the voice I hear. It is the voice of Alpin, the son of song, mourning for the dead! Bent is his head of age; red his tearful eye. Alpin, thou son of song, why alone on the silent hill? why complainest thou, as a blast in the wood; as a wave on the lonely shore?

ALPIN

MY tears, O Ryno! are for the dead; my voice for those that have passed away. Tall thou art on the hill; fair among the sons of the vale. But thou shalt fall like Morar; the mourner shall sit on thy tomb. The hills shall know thee no more; thy bow shall lie in the hall, unstrung!

THOU wert swift, O Morar! as a roe on the desart; terrible as a meteor of fire. Thy wrath was as the storm. Thy sword in battle, as lightning in the field. Thy voice was a stream after rain; like thunder on distant hills. Many fell by thy arm; they were consumed in the flames of thy wrath. But when thou didst return from war, how peaceful was thy brow! Thy face was like the sun after rain; like the moon in the silence of night; calm as the breast of the lake when the loud wind is laid.

NARROW is thy dwelling now! dark the place of thine abode! With three steps I compass thy grave, O thou who wast so great before! Four stones, with their heads of moss, are the only memorial of thee. A tree with scarce a leaf, long grass, which whistles in the wind, mark to the hunter's eye the grave of the mighty Morar. Morar! thou art low indeed. Thou hast no mother to mourn thee; no maid with her tears of love. Dead is she that brought thee forth. Fallen is the daughter of Morglan.

WHO on his staff is this? who is this, whose head is white with age? whose eyes are red with tears? who quakes at every step? It is thy father, O Morar! the father of no son but thee. He heard of thy fame in war; he heard of foes dispersed. He heard of Morar's renown; why did he not hear of his wound? Weep, thou father of Morar! weep; but thy son heareth thee not. Deep is the sleep of the dead; low their pillow of dust. No more shall he hear thy voice; no more awake at thy call. When shall it be morn in the grave, to bid the slumberer awake? Farewel, thou bravest of men! thou conqueror in the field! but the field shall see thee no more; nor the dark wood be lightened with the splendor of thy steel. Thou hast left no son. The song shall preserve thy name. Future times shall hear of thee; they shall hear of the fallen Morar!

THE grief of all arose, but most the bursting sigh of Armin. He remembers the death of his son, who fell in the days of his youth. Carmor was near the hero, the chief of the echoing Galmal. Why bursts the sigh of Armin, he said? Is there a cause to mourn? The song comes, with its music, to melt and please the soul. It is like soft mist, that, rising from a lake, pours on the silent vale; the green flowers are filled with dew, but the sun returns in his strength, and the mist is gone. Why art thou sad, O Armin! chief of sea-surrounded Gorma?

SAD! I am! nor small is my cause of woe! Carmor, thou hast lost no son; thou hast lost no daughter of beauty. Colgar the valiant lives; and Annira fairest maid. The boughs of thy house ascend, O Carmor! but Armin is the last of his race. Dark is thy bed, O Daura! deep thy sleep in the tomb! When shalt thou awake with thy songs? with all thy voice of music?

ARISE, winds of autumn, arise; blow along the heath! streams of the mountains roar! roar, tempests, in the groves of my oaks! walk through broken clouds, O moon! show thy pale face, at intervals! bring to my mind the night, when all my children fell; when Arindal the mighty fell; when Daura the lovely failed! Daura, my daughter! thou wert fair; fair as the moon on Fura; white as the driven snow; sweet as the breathing gale. Arindal, thy bow was strong. Thy spear was swift in the field. Thy look was like mist on the wave: thy shield, a red cloud in a storm. Armar, renowned in war, came, and sought Daura's love. He was not long refused: fair was the hope of their friends!

ERATH, son of Odgal, repined: his brother had been slain by Armor. He came disguised like a son of the sea: fair was his skiff on the wave; white his locks of age; calm his serious brow. Fairest of women, he said, lovely daughter of Armin! a rock not distant in the sea, bears a tree on its side; red shines the fruit afar! There Armor waits for Daura. I come to carry his love! She went; she called on Armar. Nought answered, but the son of the rock, Armor, my love! my love! why tormentest thou me with fear? hear, son of Arnart, hear: it is Daura who calleth thee! Erath the traitor fled laughing to the land. She lifted up her voice; she called for her brother and her father. Arindal! Armin! none to relieve your Daura!

HER voice came over the sea. Arindal my son descended from the hill; rough in the spoils of the chace. His arrows rattled by his side; his bow was in his hand: five dark grey dogs attend his steps. He saw fierce Erath on the shore: he seized and bound him to an oak. Thick wind the thongs of the hide around his limbs; he loads the wind with his groans. Arindal ascends the deep in his boat, to bring Daura to land. Armar came in his wrath, and let fly the grey-feathered shaft. It sung; it sunk in thy heart, O Arindal my son! for Erath the traitor thou diedst. The oar is stopped at once; he panted on the rock and expired. What is thy grief, O Daura, when round thy feet is poured thy brother's blood! the boat is broken in twain. Armar plunges into the sea, to rescue his Daura, or die. Sudden a blast from the hill came over the waves. He sunk, and he rose no more.

ALONE, on the sea-beat rock, my daughter was heard to complain. Frequent and loud were her cries. What could her father do? All night I stood on the shore. I saw her by the faint beam of the moon. All night I heard her cries. Loud was the wind; the rain beat hard on the hill. Before morning appeared, her voice was weak. It died away, like the evening-breeze among the grass of the rocks. Spent with grief she expired; and left thee Armin alone. Gone is my strength in war! fallen my pride among women! When the storms aloft arise: when the north lifts the wave on high; I sit by the sounding shore, and look on the fatal rock. Often by the setting moon, I see the ghosts of my children. Half-viewless, they walk in mournful conference together. Will none of you speak in pity? They do not regard their father. I am sad, O Carmor, nor small is my cause of woe!

SUCH were the words of the bards in the days of song; when the king heard the music of harps, the tale of other times! The chiefs gathered from all their hills, and heard the lovely sound. They praised the voice of Cona! the first among a thousand bards! But age is now on my tongue; my soul has failed! I hear, at times, the ghosts of bards, and learn their pleasant song. But memory fails on my mind. I hear the call of years! They say, as they pass along, why does Ossian sing? Soon shall he lie in the narrow house, and no bard shall raise his fame! Roll on, ye dark-brown years; ye bring no joy on your course! Let the tomb open to Ossian, for his strength has failed. The sons of song are gone to rest. My voice remains, like a blast, that roars, lonely, on a sea-surrounded rock, after the winds are laid. The dark moss whistles there; the distant mariner sees the waving trees!

AUGUSTUS MONTAGU TOPLADY

(1740-1759-1778)

A Prayer, Living and Dying[1]

ROCK of ages, cleft for me,
Let me hide myself in Thee!
Let the Water and the Blood,
From thy riven Side which flow'd,
Be of sin the double cure;
Cleanse me from it's guilt and pow'r.

Not the labors of my hands
Can fulfill thy Law's demands:
Could my zeal no respite know,
Could my tears for ever flow,
All for sin could not atone:
Thou must save, and Thou alone.

Nothing in my hand I bring;
Simply to thy Cross I cling;
Naked, come to Thee for dress;
Helpless, look to Thee for grace;

[1] Published in *Psalms and Hymns*, 1776. Text of first edition.

Foul, I to the Fountain fly:
Wash me, SAVIOR, or I die!

While I draw this fleeting breath—
When my eye-strings break in death—
When I soar to worlds unknown—
See Thee on thy judgment-throne—
ROCK of ages, cleft for me,
Let me hide myself in Thee!

CHARLES CHURCHILL

(1731-1761-1764)

The Farewell[1]

P. FAREWELL to Europe, and at once farewell
To all the follies which in Europe dwell,
To Eastern India now, a richer clime,
Richer alas in ev'ry thing but Rime,
The Muses steer their course, and, fond of change,
At large, in other worlds, desire to range,
Resolv'd at least, since They the fool must play,
To do it in a diff'rent place, and way.
F. What whim is this, what errour of the brain,
What madness worse than in the dog-star's reign?
Why into foreign countries would You roam,
Are there not knaves and fools enough at home?
If Satire be thy object, and thy lays
As yet have shewn no talents fit for praise,
If Satire be thy object, search all round,
Nor to thy purpose can one spot be found
Like England, where to rampant vigour grown
Vice choaks up ev'ry Virtue, where, self-sown,
The seeds of Folly shoot forth rank and bold,
And ev'ry seed brings forth a hundred fold.
P. No more of this—tho' Truth (the more our shame,
The more our guilt) tho' Truth perhaps may claim,
And justify her part in this, yet here,
For the first time, e'en Truth offends my ear.
Declaim from morn to night, from night to morn,
Take up the theme a new, when day's new-born,

[1] Published in 1764. Text of *Works*, third edition, 1766.

I hear, and hate—be England what She will,
With all her faults She is my Country still.
F. Thy Country, and what then? Is that mere word
Against the voice of Reason to be heard?
Are prejudices, deep imbib'd in youth,
To counter-act, and make thee hate the truth?
'Tis the sure symptom of a narrow soul
To draw its grand attatchment from the whole,
And take up with a part; Men, not confin'd
Within such paltry limits, Men design'd
Their nature to exalt; where'er they go,
Wherever waves can roll, and winds can blow,
Where'er the blessed Sun, plac'd in the sky
To watch this subject world, can dart his eye,
Are still the same, and, prejudice out-grown,
Consider ev'ry country as their own.
At one grand view They take in Nature's plan,
Not more at home in England, than Japan.
P. My good, grave Sir of Theory, whose wit,
Grasping at shadows, ne'er caught substance yet,
'Tis mighty easy o'er a glass of wine
On vain refinements vainly to refine,
To laugh at poverty in plenty's reign,
To boast of Apathy when out of pain,
And in each sentence, worthy of the Schools,
Varnish'd with sophistry, to deal out rules
Most fit for practice, but for one poor fault
That into practice they can ne'er be brought.
At home, and sitting in your elbow-chair
You praise Japan, tho' you was never there.
But was the Ship this moment under sail,
Would not your mind be chang'd, your Spirits fail,
Would you not cast one longing eye to shore,
And vow to deal in such wild schemes no more?
Howe'er our pride may tempt us to conceal
Those passions, which we cannot chuse but feel,
There's a strange Something, which without a brain
Fools feel, and with one wise men can't explain,
Planted in Man, to bind him to that earth,
In dearest ties, from whence he drew his birth.
If Honour calls, where'er She points the way,
The Sons of Honour follow, and obey;
If Need compels, wherever we are sent,
'Tis want of courage not to be content;
But, if we have the liberty of choice,
And all depends on our own single voice,
To deem of ev'ry Country as the same
Is rank rebellion 'gainst the lawful claim

Of Nature, and such dull indifference
May be PHILOSOPHY, but can't be SENSE.
F. Weak and unjust Distinction, strange design,
Most peevish, most perverse, to undermine
PHILOSOPHY, and throw her empire down
By means of SENSE, from whom she holds her crown.
Divine PHILOSOPHY, to Thee we owe
All that is worth possessing here below;
Virtue and Wisdom consecrate thy reign,
Doubled each joy, and Pain no longer Pain.
When, like a Garden, where for want of toil,
And wholesome discipline, the rich, rank soil
Teems with incumbrances, where all around
Herbs noxious in their nature make the Ground,
Like the good Mother of a thankless Son,
Curse her own womb, by fruitfulness undone,
Like such a garden, when the human soul,
Uncultur'd, wild, impatient of controul,
Brings forth those passions of luxuriant race,
Which spread, and stifle ev'ry herb of grace,
Whilst Virtue, check'd by the cold hand of scorn,
Seems with'ring on the bed where she was born,
PHILOSOPHY steps in, with steady hand
She brings her aid, she clears th' encumber'd land,
Too virtuous, to spare vice one stroke, too wise
One moment to attend to Pity's cries,
See with what Godlike, what relentless pow'r
She roots up ev'ry weed
P. and ev'ry flow'r.
PHILOSOPHY, a name of meek degree,
Embrac'd, in token of humility,
By the proud Sage, who, whilst he strove to hide,
In that vain artifice, reveal'd his pride.
PHILOSOPHY, whom Nature had design'd
To purge all errours from the human mind,
Herself misled by the Philosopher,
At once her Priest and Master, made us err;
Pride, Pride, like leaven in a mass of flour,
Tainted her laws, and made e'en Virtue sowre.
Had she, content within her proper sphere,
Taught lessons suited to the human ear,
Which might fair Virtue's genuine fruits produce,
Made not for ornament, but real use,
The heart of Man unrival'd she had sway'd;
Prais'd by the good, and by the bad obey'd.
But when She, overturning Reason's throne,

Strove proudly in its place to plant her own,
When she with Apathy the breast would steel,
And teach us, deeply feeling, not to feel,
When she would wildly all her force employ,
Not to correct our passions, but destroy,
When, not content our nature to restore,
As made by God, she made it all new o'er,
When, with a strange and criminal excess,
To make us more than Men, she made us less,
The Good her dwindled pow'r with pity saw,
The Bad with joy, and none but fools with awe.
  Truth, with a simple and unvarnish'd tale,
E'en from the mouth of N—might prevail,
Could she get there; but Falshood's sugar'd strain
Should pour her fatal Blandishments in vain,
Nor make one convert, tho' the Siren hung,
Where she too often hangs, on M—— tongue.
Should all the SOPHS, whom in his course the Sun
Hath seen, or past or present, rise in One,
Should He, whilst pleasure in each sentence flows,
Like PLATO, give us Poetry in Prose,
Should He, full Orator at once impart
Th' ATHENIAN's Genius, with the ROMAN's Art,
Genius and Art should in this instance fail,
Nor Rome tho' join'd with Athens here prevail.
'Tis not in Man, 'tis not in more than man
To make me find one fault in Nature's plan.
Plac'd low ourselves, we censure those above,
And, wanting judgment, think that She wants love,
Blame, where we ought in reason to commend,
And think her most a foe, when most a friend.
Such be PHILOSOPHERS—their specious art,
Tho' Friendship pleads, shall never warp my heart;
Ne'er make me from this breast one passion tear,
Which Nature, my best friend, hath planted there.
  F. Forgiving as a Friend, what, whilst I live,
As a Philosopher I can't forgive,
In this one point at last I join with You;
To Nature pay all that is Nature's due,
But let not clouded Reason sink so low,
To fancy debts she does not, cannot owe.
Bear, to full Manhood grown, those shackles bear,
Which Nature meant us for a time to wear,
As we wear leading-strings, which, useless grown,
Are laid aside, when we can walk alone.
But on thyself, by peevish humour sway'd,

Wilt thou lay burdens Nature never laid?
Wilt Thou make faults, whilst Judgment weakly errs,
And then defend, mistaking them for her's?
Dar'st Thou to say, in our enlight'ned age,
That this grand Master Passion, this brave rage,
Which flames out for thy country, was imprest,
And fix'd by Nature in the human breast?
If you prefer the place where you was born,
And hold all others in contempt and scorn
On fair Comparison; If on that land
With lib'ral, and a more than equal hand
Her gifts, as in profusion Plenty sends;
If Virtue meets with more and better friends;
If Science finds a Patron 'mongst the great;
If Honesty is Minister of State;
If Pow'r the guardian of our rights design'd,
Is to that great, that only end confin'd;
If Riches are employ'd to bless the poor;
If Law is sacred, Liberty secure;
Let but these facts depend on proofs of weight,
Reason declares, thy Love can't be too great,
And, in this light could he our Country view,
A very HOTTENTOT must love it too.
But if, by Fate's decrees, you owe your birth
To some most barren and penurious earth,
Where, ev'ry comfort of this life denied,
Her real wants are scantily supplied,
Where Pow'r is Reason, Liberty a Joke,
Laws never made, or made but to be broke,
To fix thy love on such a wretched spot
Because, in lust's wild fever, there begot,
Because, thy weight no longer fit to bear,
By chance, not choice, thy Mother dropt thee there,
Is Folly which admits not of defence;
It can't be Nature, for it is not Sense.
By the same argument which here you hold,
(When Falshood's insolent let truth be bold)
If Propagation can in torments dwell,
A Devil must, if born there, love his hell.
P. Had Fate, to whose decrees I lowly bend,
And e'en in punishment confess a friend,
Ordain'd my birth in some place yet untried,
On purpose made to mortify my pride,
Where the Sun never gave one glimpse of day,
Where Science never yet could dart one ray,
Had I been born on some bleak, blasted plain

Of barren Scotland, in a STUART's reign,
Or in some kingdom, where Men, weak or worse,
Turn'd Nature's ev'ry blessing to a curse,
Where crowns of Freedom, by the Fathers won,
Dropp'd leaf by leaf from each degen'rate Son,
In spite of all the wisdom you display,
All you have said, and yet may have to say,
My weakness here, if weakness, I confess,
I, as my country, had not lov'd her less.
Whether strict Reason bears me out in this,
Let those who, always seeking, always miss
The ways of Reason, doubt with precious zeal;
Their's be the praise to argue, mine to feel.
Wish we to trace this passion to the root,
We, like a tree, may know it by its fruit,
From its rich stem ten thousand virtues spring,
Ten thousand blessings on its branches cling,
Yet in the circle of revolving years,
Not one misfortune, not one vice appears.
Hence then, and what you Reason call adore;
This, if not Reason, must be something more.
But (for I wish not others to confine,
Be their opinions unrestrain'd as mine)
Whether this Love's of good, or evil growth,
A Vice, a Virtue, or a spice of both,
Let men of nicer argument decide;
If it is virtuous, sooth an honest pride
With lib'ral praise; if vicious, be content,
It is a Vice I never can repent;
A Vice which, weigh'd in Heav'n, shall more avail
Than ten cold virtues in the other scale.
F. This wild, untemper'd zeal (which after all
We, Candour unimpeach'd, might madness call)
Is it a Virtue? that You scarce pretend;
Or can it be a Vice, like Virtue's friend,
Which draws us off from and dissolves the force
Of private ties, nay, stops us in our course
To that grand object of the human soul,
That nobler Love which comprehends the whole.
Coop'd in the limits of this petty isle,
This nook, which scarce deserves a frown, or smile,
Weigh'd with Creation, You, by whim undone,
Give all your thoughts to what is scarce worth one.
The gen'rous Soul, by Nature taught to soar,
Her strength confirm'd in Philosophic lore,
At one grand view takes in a world with ease,
And, seeing all mankind, loves all she sees.

P. Was it most sure, which yet a doubt endures,
Not found in Reason's Creed, though found in your's
That these two services, like what we're told
And know of God's and Mammon's, cannot hold
And draw together, that, however loth,
We neither serve, attempting to serve both,
I could not doubt a moment which to chuse,
And which in common Reason to refuse.
Invented oft for purposes of Art,
Born of the head, tho' father'd on the heart,
This grand love of the world must be confest
A barren speculation at the best.
Not one Man in a thousand, should he live
Beyond the usual term of life, could give,
So rare Occasion comes, and to so few,
Proof whether his regards are feign'd, or true.
The Love we bear our Country, is a root
Which never fails to bring forth golden fruit,
'Tis in the mind an everlasting Spring
Of glorious actions, which become a King
Nor less become a Subject; 'tis a debt
Which bad Men, tho' they pay not, can't forget;
A duty, which the Good delight to pay,
And ev'ry Man can practice ev'ry day.
Nor, for my life (so very dim my eye,
Or dull your argument) can I descry
What you with faith assert, how that dear love
Which binds me to my Country, can remove
And make me of necessity forego,
That gen'ral love which to the world I owe.
Those ties of private nature, small extent,
In which the mind of narrow cast is pent,
Are only steps on which the gen'rous soul
Mounts by degrees till She includes the whole.
That spring of Love, which in the human mind,
Founded on self, flows narrow and confin'd,
Enlarges as it rolls, and comprehends
The social Charities of blood, and friends,
Till smaller streams included, not o'erpast,
It rises to our Country's love at last,
And He, with lib'ral and enlarged mind,
Who loves his Country, cannot hate mankind.
F. Friend as You would appear to Common Sense,
Tell me, or think no more of a defence,
Is it a proof of love by choice to run
A vagrant from Your country?
P. Can the Son,
(Shame, Shame on all such sons) with ruthless eye,

And heart more patient than the flint, stand by,
And by some ruffian, from all shame divorc'd,
All Virtue, see his honour'd Mother forc'd;
Then, no, by Him that made me, not e'en then,
Could I with patience, by the worst of Men,
Behold my Country plunder'd, beggar'd, lost
Beyond Redemption, all her glories cross'd
E'en when Occasion made them ripe, her fame
Fled like a dream, while She awakes to shame.
F. Is it not more the office of a friend,
The office of a Patron, to defend
Her sinking state, than basely to decline
So great a cause, and in despair resign?
P. Beyond my reach, alas! the grievance lies,
And, whilst more able Patriots doubt, she dies.
From a foul source, more deep than we suppose,
Fatally deep and dark, this grievance flows.
'Tis not that Peace our glorious hopes defeats,
'Tis not the Voice of Faction in the streets,
'Tis not a gross attack on Freedom made,
'Tis not the arm of Privilege display'd
Against the Subject, whilst She wears no sting
To disappoint the purpose of a King,
These are no ills, or trifles, if compar'd
With those, which are contriv'd, tho' not declar'd.
Tell me, Philosopher, is it a crime
To pry into the secret womb of Time,
Or, born in ignorance, must we despair
To reach events, and read the future there?
Why, be it so—still 'tis the right of Man,
Imparted by his Maker, where he can,
To former times and men his eye to cast,
And judge of what's to come, by what is past.
Should there be found in some not distant year
(O how I wish to be no Prophet here)
Amongst our British Lords should there be found
Some great in pow'r, in principles unsound,
Who look on Freedom with an evil eye,
In whom the springs of Loyalty are dry,
Who wish to soar on wild Ambition's wings,
Who hate the Commons, and who love not Kings,
Who would divide the people and the throne
To set up sep'rate int'rests of their own,
Who hate whatever aids their wholsome growth,
And only join with, to destroy them both,
Should there be found such men in after-times,

May Heav'n in mercy to our grievous crimes
Allot some milder vengeance, nor to them,
And to their rage this wretched land condemn.
  Thou God above, on whom all States depend,
Who knowest from the first their rise, and end,
If there's a day mark'd in the book of fate
When ruin must involve our equal state,
When Law alas! must be no more, and we,
To Freedom born, must be no longer free,
Let not a Mob of Tyrants seize the helm,
Nor titled upstarts league to rob the realm,
Let not, whatever other ills assail,
A damned ARISTOCRACY prevail.
If, all too short, our course of Freedom run,
'Tis thy good pleasure we should be undone,
Let us, some comfort in our griefs to bring,
Be slaves to one, and be that one a King.
  F. Poets, accustom'd by their trade to feign,
Oft substitute creations of the brain
For real substance, and, themselves deceiv'd,
Would have the fiction by mankind believ'd.
Such is your case—but grant, to sooth your pride,
That You know more than all the world beside,
Why deal in hints, why make a moment's doubt,
Resolv'd, and like a Man, at once speak out,
Shew us our danger, tell us where it lies,
And, to ensure our safety, make us wise.
  P. Rather than bear the pain of thought, fools stray;
The Proud will rather loose than ask their way;
To men of Sense what needs it to unfold,
And tell a tale which they must know untold?
In the bad, int'rest warps the canker'd heart,
The Good are hood-wink'd by the tricks of art;
And whilst Arch, subtle Hypocrites contrive
To keep the flames of discontent alive,
Whilst They, with arts to honest men unknown,
Breed doubts between the People and the Throne,
Making us fear, where Reason never yet
Allow'd one fear, or could one doubt admit,
Themselves pass unsuspected in disguise,
And 'gainst our real danger seal our eyes.
  F. Mark them, and let their names recorded stand
On shame's black roll, and stink thro' all the land.
  P. That might some Courage, but no Prudence be;
No hurt to them, and jeopardy to me.
  F. Leave out their names.

P. For that kind caution thanks,
But may not Judges sometimes fill up blanks?
F. Your Country's laws in doubt then you reject:
P. The Laws I love, the Lawyers I suspect:
Amongst twelve judges may not One be found,
(On bare, bare possibility I ground
This wholsome doubt) who may Enlarge, Retrench,
Create, and Uncreate, and from the Bench,
With winks, smiles, nods, and such like paltry arts,
May work and worm into a jury's hearts,
Or, baffled there, may, turbulent of soul,
Cramp their high office, and their rights controul,
Who may, tho' Judge, turn Advocate at large,
And deal replies out by the way of charge,
Making Interpretation all the way,
In spite of Facts, his wicked will obey,
And, leaving Law without the least defence,
May damn his Conscience to approve his Sense.
F. Whilst, the true guardians of this charter'd land,
In full and perfect vigour, Juries stand,
A Judge in vain shall awe, cajole, perplex.
P. Suppose I should be tried in MIDDLESEX.
F. To pack a Jury they will never dare.
P. There's no occasion to pack juries there.
F. 'Gainst Prejudice all arguments are weak,
Reason herself without effect must speak.
Fly then thy Country, like a Coward fly,
Renounce her int'rest, and her laws defy.
But why, bewitch'd, to India turn thy eyes?
Cannot our Europe thy vast wrath suffice?
Cannot thy misbegotten Muse lay bare
Her brawny arm, and play the Butcher there?
P. Thy Counsel, taken, what should Satire do?
Where could she find an object that is new?
Those travell'd Youths, whom tender Mothers wean,
And send abroad to see, and to be seen,
With whom, lest they should fornicate, or worse,
A Tutor's sent by way of a dry nurse,
Each of whom just enough of Spirit bears,
To shew our follies, and to bring home their's,
Have made all Europe's vices so well known,
They seem almost as nat'ral as our own.
F. Will India for thy purpose better do?
P. In one respect at least—there's something New.
F. A harmless People, in whom Nature speaks
Free and untainted, 'mongst whom Satire seeks,

But vainly seeks, so simply plain their hearts,
One bosom where to lodge her poison'd darts.
P. From knowledge speak You this, or, doubt on doubt
Weigh'd and resolv'd, hath Reason found it out?
Neither from knowledge, nor by Reason taught,
You have Faith ev'ry where but where You ought.
India or Europe—What's there in a name?
Propensity to vice in both the same,
Nature alike in both works for Man's good,
Alike in both by Man himself withstood.
Nabobs, as well as those who hunt them down,
Deserve a cord much better than a crown,
And a Mogul can thrones as much debase
As any polish'd Prince of Christian race.
F. Could You, a task more hard than You suppose,
Could You, in ridicule whilst Satire glows,
Make all their follies to the life appear,
'Tis ten to one You gain no credit here.
Howe'er well-drawn, the Picture after all,
Because we know not the Original,
Would not find favour in the public eye.
P. That, having your good leave, I mean to try.
And if Your observations sterling hold,
If the Piece should be heavy, tame, and cold,
To make it to the side of Nature lean,
And, meaning nothing, something seem to mean,
To make the whole in lively colours glow,
To bring before us something that we know,
And from all honest men applause to win,
I'll group the Company, and put them in.
F. Be that ungen'rous thought by shame suppress'd,
Add not distress to those too much distress'd.
Have They not, by blind Zeal misled, laid bare
Those sores which never might endure the air?
Have They not brought their mysteries so low
That what the Wise suspected not, Fools know?
From their first rise e'en to the present hour
Have They not prov'd their own abuse of pow'r,
Made it impossible, if fairly view'd,
Ever to have that dang'rous pow'r renew'd,
Whilst, unseduc'd by Ministers, the throne
Regards our Interest, and knows its own.
P. Should ev'ry other subject chance to fail,
Those who have sail'd, and those who wish'd to sail
In the last Fleet, afford an ample field
Which must beyond my hopes a harvest yield.
F. On such vile food Satire can never thrive,
P. She cannot starve, if there was only Clive.

JAMES BEATTIE

(1735-1761-1803)

The Minstrel; or, The Progress of Genius[1]

The First Book

I.

AH! WHO can tell how hard it is to climb
The steep where Fame's proud temple shines afar!
Ah! who can tell how many a soul sublime
Hath felt the influence of malignant star,
And waged with Fortune an eternal war!
Check'd by the scoff of Pride, by Envy's frown,
And Poverty's unconquerable bar,
In life's low vale remote hath pined alone
Then dropt into the grave, unpitied and unknown!

II.

And yet, the languor of inglorious days
Not equally oppressive is to all.
Him, who ne'er listen'd to the voice of praise,
The silence of neglect can ne'er appal.
There are, who, deaf to mad Ambition's call,
Would shrink to hear th' obstreperous trump of Fame;
Supremely blest, if to their portion fall
Health, competence, and peace. Nor higher aim
Had HE, whose simple tale these artless lines proclaim.

III.

This sapient age disclaims all classic lore;
Else I should here in cunning phrase display,
How forth THE MINSTREL fared in days of yore,
Right glad of heart, though homely in array;
His waving locks and beard all hoary grey:
And, from his bending shoulder, decent hung
His harp, the sole companion of his way,
Which to the whistling wind responsive rung:
And ever as he went some merry lay he sung.

[1] Published in 1771. Text of fourth edition, 1774.

IV.

Fret not yourselves, ye silken sons of pride,
That a poor Wanderer should inspire my strain.
The Muses fortune's fickle smile deride,
Nor ever bow the knee in Mammon's fane;
For their delights are with the village-train,
Whom Nature's laws engage, and Nature's charms:
They hate the sensual, and scorn the vain;
The parasite their influence never warms,
Nor him whose sordid soul the love of wealth alarms.

V.

Though richest hues the peacock's plumes adorn,
Yet horror screams from his discordant throat.
Rise, sons of harmony, and hail the morn,
While warbling larks on russet pinions float;
Or seek at noon the woodland scene remote,
Where the grey linnets carol from the hill.
O let them ne'er with artificial note,
To please a tyrant, strain the little bill,
But sing what heaven inspires, and wander where they will.

VI.

Liberal, not lavish, is kind Nature's hand;
Nor was perfection made for man below.
Yet all her schemes with nicest art are plann'd,
Good counteracting ill, and gladness wo.
With gold and gems if Chilian mountains glow,
If bleak and barren Scotia's hills arise;
There plague and poison, lust and rapine grow;
Here peaceful are the vales, and pure the skies,
And freedom fires the soul, and sparkles in the eyes.

VII.

Then grieve not, thou to whom th' indulgent Muse
Vouchsafes a portion of celestial fire;
Nor blame the partial Fates, if they refuse
Th' imperial banquet, and the rich attire.
Know thine own worth, and reverence the lyre.
Wilt thou debase the heart which God refined?
No; let thy heaven-taught soul to heaven aspire,
To fancy, freedom, harmony, resign'd;
Ambition's groveling crew for ever left behind.

VIII.

Canst thou forego the pure ethereal soul
In each fine sense so exquisitely keen,
On the dull couch of Luxury to loll,
Stung with disease, and stupefied with spleen;
Fain to implore the aid of Flattery's screen,
Even from thyself thy loathsome heart to hide,
(The mansion then no more of joy serene),
Where fear, distrust, malevolence, abide,
And impotent desire, and disappointed pride?

IX.

O how canst thou renounce the boundless store
Of charms which Nature to her votary yields!
The warbling woodland, the resounding shore,
The pomp of groves, and garniture of fields;
All that the genial ray of morning gilds,
And all that echoes to the song of even,
All that the mountain's sheltering bosom shields,
And all the dread magnificence of heaven,
O how canst thou renounce, and hope to be forgiven!

X.

These charms shall work thy soul's eternal health,
And love, and gentleness, and joy, impart.
But these thou must renounce, if lust of wealth
E'er win its way to thy corrupted heart;
For, ah! it poisons like a scorpion's dart;
Prompting th' ungenerous wish, the selfish scheme,
The stern resolve unmoved by pity's smart,
The troublous day, and long distressful dream.—
Return, my roving Muse, resume they purposed theme.

XI.

There lived in Gothic days, as legends tell,
A shepherd-swain, a man of low degree;
Whose sires, perchance, in Fairyland might dwell,
Sicilian groves, or vales of Arcady;
But he, I ween, was of the north countrie:
A nation famed for song, and beauty's charms;
Zealous, yet modest; innocent, though free;
Patient of toil; serene amidst alarms;
Inflexible in faith; invincible in arms.

XII.

The shepherd-swain of whom I mention made,
On Scotia's mountains fed his little flock;
The sickle, scythe, or plough, he never sway'd;
An honest heart was almost all his stock;
His drink the living water from the rock:
The milky dams supplied his board, and lent
Their kindly fleece to baffle winter's shock;
And he, though oft with dust and sweat besprent,
Did guide and guard their wanderings, wheresoe'er they went.

XIII.

From labour health, from health contentment springs.
Contentment opes the source of every joy.
He envied not, he never thought of kings;
Nor from those appetites sustain'd annoy,
Which chance may frustrate, or indulgence cloy:
Nor Fate his calm and humble hopes beguiled;
He mourn'd no recreant friend, nor mistress coy,
For on his vows the blameless Phebe smiled,
And her alone he loved, and loved her from a child.

XIV.

No jealousy their dawn of love o'ercast,
Nor blasted were their wedded days with strife;
Each season look'd delightful, as it past,
To the fond husband, and the faithful wife.
Beyond the lowly vale of shepherd life
They never roam'd; secure beneath the storm
Which in Ambition's lofty land is rife,
Where peace and love are canker'd by the worm
Of pride, each bud of joy industrious to deform.

XV.

The wight whose tale these artless lines unfold,
Was all the offspring of this simple pair.
His birth no oracle or seer foretold:
No prodigy appear'd in earth or air,
Nor aught that might a strange event declare.
You guess each circumstance of EDWIN's birth;
The parent's transport, and the parent's care;
The gossip's prayer for wealth, and wit, and worth;
And one long summer-day of indolence and mirth.

XVI.

And yet poor Edwin was no vulgar boy;
Deep thought oft seem'd to fix his infant eye,
Dainties he heeded not, nor gaude, nor toy,
Save one short pipe of rudest minstrelsy.
Silent when glad; affectionate, though shy;
And now his look was most demurely sad,
And now he laugh'd aloud, yet none knew why.
The neighbours stared and sigh'd, yet bless'd the lad:
Some deem'd him wondrous wise, and some believed him mad.

XVII.

But why should I his childish feats display?
Concourse, and noise, and toil, he ever fled;
Nor cared to mingle in the clamorous fray
Of squabbling imps; but to the forest sped,
Or roam'd at large the lonely mountain's head;
Or, where the maze of some bewilder'd stream
To deep untrodden groves his footsteps led,
There would he wander wild, 'till Phebus' beam,
Shot from the western cliff, released the weary team.

XVIII.

Th' exploit of strength, dexterity, or speed,
To him nor vanity nor joy could bring.
His heart, from cruel sport estranged, would bleed
To work the wo of any living thing,
By trap, or net; by arrow, or by sling;
These he detested, those he scorn'd to wield:
He wish'd to be the guardian, not the king,
Tyrant far less, or traitor of the field.
And sure the sylvan reign unbloody joy might yield.

XIX.

Lo! where the stripling, wrapt in wonder, roves
Beneath the precipice o'erhung with pine;
And sees, on high, amidst th' encircling groves,
From cliff to cliff the foaming torrents shine:
While waters, woods, and winds, in concert join,
And Echo swells the chorus to the skies.
Would Edwin this majestic scene resign
For aught the huntsman's puny craft supplies?
Ah! no: he better knows great Nature's charms to prize.

XX.

And oft he traced the uplands, to survey,
When o'er the sky advanced the kindling dawn,
The crimson cloud, blue main, and mountain grey,
And lake, dim-gleaming on the smoky lawn;
Far to the west the long long vale withdrawn,
Where twilight loves to linger for a while;
And now he faintly kens the bounding fawn,
And villager abroad at early toil.—
But, lo! the sun appears! and heaven, earth, ocean, smile.

XXI.

And oft the craggy cliff he loved to climb,
When all in mist the world below was lost.
What dreadful pleasure! there to stand sublime,
Like shipwreck'd mariner on desert coast,
And view th' enormous waste of vapour, tost
In billows, lengthening to th' horizon round,
Now scoop'd in gulfs, with mountains now emboss'd!
And hear the voice of mirth and song rebound,
Flocks, herds, and waterfalls, along the hoar profound!

XXII.

In truth he was a strange and wayward wight,
Fond of each gentle, and each dreadful scene.
In darkness, and in storm, he found delight:
Nor less, than when on ocean-wave serene
The southern sun diffused his dazzling shene.
Even sad vicissitude amused his soul:
And if a sigh would sometimes intervene,
And down his cheek a tear of pity roll,
A sigh, a tear, so sweet, he wish'd not to control.

XXIII.

"O ye wild groves, O where is now your bloom!"
(The Muse interprets thus his tender thought.)
"Your flowers, your verdure, and your balmy gloom,
"Of late so grateful in the hour of drought!
"Why do the birds, that song and rapture brought
"To all your bowers, their mansions now forsake?
"Ah! why hath fickle chance this ruin wrought?
"For now the storm howls mournful through the brake,
"And the dead foliage flies in many a shapeless flake.

XXIV.

"Where now the rill, melodious, pure, and cool,
"And meads, with life, and mirth, and beauty, crown'd!
"Ah! see, th' unsightly slime, and sluggish pool,
"Have all the solitary vale imbrown'd;
"Fled each fair form, and mute each melting sound.
"The raven croaks forlorn on naked spray;
"And, hark! the river, bursting every mound,
"Down the vale thunders; and, with wasteful sway,
"Uproots the grove, and rolls the shatter'd rocks away.

XXV.

"Yet such the destiny of all on earth:
"So flourishes and fades majestic man.
"Fair is the bud his vernal morn brings forth,
"And fostering gales a while the nursling fan.
"O smile, ye heavens, serene; ye mildews wan,
"Ye blighting whirlwinds, spare his balmy prime,
"Nor lessen of his life the little span.
"Born on the swift, though silent, wings of Time,
"Old-age comes on apace to ravage all the clime.

XXVI.

"And be it so. Let those deplore their doom,
"Whose hope still grovels in this dark sojourn.
"But lofty souls, who look beyond the tomb,
"Can smile at Fate, and wonder how they mourn.
"Shall spring to these sad scenes no more return?
"Is yonder wave the sun's eternal bed?—
"Soon shall the orient with new lustre burn,
"And spring shall soon her vital influence shed,
"Again attune the grove, again adorn the mead.

XXVII.

"Shall I be left abandon'd in the dust,
"When Fate, relenting, lets the flower revive?
"Shall Nature's voice, to man alone unjust,
"Bid him, though doom'd to perish, hope to live?
"Is it for this fair Virtue oft must strive
"With disappointment, penury, and pain?—
"No: Heaven's immortal spring shall yet arrive;
"And man's majestic beauty bloom again,
"Bright through th' eternal year of Love's triumphant reign."

XXVIII.

This truth sublime his simple sire had taught.
In sooth, 'twas almost all the shepherd knew.
No subtle nor superfluous lore he sought,
Nor ever wish'd his Edwin to pursue.
"Let man's own sphere (quoth he) confine his view,
"Be man's peculiar work his sole delight."
And much, and oft, he warn'd him, to eschew
Falsehood and guile, and aye maintain the right,
By pleasure unseduced, unawed by lawless might.

XXIX.

"And, from the prayer of Want, and plaint of Wo,
"O never, never turn away thine ear.
"Forlorn, in this bleak wilderness below,
"Ah! what were man, should Heaven refuse to hear!
"To others do (the law is not severe)
"What to thyself thou wishest to be done.
"Forgive thy foes; and love thy parents dear,
"And friends, and native land; nor those alone;
"All human weal and wo learn thou to make thine own."

XXX.

See, in the rear of the warm sunny shower,
The visionary boy from shelter fly!
For now the storm of summer-rain is o'er,
And cool, and fresh, and fragrant, is the sky.
And, lo! in the dark east, expanded high,
The rainbow brightens to the setting sun!
Fond fool, that deem'st the streaming glory nigh,
How vain the chace thine ardour has begun!
'Tis fled afar, ere half thy purposed race be run.

XXXI.

Yet couldst thou learn, that thus it fares with age,
When pleasure, wealth, or power, the bosom warm,
This baffled hope might tame thy manhood's rage,
And Disappointment of her sting disarm.—
But why should foresight thy fond heart alarm?
Perish the lore that deadens young desire!
Pursue, poor imp, th' imaginary charm,
Indulge gay Hope, and Fancy's pleasing fire:
Fancy and Hope too soon shall of themselves expire.

XXXII.

When the long-sounding curfew from afar
Loaded with loud lament the lonely gale,
Young Edwin, lighted by the evening star,
Lingering and listening, wander'd down the vale.
There would he dream of graves, and corses pale;
And ghosts, that to the charnel-dungeon throng,
And drag a length of clanking chain, and wail,
Till silenced by the owl's terrific song,
Or blast that shrieks by fits the shuddering isles along.

XXXIII.

Or, when the setting moon, in crimson dyed,
Hung o'er the dark and melancholy deep,
To haunted stream, remote from man, he hied,
Where Fays of yore their revels wont to keep;
And there let Fancy roam at large, till sleep
A vision brought to his intranced sight.
And first, a wildly-murmuring wind 'gan creep
Shrill to his ringing ear; then tapers bright,
With instantaneous gleam, illumed the vault of Night.

XXXIV.

Anon in view a portal's blazon'd arch
Arose; the trumpet bids the valves unfold;
And forth an host of little warriors march,
Grasping the diamond lance, and targe of gold.
Their look was gentle, their demeanour bold,
And green their helms, and green their silk attire;
And here and there, right venerably old,
The long-robed minstrels wake the warbling wire,
And some with mellow breath the martial pipe inspire.

XXXV.

With merriment, and song, and timbrels clear,
A troop of dames from myrtle bowers advance;
The little warriors doff the targe and spear,
And loud enlivening strains provoke the dance.
They meet, they dart away, they wheel askance;
To right, to left, they thrid the flying maze;
Now bound aloft with vigorous spring, then glance
Rapid along: with many-colour'd rays
Of tapers, gems, and gold, the echoing forests blaze.

XXXVI.

The dream is fled. Proud harbinger of day,
Who scaredst the vision with thy clarion shrill,
Fell chanticleer! who oft hast reft away
My fancied good, and brought substantial ill!
O to thy cursed scream, discordant still,
Let Harmony aye shut her gentle ear:
Thy boastful mirth let jealous rivals spill,
Insult thy crest, and glossy pinions tear,
And ever in thy dreams the ruthless fox appear.

XXXVII.

Forbear, my Muse. Let Love attune thy line.
Revoke the spell. Thine Edwin frets not so.
For how should he at wicked chance repine,
Who feels from every change amusement flow?
Even now his eyes with smiles of rapture glow,
As on he wanders through the scenes of morn,
Where the fresh flowers in living lustre blow,
Where thousand pearls the dewy lawns adorn,
A thousand notes of joy in every breeze are born.

XXXVIII.

But who the melodies of morn can tell?
The wild brook babbling down the mountain-side;
The lowing herd; the sheepfold's simple bell;
The pipe of early shepherd dim descried
In the lone valley; echoing far and wide
The clamorous horn along the cliffs above;
The hollow murmur of the ocean-tide;
The hum of bees, and linnet's lay of love,
And the full choir that wakes the universal grove.

XXXIX.

The cottage-curs at early pilgrim bark;
Crown'd with her pail the tripping milkmaid sings;
The whistling plowman stalks afield; and, hark!
Down the rough slope the ponderous waggon rings;
Through rustling corn the hare astonish'd springs;
Slow tolls the village-clock the drowsy hour;
The partridge bursts away on whirring wings;
Deep mourns the turtle in sequester'd bower,
And shrill lark carols clear from her aereal tour.

XL.

O Nature, how in every charm supreme!
Whose votaries feast on raptures ever new!
O for the voice and fire of seraphim,
To sing thy glories with devotion due!
Blest be the day I scap'd the wrangling crew,
From Pyrrho's maze, and Epicurus' sty;
And held high converse with the godlike few,
Who to th' enraptured heart, and ear, and eye,
Teach beauty, virtue, truth, and love, and melody.

XLI.

Hence! ye, who snare and stupefy the mind,
Sophists, of beauty, virtue, joy, the bane!
Greedy and fell, though impotent and blind,
Who spread your filthy nets in Truth's fair fane,
And ever ply your venom'd fangs amain!
Hence to dark Error's den, whose rankling slime
First gave you form! hence! lest the Muse should deign,
(Though loth on theme so mean to waste a rhyme),
With vengeance to pursue your sacrilegious crime.

XLII.

But hail, ye mighty masters of the lay,
Nature's true sons, the friends of man and truth!
Whose song, sublimely sweet, serenely gay,
Amused my childhood, and inform'd my youth.
O let your spirit still my bosom sooth,
Inspire my dreams, and my wild wanderings guide.
Your voice each rugged path of life can smooth;
For well I know, where-ever ye reside,
There harmony, and peace, and innocence, abide.

XLIII.

Ah me! abandon'd on the lonesome plain,
As yet poor Edwin never knew your lore,
Save when against the winter's drenching rain,
And driving snow, the cottage shut the door.
Then, as instructed by tradition hoar,
Her legends when the Beldam 'gan impart,
Or chant the old heroic ditty o'er,
Wonder and joy ran thrilling to his heart;
Much he the tale admired, but more the tuneful art.

XLIV.

Various and strange was the long-winded tale;
And halls, and knights, and feats of arms, display'd;
Or merry swains, who quaff the nut-brown ale,
And sing, enamour'd of the nut-brown maid;
The moonlight-revel of the fairy glade;
Or hags, that suckle an infernal brood,
And ply in caves th' unutterable trade,
'Midst fiends and spectres, quench the moon in blood,
Yell in the midnight storm, or ride th' infuriate flood.

XLV.

But when to horror his amazement rose,
A gentler strain the Beldam would rehearse,
A tale of rural life, a tale of woes,
The orphan-babes, and guardian uncle fierce.
O cruel! will no pang of pity pierce
That heart by lust of lucre sear'd to stone!
For sure, if aught of virtue last, or verse,
To latest times shall tender souls bemoan
Those helpless orphan-babes by thy fell arts undone.

XLVI.

Behold, with berries smear'd, with brambles torn,
The babes now famish'd lay them down to die,
'Midst the wild howl of darksome woods forlorn,
Folded in one another's arms they lie;
Nor friend, nor stranger, hears their dying cry:
"For from the town the man returns no more."
But thou, who Heaven's just vengeance darest defy,
This deed with fruitless tears shalt soon deplore,
When Death lays waste thy house, and flames consume thy store.

XLVII.

A stifled smile of stern vindictive joy
Brighten'd one moment Edwin's starting tear.—
"But why should gold man's feeble mind decoy,
"And Innocence thus die by doom severe?"
O Edwin, while thy heart is yet sincere,
Th' assaults of discontent and doubt repel:
Dark even at noontide is our mortal sphere;
But let us hope,—to doubt, is to rebel,—
Let us exult in hope, that all shall yet be well.

XLVIII.

Nor be thy generous indignation check'd,
Nor check'd the tender tear to Misery given;
From Guilt's contagious power shall that protect,
This soften and refine the soul for heaven.
But dreadful is their doom, whom doubt hath driven
To censure Fate, and pious hope forego;
Like yonder blasted boughs by lightning riven,
Perfection, beauty, life, they never know,
But frown on all that pass, a monument of wo.

XLIX.

Shall he, whose birth, maturity, and age,
Scarce fill the circle of one summer-day,
Shall the poor gnat with discontent and rage
Exclaim, that Nature hastens to decay,
If but a cloud obstruct the solar ray,
If but a momentary shower descend!
Or shall frail man Heaven's dread decree gainsay,
Which bade the series of events extend
Wide through unnumber'd worlds, and ages without end!

L.

One part, one little part, we dimly scan
Through the dark medium of life's feverish dream;
Yet dare arraign the whole stupendous plan,
If but that little part incongruous seem.
Nor is that part perhaps what mortals deem;
Oft from apparent ill our blessings rise.
O then renounce that impious self-esteem,
That aims to trace the secrets of the skies:
For thou art but of dust; be humble, and be wise.

LI.

Thus Heaven enlarged his soul in riper years.
For Nature gave him strength, and fire, to soar,
On Fancy's wing, above this vale of tears;
Where dark cold-hearted sceptics, creeping, pore
Through microscope of metaphysic lore:
And much they grope for truth, but never hit.
For why? their powers, inadequate before,
This art preposterous renders more unfit;
Yet deem they darkness light, and their vain blunders wit.

LII.

Nor was this ancient dame a foe to mirth.
Her ballad, jest, and riddle's quaint device
Oft chear'd the shepherds round their social hearth;
Whom levity or spleen could ne'er entice
To purchase chat or laughter at the price
Of decency. Nor let it faith exceed,
That Nature forms a rustic taste so nice.—
Ah! had they been of court or city breed,
Such delicacy were right marvellous indeed.

LIII.

Oft when the winter-storm had ceas'd to rave,
He roam'd the snowy waste at even, to view,
The cloud stupendous, from th' Atlantic wave
High-towering, sail along th' horizon blue:
Where midst the changeful scenery ever new
Fancy a thousand wondrous forms descries
More wildly great than ever pencil drew,
Rocks, torrents, gulfs, and shapes of giant size,
And glittering cliffs on cliffs, and fiery ramparts rise.

LIV.

Thence musing onward to the sounding shore,
The lone enthusiast oft would take his way,
Listening with pleasing dread to the deep roar
Of the wide-weltering waves. In black array
When sulphurous clouds roll'd on the vernal day,
Even then he hasten'd from the haunt of man,
Along the darkening wilderness to stray,
What time the lightning's fierce career began,
And o'er heaven's rending arch the rattling thunder ran.

LV.

Responsive to the sprightly pipe when all
In sprightly dance the village-youth were join'd,
Edwin, of melody aye held in thrall,
From the rude gambol far remote reclined,
Sooth'd with the soft notes warbling in the wind.
Ah then, all jollity seem'd noise and folly.
To the pure soul by Fancy's fire refined
Ah what is mirth, but turbulence unholy,
When with the charm compared of heavenly melancholy!

LVI.

Is there a heart that music cannot melt?
Ah me! how is that rugged heart forlorn!
Is there, who ne'er those mystic transports felt
Of solitude and melancholy born?
He needs not woo the Muse; he is her scorn.
The sophist's rope of cobweb he shall twine;
Mope o'er the schoolman's peevish page; or mourn,
And delve for life, in Mammon's dirty mine;
Sneak with the scoundrel fox, or grunt with glutton swine.

LVII.

For Edwin Fate a nobler doom had plann'd;
Song was his favourite and first pursuit.
The wild harp rang to his adventurous hand,
And languish'd to his breath the plaintive flute.
His infant muse, though artless, was not mute:
Of elegance as yet he took no care;
For this of time and culture is the fruit;
And Edwin gain'd at last this fruit so rare:
As in some future verse I purpose to declare.

LVIII.

Meanwhile, whate'er of beautiful, or new,
Sublime, or dreadful, in earth, sea, or sky,
By chance, or search, was offer'd to his view,
He scann'd with curious and romantic eye.
Whate'er of lore tradition could supply
From Gothic tale, or song, or fable old,
Rous'd him, still keen to listen and to pry.
At last, though long by penury control'd,
And solitude, his soul her graces 'gan unfold.

LIX.

Thus on the chill Lapponian's dreary land,
For many a long month lost in snow profound,
When Sol from Cancer sends the season bland,
And in their northern cave the storms hath bound;
From silent mountains, straight, with startling sound,
Torrents are hurl'd; green hills emerge; and lo,
The trees with foliage, cliffs with flowers are crown'd;
Pure rills through vales of verdure warbling go;
And wonder, love, and joy, the peasant's heart o'erflow.

LX.

Here pause, my Gothic lyre, a little while,
The leisure hour is all that thou canst claim.
But if ***** on this labour smile,
New strains erelong shall animate thy frame.
And his applause to me is more than fame;
For still with truth accords his taste refined.
At lucre or renown let others aim,
I only wish to please the gentle mind,
Whom Nature's charms inspire, and love of humankind.

WILLIAM JULIUS MICKLE

(1735-1761-1788)

Cumnor Hall[1]

THE dews of summer nighte did falle,
The moone (sweete regente of the skye)
Silver'd the walles of Cumnor Halle,
And manye an oake that grewe therebye.

Nowe noughte was hearde beneath the skies,
(The soundes of busye lyfe were stille,)
Save an unhappie ladie's sighes,
That issued from that lonelye pile.

'Leicester,' shee cried, 'is thys thy love
'That thou so oft has sworne to mee,
'To leave mee in thys lonelye grove,
'Immurr'd in shameful privitie?

'No more thou com'st with lover's speede,
'Thy once-beloved bryde to see;
'But bee shee alive, or bee shee deade,
'I feare (sterne earle's) the same to thee.

'Not so the usage I receiv'd,
'When happye in my father's halle;
'No faithlesse husbande then me griev'd,
'No chilling feares did mee appall.

[1] Published in Evans's *Old Ballads*, Volume IV, 1784. Text of first edition.

'I rose up with the chearful morne,
'No lark more blith, no flow'r more gaye;
'And, like the birde that hauntes the thorne,
'So merrylie sung the live-long daye.

'If that my beautye is but smalle,
'Among court ladies all despis'd;
'Why didst thou rend it from that halle,
'Where (scorneful earle) it well was priz'de?

'And when you first to mee made suite,
'How fayre I was you oft would saye!
'And, proude of conquest—pluck'd the fruite,
'Then lefte the blossom to decaye.

'Yes, nowe neglected and despis'd,
'The rose is pale—the lilly's deade—
'But hee that once their charmes so priz'd,
'Is sure the cause those charms are fledde.

'For knowe, when sick'ning griefe doth preye
'And tender love's repay'd with scorne,
'The sweetest beautye will decaye—
'What flow'ret can endure the storme?

'At court I'm tolde is beauty's throne,
'Where everye lady's passing rare;
'That eastern flow'rs, that shame the sun,
'Are not so glowing, not soe fayre.

'Then, earle, why didst thou leave the bedds
'Where roses and where lillys vie,
'To seek a primrose, whose pale shades
'Must sicken—when those gaudes are bye?

''Mong rural beauties I was one,
'Among the fields wild flow'rs are faire;
'Some countrye swayne might mee have won,
'And thoughte my beautie passing rare.

'But, Leicester, (or I much am wronge)
'Or tis not beautye lures thy vowes;
'Rather ambition's gilded crowne
'Makes thee forget thy humble spouse.

'Then, Leicester, why, again I pleade,
'(The injur'd surelye may repyne,)

'Why didst thou wed a countrye mayde,
'When some fayre princesse might be thyne?

'Why didst thou praise my humble charmes,
'And, oh! then leave them to decaye?
'Why didst thou win me to thy armes,
'Then leave me to mourne the live-long daye?

'The village maidens of the plaine
'Salute me lowly as they goe;
'Envious they marke my silken trayne,
'Nor thinke a countesse can have woe.

'The simple nymphs! they little knowe,
'How farre more happy's their estate—
'—To smile for joye—than sigh for woe—
'—To be contente—than to be greate.

'Howe farre lesse bleste am I than them?
'Dailye to pyne and waste with care!
'Like the poore plante, that from its stem
'Divided—feeles the chilling ayre.

'Nor (cruel earl!) can I enjoye
'The humble charmes of solitude;
'Your minions proude my peace destroye,
'By sullen frownes or pratings rude.

'Laste nyghte, as sad I chanc'd to straye,
'The village deathe-bell smote my eare;
'They wink'd asyde, and seem'd to saye,
'Countesse, prepare—thy end is neare.

'And nowe, while happye peasantes sleepe,
'Here I set lonelye and forlorne;
'No one to soothe mee as I weepe,
'Save phylomel on yonder thorne.

'My spirits flag—my hopes decaye—
'Still that dreade deathe-bell smites my eare;
'And many a boding seems to saye,
'Countess, prepare—thy end is neare.'

Thus sore and sad that ladie griev'd,
In Cumnor Halle so lone and dreare;
And manye a heartefelte sighe shee heav'd,
And let falle manye a bitter teare.

And ere the dawne of daye appear'd,
  In Cumnor Hall so lone and dreare,
Full manye a piercing screame was hearde,
  And manye a crye of mortal feare.

The death-belle thrice was hearde to ring,
  An aërial voyce was hearde to call,
And thrice the raven flapp'd its wyng
  Arounde the tow'rs of Cumnor Hall.

The mastiffe howl'd at village doore,
  The oaks were shatter'd on the greene;
Woe was the houre—for never more
  That haplesse countesse e'er was seene.

And in that manor now no more
  Is chearful feaste and sprightly balle;
For ever since that dbearye houre
  Have spirits haunted Cumnor Hall.

The village maides, with fearful glance,
  Avoid the antient mossgrowne walle;
Nor ever leade the merrye dance,
  Among the groves of Cumnor Halle.

Full manye a travellor oft hath sigh'd,
  And pensive wepte the countess' falle,
As wand'ring onwards they've espied
  The haunted tow'rs of Cumnor Halle.

THOMAS CHATTERTON

(1752-1763-1770)

Bristowe Tragedie: or, The Dethe of Syr Charles Bawdin[1]

THE featherd songster chaunticleer
  Han wounde hys bugle horne,
And tolde the earlie villager
  The commynge of the morne:

[1] Published in 1772. Text of *Poems*, ed. Tyrwhitt, third edition, 1778.

Kynge EDWARDE sawe the ruddie streakes
  Of lyghte eclypse the greie;
And herde the raven's crokynge throte
  Proclayme the fated daie.

"Thou'rt ryght," quod hee, "for, by the Godde
  "That syttes enthron'd on hyghe!
"CHARLES BAWDIN, and hys fellowes twaine,
  "To-daie shall surelie die."

Thenne wythe a jugge of nappy ale
  Hys Knyghtes dydd onne hymm waite;
"Goe tell the traytour, thatt to-daie
  "Hee leaves thys mortall state."

Syr CANTERLONE thenne bendedd lowe,
  Wythe harte brymm-fulle of woe;
Hee journey'd to the castle-gate,
  And to Syr CHARLES dydd goe.

Butt whenne hee came, hys children twaine,
  And eke hys lovynge wyfe,
Wythe brinie tears dydd wett the floore,
  For goode Syr CHARLESES lyfe.

"O goode Syr CHARLES!" sayd CANTERLONE,
  "Badde tydyngs I doe brynge."
"Speke boldlie, manne," sayd brave Syr CHARLES,
  "Whatte says thie traytor kynge?"

"I greeve to telle, before yonne sonne
  "Does fromme the welkinn flye,
"Hee hath uponne hys honour sworne,
  "Thatt thou shalt surelie die."

"Wee all must die," quod brave Syr CHARLES;
  "Of thatte I'm not affearde;
"Whatte bootes to lyve a little space?
  "Thanke JESU, I'm prepar'd:

"Butt telle thye kynge, for myne hee's not,
  "I'de sooner die to-daie
"Thanne lyve hys slave, as manie are,
  "Tho' I shoulde lyve for aie."

Thenne CANTERLONE hee dydd goe out,
  To telle the maior straite

To gett all thynges ynne reddyness
  For goode Syr CHARLESES fate.

Thenne Maisterr CANYNGE saughte the kynge,
  And felle down onne hys knee;
"I'm come," quod hee, "unto your grace
  "To move your clemencye."

Thenne quod the kynge, "Youre tale speke out,
  "You have been much oure friende;
"Whatever youre request may bee,
  "Wee wylle to ytte attende."

"My nobile leige! alle my request
  "Ys for a nobile knyghte,
"Who, tho' may hap hee has donne wronge,
  "He thoghte ytte stylle was ryghte:

"Hee has a spouse and children twaine,
  "Alle rewyn'd are for aie;
"Yff thatt you are resolv'd to lett
  "CHARLES BAWDIN die to-daie."

"Speke nott of such a traytour vile,"
  The kynge ynne furie sayde;
"Before the evening starre doth sheene,
  "BAWDIN shall loose hys hedde:

"Justice does loudlie for hym calle,
  "And hee shalle have hys meede:
"Speke, Maister CANYNGE! Whatte thynge else
  "Att present doe you neede?"

"My nobile leige!" goode CANYNGE sayde,
  "Leave justice to our Godde,
"And laye the yronne rule asyde;
  "Be thyne the olyve rodde.

"Was Godde to serche our hertes and reines,
  "The best were synners grete;
"CHRIST's vycarr only knowes ne synne,
  "Ynne alle thys mortall state.

"Lett mercie rule thyne infante reigne,
  " 'Twylle faste thye crowne fulle sure;
"From race to race thy familie
  "Alle sov'reigns shall endure:

"But yff wythe bloode and slaughter thou
"Beginne thy infante reigne,
"Thy crowne uponne thy childrennes brows
"Wylle never long remayne."

"CANYNGE, awaie! thys traytour vile
"Has scorn'd my power and mee;
"Howe canst thou thenne for such a manne
"Intreate my clemencye?"

"My nobile leige! the trulie brave
"Wylle val'rous actions prize,
"Respect a brave and nobile mynde,
"Altho' ynne enemies."

"CANYNGE, awaie! By Godde ynne Heav'n
"Thatt dydd mee beinge gyve,
"I wylle nott taste a bitt of breade
"Whilst thys Syr CHARLES dothe lyve.

"By MARIE, and alle Seinctes ynne Heav'n,
"Thys sunne shall be hys laste."
Thenne CANYNGE dropt a brinie teare,
And from the presence paste.

Wyth herte brymm-fulle of gnawynge grief,
Hee to Syr CHARLES dydd goe,
And satt hymm downe uponne a stoole,
And teares beganne to flowe.

"Wee all must die," quod brave Syr CHARLES;
"Whatte bootes ytte howe or whenne;
"Dethe ys the sure, the certaine fate
"Of all wee mortall menne.

"Saye why, my friend, thie honest soul
"Runns overr att thyne eye;
"Is ytte for my most welcome doome
"Thatt thou dost child-lyke crye?"

Quod godlie CANYNGE, "I doe weepe,
"Thatt thou so soone must dye,
"And leave thy sonnes and helpless wyfe;
"'Tys thys thatt wettes myne eye."

"Thenne drie the tears thatt out thyne eye
"From godlie fountaines sprynge;

"Dethe I despise, and alle the power
"Of EDWARDE, traytor kynge.

"Whan throgh the tyrant's welcom means
"I shall resigne my lyfe,
"The Godde I serve wylle soone provyde
"For bothe mye sonnes and wyfe.

"Before I sawe the lyghtsome sunne,
"Thys was appointed mee;
"Shall mortal manne repyne or grudge
"Whatt Godde ordeynes to bee?

"Howe oft ynne battaile have I stoode,
"Whan thousands dy'd arounde;
"Whan smokynge streemes of crimson bloode
"Imbrew'd the fatten'd grounde:

"How dydd I knowe thatt ev'ry darte,
"Thatt cutte the airie waie,
"Myghte nott fynde passage toe my harte,
"And close myne eyes for aie?

"And shall I nowe, forr feere of dethe,
"Looke wanne and bee dysmayde?
"Ne! fromm my herte flie childyshe feere,
"Bee alle the manne display'd.

"Ah, goddelyke HENRIE! Godde forefende,
"And guarde thee and thye sonne,
"Yff 'tis hys wylle; but yff 'tis nott,
"Why thenne hys wylle bee donne.

"My honest friende, my faulte has beene
"To serve Godde and mye prynce;
"And thatt I no tyme-server am,
"My dethe wylle soone convynce.

"Ynne Londonne citye was I borne,
"Of parents of grete note;
"My fadre dydd a nobile armes
"Emblazon onne hys cote:

"I make ne doubte butt hee ys gone
"Where soone I hope to goe;
"Where wee for ever shall bee blest,
"From oute the reech of woe:

"Hee taughte mee justice and the laws
"Wyth pitie to unite;
"And eke hee taughte mee howe to knowe
"The wronge cause fromm the ryghte:

"Hee taughte mee wythe a prudent hande
"To feede the hungrie poore,
"Ne lett mye sarvants dryve awaie
"The hungrie fromme my doore:

"And none can saye, butt alle mye lyfe
"I have hys wordyes kept;
"And summ'd the actyonns of the daie
"Eche nyghte before I slept.

"I have a spouse, goe aske of her,
"Yff I defyl'd her bedde?
"I have a kynge, and none can laie
"Blacke treason onne my hedde.

"Ynne Lent, and onne the holie eve,
"Fromm fleshe I dydd refrayne;
"Whie should I thenne appeare dismay'd
"To leave thys worlde of payne?

"Ne! hapless HENRIE! I rejoyce,
"I shalle ne see thye dethe;
"Moste willynglie ynne thye just cause
"Doe I resign my brethe.

"Oh, fickle people! rewyn'd londe!
"Thou wylt kenne peace ne moe;
"Whyle RICHARD's sonnes exalt themselves,
"Thye brookes wythe bloude wylle flowe.

"Saie, were ye tyr'd of godlie peace,
"And godlie HENRIE's reigne,
"Thatt you dydd choppe youre easie daies
"For those of bloude and peyne?

"Whatte tho' I onne a sledde bee drawne,
"And mangled by a hynde,
"I doe defye the traytor's pow'r,
"Hee can ne harm my mynde;

"Whatte tho', uphoisted onne a pole,
"Mye lymbes shall rotte ynne ayre,

"And ne ryche monument of brasse
"CHARLES BAWDIN's name shall bear;

"Yett ynne the holie booke above,
"Whyche tyme can't eate awaie,
"There wythe the sarvants of the Lorde
"Mye name shall lyve for aie.

"Thenne welcome dethe! for lyfe eterne
"I leave thys mortall lyfe:
"Farewell, vayne worlde, and alle that's deare,
"Mye sonnes and lovynge wyfe!

"Nowe dethe as welcome to mee comes,
"As e'er the moneth of Maie;
"Nor woulde I even wyshe to lyve,
"Wyth my dere wyfe to staie."

Quod CANYNGE, "'Tys a goodlie thynge
"To bee prepar'd to die;
"And from thys world of peyne and grefe
"To Godde ynne Heav'n to flie."

And nowe the bell beganne to tolle,
And claryonnes to sounde;
Syr CHARLES hee herde the horses feete
A prauncyng onne the grounde:

And just before the officers,
His lovynge wyfe came ynne,
Weepynge unfeigned teeres of woe,
Wythe loude and dysmalle dynne.

"Sweet FLORENCE! nowe I praie forbere,
"Ynne quiet lett mee die;
"Praie Godde, thatt ev'ry Christian soule
"Maye looke onne dethe as I.

"Sweet FLORENCE! why these brinie teeres?
"Theye washe my soule awaie,
"And almost make mee wyshe for lyfe,
"Wyth thee, sweete dame, to staie.

"'Tys butt a journie I shalle goe
"Untoe the lande of blysse;
"Nowe, as a proofe of husbande's love,
"Receive thys holie kysse."

Thenne FLORENCE, fault'ring ynne her saie,
  Tremblynge these wordyes spoke,
"Ah, cruele EDWARDE! bloudie kynge!
  "My herte ys welle nyghe broke:

"Ah, sweete Syr CHARLES! why wylt thou goe,
  "Wythoute thye lovynge wyfe?
"The cruelle axe thatt cuttes thye necke,
  "Ytte eke shall ende mye lyfe."

And nowe the officers came ynne
  To brynge Syr CHARLES awaie,
Whoe turnedd toe his lovynge wyfe,
  And thus toe her dydd saie:

"I goe to lyfe, and nott to dethe;
  "Truste thou ynne Godde above,
"And teache thye sonnes to feare the Lorde,
  "And ynne theyre hertes hym love:

"Teache them to runne the nobile race
  "Thatt I theyre fader runne:
"FLORENCE! shou'd dethe thee take—adieu!
  "Yee officers, leade onne."

Thenne FLORENCE rav'd as anie madde,
  And dydd her tresses tere;
"Oh! staie, mye husbande! lorde! and lyfe!"—
  Syr CHARLES thenne dropt a teare.

'Tyll tyredd oute wythe ravynge loud,
  Shee fellen onne the flore;
Syr CHARLES exerted alle hys myghte,
  And march'd fromm oute the dore.

Uponne a sledde hee mounted thenne,
  Wythe lookes fulle brave and swete;
Lookes, thatt enshone ne moe concern
  Thanne anie ynne the strete.

Before hym went the council-menne,
  Ynne scarlett robes and golde,
And tassils spanglynge ynne the sunne,
  Muche glorious to beholde:

The Freers of Seincte AUGUSTYNE next
  Appeared to the syghte,

Alle cladd ynne homelie russett weedes,
  Of godlie monkysh plyghte:

Ynne diffraunt partes a godlie psaume
  Moste sweetlie theye dydd chaunt;
Behynde theyre backes syx mynstrelles came,
  Who tun'd the strunge bataunt.

Thenne fyve-and-twentye archers came;
  Echone the bowe dydd bende,
From rescue of kynge HENRIES friends
  Syr CHARLES forr to defend.

Bolde as a lyon came Syr CHARLES,
  Drawne onne a clothe-layde sledde,
Bye two blacke stedes ynne trappynges white,
  Wyth plumes uponne theyre hedde:

Behynde hym fyve-and-twentye moe
  Of archers stronge and stoute,
Wyth bended bowe echone ynne hande,
  Marched ynne goodlie route:

Seincte JAMESES Freers marched next,
  Echone hys parte dydd chaunt;
Behynde theyre backs syx mynstrelles came,
  Who tun'd the strunge bataunt:

Thenne came the maior and eldermenne,
  Ynne clothe of scarlett deck't;
And theyre attendyng menne echone,
  Lyke Easterne princes trickt:

And after them, a multitude
  Of citizenns dydd thronge;
The wyndowes were alle fulle of heddes,
  As hee dydd passe alonge.

And whenne hee came to the hyghe crosse,
  Syr CHARLES dydd turne and saie,
"O Thou, thatt savest manne fromme synne,
  "Washe mye soule clean thys daie!"

Att the grete mynsterr wyndowe sat
  The kynge ynne myckle state,
To see CHARLES BAWDIN goe alonge
  To hys most welcom fate.

Soone as the sledde drewe nyghe enowe,
  Thatt EDWARDE hee myghte heare,
The brave Syr CHARLES hee dydd stande uppe,
  And thus hys wordes declare:

"Thou seest mee, EDWARDE! traytour vile!
  "Expos'd to infamie;
"Butt bee assur'd, disloyall manne!
  "I'm greaterr nowe thanne thee.

"Bye foule proceedyngs, murdre, bloude,
  "Thou wearest nowe a crowne;
"And hast appoynted mee to dye,
  "By power nott thyne owne.

"Thou thynkest I shall dye to-daie;
  "I have beene dede 'till nowe,
"And soone shall lyve to weare a crowne
  "For aie uponne my browe:

"Whylst thou, perhapps, for som few yeares,
  "Shalt rule thys fickle lande,
"To lett them knowe howe wyde the rule
  " 'Twixt kynge and tyrant hande:

"Thye pow'r unjust, thou traytour slave!
  "Shall falle onne thye owne hedde"—
Fromm out of hearyng of the kynge
  Departed thenne the sledde.

Kynge EDWARDE's soule rush'd to hys face,
  Hee turn'd hys hedde awaie,
And to hys broder GLOUCESTER
  Hee thus dydd speke and saie:

"To hym that soe-much-dreaded dethe
  "Ne ghastlie terrors brynge,
"Beholde the manne! hee spake the truthe,
  "Hee's greater thanne a kynge!"

"Soe lett hym die!" Duke RICHARD sayde;
  "And maye echone oure foes
"Bende downe theyre neckes to bloudie axe,
  "And feede the carryon crowes."

And nowe the horses gentlie drewe
  Syr CHARLES uppe the hyghe hylle;

The axe dydd glysterr ynne the sunne,
  Hys pretious bloude to spylle.

Syrr CHARLES dydd uppe the scaffold goe,
  As uppe a gilded carre
Of victorye, bye val'rous chiefs
  Gayn'd ynne the bloudie warre:

And to the people hee dydd saie,
  "Beholde you see mee dye,
"For servynge loyally mye kynge,
  "Mye kynge most rightfullie.

"As longe as EDWARDE rules thys lande,
  "Ne quiet you wylle knowe;
"Youre sonnes and husbandes shalle bee slayne,
  "And brookes wythe bloude shalle flowe.

"You leave youre goode and lawfulle kynge,
  "Whenne ynne adversitye;
"Lyke mee, untoe the true cause stycke,
  "And for the true cause dye."

Thenne hee, wyth preestes, uponne hys knees,
  A pray'r to Godde dydd make,
Beseechynge hym unto hymselfe
  Hys partynge soule to take.

Thenne, kneelynge downe, hee layd his hedde
  Most seemlie onne the blocke;
Whyche fromme hys bodie fayre at once
  The able heddes-manne stroke:

And oute the bloude beganne to flowe,
  And rounde the scaffolde twyne;
And teares, enow to washe't awaie,
  Dydd flowe fromme each mann's eyne.

The bloudie axe hys bodie fayre
  Ynnto foure parties cutte;
And ev'rye parte, and eke hys hedde,
  Uponne a pole was putte.

One parte dydd rotte onne Kynwulph-hylle,
  One onne the mynster-tower,
And one from off the castle-gate
  The crowen dydd devoure:

The other onne Seyncte Powle's goode gate,
  A dreery spectacle;
Hys hedde was plac'd onne the hyghe crosse,
  Ynne hyghe-streete most nobile.

Thus was the ende of BAWDIN's fate:
  Godde prosper longe oure kynge,
And grante hee maye, wyth BAWDIN's soule,
  Ynne heav'n Godd's mercie synge!

Mynstrelles Songe[1]

O! SYNGE untoe mie roundelaie,
O! droppe the brynie teare wythe mee,
Daunce ne moe atte hallie daie,
Lycke a reynynge ryver bee;
    Mie love ys dedde,
    Gon to hys death-bedde,
    Al under the wyllowe tree.

Blacke hys cryne[2] as the wyntere nyghte,
Whyte hys rode[3] as the sommer snowe,
Rodde hys face as the mornynge lyghte,
Cale[4] he lyes ynne the grave belowe;
    Mie love ys dedde,
    Gon to hys deathe-bedde,
    Al under the wyllowe tree.

Swote hys tyngue as the throstles note,
Quycke ynn daunce as thoughte canne bee,
Defte hys taboure, codgelle stote,
O! hee lyes bie the wyllowe tree:
    Mie love ys dedde,
    Gonne to hys deathe-bedde,
    Alle underre the wyllowe tree.

Harke! the ravenne flappes hys wynge,
In the briered delle belowe;
Harke! the dethe-owle loude dothe synge,

[1] Published in *Ælla, a Tragycal Enterlude,* 1777. Text of *Poems,* ed. Tyrwhitt, third edition, 1778. The notes are from this edition.

[2] hair.

[3] complexion.

[4] cold.

To the nyghte-mares as heie[5] goe;
Mie love ys dedde,
Gon to hys deathe-bedde,
Al under the wyllowe tree.

See! the whyte moone sheenes onne hie;
Whyterre ys mie true loves shroude;
Whyterre yanne the mornynge skie,
Whyterre yanne the evenynge cloude;
Mie love ys dedde,
Gon to hys deathe-bedde,
Al under the wyllowe tree.

Heere, uponne mie true loves grave,
Schalle the baren fleurs be layde,
Nee one hallie Seyncte to save
Al the celness[6] of a mayde.
Mie love ys dedde,
Gonne to hys death-bedde,
Alle under the wyllowe tree.

Wythe mie hondes I'lle dente the brieres
Rounde his hallie corse to gre,
Ouphante fairie, lyghte youre fyres,
Heere mie boddie stylle schalle bee.
Mie love ys dedde,
Gon to hys deathe-bedde,
Al under the wyllowe tree.

Comme, wythe acorne-coppe & thorne,
Drayne mie hartys blodde awaie;
Lyfe and all yttes goode I scorne,
Daunce bie nete, or feaste by daie.
Mie love ys dedde,
Gon to hys death-bedde,
Al under the wyllowe tree.

Waterre wytches, crownede wythe reytes,[7]
Bere mee to yer leathalle tyde.
I die; I comme; mie true love waytes.
Thos the damselle spake, and dyed.

[5] they.
[6] coldness.
[7] water-flags.

An Excelente Balade of Charitie: As Wroten bie the Gode Prieste Thomas Rowley,[1] 1464[2]

IN VIRGYNE the sweltrie sun gan sheene,
And hotte upon the mees[3] did caste his raie;
The apple rodded[4] from its palie greene,
And the mole[5] peare did bende the leafy spraie;
The peede chelandri[6] sunge the livelong daie;
'Twas nowe the pride, the manhode of the yeare,
And eke the grounde was dighte[7] in its mose defte[8] aumere.[9]

The sun was glemeing in the midde of daie,
Deadde still the aire, and eke the welken[10] blue,
When from the sea arist[11] in drear arraie
A hepe of cloudes of sable sullen hue,
The which full fast unto the woodlande drewe,
Hiltring[12] attenes[13] the sunnis fetive[14] face,
And the blacke tempeste swolne and gatherd up apace.

Beneathe an holme, faste by a pathwaie side,
Which dide unto Seyncte Godwine's covent[15] lede,
A hapless pilgrim moneynge did abide.
Pore in his viewe, ungentle[16] in his weede,
Longe bretful[17] of the miseries of neede,
Where from the hail-stone coulde the almer[18] flie?
He had no housen theere, ne anie covent nie.

---

[1] Thomas Rowley, the author, was born at Norton Mal-reward in Somersetshire, educated at the Convent of St. Kenna at Keynesham, and died at Westbury in Gloucestershire.

[2] Published in *Poems*, 1777. Text of *Poems*, ed. Tyrwhitt, third edition, 1778. The preceding note and those that follow are Chatterton's.

[3] meads.

[4] reddened, ripened.

[5] soft.

[6] pied goldfinch.

[7] drest, arrayed.

[8] neat, ornamental.

[9] a loose robe or mantle.

[10] the sky, the atmosphere.

[11] arose.

[12] hiding, shrouding.

[13] at once.

[14] beauteous.

[15] It would have been *charitable*, if the author had not pointed at personal characters in this Ballad of Charity. The Abbot of St. Godwin's at the time of the writing of this was Ralph de Bellomont, a great stickler for the Lancastrian family. Rowley was a Yorkist.

[16] beggarly.

[17] filled with.

[18] beggar.

Look in his glommed[19] face, his sprighte there scanne;
Howe woe-be-gone, how withered, forwynd,[20] deade!
Haste to thie church-glebe-house[21], asshrewed[22] manne!
Haste to thie kiste,[23] thie onlie dortoure[24] bedde.
Cale, as the claie whiche will gre on thie hedde,
Is Charitie and Love aminge highe elves;
Knightis and Barons live for pleasure and themselves.

The gatherd storme is rype; the bigge drops falle;
The forswat[25] meadowes smethe,[26] and drenche[27] the raine;
The comyng ghastness do the cattle pall,[28]
And the full flockes are drivynge ore the plaine;
Dashde from the cloudes the waters flott[29] againe;
The welkin opes; the yellow levynne[30] flies;
And the hot fierie smothe[31] in the wide lowings[32] dies.

Liste! now the thunder's rattling clymmynge[33] sound
Cheves[34] slowlie on, and then embollen[35] clangs,
Shakes the hie spyre, and losst, dispended, drown'd,
Still on the gallard[36] eare of terroure hanges;
The windes are up; the lofty elmen swanges;
Again the levynne and the thunder poures,
And the full cloudes are braste[37] attenes in stonen showers.

Spurreynge his palfrie oere the watrie plaine,
The Abbote of Seyncte Godwynes convente came;
His chapournette[38] was drented with the reine,
And his pencte[39] gyrdle met with mickle shame;

[19] clouded, dejected. A person of some note in the literary world is of opinion, that *glum* and *glom* are modern cant words; and from this circumstance doubts the authenticity of Rowley's Manuscripts. Glum-mong in the Saxon signifies twilight, a dark or dubious light: and the modern word *gloomy* is derived from the Saxon *glum*.

[20] dry, sapless.

[21] the grave.

[22] accursed, unfortunate.

[23] coffin.

[24] a sleeping room.

[25] sun-burnt.

[26] smoke.

[27] drink.

[28] *pall*, a contraction from *appall*, to fright.

[29] fly.

[30] lightning.

[31] steam, or vapours.

[32] flames.

[33] noisy.

[34] moves.

[35] swelled, strengthened.

[36] frighted.

[37] burst.

[38] a small round hat, not unlike the shapournette in heraldry, formerly worn by Ecclesiastics and Lawyers.

[39] painted.

He aynewarde tolde his bederoll[40] at the same;
The storme encreasen, and he drew aside,
With the mist[41] almes craver neere to the holme to bide.

His cope[42] was all of Lyncolne clothe so fyne,
With a gold button fasten'd neere his chynne;
His autremete[43] was edged with golden twynne,
And his shoone pyke a loverds[44] mighte have binne;
Full well it shewn he thoughten coste no sinne:
The trammels of the palfrye pleasde his sighte,
For the horse-millanare[45] his head with roses dighte.

An almes, sir prieste! the droppynge pilgrim saide,
O! let me waite within your covente dore,
Till the sunne sheneth hie above our heade,
And the loude tempeste of the aire is oer;
Helpless and ould am I alas! and poor;
No house, ne friend, ne moneie in my pouche;
All yatte I call my owne is this my silver crouche.

Varlet, replyd the Abbatte, cease your dinne;
This is no season almes and prayers to give;
Mie porter never lets a faitour[46] in;
None touch mie rynge who not in honour live.
And now the sonne with the blacke cloudes did stryve,
And shettynge on the grounde his glairie raie,
The Abbatte spurrde his steede, and eftsoones roadde awaie.

Once moe the skie was blacke, the thunder rolde;
Faste reyneynge oer the plaine a prieste was seen;
Ne dighte full proude, ne buttoned up in golde;
His cope and jape[47] were graie, and eke were clene;
A Limitoure he was of order seene;
And from the pathwaie side then turned hee,
Where the pore almer laie binethe the holmen tree.

An almes, sir priest! the droppynge pilgrim sayde,
For sweete Seyncte Marie and your order sake.
The Limitoure then loosen'd his pouche threade,
And did thereoute a groate of silver take;
The mister pilgrim dyd for halline[48] shake.

[40] He told his beads backwards; a figurative expression to signify cursing.
[41] poor, needy.
[42] a cloke.
[43] a loose white robe, worn by Priests.
[44] a lord.
[45] I believe this trade is still in being, though but seldom employed.
[46] a beggar, or vagabond.
[47] a short surplice, worn by Friars of an inferior class, and secular priests.
[48] joy.

Here take this silver, it maie eathe[49] thie care;
We are Goddes stewards all, nete[50] of oure owne we bare.

But ah! unhailie[51] pilgrim, lerne of me,
Scathe anie give a rentrolle to their Lorde.
Here take my semecope,[52] thou arte bare I see;
Tis thyne; the Seynctes will give me mie rewarde.
He left the pilgrim, and his waie aborde.
Virgynne and hallie Seyncte, who sitte yn gloure,[53]
Or give the mittee[54] will, or give the gode man power.

JOHN LANGHORNE

(1753-1764-1779)

A Farewell Hymn to the Valley of Irwan[1]

FAREWEL the fields of Irwan's vale,
My infant years where fancy led;
And sooth'd me with the western gale,
Her wild dreams waving round my head;
While the blythe blackbird told his tale.
Farewel, the fields of Irwan's vale!

The primrose on the valley's side,
The green thyme on the mountain's head;
The wanton rose, the daisy pied,
The wilding's blossom blushing red:
No longer I their sweets inhale.
Farewel, the fields of Irwan's vale!

How oft, within yon vacant shade,
Has ev'ning clos'd my careless eye!
How oft, along those banks, I've stray'd,
And watch'd the wave that wander'd by!
Full long their loss shall I bewail.
Farewel, the fields of Irwan's vale!

---

[49] ease.
[50] nought.
[51] unhappy.
[52] a short under-cloke.
[53] glory.
[54] mighty, rich.
[1] Published in *Solyman and Almena*, 1762. Text of *The Novelist's Magazine*, Volume II, 1780.

Yet still within yon vacant grove,
  To mark the close of parting day;
Along yon flow'ry banks to rove,
  And watch the wave that winds away;
Fair fancy sure shall never fail,
Though far from these, and Irwan's vale!

The Evening Primrose[1]

THERE are that love the shades of life,
  And shun the splendid walks of fame;
There are that hold it rueful strife
  To risque AMBITION's losing game:

That far from ENVY's lurid eye
  The fairest fruits of GENIUS rear,
Content to see them bloom and die
  In Friendship's small but kindly sphere.

Than vainer flowers tho' sweeter far,
  The Evening Primrose shuns the day;
Blooms only to the western star,
  And loves its solitary ray.

In EDEN's vale an aged hind,
  At the dim twilight's closing hour,
On his time-smoothed staff reclin'd,
  With wonder view'd the opening flower.

'Ill-fated flower, at eve to blow,'
  In pity's simple thought he cries,
'Thy bosom must not feel the glow
  'Of splendid suns, or smiling skies.

'Nor thee, the vagrants of the field,
  'The hamlet's little train behold;
'Their eyes to sweet oppression yield,
  'When thine the falling shades unfold.

'Nor thee the hasty shepherd heeds,
  'When love has fill'd his heart with cares,
'For flowers he rifles all the meads,
  'For waking flowers—but thine forbears.

[1] Published in *Fables of Flora*, 1771. Text of edition of 1794.

'Ah! waste no more that beauteous bloom
'On night's chill shade, that fragrant breath,
'Let smiling suns those gems illume!
'Fair flower, to live unseen is death.'

Soft as the voice of vernal gales
That o'er the bending meadow blow,
Or streams that steal thro' even vales,
And murmur that they move so slow:

Deep in her unfrequented bower,
Sweet Philomela pour'd her strain;
The bird of eve approv'd her flower,
And answer'd thus the anxious swain.

Live unseen!
By moonlight shades, in valleys green,
Lovely flower, we'll live unseen.
Of our pleasures deem not lightly,
Laughing day may look more sprightly,
But I love the modest mien,
Still I love the modest mien,
Of gentle evening fair, and her star-trained queen.

Didst thou, shepherd, never find,
Pleasure is of pensive kind?
Has thy cottage never known
That she loves to live alone?
Dost thou not at evening hour
Feel some soft and secret power,
Gliding o'er thy yielding mind,
Leave sweet serenity behind;
While all disarm'd, the cares of day
Steal thro' the falling gloom away?
Love to think thy lot was laid
In this undistinguish'd shade.
Far from the world's infectious view,
Thy little virtues safely blew.
Go, and in day's more dangerous hour,
Guard thy emblematic flower.

CHRISTOPHER ANSTEY

(1724-1766-1805)

The New Bath Guide[1]

Letter X

Taste and Spirit.—Mr. B-n-r-d commences A Beau Garçon

So LIVELY, so gay, my dear Mother, I'm grown,
I long to do something to make myself known;
For Persons of *Taste* and true *Spirit*, I find,
Are fond of attracting the Eyes of Mankind:
What Numbers one sees, who, for that very Reason
Come to make such a Figure at *Bath* ev'ry Season!
'Tis this that provokes Mrs. SHENKIN AP-LEEK
To dine at the Ord'nary twice in a Week,
Tho' at Home she might eat a good Dinner in Comfort,
Nor pay such a cursed extravagant Sum for't:
But then her Acquaintance would never have known
Mrs. SHENKIN AP-LEEK had acquir'd a *Bon Ton:*
Ne'er shewn how in *Taste* the AP-LEEKS can excel
The Dutchess of TRUFFLES, and Lady MORELL;
Had ne'er been ador'd by Sir PYE MACARONI,
And Count VERMICELLI, his intimate Crony;
Both Men of such *Taste*, their Opinions are taken
From an Ortolan down to a Rasher of Bacon.
 What makes KITTY SPICER, and little Miss SAGO,
To Auctions and Milliner's Shops ev'ry Day go?
What makes them to vie with each other and quarrel
Which spends the most Money for splendid Apparel?
Why, *Spirit*—to shew they have much better Sense
Than their Fathers, who rais'd it by Shillings and Pence.
What sends PETER TEWKSBURY every Night
To the Play with such infinite Joy and Delight?
Why, PETER's a Critic, with true Attic Salt,
Can damn the Performers, can hiss, and find fault,
And tell when we ought to express Approbation,
By thumping, and clapping, and Vociferation;
So he gains our Attention, and all must admire
Young TEWKSBURY's Judgment, his *Spirit* and Fire.
But JACK DILETTANTE despises the Play'rs,
To Concerts and musical Parties repairs,

[1] Published in 1766. Text of the third edition, 1766.

With Benefit-Tickets his Pockets he fills,
Like a Mountebank Doctor distributes his Bills;
And thus his Importance and Interest shews,
By conferring his Favours wherever he goes:
He's extremely polite both to me and my Cousin,
For he often desires us to take off a Dozen:
He has Taste, without doubt, and a delicate Ear,
No vile Oratorios ever could bear;
But talks of the Op'ras and his *Signiora*,
Cries *Bravo, Benissimo, Bravo, Encora!*
And oft is so kind as to thrust in a Note
While old Lady CUCKOW is straining her Throat,
Or little Miss WREN, who's an excellent Singer;
Then he points to the Notes, with a Ring on his Finger,
And shews her the Crotchet, the Quaver, and Bar,
All the Time that she warbles, and plays the *Guitar:*
Yet I think, tho' she's at it from Morning till Noon,
Her queer little Thingumbob's never in Tune.
 Thank Heaven! of late, my dear Mother, my Face is
Not a little regarded at all public Places;
For I ride in a Chair with my Hands in a Muff,
And have bought a Silk Coat and embroider'd the Cuff;
But the Weather was cold, and the Coat it was thin,
So the Taylor advis'd me to line it with Skin:
But what with my *Nivernois'* Hat can compare,
Bag-Wig, and lac'd Ruffles, and black Solitaire?
And what can a Man of true Fashion denote,
Like an Ell of good Ribbon ty'd under the Throat?
My Buckles and Box are in exquisite Taste;
The one is of Paper, the other of Paste;
And sure no *Camayeu* was ever yet seen
Like that which I purchas'd at WICKSTED's Machine:
My Stockings, of Silk, are just come from the Hosier,
For To-night I'm to dance with the charming Miss TOZIER:
So I'd have them to know when I go to the Ball,
I shall shew as much *Taste* as the best of them all:
For a Man of great Fashion was heard to declare
He never beheld so engaging an Air,
And swears all the World must my Judgment confess,
My *Solidity, Sense, Understanding* in Dress,
My Manners so form'd, and my Wig so well curl'd,
I look like a Man *of the very first World:*
But my Person and Figure you'll best understand
From the Picture I've sent, by an eminent Hand:
Shew it young Lady BETTY, by way of Endearance,
And to give her a Spice of my Mien and Appearance:
Excuse any more, I'm in Haste to depart,

For a Dance is the Thing that I love at my Heart.
So now my dear Mother, *&c., &c., &c.*

ROBERT FERGUSSON

(1750-1771-1774)

The Daft-Days[1]

Now mirk December's dowie face
Glours our the rigs wi' sour grimace,
While, thro' his *minimum* of space,
    The bleer-ey'd sun,
Wi' blinkin light and stealing pace,
    His race doth run.

From naked groves nae birdie sings,
To shepherd's pipe nae hillock rings,
The breeze nae od'rous flavour brings
    From *Borean* cave,
And dwyning nature droops her wings,
    Wi' visage grave.

Mankind but scanty pleasure glean
Frae snawy hill or barren plain,
Whan Winter, 'midst his nipping train,
    Wi' frozen spear,
Sends drift owr a' his bleak domain,
    And guides the weir.

Auld Reikie! thou'rt the canty hole,
A bield for mony caldrife soul,
Wha snugly at thine ingle loll,
    Baith warm and couth;
While round they gar the bicker roll
    To weet their mouth.

When merry *Yule-day* comes, I trow
You'll scantlins find a hungry mou;
Sma' are our cares, our stamacks fou
    O' gusty gear,
And kickshaws, strangers to our view,
    Sin Fairn-year.

[1] Published in *Weekly Magazine, or Edinburgh Amusement,* January 2, 1772. Text of *Poems by Robert Fergusson,* 1773.

Ye browster wives, now busk ye bra,
And fling your sorrows far awa';
Then come and gies the tither blaw
            Of reaming ale,
Mair precious than the well of *Spa*,
            Our hearts to heal.

Then, tho' at odds wi' a' the warl',
Amang oursells we'll never quarrel;
Tho' Discord gie a canker'd snarl
            To spoil our glee,
As lang's there's pith into the barrel
            We'll drink and 'gree.

Fidlers, your pins in temper fix,
And roset weel your fiddle-sticks,
But banish vile Italian tricks
            From out your quorum,
Nor *fortes* wi' *pianos* mix,
            Gie's *Tulloch Gorum*.

For nought can cheer the heart sae weil
As can a canty Highland reel,
It even vivifies the heel
            To skip and dance:
Lifeless is he what canna feel
            Its influence.

Let mirth abound, let social cheer
Invest the dawning of the year;
Let blithesome innocence appear
            To crown our joy,
Nor envy wi' sarcastic sneer
            Our bliss destroy.

And thou, great god of *Aqua Vitæ!*
Wha sways the empire of this city,
When fou we're sometimes capernoity,
            Be thou prepar'd
To hedge us frae that black banditti,
            The City-Guard.

Braid Claith[1]

YE WHA are fain to hae your name
Wrote in the bonny book of fame,
Let merit nae pretension claim
To laurel'd wreath,
But hap ye weel, baith back and wame,
In gude Braid Claith.

He that some ells o' this may fa,
An' slae-black hat on pow like snaw,
Bids bauld to bear the gree awa',
Wi' a' this graith,
Whan bienly clad wi' shell fu' braw
O' gude Braid Claith.

Waesuck for him wha has na fek o't!
For he's a gowk they're sure to geck at,
A chiel that ne'er will be respekit
While he draws breath,
Till his four quarters are bedeckit
Wi' gude Braid Claith.

On Sabbath-days the barber spark,
When he has done wi' scrapin wark,
Wi' siller broachie in his sark,
Gangs trigly, faith!
Or to the Meadow, or the Park,
In gude Braid Claith.

Weel might ye trow, to see them there,
That they to shave your haffits bare,
Or curl an' sleek a pickly hair,
Wou'd be right laith,
Whan pacing wi' a gawsy air
In gude Braid Claith.

If ony mettl'd stirrah green
For favour frae a lady's ein,
He maunna care for being seen
Before he sheath
His body in a scabbard clean
O' gude Braid Claith.

[1] Published in *Weekly Magazine, or Edinburgh Amusement,* October 15, 1772. Text of *Poems by Robert Fergusson,* 1773.

For, gin he come wi' coat thread-bare,
A feg for him she winna care,
But crook her bonny mou' fu' sair,
And scald him baith.
Wooers shou'd ay their travel spare
Without Braid Claith.

Braid Claith lends fock an unco heese,
Makes mony kail-worms butter-flies,
Gies mony a doctor his degrees
For little skaith:
In short, you may be what you please
Wi' gude Braid Claith.

For thof ye had as wise a snout on
As *Shakespeare* or Sir *Isaac Newton*,
Your judgment fouk wou'd hae a doubt on,
I'll tak my aith,
Till they cou'd see ye wi' a suit on
O' gude Braid Claith.

The Farmer's Ingle[1]

Et multo in primis hilarans convivia Baccho,
Ante focum, si frigus erit. Virg. Buc.

WHAN gloming grey out o'er the welkin keeks,
Whan *Batie* ca's his owsen to the byre,
Whan *Thrasher John*, sair dung, his barn-door steeks,
And lusty lasses at the dighting tire:
What bangs fu' leal the e'enings coming cauld,
And gars snaw-tapit winter freeze in vain;
Gars dowie mortals look baith blyth and bauld,
Nor fley'd wi' a' the poortith o' the plain;
Begin, my Muse, and chant in hamely strain.

Frae the big stack, weel winnow't on the hill,
Wi' *divets* theekit frae the weet and drift,
Sods, peats, and *heath'ry trufs* the chimley fill,
And gar their thick'ning smeek salute the lift;
The *gudeman*, new come hame, is blyth to find
Whan he out o'er the *halland* flings his een,
That ilka turn is handled to his mind,

[1] Published in *Weekly Magazine, or Edinburgh Amusement*, May 13, 1773. Text of first edition.

That a' his housie looks sae cosh and clean;
For cleanly house looes he, tho' e'er sae mean.

Weel kens the *gudewife* that the pleughs require
A heartsome *meltith*, and refreshing synd
O' nappy liquor, o'er a bleezing fire:
Sair wark and poortith douna weel be join'd.
Wi' butter'd *bannocks* now the *girdle* reeks,
I' the far nook the *bowie* briskly reams;
The readied *kail* stand by the chimley cheeks,
And had the riggin het wi' welcome steams,
Whilk than the daintiest kitchen nicer seems.

Frae this lat gentler gabs a lesson lear;
Wad they to labouring lend an eidant hand,
They'd rax fell strang upo' the simplest fare,
Nor find their stamacks ever at a stand.
Fu' hale and healthy wad they pass the day,
At night in calmest slumbers dose fu' sound,
Nor doctor need their weary life to spae,
Nor drogs their noddle and their sense confound,
Till death slip sleely on, and gi'e the hindmost wound.

On sicken food has mony a doughty deed
By Caledonia's ancestors been done;
By this did mony wight fu' weirlike bleed
In *brulzies* frae the dawn to set o' sun:
'Twas this that brac'd their *gardies*, stiff and strang,
That bent the deidly yew in antient days,
Laid Denmark's daring sons on yird alang,
Gar'd Scottish *thristles* bang the Roman *bays*;
For near our *crest* their heads they doughtna raise.

The couthy cracks begin whan supper's o'er,
The cheering *bicker* gars them glibly gash
O' simmer's *showery blinks* and winters sour,
Whase floods did erst their mailins produce hash:
'Bout *kirk* and *market* eke their tales gae on,
How *Jock* woo'd *Jenny* here to be his bride,
And there how *Marion*, for a bastard son,
Upo' the *cutty-stool* was forc'd to ride,
The waefu' scald o' our *Mess John* to bide.

The fient a chiep's amang the bairnies now;
For a' their anger's wi' their hunger gane:
Ay maun the childer, wi' a fastin mou',
Grumble and greet, and make an unco mane,
In rangles round before the ingle's low:

Frae *gudame's* mouth auld warld tales they hear,
O' *Warlocks* louping round the *Wirrikow*,
O' gaists that win in glen and kirk-yard drear,
Whilk touzles a' their tap, and gars them shak wi' fear.

For weel she trows that fiends and fairies be
Sent frae the de'il to fleetch us to our ill;
That ky hae tint their milk wi' evil eie,
And corn been scowder'd on the glowing kill.
O mock na this, my friends! but rather mourn,
Ye in life's brawest spring wi' reason clear,
Wi' eild our idle fancies a' return,
And dim our dolefu' days wi' bairnly fear;
The mind's ay *cradled* whan the *grave* is near.

Yet *thrift*, industrious, bides her latest days,
Tho' age her sair dow'd front wi' runcles wave,
Yet frae the russet lap the *spindle* plays,
Her e'enin stent reels she as weel's the lave.
On some feast-day, the *wee-things* buskit braw
Shall heeze her heart up wi' a silent joy,
Fu' cadgie that her head was up and saw
Her ain spun cleething on a darling oy,
Careless tho' death shou'd make the feast her foy.

In its auld *lerroch* yet the *deas* remains,
Whare the gudeman aft streeks him at his ease,
A warm and canny lean for weary banes
O' lab'rers doil'd upo' the wintry leas:
Round him will *badrins* and the *colly* come,
To wag their tail, and cast a thankfu' eie
To him wha kindly flings them mony a crum
O' kebbock whang'd, and dainty fadge to prie;
This a' the boon they crave, and a' the fee.

Frae him the *lads* their morning counsel tak,
What stacks he wants to thrash, what rigs to till;
How big a birn maun lie on *bassie's* back,
For meal and multure to the *thirling mill.*
Niest the gudewife her hireling damsels bids
Glowr thro' the byre, and see the hawkies bound,
Take tent case *Crummy* tak her wonted tids,
And ca' the leglin's treasure on the ground,
Whilk spills a *kebbuck* nice, or yellow *pound*.

Then a' the house for sleep begin to grien,
Their joints to slack frae industry a while;
The leaden God fa's heavy on their ein,

And hafflins steeks them frae their daily toil:
The cruizy too can only blink and bleer,
The restit ingle's done the maist it dow;
Tacksman and cottar eke to bed maun steer,
Upo' the cod to clear their drumly pow,
Till wauken'd by the dawning's ruddy glow.

Peace to the husbandman and a' his tribe,
Whase care fells a' our wants frae year to year;
Lang may his sock and couter turn the gleyb,
And bauks o' corn bend down wi' laded ear.
May SCOTIA's simmers ay look gay and green,
Her yellow har'sts frae scowry blasts decreed;
May a' her tenants sit fu' snug and bien,
Frae the hard grip of ails and poortith freed,
And a lang lasting train o' peaceful hours succeed.

RICHARD BRINSLEY SHERIDAN

(1751-1771-1816)

Song[1]

IF A daughter you have, she's the plague of your life,
No peace shall you know, tho' you've buried your wife,
At twenty she mocks at the duty you taught her,
O, what a plague is an obstinate daughter.
Sighing and whining,
Dying and pining,
O, what a plague is an obstinate daughter.

When scarce in their teens, they have wit to perplex us,
With letters and lovers for ever they vex us,
While each still rejects the fair suitor you've brought her,
O, what a plague is an obstinate daughter.
Wrangling and jangling,
Flouting and pouting,
O, what a plague is an obstinate daughter.

[1] Published in *Songs in the Duenna*, 1775. Text of *The Duenna*, 1794, Act I. Scene iii.

Song[1]

HAD I a heart for falsehood framed,
  I ne'er could injure you,
For tho' your tongue no promise claimed,
  Your charms wou'd make me true.
To you no soul shall bear deceit,
  No stranger offer wrong,
But friends in all the aged you'll meet;
  And lovers in the young.

But when they learn that you have blest
  Another with your heart,
They'll bid aspiring passions rest,
  And act a brother's part;
Then, lady, dread not here deceit,
  Nor fear to suffer wrong;
For friends in all the aged you'll meet,
  And brothers in the young.

Song[2]

HERE's to the maiden of bashful fifteen;
  Here's to the widow of fifty;
Here's to the flaunting extravagant quean,
  And here's to the housewife that's thrifty.

Chorus

  Let the toast pass,—
  Drink to the lass,
I'll warrant she'll prove an excuse for the glass.

Here's to the charmer whose dimples we prize;
  Now to the maid who has none, sir:
Here's to the girl with a pair of blue eyes,
  And here's to the nymph with but *one*, sir.
    Chorus. Let the toast pass, &c.

Here's to the maid with a bosom of snow;
  Now to her that's as brown as a berry:
Here's to the wife with her face full of woe,

[1] Published in *Songs in the Duenna*, 1775. Text of *The Duenna*, 1794, Act I, Scene v.

[2] Published in *The School for Scandal*, 1777, Act III, Scene iii. Text of edition of 1823. See Preface.

And now to the damsel that's merry.
Chorus. Let the toast pass, &c.

For let 'em be clumsy, or let 'em be slim,
Young or ancient, I care not a feather;
So fill a pint bumper quite up to the brim,
And let us e'en toast them together.
Chorus. Let the toast pass, &c.

GEORGE CRABBE

(1754-1772-1832)

The Village[1]

Book I

The Subject proposed—Remarks upon Pastoral Poetry—A Tract of Country near the Coast described—An impoverished Borough—Smugglers and their Assistants—Rude Manners of the Inhabitants—Ruinous Effects of a high Tide—The Village Life more generally considered: Evils of it—The youthful Labourer—The old Man: his Soliloquy—The Parish Workhouse: its Inhabitants—The sick Poor: their Apothecary—The dying Pauper—The Village Priest.

THE Village Life, and every care that reigns
O'er youthful peasants and declining swains;
What labour yields, and what, that labour past,
Age, in its hour of languor, finds at last;
What form the real picture of the poor,
Demand a song—the Muse can give no more.
Fled are those times when, in harmonious strains,
The rustic poet praised his native plains.
No shepherds now, in smooth alternate verse,
Their country's beauty or their nymphs' rehearse;
Yet still for these we frame the tender strain,
Still in our lays fond Corydons complain,
And shepherds' boys their amorous pains reveal,
The only pains, alas! they never feel.
On Mincio's banks, in Cæsar's bounteous reign,
If Tityrus found the Golden Age again,
Must sleepy bards the flattering dream prolong,
Mechanic echoes of the Mantuan song?
From Truth and Nature shall we widely stray,

[1] Published in 1783. Text of *Works*, 1823, with some modifications in punctuation.

Where Virgil, not where Fancy, leads the way?
Yes, thus the Muses sing of happy swains,
Because the Muses never knew their pains.
They boast their peasants' pipes; but peasants now
Resign their pipes and plod behind the plough;
And few, amid the rural-tribe, have time
To number syllables, and play with rhyme;
Save honest Duck, what son of verse could share
The poet's rapture, and the peasant's care?
Or the great labours of the field degrade,
With the new peril of a poorer trade?
From this chief cause these idle praises spring,
That themes so easy few forbear to sing;
For no deep thought the trifling subjects ask:
To sing of shepherds is an easy task.
The happy youth assumes the common strain,
A nymph his mistress, and himself a swain;
With no sad scenes he clouds his tuneful prayer,
But all, to look like her, is painted fair.
I grant indeed that fields and flocks have charms
For him that grazes or for him that farms;
But when amid such pleasing scenes I trace
The poor laborious natives of the place,
And see the mid-day sun, with fervid ray,
On their bare heads and dewy temples play;
While some, with feebler heads and fainter hearts,
Deplore their fortune, yet sustain their parts:
Then shall I dare these real ills to hide
In tinsel trappings of poetic pride?
No; cast by Fortune on a frowning coast,
Which neither groves nor happy valleys boast;
Where other cares than those the Muse relates,
And other shepherds dwell with other mates;
By such examples taught, I paint the Cot,
As Truth will paint it, and as Bards will not:
Nor you, ye poor, of letter'd scorn complain,
To you the smoothest song is smooth in vain;
O'ercome by labour, and bow'd down by time,
Feel you the barren flattery of a rhyme?
Can poets soothe you, when you pine for bread,
By winding myrtles round your ruin'd shed?
Can their light tales your weighty griefs o'erpower,
Or glad with airy mirth the toilsome hour?
Lo! where the heath, with withering brake grown o'er,
Lends the light turf that warms the neighbouring poor;
From thence a length of burning sand appears,
Where the thin harvest waves its wither'd ears;
Rank weeds, that every art and care defy,

Reign o'er the land, and rob the blighted rye:
There thistles stretch their prickly arms afar,
And to the ragged infant threaten war;
There poppies, nodding, mock the hope of toil;
There the blue bugloss paints the sterile soil;
Hardy and high, above the slender sheaf,
The slimy mallow waves her silky leaf;
O'er the young shoot the charlock throws a shade,
And clasping tares cling round the sickly blade;
With mingled tints the rocky coasts abound,
And a sad splendour vainly shines around.
So looks the nymph whom wretched arts adorn,
Betray'd by man, then left for man to scorn;
Whose cheek in vain assumes the mimic rose,
While her sad eyes the troubled breast disclose;
Whose outward splendour is but folly's dress,
Exposing most, when most it gilds distress.
  Here joyless roam a wild amphibious race,
With sullen wo display'd in every face;
Who far from civil arts and social fly,
And scowl at strangers with suspicious eye.
  Here too the lawless merchant of the main
Draws from his plough th' intoxicated swain;
Want only claim'd the labour of the day,
But vice now steals his nightly rest away.
  Where are the swains, who, daily labour done,
With rural games play'd down the setting sun;
Who struck with matchless force the bounding ball,
Or made the pond'rous quoit obliquely fall;
While some huge Ajax, terrible and strong,
Engaged some artful stripling of the throng,
And fell beneath him, foil'd, while far around
Hoarse triumph rose, and rocks return'd the sound?
Where now are these?—Beneath yon cliff they stand,
To show the freighted pinnace where to land;
To load the ready steed with guilty haste;
To fly in terror o'er the pathless waste;
Oh, when detected in their straggling course,
To foil their foes by cunning or by force;
Or, yielding part (which equal knaves demand),
To gain a lawless passport through the land.
  Here, wand'ring long amid these frowning fields,
I sought the simple life that Nature yields;
Rapine and Wrong and Fear usurp'd her place,
And a bold, artful, surly, savage race;
Who, only skill'd to take the finny tribe,
The yearly dinner, or septennial bribe,
Wait on the shore, and, as the waves run high,

On the tost vessel bend their eager eye,
Which to their coast directs its vent'rous way;
Theirs, or the ocean's, miserable prey.
As on their neighbouring beach yon swallows stand,
And wait for favouring winds to leave the land,
While still for flight the ready wing is spread:
So waited I the favouring hour, and fled—
Fled from these shores where guilt and famine reign,
And cried, Ah! hapless they who still remain;
Who still remain to hear the ocean roar,
Whose greedy waves devour the lessening shore;
Till some fierce tide, with more imperious sway,
Sweeps the low hut and all it holds away;
When the sad tenant weeps from door to door,
And begs a poor protection from the poor!
But these are scenes where Nature's niggard hand
Gave a spare portion to the famish'd land;
Hers is the fault, if here mankind complain
Of fruitless toil and labour spent in vain.
But yet in other scenes, more fair in view,
Where Plenty smiles—alas! she smiles for few—
And those who taste not, yet behold her store,
Are as the slaves that dig the golden ore,
The wealth around them makes them doubly poor.
Or will you deem them amply paid in health,
Labour's fair child, that languishes with wealth?
Go, then! and see them rising with the sun,
Through a long course of daily toil to run;
See them beneath the dog-star's raging heat,
When the knees tremble and the temples beat;
Behold them, leaning on their scythes, look o'er
The labour past, and toils to come explore;
See them alternate suns and showers engage,
And hoard up aches and anguish for their age;
Through fens and marshy moors their steps pursue,
When their warm pores imbibe the evening dew;
Then own that labour may as fatal be
To these thy slaves, as thine excess to thee.
Amid this tribe too oft a manly pride
Strives in strong toil the fainting heart to hide;
There may you see the youth of slender frame
Contend with weakness, weariness, and shame;
Yet, urged along, and proudly loth to yield,
He strives to join his fellows of the field;
Till long-contending nature droops at last,
Declining health rejects his poor repast,
His cheerless spouse the coming danger sees,
And mutual murmurs urge the slow disease.

Yet grant them health, 'tis not for us to tell,
Though the head droops not, that the heart is well;
Or will you praise that homely, healthy fare,
Plenteous and plain, that happy peasants share?
Oh! trifle not with wants you cannot feel,
Nor mock the misery of a stinted meal—
Homely, not wholesome; plain, not plenteous; such
As you who praise would never deign to touch.
Ye gentle souls, who dream of rural ease,
Whom the smooth stream and smoother sonnet please;
Go! if the peaceful cot your praises share,
Go, look within, and ask if peace be there:
If peace be his—that drooping weary sire,
Or theirs, that offspring round their feeble fire;
Or hers, that matron pale, whose trembling hand
Turns on the wretched hearth th' expiring brand!
Nor yet can Time itself obtain for these
Life's latest comforts, due respect and ease:
For yonder see that hoary swain, whose age
Can with no cares except his own engage;
Who, propp'd on that rude staff, looks up to see
The bare arms broken from the withering tree,
On which, a boy, he climb'd the loftiest bough,
Then his first joy, but his sad emblem now.
He once was chief in all the rustic trade;
His steady hand the straightest furrow made;
Full many a prize he won, and still is proud
To find the triumphs of his youth allow'd.
A transient pleasure sparkles in his eyes;
He hears and smiles, then thinks again and sighs:
For now he journeys to his grave in pain;
The rich disdain him, nay, the poor disdain;
Alternate masters now their slave command,
Urge the weak efforts of his feeble hand;
And, when his age attempts its task in vain,
With ruthless taunts, of lazy poor complain.
Oft may you see him, when he tends the sheep,
His winter-charge, beneath the hillock weep;
Oft hear him murmur to the winds that blow
O'er his white locks and bury them in snow,
When, roused by rage and muttering in the morn,
He mends the broken hedge with icy thorn:—
"Why do I live, when I desire to be
"At once from life and life's long labour free?
"Like leaves in spring, the young are blown away,
"Without the sorrows of a slow decay;
"I, like yon wither'd leaf, remain behind,
"Nipp'd by the frost, and shivering in the wind;

"There it abides till younger buds come on,
"As I, now all my fellow-swains are gone;
"Then, from the rising generation thrust,
"It falls, like me, unnoticed to the dust.
"These fruitful fields, these numerous flocks I see,
"Are others' gain, but killing cares to me:
"To me the children of my youth are lords,
"Cool in their looks, but hasty in their words:
"Wants of their own demand their care; and who
"Feels his own want and succours others too?
"A lonely, wretched man, in pain I go,
"None need my help, and none relieve my wo;
"Then let my bones beneath the turf be laid,
"And men forget the wretch they would not aid!"
Thus groan the old, till, by disease oppress'd,
They taste a final wo, and then they rest.
Theirs is yon house that holds the parish poor,
Whose walls of mud scarce bear the broken door;
There, where the putrid vapours, flagging, play,
And the dull wheel hums doleful through the day—
There children dwell, who know no parents' care;
Parents, who know no children's love, dwell there!
Heart-broken matrons on their joyless bed,
Forsaken wives, and mothers never wed;
Dejected widows with unheeded tears,
And crippled age with more than childhood fears;
The lame, the blind, and, far the happiest they!
The moping idiot and the madman gay.
Here too the sick their final doom receive,
Here brought, amid the scenes of grief, to grieve,
Where the loud groans from some sad chamber flow,
Mix'd with the clamours of the crowd below;
Here, sorrowing, they each kindred sorrow scan,
And the cold charities of man to man:
Whose laws indeed for ruin'd age provide,
And strong compulsion plucks the scrap from pride;
But still that scrap is bought with many a sigh,
And pride embitters what it can't deny.
Say ye, oppress'd by some fantastic woes,
Some jarring nerve that baffles your repose;
Who press the downy couch, while slaves advance
With timid eye to read the distant glance;
Who with sad prayers the weary doctor tease,
To name the nameless ever-new disease;
Who with mock patience dire complaints endure,
Which real pain, and that alone, can cure—
How would ye bear in real pain to lie,
Despised, neglected, left alone to die?

How would ye bear to draw your latest breath,
Where all that's wretched paves the way for death?
  Such is that room which one rude beam divides,
And naked rafters form the sloping sides;
Where the vile bands that bind the thatch are seen,
And lath and mud are all that lie between,
Save one dull pane, that, coarsely patch'd, gives way
To the rude tempest, yet excludes the day.
Here, on a matted flock, with dust o'erspread,
The drooping wretch reclines his languid head;
For him no hand the cordial cup applies,
Or wipes the tear that stagnates in his eyes;
No friends with soft discourse his pain beguile,
Or promise hope till sickness wears a smile.
  But soon a loud and hasty summons calls,
Shakes the thin roof, and echoes round the walls.
Anon, a figure enters, quaintly neat,
All pride and business, bustle and conceit;
With looks unalter'd by these scenes of wo,
With speed that, entering, speaks his haste to go,
He bids the gazing throng around him fly,
And carries fate and physic in his eye:
A potent quack, long versed in human ills,
Who first insults the victim whom he kills;
Whose murd'rous hand a drowsy Bench protect,
And whose most tender mercy is neglect.
  Paid by the parish for attendance here,
He wears contempt upon his sapient sneer;
In haste he seeks the bed where Misery lies,
Impatience mark'd in his averted eyes;
And, some habitual queries hurried o'er,
Without reply, he rushes on the door.
His drooping patient, long inured to pain,
And long unheeded, knows remonstrance vain;
He ceases now the feeble help to crave
Of man; and silent sinks into the grave.
  But ere his death some pious doubts arise,
Some simple fears, which "bold bad" men despise:
Fain would he ask the parish-priest to prove
His title certain to the joys above;
For this he sends the murmuring nurse, who calls
The holy stranger to these dismal walls;
And doth not he, the pious man, appear,
He, "passing rich with forty pounds a year"?
Ah! no; a shepherd of a different stock,
And far unlike him, feeds this little flock:
A jovial youth, who thinks his Sunday's task
As much as God or man can fairly ask;

The rest he gives to loves and labours light,
To fields the morning, and to feasts the night;
None better skill'd the noisy pack to guide,
To urge their chase, to cheer them or to chide;
A sportsman keen, he shoots through half the day,
And, skill'd at whist, devotes the night to play.
Then, while such honours bloom around his head,
Shall he sit sadly by the sick man's bed,
To raise the hope he feels not, or with zeal
To combat fears that e'en the pious feel?
  Now once again the gloomy scene explore,
Less gloomy now; the bitter hour is o'er,
The man of many sorrows sighs no more.—
Up yonder hill, behold how sadly slow
The bier moves winding from the vale below;
There lie the happy dead, from trouble free,
And the glad parish pays the frugal fee.
No more, O Death! thy victim starts to hear
Churchwarden stern, or kingly overseer;
No more the farmer claims his humble bow,
Thou art his lord, the best of tyrants thou!
  Now to the church behold the mourners come,
Sedately torpid and devoutly dumb;
The village children now their games suspend,
To see the bier that bears their ancient friend:
For he was one in all their idle sport,
And like a monarch ruled their little court;
The pliant bow he form'd, the flying ball,
The bat, the wicket, were his labours all;
Him now they follow to his grave, and stand
Silent and sad, and gazing, hand in hand;
While bending low, their eager eyes explore
The mingled relics of the parish poor.
The bell tolls late, the moping owl flies round,
Fear marks the flight and magnifies the sound;
The busy priest, detain'd by weightier care,
Defers his duty till the day of prayer;
And, waiting long, the crowd retire distress'd,
To think a poor man's bones should lie unbless'd.

Book II

There are found, amid the Evils of a laborious Life, some Views of Tranquillity and Happiness—The Repose and Pleasure of a Summer Sabbath: interrupted by Intoxication and Dispute—Village Detraction—Complaints of the 'Squire—The Evening Riots—Justice—Reasons for this unpleasant View of Rustic Life: the Effect it should have upon the Lower Classes; and the Higher—These last have their peculiar Distresses: Exemplified in the Life and heroic Death of Lord Robert Manners—Concluding Address to His Grace the Duke of Rutland.

No longer truth, though shown in verse, disdain,
But own the Village Life a life of pain.
I too must yield, that oft amid these woes
Are gleams of transient mirth and hours of sweet repose,
Such as you find on yonder sportive Green,
The 'squire's tall gate and churchway-walk between;
Where loitering stray a little tribe of friends,
On a fair Sunday when the sermon ends.
Then rural beaux their best attire put on,
To win their nymphs, as other nymphs are won;
While those long wed go plain, and, by degrees,
Like other husbands, quit their care to please.
Some of the sermon talk, a sober crowd,
And loudly praise, if it were preach'd aloud;
Some on the labours of the week look round,
Feel their own worth, and think their toil renown'd;
While some, whose hopes to no renown extend,
Are only pleased to find their labours end.
Thus, as their hours glide on, with pleasure fraught,
Their careful masters brood the painful thought;
Much in their mind they murmur and lament,
That one fair day should be so idly spent;
And think that Heaven deals hard, to tithe their store
And tax their time for preachers and the poor.
Yet still, ye humbler friends, enjoy your hour,
This is your portion, yet unclaim'd of power;
This is Heaven's gift to weary men oppress'd,
And seems the type of their expected rest.
But yours, alas! are joys that soon decay;
Frail joys, begun and ended with the day;
Or yet, while day permits those joys to reign,
The village vices drive them from the plain.
See the stout churl, in drunken fury great,
Strike the bare bosom of his teeming mate!
His naked vices, rude and unrefined,
Exert their open empire o'er the mind;
But can we less the senseless rage despise,
Because the savage acts without disguise?
Yet here disguise, the city's vice, is seen,
And Slander steals along and taints the Green:
At her approach domestic peace is gone,
Domestic broils at her approach come on;
She to the wife the husband's crime conveys,
She tells the husband when his consort strays,
Her busy tongue through all the little state
Diffuses doubt, suspicion, and debate;
Peace, tim'rous goddess! quits her old domain,
In sentiment and song content to reign.
Nor are the nymphs that breathe the rural air

So fair as Cynthia's, nor so chaste as fair:
These to the town afford each fresher face,
And the clown's trull receives the peer's embrace;
From whom, should chance again convey her down,
The peer's disease in turn attacks the clown.
  Here too the 'squire, or 'squire-like farmer, talk,
How round their regions nightly pilferers walk;
How from their ponds the fish are borne, and all
The rip'ning treasures from their lofty wall;
How meaner rivals in their sports delight,
Just rich enough to claim a doubtful right;
Who take a licence round their fields to stray,
A mongrel race! the poachers of the day.
  And hark! the riots of the Green begin,
That sprang at first from yonder noisy inn;
What time the weekly pay was vanish'd all,
And the slow hostess scored the threat'ning wall;
What time they ask'd, their friendly feast to close,
A final cup, and that will make them foes;
When blows ensue that break the arm of toil,
And rustic battle ends the boobies' broil.
  Save when to yonder Hall they bend their way,
Where the grave justice ends the grievous fray;
He who recites, to keep the poor in awe,
The law's vast volume—for he knows the law:—
To him with anger or with shame repair
The injured peasant and deluded fair.
  Lo! at his throne the silent nymph appears,
Frail by her shape, but modest in her tears;
And while she stands abash'd, with conscious eye,
Some favourite female of her judge glides by,
Who views with scornful glance the strumpet's fate,
And thanks the stars that made her keeper great;
Near her the swain, about to bear for life
One certain evil, doubts 'twixt war and wife;
But, while the falt'ring damsel takes her oath,
Consents to wed, and so secures them both.
  Yet, why, you ask, these humble crimes relate,
Why make the poor as guilty as the great?
To show the great, those mightier sons of pride,
How near in vice the lowest are allied;
Such are their natures and their passions such,
But these disguise too little, those too much:
So shall the man of power and pleasure see
In his own slave as vile a wretch as he;
In his luxurious lord the servant find
His own low pleasures and degenerate mind:
And each in all the kindred vices trace

Of a poor, blind, bewilder'd, erring race;
Who, a short time in varied fortune past,
Die, and are equal in the dust at last.
And you, ye poor, who still lament your fate,
Forbear to envy those you call the great;
And know, amid those blessings they possess,
They are, like you, the victims of distress;
While sloth with many a pang torments her slave,
Fear waits on guilt, and danger shakes the brave.
Oh! if in life one noble chief appears,
Great in his name, while blooming in his years;
Born to enjoy whate'er delights mankind,
And yet to all you feel or fear resign'd;
Who gave up joys and hopes, to you unknown,
For pains and dangers greater than your own:
If such there be, then let your murmurs cease,
Think, think of him, and take your lot in peace.
And such there was:—Oh! grief, that checks our pride!
Weeping we say, there was—for Manners died:
Beloved of Heaven, these humble lines forgive,
That sing of Thee, and thus aspire to live.
As the tall oak, whose vigorous branches form
An ample shade and brave the wildest storm,
High o'er the subject wood is seen to grow,
The guard and glory of the trees below;
Till on its head the fiery bolt descends,
And o'er the plain the shatter'd trunk extends;
Yet then it lies, all wond'rous as before,
And still the glory, though the guard no more:
So THOU, when every virtue, every grace,
Rose in thy soul, or shone within thy face;
When, though the son of Granby, thou wert known
Less by thy father's glory than thy own;
When Honour loved and gave thee every charm,
Fire to thy eye and vigour to thy arm;
Then from our lofty hopes and longing eyes,
Fate and thy virtues call'd thee to the skies;
Yet still we wonder at thy tow'ring fame,
And, losing thee, still dwell upon thy name.
Oh! ever honour'd, ever valued! say,
What verse can praise thee, or what work repay?
Yet verse (in all we can) thy worth repays,
Nor trusts the tardy zeal of future days;—
Honours for thee thy country shall prepare,
Thee in their hearts, the good, the brave shall bear;
To deeds like thine shall noblest chiefs aspire,
The Muse shall mourn thee, and the world admire.
In future times, when, smit with Glory's charms,

The untried youth first quits a father's arms;—
"Oh! be like him," the weeping sire shall say;
"Like Manners walk, who walk'd in Honour's way;
"In danger foremost, yet in death sedate,
"Oh! be like him in all things, but his fate!"
If for that fate such public tears be shed,
That Victory seems to die now THOU art dead;
How shall a friend his nearer hope resign,
That friend a brother, and whose soul was thine?
By what bold lines shall we his grief express,
Or by what soothing numbers make it less?
'Tis not, I know, the chiming of a song,
Nor all the powers that to the Muse belong,
Words aptly cull'd and meanings well express'd,
Can calm the sorrows of a wounded breast;
But Virtue, soother of the fiercest pains,
Shall heal that bosom, Rutland, where she reigns.
Yet hard the task to heal the bleeding heart,
To bid the still-recurring thoughts depart,
Tame the fierce grief and stem the rising sigh,
And curb rebellious passion with reply;
Calmly to dwell on all that pleased before,
And yet to know that all shall please no more—
Oh! glorious labour of the soul, to save
Her captive powers, and bravely mourn the brave.
To such these thoughts will lasting comfort give—
Life is not measured by the time we live:
'Tis not an even course of threescore years,
A life of narrow views and paltry fears,
Gray hairs and wrinkles and the cares they bring,
That take from death the terrors or the sting;
But 'tis the gen'rous spirit, mounting high
Above the world, that native of the sky;
The noble spirit, that, in dangers brave,
Calmly looks on, or looks beyond the grave:—
Such Manners was, so he resign'd his breath,
If in a glorious, then a timely death.
Cease then that grief, and let those tears subside;
If Passion rule us, be that passion pride;
If Reason, Reason bids us strive to raise
Our fallen hearts, and be like him we praise;
Or, if Affection still the soul subdue,
Bring all his virtues, all his worth in view,
And let Affection find its comfort too:
For how can Grief so deeply wound the heart,
When Admiration claims so large a part?
Grief is a foe; expel him, then, thy soul;

Let nobler thoughts the nearer views control!
Oh! make the age to come thy better care;
See other Rutlands, other Granbys there!
And, as thy thoughts through streaming ages glide,
See other heroes die as Manners died:
And, from their fate, thy race shall nobler grow,
As trees shoot upwards that are pruned below;
Or as old Thames, borne down with decent pride,
Sees his young streams run warbling at his side;
Though some, by art cut off, no longer run,
And some are lost beneath the summer's sun—
Yet the pure stream moves on, and, as it moves,
Its power increases and its use improves;
While plenty round its spacious waves bestow,
Still it flows on, and shall for ever flow.

SIR JOHN HENRY MOORE

(1756-1777-1780)

The Duke of Benevento
A Tale[1]

I HATE a prologue to a story
Worse than the tuning of a fiddle,
  Squeaking and dinning;
Hang order and connection,
I love to dash into the middle;
  Exclusive of the fame and glory,
There is a comfort on reflection
  To think you've done with the beginning.

And so at supper one fine night,
  Hearing a cry of Alla, Alla,
The Prince was damnably confounded,
    And in a fright,
But more so when he saw himself surrounded
By fifty Turks; and at their head the fierce Abdalla.

And then he look'd a little grave
To find himself become a slave,

[1] Published in *Poetical Trifles*, 1778. Text of first edition.

And thought the Corsair rather in a hurry,
Out of all rules,
To make the Duke of Benevento curry
And take care of his mules:
But as 'twas vain to make a riot,
Without grimace,
Or a wry face,
He gave a shrug, and rubb'd his mules in quiet.

It would have been great sport
To all the puppies of the court
To view these changes, and disasters;
But their enjoyments
Were damp'd by certain slovenly employments,
Not more amusing than their master's.

But who can paint his grief,
Who can describe the transports of his sorrow
When he beheld Almida's charms
Conducted to Abdalla's arms,
And saw no prospect of relief?
But that the blooming Maid,
By cruel destiny betray'd,
Must no more triumph in that name to-morrow.

Not understanding what he said,
Seeing him caper like an antic,
And tear his hair, and beat his head,
The Eunuch wisely judg'd him to be frantic.

But she, the lovely cause of all his care,
Darting a look to his enraptur'd soul,
Might soften e'en the madness of despair;
Bade him his weak, unmanly rage controul,
Each favouring opportunity improve;
And bade him dare to hope, and bade him dare to love.

The Corsair in a transport of surprise,
When he beheld Almida's sparkling eyes,
Her faultless figure, her majestic air,
The graceful ringlets of her auburn hair,
That twin'd in many a fold to deck,
Not hide, the dazzling whiteness of her neck;
The various charms her flowing robe reveal'd,
While fancy whisper'd to his throbbing heart
Each nameless beauty, that well-judging art,
To fix the roving mind, had carefully conceal'd.

'O Mahomet! I thank thee,' he exclaim'd,
'That to thy servant thou hast given
'This bright inhabitant of heaven,
'To gild the progress of his life below,
'For him this beauteous Houri fram'd;
'Enjoyment I have known, but never lov'd till now.'

Then with a smile
Might ev'n a Stoic's heart beguile,
The fair one with a little flattery
To his charm'd ears address'd her battery.

'Still may my Lord (said she) approve
'The happy object of his love,
'Then when Almida sues,
'Let not Abdalla's heart her first request refuse:
'Deign to suspend but for three days
'The progress of your amorous flame,
'And to console my heart for these delays,
'Grant me two small requests that I shall name.
'The first is to desire,
'If you incline,
'Five hundred lashes for two friends of mine,
'And just as many for a Fry'r;
'The next a litter, and two mules,
'The heavy hours of absence to amuse,
'Besides a Muleteer that I shall chuse,
'At my disposal, subject to my rules.'

So said, the culprit knaves appear,
Upon each rascal's pamper'd hide
The stripes are in due form applied,
Which done, she chose,
You may suppose,
Her lover for her Muleteer.

Then with a voice sweet as an angel's song,
While Tancred with attentive ear
In silent rapture stoop'd to hear,
The Beauteous Maid the silence broke,
Conviction follow'd as she spoke,
And truth, and soft persuasion, dwelt on her enchanting tongue.

'With grief those scenes unwilling I disclose,
'Whence every error, each misfortune, rose;
'When pleasures, of the lowest, meanest kind,

'Unnerv'd your feeble frame, and checked the progress of your mind.
'In vain your people's curses, or their tears,
'Your heart assail'd,
'Two flattering knaves had charm'd your ears,
'And Raymond vainly counsel'd, or as vainly rail'd;
'He was your father's friend, wise, honest, brave,
'Him you displac'd,
'And listening to the malice of a slave,
'The Guardian of your Crown was banish'd, and disgrac'd.

'Me too you lov'd, and I approv'd the flame
'In hopes my counsels might have weight,
'To prompt you to redress the state,
'And save from infamy your sinking name.

'But soon your Confessor, the crafty Priest,
'Rage, hate, and malice, rankling in his breast,
'With timorous scruples fill'd your wavering mind;
'In vain each finer feeling strove
'To guard your heart, and court it to be kind,
'While haggard superstition triumph'd over love.

'But justice still pursues betimes,
'E'en now, for she directs the hour,
'The Priest, and the vile partners of his pow'r,
'Feel vengeance overtake their crimes.

'The Turks' unnotic'd march, last night's surprise,
'The foe unthought-of thundering at the gate,
'At length have clear'd your eyes,
Their treacherous negligence is found, is felt too late.

'No more of this unpleasing strain—
'If thinking, acting like a man,
'Reform'd by slavery's painful chain,
'Virtue within your breast resume her reign,
'Inspire your thoughts, and guide your future plan,

'My heart will still be your's: e'en Raymond too
'Still loves his Prince, to him repair,
'Confess your faults, his aid demand,
The gallant veteran waits but your command
'To spread his conquering banners to the air,
'To sacrifice his life with you,
'Or rescue and relieve his native land.

'Abdalla claims my promise in three days.
'Think then on me,
'Danger and death attend delays,
'Be virtuous, be daring, and be free.'

The Lady's sermon was a little long,
Not but she talk'd both well and wittily,
And then she look'd so prettily,
Her eyes excus'd the freedoms of her tongue.

For when a favourite mistress speaks,
We always think her in the right,
E'en though she talks for days, or weeks,
Or in the middle of the night.

To say the truth, her speech was rather rough,
But as she promis'd him her heart,
Upon the whole he took it in good part,
And as he lov'd her, lik'd it well enough.

So thank'd her for the good advice,
And took his leave; and ere he went,
By way of compliment,
Call'd her his guardian angel, his sweet tutor,
And kiss'd her fair hand, once, or twice,
And swore to be a good boy for the future.

In short, it was so settled; the third night,
By good luck too 'twas dark as hell,
Tancred with Raymond and a chosen band
Surprise the guards, who in their fright
Make but a shabby stand,
And enter at the gates pell-mell.

Mean time Abdalla, snug in bed,
Finding Almida staid away so long,
Suspecting there was something wrong,
Look'd out; and found his troops were kill'd or gone,
Himself a prisoner, and alone,
And Tancred reigning in his stead.

And now the sore-back'd scoundrels in a trice
Came kindly with their counsels, and advice,
Proposing as a pious work
Just to impale
Or stick a hedge-stake through the tail
Of the poor Turk.

Indignant fury flash'd from Tancred's eye—
'Ye vile corruptors of my youth,
'Ye foes to honour, honesty, and truth,
'Hence from my sight, nor offer a reply:
'If the third day
'Within the limits of this state
'Disclose your stay,
'Not e'en Almida's self shall save you from your fate.

'Go, brave Abdalla, to your native shore;
'From sloth, from vice, from infamy,
'Your kind instructions and assistance
'Have haply set me free;
'Thanks for your visit, pray return no more,
'Let us be always friends, but at a distance.

'And now, my better angel, whose kind care
'The mists of error from my sight dispell'd,
'Burst the vile fetters that my reason held,
'Restor'd fair wisdom's gentle sway,
'Guided my steps to her, and pointed out the way;
'Now, while my people's eager voice,
'And Raymond too confirms my choice,
'O come, my heavenly fair!
'Ascend, adorn, and bless my throne;
'Still with that cheering influence preside,
'My life, my future conduct, guide,
'Inspire my raptur'd heart, and make it virtuous as your own.'

WILLIAM COWPER

(1731-1779-1800)

Olney Hymns[1]

Walking With God. Gen. v. 24

OH! for a closer walk with GOD,
A calm and heav'nly frame;
A light to shine upon the road
That leads me to the Lamb!

[1] Published in 1779, in collaboration with the Rev. John Newton. Text of first edition.

Where is the blessedness I knew
  When first I saw the Lord?
Where is the soul-refreshing view
  Of Jesus, and his word?

What peaceful hours I once enjoy'd!
  How sweet their mem'ry still!
But they have left an aching void,
  The world can never fill.

Return, O holy Dove, return,
  Sweet messenger of rest;
I hate the sins that made thee mourn,
  And drove thee from my breast.

The dearest idol I have known,
  Whate'er that idol be;
Help me to tear it from thy throne,
  And worship only thee.

So shall my walk be close with God,
  Calm and serene my frame;
So purer light shall mark the road
  That leads me to the Lamb.

Praise for the Fountain Opened. Zech. xiii. 1

There is a fountain fill'd with blood
  Drawn from Emmanuel's veins;
And sinners, plung'd beneath that flood,
  Lose all their guilty stains.

The dying thief rejoic'd to see
  That fountain in his day;
And there have I, as vile as he,
  Wash'd all my sins away.

Dear dying Lamb, thy precious blood
  Shall never lose its pow'r;
Till all the ransom'd church of God
  Be sav'd, to sin no more.

E'er since, by faith, I saw the stream
  Thy flowing wounds supply:
Redeeming love has been my theme,
  And shall be till I die.

Then in a nobler sweeter song
  I'll sing thy power to save;
When this poor lisping stamm'ring tongue
  Lies silent in the grave.

Lord, I believe thou hast prepar'd
  (Unworthy tho' I be)
For me a blood-bought free reward,
  A golden harp for me!

'Tis strung, and tun'd, for endless years,
  And form'd by pow'r divine;
To sound in God the Father's ears,
  No other name but thine.

Contentment. Phil. iv. 11

Fierce passions discompose the mind,
  As tempests vex the sea;
But calm content and peace we find,
  When, Lord, we turn to thee.

In vain by reason and by rule,
  We try to bend the will;
For none, but in the Saviour's school,
  Can learn the heav'nly skill.

Since at his feet my soul has sat,
  His gracious words to hear;
Contented with my present state,
  I cast, on him, my care.

"Art thou a sinner, soul?" he said,
  "Then how canst thou complain?
How light thy troubles here, if weigh'd
  With everlasting pain!

If thou of murmuring wouldst be cur'd,
  Compare thy griefs with mine;
Think what my love for thee endur'd,
  And thou wilt not repine.

'Tis I appoint thy daily lot,
  And I do all things well:
Thou soon shalt leave this wretched spot,
  And rise with me to dwell.

In life my grace shall strength supply,
  Proportion'd to thy day;
At death thou still shalt find me nigh,
  To wipe thy tears away."

Thus I who once my wretched days
  In vain repinings spent;
Taught in my Saviour's school of grace,
  Have learn'd to be content.

The Happy Change

How blest thy creature is, O GOD,
  When with a single eye,
He views the lustre of thy word,
  The day-spring from on high!

Thro' all the storms that veil the skies,
  And frown on earthly things;
The Sun of righteousness he eyes,
  With healing on his wings.

Struck by that light, the human heart,
  A barren soil no more;
Sends the sweet smell of grace abroad,
  Where serpents lurk'd before.

The soul, a dreary province once
  Of Satan's dark domain;
Feels a new empire form'd within,
  And owns a heav'nly reign.

The glorious orb, whose golden beams
  The fruitful year control;
Since first, obedient to thy word,
  He started from the goal;

Has cheer'd the nations, with the joys
  His orient rays impart;
But JESUS, 'tis thy light alone,
  Can shine upon the heart.

I Will Praise the Lord at All Times

Winter has a joy for me,
While the Saviour's charms I read,
Lowly, meek, from blemish free,
In the snow-drop's pensive head.

Spring returns, and brings along
Life-invigorating suns:
Hark! the turtle's plaintive song,
Seems to speak his dying grones!

Summer has a thousand charms,
All expressive of his worth;
'Tis his sun that lights and warms,
His the air that cools the earth.

What, has autumn left to say
Nothing, of a Saviour's grace?
Yes, the beams of milder day
Tell me of his smiling face.

Light appears with early dawn,
While the sun makes haste to rise,
See his bleeding beauties, drawn
On the blushes of the skies.

Ev'ning, with a silent pace,
Slowly moving in the west,
Shews an emblem of his grace,
Points to an eternal rest.

The Shrubbery, Written in a Time of Affliction[1]

OH, HAPPY shades—to me unblest!
  Friendly to peace, but not to me!
How ill the scene that offers rest,
  And heart that cannot rest, agree!

This glassy stream, that spreading pine,
  Those alders quiv'ring to the breeze,
Might sooth a soul less hurt than mine,
  And please, if any thing could please.

But fix'd unalterable care
  Foregoes not what she feels within,
Shows the same sadness ev'ry where,
  And slights the season and the scene.

---

[1] Published in *Poems*, 1782. Text of *Poems*, 1800.

For all that pleas'd in wood or lawn,
While peace posses'd these silent bow'rs,
Her animating smile withdrawn,
Has lost its beauties and its pow'rs.

The saint or moralist should tread
This moss-grown alley, musing, slow;
They seek, like me, the secret shade,
But not, like me, to nourish woe!

Me fruitful scenes and prospects waste
Alike admonish not to roam;
These tell me of enjoyments past,
And those of sorrows yet to come.

Verses
Supposed to be Written by Alexander Selkirk, During His Solitary Abode in the Island of Juan Fernandez[1]

I AM monarch of all I survey,
My right there is none to dispute;
From the centre all round to the sea,
I am lord of the fowl and the brute.
Oh, solitude! where are the charms
That sages have seen in thy face?
Better dwell in the midst of alarms,
Than reign in this horrible place.

I am out of humanity's reach,
I must finish my journey alone,
Never hear the sweet music of speech;
I start at the sound of my own.
The beasts, that roam over the plain,
My form with indifference see;
They are so unacquainted with man,
Their tameness is shocking to me.

Society, friendship, and love,
Divinely bestow'd upon man,
Oh, had I the wings of a dove,
How soon would I taste you again!
My sorrows I then might assuage
In the ways of religion and truth,

[1] Published in *Poems*, 1782. Text of *Poems*, 1800.

Might learn from the wisdom of age,
  And be cheer'd by the sallies of youth.

Religion! what treasure untold
  Resides in that heavenly word!
More precious than silver and gold,
  Or all that this earth can afford.
But the sound of the church-going bell
  These vallies and rocks never heard,
Ne'er sigh'd at the sound of a knell,
  Or smil'd when a sabbath appear'd.

Ye winds, that have made me your sport,
  Convey to this desolate shore
Some cordial endearing report
  Of a land I shall visit no more.
My friends, do they now and then send
  A wish or a thought after me?
O tell me I yet have a friend,
  Though a friend I am never to see.

How fleet is a glance of the mind!
  Compar'd with the speed of its flight,
The tempest itself lags behind,
  And the swift wing'd arrows of light.
When I think of my own native land,
  In a moment I seem to be there;
But alas! recollection at hand
  Soon hurries me back to despair.

But the sea-fowl is gone to her nest,
  The beast is laid down in his lair,
Ev'n here is a season of rest,
  And I to my cabin repair.
There's mercy in every place;
  And mercy, encouraging thought!
Gives even affliction a grace,
  And reconciles man to his lot.

The Diverting History of John Gilpin, Showing How He Went Farther Than he Intended, and Came Safe Home Again[1]

JOHN GILPIN was a citizen
  Of credit and renown,
A train-band captain eke was he
  Of famous London town.

John Gilpin's spouse said to her dear—
  Though wedded we have been
These twice ten tedious years, yet we
  No holiday have seen.

To-morrow is our wedding-day,
  And we will then repair
Unto the Bell at Edmonton
  All in a chaise and pair.

My sister, and my sister's child,
  Myself, and children three,
Will fill the chaise; so you must ride
  On horseback after we.

He soon replied—I do admire
  Of womankind but one,
And you are she, my dearest dear,
  Therefore it shall be done.

I am a linen-draper bold,
  As all the world doth know,
And my good friend the calender
  Will lend his horse to go.

Quoth Mrs. Gilpin—That's well said;
  And, for that wine is dear,
We will be furnish'd with our own,
  Which is both bright and clear.

John Gilpin kiss'd his loving wife;
  O'erjoy'd was he to find
That, though on pleasure she was bent,
  She had a frugal mind.

[1] Written in October, 1782. Published in the *Public Advertiser*, November 14, 1782. Text of *Poems*, 1800.

The morning came, the chaise was brought,
  But yet was not allow'd
To drive up to the door, lest all
  Should say that she was proud.

So three doors off the chaise was stay'd,
  Where they did all get in;
Six precious souls, and all agog
  To dash through thick and thin!

Smack went the whip, round went the wheels,
  Were never folk so glad,
The stones did rattle underneath,
  As if Cheapside were mad.

John Gilpin at his horse's side
  Seiz'd fast the flowing mane,
And up he got, in haste to ride,
  But soon came down again;

For saddle-tree scarce reach'd had he,
  His journey to begin,
When, turning round his head, he saw
  Three customers come in.

So down he came; for loss of time,
  Although it griev'd him sore,
Yet loss of pence, full well he knew,
  Would trouble him much more.

'Twas long before the customers
  Were suited to their mind,
When Betty screaming came down stairs—
  "The wine is left behind!"

Good lack! quoth he—yet bring it me,
  My leathern belt likewise,
In which I bear my trusty sword
  When I do exercise.

Now mistress Gilpin (careful soul!)
  Had two stone bottles found,
To hold the liquor that she lov'd,
  And keep it safe and sound.

Each bottle had a curling ear,
  Through which the belt he drew,

And hung a bottle on each side,
  To make his balance true.

Then, over all, that he might be
  Equipp'd from top to toe,
His long red cloak, well brush'd and neat,
  He manfully did throw.

Now see him mounted once again
  Upon his nimble steed,
Full slowly pacing o'er the stones,
  With caution and good heed!

But, finding soon a smoother road
  Beneath his well-shod feet,
The snorting beast began to trot,
  Which gall'd him in his seat.

So, Fair and softly, John he cried,
  But John he cried in vain;
That trot became a gallop soon,
  In spite of curb and rein.

So stooping down, as needs he must
  Who cannot sit upright,
He grasp'd the mane with both his hands,
  And eke with all his might.

His horse, who never in that sort
  Had handled been before,
What thing upon his back had got
  Did wonder more and more.

Away went Gilpin, neck or nought;
  Away went hat and wig!—
He little dreamt, when he set out,
  Of running such a rig!

The wind did blow, the cloak did fly,
  Like streamer long and gay,
Till, loop and button failing both,
  At last it flew away.

Then might all people well discern
  The bottles he had slung;
A bottle swinging at each side,
  As hath been said or sung.

The dogs did bark, the children scream'd,
  Up flew the windows all;
And ev'ry soul cried out—Well done!
  As loud as he could bawl.

Away went Gilpin—who but he?
  His fame soon spread around—
He carries weight! he rides a race!
  'Tis for a thousand pound!

And still, as fast as he drew near,
  'Twas wonderful to view
How in a trice the turnpike-men
  Their gates wide open threw.

And now, as he went bowing down
  His reeking head full low,
The bottles twain behind his back
  Were shatter'd at a blow.

Down ran the wine into the road,
  Most piteous to be seen,
Which made his horse's flanks to smoke
  As they had basted been.

But still he seem'd to carry weight,
  With leathern girdle brac'd;
For all might see the bottle-necks
  Still dangling at his waist.

Thus all through merry Islington
  These gambols he did play,
And till he came upon the Wash
  Of Edmonton so gay.

And there he threw the wash about
  On both sides of the way,
Just like unto a trundling mop,
  Or a wild goose at play.

At Edmonton his loving wife
  From the balcony spied
Her tender husband, wond'ring much
  To see how he did ride.

Stop, stop, John Gilpin!—Here's the house—
  They all at once did cry;

The dinner waits, and we are tir'd:
  Said Gilpin—So am I!

But yet his horse was not a whit
  Inclin'd to tarry there;
For why?—his owner had a house
  Full ten miles off, at Ware.

So like an arrow swift he flew,
  Shot by an archer strong;
So did he fly—which brings me to
  The middle of my song.

Away went Gilpin, out of breath,
  And sore against his will,
Till at his friend the calender's
  His horse at last stood still.

The calender, amaz'd to see
  His neighbour in such trim,
Laid down his pipe, flew to the gate,
  And thus accosted him:—

What news? what news? your tidings tell;
  Tell me you must and shall—
Say why bare-headed you are come,
  Or why you come at all?

Now Gilpin had a pleasant wit,
  And lov'd a timely joke;
And thus unto the calender
  In merry guise he spoke:—

I came because your horse would come;
  And, if I well forebode,
My hat and wig will soon be here—
  They are upon the road.

The calender, right glad to find
  His friend in merry pin,
Return'd him not a single word,
  But to the house went in;

Whence straight he came with hat and wig;
  A wig that flow'd behind,
A hat not much the worse for wear,
  Each comely in its kind.

He held them up, and, in his turn,
  Thus show'd his ready wit—
My head is twice as big as your's,
  They therefore needs must fit.

But let me scrape the dirt away
  That hangs upon your face;
And stop and eat, for well you may
  Be in a hungry case.

Said John—It is my wedding-day,
  And all the world would stare,
If wife should dine at Edmonton
  And I should dine at Ware!

So, turning to his horse, he said—
  I am in haste to dine;
'Twas for your pleasure you came here,
  You shall go back for mine.

Ah, luckless speech, and bootless boast!
  For which he paid full dear;
For, while he spake, a braying ass
  Did sing most loud and clear;

Whereat his horse did snort, as he
  Had heard a lion roar,
And gallop'd off with all his might,
  As he had done before.

Away went Gilpin, and away
  Went Gilpin's hat and wig!
He lost them sooner than at first—
  For why?—they were too big!

Now, mistress Gilpin, when she saw
  Her husband posting down
Into the country far away,
  She pull'd out half a crown;

And thus unto the youth she said
  That drove them to the Bell—
This shall be yours when you bring back
  My husband safe and well.

The youth did ride, and soon did meet
  John coming back amain;

Whom in a trice he tried to stop,
  By catching at his rein;

But, not performing what he meant,
  And gladly would have done,
The frighted steed he frighted more,
  And made him faster run.

Away went Gilpin, and away
  Went post-boy at his heels!—
The post-boy's horse right glad to miss
  The lumb'ring of the wheels.

Six gentlemen upon the road,
  Thus seeing Gilpin fly,
With post-boy scamp'ring in the rear,
  They rais'd the hue and cry:

Stop thief! stop thief!—a highwayman!
  Not one of them was mute;
And all and each that pass'd that way
  Did join in the pursuit.

And now the turnpike gates again
  Flew open in short space;
The toll-men thinking, as before,
  That Gilpin rode a race.

And so he did—and won it too!—
  For he got first to town;
Nor stopp'd till where he had got up
  He did again get down.

Now let us sing—Long live the king,
  And Gilpin long live he;
And, when he next doth ride abroad,
  May I be there to see!

The Task[1]

Book I

The Sofa

ARGUMENT OF THE FIRST BOOK.—Historical deduction of seats, from the stool to the Sofa—A School-boy's ramble—A walk in the country—The scene

[1] Published in 1785. Text of *Poems*, 1800.

described—Rural sounds as well as sights delightful—Another walk—Mistake concerning the charms of solitude corrected—Colonnades commended—Alcove, and the view from it—The wilderness—The grove—The thresher—The necessity and the benefits of exercise—The works of nature superior to, and in some instances inimitable by, art—The wearisomeness of what is commonly called a life of pleasure—Change of scene sometimes expedient—A common described, and the character of crazy Kate introduced—Gipsies—The blessings of civilized life—That state most favourable to virtue—The South Sea islanders compassionated, but chiefly Omai—His present state of mind supposed—Civilized life friendly to virtue, but not great cities—Great cities, and London in particular, allowed their due praise, but censured—Fete champetre—The book concludes with a reflection on the fatal effects of dissipation and effeminacy upon our public measures.

I SING the SOFA. I, who lately sang
Truth, Hope, and Charity, and touch'd with awe
The solemn chords, and with a trembling hand,
Escap'd with pain from that advent'rous flight,
Now seek repose upon an humbler theme:
The theme though humble, yet august and proud
Th' occasion—for the Fair commands the song.
  Time was, when clothing sumptuous or for use,
Save their own painted skins, our sires had none.
As yet black breeches were not; satin smooth,
Or velvet soft, or plush with shaggy pile:
The hardy chief upon the rugged rock
Wash'd by the sea, or on the grav'ly bank
Thrown up by wintry torrents roaring loud,
Fearless of wrong, repos'd his weary strength.
Those barb'rous ages past, succeeded next
The birth-day of invention; weak at first,
Dull in design, and clumsy to perform.
Joint-stools were then created; on three legs
Upborn they stood. Three legs upholding firm
A massy slab, in fashion square or round.
On such a stool immortal Alfred sat,
And sway'd the sceptre of his infant realms:
And such in ancient halls and mansions drear
May still be seen; but perforated sore,
And drill'd in holes, the solid oak is found,
By worms voracious eating through and through.
  At length a generation more refin'd
Improv'd the simple plan; made three legs four,
Gave them a twisted form vermicular,
And o'er the seat, with plenteous wadding stuff'd,
Induc'd a splendid cover, green and blue,
Yellow and red, of tap'stry richly wrought,
And woven close, or needle-work sublime.
There might ye see the piony spread wide,

The full-blown rose, the shepherd and his lass,
Lap-dog and lambkin with black staring eyes,
And parrots with twin cherries in their beak.
  Now came the cane from India, smooth and bright
With Nature's varnish; sever'd into stripes
That interlac'd each other, these supplied
Of texture firm a lattice-work, that brac'd
The new machine, and it became a chair.
But restless was the chair; the back erect
Distress'd the weary loins, that felt no ease;
The slipp'ry seat betray'd the sliding part
That press'd it, and the feet hung dangling down,
Anxious in vain to find the distant floor.
These for the rich: the rest, whom fate had plac'd
In modest mediocrity, content
With base materials, sat on well-tann'd hides,
Obdurate and unyielding, glassy smooth,
With here and there a tuft of crimson yarn,
Or scarlet crewel, in the cushion fixt;
If cushion might be call'd, what harder seem'd
Than the firm oak of which the frame was form'd.
No want of timber then was felt or fear'd
In Albion's happy isle. The lumber stood
Pond'rous and fixt by its own massy weight.
But elbows still were wanting; these, some say,
An alderman of Cripplegate contriv'd:
And some ascribe th' invention to a priest
Burly and big, and studious of his ease.
But, rude at first, and not with easy slope
Receding wide, they press'd against the ribs,
And bruis'd the side; and, elevated high,
Taught the rais'd shoulders to invade the ears.
Long time elaps'd or e'er our rugged sires
Complain'd, though incommodiously pent in,
And ill at ease behind. The ladies first
'Gan murmur, as became the softer sex.
Ingenious fancy, never better pleas'd
Than when employ'd t'accommodate the fair,
Heard the sweet moan with pity, and devis'd
The soft settee; one elbow at each end,
And in the midst an elbow it receiv'd,
United yet divided, twain at once.
So sit two kings of Brentford on one throne;
And so two citizens who take the air,
Close pack'd, and smiling, in a chaise and one.
But relaxation of the languid frame,
By soft recumbency of outstretch'd limbs,
Was bliss reserv'd for happier days. So slow

The growth of what is excellent; so hard
T' attain perfection in this nether world.
Thus first necessity invented stools,
Convenience next suggested elbow-chairs,
And luxury th'accomplish'd Sofa last.
  The nurse sleeps sweetly, hir'd to watch the sick,
Whom snoring she disturbs. As sweetly he,
Who quits the coach-box at the midnight hour
To sleep within the carriage more secure,
His legs depending at the open door.
Sweet sleep enjoys the curate in his desk,
The tedious rector drawling o'er his head;
And sweet the clerk below. But neither sleep
Of lazy nurse, who snores the sick man dead,
Nor his who quits the box at midnight hour
To slumber in the carriage more secure,
Nor sleep enjoy'd by curate in his desk,
Nor yet the dozings of the clerk, are sweet,
Compar'd with the repose the Sofa yields.
  Oh may I live exempted (while I live
Guiltless of pamper'd appetite obscene)
From pangs arthritic, that infest the toe
Of libertine excess. The Sofa suits
The gouty limb, 'tis true; but gouty limb,
Though on a Sofa, may I never feel:
For I have lov'd the rural walk through lanes
Of grassy swarth, close cropt by nibbling sheep,
And skirted thick with intertexture firm
Of thorny boughs; have lov'd the rural walk
O'er hills, through valleys, and by rivers' brink,
E'er since a truant boy I pass'd my bounds
T' enjoy a ramble on the banks of Thames;
And still remember, nor without regret
Of hours that sorrow since has much endear'd,
How oft, my slice of pocket store consum'd,
Still hung'ring, pennyless and far from home,
I fed on scarlet hips and stony haws,
Or blushing crabs, or berries, that imboss
The bramble, black as jet, or sloes austere.
Hard fare! but such as boyish appetite
Disdains not; nor the palate, undeprav'd
By culinary arts, unsav'ry deems.
No Sofa then awaited my return;
Nor Sofa then I needed. Youth repairs
His wasted spirits quickly, by long toil
Incurring short fatigue; and, though our years
As life declines speed rapidly away,
And not a year but pilfers as he goes

Some youthful grace that age would gladly keep;
A tooth or auburn lock, and by degrees
Their length and colour from the locks they spare;
Th' elastic spring of an unwearied foot
That mounts the style with ease, or leaps the fence,
That play of lungs, inhaling and again
Respiring freely the fresh air, that makes
Swift pace or steep ascent no toil to me,
Mine have not pilfer'd yet; nor yet impair'd
My relish of fair prospect; scenes that sooth'd
Or charm'd me young, no longer young, I find
Still soothing and of pow'r to charm me still.
And witness, dear companion of my walks,
Whose arm this twentieth winter I perceive
Fast lock'd in mine, with pleasure such as love,
Confirm'd by long experience of thy worth
And well-tried virtues, could alone inspire—
Witness a joy that thou hast doubled long.
Thou know'st my praise of nature most sincere,
And that my raptures are not conjur'd up
To serve occasions of poetic pomp,
But genuine, and art partner of them all.
How oft upon yon eminence our pace
Has slacken'd to a pause, and we have born
The ruffling wind, scarce conscious that it blew,
While admiration, feeding at the eye,
And still unsated, dwelt upon the scene.
Thence with what pleasure have we just discern'd
The distant plough slow moving, and beside
His lab'ring team, that swerv'd not from the track,
The sturdy swain diminish'd to a boy!
Here Ouse, slow winding through a level plain
Of spacious meads with cattle sprinkled o'er,
Conducts the eye along its sinuous course
Delighted. There, fast rooted in their bank,
Stand, never overlook'd, our fav'rite elms,
That screen the herdsman's solitary hut;
While far beyond, and overthwart the stream
That, as with molten glass, inlays the vale,
The sloping land recedes into the clouds;
Displaying on its varied side the grace
Of hedge-row beauties numberless, square tow'r,
Tall spire, from which the sound of cheerful bells
Just undulates upon the list'ning ear,
Groves, heaths, and smoking villages, remote.
Scenes must be beautiful, which, daily view'd,
Please daily, and whose novelty survives

Long knowledge and the scrutiny of years.
Praise justly due to those that I describe.
  Nor rural sights alone, but rural sounds,
Exhilarate the spirit, and restore
The tone of languid Nature. Mighty winds,
That sweep the skirt of some far-spreading wood
Of ancient growth, make music not unlike
The dash of ocean on his winding shore,
And lull the spirit while they fill the mind:
Unnumber'd branches waving in the blast,
And all their leaves fast flutt'ring, all at once.
Nor less composure waits upon the roar
Of distant floods, or on the softer voice
Of neighb'ring fountain, or of rills that slip
Through the cleft rock, and, chiming as they fall
Upon loose pebbles, lose themselves at length
In matted grass, that with a livelier green
Betrays the secret of their silent course.
Nature inanimate employs sweet sounds,
But animated nature sweeter still,
To sooth and satisfy the human ear.
Ten thousand warblers cheer the day, and one
The live-long night: nor these alone, whose notes
Nice finger'd art must emulate in vain,
But cawing rooks, and kites that swim sublime
In still repeated circles, screaming loud,
The jay, the pie, and ev'n the boding owl
That hails the rising moon, have charms for me.
Sounds inharmonious in themselves and harsh,
Yet heard in scenes where peace for ever reigns,
And only there, please highly for their sake.
  Peace to the artist, whose ingenious thought
Devis'd the weather-house, that useful toy!
Fearless of humid air and gathering rains,
Forth steps the man—an emblem of myself!
More delicate, his tim'rous mate retires.
When Winter soaks the fields, and female feet,
Too weak to struggle with tenacious clay,
Or ford the rivulets, are best at home,
The task of new discov'ries falls on me.
At such a season, and with such a charge,
Once went I forth; and found, till then unknown,
A cottage, whither oft we since repair:
'Tis perch'd upon the green-hill top, but close
Environ'd with a ring of branching elms
That overhang the thatch, itself unseen
Peeps at the vale below; so thick beset
With foliage of such dark redundant growth,

I call'd the low-roof'd lodge the *peasant's nest.*
And, hidden as it is, and far remote
From such unpleasing sounds as haunt the ear
In village or in town, the bay of curs
Incessant, clinking hammers, grinding wheels,
And infants clam'rous whether pleas'd or pain'd,
Oft have I wish'd the peaceful covert mine.
Here, I have said, at least I should possess
The poet's treasure, silence, and indulge
The dreams of fancy, tranquil and secure.
Vain thought! the dweller in that still retreat
Dearly obtains the refuge it affords.
Its elevated scite forbids the wretch
To drink sweet waters of the crystal well;
He dips his bowl into the weedy ditch,
And, heavy-laden, brings his bev'rage home,
Far-fetch'd and little worth; nor seldom waits,
Dependant on the baker's punctual call,
To hear his creaking panniers at the door,
Angry and sad, and his last crust consum'd.
So farewell envy of the *peasant's nest!*
If solitude make scant the means of life,
Society for me!—thou seeming sweet,
Be still a pleasing object in my view;
My visit still, but never mine abode.
  Not distant far, a length of colonnade
Invites us. Monument of ancient taste,
Now scorn'd, but worthy of a better fate.
Our fathers knew the value of a screen
From sultry suns; and, in their shaded walks
And long protracted bow'rs, enjoy'd at noon
The gloom and coolness of declining day.
We bear our shades about us; self-depriv'd
Of other screen, the thin umbrella spread,
And range an Indian waste without a tree.
Thanks to Benevolus—he spares me yet
These chesnuts rang'd in corresponding lines;
And, though himself so polish'd, still reprieves
The obsolete prolixity of shade.
  Descending now (but cautious, lest too fast)
A sudden steep, upon a rustic bridge
We pass a gulph, in which the willows dip
Their pendent boughs, stooping as if to drink.
Hence, ancle-deep in moss and flow'ry thyme,
We mount again, and feel at ev'ry step
Our foot half sunk in hillocks green and soft,
Raised by the mole, the miner of the soil.
He, not unlike the great ones of mankind,

Disfigures earth; and, plotting in the dark,
Toils much to earn a monumental pile,
That may record the mischiefs he has done.
The summit gain'd, behold the proud alcove
That crowns it! yet not all its pride secures
The grand retreat from injuries impress'd
By rural carvers, who with knives deface
The pannels, leaving an obscure, rude name,
In characters uncouth, and spelt amiss.
So strong the zeal t' immortalize himself
Beats in the breast of man, that ev'n a few
Few transient years, won from th' abyss abhorr'd
Of blank oblivion, seem a glorious prize,
And even to a clown. Now roves the eye;
And, posted on this speculative height,
Exults in its command. The sheep-fold here
Pours out its fleecy tenants o'er the glebe.
At first, progressive as a stream, they seek
The middle field; but, scatter'd by degrees,
Each to his choice, soon whiten all the land.
There from the sun-burnt hay-field, homeward creeps
The loaded wain; while, lighten'd of its charge,
The wain that meets it passes swiftly by;
The boorish driver leaning o'er his team
Vocif'rous, and impatient of delay.
Nor less attractive is the woodland scene,
Diversified with trees of ev'ry growth,
Alike, yet various. Here the gray smooth trunks
Of ash, or lime, or beech, distinctly shine,
Within the twilight of their distant shades;
There, lost behind a rising ground, the wood
Seems sunk, and shorten'd to its topmost boughs.
No tree in all the grove but has its charms,
Though each its hue peculiar; paler some,
And of a wannish gray; the willow such,
And poplar, that with silver lines his leaf,
And ash far-stretching his umbrageous arm;
Of deeper green the elm; and deeper still,
Lord of the woods, the long-surviving oak.
Some glossy-leav'd, and shining in the sun,
The maple, and the beech of oily nuts
Prolific, and the lime at dewy eve
Diffusing odours: nor unnoted pass
The sycamore, capricious in attire,
Now green, now tawny, and, ere autumn yet
Have chang'd the woods, in scarlet honours bright.
O'er these, but far beyond (a spacious map
Of hill and valley interpos'd between),

The Ouse, dividing the well-water'd land,
Now glitters in the sun, and now retires,
As bashful, yet impatient to be seen.
  Hence the declivity is sharp and short,
And such the re-ascent; between them weeps
A little naiad her impov'rish'd urn
All summer long, which winter fills again.
The folded gates would bar my progress now,
But that the lord of this enclos'd demesne,
Communicative of the good he owns,
Admits me to a share; the guiltless eye
Commits no wrong, nor wastes what it enjoys.
Refreshing change! where now the blazing sun?
By short transition we have lost his glare,
And stepp'd at once into a cooler clime.
Ye fallen avenues! once more I mourn
Your fate unmerited, once more rejoice
That yet a remnant of your race survives.
How airy and how light the graceful arch,
Yet awful as the consecrated roof
Re-echoing pious anthems! while beneath
The chequer'd earth seems restless as a flood
Brush'd by the wind. So sportive is the light
Shot through the boughs, it dances as they dance,
Shadow and sunshine intermingling quick,
And dark'ning and enlight'ning, as the leaves
Play wanton, ev'ry moment, ev'ry spot.
  And now, with nerves new-brac'd and spirits cheer'd,
We tread the wilderness, whose well-roll'd walks,
With curvature of slow and easy sweep—
Deception innocent—give ample space
To narrow bounds. The grove receives us next;
Between the upright shafts of whose tall elms
We may discern the thresher at his task.
Thump after thump resounds the constant flail,
That seems to swing uncertain, and yet falls
Full on the destin'd ear. Wide flies the chaff.
The rustling straw sends up a frequent mist
Of atoms, sparkling in the noon-day beam.
Come hither, ye that press your beds of down,
And sleep not: see him sweating o'er his bread
Before he eats it.—'Tis the primal curse,
But soften'd into mercy; made the pledge
Of cheerful days, and nights without a groan.
  By ceaseless action all that is subsists.
Constant rotation of th' unwearied wheel
That nature rides upon maintains her health,
Her beauty, her fertility. She dreads

An instant's pause, and lives but while she moves.
Its own revolvency upholds the world.
Winds from all quarters agitate the air,
And fit the limpid element for use,
Else noxious: oceans, rivers, lakes, and streams,
All feel the fresh'ning impulse, and are cleans'd
By restless undulation: ev'n the oak
Thrives by the rude concussion of the storm:
He seems indeed indignant, and to feel
Th' impression of the blast with proud disdain,
Frowning as if in his unconscious arm
He held the thunder: but the monarch owes
His firm stability to what he scorns—
More fixt below, the more disturb'd above.
The law, by which all creatures else are bound,
Binds man the lord of all. Himself derives
No mean advantage from a kindred cause,
From strenuous toil his hours of sweetest ease.
The sedentary stretch their lazy length
When custom bids, but no refreshment find,
For none they need: the languid eye, the cheek
Deserted of its bloom, the flaccid, shrunk,
And wither'd muscle, and the vapid soul,
Reproach their owner with that love of rest
To which he forfeits ev'n the rest he loves.
Not such th' alert and active. Measure life
By its true worth, the comforts it affords,
And their's alone seems worthy of the name.
Good health, and, its associate in most,
Good temper; spirits prompt to undertake,
And not soon spent, though in an arduous task;
The pow'rs of fancy and strong thought are their's;
Ev'n age itself seems privileg'd in them,
With clear exemption from its own defects.
A sparkling eye beneath a wrinkled front
The vet'ran shows, and, gracing a gray beard
With youthful smiles, descends toward the grave
Sprightly, and old almost without decay.
  Like a coy maiden, ease, when courted most,
Farthest retires—an idol, at whose shrine
Who oft'nest sacrifice are favour'd least.
The love of Nature, and the scenes she draws,
Is Nature's dictate. Strange! there should be found,
Who, self-imprison'd in their proud saloons,
Renounce the odours of the open field
For the unscented fictions of the loom;
Who, satisfied with only pencil'd scenes,
Prefer to the performance of a God

Th' inferior wonders of an artist's hand!
Lovely indeed the mimic works of art;
But Nature's works far lovelier. I admire—
None more admires—the painter's magic skill,
Who shows me that which I shall never see,
Conveys a distant country into mine,
And throws Italian light on English walls:
But imitative strokes can do no more
Than please the eye—sweet Nature ev'ry sense.
The air salubrious of her lofty hills,
The cheering fragrance of her dewy vales,
And music of her woods—no works of man
May rival these; these all bespeak a pow'r
Peculiar, and exclusively her own.
Beneath the open sky she spreads the feast;
'Tis free to all—'tis ev'ry day renew'd;
Who scorns it starves deservedly at home.
He does not scorn it, who, imprison'd long
In some unwholesome dungeon, and a prey
To sallow sickness, which the vapours, dank
And clammy, of his dark abode have bred,
Escapes at last to liberty and light:
His cheek recovers soon its healthful hue;
His eye relumines its extinguish'd fires;
He walks, he leaps, he runs—is wing'd with joy,
And riots in the sweets of ev'ry breeze.
He does not scorn it, who has long endur'd
A fever's agonies, and fed on drugs.
Nor yet the mariner, his blood inflam'd
With acrid salts; his very heart athirst
To gaze at Nature in her green array,
Upon the ship's tall side he stands, possess'd
With visions prompted by intense desire:
Fair fields appear below, such as he left,
Far distant, such as he would die to find—
He seeks them headlong, and is seen no more.
  The spleen is seldom felt where Flora reigns;
The low'ring eye, the petulance, the frown,
And sullen sadness, that o'ershade, distort,
And mar the face of beauty, when no cause
For such immeasurable woe appears,
These Flora banishes, and gives the fair
Sweet smiles, and bloom less transient than her own.
It is the constant revolution, stale
And tasteless, of the same repeated joys,
That palls and satiates, and makes languid life
A pedlar's pack, that bows the bearer down.
Health suffers, and the spirits ebb; the heart

Recoils from its own choice—at the full feast
Is famish'd—finds no music in the song,
No smartness in the jest; and wonders why.
Yet thousands still desire to journey on,
Though halt, and weary of the path they tread.
The paralytic, who can hold her cards,
But cannot play them, borrows a friend's hand
To deal and shuffle, to divide and sort,
Her mingled suits and sequences; and sits,
Spectatress both and spectacle, a sad
And silent cypher, while her proxy plays.
Others are dragg'd into the crowded room
Between supporters; and, once seated, sit,
Through downright inability to rise,
Till the stout bearers lift the corpse again.
These speak a loud memento. Yet ev'n these
Themselves love life, and cling to it, as he
That overhangs a torrent to a twig.
They love it, and yet loath it; fear to die,
Yet scorn the purposes for which they live.
Then wherefore not renounce them? No—the dread,
The slavish dread of solitude, that breeds
Reflection and remorse, the fear of shame,
And their invet'rate habits, all forbid.
  Whom call we gay? That honour has been long
The boast of mere pretenders to the name.
The innocent are gay—the lark is gay,
That dries his feathers, saturate with dew,
Beneath the rosy cloud, while yet the beams
Of day-spring overshoot his humble nest.
The peasant too, a witness of his song,
Himself a songster, is as gay as he.
But save me from the gaiety of those
Whose head-aches nail them to a noon-day bed;
And save me too from their's whose haggard eyes
Flash desperation, and betray their pangs
For property stripp'd off by cruel chance;
From gaiety that fills the bones with pain,
The mouth with blasphemy, the heart with woe.
  The earth was made so various, that the mind
Of desultory man, studious of change,
And pleas'd with novelty, might be indulg'd.
Prospects, however lovely, may be seen
Till half their beauties fade; the weary sight,
Too well acquainted with their smiles, slides off,
Fastidious, seeking less familiar scenes.
Then snug enclosures in the shelter'd vale,
Where frequent hedges intercept the eye,

Delight us; happy to renounce awhile,
Not senseless of its charms, what still we love,
That such short absence may endear it more.
Then forests, or the savage rock, may please,
That hides the sea-mew in his hollow clefts
Above the reach of man. His hoary head,
Conspicuous many a league, the mariner
Bound homeward, and in hope already there,
Greets with three cheers exulting. At his waist
A girdle of half-wither'd shrubs he shows,
And at his feet the baffled billows die.
The common, overgrown with fern, and rough
With prickly gorse, that, shapeless and deform'd,
And dang'rous to the touch, has yet its bloom,
And decks itself with ornaments of gold,
Yields no unpleasing ramble; there the turf
Smells fresh, and, rich in odorif'rous herbs
And fungous fruits of earth, regales the sense
With luxury of unexpected sweets.
  There often wanders one, whom better days
Saw better clad, in cloak of satin trimm'd
With lace, and hat with splendid ribband bound.
A serving maid was she, and fell in love
With one who left her, went to sea, and died.
Her fancy follow'd him through foaming waves
To distant shores; and she would sit and weep
At what a sailor suffers; fancy, too,
Delusive most where warmest wishes are,
Would oft anticipate his glad return,
And dream of transports she was not to know.
She heard the doleful tidings of his death—
And never smil'd again! And now she roams
The dreary waste; there spends the livelong day,
And there, unless when charity forbids,
The livelong night. A tatter'd apron hides,
Worn as a cloak, and hardly hides, a gown
More tatter'd still; and both but ill conceal
A bosom heav'd with never-ceasing sighs.
She begs an idle pin of all she meets,
And hoards them in her sleeve; but needful food,
Though press'd with hunger oft, or comelier clothes,
Though pinch'd with cold, asks never.—Kate is craz'd!
  I see a column of slow rising smoke
O'ertop the lofty wood that skirts the wild.
A vagabond and useless tribe there eat
Their miserable meal. A kettle, slung
Between two poles upon a stick transverse,
Receives the morsel—flesh obscene of dog,

Or vermin, or, at best, of cock purloin'd
From his accustom'd perch. Hard faring race!
They pick their fuel out of ev'ry hedge,
Which, kindled with dry leaves, just saves unquench'd
The spark of life. The sportive wind blows wide
Their flutt'ring rags, and shows a tawny skin,
The vellum of the pedigree they claim.
Great skill have they in palmistry, and more
To conjure clean away the gold they touch,
Conveying worthless dross into its place;
Loud when they beg, dumb only when they steal.
Strange! that a creature rational, and cast
In human mould, should brutalize by choice
His nature; and, though capable of arts
By which the world might profit, and himself,
Self-banish'd from society, prefer
Such squalid sloth to honourable toil!
Yet even these, though, feigning sickness oft,
They swathe the forehead, drag the limping limb,
And vex their flesh with artificial sores,
Can change their whine into a mirthful note
When safe occasion offers; and, with dance,
And music of the bladder and the bag,
Beguile their woes, and make the woods resound.
Such health and gaiety of heart enjoy
The houseless rovers of the sylvan world;
And, breathing wholesome air, and wand'ring much,
Need other physic none to heal th' effects
Of loathsome diet, penury, and cold.
  Blest he, though undistinguish'd from the crowd
By wealth or dignity, who dwells secure,
Where man, by nature fierce, has laid aside
His fierceness, having learnt, though slow to learn,
The manners and the arts of civil life.
His wants, indeed, are many; but supply
Is obvious, plac'd within the easy reach
Of temp'rate wishes and industrious hands.
Here virtue thrives as in her proper soil;
Not rude and surly, and beset with thorns,
And terrible to sight, as when she springs
(If e'er she spring spontaneous) in remote
And barb'rous climes, where violence prevails,
And strength is lord of all; but gentle, kind,
By culture tam'd, by liberty refresh'd,
And all her fruits by radiant truth matur'd.
War and the chase engross the savage whole;
War follow'd for revenge, or to supplant
The envied tenants of some happier spot,

The chase for sustenance, precarious trust!
His hard condition with severe constraint
Binds all his faculties, forbids all growth
Of wisdom, proves a school in which he learns
Sly circumvention, unrelenting hate,
Mean self-attachment, and scarce aught beside.
Thus fare the shiv'ring natives of the north,
And thus the rangers of the western world,
Where it advances far into the deep,
Towards th' antarctic. Ev'n the favour'd isles,
So lately found, although the constant sun
Cheer all their seasons with a grateful smile,
Can boast but little virtue; and, inert
Through plenty, lose in morals what they gain
In manners—victims of luxurious ease.
These therefore I can pity, plac'd remote
From all that science traces, art invents,
Or inspiration teaches; and enclosed
In boundless oceans, never to be pass'd
By navigators uninform'd as they,
Or plough'd perhaps by British bark again:
But, far beyond the rest, and with most cause,
Thee, gentle savage! whom no love of thee
Or thine, but curiosity perhaps,
Or else vain glory, prompted us to draw
Forth from thy native bow'rs, to show thee here
With what superior skill we can abuse
The gifts of Providence, and squander life.
The dream is past; and thou hast found again
Thy cocoas and bananas, palms and yams,
And homestall thatch'd with leaves. But hast thou found
Their former charms? And, having seen our state,
Our palaces, our ladies, and our pomp
Of equipage, our gardens, and our sports,
And heard our music; are thy simple friends,
Thy simple fare, and all thy plain delights,
As dear to thee as once? And have thy joys
Lost nothing by comparison with our's?
Rude as thou art, (for we return'd thee rude
And ignorant, except of outward show)
I cannot think thee yet so dull of heart
And spiritless, as never to regret
Sweets tasted here, and left as soon as known.
Methinks I see thee straying on the beach,
And asking of the surge that bathes thy foot
If ever it has wash'd our distant shore.
I see thee weep, and thine are honest tears,
A patriot's for his country: thou art sad

At thought of her forlorn and abject state,
From which no pow'r of thine can raise her up.
Thus fancy paints thee, and, though apt to err,
Perhaps errs little when she paints thee thus.
She tells me, too, that duly ev'ry morn
Thou climb'st the mountain top, with eager eye
Exploring far and wide the wat'ry waste
For sight of ship from England. Ev'ry speck
Seen in the dim horizon turns thee pale
With conflict of contending hopes and fears.
But comes at last the dull and dusky eve,
And sends thee to thy cabin, well prepar'd
To dream all night of what the day denied.
Alas! expect it not. We found no bait
To tempt us in thy country. Doing good,
Disinterested good, is not our trade.
We travel far, 'tis true, but not for nought;
And must be brib'd, to compass earth again,
By other hopes and richer fruits than your's.
  But, though true worth and virtue in the mild
And genial soil of cultivated life
Thrive most, and may perhaps thrive only there,
Yet not in cities oft: in proud and gay
And gain-devoted cities. Thither flow,
As to a common and most noisome sew'r,
The dregs and feculence of ev'ry land.
In cities foul example on most minds
Begets its likeness. Rank abundance breeds
In gross and pamper'd cities sloth and lust,
And wantonness and gluttonous excess.
In cities vice is hidden with most ease,
Or seen with least reproach; and virtue, taught
By frequent lapse, can hope no triumph there
Beyond th' achievement of successful flight.
I do confess them nurs'ries of the arts,
In which they flourish most; where, in the beams
Of warm encouragement, and in the eye
Of public note, they reach their perfect size.
Such London is, by taste and wealth proclaim'd
The fairest capital of all the world,
By riot and incontinence the worst.
There, touch'd by Reynolds, a dull blank becomes
A lucid mirror, in which Nature sees
All her reflected features. Bacon there
Gives more than female beauty to a stone,
And Chatham's eloquence to marble lips.
Nor does the chissel occupy alone
The pow'rs of sculpture, but the style as much;

Each province of her art her equal care.
With nice incision of her guided steel
She ploughs a brazen field, and clothes a soil
So sterile with what charms soe'er she will,
The richest scen'ry and the loveliest forms.
Where finds philosophy her eagle eye,
With which she gazes at yon burning disk
Undazzled, and detects and counts his spots?
In London: where her implements exact,
With which she calculates, computes, and scans,
All distance, motion, magnitude, and now
Measures an atom, and now girds a world?
In London. Where has commerce such a mart,
So rich, so throng'd, so drain'd, and so supplied,
As London—opulent, enlarg'd, and still
Increasing, London? Babylon of old
Not more the glory of the earth than she,
A more accomplish'd world's chief glory now.
She has her praise. Now mark a spot or two,
That so much beauty would do well to purge;
And show this queen of cities, that so fair
May yet be foul; so witty, yet not wise.
It is not seemly, nor of good report,
That she is slack in discipline; more prompt
T' avenge than to prevent the breach of law:
That she is rigid in denouncing death
On petty robbers, and indulges life
And liberty, and oft-times honour too,
To peculators of the public gold:
That thieves at home must hang; but he, that puts
Into his overgorg'd and bloated purse
The wealth of Indian provinces, escapes.
Nor is it well, nor can it come to good,
That, through profane and infidel contempt
Of holy writ, she has presum'd t' annul
And abrogate, as roundly as she may,
The total ordinance and will of God;
Advancing fashion to the post of truth,
And cent'ring all authority in modes
And customs of her own, till sabbath rites
Have dwindled into unrespected forms,
And knees and hassocs are well-nigh divorc'd.
God made the country, and man made the town.
What wonder then that health and virtue, gifts
That can alone make sweet the bitter draught
That life holds out to all, should most abound
And least be threaten'd in the fields and groves?
Possess ye, therefore, ye, who, borne about

In chariots and sedans, know no fatigue
But that of idleness, and taste no scenes
But such as art contrives, possess ye still
Your element; there only can ye shine;
There only minds like your's can do no harm.
Our groves were planted to console at noon
The pensive wand'rer in their shades. At eve
The moon-beam, sliding softly in between
The sleeping leaves, is all the light they wish,
Birds warbling all the music. We can spare
The splendour of your lamps; they but eclipse
Our softer satellite. Your songs confound
Our more harmonious notes: the thrush departs
Scar'd, and th' offended nightingale is mute.
There is a public mischief in your mirth;
It plagues your country. Folly such as your's,
Grac'd with a sword, and worthier of a fan,
Has made, what enemies could ne'er have done,
Our arch of empire, stedfast but for you,
A mutilated structure, soon to fall.

Book III

The Garden

Argument of the Third Book.—Self-recollection and reproof—Address to domestic happiness—some account of myself—The vanity of many of their pursuits who are reputed wise—Justification of my censures—Divine illumination necessary to the most expert philosopher—The question, What is truth? answered by other questions—Domestic happiness addressed again—Few lovers of the country—My tame hare—Occupations of a retired gentleman in his garden—Pruning—Framing—Greenhouse—Sowing of flower-seeds—The country preferable to the town even in the winter—Reasons why it is deserted at that season—Ruinous effects of gaming and of expensive improvement—Book concludes with an apostrophe to the metropolis.

As one who, long in thickets and in brakes
Entangled, winds now this way and now that
His devious course uncertain, seeking home;
Or, having long in miry ways been foil'd
And sore discomfited, from slough to slough
Plunging, and half despairing of escape;
If chance at length he find a greensward smooth
And faithful to the foot, his spirits rise,
He chirrups brisk his ear-erecting steed,
And winds his way with pleasure and with ease;
So I, designing other themes, and call'd
T' adorn the Sofa with eulogium due,
To tell its slumbers, and to paint its dreams,
Have rambled wide. In country, city, seat

Of academic fame (howe'er deserv'd),
Long held, and scarcely disengag'd at last.
But now, with pleasant pace, a cleanlier road
I mean to tread. I feel myself at large,
Courageous, and refresh'd for future toil,
If toil await me, or if dangers new.
  Since pulpits fail, and sounding-boards reflect
Most part an empty ineffectual sound,
What chance that I, to fame so little known,
Nor conversant with men or manners much,
Should speak to purpose, or with better hope
Crack the satiric thong? 'Twere wiser far
For me, enamour'd of sequester'd scenes,
And charm'd with rural beauty, to repose,
Where chance may throw me, beneath elm or vine,
My languid limbs, when summer sears the plains;
Or, when rough winter rages, on the soft
And shelter'd Sofa, while the nitrous air
Feeds a blue flame, and makes a cheerful hearth;
There, undisturb'd by folly, and appriz'd
How great the danger of disturbing her,
To muse in silence, or at least confine
Remarks that gall so many to the few
My partners in retreat. Disgust conceal'd
Is oft-times proof of wisdom, when the fault
Is obstinate, and cure beyond our reach.
  Domestic happiness, thou only bliss
Of Paradise that has surviv'd the fall!
Though few now taste thee unimpair'd and pure,
Or, tasting, long enjoy thee; too infirm,
Or too incautious, to preserve thy sweets
Unmixt with drops of bitter, which neglect
Or temper sheds into thy crystal cup.
Thou art the nurse of virtue—in thine arms
She smiles, appearing, as in truth she is,
Heav'n-born, and destin'd to the skies again.
Thou art not known where pleasure is ador'd,
That reeling goddess with the zoneless waist
And wand'ring eyes, still leaning on the arm
Of novelty, her fickle frail support;
For thou art meek and constant, hating change,
And finding, in the calm of truth-tried love,
Joys that her stormy raptures never yield.
Forsaking thee, what shipwreck have we made
Of honour, dignity, and fair renown!
Till prostitution elbows us aside
In all our crowded streets; and senates seem
Conven'd for purposes of empire less

Than to release th' adultress from her bond.
Th' adultress! what a theme for angry verse!
What provocation to th' indignant heart
That feels for injur'd love! but I disdain
The nauseous task to paint her as she is,
Cruel, abandon'd, glorying in her shame!
No:—let her pass, and, chariotted along
In guilty splendour, shake the public ways;
The frequency of crimes has wash'd them white!
And verse of mine shall never brand the wretch,
Whom matrons now, of character unsmirch'd,
And chaste themselves, are not asham'd to own.
Virtue and vice had bound'ries in old time,
Not to be pass'd: and she, that had renounc'd
Her sex's honour, was renounc'd herself
By all that priz'd it; not for prud'ry's sake,
But dignity's, resentful of the wrong.
'Twas hard, perhaps, on here and there a waif,
Desirous to return, and not receiv'd;
But was an wholesome rigour in the main,
And taught th' unblemish'd to preserve with care
That purity, whose loss was loss of all.
Men, too, were nice in honour in those days,
And judg'd offenders well. Then he that sharp'd,
And pocketted a prize by fraud obtain'd,
Was mark'd and shunn'd as odious. He that sold
His country, or was slack when she requir'd
His ev'ry nerve in action and at stretch,
Paid, with the blood that he had basely spar'd,
The price of his default. But now—yes, now
We are become so candid and so fair,
So lib'ral in construction, and so rich
In Christian charity, (good-natur'd age!)
That they are safe, sinners of either sex,
Transgress what laws they may. Well dress'd, well bred,
Well equipag'd, is ticket good enough
To pass us readily through ev'ry door.
Hypocrisy, detest her as we may,
(And no man's hatred ever wrong'd her yet)
May claim this merit still—that she admits
The worth of what she mimics with such care,
And thus gives virtue indirect applause;
But she has burnt her mask, not needed here,
Where vice has such allowance, that her shifts
And specious semblances have lost their use.
  I was a stricken deer, that left the herd
Long since; with many an arrow deep infixt,
My panting side was charg'd, when I withdrew

To seek a tranquil death in distant shades.
There was I found by one who had himself
Been hurt by th' archers. In his side he bore,
And in his hands and feet, the cruel scars.
With gentle force soliciting the darts,
He drew them forth, and heal'd, and bade me live.
Since then, with few associates, in remote
And silent woods I wander, far from those
My former partners of the peopled scene;
With few associates, and not wishing more.
Here much I ruminate, as much I may,
With other views of men and manners now
Than once, and others of a life to come,
I see that all are wand'rers, gone astray
Each in his own delusions; they are lost
In chase of fancied happiness, still woo'd
And never won. Dream after dream ensues;
And still they dream that they shall still succeed,
And still are disappointed. Rings the world
With the vain stir. I sum up half mankind,
And add two thirds of the remaining half,
And find the total of their hopes and fears
Dreams, empty dreams. The million flit as gay
As if created only like the fly,
That spreads his motley wings in th' eye of noon,
To sport their season, and be seen no more.
The rest are sober dreamers, grave and wise,
And pregnant with discov'ries new and rare.
Some write a narrative of wars, and feats
Of heroes little known; and call the rant
An history: describe the man, of whom
His own coevals took but little note;
And paint his person, character, and views,
As they had known him from his mother's womb.
They disentangle from the puzzled skein,
In which obscurity has wrapp'd them up,
The threads of politic and shrewd design,
That ran through all his purposes, and charge
His mind with meanings that he never had,
Or, having, kept conceal'd. Some drill and bore
The solid earth, and from the strata there
Extract a register, by which we learn,
That he who made it, and reveal'd its date
To Moses, was mistaken in its age.
Some, more acute, and more industrious still,
Contrive creation; travel nature up
To the sharp peak of her sublimest height,
And tell us whence the stars; why some are fix'd,

And planetary some; what gave them first
Rotation, from what fountain flow'd their light.
Great contest follows, and much learned dust
Involves the combatants; each claiming truth,
And truth disclaiming both. And thus they spend
The little wick of life's poor shallow lamp,
In playing tricks with nature, giving laws
To distant worlds, and trifling in their own.
Is't not a pity now, that tickling rheums
Should ever tease the lungs and blear the sight
Of oracles like these? Great pity too,
That, having wielded th' elements, and built
A thousand systems, each in his own way,
They should go out in fume, and be forgot?
Ah! what is life thus spent? and what are they
But frantic who thus spend it? all for smoke—
Eternity for bubbles, proves at last
A senseless bargain. When I see such games
Play'd by the creatures of a pow'r who swears
That he will judge the earth, and call the fool
To a sharp reck'ning that has liv'd in vain;
And when I weigh this seeming wisdom well,
And prove it in th' infallible result
So hollow and so false—I feel my heart
Dissolve in pity, and account the learn'd,
If this be learning, most of all deceiv'd.
Great crimes alarm the conscience, but it sleeps
While thoughtful man is plausibly amus'd.
Defend me, therefore, common sense, say I,
From reveries so airy, from the toil
Of dropping buckets into empty wells,
And growing old in drawing nothing up!
'Twere well, says one sage erudite, profound,
Terribly arch'd and aquiline his nose,
And overbuilt with most impending brows,
'Twere well, could you permit the world to live
As the world pleases. What's the world to you?—
Much. I was born of woman, and drew milk,
As sweet as charity, from human breasts.
I think, articulate, I laugh and weep,
And exercise all functions of a man.
How then should I and any man that lives
Be strangers to each other? Pierce my vein,
Take of the crimson stream meand'ring there,
And catechise it well; apply thy glass,
Search it, and prove now if it be not blood
Congenial with thine own: and, if it be,
What edge of subtlety canst thou suppose

Keen enough, wise and skilful as thou art,
To cut the link of brotherhood, by which
One common Maker bound me to the kind?
True; I am no proficient, I confess,
In arts like your's. I cannot call the swift
And perilous lightnings from the angry clouds,
And bid them hide themselves in earth beneath;
I cannot analyse the air, nor catch
The parallax of yonder luminous point,
That seems half quench'd in the immense abyss:
Such pow'rs I boast not—neither can I rest
A silent witness of the headlong rage
Or heedless folly by which thousands die,
Bone of my bone, and kindred souls to mine.
  God never meant that man should scale the heav'ns
By strides of human wisdom. In his works
Though wondrous, he commands us in his word
To seek *him* rather, where his mercy shines.
The mind indeed, enlighten'd from above,
Views him in all; ascribes to the grand cause
The grand effect; acknowledges with joy
His manner, and with rapture tastes his style.
But never yet did philosophic tube,
That brings the planets home into the eye
Of observation, and discovers, else
Not visible, his family of worlds,
Discover him that rules them; such a veil
Hangs over mortal eyes, blind from the birth,
And dark in things divine. Full often, too,
Our wayward intellect, the more we learn
Of nature, overlooks her author more;
From instrumental causes proud to draw
Conclusions retrograde, and mad mistake.
But if his word once teach us, shoot a ray
Through all the heart's dark chambers, and reveal
Truths undiscern'd but by that holy light,
Then all is plain. Philosophy, baptiz'd
In the pure fountain of eternal love,
Has eyes indeed; and, viewing all she sees
As meant to indicate a God to man,
Gives *him* his praise, and forfeits not her own.
Learning has borne such fruit in other days
On all her branches: piety has found
Friends in the friends of science, and true pray'r
Has flow'd from lips wet with Castalian dews.
Such was thy wisdom, Newton, childlike sage!
Sagacious reader of the works of God,
And in his word sagacious. Such too thine,

Milton, whose genius had angelic wings,
And fed on manna! And such thine, in whom
Our British Themis gloried with just cause,
Immortal Hale! for deep discernment prais'd
And sound integrity, not more than fam'd
For sanctity of manners undefil'd.
  All flesh is grass, and all its glory fades
Like the fair flow'r dishevell'd in the wind;
Riches have wings, and grandeur is a dream:
The man we celebrate must find a tomb,
And we that worship him ignoble graves.
Nothing is proof against the gen'ral curse
Of vanity, that seizes all below.
The only amaranthine flow'r on earth
Is virtue; th' only lasting treasure, truth.
But what is truth? 'twas Pilate's question, put
To Truth itself, that deign'd him no reply.
And wherefore? will not God impart his light
To them that ask it?—Freely—'tis his joy,
His glory, and his nature, to impart.
But to the proud, uncandid, insincere,
Or negligent inquirer, not a spark.
What's that which brings contempt upon a book,
And him who writes it; though the style be neat,
The method clear, and argument exact?
That makes a minister in holy things
The joy of many, and the dread of more,
His name a theme for praise and for reproach?—
That, while it gives us worth in God's account,
Depreciates and undoes us in our own?
What pearl is it that rich men cannot buy,
That learning is too proud to gather up;
But which the poor, and the despis'd of all,
Seek and obtain, and often find unsought?
Tell me—and I will tell thee what is truth.
  O, friendly to the best pursuits of man,
Friendly to thought, to virtue, and to peace,
Domestic life in rural leisure pass'd!
Few know thy value, and few taste thy sweets;
Though many boast thy favours, and affect
To understand and choose thee for their own.
But foolish man foregoes his proper bliss,
Ev'n as his first progenitor, and quits,
Though placed in paradise, (for earth has still
Some traces of her youthful beauty left)
Substantial happiness for transient joy.
Scenes form'd for contemplation, and to nurse
The growing seeds of wisdom; that suggest,

By ev'ry pleasing image they present,
Reflections such as meliorate the heart,
Compose the passions, and exalt the mind;
Scenes such as these 'tis his supreme delight
To fill with riot, and defile with blood.
Should some contagion, kind to the poor brutes
We persecute, annihilate the tribes
That draw the sportsman over hill and dale,
Fearless, and rapt away from all his cares;
Should never game-fowl hatch her eggs again,
Nor baited hook deceive the fish's eye;
Could pageantry and dance, and feast and song,
Be quell'd in all our summer-months' retreat;
How many self-deluded nymphs and swains,
Who dream they have a taste for fields and groves,
Would find them hideous nurs'ries of the spleen,
And crowd the roads, impatient for the town!
They love the country, and none else, who seek
For their own sake its silence and its shade.
Delights which who would leave, that has a heart
Susceptible of pity, or a mind
Cultur'd and capable of sober thought,
For all the savage din of the swift pack,
And clamours of the field?—Detested sport,
That owes its pleasures to another's pain;
That feeds upon the sobs and dying shrieks
Of harmless nature, dumb, but yet endu'd
With eloquence, that agonies inspire,
Of silent tears and heart-distending sighs!
Vain tears, alas, and sighs, that never find
A corresponding tone in jovial souls!
Well—one at least is safe. One shelter'd hare
Has never heard the sanguinary yell
Of cruel man, exulting in her woes.
Innocent partner of my peaceful home,
Whom ten long years' experience of my care
Has made at last familiar; she has lost
Much of her vigilant instinctive dread,
Not needful here, beneath a roof like mine.
Yes—thou may'st eat thy bread, and lick the hand
That feeds thee; thou may'st frolic on the floor
At evening, and at night retire secure
To thy straw couch, and slumber unalarm'd;
For I have gain'd thy confidence, have pledg'd
All that is human in me to protect
Thine unsuspecting gratitude and love.
If I survive thee I will dig thy grave;
And, when I place thee in it, sighing, say,

I knew at least one hare that had a friend.
  How various his employments, whom the world
Calls idle; and who justly, in return,
Esteems that busy world an idler too!
Friends, books, a garden, and perhaps his pen,
Delightful industry enjoy'd at home,
And nature in her cultivated trim
Dress'd to his taste, inviting him abroad—
Can he want occupation who has these?
Will he be idle who has much t' enjoy?
Me, therefore, studious of laborious ease,
Not slothful; happy to deceive the time,
Not waste it; and aware that human life
Is but a loan to be repaid with use,
When He shall call his debtors to account
From whom are all our blessings; bus'ness finds
Ev'n here: while sedulous I seek t' improve,
At least neglect not, or leave unemploy'd,
The mind he gave me; driving it, though slack
Too oft, and much impeded in its work
By causes not to be divulg'd in vain,
To its just point—the service of mankind.
He that attends to his interior self,
That has a heart, and keeps it; has a mind
That hungers, and supplies it; and who seeks
A social, not a dissipated life;
Has business; feels himself engag'd t' achieve
No unimportant, though a silent, task.
A life all turbulence and noise may seem,
To him that leads it, wise, and to be prais'd;
But wisdom is a pearl with most success
Sought in still water, and beneath clear skies.
He that is ever occupied in storms,
Or dives not for it, or brings up instead,
Vainly industrious, a disgraceful prize.
  The morning finds the self-sequester'd man
Fresh for his task, intend what task he may.
Whether inclement seasons recommend
His warm but simple home, where he enjoys,
With her who shares his pleasures and his heart,
Sweet converse, sipping calm the fragrant lymph
Which neatly she prepares; then to his book,
Well chosen, and not sullenly perus'd
In selfish silence, but imparted oft
As aught occurs that she may smile to hear,
Or turn to nourishment, digested well.
Or, if the garden with its many cares,
All well repaid, demand him, he attends

The welcome call, conscious how much the hand
Of lubbard labour needs his watchful eye,
Oft loit'ring lazily, if not o'erseen,
Or misapplying his unskilful strength.
Nor does he govern only or direct,
But much performs himself. No works indeed
That ask robust tough sinews, bred to toil,
Servile employ; but such as may amuse,
Not tire, demanding rather skill than force.
Proud of his well-spread walls, he views his trees
That meet (no barren interval between)
With pleasure more than ev'n their fruits afford,
Which, save himself who trains them, none can feel:
These, therefore, are his own peculiar charge;
No meaner hand may discipline the shoots,
None but his steel approach them. What is weak,
Distemper'd, or has lost prolific pow'rs,
Impair'd by age, his unrelenting hand
Dooms to the knife: nor does he spare the soft
And succulent, that feeds its giant growth,
But barren, at th' expence of neighb'ring twigs
Less ostentatious, and yet studded thick
With hopeful gems. The rest, no portion left
That may disgrace his art, or disappoint
Large expectation, he disposes neat
At measur'd distances, that air and sun,
Admitted freely, may afford their aid,
And ventilate and warm the swelling buds.
Hence summer has her riches, autumn hence,
And hence ev'n winter fills his wither'd hand
With blushing fruits, and plenty, not his own.
Fair recompense of labour well bestow'd,
And wise precaution; which a clime so rude
Makes needful still, whose spring is but the child
Of churlish winter, in her froward moods
Discov'ring much the temper of her sire.
For oft, as if in her the stream of mild
Maternal nature had revers'd its course,
She brings her infants forth with many smiles;
But, once deliver'd, kills them with a frown.
He, therefore, timely warn'd, himself supplies
Her want of care, screening and keeping warm
The plenteous bloom, that no rough blast may sweep
His garlands from the boughs. Again, as oft
As the sun peeps and vernal airs breathe mild,
The fence withdrawn, he gives them ev'ry beam,
And spreads his hopes before the blaze of day.
  To raise the prickly and green-coated gourd,

So grateful to the palate, and when rare
So coveted, else base and disesteem'd—
Food for the vulgar merely—is an art
That toiling ages have but just matur'd,
And at this moment unassay'd in song.
Yet gnats have had, and frogs and mice, long since,
Their eulogy; those sang the Mantuan bard,
And these the Grecian, in ennobling strains;
And in thy numbers, Phillips, shines for aye
The solitary shilling. Pardon then,
Ye sage dispensers of poetic fame,
Th' ambition of one, meaner far, whose pow'rs,
Presuming an attempt not less sublime,
Pant for the praise of dressing to the taste
Of critic appetite, no sordid fare,
A cucumber, while costly yet and scarce.
  The stable yields a stercoraceous heap,
Impregnated with quick fermenting salts,
And potent to resist the freezing blast:
For, ere the beech and elm have cast their leaf
Deciduous, when now November dark
Checks vegetation in the torpid plant
Expos'd to his cold breath, the task begins.
Warily, therefore, and with prudent heed,
He seeks a favour'd spot; that where he builds
Th' agglomerated pile his frame may front
The sun's meridian disk, and at the back
Enjoy close shelter, wall, or reeds, or hedge
Impervious to the wind. First he bids spread
Dry fern or litter'd hay, that may imbibe
Th' ascending damps; then leisurely impose,
And lightly, shaking it with agile hand
From the full fork, the saturated straw.
What longest binds the closest forms secure
The shapely side, that as it rises takes,
By just degrees, an overhanging breadth,
Shelt'ring the base with its projected eaves:
Th' uplifted frame, compact at ev'ry joint,
And overlaid with clear translucent glass,
He settles next upon the sloping mount,
Whose sharp declivity shoots off secure
From the dash'd pane the deluge as it falls.
He shuts it close, and the first labour ends.
Thrice must the voluble and restless earth
Spin round upon her axle, ere the warmth,
Slow gathering in the midst, through the square mass
Diffus'd, attain the surface: when, behold!
A pestilent and most corrosive steam,

Like a gross fog Bœotian, rising fast,
And fast condens'd upon the dewy sash,
Asks egress; which obtain'd, the overcharg'd
And drench'd conservatory breathes abroad,
In volumes wheeling slow, the vapour dank;
And, purified, rejoices to have lost
Its foul inhabitant. But to assuage
Th' impatient fervour which it first conceives
Within its reeking bosom, threat'ning death
To his young hopes, requires discreet delay.
Experience, slow preceptress, teaching oft
The way to glory by miscarriage foul,
Must prompt him, and admonish how to catch
Th' auspicious moment, when the temper'd heat,
Friendly to vital motion, may afford
Soft fomentation, and invite the seed.
The seed, selected wisely, plump, and smooth,
And glossy, he commits to pots of size
Diminutive, well fill'd with well-prepar'd
And fruitful soil, that has been treasur'd long,
And drank no moisture from the dripping clouds:
These on the warm and genial earth, that hides
The smoking manure that o'erspreads it all,
He places lightly, and, as time subdues
The rage of fermentation, plunges deep
In the soft medium, till they stand immers'd.
Then rise the tender germs, upstarting quick,
And spreading wide their spongy lobes; at first
Pale, wan, and livid; but assuming soon,
If fann'd by balmy and nutritious air,
Strain'd through the friendly mats, a vivid green.
Two leaves produc'd, two rough indented leaves,
Cautious he pinches from the second stalk
A pimple, that portends a future sprout,
And interdicts its growth. Thence straight succeed
The branches, sturdy to his utmost wish;
Prolific all, and harbingers of more.
The crowded roots demand enlargement now,
And transplantation in an ampler space.
Indulg'd in what they wish, they soon supply
Large foliage, overshadowing golden flow'rs,
Blown on the summit of th' apparent fruit.
These have their sexes; and, when summer shines,
The bee transports the fertilizing meal
From flow'r to flow'r, and ev'n the breathing air
Wafts the rich prize to its appointed use.
Not so when winter scowls. Assistant art
Then acts in nature's office, brings to pass

The glad espousals, and ensures the crop.
 Grudge not, ye rich, (since luxury must have
His dainties, and the world's more num'rous half
Lives by contriving delicates for you)
Grudge not the cost. Ye little know the cares,
The vigilance, the labour, and the skill,
That day and night are exercis'd, and hang
Upon the ticklish balance of suspense,
That ye may garnish your profuse regales
With summer fruits brought forth by wintry suns.
Ten thousand dangers lie in wait to thwart
The process. Heat and cold, and wind, and steam,
Moisture and drought, mice, worms, and swarming flies,
Minute as dust, and numberless, oft work
Dire disappointment that admits no cure,
And which no care can obviate. It were long,
Too long, to tell th' expedients and the shifts
Which he that fights a season so severe
Devises, while he guards his tender trust;
And oft, at last, in vain. The learn'd and wise
Sarcastic would exclaim, and judge the song
Cold as its theme, and, like its theme, the fruit
Of too much labour, worthless when produced.
 Who loves a garden loves a green-house too.
Unconscious of a less propitious clime,
There blooms exotic beauty, warm and snug,
While the winds whistle and the snows descend.
The spiry myrtle with unwith'ring leaf
Shines there, and flourishes. The golden boast
Of Portugal and western India there,
The ruddier orange, and the paler lime,
Peep through their polish'd foliage at the storm,
And seem to smile at what they need not fear.
Th' amomum there with intermingling flow'rs
And cherries hangs her twigs. Geranium boasts
Her crimson honours, and the spangled beau,
Ficoides, glitters bright the winter long.
All plants, of ev'ry leaf, that can endure
The winter's frown, if screen'd from his shrewd bite,
Live there, and prosper. Those Ausonia claims,
Levantine regions these; th' Azores send
Their jessamine, her jessamine remote
Caffraia: foreigners from many lands,
They form one social shade, as if conven'd
By magic summons of th' Orphean lyre.
Yet just arrangement, rarely brought to pass
But by a master's hand, disposing well
The gay diversities of leaf and flow'r,

Must lend its aid t' illustrate all their charms,
And dress the regular yet various scene.
Plant behind plant aspiring, in the van
The dwarfish, in the rear retir'd, but still
Sublime above the rest, the statelier stand.
So once were rang'd the sons of ancient Rome,
A noble show! while Roscius trod the stage;
And so, while Garrick, as renown'd as he,
The sons of Albion; fearing each to lose
Some note of Nature's music from his lips,
And covetous of Shakespeare's beauty, seen
In ev'ry flash of his far-beaming eye.
Nor taste alone and well-contriv'd display
Suffice to give the marshall'd ranks the grace
Of their complete effect. Much yet remains
Unsung, and many cares are yet behind,
And more laborious; cares on which depends
Their vigour, injur'd soon, not soon restor'd.
The soil must be renew'd, which, often wash'd,
Loses its treasure of salubrious salts,
And disappoints the roots; the slender roots
Close interwoven, where they meet the vase,
Must smooth be shorn away; the sapless branch
Must fly before the knife; the wither'd leaf
Must be detach'd, and where it strews the floor
Swept with a woman's neatness, breeding else
Contagion, and disseminating death.
Discharge but these kind offices, (and who
Would spare, that loves them, offices like these?)
Well they reward the toil. The sight is pleas'd,
The scent regal'd, each odorif'rous leaf,
Each op'ning blossom, freely breathes abroad
Its gratitude, and thanks him with its sweets.
  So manifold, all pleasing in their kind,
All healthful, are th' employs of rural life,
Reiterated as the wheel of time
Runs round; still ending, and beginning still.
Nor are these all. To deck the shapely knoll,
That, softly swell'd and gaily dress'd, appears
A flow'ry island, from the dark green lawn
Emerging, must be deem'd a labour due
To no mean hand, and asks the touch of taste.
Here also grateful mixture of well-match'd
And sorted hues (each giving each relief,
And by contrasted beauty shining more)
Is needful. Strength may wield the pond'rous spade,
May turn the clod, and wheel the compost home;
But elegance, chief grace the garden shows,

And most attractive, is the fair result
Of thought, the creature of a polish'd mind.
Without it all is gothic as the scene
To which th' insipid citizen resorts
Near yonder heath, where industry mispent,
But proud of his uncouth ill-chosen task,
Has made a heav'n on earth; with suns and moons
Of close-ramm'd stones has charg'd th' encumber'd soil,
And fairly laid the zodiac in the dust.
He, therefore, who would see his flow'rs dispos'd
Sightly and in just order, ere he gives
The beds the trusted treasure of their seeds,
Forecasts the future whole; that, when the scene
Shall break into its preconceiv'd display,
Each for itself, and all as with one voice
Conspiring, may attest his bright design.
Nor even then, dismissing as perform'd
His pleasant work, may he suppose it done.
Few self-supported flow'rs endure the wind
Uninjur'd, but expect th' upholding aid
Of the smooth-shaven prop, and, neatly tied,
Are wedded thus, like beauty to old age,
For int'rest sake, the living to the dead.
Some clothe the soil that feeds them, far diffus'd
And lowly creeping, modest and yet fair,
Like virtue, thriving most where little seen:
Some, more aspiring, catch the neighbour shrub
With clasping tendrils, and invest his branch,
Else unadorn'd, with many a gay festoon
And fragrant chaplet, recompensing well
The strength they borrow with the grace they lend.
All hate the rank society of weeds,
Noisome, and ever greedy to exhaust
Th' impov'rish'd earth; an overbearing race,
That, like the multitude made faction-mad,
Disturb good order, and degrade true worth.
Oh, blest seclusion from a jarring world,
Which he, thus occupied, enjoys! Retreat
Cannot indeed to guilty man restore
Lost innocence, or cancel follies past;
But it has peace, and much secures the mind
From all assaults of evil; proving still
A faithful barrier, not o'erleap'd with ease
By vicious custom, raging uncontroll'd
Abroad, and desolating public life.
When fierce temptation, seconded within
By traitor appetite, and arm'd with darts
Temper'd in hell, invades the throbbing breast,

To combat may be glorious, and success
Perhaps may crown us; but to fly is safe.
Had I the choice of sublunary good,
What could I wish that I possess not here?
Health, leisure, means t' improve it, friendship, peace,
No loose or wanton, though a wand'ring, muse,
And constant occupation without care.
Thus blest, I draw a picture of that bliss;
Hopeless, indeed, that dissipated minds,
And profligate abusers of a world
Created fair so much in vain for them,
Should seek the guiltless joys that I describe,
Allur'd by my report: but sure no less,
That, self-condemn'd, they must neglect the prize,
And what they will not taste must yet approve.
What we admire we praise; and, when we praise,
Advance it into notice, that, its worth
Acknowledg'd, others may admire it too.
I therefore recommend, though at the risk
Of popular disgust, yet boldly still,
The cause of piety and sacred truth,
And virtue, and those scenes which God ordain'd
Should best secure them and promote them most;
Scenes that I love, and with regret perceive
Forsaken, or through folly not enjoy'd.
Pure is the nymph, though lib'ral of her smiles,
And chaste, though unconfin'd, whom I extol.
Not as the prince in Shushan, when he call'd,
Vain-glorious of her charms, his Vashti forth
To grace the full pavilion. His design
Was but to boast his own peculiar good,
Which all might view with envy, none partake.
My charmer is not mine alone; my sweets,
And she that sweetens all my bitters too,
Nature, enchanting Nature, in whose form
And lineaments divine I trace a hand
That errs not, and find raptures still renew'd,
Is free to all men—universal prize.
Strange that so fair a creature should yet want
Admirers, and be destin'd to divide
With meaner objects ev'n the few she finds!
Stripp'd of her ornaments, her leaves and flow'rs,
She loses all her influence. Cities then
Attract us, and neglected Nature pines,
Abandon'd, as unworthy of our love.
But are not wholesome airs, though unperfum'd
By roses; and clear suns, though scarcely felt;
And groves, if unharmonious, yet secure

From clamour, and whose very silence charms;
To be preferr'd to smoke, to the eclipse
That Metropolitan volcanos make,
Whose Stygian throats breathe darkness all day long;
And to the stir of commerce, driving slow,
And thund'ring loud, with his ten thousand wheels?
They would be, were not madness in the head,
And folly in the heart; were England now
What England was; plain, hospitable, kind,
And undebauch'd. But we have bid farewell
To all the virtues of those better days,
And all their honest pleasures. Mansions once
Knew their own masters; and laborious hinds
Who had surviv'd the father, serv'd the son.
Now the legitimate and rightful lord
Is but a transient guest, newly arriv'd,
And soon to be supplanted. He that saw
His patrimonial timber cast its leaf,
Sells the last scantling, and transfers the price
To some shrewd sharper, ere it buds again.
Estates are landscapes, gaz'd upon a while,
Then advertis'd, and auctioneer'd away.
The country starves, and they that feed th' o'ercharg'd
And surfeited lewd town with her fair dues,
By a just judgment strip and starve themselves.
The wings that waft our riches out of sight
Grow on the gamester's elbows; and th' alert
And nimble motion of those restless joints,
That never tire, soon fans them all away.
Improvement too, the idol of the age,
Is fed with many a victim. Lo, he comes!
Th' omnipotent magician, Brown, appears!
Down falls the venerable pile, th' abode
Of our forefathers—a grave whisker'd race,
But tasteless. Springs a palace in its stead,
But in a distant spot; where, more expos'd,
It may enjoy th' advantage of the north,
And aguish east, till time shall have transform'd
Those naked acres to a shelt'ring grove.
He speaks. The lake in front becomes a lawn;
Woods vanish, hills subside, and vallies rise:
And streams, as if created for his use,
Pursue the track of his directing wand,
Sinuous or straight, now rapid and now slow,
Now murm'ring soft, now roaring in cascades—
Ev'n as he bids! Th' enraptur'd owner smiles.
'Tis finish'd, and yet, finish'd as it seems,
Still wants a grace, the loveliest it could show,

A mine to satisfy th' enormous cost.
Drain'd to the last poor item of his wealth,
He sighs, departs, and leaves th' accomplish'd plan
That he has touch'd, retouch'd, many a long day
Labour'd, and many a night pursu'd in dreams,
Just when it meets his hopes, and proves the heav'n
He wanted, for a wealthier to enjoy!
And now perhaps the glorious hour is come,
When, having no stake left, no pledge t' endear
Her int'rests, or that gives her sacred cause
A moment's operation on his love,
He burns with most intense and flagrant zeal
To serve his country. Ministerial grace
Deals him out money from the public chest;
Or, if that mine be shut, some private purse
Supplies his need with an usurious loan,
To be refunded duly when his vote,
Well-manag'd, shall have earn'd its worthy price.
Oh innocent, compar'd with arts like these,
Crape, and cock'd pistol, and the whistling ball
Sent through the trav'ller's temples! He that finds
One drop of heav'n's sweet mercy in his cup,
Can dig, beg, rot, and perish, well content,
So he may wrap himself in honest rags
At his last gasp; but could not for a world
Fish up his dirty and dependent bread
From pools and ditches of the commonwealth,
Sordid and sick'ning at his own success.
  Ambition, av'rice, penury incurr'd
By endless riot, vanity, the lust
Of pleasure and variety, dispatch,
As duly as the swallows disappear,
The world of wand'ring knights and squires to town.
London ingulphs them all! The shark is there,
And the shark's prey; the spendthrift, and the leech
That sucks him. There the sycophant, and he
Who, with bare-headed and obsequious bows,
Begs a warm office, doom'd to a cold jail
And groat per diem, if his patron frown.
The levee swarms, as if, in golden pomp,
Were character'd on ev'ry statesman's door,
"Batter'd and bankrupt fortunes mended here."
These are the charms that sully and eclipse
The charms of nature. 'Tis the cruel gripe
That lean hard-handed poverty inflicts,
The hope of better things, the chance to win,
The wish to shine, the thirst to be amus'd,
That at the sound of winter's hoary wing

Unpeople all our counties of such herds
Of flutt'ring, loit'ring, cringing, begging, loose
And wanton vagrants, as make London, vast
And boundless as it is, a crowded coop.
  Oh thou, resort and mart of all the earth,
Chequer'd with all complexions of mankind,
And spotted with all crimes; in whom I see
Much that I love, and more that I admire,
And all that I abhor; thou freckled fair,
That pleasest and yet shock'st me, I can laugh
And I can weep, can hope, and can despond,
Feel wrath and pity, when I think on thee!
Ten righteous would have sav'd a city once,
And thou hast many righteous.—Well for thee—
That salt preserves thee; more corrupted else,
And therefore more obnoxious, at this hour
Than Sodom in her day had pow'r to be,
For whom God heard his Abr'am plead in vain.

Sonnet to William Wilberforce, Esq.[1]

THY country, Wilberforce, with just disdain,
Hears thee, by cruel men and impious call'd
Fanatic, for thy zeal to loose th' enthrall'd
From exile, public sale, and slav'ry's chain.
Friend of the poor, the wrong'd, the fetter-gall'd,
Fear not lest labour such as thine be vain.
Thou hast achiev'd a part; hast gain'd the ear
Of Britain's senate to thy glorious cause;
Hope smiles, joy springs, and though cold caution pause
And weave delay, the better hour is near
That shall remunerate thy toils severe
By peace for Afric, fenced with British laws.
  Enjoy what thou hast won, esteem and love
  From all the Just on earth, and all the Blest above.

On the Receipt of My Mother's Picture Out of Norfolk The Gift of My Cousin Ann Bodham[2]

OH THAT those lips had language! Life has pass'd
With me but roughly since I heard thee last.

[1] Published in the *Northampton Mercury*, April, 1792. Text of *Poems*, 1815.
[2] Published in 1798. Text of *Poems*, 1800.

Those lips are thine—thy own sweet smiles I see,
The same that oft in childhood solaced me;
Voice only fails, else, how distinct they say,
"Grieve not, my child, chase all thy fears away!"
The meek intelligence of those dear eyes
(Blest be the art that can immortalize,
The art that baffles time's tyrannic claim
To quench it) here shines on me still the same.
  Faithful remembrancer of one so dear,
Oh welcome guest, though unexpected, here!
Who bidd'st me honour with an artless song,
Affectionate, a mother lost so long,
I will obey, not willingly alone,
But gladly, as the precept were her own;
And, while that face renews my filial grief,
Fancy shall weave a charm for my relief—
Shall steep me in Elysian reverie,
A momentary dream, that thou art she.
  My mother! when I learn'd that thou wast dead,
Say, wast thou conscious of the tears I shed?
Hover'd thy spirit o'er thy sorrowing son,
Wretch even then, life's journey just begun?
Perhaps thou gav'st me, though unseen, a kiss;
Perhaps a tear, if souls can weep in bliss—
Ah that maternal smile! it answers—Yes.
I heard the bell toll'd on thy burial day,
I saw the hearse that bore thee slow away,
And, turning from my nurs'ry window, drew
A long, long sigh, and wept a last adieu!
But was it such?—It was.—Where thou art gone
Adieus and farewells are a sound unknown.
May I but meet thee on that peaceful shore,
The parting sound shall pass my lips no more!
Thy maidens griev'd themselves at my concern,
Oft gave me promise of a quick return.
What ardently I wish'd, I long believ'd,
And, disappointed still, was still deceiv'd;
By disappointment every day beguil'd,
Dupe of *to-morrow* even from a child.
Thus many a sad to-morrow came and went,
Till, all my stock of infant sorrow spent,
I learn'd at last submission to my lot;
But, though I less deplor'd thee, ne'er forgot.
  Where once we dwelt our name is heard no more,
Children not thine have trod my nurs'ry floor;
And where the gard'ner Robin, day by day,
Drew me to school along the public way,
Delighted with my bauble coach, and wrapt

In scarlet mantle warm, and velvet capt,
'Tis now become a history little known,
That once we call'd the past'ral house our own.
Short-liv'd possession! but the record fair
That mem'ry keeps of all thy kindness there,
Still outlives many a storm that has effac'd
A thousand other themes less deeply trac'd.
Thy nightly visits to my chamber made,
That thou might'st know me safe and warmly laid;
Thy morning bounties ere I left my home,
The biscuit, or confectionary plum;
The fragrant waters on my cheeks bestow'd
By thy own hand, till fresh they shone and glow'd;
All this, and more endearing still than all,
Thy constant flow of love, that knew no fall,
Ne'er roughen'd by those cataracts and breaks
That humour interpos'd too often makes;
All this still legible in mem'ry's page,
And still to be so, to my latest age,
Adds joy to duty, makes me glad to pay
Such honours to thee as my numbers may;
Perhaps a frail memorial, but sincere,
Not scorn'd in heav'n, though little notic'd here.
  Could time, his flight revers'd, restore the hours,
When, playing with thy vesture's tissued flow'rs,
The violet, the pink, and jessamine,
I prick'd them into paper with a pin,
(And thou wast happier than myself the while,
Would'st softly speak, and stroke my head and smile)
Could those few pleasant hours again appear,
Might one wish bring them, would I wish them here?
I would not trust my heart—the dear delight
Seems so to be desir'd, perhaps I might.—
But no—what here we call our life is such,
So little to be lov'd, and thou so much,
That I should ill requite thee to constrain
Thy unbound spirit into bonds again.
  Thou, as a gallant bark from Albion's coast
(The storms all weather'd and the ocean cross'd)
Shoots into port at some well-haven'd isle,
Where spices breathe and brighter seasons smile,
There sits quiescent on the floods that show
Her beauteous form reflected clear below,
While airs impregnated with incense play
Around her, fanning light her streamers gay;
So thou, with sails how swift! hast reach'd the shore
"Where tempests never beat nor billows roar,"
And thy lov'd consort on the dang'rous tide

Of life, long since, has anchor'd at thy side.
But me, scarce hoping to attain that rest,
Always from port withheld, always distress'd—
Me howling winds drive devious, tempest toss'd,
Sails ript, seams op'ning wide, and compass lost,
And day by day some current's thwarting force
Sets me more distant from a prosp'rous course.
But oh the thought, that thou art safe, and he!
That thought is joy, arrive what may to me.
My boast is not that I deduce my birth
From loins enthron'd, and rulers of the earth;
But higher far my proud pretensions rise—
The son of parents pass'd into the skies.
And now, farewell—time, unrevok'd, has run
His wonted course, yet what I wish'd is done.
By contemplation's help, not sought in vain,
I seem t' have liv'd my childhood o'er again;
To have renew'd the joys that once were mine,
Without the sin of violating thine:
And, while the wings of fancy still are free,
And I can view this mimic shew of thee,
Time has but half succeeded in his theft—
Thyself remov'd, thy power to soothe me left.

The Castaway[1]

Obscurest night involv'd the sky,
  Th' Atlantic billows roar'd,
When such a destin'd wretch as I,
  Wash'd headlong from on board,
Of friends, of hope, of all bereft,
His floating home for ever left.

No braver chief could Albion boast
  Than he with whom he went,
Nor ever ship left Albion's coast,
  With warmer wishes sent.
He lov'd them both, but both in vain,
Nor him beheld, nor her again.

Not long beneath the 'whelming brine,
  Expert to swim, he lay;

[1] Written in 1799. Published in Hayley's *Life and Posthumous Writings*, 1803. Text of edition of 1806.

Nor soon he felt his strength decline,
  Or courage die away;
But wag'd with death a lasting strife,
Supported by despair of life.

He shouted: nor his friends had fail'd
  To check the vessel's course,
But so the furious blast prevail'd,
  That, pitiless perforce,
They left their outcast mate behind,
And scudded still before the wind.

Some succour yet they could afford;
  And, such as storms allow,
The cask, the coop, the floated cord,
  Delay'd not to bestow.
But he (they knew) nor ship, nor shore,
Whate'er they gave, should visit more.

Nor, cruel as it seem'd, could he
  Their haste himself condemn,
Aware that flight, in such a sea,
  Alone could rescue them;
Yet bitter felt it still to die
Deserted, and his friends so nigh.

He long survives, who lives an hour
  In ocean, self-upheld;
And so long he, with unspent pow'r,
  His destiny repell'd;
And ever, as the minutes flew,
Entreated help, or cried—"Adieu!"

At length, his transient respite past,
  His comrades, who before
Had heard his voice in ev'ry blast,
  Could catch the sound no more.
For then, by toil subdued, he drank
The stifling wave, and then he sank.

No poet wept him: but the page
  Of narrative sincere,
That tells his name, his worth, his age,
  Is wet with Anson's tear.
And tears by bards or heroes shed
Alike immortalize the dead.

I therefore purpose not, or dream,
  Descanting on his fate,
To give the melancholy theme
  A more enduring date:
But misery still delights to trace
Its 'semblance in another's case.

No voice divine the storm allay'd,
  No light propitious shone;
When, snatch'd from all effectual aid,
  We perish'd, each alone:
But I beneath a rougher sea,
And whelm'd in deeper gulphs than he.

THOMAS RUSSELL

(1762-1782-1788)

Sonnet
To Oxford[1]

OXFORD, since late I left thy peaceful shore,
  Much I regret thy domes with turrets crown'd,
  Thy crested walls with twining ivy bound,
  Thy Gothic fanes, dim isles, and cloysters hoar,
And treasur'd rolls of Wisdom's ancient lore;
  Nor less thy varying bells, which hourly sound
  In pensive chime, or ring in lively round,
  Or toll in the slow Curfeu's solemn roar;
Much too thy moonlight walks, and musings grave
  Mid silent shades of high-embowering trees,
  And much thy Sister-Streams, whose willows wave
In whispering cadence to the evening breeze;
  But most those Friends, whose much-lov'd converse gave
  Thy gentle charms a tenfold power to please.

[1] Published in *Sonnets and Miscellaneous Poems*, 1789. Text of first edition.

Sonnet
To Valclusa[1]

WHAT tho', VALCLUSA, the fond Bard be fled
  That woo'd his Fair in thy sequester'd bowers,
Long lov'd her living, long bemoan'd her dead,
  And hung her visionary shrine with flowers!
What tho' no more he teach thy shades to mourn
  The hapless chances that to Love belong,
As erst, when drooping o'er her turf forlorn
  He charm'd wild ECHO with his plaintive song!
Yet still, enamour'd of the tender tale,
  Pale Passion haunts thy grove's romantic gloom,
Yet still soft Music breathes in every gale,
  Still undecay'd the Fairy-garlands bloom,
Still heavenly incense fills each fragrant vale,
Still PETRARCH'S GENIUS weeps o'er LAURA'S tomb.

Sonnet
Suppos'd to be Written at Lemnos[2]

ON THIS lone Isle, whose rugged rocks affright
  The cautious pilot, ten revolving years
  Great Pæan's Son, unwonted erst to tears,
  Wept o'er his wound: alike each rolling light
Of heaven he watch'd, and blam'd it's lingering flight,
  By day the sea-mew screaming round his cave
  Drove slumber from his eyes, the chiding wave,
  And savage howlings chas'd his dreams by night.
HOPE still was his: in each low breeze, that sigh'd
  Thro' his rude grot, he heard a coming oar,
  In each white cloud a coming sail he spied;
Nor seldom listen'd to the fancied roar
  Of Oeta's torrents, or the hoarser tide
  That parts fam'd Trachis from th' Euboic shore.

[1] Published in *Sonnets and Miscellaneous Poems*, 1789. Text of first edition.
[2] Published in *Sonnets and Miscellaneous Poems*, 1789. Text of first edition.

WILLIAM BLAKE

(1757-1783-1827)

Poetical Sketches[1]

To Spring

O THOU with dewy locks, who lookest down
Thro' the clear windows of the morning, turn
Thine angel eyes upon our western isle,
Which in full choir hails thy approach, O Spring!

The hills tell each other, and the list'ning
Vallies hear; all our longing eyes are turned
Up to thy bright pavillions: issue forth,
And let thy holy feet visit our clime.

Come o'er the eastern hills, and let our winds
Kiss thy perfumed garments; let us taste
Thy morn and evening breath; scatter thy pearls
Upon our love-sick land that mourns for thee.

O deck her forth with thy fair fingers; pour
Thy soft kisses on her bosom; and put
Thy golden crown upon her languish'd head,
Whose modest tresses were bound up for thee!

To Summer

O THOU, who passest thro' our vallies in
Thy strength, curb thy fierce steeds, allay the heat
That flames from their large nostrils! thou, O Summer,
Oft pitched'st here thy golden tent, and oft
Beneath our oaks hast slept, while we beheld
With joy thy ruddy limbs and flourishing hair.

Beneath our thickest shades we oft have heard
Thy voice, when noon upon his fervid car
Rode o'er the deep of heaven; beside our springs
Sit down, and in our mossy vallies, on
Some bank beside a river clear, throw thy

[1] Published in 1783. Text of *Poetry and Prose of William Blake*, ed. Geoffrey Keynes, 1927. By permission.

Silk draperies off, and rush into the stream:
Our vallies love the Summer in his pride.

Our bards are fam'd who strike the silver wire:
Our youth are bolder than the southern swains:
Our maidens fairer in the sprightly dance:
We lack not songs, nor instruments of joy,
Nor echoes sweet, nor waters clear as heaven,
Nor laurel wreaths against the sultry heat.

To the Evening Star

THOU fair-hair'd angel of the evening,
Now, whilst the sun rests on the mountains, light
Thy bright torch of love; thy radiant crown
Put on, and smile upon our evening bed!
Smile on our loves, and, while thou drawest the
Blue curtains of the sky, scatter thy silver dew
On every flower that shuts its sweet eyes
In timely sleep. Let thy west wind sleep on
The lake; speak silence with thy glimmering eyes,
And wash the dusk with silver. Soon, full soon,
Dost thou withdraw; then the wolf rages wide,
And the lion glares thro' the dun forest:
The fleeces of our flocks are cover'd with
Thy sacred dew: protect them with thine influence.

Song

MY SILKS and fine array,
  My smiles and languish'd air,
By love are driv'n away;
  And mournful lean Despair
Brings me yew to deck my grave:
Such end true lovers have.

His face is fair as heav'n,
  When springing buds unfold;
O why to him was't giv'n,
  Whose heart is wintry cold?
His breast is love's all worship'd tomb,
Where all love's pilgrims come.

Bring me an axe and spade,
  Bring me a winding sheet;
When I my grave have made,
  Let winds and tempests beat:

Then down I'll lie, as cold as clay.
True love doth pass away!

Mad Song

THE wild winds weep,
  And the night is a-cold;
Come hither, Sleep,
  And my griefs unfold:
But lo! the morning peeps
  Over the eastern steeps,
And the rustling birds of dawn
The earth do scorn.

Lo! to the vault
  Of paved heaven,
With sorrow fraught
  My notes are driven:
They strike the ear of night,
  Make weep the eyes of day;
They make mad the roaring winds,
  And with tempests play.

Like a fiend in a cloud,
  With howling woe,
After night I do croud,
  And with night will go;
I turn my back to the east,
From whence comforts have increas'd;
For light doth seize my brain
With frantic pain.

To the Muses

WHETHER on Ida's shady brow,
  Or in the chambers of the East,
The chambers of the sun, that now
  From antient melody have ceas'd;

Whether in Heav'n ye wander fair,
  Or the green corners of the earth,
Or the blue regions of the air,
  Where the melodious winds have birth;

Whether on chrystal rocks ye rove,
  Beneath the bosom of the sea
Wand'ring in many a coral grove,
  Fair Nine, forsaking Poetry!

How have you left the antient love
 That bards of old enjoy'd in you!
The languid strings do scarcely move!
 The sound is forc'd, the notes are few!

Songs of Innocence[1]

Introduction

PIPING down the valleys wild,
Piping songs of pleasant glee,
On a cloud I saw a child,
And he laughing said to me:

"Pipe a song about a Lamb!"
So I piped with merry chear.
"Piper, pipe that song again;"
So I piped: he wept to hear.

"Drop thy pipe, thy happy pipe;
"Sing thy songs of happy chear:"
So I sung the same again,
While he wept with joy to hear.

"Piper, sit thee down and write
"In a book, that all may read."
So he vanish'd from my sight,
And I pluck'd a hollow reed,

And I made a rural pen,
And I stain'd the water clear,
And I wrote my happy songs
Every child may joy to hear.

The Ecchoing Green

THE Sun does arise,
And make happy the skies;
The merry bells ring
To welcome the Spring;
The skylark and thrush,
The birds of the bush,
Sing louder around

[1] Engraved in 1789. Text of *Poetry and Prose of William Blake*, ed. Geoffrey Keynes, 1927. By permission.

To the bells' chearful sound,
While our sports shall be seen
On the Ecchoing Green.

Old John, with white hair,
Does laugh away care,
Sitting under the oak,
Among the old folk.
They laugh at our play,
And soon they all say:
"Such, such were the joys
"When we all, girls & boys,
"In our youth time were seen
"On the Ecchoing Green."

Till the little ones, weary,
No more can be merry;
The sun does descend,
And our sports have an end.
Round the laps of their mothers
Many sisters and brothers,
Like birds in their nest,
Are ready for rest,
And sport no more seen
On the darkening Green.

The Lamb

Little Lamb, who made thee?
Dost thou know who made thee?
Gave thee life, & bid thee feed
By the stream & o'er the mead;
Gave thee clothing of delight,
Softest clothing, wooly, bright;
Gave thee such a tender voice,
Making all the vales rejoice?
Little Lamb, who made thee?
Dost thou know who made thee?

Little Lamb, I'll tell thee,
Little Lamb, I'll tell thee:
He is called by thy name,
For he calls himself a Lamb.
He is meek, & he is mild;
He became a little child.
I a child, & thou a lamb,

We are called by his name.
Little Lamb, God bless thee!
Little Lamb, God bless thee!

The Little Black Boy

My mother bore me in the southern wild,
And I am black, but O! my soul is white;
White as an angel is the English child,
But I am black, as if bereav'd of light.

My mother taught me underneath a tree,
And sitting down before the heat of day,
She took me on her lap and kissed me,
And pointing to the east, began to say:

"Look on the rising sun: there God does live,
"And gives his light, and gives his heat away;
"And flowers and trees and beasts and men receive
"Comfort in morning, joy in the noonday.

"And we are put on earth a little space,
"That we may learn to bear the beams of love;
"And these black bodies and this sunburnt face
"Is but a cloud, and like a shady grove.

"For when our souls have learn'd the heat to bear,
"The cloud will vanish; we shall hear his voice,
"Saying: 'Come out from the grove, my love & care,
" 'And round my golden tent like lambs rejoice.' "

Thus did my mother say, and kissed me;
And thus I say to little English boy:
When I from black and he from white cloud free,
And round the tent of God like lambs we joy,

I'll shade him from the heat, till he can bear
To lean in joy upon our father's knee;
And then I'll stand and stroke his silver hair,
And be like him, and he will then love me.

The Chimney Sweeper

When my mother died I was very young,
And my father sold me while yet my tongue
Could scarcely cry " 'weep! 'weep! 'weep! 'weep!"
So your chimneys I sweep, & in soot I sleep.

There's little Tom Dacre, who cried when his head,
That curl'd like a lamb's back, was shav'd: so I said
"Hush, Tom! never mind it, for when your head's bare
"You know that the soot cannot spoil your white hair."

And so he was quiet, & that very night,
As Tom was a-sleeping, he had such a sight!
That thousands of sweepers, Dick, Joe, Ned, & Jack,
Were all of them lock'd up in coffins of black.

And by came an Angel who had a bright key,
And he open'd the coffins & set them all free;
Then down a green plain, leaping, laughing, they run,
And wash in a river, and shine in the Sun.

Then naked & white, all their bags left behind,
They rise upon clouds and sport in the wind;
And the Angel told Tom, if he'd be a good boy,
He'd have God for his father, & never want joy.

And so Tom awoke; and we rose in the dark,
And got with our bags & our brushes to work.
Tho' the morning was cold, Tom was happy & warm;
So if all do their duty they need not fear harm.

The Divine Image

To MERCY, Pity, Peace, and Love
All pray in their distress;
And to these virtues of delight
Return their thankfulness.

For Mercy, Pity, Peace, and Love
Is God, our father dear,
And Mercy, Pity, Peace, and Love
Is Man, his child and care.

For Mercy has a human heart,
Pity a human face,
And Love, the human form divine,
And Peace, the human dress.

Then every man, of every clime,
That prays in his distress,
Prays to the human form divine,
Love, Mercy, Pity, Peace.

And all must love the human form,
In heathen, turk, or jew;
Where Mercy, Love, & Pity dwell
There God is dwelling too.

Holy Thursday

'TWAS on a Holy Thursday, their innocent faces clean,
The children walking two & two, in red & blue & green,
Grey-headed beadles walk'd before, with wands as white as snow,
Till into the high dome of Paul's they like Thames' waters flow.

O what a multitude they seem'd, these flowers of London town!
Seated in companies they sit with radiance all their own.
The hum of multitudes was there, but multitudes of lambs,
Thousands of little boys & girls raising their innocent hands.

Now like a mighty wind they raise to heaven the voice of song,
Or like harmonious thunderings the seats of Heaven among.
Beneath them sit the aged men, wise guardians of the poor;
Then cherish pity, lest you drive an angel from your door.

Night

THE sun descending in the west,
The evening star does shine;
The birds are silent in their nest,
And I must seek for mine.
The moon like a flower
In heaven's high bower,
With silent delight
Sits and smiles on the night.

Farewell, green fields and happy groves,
Where flocks have took delight.
Where lambs have nibbled, silent moves
The feet of angels bright;
Unseen they pour blessing
And joy without ceasing,
On each bud and blossom,
And each sleeping bosom.

They look in every thoughtless nest,
Where birds are cover'd warm;
They visit caves of every beast,
To keep them all from harm.
If they see any weeping
That should have been sleeping,

They pour sleep on their head,
And sit down by their bed.

When wolves and tygers howl for prey,
They pitying stand and weep;
Seeking to drive their thirst away,
And keep them from the sheep;
But if they rush dreadful,
The angels, most heedful,
Receive each mild spirit,
New worlds to inherit.

And there the lion's ruddy eyes
Shall flow with tears of gold,
And pitying the tender cries,
And walking round the fold,
Saying "Wrath, by his meekness,
"And by his health, sickness
"Is driven away
"From our immortal day.

"And now beside thee, bleating lamb,
"I can lie down and sleep;
"Or think on him who bore thy name,
"Graze after thee and weep.
"For, wash'd in life's river,
"My bright mane for ever
"Shall shine like the gold
"As I guard o'er the fold."

Nurse's Song

WHEN the voices of children are heard on the green
And laughing is heard on the hill,
My heart is at rest within my breast
And everything else is still.

"Then come home, my children, the sun is gone down
"And the dews of night arise;
"Come, come, leave off play, and let us away
"Till the morning appears in the skies."

"No, no, let us play, for it is yet day
"And we cannot go to sleep;
"Besides, in the sky the little birds fly
"And the hills are all cover'd with sheep."

"Well, well, go & play till the light fades away
"And then go home to bed."
The little ones leaped & shouted & laugh'd
And all the hills ecchoed.

On Another's Sorrow

CAN I see another's woe,
And not be in sorrow too?
Can I see another's grief,
And not seek for kind relief?

Can I see a falling tear,
And not feel my sorrow's share?
Can a father see his child
Weep, nor be with sorrow fill'd?

Can a mother sit and hear
An infant groan an infant fear?
No, no! never can it be!
Never, never can it be!

And can he who smiles on all
Hear the wren with sorrows small,
Hear the small bird's grief & care,
Hear the woes that infants bear,

And not sit beside the nest,
Pouring pity in their breast;
And not sit the cradle near,
Weeping tear on infant's tear;

And not sit both night & day,
Wiping all our tears away?
O, no! never can it be!
Never, never can it be!

He doth give his joy to all;
He becomes an infant small;
He becomes a man of woe;
He doth feel the sorrow too.

Think not thou canst sigh a sigh
And thy maker is not by;
Think not thou canst weep a tear
And thy maker is not near.

O! he gives to us his joy
That our grief he may destroy;
Till our grief is fled & gone
He doth sit by us and moan.

The Book of Thel[1]

Thel's Motto

Does the Eagle know what is in the pit?
Or wilt thou go ask the Mole?
Can Wisdom be put in a silver rod?
Or Love in a golden bowl?

I

THE daughters of the Seraphim led round their sunny flocks,
All but the youngest: she in paleness sought the secret air,
To fade away like morning beauty from her mortal day:
Down by the river of Adona her soft voice is heard,
And thus her gentle lamentation falls like morning dew:

"O life of this our spring! why fades the lotus of the water,
"Why fade these children of the spring, born but to smile & fall?
"Ah! Thel is like a wat'ry bow, and like a parting cloud;
"Like a reflection in a glass; like shadows in the water;
"Like dreams of infants, like a smile upon an infant's face;
"Like the dove's voice; like transient day; like music in the air.
"Ah! gentle may I lay me down, and gentle rest my head,
"And gentle sleep the sleep of death, and gentle hear the voice
"Of him that walketh in the garden in the evening time."

The Lilly of the valley, breathing in the humble grass,
Answer'd the lovely maid and said: "I am a wat'ry weed,
"And I am very small and love to dwell in lowly vales;
"So weak, the gilded butterfly scarce perches on my head.
"Yet I am visited from heaven, and he that smiles on all
"Walks in the valley and each morn over me spreads his hand,
"Saying, 'Rejoice, thou humble grass, thou new-born lilly flower,
" 'Thou gentle maid of silent valleys and of modest brooks;
" 'For thou shalt be clothed in light, and fed with morning manna,
" 'Till summer's heat melts thee beside the fountains and the springs

[1] Engraved in 1789. Text of *Poetry and Prose of William Blake*, ed. Geoffrey Keynes, 1927. By permission.

"'To flourish in eternal vales.' Then why should Thel complain?
"Why should the mistress of the vales of Har utter a sigh?"

She ceas'd & smil'd in tears, then sat down in her silver shrine.

Thel answer'd: "O thou little virgin of the peaceful valley,
"Giving to those that cannot crave, the voiceless, the o'ertired;
"Thy breath doth nourish the innocent lamb, he smells thy milky garments,
"He crops thy flowers while thou sittest smiling in his face,
"Wiping his mild and meekin mouth from all contagious taints.
"Thy wine doth purify the golden honey; thy perfume,
"Which thou dost scatter on every little blade of grass that springs,
"Revives the milked cow, & tames the fire-breathing steed.
"But Thel is like a faint cloud kindled at the rising sun:
"I vanish from my pearly throne, and who shall find my place?"

"Queen of the vales," the Lilly answer'd, "ask the tender cloud,
"And it shall tell thee why it glitters in the morning sky,
"And why it scatters its bright beauty thro' the humid air.
"Descend, O little Cloud, & hover before the eyes of Thel."

The Cloud descended, and the Lilly bow'd her modest head
And went to mind her numerous charge among the verdant grass.

II

"O little Cloud," the virgin said, "I charge thee tell to me
"Why thou complainest not when in one hour thou fade away:
"Then we shall seek thee, but not find. Ah! Thel is like to thee:
"I pass away: yet I complain, and no one hears my voice."

The Cloud then shew'd his golden head & his bright form emerg'd,
Hovering and glittering on the air before the face of Thel.

"O Virgin, know'st thou not our steeds drink of the golden springs
"Where Luvah doth renew his horses? Look'st thou on my youth,
"And fearest thou, because I vanish and am seen no more,
"Nothing remains? O maid, I tell thee, when I pass away
"It is to tenfold life, to love, to peace and raptures holy:
"Unseen descending, weigh my light wings upon balmy flowers,
"And court the fair-eyed dew to take me to her shining tent:
"The weeping virgin, trembling kneels before the risen sun,
"Till we arise link'd in a golden band and never part,
"But walk united, bearing food to all our tender flowers."

"Dost thou, O little Cloud? I fear that I am not like thee,
"For I walk thro' the vales of Har, and smell the sweetest flowers,
"But I feed not the little flowers; I hear the warbling birds,
"But I feed not the warbling birds; they fly and seek their food:
"But Thel delights in these no more, because I fade away;
"And all shall say, 'Without a use this shining woman liv'd,
" 'Or did she only live to be at death the food of worms?' "

The Cloud reclin'd upon his airy throne and answer'd thus:

"Then if thou art the food of worms, O virgin of the skies,
"How great thy use, how great thy blessing! Every thing that lives
"Lives not alone nor for itself. Fear not, and I will call
"The weak worm from its lowly bed, and thou shalt hear its voice.
"Come forth, worm of the silent valley, to thy pensive queen."

The helpless worm arose, and sat upon the Lilly's leaf,
And the bright Cloud sail'd on, to find his partner in the vale.

III

Then Thel astonish'd view'd the Worm upon its dewy bed.

"Art thou a Worm? Image of weakness, art thou but a Worm?
"I see thee like an infant wrapped in the Lilly's leaf.
"Ah! weep not, little voice, thou canst not speak, but thou canst weep.
"Is this a Worm? I see thee lay helpless & naked, weeping,
"And none to answer, none to cherish thee with mother's smiles.

The Clod of Clay heard the Worm's voice & rais'd her pitying head:
She bow'd over the weeping infant, and her life exhal'd
In milky fondness: then on Thel she fix'd her humble eyes.

"O beauty of the vales of Har! we live not for ourselves.
"Thou seest me the meanest thing, and so I am indeed.
"My bosom of itself is cold, and of itself is dark;
"But he, that loves the lowly, pours his oil upon my head,
"And kisses me, and binds his nuptial bands around my breast,
"And says: 'Thou mother of my children, I have loved thee
" 'And I have given thee a crown that none can take away.'
"But how this is, sweet maid, I know not, and I cannot know;
"I ponder, and I cannot ponder; yet I live and love."

The daughter of beauty wip'd her pitying tears with her white veil,
And said: "Alas! I knew not this, and therefore did I weep.

"That God would love a Worm I knew, and punish the evil foot
"That wilful bruis'd its helpless form; but that he cherish'd it
"With milk and oil I never knew, and therefore did I weep;
"And I complain'd in the mild air, because I fade away,
"And lay me down in thy cold bed, and leave my shining lot."

"Queen of the vales," the matron Clay answer'd, "I heard thy sighs,
"And all thy moans flew o'er my roof, but I have call'd them down.
"Wilt thou, O Queen, enter my house? 'Tis given thee to enter
"And to return: fear nothing, enter with thy virgin feet."

IV

The eternal gates' terrific porter lifted the northern bar:
Thel enter'd in & saw the secrets of the land unknown.
She saw the couches of the dead, & where the fibrous roots
Of every heart on earth infixes deep its restless twists:
A land of sorrows & of tears where never smile was seen.

She wander'd in the land of clouds thro' valleys dark, list'ning
Dolours & lamentations; waiting oft beside a dewy grave
She stood in silence, list'ning to the voices of the ground,
Till to her own grave plot she came, & there she sat down,
And heard this voice of sorrow breathed from the hollow pit.

"Why cannot the Ear be closed to its own destruction?
"Or the glist'ning Eye to the poison of a smile?
"Why are Eyelids stor'd with arrows ready drawn,
"Where a thousand fighting men in ambush lie?
"Or an Eye of gifts & graces show'ring fruits & coined gold?
"Why a Tongue impress'd with honey from every wind?
"Why an Ear, a whirlpool fierce to draw creations in?
"Why a Nostril wide inhaling terror, trembling, & affright?
"Why a tender curb upon the youthful burning boy?
"Why a little curtain of flesh on the bed of our desire?"

The Virgin started from her seat, & with a shriek
Fled back unhinder'd till she came into the vales of Har.

The Marriage of Heaven and Hell[1]

The Argument

RINTRAH roars & shakes his fires in the burden'd air;
Hungry clouds swag on the deep.

Once meek, and in a perilous path,
The just man kept his course along
The vale of death.
Roses are planted where thorns grow,
And on the barren heath
Sing the honey bees.

Then the perilous path was planted,
And a river and a spring
On every cliff and tomb,
And on the bleached bones
Red clay brought forth;

Till the villain left the paths of ease,
To walk in perilous paths, and drive
The just man into barren climes.

Now the sneaking serpent walks
In mild humility,
And the just man rages in the wilds
Where lions roam.

Rintrah roars & shakes his fires in the burden'd air;
Hungry clouds swag on the deep.

As a new heaven is begun, and it is now thirty-three years since its advent, the Eternal Hell revives. And lo! Swedenborg is the Angel sitting at the tomb: his writings are the linen clothes folded up. Now is the dominion of Edom, & the return of Adam into Paradise. See Isaiah xxxiv & xxxv Chap.

Without Contraries is no progression. Attraction and Repulsion, Reason and Energy, Love and Hate, are necessary to Human existence.

From these contraries spring what the religious call Good & Evil. Good is the passive that obeys Reason. Evil is the active springing from Energy.

Good is Heaven. Evil is Hell.

---

[1] Engraved cir. 1793. Text of *Poetry and Prose of William Blake*, ed. Geoffrey Keynes, 1927. By permission.

The Voice of the Devil

ALL Bibles or sacred codes have been the causes of the following Errors:

1. That Man has two real existing principles: Viz: a Body & a Soul.

2. That Energy, call'd Evil, is alone from the Body; & that Reason, call'd Good, is alone from the Soul.

3. That God will torment Man in Eternity for following his Energies.

But the following Contraries to these are True:

1. Man has no Body distinct from his Soul; for that call'd Body is a portion of Soul discern'd by the five Senses, the chief inlets of Soul in this age.

2. Energy is the only life, and is from the Body; and Reason is the bound or outward circumference of Energy.

3. Energy is Eternal Delight.

THOSE who restrain desire, do so because theirs is weak enough to be restrained; and the restrainer or reason usurps its place & governs the unwilling.

And being restrain'd, it by degrees becomes passive, till it is only the shadow of desire.

The history of this is written in Paradise Lost, & the Governor or Reason is call'd Messiah.

And the original Archangel, or possessor of the command of the heavenly host, is call'd the Devil or Satan, and his children are call'd Sin & Death.

But in the Book of Job, Milton's Messiah is call'd Satan.

For this history has been adopted by both parties.

It indeed appear'd to Reason as if Desire was cast out; but the Devil's account is, that the Messiah fell, & formed a heaven of what he stole from the Abyss.

This is shewn in the Gospel, where he prays to the Father to send the comforter, or Desire, that Reason may have Ideas to build on; the Jehovah of the Bible being no other than he who dwells in flaming fire.

Know that after Christ's death, he became Jehovah.

But in Milton, the Father is Destiny, the Son a Ratio of the five senses, & the Holy-ghost Vacuum!

Note: The reason Milton wrote in fetters when he wrote of Angels & God, and at liberty when of Devils & Hell, is because he was a true Poet and of the Devil's party without knowing it.

A Memorable Fancy

As I was walking among the fires of hell, delighted with the enjoyments of Genius, which to Angels look like torment and insanity, I collected some of their Proverbs; thinking that as the sayings used in a nation mark its character, so the Proverbs of Hell show the nature of Infernal wisdom better than any description of buildings or garments.

When I came home: on the abyss of the five senses, where a flat sided steep frowns over the present world, I saw a mighty Devil folded in black clouds, hovering on the sides of the rock: with corroding fires he wrote the following sentence now percieved by the minds of men, & read by them on earth:

How do you know but ev'ry Bird that cuts the airy way,
Is an immense world of delight, clos'd by your senses five?

Proverbs of Hell

IN seed time learn, in harvest teach, in winter enjoy.

Drive your cart and your plow over the bones of the dead.

The road of excess leads to the palace of wisdom.

Prudence is a rich, ugly old maid courted by Incapacity.

He who desires but acts not, breeds pestilence.

The cut worm forgives the plow.

Dip him in the river who loves water.

A fool sees not the same tree that a wise man sees.

He whose face gives no light, shall never become a star.

Eternity is in love with the productions of time.

The busy bee has no time for sorrow.

The hours of folly are measur'd by the clock; but of wisdom, no clock can measure.

All wholesome food is caught without a net or a trap.

Bring out number, weight & measure in a year of dearth.

No bird soars too high, if he soars with his own wings.

A dead body revenges not injuries.

The most sublime act is to set another before you.

If the fool would persist in his folly he would become wise.

Folly is the cloke of knavery.

Shame is Pride's cloke.

Prisons are built with stones of Law, Brothels with bricks of Religion.

The pride of the peacock is the glory of God.

The lust of the goat is the bounty of God.

The wrath of the lion is the wisdom of God.

The nakedness of woman is the work of God.

Excess of sorrow laughs. Excess of joy weeps.

The roaring of lions, the howling of wolves, the raging of the stormy sea, and the destructive sword, are portions of eternity, too great for the eye of man.

The fox condemns the trap, not himself.

Joys impregnate. Sorrows bring forth.

Let man wear the fell of the lion, woman the fleece of the sheep.

The bird a nest, the spider a web, man friendship.

The selfish, smiling fool, & the sullen, frowning fool shall be both thought wise, that they may be a rod.

What is now proved was once only imagin'd.

The rat, the mouse, the fox, the rabbet watch the roots; the lion, the tyger, the horse, the elephant watch the fruits.

The cistern contains: the fountain overflows.

One thought fills immensity.

Always be ready to speak your mind, and a base men will avoid you.

Every thing possible to be believ'd is an image of truth.

The eagle never lost so much time as when he submitted to learn of the crow.

The fox provides for himself, but God provides for the lion.

Think in the morning. Act in the noon. Eat in the evening. Sleep in the Night.

He who has suffer'd you to impose on him, knows you.

As the plow follows words, so God rewards prayers.

The tygers of wrath are wiser than the horses of instruction.

Expect poison from the standing water.

You never know what is enough unless you know what is more than enough.

Listen to the fool's reproach! it is a kingly title!

The eyes of fire, the nostrils of air, the mouth of water, the beard of earth.

The weak in courage is strong in cunning.

The apple tree never asks the beech how he shall grow; nor the lion, the horse, how he shall take his prey.

The thankful reciever bears a plentiful harvest.

If others had not been foolish, we should be so.

The soul of sweet delight can never be defil'd.

When thou seest an Eagle, thou seest a portion of Genius; lift up thy head!

As the caterpiller chooses the fairest leaves to lay her eggs on, so the priest lays his curse on the fairest joys.

To create a little flower is the labour of ages.

Damn braces. Bless relaxes.

The best wine is the oldest, the best water the newest.

Prayers plow not! Praises reap not!

Joys laugh not! Sorrows weep not!

The head Sublime, the heart Pathos, the genitals Beauty, the hands & feet Proportion.

As the air to a bird or the sea to a fish, so is contempt to the contemptible.

The crow wish'd every thing was black, the owl that every thing was white.

Exuberance is Beauty.

If the lion was advised by the fox, he would be cunning.

Improvement makes strait roads; but the crooked roads without Improvement are roads of Genius.

Sooner murder an infant in its cradle than nurse unacted desires.

Where man is not, nature is barren.

Truth can never be told so as to be understood, and not be believ'd.

Enough! or Too much.

THE ancient Poets animated all sensible objects with Gods or Geniuses, calling them by the names and adorning them with the properties of woods, rivers, mountains, lakes, cities, nations, and whatever their enlarged & numerous senses could percieve.

And particularly they studied the genius of each city & country, placing it under its mental deity;

Till a system was formed, which some took advantage of, & enslav'd the vulgar by attempting to realize or abstract the mental deities from their objects: thus began Priesthood;

Choosing forms of worship from poetic tales.

And at length they pronounc'd that the Gods had order'd such things.

Thus men forgot that All deities reside in the human breast.

A Memorable Fancy

THE Prophets Isaiah and Ezekiel dined with me, and I asked them how they dared so roundly to assert that God spoke to them; and whether they did not think at the time that they would be misunderstood, & so be the cause of imposition.

Isaiah answer'd: "I saw no God, nor heard any, in a finite "organical perception; but my senses discover'd the infinite in "everything, and as I was then perswaded, & remain confirm'd, "that the voice of honest indignation is the voice of God, I cared "not for consequences, but wrote."

Then I asked: "does a firm perswasion that a thing is so, make "it so?"

He replied: "All poets believe that it does, & in ages of "imagination this firm perswasion removed mountains; but many "are not capable of a firm perswasion of any thing."

Then Ezekial said: "The philosophy of the east taught the "first principles of human perception: some nations held one "principle for the origin, and some another: we of Israel taught "that the Poetic Genius (as you now call it) was the first prin-"ciple and all the others merely derivative, which was the cause "of our despising the Priests & Philosophers of other countries, "and prophecying that all Gods would at last be proved to orig-"inate in ours & to be the tributaries of the Poetic Genius; it was "this that our great poet, King David, desired so fervently &

"invokes so pathetic'ly, saying by this he conquers enemies & "governs kingdoms; and we so loved our God, that we cursed in "his name all the deities of surrounding nations, and asserted that "they had rebelled: from these opinions the vulgar came to think "that all nations would at last be subject to the jews."

"This," said he, "like all firm perswasions, is come to pass; "for all nations believe the jews' code and worship the jews' god, "and what greater subjection can be?"

I heard this with some wonder, & must confess my own conviction. After dinner I ask'd Isaiah to favour the world with his lost works; he said none of equal value was lost. Ezekiel said the same of his.

I also asked Isaiah what made him go naked and barefoot three years? he answer'd: "the same that made our friend Diogenes, "the Grecian."

I then asked Ezekiel why he eat dung, & lay so long on his right & left side? he answer'd, "the desire of raising other men "into a perception of the infinite: this the North American tribes "practise, & is he honest who resists his genius or conscience only "for the sake of present ease or gratification?"

THE ancient tradition that the world will be consumed in fire at the end of six thousand years is true, as I have heard from Hell.

For the cherub with his flaming sword is hereby commanded to leave his guard at tree of life; and when he does, the whole creation will be consumed and appear infinite and holy, whereas it now appears finite & corrupt.

This will come to pass by an improvement of sensual enjoyment.

But first the notion that man has a body distinct from his soul is to be expunged; this I shall do by printing in the infernal method, by corrosives, which in Hell are salutary and medicinal, melting apparent surfaces away, and displaying the infinite which was hid.

If the doors of perception were cleansed every thing would appear to man as it is, infinite.

For man has closed himself up, till he sees all things thro' narrow chinks of his cavern.

A Memorable Fancy

I WAS in a Printing house in Hell, & saw the method in which knowledge is transmitted from generation to generation.

In the first chamber was a Dragon-Man, clearing away the rubbish from a cave's mouth; within, a number of Dragons were hollowing the cave.

In the second chamber was a Viper folding round the rock &

the cave, and others adorning it with gold, silver and precious stones.

In the third chamber was an Eagle with wings and feathers of air: he caused the inside of the cave to be infinite; around were numbers of Eagle-like men who built palaces in the immense cliffs.

In the fourth chamber were Lions of flaming fire, raging around & melting the metals into living fluids.

In the fifth chamber were Unnam'd forms, which cast the metals into the expanse.

There they were reciev'd by Men who occupied the sixth chamber, and took the forms of books & were arranged in libraries.

THE Giants who formed this world into its sensual existence, and now seem to live in it in chains, are in truth the causes of its life & the sources of all activity; but the chains are the cunning of weak and tame minds which have power to resist energy; according to the proverb, the weak in courage is strong in cunning.

Thus one portion of being is the Prolific, the other the Devouring: to the Devourer it seems as if the producer was in his chains; but it is not so, he only takes portions of existence and fancies that the whole.

But the Prolific would cease to be Prolific unless the Devourer, as a sea, received the excess of his delights.

Some will say: "Is not God alone the Prolific?" I answer: "God only Acts & Is, in existing beings or Men."

These two classes of men are always upon earth, & they should be enemies: whoever tries to reconcile them seeks to destroy existence.

Religion is an endeavour to reconcile the two.

Note: Jesus Christ did not wish to unite, but to seperate them, as in the Parable of sheep and goats! & he says: "I came not to send Peace, but a Sword."

Messiah or Satan or Tempter was formerly thought to be one of the Antediluvians who are our Energies.

A Memorable Fancy

AN Angel came to me and said: "O pitiable foolish young man! "O horrible! O dreadful state! consider the hot burning dungeon "thou art preparing for thyself to all eternity, to which thou art "going in such career."

I said: "Perhaps you will be willing to shew me my eternal "lot, & we will contemplate together upon it, and see whether "your lot or mine is most desirable."

So he took me thro' a stable & thro' a church & down into the church vault, at the end of which was a mill: thro' the mill we went, and came to a cave: down the winding cavern we groped our tedious way, till a void boundless as a nether sky appear'd beneath us, & we held by the roots of trees and hung over this immensity; but I said: "if you please, we will commit ourselves "to this void, and see whether providence is here also: if you will "not, I will:" but he answer'd: "do not presume, O young man, "but as we here remain, behold thy lot which will soon appear "when the darkness passes away."

So I remain'd with him, sitting in the twisted root of an oak; he was suspended in a fungus, which hung with the head downward into the deep.

By degrees we beheld the infinite Abyss, fiery as the smoke of a burning city; beneath us, at an immense distance, was the sun, black but shining; round it were fiery tracks on which revolv'd vast spiders, crawling after their prey, which flew, or rather swum, in the infinite deep, in the most terrific shapes of animals sprung from corruption; & the air was full of them, & seem'd composed of them: these are Devils, and are called Powers of the air. I now asked my companion which was my eternal lot? he said: "between the black & white spiders."

But now, from between the black & white spiders, a cloud and fire burst and rolled thro' the deep, black'ning all beneath, so that the nether deep grew black as a sea, & rolled with a terrible noise; beneath us was nothing now to be seen but a black tempest, till looking east between the clouds & the waves, we saw a cataract of blood mixed with fire, and not many stones' throw from us appear'd and sunk again the scaly fold of a monstrous serpent; at last, to the east, distant about three degrees, appear'd a fiery crest above the waves; slowly it reared like a ridge of golden rocks, till we discover'd two globes of crimson fire, from which the sea fled away in clouds of smoke; and now we saw it was the head of Leviathan; his forehead was divided into streaks of green & purple like those on a tyger's forehead: soon we saw his mouth & red gills hang just above the raging foam, tinging the black deep with beams of blood, advancing toward us with all the fury of a spiritual existence.

My friend the Angel climb'd up from his station into the mill: I remain'd alone; & then this appearance was no more, but I found myself sitting on a pleasant bank beside a river by moonlight, hearing a harper, who sung to the harp; & his theme was: "The man who never alters his opinion is like standing water, & "breeds reptiles of the mind."

But I arose and sought for the mill, & there I found my Angel, who, surprised, asked me how I escaped?

I answer'd: "All that we saw was owing to your metaphysics; "for when you ran away, I found myself on a bank by moonlight "hearing a harper. But now we have seen my eternal lot, shall "I shew you yours?" he laugh'd at my proposal; but I by force suddenly caught him in my arms, & flew westerly thro' the night, till we were elevated above the earth's shadow; then I flung myself with him directly into the body of the sun; here I clothed myself in white, & taking in my hand Swedenborg's volumes, sunk from the glorious clime, and passed all the planets till we came to saturn: here I stay'd to rest, & then leap'd into the void between saturn & the fixed stars.

"Here," said I, "is your lot, in this space—if space it may be "call'd." Soon we saw the stable and the church, & I took him to the altar and open'd the Bible, and lo! it was a deep pit, into which I descended, driving the Angel before me; soon we saw seven houses of brick; one we enter'd; in it were a number of monkeys, baboons, & all of that species, chain'd by the middle, grinning and snatching at one another, but withheld by the shortness of their chains: however, I saw that they sometimes grew numerous, and then the weak were caught by the strong, and with a grinning aspect, first coupled with, & then devour'd, by plucking off first one limb and then another, till the body was left a helpless trunk; this, after grinning & kissing it with seeming fondness, they devour'd too; and here & there I saw one savourily picking the flesh off his own tail; as the stench terribly annoy'd us both, we went into the mill, & I in my hand brought the skeleton of a body, which in the mill was Aristotle's Analytics.

So the Angel said: "thy phantasy has imposed upon me, & thou "oughtest to be ashamed."

I answer'd: "we impose on one another, & it is but lost time "to converse with you whose works are only Analytics."

OPPOSITION is true Friendship.

I HAVE always found that Angels have the vanity to speak of themselves as the only wise; this they do with a confident insolence sprouting from systematic reasoning.

Thus Swedenborg boasts that what he writes is new: tho' it is only the Contents or Index of already publish'd books.

A man carried a monkey about for a shew, & because he was a little wiser than the monkey, grew vain, and conciev'd himself as much wiser than seven men. It is so with Swedenborg: he shews the folly of churches, & exposes hypocrites, till he imagines that all are religious, & himself the single one on earth that ever broke a net.

Now hear a plain fact: Swedenborg has not written one new truth. Now hear another: he has written all the old falsehoods.

And now hear the reason. He conversed with Angels who are all religious, & conversed not with Devils who all hate religion, for he was incapable thro' his conceited notions.

Thus Swedenborg's writings are a recapitulation of all superficial opinions, and an analysis of the more sublime—but no further.

Have now another plain fact. Any man of mechanical talents may, from the writings of Paracelsus or Jacob Behmen, produce ten thousand volumes of equal value with Swedenborg's, and from those of Dante or Shakespear an infinite number.

But when he has done this, let him not say that he knows better than his master, for he only holds a candle in sunshine.

A Memorable Fancy

ONCE I saw a Devil in a flame of fire, who arose before an Angel that sat on a cloud, and the Devil utter'd these words:

"The worship of God is: Honouring his gifts in other men, "each according to his genius, and loving the greatest men best: "those who envy or calumniate great men hate God; for there is "no other God."

The Angel hearing this became almost blue; but mastering himself he grew yellow, & at last white, pink, & smiling, and then replied:

"Thou Idolater! is not God One? & is not he visible in Jesus "Christ? and has not Jesus Christ given his sanction to the law "of ten commandments? and are not all other men fools, sinners, "& nothings?"

The Devil answer'd: "bray a fool in a morter with wheat, yet "shall not his folly be beaten out of him; if Jesus Christ is the "greatest man, you ought to love him in the greatest degree; "now hear how he has given his sanction to the law of ten com- "mandments: did he not mock at the sabbath, and so mock the "sabbath's God? murder those who were murder'd because of "him? turn away the law from the woman taken in adultery? "steal the labor of others to support him? bear false witness "when he omitted making a defence before Pilate? covet when he "pray'd for his disciples, and when he bid them shake off the "dust of their feet against such as refused to lodge them? I tell "you, no virtue can exist without breaking these ten command- "ments. Jesus was all virtue, and acted from impulse, not from "rules."

When he had so spoken, I beheld the Angel, who stretched out his arms, embracing the flame of fire, & he was consumed and arose as Elijah.

Note: This Angel, who is now become a Devil, is my particular friend; we often read the Bible together in its infernal or diabolical sense, which the world shall have if they behave well.

I have also The Bible of Hell, which the world shall have whether they will or no.

ONE Law for the Lion & Ox is Oppression.

A Song of Liberty

I.

THE Eternal Female groan'd! it was heard over all the Earth.

2. Albion's coast is sick, silent; the American meadows faint!

3. Shadows of Prophecy shiver along by the lakes and the rivers, and mutter across the ocean: France, rend down thy dungeon!

4. Golden Spain, burst the barriers of old Rome!

5. Cast thy keys, O Rome, into the deep down falling, even to eternity down falling,

6. And weep.

7. In her trembling hands she took the new born terror, howling.

8. On those infinite mountains of light, now barr'd out by the atlantic sea, the new born fire stood before the starry king!

9. Flag'd with grey brow'd snows and thunderous visages, the jealous wings wav'd over the deep.

10. The speary hand burned aloft, unbuckled was the shield; forth went the hand of jealousy among the flaming hair, and hurl'd the new born wonder thro' the starry night.

11. The fire, the fire is falling!

12. Look up! look up! O citizen of London, enlarge thy countenance! O Jew, leave counting gold! return to thy oil and wine. O African! black African! (go, winged thought, widen his forehead.)

13. The fiery limbs, the flaming hair, shot like the sinking sun into the western sea.

14. Wak'd from his eternal sleep, the hoary element roaring fled away.

15. Down rush'd, beating his wings in vain, the jealous king; his grey brow'd councellors, thunderous warriors, curl'd veterans, among helms, and shields, and chariots, horses, elephants, banners, castles, slings, and rocks.

16. Falling, rushing, ruining! buried in the ruins, on Urthona's dens;

17. All night beneath the ruins; then, their sullen flames faded, emerge round the gloomy king.

18. With thunder and fire, leading his starry hosts thro' the waste wilderness, he promulgates his ten commands, glancing his beamy eyelids over the deep in dark dismay,

19. Where the son of fire in his eastern cloud, while the morning plumes her golden breast,

20. Spurning the clouds written with curses, stamps the stony law to dust, loosing the eternal horses from the dens of night, crying:

EMPIRE IS NO MORE! AND NOW THE LION & WOLF SHALL CEASE.

CHORUS

Let the Priests of the Raven of dawn no longer, in deadly black, with hoarse note curse the sons of joy. Nor his accepted brethren —whom, tyrant, he calls free—lay the bound or build the roof. Nor pale religious letchery call that virginity that wishes but acts not!

For every thing that lives is Holy.

Songs of Experience[1]

Holy Thursday

Is THIS a holy thing to see
In a rich and fruitful land,
Babes reduc'd to misery,
Fed with cold and usurous hand?

Is that trembling cry a song?
Can it be a song of joy?
And so many children poor?
It is a land of poverty!

And their sun does never shine,
And their fields are bleak & bare,
And their ways are fill'd with thorns:
It is eternal winter there.

For where-e'er the sun does shine,
And where-e'er the rain does fall,
Babe can never hunger there,
Nor poverty the mind appall.

Nurse's Song

WHEN the voices of children are heard on the green
And whisp'rings are in the dale,
The days of my youth rise fresh in my mind,
My face turns green and pale.

Then come home, my children, the sun is gone down,
And the dews of night arise;

[1] Engraved in 1794. Text of *Poetry and Prose of William Blake*, ed. Geoffrey Keynes, 1927. By permission.

Your spring & your day are wasted in play,
And your winter and night in disguise.

The Tyger

TYGER! Tyger! burning bright
In the forests of the night,
What immortal hand or eye
Could frame thy fearful symmetry?

In what distant deeps or skies
Burnt the fire of thine eyes?
On what wings dare he aspire?
What the hand dare sieze the fire?

And what shoulder, & what art,
Could twist the sinews of thy heart?
And when thy heart began to beat,
What dread hand? & what dread feet?

What the hammer? what the chain?
In what furnace was thy brain?
What the anvil? what dread grasp
Dare its deadly terrors clasp?

When the stars threw down their spears,
And water'd heaven with their tears,
Did he smile his work to see?
Did he who made the Lamb make thee?

Tyger! Tyger! burning bright
In the forests of the night,
What immortal hand or eye,
Dare frame thy fearful symmetry?

The Little Vagabond

DEAR Mother, dear Mother, the Church is cold,
But the Ale-house is healthy & pleasant & warm;
Besides I can tell where I am used well,
Such usage in Heaven will never do well.

But if at the Church they would give us some Ale,
And a pleasant fire our souls to regale,
We'd sing and we'd pray all the live-long day,
Nor ever once wish from the Church to stray.

Then the Parson might preach, & drink, & sing,
And we'd be as happy as birds in the spring;

And modest Dame Lurch, who is always at Church,
Would not have bandy children, nor fasting, nor birch.

And God, like a father rejoicing to see
His children as pleasant and happy as he,
Would have no more quarrel with the Devil or the Barrel,
But kiss him, & give him both drink and apparel.

London

I WANDER thro' each charter'd street,
Near where the charter'd Thames does flow,
And mark in every face I meet
Marks of weakness, marks of woe.

In every cry of every Man,
In every Infant's cry of fear,
In every voice, in every ban,
The mind-forg'd manacles I hear.

How the Chimney-sweeper's cry
Every black'ning Church appalls;
And the hapless Soldier's sigh
Runs in blood down Palace walls.

But most thro' midnight streets I hear
How the youthful Harlot's curse
Blasts the new born Infant's tear,
And blights with plagues the Marriage hearse.

A Little Boy Lost

"NOUGHT loves another as itself,
"Nor venerates another so,
"Nor is it possible to Thought
"A greater than itself to know:

"And Father, how can I love you
"Or any of my brothers more?
"I love you like the little bird
"That picks up crumbs around the door."

The Priest sat by and heard the child,
In trembling zeal he siez'd his hair:
He led him by his little coat,
And all admir'd the Priestly care.

And standing on the altar high,
"Lo! what a fiend is here!" said he,

"One who sets reason up for judge
"Of our most holy Mystery."

The weeping child could not be heard,
The weeping parents wept in vain;
They strip'd him to his little shirt,
And bound him in an iron chain;

And burn'd him in a holy place,
Where many had been burn'd before:
The weeping parents wept in vain.
Are such things done on Albion's shore?

Preface to Milton, A Poem in 2 Books To Justify the Ways of God to Men[1]

AND did those feet in ancient time
Walk upon England's mountains green?
And was the holy Lamb of God
On England's pleasant pastures seen?

And did the Countenance Divine
Shine forth upon our clouded hills?
And was Jerusalem builded here
Among these dark Satanic Mills?

Bring me my Bow of burning gold:
Bring me my Arrows of desire:
Bring me my Spear: O clouds unfold!
Bring me my Chariot of fire.

I will not cease from Mental Fight,
Nor shall my Sword sleep in my hand
Till we have built Jerusalem
In England's green & pleasant Land.

[1] Engraved in 1804. Text of *Poetry and Prose of William Blake*, ed. Geoffrey Keynes, 1927. By permission.

ROBERT BURNS

(1759-1786-1796)

The Twa Dogs, A Tale[1]

'TWAS in that place o' Scotland's isle,
That bears the name o' auld king COIL,
Upon a bonie day in June,
When wearing thro' the afternoon,
Twa Dogs, that were na thrang at hame,
Forgather'd ance upon a time.
  The first I'll name, they ca'd him *Cæsar,*
Was keepet for His Honor's pleasure;
His hair, his size, his mouth, his lugs,
Shew'd he was nane o' Scotland's dogs,
But whalpet some place far abroad,
Where sailors gang to fish for Cod.
  His locked, letter'd, braw brass-collar
Shew'd him the *gentleman* an' *scholar;*
But tho' he was o' high degree,
The fient a pride na pride had he,
But wad hae spent an hour caressan,
Ev'n wi' a Tinkler-gipsey's *messan:*
At Kirk or Market, Mill or Smiddie,
Nae tawted *tyke,* tho' e'er sae duddie,
But he wad stan't, as glad to see him,
An' stroan't on stanes an' hillocks wi' him.
  The tither was a *ploughman's collie,*
A rhyming, ranting, raving billie,
Wha for his friend an' comrade had him,
And in his freaks had *Luath* ca'd him,
After some dog in *Highland sang,*
Was made lang syne, lord knows how lang.
  He was a gash an' faithfu' *tyke,*
As ever lap a sheugh or dyke.
His honest, sonsie, baws'nt face,
Ay gat him friends in ilka place;
His breast was white, his towzie back,
Weel clad wi' coat o' glossy black;
His gawsie tail, wi' upward curl,
Hung owre his hurdies wi' a swirl.
  Nae doubt but they were fain o' ither,
An' unco pack an' thick thegither;

[1] Published in *Poems,* Kilmarnock, 1786. Text of first edition.

Wi' social nose whyles snuff'd an' snowket;
Whyles mice and modewurks they howket;
Whyles scour'd awa in lang excursion,
An' worry'd ither in diversion;
Till tir'd at last wi' mony a farce,
They set them down upon their arse,
An' there began a lang digression
About the *lords o' the creation.*

CAESAR

I've aften wonder'd, honest *Luath,*
What sort o' life poor dogs like you have;
An' when the *gentry's* life I saw,
What way *poor bodies* liv'd ava.
Our *Laird* gets in his racked rents,
His coals, his kane, an' a' his stents:
He rises when he likes himsel;
His flunkies answer at the bell;
He ca's his coach; he ca's his horse;
He draws a bonie, silken purse
As lang's my tail, whare thro' the steeks,
The yellow letter'd *Geordie* keeks.
Frae morn to een it's nought but toiling,
At baking, roasting, frying, boiling;
An' tho' the gentry first are steghan,
Yet ev'n the *ha' folk* fill their peghan
Wi' sauce, ragouts, an' sic like trashtrie,
That's little short o' downright wastrie.
Our *Whipper-in,* wee, blastet wonner,
Poor, worthless elf, it eats a dinner,
Better than ony *Tenant-man*
His Honor has in a' the lan':
An' what poor *Cot-folk* pit their painch in,
I own it's past my comprehension.

LUATH

Trowth, Cæsar, whyles their fash't enough;
A *Cotter* howkan in a sheugh,
Wi' dirty stanes biggan a dyke,
Bairan a quarry, an' sic like,
Himsel, a wife, he thus sustains,
A smytrie o' wee, duddie weans,
An' nought but his han'-daurk, to keep
Them right an' tight in thack an' raep.
An' when they meet wi' fair disasters,
Like loss o' health or want o' masters,

Ye maist wad think, a wee touch langer,
An' they maun starve o' cauld and hunger:
But how it comes, I never kent yet,
They're maistly wonderfu' contented;
An' buirdly chiels, and clever hizzies,
Are bred in sic a way as this is.

CAESAR

But then, to see how ye're negleket,
How huff'd, an' cuff'd, an' disrespeket!
L—d man, our gentry care as little
For *delvers*, *ditchers*, an' sic cattle;
They gang as saucy by poor folk,
As I wad by a stinkan brock.
I've notic'd, on our Laird's *court-day*,
An' mony a time my heart's been wae,
Poor *tenant bodies*, scant o' cash,
How they maun thole a *factor's* snash;
He'll stamp an' threaten, curse an' swear,
He'll *apprehend* them, *poind* their gear;
While they maun stan', wi' aspect humble,
An' hear it a', an' fear an' tremble!
I see how folk live that hae riches;
But surely poor-folk maun be wretches!

LUATH

They're no sae wretched 's ane wad think;
Tho' constantly on poortith's brink,
They're sae accustom'd wi' the sight,
The view o't gies them little fright.
Then chance and fortune are sae guided,
They're ay in less or mair provided;
An' tho' fatigu'd wi' close employment,
A blink o' rest 's a sweet enjoyment.
The dearest comfort o' their lives,
Their grushie weans an' faithfu' wives;
The *prattling things* are just their pride,
That sweetens a' their fire side.
An' whyles twalpennie-worth o' *nappy*
Can mak the bodies unco happy;
They lay aside their private cares,
To mind the Kirk and State affairs;
They'll talk o' *patronage* an' *priests*,
Wi' kindling fury i' their breasts,
Or tell what new taxation's comin,
An' ferlie at the folk in LON'ON.

As bleak-fac'd Hallowmass returns,
They get the jovial, rantan *Kirns*,
When *rural life*, of ev'ry station,
Unite in common recreation;
Love blinks, Wit slaps, an' social Mirth
Forgets there's *care* upo' the earth.
That *merry day* the year begins,
They bar the door on frosty win's;
The nappy reeks wi' mantling ream,
An' sheds a heart-inspiring steam;
The luntan pipe, an' sneeshin mill,
Are handed round wi' right guid will;
The cantie, auld folks, crackan crouse,
The young anes rantan thro' the house—
My heart has been sae fain to see them,
That I for joy hae barket wi' them.
Still it's owre true that ye hae said,
Sic game is now owre aften play'd;
There's monie a creditable *stock*
O' decent, honest, fawsont folk,
Are riven out baith root an' branch,
Some rascal's pridefu' greed to quench,
Wha thinks to knit himsel the faster
In favor wi' some *gentle Master*,
Wha aiblins thrang a *parliamentin*,
For Britain's guid his saul indentin——

CAESAR

Haith lad ye little ken about it;
For Britain's guid! guid faith! I doubt it.
Say rather, gaun as PREMIERS lead him,
An' saying *aye* or *no*'s they bid him:
At Operas an' Plays parading,
Mortgaging, gambling, masquerading:
Or maybe, in a frolic daft,
To HAGUE or CALAIS takes a waft,
To make a *tour* an' tak a whirl,
To learn *bon ton* an' see the worl'.
There, at VIENNA or VERSAILLES,
He rives his father's auld entails;
Or by MADRID he takes the rout,
To thrum *guittars* an' fecht wi' nowt;
Or down *Italian Vista* startles,
Wh—re-hunting amang groves o' myrtles:
Then bowses drumlie *German-water*,
To mak himsel look fair and fatter,
An' purge the bitter ga's an' cankers,

O' curst *Venetian* b—res an' ch—ncres.
For Britain's guid! for her destruction!
Wi' dissipation, feud an' faction!

LUATH

Hech man! dear sirs! is that the gate,
They waste sae mony a braw estate!
Are we sae foughten and harass'd
For gear to gang that gate at last!
O would they stay aback frae courts,
An' please themsels wi' countra sports,
It wad for ev'ry ane be better,
The *Laird*, the *Tenant*, an' the *Cotter!*
For thae frank, rantan, ramblan billies,
Fient haet o' them 's ill hearted fellows;
Except for breakin o' their timmer,
Or speakin lightly o' their *Limmer*,
Or shootin of a hare or moorcock,
The ne'er-a-bit they're ill to poor folk.
But will ye tell me, master *Cæsar*,
Sure *great folk's* life's a life o' pleasure?
Nae cauld nor hunger e'er can steer them,
The vera thought o't need na fear them.

CAESAR

L—d man, were ye but whyles where I am,
The *gentles* ye wad neer envy them!
It's true, they need na starve or sweat,
Thro' Winter's cauld, or Summer's heat;
They've nae sair-wark to craze their banes,
An' fill *auld-age* wi' grips an' granes;
But *human-bodies* are sic fools,
For a' their colledges an' schools,
That when nae *real* ills perplex them,
They *mak* enow themsels to vex them;
An' ay the less they hae to sturt them,
In like proportion, less will hurt them.
A country fellow at the pleugh,
His *acre's* till'd, he's right eneugh;
A country girl at her wheel,
Her *dizzen's* done, she's unco weel;
But Gentlemen, an' Ladies warst,
Wi' ev'n down *want o' wark* are curst.
They loiter, lounging, lank an' lazy;
Tho' deil-haet ails them, yet uneasy;
Their days, insipid, dull an' tasteless,

Their nights, unquiet, lang an' restless.
  An' ev'n their sports, their balls an' races,
Their galloping thro' public places,
There's sic parade, sic pomp an' art,
The joy can scarcely reach the heart.
  The *Men* cast out in *party-matches*,
Then sowther a' in deep debauches.
Ae night, they're mad wi' drink an' wh—ring,
Niest day their life is past enduring.
  The *Ladies* arm-in-arm in clusters,
As great an' gracious a' as sisters;
But hear their *absent thoughts* o' ither,
They're a run deils an' jads thegither.
Whyles, owre the wee bit cup an' platie,
They sip the *scandal-potion* pretty;
Or lee-lang nights, wi' crabbet leuks,
Pore owre the devil's *pictur'd beuks*;
Stake on a chance a farmer's stackyard,
An' cheat like ony *unhang'd blackguard*.
  There's some exceptions, man an' woman;
But this is Gentry's life in common.

  By this, the sun was out o' sight,
 An' darker gloamin' brought the night:
The *bum-clock* humm'd wi' lazy drone,
The kye stood rowtan i' the loan;
When up they gat an' shook their lugs,
Rejoic'd they were na *men* but *dogs*;
An' each took off his several way,
Resolv'd to meet some ither day.

The Holy Fair[1]

A robe of seeming truth and trust
  Hid crafty observation;
And secret hung, with poison'd crust,
  The dirk of Defamation:
A mask that like the gorget show'd,
  Dye-varying, on the pigeon;
And for a mantle large and broad,
  He wrapt him in Religion.

Hypocrisy a-la-Mode.

Upon a simmer Sunday morn,
  When Nature's face is fair,

[1] Published in *Poems*, Kilmarnock, 1786. Text of first edition.

I walked forth to view the corn,
  An' snuff the callor air.
The rising sun, our GALSTON Muirs,
  Wi' glorious light was glintan;
The hares were hirplan down the furrs,
  The lav'rocks they were chantan
                Fu' sweet that day.

As lightsomely I glowr'd abroad,
  To see a scene sae gay,
Three *hizzies*, early at the road,
  Cam skelpan up the way.
Twa had manteeles o' dolefu' black,
  But ane wi' lyart lining;
The third, that gaed a wee a-back,
  Was in the fashion shining
                Fu' gay that day.

The *twa* appear'd like sisters twin,
  In feature, form an' claes;
Their visage wither'd, lang an' thin,
  An' sour as ony slaes:
The *third* cam up, hap-step-an'-loup,
  As light as ony lambie,
An' wi' a curchie low did stoop,
  As soon as e'er she saw me,
                Fu' kind that day.

Wi' bonnet aff, quoth I, "Sweet lass,
  "I think ye seem to ken me;
"I'm sure I've seen that bonie face,
  "But yet I canna name ye."
Quo' she, an' laughan as she spak,
  An' taks me by the han's,
"Ye, for my sake, hae gien the feck
  "Of a' the *ten comman's*
                A screed some day."

"My name is FUN—your cronie dear,
  "The nearest friend ye hae;
"An' this is SUPERSTITION here,
  "An' that's HYPOCRISY.
"I'm gaun to * * * * * * *holy fair,*
  "To spend an hour in daffin:
"Gin ye'll go there, yon runkl'd pair,
  "We will get famous laughin
                At them this day."

Quoth I, "With a' my heart, I'll do't;
"I'll get my sunday's sark on,
"An' meet you on the holy spot;
"Faith, we'se hae fine remarkin!"
Then I gaed hame at crowdie-time,
An' soon I made me ready;
For roads were clad, frae side to side,
Wi' monie a wearie body,
In droves that day.

Here, farmers gash, in ridin graith,
Gaed hoddan by their cotters;
There, swankies young, in braw braid-claith,
Are springan owre the gutters.
The lasses, skelpan barefit, thrang,
In silks an' scarlets glitter;
Wi' *sweet-milk cheese*, in monie a whang,
An' *farls*, bak'd wi' butter,
Fu' crump that day.

When by the *plate* we set our nose,
Weel heaped up wi' ha'pence,
A greedy glowr *black-bonnet* throws,
An' we maun draw our tippence.
Then in we go to see the show,
On ev'ry side they're gath'ran;
Some carryan dails, some chairs an' stools,
An' some are busy bleth'ran
Right loud that day.

Here stands a shed to fend the show'rs,
An' screen our countra Gentry;
There, *racer Jess*, an' twathree wh—res,
Are blinkan at the entry.
Here sits a raw o' tittlan jads,
Wi' heaving breasts an' bare neck;
An' there, a batch o' *Wabster lads*,
Blackguarding frae K * * * * * ck
For *fun* this day.

Here, some are thinkan on their sins,
An' some upo' their claes;
Ane curses feet that fyl'd his shins,
Anither sighs an' prays:
On this hand sits an *Elect* swatch,
Wi' screw'd-up, grace-proud faces;

On that, a set o' chaps, at watch,
  Thrang winkan on the lasses
            To *chairs* that day.

O happy is that man, an' blest!
  Nae wonder that it pride him!
Whase ain dear lass, that he likes best,
  Comes clinkan down beside him!
Wi' arm repos'd on the *chair-back*,
  He sweetly does compose him;
Which, by degrees, slips round her *neck*,
  An's loof upon her *bosom*
            Unkend that day.

Now a' the congregation o'er
  Is silent expectation;
For * * * * * * speels the holy door,
  Wi' tidings o' s—lv—t—n.
Should *Hornie*, as in ancient days,
  'Mang sons o' G— present him,
The vera sight o' * * * * * *'s face,
  To's ain *het hame* had sent him
            Wi' fright that day.

Hear how he clears the points o' Faith
  Wi' rattlin' an' thumpin!
Now meekly calm, now wild in wrath,
  He's stampan, an' he's jumpan!
His lengthen'd chin, his turn'd up snout,
  His eldritch squeel an' gestures,
O how they fire the heart devout,
  Like *cantharidian* plaisters
            On sic a day!

But hark! the *tent* has chang'd it's voice;
  There's peace an' rest nae langer;
For a' the *real judges* rise,
  They canna sit for anger.
* * * * * opens out his cauld harangues,
  On *practice* and on *morals*;
An' aff the *godly* pour in thrangs,
  To gie the jars an' barrels
            A lift that day.

What signifies his barren shine,
  Of *moral pow'rs* an' *reason?*
His English style, an' gesture fine,
  Are a' clean out o' season.

Like SOCRATES or ANTONINE,
  Or some auld pagan heathen,
The *moral man* he does define,
  But ne'er a word o' *faith* in
          That's right that day.

In guid time comes an antidote
  Against sic poosion'd nostrum;
For * * * * * * *, frae the water-fit,
  Ascends the *holy rostrum:*
See, up he's got the word o' G—,
  An' meek an' mim has view'd it,
While COMMON-SENSE has taen the road,
  An' aff, an' up the *Cowgate*
          Fast, fast that day.

Wee * * * * * * niest, the Guard relieves,
  An' Orthodoxy raibles,
Tho' in his heart he weel believes,
  An' thinks it auld wives' fables:
But faith! the birkie wants a *Manse*,
  So, cannilie he hums them;
Altho' his *carnal* Wit an' Sense
  Like hafflins-wise o'ercomes him
          At times that day.

Now, butt an' ben, the Change-house fills,
  Wi' *yill-caup* Commentators:
Here's crying out for bakes an' gills,
  An' there the pint-stowp clatters;
While thick an' thrang, an' loud an' lang,
  Wi' *Logic*, an' wi' *Scripture*,
They raise a din, that, in the end,
  Is like to breed a rupture
          O' wrath that day.

Leeze me on Drink! it gies us mair
  Than either School or Colledge:
It kindles Wit, it waukens Lear,
  It pangs us fou o' Knowledge.
Be't *whisky-gill* or *penny-wheep*,
  Or ony stronger potion,
It never fails, on drinkin deep,
  To kittle up our *notion*,
          By night or day.

The lads an' lasses, blythely bent
  To mind baith *saul* an' *body*,

Sit round the table, weel content,
  An' steer about the *toddy.*
On this ane's dress, an' that ane's leuk,
  They're makin observations;
While some are cozie i' the neuk,
  An' forming *assignations*
    To meet some day.

But now the L—'s ain trumpet touts,
  Till a' the hills are rairan,
An' echos back return the shouts;
  Black * * * * * * is na spairan:
His piercin words, like Highlan swords,
  Divide the joints an' marrow;
His talk o' H—ll, whare devils dwell,
  Our vera "Sauls does harrow"
    Wi' fright that day!

A vast, unbottom'd, boundless *Pit*,
  Fill'd fou o' *lowan brunstane*,
Whase raging flame, an' scorching heat,
  Wad melt the hardest whun-stane!
The *half asleep* start up wi' fear,
  An' think they hear it roaran,
When presently it does appear,
  'Twas but some neebor *snoran*
    Asleep that day.

'Twad be owre lang a tale to tell,
  How monie stories past,
An' how they crouded to the yill,
  When they were a' dismist:
How drink gaed round, in cogs an' caups,
  Amang the furms an' benches;
An' *cheese* an' *bread*, frae women's laps,
  Was dealt about in lunches,
    An' dawds that day.

In comes a gawsie, gash *Guidwife*,
  An' sits down by the fire,
Syne draws her *kebbuck* an' her knife;
  The lasses they are shyer.
The auld *Guidmen*, about the *grace*,
  Frae side to side they bother,
Till some ane by his bonnet lays,
  An' gies them't, like a *tether*,
    Fu' lang that day.

Waesucks! for him that gets nae lass,
  Or lasses that hae naething!
Sma' need has he to say a grace,
  Or melvie his braw claithing!
O *Wives* be mindfu', ance yoursel,
  How bonie lads ye wanted,
An' dinna, for a *kebbuck-heel*,
  Let lasses be affronted
          On sic a day!

Now *Clinkumbell*, wi' rattlan tow,
  Begins to jow an' croon;
Some swagger hame, the best they dow,
  Some wait the afternoon.
At slaps the billies halt a blink,
  Till lasses strip their shoon:
Wi' *faith* an' *hope*, an' *love* an' *drink*,
  They're a' in famous tune
          For crack that day.

How monie hearts this day converts,
  O' sinners and o' Lasses!
Their hearts o' stane, gin night are gane,
  As saft as ony flesh is.
There's some are fou o' *love divine*;
  There's some are fou o' *brandy*;
An' monie jobs that day begin,
  May end in *Houghmagandie*
          Some ither day.

Address to the Deil[1]

O Prince, O chief of many throned pow'rs,
That led th'embattl'd Seraphim to war—
MILTON.

O Thou, whatever title suit thee!
Auld Hornie, Satan, Nick, or Clootie,
Wha in yon cavern grim an' sootie,
          Clos'd under hatches,
Spairges about the brunstane cootie,
          To scaud poor wretches!

[1] Published in *Poems*, Kilmarnock, 1786. Text of first edition.

Hear me, *auld Hangie,* for a wee,
An' let poor, *damned bodies* bee;
I'm sure sma' pleasure it can gie,
Ev'n to a *deil,*
To skelp an' scaud poor dogs like me,
An' hear us squeel!

Great is thy pow'r, an' great thy fame;
Far kend an' noted is thy name;
An' tho' yon *lowan heugh's* thy hame,
Thou travels far;
An' faith! thou's neither lag nor lame,
Nor blate nor scaur.

Whyles, ranging like a roaran lion,
For prey, a' holes an' corners tryin;
Whyles, on the strong-wing'd Tempest flyin,
Tirlan the *kirks*;
Whyles, in the human bosom pryin,
Unseen thou lurks.

I've heard my rev'rend *Graunie* say,
In lanely glens ye like to stray;
Or where auld, ruin'd castles, gray,
Nod to the moon,
Ye fright the nightly wand'rer's way,
Wi' eldritch croon.

When twilight did my *Graunie* summon,
To say her pray'rs, douse, honest woman!
Aft 'yont the dyke she's heard you bumman,
Wi' eerie drone;
Or, rustling, thro' the boortries coman,
Wi' heavy groan.

Ae dreary, windy, winter night,
The stars shot down wi' sklentan light,
Wi' you, *mysel,* I gat a fright,
Ayont the lough;
Ye, like a *rash-buss,* stood in sight,
Wi' waving sugh.

The cudgel in my nieve did shake,
Each bristl'd hair stood like a stake,
When wi' an eldritch, stoor *quaick, quaick,*
Amang the springs.
Awa ye squatter'd like a *drake,*
On whistling wings.

Let *Warlocks* grim, an' wither'd *Hags*,
Tell how wi' you on ragweed nags,
They skim the muirs an' dizzy crags,
Wi' wicked speed;
And in kirk-yards renew their leagues,
Owre howcket dead.

Thence, countra wives, wi' toil an' pain,
May plunge an' plunge the *kirn* in vain;
For Oh! the yellow treasure's taen
By witching skill;
An' dawtet, twal-pint *Hawkie's* gane
As yell's the Bill.

Thence, mystic knots mak great abuse,
On *Young-Guidmen*, fond, keen an' croose;
When the best *wark-lume* i' the house,
By contraip wit,
Is instant made no worth a louse,
Just at the bit.

When thowes dissolve the snawy hoord,
An' float the jinglan icy boord,
Then, *Water-kelpies* haunt the foord,
By your direction,
An' nighted Trav'llers are allur'd
To their destruction.

An' aft your moss-traversing *Spunkies*
Decoy the wight that late an' drunk is:
The bleezan, curst, mischievous monkies
Delude his eyes,
Till in some miry slough he sunk is,
Ne'er mair to rise.

When MASONS' mystic *word* an' *grip*,
In storms an' tempests raise you up,
Some cock or cat, your rage maun stop,
Or, strange to tell!
The *youngest Brother* ye wad whip
Aff straught to *H—ll.*

Lang syne in EDEN'S bonie yard,
When youthfu' lovers first were pair'd,
An' all the Soul of Love they shar'd,
The raptur'd hour,
Sweet on the fragrant, flow'ry swaird,
In shady bow'r.

Then you, ye auld, snick-drawing dog!
Ye cam to Paradise incog,
An' play'd on man a cursed brogue,
(Black be your fa'!)
An' gied the infant warld a shog,
'Maist ruin'd a'.

D'ye mind that day, when in a bizz,
Wi' reeket duds, an' reestet gizz,
Ye did present your smoutie phiz,
'Mang better folk,
An' sklented on the *man of Uzz*,
Your spitefu' joke?

An' how ye gat him i' your thrall,
An' brak him out o' house an' hal',
While scabs an' botches did him gall,
Wi' bitter claw,
An' lows'd his ill-tongu'd, wicked *Scawl*
Was warst ava?

But a' your doings to rehearse,
Your wily snares an' fechtin fierce,
Sin' that day MICHAEL did you pierce,
Down to this time,
Wad ding a' *Lallan* tongue, or *Erse*,
In Prose or Rhyme.

An' now, auld *Cloots*, I ken ye're thinkan,
A certain *Bardie's* rantin, drinkin,
Some luckless hour will send him likan,
To your black pit;
But faith! he'll turn a corner jinkan,
An' cheat you yet.

But fare-you-weel, auld *Nickie-ben*!
O wad ye tak a thought an' men'!
Ye aiblins might—I dinna ken—
Still hae a *stake*—
I'm wae to think upo' yon den,
Ev'n for your sake!

The Cotter's Saturday Night

Inscribed to R. A. ——, Esq.[1]

Let not Ambition mock their useful toil,
Their homely joys, and destiny obscure;
Nor Grandeur hear, with a disdainful smile,
The short and simple annals of the Poor.
GRAY.

I.

MY LOV'D, my honor'd, much respected friend,
No mercenary Bard his homage pays;
With honest pride, I scorn each selfish end,
My dearest meed, a friend's esteem and praise:
To you I sing, in simple Scottish lays,
The *lowly train* in life's sequester'd scene;
The native feelings strong, the guileless ways,
What A * * * * in a *Cottage* would have been;
Ah! tho' his worth unknown, far happier there I ween!

II.

November chill blaws loud wi' angry sugh;
The short'ning winter-day is near a close;
The miry beasts retreating frae the pleugh;
The black'ning trains o' craws to their repose:
The toil-worn COTTER frae his labor goes,
This night his weekly moil is at an end,
Collects his *spades*, his *mattocks* and his *hoes*,
Hoping the *morn* in ease and rest to spend,
And weary, o'er the moor, his course does hameward bend.

III.

At length his lonely *Cot* appears in view,
Beneath the shelter of an aged tree;
The expectant *wee-things*, toddlan, stacher through
To meet their *Dad*, wi' flichterin noise and glee.
His wee-bit ingle, blinkan bonilie,
His clean hearth-stane, his thrifty *Wifie's* smile,
The *lisping infant*, prattling on his knee,
Does a' his weary *kiaugh* and care beguile,
And makes him quite forget his labor and his toil.

[1] Published in *Poems*, Kilmarnock, 1786. Text of first edition.

IV.

Belyve, the *elder bairns* come drapping in,
At *Service* out, amang the Farmers roun';
Some ca' the pleugh, some herd, some tentie rin
A cannie errand to a neebor town:
Their eldest hope, their *Jenny*, woman-grown,
In youthfu' bloom, Love sparkling in her e'e,
Comes hame, perhaps, to shew a braw new gown,
Or deposite her sair-won penny-fee,
To help her *Parents* dear, if they in hardship be.

V.

With joy unfeign'd, *brothers* and *sisters* meet,
And each for other's weelfare kindly spiers:
The social hours, swift-wing'd, unnotic'd fleet;
Each tells the uncos that he sees or hears.
The Parents partial eye their hopeful years;
Anticipation forward points the view;
The *Mother*, wi' her needle and her sheers,
Gars auld claes look amaist as weel's the new;
The *Father* mixes a' wi' admonition due.

VI.

Their Master's and their Mistress's command,
The *youngkers* a' are warned to obey;
And mind their labors wi' an eydent hand,
And ne'er, tho' out o' sight, to jauk or play:
"And O! be sure to fear the LORD alway!
"And mind your *duty*, duely, morn and night!
"Lest in temptation's path ye gang astray,
"Implore his *counsel* and assisting *might:*
"They never sought in vain that sought the LORD aright."

VII.

But hark! a rap comes gently to the door;
Jenny, wha kens the meaning o' the same,
Tells how a neebor lad came o'er the moor,
To do some errands, and convoy her hame.
The wily Mother sees the *conscious flame*
Sparkle in *Jenny's* e'e, and flush her cheek,
With heart-struck, anxious care enquires his name,
While *Jenny* hafflins is afraid to speak;
Weel-pleas'd the Mother hears, it's nae wild, worthless *Rake*.

VIII.

With kindly welcome, *Jenny* brings him ben;
  A *strappan youth*; he takes the Mother's eye;
Blythe *Jenny* sees the *visit's* no ill taen;
  The Father cracks of horses, pleughs and kye.
The *Youngster's* artless heart o'erflows wi' joy,
  But blate and laithfu', scarce can weel behave;
The Mother, wi' a woman's wiles, can spy
  What makes the *youth* sae bashfu' and sae grave;
Weel-pleas'd to think her *bairn's* respected like the lave.

IX.

O happy love! where love like this is found!
  O heart-felt raptures! bliss beyond compare!
I've paced much this weary, *mortal round*,
  And sage EXPERIENCE bids me this declare—
"If Heaven a draught of heavenly pleasure spare,
  "One *cordial* in this melancholy *Vale*,
" 'Tis when a youthful, loving, *modest* Pair,
  "In other's arms, breathe out the tender tale,
"Beneath the milk-white thorn that scents the ev'ning gale."

X.

Is there, in human form, that bears a heart—
  A Wretch! a Villain! lost to love and truth!
That can, with studied, sly, ensnaring art,
  Betray sweet Jenny's unsuspecting youth?
Curse on his perjur'd arts! dissembling smooth!
  Are *Honor*, *Virtue*, *Conscience*, all exil'd?
Is there no Pity, no relenting Ruth,
  Points to the Parents fondling o'er their Child?
Then paints the *ruin'd Maid*, and *their* distraction wild!

XI.

But now the Supper crowns their simple board,
  The healsome *Porritch*, chief of SCOTIA'S food:
The soupe their *only Hawkie* does afford,
  That 'yont the hallan snugly chows her cood;
The *Dame* brings forth, in complimental mood,
  To grace the lad, her weel-hain'd kebbuck, fell,
And aft he's prest, and aft he ca's it guid;
  The frugal *Wifie*, garrulous, will tell,
How 'twas a towmond auld, sin' Lint was i' the bell.

XII.

The chearfu' Supper done, wi' serious face,
  They, round the ingle, form a circle wide;
The Sire turns o'er, with patriarchal grace,
  The big *ha'-Bible*, ance his *Father's* pride:
His bonnet rev'rently is laid aside,
  His *lyart haffets* wearing thin and bare;
Those strains that once did sweet in ZION glide,
  He wales a portion with judicious care;
"And let us worship GOD!" he says with solemn air.

XIII.

They chant their artless notes in simple guise;
  They tune their *hearts*, by far the noblest aim:
Perhaps *Dundee's* wild warbling measures rise,
  Or plaintive *Martyrs*, worthy of the name;
Or noble *Elgin* beets the heaven-ward flame,
  The sweetest far of SCOTIA'S holy lays:
Compar'd with these, *Italian trills* are tame;
  The tickl'd ears no heart-felt raptures raise;
Nae unison hae they, with our CREATOR'S praise.

XIV.

The priest-like Father reads the sacred page,
  How *Abram* was the Friend of GOD on high;
Or, *Moses* bade eternal warfare wage,
  With *Amalek's* ungracious progeny;
Or how the *royal Bard* did groaning lye,
  Beneath the stroke of Heaven's avenging ire;
Or *Job's* pathetic plaint, and wailing cry;
  Or rapt *Isaiah's* wild, seraphic fire;
Or other *Holy Seers* that tune the *sacred lyre*.

XV.

Perhaps the *Christian Volume* is the theme,
  How *guiltless blood* for *guilty man* was shed;
How HE, who bore in heaven the second name,
  Had not on Earth whereon to lay His head:
How His first *followers* and *servants* sped;
  The *Precepts sage* they wrote to many a land:
How *he*, who lone in *Patmos* banished,
  Saw in the sun a mighty angel stand;
And heard great *Bab'lon's* doom pronounc'd by Heaven's command.

XVI.

Then kneeling down to HEAVEN'S ETERNAL KING,
  The *Saint*, the *Father*, and the *Husband* prays:
Hope "springs exulting on triumphant wing,"
  That *thus* they all shall meet in future days:
There, ever bask in *uncreated rays*,
  No more to sigh, or shed the bitter tear,
Together hymning their CREATOR'S praise,
  In *such society*, yet still more dear;
While circling Time moves round in an eternal sphere.

XVII.

Compar'd with *this*, how poor Religion's pride,
  In all the pomp of *method*, and of *art*,
When men display to congregations wide,
  Devotion's ev'ry grace, except the *heart!*
The POWER, incens'd, the Pageant will desert,
  The pompous strain, the sacredotal stole;
But haply, in some *Cottage* far apart,
  May hear, well pleas'd, the language of the *Soul*;
And in His *Book of Life* the Inmates poor enroll.

XVIII.

Then homeward all take off their sev'ral way;
  The youngling *Cottagers* retire to rest:
The Parent-pair their *secret homage* pay,
  And proffer up to Heaven the warm request,
That HE who stills the *raven's* clam'rous nest,
  And decks the *lily* fair in flow'ry pride,
Would, in the way *His Wisdom* sees the best,
  For *them* and for their *little ones* provide;
But chiefly, in their hearts with *Grace divine* preside.

XIX.

From scenes like these, old SCOTIA'S grandeur springs,
  That makes her lov'd at home, rever'd abroad:
Princes and lords are but the breath of kings,
  "An honest man's the noble[st] work of GOD."
And *certes*, in fair Virtue's heavenly road,
  The *Cottage* leaves the *Palace* far behind:
What is a lordling's pomp? a cumbrous load,
  Disguising oft the *wretch* of human kind,
Studied in arts of Hell, in wickedness refin'd!

XX.

O SCOTIA! my dear, my native soil!
  For whom my warmest wish to heaven is sent!
Long may thy hardy sons of *rustic toil*,
  Be blest with health, and peace, and sweet content!
And O may Heaven their simple lives prevent
  From *Luxury's* contagion, weak and vile!
Then howe'er *crowns* and *coronets* be rent,
  A *virtuous Populace* may rise the while,
And stand a wall of fire around their much-lov'd ISLE.

XXI.

O THOU! who pour'd the *patriotic tide*,
  That stream'd thro' great, unhappy WALLACE' heart;
Who dar'd to, nobly, stem tyrannic pride,
  Or *nobly die*, the second glorious part:
(The Patriot's GOD, peculiarly thou art,
  His *friend, inspirer, guardian* and *reward!*)
O never, never SCOTIA'S realm desert,
  But still the *Patriot*, and the *Patriot-Bard*,
In bright succession raise, her *Ornament* and *Guard!*

To a Mouse, On turning her up in her Nest, with the Plough, November, 1785.[1]

WEE, sleeket, cowran, tim'rous *beastie*,
O, what a panic's in thy breastie!
Thou need na start awa sae hasty,
        Wi' bickering brattle!
I wad be laith to rin an' chase thee,
        Wi' murd'ring *pattle!*

  I'm truly sorry Man's dominion
Has broken Nature's social union,
An' justifies that ill opinion,
        Which makes thee startle,
At me, thy poor, earth-born companion,
        An' *fellow-mortal!*

  I doubt na, whyles, but thou may *thieve*;
What then? poor beastie, thou maun live!

[1] Published in *Poems*, Kilmarnock, 1786. Text of first edition.

A *daimen-icker* in a *thrave*
'S a sma' request:
I'll get a blessin wi' the lave,
An' never miss't!

Thy wee-bit *housie*, too, in ruin!
It's silly wa's the win's are strewin!
An' naething, now, to big a new ane,
O' foggage green!
An' bleak *December's winds* ensuin,
Baith snell an' keen!

Thou saw the fields laid bare an' wast,
An' weary *Winter* comin fast,
An' cozie here, beneath the blast,
Thou thought to dwell,
Till crash! the cruel *coulter* past
Out thro' thy cell.

That wee-bit heap o' leaves an' stibble,
Has cost thee monie a weary nibble!
Now thou's turn'd out, for a' thy trouble,
But house or hald,
To thole the Winter's *sleety dribble*,
An' *cranreuch* cauld!

But Mousie, thou art no thy-lane,
In proving *foresight* may be vain:
The best laid schemes o' *Mice* an' *Men*,
Gang aft agley,
An' lea'e us nought but grief an' pain,
For promis'd joy!

Still, thou art blest, compar'd wi' *me!*
The *present* only toucheth thee:
But Och! I *backward* cast my e'e,
On prospects drear!
An' *forward*, tho' I canna *see*,
I *guess* an' *fear!*

Man was Made to Mourn, A Dirge[1]

WHEN chill November's surly blast
  Made fields and forests bare,
One ev'ning, as I wand'red forth,
  Along the banks of AIRE,
I spy'd a man, whose aged step
  Seem'd weary, worn with care;
His face was furrow'd o'er with years,
  And hoary was his hair.

Young stranger, whither wand'rest thou?
  Began the rev'rend Sage;
Does thirst of wealth thy step constrain,
  Or youthful Pleasure's rage?
Or haply, prest with cares and woes,
  Too soon thou hast began,
To wander forth, with me, to mourn
  The miseries of Man.

The Sun that overhangs yon moors,
  Out-spreading far and wide,
Where hundreds labour to support
  A haughty lordling's pride;
I've seen yon weary winter-sun
  Twice forty times return;
And ev'ry time has added proofs,
  That Man was made to mourn.

O Man! while in thy early years,
  How prodigal of time!
Mispending all thy precious hours,
  Thy glorious, youthful prime!
Alternate Follies take the sway;
  Licentious Passions burn;
Which tenfold force gives Nature's law,
  That Man was made to mourn.

Look not alone on youthful Prime,
  Or Manhood's active might;
Man then is useful to his kind,
  Supported is his right:
But see him on the edge of life,
  With Cares and Sorrows worn,

[1] Published in *Poems*, Kilmarnock, 1786. Text of first edition.

Then Age and Want, Oh! ill-match'd pair!
Show Man was made to mourn.

A few seem favourites of Fate,
In Pleasure's lap carest;
Yet, think not all the Rich and Great,
Are likewise truly blest.
But Oh! what crouds in ev'ry land,
All wretched and forlorn,
Thro' weary life this lesson learn,
That Man was made to mourn!

Many and sharp the num'rous Ills
Inwoven with our frame!
More pointed still we make ourselves,
Regret, Remorse and Shame!
And Man, whose heav'n-erected face,
The smiles of love adorn,
Man's inhumanity to Man
Makes countless thousands mourn!

See, yonder poor, o'erlabour'd wight,
So abject, mean and vile,
Who begs a brother of the earth
To give him leave to toil;
And see his lordly *fellow-worm*,
The poor petition spurn,
Unmindful, tho' a weeping wife,
And helpless offspring mourn.

If I'm design'd yon lordling's slave,
By Nature's law design'd,
Why was an independent wish
E'er planted in my mind?
If not, why am I subject to
His cruelty, or scorn?
Or why has Man the will and pow'r
To make his fellow mourn?

Yet, let not this too much, my Son,
Disturb thy youthful breast:
This partial view of human-kind
Is surely not the *last!*
The poor, oppressed, honest man
Had never, sure, been born,
Had there not been some recompence
To comfort those that mourn!

O Death! the poor man's dearest friend,
The kindest and the best!
Welcome the hour, my aged limbs
Are laid with thee at rest!
The Great, the Wealthy fear thy blow,
From pomp and pleasure torn;
But Oh! a blest relief for those
That weary-laden mourn!

To a Mountain-Daisy, On turning one down, with the Plough, in April – 1786[1]

WEE, modest, crimson-tipped flow'r,
Thou's met me in an evil hour;
For I maun crush amang the stoure
Thy slender stem:
To spare thee now is past my pow'r,
Thou bonie gem.

Alas! it's no thy neebor sweet,
The bonie *Lark*, companion meet!
Bending thee 'mang the dewy weet!
Wi's spreckl'd breast,
When upward-springing, blythe, to greet
The purpling East.

Cauld blew the bitter-biting *North*
Upon thy early, humble birth;
Yet chearfully thou glinted forth
Amid the storm,
Scarce rear'd above the *Parent-earth*
Thy tender form.

The flaunting *flow'rs* our Gardens yield,
High-shelt'ring woods and wa's maun shield,
But thou, beneath the random bield
O' clod or stane,
Adorns the histie *stibble-field*,
Unseen, alane.

There, in thy scanty mantle clad,
Thy snawie bosom sun-ward spread,

[1] Published in *Poems*, Kilmarnock, 1786. Text of first edition.

Thou lifts thy unassuming head
In humble guise;
But now the *share* uptears thy bed,
And low thou lies!

Such is the fate of artless Maid,
Sweet *flow'ret* of the rural shade!
By Love's simplicity betray'd,
And guileless trust,
Till she, like thee, all soil'd, is laid
Low i' the dust.

Such is the fate of simple Bard,
On Life's rough ocean luckless starr'd!
Unskilful he to note the card
Of *prudent Lore*,
Till billows rage, and gales blow hard,
And whelm him o'er!

Such fate to *suffering worth* is giv'n,
Who long with wants and woes has striv'n,
By human pride or cunning driv'n
To Mis'ry's brink,
Till wrench'd of ev'ry stay but HEAV'N,
He, ruin'd, sink!

Ev'n thou who mourn'st the *Daisy's* fate,
That fate is thine—no distant date;
Stern Ruin's *plough-share* drives, elate,
Full on thy bloom,
Till crush'd beneath the *furrow's* weight,
Shall be thy doom!

To a Louse, On Seeing One on a Lady's Bonnet at Church[1]

Ha! whare ye gaun, ye crowlan ferlie!
Your impudence protects you sairly:
I canna say but ye strunt rarely,
Owre *gawze* and *lace*;
Tho' faith, I fear ye dine but sparely,
On sic a place.

[1] Published in *Poems*, Kilmarnock, 1786. Text of first edition.

Ye ugly, creepan, blastet wonner,
Detested, shunn'd, by saunt an' sinner,
How daur ye set your fit upon her,
Sae fine a *Lady!*
Gae somewhere else and seek your dinner,
On some poor body.

Swith, in some beggar's haffet squattle;
There ye may creep, and sprawl, and sprattle,
Wi' ither kindred, jumping cattle,
In shoals and nations;
Whare *horn* nor *bane* ne'er daur unsettle,
Your thick plantations.

Now haud you there, ye're out o' sight,
Below the fatt'rels, snug and tight,
Na faith ye yet! ye'll no be right,
Till ye've got on it,
The vera tapmost, towrin height
O' *Miss's bonnet.*

My sooth! right bauld ye set your nose out,
As plump an' gray as onie grozet:
O for some rank, mercurial rozet,
Or fell, red smeddum,
I'd gie you sic a hearty dose o't,
Wad dress your droddum!

I wad na been surpriz'd to spy
You on an auld wife's *flainen toy*;
Or aiblins some bit duddie boy,
On's *wylecoat*;
But Miss's fine *Lunardi*, fye!
How daur ye do't?

O *Jenny* dinna toss your head,
An' set your beauties a' abread!
Ye little ken what cursed speed
The blastie's makin!
Thae *winks* and *finger-ends*, I dread,
Are notice takin!

O wad some Pow'r the giftie gie us
To see oursels as others see us!
It wad frae monie a blunder free us
An' foolish notion:
What airs in dress an' gait wad lea'e us,
And ev'n Devotion!

Epistle to J. Lapraik[1]

WHILE briers an' woodbines budding green,
An' Paitricks scraichan loud at e'en,
And morning Poossie whiddan seen,
Inspire my Muse,
This freedom, in an *unknown* frien',
I pray excuse.

On Fasteneen we had a rockin,
To ca' the crack and weave our stockin;
And there was muckle fun and jokin,
Ye need na doubt;
At length we had a hearty yokin,
At *sang about.*

There was ae *sang*, amang the rest,
Aboon them a' it pleas'd me best,
That some kind husband had addrest,
To some sweet wife:
It thirl'd the heart-strings thro' the breast,
A' to the life.

I've scarce heard ought describ'd sae weel,
What gen'rous, manly bosoms feel;
Thought I, "Can this be *Pope*, or *Steele*,
Or *Beattie's* wark;"
They tald me 'twas an odd kind chiel
About *Muirkirk.*

It pat me fidgean-fain to hear't,
An' sae about him there I spier't;
Then a' that kent him round declar'd,
He had *ingine*,
That nane excell'd it, few cam near't,
It was sae fine.

That set him to a pint of ale,
An' either douse or merry tale,
Or rhymes an' sangs he'd made himsel,
Or witty catches,
'Tween Inverness and Tiviotdale,
He had few matches.

[1] Published in *Poems*, Kilmarnock, 1786. Text of first edition.

Then up I gat, an swoor an aith,
Tho' I should pawn my pleugh an' graith,
Or die a cadger pownie's death,
At some dyke-back,
A *pint* an' *gill* I'd gie them *baith*,
To hear your crack.

But first an' foremost, I should tell,
Amaist as soon as I could spell,
I to the *crambo-jingle* fell,
Tho' rude an' rough,
Yet crooning to a body's sel,
Does weel eneugh.

I am nae *Poet*, in a sense,
But just a *Rhymer* like by chance,
An' hae to Learning nae pretence,
Yet, what the matter?
Whene'er my Muse does on me glance,
I jingle at her.

Your Critic-folk may cock their nose,
And say, "How can you e'er propose,
"You wha ken hardly *verse* frae *prose*,
"To mak a *sang?*"
But by your leaves, my learned foes,
Ye're maybe wrang.

What's a' your jargon o' your Schools,
Your Latin names for horns an' stools;
If honest Nature made you *fools*,
What sairs your Grammars?
Ye'd better taen up *spades* and *shools*,
Or *knappin-hammers*.

A set o' dull, conceited Hashes,
Confuse their brains in *Colledge-classes!*
They *gang in* Stirks, and *come out* Asses,
Plain truth to speak;
An' syne they think to climb Parnassus
By dint o' Greek!

Gie me ae spark o' Nature's fire,
That's a' the learning I desire;
Then tho' I drudge thro' dub an' mire
At pleugh or cart,
My Muse, tho' hamely in attire,
May touch the heart.

O for a spunk o' ALLAN'S glee,
Or FERGUSON'S, the bauld an' slee,
Or bright L * * * * * K'S, my friend to be,
If I can hit it!
That would be *lear* eneugh for me,
If I could get it.

Now, Sir, if ye hae friends enow,
Tho' *real friends* I b'lieve are few,
Yet if your catalogue be fow,
I'se no insist;
But gif ye want ae friend that's true,
I'm on your list.

I winna blaw about *mysel*,
As ill I like my fauts to tell;
But friends an' folk that wish me well,
They sometimes roose me;
Tho' I maun own, as monie still,
As far abuse me.

There's ae *wee faut* they whiles lay to me,
I like the lasses—Gude forgie me!
For monie a Plack they wheedle frae me,
At dance or fair:
Maybe some *ither thing* they gie me
They weel can spare.

But MAUCHLINE Race or MAUCHLINE Fair,
I should be proud to meet you there;
We'se gie ae night's discharge to *care*,
If we forgather,
An' hae a swap o' *rhymin-ware*,
Wi' ane anither.

The *four-gill chap*, we'se gar him clatter,
An' kirs'n him wi' reekin water;
Syne we'll sit down an' tak our whitter,
To chear our heart;
An' faith, we'se be *acquainted* better
Before we part.

Awa ye selfish, warly race,
Wha think that havins, sense an' grace,
Ev'n love an' friendship should give place
To *catch-the-plack!*
I dinna like to see your face,
Nor hear your crack.

But ye whom social pleasure charms,
Whose hearts the *tide of kindness* warms,
Who hold your *being* on the terms,
"Each aid the others,"
Come to my bowl, come to my arms,
My friends, my brothers!

But to conclude my lang epistle,
As my auld pen's worn to the grissle;
Twa lines frae you wad gar me fissle,
Who am, most fervent,
While I can either sing, or whistle,
Your friend and servant.

Address to the Unco Guid, or the Rigidly Righteous[1]

My Son, these maxims make a rule,
And lump them ay thegither;
The Rigid Righteous *is a fool,*
The Rigid Wise *anither:*
The cleanest corn that e'er was dight
May hae some pyles o' caff in;
So ne'er a fellow-creature slight
For random fits o' daffin.
SOLOMON.—Eccles. ch. vii. vers. 16.

A YE wha are sae guid yoursel,
Sae pious and sae holy,
Ye've nought to do but mark and tell
Your Neebours' fauts and folly!
Whase life is like a weel-gaun mill,
Supply'd wi' store o' water,
The heaped happer's ebbing still,
And still the clap plays clatter.

Hear me, ye venerable Core,
As counsel for poor mortals,
That frequent pass douce Wisdom's door
For glaikit Folly's portals;
I, for their thoughtless, careless sakes
Would here propone defences,
Their donsie tricks, their black mistakes,
Their failings and mischances.

[1] Published in *Poems, Chiefly in the Scottish Dialect,* Edinburgh, 1787. Text of first edition.

Ye see your state wi' theirs compar'd,
  And shudder at the niffer,
But cast a moment's fair regard
  What maks the mighty differ;
Discount what scant occasion gave,
  That purity ye pride in,
And (what's aft mair than a' the lave)
  Your better art o' hiding.

Think, when your castigated pulse
  Gies now and then a wallop,
What ragings must his veins convulse,
  That still eternal gallop:
Wi' wind and tide fair i' your tail,
  Right on ye scud your sea-way;
But, in the teeth o' baith to sail,
  It makes an unco leeway.

See Social-life and Glee sit down,
  All joyous and unthinking,
Till, quite transmugrify'd, they're grown
  Debauchery and Drinking:
O would they stay to calculate
  Th' eternal consequences;
Or your more dreaded h—ll to state,
  D—mnation of expences!

Ye high, exalted, virtuous Dames,
  Ty'd up in godly laces,
Before ye gie poor *Frailty* names,
  Suppose a change o' cases;
A dear-lov'd lad, convenience snug,
  A treacherous inclination——
But, let me whisper i' your lug,
  Ye're aiblins nae temptation.

Then gently scan your brother Man,
  Still gentler sister Woman;
Tho' they may gang a kennin wrang,
  To step aside is human:
One point must still be greatly dark,
  The moving *Why* they do it;
And just as lamely can ye mark,
  How far perhaps they rue it.

Who made the heart, 'tis *He* alone
  Decidedly can try us,

He knows each chord its various tone,
  Each spring its various bias:
Then at the balance let's be mute,
  We never can adjust it;
What's *done* we partly may compute,
  But know not what's *resisted.*

Green Grow the Rashes. A Fragment[1]

Chorus

Green grow the rashes, O;
Green grow the rashes, O;
The sweetest hours that e'er I spend,
  Are spent amang the lasses, O.

THERE's nought but care on ev'ry han',
  In ev'ry hour that passes, O:
What signifies the life o' man,
  An' 'twere na for the lasses, O.
      Green grow, &c.

The warly race may riches chase,
  An' riches still may fly them, O;
An' tho' at last they catch them fast,
  Their hearts can ne'er enjoy them, O.
      Green grow, &c.

But gie me a canny hour at e'en,
  My arms about my Dearie, O;
An' warly cares, an' warly men,
  May a' gae tapsalteerie, O!
      Green grow, &c.

For your sae douse, ye sneer at this,
  Ye're nought but senseless asses, O:
The wisest Man the warl' saw,
  He dearly lov'd the lasses, O.
      Green grow, &c.

Auld Nature swears, the lovely Dears
  Her noblest work she classes, O:

[1] Published in *Poems, Chiefly in the Scottish Dialect,* Edinburgh, 1787. Text of first edition.

Her prentice han' she try'd on man,
An' then she made the lasses, O.
Green grow, &c.

I Love My Jean[1]

Of a' the airts the wind can blaw,
I dearly like the west,
For there the bony Lassie lives,
The Lassie I lo'e best:
There's wild-woods grow, and rivers row,
And mony a hill between;
But day and night my fancy's flight
Is ever wi' my Jean.

I see her in the dewy flowers,
I see her sweet and fair;
I hear her in the tunefu' birds,
I hear her charm the air:
There's not a bony flower, that springs
By fountain, shaw, or green,
There's not a bony bird that sings,
But minds me o' my Jean.

Whistle o'er the Lave o't[2]

First when Maggy was my care,
Heaven, I thought, was in her air;
Now we're married, spier nae mair,
But Whistle o'er the lave o't.

Meg was meek and Meg was mild,
Sweet and harmless as a child;
Wiser men than me's beguil'd,
So Whistle o'er the lave o't.

How we live, my Meg and me,
How we love and how we gree;
I carena by how few may see,
Whistle o'er the lave o't.

---

[1] Published in *The Scots Musical Museum*, Vol. III, 1790. Text of first edition.
[2] Published in *The Scots Musical Museum*, Vol. III, 1790. Text of first edition.

Wha I wish were maggots meat,
  Dish'd up in her winding sheet;
I could write, but Meg maun see't,
  Whistle o'er the lave o't.

My Heart's in the Highlands[1]

My heart's in the Highlands, my heart is not here;
My heart's in the Highlands a chasing the deer;
A chasing the wild deer, and following the roe,
My heart's in the Highlands, wherever I go.
Farewell to the Highlands, farewell to the north,
The birth place of Valour, the country of Worth,
Wherever I wander, wherever I rove,
The hills of the Highlands for ever I love.

Farewell to the mountains high cover'd with snow;
Farewell to the straths and green vallies below:
Farewell to the forests and wild hanging woods;
Farewell to the torrents and loud pouring floods.
My heart's in the Highlands, my heart is not here,
My heart's in the Highlands a chasing the deer:
Chasing the wild deer, and following the roe;
My heart's in the Highlands, wherever I go.

John Anderson My Jo[2]

John Anderson my jo, John,
  When we were first Acquent;
Your locks were like the raven,
  Your bony brow was brent;
But now your brow is beld, John,
  Your locks are like the snaw;
But blessings on your frosty pow,
John Anderson my jo, John,

John Anderson my jo, John,
  We clamb the hill the gither;
And mony a canty day John,
  We've had wi' ane anither:

[1] Published in *The Scots Musical Museum*, Vol. III, 1790. Text of first edition.
[2] Published in *The Scots Musical Museum*, Vol. III, 1790. Text of first edition.

Now we maun totter down, John,
And hand in hand we'll go;
And sleep the gither at the foot,
John Anderson my Jo.

Willie Brew'd a Peck o' Maut[1]

O WILLIE brew'd a peck o' maut,
And Rob and Allan cam to see;
Three blyther hearts, that lee lang night,
Ye wad na found in Christendie.
We are na fou, We're nae that fou,
But just a drappie in our e'e;
The cock may craw, the day may daw,
And ay we'll taste the barley bree.

Here are we met, three merry boys,
Three merry boys I trow are we;
And mony a night we've merry been,
And mony mae we hope to be!
We are na fou, &c.

It is the moon, I ken her horn,
That's blinkin in the lift sae hie;
She shines sae bright to wyle us hame,
But by my sooth she'll wait a wee!
We are na fou, &c.

Wha first shall rise to gang awa,
A cuckold, coward loun is he!
Wha first beside his chair shall fa',
He is the king amang us three!
We are na fou, &c.

Tam Glen[2]

MY HEART is a breaking, dear Tittie,
Some counsel unto me come len',
To anger them a' is a pity,
But what will I do wi' Tam Glen.

[1] Published in *The Scots Musical Museum*, Vol. III, 1790. Text of first edition.
[2] Published in *The Scots Musical Museum*, Vol. III, 1790. Text of first edition.

I'm thinking, wi' sic a braw fellow,
  In poortith I might mak a fen:
What care I in riches to wallow,
  If I mauna marry Tam Glen.

There's Lowrie the laird o' Dumeller,
  "Gude day to you brute" he comes ben:
He brags and he blaws o' his siller,
  But when will he dance like Tam Glen.

My Minnie does constantly deave me,
  And bids me beware o' young men;
They flatter, she says, to deceive me,
  But wha can think sae o' Tam Glen.

My Daddie says, gin I'll forsake him,
  He'll gie me gude hunder marks ten:
But, if it's ordain'd I maun take him,
  O wha will I get but Tam Glen.

Yestreen at the Valentines' dealing,
  My heart to my mou gied a sten;
For thrice I drew ane without failing,
  And thrice it was written, Tam Glen.

The last Halloween I was waukin
  My droukit sark-sleeve, as ye ken;
His likeness cam up the house staukin,
  And the very grey breeks o' Tam Glen!

Come counsel, dear Tittie, don't tarry;
  I'll gie you my bonie black hen,
Gif ye will advise me to Marry
  The lad I lo'e dearly, Tam Glen.

Tam o' Shanter[1]

WHEN chapman billies leave the street,
And drouthy neebors, neebors meet,
As market-days are wearing late,
An' folk begin to tak the gate;
While we sit bousing at the nappy,
An' getting fou and unco happy,

[1] Published in the *Edinburgh Magazine*, March, 1791. Text of *Life and Works*, ed. Alexander Peterkin, Edinburgh, 1815.

We think na on the lang Scots miles,
The mosses, waters, slaps, and styles,
That lie between us and our hame,
Whare sits our sulky sullen dame,
Gathering her brows like gathering storm,
Nursing her wrath to keep it warm.
This truth fand honest *Tam o' Shanter*,
As he frae Ayr ae night did canter,
(Auld Ayr, wham ne'er a town surpasses,
For honest men and bonny lasses.)
O *Tam!* hadst thou but been sae wise,
As ta'en thy ain wife *Kate's* advice!
She tauld thee weel thou was a skellum,
A blethering, blustering, drunken blellum;
That frae November till October,
Ae market-day thou was nae sober;
That ilka melder, wi' the miller,
Thou sat as lang as thou had siller;
That ev'ry naig was ca'd a shoe on,
The smith and thee gat roaring fou on;
That at the L—d's house, ev'n on Sunday,
Thou drank wi' Kirton Jean till Monday.
She prophesy'd, that late or soon,
Thou would be found deep drown'd in *Doon*;
Or catch'd wi' warlocks in the mirk,
By *Alloway's* auld haunted kirk.
Ah, gentle dames! it gars me greet,
To think how mony counsels sweet,
How mony lengthen'd sage advices,
The husband frae the wife despises!
But to our tale: Ae market night,
Tam had got planted unco right;
Fast by an ingle, bleezing finely,
Wi' reaming swats, that drank divinely;
And at his elbow, souter *Johnny*,
His ancient, trusty, drouthy crony;
Tam lo'ed him like a vera brither;
They had been fou for weeks thegither.
The night drave on wi' sangs and clatter;
And ay the ale was growing better:
The landlady and *Tam* grew gracious,
Wi' favours, secret, sweet, and precious:
The souter tauld his queerest stories;
The landlord's laugh was ready chorus:
The storm without might rair and rustle,
Tam did na mind the storm a whistle.
Care, mad to see a man sae happy,
E'en drown'd himself amang the nappy;

As bees flee hame wi' lades o' treasure,
The minutes wing'd their way wi' pleasure:
Kings may be blest, but *Tam* was glorious,
O'er a' the ills o' life victorious!
  But pleasures are like poppies spread,
You seize the flow'r, its bloom is shed!
Or like the snow-falls in the river,
A moment white—then melts for ever;
Or like the borealis race,
That flit ere you can point their place;
Or like the rainbow's lovely form
Evanishing amid the storm.—
Nae man can tether time or tide:
The hour approaches *Tam* maun ride;
That hour, o' night's black arch the key-stane,
That dreary hour he mounts his beast in;
And sic a night he taks the road in,
As ne'er poor sinner was abroad in.
  The wind blew as 'twad blawn its last;
The rattlin' showers rose on the blast:
The speedy gleams the darkness swallow'd;
Loud, deep, and lang, the thunder bellow'd;
That night, a child might understand,
The deil had business on his hand.
  Weel mounted on his gray mare, *Meg*—
A better never lifted leg—
Tam skelpit on thro' dub and mire,
Despising wind, and rain, and fire;
Whiles holding fast his guid blue bonnet;
Whiles crooning o'er some auld Scots sonnet;
Whiles glow'ring round wi' prudent cares,
Lest bogles catch him unawares:
Kirk-Alloway was drawing nigh,
Whare ghaists and houlets nightly cry—
  By this time he was cross the ford,
Whare in the snaw the chapman smoor'd;
And past the birks and meikle stane,
Whare drunken *Charlie* brak 's neck-bane;
And thro' the whins, and by the cairn,
Whare hunters fand the murder'd bairn;
And near the thorn, aboon the well,
Whare *Mungo's* mither hang'd hersel.—
Before him *Doon* pours all his floods;
The doubling storm roars thro' the woods;
The lightnings flash from pole to pole;
Near and more near the thunders roll;
When, glimmering thro' the groaning trees,
Kirk-Alloway seem'd in a bleeze;

Thro' ilka bore the gleams were glancing;
And loud resounded mirth and dancing.—
  Inspiring bold *John Barleycorn!*
What dangers thou canst make us scorn!
Wi' tippenny, we fear nae evil;
Wi' usquabae we'll face the devil!—
The swats sae ream'd in *Tammie's* noddle,
Fair play, he car'd na deils a boddle.
But *Maggie* stood right sair astonish'd,
Till, by the heel and hand admonish'd,
She ventur'd forward on the light;
And, vow! *Tam* saw an unco sight!
Warlocks and witches in a dance;
Nae cotillion brent new frae *France*,
But hornpipes, jigs, strathspeys, and reels,
Put life and mettle in their heels.
A winnock-bunker in the east,
There sat auld Nick, in shape o' beast;
A towzie tyke, black, grim, and large,
To gie them music was his charge:
He screw'd the pipes and gart them skirl,
Till roof and rafters a' did dirl.—
Coffins stood round, like open presses,
That shaw'd the dead in their last dresses;
And by some devilish cantrip slight,
Each in its cauld hand held a light,—
By which heroic *Tam* was able
To note upon the haly table,
A murderer's banes in gibbet airns;
Twa span-lang, wee, unchristen'd bairns;
A thief new-cutted frae a rape,
Wi' his last gasp his gab did gape:
Five tomahawks, wi' blude red-rusted;
Five scimitars wi' murder crusted;
A garter, which a babe had strangled;
A knife, a father's throat had mangled,
Whom his ain son o' life bereft,
The grey hairs yet stack to the heft;
Wi' mair o' horrible and awfu',
Which ev'n to name wad be unlawfu'.
  As *Tammie* glowr'd, amaz'd, and curious,
The mirth and fun grew fast and furious:
The piper loud and louder blew;
The dancers quick and quicker flew;
They reel'd, they set, they cross'd, they cleekit,
Till ilka carlin swat and reekit,
And coost her duddies to the wark,
And linket at it in her sark!

Now *Tam*, O *Tam!* had thae been queens
A' plump an' strapping, in their teens,
Their sarks, instead o' creeshie flannen,
Been snaw-white seventeen hunder linen!
Thir breeks o' mine, my only pair,
That ance were plush, o' gude blue hair,
I wad hae gi'en them off my hurdies,
For ae blink o' the bonie burdies!
But wither'd beldams, auld and droll,
Rigwoodie hags wad spean a foal,
Lowping and flinging on a crummock,
I wonder didna turn thy stomach.
But *Tam* kenn'd what was what fu' brawlie,
There was ae winsome wench and walie,
That night enlisted in the core,
(Lang after kenn'd on *Carrick* shore!
For mony a beast to dead she shot,
And perish'd mony a bonnie boat,
And shook baith meikle corn and bear,
And kept the country-side in fear),
Her cutty sark, o' Paisley harn,
That while a lassie she had worn,
In longitude tho' sorely scanty,
It was her best, and she was vauntie,—
Ah! little kenn'd thy reverend grannie,
That sark she coft for her wee *Nannie*,
Wi' twa pund Scots ('twas a' her riches),
Wad ever grac'd a dance of witches!
But here my Muse her wing maun cour;
Sic flights are far beyond her pow'r!
To sing how *Nannie* lap and flang,
(A souple jade she was and strang)
And how *Tam* stood, like ane bewitch'd,
And thought his very een enrich'd;
Even Satan glowr'd, and fidg'd fu' fain,
And hotch'd and blew wi' might and main:
Till first ae caper, syne anither,
Tam tint his reason a' thegither,
And roars out, "Weel done, Cutty-sark!"
And in an instant all was dark:
And scarcely had he *Maggie* rallied,
When out the hellish legion sallied.
As bees bizz out wi' angry fyke,
When plundering herds assail their byke;
As open pussie's mortal foes,
When, pop! she starts before their nose;
As eager runs the market-crowd,
When "Catch the thief!" resounds aloud;

So *Maggie* runs, the witches follow,
Wi' mony an eldritch skreech and hollow.
Ah, *Tam!* Ah, *Tam!* thou'll get thy fairin!
In hell they'll roast you like a herrin!
In vain thy *Kate* awaits thy comin!
Kate soon will be a woefu' woman!
Now, do thy speedy utmost, *Meg,*
And win the key-stane of the brig;
There at them thou thy tail may toss,
A running stream they dare na cross.
But ere the key-stane she could make,
The fient a tail she had to shake!
For *Nannie*, far before the rest,
Hard upon noble *Maggie* prest,
And flew at *Tam* wi' furious ettle;
But little wist she *Maggie's* mettle—
Ae spring brought off her master hale,
But left behind her ain gray tail:
The carlin claught her by the rump,
And left poor *Maggie* scarce a stump.
Now, wha this tale o' truth shall read,
Ilk man and mother's son take heed:
Whene'er to drink you are inclin'd,
Or cutty-sarks run in your mind,
Think ye may buy the joys o'er dear,
Remember *Tam o' Shanter's* mare.

Ae Fond Kiss[1]

AE FOND kiss, and then we sever;
Ae farewell and then for ever!
Deep in heart-wrung tears I'll pledge thee,
Warring sighs and groans I'll wage thee.
Who shall say that fortune grieves him
While the star of hope she leaves him?
Me, nae chearfu' twinkle lights me;
Dark despair around benights me.

I'll ne'er blame my partial fancy,
Naething could resist my Nancy:
But to see her, was to love her;
Love but her, and love for ever.
Had we never lov'd sae kindly,
Had we never lov'd sae blindly,

[1] Published in *The Scots Musical Museum*, Vol. IV, 1792. Text of first edition.

Never met or never parted,
  We had ne'er been broken-hearted.

Fare thee weel, thou first and fairest!
  Fare thee weel, thou best and dearest!
Thine be ilka joy and treasure,
  Peace, Enjoyment, Love and Pleasure!
Ae fond kiss, and then we sever;
  Ae fareweel, Alas! for ever!
Deep in heart-wrung tears I'll pledge thee,
  Warring sighs and groans I'll wage thee.

The Banks o' Doon[1]

Ye Banks and braes o' bonie Doon,
  How can ye bloom sae fresh and fair;
How can ye chant, ye little birds,
  And I sae weary fu' o' care!
Thou'll break my heart thou warbling bird,
  That wantons thro' the flowering thorn:
Thou minds me o' departed joys,
  Departed never to return.

Oft hae I rov'd by bonie Doon,
  To see the rose and woodbine twine;
And ilka bird sang o' its luve,
  And fondly sae did I o' mine.
Wi' lightsome heart I pu'd a rose,
  Fu' sweet upon its thorny tree;
And my fause lover staw my rose,
  But, ah! he left the thorn wi' me.

Afton Water[2]

Flow gently sweet Afton among thy green braes,
Flow gently, I'll sing thee a song in thy praise;
My Mary's asleep by thy murmuring stream,
Flow gently, sweet Afton, disturb not her dream.

Thou stock dove whose echo resounds thro' the glen,
Ye wild whistling blackbirds in yon thorny den,

[1] Published in *The Scots Musical Museum*, Vol. IV, 1792. Text of first edition.
[2] Published in *The Scots Musical Museum*, Vol. IV, 1792. Text of first edition.

Thou green crested lapwing thy screaming forbear,
I charge you disturb not my slumbering Fair.

How lofty, sweet Afton, thy neighbouring hills,
Far mark'd with the courses of clear, winding rills;
There daily I wander as noon rises high,
My flocks and my Mary's sweet Cot in my eye.

How pleasant thy banks and green vallies below,
Where wild in the woodlands the primroses blow;
There oft as mild ev'ning weeps over the lea,
The sweet scented birk shades my Mary and me.

Thy chrystal stream, Afton, how lovely it glides,
And winds by the cot where my Mary resides;
How wanton thy waters her snowy feet lave,
As gathering sweet flowerets she stems thy clear wave.

Flow gently, sweet Afton, among thy green braes,
Flow gently, sweet River, the theme of my lays;
My Mary's asleep by thy murmuring stream,
Flow gently, sweet Afton, disturb not her dream.

Scots Wha Hae[1]

SCOTS, wha hae wi' WALLACE bled,
Scots, wham Bruce has aften led;
Welcome to your gory bed,
  Or to victorie.

Now's the day, and now's the hour;
See the front o' battle lour;
See approach proud Edward's power—
  Chains and slaverie!

Wha will be a traitor-knave?
Wha can fill a coward's grave?
Wha sae base as be a slave?
  Let him turn and flee!

Wha for SCOTLAND's king and law
Freedom's sword will strongly draw,

[1] Published in the *Morning Chronicle*, May 8, 1794. Text of *Life and Works*, ed. Alexander Peterkin, Edinburgh, 1815.

FREEMAN stand, or FREEMAN fa',
Let him follow me!

By oppression's woes and pains!
By your sons in servile chains!
We will drain our dearest veins,
But they shall be free!

Lay the proud usurpers low!
Tyrants fall in every foe!
LIBERTY's in every blow!
Let us DO, or DIE!

For A' That and A' That[1]

Is THERE, for honest poverty,
That hangs his head, and a' that;
The coward-slave, we pass him by,
We dare be poor for a' that!
For a' that, and a' that,
Our toils obscure, and a' that,
The rank is but the guinea's stamp,
The man's the gowd for a' that.

What though on hamely fare we dine,
Wear hoddin grey, and a' that;
Gie fools their silks, and knaves their wine,
A man's a man for a' that:
For a' that, and a' that,
Their tinsel show, and a' that;
The honest man, though e'er sae poor,
Is king o' men for a' that.

Ye see yon birkie, ca'd a lord,
Wha struts, and stares, and a' that;
Though hundreds worship at his word,
He's but a coof for a' that:
For a' that, and a' that:
His ribband, star, and a' that,
The man of independent mind,
He looks and laughs at a' that.

[1] Published in the *Glasgow Magazine*, August, 1795. Text of *Life and Works*, ed. Alexander Peterkin, Edinburgh, 1815.

A prince can mak a belted knight,
  A marquis, duke, and a' that;
But an honest man's aboon his might,
  Guid faith, he maunna fa' that!
    For a' that, and a' that,
      Their dignities, and a' that,
    The pith o' sense and pride o' worth,
      Are higher ranks than a' that.

Then let us pray that come it may,
  As come it will for a' that,
That sense and worth, o'er a' the earth,
  May bear the gree, and a' that.
    For a' that, and a' that,
      Its comin' yet for a' that,
    That man to man, the warld o'er,
      Shall brothers be for a' that.

A Red Red Rose[1]

O MY Luve's like a red, red rose,
  That's newly sprung in June;
O My Luve's like the melodie
  That's sweetly play'd in tune.

As fair are thou, my bonie lass,
  So deep in luve am I;
And I will luve thee still, my dear,
  Till a' the seas gang dry.

Till a' the seas gang dry, my Dear,
  And the rocks melt wi' the sun:
O I will love thee still my dear,
  While the sands o' life shall run.

Auld Lang Syne[2]

SHOULD auld acquaintance be forgot
  And never brought to mind?
Should auld acquaintance be forgot,
  And auld lang syne!

[1] Published in *The Scots Musical Museum*, Vol. V, 1796. Text of first edition.
[2] Published in *The Scots Musical Museum*, Vol. V, 1796. Text of first edition.

For auld lang syne, my jo,
For auld lang syne,
We'll tak a cup o' kindness yet
For auld lang syne.

And surely ye'll be your pint stowp!
And surely I'll be mine!
And we'll tak a cup o' kindness yet,
For auld lang syne.
For auld, &c.

We twa hae run about the braes,
And pou'd the gowans fine;
But we've wander'd mony a weary fitt,
Sin auld lang syne.
For auld, &c.

We twa hae paidl'd in the burn,
Frae morning sun till dine;
But seas between us braid hae roar'd,
Sin auld lang syne.
For auld, &c.

And there's a hand, my trusty fiere!
And gie's a hand o' thine!
And we'll tak a right gude-willie-waught,
For auld lang syne.
For auld, &c.

Duncan Gray[1]

DUNCAN GRAY came here to woo,
Ha, ha, the wooing o't!
On blythe Yule-night when we were fou,
Ha, ha, the wooing o't!
Maggie coost her head fu' high,
Look'd asklent and unco skeigh,
Gart poor Duncan stand abeigh—
Ha, ha, the wooing o't!

Duncan fleech'd, and Duncan pray'd,
Ha, ha, the wooing o't!

[1] Published in *Select Collection of Original Scottish Airs,* Vol. I, 1798. Text of first edition.

Meg was deaf as Ailsa Craig,
  Ha, ha, the wooing o't!
Duncan sigh'd baith out and in,
Grat his een baith bleer't and blin',
Spak o' lowpin o'er a linn—
  Ha, ha, the wooing o't!

Time and chance are but a tide,
  Ha, ha, the wooing o't!
Slighted love is sair to bide,
  Ha, ha, the wooing o't!
"Shall I, like a fool," quoth he,
"For a haughty hizzie die?
She may gae to—France for me!"—
  Ha, ha, the wooing o't!

How it comes let doctors tell,
  Ha, ha, the wooing o't!
Meg grew sick as he grew haill,
  Ha, ha, the wooing o't!
Something in her bosom wrings;
For relief a sigh she brings;
And O, her een they spak sic things!—
  Ha, ha, the wooing o't!

Duncan was a lad o' grace,
  Ha, ha, the wooing o't!
Maggie's was a piteous case,
  Ha, ha, the wooing o't!
Duncan couldna be her death,
Swelling pity smoor'd his wrath;
Now they're crouse and cantie baith—
  Ha, ha, the wooing o't!

Highland Mary[1]

YE BANKS and braes and streams around
  The castle o' Montgomery,
Green be your woods, and fair your flowers,
  Your waters never drumlie!
Their simmer first unfauld her robes,
  And there the langest tarry;

[1] Published in *Select Collection of Original Scottish Airs*, Vol. II, 1799. Text of first edition.

For there I took the last fareweel
O' my sweet Highland Mary.

How sweetly bloom'd the gay green birk,
How rich the hawthorn's blossom,
As underneath their fragrant shade
I clasp'd her to my bosom!
The golden hours on angel wings
Flew o'er me and my dearie;
For dear to me as light and life
Was my sweet Highland Mary.

Wi' mony a vow and lock'd embrace
Our parting was fu' tender;
And, pledging aft to meet again,
We tore oursels asunder;
But oh! fell Death's untimely frost,
That nipt my flower sae early!
Now green's the sod, and cauld's the clay,
That wraps my Highland Mary!

O pale, pale now, those rosy lips,
I aft have kiss'd sae fondly!
And closed for aye the sparkling glance,
That dwelt on me sae kindly!
And mould'ring now in silent dust,
That heart that lo'ed me dearly!
But still within my bosom's core
Shall live my Highland Mary.

The Jolly Beggars. A Cantata[1]

Recitativo

When lyart leaves bestrow the yird,
Or wavering like the Bauckie-bird,
Bedim cauld Boreas' blast;
When hailstanes drive wi' bitter skyte,
And infant frosts begin to bite,
In hoary cranreuch drest;
Ae night at e'en a merry core
O' randie, gangrel bodies,

[1] Published in Stewart and Meikle, *Poetical Miscellany,* 1799. Text of *Life and Works,* ed. Alexander Peterkin, Edinburgh, 1815.

In Poosie-Nansie's held the splore,
  To drink their orra duddies:
    Wi' quaffing and laughing,
      They ranted and they sang;
    Wi' jumping and thumping,
      The vera girdle rang.

First, neist the fire, in auld red rags,
Ane sat, weel brac'd wi' mealy bags,
  And knapsack a' in order;
His doxy lay within his arm,
Wi' usquebae an' blankets warm—
  She blinket on her sodger:
An' ay he gies the tozie drab
  The tither skelpin' kiss,
While she held up her greedy gab
  Just like an aumos dish.
    Ilk smack still, did crack still,
      Just like a cadger's whip,
    Then staggering and swaggering
      He roar'd this ditty up—

Air

Tune—"SOLDIERS' JOY"

I am a son of Mars who have been in many wars,
And show my cuts and scars wherever I come;
This here was for a wench, and that other in a trench,
When welcoming the French at the sound of the drum.
Lal de daudle, &c.

My 'prenticeship I past where my leader breath'd his last,
When the bloody die was cast on the heights of Abram;
I served out my trade when the gallant game was play'd,
And the Moro low was laid at the sound of the drum.
Lal de daudle, &c.

I lastly was with Curtis, among the floating batt'ries,
And there I left for witness an arm and a limb;
Yet let my country need me, with Elliot to head me,
I'd clatter on my stumps at the sound of a drum.
Lal de daudle, &c.

And now tho' I must beg with a wooden arm and leg,
And many a tatter'd rag hanging over my bum,

I'm as happy with my wallet, my bottle and my callet,
As when I us'd in scarlet to follow a drum.
Lal de daudle, &c.

What tho' with hoary locks, I must stand the winter shocks,
Beneath the woods and rocks oftentimes for a home,
When the tother bag I sell, and the tother bottle tell,
I could meet a troop of hell, at the sound of the drum.
Lal de daudle, &c.

Recitativo

He ended; and the kebars sheuk,
Aboon the chorus roar;
While frighted rattons backward leuk,
And seek the benmost bore;
A fairy fiddler frae the neuk,
He skirl'd out encore!
But up arose the martial chuck
And laid the loud uproar.

Air

Tune—"Soldier Laddie"

I once was a maid, tho' I cannot tell when,
And still my delight is in proper young men;
Some one of a troop of dragoons was my daddie,
No wonder I'm fond of a sodger laddie.
Sing, Lal de lal, &c.

The first of my loves was a swaggering blade,
To rattle the thundering drum was his trade;
His leg was so tight, and his cheek was so ruddy,
Transported I was with my sodger laddie.
Sing, Lal de lal, &c.

But the godly old chaplain left him in the lurch,
The sword I forsook for the sake of the church;
He ventur'd the *soul*, and I risked the *body*,
'Twas then I prov'd false to my sodger laddie.
Sing, Lal de lal, &c.

Full soon I grew sick of my sanctified sot,
The regiment at large for a husband I got;
From the gilded spontoon to the fife I was ready,
I asked no more but a sodger laddie.
Sing, Lal de lal, &c.

But the peace it reduc'd me to beg in despair,
Till I met my old boy at Cunningham fair;
His *rags regimental* they flutter'd so gaudy,
My heart it rejoic'd at my sodger laddie.
Sing, Lal de lal, &c.

And now I have liv'd—I know not how long,
And still I can join in a cup or a song;
But whilst with both hands I can hold the glass steady,
Here's to thee, my hero, my sodger laddie.
Sing, Lal de lal, &c.

Recitativo

Then neist outspak a raucle carlin,
Wha kent fu' weel to cleek the sterling,
For mony a pursie she had hooked,
And had in mony a well been ducked.
Her dove had been a Highland laddie,
But weary fa' the waefu' woodie!
Wi' sighs and sobs she thus began
To wail her braw John Highlandman.

Air

Tune—"O an ye were dead, Gudeman"

A Highland lad my love was born,
The Lalland laws he held in scorn;
But he still was faithfu' to his clan,
My gallant braw John Highlandman.

Chorus

Sing, hey my braw John Highlandman!
Sing, ho my braw John Highlandman!
There's not a lad in a' the lan'
Was match for my John Highlandman.

With his philibeg an' tartan plaid,
An' gude claymore down by his side,
The ladies hearts he did trepan,
My gallant braw John Highlandman.
Sing, hey, &c.

We ranged a' from Tweed to Spey,
An' liv'd like lords and ladies gay;

For a Lalland face he feared none,
My gallant braw John Highlandman.
Sing, hey, &c.

They banish'd him beyond the sea,
But ere the bud was on the tree,
Adown my cheeks the pearls ran,
Embracing my John Highlandman.
Sing, hey, &c.

But, oh! they catch'd him at the last,
And bound him in a dungeon fast;
My curse upon them every one,
They've hang'd my braw John Highlandman.
Sing, hey, &c.

And now a widow, I must mourn
The pleasures that will ne'er return;
No comfort but a hearty can,
When I think on John Highlandman.
Sing, hey, &c.

Recitativo

A pigmy scraper, wi' his fiddle,
Wha us'd to trysts and fairs to driddle,
Her strappan limb and gausy middle
He reach'd nae higher,
Had hol'd his heartie like a riddle,
An' blawn't on fire.

Wi' hand on haunch, an' upward e'e,
He croon'd his gamut, one, two, three,
Then in an Arioso key,
The wee Apollo
Set off wi' *Allegretto* glee
His giga solo.

Air

Tune—"WHISTLE OWRE THE LAVE O'T"

LET me ryke up to dight that tear,
An' go wi' me to be my dear,
An' then your every care and fear
May whistle owre the lave o't.

Chorus

I am a fiddler to my trade,
An' a' the tunes that e're I play'd,
The sweetest still to wife or maid,
Was whistle owre the lave o't.

At kirns and weddings we'se be there,
An' O! sae nicely's we will fare;
We'll bouse about till Daddie Care
Sing whistle owre the lave o't.
I am, &c.

Sae merrily the banes we'll pyke,
An' sun oursels about the dyke,
An' at our leisure, when we like,
We'll whistle owre the lave o't.
I am, &c.

But bless me wi' your heaven o' charms,
And while I kittle hair on thairms,
Hunger, cauld, an' a' sic harms,
May whistle owre the lave o't.
I am, &c.

Recitativo

Her charms had struck a sturdy Caird,
As weel as poor Gutscraper;
He taks the fiddler by the beard,
And draws a rusty rapier.—
He swoor by a' was swearing worth,
To speet him like a pliver,
Unless he would from that time forth,
Relinquish her for ever.

Wi' ghastly e'e, poor tweedle-dee
Upon his hunkers bended,
And pray'd for grace wi' ruefu' face,
And so the quarrel ended.
But though his little heart did grieve,
When round the tinker prest her,
He feign'd to snirtle in his sleeve,
When thus the caird address'd her.

Air

Tune—"CLOUD THE CAUDRON."

My bonnie lass, I work in brass,
  A tinker is my station;
I've travell'd round all Christian ground
  In this my occupation.
I've ta'en the gold, I've been enroll'd
  In many a noble squadron;
But vain they search'd, when off I march'd
  To go and clout the caudron.
                I've ta'en the gold, &c.

Despise that shrimp, that wither'd imp,
  Wi' a' his noise and caprin',
An' tak' a share wi' those that bear
  The *budget* an' the *apron*.
An' *by* that stowp! my faith an' houpe,
  An' *by* that dear Keilbagie,
If e'er ye want, or meet wi' scant,
  May I ne'er weet my craigie.
                An' by that stowp, &c.

Recitativo

The caird prevail'd—the unblushing fair
  In his embraces sunk,
Partly wi' love o'ercome sae sair,
  An' partly she was drunk.
Sir Violino, with an air
  That show'd a man of spunk,
Wish'd *unison* between the pair,
  An' made the bottle clunk
          To their health that night.

But hurchin Cupid shot a shaft
  That play'd a dame a shavie,
The fiddler rak'd her fore and aft,
  Behint the chicken cavie,
Her lord, a wight o' Homer's craft,
  Tho' limping wi' the spavie,
He hirpl'd up, and lap like daft,
  An shor'd them Dainty Davie
          O boot that night.

He was a care-defying blade
  As ever Bacchus listed,

Tho' Fortune sair upon him laid,
  His heart she ever miss'd it.
He had no wish but—to be glad,
  Nor want but—when he thirsted;
He hated nought but—to be sad,
  And thus the Muse suggested,
      His sang that night.

Air

Tune—"FOR A' THAT, AN' A' THAT."

I am a bard of no regard,
  Wi' gentle folks, an' a' that;
But *Homer-like*, the glowran byke,
  Frae town to town I draw that.

Chorus

For a' that, an' a' that,
  An' twice as muckle's a' that;
I've lost but ane, I've twa behin',
  I've wife enough *for a' that.*

I never drank the Muses' stank,
  Castalia's burn, an' a' that;
But there it streams, and richly reams,
  My *Helicon* I ca' that,
      For a' that, &c.

Great love I bear to a' the fair,
  Their humble slave, an' a' that;
But lordly will, I hold it still
  A mortal sin to thraw that.
      For a' that, &c.

In raptures sweet, this hour we meet,
  Wi' mutual love an a' that;
But for how lang the *flie may stang*,
  Let *inclination* law that.
      For a' that, &c.

Their tricks and craft have put me daft,
  They've ta'en me in, an' a' that;
But clear your decks, and here's the *sex!*
  I like the jads for a' that.
    For a' that, an' a' that,
      An' twice as muckle's a' that;
    My dearest bluid, to do them guid,
      They're welcome till't for a' that.

Recitativo

So sung the bard—and Nansie's wa's
  Shook with a thunder of applause,
Re-echo'd from each mouth;
  They toom'd their pocks, an' pawn'd their duds,
They scarcely left to co'er their fuds,
  To quench their lowan drouth.

Then owre again, the jovial thrang,
  The poet did request,
To loose his pack an' wale a sang,
  A ballad o' the best:
    He rising, rejoicing,
      Between his twa *Deborahs*,
    Looks round him, an' found them
      Impatient for the chorus.

Air

Tune—"JOLLY MORTALS FILL YOUR GLASSES."

SEE! the smoking bowl before us,
  Mark our jovial ragged ring!
Round and round take up the chorus,
And in raptures let us sing.

Chorus

A fig for those by law protected!
  Liberty's a glorious feast!
Courts for cowards were erected,
  Churches built to please the priest.

What is title? what is treasure?
  What is reputation's care?
If we lead a life of pleasure,
  'Tis no matter *how* or *where!*
            A fig, &c.

With the ready trick and fable,
  Round we wander all the day;
And at night, in barn or stable,
  Hug our doxies on the hay.
            A fig, &c.

Does the train-attended *carriage*
  Through the country lighter rove?

Does the sober bed of marriage
  Witness brighter scenes of love?
      A fig, &c.

Life is all a *variorum*,
  We regard not how it goes;
Let them cant about *decorum*
  Who have characters to lose.
      A fig, &c.

Here's to budgets, bags and wallets!
  Here's to all the wandering train!
Here's our ragged *brats and callets!*
  One and all cry out, Amen!

A fig for those by law protected!
  Liberty's a glorious feast!
Courts for cowards were erected,
  Churches built to please the priest.

Holy Willie's Prayer[1]

O THOU, wha in the heavens dost dwell,
Wha, as it pleases best thysel',
Sends ane to heaven and ten to hell,
      A' for thy glory,
And no for ony guid or ill
      They've done afore thee!

I bless and praise thy matchless might,
Whan thousands thou hast left in night,
That I am here afore thy sight,
      For gifts an' grace,
A burnin' an' a shinin' light,
      To a' this place.

What was I, or my generation,
That I should get such exaltation,
I, wha deserve sic just damnation,
      For broken laws,
Five thousand years 'fore my creation,
      Thro' Adam's cause.

[1] Published in Stewart and Meikle, *Poetical Miscellany,* 1799. Text of *Life and Works,* ed. Alexander Peterkin, Edinburgh, 1815.

When frae my mither's womb I fell,
Thou might ha'e plunged me in hell,
To gnash my gums, to weep and wail,
In burnin' lake,
Whar damned devils roar and yell,
Chain'd to a stake.

Yet I am here a chosen sample,
To show thy grace is great an' ample;
I'm here a pillar in thy temple,
Strong as a rock,
A guide, a buckler, an' example
To a' thy flock.

But yet, O L—d! confess I must,
At times I'm fash'd wi' fleshly lust
An' sometimes too, wi' warldly trust,
Vile self gets in;
But thou remembers we are dust,
Defil'd in sin.

O L—d! yestreen, thou kens, wi' Meg,
Thy pardon I sincerely beg,
O! may it ne'er be a livin' plague
To my dishonour,
An' I'll ne'er lift a lawless l-g
Again upon her.

Besides, I farther maun allow,
Wi' Lizzie's lass, three times I trow;
But, L—d, that Friday I was fou,
When I came near her,
Or else, thou kens, thy *servant true*
Wad ne'er ha'e steer'd her.

Maybe thou lets this *fleshly thorn*,
Beset thy servant e'en and morn,
Lest he owre high and proud shou'd turn,
'Cause he's sae *gifted;*
If sae, thy han' maun e'en be borne,
Until thou lift it.

L—d, bless thy chosen in this place,
For *here* thou hast a *chosen race;*
But G-d confound their stubborn face,
And blast their name,
Wha bring thy elders to disgrace,
An' public shame.

L—d, mind G—n H—n's deserts,
He drinks, an' swears, an' plays at carts,
Yet has sae mony takin' arts,
Wi' grit an' sma',
Frae G—d's ain priest the people's hearts
He steals awa'.

An' whan we chasten'd him therefore,
Thou kens how he bred sic a splore,
As set the warld in a roar
O' laughin' at us;
Curse thou his basket and his store,
Kail an' potatoes.

L—d, hear my earnest cry an' pray'r,
Against that presbyt'ry o' Ayr;
Thy strong right hand, L—d make it bare,
Upo' their heads,
L—d weigh it down, and dinna spare.
For their misdeeds.

O L—d my G—d, that glib-tongu'd A—n,
My very heart an' saul are quakin',
To think how we stood sweatin', shakin',
An p—d wi dread,
While he, wi' hingrin' lips and snakin',
Held up his head.

L—d, in the day of vengeance try him,
L—d, visit them wha did employ him,
An' pass not in thy mercy by 'em,
Nor hear their pray'r;
But, for thy people's sake, destroy 'em,
And dinna spare.

But, L—d, remember me and mine
Wi' mercies temp'ral and divine,
That I for gear and grace may shine,
Excell'd by nane,
An' a' the glory shall be thine,
Amen, Amen.

Mary Morison[1]

O MARY, at thy window be,
  It is the wish'd, the trysted hour;
Those smiles and glances let me see,
  That makes the miser's treasure poor:
How blythly wad I bide the stoure,
  A weary slave frae sun to sun,
Could I the rich reward secure,
  The lovely Mary Morison.

Yestreen, when to the trembling string,
  The dance gaed thro' the lighted ha',
To thee my fancy took its wing,
  I sat, but neither heard nor saw:
Tho' this was fair, and that was braw,
  And yon the toast of a' the town,
I sigh'd, and said amang them a',
  "Ye are na Mary Morison."

O Mary, canst thou wreck his peace,
  Wha for thy sake wad gladly die!
Or canst thou break that heart of his,
  Whase only faut is loving thee.
If love for love thou wilt na gie,
  At least be pity to me shown;
A thought ungentle canna be
  The thought o' Mary Morison.

Address to a Lady[2]

OH WERT thou in the cauld blast,
  On yonder lea, on yonder lea;
My plaidie to the angry airt,
  I'd shelter thee, I'd shelter thee:
Or did misfortune's bitter storms
  Around thee blaw, around thee blaw,
Thy bield should be my bosom,
  To share it a', to share it a'.

Or were I in the wildest waste,
  Sae black and bare, sae black and bare,

[1] Published in *Works*, ed. Currie, Vol. IV, 1800. Text of first edition.
[2] Published in *Works*, ed. Currie, 1800. Text of *Life and Works*, ed. Alexander Peterkin, Edinburgh, 1815.

The desert were a paradise,
  If thou wert there, if thou wert there.
Or were I monarch o' the globe,
  Wi' thee to reign, wi' thee to reign;
The brightest jewel in my crown,
  Wad be my queen, wad be my queen.

Ye Flowery Banks[1]

YE FLOWERY banks o' bonie Doon,
  How can ye blume sae fair;
How can ye chant, ye little birds,
  And I sae fu' o' care!

Thou'll break my heart thou bonie bird
  That sings upon the bough;
Thou minds me o' the happy days
  When my fause luve was true.

Thou'll break my heart, thou bonie bird
  That sings beside thy mate;
For sae I sat, and sae I sang,
  And wist na o' my fate.

Aft hae I rov'd by bonie Doon,
  To see the wood-bine twine,
And ilk brid sang o' its love,
  And sae did I o' mine.

Wi' lightsome heart I pu'd a rose
  Frae aff its thorny tree,
And my fause luver staw my rose,
  But let the thorn wi' me.

[1] Published in *Reliques*, ed. Cromek, 1808. Text of first edition.

WILLIAM LISLE BOWLES

(1762-1789-1850)

Sonnets[1]

Sonnet V

Evening, as slow thy placid shades descend,
Veiling with gentlest hush the landscape still,
The lonely battlement, and farthest hill
And wood, I think of those that have no friend,
Who now, perhaps, by melancholy led,
From the broad blaze of day, where pleasure flaunts,
Retiring, wander 'mid thy lonely haunts
Unseen; and watch the tints that o'er thy bed
Hang lovely, to their pensive fancy's eye
Presenting fairy vales, where the tir'd mind
Might rest, beyond the murmurs of mankind,
Nor hear the hourly moans of misery!
Ah! beauteous views, that Hope's fair gleams the while
Should smile like you, and perish as they smile!

Sonnet IX

At Dover Cliffs, July 20, 1787

On these white cliffs, that calm above the flood,
Uplift their shadowing heads, and, at their feet,
Scarce hear the surge that has for ages beat,
Sure many a lonely wand'rer has stood;
And, whilst the lifted murmur met his ear,
And o'er the distant billows the still Eve
Sail'd slow, has thought of all his heart must leave
To-morrow; of the friends he lov'd most dear;
Of social scenes, from which he wept to part:
But if, like me, he knew how fruitless all
The thoughts that would full fain the past recall,
Soon would he quell the risings of his heart,
And brave the wild winds and unhearing tide—
The World his country, and his God his guide.

[1] Published in 1789. Text of ninth edition, 1805.

Sonnet XIV

O Time! who know'st a lenient hand to lay
Softest on sorrow's wound, and slowly thence
(Lulling to sad repose the weary sense)
The faint pang stealest unperceiv'd away;
On Thee I rest my only hope at last,
And think, when thou hast dry'd the bitter tear
That flows in vain o'er all my soul held dear,
I may look back on every sorrow past,
And meet life's peaceful evening with a smile—
As some lone bird, at day's departing hour,
Sings in the sunbeam, of the transient show'r
Forgetful, though its wings are wet the while:—
Yet ah! how much must that poor heart endure,
Which hopes from thee, and thee alone, a cure!

Sonnet XV

Languid, and sad, and slow, from day to day
I journey on, yet pensive turn to view
(Where the rich landscape gleams with softer hue)
The streams, and vales, and hills, that steal away.
So fares it with the children of the earth:
For when life's goodly prospect opens round,
Their spirits beat to tread that fairy ground,
Where every vale sounds to the pipe of mirth.
But them vain hope and easy youth beguiles,
And soon a longing look, like me, they cast
Back on the pleasing prospect of the past:
Yet Fancy points where still far onward smiles
Some sunny spot, and her fair colouring blends,
'Till cheerless on their path the night descends.

Sonnet XVI

On a Distant View of England

Ah! from mine eyes the tears unbidden start,
As thee, my country, and the long-lost sight
Of thy own cliffs, that lift their summits white
Above the wave, once more my beating heart
With eager hope and filial transport hails!
Scenes of my youth, reviving gales ye bring,
As when erewhile the tuneful morn of spring
Joyous awoke amidst your blooming vales,

And fill'd with fragrance every painted plain:
Fled are those hours, and all the joys they gave!
Yet still I gaze, and count each rising wave
That bears me nearer to your haunts again;
If haply, 'mid those woods and vales so fair,
Stranger to Peace, I yet may meet her there.

Sonnet XXIII

Netley Abbey

FALL'N pile! I ask not what has been thy fate;
But when the weak winds, wafted from the main,
Through each rent arch, like spirits that complain,
Come hollow to my ear, I meditate
On this world's passing pageant, and the lot
Of those who once full proudly in their prime
And beauteous might have stood, till bow'd by time
Or injury, their early boast forgot,
They may have fallen like thee: Pale and forlorn,
Their brow, besprent with thin hairs, white as snow,
They lift, majestick yet; as they would scorn
This short-liv'd scene of vanity and woe;
Whilst on their sad looks smilingly they bear
The trace of creeping age, and the dim hue of care!

WRITERS FOR *The Anti-Jacobin; or, Weekly Examiner*

(1797-1798)

The Friend of Humanity and the Knife Grinder[1]

FRIEND OF HUMANITY

"NEEDY Knife-grinder! whither are you going?
Rough is the road, your wheel is out of order—
Bleak blows the blast;—your hat has got a hole in't,
So have your breeches!

"Weary Knife-grinder! little think the proud ones,
Who in their coaches roll along the turnpike-

[1] By George Canning and J. H. Frere. Published in No. II, November 27, 1797. Text of *Poetry of the Anti-Jacobin*, London, 1799.

-road, what hard work 'tis crying all day "Knives and
"Scissors to grind O!"

"Tell me, Knife-grinder, how you came to grind knives?
Did some rich man tyrannically use you?
Was it the squire? or parson of the parish?
Or the attorney?

"Was it the squire, for killing of his game? or
Covetous parson, for his tithes distraining?
Or roguish lawyer, made you lose your little
All in a lawsuit?

"(Have you not read the Rights of Man, by Tom Paine?)
Drops of compassion tremble on my eyelids,
Ready to fall, as soon as you have told your
Pitiful story."

KNIFE-GRINDER

"Story! God bless you! I have none to tell, sir,
Only last night a-drinking at the Chequers,
This poor old hat and breeches, as you see, were
Torn in a scuffle.

"Constables came up for to take me into
Custody; they took me before the justice;
Justice Oldmixon put me in the parish-
-Stocks for a vagrant.

"I should be glad to drink your Honour's health in
A pot of beer, if you will give me sixpence;
But for my part, I never love to meddle
With politics, sir."

FRIEND OF HUMANITY

"*I* give thee sixpence! I will see thee damn'd first—
Wretch! whom no sense of wrongs can rouse to vengeance—
Sordid, unfeeling, reprobate, degraded,
Spiritless outcast!"

[*Kicks the Knife-grinder, overturns his wheel, and exit in a transport of Republican enthusiasm and universal philanthropy.*]

The Progress of Man, Canto Twenty-third[1]

HAIL! beauteous lands that crown the Southern Seas;
Dear happy seats of Liberty and Ease!
Hail! whose green coasts the peaceful ocean laves,
Incessant washing with his watery waves!
Delicious islands! to whose envied shore
Thee, gallant Cook! the ship Endeavour bore.
There laughs the sky, there zephyr's frolic train,
And light-wing'd loves, and blameless pleasures reign:
There, when two souls congenial ties unite,
No hireling *Bonzes* chant the mystic rite;
Free every thought, each action unconfin'd,
And light those fetters which no rivets bind.
There in each grove, each sloping bank along,
And flow'rs and shrubs and odorous herbs among,
Each shepherd clasp'd, with undisguis'd delight,
His yielding fair one,—in the Captain's sight;
Each yielding fair, as chance or fancy led,
Preferr'd new lovers to her sylvan bed.
Learn hence, each nymph, whose free aspiring mind
Europe's cold laws, and colder customs bind—
O! learn, what Nature's genial laws decree—
What Otaheite is, let Britain be!
Of WHIST or CRIBBAGE mark th' amusing game—
The Partners *changing*, but the SPORT the *same*.
Else would the Gamester's anxious ardour cool,
Dull every deal, and stagnant every pool.
—Yet must *one* Man, with one unceasing Wife,
Play the LONG RUBBER of connubial life.
Yes! human laws, and laws esteem'd divine,
The generous passion straighten and confine;
And, as a stream, when art constrains its course,
Pours its fierce torrent with augmented force,
So, Passion narrow'd to one channel small,
Unlike the former, does not flow at all.
—For Love *then* only flaps his purple wings,
When uncontroll'd by Priestcraft or by Kings.
Such the strict rules that, in these barbarous climes,
Choke youth's fair flow'rs, and feelings turn to crimes:
And people every walk of polish'd life,
With that two-headed monster, MAN and WIFE.
Yet bright examples sometimes we observe,
Which from the general practice seem to swerve;

[1] By George Canning and J. H. Frere. Published in No. XXI, April 2, 1798. Text of *Poetry of the Anti-Jacobin*, London, 1799.

Such as, presented to Germania's view,
A Kotzbue's bold emphatic pencil drew;
Such as, translated in some future age,
Shall add new glories to the British stage;
—While the moved audience sit in dumb despair,
"Like Hottentots, *and at each other stare*."
  With look sedate, and staid beyond her years,
In matron weeds a *Housekeeper* appears.
The jingling keys her comely girdle deck—
Her 'kerchief colour'd, and her aprong *check*.
Can that be Adelaide, that "soul of whim,"
Reform'd in practice, and in manner prim?
—On household cares intent, with many a sigh
She turns the pancake, and she moulds the pie;
Melts into sauces rich the savoury ham;
From the crush'd berry strains the lucid jam;
Bids brandied cherries, by infusion slow,
Imbibe new flavour, and their own forego,
Sole cordial of her heart, sole solace of her woe!
While still, responsive to each mournful moan,
The saucepan simmers in a softer tone.

. . . .

The Rovers; or, The Double Arrangement[1]

Song by Rogero[2]

WHENE'ER with haggard eyes I view
  This dungeon that I'm rotting in,
I think of those companions true
  Who studied with me at the U—
    —niversity of Gottingen,—
    —niversity of Gottingen.

[*Weeps, and pulls out a blue kerchief, with which he wipes his eyes; gazing tenderly at it, he proceeds*—

Sweet kerchief, check'd with heav'nly blue,
  Which once my love sat knotting in!—
Alas! Matilda *then* was true!—
  At least I thought so at the U—
    —niversity of Gottingen—
    —niversity of Gottingen.

[1] Published in No. XXX, June 4, 1798. Text of *Poetry of the Anti-Jacobin*, London, 1798.

[2] By George Canning.

[*At the repetition of this Line Rogero clanks his Chains in cadence.*

Barbs! barbs! alas! how swift you flew
  Her neat post-waggon trotting in!
Ye bore Matilda from my view;
  Forlorn I languish'd at the U—
    —niversity of Gottingen—
    —niversity of Gottingen.

This faded form! this pallid hue!
  This blood my veins is clotting in,
My years are many—they were few
  When first I enter'd at the U—
    —niversity of Gottingen—
    —niversity of Gottingen.

There first for thee my passion grew,
  Sweet! sweet Matilda Pottingen!
Thou wast the daughter of my Tu—
  —tor, Law Professor at the U—
    —niversity of Gottingen—
    —niversity of Gottingen.

Sun, moon, and thou vain world, adieu,
  That kings and priests are plotting in:
Here doom'd to starve on water-gru—
  —el never shall I see the U—
    —niversity of Gottingen—
    —niversity of Gottingen.

[*During the last Stanza Rogero dashes his head repeatedly against the walls of his Prison; and, finally, so hard as to produce a visible contusion. He then throws himself on the floor in an agony. The Curtain drops—the Music still continuing to play, till it is wholly fallen.*

New Morality[1]

From mental mists to purge a nation's eyes;
To animate the weak, unite the wise;
To trace the deep infection, that pervades
The crowded town, and taints the rural shades;

[1] By George Canning, J. H. Frere, William Gifford, and George Ellis. Published in No. XXXVI, July 9, 1798. Text of *Poetry of the Anti-Jacobin*, London, 1799.

To mark how wide extends the mighty waste
O'er the fair realms of Science, Learning, Taste;
To drive and scatter all the brood of lies,
And chase the varying falsehood as it flies;
The long arrears of ridicule to pay,
To drag reluctant Dullness back to day;
Much yet remains.—To you these themes belong,
Ye favour'd sons of virtue and of song!
  Say, is the field too narrow? are the times
Barren of folly, and devoid of crimes?
  Yet, venial vices, in a milder age,
Could rouse the warmth of Pope's satiric rage:
The doating miser, and the lavish heir,
The follies, and the foibles of the fair,
Sir Job, Sir Balaam, and old Euclio's thrift,
And Sappho's diamonds with her dirty shift,
Blunt, Charteris, Hopkins,—meaner subjects fir'd
The keen-eyed Poet; while the Muse inspir'd
Her ardent child,—entwining, as he sate,
His laurell'd chaplet with the thorns of hate.
  But say,—indignant does the Muse retire,
Her shrine deserted, and extinct its fire?
No pious hand to feed the sacred flame,
No raptur'd soul a poet's charge to claim?
  Bethink thee, G—ff—rd; when some future age
Shall trace the promise of thy playful page;—
"The hand which brush'd a swarm of fools away,
"Should rouse to grasp a more reluctant prey!"—
Think then, will pleaded indolence excuse
The tame secession of thy languid Muse?
  Ah! where is now that promise? why so long
Sleep the keen shafts of satire and of song?
Oh! come, with Taste and Virtue at thy side,
With ardent zeal inflam'd, and patriot pride;
With keen poetic glance direct the blow,
And empty all thy quiver on the foe:—
No pause—no rest—till weltering on the ground
The poisonous hydra lies, and pierc'd with many a wound.
  Thou too!—the nameless Bard,—whose honest zeal
For law, for morals, for the public weal,
Pours down impetuous on thy country's foes
The stream of verse, and many-languag'd prose;
Thou too!—though oft thy ill-advis'd dislike
The guiltless head with random censure strike,—
Though quaint allusions, vague and undefin'd,
Play faintly round the ear, but mock the mind;—
Through the mix'd mass yet truth and learning shine,
And manly vigour stamps the nervous line;

And patriot warmth the generous rage inspires,
And wakes and points the desultory fires!
  Yet more remain unknown:—for who can tell
What bashful genius, in some rural cell,
As year to year, and day succeeds to day,
In joyless leisure wastes his life away?
In him the flame of early fancy shone;
His genuine worth his old companions own;
In childhood and in youth their chief confess'd,
His master's pride his pattern to the rest.
Now, far aloof retiring from the strife
Of busy talents, and of active life,
As, from the loop-holes of retreat, he views
Our stage, verse, pamphlets, politics, and news,
He loaths the world,—or, with reflection sad,
Concludes it irrecoverably mad;
Of taste, of learning, morals, all bereft,
No hope, no prospect to redeem it left.
  Awake! for shame! or e'er thy nobler sense
Sink in the' oblivious pool of indolence!
Must wit be found alone on falsehood's side,
Unknown to truth, to virtue unallied?
Arise! nor scorn thy country's just alarms;
Wield in her cause thy long-neglected arms:
Of lofty satire pour th' indignant strain,
Leagued with her friends, and ardent to maintain
'Gainst Learning's, Virtue's, Truth's, Religion's foes,
A kingdom's safety, and the world's repose.
  If Vice appal thee,—if thou view with awe
Insults that brave, and crimes that 'scape the law;—
Yet may the specious bastard brood, which claim
A spurious homage under Virtue's name,
Sprung from that parent of ten thousand crimes,
The *New Philosophy* of modern times,—
Yet, these may rouse thee!—With unsparing hand,
Oh, lash the vile impostures from the land!
  First, stern Philanthropy:—not she, who dries
The orphan's tears, and wipes the widow's eyes;
Not she, who, sainted Charity her guide,
Of British bounty pours the annual tide:—
But *French* Philanthropy;—whose boundless mind
Glows with the general love of all mankind;—
Philanthropy,—beneath whose baneful sway
Each patriot passion sinks, and dies away.
  Taught in her school to imbibe thy mawkish strain,
Condorcet, filter'd through the dregs of Paine,
Each pert adept disowns a Briton's part,
And plucks the name of England from his heart.

What shall a name, a word, a sound control
The' aspiring thought, and cramp the' expansive soul?
Shall one half-peopled Island's rocky round
A love, that glows for all Creation, bound?
And social charities contract the plan
Fram'd for thy Freedom, UNIVERSAL MAN?
—No—through the' extended globe his feelings run
As broad and general as the' unbounded sun!
No narrow bigot *he*;—*his* reason'd view
Thy interests, England, ranks with thine, Peru!
France at our doors, *he* sees no danger nigh,
But heaves for Turkey's woes the' impartial sigh;
A steady Patriot of the World alone,
The Friend of every Country—but his own.
Next comes a gentler Virtue.—Ah! beware
Lest the harsh verse her shrinking softness scare.
Visit her not too roughly;—the warm sigh
Breathes on her lips;—the tear-drop gems her eye.
Sweet Sensibility, who dwells enshrin'd
In the fine foldings of the feeling mind;—
With delicate Mimosa's sense endu'd,
Who shrinks instinctive from a hand too rude;
Or, like the *anagallis*, prescient flower,
Shuts her soft petals at the' approaching shower.
Sweet child of sickly Fancy!—her of yore
From her lov'd France Rousseau to exile bore;
And, while midst lakes and mountains wild he ran,
Full of himself, and shunn'd the haunts of man,
Taught her o'er each lone vale and Alpine steep
To lisp the story of his wrongs, and weep;
Taught her to cherish still in either eye,
Of tender tears a plentiful supply,
And pour them in the brooks that babbled by;—
—Taught by nice scale to mete her feelings strong,
False by degrees, and exquisitely wrong;—
—For the crush'd beetle *first*,—the widow'd dove,
And all the warbled sorrows of the grove;—
Next for poor suff'ring *guilt*;—and *last* of all,
For Parents, Friends, a King and Country's fall.
Mark her fair votaries, prodigal of grief,
With cureless pangs, and woes that mock relief,
Droop in soft sorrow o'er a faded flower;
O'er a dead jack-ass pour the pearly shower;—
But hear, unmov'd, of *Loire*'s ensanguin'd flood,
Chok'd up with slain;—of *Lyons* drench'd in blood;
Of crimes that blot the age, the world with shame,
Foul crimes, but sicklied o'er with Freedom's name;
Altars and thrones subverted, social life

Trampled to earth,—the husband from the wife,
Parent from child, with ruthless fury torn,—
Of talents, honour, virtue, wit, forlorn,
In friendless exile,—of the wise and good
Staining the daily scaffold with their blood,—
Of savage cruelties, that scare the mind,
The rage of madness with hell's lusts combin'd—
Of hearts torn reeking from the mangled breast,—
They hear—and hope, that ALL IS FOR THE BEST.
  Fond hope!—but JUSTICE sanctifies the pray'r—
JUSTICE!—here, Satire, strike! 'twere sin to spare!
Not she in British Courts that takes her stand,
The dawdling balance dangling in her hand,
Adjusting punishments to fraud and vice,
With scrupulous quirks, and disquisition nice:—
But firm, erect, with keen reverted glance,
The' avenging angel of regenerate France,
Who visits ancient sins on modern times,
And punishes the Pope for Cæsar's crimes.
  Such is the liberal JUSTICE which presides
In these our days, and modern patriots guides;—
JUSTICE, whose blood-stain'd book one sole decree,
One statute fills—"the People shall be Free."
Free by what means?—by folly, madness, guilt,
By boundless rapines, blood in oceans spilt;
By confiscation, in whose sweeping toils
The poor man's pittance with the rich man's spoils,
Mix'd in one common mass, are swept away,
To glut the short-liv'd tyrant of the day:—
By laws, religion, morals, all o'erthrown:—
—Rouse then, ye sovereign people, claim your own:—
The licence that enthrals, the truth that blinds,
The wealth that starves you, and the pow'r that grinds.
—So JUSTICE bids.—'Twas her enlighten'd doom,
Louis, thy holy head devoted to the tomb!
'Twas JUSTICE claim'd, in that accursed hour,
The fatal forfeit of too lenient pow'r.
—Mourn for the Man we may;—but for the King,—
Freedom, oh! Freedom's such a charming thing!
  "Much may be said on both sides."—Hark! I hear
A well-known voice that murmurs in my ear,—
The voice of CANDOUR.—Hail! most solemn sage,
Thou drivelling virtue of this moral age,
CANDOUR, which softens party's headlong rage.
CANDOUR,—which spares its foes;—nor e'er descends
With bigot zeal to combat for its friends.
CANDOUR,—which loves in see-saw strain to tell
Of *acting foolishly*, but *meaning well*;

Too nice to praise by wholesale, or to blame,
Convinc'd that *all* men's *motives* are the same;—
And finds, with keen discriminating sight,
BLACK's not *so* black;—nor WHITE *so very* white.
"Fox, to be sure, was vehement and wrong:—
"But then Pitt's words, you'll own, were *rather* strong.
"Both must be blam'd, both pardon'd;—'twas just so
"With Fox and Pitt full forty years ago;
"So Walpole, Pulteney;—factions in all times,
"Have had their follies, ministers their crimes."
Give me the' avow'd, the' erect, the manly foe,
Bold I can meet—perhaps may turn his blow;
But of all plagues, good heav'n, thy wrath can send,
Save, save, oh! save me from the *Candid Friend!*
"Barras loves plunder,—Merlin takes a bribe,—
"What then?—shall CANDOUR these good men proscribe?
"No! ere we join the loud-accusing throng,
"Prove,—not the facts,—but, that *they thought them wrong.*
"Why hang O'Quigley?—he, misguided man,
"In sober thought his country's weal *might* plan.
"And, while his deep-wrought Treason sapp'd the throne,
"*Might* act from *taste in morals*, all his own."
Peace to such Reasoners!—let them have their way;
Shut their dull eyes against the blaze of day.—
Priestley's a Saint, and Stone a Patriot still;
And La Fayette a Hero, if they will.
I love the bold uncompromising mind,
Whose principles are fix'd, whose views defin'd:
Who scouts and scorns, in canting CANDOUR's spite,
All *taste in morals*, innate sense of right,
And Nature's impulse, all uncheck'd by art,
And feelings fine, that float about the heart:
Content, for good men's guidance, bad men's awe,
On moral truth to rest, and Gospel law.
Who owns, when Traitors feel the' avenging rod,
Just retribution, and the hand of God;
Who hears the groans through Olmutz' roofs that ring,
Of him who mock'd, misled, betray'd his King—
Hears unappall'd:—though Faction's zealots preach—
Unmov'd, unsoften'd by F—tzp—tr—ck's speech.
—That speech on which the melting Commons hung,
"While truths divine came mended from *his* tongue"—
How loving husband clings to duteous wife,—
How pure religion soothes the ills of life,—
How Popish ladies trust their pious fears
And naughty actions in their chaplain's ears.—
Half novel and half sermon on it flow'd;
With pious zeal THE OPPOSITION glow'd;

And as o'er each the soft infection crept,
Sigh'd as he whin'd, and as he whimper'd wept;—
E'en C—w—n dropt a sentimental tear,
And stout St. A—dr—w yelp'd a softer "Hear!"
O! nurse of crimes and fashions! which in vain
Our colder servile spirits would attain,
How do we ape thee, France! but blundering still
Disgrace the pattern by our want of skill.
The borrow'd step our awkward gait reveals:
(As clumsy C—rtn—y mars the verse he steals.)
How do we ape thee, France!—nor claim alone
Thy arts, thy tastes, thy morals for our own,
But to thy Worthies render homage due,
Their "hair-breadth scapes" with anxious interest view;
Statesmen and heroines whom this age adores,
Tho' plainer times would call them rogues and whores.
See Louvet, patriot, pamphleteer, and sage,
Tempering with amorous fire his virtuous rage.
Form'd for all tasks, his various talents see,—
The luscious novel, the severe decree.
—Then mark him welt'ring in his nasty sty,
Bare his lewd transports to the public eye.
Not *his* the love in silent groves that strays,
Quits the rude world, and shuns the vulgar gaze.
In Lodoiska's full possession blest,
One craving void still aches within his breast;—
Plung'd in the filth and fondness of her arms,
Not to himself alone he stints her charms;
Clasp'd in each other's foul embrace they lie,
But know no joy, unless the world stands by.
—The fool of vanity, for her alone
He lives, loves, writes, and dies but to be known.
His widow'd mourner flies to poison's aid,
Eager to join her Louvet's parted shade
In those bright realms where sainted lovers stray,—
But harsh emetics tear that hope away.
—Yet hapless Louvet! where thy bones are laid,
The easy nymphs shall consecrate the shade.
There, in the laughing morn of genial spring,
Unwedded pairs shall tender couplets sing;
Eringoes, o'er the hallow'd spot shall bloom,
And flies of Spain buzz softly round the tomb.
But hold, severer virtue claims the Muse—
Roland the just, with ribands in his shoes—
And Roland's spouse who paints with chaste delight
The doubtful conflict of her nuptial night;—
Her virgin charms what fierce attacks assail'd,
And how the rigid Minister prevail'd.

And ah! what verse can grace thy stately mien,
Guide of the world, preferment's golden queen,
Neckar's fair daughter,—Stael the Epicene!
Bright o'er whose flaming cheek and pumple nose
The bloom of young desire unceasing glows!
Fain would the Muse—but ah! she dares no more,
A mournful voice from lone Guyana's shore,
—Sad Quatremer—the bold presumption checks,
Forbid to question thy ambiguous sex.
To thee, proud Barras bows;—thy charms control
Rewbell's brute rage, and Merlin's subtle soul;
Rais'd by thy hands, and fashion'd to thy will,
Thy pow'r, thy guiding influence, governs still,
Where at the blood-stain'd board expert he plies,
The lame artificer of fraud and lies;
He with the mitred head and cloven heel;—
Doom'd the coarse edge of Rewbell's jests to feel;
To stand the playful buffet, and to hear
The frequent ink-stand whizzing past his ear;
While all the five Directors laugh to see
"The limping priest so deft at his new ministry."
Last of the' ANOINTED FIVE behold, and least,
The Directorial Lama, Sovereign Priest,—
Lepaux:—whom atheists worship;—at whose nod
Bow their meek heads *the men without a God.*
Ere long, perhaps, to this astonish'd Isle,
Fresh from the shores of subjugated Nile,
Shall Buonaparte's victor fleet protect
The genuine Theo-Philanthropic sect,—
The sect of Marat, Mirabeau, Voltaire,—
Led by their Pontiff, good La Reveillere.
—Rejoic'd our CLUBS shall greet him, and install
The holy Hunch-back in thy dome, St. Paul!
While countless votaries thronging in his train
Wave their Red Caps, and hymn this jocund strain:
"*Couriers* and *Stars*, Sedition's Evening Host,
"Thou *Morning Chronicle*, and *Morning Post*,
"Whether ye make the Rights of Man your theme,
"Your Country libel, and your God blaspheme,
"Or dirt on private worth and virtue throw,
"Still blasphemous or blackguard, praise Lepaux.
"And ye five other wandering Bards, that move
"In sweet accord of harmony and love,
"C——dge and S—th—y, L—d, and L—be and Co.
"Tune all your mystic harps to praise Lepaux!
"Pr—tl—y and W—f—ld, humble, holy men,
"Give praises to his name with tongue and pen!
"Th—lw—l, and ye that lecture as ye go,

"And for your pains get pelted, praise Lepaux!
"Praise him each Jacobin, or fool, or knave,
"And your cropp'd heads in sign of worship wave!
"All creeping creatures, venomous and low,
"Paine, W—ll—ms, G—dw—n, H—lcr—ft, praise Lepaux!
"——— and ——— with ——— join'd,
"And every other beast after his kind.
"And thou *Leviathan!* on ocean's brim
"Hugest of living things that sleep and swim;
"Thou in whose nose by Burke's gigantic hand
"The hook was fix'd to drag thee to the land,
"With ——, ———, and ——— in thy train,
"And ——— wallowing in the yeasty main—
"Still as ye snort, and puff, and spout, and blow,
"In puffing, and in spouting, praise Lepaux!"
Britain, beware; nor let the' insidious foe,
Of force despairing, aim a deadlier blow.
Thy peace, thy strength, with devilish wiles assail,
And when her arms are vain, by arts prevail.
True, thou art rich, art powerful!—thro' thine Isle
Industrious skill, contented labour, smile;
Far seas are studded with thy countless sails;
What wind but wafts them, and what shore but hails!
True, thou art brave!—o'er all the busy land
In patriot ranks embattled myriads stand;
Thy foes behold with impotent amaze,
And drop the lifted weapon as they gaze!
But what avails to guard each outward part,
If subtlest poison, circling at thy heart,
Spite of thy courage, of thy pow'r, and wealth,
Mine the sound fabric of thy vital health?
So thine own Oak, by some fair streamlet's side
Waves its broad arms, and spreads its leafy pride,
Tow'rs from the earth, and rearing to the skies
Its conscious strength, the tempest's wrath defies:
Its ample branches shield the fowls of air,
To its cool shade the panting herds repair.—
The treacherous current works its noiseless way,—
The fibres loosen, and the roots decay;
Prostrate the beauteous ruin lies; and all
That shar'd its shelter, perish in its fall.
O thou!—lamented Sage!—whose prescient scan
Pierc'd through foul Anarchy's gigantic plan,
Prompt to incredulous hearers to disclose
The guilt of France, and Europe's world of woes;—
Thou, on whose name each distant age shall gaze,
The mighty sea-mark of these troubled days!
O large of soul, of genius unconfin'd,

Born to delight, instruct, and mend mankind!—
Burke! in whose breast a Roman ardour glow'd;
Whose copious tongue with Grecian richness flow'd;
Well hast thou found (if such thy Country's doom)
A timely refuge in the sheltering tomb!
  As, in far realms, where Eastern kings are laid,
In pomp of death, beneath the cypress shade,
The perfum'd lamp with unextinguish'd light
Flames thro' the vault, and cheers the gloom of night:—
So, mighty Burke! in thy sepulchral urn,
To Fancy's view, the lamp of Truth shall burn.
Thither late times shall turn their reverent eyes,
Led by thy light, and by thy wisdom wise.
  There *are*, to whom (*their* taste such pleasures cloy)
No light thy wisdom yields, thy wit no joy.
Peace to their heavy heads, and callous hearts,
Peace—such as sloth, as ignorance imparts!—
Pleas'd may they live to plan their Country's good,
And crop with calm content their flow'ry food!
  What though thy venturous spirit lov'd to urge
The labouring theme to Reason's utmost verge,
Kindling and mounting from th' enraptur'd sight;—
Still anxious wonder watch'd thy daring flight!
—While vulgar minds, with mean malignant stare,
Gaz'd up, the triumph of thy fall to share!
Poor triumph! price of that extorted praise,
Which still to daring Genius Envy pays.
  Oh! for thy playful smile,—thy potent frown,—
To' abash bold Vice, and laugh pert Folly down!
So should the Muse in Humour's happiest vein,
With verse that flow'd in metaphoric strain,
And apt allusions to the rural trade,
Tell of *what wood young* Jacobins *are made*;
How the skill'd Gardener grafts with nicest rule
The *slip* of Coxcomb, on the *stock* of Fool;—
Forth in bright blossom bursts the tender sprig,
A thing to wonder at, perhaps a *Whig*.—
Should tell, how wise each half-fledg'd pedant prates
Of weightiest matters, grave distinctions states—
—That rules of policy, and public good,
In Saxon times were rightly understood;
—That Kings are proper, *may be* useful things,
But then some Gentlemen object to Kings;
—That in all times the Minister's to blame;
—That British Liberty's an empty name,
Till each fair burgh, numerically free,
Shall choose its Members by *the Rule of Three*.
  So should the Muse, with verse in thunder cloth'd,

Proclaim the crimes by God and Nature loath'd.
Which—when fell poison revels in the veins—
(That poison fell, which frantic Gallia drains
From the crude fruit of Freedom's blasted tree)
Blots the fair records of Humanity.
  To feebler nations let proud France afford
Her damning choice,—the chalice or the sword,—
To drink or die;—or fraud! oh specious lie!
Delusive choice! for *if* they drink, they die.
  The sword we dread not:—of ourselves secure,
Firm were our strength, our Peace and Freedom sure.
Let all the world confederate all its pow'rs,
"Be they not back'd by those that should be ours,"
High on his rock shall BRITAIN'S GENIUS stand,
Scatter the crowded hosts, and vindicate the land.
  Guard we but our own hearts: with constant view
To ancient morals, ancient manners true,
True to the manlier virtues, such as nerv'd
Our fathers' breasts, and this proud Isle preserv'd
For many a rugged age:—and scorn the while,—
Each philosophic atheist's specious guile.—
The soft seductions, the refinements nice,
Of gay morality, and easy vice:—
So shall we brave the storm;—our 'stablish'd pow'r
Thy refuge, Europe, in some happier hour.—
—But, French *in heart*—tho' victory crown our brow,
Low at our feet though prostrate nations bow,
Wealth gild our cities, commerce crowd our shore,—
London may shine, but England is no more.

Materials for the Study of English Poetry, 1660-1800[1]

Bibliographies

Annual bibliography of English language and literature. Edited for the Modern Humanities Research Association. Cambridge, 1921—.

The Cambridge bibliography of English literature. In press. [Based on the bibliographies in *The Cambridge history of English literature*, but greatly enlarged and improved.]

Courtney, W. P. *Dodsley's Collection of poetry, its contents & contributors*. London, 1910.

Crane, R. S. "English literature of the Restoration and eighteenth century: a current bibliography." *PQ*, 1926-32.

Northup, C. S. *A register of bibliographies of the English language and literature*. New Haven, 1925.

Williams, I. A. *Seven XVIIIth century bibliographies*. London, 1924.

——— "Some poetical miscellanies of the early eighteenth century." *Library*, 4th series, X (1929), 233-51.

The Year's work in English studies. Edited for the English Association. London, 1922—.

Collections and Anthologies

(In chronological order)

Miscellany poems . . . by the most eminent hands. Publish'd by Mr. Dryden. London, 1684-1709. 6 vols. 5th printing, London, 1727. 6 vols.

A Collection of poems by several hands. London, 1748-58. 6 vols. [On the history and contents of this collection see W. P. Courtney, *Dodsley's Collection of poetry, its contents & contributors*, London, 1910.]

The Poetical calendar, containing a collection of scarce and valuable pieces of poetry. Ed. Francis Fawkes and William Woty. London, 1763. 12 vols. in 4.

A Select collection of poems, with notes, biographical and historical. Ed. J. Nichols. London, 1780-82. 8 vols.

Bell's classical arrangement of fugitive poetry. London, 1789-1810. 18 vols.

The Works of the British poets. Ed. Robert Anderson. London, 1795. 13 vols.

The Works of the English poets, from Chaucer to Cowper. Ed. A. Chalmers. London, 1810. 21 vols.

The English poets. Ed. T. H. Ward. London, 1880. 4 vols.

Musa proterva: love-poems of the Restoration. Ed. A. H. Bullen. London, 1889.

Book of seventeenth century lyrics. Ed. F. E. Schelling. Boston, 1899. ("Athenæum press series.")

The Dryden anthology, 1675-1700. Ed. Edward Arber. London, 1899.

The Pope anthology, 1701-1744. Ed. Edward Arber. London, 1899.

The Goldsmith anthology, 1745-1774. Ed. Edward Arber. London, 1900.

[1] List of Abbreviations:—*ES=Englische Studien; JEGP=Journal of English and Germanic philology; LM=London mercury; MLN=Modern language notes; MLR=Modern language review; MP=Modern philology; PMLA=Publications of the Modern Language Association; PQ=Philological quarterly; RAA=Revue anglo-américaine; RES=Review of English studies; SP=Studies in philology; TLS=Times literary supplement.*

The Cowper anthology, 1775-1800. Ed. Edward Arber. London, 1901.

Minor poets of the Caroline period. Ed. George Saintsbury. Oxford, 1905-21. 3 vols.

English poems. Ed. W. C. Bronson. *The Restoration and the eighteenth century (1660-1800).* Chicago, [1908].

Political ballads illustrating the administration of Sir Robert Walpole. Ed. Milton Percival. Oxford, 1916.

English poets of the eighteenth century. Ed. Ernest Bernbaum. New York, 1918.

Metaphysical lyrics and poems of the seventeenth century: Donne to Butler. Ed. H. J. C. Grierson. Oxford, 1921.

Shorter poems of the eighteenth century, an anthology. Ed. Iolo A. Williams. London, 1923.

Forgotten lyrics of the eighteenth century. Ed. Oswald Doughty. London, 1924.

The Oxford book of eighteenth century verse. Ed. David Nichol Smith. Oxford, 1926.

Poems on several occasions written in the eighteenth century. Ed. Kathleen Campbell. Oxford, 1926.

Selections from the pre-romantic movement. Ed. Ernest Bernbaum. New York, 1929.

An Anthology of English poetry: Dryden to Blake. Ed. Kathleen Campbell. London, 1930.

Restoration verse, 1660-1715. Ed. William Kerr. London and New York, 1930.

An Anthology of Augustan poetry. Ed. F. T. Wood. London and New York, 1931.

GENERAL STUDIES

Babbitt, Irving. *Rousseau and romanticism.* Boston and New York, 1919. [A brilliant but in many respects unsound work. Cf. *MLN*, XXXV, 302-08; XXXVII, 268-74.]

Beers, H. A. *A history of English romanticism in the eighteenth century.* New York, 1899; 2d ed., New York, 1910.

Beljame, A. *Le public et les hommes de lettres en Angleterre au dix-huitième siècle, 1660-1744.* Paris, 1881.

Bernbaum, Ernest. *Guide through the romantic movement.* New York, 1930.

Bredvold, L. I. "The element of art in eighteenth century poetry." In his *Selected poems of Alexander Pope*, New York, 1926. [An excellent essay.]

Broadus, E. K. *The laureateship, a study of the office of poet laureate in England.* Oxford, 1921.

The Cambridge history of English literature. Vols. VIII-XI. Cambridge and New York, 1912-14.

Cazamian, Louis. *L'évolution psychologique et la littérature en Angleterre, 1660-1914.* Paris, 1920.

Courthope, W. J. *A history of English poetry.* Vols. III, V-VI. London and New York, 1903, 1905, 1910.

Dennis, John. *The age of Pope.* London, 1894.

"The Eighteenth century in verse." *TLS*, November 10, 1927, pp. 797-98.

Elton, Oliver. *The Augustan ages.* Edinburgh and London, 1899.

——— *A survey of English literature, 1730-1780.* London, 1928. 2 vols.

——— *A survey of English literature, 1780-1830.* London, 1912. 2 vols.

Eyre-Todd, George. *Scottish poetry of the eighteenth century.* Glasgow, 1896. 2 vols.

Fairchild, H. N. *The romantic quest.* New York, 1931.

Garnett, Richard. *The age of Dryden.* London, 1895.

Gosse, Edmund. *From Shakespeare to Pope: an inquiry into the causes and phenomena of the rise of classical poetry in England.* New York, 1885.

Grierson, H. J. C. *The background of English literature and other collected essays and addresses.* London, 1925.

Grierson, H. J. C. *Cross currents in English literature of the XVIIth century.* London, 1929.

Havens, R. D. "Changing taste in the eighteenth century: a study of Dryden's and Dodsley's miscellanies." *PMLA*, XLIV (1929), 501-36.

——— "Romantic aspects of the age of Pope." *PMLA*, XXVII (1912), 297-324.

Johnson, Samuel. *Lives of the English poets.* Ed. G. B. Hill. Oxford, 1905. 3 vols.

Legouis, E., and L. Cazamian. *A history of English literature.* Translated from the French. New ed. New York, 1929.

Lovejoy, A. O. "On the discrimination of romanticisms." *PMLA*, XXXIX (1924), 229-53. [A fundamental contribution to the interpretation of eighteenth-century romanticism.]

Millar, J. H. *The mid-eighteenth century.* Edinburgh, 1902.

Minto, William. *The literature of the Georgian era.* London and New York, 1895. [An interesting anticipation of current attitudes toward the eighteenth century.]

Partridge, Eric. *Eighteenth century English romantic poetry.* Paris, 1924.

Phelps, W. L. *The beginnings of the English romantic movement.* Boston, 1893. [A pioneer work, the point of view of which is now largely antiquated.]

Saintsbury, George. *The peace of the Augustans.* London, 1916.

Schöffler, H. *Protestantismus und Literatur: neue Wege zur englischen Literatur des 18. Jahrhunderts.* Leipzig, 1922.

Seccombe, Thomas. *The age of Johnson.* London, 1900.

Stephen, Leslie. *English literature and society in the eighteenth century.* London, 1904.

Vines, Sherard. *The course of English classicism from the Tudor to the Victorian age.* London and New York, 1930.

Walker, Hugh. *Three centuries of Scottish literature.* Glasgow and New York, 1893. 2 vols.

Wendell, Barrett. *The temper of the seventeenth century in English literature.* New York, 1904.

STUDIES OF SPECIAL TOPICS

The Philosophical Background

Bredvold, L. I. "The naturalism of John Donne." *JEGP*, XXII (1923), 471-502.

Burtt, E. A. *The metaphysical foundations of modern physical science.* London and New York, 1925.

Bury, J. B. *The idea of progress; an inquiry into its origin and growth.* London, 1920.

Crofts, J. E. V. "Enthusiasm." *Eighteenth century literature: an Oxford miscellany* (Oxford, 1909), pp. 127-50.

Crum, R. B. *Scientific thought in poetry.* New York, 1931.

Duncan, C. S. *The new science and English literature in the classical period.* Menasha, Wis., 1913.

Elton, Oliver. "Reason and enthusiasm in the eighteenth century." *Essays and studies by members of the English Association*, X (1924), 122-36.

Jones, R. F. "The background of the 'Battle of the books.'" *Washington University studies*, Vol. VII, Humanistic series (1920), pp. 97-162.

Lovejoy, A. O. "Optimism and romanticism." *PMLA*, XLII (1927), 921-45.

——— "The parallel of deism and classicism." *MP*, XXIX (1932), 281-99. [The best brief statement of the dominant eighteenth-century point of view.]

——— "'Pride' in eighteenth-century thought." *MLN*, XXXVI (1921), 31-37.

Nicolson, Marjorie. "The early stage of Cartesianism in England." *SP*, XXVI (1929), 356-74.

Randall, J. H., Jr. *The making of*

the modern mind: a survey of the intellectual background of the present age. Boston, 1926.

Stephen, Leslie. *History of English thought in the eighteenth century*. 3d ed. London, 1902. 2 vols.

Thompson, E. N. S. "Mysticism in seventeenth-century English literature." *SP*, XVIII (1921), 170-231.

Whitehead, A. N. *Science and the modern world*. New York, 1926.

Theories of Poetry

Bosker, A. *Literary criticism in the age of Johnson*. Groningen, 1930. [Cf. *PQ*, X, 177-78.]

Bray, René. *La formation de la doctrine classique en France*. Paris, 1927.

Cowl, R. P. *The theory of poetry in England*. London, 1914. [A useful collection of brief extracts from critics of the sixteenth to the nineteenth centuries.]

Crane, R. S. "An early eighteenth-century enthusiast for primitive poetry." *MLN*, XXXVII (1922), 27-36.

Critical essays of the eighteenth century, 1700-1725. Ed. W. H. Durham. New Haven, 1915.

Critical essays of the seventeenth century. Ed. J. E. Spingarn. Oxford, 1908-09. 3 vols.

Draper, J. W. "Aristotelian 'mimesis' in eighteenth-century England." *PMLA*, XXXVI (1921), 372-400.

——— *Eighteenth century English æsthetics: a bibliography*. Heidelberg, 1931. [A useful list of references.]

Folkierski, W. *Entre le classicisme et le romantisme: étude sur l'esthétique et les esthéticiens du XVIIIe siècle*. Paris, 1925.

Herrick, M. T. *The Poetics of Aristotle in England*. New Haven, 1930.

Howard, W. G. "Good taste and conscience." *PMLA*, XXV (1910), 486-97.

——— "Ut pictura poesis." *PMLA*, XXIV (1909), 40-123.

Kaufman, Paul. "Heralds of original genius." *Essays in memory of Barrett Wendell* (Cambridge, Mass., 1926), pp. 191-217.

Lovejoy, A. O. " 'Nature' as æsthetic norm." *MLN*, XLII (1927), 444-50. [A valuable analysis.]

——— "The parallel of deism and classicism." *MP*, XXIX (1932), 281-99.

Robertson, J. G. *Studies in the genesis of romantic theory in the eighteenth century*. Cambridge, 1923.

Saintsbury, George. *A history of English criticism*. Edinburgh and London, 1911.

Smith, L. P. "Four romantic words" ['romantic,' 'originality,' 'creative,' and 'genius']. In his *Words and idioms*, Boston, 1925.

Van Tieghem, Paul. "La notion de vraie poésie dans le préromantisme européen." In his *Le Préromantisme: études d'histoire littéraire*, Paris, 1924.

Whitney, Lois. "English primitivistic theories of epic origins." *MP*, XXI (1924), 337-78.

——— "Thomas Blackwell, a disciple of Shaftesbury." *PQ*, V (1926), 196-211

Poetic Genres

The Art of poetry on a new plan. London, 1762. 2 vols. [Possibly revised by Goldsmith. A useful classification and discussion of the principal poetic genres recognized in the middle of the eighteenth century.]

Bett, Henry. *The hymns of Methodism in their literary relations*. London, 1913.

Bragg, Marion K. *The formal eclogue in eighteenth-century England*. Orono, Maine, 1926.

Brie, Friedrich. *Englische Rokoko-Epik (1710-1730)*. Munich, 1927.

Dixon, W. M. *English epic and heroic poetry*. London and New York, 1912.

Doughty, Oswald. "Eighteenth century song." *English studies*, VII (1925), 161-69.

Doughty, Oswald. *English lyric in the age of reason*. London, 1922.

Griffith, R. H. "The progress pieces of the eighteenth century." *Texas review*, V (1920), 218-33.

Havens, R. D. "More eighteenth-century sonnets." *MLN*, XLV (1930), 77-84.

Jones, R. F. "Eclogue types in English poetry of the eighteenth century." *JEGP*, XXIV (1925), 33-60.

Kitchin, George, *A survey of burlesque and parody in English*. Edinburgh and London, 1931.

McKillop, A. D. "Some details of the sonnet revival." *MLN*, XXXIX (1924), 438-40.

Mantz, H. E. "Non-dramatic pastoral in Europe in the eighteenth century." *PMLA*, XXXI (1916), 421-47.

Morton, E. P. "The English sonnet (1658-1750)." *MLN*, XX (1905), 97-98.

Plessow, Max. *Geschichte der Fabeldichtung in England bis zu John Gay (1726)*. Berlin, 1906.

Previté-Orton, C. W. *Political satire in English poetry*. Cambridge, 1910.

Reed, E. B. *English lyrical poetry from its origins to the present time*. New Haven, 1912.

Schelling, F. E. *The English lyric*. Boston and New York, 1913.

Shafer, Robert. *The English ode to 1660*. Princeton, 1918.

Van Tieghem, Paul. "Les idylles de Gessner et le rêve pastoral." In his *Le Préromantisme: études d'histoire littéraire*, 2d series, Paris, 1930.

Walker, Hugh. *English satire and satirists*. London, 1925.

Versification and Style

Alden, R. M. "The lyrical conceits of the 'metaphysical poets.'" *SP*, XVII (1920), 183-98.

Guest, E. *A history of English rhythms*. New ed. London, 1882.

Havens, R. D. "The poetic diction of the English classicists." *Anniversary papers by colleagues and pupils of George Lyman Kittredge* (Boston, 1913), pp. 435-44.

Morton, E. P. "Poems in the stanza of *In memoriam*." *MLN*, XXIV (1909), 67-70.

——— "The Spenserian stanza before 1700." *MP*, IV (1907), 639-54.

——— "The Spenserian stanza in the eighteenth century." *MP*, X (1913), 365-91.

Omond, T. S. *English metrists*. Oxford, 1921.

——— *English metrists in the eighteenth and nineteenth centuries*. London, 1907.

Quayle, Thomas. *Poetic diction: a study of eighteenth century verse*. London, 1924.

Saintsbury, George. *A history of English prosody from the twelfth century to the present day*. Vol. II: *From Shakespeare to Crabbe*. London, 1908.

Tatlock, J. S. P. "Origin of the closed couplet in English." *Nation* (New York), April 9, 1914, p. 390.

Wyld, H. C. *Studies in English rhymes from Surrey to Pope*. London, 1923.

The Influence of Classical Poetry

Goad, Caroline M. *Horace in the English literature of the eighteenth century*. New Haven, 1918.

Lilly, Marie L. *The georgic: a contribution to the study of the Vergilian type of didactic poetry*. Baltimore, 1919.

Mustard, W. P. "Virgil's *Georgics* and the British poets." *American journal of philology*, XXIX (1908), 1-32.

Nitchie, Elizabeth. *Vergil and the English poets*. New York, 1919.

Whitford, R. C. "Juvenal in England, 1750-1802." *PQ*, VII (1928), 9-16.

The Influence of French Poetry

Charlanne, Louis. *L'influence française en Angleterre au XVIIe siècle*. Paris, 1906.

Clark, A. F. B. *Boileau and the French classical critics in England (1660-1830)*. Paris, 1925.

West, A. H. *L'influence française dans la poésie burlesque en Angleterre entre 1660 et 1700*. Paris, 1931.

Woledge, Geoffrey. "Saint Amand, Fairfax and Marvell." *MLR*, XXV (1930), 481-83.

Wollstein, Rose H. *English opinions of French poetry, 1660-1750*. New York, 1923.

The Influence of the Poetry of the English Renaissance

Babcock, R. W. *The genesis of Shakespeare idolatry, 1766-1799*. Chapel Hill, N. C., 1931.

Cory, H. E. *The critics of Edmund Spenser*. Berkeley, Cal., 1911.

——— *Edmund Spenser, a critical study*. Berkeley, Cal., 1917.

——— "Spenser, Thomson, and romanticism." *PMLA*, XXVI (1911), 51-91.

Crane, R. S. "Imitation of Spenser and Milton in the early eighteenth century: a new document." *SP*, XV (1918), 195-206.

Gertsch, Alfred. *Der Steigende Ruhm Miltons*. Leipzig, 1927.

Havens, R. D. *The influence of Milton on English poetry*. Cambridge, Mass., 1922. [The most exhaustive study of the subject. Important for many aspects of eighteenth-century poetry.]

Maar, Harko G. de. *A history of modern English romanticism*. Vol. I: *Elizabethan and modern romanticism in the eighteenth century*. London, 1924.

Moore, C. A. "Miltoniana (1679-1741)." *MP*, XXIV (1927), 321-39.

Nethercot, A. H. "The reputation of the 'metaphysical poets' during the seventeenth century." *JEGP*, XXIII (1924), 173-98.

——— "The reputation of the 'metaphysical poets' during the age of Pope." *PQ*, IV (1925), 161-79.

——— "The reputation of the 'metaphysical poets' during the age of Johnson and the 'romantic revival.'" *SP*, XXII (1925), 81-132.

——— "The term 'metaphysical poets' before Johnson." *MLN*, XXXVII (1922), 11-17.

Schelling, F. E. "Ben Jonson and the classical school." *PMLA*, VI (1898), 221-49.

Sherburn, George. "The early popularity of Milton's minor poems." *MP*, XVII (1919-1920), 259-78, 515-40.

Smith, David Nichol. *Shakespeare in the eighteenth century*. Oxford, 1928.

Williamson, George. *The Donne tradition: a study in English poetry from Donne to the death of Cowley*. Cambridge, Mass., 1930.

The Medieval Revival

Clark, Kenneth. *The Gothic revival, an essay in the history of taste*. London, 1928.

Eastlake, C. L. *A history of the Gothic revival*. London, 1872. [The revival in architecture.]

Farley, F. E. *Scandinavian influences in the English romantic movement*. Boston, 1903.

Haferkorn, R. *Gotik und Ruine in der englischen Dichtung des 18. Jahrhunderts*. Leipzig, 1924.

Hughes, W. J. *Wales and the Welsh in English literature from Shakespeare to Scott*. London, 1924.

Hustvedt, Sigurd. *Ballad criticism in Scandinavia and Great Britain during the eighteenth century*. New York, 1916.

Longueil, A. E. "The word 'Gothic'

in eighteenth century criticism." *MLN*, XXXVIII (1923), 453-60.

Snyder, E. D. *The Celtic revival in English literature, 1760-1800.* Cambridge, Mass., 1923.

Van Tieghem, Paul. "La découverte de la mythologie et de l'ancienne poésie scandinave." In his *Le Préromantisme: études d'histoire littéraire*, Paris, 1924.

Primitivism and the Cult of the "Noble Savage"

(See also under *Theories of Poetry*)

Bissell, Benjamin. *The American Indian in English literature of the eighteenth century.* New Haven, 1925.

Burd, H. A. "The Golden Age idea in eighteenth-century poetry." *Sewanee review*, XXIII (1915), 172-85.

Fairchild, H. N. *The noble savage: a study in romantic naturalism.* New York, 1928. [Cf. *PQ*, VIII, 174-75.]

Farley, F. E. "The dying Indian." *Anniversary papers by colleagues and pupils of George Lyman Kittredge* (Boston, 1913), pp. 251-60.

——— "Three 'Lapland songs.'" *PMLA*, XXI (1906), 1-39.

Lovejoy, A. O. "The supposed primitivism of Rousseau's *Discourse on inequality*." *MP*, XXI (1923), 165-86.

Tinker, C. B. *Nature's simple plan.* Princeton, 1922. [Cf. *MLN*, XXXIX, 291-97.]

"The Return to Nature"

Beatty, J. M., Jr. "The English Lake district before Wordsworth." *South Atlantic quarterly*, XXII (1923), 331-44.

Biese, Alfred. *The development of the feeling for nature in the Middle Ages and modern times.* London and New York, 1905.

Brooke, Stopford A. *Naturalism in English poetry.* London, 1920.

Das, P. K. *Evidences of a growing taste for nature in the age of Pope.* Calcutta, 1928.

Ellis, Havelock. "The love of wild nature." *Contemporary review*, XCV (1909), 180-99.

Engel, Claire-Eliane. *La littérature alpestre en France et en Angleterre au XVIIIe et au XIXe siècle.* Chambéry, 1930. [Cf. *PQ*, XI, 175-77.]

Haas, C. E. de. *Nature and the country in English poetry of the first half of the eighteenth century.* Amsterdam, 1928.

Havens, R. D. "Nature in the early eighteenth century." *Nation* (New York), March 26, 1914, p. 329.

Hussey, Christopher. *The picturesque: studies in a point of view.* London and New York, 1927.

Manwaring, Elizabeth. *Italian landscape in eighteenth century England: a study chiefly of the influence of Claude Lorrain and Salvator Rosa on English taste, 1700-1800.* New York, 1925.

Martin, A. C. "The love of solitude in eighteenth century poetry." *South Atlantic quarterly*, XXIX (1930), 48-59.

Moore, C. A. "Berkeley's influence on popular literature." *South Atlantic quarterly*, XIV (1915), 263-78.

——— "A predecessor of Thomson's *Seasons*." *MLN*, XXXIV (1919), 278-81.

——— "The return to nature in English poetry of the eighteenth century." *SP*, XIV (1917), 243-91. [An important article.]

Palgrave, Francis T. *Landscape in poetry from Homer to Tennyson.* London, 1897.

Reynolds, Myra. *The treatment of nature in English poetry between Pope and Wordsworth.* 2d ed. Chicago, 1909.

Shairp, John C. *On poetic interpretation of nature.* London and New York, 1877.

Van Tieghem, Paul. "L'automne dans la poésie ouest-européenne de Brockes à Lamartine (1720-1820)." *Mélanges Baldensperger* (Paris, 1930), II, 327-43.

Veitch, John. *The feeling for nature*

in Scottish poetry. Edinburgh and London, 1887. 2 vols.

Williams, George G. "The beginnings of nature poetry in the eighteenth century." *SP*, XXVII (1930), 583-608.

The Cult of Melancholy

Draper, John W. *The funeral elegy and the rise of English romanticism.* New York, 1929.

Havens, R. D. "Literature of melancholy." *MLN*, XXIV (1909), 226-27.

Kalkühler, F. *Die Natur des Spleens bei den englischen Schriftstellern in der ersten Hälfte des 18. Jahrhunderts.* Leipzig, 1920.

Moore, C. A. "John Dunton: pietist and impostor." *SP*, XXII (1925), 467-99.

Reed, Amy L. *The background of Gray's Elegy: a study in the taste for melancholy poetry, 1700-1751.* New York, 1924.

Van Tieghem, Paul. "La poésie de la nuit et des tombeaux." In his *Le Préromantisme: études d'histoire littéraire*, 2d series, Paris, 1930.

Humanitarianism and Sensibility

Crane, Verner W. "The philanthropists and the genesis of Georgia." *American historical review*, XXVII (1921), 63-69.

Harwood, Dix. *Love for animals and how it developed in Great Britain.* New York, 1928.

Klingberg, F. J. *The anti-slavery movement in England: a study in English humanitarianism.* New Haven, 1926.

Moore, C. A. "Shaftesbury and the ethical poets in England, 1700-1760." *PMLA*, XXXI (1916), 264-325. [A valuable article in spite of the fact that it exaggerates somewhat the novelty of Shaftesbury's ideas and hence the importance of his influence. Cf. *PQ*, XI, 204-06.]

——— "Whig panegyric verse, 1700-1760: a phase of sentimentalism." *PMLA*, XLI (1926), 362-401.

Poetic Schools and Groups

Hesselgrave, Ruth A. *Lady Miller and the Batheaston literary circle.* New Haven, 1927.

Lewis, Saunders. *A school of Welsh Augustans.* London, 1924.

Longaker, John M. *The Della Cruscans and William Gifford.* Philadelphia, 1924.

Whibley, Charles. "The court poets." In his *Literary studies*, London, 1919.

EDITIONS AND STUDIES OF INDIVIDUAL POETS

Joseph Addison

The Works of Joseph Addison. With notes by Richard Hurd. Ed. H. G. Bohn. London, 1863-69. 6 vols.

The Miscellaneous works of Joseph Addison. Ed. A. C. Guthkelch. London, 1914. 2 vols.

Selections from the writings of Joseph Addison. Ed. Barrett Wendell and C. N. Greenough. Boston, 1905.

Aikin, Lucy. *The life of Joseph Addison.* London, 1843. 2 vols.

Courthope, W. J. *Addison.* London, 1884. ("English men of letters.")

Dobrée, Bonamy. "The first Victorian." In his *Essays in biography*, London, 1925.

Johnson, Samuel. "Addison." In his *Lives of the English poets* (ed. G. B. Hill, Oxford, 1905), II, 79-150.

McCutcheon, R. P. "Addison and the *Muses mercury*." *SP*, XX (1923), 17-28.

Mark Akenside

Williams, I. A. "Mark Akenside." In his *Seven XVIIIth century bibliographies*, London, 1924.

The Poetical works of Mark Akenside. Ed. A. Dyce. London, 1894. ("Aldine edition.")

The Poetical Works of Mark Akenside and John Dyer. Ed. R. A. Willmott. London, 1855.

Bucke, Charles. *On the life, writings, and genius of Akenside*. London, 1832.

Bundt, Otto. "Akenside's Leben und Werke, mit besonderer Berücksichtigung der 'Pleasures of imagination.'" *Anglia*, XX (1898), 1-44, 467-532; XXI (1899), 89-164.

Chapman, R. W. "A note on the first edition of *The pleasures of imagination*." *RES*, I (1925), 346-48.

Johnson, Samuel. "Akenside." In his *Lives of the English Poets* (ed. G. B. Hill, Oxford, 1905), III, 411-20.

Potter, G. R. "Mark Akenside, prophet of evolution." *MP*, XXIV (1926), 55-64.

Christopher Anstey

Williams, I. A. [Bibliography of the first editions of Anstey.] *LM*, XI (1925), 300-02, 414-17, 526-28, 643-44; XII (1925), 194, 300-01.

The Poetical works of the late Christopher Anstey, Esq. London, 1808.

Maier, Walter. *Christopher Anstey und der "New Bath guide."* Heidelberg, 1914.

The Anti-Jacobin

The Poetry of the Anti-Jacobin. Ed. Charles Edmonds. 3d ed. London, 1890.

——— Ed. L. Rice-Oxley. Oxford, 1924.

Philip Ayres

Saintsbury, George. "Philip Ayres." *Bibliographer*, II (1903), 215-24.

James Beattie

The Poetical works of James Beattie. Ed. A. Dyce. London, 1894. ("Aldine edition.")

Forbes, Margaret. *Beattie and his friends*. Westminster, 1904.

Forbes, Sir William. *An account of the life and writings of James Beattie*. London, 1807, 2 vols.

George Berkeley

The Works of George Berkeley. Ed. A. C. Fraser. Oxford, 1871. 3 vols.

Tyler, Moses Coit. "George Berkeley and his American visit." In his *Three men of letters*, New York, 1895.

Robert Blair

The Works of the English poets. Ed. A. Chalmers. London, 1810. Vol. XV.

Drake, W. A. "A note on Robert Blair." *Freeman*, VIII (1924), 516-18.

William Blake

Keynes, Geoffrey. *A bibliography of William Blake.* New York and London, 1921.

The Writings of William Blake. Ed. Geoffrey Keynes. London, 1925. 3 vols.

Poetry and prose of William Blake. Ed. Geoffrey Keynes. London, 1927. [The best one volume edition.]

The Poetical works of William Blake. Ed. John Sampson. Oxford, 1905.

The Prophetic writings of William Blake. Ed. D. J. Sloss and J. P. R. Wallis. Oxford, 1926. 2 vols.

Berger, Pierre. *William Blake, poet and mystic.* Translated from the French by D. H. Conner. London, 1914.

Bruce, Harold L. "William Blake and Gilchrist's 'remarkable coterie of advanced thinkers.'" *MP*, XXIII (1926), 285-92.

——— *William Blake in this world.* New York, 1925.

Burdett, Osbert. *William Blake.* London, 1926. ("English men of letters.")

Damon, S. Foster. *William Blake: his philosophy and symbols.* Boston, 1924.

Fehr, Bernhard. "William Blake und die Kabbala." *ES*, LIV (1920), 139-48.

Nicoll, Allardyce. *William Blake and his poetry.* London, 1922.

Plowman, Max. *An introduction to the study of Blake.* London and New York, 1927.

Saurat, Denis. *Blake and Milton.* Paris, 1920; New York, 1924.

——— *Blake & modern thought.* London and New York, 1929. [An important study of the sources of Blake's thought.]

——— "Blake et les Celtomanes." *MP*, XXIII (1925), 175-88.

Swinburne, A. C. *William Blake, a critical essay.* London, 1868.

White, Helen C. *The mysticism of William Blake.* Madison, Wis., 1927.

Wicksteed, Joseph H. *Blake's Innocence and Experience: a study of the songs and manuscripts "shewing the two contrary states of the human soul."* London and New York, 1928.

Wilson, Mona. *The life of William Blake.* London, 1927. [The best biography.]

Wright, Thomas. *The life of William Blake.* Olney, Bucks, 1929.

William Lisle Bowles

The Poetical works of William Lisle Bowles. Ed. George Gilfillan. Edinburgh, 1855. 2 vols.

A Wiltshire parson and his friends: the correspondence of William Lisle Bowles. Ed. Garland Greever. Boston and London, 1926.

William Broome

The Works of the English poets. Ed. A. Chalmers. London, 1810. Vol. XII.

Johnson, Samuel. "Broome." In his *Lives of the English poets* (ed. G. B. Hill, Oxford, 1905), III, 75-81.

John Sheffield, Duke of Buckinghamshire

The Works of the English poets. Ed. A. Chalmers. London, 1810. Vol. X.

Johnson, Samuel. "Sheffield, Buckinghamshire." In his *Lives of the English poets* (ed. G. B. Hill, Oxford, 1905), II, 167-77.

Robert Burns

The Poetry of Robert Burns. Ed. W. E. Henley and T. F. Henderson. Edinburgh, 1896-97. 4 vols. ("Centenary edition.")

The Complete poetical works of Robert Burns. Ed. J. Logie Robertson. London, 1896. 3 vols.

The Poetical works of Robert Burns. Ed. J. Logie Robertson. London, 1916. ("Oxford edition.")

Scottish poems of Robert Burns in his native dialect. Ed. Sir James Wilson. London, 1925.

The Songs of Robert Burns. Ed. J. C. Dick. London, 1903.

The Letters of Robert Burns. Ed. J. DeLancey Ferguson. Oxford, 1931. 2 vols.

Angellier, A. *Étude sur la vie et les œuvres de Robert Burns.* Paris, 1892. 2 vols.

Carlyle, Thomas. "Burns." *Edinburgh review,* XLVIII (1828), 267-312. Many later reprints.

Carswell, Catherine. *The life of Robert Burns.* London, 1930.

Craigie, William A. *A primer of Burns.* London, 1896.

Ferguson, J. DeLancey. "Some notes on Burns's reading." *MLN,* XLV (1930), 370-77.

Hecht, Hans. *Robert Burns: Leben und Wirken des schottischen Volksdichters.* Heidelberg, 1919.

McNaught, D. *The truth about Burns.* Glasgow, 1922.

Marsh, George L. "The text of Burns." *The Manly anniversary studies in language and literature* (Chicago, 1923), 219-28.

Neilson, William Allan. "Burns in English." *Anniversary papers by colleagues and pupils of George Lyman Kittredge* (Boston, 1913), pp. 165-69.

——— *Robert Burns: how to know him.* Indianapolis, Ind., 1917.

Snyder, Franklyn B. "A note on Burns's language." *MLN,* XLIII (1928), 511-18.

——— "Notes on Burns and England." *MLN,* XXXVII (1922), 76-82.

——— "Notes on Burns and the popular ballads." *JEGP,* XVII (1918), 281-88.

——— "Notes on Burns and Thomson." *JEGP,* XIX (1920), 305-17.

——— "Notes on Burns's first volume." *MP,* XVI (1919), 475-83.

——— *The life of Robert Burns.* New York, 1932.

Stevenson, Robert Louis. "Some aspects of Robert Burns." In his *Familiar studies of men and books,* London, 1882.

Wilson, Sir James. *The dialect of Robert Burns as spoken in central Ayrshire.* London, 1923.

Samuel Butler

Hudibras. Ed. Zachary Grey. London, 1744. 2 vols.

Hudibras. Ed. A. R. Waller. Cambridge, 1905. [The best modern edition.]

Characters and passages from notebooks. Ed. A. R. Waller. Cambridge, 1908.

Satires and miscellaneous poetry and prose. Ed. René Lamar. Cambridge, 1928.

Craig, Hardin. "*Hudibras,* Part I, and the politics of 1647." *The Manly anniversary studies in language and literature* (Chicago, 1923), pp. 145-55.

Curtiss, J. T. "Butler's *Sidrophel.*" *PMLA,* XLIV (1929), 1066-78.

deBeer, E. S. "The later life of Samuel Butler." *RES,* IV (1928), 159-66.

Johnson, Samuel. "Butler." In his

Lives of the English poets (ed. G. B. Hill, Oxford, 1905), I, 201-18.

Lamar, René. "Du nouveau sur l'auteur d'*Hudibras*." *RAA*, I (1924), 213-27.

Veldkamp, Jan. *Samuel Butler, the author of Hudibras.* Hilversum. 1924.

John Byrom

The Poems of John Byrom. Ed. A. W. Ward. Manchester, 1894-1912. 3 vols.

Henry Carey

The Poems of Henry Carey. Ed. F. T. Wood. London, 1930.

Thomas Chatterton

The Poetical works of Thomas Chatterton. Ed. W. W. Skeat. London, 1875. 2 vols. ("Aldine edition.")

The Rowley poems by Thomas Chatterton. Reprinted from Tyrwhitt's third edition. Ed. M. E. Hare. Oxford, 1911.

Ellinger, Esther P. *Thomas Chatterton, the marvellous boy.* Philadelphia, 1930.

Meyerstein, E. H. W. *A life of Thomas Chatterton.* London, 1930; New York, 1931.

Powell, L. F. "Thomas Tyrwhitt and the Rowley poems." *RES*, VII (1931), 314-26.

Richter, Helene. *Thomas Chatterton.* Vienna and Leipzig, 1900.

Philip Dormer Stanhope, Earl of Chesterfield

The Poetical works of Lord Chesterfield. London, 1927.

Charles Churchill

Williams, I. A. "Charles Churchill." In his *Seven XVIII*[th] *century bibliographies*, London, 1924.

The Poetical works of Charles Churchill. Ed. W. Tooke and J. Hannay. London, 1892. 2 vols. ("Aldine edition.")

Beatty, Joseph M., Jr. "An essay in critical biography — Charles Churchill." *PMLA*, XXXV (1920), 226-46.

——— "Charles Churchill's treatment of the couplet." *PMLA*, XXXIV (1919), 60-69.

——— "Churchill's influence on minor eighteenth century satirists." *PMLA*, XLII (1927), 162-76.

——— "The political satires of Charles Churchill." *SP*, XVI (1919), 303-33.

"Charles Churchill." *TLS*, February 5, 1931, pp. 85-86.

Putschi, Ferdinand. *Charles Churchill, sein Leben und seine Werke.* Vienna and Leipzig, 1909.

Colley Cibber

An Apology for the life of Mr. Colley Cibber. Written by himself. Ed. Robert W. Lowe. London, 1889. 2 vols.

William Collins

Williams, I. A. "William Collins." In his *Seven XVIIIth century bibliographies*, London, 1924.

The Poems of William Collins. Ed. W. C. Bronson. Boston, 1898. ("Athenæum Press series.") [An excellent annotated edition.]

The Poems of William Collins. Ed. Edmund Blunden. London, 1929.

Persian eclogues, 1742. London, 1925. [Type-facsimile edition.]

Odes on several descriptive and allegorical subjects, 1747. London, 1926. ("Noel Douglas replicas.")

Garrod, H. W. *Collins*. Oxford, 1928.

Johnson, Samuel. "Collins." In his *Lives of the English poets* (ed. G. B. Hill, Oxford, 1905), III, 334-42.

Legouis, Pierre. "Les amours de Dieu chez Collins et Milton." *RAA*, VIII (1930), 136-38.

McKillop, A. D. "The romanticism of William Collins." *SP*, XX (1923), 1-16.

Murry, J. M. "The poetry of William Collins." In his *Countries of the mind*, London, 1922.

White, H. O. "The letters of William Collins." *RES*, III (1927), 12-21.

——— "William Collins and his contemporary critics." *TLS*, January 5, 12, 1922, pp. 12, 28.

Woodhouse, A. S. P. "Collins and Martin Martin." *TLS*, December 20, 1928, p. 1011. [On the sources of the *Ode on the popular superstitions of the Highlands*.]

——— "Collins and the creative imagination: a study in the critical background of his odes (1746)." *Studies in English by members of University College, Toronto* (Toronto, 1931), pp. 59-130. [A valuable study.]

——— "Collins in the eighteenth century." *TLS*, October 16, 1930, p. 838.

William Congreve

The Complete works of William Congreve. Ed. Montague Summers. London, 1923. 4 vols.

The Works of Congreve. Ed. F. W. Bateson. London, 1930.

Ball, F. Elrington. "Congreve as a ballad-writer." *Notes & queries*, 12th series, VIII (1921), 301-03.

Gosse, Edmund. *Life of William Congreve*. Rev. ed. London, 1924.

Johnson, Samuel. "Congreve." In his *Lives of the English poets* (ed. G. B. Hill, Oxford, 1905), II, 212-34.

Protopopescu, D. *Un classique moderne: William Congreve, sa vie, son œuvre*. Paris, 1924.

Taylor, D. Crane. *William Congreve*. Oxford, 1931.

Charles Cotton

Poems of Charles Cotton. Ed. John Beresford. London, 1923.

Beresford, John. "The poetry of Charles Cotton." *LM*, V (1921), 57-69.

Sembower, C. J. *The life and the poetry of Charles Cotton*. Philadelphia, 1911.

Abraham Cowley

The Complete works in verse and prose of Abraham Cowley. Ed. A. B. Grosart. London, 1881. 2 vols. ("The Chertsey worthies library.")

The English writings of Abraham Cowley. Ed. A. R. Waller. Cambridge, 1905-06. 2 vols.

The Mistress, with her select poems of Abraham Cowley. Ed. John Sparrow. London, 1926.

Aldington, Richard. "Cowley and the French epicureans." In his *Literary studies and reviews*, London and New York, 1924.

"Cowley's lyrics." *TLS*, November 18, 1926, pp. 805-06.

Gosse, Edmund. "Abraham Cowley." In his *Seventeenth century studies*, London, 1883.

Johnson, Samuel. "Cowley." In his *Lives of the English poets* (ed. G. B. Hill, Oxford, 1905), I, 1-65.

Loiseau, Jean. *Abraham Cowley's reputation in England.* Paris, 1931.

——— *Abraham Cowley, sa vie, son œuvre.* Paris, 1931. [The most elaborate literary study of Cowley, with a useful bibliography.]

McBryde, J. M. "A study of Cowley's *Davideis.*" *JEGP*, II (1898), 454-527; III (1900), 24-34.

Nethercot, Arthur H. *Abraham Cowley, the muse's Hannibal.* Oxford, 1931.

——— "The relation of Cowley's 'Pindarics' to Pindar's odes." *MP*, XIX (1921), 107-09.

——— "The reputation of Abraham Cowley (1660-1800)." *PMLA*, XXXVIII (1923), 588-641.

William Cowper

The Complete poetical works of William Cowper. Ed. H. S. Milford. London, 1913. [The best modern edition.]

The Unpublished and uncollected poems of William Cowper. Ed. Thomas Wright. London, 1900.

Neve, John. *A concordance to the poetical works of William Cowper.* London, 1887.

Bagehot, Walter. "William Cowper." In his *Literary studies*, London, 1879.

Brooke, Stopford A. *Theology in the English poets: Cowper, Coleridge, Wordsworth, and Burns.* 6th ed. London, 1880.

Cecil, David. *The stricken deer, or the life of Cowper.* London, 1929.

Fausset, Hugh I'Anson. *William Cowper.* London, 1928.

Förster, Max. "Cowpers Ballade 'John Gilpin': Textgestalt, Verbreitung und Fortsetzungen." *ES*, LXIV (1929), 380-416; LXV (1930), 26-48.

Holmes, E. D. "The question of Cowper's indebtedness to Churchill." *MLN*, XIII (1898), 330-39.

Smith, Goldwin. *Cowper.* New York, 1880. ("English men of letters.")

Stephen, Leslie. "Cowper and Rousseau." In his *Hours in a library*, new ed., London, 1905, vol. III.

Wright, Thomas. *The life of William Cowper.* 2d ed. London, 1921. [The standard biography.]

George Crabbe

The Works of the Rev. George Crabbe. London, 1832. 5 vols.

The Poems of George Crabbe. Ed. A. W. Ward. Cambridge, 1905-07. 3 vols.

Ainger, Alfred. *Crabbe.* London and New York, 1903. ("English men of letters.")

Bär, Horst. *George Crabbe als Epiker.* Leipzig, 1929.

Huchon, René. *George Crabbe and his times, 1754-1832.* Translated from the French by Frederick Clarke. London, 1907.

Stephen, Leslie. "Crabbe's poetry." In his *Hours in a library*, 2d series, London, 1876.

Wylie, Laura J. "The England of George Crabbe." In her *Social studies in English literature*, New York, 1916.

John Cunningham

The Works of the English poets. Ed. A. Chalmers. London, 1810. Vol. XIV.

Sir William Davenant

The Works of the English poets. Ed. A. Chalmers. London, 1810. Vol. VI.

Gronauer, Georg. *Sir William Davenant's "Gondibert": eine literarhistorische Untersuchung.* Erlangen, 1911.

Daniel Defoe

The Shakespeare Head edition of the novels and selected works of Daniel Defoe. Oxford, 1927-28. 14 vols.

Guthkelch, A. C. "Defoe's *True-born Englishman.*" *Essays and studies by members of the English Association,* IV (1913), 101-50. [An edition of the poem with introduction and notes.]

Dottin, Paul. *Daniel De Foe et ses romans.* Paris, 1924. 3 vols.

Fischer, Walther. "Defoe und Milton." *ES,* LVIII (1924), 213-27.

Trent, W. P. *Daniel Defoe: how to know him.* Indianapolis, Ind., 1916.

Wright, Thomas. *The life of Daniel Defoe.* Bi-centenary ed. London, 1931.

Sir John Denham

The Poetical works of Sir John Denham. Ed. T. H. Banks, Jr. New Haven, 1928.

Banks, T. H., Jr. "The personal relations between Denham and Waller." *MLN,* XLII (1927), 372-78.

——— "Sir John Denham's *Cooper's Hill.*" *MLR,* XXI (1926), 269-77.

Johnson, Samuel. "Denham." In his *Lives of the English poets* (ed. G. B. Hill, Oxford, 1905), I, 70-82.

George Bubb Dodington, Lord Melcombe

Courtney, W. P. "George Bubb Dodington and his literary circle." In his *Dodsley's Collection of poetry, its contents & contributors,* London, 1910.

Robert Dodsley

The Works of the English poets. Ed. A. Chalmers, London, 1910. Vol. XV.

Straus, Ralph. *Robert Dodsley, poet, publisher & playwright.* London, 1910.

John Dryden

Dobell, P. J. *John Dryden: bibliographical memoranda.* London, 1922.

A Dryden library. A catalogue of printed books, manuscripts, and autograph letters by John Dryden. Collected by T. J. Wise. London, 1930.

The Works of John Dryden. Ed. Sir Walter Scott and George Saintsbury. Edinburgh, 1882-93. 18 vols.

The Poetical works of John Dryden. Ed. W. D. Christie. London, 1870. ("Globe edition.") [Useful for its notes.]

The Poetical works of John Dryden. Ed. G. R. Noyes. Boston and New York, 1908. ("Cambridge edition.")

The Poems of John Dryden. Ed. John Sargeaunt. London, 1910. ("Oxford edition.") [The best text.]

Annus Mirabilis, the year of wonders, 1666. Type-facsimile reprint of the first edition, 1667. Oxford, 1927.

MacFlecknoe, 1682. Oxford, 1924. [Type-facsimile edition.]

Essays of John Dryden. Ed. W. P. Ker. Oxford, 1900. 2 vols.

Babington, Percy L. "Dryden not the author of 'MacFlecknoe.'" *MLR*, XIII (1918), 25-34. [Argues that the author was John Oldham. See the replies of H. M. Belden, *MLN*, XXXIII (1918), 449-56, and G. Thorn-Drury, *MLR*, XIII (1918), 276-81.]

Bredvold, Louis I. "Dryden, Hobbes, and the Royal Society." *MP*, XXV (1928), 417-38.

Diffenbaugh, Guy L. *The rise and development of the mock heroic poem in England from 1660 to 1714: Dryden's "MacFlecknoe."* Urbana, Ill., 1926.

Eliot, T. S. *Homage to John Dryden.* London, 1924.

Ellis, Amanda M. "Horace's influence on Dryden." *PQ*, IV (1925), 39-60.

Jameson, R. D. "Notes on Dryden's lost prosodia." *MP*, XX (1923), 241-53. [On his theory of versification.]

Johnson, Samuel. "Dryden." In his *Lives of the English poets* (ed. G. B. Hill, Oxford, 1905), I, 331-481.

Jones, R. F. "The originality of *Absalom and Achitophel.*" *MLN*, XLVI (1931), 211-18.

Kaye, F. B. "La Rochefoucauld and the character of Zimri." *MLN*, XXXIX (1924), 251.

Nicoll, Allardyce. *Dryden and his poetry.* London, 1923.

Root, Robert K. "Dryden's conversion to the Roman Catholic faith." *PMLA*, XXII (1907), 298-308.

Saintsbury, George. *Dryden.* London, 1881. ("English men of letters.")

Thorn-Drury, G. "Some notes on Dryden." *RES*, I (1925), 79-83, 187-97, 324-30.

Van Doren, Mark. *The poetry of John Dryden.* New York, 1920. [Excellent literary criticism.]

Verrall, A. W. *Lectures on Dryden.* Cambridge, 1914.

Wolf, J. Q. "A note on Dryden's Zimri." *MLN*, XLVII (1932), 97-99.

John Dyer

The Poetical works of Mark Akenside and John Dyer. Ed. Robert A. Willmott. London, 1855. [The best edition.]

The Poems of John Dyer. Ed. Edward Thomas. London, 1903.

Greever, Garland. "The two versions of 'Grongar Hill.'" *JEGP*, XVI (1917), 274-81.

Hughes, Helen Sard. "John Dyer and the Countess of Hertford." *MP*, XXVII (1930), 311-20.

Johnson, Samuel. "Dyer." In his *Lives of the English poets* (ed. G. B. Hill, Oxford, 1905), III, 343-47.

Thomas Edwards

Rinaker, Clarissa. "Thomas Edwards and the sonnet revival." *MLN*, XXXIV (1919), 272-77.

Sir George Etherege

The Works of Sir George Etherege. Ed. H. F. B. Brett-Smith. Oxford, 1927—.

Dobrée, Bonamy. "His Excellency Sir George Etherege." In his *Essays in biography,* London, 1925.

Meindl, Vincenz. *Sir George Etheredge, sein Leben, seine Zeit und seine Dramen.* Vienna and Leipzig, 1901.

Robert Fergusson

The Works of Robert Fergusson. Ed. A. B. Grosart. London, 1851.

Scots poems. Ed. Bruce Dickins. Edinburgh, 1925.

Green, F. C. *Robert Fergusson's Anteil an der Literatur Schottlands.* Heidelberg, 1923.

Grosart, A. B. *Robert Fergusson.* Edinburgh and London, 1898.

Henry Fielding

The Works of Henry Fielding. Ed. Leslie Stephen. London, 1882. 10 vols.

Banerji, H. K. *Henry Fielding: playwright, journalist and master of the art of fiction, his life and works.* Oxford, 1929.

Cross, W. L. *The history of Henry Fielding.* New Haven, 1918. 3 vols.

Dobson, Austin. *Henry Fielding, a memoir.* Revised ed. New York, 1900.

Thomas Flatman

Minor poets of the Caroline period. Ed. George Saintsbury. Vol. III. Oxford, 1921.

Child, F. A. *The life and uncollected poems of Thomas Flatman.* Philadelphia, 1921.

Murry, J. M. "Thomas Flatman." In his *Countries of the mind,* 2d series, London, 1931.

Samuel Garth

The Works of the English poets. Ed. A. Chalmers. London, 1810. Vol. IX.

Garth's Dispensary. Ed. W. J. Leicht. Heidelberg, 1905.

Johnson, Samuel. "Garth." In his *Lives of the English poets* (ed. G. B. Hill, Oxford, 1905), II, 57-64.

Schenk, Theodor. *Sir Samuel Garth und seine Stellung zum komischen Epos.* Heidelberg, 1900.

John Gay

The Poetical works of John Gay. Ed. J. Underhill. London, 1893. ("The muses' library.")

The Poetical works of John Gay. Ed. G. C. Faber. London, 1926.

The Shepherd's week. Ed. H. F. B. Brett-Smith. Oxford, 1924. [A facsimile reprint of the first edition.]

Trivia: or the art of walking the streets of London. Ed. W. H. Williams. London, 1922.

Irving, W. H. *John Gay's London.* Cambridge, Mass., 1928. [On the literary and social background of *Trivia.*]

Johnson, Samuel. "Gay." In his *Lives of the English poets* (ed. G. B. Hill, Oxford, 1905), II, 267-85.

Melville, Lewis. *Life and letters of John Gay.* London, 1921. [A rather untrustworthy compilation.]

Schultz, W. E. *Gay's Beggar's Opera: its content, history and influence.* New Haven, 1923.

Swaen, A. E. H. "The airs and tunes of John Gay's Beggar's Opera." *Anglia,* XLIII (1919), 152-90.

Oliver Goldsmith

Williams, I. A. "Oliver Goldsmith." In his *Seven XVIIIth century bibliographies,* London, 1924.

The Works of Oliver Goldsmith. Ed. J. W. M. Gibbs. London, 1884-86. 5 vols.

The Complete poetical works of Oliver Goldsmith. Ed. Austin Dobson. London, 1906. [The most fully annotated edition.]

New Essays by Oliver Goldsmith. Ed. R. S. Crane. Chicago, 1927. [May be consulted for the genesis of *The Traveller* and *The Deserted village.*]

The Collected letters of Oliver Goldsmith. Ed. K. C. Balderston. Cambridge, 1928.

The Deserted village. London, 1927. ("Noel Douglas replicas.") [Facsimile of first edition, 1770.]

Balderston, K. C. "The birth of Goldsmith." *TLS*, March 7, 1929, pp. 185-86.

Dobson, Austin. *Life of Oliver Goldsmith.* London, 1888.

Forster, John. *The life and times of Oliver Goldsmith.* 2d ed. London, 1854. 2 vols.

Patton, Julia. *The English village: a literary study, 1750-1850.* New York, 1919. [On the background of *The Deserted village.*]

Prior, James. *The life of Oliver Goldsmith, M.B.* London, 1837. 2 vols.

Scott, Temple. *Oliver Goldsmith, bibliographically and biographically considered.* London, 1928.

James Grainger

The Works of the English poets. Ed. A. Chalmers. London, 1810. Vol. XIV.

Knox, R. A. "A neglected poet." *LM*, VIII (1923), 45-51.

Thomas Gray

Northup, C. S. *A bibliography of Thomas Gray.* New Haven, 1917.

The Works of Thomas Gray in prose and verse. Ed. Edmund Gosse. London, 1884. 4 vols. Revised ed. London, 1902-06.

The Poetical works of Thomas Gray, English and Latin. Ed. John Bradshaw. London, 1891. ("Aldine edition.")

Selections from the poetry and prose of Thomas Gray. Ed. W. L. Phelps. Boston, 1894. ("Athenæum press series.")

Gray's English poems. Ed. D. C. Tovey. Cambridge, 1898.

An Elegy written in a country churchyard. Ed. F. G. Stokes. Oxford, 1929.

The Letters of Thomas Gray. Ed. D. C. Tovey. London, 1900-12. 3 vols.

Cook, A. S. *A concordance to the English poems of Thomas Gray.* Boston and New York, 1908.

Fothergill, Roy. "An early influence on the poetry of Gray." *Revue de littérature comparée,* IX (1929), 565-73. [On Gray and Jean-Baptiste Gresset.]

Gosse, Edmund. *Gray.* London, 1882. ("English men of letters.")

Johnson, Samuel. "Gray." In his *Lives of the English poets* (ed. G. B. Hill, Oxford, 1905), III, 421-42.

Jones, W. Powell. "The contemporary reception of Gray's *Odes.*" *MP*, XXVIII (1930), 61-82.

Kittredge, George Lyman. "Gray's knowledge of Old Norse." In *Selections from the poetry and prose of Thomas Gray*, ed. Phelps (Boston, 1894), pp. xli-l.

Norton, C. E. *The poet Gray as a naturalist.* Boston, 1903.

Shepard, Odell. "A youth to fortune and to fame unknown." *MP*, XX (1923), 347-73.

Snyder, E. D. "Thomas Gray's interest in Celtic." *MP*, XI (1914), 559-79.

Stephen, Leslie. "Gray and his school." In his *Hours in a library* (2d ed., London, 1892), III, 101-38.

Toynbee, Paget. "A newly discovered draft of Gray's lines, 'William Shakespeare to Mrs. Anne.' " *MLR*, XXV (1930), 83-85.

Whibley, Leonard. "The foreign tour of Gray and Walpole." *Black-*

wood's magazine, CCXXVII (1930), 813-27.
——— "Gray's satirical poems." *TLS*, October 9, 1930, p. 805.
——— "Thomas Gray at Eton." *Blackwood's magazine*, CCXXV (1929), 611-23.
——— "Thomas Gray, undergraduate." *Blackwood's magazine*, CCXXVII (1930), 273-86.

Matthew Green

The Works of the English poets. Ed. A. Chalmers. London, 1910. Vol. XV.
The Spleen and other poems. Ed. R. K. Wood. London, 1926.

William Hamilton of Bangour

The Works of the English poets. Ed. A. Chalmers. London, 1810. Vol. XV.
The Poems and songs of William Hamilton of Bangour. Ed. James Paterson. Edinburgh, 1850.
Chalmers, J. "Notices of the life of William Hamilton of Bangour, and a chronological list of his poems." *Archæologia scotica*, III (1831), 255-66.

James Hammond

The Works of the English poets. Ed. A. Chalmers. London, 1810. Vol. XI.
Johnson, Samuel. "Hammond." In his *Lives of the English poets* (ed. G. B. Hill, Oxford, 1905), II, 312-16.

Richard Jago

The Works of the English poets. Ed. A. Chalmers. London, 1810. Vol. XVII.

Samuel Johnson

Courtney, W. P., and D. Nichol Smith. *A bibliography of Samuel Johnson*. Oxford, 1915; reissued, 1925.
The R. B. Adam library relating to Dr. Samuel Johnson and his era. London, 1929. 3 vols.

The Works of Samuel Johnson. London, 1825. 11 vols. ("Oxford English classics.")
London, a poem, and The vanity of human wishes. With an introductory essay by T. S. Eliot. London, 1930.
The Vanity of human wishes, 1749. Oxford, 1927. [Type-facsimile edition.]

Boswell, James. *Life of Samuel Johnson*. Ed. G. B. Hill. Oxford, 1887. 6 vols. [A new edition with notes by L. F. Powell is in preparation.]
Brown, Joseph Epes. *The critical opinions of Samuel Johnson*. Princeton, 1926.
Chapman, R. W. "Dr. Johnson and poetry." *Saturday review of literature*. August 17, 1929, pp. 49-51.
Raleigh, Walter. *Six essays on Johnson*. Oxford, 1910.
Reade, Aleyn Lyell. *Johnsonian gleanings*. London, 1909—.
Roberts, S. C. "*On the death of Dr. Robert Levet*—a note on the text." *RES*, III (1927), 442-45.
Stephen, Leslie. *Samuel Johnson*. London, 1878. ("English men of letters.")

John Langhorne

The Works of the English poets. Ed. A. Chalmers. London, 1810. Vol. XVI.

George Granville, Lord Lansdowne

The Works of the English poets. Ed. A. Chalmers. London, 1810. Vol. XI.

Johnson, Samuel. "Granville." In his *Lives of the English poets* (ed. G. B. Hill, Oxford, 1905), II, 286-96.

George Lyttelton, Baron Lyttelton

The Works of the English poets. Ed. A. Chalmers. London, 1810. Vol. XIV.

Johnson, Samuel. "Lyttelton." In his *Lives of the English poets* (ed. G. B. Hill, Oxford, 1905), III, 446-57.

Roberts, S. C. "An eighteenth-century gentleman." *LM*, XI (1925), 290-97.

James Macpherson

Black, George F. "Macpherson's Ossian and the Ossianic controversy: a contribution towards a bibliography." *Bulletin of the New York Public library*, XXX (1926), 424-39, 508-24.

The Poems of Ossian. Ed. George Eyre-Todd. London, [1888].

——— Ed. William Sharp. London, 1896. ("Centenary edition.")

James Macpherson's Fragments of ancient poetry (1760). Ed. Otto L. Jiriczek. Heidelberg, 1915.

Saunders, Thomas Bailey. *The life and letters of James Macpherson.* London, 1894.

Schnabel, Br. "Ossian in der schönen Literatur England's bis 1832." *ES*, XXIII (1897), 31-70, 366-401.

Smart, J. S. *James Macpherson; an episode in literature.* London, 1905.

Van Tieghem, Paul. *Ossian en France.* Paris, 1917. 2 vols.

——— "Ossian et l'ossianisme au XVIIIe siècle." In his *Le Préromantisme: études d'histoire littéraire*, Paris, 1924.

David Mallet

The Works of the English poets. Ed. A. Chalmers. London, 1810. Vol. XIV.

Johnson, Samuel. "Mallet." In his *Lives of the English poets* (ed. G. B. Hill, Oxford, 1905), III, 400-10.

Swaen, A. E. H. "Fair Margaret and sweet William." *Archiv für das Studium der neueren Sprachen und Literaturen*, CXXXVI (1917), 40-71.

Bernard Mandeville

Kaye, F. B. "The writings of Bernard Mandeville." *JEGP*, XX (1921), 419-67.

The Fable of the bees: or, private vices, publick benefits. Ed. F. B. Kaye. Oxford, 1924. 2 vols.

Andrew Marvell

The Poems and letters of Andrew Marvell. Ed. H. M. Margoliouth. Oxford, 1927. 2 vols.

Eliot, T. S. "Andrew Marvell." In his *Homage to John Dryden*, London, 1924.

Legouis, Pierre. *André Marvell, poète, puritain, patriote, 1621-1678.* Paris, 1928.

William Julius Mickle

The Works of the English poets. Ed. A. Chalmers. London, 1810. Vol. XVII.

Lady Mary Wortley Montagu

The Works of Lady Mary Wortley Montagu. Ed. J. Dallaway. London, 1803. 5 vols.

Melville, Lewis. *Lady Mary Wortley Montagu: her life and letters.* Boston, 1925.

Paston, George. *Lady Mary Wortley Montagu and her times.* London and New York, 1907.

Edward Moore

The Works of the English poets. Ed. A. Chalmers. London, 1810. Vol. XIV.

Caskey, John Homer. *The life and works of Edward Moore.* New Haven, 1927.

Sir John Henry Moore

The Poetical works of Sir John Henry Moore. Ed. Thomas Park. London, 1808.

John Oldham

The Poetical works of John Oldham. Ed. Robert Bell. London, 1854.

Thomas Parnell

The Poetical works of Thomas Parnell. Ed. G. A. Aitken. London, 1894. ("Aldine edition.")

Cruickshank, A. H. "Thomas Parnell, or what was wrong with the eighteenth century." *Essays and studies by members of the English Association,* VII (1921), 57-81.

Johnson, Samuel. "Parnell." In his *Lives of the English poets* (ed. G. B. Hill, Oxford, 1905), II, 49-54.

Thomas Percy

Reliques of ancient English poetry. Ed. H. B. Wheatley. London, 1886. 3 vols.

——— Ed. M. M. Arnold Schröer. Berlin, 1893. [A critical edition.]

Thomas Percy und William Shenstone; ein Briefwechsel aus der Entstehungszeit der Reliques of ancient English poetry. Ed. Hans Hecht. Strassburg, 1909.

Dennis, Leah. "The text of the Percy-Warton letters." *PMLA,* XLVI (1931), 1166-1201.

Gaussen, Alice C. C. *Percy: prelate and poet.* London, 1908.

Kittredge, G. L. "Percy and his Nancy." *Manly anniversary studies in language and literature* (Chicago, 1923), pp. 204-18.

Powell, L. F. "Percy's *Reliques.*" *Library,* 4th series, IX (1928), 113-37.

Rinaker, Clarissa, "Percy as a sonneteer." *MLN,* XXXV (1920), 56-58.

Ambrose Philips

The Works of the English poets. Ed. A. Chalmers. London, 1810. Vol. XIII.

Johnson, Samuel. "A. Philips." In his *Lives of the English poets* (ed. G. B. Hill, Oxford, 1905), III, 312-25.

John Philips

The Works of the English poets. Ed. A. Chalmers. London, 1810. Vol. VIII.

The Poems of John Philips. Ed. M. G. Lloyd Thomas. Oxford, 1927.

Johnson, Samuel. "J. Philips." In his *Lives of the English poets* (ed. G. B. Hill, Oxford, 1905), I, 312-27.

John Pomfret

The Works of the English poets. Ed. A. Chalmers. London, 1810. Vol. VIII.

Johnson, Samuel. "Pomfret." In his *Lives of the English poets* (ed. G. B. Hill, Oxford, 1905), I, 301-02.

Alexander Pope

Griffith, R. H. *Alexander Pope: a bibliography.* Vol. I, Parts i and ii. Austin, Texas, 1922, 1927.

The Works of Alexander Pope. Ed. W. Elwin and W. J. Courthope. London, 1871-89. 10 vols.

The Complete poetical works of Alexander Pope. Ed. H. W. Boynton. Boston and New York, 1903. ("Cambridge edition.") [Includes the translation of Homer.]

Selected poems of Alexander Pope. Ed. Louis I. Bredvold. New York, 1926.

Selections from Alexander Pope. Ed. George Sherburn. New York, 1929. [Excellent introduction and notes.]

The Dunciad variorum with the prolegomena of Scriblerus. Facsimile edition with an introduction by R. K. Root. Princeton, 1929.

Essay on man. Ed. Mark Pattison. Oxford, 1869.

Satires and epistles. Ed. Mark Pattison. 4th ed. cor. Oxford, 1881.

Abbott, Edwin. *A concordance to the works of Alexander Pope.* London, 1875.

Audra, E. *L'influence française dans l'œuvre de Pope.* Paris, 1931.

Case, Arthur E. "Some new poems by Pope." *LM,* X (1924), 614-23.

Chesterton, G. K. "Pope and the art of satire." In his *Twelve types,* London, 1903. Also in his *Varied types,* New York, 1903, etc.

Griffith, R. H. "Pope's satiric portrait of Addison." *Texas review,* VIII (1923), 273-84.

Johnson, Samuel. "Pope." In his *Lives of the English poets* (ed. G. B. Hill, Oxford, 1905), III, 82-272.

Jones, R. F. *Lewis Theobald.* New York, 1919.

Leather, Mary S. "Pope as a student of Milton." *ES,* XXV (1898), 398-410.

Lovejoy, A. O. " 'Pride' in eighteenth-century thought." *MLN,* XXXVI (1921), 31-37. [Important for the interpretation of the *Essay on man.*]

Mackail, J. W. *Pope.* Cambridge, 1919.

McLean, L. Mary. "The riming system of Alexander Pope." *PMLA,* VI (1891), 134-60.

Mead, W. E. *The versification of Pope in its relation to the seventeenth century.* Leipzig, 1889.

Moore, C. A. "Did Leibniz influence Pope's *Essay?*" *JEGP,* XVI (1917), 84-102.

Sitwell, Edith. *Alexander Pope.* London, 1930.

Smith, M. Ellwood. "Four hitherto

unidentified letters by Alexander Pope." *PMLA*, XXIX (1914), 236-55. [Valuable for the history of Pope's satirical portrait of Addison. The letters are probably not by Pope.]

Stephen, Leslie. *Alexander Pope.* London, 1880. ("English men of letters.")

——— "Pope as a moralist." In his *Hours in a library*, London, 1874.

Strachey, Lytton. *Pope.* Cambridge, 1925.

Tupper, James W. "A study of Pope's *Imitations of Horace*." *PMLA*, XV (1900), 181-215.

Warren, Austin. *Alexander Pope as critic and humanist.* Princeton, 1929.

Warton, Joseph. *An essay on the genius and writings of Pope.* London, 1756, 1782. 2 vols.

Wyld, H. C. "Observations on Pope's versification." *MLR*, XXV (1930), 274-85.

Matthew Prior

Aitken, G. A. "Notes on the bibliography of Matthew Prior." *Transactions of the Bibliographical society*, XIV (1919), 39-68.

The Writings of Matthew Prior. Ed. A. R. Waller. Cambridge, 1905, 1907. 2 vols.

The Shorter poems of Matthew Prior. Ed. Francis Bickley. London, 1923. ("Abbey classics.")

Occasional verses, 1702-1709. Oxford, 1927. [Type-facsimile edition.]

Dobson, Austin. "Matthew Prior." In his *Eighteenth century vignettes*, 3d series, New York, 1896.

Doughty, Oswald. "The poet of the 'familiar style.'" *English studies*, VII (1925), 5-10.

Frey, Engelbert. *Der Einfluss der englischen, französischen, italienischen und lateinischen Literatur auf die Dichtungen Matthew Priors.* Strassburg, 1915.

Johnson, Samuel. "Prior." In his *Lives of the English poets* (ed. G. B. Hill, Oxford, 1905), II, 180-211.

Legg, L. G. Wickham. *Matthew Prior, a study of his public career and correspondence.* Cambridge, 1921.

Allan Ramsay

Poems of Allan Ramsay. Selected and arranged by J. L. Robertson. London, 1887.

Chapman, R. W. "Allan Ramsay's *Poems*, 1720." *RES*, III (1927), 343-46.

Gibson, Andrew. *New light on Allan Ramsay.* Edinburgh, 1927.

Mackail, J. W. "Allan Ramsay and the romantic revival." *Essays and studies by members of the English Association*, X (1924).

Martin, Burns. *Allan Ramsay, a study of his life and works.* Cambridge, Mass., 1931.

John Wilmot, Earl of Rochester

Collected works of John Wilmot, Earl of Rochester. Ed. John Hayward. London, 1926.

Johnson, Samuel. "Rochester." In his *Lives of the English poets* (ed. G. B. Hill, Oxford, 1905), I, 219-26.

Prinz, Johannes. *John Wilmot Earl of Rochester, his life and writings.* Leipzig, 1927.

Williamson, George. "The Restoration Petronius." *University of California chronicle*, XXIX (1927), 273-80.

Thomas Russell

The Poems of Cuthbert Shaw and Thomas Russell. Ed. Eric Partridge. London, 1925.

Charles Sackville, Earl of Dorset

The Works of the English poets. Ed. A. Chalmers. London, 1810. Vol. VIII.

Johnson, Samuel. "Dorset." In his *Lives of the English poets* (ed. G. B. Hill, Oxford, 1905), I, 303-08.

Sir Charles Sedley

The Poetical and dramatic works of Sir Charles Sedley. Ed. V. de Sola Pinto. London, 1928. 2 vols.

Lissner, Max. "Sir Charles Sedley's Leben und Werke." *Anglia,* XXVIII (1905), 145-254.

Pinto, V. de Sola. *Sir Charles Sedley, 1639-1701: a study in the life and literature of the Restoration.* London, 1927.

William Shenstone

Williams, I. A. "William Shenstone." In his *Seven XVIIIth century bibliographies,* London, 1924.

The Works of the English poets. Ed. A. Chalmers. London, 1810. Vol. XIII.

Shenstone's The School-mistress, 1742. Oxford, 1924. [Type-facsimile edition.]

Bond, R. P. "Shenstone's heroi-comical poem." *SP,* XXVIII (1931), 742-49.

Hazeltine, Alice I. *A study of William Shenstone and of his critics, with fifteen of his unpublished poems.* Menasha, Wis., 1918.

Hughes, Helen Sard. "Shenstone and the Countess of Hertford." *PMLA,* XLVI (1931), 1113-27.

Johnson, Samuel. "Shenstone." In his *Lives of the English poets* (ed. G. B. Hill, Oxford, 1905), III, 348-59.

Müller, Mathilde. *William Shenstone, ein Vorläufer der englischen Romantik.* Zürich, 1909.

Richard Brinsley Sheridan

Williams, I. A. "Richard Brinsley Sheridan." In his *Seven XVIIIth century bibliographies,* London, 1924.

The Plays and poems of Richard Brinsley Sheridan. Ed. R. Crompton Rhodes. Oxford, 1928. 3 vols.

Sichel, W. S. *Sheridan, from new and original material.* London, 1909. 2 vols.

Christopher Smart

Gray, G. J. "A bibliography of the writings of Christopher Smart." *Transactions of the Bibliographical society,* VI (1903), 269-303.

The Works of the English poets. Ed. A. Chalmers. London, 1810. Vol. XVI.

A Song to David, with other poems. Ed. Edmund Blunden. London, 1924.

A Song to David. Oxford, 1926. [Type-facsimile edition.]

Abbott, C. D. "Christopher Smart's madness." *PMLA,* XLV (1930), 1014-22.

"Christopher Smart (born April 11, 1722)." *TLS,* April 6, 1922, p. 224.

Gosse, Edmund. "Smart's poems." In his *Gossip in a library,* London, 1891.

Tobias Smollett

The Works of the English poets. Ed. A. Chalmers. London, 1810. Vol. XV.

The Letters of Tobias Smollett, M. D. Ed. E. S. Noyes. Cambridge, Mass., 1926.

Buck, Howard S. *Smollett as poet.* New Haven, 1927.

Knapp, Lewis M. "Smollett's verses and their musical settings in the eighteenth century." *MLN*, XLVI (1931), 224-32.

Whitridge, Arnold. *Tobias Smollett: a study of his miscellaneous works.* [New York, 1925.]

William Somervile

The Works of the English poets. Ed. A. Chalmers. London. 1810. Vol. XI.

Johnson, Samuel. "Somervile." In his *Lives of the English poets* (ed. G. B. Hill, Oxford, 1905), II, 317-20.

Jonathan Swift

The Poems of Jonathan Swift. Ed. W. E. Browning. London, 1910.

The Correspondence of Jonathan Swift. Ed. F. Elrington Ball. London, 1910-14. 6 vols.

Vanessa and her correspondence with Swift. Ed. A. M. Freeman. London, 1921.

Ball, F. Elrington. *Swift's verse, an essay.* London, 1929.

Craik, Henry. *The life of Jonathan Swift.* London, 1882.

Davis, Herbert. "Swift's view of poetry." *Studies in English by members of University College, Toronto* (Toronto, 1931), pp. 9-58. [An illuminating essay.]

——— "Verses on the death of Dr. Swift." *Book-collector's quarterly*, No. II (March-May, 1931), pp. 57-73.

Johnson, Samuel. "Swift." In his *Lives of the English poets* (ed. G. B. Hill, Oxford, 1905), III, 1-66.

Pons, Émile. *Swift: les années de jeunesse et le "Conte du tonneau."* Strasbourg and London, 1925.

Stephen, Leslie. *Swift.* London, 1882. ("English men of letters.")

Van Doren, Carl. *Swift.* New York, 1930.

James Thomson

The Complete poetical works of James Thomson. Ed. J. Logie Robertson. London, 1908. ("Oxford edition.") [The best one volume edition.]

Thomson's Seasons. Critical edition by Otto Zippel. Berlin, 1908.

Blau, Armin. *James Thomson's "Seasons": eine genetische Stiluntersuchung.* Berlin, 1910.

Cameron, Margaret M. *L'influence des Saisons de Thomson sur la poésie descriptive en France (1759-1810).* Paris, 1927.

Cronk, Gertrude G. "Lucretius and Thomson's autumnal fogs." *American journal of philology*, LI (1930), 233-42.

Drennon, Herbert. "James Thomson and Newtonianism." University of Chicago *Abstracts of theses*, Humanistic series, VII (1930), 523-28.

Havens, R. D. "Primitivism and the idea of progress in Thomson." *SP*, XXIX (1932), 41-52.

Hughes, Helen Sard. "Thomson and the Countess of Hertford." *MP*, XXV (1928), 439-68; XXVIII (1931), 468-70.

Johnson, Samuel. "Thomson." In his *Lives of the English poets* (ed. G. B. Hill, Oxford, 1905), III, 281-301.

Macaulay, G. C. *Thomson.* London, 1908. ("English men of letters.")

Marcus, Hans. "Die Entstehung von 'Rule Britannia.'" *Beiblatt zur Anglia,* XXXVI (1925), 21-32, 54-64, 78-89, 155-59.

Moore, C. A. "A predecessor of Thomson's *Seasons.*" *MLN,* XXXIV (1919), 278-81.

Morel, Léon. *James Thomson, sa vie et ses œuvres.* Paris, 1895.

Potter, G. R. "James Thomson and the evolution of spirits." *ES,* LXI (1926), 57-65.

Preston, Keith. "Aspects of autumn in Roman poetry." *Classical philology,* XIII (1918), 272-82. [Interesting for the background of Thomson's *Autumn.*]

Wells, J. E. "James Thomson and Milton." *MLN,* XXIV (1909), 60-61.

Zippel, Otto. *Entstehungs- und Entwicklungsgeschichte von Thomsons "Winter."* Berlin, 1907.

Thomas Tickell

The Works of the English poets. Ed. A. Chalmers. London. 1810. Vol. XI.

The Poetical works of Thomas Tickell. Boston, 1854. ("British poets," ed. F. J. Child.)

Butt, J. E. "A 'first edition' of Tickell's 'Colin and Lucy.'" *Bodleian quarterly record,* VI (1930), 103-04.

Johnson, Samuel. "Tickell." In his *Lives of the English poets* (ed. G. B. Hill, Oxford, 1905), II, 304-11.

Tickell, Richard Eustace. *Thomas Tickell and the eighteenth century poets (1685-1740).* London, 1931.

Augustus Montagu Toplady

The Works of Augustus Montagu Toplady. New ed. London, 1825. 6 vols.

Wright, Thomas. *Augustus M. Toplady and contemporary hymn-writers.* London, 1911.

"The Vicar of Bray"

Ward, H. Gordon. "The authorship of the 'Vicar of Bray.'" *Notes & queries,* CLVI (1929), 152.

Edmund Waller

The Poems of Edmund Waller. Ed. G. Thorn-Drury. London, 1893. ("The muses' library.")

Aldington, Richard. "A note on Waller's poems." *Living age,* CCCXII (1912), 179-81.

Johnson, Samuel. "Waller." In his *Lives of the English poets* (ed. G. B. Hill, Oxford, 1905), I, 249-300.

Horace Walpole, Earl of Orford

Horace Walpole's fugitive verses. Ed. W. S. Lewis. New York, 1931.

The Letters of Horace Walpole. Ed. Mrs. Paget Toynbee. Oxford, 1903-05. 16 vols.

——— Supplement. Ed. Paget Toynbee. Oxford, 1918-25. 3 vols.

Dobson, Austin. *Horace Walpole, a memoir.* 4th ed., revised and enlarged by Paget Toynbee. London, 1927.

Stuart, Dorothy M. *Horace Walpole.* London, 1927. ("English men of letters.")

Yvon, Paul. *La vie d'un dilettante: Horace Walpole (1717-1797): essai de biographie psychologique et littéraire*. Paris, 1924.

——— *The poetical ideals of a gentleman author in the XVIIIth century: Horace Walpole as a poet*. Paris, 1924.

William Walsh

The Works of the English poets. Ed. A. Chalmers. London, 1810. Vol. VIII.

Johnson, Samuel. "Walsh." In his *Lives of the English poets* (ed. G. B. Hill, Oxford, 1905), I, 328-30.

Joseph Warton

The Works of the English poets. Ed. A. Chalmers. London, 1810. Vol. XVIII.

The Three Wartons, a choice of their verse. Ed. Eric Partridge. London, 1927.

Lovejoy, A. O. "On the discrimination of romanticisms." *PMLA*, XXXIX (1924), 229-53. [Discusses the significance of Warton's *The Enthusiast*.]

Smith, Audley L. "The primitivism of Joseph Warton." *MLN*, *XLII* (1927), 501-04.

Thomas Warton, Sr.

Poems on several occasions reproduced from the edition of 1748. New York, 1930. ("Facsimile text society.")

Bishop, David H. "The father of the Wartons." *South Atlantic quarterly*, XVI (1917), 357-68.

Willoughby, E. E. "The chronology of the poems of Thomas Warton, the elder." *JEGP*, XXX (1931), 87-89.

Thomas Warton, Jr.

The Works of the English poets. Ed. A. Chalmers. London, 1810. Vol. XVIII.

Verses on Sir Joshua Reynolds's painted window at New College, Oxford, 1782. Oxford, 1930. [Type-facsimile edition.]

Dennis, Leah. "The text of the Percy-Warton letters." *PMLA*, XLVI (1931), 1166-1201.

Havens, R. D. "Thomas Warton and the eighteenth-century dilemma." *SP*, XXV (1928), 36-50.

Hinton, Percival. "Thomas Warton's poems." *TLS*, April 24, 1930, p. 352.

Rinaker, Clarissa. *Thomas Warton, a biographical and critical study*. Urbana, Ill., 1916.

Woodhouse, A. S. P. "Thomas Warton and the 'Ode to horror.'" *TLS*, January 24, May 23, 1929, pp. 62, 420.

Isaac Watts

The Works of the English poets. Ed. A. Chalmers. London, 1810. Vol. XIII.

Johnson, Samuel. "Watts." In his *Lives of the English poets* (ed. G. B. Hill, Oxford, 1905), III, 302-11.

Wright, Thomas. *Isaac Watts and contemporary hymn-writers*. London, 1914.

Charles and John Wesley

The Poetical works of John and Charles Wesley. Ed. G. Osborn. London, 1868-72. 13 vols.

Hatfield, J. T. "John Wesley's translations of German hymns." *PMLA*, XI (1896), 171-99.

Anne Finch, Countess of Winchilsea

The Poems of Anne, countess of Winchilsea, from the original edition of 1713 and from unpublished manuscripts. Ed. Myra Reynolds. Chicago, 1903.

Hughes, Helen Sard. "Lady Winchilsea and her friends." *LM*, XIX (1929), 624-35.

Murry, J. M. "Anne Finch, Countess of Winchilsea (1661-1720)." *New Adelphi*, I (1927), 145-53.

Edward Young

The Poetical works of Edward Young. Ed. J. Mitford. London, 1844, etc. 2 vols. ("Aldine edition.")

Clark, H. H. "The romanticism of Edward Young." *Transactions of the Wisconsin Academy of sciences, arts and letters*, XXIV (1929), 1-45.

——— "A study of melancholy in Edward Young." *MLN*, XXXIX (1924), 129-36, 193-203.

Eliot, George. "Worldliness and other-worldliness: the poet Young." In her *Essays*, 2d ed., London, 1884.

Johnson, Samuel. "Young." In his *Lives of the English poets* (ed. G. B. Hill, Oxford, 1905), III, 361-99.

Shelley, Henry C. *The life and letters of Edward Young.* London, 1914.

Thomas, W. *Le poète Edward Young (1683-1765): étude sur sa vie et ses œuvres.* Paris, 1901.

Glossary of Scottish Words and Expressions

This glossary includes all the words or phrases in the selections from Ramsay, Fergusson, and Burns which might be expected to trouble readers not familiar with the dialects in which those poets worked.

Aboon, above
Abread, abroad
Agley, amiss
Aiblins, perhaps, possibly
Airts, points of the compass
Asklent, aslant
Auld Reikie, Edinburgh
Aumos dish, alms-dish
Ava, at all

Badrins, cats
Bairan, laying bare, stripping (of earth)
Bangs, overcomes
Bannock, thick, round cake
Bassie, an old horse
Bauckie-bird, bat
Bauks, strips, ridges
Baws'nt, streaked with white
Beet, kindle or mend the fire
Beld, bald
Belyve, by and by
Ben, inwards, inside, within
Benmost, farthest in, innermost
Bent, open field
Bicker, wooden dish
Bield, shelter
Bienly, comfortably
Big, build
Birkie, lively smart youth
Birn, burden, load
Blastet, worthless
Blate, shy
Bleez, blaze, get angry
Blellum, idle, talking fellow
Bleth'ran, talking nonsense
Boddle, copper coin of the value of one-sixth of an English penny; hence anything of trifling value
Boortries, elder-trees
Bore, hole, chink
Borrows-town, royal borough
Bousing, drinking
Bowie, milk pail
Brattle, sudden start
Brent, high and unwrinkled
Broachie, small brooch
Brock, badger
Browster wife, ale-wife
Brulzies, fights or disturbances
Buirdly, stalwart, good-looking
Bumman, humming
Busk, adorn, dress, deck
But, without
Butt an' ben, in both outer and inner rooms
Byke, swarm, crowd
Byre, cowhouse

Cadger pownie, huckster's pony
Cadgie, gay
Caff, chaff
Caldrife, chilly
Callet, prostitute
Callor, fresh
Canny, cozy, comfortable
Cantie, contented
Cantrip, magic spell
Canty, pleasant
Capernoity, bad-tempered
Carlin, old woman
Cavie, hen-coop
Chiel, fellow, person
Chiep, cheep, sound
Cleek, clutch
Cod, pillow
Coft, bought
Coof, fool or simpleton
Coost, cast, tossed
Cosh, neat, snug, comfortable
Cour, lower, let sink
Couter, coulter
Couth, social
Crack, conversation, gossip
Crackan, talking
Craigie, throat
Crambo-jingle, doggerel rime
Cranreuch, hoar-frost
Creeshie, greasy
Crouse, cheerful
Cruizy, oil lamp

Crummock, staff with a crooked head
Crump, crisp

Daffin, sport
Dails, deal boards
Daimen-icker, occasional ear (of corn)
Dawds, large pieces of bread
Dawted, petted
Deas, settle, long seat
Deave, worry, bother
Deil-haet, nothing at all
Dight, wipe off; (of wheat) freed from chaff, winnowed
Divets, divots, pieces of turf used in a thatch
Dizzen, dozen (of cuts of yarn)
Doil'd, tired out
Dorty, fastidious
Douce, douse, serious, sober
Dousie, stupid
Dow'd, worn, marked with wear
Dowf, dull
Dowie, dismal, gloomy
Doxy, sweetheart
Driddle, toddle, walk loiteringly
Droddum, breech
Droukit, drenched
Drumlie, muddy, turbid
Duddie, ragged
Duddies, clothes
Duds, ragged clothes
Dung, fatigued
Dwyning, decaying
Dyke, wall

Eidant, diligent
Eldritch, fearful, ghastly
Elson, shoemaker's awl
Ettle, effort, intent, aim
Eydent, see ***Eidant***

Fadge, flat, wheaten loaf
Fain, fond
Fairan, deserts
Farls, oat cakes
Fash'd, troubled
Fatt'rels, ribbon-ends
Fawsont, seemly, respectable
Fecht, fight
Feck, majority
Fek, quantity
Fell, tasty
Ferlie (n.), wonder (here as a term of contempt)
Ferlie (v.), wonder at, marvel
Fidgean-fain, eager and restless
Fidge'd, fidgeted
Fient, fiend, devil
Fient haet, not a whit
Fiere, companion
Fissle, bustle with pleasure
Fitsted, footprint
Fleech, fleetch, flatter, cajole
Fley'd, frightened
Foughten, oppressed
Fow, full
Foy, farewell feast
Fuds, buttocks

Gabs, palates, appetites
Gads, rods or bars (of metal)
Gangrel, vagabond, tramp-like
Gar, make, cause
Gardies, arms
Gash (v.), prattle
Gash (adj.), affable, pleasant
Gausy, gawsie, gawsy, big, jolly, plump
Gear, possessions, property
Geck, scoff, mock, deride
Geordie, gold guinea
Gizz, face
Glaikit, senseless, silly
Glowr, gaze, look
Gowd, gold
Gowk, clown, fool
Graith, tackle, equipment
Grat, wept
Gree (n.), first place, palm, prize
Gree (v.), agree
Grien, long for
Grissle, gristle
Grozet, gooseberry
Grushie, of thriving growth
Gude-willie-waught, hearty drink
Gusty, pleasing to the palate
Gyzen'd, warped

Haffets, locks of hair on the temples
Hafflins (adv.), half
Hafflins-wise, half-ways
Haith, an exclamation of surprise
Hald, dwelling
Hallan, halland, partition-wall; partition in a cottage
Han'-daurk, daily manual labor
Happer, hopper of a mill
Harn, coarse cloth of hemp or flax
Hash, damage
Haughs, low, level ground beside a stream
Hawkies, cows
Hech, an exclamation of surprise
Heese, heeze (n. or v.), lift (in the world); hoist, heave, raise
Hirplan, hobbling
Hirpl'd, limped
Histie, dry
Hizzies, girls, young women
Hoddan, "The motion of a sage

farmer on an old cart horse" (Burns)
Hoddin, homespun cloth
Hotch'd, jerked, moved clumsily
Houghmagandie, fornication
Howcket, howket, exhumed, dug up
Howkan, digging
Hurdies, buttocks
Hynds, farm-servants

Ilka, each, every
Ingine, genius
Ingle, fire

Jads, jades, worthless women

Kail-worms, caterpillars that feed on cabbage
Kane, rent in kind
Kanny, careful
Kebars, rafters
Kebbock, kebbuck, whole cheese
Keek, peep
Kiaugh, anxiety
Kill, kiln
Kirn, harvest-home
Kittle, tickle, touch lightly
Ky, cows

Laithfu', bashful
Lang-kail, cabbage unmashed
Lave, rest, remainder
Lavrocks, larks
Leal (adv.), faithfully, thoroughly; (adj.), loyal
Lean, resting place
Lee-lang, whole, entire
Leeze-me-on, commend me to
Leglin, milk-pail with upright handle
Lerroch, place, site
Leuks, looks
Lift, sky
Limmer, loose woman
Lingle, shoemaker's thread
Linket, tripped along
Linn, waterfall
Loof, palm of the hand
Lowan, flaming
Lowpin, leaping
Lucken gowans, globe flowers
Luntan, smoking, puffing
Lyart, faded, gray

Mailin, farm
Mane, moan, complaint
Marrow, mate
Meikle, much
Melder, quantity of oats ground at one time
Meltith, meal
Melvie, soil with meal
Messan, small dog
Modewurks, moles
Motie, spotted
Multure, toll of meal taken by a miller for grinding corn

Nappy, foaming ale
Nieve, fist
Niffer, exchange, barter
Nowt, cattle

Orra, spare
Owsen, oxen
Oy, grandchild

Painch, paunch
Paitricks, partridges
Pattle, plough-staff
Peghan, stomach
Penny-wheep, small beer
Philibeg, kilt
Pint-stowp, pint-measure
Plack, small coin, one-third of an English penny
Pliver, plover
Poind, impound
Poortith, poverty
Poossie, cat, hare
Pop'ling, bubbling

Raep, rope
Raibles, discourses
Randie, wild, disorderly
Rangles, groups
Rantan, frolicking
Rash-buss, clump of rushes
Ratches, hunting-dogs
Rattons, rats
Raucle, boisterous, rude
Rax, grow
Reams, froths, foams
Reeket, smoky, smelly
Reestet, shrivelled up
Restit, made up for the night
Riggin, roof, ceiling
Rigs, ridges
Rigwoodie, ill-shaped, lean, bony
Rockin, spinning bee
Roose, praise
Rozet, resin
Runcles, wrinkles
Ryke, reach

Sark, shirt
Scantlins, scarcely
Scaur, timid
Scowder'd, scorched
Scraichan, screeching
Screed, tear
Shavie, trick
Shaw, grove

Sheugh, ditch or drain, or small stream
Shor'd, threatened
Skair, share
Skaith, injury, damage
Skeigh, timid
Skellum, scamp, rascal
Skelpan, dashing
Skelpin', smacking
Skirl, sound shrilly
Sklentan, sloping, slanting
Skyte, slap
Slaes, sloes
Slaps, gaps or openings in a wall
Slee, sly
Smeddum, powder
Smeek, smoke
Smoor'd, smothered
Smytrie, group, collection
Snash, abusive language
Sneeshin mill, snuff-box
Snick-drawing, latch-lifting, stealthy
Snirtle, laugh
Snowket, snuffled, smelled
Sonsie, jolly, cheerful, pleasant
Souter, shoemaker
Sowther, make up
Spairge, sprinkle
Spean, wean
Speer, spier, ask
Speet, spit, transfix
Splore, spree, revel, frolic
Sprattle, scramble
Stacher, stagger
Starns, stars
Steek, shut, fasten
Steghan, stuffing with food
Sten, leap, spring
Stents, taxes, assessments
Stirks, young oxen
Stirrah, stripling
Stoure, dust; dusty toil
Stowp, liquid measure
Strae, straw
Straths, wide valleys
Strathspey, slow Highland dance
Stroan't, urinated
Strunt, strut
Sugh, gentle murmur or hum
Swatch, sample, batch
Swats, new ale
Sweer, slow, lazy
Swith, get away, begone
Synd, drink

Tacksman, tenant-farmer
Tapsalteerie, topsy-turvy
Tawted, with matted hair
Tent, care, heed
Tenty, careful
Thack, thatch
Thairm, cat-gut, string (of a fiddle)
Theekit, thatched, roofed
Thirl'd, pierced, caused to vibrate
Thole, bear, suffer
Thrang, crowded, busy
Thrave, two shocks of grain (24 or 28 sheaves)
Thy-lane, yourself alone
Tids, temper, ill-humor
Timmer, timber, wood
Tine, lose, forfeit
Tirlan, uncovering, unroofing
Tocher, dowry
Toofall, oncoming
Toom, empty
Touzles, dishevels
Towzie, shaggy
Tozie, tipsy
Trig, neat, tidy
Trufs, turfs
Twin, part with
Tyke, dog, cur

Unco, extremely
Unkend, unknown
Usquabae, whiskey

Vauntie, boastful, proud, vain

Waesuck, alas
Wale, pick
Walie, thriving, strapping
Wally, billowy
Wame, belly
Wark-lume, implement
Warly, worldly
Waukin, wawking, watching, waking
Waws, walls
Weans, children
Weel-gaun, working smoothly
Weel-hain'd, well kept
Weirlike, warlike
Whang'd, cut, sliced
Whiddan, whisking, darting
Whinger, short dagger
Whins, furze
Whitter, social glass
Whun-stane, hard variety of stone
Win, dwell
Winnock-bunker, window seat
Wissen'd, withered
Wonner, wonder (term of contempt)
Woodie, gallows
Wylecoat, undervest
Wyt, blame

Yill, ale
Yird, earth

Index of First Lines

Index of Authors and Titles

NOTES FOR A COLLECTION OF ENGLISH POEMS

1660—1800

By
H. W. TAYLOR
and
R. S. CRANE

NEW YORK *and* LONDON
HARPER & BROTHERS PUBLISHERS

Notes

The following notes have three aims: (1) to supply such information as will enable the student to recover the essential meaning of the texts printed in *A Collection of English Poems, 1660-1800* wherever this meaning has become obscure through lapse of time or changes in language and customs; (2) to indicate the intellectual, political, or biographical setting of such poems as depend for their intelligibility upon a knowledge of their antecedents or of other contemporary writings not represented in the anthology; (3) to provide what it is hoped will be a useful apparatus of cross-references and of references to scholarly and critical studies published since 1932 and not, therefore, listed in the bibliography. A few corrections of misprints in the texts or of errors in the bibliographical footnotes have also been included.

It is assumed that users of the anthology will have access to a good dictionary, such as Webster's *New International*, to one of the more inclusive histories of English literature, such as *The Cambridge history of English literature* or Legouis and Cazamian's *History of English literature*, and to an encyclopedia containing biographical notices of the principal poets represented in the volume. To have attempted to supply the place of such familiar helps as these would have extended the notes beyond any reasonable limit. It is likewise assumed that most teachers who may use the collection will prefer that students should rely upon their own sensibility and poetical insight in interpreting the poems rather than upon the critical analysis or appraisals of any editor.

No one has better stated the spirit in which notes such as the following should be used than one of the poets here commented upon. "Notes," wrote Johnson in the preface to his edition of Shakespeare, "are often necessary, but they are necessary evils. Let him, that is yet unacquainted with the powers of Shakespeare, and who desires to feel the highest pleasure that the drama can give, read every play from the first scene to the last, with utter negligence of all his commentators. . . . Let him read on through brightness and obscurity, through integrity and corruption; let him preserve his comprehension of the dialogue and his interest in the fable. And when the pleasures of novelty have ceased, let him attempt exactness and read the commentators."

ABRAHAM COWLEY

1. TO SIR WILLIAM DAVENANT.

18. Verona was captured by Alboin, the Lombard king, in 568. Thereafter it was one of the chief residences of the Lombard kings, and also of the Frankish kings after the Franks had driven the Lombards out of Italy (see l. 24). The action of *Gondibert* takes place partly in Verona during the time of the Lombard ascendancy.

2. ODE. OF WIT.

Cowley's purpose in this poem is not to give a definition of "wit" as a guide to the general usage of the term, but rather to picture an ideal mode for the functioning of the poetical faculty. "Wit" is virtually equated to "height of genius" (see l. 71); it signifies the qualities that make good composition. Therefore it excludes certain things: excessive ornamentation (ll. 33-40), puns or any other sort of play on the sounds or spelling of words (ll. 41-44), indecency (ll. 45-48), bombast (ll. 49-50), strained metaphors (l. 51), the extreme curtness of Senecan prose (l. 52), far-fetched comparisons (ll. 54-55). On the other hand, it includes orderliness of ideas, a harmony and proportion of all parts of the composition (ll. 57-64).

Cowley's use of "wit" as a key word is perhaps explainable by its commonness in the seventeenth century as a name for various aspects of the poetic process (see W. Lee Ustick and Hoyt H. Hudson, "Wit, 'Mixt wit,' and the bee in amber," *Huntington library bulletin,* No. 8 [Oct., 1935], pp. 103-30). Its usual meaning in previous centuries had been the broad one of "intellect" or "mind" in general. During the seventeenth, especially after the middle of the century, it came to signify more particularly what was also called "fancy," the power of seeing resemblances, of discovering analogies between things apparently unlike, hence the power of making metaphors and similes. In this sense it was contrasted to "judgment," the power of making distinctions. Near the end of the century John Locke (*An essay concerning human understanding* [1690], II, xi, 2) defined the two faculties thus: ". . . *Wit* lying most in the assemblage of *Ideas*, and putting those together with quickness and variety, wherein can be found any resemblance or congruity. . . . *Judgment,* on the contrary, lies quite on the other side, in separating carefully *Ideas* one from another, wherein can be found the least difference . . ." (quoted by Ustick and Hudson). Earlier, however, Thomas Hobbes had treated wit as consisting of both fancy and judgment, and had explained that fancy produced the ornaments of a poem, while judgment was responsible for its structure (*Human nature,* in *English works*, ed. Molesworth [1840], IV, 55-56; cited by Ustick and Hudson).

Cowley appears to have a similar distinction in mind; he shows that the faculty of conjuring up images and seeing similarities goes astray unless supported by the faculty of organizing, which of course involves the making of discriminations, and he makes true wit consist in the joining of the two faculties. The main interest of this thesis lies in its exemplifying the attack on false wit which formed an important part of neo-classic doctrine. Briefly, the point of attack was this: a tendency to cultivate ingenious conceits, to make poetry a succession of clever phrases, and to let such cleverness degenerate into strained, far-fetched metaphors and even into mere playing with sounds, had developed in the sixteenth and early seventeenth centuries; and this tendency had made poets forget the element of design and movement in poetry, to the detriment of their art. In this vein wrote the Duke of Buckinghamshire, in *An essay upon poetry* (1682):

"Their greatest fault, who in this kind [the elegy] have writ,
Is neither want of words, nor dearth of wit;
But though this Muse harmonious numbers yield,
And every Couplet be with fancy fill'd;
If yet a just coherence be not made
Between each thought, and the whole model layed
So right, that every step may higher rise,
As in a Ladder, till it reach the Skies;
Trifles like these perhaps of late have past,
And may be lik'd awhile, but never last;
'Tis Epigram, 'tis Point, 'tis what you will,
But not an Elegie, nor writ with skill."

This misleading and barren art of conceit-writing was later attacked by Addison, in the *Spectator*, No. 62; by Pope, in the *Essay on criticism*, ll. 289-96; and by Johnson, in his life of Cowley in the *Lives of the English poets* (to mention only some of the most famous texts out of many). And it is important to note that Cowley himself eventually was assigned to the company of "conceited" poets, along with Cleveland, Crashaw, and others. Johnson in fact regarded him as typical of that company.

5. THE CHRONICLE.

78. The chronicles of Holinshed (1577) and Stow (1580) are among the classics of collected information historical or fabulous.

6. THE PRAISE OF PINDAR.

"Pindarum quisquis studet æmulari." "Whoever strives to equal Pindar." Horace, *Carmina* iv, 2, 1.

8. TO THE ROYAL SOCIETY.

The Royal Society (chartered in 1662) represented to its members and friends the spirit of true physical science, i.e., the "inductive," experimental, investigative way of studying nature, as opposed to what they thought to be the barren speculative methods of ancient and medieval natural philosophy, which spun ideas about nature instead of observing it. Cowley's enthusiasm is representative of a new and growing sentiment of this period. See R. F. Jones, *Ancients and moderns, a study of the background of the "Battle of the books"* (St. Louis: Washington University, 1936).

8-36. These lines epitomize, in a broad way, the account of physical science given in the first part of Sprat's *History*.

9, 37. Sir Francis Bacon, in his *Novum organum* (1620), had set forth the principles of "Induction" and had extolled its merits. Later philosophers have found defects in his analysis of scientific method. The early members of the Royal Society, however, acknowledged his importance as the advocate of a new method and the liberator from old shackles (see Chas. R. Weld, *History of the Royal Society* [London, 1848], I, 57-64, and Jones, *Ancients and moderns, passim*). Robert Boyle (see note to p. 59, ll. 27-28), *Considerations concerning the usefulness of experimental philosophy* (1663), praised Bacon in these terms: ". . . it was owing to the sagacity and freedom of Lord Bacon, that men were then pretty well enabled both to make discoveries, and to remove the impediments that had hitherto kept physics from being useful."

42. Bacon, *Novum organum,* Book I, Aphorism lxxxiv (*Works* [New York, 1878], Vol. I, Part II, p. 117): ". . . with regard to authority, it shows a feeble mind to grant so much to authors and yet deny time his rights, who is the author of authors, nay rather of all authority. For rightly is truth called the daughter of time, not of authority. It is no wonder therefore if those enchantments of antiquity and authority and consent have so bound up men's powers that they have been made impotent (like persons bewitched) to accompany with the nature of things."

62-68. Bacon, Preface to the *Instauratio magna* (*Works,* Vol. I, Part II, pp. 33-34): "For all those who before me have applied themselves to the invention of arts have but cast a glance or two upon facts and examples and experience, and straightway proceeded . . . to invoke their own spirits to give them oracles. I, on the contrary, dwelling purely and constantly among the facts of nature, withdraw my intellect from them no further than may suffice to let the images and rays of natural objects meet in a point, as they do in the sense of vision. . . ."

69. The false notions engendered by regarding words as though they were really existent and not mere arbitrary signs, Bacon dubs Idols of the Market-place. In the *Novum organum*, Book I, Aphorism lix (*Works,* Vol. I, Part II, pp. 86-87) he says: ". . . men believe that their reason governs words; but it is also true that words react on the understanding; and this it is that has rendered philosophy and the sciences sophistical and inactive. Now words, being commonly framed and applied according to the capacity of the vulgar, follow those lines of division which are most obvious to the vulgar understanding. And whenever an understanding of

greater acuteness or a more diligent observation would alter those lines to suit the true divisions of nature, words stand in the way and resist the change. Whence it comes to pass that the high and formal discussions of learned men end oftentimes in disputes about words and names. . . ."

10, 109ff. Sprat, in his *History of the Royal Society,* Part II, Sect. XXIII-XXV, shows with much detail the high esteem in which the Society was held, and what high hopes were had for it. At the beginning of Section XXIV (text of 3rd edition, 1722) he says: ". . . the *Original* of the *Royal Society* has found a general *Approbation* within our selves, and . . . the most prudent Men of all Professions and Interests, have shewn by their Respects to these hopeful Beginnings, that there is a *Reverence* due to the first Trials and Intentions, as well as to the last Accomplishment of generous Attempts."

11, 136-47. The telescope and microscope were still novelties in the middle of the seventeenth century, and the realization of their value was a source of excitement. See Marjorie Nicolson, "The telescope and imagination," *Modern philology,* XXXII (1935), 233-60; "The 'New astronomy' and English literary imagination," *Studies in philology,* XXXII (1935), 428-62; *The microscope and English imagination,* "Smith College studies in modern languages," Vol. XVI, No. 4, July, 1935.

154. Sprat says (*History of the Royal Society,* Part II, Section XIII) that one concern of the Society was "to regard the *least* and the *plainest* Things, and those that may appear at *first* the most *inconsiderable,* as well as the *greatest Curiosities.*"

SIR WILLIAM DAVENANT

12. GONDIBERT. BOOK II, CANTO V.

The action of the poem up to the present section is as follows: Duke Gondibert and Prince Oswald are the two chief warriors of the Lombard kingdom, and as such are the most eligible for the hand of Rhodalind, the daughter of King Aribert. The King prefers Gondibert, and Rhodalind loves him secretly. Gondibert, however, whose nobility of temperament puts him beyond the reach of ordinary political ambition, fails to realize his desirability. On the other hand, Oswald has been scheming to win the affections of Rhodalind.

The armies of Oswald and Gondibert return from successful expeditions. Each army is desirous of having its leader marry Rhodalind and seize the throne. During the annual hunt to celebrate the Lombard ascendancy over the Vandals, Oswald's forces attempt to ambush Gondibert's. Failing to catch Gondibert off guard, Oswald next proposes a duel, in which he is slain. The result is a desperate battle between the two forces, in which Gondibert is badly wounded. Old Ulfin, a faithful warrior who has served Gondibert's grandfather, persuades Gondibert to seek shelter at the house of the wealthy philosopher and physician, where his wounds can be cured.

Meanwhile the news of Oswald's death is causing great turmoil among his followers, and civil war is barely averted. The story turns away from Gondibert to give an account of these matters, then returns, at the beginning of the section here reproduced, to the arrival of Gondibert with Ulfin, his son Ulfinore, the young soldier Goltho, who had performed brilliantly in the fight, and their train.

14, 73-80. It was an often repeated argument in this and the next century (see also Pope, *Essay on man,* Book I) that the pride of man in supposing himself to be the special concern of creation was not supported by a study of the nature of the universe. In particular, it was thought that the Copernican astronomy, by its demonstration that the earth is not a fixed body with the heavens revolving about it, but is itself revolving about the sun, had definitely robbed this cosmic pride of its foundation. See A. O. Lovejoy, "'Pride' in eighteenth-century thought," *MLN,* XXXVI (1921), 31-37.

15, 87. "Great Natures Office." The activities of this institution, together with others mentioned in this canto but not explicitly connected with the "office" itself, are a fair representation of the kinds of learning most in favor in the mid-seventeenth century. Worthy of note is the attention given to astronomy (ll. 61-80), to natural history (ll. 93-140), to ancient learning (ll. 145-76), and to law (ll. 177-84). In the main, the house of Astragon favors not only the investigative approach to natural phenomena (cf. p. 8, and note on Cowley's poem), but also the wide and careful study of the documents of the past.

17, 189-204. This attack upon the accumulation of theological documents seems mainly directed at scholasticism.

18, 205-12. These lines probably refer to the Arabic *Gospel of the infancy*, a narrative in which the Holy Babe declares His divine nature in the cradle. This apocryphal gospel was in existence by the sixth century, in which the action of the present poem takes place.

19, 262. "Heav'n's lov'd *Laureat.*" David.

SIR JOHN DENHAM

20. Cooper's Hill.

19. The "Muse" was Edmund Waller, who had written a poem entitled "Upon His Majesty's repairing of Paul's."

21, 67. It was a tradition dating back to the early Middle Ages that Brutus, the grandson of Aeneas, banished from Rome for accidentally killing his father, voyaged to Britain, where he founded London. Albanact was one of the sons of Brutus.

77ff. The references are to Edward III, Queen Philippa, and the Black Prince, and to the brilliant military exploits of Edward and his son. The "order" mentioned in l. 83 is the Order of the Garter.

22, 117. Henry VIII destroyed the property and confiscated the wealth of the monastic orders after he had broken with the Catholic authority.

24, 214. "the self-enamour'd youth." Narcissus, who fell in love with his own image reflected in the water.

27. NATURA NATURATA.

The phrase constituting the title occurs in scholastic philosophy, and signifies the "works of nature," the world of phenomena, nature as constituted by the Creator, who, in contrast, is called *Natura naturans*. (See Charles du Fresne, *sieur* Du Cange, *Glossarium mediae et infimae Latinitatis,* ed. Favre [Niort, 1883-87].) These terms had been in common use in the Middle Ages (see R. P. McKeon, *The philosophy of Spinoza* [New York, 1928], p. 69 n.). John Scotus Eriugena, the ninth-century philosopher and theologian, in the beginning of his *De divisione naturae* defines "nature" as the sum of all existence, embracing four types of being: (1) that which creates and is not created, or God as the source (cf. *natura naturans*); (2) that which creates and is created (called by Eriugena the primordial causes, the first creations of the Creator of all, which in turn create what exists beneath them [Maïeul Cappuyns, *Jean Scot Érigène* (Louvain, 1933), pp. 352-53]); (3) that which does not create but is created, or the world of particulars (cf. *natura naturata*); (4) that which neither creates nor is created, or God as the end or goal of all being.

In Denham's poem, of course, it is the word and not the thought which is borrowed from scholastic philosophy. The conception of nature employed by Denham is one which occasioned much unfavorable comment during the sixteenth century and the first part of the seventeenth. This view, with its moral implications, has been called "libertine naturalism" (see the article by L. I. Bredvold cited on p. 1117), and is connected with the views of the sect called Libertines, though it touched many persons not actually associated with that sect. "Nature" in the Renaissance had, among others, two mutually opposed meanings. It could mean the universal order, by contemplation of which man is able to discover a true and unshakable basis for ethics, and ascertain the laws which must bind his conduct in society; or it could mean (as in the present poem) a happy state of freedom from the restraints of society, which are mere matters of convention having no basis in the constitution of man or of the universe. In the first sense nature was law (a concept developed by the ancient Stoics and fortified by the expositions of Cicero; see *De legibus*, Book I); in the second, impulse (a notion of the skeptics and Epicureans, seen, e.g., in Lucretius, *De rerum natura*, Book V). Montaigne expressed this philosophy of "libertine naturalism" in various ways. In the essay "On custom" he said: ". . . the laws of conscience, which pretend to be derived from nature, proceed from custom; every one, having an inward veneration for the opinions and manners approved and received amongst his own people. . . ." (*Essays*, Cotton's translation, ed. Hazlitt [London, 1892], I, 119-20). Similarly, in "The apology for Raimond Sebond," he said: "It is no wonder, if people, who take their pattern from the first image of nature, should in most of their opinions, swerve from the common path. . . ." (*ibid.*, II, 460). The "nature" here mentioned is essentially the same as the divinity appealed to by Shakespeare's Edmund, in *King Lear*, I, ii, ll. 1-3:

> "Thou, nature, art my goddess; to thy law
> My services are bound. Wherefore should I
> Stand in the plague of custom. . . ."

—the "law" of this goddess being, of course, much less restraining than that of the Stoic conception.

EDMUND WALLER

30. THE BATTLE OF THE SUMMER-ISLANDS. CANTO I.

40. For "king" read "kind."

32. CANTO III.

11. Talus was the man of iron who served Artegall in the pursuit of justice. His flail was for the purpose of threshing out falsehood. See Spenser, *The Faerie Queene,* Book V, Canto I, stanza xii.

33, 62. "the pious Trojan." Aeneas (frequently called "pious" by Virgil in the *Aeneid*). In escaping from Troy, Aeneas became separated from his wife Creusa. Upon discovering his loss, he rushed back into the burning city, only to come upon her spectre.

38. ON ST. JAMES'S PARK, AS LATELY IMPROVED BY HIS MAJESTY.

91. "that antique Pile." Westminster Abbey.

99. The Chapter-House of Westminster Abbey was used as a meeting place for the Commons up to 1547.

39. OF THE LAST VERSES IN THE BOOK.

"Miratur Limen Olympi." "He marvels at the threshold of Olympus." Virgil, *Eclogae* v. 56.

JOHN DRYDEN

45. UPON THE DEATH OF THE LORD HASTINGS.

Henry, Lord Hastings, son of the Earl of Huntington, died in 1649 at the age of nineteen. The *Lachrymae Musarum*, in which this poem appeared, was a small volume of verses to his memory, by several hands. It appears that Lord Hastings was an extremely talented young man, and that Dryden's expressions of regret were not without warrant.

46, 43. Tycho Brahe (1546-1601), the Danish astronomer, was noted for his expertness in the art of observation. In one of his works he discussed his observations of the "new star" of 1572, correcting the common notion that it was an exhalation from the earth. The "new star" mentioned by Dryden in l. 46 may possibly be an allusion to this appearance. Cf. *Modern philology*, XXXII (1935), 236-37.

47. HEROICK STANZAS.

See note to p. 106.

49, 77. "*Pheretrian Jove.*" Feretrius was a surname of Jove. It has been interpreted variously to mean one who strikes down a person who has sworn falsely, or one who brings peace, or one to whom the spoils of battle are dedicated. As Dryden uses the phrase, it conveys certainly the third of the senses mentioned, and suggests also the second.

51. ASTRÆA REDUX.

The title is equivalent to "justice restored." See note to p. 106.

52, 9. "Th' Ambitious *Swede.*" Charles X of Sweden, who kept his kingdom at war during most of his reign (1654-60).

17. "the fair *Iberian* Bride." In 1659, France and Spain effected a peace treaty, which was cemented by the marriage of the Infanta of Spain to Louis XIV.

53, 67. "soft *Otho.*" The Roman emperor Otho is described as having an effeminate manner. He committed suicide after his defeat in the battle of Brixellum.

69-70. The Roman emperor Galba let esteem for ability take precedence over any consideration of blood-ties, when he made Piso his successor.

74. Dryden here alludes to the famous phrase of Francis I of France, "All is lost save honor." At the battle of Worcester (1651) Charles II had conducted himself with great valor in the midst of a rout.

79. "banish'd *David.*" Cf. p. 68, l. 59.

54, 101. "Covenanting League." The reference is to Charles's maternal grandfather Henry IV of France (1553-1610) and his war against the Catholic or Holy League. This league bore a resemblance, sufficient for Dryden's purpose, to the Solemn League and Covenant, an agreement made in 1643 between the English and Scottish Parliaments, for "the reformation and defense of religion," i.e., Presbyterianism, "the honor and happiness of the king," etc.

145. "*Booth's* forward Valour." After the death of Cromwell in 1658, Sir George Booth headed an unsuccessful uprising in Chester.

55, 151ff. General George Monk, as commander of the English forces in Scotland, took a leading part in the military movements connected with the Restoration.

56, 201. Lodovico Sforza (1451-1508) became Duke of Milan supposedly by murdering his nephew, the rightful holder of the title. As Duke, he had a brilliant political career, but was finally caught in the meshes of his own designs.

219. Scheveline was the small town in Holland from which Charles II set sail for England at the Restoration.

58. To My Honour'd Friend Dr. Charleton.

Dr. Walter Charleton was physician in ordinary to Charles II, besides being a writer upon various scholarly and philosophic subjects. In his *Chorea gigantum* he set forth the thesis concerning Stonehenge which Dryden celebrates in his poem.

1. "The longest Tyranny." See note on Cowley's "To the Royal Society," p. 8.

59, 3. "the *Stagirite*." Aristotle.

25. William Gilbert was a physician and scientist who became physician to Queen Elizabeth and was prominent in the College of Physicians, rising to the presidency of that institution. His great work on the loadstone or magnet, *De magnete magneticisque corporibus* (1600), containing observations on the importance of magnetism in navigation, enhanced his reputation.

27-28. Robert Boyle (1627-91) was a physicist and chemist of great ability in original research, who did much for his own day in improving experimental technique. To him we owe the familiar Boyle's Law. His brother Roger, the first Earl of Orrery, was a statesman and dramatist, one of several literary noblemen of the Restoration whose friendship was of assistance to such professional literary men as Dryden.

29-32. William Harvey, physician and physiologist, formulated the laws of the circulation of the blood. His treatise on the subject, *De motu cordis et sanguinis in animalibus* (1628), created much excitement, and some futile opposition, especially on the Continent. His friend George Ent, also a physician and scientist, published in 1641 a treatise defending the doctrines of Harvey.

60, 54. See note to p. 53, l. 74.

62. Epilogue.

6. Cobb and Otter were characters in Ben Jonson's *Every man in his humour* and *The silent woman*, respectively. Cobb was a water-bearer; Otter a "land and sea captain" with a quaint habit

of christening his drinking cups with the name of some animal. In a "Defence of the Epilogue" (1672) Dryden said of Jonson's comic personages: "In these low characters of vice and folly, lay the excellency of that inimitable writer."

66. Prologue.

11. This line refers to the popular ceremony of "Pope-burning," i.e., burning the Pope in effigy—an anti-Catholic gesture frequently made on the evening of November 5, the anniversary of the Gunpowder Plot.

67, 16-17. Cf. the note to these lines in Dryden's *Works*, ed. Scott-Saintsbury (1885), X, 350: "The meaning is, that the poets rebel against sense and criticism, like the Parliament, in 1641, against the King; and that the audience judge as ill as those who, in 1648, condemned Charles I to the block. The parallel between the political disputes in 1680 and 1681, and those which preceded the great civil war, was fashionable among the Tories."

67. Absalom and Achitophel.

The occasion of this poem was the approaching trial of the first Earl of Shaftesbury on the charge of treason in November, 1681. That trial, which ended in the acquittal of Shaftesbury (see below, note on *The medal*), was the climax of a series of political maneuvers in which Shaftesbury had been a principal performer, but which also involved the complicated politico-religious situation in the royal family. For several years prior to the trial, the problem of whether England was to remain Protestant or become Catholic had been a complicated one. Charles II was nominally Protestant, but was suspected of Catholic sympathies; his brother James, heir to the crown, was an acknowledged Catholic; James's daughter Mary was a Protestant and had married a Protestant prince, William of Orange. And to make the problem more tangled, the Duke of Monmouth, a favorite illegitimate son of Charles and a military leader of some distinction (see the poem, ll. 23-24), allied himself with the "Whig" faction headed by Shaftesbury, and became known as the "Protestant Duke." (The terms Whig and Tory were becoming popular about this time; Dryden refers to them in the prose preface to the poem.)

In 1678, one Titus Oates submitted evidence concerning a "Popish plot" to the magistrate Sir Edmund Bury Godfrey (the poem, ll. 108-15, 517). Though Oates turned out in the end to be a fantastic perjurer, he was taken with great seriousness for the time being, and the fact that in October, 1678, not long after he had given his testimony, Godfrey was found dead with his sword run through his body (l. 676) greatly increased Oates's temporary prestige. Shaftesbury took advantage of the excitement to arouse sentiment against the Catholics, and in May of the next year the Whigs, led by him, introduced into the House of Commons the "Exclusion Bill," designed to shut out James from the succession on the ground of his religion. At this time the popularity of Monmouth was at its height, and the Whigs were pressing his claim to the succession on the basis of his Protestantism and also on the less solid plea that, since his title was uncertain, he would be all the better king, being responsible to the people (ll. 224-27). He increased his prestige by quelling the insurrection of the Covenanters in Scotland. The situation was so troublesome that in August, 1679, Charles ordered both Monmouth and James out of the country (l. 921).

Just what Shaftesbury's motives were is a matter of speculation; but he was certainly willing to press Monmouth's claim. He endeavored to bring about a reconciliation of Charles and Monmouth by having the latter return secretly from banishment. The maneuver, however, was not pleasing to the King, and Monmouth was forbidden the Court, though he remained in England. In the next year (August, 1680) Shaftesbury arranged a royal progress for Monmouth through the west of England (ll. 682-746). The effect of this demonstration upon the populace was considerable, but the move only increased the tension at Court. The Whigs (or the Patriots, as they called themselves about this time —see ll. 179, 965-73) desired the calling of Parliament in the autumn, so that the Exclusion Bill might be voted upon. It would have been dangerous not to grant their request; but as it was, things turned out favorably for the King, for the bill, after being passed by the House of Commons, was rejected by the Lords. Shaftesbury continued the struggle through other issues, but without success. Moreover, the tide of opinion was turning against Monmouth, and in July, 1681, Shaftesbury was committed to the Tower on a charge of high treason, and the "conspiracy" came to an ignominious close. (See Louise Fargo Brown, *The first Earl of Shaftesbury* [New York, 1933], chaps. xv, xvi.)

Dryden's choice of a Biblical allegory as a means of representing these incidents is not surprising in view of the evident applicability of the Old Testament story (2 Samuel xiii-xviii). He was not the first, however, to find parallels between Charles II, Shaftesbury, and Monmouth on the one hand, and David, Achitophel, and Absalom on the other. David and Charles had been familiarly identified for several years; indeed, Dryden had referred to Charles, in *Astræa redux* (see p. 53, l. 79), as "banish'd David." The name Achitophel had been used for several decades, by Royalists and Puritans before there were Whigs and Tories, as a designation for any corrupt political leader (see R. F. Jones, *MLN*, XLVI, 211-18). In 1680 a pamphlet entitled *Absalom's conspiracy, or the tragedy of treason* had definitely linked Monmouth and Shaftesbury as Absalom and Achitophel. Dryden, then, was using material of a high allusive value, material which, as far as it concerned the three main personalities, must have met ready response. He did not, moreover, obscure his allegory by too close an adherence to the Biblical narrative; in fact, his use of certain details will be found rather inaccurate. The plot, such as it is, of *Absalom and Achitophel* treats both the Bible and the actual situation with great freedom. The Popish Plot, the Whig attitude toward the succession, the progress of Monmouth through England in the summer of 1680, are sketched briefly (see references above). Charles's multifarious efforts against Shaftesbury are reduced, in the poem, to a single long speech (ll. 939-1025).

The nature of Dryden's political philosophy has been explained in a very clear-cut manner recently by L. I. Bredvold, in *The intellectual milieu of John Dryden* (Ann Arbor, 1934). Professor Bredvold points out that Dryden does not anywhere in his writings definitely depart from a sort of conservative skepticism—a conviction that radical reforms in government lead, not to the realization of lofty ideals, but merely to confusion; that change in government is therefore always to be distrusted; that security can be gained only by having a solid central authority which, though not indifferent to the people's needs, is still not at the people's mercy. In *Absalom and Achitophel* he expresses a strong grievance against the English for their unwillingness to let well enough alone in government. They are

"God's pamper'd People, who, debauch'd with ease,
No King could govern, nor no God could please."
(ll. 47-48.)

And

"once in twenty Years, their Scribes record,
By natural Instinct they change their Lord" (ll. 218-19).

Moreover, to Dryden the English people shared the common quality of all crowds: incapacity to form anything like a stable government on democratic principles (cf. p. 91, ll. 91-94). Democracy is at the very bottom of the political barrel (ll. 226-27). To let the crowd decide is to let government sink, by a series of highly unpleasant stages, to that condition of savagery and chaos which Hobbes, in his *Leviathan* (1651), described as the "state of nature." The only protection against this disaster is, it seems, monarchy—not an arbitrary and unprincipled monarchy, yet one which, granted its decisions are just, has the power to enforce them (see ll. 753-94, 977-78; cf. p. 92, ll. 113-18; p. 95, ll. 247-51).

That Dryden's partisanship was not narrow or mean-spirited is apparent from his appreciation of the Marquis of Halifax (see ll. 882-87). Halifax was a leader among the group known as the Trimmers, who avoided committing themselves to either side of the Whig-Tory quarrel, and advocated (to use their own figure) keeping the boat on an even keel. A great deal of abuse was heaped upon the Trimmers; even Dryden, in the lines just referred to, preferred Halifax to be on the right side. Yet in respect to the importance and proper character of a monarchy, Halifax's formulation of the Trimmer attitude in his *Character of a trimmer* harmonizes with Dryden's own view as explained above. (The *Character* appeared in manuscript in 1684, and was published in 1688. See H. C. Foxcroft, *The life and letters of Sir George Savile, first Marquis of Halifax* [London, 1898], II, 269-70, 274-77.) In the opening section, on laws and government, the *Character* reads: ". . . a Prince that is so joined to his people that they seem to be his limbs, rather than his subjects; clothed with mercy and justice rightly applied in their several places; his throne supported by love as well as by power; and the warm wishes of his devoted subjects, like a never-failing incense, still ascending towards him, looketh so like the best image we can frame to ourselves of God almighty that men would have much to do not to fall down and worship him . . ." (*ibid.*, p. 290).

A useful approach to the poem—at least, one which brings the reader quickly in view of its most pleasing aspects, while at the same time revealing its limitations as a narrative composition—is suggested in Samuel Johnson's criticism in his life of Dryden (*Lives of the English poets*, ed. G. B. Hill, I, 436-37). Johnson's position is that if the poem be considered as "political and controversial it will be found to comprise all the excellences of which the subject is susceptible: acrimony of censure, elegance of praise, artful delineation of characters, variety and vigour of sentiment, happy turns of language, and pleasing harmony of numbers . . ." —which is to say, that it comprises many short pieces of very fine satire and invective, that it happily illustrates in this or that passage the art of ridicule, whether of persons or of ideas, joined with the art of argumentative eloquence, all carried out in expertly turned verse. Excellent poetic structure, however, Johnson does not find in the poem. As he says: ". . . there is . . . an unpleasing disproportion between the beginning and the end. We are alarmed by a faction formed out of many sects various in their principles, but agreeing in their purpose of mischief, formidable for their numbers, and strong by their supports, while the king's friends are few and weak. The chiefs on either part are set forth to view; but when expectation is at the height the king makes a speech, and

Henceforth a series of new times began. . . ."

89. The Medal.

The acquittal of Shaftesbury in November, 1681, on the charge of treason, caused Dryden to continue the attack begun in *Absalom and Achitophel*. Beginning with an allusion to the well-known joke about Shaftesbury's having once hoped to be elected king of Poland (ll. 3, 15), he amplified the satirical character sketch (cf. ll. 6 ff. with pp. 70-71, ll. 150-99) given in the former poem, and repeated his attack on democratic ideas of government and his plea for conservatism. The parallelism of the thoughts on government in the two poems has already been pointed out in some instances (see note to *Absalom and Achitophel*); others are evident, especially in ll. 167 to the end, which section elaborates the picture of the downfall of a democratic government as sketched in the former poem, p. 84, ll. 765-94. In his conclusion Dryden hints that even if Monmouth should become a king, he would come under suspicion for being the son of a king, just as Collatine, who helped overthrow the last of the Tarquin kings in Rome, fell under suspicion because he was himself a Tarquin (l. 317); only a "rightful monarch" (l. 322), whose place is not dependent on popular sentiment, can subdue faction and keep a country in a condition of peace.

96. MACFLECKNOE.

Richard Flecknoe seems to have been brought into the scheme of the poem merely because he was recognized to be a very bad poet, had recently died (1678?), and was enough older than Shadwell to be pictured as handing down the realm of nonsense to the latter. Heywood and Shirley (l. 29) suited Dryden's purpose because they were prolific dramatists—the former being the most prolific of the Elizabethan period—and were commonly thought to be bad; so also Dekker (l. 87) and Ogleby (ll. 102, 174). Dryden's real concern was with Shadwell alone.

The basis of that concern has for a long time been misunderstood. The traditional account of *MacFlecknoe* is that it was written as an answer to Shadwell's *The medal of John Bayes, a satire against folly and knavery* (1682), which in turn had been a reply to Dryden's *The medal.* This tradition rests, however, on no very solid ground. There is reason to doubt that *The medal of John Bayes* was Shadwell's at all (G. Thorn-Drury, in *Review of English studies*, I [1925], 191). And there are the strongest reasons to doubt that Dryden's poem was the product of the political war of 1681-82. To say the least, it is free from political reference, which circumstance would be remarkable in a satire motivated by such strong party animosity as Dryden possessed. But further evidence exists (see *ibid.*, pp. 187-90) in the shape of a transcript, found in the Bodleian Library, of a part of *Mac Flecknoe*, bearing the date 1678 and not showing the subtitle "a satire upon the true-blue Protestant poet, T. S." The date might have been a scribal error, but the absence of the subtitle certainly suggests that it was not part of Dryden's original conception, and was probably added by the printer to appeal to the current interest in political affairs. And even the publication of *Mac Flecknoe* may have preceded that of *The medal of John Bayes.* The latter supposedly appeared in May of 1682; whereas the *Loyal Protestant* for Feb. 9, 1681/2, referred to "a *MacFlecknoe*," a phrase which suggests a printed book rather than a manuscript, and makes it possible that even the publication of Dryden's poem was not motivated by the supposed attack of Shadwell.

Whether Shadwell wrote *The medal of John Bayes* or not, he had produced other pieces that were eligible for Dryden's satire. His *Psyche* (1675), which Dryden takes pains to refer to three times (ll. 54, 90, 179-80), was an ambitious piece of the operatic sort popular in the seventeenth century, with spoken dialogue, songs, dancing, and elaborate scenery. It was an adaptation from Molière, and a bad one, but with the aid of magnificent staging it had considerable success. Somewhat better, but not beyond the reach of criticism, was *The virtuoso* (1676), a comedy satirizing the Royal Society and containing some hits at Dryden himself. Dryden takes his revenge in *MacFlecknoe* by making out that Shadwell writes as foolishly as the fop character Sir Formal Trifle in *The virtuoso* speaks (ll. 168-70), and by adapting a scene from that play to bring the declamation of Flecknoe to a fitting close.

As to the mock-heroic method used by Dryden, a comparison of *MacFlecknoe* with Pope's *Dunciad* reveals some interesting resemblances. Pope was undoubtedly influenced to some extent by Dryden. See also note to p. 149.

97, 53. St. André was a dancing-master.

98, 57. Singleton was a singer noted especially for his performance of songs and of the recitatives in operatic plays.

59. Villerius was a rôle in D'Avenant's *Siege of Rhodes*. The part included much recitative.

64. "*Augusta*" is London. The allusion is to the political uncertainties of the period.

67. The Barbican was a remnant of the old fortifications of London—at the time of the poem a center for public amusements of the most vulgar order. Note the following lines.

78. Maximinus the Thracian (d. 238 A.D.) was a powerful warrior who was elevated to the throne of the Roman Empire by his soldiers, but killed by them three years later for his cruelty. He appeared as a character in Dryden's own early play *Tyrannic love* (1670).

84. "*Panton.*" Apparently there was a celebrated punster of this name.

91. "*Misers.*" Shadwell had translated Molière's *L'avare* under the title *The miser* (1672).

97. Bun-Hill and Watling Streets are not actually very far apart, so that this line becomes a good sample of mock-heroic disproportion.

99, 105. Henry Herringman was a bookseller and a prolific publisher of poems, plays, and minor pieces of various sorts.

108-11. These lines parody two passages in the *Aeneid*. Those passages, in Dryden's translation, are as follows:

"Strange to relate, from young Iülus' head
A lambent flame arose, which gently spread
Around his brows, and on his temples fed."
(Book II, ll. 930-32; text of Cambridge ed.)

"And by his side Ascanius took his place,
The second hope of Rome's immortal race."
(Book XII, ll. 253-54)

151. "Gentle *George*" is Sir George Etherege, the Restoration comic dramatist.

152-53. Dorimant, Loveit, and Sir Fopling Flutter are characters in Etherege's *The man of mode*; Cully and Cockwood, in his *Love in a tub*.

100, 179. Prince Nicander is one of the noble lovers of Psyche in Shadwell's opera.

189-92. These lines are a parody on a passage in Shadwell's Epilogue to *The humourists* (1671), which reads thus:

"A Humour is the Byass, of the Mind,
By which with Violence 'tis one way inclin'd:
It makes our Actions lean on one side still;
And in all Changes that way bends the Will."
(*Dramatic works* [London, 1720], I, 213)

101. *From* THE SECOND PART OF ABSALOM AND ACHITOPHEL.

After the success of *Absalom and Achitophel* there was demand for a sequel. Dryden was not disposed to take up the task again, and secured the services of Tate, who was a loyal young Tory and a passable versifier. Dryden himself supervised the planning and writing, and contributed many actual lines. Those given in this volume are definitely known to be by him; and his touch is apparent in various other parts of the poem.

Perhaps the best sections of the whole poem are the characterizations of Doeg and Og, i.e., Elkanah Settle and Shadwell, respectively. Dryden despised Settle as a feeble poet, a satirist without power to hurt anyone, and a turncoat (Settle had first been a Tory, then had turned Whig; some years after this poem he turned Tory again). As a Whig, Settle had replied to Dryden's *Absalom and Achitophel* with a poem entitled *Absalom senior, or Achitophel transprosed* (see the allusion thereto in ll. 444-46; l. 446 is a take-off on one of Settle's own lines), and had also made himself contemptible as far as Dryden was concerned by being a leader in the ceremony of "Pope-burning" (see ll. 451-52, also note to p. 66). As to the characterization of Shadwell, cf. *Mac Flecknoe*.

106. RELIGIO LAICI.

This poem needs to be read together with *The hind and the panther*, and perhaps with the political poems also, if its place in

Dryden's thought and hence its full meaning are to be understood. Behind all of Dryden's shifts of position there is a consistent negative philosophy. In politics it takes the form of conservatism, a stress on stability as a prime virtue in a government. The *Heroic stanzas* on Cromwell praise, not Cromwell's Puritanism, but only his power to restore peace and order (see, e.g., pp. 48-49, ll. 41-48, 61-62). Similarly, *Astræa redux* welcomes Charles II as a new restorer of peace rather than one who has triumphed over Puritanism, and it says no word against Cromwell (cf. p. 69, ll. 69-74). In religion, this way of thinking takes the form of a qualified "fideism"—i.e., a denial of the power of the natural reason to establish firmly such fundamental truths as the existence of God and the historic fact of a revelation or to guide man to faith (see *Religio laici*, ll. 1-41).

Dryden wrote a prose preface to *Religio laici* in which he set forth his main positions very plainly. He began by owning himself a skeptic in philosophy and professing his unwillingness therefore to impose his opinions in religion, which is above philosophy. From this standpoint he protested against the claims of Deism in particular: what the Deists asserted to be the universal truth as perceived by human reason, Dryden dubbed merely the remnant of "reveal'd religion in the posterity of Noah." The powers of the human mind, even in the cases of Socrates, Plato, and other great "heathen philosophers," he considered to have been overestimated. Moreover, human reason leads to differences and confusions of opinion, he thought, when it is employed at an improper task; we must be content with what the Scriptures reveal; reason can do no more than assure us that the Bible is the word of God (cf. the poem, ll. 42-125, 168-211).

As to the character of this revelation, Dryden's position involved no subtleties. The Bible "in all things needful to salvation" is sufficiently clear; anything obscure is simply "not necessary to salvation" (cf. ll. 295-300, 311-25, 431-32).

To this faith, however, there are two sorts of enemies, said Dryden: the Papists, because they have "kept the Scripture from us" and what they have delivered they have assumed a right of interpreting "under the pretense of infallibility" (cf. ll. 370-87); and the Fanatics, that is to say, the Puritans and dissenters of various other sorts, because they assume "what amounts to an infallibility in the private spirit" (cf. ll. 398-408), and turn Scripture to the uses of sedition. Of the two, he says, the Papists are the less dangerous; and when, some years later, he had reconciled himself to this same assumption of infallibility, the danger was forgotten (see *The hind and the panther*). The Fanatics, on the other hand, he denounced without restraint. They have distorted Scripture ever since it was translated into the vernacular, he said, and they have carried their rebellious spirit into politics; wherever

Calvin's discipline went, "rebellion, civil war, and misery attended it."

One impetus, apparently, behind the writing of *Religio laici* was the appearance in 1682 of Henry Dickinson's translation of Father Simon's *Histoire critique du Vieux Testament.* Whatever Dryden may previously have been thinking about the true basis of faith, Father Simon's demonstration that the text of Holy Writ was extremely hard to determine must have appealed to his naturally skeptical turn of mind (see ll. 234-51). On this occasion he rescued his belief in the sufficiency of the Bible by several ingenious turns of argument. The position of the Roman Catholic Church, he recognized, was that church tradition was necessary for correct interpretation of the Scriptures (ll. 276-81). His comment on this claim was that a church so omniscient that it can guide men rightly by tradition should be able to restore the Scripture itself (ll. 282-94). If, on the other hand, the text of Scripture was actually in such a dubious state as Father Simon had shown, how much more carelessly must tradition, which was mostly a matter of oral transmission, have been preserved (ll. 258-75)? Only one branch of tradition appealed to Dryden: the works of the early Fathers, because their antiquity put them nearer the source of knowledge and because they were written, not oral (ll. 334-55). But these, he maintained, were not the exclusive property of the Roman Church, and that body had no rightful claim to be the sole expounders of them (ll. 356-69).

The only right course, says Dryden in conclusion (ll. 427 ff.), is neither to forego Scripture entirely in favor of tradition, nor to try what is beyond our power—that is, interpret it according to our own individual lights. The things necessary for salvation are "few and plain." Beyond them, we may most safely trust the early Fathers. If the Fathers and the Scripture disagree, the points of difference may be regarded as not essential. Finally, if our own reason and our Church are in contradiction, we had best be silent, for the sake of peace.

This whole confession of a layman's faith, in short, is a plea to rest religion on a simple, solid, enduring base, and not to disturb it by any of the devices of mere human reason, which, inferior to faith as a guide to salvation, can only work harm. In *Religio laici* the foundation is the Bible; in *The hind and the panther* it is the Roman Catholic tradition. Except for the strain of skepticism, the position of *Religio laici* in its main lines was that of the Latitudinarian divines of the Established Church, who, in their effort to mediate between Puritans on the one hand and Papists on the other, had for a generation been insisting (in the words of Joseph Glanvill, *Essays* [1676], Essay vii, pp. 25-26) that "The principles which are necessary to Salvation are very few, and very plain, and generally acknowledg'd among Christians." *The hind and the panther* reveals how Dryden's skepticism of reason, combined with his desire for authority and peace (cf. the political poems), became moving causes in his intellectual conversion to Catholicism.

116. TO THE MEMORY OF MR. OLDHAM.

9. "*Nisus.*" See Virgil's *Aeneid*, Book V. In the footrace during the games between the Sicilians and the Trojans, Nisus, having slipped and fallen near the goal, tripped up the leading Sicilian runner, so that the Trojan Euryalus might win.

15-16. The verse of John Oldham (1653-83) was more noteworthy for its vigor than for its smoothness, especially in his satires. In his principal work, *Satyrs upon the Jesuits,* Oldham wrote, or affected to write, as a plain honest man rather than a skilled artist. See pp. 197-98, ll. 28-31.

117, 23. Marcellus, who like Oldham died young, was the nephew of the emperor Augustus. He gave promise of great ability, and was expected to assume the throne on the death of Augustus. He was praised by Virgil (see the *Aeneid*, VI, 860-65).

119. TO THE PIOUS MEMORY OF MRS. ANN KILLIGREW.

Anne Killigrew, daughter of a minister and niece of two minor dramatists, was a young lady of talent and promise, though Dryden's lavish praise owes more to admiration of the subject's personality than to disinterested criticism. She died at the age of twenty-five, in 1685, and her poems were published in the following year, with Dryden's ode as introduction.

124. THE HIND AND THE PANTHER. PART I.

The first part of this poem introduces the various churches under the beast-allegory (see footnotes), with several digressions in which the poet directly states his views on certain points of faith; all this serving as an introduction to the long dialogue which occupies the remaining two parts of the poem.

125, 62-71. Cf. *Religio laici.* In that poem the idea of private reason is used with a somewhat narrower application (see pp. 114-15, esp. ll. 394-97, 445-48); Dryden is there contrasting two extremes—individual interpretation of Scripture as practiced by dissenters, and submission to church authority as practiced by the Catholics—not only with each other but with the happy medium, a direct interpretation not enforced by authority, yet also free from subtleties and disputes and easy for the layman to comprehend.

128, 197-234. In these lines Dryden recurs to previously expressed ideas concerning the connection between religious dissent and political rebellion. See note to p. 106.

133, 410-29. The Anglican doctrine concerning the Eucharist offers a compromise between Catholic and Calvinist views, though it verbally rejects the former and in most respects agrees with the latter. The Catholics hold that the bread and wine are actually transformed into the body and blood of the Savior (transubstantiation); whereas the Calvinists deny entirely the corporeal presence, holding that the body and blood are present only in a spiritual way, hence present to believers only. The Anglican doctrine, as expressed in Article 28 of the *Thirty-nine articles of the Christian faith*, is ambiguous, or seemed so to Dryden, about the exact nature of the presence (see ll. 414-16). In part the Article reads as follows: ". . . to such as rightly, worthily, and with faith receive the same, the bread which we break is a partaking of the body of Christ, and likewise the cup of blessing is a partaking of the blood of Christ. Transubstantiation, or the change of the substance of bread and wine, in the Supper of the Lord, cannot be proved by Holy Writ; but is repugnant to the plain words of Scripture. . . . The body of Christ is given, taken, and eaten in the Supper only after an heavenly and spiritual manner. And the mean whereby the body of Christ is received and eaten is faith."

138. LINES PRINTED UNDER THE ENGRAVED PORTRAIT OF MILTON.

1-2. I.e., Homer, Virgil, and Milton.

143. TO MR. CONGREVE.

48. "*Tom* the first" is Thomas Shadwell (see note to p. 96), who succeeded Dryden as poet laureate after the Revolution of 1688, and also took Dryden's post of historiographer royal. "*Tom* the second" is Thomas Rymer, who succeeded Shadwell as historiographer. Rymer has since, whether with justice or not, become almost a symbol of the extreme of neo-classic dogmatism.

SAMUEL BUTLER

149. HUDIBRAS, PART I, CANTO I.

The objects of Butler's satire in this poem were several. Like Dryden, he was a conservative in religious matters and despised all the left-wing sects of Christianity. In *Hudibras* he attacked the Presbyterians through the character of the Knight himself, and the various independent sects, including the Anabaptists and the Rosicrucians, through the character of the squire Ralpho. His common-sense, empirical attitude toward intellectual problems made him reject the subtleties of metaphysics, especially those of the scholastic sort (ll. 127 ff.). In fact, pedantry of any kind seemed to him a misuse of the intellect, and pretensions to intricate and esoteric knowledge were meat for his satire (see, e.g., ll. 51 ff.).

As to the literary method of this satire, it is interesting to note that it is the exact opposite of the mock-heroic. In the mock-heroic style, trivial matters are made ridiculous by being treated as if they were great ones. See, for instance, Dryden's *Mac Flecknoe* and Pope's *Rape of the lock* and *Dunciad*. But in *Hudibras* great matters—the church, the state, philosophy, scholarship—are treated as something low and vulgar. This comic vulgarization of weighty subjects has been a characteristic method of some of the world's greatest satirists—Swift, in English literature, being its foremost exponent (see *A tale of a tub* and *Gulliver's travels*). The distinction between these two types was well observed by Peter Motteux in the seventeenth century. In his *Gentleman's journal*, January, 1692-3, pp. 26-27, he remarked that the art of what he called burlesque consisted in part in "a disproportion between the style in which we speak of a thing and its true *Idea*," and that that was "the distinguishing mark of *French* and *Italian* Burlesque, of which there seems to be two sorts; as when low and mean expressions are us'd to represent the greatest Events, as in *Scarron's Virgil Travesty*, or great and lofty terms to describe common things, as in *Boileau's Lutrin*. . . ." As a matter of fact, the development of "burlesque" poetry did tend to fall rather definitely into these two varieties (see R. P. Bond, *English burlesque poetry, 1700-1750* [Cambridge, Mass, 1932], pp. 21-22 and *passim*).

Though this poem is not essentially a personal satire, it seems evident from the reference in l. 896 that when creating the character of Hudibras, Butler had in mind Sir Samuel Luke, a rigid Presbyterian, who had been a general under Cromwell. Butler had been secretary to Luke during the Cromwell régime, and one easily imagines that he found his position unpleasant. The total personality of Hudibras, however, is a grotesque fiction that vastly exceeds any actual model.

Fuller annotations of this poem are given in the editions of Zachary Grey (1744) and of the Rev. Treadwell R. Nash (1793).

150, 66. Analytic, or analytics, is that portion of logic which describes, in an exact terminology, the general forms which reasoning takes. The term is derived from the Aristotelian *Organon*, in which "Prior Analytics" and "Posterior Analytics" dealt, respectively, with syllogisms and the construction of scientific demonstrations.

151, 120. By Erra Pater, Butler may have meant William Lilly the astrologer. He had so referred to Lilly in his *Mercurius Menippus* [*Memoirs of the years 1649 and 50*]. But there was also, apparently, a real Erra Pater—an old astrologer, who is referred to by various seventeenth-century writers (see Zachary Grey's edition of *Hudibras*). It may be, rather, that Lilly is Sidrophel "the Rosy-crucian," in Part II, Canto III of the poem (see note to p. 190, l. 15).

152, 152. Alexander of Hales (d. 1245), one of the scholastic divines, was called Doctor Irrefragible or Invincible.

153, 189. Cf. Dryden's characterization of the Presbyterians, pp. 127-28, ll. 154-96.

154, 258. The Order of the Cordeliers in France (corresponding to the Grey Friars in England) was the strictest of all the branches of the Franciscan Order.

155, 279. Taliacotius was a physician at Bologna in the sixteenth century. A facetious account is given in the *Tatler*, No. 260, of his skill and reputation in the manufacture of noses. As to the sympathetic quality of the noses, the *Tatler* relates: "The sympathy between the nose and its parent was very extraordinary. . . . An eminent instance . . . happened to three Spaniards, whose noses were all made out of the same piece of brawn. They found them one day shoot and swell extremely; upon which they sent to know how the porter did: and heard, upon enquiry, that the *parent of the noses* had been severely kicked the day before. . . ." The basis of such tales as this was Taliacotius's own treatise on surgery by grafting, *De curtorum chirurgia per insitionem* (1597).

157, 370. Bailiffs arrested persons by giving them a tap on the shoulder.

159, 461. "*Tyrian* Queen." Dido, who, upon trying to purchase land on which to build a city, was offered, for a price, as much land as she could surround with an ox-hide. By cutting the ox-hide into small strips, she was able to claim a very large tract of land. Cf. *Aeneid,* I, 365-68.

470. "*Trojan* Knight." Aeneas. Book VI of the *Aeneid* relates Aeneas's descent into hell. Hell is also a name for a tailor's waste-basket.

476. "*New light*" was in Butler's day a popular term for current doctrines in religion which broke more or less sharply with tradition, and the holders of which claimed superior enlightenment.

504. This line alludes to the practice of immersion, which the Anabaptists declared to be the only efficacious mode of baptism.

160, 533. "Sir *Agrippa.*" Cornelius Agrippa (1486-1535), a German soldier and physician, wrote *De occulta philosophia,* a defense of magic as a way to knowledge of God and nature.

535-36. Anthroposophus was a nickname for Thomas Vaughan (1622-66), who was also dubbed "the Magician." He was a brother of the poet Henry Vaughan, and an illuminatus of the first rank. He wrote a treatise entitled *Anthroposophia theomagica,* upon the state of man after death; hence the nickname. Robert Fludd (1574-1637) was an English physician, alchemist, and Rosicrucian. Among his works was an *Apologetic tract* defending the Rosicrucians. Jakob Behmen, or Böhme (1575-1624), a celebrated German mystic, wrote *The way to Christ.*

540. "*Veré adeptus.*" Cf. Zachary Grey's note in his edition of *Hudibras*: "A title assumed by such alchymists as pretended to have found out the philosopher's stone, called Adept Philosophers."

547. "Numbers." This line alludes to the Pythagorean theory of numbers, i.e., that numbers actually constituted the essence of material things.

554. "*First Matter.*" In Aristotelian and scholastic metaphysics a thing could have determinate existence only by the addition of a particular form (see l. 556) to a formless and barely existent

component. First matter was therefore what had this bare existence before the first act of creation.

162, 640. George Wither, or Withers (1588-1667), William Prynne (1600-69), and John Vicars (1580?-1652) were Puritan pamphleteers. Wither and Vicars were also poets. The latter was notorious for the badness of his verse and the violence of his polemic writings. Concerning Wither, see note to p. 455, l. 126.

164, 730. The references are to the Solemn League and Covenant of 1643 and to the "Good Old Cause," as the Puritan movement was called in Commonwealth days. Cf. p. 165, ll. 756-64.

736. "*Nare.*" From Latin *naris*, nose.

742. "*Cane & angue pejus.*" "Worse than dog and serpent." The phrase is proverbial, and alludes to the Roman method of punishing parricides by tying them up in a sack with a dog, a snake, and a monkey, and throwing them all into a river.

746. "*Cynarctomachy.*" A concoction of Butler's, meaning bear-baiting. It is derived from the Greek words for dog, bear, and fighting.

165, 774. "*mordicus.*" "With the teeth."

780. "*Boute-feus.*" Artillery term, referring to the firebrand used to set off cannon.

166, 799. "*Bear-baiting.*" The Presbyterian Assembly, which Ralpho, as an Independent, rejects.

807. Butler here refers to the three grades of assembly in the Presbyterian church: the classis (see l. 830, and note) or presbytery, the provincial synod, and the national synod.

815-26. This passage is a burlesque on the subtleties and technicalities of scholastic disputations. The argument of Hudibras runs as follows: Ralpho's *thesis*, that bear-baiting is anti-Christian, may be granted to be precisely true, according to rule of reasoning (*ad amussim*); for Hudibras agrees word for word (*totidem verbis*) with Ralpho's denial that bear-baiting is more lawful than synods, according to divine justice (*jure divino*). (The denial appears in ll. 805-07.) But Hudibras nevertheless scents a fallacy in Ralpho's argument: he suspects Ralpho of implying that if his first point were granted, that bear-baiting is unlawful because unscriptural, it would follow that synods are equally unlawful, by *homoeosis*, i.e., the formula that whatever can be predicated of a thing can be predicated of other things which resemble it in essentials (in this case, the thing predicated is lack of scriptural authority). It appears that Ralpho does actually intend such an implication; see his reply in ll. 827-38.

830. "*Classis.*" The term, like "presbytery," was used in the Reformed Church to signify a minor assembly of ministers and elders in a district. It was commonly used in England during the Puritan régime. Butler seems to mean here not only the classis proper but the provincial synod also.

841. "*Mira de lente.*" "A great stir over nothing."

168, 909. "*Phrygian* Knight." Laocoön, who thrust his spear into the Trojan Horse to see if there were any men in it. See Virgil, *Aeneid,* II, 50 ff.

JOHN WILMOT, EARL OF ROCHESTER

185. A SATYR AGAINST MANKIND.

1-7. The paradox that animals are superior to man had considerable currency in the sixteenth and seventeenth centuries. It was of ancient origin, being found, for example, in Plutarch's *Gryllus*, a dialogue between Ulysses and several beasts who were men before they had fallen under the power of Circe. It bears an obvious relation to primitivism (see p. 749, ll. 78 ff., and note), though it must be distinguished from the latter, since it does not assert *man's* natural state to be fortunate. George Boas, in *The happy beast in French thought of the seventeenth century* (Baltimore, 1933), has given it the convenient name of "theriophily."

As Boas shows, the idea was often used for satirical purposes, especially for satire or censure of man's pride. Among others, Montaigne, in "The apology for Raimond Sebond," contributed an important and influential treatment of the subject, stressing the theme that man is not so superior as he thinks, and condemning man's thirst for knowledge. A work more directly related to Rochester's poem is the Eighth Satire of Boileau (1663). This piece has been called the source of Rochester's *Satyr*; at any rate, there are certain broad parallels of thought between the two poems. Boileau begins with the idea that man is the stupidest of animals, and goes on to point out that he lacks true wisdom, that he is more murderous than other animals, that his much-prized reason only leads him into folly, and that beasts get along better without any such faculty.

186, 13-30. Cf. Montaigne, "The apology for Raimond Sebond," *Essays,* trans. Cotton (London, 1902), II, 291: "And if it be so, that he only of all the animals has this privilege of the imagination, and this irregularity of thoughts representing to him that which is, that which is not, and that he would have, the false and the true; 'tis an advantage dearly bought, and of which he has very little reason to be proud; for from that springs the principal fountain of all the evils that befall him, sin, sickness, irresolution, affliction, despair."

33-34. Cf. ll. 94-97, and note.

187, 73. Nathaniel Ingelo (1621?-83) was a divine, and the author of sermons and other religious works, including a religious romance entitled *Benvolio and Urania* (1660).

74. Simon Patrick (1626-1707), bishop of Ely, was the author of *The parable of the pilgrim* (1665). Richard Sibbes (1577-1635), a Puritan divine, wrote numerous sermons and devotional tracts.

94-97. Rochester's doctrine in these lines is an allusion to the main teaching of Epicureanism concerning the end of life and the proper means of attaining that end. Thomas Stanley, in his *History of philosophy, containing the lives . . . of the philosophers* (1655-62), had provided an account of Epicureanism which was well known and which Rochester had very likely read. As Stanley explains (*Lives of the philosophers* [4th ed.; London, 1743], p. 618), the happy life, according to Epicurus, consists in "the Tranquility of the Mind, and Indolency of the body, but especially in the former. . . ." To the attainment of such a life it is necessary that man's thinking be confined to its proper objects. In Stanley's words (*ibid.*, p. 619), "Now whereas the principal Parts of Philosophy are held to be two; one *Physick*, consisting in Contemplation of Nature; the other *Ethick*, which treats of directing of manners in order to happy Life, it is manifest, either that *Ethick* comprehends all Philosophy, or that *Physick* comes to be a Part thereof, only inasmuch as it conduceth to happy Life."

The position against which this doctrine stands in contrast is that expressed in Aristotle's *Nichomachean ethics*—that the exercise of the speculative faculty is the highest human activity, hence the contemplative life, the life of the philosopher, is the best life of all. Epicurus, on the other hand, rejects not only metaphysical speculation but also poetry (since it gives rise to useless fancies) and dialectic because ". . . it doth nothing but beget thorny Questions, being an empty Bubbling and Forge of Cavils." See Stanley, pp. 618-19.

100-01. Cf. Stanley, *Lives of the philosophers* (1743), p. 621: ". . . Sense is the first of the Criteries, to which we may appeal from the rest, but itself is self-evident, and of manifest Truth."

188, 120. Sir Thomas Meres (1635-1715) was a prominent member of Parliament and a Whig politician.

189, 159. Cf. p. 325, ll. 409-10.

190. UPON DRINKING IN A BOWL.

11. Maastricht was a frontier town and fortress, the capital of the province of Limburg, Holland. It was taken by the French in 1673.

12. "*Yarmouth* Leaguer." The phrase is an allusion to the French-English campaign against the Dutch in 1673. The English troops were gathered at Yarmouth.

15. "Sidrophel the Rosy-crucian" appears in Butler's *Hudibras*, Part II, Canto III. He is an astrologer of great note, whom men consult on all sorts of problems. It has been supposed that Butler was satirizing William Lilly, a famous astrologer and almanac-maker who was consulted by both Cavaliers and Puritans at different times during the revolutionary period. Possibly Rochester is here alluding to Lilly rather than to the fictitious character in *Hudibras*.

JOHN OLDHAM

197. SATYRS UPON THE JESUITS. PROLOGUE.

Cf. note to p. 116, ll. 15-16. This poem was occasioned by the Popish Plot (see note to p. 67).

17. Francisco Suarez was a Jesuit theologian, whose *Defensio fidei* (1613) was burned in England and France. Antonio Escobar y Mendoza, another Jesuit, was identified with the doctrine that purity of intention justifies criminal acts.

20. "*Ignatian.*" A Jesuit; from St. Ignatius Loyola, the founder of the Society.

198, 31. The Royalist leanings of Robert Wild (1609-79), Puritan divine and poet, did not prevent his being coupled with the then notorious Withers, or Wither, one of the spokesmen of the Commonwealth cause (see note to p. 162, l. 640).

35. St. Omer's was a famous Jesuit college founded *c.* 1593 for the purpose of propagating Catholic doctrine in England. Since at that time such an institution was forbidden on English soil, the College was established near Calais, to be as near England as possible. The "dose" evidently means the body of doctrine and propaganda sent out by the College.

199. THE CARELESS GOOD FELLOW.

26. Sir Algernon Sidney was a veteran politician and intriguer, who had been involved in shady intrigues with the French. In 1682 he was beheaded for treason. Jean-Antoine, Comte D'Avaux, was for many years a diplomatic official, an ambassador and counselor, who took part in all the main negotiations of his time.

40. "Mr. *Fox.*" The "careless good fellow" had evidently heard of John Foxe's *Actes and monuments* (1563), generally known as the Book of the Martyrs.

MATTHEW PRIOR

207. ODE WRITTEN IN 1688.

26-58. Cf. p. 8.

209, 100. "Reason's glimmering Light." Cf. p. 106, l. 5, and context.

209. THE SECRETARY.

Prior was for several years (1690-97) the secretary of the English ambassador at the Hague, in which post he established a reputation as a diplomatist, while not neglecting society or the poetic art.

211. TO A LADY.

29. The Parthians were traditionally noted for their ability to

inflict damage on an enemy while actually retreating, and are supposed to have used this skill as a means of offense.

216. Written in the Beginning of Mezeray's History of France.

14. Pharamond was a legendary king, supposedly the first king of France; his reign has been placed in the early fifth century.

217, 18. *"Cambray"* signifies the celebrated French author and "philosophe" Fénelon, Archbishop of Cambrai, whose worldly wisdom might have been equal to the difficulties of Prior's question. The famous *Fables* of Jean de La Fontaine qualified him also to speak of human nature.

223. An Epitaph.

The motto: "Let who will stand firm upon the slippery pinnacle of princely power." Seneca, *Thyestes* 391-92.

DANIEL DEFOE

235. The True-Born Englishman. Part I.

This satire was occasioned by a piece by John Tutchin (1661?-1707) called *The foreigners* (1700), which had expressed discontent with the fact that England was at that time ruled by a foreign-born king, William, who had been the Prince of Orange, and that William was bestowing favors and offices on his countrymen. Defoe, being a loyal supporter of William, responded with this poem in ridicule of English pretensions to, and pride in, racial purity. See, e.g., ll. 317-18, 349-53.

238, 147. Charles Davenant, son of the poet Sir William D'Avenant, published in 1700 a *Discourse upon grants and resumptions*, in which he protested against the way in which forfeited estates had been given away by the Crown instead of being applied (as he thought they should have been) to the payment of the public debt.

240, 213. See I Samuel xxvi. David showed his generosity when he refused an opportunity to kill his pursuer and persecutor Saul at Hackilah. He thereby won Saul's affection.

218. *"Pict-land."* A name for the Scottish Highlands, or that part of Scotland lying north of the Forth River.

249-50. *"Italian Castlemain"* was Barbara Villiers, later the Countess of Castlemain. *"French Portsmouth"* was Louise de Kérouaille, who became Duchess of Portsmouth. By *"Taby Scot"* Defoe may have meant Lucy Walter, mother of the Duke of Monmouth (see note to p. 67). The *"Cambrian,"* i.e., Welshwoman, may then signify Nell Gwyn, whose name at least was Welsh, though her parentage was a matter of doubt.

256. Frederick Herman Schomberg, an old military commander who at various times had served the Germans, French, Portuguese, and English, eventually had the honor of helping William

of Orange enter England in 1688. He became naturalized and received several titles, among them that of Duke of Schomberg. William Bentinck, a Dutchman, diplomatic agent of William of Orange, was made Earl of Portland when William became King of England.

243, 354-55. The Bohn Library edition (adapted from Sir Walter Scott's edition) of Defoe's *Works* (1896), V, 443, supplies the names as follows:

"Her Sackvills, Savils, Cecils, Delamers,
Mohuns, Montagues, Duras, and Veeres. . . ."

JONATHAN SWIFT

254. HORACE. EPISTLE VII. BOOK I.

1. *"HARLEY."* See note on p. 450.

16. Erasmus Lewis was Harley's secretary.

255, 36. Thomas, first Marquis of Wharton, was the guiding hand of the Whig faction during the years when it was opposing Harley. From 1710 to 1714, while Harley was in power, Wharton was a constant source of annoyance.

256, 111. Parvisol was Swift's agent in Ireland. He was apparently not a servant of scrupulous honesty.

257, 120. Read was Harley's porter.

257. STELLA'S BIRTH-DAY.

"Stella" was Esther Johnson, whom Swift met while he was living in the house of Sir William Temple. The meeting resulted in a friendship which terminated only with her death in 1728 and which, from the point of view of the world, has constituted one of the most famous and most mysterious of love affairs. Swift has been supposed to have been secretly married to Stella, but there is no substantial evidence on this point.

260. IN SICKNESS.

During the years just previous to the Queen's death, Swift had enjoyed an extremely happy association with Arbuthnot, both being of the company of wits and literary men who gathered round Harley as lord treasurer.

267. THE BEASTS CONFESSION.

203-06. Cf. p. 185.

268. VERSES ON THE DEATH OF DR. SWIFT.

Swift seems to have at first intended that this poem should remain in manuscript until after his death; it was published, however, with his permission.

271, 166. *"drapier."* See p. 274, ll. 291-93, and note.

272, 177. Lady Suffolk had once been counted on by the members of the opposition to Walpole (see note to ll. 187-94) as an aid to their cause at court; but by the time this poem was written, they had come to believe that she had betrayed them.

179-80. See note to p. 489, l. 61.

187. *"Chartres."* Note probably by Swift (attributed to him by W. E. Browning, ed., *The poems of Jonathan Swift,* I, vi): "Chartres is a most infamous vile scoundrel, grown from a foot-boy, or worse, to a prodigious fortune, both in England and Scotland."

187-94. After 1721, when Sir Robert Walpole stepped into government leadership, political sentiment against him began to take a drift which presently brought into existence a group known as the Opposition. This group, led after 1726 by Bolingbroke (Henry St. John) and William Pulteney (see p. 269, ll. 57-60), attracted to itself nearly all the prominent literary men of the time, including Swift, Pope, Thomson, Gay, Fielding, and Akenside. The official journal of the group was the *Craftsman* (see p. 273, ll. 271-74), fruit of the alliance of Bolingbroke and Pulteney after the latter's formal rupture with Walpole in 1726. Bolingbroke, after some unhappy attempts to cooperate with Walpole's government, had been in retirement, and now welcomed the opportunity offered in the *Craftsman.*

195. *"Curll."* See note to p. 453, l. 38.

198. Note probably by Swift (cf. note to l. 187): "Three stupid verse-writers in London; the last, to the shame of the court, and the highest disgrace to wit and learning, was made laureate. Moore, commonly called Jemmy Moore, son of Arthur Moore, whose father was jailor of Monaghan, in Ireland. See the character of Jemmy Moore, and Tibbalds, in the 'Dunciad.'"

273, 251. *"Lintot."* See p. 341, and head note.

268. While he was poet laureate, Colley Cibber discharged his duties faithfully in the matter of New-Year and birthday odes. See note to p. 272, l. 198.

270. Stephen Duck (1705-56) was conspicuous in his time as a "natural" poet, who could compose verse without benefit of formal education. His "unlettered muse" won favor with Queen Caroline.

274, 276. "Orator" Henley (John Henley, 1692-1756) was an eccentric preacher, a Cambridge graduate, who remained in the Church for some time, but eventually found himself too restricted there. In 1726 he set up a gaudy tub-pulpit in a market-place, whence he preached and lectured after his own taste, with great popular success. His ingenuity in using the lowest tricks of mob oratory seems to have been remarkable. He continued to be a public attraction for many years.

291-93. In 1724 Swift had published, in Ireland, a series of brilliant political pamphlets under the pseudonym of "M. B., drapier." The immediate occasion was the attempt of the English government to debase Irish money by introducing a huge quantity of copper coin, but there were broader implications; to Swift, the whole issue of Irish freedom was involved. His pamphlets so aroused the Irish people that the English government was obliged to give up its scheme, and Swift was hailed as the rescuer of the nation.

JOSEPH ADDISON

277. LETTER TO HALIFAX.

The motto, somewhat freely rendered: "I salute thee, Saturnian land [Italy], great mother of harvests and of men! For thee I undertake the ancient task of praise and song, having dared to uncover the sacred springs." Virgil, *Georgica* ii, 174-76. The Latin text as given is inaccurate. For *Aggredior* read *Ingredior*; for *fontes* read *fontis*.

281. THE CAMPAIGN.

The political situation back of this poem was somewhat tangled. The Tories were split into two factions: the group in power under Godolphin, to which Marlborough belonged; and the High Church group, which was trying to belittle the importance of the victory at Blenheim for the sake of their own hero Sir George Rooke, who had won naval battles at Gibraltar and Malaga. The Whigs, who had not let party spirit interfere with their genuine enthusiasm over Blenheim, now sided with Marlborough, and Godolphin was able to secure the services of Addison, who was a Whig, to write a poem celebrating the Duke's victory. The result was the present poem, which, whether it accomplished all that Godolphin hoped it would, at least won Addison an under-secretaryship. See G. M. Trevelyan, *England under Queen Anne: Blenheim* (London, 1930), pp. 418-23.

32. "CHURCHILL." The Duke of Marlborough.

283, 100. *"Eugenio."* Prince Eugene, the Austrian general whose forces were combined with those of Marlborough in the battle.

291. ODE.

Concerning the idea of this poem, Addison said, in the *Spectator*, No. 465 (in which the poem first appeared): "The Supream Being has made the best arguments for his own Existence, in the Formation of the Heavens and the Earth, and these are Arguments which a Man of Sense cannot forbear attending to, who is out of the Noise and Hurry of Human Affairs. *Aristotle* says, that should a Man live under Ground, and there converse with Works of Art and Mechanism, and should afterwards be brought up into the open Day, and see the several Glories of the Heaven and Earth, he would immediately pronounce them the Works of such a Being as we define God to be." Though in Addison's day there was nothing novel about the idea that "the heavens declare the glory of God" (see Psalm 19), certain circumstances conspired to give that idea a fresh vitality—notably the advances in astronomical investigation and theory which culminated in Sir Isaac Newton. See note to p. 564.

SAMUEL GARTH

294. The Dispensary. Canto IV.

In 1687 the College of Physicians of London passed an edict requiring its members to give gratuitous advice and assistance to the poor. The apothecaries of London made the carrying out of this edict difficult by failing in some respects to enter into the spirit of charity; and there was lack of harmony among the members of the College itself. In the Preface to the 1706 edition of the poem, Garth thus explained why he had written it: ". . . finding the Animosities among the Members of the *College of Physicians* encreasing daily . . . I was persuaded to . . . endeavour to Rally some of our disaffected Members into a Sense of their Duty, who have hitherto most obstinately opposed all manner of Union. . . ." As to the personal references in the poem, Garth said in this Preface: "If the *Satyr* may appear directed at any particular Person, 'tis at such only as are presum'd to be engag'd in Dishonourable Confederacies for mean and mercenary Ends, against the dignity of their own Profession. But if there be no such, then these Characters are but imaginary, and by consequence ought to give no Body Offence."

The outline of the story is as follows: Sloth, hearing of the plan to institute a free dispensary, feels that his rule of faction, feud, and neglect of learning is threatened. He sends an emissary to Envy, who, taking the form of an apothecary, incites his fellow apothecaries, who find their profits threatened, and some members of the College itself, to combine against the dispensary project. Their meeting of protest is portrayed in the canto here reproduced; it is followed by a violent battle, of which Garth himself said in his Preface: "The description of the battle is grounded upon a feud that happened in the dispensary, betwixt a member of the college with his retinue, and some of the servants that attended there to dispense the medicines; and is so far real, though the poetical relation be fictitious." At the end of the battle, the goddess Health appears, shames the faculty of the College for its dissensions, and shows the way to a proper fulfillment of its office.

5-6. Richard Bentley (not to be confused with the great scholar of the same name) was a bookseller who dealt largely in plays. Samuel Briscoe also printed and sold plays. The incident of his being "undone" is obscure. John Dunton, in his *Life and errors* (1705; see 1818 edition, I, 292-93), makes a cryptic mention of "revived Briscoe, who has printed for Dryden, Wycherley, Congreve, &c. and, by contracting a friendship with Tom Brown [a popular satirist and Grub Street hack], will grow rich as fast as his Author can write or hear from the Dead, so that honest Sam does, as it were, thrive by his misfortunes, and I hear has the satisfaction and goodness to forgive those enemies who are now starving, as a judgment upon them, for attempting his overthrow. . . ."

298, 211ff. The following names of Garth's friends are to be supplied: l. 211, Wycherley, Dryden; l. 214, Dorset; l. 218, Normanbys; l. 220, Addison; l. 226, Stepney; l. 227, Prior; l. 236, Montague.

AMBROSE PHILIPS

303. PASTORALS. THE SIXTH PASTORAL.

See note to p. 497, l. 179.

311. TO MISS CHARLOTTE PULTENEY IN HER MOTHER'S ARMS.

Charlotte and Margaret (see p. 312) were daughters of Daniel Pulteney. The poems to them were among those which earned for Philips the name of "Namby-pamby."

JOHN PHILIPS

314. THE SPLENDID SHILLING.

27-32. It is part of the parody to refer to the modern Welsh towns by their ancient names, thereby giving a tone of supposedly Miltonic erudition to the manner of utterance. For Cestrian read Cheshire; for Arvonian Mart, Aberavon, a small market town in Glamorganshire; for Maridunum, Caermarthen; for Brechinia, Brecon; for the Vaga, the Wye; for Ariconium, Hereford.

BERNARD MANDEVILLE

325. THE GRUMBLING HIVE.

416. *"the Benefits." The fable of the bees* (1714; augmented in 1723; further augmented by a "second part" in 1728), a potpourri of notes and essays which Mandeville wrote by way of elaborating the "moral" of this poem, had as subtitle the paradoxical catchphrase "private vices, public benefits." See p. 1134.

THOMAS TICKELL

335. TO THE EARL OF WARWICK ON THE DEATH OF MR. ADDISON.

This poem records a personal feeling amply motivated by the author's association with the subject of it. Addison had been the friendly monitor of Tickell's literary career (of which the present piece is the principal ornament); and when Addison became secretary of state (1717-19), he made Tickell his under-secretary. Tickell produced the edition of Addison's works in which this poem appeared.

336, 74. *Cato* was the title of Addison's tragedy, produced in 1713.

337, 102. See p. 503, and head note.

Colin and Lucy.

Footnote. This poem was in print before 1729. The original edition was apparently a Dublin broadside of 1725.

GEORGE BERKELEY

340. Verses on the Prospect of Planting Arts and Learning in America.

This poem was first printed in 1752. It was, however, written much earlier. Its content is apropos of Berkeley's *Proposal for the better supplying of churches in our foreign plantations, and for converting the savage Americans to Christianity, by a college to be erected in . . . Bermuda* (1725). A. A. Luce, in *Proceedings of the Royal Irish Academy*, XLII (1934), Section C, p. 116, quotes a letter of Feb. 10, 1726 (Dering to Lord Percival), which gives evidence that Berkeley had recently completed the poem at that date, though in Berkeley's own letter of the same date to Percival, the poem is attributed to "a friend."

5-12. See note to p. 749.

JOHN GAY

341. On a Miscellany of Poems to Bernard Lintott.

Lintot issued in 1712 the miscellany in which this poem appeared. As leading rival to the great Jacob Tonson (see l. 12, and note), he hoped to break Tonson's monopoly of fame as a miscellany-publisher.

12. "*Jacob*'s mighty name." Jacob Tonson the elder, sometimes called the first of the modern line of publishers, had a long and brilliant career. A man of learning as well as a publisher, he was noted for his judgment in choice of authors. Not the least of his exploits was his *Miscellany*, issued *seriatim* between 1684 and 1709 (date of the last part, first edition), which caused Wycherley to dub him the "gentleman-usher to the Muses."

343, 92. "*Pirate Hill.*" Henry Hills, Jr., was a notorious pirater of poems and sermons. In 1709 and 1710 he had issued numerous pirated editions, done cheaply and without any distinction of workmanship.

94. John Morphew was one of the principal publishers and

booksellers of this period. Popular novels, political pamphlets, and other ephemerae were his main productions.

343. A CONTEMPLATION ON NIGHT.

Cf. p. 291, "Ode."

344. THE SHEPHERD'S WEEK. THURSDAY; OR, THE SPELL.

This set of pastorals was begun as a parody on those of Ambrose Philips, but Gay did not overemphasize this original aim, and seems in fact to have lost track of it at times. The most obvious satirical touches are the names of the characters.

352. TRIVIA. BOOK I.

5. Trivia was a name applied to Diana as worshiped where three roads met. It meant also, however, simply "public streets," being the plural of *trivium*, "a place where three ways meet."

354, 72. "*White*'s." A chocolate house, famous as a gambling place. Swift called it "the common rendezvous of infamous sharpers and noble cullies."

356, 164. "tilts." Small pleasure boats on the Thames, with awnings that could be spread over hoops. These awnings were often more decorative than protective.

195. "hat unloop'd." Men of this day usually cocked or looped their hatbrims up at some point, with a fastening which could be loosened in case it was desired to let the brim down.

360. BOOK II.

98. "the post." In most London streets the edge of the pavement was marked by a line of posts.

363, 237. "*Samian.*" Pythagoras, who was born at Samos. The doctrine of transmigration of souls, here referred to, is supposed to have been taught by him.

364, 254. "*Cornavian.*" Cheshire. The *Connoisseur* for June 13, 1754, remarked about the district producing this famous delicacy: "I had rather live all my days among the cheese-mongers' shops in Thames Street, than pass such another spring in this filthy country."

288. "the thimble's cheats." Gay's note: "A cheat, commonly practic'd in the Streets, with three Thimbles and a little Ball"—the equivalent of the modern shell game.

365, 337. The New Exchange was a bazaar where milliners, seamstresses, and other women merchants did business.

366, 344-45. St. Paul's Church in Covent-Garden was supposedly designed by Inigo Jones, the famous architect of the early seventeenth century. It was regarded as a fine example of classic simplicity.

368, 475. William Fortescue (1687-1749), a friend of Gay from school days, was a capable lawyer, destined one day to become Master of the Rolls. In the year before this poem was published, he was called by the Inner Temple.

483. Arundel House, in the day of Thomas Howard, second Earl of Arundel (1586-1646), contained a fine collection of paint-

ings and other works of art, as well as a library. At the Restoration the contents of the house were variously distributed and the house itself was torn down.

370, 562. See note to p. 391, l. 270.

378. Fable XVIII.

The theory of painting with which Gay here waxes facetious was one widely accepted in the eighteenth century. An exact copying of the particulars of the subject (see ll. 15-22 of the poem) was considered inartistic, because beauty did not lie in the individuality of any object but rose from a process of modifying individual forms toward a general and ideal conception of human character (see ll. 27-32). For an elaboration of this doctrine, see Sir Joshua Reynolds's *Discourses on art* (1769-90).

381. The Beggar's Opera. Air I.

7. This line is undoubtedly an allusion to Walpole. The opera makes extensive use of the theme that statesmen are thieves and rogues on a higher plane—though the satire appears in the general trend of the plot more than in specific lines. Gay was a member of the Opposition (see note to p. 272, ll. 187-94), and the idea that Walpole was a dishonest statesman was prominent in Opposition propaganda. In the opera, this air is sung by Peachum, a gang-leader who makes money on the side by betraying his followers to the law.

ALEXANDER POPE

386. An Essay on Criticism.

The conception of the rôle of the critic and of criticism which Pope sets forth here is best understood when it is placed in the context of other conceptions to be found in the European tradition before the eighteenth century. In the dialogues of Plato the critic is identified at different points in the dialectic (1) with the inspired interpreter of inspired poets, the rhapsodist who, lacking a mastery of any art for the illustration of Homer, praises his author by being possessed by him (cf. *Ion*); (2) with the philosopher-ruler who, having attained knowledge of justice and the good, banishes the poet from the ideal state as a mere imitator (cf. *Republic*, Book X); and (3) with the censor of the possible state described in the *Laws*, whose business is to regulate the activities of ignorant poets by inquiring as to the correctness and utility of their imitations. According to Aristotle, the critic is a man disciplined in the practical science of poetics—a science concerned with differentiating the possible kinds of poetical works and with investigating the conditions of excellence in each; in his examination of particular works he seeks the justification of anything in a given poem in terms of something else in the same poem. For Longinus the critic is essentially a man of taste who assesses the greatness or "sublimity" of particular works or passages by means of touchstones supplied by the masterpieces of the past. For Horace, finally, the critic is again a man of taste, but one whose function is to be the spokesman of the best audience of his time and as such to instruct the poet in the conditions he must fulfill, or the "rules" he must obey, if he wishes to please this audience and attain lasting fame. In spite of Pope's respect for Aristotle (see, e.g., p. 388, l. 138) and his admiration for Longinus (see p. 400, ll. 675-80), it is clear that on the whole his conception of the critic's function is Horatian, and the main content of the *Essay on criticism* consists of precepts addressed to the critic concerning what knowledge he must have, and what faults, both of taste and morals, he must avoid if he desires at once to serve the good poets of his time and to protect polite society against the influence of the bad.

12. Cf. Addison, *Spectator,* No. 409: "It is very difficult to lay down Rules for the Acquirement of such a Taste as that I am here speaking of [i.e., an acute discrimination of degrees and kinds of excellence]. The Faculty must in some degree be born with us, and it very often happens, that those who have other Qualities in Perfection are wholly void of this."

387, 68 ff. The word "nature" was much used in the eighteenth century, and had a bewildering variety of meanings. Pope's use of it in this passage illustrates one of its most important significations. In Professor Lovejoy's analysis (*MLN,* XLII, 444-50) this meaning appears as definition No. 17: "The universal and immutable in thought, feeling, and taste: what has always been known, what everyone can immediately understand and enjoy." The critic who "follows Nature," therefore, is one who knows what all people, or at least what all of the best people, usually think or feel and who is consequently able, in his judgments, to discriminate between what is and what is not sure to please a polite audience because of its conformity with universal sentiment. See p. 392, ll. 297-98, and note.

88-89. A very common formula among critics of the seventeenth and eighteenth centuries who, like Pope, conceived of criticism in a Horatian sense. The meaning is simply that the precepts contained in the works of ancient critics like Aristotle, Horace, Longinus, and Quintilian, could be safely taken as guides by modern poets and critics since they were descriptions of the practice of poets who had given pleasure to many readers through a long period of time and since "Nature" (in the sense defined in the last note) is always the same. It is of course not true that the so-called "rules" in Aristotle's *Poetics* are merely "Just precepts thus from great examples giv'n"; they are propositions in an analysis of poetry which, though formulated on the basis of an inductive study of Greek tragedies and epics, has more than a merely descriptive validity. By Pope's time, however, the *Poetics* had been thoroughly assimilated to the essentially rhetorical approach of Horace, Longinus, and Quintilian, and his principles had come to be looked upon as having the same character and status as the precepts for pleasing refined audiences of the later critics.

388, 93. On this conception of "rules" as a code of literary etiquette prescribing what may and may not be safely said in a poem designed to please, cf. Longinus, *On the sublime,* chap. ii: "In all production Nature is the prime cause, the great exemplar; but as to all questions of degree, of the happy moment in each case, and again of the safest rules of practice and use, such prescriptions are the proper contribution of an art or system. . . . For genius needs the curb as often as the spur."

112-13. Textual critics. Cf. Pope's sneers at Bentley and Theobald in the *Epistle to Dr. Arbuthnot.* See p. 497, ll. 157-72.

114. "Invention" here means the faculty of discovering appropriate and interesting ideas on a subject. It implies a certain measure of originality. In the beginning a term in rhetoric, it had come to be applied to poetry and the arts in general, and meant that power of discovering new relations of ideas without which no great art (and, as Pope has it here, no great criticism either) is possible. Cf. also the discussion of "wit" and "fancy" in the note to p. 2.

115. Cf. Pope's amusing essay, "A receipt to make an epick poem," in the *Guardian,* No. 78, June 10, 1713.

129-30. "Mantuan Muse," "Maro." Names for Virgil.

138. "the Stagirite." Aristotle.

389, 140. That is, to observe the rules of the ancient critics is the safest way to "copy Nature." For an analysis of the variant meanings of this latter formula in the ancient critics, see *Modern philology,* XXXIV (1936), 1-35.

390, 208 ff. Cf. Longinus, *On the sublime,* chap. xxxiii: ". . . I am well aware that lofty genius is far removed from flawlessness; for invariable accuracy incurs the risk of pettiness, and in the sublime, as in great fortunes, there must be something which is overlooked. It may be necessarily the case that low and average natures remain as a rule free from failing and in greater safety because they never run a risk or seek to scale the heights. . . ."

391, 267. "La Mancha's Knight." Don Quixote. The incident is from the spurious *Second part of Don Quixote,* by Alonzo Fernandez de Avellaneda (pseud.), Book III, chap. x.

270. John Dennis (1657-1734), the famous critic and ambitious but unsuccessful dramatist, undoubtedly had ways of talking, as of writing, which were open to ridicule. This fact scarcely prevented him from taking offense at Pope's references to him in this line and in a passage later in the poem (p. 398, ll. 585-87). The result was one of the long-drawn literary quarrels that mark Pope's career. See note to p. 498, ll. 193-214.

392, 297-98. Cf. Boileau's declaration, in the preface to the 1701 edition of his works, that the poet achieves greatness by expressing justly the thoughts already possessed, though inarticulately, by a majority of his readers. Such a definition of "True Wit" was a reflection at once of the "classical" revulsion against the "metaphysical wit" of the earlier seventeenth century (see note to p. 2) and of the prominence among the critics of this period of the type of rhetorical approach to works of art of which Horace had been the chief representative in antiquity and of which the dominant tendency was a subjection of the poet to the taste and "thought" of the audience (see note to p. 386).

328. "Fungoso." A character in Ben Jonson's *Every man out of his humour*, who aspired to be in fashion, yet was always out of it.

393, 365 ff. The tradition of poetical criticism which Pope follows in this passage went back at least to the rhetoricians of the Alexandrian period. The best-known ancient model was contained in the treatise *On the arrangement of words* by Dionysius of Halicarnassus (*fl.* late 1st century B.C.). Cf. J. W. H. Atkins, *Literary criticism in antiquity* (Cambridge, 1934), II, 118, and note to p. 399, l. 665. Pope was doubtless familiar with the passage in Vida's *Art of poetry* (see note to l. 704, below) in which that critic applied to Virgil's *Aeneid* the principle that the sound should be an echo to the sense. Cf. Samuel Johnson's trenchant criticism of the method in the *Rambler*, Nos. 92, 94 (1751).

372. Camilla was the virgin queen of the Volscians. See the *Aeneid*, trans. Dryden, Book VII, ll. 1094 ff.:

> "Last, from the Volscians fair Camilla came,
> And led her warlike troops, a warrior dame . . .
>
> . . . .
>
> Outstripp'd the winds in speed upon the plain,
> Flew o'er the field, nor hurt the bearded grain,
> She swept the seas, and, as she skimm'd along,
> Her flying feet unbath'd on billows hung."
>
> (Text of the Cambridge edition)

394, 382-83. See p. 144, l. 20.

395, 463-65. Sir Richard Blackmore's *Satyr against wit* (1700) belittled the genius of Dryden among others. According to Blackmore, if Dryden's wit were to be put into a fire, a great stench would arise. Luke Milbourne attacked Dryden in his *Notes on Dryden's Virgil* (1698). Zoilus was the ancient critic whose strictures upon Homer have made his name a synonym for critical stupidity.

398, 585-87. The characteristics of John Dennis (see note to p. 391, l. 270) as a conversationalist are fairly well represented here, if tradition is not at fault. Dennis is called Appius from his tragedy *Appius and Virginia*, which had failed in 1709.

399, 648. "Mæonian Star." Homer, who was supposedly born in Mæonia, or Lydia.

665. Dionysius of Halicarnassus was a Greek rhetorician and historian who lived in Rome during the Augustan period. Among his important works are treatises *On ancient orators* and *On the arrangement of words*, in the second of which he made numerous analytical remarks about the style of Homer.

667. The *Satyricon*, a rambling novel by Petronius Arbiter (d. 66 A.D.), contains passages in which, in dialogue form, comments are made on the enfeebling of the arts by false standards, artistic and ethical, and criticism of both the past and the present thereby dispensed.

400, 669. The principal work of Quintilian (first century A.D.) was the *Institutes of oratory*, a comprehensive treatise on the training of men for the career of an orator. Though primarily concerned with the means of attaining eloquence, it touched, by implication if not otherwise, on many of the fundamentals of literary art in general.

675. The name "Longinus" remains a convenient designation of an unidentified writer (apparently of the first century A.D.) who composed a treatise *On the sublime*, one of the classics of literary criticism.

697. Giovanni de' Medici, or Pope Leo X (1475-1521), was a great patron of learning and the arts—befriending, among others, the poet Vida (see l. 704).

704. Marco Girolamo Vida (*c.* 1489-1566) was a scholar, poet, and ecclesiastic, who wrote, among other things, two Latin poems, the *Christiad* and an *Art of poetry*. The second of these puts him in the tradition of "arts of poetry" which stems from Horace and includes the *Essay on criticism*.

714. Nicolas Boileau-Despréaux (1636-1711) was the chief arbiter of French neo-classic taste. His *L'art poétique* (1674) won him the nickname of *Législateur du Parnasse*. It was, of course, suggestive of Horace's *Ars poetica*; hence Pope's line.

401, 723. "the Muse." John Sheffield, Duke of Buckinghamshire, who wrote a verse *Essay on poetry* (1682). Line 724 is from that poem.

725. Wentworth Dillon, Earl of Roscommon (1633?-85), was a poet, translator, and critic who, according to Samuel Johnson (in his life of Roscommon), "improved taste, if he did not enlarge knowledge." He is now remembered principally for his poetical *Essay on translated verse* (1684).

729. William Walsh (1663-1708) was said by Dryden, in the "Postscript to the Aeneis," to be "the best critic of our nation." His few writings do not incontrovertibly support this judgment; yet Pope, at least, must have found his opinions valuable, in the two or three years before Walsh's death in which they were acquainted. It is possible that the *Essay on criticism* owes much to Walsh's teaching. See George Sherburn, *The early life of Alexander Pope* (Oxford, 1934), pp. 54-59.

THE RAPE OF THE LOCK.

The occasion of this poem was a small episode in a country community: the snipping off of a lock of Miss Arabella Fermor's hair by Lord Petre. Pope's friend Caryll, a relative of Lord Petre, thought that the animosity resulting from the lord's action might be dispelled in laughter if Pope could show in poetry how inconsequential the whole matter was. Pope acted on the suggestion, but it appears that the desired end was not attained as far as Miss Fermor was concerned, and Pope did more for the world in general than for the neighborhood. There are two versions of the poem. The first, in two cantos, appeared in 1712. Two years later Pope revised the poem extensively, adding the machinery of the sylphs. This addition has been universally agreed to be a great improvement to the piece, though Joseph Addison disapproved and thought the first version good enough to be let alone. Later, at least, Pope seems to have taken this opinion of Addison's as a sign of the latter's jealousy. See note to p. 498, ll. 193-214.

418. CANTO V.

137. Pope's note: "John Partridge was a ridiculous stargazer, who in his almanacks every year never failed to predict the downfall of the Pope and the King of France, then at war with the English." In 1707-09 Swift had his fun with Partridge by issuing an almanac of his own, in which he predicted the death of Partridge himself, and later publishing demonstrations that Partridge had really died, for all that person's denials of the fact.

425. WINDSOR-FOREST.

298. "Mira." Cf. pp. 292-93.

429. PROLOGUE TO CATO.

42. "*Italian* song." The popularity of Italian opera in England at this time was a source of annoyance to more than one person of taste, both because it was a faddish importation and because it contained ridiculous features. Addison himself made several remarks upon opera, some serious and some facetious. See the *Spectator,* Nos. 5, 13, 18, 29, 314.

432. A FAREWELL TO LONDON.

The Elwin-Courthope edition of Pope's *Works*, IV, 481-83, supplies the following names: l. 5, Brocas, a minor poet, and Craggs (see p. 503); l. 7, Viscount Hinchinbroke, a young nobleman with whom Pope had done some merrymaking; ll. 31-32, Mrs. Younger and Mrs. Bicknell, two actresses who were friends of Pope.

433, 24. Pope started work on his translation of the *Iliad* in 1714, and that task remained one of his chief occupations (and one which he seems to have found very irksome) until its completion in 1720.

439. VERSES TO THE MEMORY OF AN UNFORTUNATE LADY.

This poem was thought, upon no apparent ground, to have been based on fact, and the lady to have been a lost love of Pope's.

Successive editors and commentators upon Pope kept the fiction alive for several decades after his death.

441. Eloisa to Abelard.

The version of the letters upon which Pope drew for numerous phrases was not the original, in Latin, but a translation made by John Hughes in 1714 from a romanticized French version which had appeared anonymously at Amsterdam and the Hague in 1693. Most of the ideas which Pope borrowed from the Hughes translation are not to be found in the original Latin.

449. Epistle to Martha Blount.

The title of this poem is misleading. The name of Martha Blount was a later addition on Pope's part; the verses had originally been addressed simply to a "young lady," who was evidently Teresa Blount, Martha's sister. "Zephalinda" (l. 7) was a pseudonym used by Teresa; "Parthenissa" (l. 46), a name applied to Martha. See Pope's *Works*, ed. Elwin and Courthope, III, 223-27, and George Sherburn, *The early life of Alexander Pope* (Oxford, 1934), p. 201. Martha and Teresa Blount and Lady Mary Wortley Montagu were probably the women who figured most largely in Pope's life. Of the three, Martha remained the longest in Pope's affections, and he willed most of his property to her. Lady Mary eventually became an object of his satire (see p. 501, l. 369).

450. To Robert Earl of Oxford.

Robert Harley, Earl of Oxford, was one of Pope's best friends, and a member, with Parnell (see l. 1), Pope, Swift, and others, of the Scriblerus Club, the activities of which terminated in 1714 with the death of Queen Anne and the change in the political situation. He was confined in the Tower from 1715 to 1717, and though eventually acquitted of the charges against him, ceased thereafter to be influential in political affairs.

451. To Mrs. M. B. on Her Birth-day.

Cf. p. 449.

452. The Dunciad. Book I.

The 1728 text of this poem, as also that of 1729 here reproduced, shows Pope's original conception of the subject, in which the hero is Lewis Theobald ("Tibbald"), the lawyer and scholar, and lesser rôles are given to a great number of Pope's enemies as well as to many "dunces" of other days. Theobald's offense had been to publish a volume entitled *Shakespeare restored* (1726), which contained a number of strictures on Pope's own edition of the works of Shakespeare. Some of the strictures were justified, but Pope felt himself much abused, and that too by a mere dull, grubbing pedant (cf. "pidling Tibalds," p. 497, l. 164). In 1742 Pope published *The new dunciad*, which in the following year was transformed into the fourth book of a new and much changed version of *The dunciad* itself. Before this 1743 version appeared, Pope had had a falling-out with Colley Cibber (1671-1757), the famous actor-manager-dramatist-laureate, and had determined to "elevate" him to the position of hero, reducing Theobald's rôle to a minor one. The numerous alterations necessary to effect the change of hero and the incorporation of the new fourth book into the design make the "Cibber" *Dunciad* something different from a mere final improved handling of the original idea. The 1729 *Dunciad* remains a highly polished piece, worth much on its own account.

Of the "dunces" that people this poem, some may have deserved the title in its most drastic sense, that of a mere dullard, whose mind shows little activity of any sort. But to Pope the term had also the meaning of a person who simply misapplies his mind, uses it upon unworthy subjects or in some illogical, perverse, nonsensical fashion. Theobald was (if we take Pope's judgment) a dunce of the latter sort. He did not lack mental capacity, but he insisted upon doing things which lay outside his proper talents (see l. 190).

2. "Smithfield Muses." Pope's note: "Smithfield [in the northern part of London] is the place where Bartholomew Fair was kept, whose shows, machines, and dramatical entertainments, formerly agreeable only to the taste of the rabble, were, by the hero of this poem and others of equal genius, brought to the theatres of Covent Garden, Lincoln's Inn Fields, and the Haymarket, to be the reigning pleasures of the Court and town. This happened in the reigns of King George I and II."

6. Cf. p. 143, l. 48, and note. Pope doubtless felt himself in a position similar to Dryden's, as one maligned by dunces and forced to witness their triumphs.

453, 22. See note to p. 274, ll. 291-93.

38. Edmund Curll was a publisher notorious for his low ethics, a specialist in scandal and pornography. He was also expert at pirating, and drew upon Pope's works among others. Pope and Curll had become permanent enemies by the time the *Dunciad* was composed. Pope's falling-out with Lintot (see p. 341, and head note) was over matters connected with the publication of Pope's *Odyssey* (1725-26). Pope explained the phrase "rubric post" (misprinted in the text "rubric's post") by saying that Lintot "usually adorned his shop with titles in red letters."

55. "genial Jacob." Jacob Tonson. See note to p. 341, l. 12. "Third-day" refers to the custom of devoting the proceeds of the third performance of a play to the benefit of the author.

454, 83. Sir George Thorold became Lord Mayor of London in 1719, with much ceremony. Just why Pope chose this occasion as the framework of his satire, is not apparent.

88. "Settle." See note to p. 101. Settle was city poet of London in 1719, and as such commemorated the induction of Thorold in verse.

96. The note in the 1729 version refers to John Heywood, poet

and dramatist of the time of Henry VIII, who is best known as the "father of English comedy." His non-dramatic works, by which he is supposed to have set some store, have since been rated below his comic interludes.

101. Pope links William Prynne and Defoe together as typical political writers. Prynne (1600-69) was a writer for the Puritan cause, Defoe a pamphleteer for different factions.

102. Lawrence Eusden was poet laureate at the time the poem was written. Sir Richard Blackmore (1655-1729), the author of several epics and of *The creation*, a philosophical poem (1712), was to Pope a representative bad poet. In 1728 Pope published a burlesque treatise entitled *Peri bathous; or, the art of sinking in poetry,* in which he quoted copiously from Blackmore.

103. "Philips." See note to p. 497, l. 179. Nahum Tate, minor poet, contemporary and friend of Dryden, was described by Pope as "a cold writer, of no invention."

104. See note to p. 498, ll. 193-214.

455, 112. "Sinking." See note to l. 102 above.

121-22. John Ogilby (1600-76) and the Duchess of Newcastle (1624-74) were type-instances of voluminous authors more noted for quantity than for quality. So also were De Lyra and Philemon Holland (1552-1637), mentioned in ll. 133-34.

126. George Withers, or Wither (1588-1667), and Francis Quarles (1592-1644) were poets and pamphleteers of the earlier seventeenth century. Wither, at least, was on occasion a better poet than Pope implies; yet both he and Quarles suffered from having subjects and styles which the neo-classic taste abhorred. Richard Blome (d. 1705), a compiler and publisher of the latter part of that century, was an expert at getting persons, sometimes for reasons of necessity, to write upon various subjects for him. He issued numerous volumes on geography, heraldry, and other learned subjects.

129. William Caxton is known as the first English printer. Wynkyn de Worde was his immediate successor.

142. "a little Ajax." Theobald's own translation (1714).

148. The balls used in lawn bowling are not perfectly spherical, but have two somewhat flattened sides opposite each other. This shape enables the bowler to give the ball a curved path, a trick which, when mastered, results in increased accuracy.

456, 161-68. See note to p. 452.

164. Theobald contributed notes on Shakespeare to *Mist's weekly journal* for some time after he had published his *Shakespeare restored* in 1726.

194. Mist was the publisher of a famous Tory periodical called *Mist's weekly journal* (1716-37).

200. Edward Ward (1667-1731) was a voluminous minor poet and writer of dialogues, sketches of London life, etc. Pope said

of his works that a great number "were yearly sold into the Plantations," i.e., the colonies.

457, 214. "Thulè." Pope's note: "an unfinished poem of that name, of which one sheet was printed many years ago, by Amb. Philips, a northern author [see note to p. 497, l. 179]. It is an usual method of putting out a fire, to cast wet sheets upon it."

240. Colley Cibber (see note to p. 452) was the author of several plays and the reviser of several more. His revamping of Shakespeare's *Richard III* was one of his most notable exploits. Charles Johnson (*fl.* 1724-34) was a dramatist of some ingenuity but an abject plagiarist given to understating, or forgetting acknowledgment of, his borrowings. John Ozell (d. 1743) was a prolific translator. One of his ventures had been a version of Homer which some persons declared superior to Pope's—a judgment which of course Pope resented.

244. John James Heidegger, a Swiss, succeeded in London as an opera producer, became manager of the Haymarket Opera House, and Master of the Revels under George II. He was remarkably ugly, and once won a bet with Lord Chesterfield that the latter could not, within a given number of days, find an uglier person in London.

247-48. Settle died in 1724. See note to p. 454, l. 88.

458, 250. Charles Gildon (d. 1724) had been a poet, dramatist, and critic of no great merit. He had coined for Pope the name "Sawney Dapper," and had otherwise abused Pope's reputation. John Banks had been active during the latter half of the seventeenth century as a writer of bad blank-verse tragedies. His only recommendation was a certain ability at melodramatic pathos, which prolonged the life of a few of his plays. Sir Robert Howard (1626-98) had been a friend of Dryden and had collaborated with him on the heroic drama *The Indian queen*.

260. Pope's note: "See Ogilby's Aesop's Fables, where, in the story of the Frogs and their King, this excellent hemistic is to be found."

459. EPIGRAM II.

"D———s." John Dennis. See p. 398, l. 585, and note.

EPIGRAM ON THE TOASTS OF THE KIT-KAT CLUB.

The Kit-Kat Club was a select group of Whig wits and politicians, which originated about 1699. Its name was derived from Christopher Cat, keeper of a pie-house in which the club at first met (see l. 3). The membership included Robert Walpole, Congreve, Steele, Addison, Vanbrugh; the secretary was Jacob Tonson (see note to p. 341, l. 12). In 1716 there appeared, in the fourth edition of Dryden's *Miscellanies*, Fifth Part, a set of "Verses written for the toasting-glasses of the Kit-Kat Club, in the year 1703"—which evidently constitutes the "pell-mell pack of toasts" mentioned in l. 7. See Robert J. Allen, in *Review of English studies*, VII (1931), 57.

460. AN ESSAY ON MAN.

When Pope began to plan and write this poem is not altogether clear, but he seems to have been actively engaged in its composition from at least the year 1730. Pope was at this time closely associated with Bolingbroke, who had become deeply interested in philosophical questions during his exile in France after 1714. It has often been supposed that in writing the *Essay* Pope did little more than put into verse ideas supplied to him by his friend, partly through conversations, partly through written memoranda drawn up at the poet's request. It is in every way probable that the *Essay* owes much to the immediate suggestion of the man whom Pope called (IV, 390) his "guide, philosopher, and friend," although the parallels which have been pointed out between lines of the poem and passages in Bolingbroke's posthumously published *Fragments* occasionally suggest that the philosopher may likewise have been indebted, at least for images and turns of expression, to the poet. The problem, however, is of minor importance since there are very few ideas expressed in the *Essay on man* which are not to be found widely diffused in the reflective literature of Europe throughout the whole period of the Enlightenment. Of most of them, indeed, Pope could hardly have been ignorant even if he had never known Bolingbroke.

The *Essay on man* has been characterized as "an undisguised panegyric of Reason." In one sense nothing could be farther from the truth. If by "Reason" is meant man's capacity for knowledge, his ability to construct metaphysical or physical systems, as these powers had been conceived in certain ages of the past, the whole tendency of Pope's argument is to destroy any such rationalistic pride in the human intellect. In passage after passage he insists upon man's speculative limitations, and he concludes with a pronouncement the effect of which is to confine the intellectual curiosity of mankind to questions of the most immediately useful and practical sort—"And all our Knowledge is, OURSELVES TO KNOW." (See, e.g., I, 17-32, 35-36, 61-66, 101-02, 123; II, 1-2, 19-52; IV, 19-34, 259-62, 398.) Again, if "Reason" is taken in the sense of man's practical intellect—his intellectual powers as ordered to action—the same trait is manifest: the doctrine which Pope expounds in Epistle II is not only hostile to the exalted claims of the Stoics (see II, 101-22) but, in one passage at least (II, 133-74), approximates very closely the type of extreme anti-rationalism preached by Mandeville in the early eighteenth century (see the introduction to F. B. Kaye's edition of *The fable of the bees*, Oxford, 1924). Finally, the primitivistic philosophy of history adumbrated in Epistle III has as one of its elements the idealization of a state of nature in which "pride" was not, "nor Arts, that Pride to aid" (III, 151), and as another the notion that the peculiar rôle of reformers of civilization lies not in the discovery of new truths but in the recovery of the simple "Faith and Moral" taught by Nature to the first of men (III, 283-87).

In another sense of the word "Reason," however, the statement quoted expresses an important truth about the *Essay*. Pope's announced purpose in the poem is to "vindicate the ways of God to Man," and his vindication consists in his saying over and over again that "Whatever is, is right," that is to say, that things as they are, the physical world with all its occasions of evil for man, man's nature with all its intellectual and moral limitations, constitute a universe which obeys rational necessities in all its parts. Man, Pope believes, can be urged to forego his "pride" and to "submit" because the world in which he lives has nothing arbitrary about it but is built according to principles which, when properly understood, must fully commend themselves to his reason. These principles are three in number. The first is the principle of plenitude: that God, being good, must manifest his goodness by the creation of a universe which is "full" (see I, 45) in the sense that every possible form or idea is actualized in it, subject of course to the law of contradiction. The second is the principle of continuity: that in such a universe there can be no gaps, but rather, as a late medieval writer expressed it, "such an order . . . among species that the highest species of one genus coincides with the lowest of the next higher genus, in order that the universe may be one, perfect, continuous." The third is the principle of gradation: that a full and coherent universe must necessarily be one characterized by a hierarchy or "chain" of unequal created beings and objects, ranging from the highest conceivable, short of God, to the lowest conceivable, short of nothing (see, e.g., I, 233-41). The conception of the general pattern of the universe involved in these three closely related principles was by no means a new one in the eighteenth century. Developed in antiquity by the Neo-Platonists out of doctrines expressed by Plato (particularly in the *Timaeus*) and by Aristotle, it had had a continuous life in the philosophical and theological literature of western Europe through the Middle Ages, the Renaissance, and the seventeenth century, until in the eighteenth century it attained almost (though not quite) universal diffusion and acceptance. Its history has recently been told in detail by A. O. Lovejoy in *The Great Chain of Being, a study of the history of an idea* (Cambridge: Harvard University Press, 1936); the student who wishes to understand this central aspect of Pope's poem, by virtue of which it can legitimately be described as a "panegyric of Reason," is urged to read Professor Lovejoy's volume.

469. EPISTLE II.

131. Cf. p. 492, l. 174.

475. EPISTLE III.

148. See note to p. 749.

485. EPISTLE IV.

278. "Lord Umbra, or Sir Billy." The former is Bubb Dodington, afterwards Lord Melcombe, a man of some prominence in political affairs and a patron of literary men (Pope later referred to him as Bubo—see, e.g., p. 500, l. 280; p. 512, l. 12). The latter is Sir William Yonge. He was thus described by Lord Hervey (the "Sporus" of the *Epistle to Arbuthnot*—see p. 500): [Sir W. Yonge] "had a great command of what is called parliamentary language and a talent of talking eloquently without a meaning and expatiating agreeably upon nothing beyond any man, I believe, that ever had the gift of speech" (*Memoirs,* ed. Sedgwick [London, 1931], p. 36). Pope was fond of linking the personalities of Dodington and Yonge together (see p. 500, l. 280; p. 512, ll. 12-13; p. 514, l. 68), perhaps because they were both inveterate place-seekers.

488. MORAL ESSAYS. EPISTLE I. TO LORD COBHAM.

Cobham was an army officer, a politician, and a patron of letters, Pope being one of those literary men whom he had befriended. Cobham laid out the famous gardens at Stowe (see p. 615, l. 1053).

489, 54. See note to p. 500, l. 299.

57. Manly was the name of the hero of Wycherley's comedy *The plain dealer*. The name was commonly used also to refer to Wycherley himself. See p. 142, l. 30.

59. "Umbra." Possibly Bubb Dodington. Cf. p. 485, l. 278, and note.

61. Queen Caroline seems to have been the object of some amusement for being more anxious to please people than her regal dignity required.

62. This is apparently an allusion to Swift.

490, 86. Newmarket was a famous horse-racing town.

87. The French moralists, Michel de Montaigne (1533-92) and his disciple Pierre Charron (1541-1603), were for Pope and many of his contemporaries models of penetration into human motives. The former was the author of a collection of *Essays* which had been twice translated into English. The latter composed treatises *On the three verities* and *On wisdom.*

108. Charles V of Spain (1500-58), after an unsuccessful conflict with religious factions in his realm, abdicated in 1556 and spent the few remaining years of his life in a small house attached to a monastery. Philip II of Spain (1527-98), son of Charles, is said to have been a grave, abstemious, and studious man, much given to reading and annotating. The abdication of his father, however, made him king at a time when war was essential to the preservation of the Spanish empire, and his reign was marked by continual conflict.

492, 187. Wharton, that is, feels he must rival not only Cicero but also the Earl of Rochester, the latter being perhaps the most notorious rake of the Restoration. Philip, Duke of Wharton

(1698-1731), was prominent in politics in the reign of George I. His political connections varied from support of Walpole's government to espousal of the cause of the Pretender.

493, 231. Pope's note: "An ancient nobleman, who continued this practice long after his legs were disabled by the gout. Upon the death of Prince George of Denmark, he demanded an audience of the Queen, to advise her to preserve her health and dispel her grief by dancing."

494. EPISTLE TO DR. ARBUTHNOT.

Dr. John Arbuthnot (1667-1735) and Pope had become fast friends many years before, and their association in the Scriblerus Club had made them well acquainted with each other's tastes in satire.

1. "good John." John Searl, Pope's servant.

495, 53. "Curl." Cf. p. 453, l. 38, and note. Curll's productions were multifarious, and he gave employment (for small remuneration) to many poverty-stricken writers.

62. Pope's "interest" with Lintot was at one time very considerable, the latter having published Pope's *Iliad* and *Odyssey*.

496, 97-98. Colley Cibber, the actor-manager and buffoon, "Orator" Henley, the charlatan preacher, and James Moore Smyth (cf. p. 678, ll. 31-32), the poet and witling, had been satirized in the *Dunciad*. Later (1743) Cibber was to be elevated to the rôle of hero in that poem.

100. "Philips." See p. 497, ll. 179-82, and note.

101. "Sappho." See p. 501, l. 369, and note.

135-41. In his younger days Pope met numerous men of importance, among whom the ones he names in this passage were possibly the most influential in furthering his career. George Granville, Baron Lansdowne (1667-1735), a prominent politician, doubtless increased Pope's acquaintance with affairs; William Walsh (1663-1708), poet and critic, much admired in the latter capacity by his friends, seems to have exercised a strong formative influence on Pope's notions of poetry; Sir Samuel Garth (1661-1719), physician, famous as author of *The Dispensary* (see p. 294), possessed a good-natured but pungent wit which seems to have been a source of attraction for Pope; Congreve approved of some of Pope's earlier pieces, and Swift long continued to be Pope's friendly though frank adviser; though he had but slight acquaintance with Bishop Talbot (1659?-1730) and Lord Somers (1651-1716), men in public life, he had a long friendship with John Sheffield, the Duke of Buckinghamshire (1648-1721); and he came to know the Bishop of Rochester (Francis Atterbury, 1662-1732) and Henry St. John, Viscount Bolingbroke (1678-1751), in the Scriblerus Club—forming, indeed, with the latter one of his strongest friendships (see note to p. 460, *Essay on man*).

497, 146. Thomas Burnet (1694-1753) and John Oldmixon (1673-1742) had been political place-seekers in the Whig faction, and literary hacks of no distinction. Burnet had been a favorite of Addison and one of those, apparently, whom the latter had taught to sneer (see p. 498, l. 202). Thomas ("Hesiod") Cooke (1703-56), another scribbler, had written *The battle of the poets* (1725), which represented Pope as having used shady methods with his collaborators in the translation of the *Odyssey*.

149. "gentle *Fanny*." Lord Hervey, referred to later (ll. 305-33) as Sporus.

150. The "painted mistress" is evidently Belinda, in *The rape of the lock* (see p. 404, ll. 121-48); the "purling stream" is a reference to the Lodona episode in *Windsor Forest* (see pp. 422-23). Dennis had attacked both these poems (see l. 153).

151. See note to p. 458, l. 250. Pope suspected Gildon of having been hired by the Whigs, or possibly by Addison (see p. 498, ll. 193-214, and note), to write attacks on him. One attack in particular, a *True character of Mr. Pope* (1716), issued anonymously, was attributed by Pope to Gildon and John Dennis (see the 1729 *Dunciad*, introduction to the "Testimonies of authors"). As Mr. A. E. Case has pointed out, in "Pope, Addison, and the 'Atticus' lines," *Modern philology*, XXXIII (1935-36), 187-93, common gossip plus a malicious hint from Addison's young stepson, the Earl of Warwick, would have been convincing enough to Pope. This hypothesis explains further why Gildon and Dennis are juxtaposed in the present passage.

153. "*Dennis*." See note to p. 498, ll. 193-214.

156. "the *Mint*." A district in Southwark, London, which for many years was a sanctuary for debtors, by common consent. The privilege of immunity was abolished during the reign of George I.

164. Richard Bentley (1662-1742) was Master of Trinity College at Cambridge, and one of the greatest classical scholars of his day, as well as one of the severest critics of the scholarly shortcomings of others. According to tradition, he had once said of Pope's translation of the *Iliad*, "It is a pretty poem, but it is not Homer."

"pidling *Tibalds*." See note to p. 452.

179. The "Bard" is Ambrose Philips (1675?-1749). Pope seems to have been jealous of the success of Philips's *Pastorals*, which many readers preferred to his own. He wrote anonymously for the *Guardian* (No. 40) an essay in which he praised Philips's pastorals with such obvious irony that Philips became violently angry. Pope also encouraged Gay to write *The shepherd's week* in ridicule of Philips's pastorals, but Gay as satirist turned out to be anything but severe.

180. In 1714 Philips had brought out a collection of *Persian Tales* in two volumes. See *Times literary supplement*, November 16, 1935, p. 752; December 14, 1935, p. 864.

498, 193-214. The "Atticus" of this portrait is Joseph Addison.

The quarrel between Pope and Addison is more difficult to explain than some of Pope's other quarrels. It was not an open quarrel like the one with Dennis; consequently the motives are not clear. Professor George Sherburn has given a very penetrating account of the subject in *The early career of Alexander Pope* (Oxford, 1934); see esp. chap. v.

In the beginning, Pope and Addison were friends, though not intimate ones. When, in 1713, John Dennis published a derogatory criticism of Addison's *Cato* (*Remarks upon the tragedy of Cato*), Pope responded with a pamphlet entitled *The narrative of Dr. Robert Norris, concerning the strange and deplorable frenzy of Mr. John Denn-s.* In Professor Sherburn's words, Dennis "was never called a fool more artistically than on this occasion" (p. 110). Addison, however, expressed disapproval of the vigor of the attack, indeed virtually disavowed responsibility for it, through a letter written by Steele to Lintot, who had published the pamphlet. If Pope knew of this letter (as is likely from his acquaintance with Steele), he had perhaps a right to think he had been let down. This may have been the beginning of Pope's dislike of Addison.

At any rate, the two gradually drifted apart. One cause beyond the above-mentioned incident may have been Pope's feeling that the group headed by Addison (the "little Senate" mentioned in l. 209) preferred the pastorals of Ambrose Philips to his own (see note to p. 497, l. 179). Another was that Addison seemed interested in Tickell's proposed translation of the *Iliad*, which was a potential competitor of Pope's. Besides, Pope became a member of the Scriblerus Club (with Arbuthnot, Swift, Gay, and others), the political tone of which did not fit with Addison's Whiggism.

Eventually an "overt act" was committed against Pope—not by Addison himself but by Burnet and Duckett, two members of the "little Senate," with Addison's advice (see Sherburn, pp. 133 ff.). The title was *Homerides: or, a letter to Mr. Pope occasion'd by his intended translation of Homer* (1715). About the same time appeared the *True character of Mr. Pope* (see note to p. 497, l. 151), which Pope probably thought had been written at Addison's instigation (A. E. Case, in *Modern philology*, XXXIII, 191). These pamphlets precipitated a series of attacks and counter-attacks in print, in which Pope certainly felt that Addison was his real, if hidden, opponent.

Ll. 202-03 of the present poem might be construed as an allusion to these events. It seems, however, that the "Atticus" sketch itself was conceived before, not after, the attacks—that it existed in some form in 1715 (Sherburn, p. 146). It is to be thought of as a carefully considered opinion formed at leisure, not as part of a verbal war. And ll. 202-03 express what Pope might well have known about Addison without having been a victim himself.

232. *"Bufo."* Probably Lord Halifax. Halifax had been the

patron of Tickell, whose translation of the *Iliad* had been in competition with Pope's. There is evidence that Pope originally intended these lines to refer to Bubb Dodington (see note to p. 485, l. 278). L. 230 in one of its manuscript forms reads B—b for Bufo (see Pope's *Works*, ed. Elwin and Courthope, III, 258-59). The lines about Dryden, however (p. 499, ll. 245-46), make the passage in its present form inapplicable to Dodington for chronological reasons.

500, 280. Cf. p. 485, l. 278, and note.

299-300. In his *Epistle to the Earl of Burlington* (1731) Pope had pictured a lavish estate (the "dean and silver bell" are two minor details of that picture) characterized by very bad taste. The source of his central idea may well have been certain remarks about bad architectural taste which had appeared in the Preface to Burlington's *Fabbriche antiche designate da Andrea Palladio Vicentino* (London, 1730). When Pope's *Epistle* appeared, however, it was immediately assumed to be a picture of Cannons, the estate of the Duke of Chandos. Cannons was a notably elaborate estate, but it is not possible to say now whether it significantly resembled the estate described by Pope. The fact that Pope and Chandos were very good friends makes it the less likely that the former intended to ridicule Cannons. See George Sherburn, " 'Timon's villa' and Cannons," *Huntington Library bulletin,* No. 8 (Oct., 1935).

305. "*Sporus.*" Lord Hervey (in l. 149 called "Fanny"). The original cause of Pope's animosity toward him is a matter of conjecture. By the time the present attack was written, however, sufficient motives existed, for there had been open warfare between the two. In 1733, Pope, in his *Horace, the first satire of the second book,* had ridiculed Lord Hervey under the name of Fanny. This attack was replied to in *Verses addressed to the imitator of Horace*, apparently a collaboration between Lord Hervey and Lady Mary Wortley Montagu, and in *A letter from a nobleman at Hampton Court to a doctor of divinity*, by Hervey. Pope's principal rejoinder was *A letter to a noble lord*, which has been called the prose counterpart of the *Epistle to Arbuthnot.* (See Courthope, *The life of Alexander Pope* [1889], pp. 260-67.)

501, 363. "*Japhet* in a jayl." Pope referred to this person several times in his poems. His note to the name in *Moral essays*, III, l. 86, reads thus: "Japhet Crook, alias Sir Peter Stranger, was punished with the loss of those parts [nose and ears], for having forged a conveyance of an estate to himself, upon which he took up several thousand pounds. He was at the same time sued in Chancery for having fraudulently obtained a Will, by which he possessed another considerable Estate, in wrong of the brother of the deceased. By these means he was *worth* a great sum, which (in reward for the small loss of his ears) he enjoyed in prison till his death, and quietly left to his successor." See also p. 515, l. 120; p. 517, l. 57; p. 520, ll. 185-90.

369. "*Sapho.*" Lady Mary Wortley Montagu. See note to p. 449.

373. "rhym'd for *Moor.*" See note to p. 678, ll. 31-32.

502, 375. Leonard Welsted had written a poem entitled *Of dulness and scandal*, in which he had suggested the existence of scandal behind Pope's "Verses to the memory of an unfortunate lady." See note to p. 439.

378-79. Eustace Budgell was in the company of persons who had attacked Pope. Matthew Tindal, author of a celebrated deistic work, *Christianity as old as the Creation* (1730), had apparently willed Budgell a large portion of his property, but Budgell was suspected of having forged the will himself.

380. "the two *Curls.*" Edmund Curll and Lord Hervey. See, respectively, note to p. 453, l. 38, and note to p. 500, l. 305.

503. To James Craggs, Esq.

Craggs had a brief but brilliant political career, somewhat marred by entanglement in the affairs of the South Sea Company, which collapsed in 1720. He died in 1721 of smallpox. Pope's admiration for him had a foundation in an intimate friendship, and was doubtless influenced by the fact that Craggs was an opponent of Walpole (see note to p. 272, ll. 187-94).

Imitations of Horace. The First Epistle of the Second Book of Horace, to Augustus.

1. "great Patron of Mankind." This and the succeeding compliments are of course ironical. The indifference of George II to literature was well known (see p. 511, l. 356). Moreover, at the time when this poem was written, it was a constant theme among the writers in the Opposition (see note to p. 272, ll. 187-94) that England's rights abroad, especially on the sea, were being trampled upon and that the government was pursuing a cowardly policy of peace.

504, 40. "Christ's Kirk o' the Green." Title of a comic ballad traditionally ascribed to James I of Scotland.

42. "the Devil." A tavern of Elizabethan times in London, where Ben Jonson presided over a poetical club.

505, 66. "Stowe." John Stow published *The chronicles of England, from Brute unto this present year of Christ, 1580.*

75-78. The reputation of Cowley, great during his life, suffered considerably in the eighteenth century from a widespread reaction in favor of what was considered a simple and natural manner, lucid and devoid of excess ornament. Cowley's poetry is an example (though not an extreme one) of the style which Samuel Johnson, in his life of Cowley, called the "metaphysical," characterized by an excess of "wit." Concerning this quality and its effects, Johnson says: ". . . Wit . . . may be . . . considered as . . . a combination of dissimilar images, or a discovery of occult resemblances in things apparently unlike. Of wit, thus defined, they [the metaphysical poets] have more than enough . . . they were not successful in representing or moving the affections. As they were wholly employed on something unexpected and surprising they had no regard to that uniformity of sentiment, which enables us to conceive and excite the pains and the pleasure of other minds. . . ." It does not appear that Cowley was as completely eclipsed as Pope implies in l. 75; he remained, in fact, the best-known poet of the "metaphysical" group. See A. H. Nethercot, "The reputation of the 'metaphysical poets' during the age of Pope," *Philological quarterly,* IV (1925), 161-79.

91-92. *Gammer Gurton's needle* was one of the first English comedies—1575, if not earlier. Pope describes it as "a piece of very low humour, one of the first printed plays in English, and therefore much valued by some antiquaries." *The careless husband* (1705) was a comedy by Colley Cibber. It was, as a matter of fact, very successful, though Pope's line seems to say the contrary.

98. Sir Philip Sidney, a classicist in literary theory, advocated the use of ancient metrical forms in English poetry—for example, the dactylic hexameter of Virgil's *Aeneid*. His own efforts to apply the theory were far from happy.

104. One of the less fortunate performances of the great scholar Richard Bentley was his edition of *Paradise lost* (1732) with numerous textual emendations, in which, needless to say, he failed to improve on Milton. The "desp'rate hook" probably refers to the use of brackets to set off interpolated words and phrases in the text.

507, 182. Pope describes Ward as "a famous empiric, whose pill and drop had several surprising effects."

183. The holders of the Radcliffe fellowships in University College, Oxford, were required to spend at least half of their time improving their experience and wisdom by foreign travel.

186. In the *Epistle to the Earl of Burlington* Pope placed the following note to Ripley's name (l. 18 of that poem): "This man was a carpenter, employed by a first Minister [Walpole], who raised him to be an Architect, without any genius in the art; and after some wretched proofs of his insufficiency in public buildings, made him Comptroller of the Board of Works."

508, 224. See p. 274, ll. 291-93, and note.

509, 290. Astrea was a common nickname for Mrs. Aphra Behn (1640-89), the well-known writer of scandalous plays and novels in the Restoration period.

293. "Pinky." William Penkethman, a comic actor who specialized in buffooneries which, as Colley Cibber remarked, were "more whimsical than natural." In the *Tatler*, No. 188, it is said that Penkethman "devours a cold chick with great applause." In the *Spectator*, No. 370, Steele said: "Mr. *Penkethman* is also Master of as many Faces in the Dumb-Scene as can be expected from a Man in the Circumstances of being ready to perish out of

Fear and Hunger: He wonders throughout the whole Scene very masterly, without neglecting his Victuals."

510, 309. "The coal-black joke" was the name of a very indecent popular song, the tune of which had great vogue and was doubtless used often with other words.

313. This line evidently refers to the successive rise to popularity of opera, which Pope considered to have spoiled public taste for drama proper, and of pageantry and pantomime, which carried even further the work of corruption.

511, 355. Merlin's Cave was built by the order of Queen Caroline in the royal gardens at Richmond, and adorned with astronomical figures and characters.

512, 419. "rails." The stalls of unhoused booksellers on these streets, who dealt mainly in old books. By Soho is meant, not the then fashionable Soho Square, but "Old Soho," later Wardour Street.

ONE THOUSAND SEVEN HUNDRED AND THIRTY EIGHT.

17-18. One Captain Jenkins was the person thus victimized, by his own account. This supposed outrage, among many others committed upon the English merchant marine, resulted, in 1739, in the "War of Jenkins' ear."

513, 24. The members of the Opposition (see note to p. 272, ll. 187-94) were fond of alluding to one another as "patriots." Walpole, in their propaganda, was no patriot, because he was indifferent to the welfare of the country, and was not only corrupting the government but enslaving the people. It was the duty of the patriotic Opposition, then, to revive in the English nation the spirit of liberty, which alone could resist the process of enslavement, and which had very much decayed in the régime of Walpole. See p. 515, ll. 160 ff.

27-36. The political character of Sir Robert Walpole was a frequent source of allusion in the verse and prose of this period, and the inspiration of a good deal of satire. Pope's position toward Walpole was ambiguous. He had known him and been friendly with him, as these lines state. On the other hand, he was a staunch friend of Bolingbroke, one of Walpole's most implacable foes. Ll. 151 ff. are in marked contrast to 27-36.

38-40. Pope's note: "Sir Joseph Jekyll, Master of the Rolls, a true Whig in his principles, and a man of the utmost probity. He sometimes voted against the Court, which drew upon him the laugh of ONE who bestowed it equally on religion and honesty. . . ." The "one" may mean Walpole. See Pope's *Works*, ed. Elwin and Courthope, III, 460.

45-48. Pope's note: "George Lyttleton, secretary to the Prince of Wales, distinguished both for his writings and speeches in the spirit of liberty." Cf. note to l. 24.

51. Cf. p. 519, l. 137.

65 ff. The "harmless characters" named all deserve the epithet except perhaps Lord Hervey (p. 514, ll. 71-72), who had aroused Pope to such a pitch of satiric zeal, in the *Epistle to Arbuthnot*, as would seem unlikely for a harmless person.

514, 68. Cf. p. 485, l. 278, and note.

71-72. Lord Hervey, Fox, the Senate.

74. Lord Hervey had composed an epitaph on Queen Caroline in Latin and English.

92. The Earls of Selkirk and of Delaware.

515, 120. Cf. p. 501, l. 363, and note.

135. Ralph Allen was a self-made man of wealth who was famous for his munificence. Pope's praise of him in these lines gains interest from the fact that he was also the original of the magnanimous Squire Allworthy in Fielding's *Tom Jones*.

153-54. At this time the Opposition was trying to force England into a war with Spain over the depredations committed by the latter on British shipping, while Walpole was determined to preserve peace. War was declared in 1739.

516. One Thousand Seven Hundred and Thirty Eight. Dialogue II.

11. Pope's note: "The Ordinary of Newgate, who publishes the memoirs of the malefactors, and is often prevailed upon to be so tender of their reputation as to set down no more than the initials of their name." One of Goldsmith's *Essays* (first published in 1760) is a memoir "supposed to be written by the Ordinary of Newgate," the subject being Theophilus Cibber, the son of Colley Cibber.

517, 54. *"Wild."* Jonathan Wild (1682?-1725) was an informer and a receiver of stolen goods who for a long time managed to preserve an appearance of honesty, behind which he committed various sorts of crimes. He was eventually hanged.

57. See note to p. 501, l. 363.

61. "S——k" is probably Lord Selkirk, an old courtier who had been active since the time of James II. Cf. p. 514, ll. 91-96.

67. William Kent was an artist and landscape designer. In the latter art he was something of an original genius, and had a great deal to do with advancing the informal type of landscape design. The phrase "Kent and nature" not only echoes the expression "art and nature" but suggests that Kent is an artist whose work is "natural" rather than formal. Pope had a great taste for wildness and irregularity in scenery, and carried out what he conceived to be those effects on his own estate at Twickenham. Cf. A. O. Lovejoy, "The Chinese origin of a romanticism," *Journal of English and Germanic philology*, XXXII (1933), 1-20.

69. "Craggs." Cf. p. 503, and note.

77 ff. Lord Somers and the Earl of Halifax had been friends of Pope in his younger days. Somers was deprived of his office of

Lord Keeper in 1700, while Halifax was turned out in 1710 when Harley came into power. The Duke of Shrewsbury, Lord Carleton, and James, Earl of Stanhope also hold places in Pope's earlier life. St. John (Bolingbroke), Lyttleton, Pulteney, and Chesterfield, as leaders of the opposition to Walpole, were prominent in Pope's present interest at the time of composition of the poem.

518, 82. Francis Atterbury, Bishop of Rochester, was perhaps the best preacher of his day. Upon being exiled as punishment for Jacobite activities real or supposed, he was by many regarded as a martyr.

86. This characterization of the Duke of Argyll is apt. He had been a distinguished soldier under Marlborough, and was apparently a man of vigorous manner and speech in state affairs.

88. Sir William Wyndham was a friend and political tool of Bolingbroke, whom he served capably during most of his career.

99. The "Man of Ross" was John Kyrle (1637-1724), so called from his estate at Ross, Herefordshire. He was famous for his philanthropic activities. The Lord Mayor of London at this time was Sir John Barnard, who, with Polwarth (see p. 519, l. 130), constituted an important part of the Opposition's oratorical battery. Walpole is supposed to have said that after Barnard and Polwarth had spoken, the worst part of the attack was over.

519, 129. As a writer in the pay of Walpole, Arnall was to all friends of the Opposition such as Pope an excellent exemplar of the art of lying.

130. "COBHAM." See p. 493, ll. 262-65. "POLWARTH." See note to p. 518, l. 99.

133-35. Cf. p. 513, ll. 29-30.

158. Cf. p. 514, l. 92, and note.

159. Sir Francis Page, a judge of the Common Pleas, seems to have been something of a bully in his courtroom. See Fielding, *Tom Jones,* Book VIII, chap. xi.

520, 185-90. See note to p. 501, l. 363.

521, 230-31. That is to say, the poetical skill of Waller's panegyric on Oliver Cromwell and Boileau's making a star out of the feather on a king's hat, cannot conceal the unworthiness of the subjects they treated.

237. John Anstis was king at arms of the order of the Garter. As such, he performed the ceremony of casting into the graves of peers their various insignia of honor.

238. The Elwin-Courthope edition of Pope's *Works*, III, 487, accepts the names George and Frederick for the single and double asterisks, respectively.

THE UNIVERSAL PRAYER.

This poem was apparently written as early as 1715. See George Sherburn in the *Philological quarterly*, XII (1933), 403.

522, 21-24. Cf. the *Essay on man*; see p. 465, ll. 233 ff.

ALLAN RAMSAY

533. AN ODE TO MR. F———.

"*Solvitur acris hiems.*" "Sharp winter is passing"—literally, "is being dissolved." Horace, *Carmina* i.4.1.

534. A POET'S WISH.

The Motto: "What sacred thing does the poet require of Apollo?" Horace, *Carmina* i.31.1-2.

EDWARD YOUNG

543. NIGHT-THOUGHTS. NIGHT I.

67-80. As to the ideas expressed in these lines, cf. p. 466, ll. 3-18.

73. Cf. p. 464, ll. 207 ff.

547, 234-36. Cf. p. 473, ll. 27 ff.

549, 340-43. Cf. Johnson, *The vanity of human wishes,* pp. 675-76, ll. 431 to the end.

551, 452 ff. This refers to Pope's expressed refusal, in the *Essay on man*, to explore the mysteries of the universe. See p. 466, ll. 1-2.

JOHN BYROM

553. EPIGRAM ON THE FEUDS BETWEEN HANDEL AND BONONCINI.

At the time of the first publication of this poem, the great composer Handel (1685-1759) had been engaged for some years in warm rivalry with Giovanni Battista Bononcini, or Buononcini (b. 1672), in the composition and production of operas.

LADY MARY WORTLEY MONTAGU

561. FAREWELL TO BATH.

17-24. Two of the most famous of the so-called assembly rooms at Bath were those conducted by Dame Lindsay, an opera singer, and by her sister Mrs. Hayes. (See Edith Sitwell, *Bath* [London, 1932], p. 45.) The principal amusements in these places were dancing and gambling. Dame Lindsay had a bad reputation in some quarters; Goldsmith, in his *Life of Richard Nash*, described her as having an outwardly pleasant manner but as being at heart a scoundrel who exploited helpless persons for her own profit (*Works of Oliver Goldsmith,* ed. Gibbs, IV, 94). The best of society frequented the assembly rooms. The dancers mentioned by Lady Mary were doubtless all good friends of hers; the Brownlow family, at least, she had known for some twenty years (see *The correspondence of Lady Mary Wortley Montagu*, ed. Thomas [London, 1898], I, 31-32).

25. Richard Nash (1674-1762), generally known as Beau Nash, had risen by his own ingenuity to the position of gambling entrepreneur, arbiter of fashion, and master of ceremonies at Bath. The author's solicitude here, if not ironical, must have been occasioned by a minor misfortune only.

JAMES THOMSON

564. A POEM SACRED TO THE MEMORY OF SIR ISAAC NEWTON. The enthusiasm of the early eighteenth century over Newton's discoveries and ideas was intense and widespread, and this poem of Thomson is a representative expression. Newton had rectified what seemed to be the old errors of the scholastic approach to nature (ll. 19-29, 82-90; cf. note to p. 8). He had reduced to terms of gravitation and projection not only the motions of the solar system (ll. 39-42) but those also of all other visible bodies in the universe (ll. 57-67). Besides, he had given man, through his statement of the laws of optics, a fresh guide to the beauties of nature, these beauties emanating specifically from perception of phenomena in the light of natural law (ll. 91 ff.; for an instance of "Newtonian" beauty in nature, see ll. 119-24). Such discoveries seemed evidence, not only of a perfect order in the universe, but of God's wisdom in the creation of such an order and of His constant presence as a guiding force (l. 138; cf. p. 623, ll. 29-36). As a matter of fact, Newton himself took this view of his work (see ll. 137-43).

566, 83. *"Vortices."* Descartes believed that all the particles of the universe were moving in innumerable vortices or whirlpools of varied sizes and velocities.

"Spheres." This is an allusion to the astronomical system usually called Ptolemaic, in which the motions of the heavenly bodies were explained on the hypothesis of spheres revolving variously about the earth. Ptolemaic astronomy prevailed virtually undisputed until after the time of Copernicus.

567, 157. John Conduitt, nephew of Newton by marriage, wrote a memorial sketch shortly after the latter's death, and seems to have attempted a larger biography of Newton—which, however, was not completed, though Conduitt possessed some valuable materials.

577. WINTER.

360. The practice of loading prisoners with irons, to simplify the problem of preventing escape from dilapidated prisons, became so common during the early eighteenth century that Parliament finally saw fit in 1729 to appoint a committee of investigation, which exposed many cases of excessive cruelty on the part of the wardens.

579, 441 ff. The passage on ancient governments which begins at this point reflects, in its stress on freedom against tyranny and servility, the propaganda of the Opposition. See note to p. 513, l. 24.

582, 558. James Hammond the poet, who died in 1742 at the age of thirty-two, was one of the younger men associated with the opposition to Sir Robert Walpole, and belonged to a clique that gathered around Frederick, Prince of Wales, in whom the Opposition professed to find an embodiment of their ideal conception, the patriot king.

584, 650. Monimia was the heroine of Otway's *The orphan* (1680). The rôle was a popular tear-producer.

651. Belvidera was the wife of Jaffier, the conspirator, in Otway's *Venice preserved* (1682). Actresses favored this part in the eighteenth century.

660. "Patriot-Virtues." See note to p. 513, l. 24.

590, 965. Peter the Great of Russia.

592, 1049-51. Cf. p. 485, ll. 309 ff.

594. AUTUMN.

13. "Patriot-Virtues." Cf. p. 584, l. 660, and see note to p. 513, l. 24.

607, 653-55. John Philips wrote a long blank-verse poem entitled *Cyder* (1708), in which he displayed a love of country scenes very similar to that of Thomson himself. Philips's skill in copying Milton's style was highly praised by some of his admirers.

613, 939. Cf. p. 518, ll. 86-87.

615, 1053 ff. Cf. note to p. 488.

618, 1215. Palermo had been visited by a disastrous earthquake in 1726.

622, 1363 ff. Cf. note to p. 564.

HENRY FIELDING

662. A LETTER TO SIR ROBERT WALPOLE.

Fielding was for several years an adherent of the Opposition cause (see note to p. 272, ll. 187-94), though he eventually lost patience with its internal disagreements. In 1737 Fielding had been driven out of his career as dramatist and producer by the Licensing Act, which put an end to his political satire as far as the stage was concerned. Ll. 40-41 are probably an allusion to this event.

GEORGE LYTTELTON, BARON LYTTELTON

663. ODE. IN IMITATION OF PASTOR FIDO.

Pastor Fido was an Italian pastoral tragi-comedy by Guarini, produced in 1585. It was extremely successful, and the elegance of its language was much admired.

SAMUEL JOHNSON

667. PROLOGUE SPOKEN BY MR. GARRICK.

36. A pantomime entitled *Harlequin Doctor Faustus*, produced by John Thurmond, dancing-master of Drury Lane theater, in 1723, did much to promote the fortunes of the art of pantomime, and was itself one of the most famous pieces in this genre.

668, 42. Aphra Behn (1640-89) was a somewhat scandalous playwright and romancer of the Restoration period; Thomas D'Urfey (1653-1723), a prolific dramatist and song-writer of the same period.

46. Hunt was a famous boxer; Mahomet a recently arrived rope-dancer, supposed to be a Turk.

671. THE VANITY OF HUMAN WISHES.

127. George Villiers, first Duke of Buckingham, was assassinated in 1628 by a discharged officer, after he had made himself an object of popular hatred by his determined prosecution of war to the exhaustion of his men's strength and patience.

129. Thomas Wentworth, first Earl of Strafford, was detected in a plot with Charles I to use the army for the purpose of overthrowing Parliament, and executed for treason. Edward Hyde, Earl of Clarendon, the great Royalist statesman, was exiled in 1667 after his actions had put him in the bad graces of Charles II and the House of Commons.

137. "Bodley's dome." The Bodleian Library at Oxford.

138. "Bacon's mansion." Roger Bacon, the thirteenth-century philosopher, is supposed to have lived at Oxford. The tradition was that a certain cell in a tower on Folly Bridge in Oxford (still standing in Johnson's day) had been occupied by Bacon, and that if any one greater than Bacon should ever pass beneath that cell, it would fall down upon him.

672, 162. Thomas Lydiat, the divine and chronologer, underwent some severe hardships, among others being persecution during the 1640's for his Royalist belief.

190. The Hon. Eveline Godley, in *Charles XII of Sweden: a study of kingship* (London, 1928), pp. 4-5, says: "Legends gathered round his name, in his own country, even while he lived. Half a century later, 'Swedish Charles,' as seen by Voltaire and by other leading writers of the age, had become an almost mythical figure; the symbol for all time of empty military renown."

673, 239. The "bold Bavarian" was Charles Albert, Elector of Bavaria and Roman Emperor, who died in 1745, after his plans of conquest, at first successful, had at length come to ruin.

244. Maria Theresa, Archduchess of Austria and Queen of Hungary and Bohemia, was perhaps the principal opponent of the

Bavarian Charles's ambitions, her territories being an important object of his attack, and her husband, Francis, Grand Duke of Tuscany, having been successfully opposed by Charles for election to the title of Holy Roman Emperor.

676. ON THE DEATH OF MR. ROBERT LEVET.

Levett was characterized by Boswell (*Life of Johnson,* ed. Hill, I, 243) as "an obscure practiser in physick amongst the lower people." He lived in Johnson's lodgings for many years, and Johnson respected him highly—on one occasion characterizing him thus: "Levet . . . is a brutal fellow, but I have a good regard for him; for his brutality is in his manners, not in his mind." Levett appears to have had some unusual talents, though he never became famous (*ibid.*, n.3).

MATTHEW GREEN

677. *From* THE SPLEEN.

"The spleen" was a common eighteenth-century name for a settled or recurring condition of melancholy, moroseness, and irritability. The ailment had been a subject of medical interest from Elizabethan times onward, especially under the designation of "melancholy," and had occasioned Burton's great work, *The anatomy of melancholy* (1621). Addison, in the *Spectator*, No. 387, voiced the opinion, not original with him, that melancholy or the spleen was a characteristically English malady. Many literary persons, among them Samuel Johnson, shared the medical men's notion of melancholy as simply a disease necessary to be cured for human happiness. Green's poem carries out this idea. On the other hand, the idea of melancholy as a pleasurable feeling had currency in this day; witness Young's *Night-thoughts* (p. 542), Blair's *The grave* (p. 658), Gray's *Elegy* (p. 765), Thomas Warton, Jr.'s *The pleasures of melancholy* (p. 802), and other pieces of the "graveyard school."

678, 15. Charles Gildon (1665-1724) was one of the neo-classic critics who made a great point of the "rules" of poetry. His *Complete art of poetry* (1718) is a characteristic work.

31-32. James Moore, or James Moore Smyth, once a member of the circle of friends of Alexander Pope, was accused by the latter of using, in his comedy *The rival modes*, certain lines (ll. 243-48) from Pope's *Moral essays*, Epistle II. Pope pilloried Moore in the *Dunciad* (see beginning of Book II, also the "Testimonies of authors"). L. 373 of the *Epistle to Arbuthnot* (p. 501) has been taken as an admission on Pope's part that he had permitted Moore to use the lines, though the meaning is not perfectly clear.

688, 763. "Entium Ens." Literally, "thing of things," or quintessence of being.

PHILIP DORMER STANHOPE, EARL OF CHESTERFIELD

692. VERSES WRITTEN IN A LADY'S SHERLOCK "UPON DEATH."

William Sherlock, Dean of St. Paul's (d. 1707), wrote a *Practical discourse concerning death* (1689), which became highly popular.

ADVICE TO A LADY IN AUTUMN.

Apparently the first publication of this poem was in the *Gentleman's magazine*, November, 1736.

WILLIAM SHENSTONE

695. THE SCHOOL-MISTRESS.

The motto, freely translated, is as follows: "Voices were heard, and a great noise of children at the threshold of life." Virgil, *Aeneid* vi. 426-27.

701, 255. "Dennis." See p. 398, ll. 585-87, and note.

703. A PASTORAL BALLAD.

Motto: "*Arbusta humilesque myricæ.*" "Trees and low tamarisks." Virgil, *Eclogue* iv. 2.

MARK AKENSIDE

712. HYMN TO SCIENCE.

The word "science" is here used in its broadest sense to designate all forms of rational inquiry. Akenside, after expressing the usual scorn of the eighteenth century for the "monk's philosophy" of the Middle Ages, passes in review, first mathematics and physics (ll. 19-24), then psychology, conceived more or less in Lockian terms (ll. 25-42), then metaphysics (ll. 43-54), then the practical sciences of politics and ethics (ll. 55-72). Characteristic of the time are the lines on the Chain of Being (ll. 43-48), the exaltation of ethics as the "best efforts of thy skill" (ll. 67-72), and the concluding emphasis on the practical functions of science.

714. *From* THE PLEASURES OF IMAGINATION, BOOK III.

By "imagination" Akenside means simply impressions of the phenomena of nature and the world of human activity, and reverie upon what one has seen. Addison used the term similarly in his essays on the imagination in the *Spectator*, Nos. 411-21. In the first of those essays he says: ". . . by the Pleasures of the Imagination . . . I here mean such as arise from visible Objects, either when we have them actually in our View, or when we call up their Ideas in our Minds by Paintings, Statues, Descriptions, or any the like Occasion."

716. ODE I.

The motto: "I, after the custom and the fashion of the bee of Mount Matinus." Horace, *Carmina* iv. 2, 27-28.

WILLIAM COLLINS

727. PERSIAN ECLOGUES. PREFACE.

The prevalent manner of dealing with national character in the eighteenth century was, after a possible prelude to the effect that human nature is fundamentally the same the world over, to assign some prominent and easily describable trait of temperament to a people as a whole, and to assume that the average member of that people would show the predicated trait to a marked degree. See, e.g., Goldsmith, *The traveller*. Even the most thoughtful and broadly educated persons of the day were not likely to be critical of this method.

729. ODE TO PITY.

This ode and the one that follows are an allusion to Aristotle's definition of tragedy as "the imitation of an action that is serious, complete in itself, and of a certain magnitude; in language made beautiful by different means in different parts of the work; in dramatic, not narrative, form; through scenes of pity and fear bringing about its purgation of such emotions." This famous passage has been subjected to numerous varying and conflicting interpretations. The general tendency of neo-classic critics, and one to be noticed in these poems of Collins, was to think that Aristotle had made the purgation, or catharsis, of pity and fear the principal end of tragedy, though Aristotle's own statement that the end of the tragedy is the plot is inconsistent with this construction. Sometimes the catharsis was explained in terms of direct moral edification. Rapin, in his *Reflections on Aristotle's Poetics*, Sect. XVII (*Works* [London, 1706], II, 205), said that tragedy regulates the weaknesses of undue compassion and fear by showing what objects should and should not arouse those emotions, by showing how not to pity the unworthy or to fear ordinary accidents. Similarly, Lord Kames, in his *Elements of criticism* (1762), chap. xxii, distinguished between "pathetic tragedy" and "moral tragedy." The former, he said, produces only pity; the latter, which is the higher form, raises in the beholder "an emotion of fear or terror; and it is by this emotion, frequently reiterated in a variety of moral tragedies, that the spectators are put upon their guard against the disorders of passion." On the other hand, Rapin also described the effects of tragedy in psychological, not to say medical terms. In Section XVIII of the work cited (*Works,* II, 206-07), he said: ". . . as of all Passions Fear and Pity are those that make the strongest impressions on the Heart of Man. . . . *Aristotle* has chosen these . . . when the Soul is shaken, by Motions so Natural and so Humane, all the Impressions it feels becomes [*sic*] Delightful. . . . And in this *Agitation* consists all the Pleasure that one is capable to receive from Tragedy. . . ." Cf. also Burke, in his *Inquiry into . . . the sublime and beautiful* (1757), Part IV, Sect. VII: "As common labour, which is a mode of pain, is the exercise of the grosser, a mode of terrour is the exercise of the finer parts of the system . . . if . . . terrour is not conversant about the present destruction of the person, as these emotions clear the parts . . . of a dangerous and troublesome incumbrance, they are capable of producing delight; not pleasure, but a sort of delightful horrour, a sort of tranquillity tinged with terrour; which, as it belongs to self-preservation, is one of the strongest of all the passions." It appears to be to the second of these interpretations—the medical rather than the moral—that Collins inclines, as far as one may judge from the content of these two odes.

730, 7. "*Pella's* Bard." Collins's note: "Euripides, of whom Aristotle pronounces, on a Comparison of him and Sophocles, that he was the greater Master of the tender Passions. . . ."

19-20. Otway's reputation had as one of its main supports his power to create pity—perhaps nowhere better shown than in the delineation of Monimia's sufferings in *The orphan.*

733. Ode to Simplicity.

16. "Her," etc. Collins's note: "The . . . Nightingale, for which Sophocles seems to have entertained a peculiar Fondness." Sophocles is of course "sad Electra's Poet," so called from his tragedy *Electra.*

19. Cephisus was the largest stream in ancient Attica, the state of which Athens was the chief city.

734, 35. "one distinguish'd Throne." That of Augustus, in whose period Latin poetry reached its height.

735. Ode on the Poetical Character.

This poem appears to have been very obscure to many persons in the eighteenth century. The cause of the difficulty probably lay in Collins's departure from the conventional neo-classic view of the poet's character—the view that the poet "follows nature" (see p. 387, ll. 68 ff.), and is therefore fundamentally a reproducer of things already existing though hidden from the ordinary man. As Mr. A. S. P. Woodhouse has explained in his study of Collins's view of the poetic imagination (see p. 1127), the allegory of the poem concerns the union of the Deity with Fancy (the "lov'd Enthusiast") to create the universe, with the attendant creation of the magic girdle (i.e., the poetical faculty—see ll. 19, 23-24)—the inference being, in Woodhouse's words, that "the activity of the poetic imagination is, in some sort, a counterpart of the divine act of creation, that the poet, too, is a creator . . ." and not a copyist, even in the most exalted sense of that term.

One instance of the unsympathetic reception of this ode is a poem in the *Student*, II (1751), 313-15, entitled "Ode to Horror," which ridiculed Collins, along with the Wartons, for their love of the "Gothic" and the romantically dismal. Cf. this anthology, pp. 731-33, 802 ff. Some of the lines in the satire allude obviously to the *Ode on the poetical character*, e.g., the following:

"O goddess, erst by Spenser view'd
What time th' enchanter vile embru'd
His hands in Florimel's pure heart
Till loos'd by steel-clad Britomart. . . .
. . . .
O curfeu-loving Goddess haste,
O waft me to some Scythian waste,
Where in *Gothic* solitude
Mid prospects most sublimely rude
Beneath a rough rock's gloomy chasm
Thy sister sits Enthusiasm:
Let me with her in magic trance
Hold most delirious dalliance. . . ."

(See H. O. White, in the London *Times literary supplement*, Jan. 12, 1922, p. 28.) A. S. P. Woodhouse (see p. 1141) has argued that the author of this "Ode to Horror" may have been none other than the younger Thomas Warton himself. He finds Warton addicted to "literary jests even at the expense of his own cherished interests," and reminds us that all the Wartons were as much eighteenth-century wits as early Romanticists.

736, 46. "Tarsel." The tercel, or male falcon.

742. Ode on the Popular Superstitions of the Highlands. 1. "H———." John Home, later author of *Douglas* (1757), a tragedy based partly on the old Scotch ballad "Childe Maurice." Some of Collins's knowledge of the Scottish Highlands is generally attributed to conversations with Home.

745, 155-171. See note to p. 749. In this passage Collins is indebted to Martin Martin's *Voyage to St. Kilda* (1698), a book which had some influence on eighteenth-century contemplations of primitive virtue.

746, 197. Edward Fairfax published in 1600 a translation of Tasso's *Gerusalemme liberata*, alluded to in the preceding lines.

JOSEPH WARTON

747. The Enthusiast: or, The Lover of Nature.

The term "nature" here means not only natural scenery and its accompaniments (though these figure prominently in the poem) but the innate constitution of man as opposed to the alterations in it resulting from the arts and devices of civilization. The theme of the poem is the superiority of nature to art, whatever aspect of nature be taken. Wild landscape is preferred to the finest of gardens (ll. 4-14); the warblings of birds excel the sounds of man-made instruments (ll. 36-44); the colors of nature are preferred to those of the greatest paintings (ll. 45-50); in poetry, the "natural" poet surpasses the mere artist (ll. 130-31, and note); and as regards the life of man as a whole, he was more happy and more virtuous in his original, or "natural," state, than under the conditions of civilization (ll. 78 ff., and note).

This poem has been taken as an important early expression of Romanticism—"nature" symbolizing the new, free spirit which was to characterize Romantic art. Professor Lovejoy has effectively shown that there is no foundation for this judgment (see p. 1141). Warton's general theme, far from being a novelty, had been a commonplace all through the neo-classic period, in various guises. The noble savage, for example, or the "natural" poet (see notes to ll. 78 and 131, respectively), were familiar conceptions. If there is novelty in the latter of these two, it lies, as Lovejoy suggests, in Warton's taking a bolder stand than was customary for natural wildness and departure from conventions as a criterion of excellence in poetry specifically. But a similar position in the theory of landscape gardening had already been common since the late seventeenth century. See Lovejoy in *MLN*, XLVII (1932), 419-46, and in *Journal of English and Germanic philology*, XXXII (1933), 1-20.

Indeed, all of the Wartons were probably much less in revolt against accepted standards than has often been supposed. As regards Thomas the younger, for example, D. Nichol Smith, in "Warton's history of English poetry," *Proceedings of the British Academy,* XV (1929), 97-99, points out that he was far from being a consistent rebel against neo-classicism; that whereas he could at one time deplore the loss of the extravagant and fanciful from English poetry (as in the conclusion to Volume II of his *History*), he could at another praise the art of Reynolds (see p. 815) for exhibiting just the qualities which had replaced the extravagant and fanciful; that in many parts of the *History* he disparaged the "Gothic" qualities of medieval literature in terms quite typical of neo-classic criticism.

749, 78 ff. This passage illustrates one of the constantly recurring ideas of the eighteenth century: that man was better off, and perhaps would still be better off, in a "state of nature" than in a state of civilization. This view, known as "primitivism," has been mistakenly supposed to be the invention of Jean-Jacques Rousseau; it had, as a matter of fact, an extensive history before his time, and most aspects of it, indeed, date back to antiquity. From antiquity comes the idea expressed by Warton in the present passage, that in some bygone age man lived a simple and happy life, without vices and without the miseries that accompany them in our civilized world. The idea was first set forth at length by Hesiod in his *Works and days*. He there mentioned five ages of man: the Golden Age, when a happy people lived in a pleasant environment, enjoying the bounty of nature, carrying on an indolent existence and never turning to violence and war; a Silver Age, not quite so ideal as the first; then a Bronze Age, still less so; then an Age of Heroes, in which men for a time threw off some of the baseness they had acquired; and finally, an Iron Age, or the present deteriorated state of man. See A. O. Lovejoy and George Boas, *Primitivism and related ideas in antiquity* (Baltimore, 1935), pp. 25-31. The primitivistic ideal here is of what Lovejoy calls the "soft" variety. Somewhat sterner views of primitive virtue were also current in ancient thought; a notable example is found in Lucretius, *De rerum natura*, Book V, in which the early state of both man and nature is represented as more vigorous than the present, and civilized man, for all his arts, is shown to be morally degenerate. The primitive life pictured by Lucretius is not entirely idyllic; it has its ugly spots as to both morals and outward circumstance. Yet this very passage is the main source of the details in Warton's picture of primitive man; the "hard" touches being altered or omitted (see p. 1141, article by Audley L. Smith), and the whole being romanticized in terms of a thoroughgoing golden-age idealism—though, to be sure, Warton does make some concessions to "hard" primitivism in ll. 110-29. These concessions take the form of extolling the merits of life under rigorous conditions, and making the enduring of hardship, rather than the enjoyment of ease, its central theme. Cf. Collins on the inhabitants of St. Kilda (p. 745, ll. 155-71).

Another phase of primitivism, perhaps most popular of all in the eighteenth century, was that of the "noble savage," supposedly still extant. The American Indian and, later in the century, the South Sea Islander had special prominence as noble savages. The climate and the ease of living (real or supposed) in the South Sea Isles recommended them to the fancy of parlor primitivists (see note to p. 1102, l. 1).

750, 131. It was a familiar opinion in the later seventeenth and eighteenth centuries that Shakespeare was a "natural" poet, who had not received much formal instruction and who had little need of it, being able to do instinctively what other poets had to learn to do by long application. Dryden expressed such a view in the *Essay of dramatic poesy* ("He needed not the spectacles of books to read nature"); so also did Milton, in *L'Allegro*, in a passage contrasting "art" and "nature" in comedy:

"Then to the well-trod stage anon,
If Jonson's learned sock be on,
Or sweetest Shakespeare, Fancy's child,
Warble his native wood-notes wild."

THOMAS GRAY

763. THE ALLIANCE OF EDUCATION AND GOVERNMENT.

The motto: "Begin, my friend; for surely you can in no way carry your song with you into Hades, the place where everything is forgotten." Theocritus, *Thyrsis* 62-63.

This poem presents the politico-ethical phase of the idea of nature as a changeless universal principle, expressed on its aesthetic side in Pope's *Essay on criticism*, ll. 68-79 (see p. 387). Gray's stand represents a compromise often arrived at. All peoples have a certain share of "reason's light" (ll. 26-37), hence *should* develop the same essential virtues; national differences are signs of weakness. On the other hand, within limits the environment will inevitably bring out some virtues more than others. Goldsmith, in *The traveller* (see pp. 836 ff.), enumerates at length the virtues, as well as the defects, of various nations.

773. THE PROGRESS OF POESY.

95. "He, that rode sublime." Milton, in *Paradise lost*.

105. "Two Coursers." The lines of the closed heroic couplet.

112. "what daring Spirit." Gray's note: "We have had in our language no other notes of the sublime kind, than that of Dryden on St. Cecilia's Day. . . . Mr. Mason indeed of late days has touched the true chords, and with a masterly hand, in some of his Choruses. . . ." Concerning Mason, see note to p. 784.

115. "the Theban Eagle." Pindar, the ancient writer of odes, who, as Gray says, compared himself to that bird.

778. SKETCH OF HIS OWN CHARACTER.

6. Charles Townshend was one of the most brilliant orators of the day. In 1766 he became chancellor of the exchequer. Samuel Squire became a bishop in 1761, an event at which Gray privately sneered (see letter of Gray to Wharton, May 9, 1761, in *Correspondence of Thomas Gray*, ed. Toynbee and Whibley [Oxford, 1935], II, 737).

THE FATAL SISTERS.

This and the following translations or paraphrases of Old Norse and Welsh odes were originally intended by Gray to be used as illustrations in the opening chapters of a projected history of English poetry. The original of *The fatal sisters* is an Icelandic poem of (perhaps) the eleventh century; Gray's translation was based on a Latin paraphrase accessible to him in two late seventeenth-century works of Scandinavian erudition—Thomas Bartholin's *De causis contemptae a Danis adhuc Gentilibus mortis* (1689) and Torfæus' *Historia Orcadum* (1697). See the Appendix (by G. L. Kittredge) to W. L. Phelps' *Selections from the poetry and prose of Thomas Gray* (Boston, 1894), and Roger Martin, *Essai sur Thomas Gray* (Toulouse, 1934), chap. ii.

780. THE DESCENT OF ODIN.

Translated from the Latin version in Bartholin.

783. THE TRIUMPHS OF OWEN.

In the 1768 edition of his poems, Gray adds to the title the following: "From Mr. [Evan] Evans's Specimens of the Welch poetry; London, 1764, quarto."

784. WILLIAM SHAKESPEARE TO MRS. ANNE, REGULAR SERVANT TO THE REV. MR. PRECENTOR OF NEW YORK.

The Precentor was William Mason, poet and biographer of Gray, who, with Gray and others, had been styled at Cambridge the "polite scholars." Mason responded to the raillery of this poem by saying that although it was poor, he would paste it in his Shakespeare anyway, to enhance the value thereof.

CHRISTOPHER SMART

785. A SONG TO DAVID.

See 1 and 2 Samuel and 1 Kings.

789, 175. Though the "pillars" are here entirely a matter of symbolism, the symbol derives ultimately from the use of actual pillars in a religious connection. Primitive Semitic peoples believed that rocks were deities; and later, "pillars" of a more or less conical shape were erected as emblems of divinity, and served as altars.

181-222. Cf. Genesis i. 1-11.

THOMAS WARTON, JR.

802. THE PLEASURES OF MELANCHOLY.

The motto: "Teach me funereal songs, O Melpomene!" Horace, *Carmina* i. 24. 2-3.

804, 96. Cf. p. 441.

806, 215. See Otway's *The orphan.*

220. Jaffier was the remorseful conspirator in Otway's *Venice preserved.*

226-43. See note to p. 749.

813. SONNET III.

Sir William Dugdale published between 1655 and 1673 his *Monasticon Anglicanum,* a history of English monasteries. Its tremendous store of original documents and its prosaic seriousness seem to have touched Warton's feeling for the medieval and romantic.

SONNET IV.

Of the various theories to which Warton refers, those involving the Danes (cf. p. 59, l. 45) and the Druids were the most seriously considered during the seventeenth and eighteenth centuries. William Stukeley, in his *Stonehenge, a temple restor'd to the British Druids* (1740), elaborated the theory that Stonehenge was a temple built by the Druids, and though his evidence cannot stand the test of modern criticism, this theory retained its popularity up to recent times. The Merlin theory goes back to the first definite mention of Stonehenge in writing—that by Geoffrey of Monmouth. Geoffrey's account was that the Saxon leader Hengist massacred by treachery many chiefs of the Britons at a conference on peace terms at Amber (Amesbury), and that later Uther Pendragon, the father of King Arthur, headed an expedition to Ireland, whence, with the aid of the magician Merlin, he brought back huge stones to build a memorial.

11. Brutus, grandson of Aeneas, was the legendary founder of Britain.

815. VERSES ON SIR JOSHUA REYNOLDS'S PAINTED WINDOW.

28. "Vitruvian symmetry," that is, symmetry achieved according to the rules of Marcus Vitruvius Pollio, Roman architect under Caesar and Augustus, whose treatise *De architectura* had been the classic textbook of architectural theory and practice since the Renaissance.

816, 65-68. Reynolds himself, in his third *Discourse* (1770) had written: "When the artist has by diligent attention acquired a clear and distinct idea of beauty and symmetry; when he has reduced the variety of nature to the abstract idea; his next task will be to become acquainted with the genuine habits of nature, as distinguished from those of fashion. For in the same manner, and on the same principles, as he has acquired the knowledge of the real forms of nature, distinct from accidental deformity, he must endeavour to separate simple chaste nature, from those adventitious, those affected and forced airs or actions, with which she is loaded by modern education." The peculiar qualities of Gothic art, though not strictly "modern," nevertheless were to most judges before the middle of the eighteenth century aspects of a merely local and temporary spirit in art; they represented an artistic feeling which, however quaint or romantic, did not rise to universal and timeless conceptions of beauty. Beginning in the 1740's or shortly before, a revulsion of taste had set in in certain quarters, with the result that many Englishmen (including Warton himself; see p. 806, ll. 196-210) had become enthusiastic admirers of Gothic buildings and had sought to justify their taste by insisting on the superior "naturalness" of the Gothic style as compared with the classical (see A. O. Lovejoy, "The first Gothic revival and the Return to Nature," *MLN,* XLVII [1932], 419-46). The present poem represents a return, on Warton's part, to the earlier and more exclusive taste.

TOBIAS SMOLLETT

817. The Tears of Scotland.

Dr. Alexander Carlyle (1722-1805), a friend of Smollett, in his *Memoirs* (publ. 1860), gave as the occasion of this poem the rumored English atrocities after the defeat of the Pretender at Culloden in April, 1746. He also seems to have meant to say that the poem was published in the same year. The *Gentleman's magazine* for July, 1746, advertised the publication of *The groans of Scotland*, which may have been Smollett's poem. The earliest extant text, however, is apparently a leaflet (undated) now in the Harvard Library, lacking the title page and showing some inferiorities to the standard version here given, but giving the present title on the first page of the text. In 1753 the poem was printed in *The union*. See H. S. Buck, *Smollett as poet* (New Haven, 1927), pp. 21-29.

JOHN CUNNINGHAM

822. A Landscape.

The motto: "Let my pleasure be the country, and the running streams among the dells." Virgil, *Georgica* ii. 485. The text given in the motto is inaccurate. For *irrigui* read *rigui*; for *omnes* read *amnes*.

JAMES GRAINGER

828. Solitude.

9. Tadmor, or Palmyra, was an ancient city in the desert east of Syria. Modern European interest in its ruins dates from the visit of Dr. William Halifax to the site in 1691. An elaborate study of the architecture was made by Wood and Hawkins, who published their results as *The ruins of Palmyra* (1753). Numerous other books on the history and remains had appeared in the interval.

829, 43. "Cean." Simonides, the Greek lyric poet, who was born on the island of Keos.

45. "Naso." The Roman poet Ovid.

51. Hagley was the ancestral estate of the Lyttelton family. See p. 833, l. 223, and note.

831, 130. "Ausonian." Italian.

131-33. Bion (*fl.* 280 B.C.) and Moschus (*fl.* 200 B.C.) were two Greek writers of pastoral elegy.

832, 185-86. Cf. p. 465, ll. 267-68.

833, 217. Socrates.

223. The "Lord of Hagley" was George, first Baron Lyttelton (1709-73). He was both a scholar and an orator. His effectiveness in speaking seems to have been hampered by his voice and appearance; he could be, however, very eloquent in set speeches.

234. "Allen." Cf. note to p. 515, l. 135. Brunswick was the name of the great German ruling family, to one branch of which, the Hanoverian, George II of England belonged.

834, 245. Sir Philip Sidney died of a wound received at the battle of Zutphen (1586), where he had behaved with a heroic and perhaps extravagant disregard for his own safety.

246. Anytus was one of the accusers of Socrates.

OLIVER GOLDSMITH

835. THE TRAVELLER.

The fifth paragraph of the dedicatory epistle has been thought to be an allusion to Charles Churchill. Churchill's *The farewell* had been published a few months before *The traveller* appeared (see note to p. 877). Goldsmith's insistence (ll. 63-80) on the falsity of the "patriot's boast," coupled with the remarks in this paragraph of the dedication, makes it a plausible theory that one impetus toward the publication (though not the writing) of the poem was a desire to answer Churchill. Many of the ideas of the poem had been in Goldsmith's mind for some time (see R. S. Crane, *New essays by Oliver Goldsmith,* p. xxxix), and, if Goldsmith's statement in the dedication may be believed, a portion of the text had been composed as early as 1754 or 1755, when the author was in Switzerland.

844, 401-12. Cf. p. 860, ll. 395-402.

851. THE DESERTED VILLAGE.

The parts of this poem best remembered and most often quoted are those relating to the village in its happy state. The desertion of Auburn has been less valued and has been the cause of unfavorable comment for the inconsistency and unsoundness of its economic thought. This second aspect of the poem, however, must not be forgotten if the poet's purpose is to be appreciated.

Macaulay (see his article on Goldsmith in the *Encyclopaedia Britannica,* 11th ed.) thought two unrelated pictures had been incongruously joined: "The village in its happy days is a true English village. The village in its decay is an Irish village . . . by joining the two, he has produced something which never was and never will be seen in any part of the world." But Goldsmith himself had anticipated and answered this objection in the dedication of the poem itself. There is no reason to doubt that Goldsmith's purpose was to portray the effects of one aspect of the enclosure movement (see also the poem, ll. 303-08, 395-402). His conviction of the reality and importance of that contemporary phenomenon should be evident. Whether he exaggerated, and whether his condemnation of luxury is unsound economics, we do not have to decide.

An essay in *Lloyd's evening post* for June 14-16, 1762, identified as Goldsmith's (see R. S. Crane, *New essays by Oliver Goldsmith,* pp. 116-24), describes the eviction of the inhabitants of an English village, in terms similar to those of *The deserted village,* ll. 371-84. The description is followed by this commentary: ". . . I am informed that nothing is at present more common than such revolutions. In almost every part of the kingdom the laborious husbandman has been reduced, and the lands are now either occupied by some general undertaker, or turned into enclosures destined for the purposes of amusement or luxury." Goldsmith's treatment of the subject of enclosures in this earlier piece should (if indeed any added evidence is needed) dispel the notion frequently held that *The deserted village* was an attack on the Industrial Revolution or a reminiscence of Ireland. It is evident that the enclosures were what had interested him for several years before he wrote the poem; the selfish landlord, not the slave-driving manufacturer, was the object of attack.

860, 418. "Torno," or Tornea, is a river in Sweden which flows into the Gulf of Bothnia. Pambamarca is a mountain peak in Ecuador.

THE HAUNCH OF VENISON, A POETICAL EPISTLE TO LORD CLARE.

The Lord was a hearty, jovial Irishman of considerable wealth, who had Goldsmith as house-guest on many occasions, and whose sense of the comic Goldsmith enjoyed, though it was apparently far less subtle than Goldsmith's own.

861, 16. "MR. BURNE." Lord Clare's nephew.

22. "MONROE'S." Dorothy Monroe, a famous beauty.

25. "HIFF." Paul Hiffernan, a quarrelsome Irishman, and a hack-writer. He had been a friend of Burke in his younger days, and was later a friend of Goldsmith. The identity of the others mentioned is obscure.

862, 71-72. The names in these lines are fictitious ones signed to articles appearing in newspapers of the day.

THOMAS PERCY

868. THE FRIAR OF ORDERS GRAY.

For the Shakespearean borrowings, see as follows: ll. 1-2, *The taming of the shrew,* IV, i; ll. 9-12, 18-21, 25-28, 57-60, 84, *Hamlet,* IV, v; ll. 65-72, *Much ado about nothing,* II, iii.

CHARLES CHURCHILL

877. THE FAREWELL.

Dated conjecturally July, 1764, by James Laver, ed., *The poems of Charles Churchill* (King's Printers edition, 1933), II, 388. See note to p. 835.

879, 105. Diogenes trod on Plato's robe, exclaiming, "Thus I trample under foot the pride of Plato." Plato replied, "Yes, and with greater pride, Diogenes."

880, 132. "N——." Sir Fletcher Norton, at this time Attorney General, was a persistent foe of Wilkes. See note to p. 886, l. 419.

136. "M——." The Earl of Mansfield was a brilliant lawyer, for whom Churchill had formerly expressed admiration. He had, however, become hostile to Wilkes, thereby earning Churchill's enmity.

886, 419. Not long before this poem was written, the papers of John Wilkes, Churchill's associate on the *North Briton,* an anti-ministerial journal, had been seized. The person accused of the seizure was defended by testimony which brought the giver thereof under the charge of perjury; but the jury in Middlesex acquitted the supposed perjurer.

887, 473. "the Company." The East India Company.

491. Robert Clive was a director of the East India Company. His military victory at Plassey, India, in 1757, had increased the Company's power to such an extent as to lead, in Churchill's view, to serious abuses.

JAMES BEATTIE

903. THE MINSTREL. BOOK I.

534. This line has since been altered to read:

"But on this verse if Montague should smile . . ."

See Beattie's *Poetical works*, ed. Dyce (London, 1894), p. 32.

ROBERT FERGUSSON

930. THE FARMER'S INGLE.

The motto: "—and first of all rendering gay the banquets with much wine before the hearth, if it shall be cold." Virgil, *Eclogae* v. 69.

GEORGE CRABBE

935. The Village.

Pastoral poetry was an integral part of the neo-classic tradition, and enjoyed much popularity in the early part of the eighteenth century. By the time Crabbe wrote *The village* pastoral-writing was a faded art, and Crabbe's strictures upon it could not have occasioned much surprise. Such poems as Gray's *Elegy* and Goldsmith's *Deserted village*, however, had served to keep alive some of the romanticism that had earlier been distinctive of the pastoral pieces.

Boswell reports (*Life of Johnson,* ed. Hill, IV, 175) that Samuel Johnson made several revisions in *The village* while it was in manuscript, and particularly notes that he revised ll. 15-20, which embody part of the well-known condemnation of pastorals. This report gains interest from the fact of Johnson's chronic dislike of the pastoral tradition. The references to pastoral poetry in Johnson's works are several, and none of them is without some measure of contempt. See, e.g., in the life of Milton: "Nothing can less display knowledge, or less exercise invention, than to tell how a shepherd has lost his companion, and must now feed his flocks alone, without any judge of his skill in piping; and how one god asks another god what is become of Lycidas, and how neither god can tell." In *Rasselas*, chap. xix, Johnson shows a group of shepherds whose life and way of thinking are far from the pastoral ideal, and makes the Princess comment "that she would never suffer these envious savages to be her companions, and that she should not soon be desirous of seeing any more specimens of rustick happiness. . . ."

WILLIAM COWPER

957. Alexander Selkirk.

Selkirk was a sailor and adventurer, who, as a result of quarreling aboard ship, was left on Juan Fernandez Island, four hundred miles out from Chile, for five years (1704-09). His experiences were retold in Captain Woodes Rogers's *A cruising voyage round the world* and Captain Edward Cooke's *A voyage to the south sea and round the world* (both 1712). Sir Richard Steele made him the subject of a paper in *The Englishman*, No. 26 (1713). It was apparently from these sources that Defoe drew the main ideas for *Robinson Crusoe*.

965. The Task. Book I.

Cowper suffered all his life from a tendency to melancholia, and his association with the Evangelical revival was not always the best antidote. A certain Lady Austen, whom Cowper knew during his later years, suggested that he take a lighter subject than he had been wont to write upon—to wit, a sofa (see ll. 1-7)—and develop it in blank verse. The suggestion he humorously styled his "task," and treated it at the start in a mock-serious fashion, parodying the manner of Milton.

967, 61. The "alderman" may have been either a debtor or trespasser, or a city water-bailiff. The postern at Cripplegate was used, in different periods, for a prison and for the bailiff's office.

78. The "two kings of Brentford" appear in Buckingham's famous farce at Dryden's expense, *The rehearsal* (1672). They always enter together and do exactly the same things.

971, 262. "Benevolus" was one John Courtenay Throckmorton, a great friend of Cowper.

974, 413 ff. Cf. p. 748, ll. 45-56.

980, 700. Cf. p. 816, ll. 45 ff.

702. John Bacon was a very successful sculptor of Cowper's day, who executed various public monuments and statues in London. Two of these were of William Pitt the elder, first Earl of Chatham (see l. 704).

988. BOOK III.

258. Sir Matthew Hale was a great legal scholar and antiquarian of the seventeenth century, author of numerous works on law and religion.

992, 453. "the Mantuan bard." Virgil.

454. The "Grecian" is Homer, who was supposed to have written the mock epic entitled *The battle of the frogs and mice.*

456. See p. 313.

997, 714-15. The reference is to King Ahasuerus and his queen, Vashti, mentioned in the Book of Esther. Shushan was Ahasuerus's capital.

998, 766. Lancelot Brown (1715-83) was a famous landscape gardener.

1000. SONNET TO WILLIAM WILBERFORCE, ESQ.

Wilberforce was a philanthropist who spent a long parliamentary career in the interest of humane legislation. This sonnet was occasioned by a partial success of Wilberforce in his long fight against slavery—the passage, in 1792, of a bill in the House of Commons providing for gradual abolition of the slave-trade. The event was somewhat disappointing to the abolitionists, who had been fighting against the insertion of the word "gradually" into the bill (see Earl Stanhope, *The life of William Pitt* [London, 1861], II, 142-46). Wilberforce was a friend of John Newton, the evangelist and former slave-trader who dominated Cowper's life for many years (see p. 952, footnote).

THOMAS RUSSELL

1006. SONNET TO VALCLUSA.

Valclusa was the place where Petrarch spent a number of years living a hermit's life and devoting himself to study and writing. He wrote the sonnets to Laura during this period.

SONNET SUPPOS'D TO BE WRITTEN AT LEMNOS.

3. "Great Pæan's Son." Hephaestus, the son of Zeus and Hera ("Pæan" was a surname applied to various gods), and the god of fire. He was thrown from Olympus by his mother when a child because of his frailty, and lived for nine years in a grotto by the sea (cf. ll. 2, 6). Later, he was thrown from Olympus a second time by Zeus during a quarrel, and landed upon the island of Lemnos in the Aegean. Russell appears to have combined these two incidents.

WILLIAM BLAKE

1017. THE BOOK OF THEL.

Thel has been variously described, but the sum of all descriptions seems to be that she is humanity in a state of innocence, a pagan spirit who, in the words of Swinburne, "feeds upon the sorrow that comes of beauty, the heathen weariness of heart, that is sick of life because death will come" (*William Blake, a critical essay* [new ed.; New York, 1906], p. 222). Through conversing with the Lily, the Cloud, and the Worm, she learns that "the secret of creation is sacrifice; the very act of growth is a sacrament; and through this eternal generation in which one life is given for another and shed into new veins of existence, each thing is redeemed from perpetual death by perpetual change" (*ibid.*, pp. 223-24). All this is given in the first three parts of the poem. In life as so far pictured, on an idyllic plane, the ethic of humility is pleasant enough. But when Thel goes on to inquire into the meaning of life and death, and sees the misery of life as it actually is, all complacency is lost in terror. The voice from the pit offers only problems, no solution. The poem thus ends enigmatically, the only conclusion seeming to lie in the cryptic "motto" at the beginning. The meaning of life is not easily found; the sources of knowledge are obscure, the means of expressing it subject to confusion. Concerning the symbolism of the last two lines, the following statement is given in Edwin J. Ellis, *The real Blake* (New York, 1907), p. 156: "*Silver* is, in his [Blake's] system, the metal of heart's love; *Gold,* of mind's enthusiasm."

1021. THE MARRIAGE OF HEAVEN AND HELL.

Blake's Satanistic pose must not be taken literally. He is speaking ironically and in paradox. He puts himself in the Devil's party because what he really believes to be the good is what the conventionally religious call evil. His view of life is essentially dynamic ("energy is the only life," "energy is eternal delight," etc.); perpetual conflict and resolution he postulates as necessary to any development of the human spirit. The title of the piece reflects this idea of the meeting of opposites. It is an allusion to Swedenborg's *Heaven and Hell*, in which the orthodox view was expressed. that evil must be put down if good is to prevail. Accepting the usual senses of those terms, Blake violently disagreed, and affected to be on the Devil's side, as a means of showing his contempt for the spiritual deadness, the hypocrisy which he saw in conventional morality and religion. This satire is only a mask, however, for a profoundly religious feeling. Here he is being negative: conventions and laws are tyranny; man must have free expression of his impulses if he is to realize himself. But in his work as a whole, Blake presented a positive view of the nature of man, of the world, of the universe, though in symbolism not easy to follow.

ROBERT BURNS

1051. THE COTTER'S SATURDAY NIGHT.

The "R. A. ——" of the inscription was Robert Aiken (see also l. 8 of the poem), who saw genius in Burns's work before it had become known to the public. Burns once referred to Aiken as "a great critic of songs."

1056. TO A MOUSE.

Cf. p. 1107, ll. 119 ff. In Burns, however, the sensibility pose is far from extreme.

1063. EPISTLE TO J. LAPRAIK.

John Lapraik was a Scottish poet, about sixty years old when this poem was written. Burns apparently regarded him as a fine exemplar of Scottish genius. The song (see stanza 3) which had aroused Burns's admiration for Lapraik's "spark of nature's fire" was called "When I upon thy bosom lean." The fact that it closely resembles a poem published anonymously in *Ruddiman's magazine* (1773) entitled "When on thy bosom I recline," has made Lapraik's piece look like rank plagiarism. It is possible, however, that Lapraik wrote both poems. (See Burns's *Works*, ed. Henley and Henderson [1896], I, 380-81.)

WRITERS FOR THE ANTI-JACOBIN

1100. THE ANTI-JACOBIN; OR, WEEKLY EXAMINER. This periodical ran during 1797-98, at the time when English political opinion was bitterly divided over the activities of republican

France. The liberals were inclined to apologize for the military aggressiveness shown by the French under Napoleon, but the ministry, headed by William Pitt the younger, held stoutly to the position that Napoleon was threatening the peace and safety of Europe. Needing the assistance of one capable of offsetting the eloquence of the liberal element, Pitt managed to enlist George Canning, whom Byron has described as "a genius—almost a universal one; an orator, a wit, a poet, a statesman." Canning conceived the idea of the *Anti-Jacobin*, a pot-pourri of prose and verse aimed at making ridiculous the whole intellectual basis of the French Revolution. William Gifford, later famous as an editor of the *Quarterly review*, became editor of the *Anti-Jacobin*. Prominent among the contributors were John Hookham Frere and George Ellis (see pp. 1100 ff., footnotes). For some new light on the authorship of the individual pieces, see Owen E. Holloway in the *Review of English studies*, X (1934), 3-4.

THE FRIEND OF HUMANITY AND THE KNIFE GRINDER.

The clumsiness of the meter in this poem is intentional. The authors were burlesquing a poem by Robert Southey entitled "The widow," in which the Sapphic meter had been employed very ineptly, in their opinion. In strict Sapphic meter, the first two lines of the present poem would have to be accented as follows:

> *Need*y *knife*-grind*er*! whither *are* you *go*ing?
> *Rough* is *the* road, *your* wheel is *out* of *or*der—

1101, 38. *"universal philanthropy."* Cf. p. 1106, ll. 89-114.

1102. THE PROGRESS OF MAN, CANTO TWENTY-THIRD.

Numbers XV and XVI of the *Anti-Jacobin* contained fragments of the "first canto" of this poem. The editor affected unwillingness to print the poem entire, because of various criticisms. The piece is a burlesque of Richard Payne Knight's *Progress of civil society* (1796).

1. "Southern Seas." This "canto" treats of arguments against marriage which the *Anti-Jacobin* attributed to the Revolutionaries and their English sympathizers. The arguments are based on one variety of the popular primitivism of the eighteenth century: the idealization of life as it was supposed to be led in the South Sea isles. Cf. note to p. 749.

6. James Cook, on his first voyage of exploration, made with several scientists aboard, arrived at Tahiti in 1769. His findings there, as interpreted by London popularizers, gave fresh life to the age-old and always enticing theme of the happy isles in the west. In London, interest in the South Sea Islands was raised to a high point by the arrival in 1776 of Omai, an Otaheitan savage. Omai appears to have been an affable and not unintelligent young man, and London society made much of him, He attained the dignity of an allowance from George III and of portraits by various artists, including Sir Joshua Reynolds. See C. B. Tinker, *Nature's simple plan*, pp. 75 ff.

1103, 48. The editor of the *Anti-Jacobin* annotates this line as follows: "A beautiful figure of German literature. The Hottentots remarkable for staring at each other—God knows why."

THE ROVERS; OR, THE DOUBLE ARRANGEMENT. SONG BY ROGERO.

The writers of this piece saw a connection between the emotional extravagances of German romantic literature and the subversive ideas of the Revolution—both characterized by "a wild desire of undefinable latitude and extravagance,—an aspiration after shapeless somethings that can neither be described nor understood . . ." (see the *Anti-Jacobin*, No. XXX). In this burlesque on German drama, Rogero is a high-minded youth held captive by tyrannical authority.

1104. NEW MORALITY.

The number of the *Anti-Jacobin* in which this poem appeared was the final one, so that the poem is a sort of valedictory. It is a fair collection of the general themes and personal attacks which characterized the magazine throughout its career. Representative of the vigorous conservatism of its writers is the rough handling of Louvet the political litterateur (l. 261) and of Madame de Staël the prophet of German life and culture to the rest of Europe (l. 295), for the private scandals which, in conservative opinion, showed the true corrupt nature of the new order. Representative, also, is the attempt to condemn in one sweep such diverse characters as Coleridge, Southey, Lamb, Priestley, Paine, Godwin, and Holcroft (see ll. 336-45).

1105, 29. "G—ff—rd." William Gifford.

31-32. Cf. the motto prefixed to Gifford's satire *The Baviad.*

43. "the nameless Bard." T. J. Mathias, teacher to the family of King George III.

1107, 143. This line is an allusion to the episode in Laurence Sterne's *A sentimental journey,* the section entitled "Nampont. The dead ass," in which a man sits down beside a road and weeps over the carcass of a dead donkey.

1109, 233-34. This couplet alludes to La Fayette, imprisoned at Olmütz. General Fitzpatrick (see l. 236) made a speech on his behalf to the House of Commons, in which he moved that Commons demand from the Emperor of Germany the release of La Fayette. This speech is described in ll. 237-48.

1110, 247. "C—w—n." Curwen.

248. "St. A—dr—w." St. Andrew.

254. "C—rtn—y." Courtenay.

1111, 316. "Lepaux." Louis-Marie de la Réveillière-Lépeaux was one of the five members of the Directory of France, which came into existence in 1795. The others were Rewbell (see l. 303), Barras (see l. 302), Carnot, and Letourneur. La Réveillière was the leader of a new sect, the Theophilanthropists, who were bitter foes to other religions, and to the Catholic Church in particular. When he was at the height of his power, La Réveillière turned many churches into Theophilanthropic temples. Besides being a religious fanatic, he was an ardent Republican and Jacobin in spirit. Though possibly the most powerful member of the Directory for a time, he was forced, in 1799, to resign his office.

336. "C—dge": Coleridge. "S—th—y": Southey. "L—d": Lloyd. "L—be": Lamb.

338. "Pr—tl—y": Priestley. "W—f—ld": Wakefield.

340. "Th—lw—l": Thelwall.

1112, 345. "W—ll—ms": Williams. "G—dw—n": Godwin. "H—lcr—ft": Holcroft.

346, 352, 353. The editor annotated the blanks thus: "The Reader is at liberty to fill up the blanks according to his own opinion, and after the chances and changes of the times. It would be highly unfair to hand down to posterity as followers of *Leviathan*, the names of men who may, and probably will soon, grow ashamed of their leader."